The Toxic Substances Control Act

The Toxic Substances Control Act

A Practical Guide

Miriam V. Gold and Jean Warshaw

OXFORD
UNIVERSITY PRESS

2010

OXFORD
UNIVERSITY PRESS

Oxford University Press, Inc., publishes works that further Oxford University's objective of excellence in research, scholarship, and education.

Oxford New York
Auckland Cape Town Dar es Salaam Hong Kong Karachi Kuala Lumpur Madrid Melbourne Mexico City Nairobi New Delhi Shanghai Taipei Toronto

With offices in
Argentina Austria Brazil Chile Czech Republic France Greece Guatemala Hungary Italy Japan Poland Portugal Singapore South Korea Switzerland Thailand Turkey Ukraine Vietnam

Published by Oxford University Press, Inc.
198 Madison Avenue, New York, New York 10016

Library of Congress Cataloging-in-Publication Data
Gold, Miriam V.
The Toxic Substances Control Act: A Practical Guide / Miriam V. Gold, Jean Warshaw.
p. cm.
Includes bibliographical references and index.
ISBN 978-0-19-538862-6 (pbk. : includes cd : alk. paper)
1. United States. Toxic Substances Control Act. 2. Chemicals—Law and legislation—United States. 3. Poisons—Law and legislation—United States. 4. Hazardous substances—Law and legislation—United States. I. Warshaw, Jean. II. Title.
KF3958.G65 2010
344.7304'622—dc22

2010001390

---

1 2 3 4 5 6 7 8 9

Printed in the United States of America on acid-free paper

Notice to Readers

This publication is designed to provide accurate information with respect to the subject matter covered. It is based upon sources believed to be accurate and reliable and is intended to be current as of the time it was written. To confirm that that the information herein has not been affected or changed by recent developments, legal research should be undertaken, including review of primary sources as required. The reader should not rely on this publication to address specific questions that apply to a particular set of facts. The authors and publishers make no representation or warranty, express or implied, as to the completeness or correctness of the information contained herein. In addition, the authors and the publisher assume no liability of any kind resulting from the use of, or reliance on, the contents of this book. This publication is sold with the understanding that neither the authors nor the publisher is providing legal advice on any specific matter. If legal advice is required, a lawyer should be engaged to render advice on the specific matter at issue, after a careful review of all of the relevant facts.

(Based on the Declaration of Principles jointly adopted by a Committee of the American Bar Association and a Committee of Publishers and Associations.)

This book is dedicated to:
our parents, Sam and Ruth Vogel and Irv and Thelma Laifer;
our spouses, Bob Michel and Tom Gold; and
our children, Josh, Danny, Noah, and Claire

Preface

The genesis of this treatise began when the two authors started to work together at Ciba-Geigy Corporation. For Miriam, the genesis occurred in the mid 1990s when she took a position as Vice President of Legal and Regulatory Affairs at a company division which later became a part of Ciba Specialty Chemicals Corporation. That job required more than just advising clients on the law and telling them to comply with those requirements. It included operational responsibility for compliance. She discovered that compliance best happens when legal requirements are seamlessly integrated into day to day business operations, eliminating extra steps and additional thought and work. Making it easy for people to meet regulatory requirements made compliance sustainable. That involved both a sea change in how regulatory people did their jobs, substituting transparency and teamwork for control, and how they were perceived by employees in the rest of the business. As that transformation began to occur, something unexpected and competitively advantageous happened. Compliance and role changes led to getting products to market consistently quicker and less expensively.

For Jean, the route to this sea change began in the late 1980s when she began practicing environmental law at a time when there was a constant stream of major new environmental regulations. As each new regulation came into effect the businesses needed guidance to understand the implications and integrate new practices on a continual basis. Environmental laws are often criticized for being medium specific instead of industry specific, and the challenge of bringing together all of the governing rules for the many businesses she counseled lead to the realization that each business needs to have a sustainable system for compliance that is built into the every day work procedures.

Miriam and Jean worked together as a team to integrate compliance with the Toxic Substances Control Act into the work processes of the businesses. They benefitted greatly in implementing this task by the ISO and team culture of the businesses, and succeeded with the assistance and enthusiasm of the people in those businesses. You know who you are—and we thank you all for your support.

Having succeeded in implementing a sustainable compliance system, we decided that we should share what we learned with others, and that is what makes this book unique among other books on TSCA. We are passing along to our readers the benefits of many years in the trenches and the wisdom of our successes, as well as the lessons from our failures. It took longer than perhaps we thought it would to put this treatise together—even longer than the project we originally implemented. Along the way we have had help from colleagues, and we would like especially to thank Tom Mesevage who wrote the first drafts of Chapters 7 and 11. Our husbands, Tom Gold and Bob Michel, offered their unwavering support and encouragement, especially as the deadline for turning in our manuscript got closer and closer and we spent more and more time with one another, instead of them, rehashing, updating, and correcting our work. We also thank David Balutanski, Lynne Rosenberg, Jen Nevergole and Maddalena Nappi Reidy for helping to pull the resources and manuscript together.

Thanks to Matt Gallaway, our editor, and the rest of the team at Oxford University Press for their guidance and for making this entire project a reality.

Thanks also to HeinOnline for granting permission to reproduce Federal Register notices from their service on the accompanying CD.

Contents

CHAPTER

1

Introduction

I. What is TSCA

The Toxic Substances Control Act (TSCA),[1] enacted in 1976, provided the United States Environmental Protection Agency (EPA) with the first grant of broad authority to any federal agency to gather information on chemical risks across previously unregulated activities and industries and to use that information to regulate the manufacture, importation, use, distribution in commerce, and disposal of chemical substances. It is the last of the product regulatory schemes enacted into law by Congress, long after the passage of the Federal Food, Drug, and Cosmetics Act (FFDCA) of 1938[2] and the Federal Insecticide, Fungicide, and Rodenticide Act (FIFRA) of 1947.[3] Congress intended to close the void in the regulatory scheme in which certain types of products, such as pharmaceuticals and pesticides, were heavily regulated, whereas more ordinary but ubiquitous chemical substances could be manufactured and sold with almost no governmental oversight.

TSCA cuts across all business activities, from research through end of product life, and has a far broader scope than most other environmental statutes passed in the same decade. While its greatest impact is on companies that manufacture and sell chemicals, its reach is not limited to chemical companies. Processors of chemicals are subject to many of the same intricate regulations, and a processor is just about any entity that uses chemicals, which encompasses a broad universe of companies. For example, chemical processors would include textile manufacturers, computer assemblers, paint companies, car makers, battery makers, ink cartridge and ink pen manufacturers, manufacturers of cleaning products—almost any company that makes any physical item using or containing chemicals. Even companies primarily regulated under the FFDCA[4] or FIFRA[5] could find some of their activities subject to TSCA.

While the amount of time and effort devoted to TSCA compliance depends of course on the operations and product lines of each particular company, companies should not just assume that TSCA is irrelevant to them without conducting some analysis.

---

1. 15 U.S.C. §§ 2601–2695d.
2. 21 U.S.C. §§ 301–399.
3. 7 U.S.C. § 136.
4. For example, waste from pharmaceutical manufacturing plants is regulated under TSCA, and allegations of significant adverse effects caused by a pharmaceutical plant waste would have to be recorded under § 8(c) of TSCA. *See* Chapter 7, Reporting and Recordkeeping.
5. Raw materials used in the production of pesticides are subject to all of the TSCA rules, although the final pesticide product is exempt from the statutory definition of substances that are regulated under TSCA.

II. History of TSCA

The environmental scourges of the 1960s and 70s[6] formed the backdrop for EPA administrator Russell Train to champion this legislation and to refer to the "grim game of chemical roulette" involved in innocent everyday activities:

> Most Americans had no idea, until relatively recently, that they were living so dangerously. They had no idea that when they went to work in the morning, or when they ate their breakfast—that when they did the things they had to do to earn a living and keep themselves alive and well—that when they did things as ordinary, as innocent and as essential to life as eat, drink, breathe or touch, they could, in fact, be laying their lives on the line. They had no idea that, without their knowledge or consent, they were often engaging in a grim game of chemical roulette whose result they would not know until many years later.[7]

Although the goals of the statute are quite commendable, EPA has often been criticized for its inability to gather existing toxicity data or to mandate testing of new or existing chemicals.[8]

A prominent EPA advisory committee, noting that EPA had ordered testing for only 121 chemicals in the first twenty years under TSCA, explained that this was "not an indication of how much more information might really be needed, but rather, the administrative challenges of mounting an information request."[9] Stephen Johnson, a past EPA Administrator, testified during his confirmation hearings for an earlier post in front of the Senate Environment and Public Works Committee on May 17, 2001 about reliance on voluntary

---

6. In 1962, Rachel Carson's *Silent Spring* brought to public attention the detrimental effects of widespread use of toxic pesticides such as dichlorodiphenyltrichloroethane, or DDT. In 1969, the fire-plagued Cuyahoga River, just southeast of Cleveland, erupted on fire once again, to the attention of the nation. During the 1970s, the buried wastes at Love Canal rose to the surface with a rising water table leading to the evacuation of nine-hundred-fifty families.
7. S. Rep. No. 94-698, at 3 (1976).
8. Environmental Defense (formerly the Environmental Defense Fund) has decried what it describes as TSCA's "self-defeating legal structure" regarding chemical testing, which requires that "the agency must already *have* [testing] data in order to show that it *needs* data." Environmental Defense Fund, Inc. Toxic Ignorance 20 (1997), *available at* http://www.edf.org/documents/243_toxicignorance.pdf. Under TSCA § 4, before EPA can impose a testing requirement, it must first show either (i) that the chemical may present an "unreasonable risk" or (ii) both that it is produced in major quantities and that substantial exposures, in quantitative terms, are occurring or that there is significant human exposure in qualitative terms. Even within government, the failings of TSCA have been noted repeatedly. *See, e.g.*, GAO, Toxic Substances: EPA's Chemical Safety Program Has Not Resolved Safety Concerns, GAO/RCED-91-136 (June 19, 1991).
9. Endocrine Disrupter Screening and Testing Advisory Comm., EPA, Final Report 2–11 (1999).

programs given the difficulties of rulemaking: "On the subject of industrial chemicals, voluntary partnerships on the High Production Volume chemical testing program and the Voluntary Children's Chemical Evaluation Program will continue to be key priorities."[10] Fast forward almost ten years and the promise of the voluntary initiatives has lost some of its sheen. EPA recently announced the termination of the Chemical Assessment and Management Program (ChAMP), started in 2007 to implement broader international commitments to ensure the safety of existing chemicals, and expanded to potentially include voluntary initiatives for wider categories of chemicals and chemicals present in the U.S. in lower quantities.[11] Lisa Jackson, the current EPA Administrator, has also weighed in on the need to provide the Agency with better tools to do its work. In a recent speech outlining the Obama Administration's plans for legislative reform of TSCA, she said:

> Our oversight of the 21st century chemical industry is based on the 1976 Toxic Substances Control Act. It was an important step forward at the time—part of a number of environmental wins from the 1970s, like the Clean Air Act and the Clean Water Act, not to mention the formation of the EPA. But over the years, not only has TSCA fallen behind the industry it's supposed to regulate—it's been proven an inadequate tool for providing the protection against chemical risks that the public rightfully expects.[12]

While no one can predict whether and when Congress will be able to enact new chemical management legislation, Ms. Jackson has vowed to use the regulatory tools provided by TSCA to their fullest extent until that time comes.

III. TSCA's Future

EPA Administrator Jackson has advocated strengthening TSCA to give EPA greater power to ensure "the safety of chemicals in our products, our

---

10. Statement of Stephen L. Johnson, Nominee for Assistant Administrator, Office of Prevention, Pesticides, and Toxic Substances, EPA, before the Committee on Environment and Public Works, U.S. Senate (May 17, 2001), *available at* http://epw.senate.gov/107th/joh_0517.htm.
11. *See* Chapter 10, Voluntary Initiatives.
12. Lisa P. Jackson, Administrator, EPA, Remarks to the Commonwealth Club of San Francisco (Sept. 29, 2009) [hereinafter Jackson Remarks], *available at* http://yosemite.epa.gov/opa/admpress.nsf/8d49f7ad4bbcf4ef852573590040b7f6/fc4e2a8c05343b328525764000 7081c5!OpenDocument.

environment and our bodies."[13] She has noted that EPA has the burden of proving that it has adequate data before it can restrict the use of a chemical, while industry is not obligated to develop any new test data showing safety of a chemical before that chemical is introduced into the market.[14] The principles she listed for TSCA reform include

- reviewing all chemicals, and not just chemicals going through the premanufacture notification process, against risk-based standards;
- putting the onus on manufacturers to develop data to show that new and existing chemicals are safe;
- risk-based management of chemicals that includes consideration of (i) vulnerable populations such as children, (ii) costs, and (iii) whether substitute chemicals are available;
- clear grant of authority to the EPA to review and restrict chemicals;
- green chemistry innovation, and greater public access to risk data including restricting claims of confidentiality; and
- ensuring that industry contributes financially to the costs of implementing the foregoing principles.[15]

These principles would move the United States towards incorporating the precautionary principle, which holds that as a matter of policy, the lack of sufficient information to draw safety conclusions does not justify regulatory inaction. TSCA does not embody the precautionary principle because it requires substantial information before the EPA can take action to mitigate a risk. In contrast, the Canadian Environmental Protection Act incorporates the precautionary principle. It says: "Where there are threats of serious and irreversible damage, lack of full scientific certainty shall not be used as a reason for postponing cost-effective measures to prevent environmental degradation." The European Union's recently implemented Registration, Evaluation, Authorisation, and Restrictions of Chemicals (REACH)[16] embodies the precautionary principle by requiring the chemical industry to develop a battery of tests for each chemical.

As shown by Ms. Jackson's statements, the EPA is also seeking to require industry to develop data to demonstrate the safety of a chemical before it is commercialized. Because the existing statute does not support that requirement, legislative reform is necessary if the statute is to incorporate the

---

13. Memorandum from Lisa P. Jackson entitled Seven Priorities for EPA's Future, (Jan. 12, 2010), *available at* http://blog.epa.gov/administrator/2010/01/12/seven-priorities-for-epas-future/.
14. Jackson Remarks.
15. *Id. See also* Essential Principles for Reform of Chemicals Management Legislation, (Sept. 30, 2009), *available at* http://www.epa.gov/oppt/existingchemicals/pubs/principles.pdf.
16. Parliament and Council Regulation (EC) No. 1907/2006 (Corrigendum 29 May 2007) and Directive 2006/121/EC (Corrigendum 29 May 2007) as amended.

precautionary principle. Such statutory changes are likely to focus on making test rules under TSCA § 4 easier to promulgate, ending the grandfathering of existing chemicals under TSCA § 5, requiring manufacturers and importers to develop test data before submitting premanufacture notifications under TSCA § 5, and enhancing the EPA's authority to ban or restrict chemicals under TSCA § 6.[17] The reporting and recordkeeping requirements of TSCA § 8 and the import and export requirements in TSCA §§ 12 and 13 have not been specifically mentioned as in need of change.

The experience with REACH has shown that there are substantial costs involved in implementing a program that embodies the precautionary principle. In the current economic climate it is likely that legislators will strive to balance the demands for TSCA reform against the demands from industry to keep the chemical industry viable.

The history of the Kid-Safe Chemicals Act[18] is instructive in demonstrating that even relatively uncontroversial laws may not be readily enacted. This proposed legislation, which has garnered broad support among legislators, has not been enacted as of this writing. Its elements are very similar to the TSCA reform principles set out by Ms. Jackson, in that:

- chemical companies must demonstrate the safety of their products;
- EPA would have authority to restrict the use of industrial chemicals found in human placentas;
- EPA would have broad power to require chemical testing;
- the Center for Disease Control and Prevention would conduct further analyses of pollutants;
- the public would have greater access to data; and
- there would be new funding and incentives for green chemistry.[19]

Different stakeholder groups are aligning themselves for a lively debate over the future of TSCA reform.[20] Congress has held hearings to focus the legislative issues,[21] and while it is premature to predict any outcome it is clear

17. *See, e.g.*, United States Government Accountability Office, Chemical Regulation, Options for Enhancing the Effectiveness of the Toxic Substances Control Act, Testimony Before the Subcommittee on Commerce, Trade, and Consumer Protection, Committee on Energy and Commerce, House of Representatives, GAO-09-428T (Feb. 26, 2009), *available at* http://www.gao.gov/new.items/d09428t.pdf.
18. Kid-Safe Chemicals Act of 2008, H.R. 6100, S. 3040, 110th Congress.
19. Press Release of Senator Lautenberg. May (May 20, 2008), *available at* http://lautenberg.senate.gov/newsroom/record.cfm?id=298072.
20. Entering "TSCA reform" into any search engine brings numerous policy statements from environmental and industry advocates, as well as the EPA. Debate over TSCA reform has proceeded for many years, with no action as of yet on the horizon.
21. The House Energy and Commerce Committee's Subcommittee on Commerce, Trade and Consumer Protection held hearings on February 26, 2009 and November 17, 2009, and the

that the discussions will reach fundamental questions of how Americans balance competing values.

IV. How to Use this Book and Accompanying CD

TSCA's scope makes compliance a daunting challenge. In the last nine years, EPA brought an average of 198 enforcement actions each year, or more than one every other day.[22] As these statistics indicate, companies both big and small continue to struggle in creating effective compliance solutions. The increasing speed and competitiveness of the current business climate add yet another hurdle for compliance managers.

In addition to providing a short history and summary of the requirements of the law, based on the statute, regulations, and other source materials, such as EPA guidances, this book has on the accompanying CD a broad array of resource materials and references to other supporting source materials. Chapter 20, Practice Tools, has a list of resources for each of Chapters 2 through 19 that lists the pertinent references and source materials on the CD. The CD contains numerous Federal Register notices, EPA memoranda, guidances, and enforcement policies. The version of this list of resources that is on the CD has hyperlinks to the original sources on the CD and the Internet. This list of resources is intended to be the starting point for further research to answer specific practice questions.

The CD, as well as the text of this book, has been updated to reflect developments through mid-January 2010.

Chapter 20 also provides ISO[23] format compliance procedures and checklists that can be adapted by companies to introduce or upgrade their compliance mechanisms, as well as slides for a TSCA compliance training program that can be similarly adapted. The procedures, checklists, and slides are on the CD and can be accessed by clicking on the hyperlinks on the list of resources on the CD.

All of the materials on the CD can also be accessed using Microsoft Windows Explorer, or other file management software that will show the contents of the CD.

This book's bias is that the only sustainable manner in which to ensure compliance with TSCA is to have an integrated approach, where TSCA requirements are engineered into every business activity to which those

---

Senate Committee on Environment and Public Works, Subcommittee on Superfund, Toxics and Environmental Health held hearings on December 2, 2009.

22. *See* Chapter 14, Penalties and Enforcement, Table 1.

23. ISO is the International Organization for Standardization. *See* Chapter 13, Compliance Programs.

requirements pertain. Much lip service has been paid to the concept of integrating environment, health, and safety into business activities. But many such allegedly integrated programs tend to fall short of the mark, focusing primarily on policy statements from management, generic legal training, and audits, instead of on achieving a truly unified approach. The goal is to help meet compliance objectives by offering, in this text, strategies, training materials, and procedures designed to move organizations toward effective compliance management.

CHAPTER 2

TSCA's Scope

I. Chemical Substances Subject to TSCA

Under the authority of the Toxic Substances Control Act (TSCA),[1] the United States Environmental Protection Agency (EPA) regulates the activities of many people and companies when they handle chemicals in certain ways. Under the most frequently invoked sections of TSCA, the EPA can require:

- manufacturers and processors to test chemical substances and mixtures, under TSCA § 4;
- manufacturers to file detailed forms called premanufacture notifications before they make chemical substances that are not on a list that the EPA maintains called the TSCA Inventory (the Inventory), under TSCA § 5;
- manufacturers and processors to file detailed forms called significant new use notices before they make or process a chemical for a "significant new use," under TSCA § 5;
- manufacturers, processors, or persons who distribute a chemical substance or mixture in commerce, to stop manufacturing, processing, or distributing that substance or mixture in commerce, or limit their activities, under TSCA § 6;
- manufacturers, processors, or distributors in commerce of a chemical substance or mixture to maintain records of significant adverse reactions, under TSCA § 8(c); and
- manufacturers, processors or distributors in commerce of a chemical substance to report substantial risk information to the EPA, under TSCA § 8(e).

A clear understanding of each of the terms used in the statute is necessary to understand each of these grants of statutory authority to the EPA.

A. Commercial Chemicals

TSCA has regulations concerning virtually all industrial chemicals and many chemicals that are not typically thought of as industrial chemicals, ranging from bulk commodity chemicals and PCBs[2] to writing ink. Its provisions regulate "chemical substances" and "mixtures," and both of these are defined terms that circumscribe the scope of TSCA and its regulations.

"Chemical substance" is defined in § 3(2) of the statute to include "any organic or inorganic substance of a particular molecular identity," including

---

1. 15 U.S.C. §§ 2601–2695d.
2. Polychlorinated biphenyls; *see* Chapter 11, Bans and Restrictions.

combinations that are either the result of chemical reactions or found in nature, elements, and uncombined radicals.

The EPA has interpreted this as broadly as the statute permits to include much more than the traditional smokestack chemicals in the scope of "chemical substance." Microbes and microorganisms are also considered chemical substances[3] unless they are exempt from the statutory definition because they are used only as foods, food additives, drugs, cosmetics, medical devices, or pesticides. Although most microbes and microorganisms are subject to TSCA, the only ones that the EPA has chosen to regulate under TSCA are certain intergeneric microorganisms, which are microorganisms formed by combining genetic material isolated from different genera. All non-intergeneric microorganisms are considered to be on the Inventory.[4]

Similarly, plants and animals are chemical substances subject to TSCA[5] unless they are exempt because they are used only as foods, food additives, drugs, cosmetics, medical devices, or pesticides. The EPA has specifically said it reserves the discretion to screen transgenic plants and animals under TSCA.[6] As of December of 2009 the EPA was considering whether it should regulate transgenic plants and animals.[7]

If all microorganisms and all plants and animals that are used for a TSCA-covered purpose are "chemical substances" then the EPA arguably does not have the authority to decline to regulate them without exempting them under TSCA § 5(h). In a parallel situation, the EPA declined to regulate carbon dioxide as a pollutant under the Clean Air Act.[8] The United States Supreme Court held in *Massachusetts v. EPA*[9] that the EPA did not have the discretion to fail to regulate a substance if the statutory language requires regulation. Here, there is a clear statutory mechanism for exempting classes of substances from TSCA, and that appears to be the only mechanism for declining to regulate covered chemical substances. Therefore, the EPA could be challenged for its position that it has the authority to regulate plants and animals used for TSCA purposes, but chooses not to do so.

---

3. 43 Fed. Reg. 64572, 64584–85, comment 30 (Dec. 23, 1977).
4. EPA's Draft Questions & Answers for the New Chemicals Program, 1-61, question 122-1 (undated), [hereinafter Draft PMN Q&A] *available at* http://www.epa.gov/oppt/newchems/pubs/qanda-newchems.pdf.
5. *Id.* at 1-61, question 122-2.
6. *Id.*
7. Regulatory Plan and Semiannual Regulatory Agenda, EPA-230-Z-09-002, 111-112 (Fall 2009), [hereinafter Fall 2009 Regulatory Agenda], *available at* http://www.epa.gov/lawsregs/documents/regagendabook-fall09.pdf.
8. 42 U.S.C. §§ 7401–7671.
9. 549 U.S. 497 (2007).

The definition of "chemical substance" excludes:

- mixtures, although the components of a mixture are chemical substances;
- pesticides "when manufactured, processed, or distributed in commerce for use as a pesticide";
- tobacco and tobacco products;
- source material, special nuclear material or byproduct material as defined in the Atomic Energy Act of 1954;[10]
- firearms, shells and cartridges; and
- "any food, food additive, drug, cosmetic, or device" as defined in § 201 of the Federal Food, Drug and Cosmetic Act (FFDCA),[11] "when manufactured, processed, or distributed in commerce for use as a food, food additive, drug, cosmetic or device."[12]

Each of these exclusions is discussed below.

In addition to the substances that are defined to be outside of the scope of TSCA because they are not "chemical substances," there are many chemicals that are within the scope of TSCA, but exempt from some of the regulatory programs. These exemptions cause significant confusion in the regulated community. It is important to keep in mind that many chemical substances that are exempt from one or more TSCA program are still "chemical substances" and are still subject to all of the TSCA programs that do not explicitly exempt them. The list of chemical substances that are exempt from some TSCA programs but are subject to others includes impurities, byproducts, isolated intermediates, chemicals made or imported for import only, and research and development chemicals.

B. Impurities

Impurities are chemical substances, but they are not required to be listed on the Inventory.[13] Impurities are subject to reporting under § 8, and may be regulated under other sections of TSCA, including § 4 test rules.

The definition of impurity provides:

> "Impurity" means a chemical substance which is unintentionally present with another chemical substance.[14]

---

10. 42 U.S.C. §§ 2011–2297.
11. 21 U.S.C. §§ 301–399.
12. TSCA § 3(2); 15 U.S.C § 2602(2).
13. 40 C.F.R. § 710.4(d)(i).
14. 40 C.F.R. §§ 710.2(m) and 720.3(m).

There is no concentration limit or percentage limit for determining what substances can be impurities. Therefore, an impurity may constitute the majority of a reaction product, for example.

Impurities are exempt from the premanufacture notification regulations. The regulations say that impurities are "not manufactured or processed for distribution in commerce as chemical substances per se."[15] This means that the impurities are essentially hitchhikers that travel along with the chemical substance that is intentionally present. This definition leaves open substantial questions about what is intentionally present. For example, if an unpurified product functions for its purpose, but the purified product does not, then the impurities are necessary for the success of the product and can not be considered "unintentionally present." The EPA has taken the position in a Q&A document that "if an 'impurity' enhances the product or is manufactured itself for a commercial purpose, it would no longer be viewed as an impurity."[16] Similarly, if a company learns that something it had thought was an impurity in fact has some commercial value, then that substance must be put on the Inventory.[17] This presents a possible trap for even the most conscientious company. Often a chemist will assume that a minor constituent in a product is an impurity, but on occasion he or she will later learn that the product does not function without the minor constituent. At that point, the product cannot be manufactured, distributed or used unless the minor constituent is on the Inventory.[18]

The EPA said in a Q&A document that a substance which imparts the same function as the desired chemical, but is not intentionally made, is not an impurity.

C. Byproducts

Byproducts that are not used for commercial purposes do not need to be listed on the Inventory[19] and consequently are not subject to premanufacture notification requirements,[20] although they are chemical substances and are subject to other TSCA provisions. Byproduct is defined in the Inventory rules as:

> A chemical substance produced without separate commercial intent during the manufacture or processing of another chemical substance(s) or mixture(s).[21]

---

15. 40 C.F.R. §§ 710.4(d) and 720.30(h)(1).
16. TSCA Questions and Answers from the October, 1990 EPA-Industry Living with TSCA Workshop, question 5 (Oct. 1992) [hereinafter Living with TSCA Q&A].
17. *See* Draft PMN Q&A, 2-1, question 201-2. The Draft PMN Q&A has been in draft form since at least 1995, and has not been issued as formal guidance.
18. Living With TSCA Q&A, question 3. *See* Chapter 3, The Inventory.
19. 40 C.F.R. § 710.4(d)(ii). Byproducts are also considered not to be manufactured or processed for distribution in commerce "as chemical substances per se." 40 C.F.R. § 710.4(d).
20. Draft PMN Q&A, 2-6, question 204-1.
21. 40 C.F.R. § 710.3(d).

It is defined virtually identically in the premanufacture notification rules as:

> a chemical substance produced without a separate commercial intent during the manufacture, processing, use, or disposal of another chemical substance or mixture.[22]

If a byproduct has commercial value only to public or private organizations that burn it for fuel, dispose of it as waste (including landfilling and soil enrichment), use it as fertilizer, or extract valuable components from it, then it may be listed on the Inventory, although it is exempt.[23] The component extracted from the byproduct must be on the Inventory and the person who extracts it is defined as the "manufacturer" of the component.[24]

A byproduct is distinguished from an intermediate, as the EPA said:

> A byproduct may be formed and then consumed in whole or in part during the reaction sequence but is not an 'intermediate' unless it is consumed in whole or in part in chemical reactions used for the *intentional* manufacture of other chemical substances or is intended to alter the rate of such reactions.[25]

D. Isolated Intermediates

An intermediate that is "nonisolated" does not need to be on the TSCA Inventory, and is exempt from the premanufacture notification requirements.[26] It is still a chemical substance, and is subject to other TSCA regulations.

A nonisolated intermediate is any intermediate that is manufactured and consumed without intentional removal from enclosed equipment in which it is manufactured. This is confusing terminology, and it may help to think of a nonisolated intermediate as one that is not removed, or isolated, from the reaction process.

EPA has a classic example of what it means by nonisolated and isolated. In an undated letter from the former Office of Toxic Substances, the EPA explained:[27]

> Reactants A and B are charged to a reaction vessel to form a chemical substance X. Then C is added to react with X to form another substance Y which is then

---

22. 40 C.F.R. § 720.3(d).
23. *Id. See also* 42 Fed. Reg. 64572, 64587, comment 54 (Dec. 23, 1977).
24. 40 C.F.R. § 720.3(t); Draft PMN Q&A, 2-6, question 204-1.
25. 42 Fed. Reg. 64572, comment 68 (Dec. 23, 1977).
26. 40 C.F.R. §§ 710.4(d)(8) and 720.30(h)(8).
27. Letter from Edwin F. Tinsworth, Acting Director of Office of Toxic Substances, EPA to Geraldine V. Cox, captioned Nonisolated Intermediate Definition (undated) [hereinafter Tinsworth Letter]; *see also* Draft PMN Q&A, 2-4, question 203-2.

> drummed for shipment. In this example X is considered to be nonisolated since it is not intentionally removed from the process equipment of manufacture. Y will be considered to be isolated since it is intentionally removed by drumming for transport.

An intermediate is isolated if it is stored in a reaction vessel after manufacture. What constitutes storage depends on the manufacturer, processor, or distributor's intent, and not on the length of the storage time. If an intermediate is held in a piece of equipment during a continuous flow process to react or purify it or otherwise change its characteristics, that is generally not considered to be storage.[28]

It is important to note that any intermediate formed or flowed through an open reaction vessel is an isolated intermediate. The EPA has prepared draft guidance which illustrates this principle:

> Reaction in one vessel with Purification in Another and Transfer to a Second Vessel: The reaction is carried out in one enclosed reactor and the reaction mixture is then pumped through an enclosed drum filter to another vessel for the next reaction step. The reaction intermediate is considered to be nonisolated since there is no intentional removal and all transfer is mechanical and through closed equipment. However, if the filtration is not closed or if the transfer is manual (for example, involving the removal of the intermediate as a filter cake), then the intermediate would be considered to be isolated since the transfer would not be through closed equipment.[29]

A quality control sample that is removed from a nonisolated process is not considered to be isolated, and does not have to be on the Inventory.[30] An otherwise nonisolated catalyst or other intermediate that is drummed out once a year for routine equipment maintenance and then returned to the reaction process is not considered isolated.[31]

Catalysts are defined to be intermediates, and a nonisolated catalyst is exempt from Inventory listing.[32] The EPA confirmed this when it explained the differences between intermediates and byproducts:

> [T]he intermediate is consumed, in whole or in part, in a chemical reaction used for the intentional manufacture of other chemical substances, or is intentionally present for the purpose of altering the rate of such reactions(s).

---

28. *See* Draft PMN Q&A, 2-4, question 203-2.
29. *Id.* at 2-4 to 2-5. *See also* Tinsworth Letter.
30. *See* Draft PMN Q&A, 2-5 to 2-6, question 203-4. *See also* 42 Fed. Reg. 64572, 64589, comment 70 (Dec. 23, 1977).
31. *See* Draft PMN Q&A, 2-4 to 2-5, question 203-2.
32. 40 C.F.R. § 710.2(n); *see also* 42 Fed. Reg. 64572, comment 68 (Dec. 23, 1977).

> A byproduct may be formed and then consumed in whole or in part during the reaction sequence but is not an 'intermediate' unless it is consumed in whole or in part in chemical reactions used for the *intentional* manufacture of other chemical substances or is intended to alter the rate of such reactions.[33]

It is important to consider whether a substance is a byproduct or an intermediate, because byproducts do not need to be on the Inventory even if they are isolated, while intermediates must be on the Inventory if they are isolated.

At times, intermediates may be impurities. As the EPA stated:

> While intermediates often appear as trace impurities in a final product, they are in general distinguished from impurities in that they serve an intentional purpose in a reaction sequence.[34]

This is an extremely loose use of the term "impurity" because impurities are not subject to premanufacture notice requirements, yet the EPA said that an intermediate that is not fully consumed in the reaction process may be an impurity and must be listed on the Inventory:

> The Administrator does not agree that the term "intermediate" should be restricted to chemical substances that are totally consumed in chemical reaction processes. A chemical substance may be an intermediate and also appear later as a byproduct or as an impurity. In such circumstances, the substance should be reported for the inventory.[35]

If such a substance were an impurity or byproduct as defined in TSCA it would not need to be on the Inventory. Therefore, there are only two possible logical readings of this comment; first if a substance meets the definition of intermediate, but is not fully consumed in the reaction process, it cannot be either an impurity or a byproduct and must be on the Inventory, or second, the comment is simply misleading. Because there is no *de minimis* threshold for chemical substances that must be listed on the Inventory, the first interpretation would lead to a requirement to list every intermediate on the Inventory if so much as one molecule survives unreacted in the final product.

---

33. 42 Fed. Reg. 64572, comment 68 (Dec. 23, 1977). This leaves open many questions of interpretation. For example, if there are two alternative reaction routes, are the chemicals formed during one route intermediates and are the others byproducts?
34. *Id.*
35. 42 Fed. Reg. 64572, comment 68 (Dec. 23, 1977).

E. Chemicals Manufactured for Export Only

The TSCA statute has an exemption from many of the TSCA requirements for substances that are manufactured, imported,[36] processed, or distributed solely for export from the United States. The statutory language is tucked away in § 12(a), which otherwise deals with export notifications.[37] This exemption does not apply if the EPA has found that the substance "will present an unreasonable risk of injury to health within the United States or to the environment of the United States."[38] In other words, if there is a rule under TSCA § 6 then the substance is not exempt from any TSCA provisions.

A product for export only must be labeled or stamped to show that it is intended for export to qualify for this exemption. The statute goes on to state that the EPA may require testing under TSCA § 4 of a chemical manufactured solely for export.

Another source of the partial TSCA exemption for chemicals for export only is the Premanufacture Notification (PMN) regulations. The preamble to the original PMN regulations confirms that "EPA did not adopt the proposed requirement that manufacturers of new chemicals solely for export submit notices under section 5(a) of the Act."[39]

The premanufacture notice regulations are in 40 C.F.R. § 720.30, which states in part:

> The following substances are not subject to the notification requirements of this part:
>
> * * *

---

36. Substances imported for export only are also exempt from PMN requirements because the word "manufacture" is defined to include importation. TSCA § 3(7).
37. TSCA § 12(a) provides in pertinent part:

> Except as provided in paragraph (2) and subsection (b) of this section, this chapter (other than section 2607 [§ 8] of this title) shall not apply to any chemical substance, mixture, or to an article containing a chemical substance or mixture, if—
>
> (A) it can be shown that such substance, mixture, or article is being manufactured, processed, or distributed in commerce for export from the United States, unless such substance, mixture, or article was, in fact, manufactured, processed, or distributed in commerce, for use in the United States, and
> (B) such substance, mixture, or article (when distributed in commerce), or any container in which it is enclosed (when so distributed), bears a stamp or label stating that such substance, mixture, or article is intended for export.

38. TSCA § 12(a)(2).
39. 48 Fed. Reg. 21726 (May 13, 1983). It is clear that the EPA had a statutory prohibition against requiring premanufacture notices for substances manufactured solely for export.

> (e) Any new chemical substance manufactured solely for export if, when the substance is distributed in commerce:
> (1) The substance is labeled in accordance with section 12(a)(1)(B) of the Act.
> (2) The manufacturer knows that the person to whom the substance is being distributed intends to export it or process it solely for export as defined in § 721.3 of this chapter.

The definitions in § 720.3 reiterate the criteria for qualifying as solely for export, and clarify that a substance can be manufactured for export, then distributed and further processed before it is exported:[40]

> Manufacture solely for export means to manufacture or import for commercial purposes a chemical substance solely for export from the Untied States under the following restrictions on activities in the United States:
>
> (1) Distribution in commerce is limited to purposes of export or processing solely for export as defined in § 721.3 of this chapter.
> (2) The manufacturer or importer, and any person to whom the substance is distributed for purposes of export or processing solely for export (as defined in § 721.3 of this chapter), may not use the substance except in small quantities solely for research and development in accordance with § 720.36.

Section 721.3 adds that processing solely for export is limited to processing "at sites under the control of the processor."[41] Therefore, the processor should be cautious about using a toller to perform processing steps.[42]

---

40. *See also* 51 Fed. Reg. 15096, 15100 (Apr. 22, 1983).
41. 40 C.F.R. § 721.3 provides in pertinent part:

> *Process solely for export* means to process for commercial purposes solely for export from the United States under the following restrictions on activity in the United States: Processing must be performed at sites under the control of the processor; distribution in commerce is limited to purposes of export; and the processor may not use the chemical substance except in small quantities solely for research and development.

See also 48 Fed. Reg. 21722, 21726 (May 13, 1983).

42. The regulatory history is quite difficult to follow on this point. The preamble to the final rule promulgating § 720.3 in its current form states that the rule "modifies the definition of "manufacture *solely* for export" to include processing which is not under the direct control of a manufacturer or importer, as long as it occurs solely for export. . . . However, the manufacturer must know, by means of a contract or some other evidence, that the processing is occurring for export only." 51 Fed. Reg. 15096, 15100 (Apr. 22, 1986). That same Federal Register notice changed § 720.30 to require that a manufacturer know that a person to whom the substance is distributed intends to export it or process it solely for export. Therefore, tolling is permissible provided that the manufacturer has proof that the toller will only export the substance or process it for export.

Further confirmation that a substance that was manufactured for export only can be processed before exportation without requiring a premanufacture notification came from EPA's response at an October, 1992 Living With TSCA Workshop. EPA was asked: "Can a U.S. company import a non-inventory substance, relabel it or process it, and then export it? Is any Section 5, 12, or 13 [sic] applicable?" The EPA responded:

> Section 12(a) of TSCA exempts from PMN new chemical substances which are manufactured or processed solely for export and which will not be used in the U.S. . . . For substances to qualify as export-only chemicals, their processing must also be limited to activities which do not involve use.
>
> Therefore, a substance that will be relabeled or processed and will not be used in the United States may be imported "solely for export".
>
> Section 12 (export notification) and § 13 (import certification) rules are applicable. . . .

Substances manufactured, processed or distributed for export only are subject to all of the requirements of § 8, including the reporting requirements of § 8(e). The export rules promulgated pursuant to TSCA § 12 must generally be followed.[43]

In the Q&A, the EPA asserts that substances that are imported for export only are subject to the rules under §13, which require import certifications. The statutory provision states that substances imported for export are subject only to the requirements of §§ 4 and 8. It is apparent that the EPA does not have authority to require import certifications under § 13. However, it seems prudent to comply with the import requirements of § 13, although there are persuasive arguments that these requirements cannot be enforced.

A substance that is not on the TSCA Inventory and is manufactured, imported, processed, or distributed for export only may be used for research and development purposes without filing a PMN, provided that the requirements for that exemption from the PMN requirements are met.[44]

A substance may be processed for export only, but cannot be *used* and then exported. EPA guidance states that a chemical that is a reactant in the

---

43. The statute states that § 12 applies if the substance presents an unreasonable risk. Export notification requirements are triggered by a finding of unreasonable risk under § 6, and also by a test rule under § 4 or a consent order under § 5. Neither a test rule under § 4 nor a consent order under § 5 constitutes a finding of unreasonable risk. Therefore, would be statutory defenses to an EPA enforcement based on failure to submit export notifications for substances for export only if the requirement for submitting an export notification were triggered by a test rule under § 4 or a consent order under § 5.
44. *See* Chapter 5, PMN Exclusions and Exemptions.

manufacture of another chemical is used, and therefore a substance for export only cannot be reacted unless it is listed on the Inventory.[45]

F. Research & Development Chemicals

Chemicals used for research and development (R&D) are within TSCA's scope, although they are exempted from several of the TSCA programs. Unless an exclusion or exemption applies, they are subject to the recordkeeping rules applicable to allegations of adverse reactions under TSCA § 8(c) and the reporting rules governing substantial risk information under TSCA § 8(e).[46] If exacting regulations are complied with, the chemicals may be imported and made without subjecting the manufacturer or importer to the premanufacture notice requirements and requirements concerning Significant New Uses.[47]

G. Nanomaterials

Chemicals are not exempt from regulation under TSCA simply because they are manufactured as nanoscale materials. However, nanomaterials have been the focus of considerable recent debate about whether they are already on the TSCA Inventory if the chemical substances they are made of are on the Inventory.

Nanotechnology is the relatively new science of manipulating very small molecules, particles, and structures that have at least one dimension that is no more than one hundred nanometers. A nanometer is 1×10^{-9} meter, which is one billionth or 1/1,000,000,000 of a meter, and particles that are on this scale are often called nanomaterials, nanoscale materials, or nanoparticles. As an example of how small a nanometer is, a man who is the U.S. average height of five feet nine and one-half inches is 1,760,000,000 nanometers tall.

Nanoscale materials present unique physical and toxicological properties that make them a challenge for the regulatory system under TSCA. They often behave very differently from their bulk counterparts, and have physical and toxicological properties that are not predicted from the properties of their bulk counterparts. Many commentators have advocated for regulating all nanomaterials as new chemical substances because of their unique

---

45. EPA Office of Toxic Substances, 1989 TSCA Industry Seminar Questions & Answers, number 21 (undated); *see also* 51 Fed. Reg. 15096, 15100 (Apr. 22, 1986).
46. *See* Chapter 7, Reporting and Recordkeeping.
47. The R&D exemption from the premanufacture notification rule is addressed in Chapter 5, PMN Exclusions and Exemptions, and the exemption from Significant New Use Rules is addressed in Chapter 12, Significant New Use Rules.

properties. As explained in greater detail below, EPA classification of nanomaterials as new or existing depends solely on the "molecular identity" of the substance, and not on the size of the particles. The molecular identity is determined not only by the structural formula of the chemicals in the nanomaterials, but also the spatial arrangements and the isotopes of the atoms within the molecules.

1. Background on Nanomaterials and Nanotechnology

Nanomaterials and nanotechnology present a challenge to the EPA's ability to regulate the risks of this emerging technology. As with most emerging technologies, a complete understanding of the toxicological risks lags far behind the commercialization of nanomaterials.

At the nanoscale, particles' quantum properties may predominate over the properties that are predicted by classical physical chemistry. For example, titanium dioxide in bulk is an opaque white substance, but when it is made in particles of 15 nanometers or less it is clear. That makes it an ideal component for sunscreens because it absorbs ultraviolet light, and in fact sunscreens with nanoparticles of titanium dioxide can be purchased at most drug stores.[48]

Nanotechnology promises significant advances in fuel cells, environmental remediation, drug delivery systems, energy efficient lighting, and many other fields. Consumer products as diverse as sunscreens, tennis balls, food storage containers, and clothes washing machines contain nanomaterials. The Project on Emerging Nanotechnolgies (PEN) identified 1015 consumer products that contain nanomaterials as of August 2009.[49] Using the PEN database and others, the EPA estimated that there are 91 nanomaterials manufactured for commercial purposes in those products, and a total of 234 nanomaterials that have been made for either commercial or research purposes.[50]

There are naturally occurring nanoparticles in soot and volcanic ash, and nanoparticles have been used since the Middle Ages to color stained glass. When used in products, nanomaterials can be either free or fixed. Free nanomaterials are in solution or suspension, and are in products such as sunscreens and fuels. Fixed nanomaterials are in composites such as resins

48. Sunscreens are regulated under the Federal Food, Drug and Cosmetic Act and not under TSCA.
49. The Project on Emerging Nanotechnologies is a project of the Woodrow Wilson International Center for Scholars. The consumer product inventory is *available at* http://www.nanotechproject.org/inventories/consumer/.
50. Nanoscale Materials Stewardship Program Interim Report, 18 (Jan. 2009), *available at* http://www.epa.gov/oppt/nano/nmsp-interim-report-final.pdf.

and computer chips. There is relatively little exposure to fixed nanomaterials in consumer products.[51]

The toxicity of nanomaterials is not well understood, and many commentators have expressed concern that the unique properties of nanomaterials may be associated with unknown risks. Some of the concern is because of the ability of small particles to penetrate living tissue. There are conflicting study conclusions on whether inhaled nanoparticles may mimic the action of asbestos in the lungs. Some studies conclude that they do cause inflammation because they can reach the lung structures that exchange oxygen and carbon dioxide from the blood. However, other studies conclude that the results are equivocal. Similarly, titanium dioxide nanoparticles have been the subject of several studies to determine whether or not they can penetrate human skin when they are used in sunscreen formulations. While studies have shown that they do not penetrate beyond the outer layer of skin, the studies have been criticized because they were all on intact, unabraded healthy adult skin, and so the risks in actual use may not be the same as indicated by those studies. In addition, many formulations contain moisturizers that are designed to penetrate skin, and the effects of these moisturizers on the skin penetration of titanium dioxide nanoparticles are unknown.[52]

In addition to size, the toxicity of nanomaterials depends on the shape, surface chemistry, surface charge, and chemical composition of the particle, among other characteristics. For example, nanoparticles of cobalt and manganese can enter cells, although salts of cobalt and manganese cannot. These nanoparticles are significantly more toxic than their salt counterparts.[53] There is no scientific consensus about which characteristics are the most important determinants of toxicity.[54]

2. TSCA Status of Nanomaterials

Nanomaterials are subject to all of the TSCA regulatory programs. As a result, substantial risks presented by nanomaterials must be reported to the EPA under TSCA § 8(e) and allegations of significant adverse reactions must be

---

51. Stephen R. Clough, *The Potential Ecological Hazard of Nanomaterials, in* NANOTECHNOLOGY AND THE ENVIRONMENT, 15–16 (Kathleen Sellers et al. eds., 2009).
52. *See, e.g.*, presentation slides by Annette Santamaria "Nanomaterials in Consumer Products Do They Pose a Hazard?" from the International Conference on the Environmental Implications and Applications of Nanotechnology at The Environmental Institute (June 2009) *available at* http://www.umass.edu/tei/conferences/nanoconference/Nano%20Session%20PDF/Santamaria,%20Annette.pdf.
53. Clough, *supra* note 51.
54. J. Clarence Davies, Oversight of Next Generation Nanotechnology, Project on Emerging Technologies, 17 (Apr. 2009), *available at* http://www.nanotechproject.org/process/assets/files/7316/pen-18.pdf.

recorded under TSCA § 8(c).[55] The chemical substances in nanomaterials are subject to import certifications under TSCA § 13 and export notifications under TSCA § 12.[56] These examples are not exclusive; manufacturers, importers and processors of nanomaterials are subject to all of the TSCA regulations without any special consideration given to the size of the particles or the minute quantities in which they are often used.

The EPA has a variety of mechanisms to address any risks posed by nanomaterials, although it has not used them aggressively until recently. It has the statutory authority to issue test rules under TSCA § 4[57] and orders under §§ 5(e) and (f),[58] § 6[59] and § 7.[60] EPA announced it is considering issuing test rules on multiwalled carbon nanotubes and nanosized clay and alumina to determine their health effects.[61] EPA has entered into at least five § 5(e) consent orders on nanoparticles.[62] Each of these consent orders requires the company that submitted a PMN on a nanomaterial to perform a 90-day inhalation toxicity study within a specified time of commencing commercial production or reaching a manufacturing or importation threshold, and to provide workers with respirators and gloves that are impervious to nanoparticles, among other requirements.[63] These consent orders appear to follow a generic format that could be made applicable to all nanomaterials that go through the PMN process, and it is likely that a significant proportion of PMNs on nanomaterials will result in § 5(e) orders.

EPA has also issued Significant New Use Rules (SNURs) under TSCA § 5,[64] covering at least four different nanoparticles, two of which were the subject of the § 5(e) consent orders discussed above.[65] In all of the SNURs

---

55. 15 U.S.C. § 2607(e) and (c); *see* Chapter 7, Reporting and Recordkeeping. Reports of significant adverse reactions to nanomaterials have been submitted to the EPA, and are *available at* http://epa.gov/oppt/tsca8e/.
56. 15 U.S.C §§ 2612 and 2611; *see* Chapter 8, Exports and Imports.
57. 15 U.S.C. § 2603; *see* Chapter 9, Test Rules.
58. 15 U.S.C. § 2604(e) and (f), *see* Chapter 4, Premanufacture Notifications.
59. 15 U.S.C. § 2605, *see* Chapter 11, Bans and Restrictions.
60. 15 U.S.C. § 2606, *see* Chapter 14, Penalties and Enforcement.
61. Fall 2009 Regulatory Agenda, 97-98.
62. EPA Response to Freedom of Information Act request RIN-01494-09 (Dec. 12, 2009).
63. These consent orders are for: a multiwalled carbon nanotube that was the subject of PMN number P-08-0177; a single walled carbon nanotube that was the subject of PMN number P-08-0328; a multiwalled carbon nanotube that was the subject of PMN number P-08-0392; two multiwalled carbon nanotubes that were the subject of PMN numbers P-08-0733 and P-08-0734; and a multiwalled carbon nanotube that was the subject of PMN number P-09-0257.
64. 15 U.S.C. § 2604, *see* Chapter 12, Significant New Use Rules.
65. 74 Fed. Reg. 29982, 29991 (June 24, 2009) (covering the multiwalled carbon nanotube that was the subject of PMN number P-08-177 and the single walled nanotube that was the subject of PMN P-08-328) and 73 Fed. Reg. 65743, 65751-2 (Nov. 5, 2008) (covering a siloxane modified silica nanoparticle and a siloxane modified alumina nanoparticle).

that reference the nanoscale of the subject chemical substance, the EPA stated that it based its concern on "test data on analogous respirable, poorly soluble particulates" and that "[b]ased on physical properties" EPA believes the nanomaterials may cause health effects via dermal exposure. Any person who intends to use the nanomaterials that are subject to the SNURs without a specified respirator or without specified personal protective equipment must submit a Significant New Use Notice (SNUN) to the EPA. The EPA's focus on the nanoscale of the chemical substance, and not the chemical identity of the substance, would seem to indicate that it intends to promulgate SNURs for most new nanomaterials based on particle size alone.

EPA withdrew two of the SNURs[66] because they were issued as direct final rules without following the notice and comment procedure for formal rulemaking, and it received a notice that adverse comments would be submitted,[67] but EPA proposed them again three months later.[68] These two SNURs were for carbon nanotubes. While the carbon nanotube SNURs were in effect, the EPA received questions about whether they applied to all carbon nanotubes, or just the two specific carbon nanotubes that were listed in the SNUR. The EPA issued a clarification confirming that the SNURS, like all SNURS, only relate to the exact chemical substances named in the regulation, and not all nanotubes in general.[69] The EPA reminded companies that any carbon nanotube that is not already on the Inventory must be put on the Inventory through the PMN process. It appears that EPA made this point because SNURs are not issued until a substance is on the Inventory and therefore a manufacturer of a different carbon nanotube that is not on the Inventory would have to comply with the PMN rules.

EPA does not know the exact number and chemical composition of commercially available nanomaterials.[70] It has the authority to gather this information through the reporting requirements of TSCA § 8(a)[71] and has announced its intent to provide a notice of proposed rulemaking for this purpose in 2010.[72]

Where TSCA programs exempt *de minimis* concentrations of chemicals, mixtures with small concentrations of nanomaterials may be below the

---

66. 74 Fed. Reg. 42177 (Aug. 21, 2009).
67. *See* Chapter 12, Significant New Use Rules for a discussion of procedures for the issuance of SNURs.
68. 74 Fed. Reg. 57430 (Nov. 6, 2009).
69. E-mail from David E. Giamporcaro, Industry and Small Business Liaison, EPA to Listserv, Clarification of Applicability of Significant New Use Rules (July 28, 2009).
70. Nanoscale Materials Stewardship Program Interim Report, 18 (Jan. 2009), *available at* http://www.epa.gov/oppt/nano/nmsp-interim-report-final.pdf.
71. *See* Chapter 7, Reporting and Recordkeeping. EPA has issued reporting rules covering specific uses of chemical substances and has the authority under TSCA § 8 to issue rules concerning specific physical forms of chemical substances.
72. Fall 2009 Regulatory Agenda, 98.

de minimis thresholds. For example, nanomaterials are subject to export notification requirements, but when they are present in *de minimis* concentrations in mixtures they will not trigger export notification requirements.[73]

Substances that are excluded from TSCA's scope because they are pesticides or drugs, or because they qualify for any other exclusion, continue to be excluded from TSCA's scope when they are made at the nanoscale. Nanomaterials made for research and development continue to be exempt from the PMN requirements if they otherwise meet the research and development exemption criteria.

The current focus of public debate is whether nanomaterials are existing chemical substances that are already on the TSCA Inventory or whether they are new chemical substances that cannot be manufactured or imported for commercial use without going through the PMN process or qualifying for an exemption or exclusion.[74]

The EPA has issued two guidances describing which nanomaterials are considered new chemical substances and which are considered to be existing chemicals that are already on the TSCA Inventory. It is a pivotal question for the EPA to determine if it can regulate nanomaterials, because if a nanomaterial is considered to be an existing chemical then the EPA does not routinely learn if nanoscale materials are being made or imported into the United States and consequently no information to determine which nanomaterials may pose a regulatory concern.

The first guidance is entitled TSCA Inventory Status of Nanoscale Substances—General Approach (Inventory Status of Nanoscale Substances).[75] In that guidance the EPA adopted the position that a nanomaterial that has the same "molecular identity" as a substance on the Inventory is an existing chemical substance and does not need to be put on the Inventory through the PMN process.

The EPA was constrained by the statutory language of TSCA § 3(2), which says: "the term 'chemical substance' means any organic or inorganic substance of a particular molecular identity."[76] The EPA went on to say in the Inventory Status of Nanoscale Substances guidance that:

> EPA views molecular identity as being based on such structural and compositional features as the types and number of atoms in the molecule, the types and number of chemical bonds, the connectivity of the atoms in the molecule, and the spatial arrangement of the atoms within the molecule. EPA considers

---

73. *See* Chapter 8, Exports and Imports.
74. *See* Chapter 5, PMN Exclusions and Exemptions.
75. TSCA Inventory Status of Nanoscale Substances—General Approach, (Jan. 23, 2008) [hereinafter Inventory Status of Nanoscale Substances] *available at* http://www.epa.gov/oppt/nano/nmsp-inventorypaper2008.pdf. EPA circulated earlier versions of this document also.
76. 15 U.S.C. § 2602(2).

chemical substances that differ in any of these structural and compositional features to have different molecular identities.[77]

Applying this principle, in order to have the same molecular identity as a substance on the Inventory the EPA said both substances being compared must:

- have the same molecular formula;
- have the same structural formula, and be the same structural and positional isomer;
- have the same spatial arrangement of atoms; that is, they must both be cis (Z) isomers or trans (E) isomers;
- have the same crystal lattice structure;
- be the same allotrope (crystal structure, usually reserved for use in connection with elements); and
- be composed of the same isotopes.[78]

It is likely that the EPA is overreaching in maintaining that molecules with different isotopes do not have the same molecular identity, although regulated entities would be well advised to comply with the EPA guidances stating that introducing new isotopes changes the molecular identity of a substance. In *In The Matter Of Concord Trading Corporation*, the EPA Office of Administrative Law Judges addressed the question of whether compounds with different isotopes have the same molecular identity.[79] The EPA had issued a complaint against Concord Trading, claiming that Concord Trading had violated the PMN requirements when it did not file a PMN before importing depleted zinc oxide. Depleted zinc oxide is zinc oxide without its naturally occurring range of atomic isotopes; one or more of the isotopes have been removed or depleted, in this case Zn^{64}. Depleted zinc oxide was not listed on the Inventory at the time, although zinc oxide was listed. The tribunal held that the EPA was not entitled to a summary determination that depleted zinc oxide is not on the Inventory because it has different isotopes than non-depleted zinc oxide, which is on the Inventory. Concord Trading had argued that molecular identity for purposes of Inventory listing must be assessed at the molecular level, and not at the subatomic level. The tribunal found that there were issues of fact that were not proven and therefore the EPA was not entitled to an expedited decision. That procedural aspect of the holding by the administrative law judge leaves open the possibility that a

---

77. Inventory Status of Nanoscale Substances, 3.

78. *Id.* at 3–4.

79. In The Matter Of Concord Trading Corporation, Docket No. TSCA-94-H-19 (EPA Office of Administrative Law Judges July 24, 1997).

future tribunal could find that compounds with different isotopes do in fact have different molecular identities.

However, the administrative law judge determined that "[m]ore information is required before the words "molecular identity" can be regarded as adequate to distinguish [depleted zinc oxide] from zinc oxide as a matter of law." If that conclusion is correct then a change in isotopes is not necessarily a change of "molecular identity" and the EPA is incorrect in asserting in the Inventory Status of Nanoscale Substances that a nanomaterial that is composed of a different isotope than a substance on the Inventory is necessarily a new chemical substance. In other words, if a change in isotopes does not result in a new molecular identity as a matter of law, then the *Concord Trading* decision precludes the EPA from taking the position in the Inventory Status of Nanoscale Substances that a change in isotopes always results in a new molecular identity.[80]

EPA has more recently added to the debate about the meaning of *Concord Trading* and whether substituting isotopes changes the molecular identity of a substance. It noted that molecules with different isotopes have different molecular weights and therefore are "different chemical substances for TSCA Inventory listing purposes."[81] That argument supports the conclusion that a change in isotopes is manifested at the molecular level and not just the subatomic level. At this point, even though the EPA has not engaged in any formal rulemaking on isotopes it has publicized its position so often that it would be difficult to argue that there was insufficient notice of the EPA's stance. A cursory review of the Inventory reveals very few chemicals identified as isotopes and it is likely that the regulated community is not in compliance with the EPA's current interpretation.

TSCA does not authorize the EPA to distinguish between chemical substances based on the their particle size, and the EPA states clearly in the Inventory Status of Nanoscale Substances that particle size alone is not a basis for characterizing a substance as a new chemical if either the bulk form or nanoscale form of the chemical is on the Inventory.[82] Therefore, the bulk form of titanium dioxide is on the Inventory and so nanoparticles of titanium dioxide are considered to be on the Inventory. When a nanoscale form of a substance is put on the Inventory, the bulk form is also considered to be on the Inventory.

---

80. "Zinc oxide (ZnO), zinc-64 depleted" is now on the Inventory, through the PMN process. *See* http://iaspub.epa.gov/sor_internet/registry/substreg/searchandretrieve/searchbylist/search.do?synId=836796&displaySynonym=.
81. TSCA Nanoscale Materials Inventory Paper: Public Comments with EPA Responses, 8, EPA-HQ-OPPT-2004-0122-0098 (Dec. 20, 2007), *available at* http://regulations.gov in Docket ID: EPA-HQ-OPPT-2004-0122.
82. Inventory Status of Nanoscale Substances, 4–5.

At the time the Inventory Status of Nanoscale Substances was written, there were no nomenclature conventions for some nanoscale substances, carbon nanotubes in particular. The EPA said it will assist PMN filers in describing their substances until a nomenclature convention is established. It will also respond to letters requesting the Inventory status of chemicals that the submitter has a bona fide intent to make or import, so long as these letters comply with the requirements set out in 40 C.F.R. § 720.25.[83]

The EPA followed up the Inventory Status of Nanoscale Substances with a second guidance, clarifying that each specific type of carbon nanotube must be separately listed on the Inventory.[84] A carbon nanotube is a form of pure carbon in a tube structure. Carbon nanotubes are less than one hundred nanometers in diameter, although they can be longer than one hundred nanometers in length. Nanotubes can be single walled or multi-walled depending on how many concentric tubes there are. While the EPA's position on carbon nanotubes is a corollary of the Inventory Status of Nanoscale Substances, the EPA noted some confusion in the regulated community and reiterated that "[i]f a particular [carbon nanotube] is not on the TSCA Inventory, anyone who intends to manufacture or import that [carbon nanotube] is required to submit a PMN (or applicable exemption) under TSCA § 5 at least ninety days before commencing manufacture."[85]

II. Chemical Substances and Materials Not Subject to TSCA

A. Mixtures

Mixtures are regulated under TSCA, although they are not subject to all of TSCA's requirements. For example, The EPA has authority to require testing of mixtures under § 4 of TSCA, but mixtures are excluded from listing on the TSCA Inventory.[86] The individual components of mixtures must be on the Inventory[87]

83. *Id.* at 6. For a discussion of the requirements for submitting a letter stating a bona fide intent to manufacture or import a substance, *see* Chapter 3, The Inventory.
84. 73 Fed. Reg. 64946 (Oct. 31, 2008).
85. *Id.* at 64947.
86. 40 C.F.R. § 710.4(c)(2); *see also* Toxic Substances Control Act Inventory Representation For Products Containing Two Or More Substances: Formulated And Statutory Mixtures (undated) [hereinafter Formulated and Statutory Mixtures] *available at* http://regulations.gov in docket number EPA-HQ-OPPT-2007-0392.
87. 40 C.F.R. § 710.4.

but the combined formulation of a mixture is exempt from the PMN regulations.[88]

TSCA defines "mixture" to be:

> any combination of two or more chemical substances if the combination does not occur in nature and is not, in whole or in part, the result of a chemical reaction; except that such term does include any combination which occurs, in whole or in part, as a result of a chemical reaction if none of the chemical substances comprising the combination is a new chemical substance and if the combination could have been manufactured for commercial purposes without a chemical reaction at the time the chemical substances comprising the combination were combined.[89]

The Inventory regulations paraphrase the statutory language and add that mixtures include:

> Hydrates of a chemical substance or hydrated ions formed by association of a chemical substance with water.[90]

As a result, hydrates do not need to be on the Inventory, but the nonhydrated form of the substance must be on it.[91]

The EPA has issued guidances on chemical nomenclature, commonly called nomenclature papers, that provide additional insight into its interpretation of the term "mixture."[92] These guidances illustrate the EPA's definition of mixtures:

Materials that are mixtures, not "chemical substances" include:

- "A blend of two or more substances that has been physically combined without a chemical reaction."[93]

---

88. Premanufacture notification is required for "chemical substances" 40 C.F.R. § 720.22, and mixtures are excluded from the definition of "chemical substances" 40 C.F.R. § 720.3(e)(1).
89. TSCA § 3(8).
90. 40 C.F.R. §710.2(q).
91. The premanufacture notice requirements also exempt hydrates. 40 C.F.R. § 720.3(u).
92. These are Toxic Substances Control Act Inventory Representation For Products Containing Two Or More Substances: Formulated And Statutory Mixtures; Toxic Substances Control Act Inventory Representation For Combinations of Two Or More Substances: Complex Reaction Products [hereinafter Complex Reaction Products]; and Toxic Substances Control Act Inventory Representation For Chemical Substances Of Unknown Or Variable Composition, Complex Reaction Products And Biological Materials: UVCB Substances [hereinafter UVCB Substances]; Toxic Substances Control Act Inventory Representation For Polymeric Substances; and Toxic Substances Control Act Inventory Representation For Certain Chemical Substances Containing Varying Carbon Chain Lengths (Alkyl Ranges Using The CX-Y Notation).
93. Formulated And Statutory Mixtures, at § III A.

- For example, a blended gasoline to which a non-reactive corrosion inhibitor is added.[94]
- Another example is a formulated fertilizer made by mixing materials.

- Solid solutions.[95] Note however, that if the chemicals form a compound the compound is not a mixture.[96]
- A blend formed by chemical reaction that could have been formed by mixing.
    - For example, the EPA guidance states:

    > Consider a multi-nutrient "mixed fertilizer" that could have been prepared by physically blending dry products such as urea, superphosphate and potash or by chemical reaction when liquid ammonium phosphate was granulated with potash. The Agency considers this "mixed fertilizer" a mixture of urea, superphosphate and potash regardless of the method used to make it.[97]

    - Another similar example from the EPA guidance is:

    > If commercially-available pine oil, a non-ionic surfactant, and sodium soap of coconut oil acids are mixed, without chemical reaction, a combination is produced that is a mixture. Alternatively, if that same combination is prepared by mixing pine oil, the non-ionic surfactant, coconut oil acids and sodium hydroxide, and carrying out the saponification reaction to form the sodium soap of coconut oil acids, the combination would be identical to that manufactured by mixing the first set of substances without chemical reaction. The three substances in the final combination (i.e., pine oil, the surfactant and the sodium salt of coconut oil) constitute a mixture and each one is subject to Inventory reporting, regardless of the method used to manufacture the mixture.[98]

- Some alloys, glasses, ceramics, frits and cements are considered to be mixtures, although they have chemically reacted.[99] The EPA agreed to treat these groups of material differently because of their very complex chemistry. These are considered "statutory mixtures", and are on the Inventory as mixtures although each of their chemical constituents may

---

94. *Id.*
95. *Id.*
96. *Id.* at § III B.
97. *Id.* at § III A; *see also* the final Inventory Reporting Requirements, 42 Fed. Reg. 64572, 64585 comment 32 (Dec. 23, 1977).
98. Formulated And Statutory Mixtures, at § III A.
99. 40 C.F.R. § 710.4(c). Formulated And Statutory Mixtures, at § III B; *see also* the Inventory Reporting Requirements, 42 Fed. Reg. 64572, 64585, comment 33 (Dec. 23, 1977).

not be on the Inventory. These are listed on the Inventory in six categories:

Cement, Portland, Chemicals	[65997-15-1*]
Cement, Alumina, Chemicals	[65997-16-2*]
Glass, Oxide, Chemicals	[65997-17-3*]
Frits, Chemicals	[65997-18-4*]
Steel Manufacture, Chemicals	[65997-19-5*]
Ceramic Materials and Wares, Chemicals	[66402-68-4*]

The Inventory listings provide detailed definitions of each category of statutory mixture. It is important to consult the definitions to determine whether a particular material falls within the category.

Supported catalysts are considered statutory mixtures.[100] Aluminosilicate zeolites are also considered statutory mixtures, and the chemicals comprising the zeolite do not have to be on the Inventory, although the starting materials must be on the Inventory.[101]

- Hydrates of a chemical substance are considered statutory mixtures of the anhydrous chemical and water, except when water or a solvent is a reactant. The anhydrous form must be on the Inventory.[102]
- Complexes formed by hydrogen bonding are mixtures for TSCA purposes, and their components must be on the Inventory.[103]
- Surface treatments that are intended to alter physical properties, but not intended to impart chemical reactivity results in a mixture. In this case, each of the components must be on the Inventory. Surface treatments that are intended to impart reactivity result in new chemical substances and the product must be on the Inventory.
- Mixed salts of monovalent anions formed as a result of a chemical reaction are considered to be mixtures of the individual salts.[104]

Materials that are not mixtures, and are "chemical substances" include:

- A blend of two or more substances that has been physically combined with a chemical reaction that forms salts or ionic bonds.[105]
- "Intermetallic compounds of well-defined stoichiometry."[106]

---

100. Formulated And Statutory Mixtures, at § III B.
101. *Id.*
102. *Id. See also* the Inventory Reporting Requirements, 42 Fed. Reg. 64572, 64585, comment 34 (Dec. 23, 1977).
103. Formulated And Statutory Mixtures, at § III B.
104. Complex Reaction Products, at § II A 4.
105. Formulated And Statutory Mixtures, at § III A.
106. *Id.* at § III B.

- "Substances with Chemical Abstracts (CA) names containing the term 'hydrolyzed' are not hydrates."[107]
- "[M]etal hydroxides formed by reactions of metal oxides with water."[108]
- Surface treatments that are intended to impart reactivity result in new chemical substances and the product must be on the Inventory. Functionalized glasses formed by chemical reactions are not mixtures. However, if a glass with functional groups is coated with a polymer that reacts with the functionalized glass, the functionalized glass-polymer reaction product is a mixture.[109]
- In general, a naturally occurring product is a chemical substance and not a mixture.[110] Naturally occurring products are grandfathered on to the Inventory. 40 C.F.R. § 710.4(b) confirms this when it states:

> Any chemical substance which is naturally occurring and
>
> (1) Which is (i) unprocessed or (ii) processed only by manual, mechanical, or gravitational means; by dissolution in water; by flotation; or by heating solely to remove water; or
>
> (2) Which is extracted from air by any means, shall automatically be included in the Inventory under the category 'Naturally Occurring Substances.' Examples of such substances are: raw agricultural commodities; water, air, natural gas, and crude oil; and rocks, ores, and minerals.

The EPA considers electrostatic separation to be a form of processing analogous to filtration or gravitational separation, and has concluded that naturally occurring substances that are processed by electrostatic separation do not need to be on the Inventory.[111]

As a corollary, if a natural product is processed by any means other than those listed in 40 C.F.R. § 710.4(b), then the result is a chemical substance, and not a mixture. For example, natural latex from trees is a naturally occurring substance. Natural rubber is made from latex by adding chemical coagulants, and because adding coagulants is not one of the types of processing permitted by 40 C.F.R. § 710.4(b), natural rubber is not a natural substance and must be on the Inventory.[112]

---

107. *Id.*
108. *Id.*
109. *Id.* This guidance contains certain exceptions to this general rule.
110. UVCB Substances, § II A.
111. 42 Fed. Reg. 64572, 64586, comment 74 (Dec. 23, 1977).
112. *Id.* at comment 72.

The EPA may be moving away from the position that the constituents of ceramic materials and other statutory mixtures do not need to be on the Inventory. In a 2008 letter from the EPA to the American Chemistry Council, the EPA took the position that chemicals created during the formation of ceramic materials must be listed on the Inventory.113 The EPA gave the specific example of "ceramic-like" materials that are made using "relatively precise stoichiometric and compositional control," and result in products with "definite elemental ratios, and unit cell structure and atomic coordination sites." These "ceramic-like" materials should be given chemical names rather than use the broader term "ceramics."

Whether activated phosphors are mixtures or not is a current debate, and the EPA has published a proposed clarification saying that they are not mixtures and each activated phosphor must be on the Inventory.[114] EPA intended to issue a final rule late in 2009.[115]

Activated phosphors are used in fluorescent lights, older TV screens, and other light sources because they emit light when they are hit with radiation.[116] They are often made of a metal oxide with trace amounts of another substance, or dopant.[117] They appear to exist on the border between solid solutions and unique chemical substances. When the EPA was compiling the initial Inventory, it accepted some submittals for activated phosphors, but rejected others as mixtures that cannot be listed on the Inventory.[118] The EPA also issued informal guidance letters concluding that activated phosphors are solid solutions.[119] However it later concluded that activated phosphors cannot be manufactured without chemical reactions and therefore they are unique substances and are not solid solutions. Furthermore, the EPA pointed out that the ratio of starting materials is closely controlled[120] and that supports the conclusion that activated phosphors are substances with chemical formulas.

The practical effect of EPA changing its understanding of the basic chemistry of activated phosphors could be enormous. Manufacturers and importers

---

113. Letter from Tracy C. Williamson, Ph.D., Chief, Industrial Chemistry Branch, EPA, to Michael P. Walls, American Chemistry Council (May 28, 2008).
114. 73 Fed. Reg. 2854 (Jan. 16, 2008).
115. Fall 2009 Regulatory Agenda, 100.
116. Merriam-Webster online dictionary at http://www.merriam-webster.com/dictionary/phosphor.
117. *See, e.g.*, Rare-earth-activated phosphors U.S. Patent 6,783,855 (filed Sept. 14, 2001) (issued Aug. 31, 2004).
118. 73 Fed. Reg. 2854, 2856 (Jan. 16, 2008).
119. Memorandum from Linda Travers, Director, Information Management Division, EPA to Charles Elkins, Director, Office of Toxic Substances, EPA, TSCA Reportability of Doped Semiconductors (undated); letter from Dr. Vincent DeCarlo EPA to Carmen Venezia of Sylvania (Oct. 12, 1979); letter from Henry Lau, EPA to Robert Kovalak of General Electric (Mar. 5, 1982).
120. 73 Fed. Reg. 2854, 2856–57 (Jan. 16, 2008).

who have been using these substances since the inception of TSCA will have to file PMNs and wait at least ninety days for the EPA to review the PMN before they can continue their past practices if the rule is finalized. In recognition of this problem, the EPA has said it will delay the effective date of any final guidance for one year[121] so that companies can file their PMNs and wait for the ninety day review period to pass before the effective date. Industry has been vocal in saying that this is a policy change that merits more attention than a mere clarification, and has argued that a one year delay of the effective date is insufficient.[122]

B. Pesticides

Pesticides are excluded from TSCA by § 3, which provides in part that the term "chemical substance" does not include:

> any pesticide (as defined in the Federal Insecticide, Fungicide and Rodenticide Act) when manufactured, processed, or distributed in commerce for use as a pesticide.

The Federal Insecticide, Fungicide and Rodenticide Act (FIFRA)[123] definition of "pesticide" hinges on a subjective standard based on intent. It defines "pesticide," and provides in part:

> The term "pesticide" means
>
> (1) any substance or mixture of substances intended for preventing, destroying, repelling, or mitigating any pest . . .[124]

The interplay between TSCA and FIFRA is complex, and is made more complicated by the fact that the TSCA guidance has remained static on this point for twenty-five years, while the FIFRA regulations have steadily evolved.

The TSCA guidance on pesticides appears to be straightforward. To be exempt from TSCA a substance must be manufactured, processed, or distributed in commerce as a pesticide.[125] The EPA stated that substances that

121. *Id.* at 2857.
122. *See, e.g.*, the letter from Kathleen Roberts of the American Chemistry Council to EPA (Mar. 13, 2008); letter from Carmen Venezia to EPA (May 30, 2008), both *available at* http://regulations.gov in docket number EPA-HQ-OPPT-2007-0392.
123. 7 U.S.C. § 136.
124. 7 U.S.C. § 136(u).
125. The EPA gave an example of a substance functioning as a pesticide in its Living with TSCA Q&A at question 1. If a FIFRA registered pesticide is added as a preservative to a formulated

meet this requirement are not subject to TSCA if they are actually manufactured, processed, or distributed as a pesticide. If there are pesticidal uses and non-pesticidal uses, the non-pesticidal uses are subject to TSCA.[126] For example, if a substance that is a registered pesticide is used as a laboratory control sample instead of as a pesticide, then it is subject to TSCA. If a substance is manufactured, processed, or distributed for undifferentiated FIFRA or TSCA uses, then it is presumed to be governed by TSCA.[127]

The EPA takes the position that a substance is subject to TSCA up until the time its manufacturer, processor, or distributor expects it to function as a pesticide. When a substance is first made, it will generally be regulated under TSCA, and it will not enter FIFRA regulation and exit TSCA regulation until the manufacturer, processor, or distributor intends it to function as a pesticide.[128] Determining when the manufacturer, processor, or distributor has enough evidence of its intent is more difficult that it would seem at first. Under FIFRA, a person may apply for an experimental use permit (EUP) to use a substance to gather enough information to register it as a pesticide.[129] Alternatively, the substance can be the subject of an application for registration as a pesticide.[130] Under TSCA, the EPA has stated that filing an EUP or an application for registration is evidence that the substance is a pesticide for FIFRA purposes. Therefore, once an EUP or application for registration is filed, the substance is governed by FIFRA and not TSCA.

Until recently, the EPA consistently took the position that before an EUP or application for registration is filed, the substance is governed by TSCA.[131,132] The EPA has more recently moved away from this position and said that when a substance becomes classified as a pesticide depends on

---

product, it does not need to be on the Inventory because use as a preservative is considered a pesticidal use.

126. Question and Answer Summary EPA Seminar on Industry Obligations under TSCA (June 10, 1986) OTS Existing Chemicals Program, 3 (Jul. 25, 1986) [hereinafter Industry Obligations].

127. 42 Fed. Reg. 64572, 64585, comment 37 (Dec. 23, 1977).

128. *Id.* at comment 38. The EPA noted that the burden of complying with TSCA for a pre-EUP substance may be lessened if the substance falls within the research and development exemption from § 5 premanufacture notification requirements. *See* Chapter 5, PMN Exclusions and Exemptions.

129. FIFRA, 7 U.S.C. § 136c.

130. FIFRA, 7 U.S.C. § 136a.

131. *See*, 42 Fed. Reg. 64572.

132. Note that in the context of FIFRA, the EPA has required prior notice of small-scale testing on some microbial pesticides. 59 Fed. Reg. 45600 (Sept. 1, 1994). This notification is required before an EUP, and the EPA may determine that no EUP is necessary. Because the definition of pesticide is governed by the intent to use the substance as a pesticide, then the microbial pesticide notification should be a sufficient demonstration of intent to use as a pesticide. The EPA has not adopted this position for TSCA purposes. However, there may be good defenses to an enforcement action based on failure to comply with TSCA once a

the intent to use the substance as a pesticide. However, the EPA's departure from the bright line rule that a substance is subject to TSCA until an application is filed is inconsistent with other EPA statements in other program areas, and should only be taken to apply to the PMN rules. In its Questions & Answers for the New Chemicals Program, which is in draft form only, the EPA stated:

> 210-3. Q. How is it determined whether a substance is regulated under FIFRA or TSCA?
> A. If a manufacturer, processor, or distributor of a substance has intent, either by making express or implied pesticide claims for the product, or by the product's having no other significant commercially valuable use except as a pesticide, or if the seller or distributor has knowledge that the product will be used or is intended to be used as a pesticide, it would be considered a pesticide within the meaning of FIFRA. If the manufacturer is making a pesticidal claim for the material, this is evidence that a substance is a pesticide within the meaning of FIFRA. Also, if the substance bears no pesticidal claims, but has no commercially valuable use except as a pesticide, it could still be a pesticide under FIFRA.

In its first departure from the bright line test, the EPA said in a 1986 Federal Register notice[133] that research and development of pesticides is generally subject to TSCA until there is an application for an EUP or registration. It went on to say:

> While EPA recognizes that other activities may also evidence the "intent" to make a pesticide, it is very difficult to define such activities.
>
> The Agency considers the existence of a patent relating to use as a pesticide or the manufacture of the substance by a company or a laboratory wholly devoted to pesticide R&D and marketing as evidence of exclusive pesticide intent.

However, in that case, the EPA excluded substances from R&D requirements before an EUP or registration application "as a matter of policy," and not because such substances are excluded from TSCA because they are pesticides. The EPA's discussion of intent in that Federal Register notice was to pinpoint the time when a substance would, as a matter of EPA grace only, not be subject to the research and development regulations that the EPA was

---

prior notice has been submitted under FIFRA. It is always much more prudent to comply with the EPA's interpretation than to rely on an untested defense.

133. 51 Fed. Reg. 15096, 15098 (Apr. 22, 1986).

promulgating. The EPA emphasized that "The other provisions of TSCA still apply to pesticide-oriented R&D activities. . . ."

In other areas, the EPA is still stating that a substance is subject to TSCA until an application for an EUP or registration is filed. For example, the EPA revised its policy on significant adverse effects reporting under § 8(e) in 2003, and released a Q&A supporting its revisions.[134] That Q&A stated:

> COMMENT: EPA should exempt from section 8(e) reporting field tests conducted on research and development (R&D) pesticides. . ..
> RESPONSE: EPA agrees that they would not normally be reportable because the exposure is not widespread and previously unsuspected. However, if health or environmental effects are seen then reporting should be considered. Also, if the substance has started the regulatory review process under FIFRA it would not be subject to section 8(e) reporting. *A chemical substance which is in the process of R&D as a pesticide is subject to TSCA until such time as the manufacturer or importer demonstrates the intent to produce a pesticide by submitting to the Agency an application for an "Experimental Use Permit" or registration under FIFRA.*

Before a company files an EUP it may research the pesticidal properties of a chemical substance. In those cases, if the R&D activities are focused on investigating substances' potential for use as pesticides, then the company does not need to comply with TSCA's restrictions on managing of R&D chemicals.[135] If the company does other types of research in addition to research on pesticides, then it must show by some affirmative evidence that its only intent with respect to the chemical at issue is to develop it as a pesticide. As a consequence, pesticides can be exempted from the premanufacture notification requirements of TSCA § 5 even before an EUP is filed, but the substance will be subject to other TSCA requirements, such as reporting significant adverse effects under TSCA § 8(e).

Raw materials, inerts, safteners surfactants, solvents, and intermediates used in manufacturing pesticides are subject to TSCA, according to the EPA. Until one of these becomes a component of a pesticide product it is not typically a pesticide itself, and so it is not within the TSCA definition of pesticides. An inert ingredient destined for a pesticide product is regulated under TSCA until it becomes part of the pesticide product, at which point it is regulated under FIFRA.[136]

---

134. Comment and Response Document for Revised Policy Statement of Section 8(e) of TSCA, OPPT-2002-0067-0002, 5 (Feb. 2003) (italics added).
135. 40 C.F.R. § 720.36(g).
136. Living with TSCA Q&A, question 2.

Effluents from pesticide manufacturing facilities are subject to TSCA, and the practical effect is that allegations that pesticide plant effluents have caused a significant adverse effect must be recorded under TSCA § 8(c).[137]

FIFRA regulates inerts and other substances contained in pesticides. In 1998 a FIFRA regulation went into effect defining the term "pesticide" in the regulations requiring reporting of unreasonable adverse effects of a substance. That regulation provides:

> *Pesticide* means a pesticide product which is or was registered by EPA, and each active ingredient, inert ingredient, impurity, metabolite, contaminant or degradate contained in, or derived from, such pesticide product.[138]

Because TSCA regulations define the word "pesticide" to be the same as in FIFRA and "the regulations issued thereunder,"[139] inerts should not be subject to TSCA. However, TSCA has not kept up with this relatively new FIFRA definition of "pesticide," and the TSCA program still considers inerts, impurities, metabolites, and contaminants to be regulated under TSCA, so it is advisable to comply with the TSCA program's guidances.

At least one commentator has taken the position that TSCA does not apply to a pre-EUP substance that is intended for use or testing as a pesticide and is manufactured, processed or distributed as a pesticide.[140] In large part because of TSCA's clear and very current statements that inerts are governed by TSCA in the face of the FIFRA program's assertion of jurisdiction over inerts, it seems prudent nonetheless to focus solely on TSCA guidances in interpreting TSCA, and to disregard the FIFRA program's inconsistent regulations and guidances when interpreting TSCA. As noted above, the statutory TSCA exemption for pesticides refers to the FIFRA statute, which looks to the intended use in defining a pesticide. It would be much better if the TSCA guidances kept pace with the FIFRA regulations.

If an intermediate is a registered "manufacturing use pesticide" under FIFRA, it is considered to be a pesticide and is exempt from TSCA.[141]

---

137. Questions and Answers Concerning the TSCA Section 8(c) Rule (July 1984), 38. *See* Chapter, 7, Reporting and Recordkeeping.
138. 40 C.F.R. § 159.153(b). The rule was promulgated at 62 Fed. Reg. 49369 (Sept. 19, 1997).
139. 40 C.F.R. § 710.2(b); 40 C.F.R. § 720.3(a)(2).
140. Kenneth Weinstein, *Does TSCA § 8(e) Reporting Apply to Candidate Pesticides?* Pesticides, Chemical Regulation, and Right-to-Know Committee Newsletter, (ABA, Washington, D.C.) Feb. 2008.
141. 42 Fed. Reg. 64572, 64585, comment 39 (Dec. 23, 1977).

C. Nuclear Material

The TSCA statute exempts certain radioactive substances from the definition of "chemical substance" when it exempts:

> any source material, special nuclear material, or byproduct material (as such terms are defined in the Atomic Energy Act of 1954[142] and regulations issued under such Act).[143]

In turn, the Atomic Energy Act of 1954 defines these terms as follows:

> (e) The term "byproduct material" means (1) any radioactive material (except special nuclear material) yielded in or made radioactive by exposure to the radiation incident to the process of producing or utilizing special nuclear material, and (2) the tailings or wastes produced by the extraction or concentration of uranium or thorium from any ore processed primarily for its source material content.
>
> (z) The term "source material" means (1) uranium, thorium, or any other material which is determined by the Commission pursuant to the provisions of section 2091[144] of this title to be source material; or (2) ores containing one or more of the foregoing materials, in such concentration as the Commission may by regulation determine from time to time.
>
> (aa) The term "special nuclear material" means (1) plutonium, uranium enriched in the isotope 233 or in the isotope 235, and any other material which the Commission, pursuant to the provisions of section 2071[145] of

---

142. 42 U.S.C. § 2011–2297.
143. TSCA § 3(2)(iv) (footnote added).
144. 42 U.S.C. § 2091, entitled *Determination of source material*, provides in pertinent part:

> The Commission may determine from time to time that other material is source material in addition to those specified in the definition of source material. Before making such determination, the Commission must find that such material is essential to the production of special nuclear material and must find that the determination that such material is source material is in the interest of the common defense and security, and the President must have expressly assented in writing to the determination . . .

145. 42 U.S.C. § 2071, entitled *Determination of other material as special nuclear material; Presidential assent; effective date*, provides in pertinent part:

> The Commission may determine from time to time that other material is special nuclear material in addition to that specified in the definition as special nuclear material. Before making any such determination, the Commission must find that such material is capable of releasing substantial quantities of atomic energy and must find that the determination that such material is special nuclear material is in the interest of the common defense and security, and the President must have expressly assented in writing to the determination . . .

> this title, determines to be special nuclear material, but does not include source material; or (2) any material artificially enriched by any of the foregoing, but does not include source material.[146]

Therefore, these radioactive materials are exempt from TSCA.

D. Firearms

The exemption for firearms is based on the provision of the TSCA statute that says that the term "chemical substance" does not include:

> any article the sale of which is subject to the tax imposed by section 4181 of the Internal Revenue Code of 1986 (26 U.S.C. 4181) (determined without regard to any exemptions from such tax provided by section 4182 or 4221 or any other provision of such Code). . .[147]

The referenced provision of the Internal Revenue Code imposes a tax on pistols, revolvers, firearms, shells, and cartridges.[148] Therefore, these articles are exempt from TSCA.

While the statute itself does not use the word "firearm," the regulations do specifically exempt "any pistol, firearm, revolver, shells and cartridges" from the definition of "chemical substance."[149] Presumably, because only the listed articles are exempted from TSCA, the gunpowder used to fill the shells is subject to all of the TSCA regulations.

---

146. 42 U.S.C. § 2014.
147. TSCA § 3(1)(B)(v).
148. The full text of 26 U.S.C. § 4181 provides:

> There is hereby imposed upon the sale by the manufacturer, producer, or importer of the following articles a tax equivalent to the specified percent of the price for which so sold:
> Articles taxable at 10 percent -
> Pistols.
> Revolvers.
> Articles taxable at 11 percent -
> Firearms (other than pistols and revolvers).
> Shells, and cartridges.

149. 40 C.F.R. § 710.2(h).

E. Foods, Drugs, and Cosmetics

The TSCA statute excludes foods, drugs, and cosmetics from the definition of "chemical substance" when it excludes:

> Any food, food additive, drug, cosmetic, or device (as such terms are defined in section 201 of the Federal Food, Drug, and Cosmetic Act) when manufactured, processed, or distributed in commerce for use as a food, food additive, drug, cosmetic, or device.[150]

The statute further clarifies that meat, poultry, and eggs, while generally not regulated under the Federal Food, Drug, and Cosmetics Act are foods if they meet definitions in other referenced statutes.[151]

If a substance is manufactured, distributed, or processed for use as a food, drug, or cosmetic, and for some other use that is governed by TSCA, then portion made for a TSCA use is always subject to TSCA.[152] The portion made for a food, drug or cosmetic use is only excluded from TSCA if it is manufactured, processed or distributed separately from the portion destined for a TSCA use. If it is manufactured, distributed, or processed for undifferentiated food, drug, or cosmetic use *and* other uses, then the total amount of substance will be presumed to be subject to TSCA.[153]

The EPA follows the general principle that a substance is exempt from TSCA when the Food and Drug Administration (FDA) first regulates it.[154] The EPA defers to the FDA in this determination.[155] The EPA follows the FDA's examples of when the FDA begins regulating a product; this occurs when an application for exemption for an investigational use of a new drug, animal drug, or device is submitted.[156]

Intermediates and catalysts that are solely for use in production of a food, food additive, drug, cosmetic, or device are outside the scope of TSCA.

---

150. TSCA § 3(2)(B)(vi).

151. TSCA § 3(2)(B) states:

> The term "food" as used in clause (vi) of this subparagraph includes poultry and poultry products (as defined in sections 4(e) and 4(f) of the Poultry Products Inspection Act), meat and meat food products (as defined in section 1(j) of the Federal Meat Inspection Act), and eggs and egg products (as defined in section 4 of the Egg Products Inspection Act).

152. Draft PMN Q&A, 2-20 to 2-21, question 214-1. *See also*, EPA's "A Guide for Chemical Importers/Exporters," question 42 (Apr. 1991) and 48 Fed. Reg. 21722, 21726 (May 13, 1983).

153. 42 Fed. Reg. 64572, 64585, comment 37 (Dec. 23, 1977).

154. *Id.* at 64586, comment 40.

155. Industry Obligations, 3.

156. *Id.*

The EPA came to this conclusion because the FFDCA defines components of foods, food additives, drugs, cosmetics, and devices to be themselves foods, food additives, drugs, cosmetics, or devices. Intermediates, precursors, and catalysts are considered to be components, and components are excluded from TSCA if they are manufactured, processed, or distributed as components as defined under the FFDCA.[157]

Effluents and wastes from pharmaceutical or other FDA regulated manufacturing facilities are subject to TSCA, and the practical effect is that allegations that pesticide and pharmaceutical plant effluents have caused a significant adverse effect must be recorded under TSCA § 8(c).[158]

Soaps are not included in the FFDCA's definition of cosmetics, and so soaps are regulated under TSCA. The FFDCA does not define "soap," but the FDA interprets "soap" to be narrowly limited to old-fashioned soaps made from reacting fats with alkali. A product is considered a soap only if:

- The bulk of the nonvolatile matter in the product consists of an alkali salt of fatty acids and the product's detergent properties are due to the alkali-fatty acid compounds, and
- The product is labeled, sold, and represented solely as soap.[159]

Only soaps meeting this narrow definition are subject to TSCA, because they are not regulated by the FDA. Any cleansing product that is a detergent, or that is sold as a beauty product or to cure a health condition will be either a drug or a cosmetic and will be regulated by the FDA.[160]

A company that distributes chemicals solely for use as drug intermediates does not need to list the intermediates on the Inventory, but does need to limit sales to drug manufacturers and inform the manufacturers that the substance is not on the Inventory and may only be used to manufacture a drug.[161]

Additives used solely in packaging for FDA regulated products are governed by the FFDCA and not by TSCA.[162]

---

157. 42 Fed. Reg. 64572, 64586, comment 41 (Dec. 23, 1977). *See also* Living with TSCA Q&A, question 16.
158. Questions and Answers Concerning the TSCA Section 8(c) Rule, 38 (July 1984). *See* Chapter, 7, Reporting and Recordkeeping.
159. *See* FDA Is It a Cosmetic, a Drug, or Both? (or Is It Soap?), *available at* http://www.fda.gov/Cosmetics/GuidanceComplianceRegulatoryInformation/ucm074201.htm.
160. *Id.*
161. Industry Obligations, 11.
162. Living with TSCA Q&A, question 15.

F. Articles

Articles are not listed on the TSCA Inventory, and no PMN is required for an article.[163] Articles are not exempted from TSCA programs other than the PMN, Inventory and part of the SNUR programs. An article is defined as:

> a manufactured item (1) which is formed to a specific shape or design during manufacture, (2) which has end use function(s) dependent in whole or in part upon its shape or design during end use, and (3) which has either no change of chemical composition during its end use or only those changes of composition which have no commercial purpose separate from that of the article and that may occur as described in § 720.36(g)(5),[164] except that fluids and particles are not considered articles regardless of shape or design.[165]

EPA's former Office of Toxic Substances (OTS) issued guidance on what constitutes an article. In its October 1, 1985 "Clarification of the Interpretation of 'Article' Under TSCA," OTS said:

> For purposes of compliance with section 5 and section 13, OTS will consider items being imported as articles if they are manufactured in a specific shape or design for a particular end use application, and this design is maintained as an essential feature in the finished product. Thus, materials such as metal or plastic sheets, wire, coated fabric, rolled carpet, sheets of plywood and other similar materials will be viewed as articles by OTS, even if, for example, subsequent to import they are rolled or drawn thinner, cut, printed, laminated, or thermo-formed, as long as they meet the above criteria. . ..
>
> However, if an item is manufactured in a particular shape for the purpose of shipping convenience and the shape of the item has no function in the end use, it would not be considered an article. Thus, items such as metal ingots, billets, and blooms would continue to be viewed by OTS as chemical substances . . .

The EPA reiterated in its current Draft PMN Q&A that metal ingots and pellets that are intended to be melted and extruded are not articles.[166]

These guidances are quite helpful when addressing one of the listed types of items. However, there are significant gray areas. For example, there is a fine line between items that are manufactured in a particular shape for shipping convenience, and items such as plastic sheets that will be cut and

163. Chemical substances from which an article is made must be on the Inventory, or a PMN must be filed before those substances are made.
164. The correct cross reference must be § 720.30(h)(5).
165. 40 C.F.R. § 720.3(c) (footnotes added).
166. Draft PMN Q&A, 2-10, question 207-8.

laminated. Arguably, the plastic sheets are shipped in the form of sheets for convenience.

It is also difficult to determine what the "end use" of an item such as a plastic sheet is. If the end use is as a thermoformed three-dimensional bowl, then it is difficult to conclude that the design of the plastic sheet "is maintained as an essential feature in the finished product." It is best to review the EPA's guidances on a case by case basis when the item in question is in a gray area.[167]

In order to be categorized as an article, there can be no change of chemical composition during end use, except changes that have no commercial purpose apart from the purpose of the article. For example, when a candle is burned the combustion products have no commercial purpose. Therefore, the EPA has concluded that a candle is an article, and under an explicit regulatory exemption the combustion products are not required to be put on the Inventory.[168]

There are several regulatory provisions which must be consulted to determine if substances in an article must be listed on the Inventory. Taken together these exempt from Inventory listing and PMN requirements a wide range of substances that are in articles. Chemical substances are not subject to Inventory and PMN requirements if they:

- result from a chemical reaction that occurs upon end use of another chemical substance, mixture, or article such as an adhesive, paint, miscellaneous cleanser or other housekeeping product, fuel additive, water softening and treatment agent, photographic film, battery, match, or safety flare, and which is not itself manufactured or imported for distribution in commerce or for use as an intermediate;[169]
- result from a chemical reaction that occurs upon use of curable plastic or rubber molding compounds, inks, drying oils, metal finishing compounds, adhesives, or paints, or any other chemical substance formed during the manufacture of an article destined for the marketplace without further chemical change of the chemical substance except for those chemical changes that occur as described elsewhere in this paragraph;[170]

---

167. A good case can be made that many items fit within the guidance on what constitutes an "article." In particular, the examples seem to stand for the proposition that an article can be an intermediate product that is re-shaped for its finished use. None of the EPA's examples involve intermediate products that will be chemically reacted as they are re-shaped, but that seems to be within the scope of chemical substances that will be formed upon end use of an article. *See* Chapter 4, Premanufacture Notifications.
168. Draft PMN Q&A, 2-9, question 207-4. The regulatory exemption is found at 40 C.F.R. § 720.20(h)(5).
169. 40 C.F.R. §§ 720.30(h)(5) and 710.4(d)(5).
170. 40 C.F.R. §§ 720.30(h)(6) and 710.4(d)(6) (emphasis added).

- results from a chemical reaction that occurs when (i) a stabilizer, colorant, odorant, antioxidant, filler, solvent carrier, surfactant, plasticizer, corrosion inhibitor, antifoamer or defoamer, dispersant, precipitation inhibitor, binder, emulsifier, deemulsifier, dewatering agent, agglomerating agent, adhesion promoter, flow modifier, pH neutralizer, sequestrant, coagulant, flocculant, fire retardant, lubricant, chelating agent, or quality control reagent functions as intended or (ii) a chemical substance, which is intended solely to impart a specific physiochemical characteristic, functions as intended.[171]

Each of these regulatory sections could provide an exemption for different kinds of substances in articles. With some exceptions, these sections result in the conclusion that substances formed during the manufacture of an article do not need to be on the Inventory, and no PMN is required before making them.

"Fluid" and "particle" are critical undefined terms in 40 C.F.R. § 720.3(c). Fluids and particles cannot themselves be articles, so they must be on the Inventory, or be part of an article from which they are not intended to be released, or else the manufacturer needs to file a PMN.[172] It is not clear if there is any size limit on a particle, although the typical dictionary definition implies that particles must be minute.

In Q&A the EPA said that fibers can be articles if their end use depends entirely or partly on their shape or design, and there are no chemical changes on end use apart from "changes without commercial purpose separate from the articles of which they are a part." If the fiber were made for use as an intermediate, the fiber would be a chemical substance. Further, if a fiber or whisker were "used as a particle" then the fiber or whisker does not qualify as an article, presumably because its end use does not depend on its shape as a fiber.[173] Therefore a fiber, filament, or whisker can be an article or not, depending on its intended use.

The EPA acknowledged that some substances that are not on the Inventory, and which cannot be processed in the United States, may be incorporated into articles outside of the United States and then imported.[174] This gives importers and foreign manufacturers an advantage over domestic manufacturers.

Chemical substances imported in drums are not articles, although the drums are articles, because the chemicals have a commercial use distinct from the drum.[175] If the chemical is intended to be removed from the container or

---

171. 40 C.F.R. §§ 720.30(h)(7) and 710.4(d)(7).
172. EPA Draft Instruction Manual for Reporting Under The TSCA § 5 New Chemicals Program, 4 (2003), *available at* http://www.epa.gov/oppt/newchems/.
173. Draft PMN Q&A, 2-9 to 2-10, question 207-6. *See also* 42 Fed. Reg. 64572, 64587, comment 59 (Dec. 23, 1977).
174. 42 Fed. Reg. 64572, 64583 comment 22 (Dec. 23, 1977).
175. Draft PMN Q&A, 2-8 to 2-9, question 207-2; *see also* question 207.

article that holds it, then the chemical is not part of the article.[176] The EPA confirmed that hydraulic fluids in sealed units, and refrigeration fluids sealed inside air conditioners are part of an article because they are not intended to be released.[177] Similarly, brake fluid is a component of an article if it is imported in a brake system, assuming that the brake system is not merely a way to transport the brake fluid, the brake fluid is not intended to be released from the brake system, and the brake fluid has no function that requires release from the brake system.[178] Presumably, the fact that all these fluids are predictably released during accidents and on equipment aging does not require a conclusion that they are not part of an article.

Examples of substances that are part of articles include:[179]

- motor oil in a car, because it functions only within the car, and a release does not serve a commercial purpose; and
- transformer fluids in a transformer.

Examples of materials that are not part of an article include:[180]

- motor oil in cans or bottles;
- copy machine toner in a cartridge, because the toner is intentionally released onto paper;
- inks in a ball-point pen[181] and typewriter ribbons, because they are intentionally released onto paper; and
- caulking mixture contained in a caulking cylinder, because it is intentionally released from the cylinder.

III. Activities Governed by TSCA

TSCA's scope is circumscribed both by the types of chemicals that are involved in an activity, and by the activity itself. Different sets of regulatory programs will come into play depending on the whether the chemical substance will be used, processed, distributed, manufactured, imported, or disposed of. Each of these activities will be addressed below.

---

176. 42 Fed. Reg. 64572, 64583, comment 21 (Dec. 23, 1977).
177. Living with TSCA Q&A, question 4.
178. Draft PMN Q&A, 2-8 to 2-9, question 207-2.
179. All of these examples are from an EPA letter from Charles L. Elkins, Director of the Office of Toxic Substances, EPA to redacted (date illegible).
180. *Id.*
181. *See also* Draft PMN Q&A, 2-9, question 207-3.

A. Use and Process

"Use" and "process" need to be addressed together because sometimes they are mutually exclusive and sometimes they overlap. The TSCA statute defines "process" as:

> the preparation of a chemical substance or mixture, after its manufacture, for distribution in commerce—
>
> (A) in the same form or physical state as, or in a different form or physical state from, that in which it was received by the person so preparing such substance or mixture, or
> (B) as part of an article containing the chemical substance or mixture.[182]

TSCA does not explicitly define "use," but it is a very important concept throughout the statutory scheme. It is intertwined with the term "process." Unfortunately for anyone interested in clarity, the EPA has issued guidances that define the terms "use" and "process" differently for different sections of the statute. Sometimes "use" encompasses "processing" and sometimes it does not.

In the context of manufacture for export only, the EPA has indicated that "use" and "process" are mutually exclusive, when it said:

> [F]or substances to qualify as "solely for export" chemicals, their manufacture and processing must be limited to activities which do not involve use, except in small quantities solely for R&D in accordance with 40 CFR 720.36. Blending into a finished product does not involve use. However, the use of a new chemical substance as an intermediate in the chemical production of another chemical substance would require reporting of the intermediate.[183]

For the purposes of the "solely for export" exemption, then, an intermediate or reactant is "used" and not "processed," and "use" and "process" do not overlap.

In contrast, in the context of § 4 test rules, the EPA may require only "manufacturers" and "processors" to conduct testing, and so in this context the EPA's definition of "process" is predictably expansive, and the terms "use" and "process" overlap. In a proposed test rule from 1980,[184] the EPA stated that chemically reacting a substance is "processing":

> It should be noted that the term "processor" under TSCA has a much broader meaning than the common or industry's meaning. The following examples

182. TSCA § 3.
183. *See also* Draft PMN Q&A, 2-9, question 207-3.
184. 45 Fed. Reg. 48524, 48534 (July 18, 1980).

illustrate activities that would cause a person to be considered a processor under TSCA.

Example 1. A person reacts chemicals X and Y to produce a new chemical substance, Z. This person is a processor of X and Y and a manufacturer of Z. This example is closest to industry's meaning of the term.

Example 2. A person who purchases or manufactures chemicals and then mixes or reacts them is a processor of each chemical if the mixtures or compounds are distributed in commerce. Processors that fall within this example include producers of paints, automotive products (e.g., antifreeze, oil additives, etc.) and specialty cleaners and floor wax preparations. This example covers a large segment of the processor class.

Example 3. A person who heats and mixes powdered resins, fillers, pigments, and plasticizers to form a homogeneous mix which is then formed into sheets of a desired thickness would be a processor of each component because the components are distributed in commerce as part of an article. Tire manufacturers and producers of rubber and plastic articles would fall within this example. Processors in this example are similar to those in example 2, except that the products that are distributed in commerce are articles rather than chemicals.

Example 4. A person who purchases steel cans and then coats the cans with a resin would be a processor of the resin, since the resin is now a part of an article which is distributed in commerce. Similarly, a person who purchases printing ink and then applies the ink to paper or boxes would be a processor of the ink which has become a part of an article. Also tanneries and textile mills would be processors of the dyes used to color the leather and fabric. Persons in these examples add chemicals to previously produced articles.

The above examples are not meant to be inclusive. They are only provided to illustrate the breadth of the TSCA definition of processor and assist persons in determining whether their activities fall within the TSCA meaning of "process".

Similarly, EPA has defined "process" to include reacting a substance when it stated that R&D samples may be "processed" to form new chemical substances.[185]

Because of the variable definition of "process" and "use," is important to check the definitions for each regulatory program.

---

185. 51 Fed. Reg. 10596, 10598 (Apr. 22, 1986).

B. Manufacture and Toll Manufacture

"Manufacture" is circularly defined in the TSCA statute to mean to import, produce, or manufacture.[186] "Produce" is not separately defined, and the statute offers little more insight into the meaning of "manufacture."

"Manufacture" always includes importation wherever it appears in TSCA. This definition has profound implications for TSCA's application to importers. All of the restrictions and requirements that apply to manufacturers also apply to importers.

Any person who manufactures a new chemical substance must comply with the premanufacture notification requirements of TSCA § 5, the reporting and recordkeeping requirements of § 8, and the testing requirements of § 4.

The definition of "manufacturer" varies from section to section. The definitions applicable to TSCA § 8(c) and (d) the definitions under the TSCA § PMN and SNUR requirements are consistent in that all of them define a manufacturer to be:

> a person who imports, produces, or manufactures a chemical substance. A person who extracts a component chemical substance from a previously existing chemical substance or a complex combination of substances is a manufacturer of that component chemical substance.[187]

However, the PMN rules add toll manufacturers to the definition of "manufacturer." Toll manufacturing is the relatively common practice when one chemical manufacturer has certain processing steps performed by another manufacturer. Toll manufacturing also includes arrangements in which one company makes a chemical for another company. The company that actually does the manufacturing is defined in all of the regulations that supply a definition as a "manufacturer." In the PMN rules, in some circumstances the company that places the order is also a "manufacturer." If company A engages company B to manufacture a chemical, then company A is defined as a "manufacturer" if several conditions are met. Company B must be making the chemical exclusively for company A. Company A must control the chemical composition of the chemical, the amount made, and provide the basic manufacturing process.[188] As a result of defining company A to be a "manufacturer," company A is subject to the premanufacture notification requirements of TSCA § 5.

186. TSCA § 3(7).
187. 40 C.F.R. §§ 704.3, 716.3 and 720.3(t).
188. Premanufacture Notice Requirements, 48 Fed. Reg. 21722, 21725–26 (May 13, 1983).

If a company controls all the distribution of a chemical made by another firm, and the company that does the distribution does not process the chemical, then it is a distributor and not a toll manufacturer or processor.[189]

C. Importation

All of the TSCA provisions that apply to manufacturers also apply, by definition, to importers of chemical substances. Therefore, importers are subject to the premanufacture notification requirements of TSCA § 5, the reporting and recordkeeping requirements of § 8, and the testing requirements of § 4, as well as all the other TSCA provisions.

"Manufacture" includes to "import into the customs territory of the United States (as defined in general note 2 of the Harmonized Tariff Schedule of the United States)."[190] "Customs Territory of the United States" as used in general note 2 of the Harmonized Tariff refers to only the States, The District of Columbia and Puerto Rico.[191] Therefore, importation into Guam, American Samoa, or other U.S. possessions or territories does not constitute manufacturing. Importers of chemicals into these possessions and territories are not bound by the regulations governing manufacturers unless they are subject to TSCA for some other reason.

The importer can be "the person primarily liable for the payment of any duties on the merchandise" or "an authorized agent" as defined in the customs regulations.[192]

An importer can arrange with its foreign supplier to have the foreign supplier provide information directly to the EPA.[193]

D. Manufacture or Distribution in Commerce

There are very few activities in the United States that do not affect commerce and therefore TSCA covers many activities. TSCA states:

> The terms "distribute in commerce" and "distribution in commerce" when used to describe an action taken with respect to a chemical substance or mixture or article containing a substance or mixture mean to sell, or the sale of, the substance, mixture, or article in commerce; to introduce or deliver for introduction into commerce, or the introduction or delivery for introduction into commerce

---

189. Industry Obligations, 2.
190. TSCA § 3(7).
191. Harmonized Tariff Schedule of the United States, 3 (2008) (Rev. 1).
192. 40 C.F.R. § 710.2(e).
193. 42 Fed. Reg. 64572, 64582, comment 18 (Dec. 23, 1977).

of, the substance, mixture, or article; or to hold, or the holding of, the substance, mixture, or article after its introduction into commerce.[194]

Substances that are manufactured for R&D purposes are manufactured in commerce. Although there are specific exclusions for R&D substances from the PMN requirements of TSCA § 5,[195] they remain subject to other TSCA provisions.

IV. TSCA's Interrelationship with Other Laws

Section 9 of TSCA is entitled "Relationship to Other Federal Laws" and provides that the EPA may, if it chooses, defer to another agency to address unreasonable risks posed by chemical substances. If the EPA determines that a risk can be adequately managed using another statute it administers, it may rely on that statute instead of TSCA.

In *EPA v. Alyeska Pipeline Service Co.*,[196] the Court held that § 9 does not require the EPA to invoke other statutes to investigate potential problems that may fall within TSCA's scope, and a subpoena under TSCA is appropriate for that purpose.

A. Resource Conservation and Recovery Act

TSCA does not preempt any of the regulations governing hazardous waste disposal and remediation in the Resource Conservation and Recovery Act (RCRA).[197] Both statutes regulate cleanup and disposal of certain chemicals. There is overlap between the two statutory schemes because RCRA regulates hazardous wastes, and TSCA regulates PCBs and other chemicals subject to regulations under § 6 or the significant new use rules of § 5, and the same chemical can fall within two or more of these categories. One significant overlap is the regulation of PCBs.

In *U.S. v. Union Corp.*,[198] the court held that TSCA's regulation of PCBs does not preempt RCRA regulation of PCBs. The court stated:

> nothing in the text of the Toxic Substances Control Act ("TSCA"), which also regulates PCBs, evinces Congress' intention to preempt RCRA. Instead, TSCA

---

194. TSCA § 3(4).
195. 42 Fed. Reg. 64572, 64584, comment 29 (Dec. 23, 1977).
196. 836 F.2d 443 (9th Cir. 1988).
197. 42 U.S.C. §§ 6901–6992.
198. 277 F. Supp. 2d 478 (E.D.Pa. 2003).

specifically provides that it is not intended to "limit the authority of the Administrator, under any other provision of this chapter or any other Federal law, to take action respecting any polychlorinated biphenyl." 15 U.S.C. § 2605(e)(5).

B. Federal Food, Drug, and Cosmetic Act

Foods, drugs, and cosmetics are excluded from TSCA, as discussed above, and therefore it would seem that there should not be any overlap between the FFDCA and TSCA. However § 408(p) of the FFDCA[199] requires the establishment of a testing program to determine if pesticides and other chemicals mimic the effects of estrogen and other endocrine system hormones. The program is called the Endocrine Disruptor Screening Program, or EDSP. The EPA is conducting the EDSP, which has many similarities to the § 4 test rule program available under TSCA.

The first group of chemicals that the EPA intends to have screened under the ESP are certain pesticide active ingredients and high production volume pesticide inert ingredients.[200] The FFDCA requires screening of all pesticides eventually.[201] Because pesticides are excluded from TSCA there would not have been any statutory authority to conduct the EDSP testing for pesticide active ingredients under TSCA. Pesticide inerts are not excluded from TSCA, and their testing can be required under TSCA.[202]

If an importer or manufacturer of a pesticide inert fails to comply with a test order under FFDCA § 408(p), the FFDCA calls for the same penalties and sanctions as provided for in TSCA § 16.[203]

C. Tort Law

Many tort plaintiffs have tried to assert claims for damages under TSCA, and courts have uniformly held that TSCA does not support a private right of action for damages.[204]

It is likely that tort plaintiffs will point to TSCA violations as evidence of negligence. A TSCA violation alone is not sufficient to claim negligence.

---

199. 21 U.S.C. § 346a.
200. 74 Fed. Reg. 17579 (Apr. 15, 2009).
201. FFDCA Section 408(p)(3)(A).
202. Section 408(f)(1)(B) of the FFDCA specifically contemplates use of TSCA § 4 test rules to gather data on endocrine effects of pesticide residue chemicals. However, this portion of the FFDCA is not an independent grant of authority to use TSCA to gather information on a pesticide that is excluded from TSCA's scope.
203. *See* Chapter 14, Penalties and Enforcement.
204. *See, e.g.*, Abarca v. Chevron U.S.A., Inc., 75 F. Supp.2d 566 (E.D.Tex. 1999).

When a statute provides the minimum standard of care applicable to a particular situation, violation of that standard of care can be negligence *per se* without any additional evidence of negligence. A TSCA violation cannot be negligence *per se*, because that would be a back-door way to assert a private right of action for damages under TSCA, in violation of Congress' determination not to provide a private right of action for damages.[205]

D. Others

The labeling provisions of the Occupational Health and Safety Administration's Hazard Communication Standard do not apply to any chemical substance or mixture that is subject to a specific labeling requirement under TSCA.[206]

---

205. Sanford Street Local Dev. v. Textron, Inc., 768 F. Supp. 1218 (W.D. Mich. 1991), vacated on other grounds; 805 F. Supp. 29 (W.D. Mich. 1991), cited with approval in Schwartzman, v. Atchison Topeka Sta. Fe Ry., 857 F. Supp. 838 (N.M. 1994); and Miller v. du Pont, 880 F. Supp. 474 (S.D. Miss. 1994).

206. 29 C.F.R. § 1910.1200(b)(5)(ii).

CHAPTER 3

The Inventory

I. Compilation of the Inventory

A. Purpose of the Inventory

Section 8(b) of the Toxic Substances Control Act (TSCA)[1] requires the United States Environmental Protection Agency (EPA) to "compile, keep current, and publish a list of each chemical substance which is manufactured or processed in the United States."[2] This list of chemical substances is referred to as the TSCA Inventory or the Inventory. The purpose of the Inventory was to list in one place all chemical substances that were in commerce in the country and were not otherwise regulated. At the time TSCA was enacted, foods, food additives, drugs, medical devices, and cosmetics were regulated under the Federal Food, Drug, and Cosmetics Act (FFDCA);[3] pesticides, but not pesticide raw materials, precursors or inert ingredients, were regulated under the Federal Insecticide, Fungicide, and Rodenticide Act (FIFRA);[4] and nuclear material was regulated under the Atomic Energy Act of 1954 (AEA).[5] Left unregulated under FFDCA, FIFRA, and AEA was an unknown number of chemicals. To compile the Inventory, the EPA issued an Inventory Reporting Rule in 1977 requiring companies to report all the chemicals they had manufactured or imported in the previous three years, and the result was the inclusion of approximately sixty-two thousand chemicals on the Inventory.[6] Since that time, over twenty-one thousand more chemicals have been added to the Inventory,[7] for a total of approximately eighty-three thousand chemicals.

The Inventory was intended to provide the EPA with the identities of the chemical substances it would have the authority to regulate under TSCA. TSCA § 3(2)(A) defines chemical substance as "any organic or inorganic substance of a particular molecular identity, including—(i) any combination of such substances occurring in whole or in part as a result of a chemical reaction or occurring in nature, and (ii) any element or uncombined radical,"[8] except for the exclusions noted in TSCA § 3(2)(B).[9] TSCA excludes from the

1. 15 U.S.C. § 2607(b).
2. *Id.*
3. 21 U.S.C. §§ 301–399.
4. 7 U.S.C. § 136.
5. 42 U.S.C. §§ 2011–2297.
6. 42 Fed. Reg. 64572 (Dec. 23, 1977), referring to proposed rules of Mar. 9, 1977 and Aug. 2, 1977; 73 Fed. Reg. 20921 (Apr. 17, 2008).
7. 73 Fed. Reg. 20921, 20923 (Apr. 17, 2008).
8. 15 U.S.C.§ 2602(2)(A).
9. 15 U.S.C.§ 2602(2)(B).

definition of chemical substances foods and food additives, pesticides, drugs, cosmetics, tobacco, firearms, and nuclear materials.[10]

Chemicals not on the Inventory and not otherwise exempted cannot be imported, manufactured, or processed in the United States for commercial purposes without filing a premanufacture notice (PMN) under TSCA § 5.[11] Filing a PMN can be a lengthy and relatively expensive process.

The civil and criminal penalties for making, importing, or processing a chemical that is not on the Inventory can be severe, not to mention the potential for business disruption that could result if a company finds that one of its products should be on the Inventory but is not there. Therefore searching the Inventory to determine whether chemicals that will be manufactured, imported, or processed are listed is a central function in TSCA compliance. This task is greatly complicated by the fact that there is also a confidential Inventory, composed of chemicals whose identities are not released to the public.

All companies must have systems in place to ensure that the chemicals that they manufacture, import, or process are on the TSCA Inventory.

B. Public and Confidential Inventories

The Inventory was established in two versions, a public Inventory available and searchable by the public, and a confidential Inventory. The initial public Inventory was published in 1979 and has been continually supplemented.[12]

TSCA § 14 allows the submission of information under a claim of confidentiality.[13] Manufacturers and processors were allowed in making initial submissions to the Inventory, and are allowed in submitting PMNs, to claim as confidential certain business information, including specific chemical identity, composition, and process details. If the chemical identity is claimed as confidential, a generic name is used for filing the Notice of Commencement (NOC). A NOC must be filed after the first manufacture or import of the substance after the PMN process is complete, in order to put the substance on the Inventory. Only the name on the NOC goes on the public Inventory.

---

10. For a complete discussion on the scope of TSCA, *see* Chapter 2, TSCA's Scope.
11. 15 U.S.C. § 2604. A detailed explanation of the PMN process is located in Chapter 4, Premanufacture Notifications.
12. The official version is available for purchase at http://www.ntis.gov. Use the product search function to locate the Inventory. The public Inventory can be partially accessed without charge at the EPA's Substance Registry Service at http://iaspub.epa.gov/sor_internet/registry/substreg/home/overview/home.do. Commercial services also sell the Inventory, such as that maintained by the Chemical Abstract Service at http://www.cas.org.
13. 15 U.S.C. § 2613.

C. Inventory Corrections

EPA announced in 1980 that it would accept corrections to a company's submissions for the initial Inventory if the corrections met specific criteria.[14] EPA recognized that uncorrected errors impaired the integrity of the Inventory and diminished its reliability as an accurate compilation of commercial substances for regulatory purposes.[15] Mechanisms for correcting the Inventory provided an important means to correct an error in reporting without having to file a PMN. EPA continues to accept such corrections, receiving a few dozen requests each year, even though the initial Inventory is approximately thirty years old.[16] While no separate guidance was ever published for making corrections to Inventory listings that occurred through the PMN submission process, the 1980 procedures have been adapted for that purpose.[17] For a PMN correction to be approved, there is the additional requirement that the correctly identified chemical identity does not present more risk than the originally identified chemical.[18]

1. Correction Categories

There are three categories of corrections that can be submitted for EPA review. The first category includes corrections of the chemical identity, some of which are required because of advances in the state of the art of chemical analysis. Corrections of this type include:[19]

- errors made through typographical or transcription errors;
- refinement of the identity of the substance, such as by narrowing the range of values of a polymer or specifying the precise location of a substituent on an aromatic ring that was originally unspecified or unknown;
- identification of new components, such as determining that substance A is really a mixture of A and B, or finding that there is an additional isomer of the substance or an asymmetrical form of a substance that was originally reported as symmetrical only; or

14. 45 Fed. Reg. 50544 (July 29, 1980).
15. 59 Fed. Reg. 53461 (Oct. 24, 1994).
16. E-mail from Tracy Williamson, Chief, Industrial Chemistry Branch Office of Pollution Prevention and Toxics, U.S. EPA to Miriam V. Gold, Attorney at Law (Mar. 19, 2009, 12:09 EST)(on file with author) [hereinafter Williamson E-mail].
17. *Id.*
18. *Id.*
19. 45 Fed. Reg. 50544 (July 29, 1980).

- discovering that a substance reported as A is really C, such as finding that a polymer was reported originally as including trimethylolpropane as a monomer when trimethylolethane is the monomer actually used.

Documentation to support a category one correction request should include a copy of the original Inventory reporting form (or the original PMN form), a corrected Inventory reporting form (or PMN form), with information exactly as it appeared on the original form (such as plant site, confidentiality claims, and the like) and a description of the nature of the correction and how the need for it was identified.[20] In a subsequent guidance document, EPA identified documentation that it considers preferable in reviewing these requests, including:[21]

- commercial batch production records pertaining to the corrected substance as manufactured after January 1, 1975;[22]
- customer invoices identifying the corrected substance chemically or by trade name/product designation linked to the production records;
- material safety data sheets[23] or product bulletins that identify the substance as manufactured during the period claimed;
- manufacturing process descriptions; and
- data sheets from raw material suppliers and analytical data that accurately characterize the corrected substance identity.

The second category of corrections consists of previously unrecognized isolated intermediates formed during the manufacture of a substance already on the Inventory.[24] Documentation to support a category two correction request should include a copy of the original Inventory reporting form (or the original PMN form) for the final substance and any other related intermediates, a new Inventory reporting form (or PMN form) for the now isolated intermediate and documented proof that the intermediate was isolated after July 1, 1975.[25] Additionally, the documentation should include a

---

20. *Id.*
21. EPA The TSCA Inventory, Submitting Successful Corrections, 3 (undated) [hereinafter Corrections].
22. The guidance document brackets the manufacturing dates as between January 1, 1975 and July 1, 1979, dealing with corrections to the initial Inventory only. Since EPA has adapted this document for dealing with corrections to PMN submissions as well, one can assume that EPA would want all manufacturing information to the date of the correction.
23. *See*, 29 C.F.R. § 1919.1200 for regulations concerning material safety data sheets issued by the Occupational Safety & Health Administration.
24. 45 Fed. Reg. 50544 (July 29, 1980).
25. *Id*, at 50545. The Federal Register notice brackets the date of isolation as between January 1, 1975 and July 1, 1979, dealing with corrections to the initial Inventory only. Since EPA has adapted this process for dealing with corrections to PMN submissions as well, one can

demonstration of the chemical relationship between all of the isolated intermediates and the final substance, preferably in the form of a detailed commercial manufacturing process description.[26] An engineering flow diagram indicating the stage of manufacture during which the intermediate is isolated is acceptable.[27] Whatever is submitted should be dated to indicate when the substance was isolated.[28]

The third category of corrections consists of potential issues that were identified by EPA in problem letters sent to submitters of substances for inclusion on the original Inventory in 1978 and 1979. Problem letters were letters sent by the EPA to submitters asking for additional or clarifying information. Many such letters were never answered. Documentation to support this type of correction requires only a copy of the original problem letter and a new Inventory report form including the correction requested in the problem letter.[29]

2. Potential Outcomes

When EPA rejects a request for a correction, it sends the submitter a denial letter with the reasons for the denial. In some situations, EPA will specify what additional information will be needed for it to reevaluate the request, and a second submittal may lead to an acceptance.[30] If the correction is accepted, the correct substance identity is considered to be legally included in the TSCA Inventory retroactively to the time of the initial Inventory, or to the time when the substance was placed on the Inventory through submission of a Notice of Commencement.[31] When an Inventory correction is accepted, the erroneously listed chemical remains on the Inventory until EPA makes a formal Federal Register announcement of its removal from the Inventory to avoid disrupting commercial activity by the unpublished deletion of a chemical listing upon which some companies may be relying.[32]

An example of the process through which substances might be removed from the Inventory can be illustrated by a proposed delisting of 38 substances

---

assume that EPA would want the actual date of isolation, so long as it occurred after January 1, 1975.

26. Corrections, 4.
27. *Id.*
28. *Id.*
29. 45 Fed. Reg. 50544, 50545 (July 29, 1980).
30. Corrections, 5.
31. Williamson E-mail. The e-mail makes this statement with respect to the initial Inventory only, but later adds that the corrections process has been adapted to deal with substances that were put on the Inventory by the PMN route.
32. Williamson e-mail.

announced by the EPA in 1994.[33] Each of the substances contained in the announcement had been reported for the Inventory by persons who later submitted a request to correct the submission. The correctly named substances were placed on the Inventory through the correction process.[34] The Federal Register notice requested information as to whether any of the improperly reported candidate substances had been manufactured, imported, or processed for TSCA commercial purposes, other than research and development, between January 1, 1975 and the date of the notice, October 24, 1994, and whether any of such substances could have been initially properly reported for the Inventory.[35] More broadly, EPA also wanted to hear from anyone who believed that any of those substances should not be removed from the Inventory for any reason.[36] EPA made clear that any ongoing commercial activity begun before the date of the notice could continue.[37] If EPA determined that any substance should not be removed from the Inventory, manufacturers and importers of the specific substance could submit an Inventory Report[38] to retain the substance on the Inventory.[39] If EPA determined that the substance was not eligible for inclusion for the Inventory, the substance would be removed from the Inventory effective on the date of the Federal Register notice announcing that decision, and anyone wanting to manufacture or import that substance for a commercial purpose would have to file a PMN to do so.[40]

After reviewing the nine comments submitted in response to its announcement, EPA determined that two of the substances should not be removed from the Inventory because they had been in commercial production or importation prior to October 24, 1994.[41] The other 36 substances were deleted from the TSCA Inventory as of June 27, 1995.[42]

While not an Inventory correction, and not involving removals of chemicals from the Inventory, the EPA provided similar relief to affected industry members in the case of monomer acid and its derivatives and Tall Oil Fatty Acid and its derivatives. The EPA concluded that it, and not a private party, had erroneously equated monomer acid with Tall Oil Fatty Acid in a 1985 letter to industry, and manufacturers had relied on the Inventory listings for

33. 59 Fed. Reg. 53461 (Oct. 24, 1994). *See also* the discussion of activated phospors in Chapter 2, TSCA's Scope.
34. 59 Fed. Reg. 53461, 53462 (Oct. 24, 1994).
35. *Id.*
36. *Id.*
37. *Id.*
38. An Inventory Report is the report initially required to be submitted to put substances on the Inventory when it was first established.
39. 59 Fed. Reg. 53461, 53462 (Oct. 24, 1994).
40. *Id.*
41. 60 Fed. Reg. 33201 (June 25, 1995).
42. *Id.* at 33203.

Tall Oil Fatty Acid derivatives to make monomer acid derivatives. Because the monomer acid derivatives had not been made during the initial Inventory reporting period they did not qualify for an Inventory correction. Instead, the EPA announced that it would delay the effective date of its new interpretation for one year, during which time affected industry members could file PMNs for monomer acid derivatives.[43]

3. Third Party Corrections

Very infrequently a company that wants to commercially manufacture or import a chemical substance that it did not originally report for the Inventory might believe that substance is not properly described in the Inventory. While the non-reporting company is not allowed to use the normal Inventory correction process, EPA may agree to amend the identity of the substance based on information provided by the non-reporting company.[44]

The original submitter needs to be approached to determine if it agrees to the change of chemical identity. The non-reporting company can submit a Freedom of Information Act request to obtain the identity of the reporting company and then discuss the situation with it.[45] If the identity of the reporting company is confidential, the non-reporting company can contact the Chemical Inventory Section (CIS) within the EPA's Information Management Division with all pertinent information and CIS will bring this issue to the attention of the reporting company.[46] In either case, the reporting company and CIS have to agree with the recommended correction or it will not be accepted. If the suggestion is accepted, the reporting company must submit the request for a correction.[47]

In some special circumstances, such as if the substance is no longer of commercial interest to the reporting company, the non-reporting company may not be able to obtain the cooperation of the reporting company to submit the correction request.[48] In such limited circumstances, EPA may allow the non-reporting company to make the correction request to avoid placing it in an untenable situation.[49]

---

43. 66 Fed. Reg. 34193 (June 27, 2001).
44. Corrections, 6. EPA points out that at the time of the publication of this guidance document, there had been fewer than five correction requests of this type.
45. *Id.* at 6.
46. *Id.* at 6–7.
47. *Id.* at 7.
48. *Id.*
49. *Id.* at 8.

II. Searching the Inventory

As noted above, the public Inventory is available for search both on governmental websites and through commercial services. Most public searches can be accomplished using a specific chemical name (either a Chemical Abstracts (CA) Index Name or a CA Preferred Name) and a Chemical Abstracts Service (CAS) Registry Number, but see the nomenclature discussion noted below for some particular naming issues. Substances claimed as confidential only appear on the public Inventory under their generic names. Prior to manufacturing or importing a substance that appears only by generic name on the public Inventory, the manufacturer or importer must request EPA to conduct a search of the confidential Inventory.[50]

To request a search of the confidential Inventory, the requestor must demonstrate that it has a bona fide intent to manufacture or import the chemical for commercial purposes.[51] Because this information is only available to potential manufacturers and importers, downstream processors and users cannot request a search, and must rely on suppliers for compliance information.

To establish the bona fide intent, the potential manufacturer or importer must supply the following information to the EPA in a submittal usually referred to as a bona fide notice or letter:

- the specific chemical identity of the substance;[52]
- a signed statement that the person intends to manufacture or import the substance for commercial purposes;[53]
- a description of R&D activities conducted, including year begun, nature of the activities, and whether or not pilot plant or production scale evaluations have been conducted;[54]
    - if an importer cannot provide the above information, it can state for how long and in what country(s) the substance has been used commercially and whether it was for the same use or application as contemplated by the importer;[55]
- a specific description of the major intended application or use;[56]

---

50. A similar request may be made under 40 C.F.R. §721.11 for determining the applicability of a significant new use rule. *See* Chapter 12, Significant New Use Rules.
51. 40 C.F.R. § 720.25(b)(1).
52. 40 C.F.R. § 720.25(b)(2)(i).
53. 40 C.F.R. § 720.25(b)(2)(ii).
54. 40 C.F.R. § 720.25(b)(2)(iii)(A).
55. 40 C.F.R. § 720.25(b)(2)(iii)(B).
56. 40 C.F.R. § 720.25(b)(2)(iv).

- an infrared spectrum of the substance, or alternative spectra or other data that identify the substance if needed;[57]
- the estimated date (month and year) a PMN will be submitted if the substance is not on the Inventory;[58]
- the address of the facility at which the manufacturing or processing would most likely occur;[59] and
- a description of the most probable manufacturing process,[60] or for importers a description of how the substance is most likely to be processed or used.[61] If the substance is not expected to be processed or used at any facility under the importer's control, a statement to this effect must be included along with a description of how the substance will be processed or used at sites controlled by others, if this information is known or reasonably ascertainable.[62]

If an importer cannot provide the chemical identity information because the identity is claimed as confidential, it can request that the foreign supplier send the information directly to EPA, referencing the importer's notice.[63] If the information is not received within thirty days after receipt of the importer's notice, EPA will consider the bona fide notice incomplete.[64] If the chemical substance is manufactured with a reactant that has a specific chemical identity claimed as confidential by the supplier, the manufacturer must provide the best chemical identity information it has and must have the supplier of the chemical reactant provide directly to EPA a letter of support with the specific chemical identity of the reactant, referencing the manufacturer's notice.[65] If the information is not received within thirty days after receipt of the importer's notice, EPA will consider the bona fide notice incomplete.[66]

The regulations require the EPA to determine if the submittal adequately documents a bona fide intent to manufacture or import,[67] and if so the EPA must conduct the search of the confidential Inventory and respond within thirty days of receipt of a complete submission.[68] EPA will also notify the original submitter of the Inventory submission that another party has

57. 40 C.F.R. § 720.25(b)(2)(v).
58. 40 C.F.R. § 720.25(b)(2)(vi).
59. 40 C.F.R. § 720.25(b)(2)(vii).
60. 40 C.F.R. § 720.25(b)(2)(viii)(A).
61. 40 C.F.R. § 720.25(b)(2)(viii)(B).
62. 40 C.F.R. § 720.25(b)(2)(viii)(B).
63. 40 C.F.R. § 720.25(b)(3)(i).
64. 40 C.F.R. § 720.25(b)(3)(i).
65. 40 C.F.R. § 720.25(b)(3)(ii).
66. 40 C.F.R. § 720.25(b)(3)(ii).
67. 40 C.F.R. § 720.25(b)(5).
68. 40 C.F.R. § 720.25(b)(7). It would be prudent to allow more time, and to contact the EPA personally.

demonstrated a bona fide intent to manufacture or import the substance and has been told that the substance in on the Inventory.[69] If any information has not been submitted or is not complete or accurate, EPA will notify the submitter that the notice will not be considered and needs to be refiled properly if it is to be considered.[70]

III. Inventory Update Rules

In 1986, pursuant to § 8(a) of TSCA,[71] EPA promulgated the first Inventory Update Rule (IUR)[72] requiring companies to update the TSCA Inventory Data Base. The IUR provides data to assist EPA and other federal agencies with health, safety, and environmental protection activities.[73] Under the IUR, manufacturers and importers must report basic data such as production volume and exposure information concerning chemicals they make or import above threshold quantities, set at twenty-five thousand pounds per year as of 2006. More extensive data submission is required for chemicals made or imported above three-hundred thousand pounds per year. Subsequently, EPA issued rules requiring the Inventory to be updated in four year cycles, with reporting periods in 1990, 1994, 1998, 2002, and 2006 for information from the year immediately prior to the reporting periods. In the 2006 IUR, EPA changed the reporting cycle to five years and set the next reporting period, which will be from June 1 through September 30, 2011.[74] However, the EPA in its Fall semiannual regulatory agenda said that it will be proposing a rule to return the reporting cycle back to four years.[75] The EPA also announced that it intends to seek additional changes such as collecting production volume data for multiple years, requiring electronic reporting, and new confidentiality requirements. It plans to issue a notice of proposed rulemaking in mid-2011, but it is unclear whether such additional changes will be effective for the 2011 reporting period.

Reports are required for any chemical substance that is on the Inventory at the beginning of the reporting period,[76] which is June 1, 2011 for the 2011

69. 40 C.F.R. § 720.25(b)(6).
70. 40 C.F.R. § 720.25(b)(9).
71. 15 U.S.C. § 2607(a).
72. 51 Fed. Reg. 21438 (June 12, 1986).
73. 70 Fed. Reg. 75059, 75061 (Dec. 19, 2005).
74. 40 C.F.R. § 710.53.
75. Regulatory Plan and Semiannual Regulatory Agenda, EPA-230-Z-09-002, 96 (Fall 2009), *available at* http://www.epa.gov/lawsregs/documents/regagendabook-fall09.pdf.
76. 40 C.F.R. § 710.45.

reporting period, provided that twenty-five thousand pounds or more of the substance is made or imported.[77]

A. Chemical Substances Excluded From the IUR

The IUR rules exempt four categories of substances, discussed below. However those exemptions do not apply if the substance is subject to a rule proposed or promulgated under TSCA §§ 4, 5(a)(2), 5(b)(4), or is the subject of an order issued under §§ 5(e) or 5(f), or is the subject of relief that has been granted under a civil action under §§ 5 or 7.[78,79] In the past, EPA has labeled most of the substances that are fully exempt from reporting under the IUR regulation with an "XU" flag on the TSCA Inventory as a guide to submitters. Submitters are responsible for verifying exemptions and should be mindful that if a flagged substance subsequently becomes the subject of any of the TSCA actions noted in this paragraph, the substance is subject to the reporting requirements notwithstanding the XU flag.[80]

1. Polymers

Excluded polymers are either (i) chemical substances described with the word fragments "*polym*," "*alkyd," or "*oxylated" in the Chemical Abstracts Service Index or Preferred Nomenclature in the Chemical Substance Identities section of the Inventory[81,82] or (ii) chemical substances identified in the

---

77. The trigger quantity was raised from ten thousand pounds to twenty-five thousand pounds for the 2006 submissions and could be altered for future reporting cycles.
78. 40 C.F.R. § 740.46. Section 4 deals with testing rules. Section 5(a)(2) deals with significant new use rules. Section 5(b)(4) deals with substances identified and listed as posing an unreasonable risk of injury to health or the environment. Section 6 deals with rules proscribing the manufacture, processing, distribution, use, or disposal of a substance that might present an unreasonable risk of injury to health or the environment. Section 5(e) deals with consent orders entered into in connection with the PMN process. Section 5(f) deals with proposed rules issued in connection with the PMN process for substances that might present an unreasonable risk of injury to health or the environment. Section 5 deals with manufacturing and processing notices and § 7 deals with imminent hazards.
79. A list of substances that were subject to TSCA actions at the time of the 2006 Inventory was contained in Appendix C to the Instructions for Reporting for the 2006 Partial Updating of the TSCA Chemical Inventory Database. (Nov. 2006) [hereinafter 2006 Instructions]. However, EPA makes clear in that Appendix that the Appendix is intended to be only an information resource. The list should not be relied upon in lieu of relevant orders, Federal Register documents, or the Code of Federal Regulations.
80. 2006 Instructions, 2-3–2-4.
81. The asterisk (*) indicates that any sets of characters may precede, or follow, the character string defined.
82. 40 C.F.R. § 710.46(a)(1)(i).

Inventory as siloxane and silicone, silsesquioxane, a protein (albumin, casein, gelatin, gluten, hemoglobin), an enzyme, a polysaccharide (starch, cellulose, gum), rubber, or lignin.[83] This exclusion does not apply to a polymeric substance that has been hydrolyzed, depolymerized, or otherwise chemically modified, except in cases where the intended product of this reaction is totally polymeric in structure.[84]

2. Microorganisms

Excluded microorganisms are any combination of chemical substances that are living organisms and meet the regulatory definition of "microorganism."[85] But a chemical substance produced from a living microorganism is reportable unless it is otherwise excluded.[86]

3. Naturally Occurring Chemical Substances

Naturally occurring substances are excluded from the IUR. To be considered naturally occurring a substance must exist in nature, and must be: "(i) unprocessed or (ii) processed only by manual, mechanical, or gravitational means; by dissolution in water; by flotation; or by heating solely to remove water." Any substance "extracted from air by any means will automatically be included in the inventory under the category 'Naturally Occurring Chemical Substances.'" The regulations provide examples of naturally occurring substances, which include "raw agricultural commodities; water, air, natural gas, and crude oil; and rocks, ores, and minerals."[87]

Since some chemicals substances described by this exclusion can be manufactured both under the terms of the exclusion and by other means, the applicability of this exclusion is determined by how the substance was actually manufactured. A person required to report for the IUR must report a chemical substance that it manufactures by other means, even if the chemical substance could have also been produced in a manner described in this exemption. Any chemical substance produced from an exempt naturally occurring chemical substance is reportable unless it is otherwise excluded.[88]

---

83. 40 C.F.R. § 710.46(a)(1)(ii).
84. 40 C.F.R. § 710.46(a)(1)(iii).
85. *See* Chapter 6, Microorganisms.
86. 40 C.F.R. § 710.46(a)(2).
87. 40 C.F.R. § 710.4(b).
88. 40 C.F.R. § 710.46(a)(3).

4. Certain Forms of Natural Gas

Excluded from the IUR are:

> Chemical substances with the following Chemical Abstract Service (CAS) Registry Numbers: CAS No. 64741–48–6, Natural gas (petroleum), raw liquid mix; CAS No. 68919–39–1, Natural gas condensates; CAS No. 8006–61–9, Gasoline natural; CAS No. 68425–31–0, Gasoline (natural gas), natural; CAS No. 8006–14–2, Natural gas; and CAS No. 68410–63–9, Natural gas, dried.[89]

5. Special Cases

a. Hydrates

While hydrates are not listed in the TSCA Inventory, hydrates must be reported, if they meet the other criteria for reporting, using the CAS registry number of the corresponding anhydrous form, adjusted for water content.[90] EPA provided an example of how this would be done in its training materials for the 2006 update. A company manufactured one million pounds of sodium hypochlorite pentahydrate, NaOCl•5 H_2O (CAS# 10022-70-5). It should report the amount of anhydrous NaOCl (CAS# 7681-52-9) calculated to be in the product that was manufactured. The molecular weight of NaOCl is 74.44 and the molecular weight of NaOCl•5 H_2O is 164.52. 74.44 ÷164.52 = 45.25% NaOCl in NaOCl•5 H_2O. Therefore, 45.25% x 1,000,000 lbs = 452,500 lbs NaOCl is required to be reported.[91]

b. Mixtures

Mixtures are not subject to the IUR, but each chemical substance that is part of a mixture must be evaluated to determine whether it meets the reporting thresholds. A company does not have to report the components of a mixture if it does not import those components or manufacture them. EPA provided two examples to illustrate how to deal with mixtures. In the first example, a company imports fifty thousand pounds of Mixture Z which contains twenty thousand pounds of Chemical X and thirty thousand pounds of Chemical Y. The company sells Mixture Z directly to consumers. EPA concluded that the company is required to report. The company needs to consider whether it

89. 40 C.F.R. § 710.46(a)(4).
90. 2006 Instructions. 2-3–2-4.
91. Instructions for Reporting for the 2006 Partial Updating of the TSCA Chemical Inventory Fred Arnold, EPA Economics, Exposure and Technology Division, Office of Pollution Prevention and Toxics, Aaron Osborne, ERG, slide 16 (undated) [hereinafter Slide Instructions].

imports or manufactures additional Chemical X at the same site to which Mixture Z was imported, so as to reach the twenty-five thousand-pound reporting threshold. Company A must report Chemical Y since it is imported at more than twenty-five thousand pounds.[92] In the second example explaining the rules relating to mixtures, Company A purchases twenty-five thousand pounds of Chemical X and twenty-five thousand pounds of Chemical Y from Domestic Manufacturer B. Company A mixes the two chemicals to form Mixture Z with no chemical reaction and sells the mixture directly to consumers. In this example, EPA concluded that Company A is not required to report because it formulates a mixture and does not manufacture the component chemical substances. Domestic Manufacturer B must report both chemicals.[93]

c. Alloys

An alloy is a solid mixture containing two or more elements, at least one of which is a metal. Entities that blend chemical substances to create an alloy, but do not manufacture or import any of the component substances, are not subject to IUR reporting.[94] EPA gives the example of a circuit board manufacturer that imports one-hundred thousand pounds of lead solder, consisting of 40 percent tin and 60 percent lead. It is received as wire or bars. The circuit board manufacturer uses the solder in its manufacture and should report the importation of forty thousand pounds of tin and sixty thousands pounds of lead. The solder does not qualify as an exempt article because it is melted during use and does not retain its original shape.[95]

B. Chemical Substances Partially Exempt from the IUR

The rules provide two categories of chemical substances, petroleum process streams, and chemical substances of low interest, with relief from certain information requirements. Manufacturers and importers of chemicals subject to this partial exemption are required to submit IUR data but are not required to submit industrial processing and use information and commercial and consumer use information otherwise required for manufacturers or importers of products in excess of three-hundred thousand pounds at any one site.[96] Inorganic chemical substances had also benefitted from this partial

---

92. *Id.* at 32.
93. *Id.* at 33.
94. *Id.* at 34.
95. *Id.* at 35.
96. 40 C.F.R. § 710.52(c)(4).

exemption through the IUR reporting cycle of 2006, but will be subject to full reporting starting with the 2011 reporting period, absent further changes.[97]

1. Petroleum Process Streams

EPA has designated a list of specific petroleum process stream chemicals by CAS Number in the rule as exempt from certain information requirements under the IUR.[98] That specific list should be consulted to determine the status of any particular petroleum process stream. The petroleum process stream partial exemption was established by the 2003 Amendments to the IUR[99] and was based upon expected exposures and uses. EPA determined that those chemicals were transported, processed, and stored in well controlled vessels because they are flammable. For that reason, EPA believed worker exposure was diminished, so the substances would not warrant the full set of reporting data.[100] In the final rule dealing with petroleum process streams for the 2006 IUR, EPA made clear its intention to revisit the list for the next reporting cycle.[101]

2. Chemical Substances of Low Interest

EPA has also designated a list of specific chemical substances, by CAS Number, as exempt from certain information requirements under the IUR because that information would be of low interest.[102] In developing this list, EPA considered, among other things, whether the volume at any site exceeded the three-hundred thousand pound threshold where extensive data submission requirements become applicable;[103] the substance's physical and chemical properties and potential for persistence, bioaccumulation, health effects, or environmental effects;[104] information needs of various constituencies;[105] availability of other complementary risk screening information;[106] comparable processing and use information;[107] and whether the potential risks of the substance are adequately managed.[108]

---

97. 40 C.F.R. § 710.46(c).
98. 40 C.F.R. § 710.46(b)(1).
99. 68 Fed. Reg. 848 (Jan. 7, 2003).
100. 70 Fed. Reg. 75059, 75061 (Dec. 19, 2005).
101. *Id.* at 75062.
102. 40 C.F.R. § 710.46(b)(2).
103. 40 C.F.R. § 710.46(b)(2)(ii)(A).
104. 40 C.F.R. § 710.46(b)(2)(ii)(B).
105. 40 C.F.R. § 710.46(b)(2)(ii)(C).
106. 40 C.F.R. § 710.46(b)(2)(ii)(D).
107. 40 C.F.R. § 710.46(b)(2)(ii)(E).
108. 40 C.F.R. § 710.46(b)(2)(ii)(F).

EPA reserved the right to amend the list on its own initiative or in response to a request by the public[109] by initiating rulemaking.[110] Requests by the public must be made at least one year prior to the start of the year for which reporting is required, for example, for the 2011 reporting period, the reporting is required for manufacture and import during the 2010 year and so the request should have been made by January 1, 2009.[111] Such a request for future IURs must identify the chemical and must contain a written rationale that addresses the noted considerations and must demonstrate that the collection of the information either is or is not of low current interest.[112] EPA is required to issue a written response to each request within one-hundred twenty days of receipt of the request, and will maintain copies of these responses in a public docket established for each reporting cycle.[113]

C. Who Must Report for the IUR

Any person who manufactured or imported for commercial purposes a reportable chemical substance in the amount of twenty-five thousand pounds or more at any one owned or controlled site during the calendar year is subject to reporting for that chemical substance.[114] For importers, the site of importation is the site of the operating unit that is directly responsible for importing the substance and controls the import transaction, which can in some instances be the organization's domestic headquarters.[115]

Excluded from the reporting requirement are small manufacturers or importers. Small means having total annual sales, when combined with its parent company, if any, of less than $40,000,000, except that if a substance is manufactured or imported at any one site in excess of one-hundred thousand pounds, the entity and parent company must have combined sales of under $4,000,000 to be exempt from reporting.[116] However, the exemption does not apply if the substance is subject to a rule proposed or promulgated under TSCA §§ 4, 5(a)(2), 5(b)(4), or 6, or is the subject of an order issued under

109. 40 C.F.R. § 710.46(b)(2)(iii).
110. 40 C.F.R. § 710.46(b)(2)(iii)(B).
111. 40 C.F.R. § 710.46(b)(2)(iii)(C).
112. 40 C.F.R. § 710.46(b)(2)(iii)(D).
113. *Id.*
114. 40 C.F.R. § 710.48(a).
115. 40 C.F.R. § 710.48(b).
116. 40 C.F.R. § 704.3. The rules allows EPA to adjust these sales volumes for inflation.

section TSCA § 5(e), or is the subject of relief that has been granted under a civil action under TSCA §§ 5 or 7.[117,118]

Any person who submitted the information required by the IUR in compliance with a TSCA § 8(a) rule within one year of the start of a reporting period is not again required to report on the manufacture of that substance at that site during that submission period.[119] When two or more importers are involved in a particular import transaction, they may determine among themselves who should submit the required report.[120] However, each such importer will be liable for failure to report if no report is filed.[121]

Reporting is not required for substances which were manufactured or imported in small quantities solely for research and development,[122,123] imported as part of an article,[124] and byproducts used commercially only to burn for fuel, dispose of as waste or extract component chemicals from it for commercial purposes.[125] Reporting is also not required for chemical substances manufactured for commercial purposes that have no purpose separate from the substance, mixture or article of which they are a part,[126] such as:

(1) any impurity;
(2) any byproduct which is not used for commercial purposes;

---

117. 40 C.F.R. § 710.49. Section 4 deals with testing rules. Section 5(a)(2) deals with significant new use rules. Section 5(b)(4) deals with substances identified and listed as posing an unreasonable risk of injury to health or the environment. Section 6 deals with rules proscribing the manufacture, processing, distribution, use, or disposal of a substance that might present an unreasonable risk of injury to health or the environment. Section 5(e) deals with consent orders entered into in connection with the PMN process. Section 5 deals with manufacturing and processing notices and § 7 deals with imminent hazards.
118. A list of substances that were subject to TSCA actions at the time of the 2006 Inventory was contained in Appendix C to the 2006 Instructions. However, EPA makes clear in that Appendix that the Appendix is intended to be only an information resource. The list should not be relied upon in lieu of relevant orders, Federal Register documents, or the Code of Federal Regulations.
119. 40 C.F.R. § 710.55(a).
120. 40 C.F.R. § 710.55(b).
121. *Id.*
122. 40 C.F.R. § 710.50(a).
123. A manufacturer who makes twenty-six thousand pounds of a chemical, uses two thousand pounds for research and development, and sells the remaining chemical for industrial uses must report. The total amount of the chemical manufactured must be reported because the reporting threshold is exceeded. Questions and Answers for Reporting for the 2006 Partial Updating of the TSCA Chemical Inventory Database EPA Office of Pollution Prevention and Toxics Economics, Exposure and Technology Division, 84, Question 55 (Nov. 2006).
124. 40 C.F.R. § 710.50(b).
125. 40 C.F.R. § 720.30(g), referenced in 40 C.F.R. § 710.50(b).
126. 40 C.F.R. § 720.30(h), referenced in 40 C.F.R. § 710.50(c).

(3) any chemical substance which results from a chemical reaction that occurs incidental to exposure of another chemical substance, mixture, or article to environmental factors such as air, moisture, microbial organisms, or sunlight;

(4) any chemical substance which results from a chemical reaction that occurs incidental to storage or disposal of another chemical substance, mixture, or article;

(5) any chemical substance which results from a chemical reaction that occurs upon end use of another chemical substance, mixture, or article such as an adhesive, paint, miscellaneous cleanser or other housekeeping product, fuel additive, water softening and treatment agent, photographic film, battery, match, or safety flare, and which is not itself manufactured or imported for distribution in commerce or for use as an intermediate;

(6) Any chemical substance which results from a chemical reaction that occurs upon use of curable plastic or rubber molding compounds, inks, drying oils, metal finishing compounds, adhesives, or paints, or any other chemical substance formed during the manufacture of an article destined for the marketplace without further chemical change of the chemical substance except for those chemical changes that occur as described elsewhere in this paragraph;

(7) any chemical substance which results from a chemical reaction that occurs when (i) a stabilizer, colorant, odorant, antioxidant, filler, solvent, carrier, surfactant, plasticizer, corrosion inhibitor, antifoamer or defoamer, dispersant, precipitation inhibitor, binder, emulsifier, deemulsifier, dewatering agent, agglomerating agent, adhesion promoter, flow modifier, pH neutralizer, sequesterant, coagulant, flocculant, fire retardant, lubricant, chelating agent, or quality control reagent functions as intended, or (ii) a chemical substance, which is intended solely to impart a specific physiochemical characteristic, functions as intended; and

(8) any nonisolated intermediate.[127]

D. What to Report for the IUR

Information must be reported for each reportable chemical substance on a separate form for each site for which the submitter is required to report. Information must be submitted to the extent the information is "known to or reasonably ascertainable by"[128] that person. The additional information that is required to be submitted for substances manufactured or imported at any site in quantities of three-hundred pounds or more during the reporting

127. Each of these categories is discussed in Chapter 5, PMN Exclusions and Exemptions.
128. 40 C.F.R. § 710.52.

period must be reported only to the extent that additional information is "readily obtainable"[129] by the submitter. Information can be submitted in writing using EPA's Form U[130] or on magnetic media.[131] The report must be dated and certified by an authorized official of the reporting company.[132] Submitted information may be claimed as confidential and substantiation of any confidentiality claims must be submitted with the IUR report.[133]

1. Information Requirements for All Reportable Chemical Substances Made or Imported in Quantities of Twenty-five Thousand Pounds or More

Each report must contain the company name and Dun and Bradstreet Number;[134] the name, mailing address, phone number, and e-mail address of a technical contact; and for each plant site, the name and full street address of each site, Dun and Bradstreet number of each site, and the county (or other jurisdictional indicator) in which the plant site is located.[135]

For each chemical substance, the report must contain the specific chemical name and CAS Number or a PMN case number if a CAS Number is not known to or reasonably ascertainable by the submitter; or, for confidential substances, an EPA-designated Accession Number; and a code designating which identification number is being used.[136] The report must state whether the substance, by site, is made in or imported into the United States or both[137] and whether it is site-limited.[138] The total volume, in pounds, must be reported for each substance at each site, separately for manufacture and for importation.[139] The rule specifies that the amount must be reported to two significant figures provided that the reported figures are within 10 percent of the actual volume.[140]

---

129. *Id.*
130. 40 C.F.R. § 710.52(a). Copies of Form U for the IURs after 2006 should be available from EPA.
131. 40 C.F.R. § 710.52(b). The magnetic media must meet EPA specifications, although EPA is considering requiring electronic reporting. Regulatory Plan and Semiannual Regulatory Agenda, EPA-230-Z-09-002, 96 (Fall 2009), *available at* http://www.epa.gov/lawsregs/documents/regagendabook-fall09.pdf.
132. 40 C.F.R. § 710.52(c)(1).
133. 40 C.F.R. 710.58.
134. 40 C.F.R. § 710.52(c)(2)(i).
135. 40 C.F.R. § 710.52(c)(2)(ii).
136. 40 C.F.R. § 710.52(c)(3)(i).
137. 40 C.F.R. § 710.52(c)(3)(ii).
138. 40 C.F.R. § 710.52(c)(3)(iii).
139. 40 C.F.R. § 710.52(c)(3)(iv).
140. 40 C.F.R. § 710.52(c)(3)(iv).

The submitter must report the total number of workers likely to be exposed to each substance at each site, according to one of eight specified ranges.[141] The worker exposure ranges start with fewer than ten workers and end with greater than one thousand workers. By designated range, the submitter must report the maximum concentration, measured by percentage of weight, for each substance at the time it is sent off-site from each site.[142] The calculation as to concentration must be made at the time of reaction for site-limited substances.[143] There are five concentration ranges, starting from less than 1 percent to more than 90 percent.

The report must state the physical forms of the substance as it is sent off-site or reacted on site. The specified forms that can be selected are: dry powder, pellets, or large crystals; water or solvent-wet liquid; other solid, gas or vapor, or liquid;[144] and the percentage of each physical form to the total volume, rounded off to the nearest 10 percent.[145]

2. Information Requirements for Substances Made or Imported in Quantities of Three-hundred Thousand Pounds or More

Substances manufactured or imported at any site in quantities of three-hundred thousand pounds or more, and which are not partially exempt, require additional information. Site includes locations that receive a reportable chemical substance from the submitter directly or indirectly, including through a broker/distributor or from a customer of the submitter. Information required is limited to domestic processing and use activities that are readily obtainable by the submitter.[146]

For each substance, the submitter must report the type of industrial processing or use operations at each site, using the designations provided in the rule,[147] the applicable North American Industrial Classification System (NAICS) codes,[148] the industrial function category or categories, from the list specified, that best represents the specific manner in which the chemical substance is used,[149] the estimated percentage, rounded off to the closest 10 percent (except if the total associated volume is three-hundred thousand pounds or more, and the percentage for such category would be less than 5 percent, it should be rounded off to the nearest 1 percent) of total production or

141. 40 C.F.R. § 710.52(c)(3)(v).
142. 40 C.F.R. § 710.52(c)(3)(vi).
143. 40 C.F.R. § 710.52(c)(3)(vi).
144. 40 C.F.R. § 710.52(c)(3)(vii).
145. 40 C.F.R. § 710.52(c)(3)(viii).
146. 40 C.F.R. § 710.52(c)(4).
147. 40 C.F.R. § 710.52(c)(4)(i)(A).
148. 40 C.F.R. § 710.52(c)(4)(i)(B).
149. 40 C.F.R. § 710.52(c)(4)(i)(C).

importation associated with each combination of operations, NAICS code, and industrial function category,[150] the number of sites associated with each such combination,[151] and the number of workers likely to be exposed to each chemical substance for each such combination, by range.[152]

For each substance, the submitter must report the commercial and consumer product category, using the designations contained in the rule,[153] the percentage, rounded off to the closest 10 percent (except if the production volume for any commercial or consumer product category is three-hundred thousand pounds or more, and the percentage for such category would be less than 5 percent, rounded off to 1percent) of the total production volume associated with each commercial and consumer category[154] and the typical maximum concentration, measured by weight, in each commercial and consumer product category, by range.[155] Submitters must also report (a) whether or not any amount of the chemical substance is to be present in or on any consumer products used for children up to the age of 14,[156] or (b) if they cannot readily obtain that information.[157]

3. Importers Without Knowledge of Chemical Identity

Sometimes importers may not know the specific chemical identity of a chemical substance. Those importers are still responsible for ensuring that the applicable information is provided by the foreign supplier. EPA has established a procedure to allow the foreign supplier to report the chemical identity as confidential without providing it to the importer.[158] The importer must advise the EPA, in a cover letter, that the chemical identity and the technical contact will be submitted by the foreign supplier. For each foreign supplier with a substance with an unknown chemical identity, the importer must fill out a separate report on Form U. The importer should make a photocopy of the blank form for submission to the foreign supplier. The instructions

150. 40 C.F.R. § 710.52(c)(4)(i)(D).
151. 40 C.F.R. § 710.52(c)(4)(i)(E).
152. 40 C.F.R. § 710.52(c)(4)(i)(F).
153. 40 C.F.R. § 710.52(c)(4)(ii)(A).
154. 40 C.F.R. § 710.52(c)(4)(ii)(C).
155. 40 C.F.R. § 710.52(c)(4)(ii)(D).
156. EPA suggests three questions to consider in making a determination as to whether a consumer product is intended to be used for children up to the age of 14. They are: "1. Is the product commonly recognized (i.e., by a reasonable person) as being intended for children age 14 or younger? 2. Does the manufacturer of the product state through product labeling or other written materials that the product is intended or will be used by children age 14 or younger? Or 3. Is the advertising, promotion, or marketing of the product aimed at children age 14 or younger?" 2006 Instructions, 4-18.
157. 40 C.F.R. § 710.52(c)(4)(ii)(B).
158. 2006 Instructions, 6-4–6-5.

mandate that the importer sign the certification statement, enter the technical contact and complete parts I though III as applicable. In Part II, Section A, Block 2.A.1, the importer should enter the identifying number, the trade name or other designation by which it refers to each chemical substance. Leave Block 2.A.2 blank. This original form should be sent by the importer to EPA.

The instructions further advise the importer to enter only the plant site information on the photocopy of the blank form and then send it to the foreign supplier to complete and forward to EPA. The foreign supplier must enter its technical contact and company information on the copy, complete Parts I through III, and enter the appropriate specific chemical identities in Part II, Section A. The foreign supplier can claim the chemical identities as confidential by checking the "CBI" box and submitting substantiation of its claim. The supplier should also include with its report on Form U a letter advising that the information is being submitted by a foreign supplier on behalf of the identified importer. Information in the letter may be claimed as confidential by circling or bracketing the text to be protected and marking the page "CONFIDENTIAL."

4. Recordkeeping Requirements

Records relevant to reporting are required to be kept for five years from the last day of the IUR submission period. EPA encourages submitters to keep such records for a longer period as a useful reference for succeeding reporting periods.[159] EPA advises that required records include those that show the production volume, plant site, and site-limited status of each substance reported.[160] It further suggests that if a substance is not reported because its site-specific annual production is less than twenty-five thousand pounds, records should be kept to substantiate that production level.[161]

5. IUR Corrections

Corrections can be made to the IUR in a letter, mailed to the EPA, containing only the incorrect and the correct information. The entire submission form does not have to be resubmitted. For identification, the letter should include (1) the EPA Report Number, if it has been received, or the company number developed using the eIUR software, or if neither of these numbers are available, state that in the letter and, (2) exactly as written in the original submission, the company name, site name and address, and chemical name and

---

159. 40 C.F.R. § 710.57.
160. 2006 Instructions, 6-4.
161. *Id.*

identifying number. To correct the IUR submission, identify (a) the block number on Form U where the information is, and (b) both the specific, incorrect information that is to be replaced and the correct, replacement information.[162] The following certification must also be included:

> I hereby certify to the best of my knowledge and belief that Parts I and II have been completed in compliance with the requirements of 40 CFR 710.52(c)(1),(2), and (3); Part III of this form has been completed in compliance with the requirements of 40 CFR 710.52(c)(4); and any confidentiality claims are true and correct as to that information for which they have been asserted.[163]

IV. Inventory Representation Issues

Because of varying interpretations as to how to name a chemical substance for placement on the Inventory, the EPA issued a series of documents that give guidance on how to list substances for the Inventory. Failure to identify a substance properly can result in compliance and commercial issues for manufacturers, processors, and other users. Guidance documents[164] have been issued for polymers, chemicals with varying carbon chain lengths (alkyls), chemicals of unknown or variable composition, complex reaction products, and mixtures.[165] One common theme in the guidances is that the EPA considers how a substance is named, or the nomenclature, to be different from how it is represented on the Inventory. These guidances all give information about how to refer to the substance on the Inventory, which is its

---

162. EPA Office of Pollution Prevention and Toxics, Correcting IUR Submissions, 1 (Mar. 2006) [hereinafter IUR Corrections].
163. *Id.* at A-2. For more information, see also http://www.epa.gov/oppt/iur/pubs/guidance/correctingsubs.html.
164. Each guidance document contains a notice that the policies in the document are not final EPA action, are intended for guidance only and cannot be relied upon by any party in litigation with the U.S. Further, the notices make clear that EPA can decide to act at variance with the guidance document.
165. The EPA guidances are respectively: "Toxic Substances Control Act Inventory Representation For Polymeric Substances," "Toxic Substances Control Act Inventory Representation For Certain Chemical Substances Containing Varying Carbon Chain Lengths (Alkyl Ranges Using The CX-Y Notation)," "Toxic Substances Control Act Inventory Representation For Chemical Substances Of Unknown or Variable Composition, Complex Reaction Products And Biological Materials: UVCB Substances," "Toxic Substances Control Act Inventory Representation For Combinations Of Two Or More Substances: Complex Reaction Products," and "Toxic Substances Control Act Inventory Representation For Products Containing Two Or More Substances: Formulated And Statutory Mixtures." The first four of these guidance documents are discussed in this section. The last, dealing with formulated and statutory mixtures, is discussed in Chapter 2, TSCA's Scope. All except the first are available through http://www.epa.gov/opptintr/newchems/pubs/guideman.htm.

"representation" and not how to give chemical names to a substance. This is a somewhat metaphysical difference, and so it is best to quote the Agency. In referring to the fact that one chemical may be present on the Inventory under multiple names, the EPA said:

> Although these chemically indistinguishable substances are named differently on the Inventory, this is not a "nomenclature" issue, but an issue of substance representation.[166]

The nomenclature papers all provide guidance in interpreting the chemical names on the Inventory so that prospective manufacturers and importers can determine if they must file a PMN before they commence manufacturing or importation. They also assist PMN filers with selecting the proper name of their chemicals.

All of the guidances classify chemicals into classes:

- Class 1: "chemicals that can be represented by a definite chemical structural diagram and molecular formula," such as "acetone, iron, benzene and sodium chloride"; and
- Class 2: "product substances which are combinations of different known or unknown species or whose composition cannot be represented by a definite chemical structure diagram," such as "cresol, crude oil, superphosphate (fertilizer), tall oil and coconut oil fatty acids."[167]

A. Polymers

1. Listing Polymers

Polymers are a large class of organic chemicals that have widely varying properties. The plastics that surround us every day are all polymers, and so are many other chemicals that we do not typically think of as being polymers, such as deoxyribonucleic acid (which is commonly known as DNA), enzymes, cellulose, Teflon® fluoropolymers, and silk. They all have in common a chemical backbone made of repeating units of sets of atoms, and these repeating units are called monomers. Different monomers form different polymers. To give some examples, the monomers in cellulose are derived from sugar, and the monomers in the polyethylene used to make plastic bags are derived from

---

166. U.S. EPA, Toxic Substances Control Act Inventory Representation for Polymeric Substances, 1 (Mar. 29, 1995).

167. *See, e.g.*, Toxic Substances Control Act Inventory Representation for Combinations of Two or More Substances: Complex Reaction Products, *available at* http://www.epa.gov/oppt/newchems/pubs/rxnprods.txt.

ethylene molecules.[168] Some polymers like Teflon® fluoropolymers are relatively inert and others like DNA are biologically quite active.

The EPA explained its preferred methods for representing polymers on the Inventory in its 1995 Toxic Substances Control Act Inventory Representation for Polymeric Substances, and began by defining what substances can be listed on the Inventory as polymers.[169] For this purpose, EPA defined polymers as sequences of one or more types of monomer units, where a monomer unit is the reacted form of a monomer bonded to two or more other molecules. A polymer must also have a distribution of molecules of different molecular weights attributable primarily to different numbers of monomer units in the molecules.[170] If all the molecules of a specific substance always have the same chain length then that substance is described on the Inventory as a specific substance with a defined structure and molecular weight, and not as a polymer.[171] There are limited exceptions to this rule. Some chemicals that chemists may consider to be polymers do not fall within this definition because they do not have a distribution of molecular weights. For example, any given enzyme will have a fixed molecular weight and will not have a range of numbers of monomer units. As a result an enzyme is not a polymer for the purposes of this definition and for Inventory listing. Similarly, the EPA gave the example of resinous substances that some chemists consider to be polymers but which have neither monomers nor variable molecular weights.[172]

There are two ways to represent polymers on the Inventory. The first is by reference to the monomers and other starting reactants, and the second is by reference to the structural repeating units (SRUs).

Most polymers are listed by their monomers and other starting materials, which the EPA calls monomer-based representation. The EPA succinctly summarized this method in the Toxic Substances Control Act Inventory Representation for Polymeric Substances in section II A:

> Polymers that use monomer-based representation are described according to the starting monomers used in their manufacture as well as other reactants including free-radical initiators, cross-linking agents, chain transfer agents, mono-functional groups that act as modifiers and other end groups that become chemically incorporated into the polymer structure, subject to the two percent

168. *See, e.g.*, John, D. Roberts et al., ORGANIC CHEMISTRY 410, 745 (1971).
169. *Available at* http://www.epa.gov/opptintr/newchems/pubs/polymers.txt [hereinafter Polymeric Substances.
170. *Id.* at section I A.
171. Polymer Exemption Guidance Manual, EPA 744-B-97-001, 36, question 1 (June 1997), *available at* http://www.epa.gov/oppt/newchems/pubs/polyguid.pdf [hereinafter Polymer Exemption Guidance Manual].
172. These are the glycerol or pentaerythritol esters of rosin. Polymeric Substances, section I A.

rule (citation omitted). The basic form of a typical monomer-based polymer name is Reactant A, polymer with reactant B and reactant C.

Monomer-based representation is appropriate when the polymer does not have a definite structural diagram and either (i) has only one monomer with an unknown degree of polymerization, or (ii) has more than one type of monomer in no particular pattern. It is also appropriate for homopolymers with more than ten monomers even if the substance has a definite structural diagram, and this is the sole exception to requirement that polymers have a distribution of molecular weights.[173]

An example of a monomer-based Inventory listing is "Castor oil, polymer with hydroxyethyl methacrylate, Me methacrylate, methacrylic acid and styrene," CAS # 68551-73-5.

SRU representation is appropriate only for polymers with structures known to have repeating units. Naming the repeating units gives more information than just naming the starting monomers, and so this is a more precise way of representing substances on the Inventory.[174] There can be an average number of repeating units in the polymer backbone, a range, or an unknown number so long as there are repeating units. Certain polymers including some polyethylene glycols, polypropylene glycols, siloxanes, and silicones are named by this method.[175]

An example of a polymer using SRU representation is CAS # 25190-06-1, represented on the Inventory as poly(oxy-1,4-butanediyl), .alpha.-hydro-.omega.-hydroxy-.[176]

SRU representation is not used for polymers with ten or fewer repeating units. Polymers with ten or fewer repeating units are named as discrete substances and not as polymers.[177]

2. The Two Percent Rule

The "two percent rule" is a rule that details how to describe a polymer and what starting materials are relevant to describing a polymer for Inventory, PMN and recordkeeping purposes. Basically, the two percent rule permits a manufacturer or importer to disregard starting materials used in making a polymer if the starting materials are charged to the reaction vessel at two

173. Polymeric Substances, §§ II A 1 and II B 1.
174. *Id.* at § II A 2.
175. *Id.*
176. *Id.*; for the Inventory description *see* the EPA Substance Registry Services Web site at http://iaspub.epa.gov/sor_internet/registry/substreg/searchandretrieve/searchbylist/search.do and search the Inventory for CAS # 25190-06-1.
177. Polymeric Substances, section II A 2.

weight percent or less of the final polymer, or incorporated into the final polymer at two weight percent or less of the final reaction polymer.[178]

Polymers are generally described on the Inventory by their composition and starting materials. Therefore, a manufacturer may make or import a polymer with two percent or less of a starting material that is not listed as part of a polymer's Inventory description.[179] As with most TSCA rules, the two percent rule cannot be summarized so neatly and there are exceptions and peculiarities to the rule.

The two percent rule appears in two places in the regulations. First, it is embodied in 40 C.F.R. § 720.45(a)(2) where it defines how a polymer must be described in a PMN and how the polymer will be described on the Inventory. The two percent rule also defines how broadly Inventory listings of polymers may be interpreted. The second place it makes its appearance is in the polymer exemption rule where it is used as part of the definition of polymers exempt from the PMN requirements of TSCA § 5.[180]

When a manufacturer or importer files a PMN for a polymer, all of the starting materials must be described on the PMN form.[181] The manufacturer must also list the percent by weight of each reactant. However, when the polymer is listed on the Inventory, it will only be listed by reference to the reactants that are either charged to the reaction vessel or incorporated into the final polymer at greater than two percent by weight unless the submitter chooses to list the reactants that are used at two percent or less.

A PMN submitter may choose to list reactants that are charged or incorporated at less than two percent so that the polymer will be described on the Inventory as including that reactant. That way if the submitter chooses at a later time to increase the proportion of that reactant above two percent the resulting polymer will already be on the Inventory and the submitter will not have to go through the PMN process again.[182] Competitors who do not use the reactant will have to file a new PMN.

If a polymer is described on the Inventory as the reaction product of X, Y, and Z, then any additional raw materials, say for example A, B, and C, may be used in the reaction to form the listed polymer, so long as they are either charged to the reaction vessel or incorporated into the final polymer at two

---

178. Prior to 1995 the two percent rule only allowed measurement of the weight percent of reactants charged to the reaction vessel. Rule amendments in 1995 permitted the alternative of determining the weight percent of a reactant incorporated into the resulting polymer. 60 Fed. Reg. 16298 (Mar. 29, 1995); 60 Fed. Reg. 16316 (Mar. 29, 1995).

179. The EPA refers to a polymer's description for Inventory purposes as its "chemical identity." In practice the "chemical identity" can be very different from the polymer's chemical composition, and so this term is confusing and misleading and will not be used here.

180. 40 C.F.R. § 720.250. *See* Chapter 5, PMN Exclusions and Exemptions.

181. 40 C.F.R. § 720.45(a)(2).

182. 60 Fed. Reg. 16298, 16304 (Mar. 29, 1995).

weight percent or less.[183] The polymer that results from the reaction will be considered to be listed on the Inventory. The two percent rule greatly expands the breadth of polymers that can be made without going through the PMN process again. However, if a monomer is listed as one of the starting materials in a polymer, it must always be present in some amount in a polymer made under that Inventory listing. A polymer that is described as the reaction product of X, Y, Z, and A must always have A in it, even if A is less than or equal to two percent.[184]

To determine whether a reactant is charged to the reaction vessel at less than or equal to two percent by weight, the dry weight of the resulting polymer is used.[185] Determining the weight percent charged is basically just "bookkeeping" according to the EPA. To determine the percent incorporated, the EPA prefers that PMN submitters use analytical methods. This analysis may be both extensive and expensive.[186] Alternatively, theoretical calculations may be used to determine the percent incorporated if there are no technically feasible analytical methods.[187] In either case, there is a requirement to maintain records to demonstrate that less than two percent of the starting material is incorporated, and take into account variations from one batch to the next.[188] Finally, if there are no appropriate analytical methods and no theoretical methods, the submitter must use the percent charged method.[189]

The percent incorporated into the polymer may give a better indication of the toxicity of the resulting polymer because some reactants are taken up by the polymer in much smaller amounts than other reactants. Some reactants

---

183. The charged or incorporated method of determining two percent must be used consistently for each polymer.
184. 60 Fed. Reg. 16298, 16304 (Mar. 29, 1995).
185. *Id.* The Polymer Exemption Guidance Manual, 20, explains that the percent charged is the grams of the reactant charged divided by the total grams of dry polymer formed, multiplied by 100. This leads to real peculiarities when a part of the reactant molecule is not incorporated into the polymer. The EPA gives the formation of polyvinyl alcohol as an example. The starting material for polyvinyl alcohol is a vinyl acetate molecule, which has a molecular weight of 86 daltons. Only a part of the vinyl acetate molecule is incorporated into the resulting polymer repeating units, and those repeating units have a weight of 44 daltons. As a result, the percent incorporated is (86/44) x 100, or 195%. Similarly, when there are unreacted starting materials, the total of all of the reactants' percent charged will exceed 100.
186. 40 C.F.R. §720.45(a)(iii)(B); 60 Fed. Reg. 16298, 16304 (Mar. 29, 1995). The Polymer Exemption Guidance Manual, 21, sets out the method of determining the percent incorporated, using three values as a starting point. These values are "the molecular weight of the reactant charged; the molecular weight of the fragment that is incorporated into the polymer (if the feedstock is not entirely incorporated); and the analytically determined amount of the incorporated reactant that is present in the polymer (the weight percent of the polymer that consists of the fragment)."
187. 60 Fed. Reg. 16298, 16305 (Mar. 29, 1995).
188. Draft PMN Q&A, 2-14, question 208–9.
189. Polymer Exemption Guidance Manual, 21.

must be charged to the reaction vessel in amounts much more than two percent, but less than two percent is incorporated during polymer formation.[190]

The charged or incorporated methods must be used consistently for each PMN. If one starting material is calculated using the charged method, all the starting materials must be calculated using the charged method, and if one is calculated using the incorporated method, they all must be calculated using the incorporated method.

Additives that do not chemically react to become part of the polymer are disregarded for purposes of the two percent rule, and do not have to be named as part of the polymer. Examples of these additives include colorants and UV adsorbers, among others.[191] Similarly, emulsifiers and plasticizers do not become part of the polymer's chemical composition and are not part of the polymer's description.[192] Catalysts are not consumed in reactions and therefore do not have to be part of the polymer representation.

Free radical initiators pose a special problem in interpreting the two percent rule. They are chemicals that are used to start polymerization reactions. Some of the free radical initiators become part of the resulting polymer, and at least a fragment of the free radical initiator is almost always incorporated into the polymer as an end group.[193] Free radical initiators are not true catalysts because catalysts are unaffected by the reactions they facilitate.[194] Free radical initiators are often charged to the reaction vessel at much greater than two percent by weight, but are often incorporated into the resulting polymer at a much lower percentage. Either the charged method or incorporated method may be used to determine whether a free radical initiator must be part of the polymer representation for Inventory purposes.[195]

However, before 1989 manufacturers were not consistently reporting all free radical initiators that were charged to the reaction vessel because it was unclear whether they were intended to become part of the final polymer. The EPA clarified its position on representation of free radical initiators in the June 28, 1989 Federal Register and said that all free radical initiators charged at greater than two percent by weight of the starting reactants must be listed as part of the polymer representation, unless the manufacturer could prove

---

190. 60 Fed. Reg. 16298, 16305 (Mar. 29, 1995). For example, an excess of neutralizer is often used as a starting reactant in the manufacture of a polymer. Although the weight of the neutralizer may be much more than two percent of the final dry weight of the polymer, only a very small portion of the neutralizer may be incorporated into the polymer. Polymer Exemption Guidance Manual, 22. In this example, the percent charged method of calculating the two percent rule would result in a figure of more than two percent, but the incorporated method would result in a figure of less than two percent.
191. Polymeric Substances, section II D 1 a.
192. 54 Fed. Reg. 27174 (June 28, 1989).
193. *Id.* at 27175.
194. *See, e.g.*, http://www.arkema-inc.com/index.cfm?pag=1084.
195. 58 Fed. Reg. 7661, 7664 (Feb. 8, 1993).

that none of the free radical initiator was incorporated into the polymer.[196] That policy statement was issued before manufacturers were permitted to use the percent incorporated method, which was effective in 1995. Now that manufacturers can use either method of applying the two percent rule, they can either use the percent charged method if any of the free radical initiator becomes part of the polymer structure, use the percent incorporated method, or bear the burden of proving that none of the free radical initiator becomes part of the polymer structure.

Prior to the EPA's clarification, there had been different interpretations of whether free radical initiators must be listed in the Inventory description for polymers. As a result, the EPA had to adopt a policy to prevent unfair burdens on people who had consulted the Inventory prior to the June 28, 1989 clarification. In the clarification, the EPA stated that all polymers that were put on the Inventory or were the subject of a Notice of Commencement filed on before June 28, 1989 can be made with any amount of free radical initiator, whether or not the free radical initiator is part of the polymer description on the Inventory.[197] Of course, if the free radical initiator is listed in the Inventory representation of the polymer, that free radical initiator must be used, but it may be in any amount.

One drawback of using the percent incorporated method to determine whether a reactant must be listed in the Inventory description of the polymer is that as analytical methods improve a manufacturer may find that a reactant is actually incorporated at greater than two percent, even if the manufacturer previously believed the reactant was incorporated at less than two percent.[198]

B. UVCB Substances

UVCB substances are substances of unknown or variable composition, complex reaction products, and biological materials that cannot be represented by unique structures and molecular formulas. Some UVCB substances are not adequately described by their CA Names and have supplemental definitions that are considered integral parts of the names for TSCA purposes. The guidance, entitled Toxic Substances Control Act Inventory Representation For Chemical Substances Of Unknown Or Variable Composition, Complex Reaction Products And Biological Materials: UVCB Substances[199] points out that any substance that matches a CA Name but is not covered by the substance description is not considered to be covered by that Inventory listing.

---

196. 54 Fed. Reg. 27174, 27176 (June 28, 1989).
197. Draft PMN Q&A, 1-58, question 119-8.
198. 54 Fed. Reg. 27174, 27175-76 (June 28, 1989).
199. *Available at* http://www.epa.gov/oppt/newchems/pubs/uvcb.txt.

An example of this would be Soybean, flour CASRN 68513-95-1*†,[200] which is defined as: "[a] fine-ground powder made by steaming soybeans, followed by removal of hulls and mechanical grinding."[201] EPA points out that if another type of soybean flour were made without steaming the soybeans or removing the hulls, it would not be covered by this definition. Similarly, Gelatins, hydrolyzates CASRN 68410-45-7*†, defined as "enzymatic digest produced by hydrolysis of gelatin" would not cover a gelatin that was hydrolyzed chemically rather than enzymatically.[202]

The Inventory includes a large variety of substances of unknown composition. To be eligible for inclusion on the Inventory, the substance must have a commercial purpose, otherwise it would be classified as an impurity, a byproduct, or a waste. EPA discourages the use of substances named as "reaction products with," reserving that naming only for those substances for which there is not enough information to identify the products completely or for which the products are comprised of a combination of different chemical classes.[203] Only the substances intentionally present with commercial value should be included in the name. The reactants must always be the same as on the listing. For example, the name "reaction products with A, B, C, and D" would not include an identical product made with reaction products A, B, C, and E. The term "compounds with" is generally used for acid/base salts, adducts, inclusion compounds, and the like and is distinguishable from "reaction products with," which is used when a product-based name cannot be developed. An example of "compounds with" is "fatty acids, linseed-oil, compds. with triethylamine," CASRN 68605-07-2*, which is "the triethylamine salt of linseed oil fatty acids. It a UVCB substance because linseed oil fatty acids are biological materials."[204]

EPA gives several illustrations of nomenclature for substances of variable composition, including:

Rutile, neodymium CASRN 68516-14-3*

The UVCB definition for this substance is: "An inorganic pigment that is the reaction product of high temperature calcination in which neodymium (III)

200. "A dagger(†) is found next to the CASRN in the printed TSCA Inventory to indicate that a definition exists for that chemical substance. These definitions appear in Appendix A of volume 1 of the 1985 Edition of the TSCA Chemical Substances Inventory. Persons using various online versions need to be certain that they obtain any definitions that may pertain to UVCB substances of interest before they make Inventory determinations. The definitions are usually found in fields separate from the main CA names, and so may be overlooked." UVCB Substances, 3.UVCB Substances, § II D.

201. *Id.*

202. *Id.*

203. *Id.* at § III A 2. The EPA generally uses the "reaction products with" names only as a last resort. Complex Reaction Products, § II A 2.

204. UVCB Substances, § III A 2.

oxide and titanium (IV) oxide in varying amounts are homogeneously and ionically interdiffused to form a crystalline matrix of rutile."[205]

Natural gas (petroleum), raw liq. Mix CASRN 64741-48-6*

The UVCB definition for this substance is: "A complex combination of hydrocarbons separated as a liquid from natural gas in a gas recycling plant by processes such as refrigeration or absorption. It consists mainly of saturated aliphatic hydrocarbons having carbon numbers in the range of C2 through C8." This substance includes variable carbon chain lengths.[206]

Substances that are either biological materials or made from biological materials may be listed as UVCB products on the Inventory if they are not natural products. Natural products do not have to be listed on the Inventory. Natural products are those that occur in nature and are either unprocessed or "processed only by manual, mechanical, or gravitational means; by dissolution in water; by flotation; or by heating solely to remove water; or which is extracted from air by any means."[207] EPA gives beeswax CAS Number 12-89-3* as an example of a product that is not natural and explains:

> The UVCB definition for this substance is: 'The wax obtained from the honeycomb of the bee. It consists primarily of myricyl palmitate, cerotic acid and esters and some high-carbon paraffins.' Although the method of isolation or purification is not stated in the definition, the listing assumes that other than mechanical means were used; this substance is not a natural product for purposes of TSCA.[208]

Essential oils generally contain the phrase "[e]xtractives and their physically modified derivatives" followed by the genus and species of the biological source, and might also contain a list of the primary components of the oil. Use of another biological source would require a separate Inventory listing. EPA gives Oils, eucalyptus CAS Number 8000-48-4* as a representation of an essential oil, with a definition of "[e]xtractives and their physically modified derivatives. Eucalyptus, Myrtaceae."[209]

Polymers containing biological materials are frequently named starting with the biological, using the singular "polymer with" when the first term is singular and the "polymers with" if the first terms are plural. For example, "[r]osin, polymer with formaldehyde, methanol and phenol CAS Number

205. *Id.* at § III B.
206. *Id.*
207. *Id.* at § II B.
208. *Id.* at § III D 1.
209. *Id.* at § III D 2.

68333-68-6*" is a UVCB polymer as is "[f]atty acids, tall-oil, polymers with glycerol, isophthalic acid and rosin CASRN 68956-34-3*"[210]

C. Substances Containing Varying Carbon Lengths

The guidance on how to name carbon chains of varying lengths is entitled Toxic Substances Control Act Inventory Representation for Certain Chemical Substances Containing Varying Carbon Chain Lengths (Alkyl Ranges Using the CX-Y Notation).[211] Alkyl groups are chains of carbon atoms, and they are one of the basic building blocks of organic molecules. Often, the length of the chain is not uniform throughout a chemical product, and the Cx-y notation describes a chain of a minimum length of x carbon atoms, and a maximum length of y carbon atoms. There are other ways of representing alkyl groups of various lengths for Inventory purposes, and this guidance does not supplant or apply to them, other than describing them briefly. These other representations include those developed by the Soap and Detergent Manufacturers Association for fats and oils from specific plant and animal sources and synthetic equivalents, natural source descriptions for substances derived from a single type of animal or plant, and others including the EPA-American Petroleum Institute representations for petroleum refinery process streams.

In a carbon chain using the Cx-y convention Cx and Cy and all the lengths in between must be present, and no shorter or longer chains may be present. For example, for the representation "alkanes, C4-12" C4, C6, C8, C10 and C12 must be present, and no chains shorter than four carbons or longer than twelve carbons can be present. As a result, this Inventory listing does not permit the manufacture of C6 as a pure substance because it only covers mixtures of carbon chains with variable lengths,

Using the Cx-y convention, if one or both of x and y are odd numbers, the range will include all the even and odd numbers between and including x and y. If both x and y are even, the range will include all of the even numbers between and including x and y, but may not include the odd numbers, depending on the source and the manufacturer's intent. If the source of the carbon chain was a natural fat or oil, only the even numbers between x and y would be included because those sources typically only include carbon chains with even numbers of carbon atoms. For example, "fatty acids, C8-18, ethoxylated" only includes carbon chains with even numbers of carbon atoms, from eight to eighteen, because the starting material was a natural fat. Except in the instance of natural fats and oils, if the manufacturer intended to

210. *Id.* at § III D 3.
211. *Available at* http://www.epa.gov/oppt/newchems/pubs/alkyl-rg.txt.

include carbon chains with odd numbers of carbon atoms, then they would be included in the representation.

If all of the carbon chains in a mixture are already independently listed on the Inventory, the mixture does not need to be on the inventory as a Cx-y range.

D. Complex Reaction Products

The guidance on how to name complex reaction products is entitled Toxic Substances Control Act Inventory Representation for Combinations of Two or More Substances: Complex Reaction Products.[212] It applies only to chemicals made by a chemical reaction, and not to formulated mixtures, which are made simply by mixing with no chemical reaction. Its primary purpose is to explain when complex reaction products should be named as one reaction product, or as a series of individual components.

In general, a complex reaction product should be given a single substance name if it is not a polymer and it is a Class 2 substance. Even if the reaction product is composed of numerous types of molecules, one name should encompass all of them. If there is uncertainty about the components of a reaction product, or if the components may vary for each batch, the reaction product is generally named by reference to the products of a reaction or by reference to the reactants, with specified exceptions given in the guidance. If each of the reaction products can be unambiguously identified, and form each time the reaction is run, then the reaction product is classified as a mixture and each component should be separately named and listed on the Inventory.

The EPA treats mixed salts of monovalent[213] anions as mixtures of the individual salts, and each salt should be named and put on the Inventory separately. This policy, which has certain exceptions, was implemented in recognition of the burdens that would be placed on soap and detergent manufacturers if they had to report the reaction products of every possible reaction. However, the EPA does not extend this policy to salts of any anions other than monovalent anions, and those generally do need to be listed on the Inventory by reference to the reaction that forms them.

This guidance has many practical ramifications. If a manufacturer chooses to identify a complex reaction product as a mixture and list each component of the reaction product separately, impurities and byproducts do not have to be separately identified. However, if it subsequently learns that a component

---

212. *Available at* http://www.epa.gov/oppt/newchems/pubs/rxnprods.txt.

213. Valence is a term used to describe the number of electrons available for forming bonds. The guidance gives several examples of reactions of monovalent anions.

it thought was an impurity actually had some commercial value, then it must file a PMN for that component if it is not already listed on the Inventory. If a reaction product is named using the "reaction product with" format, naming each of the reactants, then there cannot be any substitution of reactants even if the resulting reaction products are identical. In addition, if a "reaction product with" name is developed, then one component of the reaction product cannot be isolated and used or sold separately by either the manufacturer or a downstream customer unless it is on the Inventory as a Class 1 substance. The consequences of inadvertently causing a customer or other downstream user to violate TSCA's Inventory and PMN requirements are sufficiently onerous that the "reaction product with" type of representation should be used as rarely as possible.

V. Inventory Reset

In accordance with the requirements of TSCA § (8)b to "compile, keep current, and publish a list of each chemical substance which is manufactured or processed in the United States," EPA had announced a new initiative in 2008 to maintain the integrity and utility of the Inventory. Named the Inventory Reset, it would have required in some fashion the certification that chemical substances on the Inventory are still, or have recently been, in commerce in the United States. Chemicals that were taken off the Inventory because they had not been in commerce in the recent past would have required PMN review before manufacturing or importing resume. EPA had indicated that it wanted to make the reset Inventory available in time for the next IUR reporting period for chemicals manufactured during 2010, and to time subsequent periodic Inventory resets to occur in conjunction with future IUR reporting cycles. This program was included under the Chemical Assessment and Management Program (ChAMP) initiative, which has now been suspended.[214] It seems logical to assume that there is no need for the Inventory Reset if the EPA and Congress are considering a broader review of existing chemicals.

VI. Enforcement

The enforcement response policy applicable to § 5 is entitled The Enforcement Response Policy for Reporting and Recordkeeping Rules and Requirements

214. *See* Chapter 10, Voluntary Initiatives.

for TSCA Sections 8, 12, and 13 (the Reporting Rule ERP).[215] Under this policy, the EPA may seek civil penalties, refer a violation for criminal penalties under TSCA § 16, seek to enjoin a violation, issue a Notice of Noncompliance if the violation was minor, or a combination of these.[216]

Like all of the ERPs,[217] the Reporting Rule ERP calls for determining the nature, circumstances, extent, and gravity of the violation to determine the gravity based penalty. Each individual component is given a score, based on a matrix. The penalty is then adjusted up or down based on factors such as history of prior violations, culpability, ability to pay, and such other matters as justice may require.[218] The nature of all Reporting Rule violations is hazard assessment.[219] The circumstances reflect the possibility that harm will result from the violation[220] while the extent of a violation depends on the extent of the potential harm.[221]

A failure to report under § 8(a) for the IUR is a circumstance Level 1. Violations are assessed for only one day for failure to report for the IUR.[222] A failure to maintain records or submit reports in strict compliance with the regulations is a circumstance Level 2 violation, and penalties are assessed for one day of violation.[223] If information is submitted late, the EPA will categorize that as circumstance Level 4 and impose penalties for each day that the report is late.[224]

Minor violations are circumstance Level 6, and these include sending a report to the wrong EPA office and not identifying the report as being submitted under TSCA § 8, sending a report to the wrong EPA office after receiving a prior notice of noncompliance for the same type of report, not identifying a report as being submitted subject to § 8 after receiving a notice of noncompliance for the same type of report and failing to keep records showing that a manufacturer is not subject to IUR reporting. The Reporting Rule ERP calls for imposing a one day penalty for each of these violations.[225]

---

215. Toxic and Pesticides Enforcement Division, Office of Regulatory Enforcement, Office of Enforcement and Compliance Assurance, U.S. E.P.A., Revised March 31, 1999, Effective June 1, 1999 [hereinafter Reporting Rule ERP].
216. Reporting Rule ERP, 2.
217. For a complete discussion on how ERPs operate, *see* Chapter 14, Penalties and Enforcement.
218. Reporting Rule ERP, 6.
219. *Id.* at 5.
220. *Id.* at 9.
221. *Id.* at 11.
222. *Id.* at 9.
223. *Id.* at 10.
224. *Id.*
225. *Id.*

A violation is significant in extent if it is a Level 1, 2, 3 or 4 violation of § 8(a) IUR rule.[226]

Section 8(a) inventory violations are assessed per chemical and § 8(a) IUR violations are assessed per chemical per site.[227] The Consent Agreement in *In the Matter of Kanto Corporation*[228] provides an example of violations being assessed per chemical per site for violations of the IUR. Kanto Corporation (Kanto) was penalized for failing to file a form U IUR report for six chemical substances on time. The form was required to be filed by December 23, 2002. EPA conducted an inspection at the Kanto plant on July 13, 2006 and on July 26, 2006 Kanto filed a continuation/correction 2002 Form U (the "July 2006 Form U) for the six chemical substances. Based on these stipulated facts, the Consent Agreement recited a penalty of $18,700 for each of the six chemical substances that were the subject of the July 2006 Form U. The gravity based penalty was reduced by 15 percent because Kanto had cooperated with the EPA, had demonstrated a general attitude to comply with TSCA, and had promptly corrected violations. While Kanto neither admitted nor denied the allegations, the Consent Decree makes clear that these violations will count toward establishing Kanto's compliance history in any future enforcement proceeding brought by the EPA against Kanto for the following five years.

At the time the penalty matrix was drafted, for violations after January 30, 1997 penalties ranged from a high of $27,500 to a low of $220, per day or per violation. Pursuant to the Debt Collection Improvement Act of 1996, EPA is required to increase penalties at least every four years to ensure that inflation does not erode the deterrent effect of the penalties. The penalty for a particular violation depends on the date of the violation, so the Code of Federal Regulations should be consulted to determine the appropriate penalty.[229]

Gravity based penalties can be reduced based on the Reporting Rule ERP up to 50 percent for self-reporting within thirty days, and another 15 percent for attitude, and more for taking all steps to mitigate the violation,[230] but in no event can the gravity based penalty be less than the economic benefit to

226. *Id.* at 12. The Reporting Rule ERP states that a failure to keep records showing that a manufacturer is not subject to reporting is penalized as a minor violation, but the requirement to keep such records was eliminated from the IUR rules in 2003. 68 Fed. Reg. 848, 857 (Jan. 7, 2003).
227. Reporting Rule ERP, 13.
228. Consent Agreement, TSCA-HQ-2007-5011. Environmental Appeals Board (Entered Oct. 5, 2007).
229. 40 C.F.R. Part 19. Penalty increases are announced in the Federal Register. 69 Fed. Reg. 7121 (Feb. 13, 2004); 73 Fed. Reg. 75340 (Dec. 11, 2008). *See* Chapter 14, Penalties and Enforcement, for a discussion of relevant dates and how to calculate the applicable maximum penalties for the relevant time periods.
230. Reporting Rule ERP, 15–16.

the violator.[231] The gravity based penalties can be increased for prior violations and poor attitude.

If the violations were discovered and reported to the EPA in compliance with the EPA's Audit Policy, complete or 75 percent penalty mitigation may be available.[232]

The Presiding Officer in a penalty case does not have to adhere rigidly to the framework present in the Reporting Rule ERP, but may do so. In *In Re Dic Americas, Inc.*,[233] DIC Americas, Inc. (DICA), on appeal, argued that the assessment of a penalty against it for five violations of failing to report for the IUR was excessive because the Presiding Officer failed to exercise independent judgment as to the appropriateness of the fine and adhered too rigidly to the Reporting Rule ERP in determining the penalty amount. DICA did not argue that it did not violate the statute by failing to file the reports required by the IUR on time. The Board referred to the express language of the statute, which requires that the Presiding Officer "must consider any civil penalty guidelines issued under the Act," and found that the clear implication of this direction is that a Presiding Officer has the "discretion either to adopt the rationale of an applicable penalty policy where appropriate or to deviate from it where circumstances warrant."[234] The Board noted that the record demonstrated that the Presiding Officer was open to hearing any justification from DICA as to why she should deviate from the penalty guidelines. She had said: "I am willing to listen to any reasonable assertions with respect to why, in the interests of justice particularly, the penalty ought to be reduced."[235] The Appeals Board affirmed the judgment of the Presiding Officer.

---

231. *Id.* at 16.
232. *See* Chapter 14, Penalties and Enforcement.
233. TSCA Appeal No. 94-2, Final Decision and Order, Environmental Appeals Board (Sept. 27, 1995) 184.
234. *Id.* at 189.
235. *Id.* at 190.

CHAPTER 4

Premanufacture Notifications

I. Introduction to the Premanufacture Notification Program

The Toxic Substances Control Act (TSCA)[1] called for the creation of a massive list of all the chemicals in commerce in the United States.[2] The list is the TSCA Inventory, or more simply, the Inventory. To compile the Inventory, the United States Environmental Protection Agency (EPA) issued an Inventory Reporting Rule in 1977 requiring companies to report all the chemicals they had manufactured or imported in the previous three years, and the result was inclusion of approximately sixty-two thousand chemicals on the Inventory.[3] Since that time, over twenty-one thousand more chemicals have been added to the Inventory.[4]

All of the chemicals that are on the Inventory are called "existing" chemicals. The chemicals that have yet not been put on the Inventory are called "new" chemicals. In general, companies may import and manufacture existing chemicals,[5] but unless there is an exception to the general rule no one may manufacture or import a new chemical that is not on the Inventory.

New chemicals are added to the Inventory through the premanufacture notification (PMN) procedure. The Inventory and the PMN procedures are closely related; if a substance must be on the Inventory it must get there through the PMN procedure, and if a substance goes through the PMN procedure the ultimate objective is Inventory listing, or an EPA approved exemption. For this reason, the Inventory regulations and the PMN regulations have parallel requirements.

Anyone who submits a PMN must disclose known information concerning the manufacturing, physical, and toxicological properties of the chemical. The EPA typically has a ninety day opportunity to review the PMN and determine if restrictions should be placed on the substance's use or manufacture or handling.

The PMN process is in many ways the heart of the entire TSCA regulatory program. PMNs, together with applications for exemptions from the PMN rules (the Test Marketing Exemption,[6] Low Volume Exemption, and low release and exposure exemption (LoREX)) are the main way for the EPA to

1. 15 U.S.C. §§ 2601–2695d.
2. *See* Chapter 3, The Inventory.
3. 42 Fed. Reg. 64572 (Dec. 23, 1977), referring to proposed rules of Mar. 9, 1977 and Aug. 2, 1977; *see also* 73 Fed. Reg. 20921 (Apr. 17, 2008).
4. 73 Fed. Reg. 20921, 20923 (Apr. 17, 2008).
5. There may be significant limitations on a company's right to manufacture or import an existing chemical, as discussed in more detail in this chapter. Some of these limitations may be the result of a Significant New Use Rule, an order under Section 5(e), a consent order, or a product restriction under § 6.
6. Use of the PMN form is not mandatory for the Test Marketing Exemption.

learn of chemicals that are about to be manufactured in or imported into the United States.[7] The PMN process is therefore the main portal into TSCA's regulatory system.

PMNs give EPA the opportunity to regulate the manufacture, import, processing, and use of new chemicals before they are introduced into commerce. Once EPA receives a PMN it has many options for regulating the substance that was the subject of the PMN, either through an order to the PMN submitter, an administrative consent order with the PMN submitter, court issued injunctions, or requirements to file new notifications when the substance is put to certain significant new uses.

Once the PMN review period is over, the company that filed the PMN must notify the EPA again when it completes its first commercial manufacturing or importation.[8] This notification is called a Notice of Commencement (NOC). As soon as the NOC is filed, the substance is automatically put on the Inventory, and any other company or person may manufacture or import it, subject to the EPA's authority to restrict its use.

Over thirty-two thousand PMNs were filed in the first twenty-five years of the program.[9] As noted above, there have been about twenty-one thousand chemicals added to the Inventory in this time period. This means that there were about eleven thousand PMN filings that did not end with listing of the subject chemical on the Inventory. This could be for any number of reasons, such as if the filer withdrew the PMN or if the filer decided not to manufacture the substance and did not file the NOC[10] necessary to place the substance on the Inventory. Multiple PMNs could be filed on the same substance if the earlier PMNs did not result in Inventory listings.

II. History

Before TSCA was enacted, the government only had authority to require testing of pesticides, drugs, and food additives.[11] While TSCA was being debated

7. The EPA does obtain some, more limited, information about chemicals that are exempt from the PMN process. For example, there are notifications required under TSCA § 8(e) to report adverse effects of chemicals that are not subject to PMN requirements, and there are annual submittal reports required for polymers that are exempt from the PMN process.
8. 40 C.F.R. § 720.102.
9. EPA's New Chemicals Program Summary of Accomplishments, *available at* http://www.epa.gov/oppt/newchems/pubs/accomplishments.htm.
10. A notice of commencement is a notice filed with the EPA to inform the EPA that import or manufacture has commenced. It automatically results in listing of the substance on the TSCA Inventory.
11. Chemistry Assistance Manual for Premanufacture Notification Submitters, 105, EPA 744-R-97-003 (1997) [hereinafter Chemistry Manual], *available at* http://www.epa.gov/oppt/newchems/pubs/chem-pmn/.

there was a political debate concerning balancing a premanufacture approval program and public safety. Congress ultimately struck a compromise and found that a premanufacture notification program, instead of an approval process, would:

> provide the administrator with an opportunity to review and evaluate information with respect to the substance to determine if manufacture, processing, distribution in commerce, use or disposal should be limited, delayed or prohibited because data is [sic] insufficient to evaluate the health and environmental effects or because the substance or the new use presents or will present an unreasonable risk of injury to health or the environment.[12]

In requiring notification before commercialization, Congress said:

> the most desirable time to determine the health and environmental effects of the substance, and to take action to protect against any potential adverse effects, occurs before commercial production begins. Not only is human and environmental harm avoided or alleviated, but the cost of any regulatory action in terms of loss of jobs and capital investment is minimized.[13]

The EPA has repeatedly pointed out that the PMN requirement is only a notification requirement, and there is no obligation to develop new test data in order to file a PMN. Permitting the PMN review period to expire without taking action to restrict use of the chemical does not imply any EPA approval of substances.[14] In contrast, the Federal Food, Drug, and Cosmetics Act[15] has a registration program that requires the development of a significant battery of tests to prove the safety and efficacy of a new drug.[16] Similarly, the regulations that recently became effective in the European Union under Registration, Evaluation, Authorisation, and Restrictions of Chemicals (REACH)[17] also require a battery of physical and toxicological tests before most chemicals are made or imported. Both these schemes embody the precautionary principle, which holds that when there is uncertainty about potential risks, a potential for irreversible harm, or the possibility of catastrophic harm, the uncertainty does not justify inaction and the potential for harm should be factored into

12. *Id.* at 108.
13. *Id.*
14. 48 Fed. Reg. 21722, 21724 (May 13, 1983).
15. 21 U.S.C. §§ 301–399.
16. Chemistry Manual at 110.
17. Parliament and Council Regulation (EC) No. 1907/2006 (Corrigendum 29 May 2007) and Directive 2006/121/EC (Corrigendum 29 May 2007) as amended.

regulatory decision making.[18] The Federal Food, Drug, and Cosmetics Act (FFDCA)[19] embodies the protective principle by seeking to minimize uncertainty, and REACH seeks to gain sufficient data to make reasonable safety choices. Because TSCA only requires reporting existing information in the submitter's possession or control, which may be little or nothing, it does not embody the precautionary principle. The presumption in the premanufacture notification program is that if there is no data leading to a conclusion that a substance poses a substantial risk, then it does not require regulatory restriction.

Over the twenty-five years of administering TSCA, EPA has moved the program more towards the precautionary principle. Prior to the 1998 initiation of the EPA's High Production Volume (HPV) Challenge, which called for voluntary industry testing of all chemicals manufactured or imported in volumes of one million pounds or more per year, the EPA conducted a survey that showed just how little meaningful test data the EPA had. It found that of the three thousand high production volume chemicals made or imported in quantities of one million pounds or more per year, 43 percent or one thousand two hundred ninety had none of the testing that is widely considered important for a full risk characterization, and only 7 percent, or two hundred ten chemicals, had the full set of recommended basic tests.[20] The HPV Challenge was a response to this significant gap, and resulted in voluntary submission of data on twenty two hundred chemicals.

Other voluntary challenge programs mirror the HPV program for chemicals that children may be exposed to and for inorganic chemicals made or imported in volumes of one million pounds or more per year.[21] The plethora of programs for specific classes of chemicals highlights the lack of a systematic requirement under the PMN program that would apply the precautionary principle to all chemicals.

The requirement to file PMNs is statutory, but the EPA did not issue final regulations until 1983,[22] six years after TSCA went into effect.

---

18. *See* Jonathan Remy Nash, *Standing and the Precautionary Principle*, 108 COLUM. L. REV. 494, 496–500 (2008).
19. 21 U.S.C. §§ 301–399.
20. Summary of EPA's HPV Chemical Hazard Data Availability Study, *available at* http://www.epa.gov/HPV/pubs/general/hazchem.htm.
21. *See* Chapter 10, Voluntary Initiatives.
22. 48 Fed. Reg. 21722, 21723 (May 13, 1983). Until then, the EPA had applied an interim policy concerning PMN submittals.

III. Entities That Must File PMNs

A. Manufacturers and Importers

Manufacturers and importers of "new chemical substances" are required to follow premanufacture notification procedures before manufacturing or importing those new chemicals.[23]

Importers are not specifically mentioned in the statutory or regulatory statements of the PMN requirement, but in both the statute and the regulations[24] "manufacture" is defined to include both "manufacture" and "import" and so all of the premanufacture notification rules that apply to manufacturers also apply to importers. Importers do not need to ensure that substances in articles are on the Inventory because articles are exempt from the PMN process. However, it is important to review the definition of "article" to check that all of the substances in the article meet the definition.[25] Importers must file PMNs on all new chemicals that they import in bulk or as part of a mixture.[26]

People who only process or use chemicals without manufacturing or importing them are not required to file PMNs, although processing or using a substance that a person knew or had reason to know was made or imported in violation of the PMN rules is a violation of TSCA.[27] Drawing a distinction between use and processing can be challenging because the EPA has described what constitutes processing differently for different programs. This distinction is important because people who process chemicals are subject to the significant new use notification rules, but people who merely use chemicals are not. The discussion of the distinction in this chapter is limited to the EPA's description of processing in the context of the PMN and Significant New Use Rule (SNUR)[28] requirements, and does not apply to any other TSCA program.

In the context of the PMN program processing is a subset of use, because the EPA took the position in a Q&A that "a person processing an illegally manufactured new chemical substance would not be in violation of TSCA unless the person knew or had reason to know that the substance had been illegally manufactured. See §15(2) of TSCA."[29] If processing were not a subset

---

23. TSCA § 5(a); 40 C.F.R. § 720.22(a)(1).
24. TSCA § 3(7); 40 C.F.R. § 720.3(q). *See* Chapter 2, TSCA's Scope.
25. *See* Chapter 2, TSCA's Scope for a discussion of the term "article."
26. EPA Draft Instruction Manual for Reporting under the TSCA § 5 New Chemicals Program, 4 (2003) [hereinafter PMN Instruction Manual] *available at* http://www.epa.gov/oppt/newchems/.
27. 40 C.F.R. § 720.22. *See* the Scope Chapter for a discussion of "process" and "use."
28. See Chapter 12, Significant New Use Rules.
29. EPA's Draft Questions & Answers for the New Chemicals Program 1-65 to 1-66, question 125-1 (undated) [Draft PMN Q&A], *available at* http://www.epa.gov/oppt/newchems/pubs/qanda-newchems.pdf. There is a superseded version of this document available on the EPA

of use, then processing an illegally manufactured substance would not be a violation of TSCA § 15(2). TSCA § 15(2) makes use of an illegally manufactured substance illegal because it says:

> It shall be unlawful for any person to –
>
> . . .
>
> (2) use for commercial purposes a chemical substance or mixture which such person knew or had reason to know was manufactured, processed, or distributed in commerce in violation of section [5] or [6] of this title....

The following activities are processing in the context of the PMN rules:

- manually grinding recyclable plastics without chemical reactions;[30]
- melting recyclable plastics without chemical reactions;[31]
- shaping a chemical into a filament or fiber;[32] and
- grinding legally produced off-spec polymer into a powder and using it as filler in injection molding.[33]

The word "use" is not defined in the PMN regulations, but the definition of "manufacture or import for commercial purposes" gives two examples of activities that are considered to be use. A substance is "used" for product research and development.[34] An intermediate is "used,"[35] and "intermediate" is defined as either a catalyst or as "any chemical substance that is consumed, in whole or in part, in chemical reactions used for the intentional manufacture of another chemical substance(s) or mixture(s)."[36]

The following activities are not considered processing, and are instead classified as manufacturing (which may or may not be use depending on the circumstances):

- "if the substance is deliberately converted to a water-absorbing polymer by neutralization, that conversion constitutes manufacture for commercial purposes as a chemical substance, rather than processing;"[37]

---

website that should not be used for anything other than historical purposes. The superseded version does not have the word "draft" in the background of each page. The metadata in the more current version reveals that it was created on January 20, 2004 and modified on August 22, 2005.

30. Draft PMN Q&A, 1-65 to 1-66, question 125-1.
31. *Id.*
32. *Id. at* 2-9, question 207-6.
33. Chemical Processing Under TSCA 28 (1992).
34. 40 C.F.R. §§ 720.3(r) and 720.3(s).
35. 40 C.F.R. §§ 720.3(r).
36. 40 C.F.R. § 720.3(n).
37. Draft PMN Q&A, 2-24 to 2-25, question 218-2.

- extraction of a new chemical from a previously existing substance or from a complex combination of substances is manufacturing and not processing; the extracted substance must be on the Inventory, and the entity performing the extraction is subject to the PMN rules;[38] in particular, all substances extracted from a plant or animal[39] and all substances extracted from byproducts by anyone other than a public or private organization[40] are subject to PMN requirements; as a result the entity performing the extraction of any such substances must file a PMN unless the substance is already on the Inventory, exempt or excluded from TSCA.[41]

B. Entities Must Have a Commercial Purpose for Their Activities

PMNs are only required for substances that are manufactured or imported "for commercial purposes,"[42] which is defined in the regulations to mean "to import, produce, or manufacture with the purpose of obtaining an immediate or eventual commercial advantage for the manufacturer or importer."[43] Any amount of manufacture or import, no matter how small, can be for a "commercial purpose" if it is for commercial distribution, test marketing, product research and development, or use as an intermediate. Byproducts and impurities that have no commercial value are made or imported for a commercial purpose if they are made with or present in a product with commercial value that was made or imported for a commercial advantage,[44] although they may qualify for exemptions from PMN and SNUR requirements.

Purely academic researchers are not subject to the PMN requirements because the substances they make or import are not made or imported for "commercial purposes." However, research that is funded under a contract that anticipates commercialization, or is conducted by a researcher who holds patents or has asserted trade secret rights, is not considered academic.[45]

38. 48 Fed. Reg. 21722, 21725 (May 13, 1983); 40 C.F.R. § 720.3(t).
39. Draft PMN Q&A, 1-61, question 122-2.
40. 40 C.F.R. § 720.30(g); Draft PMN Q&A, 2-6, question 204-1.
41. As early as 1977 the EPA had concluded that entities that extracted substances from byproducts were processors and not manufacturers, and were not primarily responsible for listing the extracted substances. 42 Fed. Reg. 64572, 64587, comment 55 (Dec. 13, 1977). In the final PMN regulations the EPA reversed this by defining manufacturers to include extraction. 40 C.F.R. § 720.3(t).
42. 40 C.F.R. § 720.22(a)(1).
43. 40 C.F.R § 720.3(r).
44. *Id.*
45. *See* the discussion of the research and development exemption from the PMN requirement, *infra.*

Therefore, even university researchers must be sure their substances are on the Inventory or qualify for an exemption from the PMN rules. Most university research that is not strictly academic and most industrial research can qualify for the research and development exemption from the PMN requirement if the laboratories comply with strict requirements that apply to the exemption.[46]

Chemicals that are handled in accordance with the research and development exemption from the PMN rules cannot be listed on the Inventory because § 8(b) of TSCA, which requires the Inventory to be compiled, says:

> The Administrator shall not include in such list any chemical substance which is manufactured or processed only in small quantities (as defined by the Administrator by rule) solely for purposes of scientific experimentation or analysis or chemical research on, or analysis of, such substance or another substance, including such research or analysis for the development of a product.

Since R&D substances cannot be put on the Inventory, there is no reason to file a PMN for them.

C. U.S. Entities and "Principal Importers"

The EPA should not accept a PMN from an entity that is not incorporated, licensed or doing business in the United States.[47]

Foreign manufacturers that are not doing business in the United States or licensed to do business here may not file a PMN, and so the obligation to file a PMN is imposed on the first U.S. based company in the supply chain that meets the definition of "principal importer." If there are several people involved in importing a substance, then only the principal importer, as determined by the EPA, needs to file the PMN.[48] "Principal importer" is defined as an entity incorporated, licensed, or doing business in the United States that is "the first importer who, knowing that a new chemical substance will be imported rather than manufactured domestically, specifies the identity of the chemical substance and the total amount to be imported." The "principal importer" must also meet the definition of an "importer," which is "any person who imports a chemical substance, including a chemical substance as part of a mixture or article, into the customs territory of the United States," and includes the person who is liable for paying duties or an authorized agent, the consignee, the importer of record, the owner if that person has filed an

---

46. *See* the discussion of the R&D exemption, *infra*.
47. 40 C.F.R. § 720.22(a)(3).
48. 40 C.F.R. §§ 720.22(b)(2) and 720.57.

owner's declaration and superseding bond,[49] or the transferee if the right to draw merchandise in a bonded warehouse has been transferred in accordance the applicable regulations.[50] The sole U.S. customer for an imported product may choose to become the importer, and in that case may be the "principal importer."[51] "Customs territory of the United States" refers only to the States, The District of Columbia and Puerto Rico.[52]

If no entity clearly meets the definition of principal importer, the EPA will designate the company that must file the PMN, with all its attendant responsibilities.[53]

D. Toll Manufacturers

A toll manufacturer is a company that performs some or all of the manufacturing steps involved in making a chemical on behalf of another company.[54] There are many reasons that a company will engage a toll manufacturer. For example, if a chemical manufacturer does not have a specialized piece of equipment necessary for one step in a production process, it may engage a toll manufacturer to perform that step, or it may place an order to have a toll manufacturer perform all of the manufacturing steps if simply does not have the capacity to make a product. In the PMN rules, in some circumstances the company that places the order is a "manufacturer" required to file a PMN. If company A engages company B to manufacture a chemical, then company A is defined as a "manufacturer" if several conditions are met. Company B must be making the chemical exclusively for company A. Company A must control the chemical composition of the chemical, the amount made, and provide the basic manufacturing process.[55] These conditions ensure that a company that simply purchases a stock chemical is not engaging a toll manufacturer, and is not the entity responsible for filing a PMN.

The regulations place the responsibility for filing a PMN with the company that orders the toll manufacturing, but does not relieve the company that is actually doing the synthesis from compliance with the PMN rules.

49. The declaration and bond are described in 19 C.F.R. § 141.20.
50. The Customs regulation is 19 C.F.R. Part 144, subpart C. The TSCA requirement is 40 C.F.R. § 720.3(l).
51. *Cf.*, Draft PMN Q&A, 1-60, question 120-2.
52. TSCA § 3(7) refers to the Harmonized Tariff Schedule of the United States 3, general note 2 (2008) (Rev. 1). *See* Chapter 2, TSCA's Scope.
53. 40 C.F.R. § 720.57(b).
54. *See also* the Chapter 2, TSCA's Scope for a discussion of toll manufacturing.
55. 48 Fed. Reg. 21722, 21725-26 (May 13, 1983).

Both companies have an obligation to ensure that any substance made is on the Inventory.[56]

If a company controls all the distribution of a chemical made by another firm, and the company that does the distribution does not process the chemical, then the second company is a distributor and not a toll manufacturer or processor.[57]

IV. Filing a PMN

A. When Filing Is Required

A proposed manufacturer or importer only needs to file a PMN after it has answered all of these questions:

- Is the substance on the public Inventory? If it is on the Inventory no PMN is necessary.
- Is the substance on the confidential Inventory? This can be answered by filing a bona fide request with the EPA if there is any possibility that the substance falls within the publicly available generic description of a substance on the confidential Inventory.[58] If it is on the confidential Inventory no PMN is necessary.
- Is the substance excluded from coverage under TSCA because of a statutory exclusion such as those for pesticides, drugs, and food?[59] If it is excluded from the definition of "chemical substances" that are subject to TSCA, no PMN is necessary. The definition of "chemical substance" appears in the TSCA statute and applies to all programs under TSCA.[60]
- Is the substance exempt from coverage under the PMN program because of a self-executing exemption such as the R&D exemption or the polymer exemption? If it is exempt pursuant to a self-executing exemption, no PMN is necessary.
- Is the substance exempt from coverage under the PMN program only if an exemption request is approved by the EPA? If it is exempt under an exemption that requires EPA approval, then the proposed manufacturer

---

56. *Id.* 21726 (May 13, 1983).
57. *See* Question and Answer Summary, EPA Seminar on Industry Obligations Under TSCA, 2 (June 10, 1986).
58. *See* Chapter 3, The Inventory.
59. *See* Chapter 2, TSCA's Scope.
60. TSCA § (3)(2). *See* Chapter 2, TSCA's Scope, for a full discussion of the chemicals that are subject to TSCA because of the definition of "chemical substance."

or importer must submit an application to the EPA using the PMN form. These exemptions are the TME,[61] LVE, LoREX and Polaroid[62] exemptions. The PMN form is also required for Significant New Use Notices (SNUNs).

The EPA has Prenotice Coordinators who can answer questions about filing requirements and resolve ambiguities before a PMN is filed. The Prenotice Coordinators can consider the specific facts presented. They can also assist in determining which entity in the import process is responsible for filing a PMN if there is no one entity that is clearly the principal importer.[63]

B. How to File a PMN

When preparing a PMN a filer should keep in mind the ultimate objective of manufacturing or importing the subject chemical. If the filer can make the review process easier for the EPA then the PMN has a greater chance of going through the review period in the allotted ninety days. If the PMN includes all the information that the forms require, that will keep the review process on schedule. The filer should also explain any apparent inconsistencies and issues that are red flags so that the EPA reviewer will not need to call the submitter for further explanations. If the PMN leaves open questions that the EPA must contact the filer to resolve, then the review schedule can be disrupted and the EPA may ask for the PMN review period to be suspended. Think of this process as having a heavy box on a conveyor belt. If the box is complete and continues without disruption, it will get to the end of its journey in a timely fashion. However, if the box is removed from the conveyor belt for inspection, it will take extra effort to lift it and put it back in place.

PMNs must be submitted on the approved EPA form 7710-25 (the PMN form),[64] or a copy of the PMN form generated by EPA approved commercially available software.[65] EPA is phasing out paper filing and has

61. Use of the PMN form is not mandatory but is preferred by the EPA.
62. The Polaroid exemption requires an initial notification to the EPA followed by a PMN.
63. 48 Fed. Reg. 21722, 21726 (May 13, 1983). Contact information for the Prenotice Coordinators is *available at* http://www.epa.gov/oppt/newchems/pubs/roster.htm.
64. The form in use as of 2003 [hereinafter PMN Form] is on the accompanying CD and can be downloaded from https://cdx.epa.gov/ssl/pmn/download.asp and http://www.epa.gov/opptintr/newchems/pubs/pmnpart1.pdf and http://www.epa.gov/opptintr/newchems/pubs/pmnpart2.pdf. The TSCA Hotline can also provide a copy of the PMN Form; the Hotline phone number is (212) 554-1404. EPA has posted its electronic filing software at http://www.epa.gov/oppt/newchems/epmn/epmn-index.htm and plans to distribute CDs or DVDs on request.
65. 40 C.F.R. § 720.40(a).

issued regulations governing electronic filing.[66] Effective April 6, 2010, all PMNs and other notices required by § 5, including NOCs, must be generated using the e-PMN software.[67] Until April 6, 2011 the EPA will accept paper printouts of PMNs, files on CDs or DVDs, and electronic submissions using the Central Data Exchange (CDX).[68] After that, no paper submissions will be accepted, and after April 6, 2012 only electronic submissions using CDX will be accepted.

The original plus two duplicate complete copies of all paper submissions, including attachments and enclosures, must be filed with a PMN or SNUR; no duplicate copies are required if the filing is for a TME, LVE, or LoREX exemption.[69] If any information is claimed as confidential then a full set with the confidential information "sanitized" or blanked out, must also be submitted.[70] Everything has to be in English except for reports in the open scientific literature.[71]

Every PMN requires a signature of an "authorized official."[72] Unlike most of the other environmental regulations, TSCA does not define who can be an "authorized official" in order to sign submissions,[73] and typically the person in charge of data collection for the PMN signs the forms. The authorized official must enter into an electronic signature agreement with the EPA before submitting an electronic PMN using CDX.[74]

The PMN form requires a certification by the authorized official who signs it or submits it through CDX that:

> I certify that to the best of my knowledge and belief:
>
> 1. The company ... *[submitting this form]* intends to manufacture or import for a commercial purpose, other than in small quantities solely for research and development, the substance identified in ... *[this form]*.
> 2. All information provided in this notice is complete and truthful as of the date of submission.
> 3. I am submitting with this notice all test data in my possession or control and a description of all other data known to or reasonably ascertainable by me as required by §720.50 of the Premanufacture Notification Rule.

---

66. 40 C.F.R. § 720.40; 75 Fed. Reg. 773 (Jan. 26, 2010).
67. The e-PMN software is described at http://www.epa.gov/oppt/newchems/epmn/epmn-index.htm.
68. The CDX system is described at http://www.epa.gov/cdx/.
69. Draft PMN Q&A, 1-13, question 101-9.
70. 40 C.F.R. § 720.40.(d)(2).
71. 40 C.F.R. §§ 720.40(a) and (d).
72. *See* the PMN Form.
73. 60 Fed. Reg. 16298, 16307 (Mar. 29, 1995).
74. 75 Fed. Reg. 773, 776 (Jan. 26, 2010).

This certification should not be taken lightly. The penalties for a false statement to the U.S. government can be severe under federal statutes that make knowing or willful false statements of a material fact to the government a felony. As the Sixth Circuit noted in a case involving falsification of records under the Safe Drinking Water Act, "18 U.S.C. § 1001 criminalizes the willful making of materially false statements 'in any matter within the jurisdiction of the executive, legislative, or judicial branch of the Government of the United States.'"[75] The requirement that the false statement be "material" means that the statement has a tendency to influence or is capable of influencing a government agency. A false statement that in fact did not influence the EPA may still be "material" so long as it was a statement that could have influenced the agency.[76] The person who signs the certification takes personal responsibility for an exhaustive search of data in the submitter's "possession or control" and information that is "reasonably ascertainable."[77]

The seriousness of the certification prompted PMN submitters who were concerned about good faith searches that failed to uncover available information to express their concerns to the EPA. The EPA suggests documenting the search process and in particular keeping records identifying company locations where relevant information might be located, written requests to each such location, and follow up until the location responds. Records should be kept of having reviewed all sources of relevant information such as Material Data Safety Sheets. The EPA recommends that businesses have corporate policies geared towards making relevant information available.[78]

If the PMN form is submitted because the submitter is applying for an LVE or LoREX exemption then the person who signs the form also takes personal responsibility for these additional certification statements:

> The manufacturer submitting this notice intends to manufacture or import the new chemical substance for commercial purposes, other than in small quantities solely for research and development, under the terms of 40 C.F.R. § 723.50.
>
> The manufacturer is familiar with the terms of this section and will comply with those terms; and
>
> The new chemical substance for which the notice is submitted meets all applicable exemption conditions.
>
> If this application is for an LVE in accordance with 40 C.F.R. 723.50(c)(1), the manufacturer intends to commence manufacture of the exempted substance

---

75. U.S. v. White, 270 F.3d 356, 363 (6th Cir. 2001).
76. *Id.* at 365.
77. Both the terms "possession or control" and "reasonably ascertainable" are defined terms that will be discussed *infra*.
78. PMN Instruction Manual, 8-9.

> for commercial purposes within 1 year of the date of the expiration of the 30 day review period.[79]

The certification also says that the required fee has been paid, and that any small business that pays a reduced fee qualifies as a small business.

The EPA's EPA Draft Instruction Manual for Reporting under the TSCA § 5 New Chemicals Program has page by page instructions for filling out the PMN form.[80] The e-PMN form has guided instructions throughout. The PMN form requires an alphanumeric called a TS-number that is generated by the filer.[81] The TS-number must be put on the first page of the PMN form and written on the payment, which is sent directly to the EPA's bank.

C. Data That Must Be Included in the PMN

1. Where to Look for Data

The PMN form and regulations require submission of a range of available data. Although there is no requirement to develop new data to fill out the PMN form, the PMN must include conclusive identification of the subject chemical.

A cursory reading of the regulations is misleading, and a much broader range of data must be submitted than would appear without cross checking the definitions in the regulations. Part I of the PMN form requires, in brief, submission of all data relating to chemical identity, certain information concerning impurities, synonyms, trade names, manufacturing or importation quantities, uses of the PMN substance, applications to which the PMN substance will be put, certain information concerning the processes for manufacturing, processing and use of the PMN substance, and worker exposure and environmental releases.[82] The PMN submitter is to required to submit, or in some cases describe, all information on these topics that is "known to or reasonably ascertainable by" it. All data in the submitter's "possession or control" that is "test data" must be submitted, together with descriptions of data that are "known to or reasonably ascertainable by" the submitter and concern health and environmental effects.[83] Each of the terms in quotation marks is a defined term.

---

79. PMN Form, 2; e-PMN form, certification section.
80. http://www.epa.gov/oppt/newchems/.
81. PMN Instruction Manual, 21.
82. These are the categories of information required by 40 C.F.R. § 720.45 to be submitted with a PMN.
83. 40 C.F.R. § 720.40(d).

"Known to or reasonably ascertainably by" is defined as "all information in a person's possession or control, plus all information that a reasonable person similarly situated might be expected to possess, control, or know."[84] This definition does not require that "reasonably ascertainable" information be readily available; it only requires that the information be of a sort that similarly situated people or entities "might" be expected to have or know. Costs and burdens of finding information, the nature of the PMN substance, anticipated manufacturing quantities, anticipated profits, and the size of the entity submitting the PMN are factors that can be considered in determining whether information is "reasonably ascertainable." Because these are all subjective criteria, there is no definition of "reasonably ascertainable" that is applicable in all situations.[85] As a practical matter, the potential risks to a submitter are sufficiently high in terms of tort liability, TSCA penalties and adverse publicity, that the most diligent search possible is warranted.

Information "known to or reasonably ascertainable by" the submitter also includes information in its "possession or control," which goes beyond the standard meaning:

> Possession or control means in possession or control of the submitter, or of any subsidiary, partnership in which the submitter is a general partner, parent company, or any company or partnership which the parent company owns or controls, if the subsidiary, parent company, or other company or partnership is associated with the submitter in the research, development, test marketing, or commercial marketing of the chemical substance in question. (A parent company owns or controls another company if the parent owns or controls 50 percent or more of the other company's voting stock. A parent company owns or controls any partnership in which it is a general partner). Information is included within this definition if it is:
>
> (1) In files maintained by submitter's employees who are:
>   (a) Associated with research, development, test marketing, or commercial marketing of the chemical substance in question.
>   (b) Reasonably likely to have such data.
>
> (2) Maintained in the files of other agents of the submitter who are associated with research, development, test marketing, or commercial marketing of the chemical substance in question in the course of their employment as such agents.[86]

Under this definition, a person submitting a PMN must search for all relevant information in its "possession or control" in the following places:

---

84. 40 C.F.R. § 720.3(p).
85. 48 Fed. Reg. 21722, 21730 (May 13, 1983).
86. 40 C.F.R. § 720.3(y).

- the submitter's files, including files maintained by:
  - its employees who do research, development, test marketing or commercial marketing of the PMN substance;
  - its employees who are reasonably likely to have relevant data;
  - its agents who do research, development, test marketing or commercial marketing of the PMN substance (agents are working under contract or other special arrangements with the submitter);[87]
- corporate subsidiary companies if the subsidiaries are associated with the submitter in the research, development, test marketing, or commercial marketing of the PMN substance;
- corporate parent companies if the parent companies are associated with the submitter in the research, development, test marketing, or commercial marketing of the PMN substance;
- partnerships in which the submitter is a general partner if the partnerships are associated with the submitter in the research, development, test marketing, or commercial marketing of the PMN substance;
- all companies in which a parent company owns or controls fifty percent or more of the voting stock, if those companies are associated with the submitter in the research, development, test marketing, or commercial marketing of the PMN substance;
- all partnerships in which a parent company is a general partner, if the partnerships are associated with the submitter in the research, development, test marketing, or commercial marketing of the PMN substance; and
- all entities that stand in one of the described relationships with a covered subsidiary, partnership or parent of the submitter, provided they are involved in the research, development, test marketing, or commercial marketing of the PMN substance.

This regulatory definition was drafted before limited liability companies were widely used. State laws tend to treat limited liability companies like partnerships and so the rules applicable to partnerships should include limited liability companies. There is often no equivalent of a general partner in a limited liability company and it would be prudent to search the files of all limited liability companies in which the submitter has an interest.

Any entity that has a research agreement with the submitter or one of the entities that has information in the "possession or control" of the submitter should be considered an entity that is associated with the submitter, although there is no formal guidance on this point.

---

87. 51 Fed. Reg. 15096, 15100 (Apr. 22, 1986).

Information that is only in the possession of the submitter's customers is not considered in the "possession or control" of the submitter.[88]

"Test data" in the submitter's possession or control must be submitted with the PMN.[89] That term is defined as "data from a formal or informal test or experiment, including information concerning the objectives, experimental methods and materials, protocols, results, data analyses, recorded observations, monitoring data, measurements, and conclusions from a test or experiment."[90] Test data that is not in the submitter's "possession or control" must be described in the PMN if it is "reasonably ascertainable."[91]

2. Chemistry

All of the information required by the PMN form must be submitted if it is "known or reasonably ascertainable," and this includes a significant amount of information on the PMN substance's chemistry.

Although as a general rule no new information is required to file a PMN, the PMN cannot be filed without basic information on the substance's chemical identity. The substance's chemical identity must be described in Part I of the PMN form. The requirements for describing the chemical identity vary depending on whether the PMN substance can be categorized as a Class 1 substance, a Class 2 substance, or a polymer. Class 1 substances are chemicals that can be represented by a complete chemical structure diagram, and Class 2 substances are chemicals that can not be represented by a complete chemical structure diagram.

- To describe the chemical identity of a Class 1 or Class 2 substance, the PMN submitter must include:[92]
  - the Chemical Abstracts (CA)[93] name of the substance;
  - a CA Index Name for Class 1 substances;
  - a CA Index Name or CA Preferred Name for Class 2 substances—the choice of a CA Index Name or a CA Preferred Name must be based on CA rules and conventions;
  - for Class 2 substances the submitter must identify the chemical precursors and reactants by specific chemical name (no tradenames or

88. 48 Fed. Reg. 21722, 21730 (May 13, 1983).
89. 40 C.F.R. § 720.40(d).
90. 40 C.F.R. § 720.3(ff).
91. 40 C.F.R. § 720.45(a)(1).
92. *Id.*
93. The Chemical Abstracts Service is a division of the American Chemical Society. It maintains the CAS Registry^SM^ of chemicals, with associated CAS Registry Numbers, abbreviated as CAS Number, CASRN or CAS #. The CAS website is http://www.cas.org.

generic names) and Chemical Abstract Service (CAS) Registry Number if it is available;
  - the CAS Number of the PMN substance, if it is available;
  - the correct molecular formula for all Class 1 substances and any Class 2 substance that has a definite molecular formula that is "known or reasonably ascertainable";
  - a complete and correct chemical structure diagram for all Class 1 substances; and
  - a "correct representative or partial chemical structure diagram" for all Class 2 substances and polymers "as complete as can be known, if one can be reasonably ascertained."[94]
- To describe the chemical identity of a polymer, which may be a Class 1 or Class 2 substance also, the PMN submitter must include the information required for a Class 1 or Class 2 substance plus:
  - a CA Index Name or CA Preferred Name—the choice of a CA Index Name or a CA Preferred Name must be based on CA rules and conventions;[95]
  - the specific chemical name and CAS Number (if available) of each monomer and reactant used to make the polymer, even if it is used at less than two percent (no tradenames or generic names);[96]
  - the typical weight percent of each monomer and reactant incorporated in the polymer and the maximum residual amount of the monomer in the polymer;[97]
  - if a monomer or reactant falls under the two percent rule, either using the charged or incorporated methods of calculating the two percent rule, the PMN submitter must state on the PMN form whether the monomer or reactant should be included in as part of the description of the polymer on the Inventory;[98]
  - measurements or estimates of the minimum number-average molecular weight of the polymer with a description of how the measurements or estimates were obtained;[99] and
  - measurements or estimates of the amount of species with molecular weights below 500 and 1000, with a description of how the measurements or estimates were obtained.[100]

---

94. 40 C.F.R. § 720.45(a)(1).
95. *Id.*
96. 40 C.F.R. § 720.45(a)(2).
97. *Id.*
98. *Id.*
99. *Id.*
100. *Id.*

If the PMN submitter uses the incorporated method of applying the two percent rule for polymers, it must keep records to support its determination, either by analysis or calculation. A theoretical calculation is only acceptable if the PMN submitter can document that analytical methods are either not necessary or not feasible.[101]

The identity information required for all chemicals may be obtained from the Chemical Abstracts Service Inventory Expert Service,[102] or it may be developed independently by the PMN submitter or another commercial service.[103] The EPA "strongly recommends" that submitters use CAS's service to obtain the chemical identity information necessary for the PMN.[104]

If a supplier will not divulge confidential information to a person who intends to file a PMN, the supplier can submit the confidential information directly to the EPA.[105] That way the PMN submitter will not learn any of the trade secrets of its supplier, but can still put its substances on the Inventory. This is a joint submission by the entities that are supplying the information needed for the PMN submission, and each joint submitter must sign the certifications on the PMN form.[106] A foreign manufacturer can file a joint submission with an importer who is filing a PMN, or it can write a letter of support to the EPA. The supplier of a reactant used in making the PMN substance can write a letter of support to provide the confidential information to the EPA.

3. Manufacturing, Processing, and Use Information

In addition to providing data on the chemical identity, all PMN filers must include "reasonably ascertainable" information on the following topics in Part I of the PMN form:[107]

- the name, CAS Number and weight percent of all impurities in the PMN substance;
- the known synonyms and trade names of the PMN substance;
- a description of all the byproducts from manufacturing, processing, use and disposal of the PMN substance;
- an estimate of the maximum amount of the PMN substance that will be made or imported during the first year of manufacture or importation

101. *Id.*
102. http://www.cas.org/products/client/expert/index.html.
103. 40 C.F.R. § 720.45(a)(3).
104. 60 Fed. Reg. 16298, 16299 (Mar. 29, 1995).
105. 40 C.F.R. §§ 720.40(e)(2), 720.45(a)(4) and 720.45(a)(5).
106. PMN Instruction Manual, 15 (2003).
107. 40 C.F.R. § 720.45(b)-(h).

and the maximum during any twelve month period during the first three years of manufacture or importation;

- a description of the functions and applications for the PMN substance and an estimate of the percentage of the total production that will be used for each function and application;
- for each formulation for commercial and consumer use, an estimate of the percent of the total formulation that consists of the PMN substance;
- for sites controlled by the PMN submitter where the PMN substance will be manufactured, processed or used:
    - the identity of the sites;
    - process descriptions for manufacturing, processing and use, including a diagram of the operations and chemical synthesis steps, the feedstocks and where they are introduced, and the areas where the PMN substance is removed from the process;
    - worker exposure information, including the form of the PMN substance to which workers may be exposed, the activities worker will engage in, the number of workers and how long they may be exposed;
    - information about the expected environmental releases, including the quantity to be released, the environmental media to which the substance will be released, and the control technology to be used;
- for sites that are not controlled by the PMN submitter where the PMN substance will be processed or used:
    - a description of each type of processing or use of the PMN substance;
    - an estimate of the number of processing or use sites;
    - a description of the worker exposures and environmental releases;
    - the number of workers exposed to the PMN substance and the duration of the exposures; and
    - controls employed to limit worker exposure and environmental release.

Sometimes the PMN substance will be in a category of chemicals that is subject to a test rule under § 4 of TSCA.[108] When that happens, the tests required by the test rule must be submitted with the PMN.[109] If EPA grants the submitter an exemption from compliance with the test rule because equivalent data is being developed under another test rule, the PMN cannot be filed until that data has been submitted.[110] Note that this could be at least

108. *See* Chapter 9, Test Rules.
109. 40 C.F.R. § 720.40(g).
110. 40 C.F.R. § 720.40(g)(2).

several months. If the EPA has exempted the submitter because equivalent data has already been submitted then the submitter may either provide the test data to the EPA with the PMN or refer the EPA to the date the data was submitted, the citation for the test rule and describe the exemption and give a reference to identify the exemption.[111]

If the EPA has issued a rule under TSCA § 5(b)(4) designating the PMN substance as one that may present an unreasonable risk of injury to health or the environment, then the PMN submitter must include data showing that the "manufacture, processing, distribution in commerce, use and disposal of the substance, or any combination of such activities, will not present an unreasonable risk of injury to health or the environment."[112] Presumably if there is data that disproves this conclusion it should be submitted also.

4. Test Data and Other Data

As noted above, "test data" can be from a formal or informal test or experiment, and when test data must be submitted information about the objectives, methods, materials, and protocols must be included, as well as results, analyses, observations, monitoring data, measurements, and conclusions.[113]

All test data in the PMN submitter's possession or control, as that term is defined in the regulations,[114] that relate to effects on health or the environment caused by manufacturing, processing, distributing in commerce, use, or disposal of the PMN substance or any mixture, formulation, or article containing it must be submitted with the PMN form, with some limited exceptions discussed below. Note that test data must only be submitted if it is within the submitter's "possession or control" and there is no obligation to search for all information that a reasonable person in the same situation might be expected to know. Test data that must be submitted with a PMN includes:

- health effects data;
- ecological effects data;
- physical and chemical properties;[115]
- environmental fate characteristics; and
- monitoring data and other data related to human exposure to the PMN substance or environmental release.

---

111. 40 C.F.R. § 720.40(g)(3).
112. 40 C.F.R. § 720.40(h)(2).
113. 40 C.F.R. § 720.50(a).
114. *See supra* this chapter for the definition of "possession and control." *See generally*, PMN Instruction Manual, 11–12.
115. Chemistry Manual, Chapter 2, 44.

If the test data is in the open scientific literature, only a standard literature citation, including the author's name, periodical name, date, volume, and page number needs to be submitted. If the test data is not published, then the full report that must be submitted must include the experimental methods, materials and results, together with a discussion and analysis, conclusions, references, and the name and address of the laboratory where the data was developed.

The EPA Draft Instruction Manual for Reporting under the TSCA § 5 New Chemicals Program[116] lists the types of test data that must be submitted with a PMN. The EPA cautions that the list is "illustrative, not exhaustive." The physical, chemical and environmental fate test data that must be submitted include: chromatograms; spectra (ultraviolet, visible, infrared); density/relative density; solubility in water; melting temperature; boiling/sublimation temperature; softening point; vapor pressure; dissociation constant; particle size distribution; octanol/water partition coefficient; Henry's law constant; volatilization from soil; pH; flammability; explodability; adsorption/desorption characteristics; photochemical degradation; viscosity; odor; thermal analysis; chemical analysis; chemical oxidation; chemical reduction; biodegradation; and transformation to persistent or toxic products.

Examples of health effects data include: mutagenicity; carcinogenicity; teratogenicity; neurotoxicity/behavioral effects; pharmocological effects; mammalian absorption; distribution; metabolism and excretion; cumulative, additive and synergistic effects; acute, subchronic and chronic effects; structure/activity relationships; epidemiology; reproductive effects; clinical studies; dermatoxicity; phototoxicity; irritation; sensitization; allergy; and skin staining.

Examples of environmental effects data include: microbial bioassay; algal bioassay; aquatic macrophyte bioassay; seed germination and root elongation; seedling growth; plant uptake; acute toxicity to invertebrates; life cycle test on invertebrates; acute toxicity to fish; early life stage (fish); avian dietary/reproduction; bioaccumulation/bioconcentration; model ecosystem studies; physical environment impairment effects; and flesh staining of aquatic organisms.

A study that is incomplete at the time of filing must be disclosed to the EPA, together with any preliminary results, a description of the nature and purpose of the study, name and address of the laboratory, progress, types of data collected, and anticipated completion date. The PMN submitter must submit the study if it is completed during the ninety day PMN review period. The PMN submitter must submit it within ten days of receiving it, but no later than five days before the end of the PMN review period. If the study is

---

116. *Id.* at Appendix.

completed within the last five days of the PMN review period then the PMN submitter must call the EPA immediately.[117]

In addition to test data that must be submitted, PMN submitters must describe all data "related to the effects on health or the environment of any manufacture, processing, distribution in commerce, use, or disposal of the new chemical substance, of any mixture or article containing the new chemical substance, or of any combination of such activities" that has not already been submitted because it qualifies as test data.[118] All data, whether or not it is test data, relating to health or environmental effects that is in the "possession or control" of the submitter or "known to any of its employees or other agents who are associated with the research and development, test marketing, or commercial marketing of the substance" must be described in the PMN submission even though the data does not have to be submitted.[119] The EPA may request test data in the submitter's possession or control.[120]

If data has already been submitted to the EPA without any claims of confidentiality, it does not need to be included with the PMN and instead the PMN submitter can identify the recipient by name or office, the date of the prior submission, and any standard literature citation to the report.[121] Data on exposure pathways outside of the United States does not need to be submitted with a PMN,[122] but all data on health, environmental effects, physical and chemical properties, and environmental fate must be reported no matter where the data was generated.

5. Optional Pollution Prevention Information

PMN submitters have the option of submitting information on the pollution prevention benefits of the PMN substance with the PMN form. This is an opportunity to tell the EPA about the environmental benefits expected from the new chemical. These could be more efficient use of natural resources, reductions in the amount of waste generated by use of the substance, whether it can be used instead of a more toxic substance, and any other environmental advantages from use of the PMN substance.

---

117. 40 C.F.R. § 720.50(a)(4).
118. 40 C.F.R. § 720.50(b).
119. *Id.* Very confusingly, the regulations define "known to or reasonably ascertainable by the submitter" to be "known to any of its employees or other agents who are associated with the research and development, test marketing, or commercial marketing of the substance" for the purposes of this section only.
120. 40 C.F.R. § 720.50(a)(5).
121. 40 C.F.R. § 720.50(d).
122. *Id.*; 48 Fed. Reg. 21722, 21726 (May 13, 1983).

The EPA strongly encourages submitters to include the optional pollution prevention information so that it can balance the benefits of using a substance against the potential risks.[123]

6. Binding Boxes

The PMN form has check-off boxes in several places called binding boxes. If the filer is submitting a PMN, checking a binding box indicates that the submitter is willing to be bound by the process description, production quantities, manufacturing site, or other specific information listed next to the binding box. Checking a binding box does not limit a PMN filer to the practices in the PMN, but does give the EPA an advance indication of what kinds of restrictions the filer would agree to if restrictions are necessary.[124] As a result, checking a binding box has negatives and positives for a PMN filer who must decide if that would precipitate a restriction or offer a restriction that would not present any burden. If the product is one that the EPA is likely to restrict then this option may be helpful in suggesting acceptable restrictions.

The binding boxes have a different function for TMEs, LVEs, and LoREX applications because those exemptions require the filer to abide by the limitations in the applications. For example, a LVE filer can be bound to a production limit lower than ten thousand kilograms per year by listing a lower quantity and checking the binding box.[125]

7. Continuing Obligations

There is a continuing obligation to submit new information during the PMN review period. The regulations[126] require submission of information that "materially adds to, changes, or otherwise makes significantly more complete the information included in the notice." This standard encompasses most information that is relevant to the PMN substance. Only new information that the submitter "possesses, controls, or knows" must be submitted during the PMN review period, which means that the submitter does not need to continue to search for information that is "reasonably ascertainable" but that it does not already have. However, information in the possession of one of the companies that the filer must search or in an outside laboratory performing work for the filer is under the control of the filer. The filer should call the

---

123. Chemistry Manual, Chapter 3, 98 (1997). This chapter of the Manual also provides guidance for describing the pollution prevention benefits on the PMN Form.
124. *See* PMN Instruction Manual, 11.
125. *See* Chapter 5, PMN Exclusions and Exemptions for a discussion of why LoREX applicants should not check a binding box on volume limits.
126. 40 C.F.R. § 720.40(f).

other companies and outside laboratories before the end of the PMN review period so that it can submit updated information to the EPA on a timely basis. New information must be submitted within ten days of its receipt by the PMN submitter, but if the remaining review period is less than ten days then it must be submitted at least five days from the end of the review period. If new information comes in during the last five days of the review period then the submitter must call the EPA contact immediately.[127]

The Administrative Law Judge in *In The Matter of E. I. Dupont De Nemours & Co.*[128] found that a change of manufacturing site is material and must be reported during the PMN review period. The ALJ's decision states that "[i]t is apparent from the face of the rule that eight items of information in § 720.45—which are all enumerated in separate alphabetical sections of the rule—are material to the premanufacture review." These eight material facts that must be updated are (1) the chemical identity, (2) impurities, (3) synonyms and trade names, (4) byproducts, (5) manufacturing volumes, (6) categories of use, (7) manufacturing sites, and (8) sites where the substance will be processed or used. The ALJ's reference to eight categories of information is not exhaustive, and the ALJ did not limit the scope of what can be considered material to the eight categories noted above. The ALJ also noted that information in the PMN must be updated even though one of the PMN substances could have qualified for an exemption from the PMN requirements. This is consistent with the generally applicable environmental principle that anyone who files notices with the EPA must comply with all requirements governing those notices even if the submitter was not obligated to file.

8. Confidential Business Information

PMN submitters may claim that information in the PMN is confidential business information (CBI).[129] If there is CBI in the PMN the submitter must prepare a "sanitized" copy which does not disclose CBI, and file it together with the PMN.

Although there is no prohibition on claiming that health and safety studies are CBI, the EPA may not refuse a Freedom of Information Act request for health and safety studies that were submitted with PMNs.[130] Confidential process information and confidential information concerning the composition of mixtures may not be released, but other than that health and safety studies may not be withheld on the ground that they are CBI. Even if the

---

127. *Id.*
128. Docket No. TSCA-III-731 (ALJ 1998), *available at* http://www.epa.gov/oalj/orders/denemour.htm.
129. 40 C.F.R. § 720.80.
130. TSCA § 14(b).

chemical identity is claimed as confidential, the EPA will release it in response to a Freedom of Information Act request if it is necessary for interpretation of the study and will not reveal CBI concerning the process or mixture composition.[131]

9. PMNs on Related Substances

There are two situations in which the EPA will review several new chemicals together. The first is when up to six substances have similar chemistry, toxicology, uses, and expected manufacturing or importation quantities. The EPA will accept a single consolidated PMN that covers all of the substances, provided a Prenotice Coordinator has agreed that the substances are sufficiently similar.[132] There are reduced filing fees for consolidated PMNs. Consolidated PMNs can be filed on two related polymers, one with a specific monomer or other reactant above the two percent rule level so that monomer or reactant is part of the polymer's chemical identity and the other with the same monomer or other reactant below the two percent rule level so that monomer or reactant is excluded from the polymer's chemical identity.[133]

The second situation is when the end product and the intermediate chemicals used in synthesizing the end product are new chemicals. In this case each substance requires its own PMN, but all of the PMNs can be submitted together to enable the EPA to achieve economies of scale and get a better idea of the risks posed by the manufacturing process as a whole. The PMNs for the intermediates are referred to as "intermediate PMNs." Reduced fees are available only for large businesses.

A hybrid consolidated and intermediate PMN is possible if there are up to six related new chemical end products (D), together with new chemicals used in their synthesis (A, B, and C). The EPA gives the example of four closely related syntheses:

A → B → C → D
A′ → B′ → C′ → D′
A″ → B″ → C″ → D″
A‴ → B‴ → C‴ → D‴

In this case, a consolidated PMN can be submitted for end products D, D′, D″ and D‴. Another consolidated PMN can be submitted for intermediates A, A′, A″ and A‴, another for intermediates B, B′, B″ and B‴, and another for

131. 40 C.F.R. § 720.90; 48 Fed. Reg. 21722, 21739 (May 13, 1983).
132. 48 Fed. Reg. 21722, 21735 (May 13, 1983).
133. 60 Fed. Reg. 16298, 16304 (Mar. 29, 1995).

intermediates C, C′, C″ and C‴.[134] It is not appropriate to consolidate A, B, C, and D in a single consolidated PMN.[135]

10. Fees

The fees for filing PMNs are straightforward. Small business concerns, defined as people or entities that together with any parent entities had sales of less than $40,000,000 in the prior fiscal year,[136] pay $100 for filing a PMN. All other entities pay $2500.[137]

If a Prenotice Coordinator has preapproved a consolidated PMN the total fee for up to six new substances described in a single consolidated PMN is $100 for a small business and $2500 for all others.

If PMNs cover one or more intermediates and the end product, small businesses must pay $100 for each substance. Large businesses must pay $2500 for the end product and $1000 for each intermediate.

There is no fee for filing TME applications, LVEs, or LoREXs or exemptions from the microorganism regulations.[138]

The EPA will refund fees if the PMN substance is already on the Inventory, if the PMN is incomplete, if the PMN form was used for a SNUN that is not required, or if the PMN form was used for a microorganism that is not new.[139]

11. Recordkeeping

The PMN regulations require that PMN submitters retain for five years (i) documentation supporting information provided in the PMN, (ii) documentation supporting the date of commencement of manufacture or import; and (iii) production volume records for the first three years of manufacture or import.[140] However, the statute of limitations for enforcement actions is five years and so it is important to be able to support the PMN submission for at least five years. It is prudent to retain this data much longer—for five years after the last manufacture or importation of the PMN substance—because there are continuing violations that relate back to the PMN submission, and the complete file and backup information will be important to defend against an enforcement action even it is brought many years after the PMN is filed.

---

134. www.epa.gov/opptintr/newchems/pubs/pmnintr.htm.
135. PMN Instruction Manual, 14-15. Note that this is primarily an issue of applying the fee for intermediate PMNs instead of consolidated PMNs.
136. 40 C.F.R. § 700.43.
137. 40 C.F.R. § 700.45.
138. *Id.*
139. *Id.*
140. 40 C.F.R. § 720.78.

For example, each new act of manufacturing a substance could be a TSCA violation if the substance is not on the Inventory, and so it may be critical to refer back to the original PMN to prove that the substance was correctly described in the PMN.

D. What Happens after a PMN Is Submitted

The ninety day review period starts when the EPA receives a complete PMN form. The EPA assigns a receipt number, acknowledges receipt of the PMN, and informs the submitter of the date the PMN was received.[141] If the information is not complete then the ninety day review period does not begin until the gaps are filled.[142] If another person is supplying confidential information then the review period begins when the EPA receives all the necessary information.[143] A Document Control Number is assigned if the PMN is complete.[144]

After that, the EPA checks the Inventory to determine if the substance is already on it, which would eliminate the need to go through the PMN process.[145] It also reviews the circumstances of the substance's manufacture and use to determine if the substance is exempt from the PMN process.[146]

The EPA publishes notices in the Federal Register announcing the receipt of PMNs, and gives brief descriptions of the name of the chemical, the use, the identity of the submitter and the chemical name, unless any of this information is claimed to be confidential.[147]

During its initial review of the PMN, the EPA uses the data submitted in the PMN form to assess risks associated with the entire life cycle of the subject chemical.[148] It considers information about related chemicals and the chemistry involved in synthesizing the subject chemical as well as impurities, byproducts and degradation products. The EPA may conduct a literature search during the initial review of a PMN, but there is no requirement for it to do so. The EPA may also ask the PMN submitter questions.

---

141. 73 Fed. Reg. 78261, 78263 (Dec. 22, 2008); 48 Fed. Reg. 21722, 21724 (May 13, 1983); *c.f.*, 40 C.F.R. § 720.65(a). The EPA's Chemistry Assistance Manual for Premanufacture Notification Submittters contains a detailed and clear description of the EPA's review process. Chemistry Manual, Chapter 1.
142. 40 C.F.R. § 720.65(c). The submitter can contest the EPA's determination that the information is not complete.
143. 40 C.F.R. § 720.40(e)(3).
144. 73 Fed. Reg. 78261, 78263 (Dec. 22, 2008).
145. 40 C.F.R. § 720.62; Draft PMN Q&A, 1-32 to 1-33, question 106-1.
146. 48 Fed. Reg. 21722, 21724 (May 13, 1983).
147. 40 C.F.R. § 720.70.
148. 48 Fed. Reg. 21722, 21724 (May 13, 1983).

To expedite reviews, the EPA has designated 55 categories of chemicals that are all previously identified candidates for restriction through TSCA § 5(e) orders, and in the case of persistent, bioaccumulative, and toxic (PBT) chemicals some are also candidates for outright bans.[149] The chemicals within each category have similar hazard profiles and chemical properties, and the EPA has listed recommended tests for each category that will assist in determining whether § 5(e) orders are necessary, depending on the potential exposures to the chemicals. The categories are chemical groups that the EPA has had the most experience with, and are not necessarily the most hazardous chemicals. Consideration should be given to the potential testing requirements before filing a PMN on a substance in one of these categories. The EPA encourages filers to contact it to discuss any new testing before starting. In addition, it may be worthwhile to consider whether the likely restrictions will make the product noncompetitive. The 55 chemical categories are:[150]

- acid chlorides;
- acid dyes and amphoteric dyes;
- acrylamides;
- acrylates/methacrylates;
- aldehydes;
- aliphatic amines;
- alkoxysilanes;
- aluminum compounds;
- aminobenzothiazole azo dyes;
- anhydrides, carboxylic acid;
- anilines;
- dianilines;
- anionic surfactants;
- azides;
- benzotriazoles;
- benzotriazole-hindered phenols;
- boron compounds;
- cationic dyes;
- cationic (quaternary ammonium) surfactants;
- cobalt;
- diazoniums;
- dichlorobenzidine-based pigments;
- dithiocarbamates;
- epoxides;
- esters;

149. http://www.epa.gov/oppt/newchems/pubs/cat02.htm.
150. *Id.*

- ethylene glycol ethers;
- hydrazines and related compounds;
- hindered amines;
- imides;
- diisocyanates;
- ß-naphthylamines, sulfonated;
- lanthanides or rare earth metals;
- neutral organics;
- nickel compounds;
- nonionic surfactants;
- organotins;
- peroxides;
- persistent, bioaccumulative, and toxic (PBT) chemicals;
- phenolphthaleins;
- phenols;
- phosphates, inorganic;
- phosphinate esters;
- polyanionic polymers & monomers;
- polycationic polymers;
- polynitroaromatics;
- respirable, poorly soluble particulates;
- rosin;
- stilbene, derivatives of 4,4-bis(triazin-2-ylamino)-;
- thiols;
- substituted triazines;
- triarylmethane pigments/dyes with non-solubilizing groups;
- vinyl esters;
- vinyl sulfones;
- soluble complexes of zinc; and
- zirconium compounds.

Although not one of the EPA's designated categories, certain high molecular weight polymers that are not soluble in water are also likely to result in §5(e) orders.[151]

In addition to the chemical categories that are candidates for § 5(e) orders, EPA has also provided guidance on production quantity and exposure levels that will trigger § 5(e) orders. These triggers are:

- production of 100,000 kilograms/year;
- more than 1000 workers exposed;

151. These polymers are eligible for the polymer exemption, but companies have the option of filing PMNs for them. http://www.epa.gov/oppt/newchems/pubs/hmwtpoly.htm

- more than 100 workers exposed by inhalation to more than 10 milligrams/day (acute exposure);
- more than 100 workers exposed by inhalation to 1 to 10 milligrams/day for more than 100 days per year (chronic exposure);
- more than 250 workers exposed by dermal contact for more than 100 days/year (chronic exposure);
- incorporation into consumer products to which exposure is likely;
- exposure to the general population of more than 0.003 milligrams/kilogram body weight/day via drinking water, air or groundwater;
- release of more than 10,000 kilograms/year to the environment; or
- release to surface water of more than 1,000 kilograms/year, taking removal in wastewater treatment into account.[152]

The initial review phase ends when the EPA holds a "Focus" meeting and determines whether further review is necessary, or if the substance can be dropped from further review. This occurs roughly around the twentieth day after the filing date.[153] A further review can include consideration of issuing a TSCA § 5(e) or 5(f) order.[154]

The EPA has developed criteria for determining when polymers are low risk, and will drop those polymers from further review even before the Focus meeting.[155]

The EPA has a search tool that shows the initial determinations it reaches on PMNs. Anyone can use this tool to see what conclusions the EPA has reached on it its initial review of a PMN at the Focus meeting.[156] Of the 9742 PMNs reviewed between October 15, 1998 and December 15, 2008:

- 6216 were dropped from further review, which means that the EPA did not consider the substance to be a candidate for restrictions;
- 1397 were pending regulation under 5(e), which means that the substance is in a category that triggers risk concerns, and the EPA may issue a 5(e) SNUR;
- 917 were rejected as invalid, which means that the substance was on the Inventory already, was exempt from the PMN process, not subject to TSCA, or the PMNs were incomplete;

---

152. http://www.epa.gov/oppt/newchems/pubs/expbased.htm.
153. *See* http://www.epa.gov/oppt/newchems/tools/dropstat.htm; Draft PMN Q&A, 1-32–1-33, question 106-1 says the Focus meeting is held between the twenty-third and twenty-seventh day while EPA's Sustainable Futures training introduction slides say in various places that the Focus Meeting is held between the fifteenth and nineteenth (slide 16) or twentieth (slide 11) day, *available at* http://www.epa.gov/oppt/sf/presentations/sf/sfintro1.pdf (2005).
154. 48 Fed. Reg. 21722, 21724–25 (May 13, 1983).
155. Chemistry Manual, Chapter 1, 13–14, (1997).
156. http://www.epa.gov/oppt/newchems/tools/dropstat.htm.

- 630 were dropped with letters, which means that the substances were dropped from further review and were not candidates for regulation, but the EPA had concerns about the substance;
- 283 were in the standard review process;
- 273 were dropped and non-5(e) SNURS were planned, which means that the PMN submitter's use did not pose significant risks, but other uses may pose risks and the EPA intended to issue SNURs for those substances without restricting the uses disclosed in the PMN;
- eighteen were withdrawn by the submitters;
- six were given limited further review; and
- at least two were the subject of follow-up questions by the EPA before further review.[157]

Some of this data may not be fully representative because the EPA updates some of the data after the Focus meeting.

The Focus Meeting is when the EPA makes its determinations on TMEs, LVEs, and LoREX exemption applications.[158]

After the initial review, the EPA conducts a detailed review of the PMN, provided the PMN has not been dropped. The ninety day review period may be extended for up to another ninety days under TSCA § 5(c) to permit the EPA to complete its analysis of the PMN, or for any "good cause." The PMN submitter may suspend the review period if the EPA approves,[159] and EPA at times requests the PMN submitter to suspend the PMN review period[160] or it can be extended by mutual agreement[161] for any length of time. As a practical matter, unless there is some urgent reason not to agree to a request to suspend the review period it is always better to work cooperatively with the Agency. Suspension requests for more than 15 days for PMNs filed after the April 6, 2010 effective date of the ePMN rules must be made using the electronic submittal software, and may be filed on paper, or via CD, DVD, or CDX. After the first anniversary of the effective date of the new rules, they must be submitted via CD, DVD, or CDX, and after the second anniversary they may be submitted only via CDX.[162] Suspension requests for PMNs filed

157. Analysis of the results of a search (Dec. 22, 2008) of PMN status on the EPA's website at http://www.epa.gov/oppt/newchems/tools/dropstat.htm. These data may not be correct because after a follow-up question is answered the database is updated to also include the subsequent action, so a single PMN may be entered more than once.
158. Draft PMN Q&A, 1-32–1-33, question 106-1.
159. 40 C.F.R. § 720.75(b).
160. 40 C.F.R. § 720.75(c).
161. 67 Fed. Reg. 76282, 76285 (Dec. 11, 2002).
162. 40 C.F.R. § 720.75(b)(2)(ii).

before April 6, 2010 must be on paper.[163] The same procedures hold for withdrawing a PMN.[164]

"Standard review" is not the standard process, despite its name, because only a relatively small percentage of PMNs follow this path. For those chemicals in the standard review process, the EPA holds an interdisciplinary meeting around the seventy-ninth to eighty-second day after it received the PMN. That meeting is a Decision Meeting, at which the participants review hazard, exposure, and risk assessments and reach a decision on whether the substance should be further regulated.[165]

If the EPA determines that there may be a risk associated with the substance, it has several options for imposing restrictions.[166] These include regulating the manufacturing, processing, distribution, use, or disposal of the substance with orders under TSCA §§ 5(e) or 5(f), issuing a SNUR, or requiring follow up reporting under § (5)(a)(2) or § 8(a).[167]

If the EPA does not take any affirmative steps to restrict the substance during the PMN review period, the submitter is free to manufacture or import the substance without any restrictions. The submitter must file an NOC within thirty days after it begins to manufacture or import the PMN substance. After the submitter files an NOC, the substance is automatically added to the Inventory and anyone may manufacture or import it for any purpose without notifying the EPA, again assuming that the EPA has not taken affirmative steps to impose restrictions.

E. Expedited PMNs—Sustainable Futures

There is a joint industry/EPA program called Sustainable Futures that confers benefits on both PMN filers and the EPA by expediting the PMN review process.[168] Qualified Sustainable Futures participants can file a TME and PMN simultaneously and commence manufacturing or importing forty five days after filing. Between the 45th day and the 90th day after filing, any manufacture or importation must be under the TME rules, and after the 90th day the manufacture or importation is under the PMN rules.[169]

---

163. 40 C.F.R. § 720.75(b)(2)(i).
164. 40 C.F.R. § 720.75(e)(1).
165. Draft PMN Q&As, 1-32–1-33, question 106-1.
166. 48 Fed. Reg. 21722, 21724 (May 13, 1983). Draft PMN Q&A, 1-32–1-33, question 106-1.
167. 48 Fed. Reg. 21722, 21724 (May 13, 1983).
168. www.epa.gov/oppt/sf/.
169. *See* EPA training materials on Sustainable Futures, *available through* www.epa.gov/oppt/sf/.

The Sustainable Futures program was announced in 2002 with the goal of encouraging companies to determine the risks presented by PMN substances and to develop low hazard chemicals.[170]

Companies that enter the Sustainable Futures program must go through a training program to learn the process of prescreening their substances for human health and environmental risks. Before filing a PMN they must apply models developed by the EPA to predict physical and chemical properties, environmental fate and degradation, toxicity, carcinogenicity, bioaccumulation, exposure, and risk. These computer models are referred to as the P2 Framework.[171] An analysis of the hazards and risk evaluations generated by these screening tools must be submitted with the PMN. After a company has submitted five PMNs or LVE applications[172] under the Sustainable Futures program, it can petition the EPA to permit expedited review of future PMNs that they submit under this program. However, each of the five qualifying PMNs or LVE applications must result in EPA's determination that restrictions are not required for the subject substance, and the submitter must have correctly used the models to predict that conclusion.

Qualified companies are referred to as graduates, and as of EPA's last update on its Web site five companies graduated.[173] Over thirty companies attended training sessions in 2007.[174] It is apparent from these statistics that the resource intensive nature of this program puts it outside the reach of most small companies and individuals.

F. Outcomes of the PMN process

1. Section 5(e) Orders

The EPA may issue an order under TSCA § 5(e) if there is not enough information to evaluate the risks posed by the PMN substance and if the PMN substance either (i) may present a risk or (ii) there will be substantial

170. 67 Fed. Reg. 76282 (Dec. 11, 2002). This Federal Register notice states that the PMN form must be used for TMEs, and that "[i]f EPA has not taken action to deny the exemption application, under section 5(h)(1) for TMEs … the notice submitter may manufacture or import the new chemical substance when the respective review period for those notices expires (i.e., day 45 for TME …)." *Id.* at 76284-85. This is not consistent with statements EPA has made elsewhere about TMEs. For a discussion of TMEs see Chapter 5, PMN Exclusions and Exemptions.
171. 67 Fed. Reg. 76282, 76285 (Dec. 11, 2002).
172. http://www.epa.gov/oppt/sf/pubs/faqs.htm.
173. http://www.epa.gov/oppt/sf/.
174. EPA, Office of Prevention and Pollution Control, Accomplishments Report (Jan. 2007–June 2008), *available at* http://www.epa.gov/oppt/ar/2007-2008/working/sustainable.htm.

quantities made and there will be either substantial environmental releases or substantial or significant human exposure.

The EPA has nonbinding guidelines for the types of tests it will typically require in a § 5(e) order if any of the production volume and exposure triggers discussed *supra* are met.[175] The tests that the EPA may require if the human exposure triggers are met include bacterial reverse mutation, mammalian erythrocyte micronucleus, repeated dose 28-day oral toxicity in rodents, and acute oral toxicity. For high production volume chemicals with high exposure potential the EPA may also require a prenatal developmental toxicity test and a reproduction/developmental toxicity screening test. For chemicals that meet the release to surface water trigger, the EPA may require algal toxicity, aquatic invertebrate acute toxicity, and fish acute toxicity testing. If the environmental release or concentration triggers are met, the EPA may require water solubility, fate in wastewater treatment, semi-continuous activated sludge, modified Zahn-Wellens/EMPA, activated sludge sorption isotherm, aerobic biodegradation, sealed vessel CO_2 production, anaerobic biodegradation, soil biodegradation, photolysis, and hydrolysis testing.

Rather than routinely issue unilateral orders under TSCA § 5(e), the EPA typically is willing to negotiate an order with the PMN submitter. The EPA has several model TSCA § 5(e) consent orders depending on the type of risks, releases, or exposures that may be presented.[176] As an example, there is one model based on risks to the environment that may be posed by the PMN substance.[177] This risk-based ecotoxicity model provides for an array of restrictions on the signatory, which may include an obligation to submit toxicity testing before exceeding a production volume that will be established for the specific chemical. The model permits the EPA to suggest other tests that would be helpful to evaluate the risks posed by the substance. Additional restrictions may include manufacturing, processing, use, and other restrictions tailored to the risks posed by the chemical. Like most of the model orders, the risk-based ecotoxicity model permits the EPA to allow distribution of the substance only to entities that have agreed to be bound by the conditions in the order.

The model risk-based ecotoxicity order includes provisions that are found in most of the model orders:

- requiring the signatory to notify the EPA before starting studies required by the order;

175. http://www.epa.gov/oppt/newchems/pubs/expbasedtesting.htm.

176. The set of model TSCA § 5(e) orders is *available at* http://www.epa.gov/opptintr/newchems/pubs/boilerpl.htm.

177. *Id.*

- requiring compliance with Good Laboratory Practice Standards;[178]
- requiring submission of interim reports as well as final reports;
- allowing signatories to seek waivers of testing requirements;
- requiring establishment or continuation of a preexisting hazard communication system, including labels, Material Safety Data Sheets, employee training,
- prohibiting signatories from suggesting or encouraging that others make or import the substance (the reason that the signatory to a 5(e) order cannot suggest that another company make the regulated substance is based on the nature of a 5(e) order; 5(e) orders only apply to the signatory, and any other person may manufacture or import the substance without restriction between the time it is placed on the Inventory and the time the EPA issues a SNUR; this prohibition in the model orders prevents a signatory from circumventing the restrictions in the 5(e) order by having another person manufacture the substance);
- terminating the 5(e) order when a SNUR is fully enforceable;
- requiring the signatory, upon termination of the 5(e) order because a SNUR is fully enforceable, to inform any person that it has caused, encouraged or suggested to manufacture or import the substance about the existence of the SNUR;
- requiring the signatory, upon termination of the 5(e) order because a SNUR is fully enforceable, to inform any person to whom it distributes the substance about the existence of the SNUR;
- requiring the signatory to obtain written agreements governing handling of the substance from any person to which it distributes the substance;
- requiring the signatory to cease distribution to any person who receives the substance and does not comply with the written agreement governing handling, unless certain procedures are followed;
- specifying the circumstances under which the right to manufacture or import the substance may be transferred to another person;[179]
- stating that the order does not apply to:
  - quantities of the substance that are completely reacted;
  - mixtures that contain the PMN substance in de minimis concentrations, which are defined as one percent or less by weight or volume for a noncarcinogen and 0.1% or less by weight or volume for a potential carcinogen;

---

178. 40 C.F.R. Part 492.

179. *See* Chapter 15, Acquisitions and Divestitures, for a discussion of successor transfer of TSCA § 5(e) orders.

- substances manufactured solely for export provided that no quantities of the substance are also produced for domestic use;
- R&D quantities;
- byproducts that are exempt from PMN requirements because the only commercial use for them is by a public or private organization that burns them as a fuel, disposes of them as waste including landfilling or use for soil enrichment, or extracting component substances from them;[180]
- impurities;[181]
- chemicals formed incidentally when a chemical is exposed to another chemical or to the environment;
- chemicals formed incidentally when a chemical is stored or disposed of;
- chemicals formed on end use of products such as adhesives and cleansers;
- chemicals formed during the manufacture of certain articles;
- chemicals formed when specified chemicals used to alter physical properties, such as stabilizers and plasticizers function as intended; and
- nonisolated intermediates.

Some of the model 5(e) orders have provisions for new chemical exposure limits, (NCELs) that can be implemented instead of using respirators to limit risks from inhalation of the PMN substance.[182] NCELs are specific numerical limits on the airborne concentrations of the PMN substance. The EPA may develop a maximum concentration for eight hour exposures, a maximum concentration for work shifts that are shorter or longer than eight hours, and a short term exposure limit (STEL) for fifteen minute exposure periods. In order to use NCELs instead of respirators, the signatory must develop a sampling and analytical plan and have it verified by an independent third party laboratory. As of 2002 the EPA had developed thirty four NCELs.[183]

The model 5(e) orders do not permit any direct judicial review of EPA actions pursuant to the orders. Instead, they permit a signatory to petition the EPA for a modification, but the EPA has wide discretion in reaching a conclusion. A signatory may also petition the EPA for a modification of an order

180. The model orders reference 40 C.F.R. §§ 720.3(d) and 720.30(g).
181. The model order cross-references the exemptions at 40 C.F.R. § 720.30(h), which includes impurities and the remaining items in this bulleted list.
182. *See for example*, the model order for risk based human health effects with NCELs, *available at* http://www.epa.gov/opptintr/newchems/pubs/corbhncl1.txt.
183. The EPA's most recent list is from 2002 and is *available at* http://www.epa.gov/oppt/newchems/pubs/nceltbl.htm.

pursuant to TSCA § 21(a).[184] A § 21 petition can take a significant amount of time because the EPA has ninety days to respond to the petition and only then can an action be commenced in a federal district court. The court will not conduct a de novo review of the EPA's decision, and will only determine whether the EPA violated the lenient standards in the Administrative Procedure Act[185] in reaching a decision.[186] As the Court said in *EDF v. Thomas*, "[r]eview of agency action under the APA is of course highly deferential; courts may not substitute their judgment for that of the agency and may only set aside an administrative decision that is arbitrary, capricious or not in accordance with the law."[187]

2. Section 5(f) Orders

Section 5(f) of TSCA gives the EPA the authority to issue proposed rules under TSCA § 6[188] limiting volumes or otherwise restricting the manufacture, importation, processing, or distribution of a substance if there is a "reasonable basis to conclude" that a PMN substance presents or will present an unreasonable risk of injury to human health or the environment. Proposed rules under § 5(f) must be published before the PMN review period is over, and are effective immediately. The EPA selects this route when restrictions under TSCA § 6 cannot be put in place in time to prevent a risk from occurring.[189] To date, there have been only three § 5(f) proposed rules.[190]

Section 5(f) also authorizes the EPA to seek an injunction in Federal District Court prohibiting manufacturing, importing, processing or distribution of the PMN substance. The EPA may issue an order pending the court's action. The EPA has not pursued this option.[191]

---

184. Section 21(a) of TSCA provides in full:

> (a) In general
>
> Any person may petition the Administrator to initiate a proceeding for the issuance, amendment, or repeal of a rule under section 2603 [Section 4], 2605 [Section 6], or 2607 [Section 8] of this title or an order under section 2604(e) [Section 5(e)] or 2605(b)(2) [Section 6(b)(2)] of this title.

185. 5 U.S.C. § 701.
186. Environmental Defense Fund v. Reilly, 909 F.2d 1497, 1503 (D.C. Cir. 1990).
187. 657 F.Supp. 302, 311 (D.D.C. 1987).
188. TSCA § 6 concerns restrictions on chemicals, and is addressed in Chapter 11, Bans and Restrictions.
189. http://www.epa.gov/opptintr/newchems/pubs/possible.htm.
190. EPA Response to Freedom of Information Act request HQ RIN-00602-09 (Jan. 30, 2009). The three § 5(f) orders, covering four substances, have resulted in restrictions under § 6 which are found at 40 C.F.R. §§ 747.115, 747.195 and 747.200.
191. EPA Response to Freedom of Information Act request HQ RIN-00602-09 (Jan. 30, 2009).

3. Practical Implications

The EPA has authority to issue § 5(e) orders unilaterally. If there is any need to bring a PMN substance to market, it is much faster to negotiate a § 5(e) order cooperatively. Specific terms of the model order may be negotiated, but the negotiations will start from the appropriate model § 5(e) order.

Any time a § 5(e) order is issued, or any time an action is started for a unilateral § 5(e) order, the export notice requirements are triggered.[192]

G. Notice of Commencement

After the PMN period has expired, manufacturers and importers who have filed a PMN must notify the EPA within thirty calendar days of commencing manufacture or import of the PMN substance.[193] The notification must be made on the NOC form, which is EPA form 7710–56.[194] The thirty day period begins to run on completion of manufacture of the first amount of the PMN substance made for a nonexempt purpose, i.e., when it is made for commercial purposes and not for research and development, test marketing, or another purpose exempt from the PMN filing requirements.[195] For an import, the thirty day period begins to run after the PMN substance has cleared U.S. Customs.[196]

An NOC may not be filed when a manufacturer uses surplus stocks of a chemical handled under the R&D exemption from the PMN requirements. The NOC may only be based on manufacture of substances for a purpose that is not exempt from the PMN requirements, and so a manufacturer must wait until it makes the substance for non-R&D purposes before it files the NOC.[197]

The NOC itself requires submission of the following information:

- the chemical identity of the PMN substance;
- a generic chemical name if the chemical identity is confidential;
- the PMN number assigned by the EPA when the PMN was filed;
- the date of commencement, which is the date of completion of manufacture of the first amount for nonexempt purposes, or the date the first imported amount cleared U.S. Customs;
- the name and address of the submitter;

---

192. TSCA § 12.
193. 40 C.F.R. § 720.102.
194. http://www.epa.gov/opptintr/newchems/pubs/filenoc.htm.
195. 40 C.F.R. § 720.102; *see also*, the PMN Form, Part III.
196. *Id.*
197. 51 Fed. Reg. 15096, 15100-01 (Apr. 22, 1986).

- the name of the signatory, who must be an authorized official of the PMN submitter;
- the name and telephone number of a technical contact in the U.S.;
- the address where the first manufacture of the PMN substance for a nonexempt purpose took place or the destination address of the first import for a nonexempt purpose; and
- an indication of whether information is claimed as confidential, and a reassertion of the confidentiality of the chemical identity if appropriate.[198]

The NOC results in the substance's listing on the Inventory. If the chemical identity is claimed as confidential on the NOC and the EPA does not challenge this claim, the substance will be put on the confidential Inventory and only the generic name will be made public. If there is no confidentiality then the substance will be put on the public Inventory and the chemical identity will be published.

NOCs for PMNs filed after the April 6, 2010 effective date of the new electronic filing regulations must be made using the electronic submission software, and may be filed on paper, via CD, DVD, or CDX for one year after the effective date of the new rules, and thereafter must be submitted via CD, DVD, or CDX for the next year, and then only via CDX. NOCs for PMNs filed before the effective date must be on paper.[199]

There is no personal certification on the NOC form. However, willful false statements of material facts to the U.S. government are felonies, even in the absence of the additional statements required by the certification on the PMN form.[200]

NOCs are not made public and therefore there is no need to file a separate sanitized copy if any of the information on it is CBI.[201]

V. Enforcement

EPA can and does conduct inspections regarding compliance with TSCA § 5, under its general inspection authorities and under specific regulatory authority for § 5 inspections.[202]

When the EPA finds violations and when violations are self-reported, the initial penalty assessments are calculated using the Amended TSCA § 5

198. 40 C.F.R. § 720.102; *see also*, the PMN Form, Part III.
199. 40 C.F.R. §§ 720.102(c) and (d).
200. 18 U.S.C. § 1001.
201. 60 Fed. Reg. 16298, 16307 (Mar. 29, 1995).
202. The authorization in the PMN regulations is at 40 C.F.R. § 720.122.

Enforcement Response Policy (§ 5 ERP).[203] Like all the ERPs, the § 5 ERP assigns a "nature," "circumstance," and "extent" to each violation to calculate a "gravity based penalty" which is then adjusted up or down based on the violator's attitude, violation history, and other similar factors.[204]

To determine the circumstances of a violation, it may be necessary to file a so-called "mock PMN." A mock PMN is a PMN that is submitted in the context of an enforcement proceeding when the violator is no longer manufacturing or importing the substance. The EPA uses mock PMNs to determine if the substance that is the subject of the violation would have posed a risk to humans or the environment, or whether it would have been the subject of an order restricting its handling under TSCA § 5(e) or 5(f). Mock PMNs are submitted using the PMN form. They do not result in Inventory listing of the substance. If a violator wants to have the substance placed on the Inventory, it will file a PMN using the same form, but will not designate it as a mock PMN.

There are a few anachronisms in the § 5 ERP to watch out for. The dollar values of the gravity based penalties are out of date because the maximum daily penalty has gone up from $25,000 to $37,500.[205] To determine the correct penalties for violations occurring after January 12, 2009 each dollar value given in the § 5 ERP must be multiplied by the ratio of the current maximum to the maximum in effect when the § 5 ERP was written. That ratio is currently $37,500 divided by $25,000, or 1.5. For violations between January 31, 1997 and March 15, 2004, the gravity based penalties must be increased by a factor of 1.1. For violations between March 16, 2004 and January 12, 2009 the gravity based penalties must be increased by a factor of 1.3.

The § 5 ERP also has examples that calculate penalties for more than five years of violation, contrary to *3M v. Browner*,[206] which found that there is a five year statute of limitations for TSCA violations. It also discusses a one thousand kg limit for LVEs, although the limit was raised to ten thousand kg in 1985.

One hypothetical will illustrate the application of the § 5 ERP. Assume a company manufactured substance A for four years without filing a PMN and substance A is not on the Inventory, is not excluded from TSCA, and does not qualify for an exemption from the PMN requirements. In each of 2006,

---

203. Amended TSCA § 5 Enforcement Response Policy [hereinafter § 5 ERP] as amended and restated (June 8, 1989) and further amended in Memorandum from John J. Neylan, Director, Policy and Grants Division, Office of Compliance Monitoring, to Michael J. Walker, Enforcement Counsel, Toxics Litigation Division, (July 1, 1993), *available through* http://cfpub.epa.gov/compliance/resources/policies/civil/tsca/.

204. For a full discussion of ERPs, see Chapter 14, Penalties and Enforcement. The discussion in this chapter is limited to the ERP issues that are unique to TSCA § 5.

205. *See* Chapter 14, Penalties and Enforcement, for a discussion of the penalty increases.

206. 17 F.3d 1453 (D.C. Cir. 1994).

2007, 2008, and 2009, the company made fifty batches of substance A, and each batch took five days to complete. Each batch was three thousand pounds. The company further processed substance A and sold it in a product for consumer use. The company discovered the violation and self-reported it to the EPA within thirty days of its discovery, but the discovery was not made in the context of an audit or application of a compliance management system. The company filed a PMN and the EPA found that substance A may pose an environmental risk. The Company and the EPA entered into a § 5(e) Consent Order restricting the environmental release of substance A. The EPA issued an administrative complaint charging the company with failure to submit a PMN, categorized the extent as major, and seeks penalties for each day of violation.[207]

The first step in calculating any penalty is to determine the nature, circumstance, and extent of the violation by analyzing the ERP. The § 5 ERP provides that the nature of all failures to submit required notices to the EPA is a hazard assessment violation because the violations interfere with the EPA's ability to determine whether the substance poses any risks. This hypothetical violation is also a commercial use of a substance produced without a PMN, which is also a hazard assessment violation.[208] The ERP states that circumstance of this hypothetical violation is Level 1, with penalties to be assessed for each day of violation because substance A did merit restrictions through a TSCA § 5(e) order and it was further processed and distributed to others.[209]

The EPA has the authority to charge commercial use violations in addition to the PMN violations, but in the circumstances of this hypothetical it would not generally seek commercial use penalties. Commercial use penalties are generally only sought (i) when the substance was processed but was not manufactured by the violator, and (ii) when the substance was made or imported on few occasions but processing occurred over a longer period of time, could have caused substantial endangerment to human health or the environment, and would have been the subject of a TSCA § 5(e) or 5(f) order.[210] In these circumstances the penalties available to the EPA would be small relative to the potential for harm without these additional penalties.

The extent of the violation is determined by consulting a matrix in the § 5 ERP,[211] using the nature and production quantity to look up the classification. For a hazard assessment violation where three thousand pounds of substance A were made in each production batch, the extent classification is "significant." If a batch takes several days to complete, the day of completion

---

207. *See* § 5 ERP, Appendix 1, 2, Example 2.
208. § 5 ERP, 7.
209. § 5 ERP, 8.
210. § 5 ERP, 10.
211. § 5 ERP, 13.

is the day of violation, and the quantity completed that day is the quantity to use for determining extent.[212]

Another matrix supplies the gravity based penalties for each combination of nature, circumstances and extent.[213] For the hypothetical Level 1, significant violation the daily penalty in the § 5 ERP is $17,000. However, the penalties applicable to the violations in 2006, 2007, and 2008 must be increased by a factor of 1.3, and the penalties applicable to the 2009 violations must be increased by a factor of 1.5 (assuming the manufacturing took place after January 12, 2009). Therefore the gravity based penalties for the hypothetical are:

150 total batches in 2006, 2007 and 2008 = 150 x 17,000 x 1.3 = $3,315.000
50 batches in 2009 = 50 x 17,000 x 1.5 = $1,275,000
Total gravity based penalty = $4,590,000

The total gravity based penalty in this hypothetical can be reduced by a factor of 50 percent for voluntary self reporting within thirty days of discovery, another 15 percent for mitigating the violation by filing a PMN and entering into a § 5(e) order, and another 15 percent for a cooperative attitude. The total possible penalty reduction is 80 percent, which results in an adjusted penalty of $918,000.

Note that this penalty reduction is greater than the 75 percent penalty reduction that would have been available under the Audit Policy[214] for a violation that was self-reported but was not discovered as the result of an audit or application of a compliance monitoring program.

Penalties for most other potential violations can be calculated using the § 5 ERP similarly. However, the 1993 amendment[215] reduces the penalties for failing to submit NOCs on time and must be consulted in conjunction with the § 5 ERP for this subset of TSCA § 5 violations.

When substances are imported in violation of the PMN rules, the import certification under TSCA § 13 will inevitably be incorrect, and penalties can be assessed for the import certification violations in addition to the penalties for the PMN violations. Each nonexempt chemical import must be accompanied by either a positive or negative declaration. The positive declaration states that the substance is subject to TSCA and complies with its rules, and

212. § 5 ERP, 15.
213. § 5 ERP, 16.
214. *See* Chapter 14, Penalties and Enforcement for a discussion of the penalty waiver and penalty mitigation available under the Audit Policy, 65 Fed. Reg. 19618 (Apr. 11, 2000) as further interpreted, 73 Fed. Reg. 44991 (Aug. 1, 2008).
215. Memorandum from John J. Neylan, Director, Policy and Grants Division, Office of Compliance Monitoring, EPA, to Michael J. Walker, Enforcement Counsel, Toxics Litigation Division, EPA (July 1, 1993).

the negative declaration states that the substance is not subject to TSCA. The Consent Agreement entered by the parties in *In the Matter of Fujifilm Manufacturing, U.S.A., Inc.*[216] is an example of an enforcement proceeding where penalties were assessed for both PMN violations and import certification violations. In this case, the EPA found that there were 38 importations of a substance that was not on the Inventory. The gravity based penalty for failure to file a PMN was $47,690, and the gravity based penalties for failing to submit correct import certifications was another $47,690. The total penalty was reduced by 50 percent for self reporting within thirty days of discovery, another 15 percent for good attitude and cooperation with the EPA, and another 15 percent for taking steps to mitigate the violation.

In the Matter of Ashland, Inc.[217] is an example of a company resolving EPA's finding that an NOC violation had occurred; this was achieved by payment of a fine and the conducting of an audit of compliance with the TSCA § 5 rules and the import certification rules.

---

216. Docket No. TSCA-HQ-2008-5029 (Oct. 20, 2008), *available* through http://yosemite.epa.gov/oa/EAB_Web_Docket.nsf/Unpublished~Final~Orders?OpenView.

217. EAB Order in Docket Number TSCA-HQ-2007-5013 (Aug. 16, 2007), *available through* http://yosemite.epa.gov/oa/EAB_Web_Docket.nsf/Unpublished~Final~Orders?OpenView. This Consent Agreement is a useful model of an agreement requiring a compliance audit.

CHAPTER 5

PMN Exclusions and Exemptions

I. Introduction

There are numerous exclusions and exemptions from the premanufacture notification (PMN) process. Chemicals that are excluded from the Toxic Substances Control Act (TSCA)[1] definition of "chemical substances" are excluded from the PMN requirements, as well as all TSCA programs.[2] Chemicals that are excluded from the definition of "chemical substances" include mixtures (but not the constituents of a mixture, each of which is a "chemical substance"), pesticides, tobacco, firearms, nuclear materials, food, food additives, drugs, cosmetics, and "devices" under the Federal Food, Drug, and Cosmetic Act.[3]

In contrast to the excluded chemicals that are outside the scope of all the TSCA programs, there are numerous exemptions that only exempt the subject chemical from the PMN rules. Before describing each of these exemptions, it is important to note that when the regulations exempt a chemical from the PMN process, it does not necessarily follow that the chemical is exempt from any other TSCA program. For example, most of the chemicals that qualify for one of the exemptions discussed in this chapter are not exempt from the adverse effects reporting requirements of TSCA § 8(e).

The PMN program exempts the following chemicals and activities:

- byproducts that have no commercial use, or that are commercially used by public or private organizations only (i) to burn as a fuel, (ii) for disposal as a waste including landfilling and to enrich soil, or (iii) to extract components for commercial purposes;[4]
- chemicals manufactured or imported solely for export;[5]
- impurities;[6]
- nonisolated intermediates;[7]
- research and development (R&D) substances;[8]
- certain polymers that are not likely to pose risks to health or the environment;[9]
- chemicals formed incidentally when a chemical is exposed to the environment;[10]

1. 15 U.S.C. §§ 2601–2695d.
2. *See* TSCA § 3(2), 40 C.F.R § 720.30(a).
3. 21 U.S.C. § 301–399.
4. 40 C.F.R. §§ 720.30(g) and 720.30(h)(2).
5. 40 C.F.R. § 720.30(e).
6. 40 C.F.R. § 720.30(h)(1).
7. 40 C.F.R. § 720.30(h)(8).
8. 40 C.F.R. §§ 720.30(c) and 720.30(i).
9. 40 C.F.R. § 723.250.
10. 40 C.F.R. § 720.30(h)(3).

- chemicals formed incidentally when a chemical is stored or disposed of;[11]
- chemicals formed on end use products such as adhesives and cleansers–this is often referred to as the (h)(5) exemption because it appears at 40 C.F.R. § 720(h)(5);
- chemicals formed during the manufacture of certain articles;[12]
- chemicals formed when specified chemicals used to alter physical properties, such as stabilizers and plasticizers function as intended—this is often referred to as the (h)(7) exemption because it appears at 40 C.F.R. § 720(h)(7);
- certain test marketing activities;[13]
- certain chemicals made or imported in quantities of 10,000 kilograms or less per year under the Low Volume Exemption (LVE);[14]
- certain chemicals with low environmental releases and human exposures (LoREX);[15] and
- chemicals used for instant photographic and peel-apart film (the Polaroid exemption).[16]

The United States Environmental Protection Agency (EPA) has authority under the statute to grant additional exemptions under TSCA § 5(h)(4) if the "manufacture, processing, distribution in commerce, use or disposal" of a substance "will not present an unreasonable risk of injury to health or the environment." Several exemptions have been promulgated under this authority, including the polymer exemption, the LVE and LoREX exemptions, and the Polaroid exemption.

PMNs do not need to be filed on mixtures,[17] but a PMN must be filed on each component of a mixture, unless that component is on the Inventory or qualifies for an exemption.[18]

11. 40 C.F.R. § 720.30(h)(4).
12. 40 C.F.R. § 720.30(h)(6). *See* Chapter 2, TSCA's Scope.
13. 40 C.F.R. § 720.30(d).
14. 40 C.F.R. § 723.50(a)(i).
15. 40 C.F.R. § 723.50(a)(ii).
16. 40 C.F.R. § 723.175.
17. TSCA § 2(B)(i) 40 C.F.R. §§ 720.3(e)(1), 720.3(u) and 720.30(b).
18. *See* Chapter 2, TSCA's Scope.

II. Exemptions Not Requiring Prior Notice to the EPA

A. Byproducts

Byproducts that have no commercial use, or that are commercially used by public or private organizations only (i) to burn as a fuel, (ii) for disposal as a waste including landfilling and to enrich soil, or (iii) to extract components for commercial purposes are exempt from the PMN and significant new use rule (SNUR) requirements.[19]

Manufacturers of byproducts must be especially wary about distributing their byproducts. If there are no non-exempt commercial uses, the byproducts are not required to be on the Inventory, but it may be difficult for a manufacturer that is distributing a byproduct for an exempt use to ensure that all the uses to which the byproduct is put are exempt. If there are any non-exempt uses, the manufacturer is responsible for filing a PMN[20] and subject to potentially significant penalties for failure to file one. As a result, manufacturers should contractually restrict the uses to which their byproducts are put unless the byproducts are on the Inventory.

B. Research & Development

The TSCA statute exempts chemicals from the Inventory and PMN requirements if the chemicals are made or imported only for R&D.[21] In fact, R&D substances cannot be listed on the Inventory at all.[22] In order for a substance

---

19. 40 C.F.R. §§ 720.30(g) and 720.30(h)(2).
20. 48 Fed. Reg. 21722, 21727 (May 13, 1983).
21. TSCA § 5(h)(3) provides:

> The requirements of subsections (a) and (b) of this section do not apply with respect to the manufacturing or processing of any chemical substance which is manufactured or processed, or proposed to be manufactured or processed, only in small quantities (as defined by the Administrator by rule) solely for purposes of—
>
> (A) scientific experimentation or analysis, or
> (B) chemical research on, or analysis of such substance or another substance, including such research or analysis for the development of a product,
>
> if all persons engaged in such experimentation, research, or analysis for a manufacturer or processor are notified (in such form and manner as the Administrator may prescribe) of any risk to health which the manufacturer, processor, or the Administrator has reason to believe may be associated with such chemical substance.

22. TSCA § 8(b).

to qualify as an R&D substance, a manufacturer or importer must follow the regulatory requirements that are explained below. If a manufacturer or importer does not meet these regulatory requirements then it must go through the PMN process and list the substance on the Inventory before it manufactures or imports the substance.

The statute also exempts R&D substances from SNURs.[23] The R&D exemption for SNURs is very similar to the R&D exemption from the Inventory and PMN rules. However, unless the context is clear otherwise, this discussion only relates to the R&D exemption from the Inventory and PMN requirements.

There is an R&D exemption for microorganisms, but it is substantially different in recognition of the fact that living organisms pose unique regulatory issues.[24]

The regulatory requirements for the R&D exemption fall into three categories. First, the chemical substance must be made "only in small quantities solely for research and development."[25] Second, the manufacturer or importer must evaluate the known health and environmental risks associated with the substance and notify anyone who handles the chemical about those health risks.[26] Third and finally, the R&D chemical must only be used by a "technically qualified individual" or under that individual's direct supervision.[27]

The R&D exemption is only an exemption from the PMN, Inventory, and SNUR requirements of TSCA. R&D substances are subject to the substantial risk reporting requirements of TSCA § 8(e), any restrictions that may be issued under §§ 4 or 6, import certifications, export notifications, and all other TSCA programs.

Research and development that is not for a commercial purpose is not subject to the PMN and Inventory rules at all, and the manufacturer, importer, or processor does not have to comply with the R&D exemption.[28] So, for example, a researcher who makes a chemical for purely academic research does not have to comply with the R&D exemption.[29] R&D is not considered purely academic if it is funded under a contract that anticipates commercialization, or if the researcher holds a patent in the field or has asserted trade secret rights.[30]

---

23. TSCA § 5(a)(1)(b); 40 C.F. R. Part 721.
24. 40 C.F.R. § 725.200; 62 Fed. Reg. 17910, 17921 (Apr. 11, 1997). The R&D exemption for microorganisms is addressed in Chapter 6, Microoorganisms.
25. 40 C.F.R. § 720.36(a)(1).
26. 40 C.F.R. § 720.36(a)(2).
27. 40 C.F.R. § 720.36(a)(3).
28. 40 C.F.R. § 720.30(i).
29. 51 Fed. Reg. 15096, 15098–99 (Apr. 22, 1986).
30. *Id.* at 15099 (Apr. 22, 1986).

1. Small Quantities for R&D

"Small quantities solely for research and development" is defined as "quantities of a chemical substance manufactured, imported, or processed or proposed to be manufactured, imported, or processed solely for research and development that are not greater than reasonably necessary for such purposes."[31]

There is no quantitative limit on "small quantities"[32] and so the interpretation is left to a common sense judgment of what is appropriate for a lab scale or pilot scale testing program. In an early proposed rule, the EPA noted that a numerical limit would be arbitrary because different types of R&D involve different quantities of R&D materials. For example, bench level research, pilot plant development, and production testing all require different quantities of R&D material. The EPA noted that 80,000 gallons of crude oil has been categorized as a small quantity in a pilot plant that operated over several months.[33]

R&D activities include physical and chemical analysis of the substance and experimentation, as well as research on the substance's production and performance characteristics.[34] The statute says that R&D includes research on another substance, and the EPA has interpreted this to mean that the R&D substance may be used as a reagent, a standard or an intermediate.[35] Production testing and pilot plant development as well as efficacy and performance testing are also R&D activities.[36]

2. Post-R&D Substances

After the R&D activities are complete, a manufacturer or importer may further react, process, or extract component chemicals from an R&D substance without jeopardizing the R&D exemption. R&D substances may also be disposed of as waste, in accordance with all federal, state, and local laws governing waste disposal, or burned for fuel.[37] If the end product of the R&D is a substance that is on the Inventory, it may be used for non-R&D purposes without submitting a PMN.

If the end product of the R&D process is a product in which the R&D substance is only present as an impurity, or if the end product of the R&D process is an article, then that product or article may be processed,

---

31. 40 C.F.R. § 720.3(cc).
32. 51 Fed. Reg. 15096, 15097 (Apr. 22, 1986).
33. 49 Fed. Reg. 50201, 50202–03 (Dec. 27, 1984).
34. TSCA § 5(h)(3); 51 Fed. Reg. 15096, 15097 (Apr. 22, 1986).
35. EPA New Chemical Information Bulletin, Exemptions for Research and Development and Test Marketing, 2 (Nov. 1986)[hereinafter Chemical Bulletin Exemptions].
36. Chemical Bulletin Exemptions, 3.
37. 40 C.F.R. § 720.36(e).

distributed, or used without filing a PMN.[38] The subsequent processing, distribution, or use does not need to be for R&D purposes.[39] The EPA gave an example of a catalyst that is the subject of R&D testing, and which remains in the final product as an impurity. The final product may be distributed without violating the R&D exemption.[40] No other processing, distribution, or use for any purpose other than R&D is permitted under the R&D exemption. An R&D substance may not be distributed to a consumer without filing a PMN,[41] but under controlled circumstances consumer panel testing of substances may qualify for the R&D exemption.[42]

If a manufacturer, importer, or processor wants to use surplus R&D material for a non-R&D purpose, it may file a PMN, a Low Volume Exemption[43] or a LoREX exemption application. Interestingly, the substance will not be put on the Inventory unless it is manufactured or imported subsequently for a non-exempt purpose because no Notice of Commencement (NOC) can be filed for a batch that was manufactured for R&D purposes.[44]

An R&D substance may be commercially sold, so long as that sale is for R&D purposes. So, for example, a manufacturer may sell an R&D reagent or chemical standard.[45] The seller must provide a notice to the purchaser about the R&D status of the product.

3. Risk Evaluation and Notification Requirements

If there are any known health risks associated with the R&D substance, the manufacturer or importer must notify its employees and anyone to whom it distributes the substance. The notifications must go to anyone who is performing experiments, research, analyses, and anyone who is manufacturing, processing, using, transporting, storing, or disposing of the substance.[46]

Unless all R&D is conducted in a laboratory that meets certain criteria addressed below, a manufacturer must evaluate all of the information in its possession or control that might support a finding of potential health or environmental risk to decide if a notification is required.[47] A manufacturer must clearly look in its own files for risk information. It must also evaluate information that third parties such as suppliers have given to the manufacturer,

---

38. 40 C.F.R. § 720.36(d); 51 Fed. Reg. 15096, 15097 (Apr. 22, 1986).
39. 40 C.F.R. § 720.36(d).
40. 51 Fed. Reg. 15096, 15097 (Apr. 22, 1986).
41. *Id.*
42. Chemical Bulletin Exemptions, 3.
43. 51 Fed. Reg. 15096, 15097 (Apr. 22, 1986).
44. *Id.* at 15100–01.
45. Chemical Bulletin Exemptions, 6.
46. 40 C.F.R. § 720.36(a)(2).
47. 40 C.F.R. § 720.36(b).

and information supporting EPA rules or orders restricting use of the substance.[48] However, "possession or control" is so broadly defined that a manufacturer must also ask for risk information from its subsidiaries, partnerships in which it is a general partner, parent companies, and any companies controlled by its parent company, so long as the parent or other company is working with the manufacturer on R&D, test marketing, or commercial marketing of the substance. The parent company is deemed to control another company so long as it owns 50 percent or more of the voting stock or is a general partner in a partnership. A manufacturer is also responsible for collecting risk information from its agents if they are working with the manufacturer on R&D, test marketing, or commercial marketing of the substance. [49] Presumably "agents" includes third party consultants, brokers, and probably attorneys. Risk information is in the possession or control of an entity whether its files are in the United States or not, but it does not have to provide data if doing so would violate the laws of its home country.[50]

A manufacturer or importer does not need to evaluate risk information if all R&D is conducted in a laboratory that meets stringent conditions. EPA has said in draft guidance that if a laboratory complies with the Occupational Safety and Health Administration (OSHA) laboratory standard it will be deemed to be in compliance with the conditions set out in the TSCA R&D regulations for an exemption from the risk evaluation requirement.[51] The conditions in the TSCA R&D regulations require a laboratory that is exempt from evaluating risks to follow prudent laboratory practices to control exposure to substances of unknown toxicity; the laboratory must be contained; it must make chemicals on a "non-production basis;"[52] the laboratory must be set up so one person can manipulate containers for reactions, transfers, and handling chemicals; and finally, the substance may only be distributed for disposal or to similarly qualified laboratories. Using recognized laboratory standards and handbooks is evidence that a laboratory is following prudent practices.[53] Pilot plants cannot meet this exemption from the requirement to evaluate risk data because the EPA noted that pilot plants have larger quantities of chemicals, larger research teams, and operate under looser controls.[54]

---

48. *Id.*
49. 40 C.F.R. § 720.3(y).
50. 51 Fed. Reg. 15096, 15100 (Apr. 22, 1986).
51. EPA, Draft Questions & Answers for the New Chemicals Program, 3-2–3-3, question 301-2 (undated), [hereinafter Draft PMN Q&A], *available at* http://www.epa.gov/oppt/newchems/pubs/qanda-newchems.pdf. The OSHA laboratory standards are in 29 C.F.R. §1910.1450, and require the formulation and implementation of a Chemical Hygiene Plan.
52. A "non-production basis" manufacture of chemicals must be interpreted using common sense to mean the type of manufacture typically performed in a laboratory, and not primarily for commercial sale. Technically, anything made in a laboratory is "produced" on a lab scale.
53. 51 Fed. Reg. 15096, 15099 (Apr. 22, 1986); 49 Fed. Reg. 50201, 50204 (Dec. 27, 1984).
54. 51 Fed. Reg. 15096, 15099 (Apr. 22, 1986).

As a practical matter, it makes much more sense to perform R&D in a laboratory that meets these requirements. A researcher in a non-qualifying laboratory needs to conduct a thorough evaluation of risk information in the company's possession or control for each new R&D substance before it makes or imports (or processes if there is a SNUR) the substance. So long as the chemical identity of the R&D substance is known, it will be possible to conduct that risk evaluation and determine if a SNUR applies.

A researcher who synthesizes an R&D substance in a non-qualifying laboratory without knowing in advance what that resulting substance will be faces a regulatory Catch-22. The act of manufacturing the substance will be a TSCA violation unless the manufacturer complies with the R&D exemption. However, it may not be possible to determine if SNUR applies or if there are associated health risks until the substance has been characterized by further research. Common sense would indicate that a researcher would be able to characterize a new R&D substance before conducting a risk evaluation, but there are no guidances on this problem. TSCA § 15 prohibits using a chemical that the manufacturer "knew or had reason to know" was manufactured in violation of TSCA, but it is often very difficult in retrospect to determine what a researcher had reason to know he or she was making in the lab.

A manufacturer can notify its employees of any known risks associated with the R&D chemical by using labels on the containers holding the R&D chemical, conspicuous signs, written notices to each R&D employee, or any other written notice that adequately advises of the health risks.[55] As a practical matter, it is advisable to use container labeling, conspicuous signs, or written notices to each R&D employee because these communication methods are explicitly listed in the regulations and the manufacturer will have the burden of proving that an alternative method is adequate.

If a manufacturer is going to distribute the R&D substance to anyone who is not an employee of that manufacturer, the written notice must also state that the substance may only be used for R&D purposes. The notice must describe health risks associated with the chemical except if the recipient is a R&D laboratory that otherwise qualifies for an exemption from the requirement to evaluate chemical-specific risks.[56]

4. Technically Qualified Individuals

The regulations describe a "technically qualified individual" who can use or supervise the use of an exempt R&D substance. That person is one who has the education, training, or experience to understand the risks associated with the R&D substance, is responsible for minimizing the risks, and is also

55. 40 C.F.R. § 720.36(c)(1).
56. 51 Fed. Reg. 15096, 15099 (Apr. 22, 1986).

responsible for safety assessments and safe handling of the substance.[57] There is no certification or degree a "technically qualified individual" must have, and there is no requirement that he or she be physically present during the R&D activities.[58]

5. Recordkeeping

Any person who takes advantage of the R&D exemption must retain records showing that the exemption applies.[59] These recordkeeping requirements should be followed carefully because the EPA can audit manufacturers and importers to evaluate compliance for five years after the R&D is complete. EPA can assess penalties if the records are inadequate.

The records that must be created and maintained are:

- copies of or citations to the records that the manufacturer reviewed to evaluate whether the R&D substance poses a health risk;
- copies of the written notifications made to inform employees and others of any health risks, and records of how the notices were disseminated;
- documentation of the prudent laboratory practices that were instituted in lieu of making health risk notifications;
- names and addresses of any person to whom the R&D substances were sent, amount sent, and copies of the written notification of health risks posed by the substance; and
- if more than one hundred kilograms of the R&D substance is manufactured or imported in any one year, the manufacturer or importer must keep records of what the substance is, the production volume, and how the manufacturer or importer disposed of the R&D substance

No records need to be retained about the disposition or distribution of R&D substances as impurities or as part of articles.[60]

The regulations require retaining all records relating to an R&D exemption for five years after the records are developed. In practice, it is necessary to retain these records for five years after the R&D substance is either put on the Inventory or no longer used. The statute of limitations for TSCA violations is five years, and a manufacturer bears the burden of proving compliance with the R&D exemption for five years after it ceases to rely on the R&D exemption.

57. 40 C.F.R. § 720.3(ee).
58. Chemical Bulletin Exemptions, 6.
59. 40 C.F.R. § 720.78(b).
60. 51 Fed. Reg. 15096, 15100 (Apr. 22, 1986).

6. Research on Pesticides

A substance that is made or imported in small quantities for R&D solely to determine if it can be used as a pesticide is exempt from Inventory and PMN requirements. The manufacturer or importer does not have to follow the notification and "technically qualified individual" requirements of the R&D exemption.[61] The manufacturer must be able to prove that the R&D is solely to determine if the substance can function as a pesticide. The manufacturer can either show that there is a patent for using the substance as a pesticide, or that the manufacturer or laboratory is solely devoted to pesticide research and marketing, or some other equally convincing evidence of exclusive pesticidal intent. If the manufacturer cannot make this showing, then the notification and "technically qualified individual" requirements apply.[62]

C. The Polymer Exemption

Toxicologists recognized that there are broad categories of polymers that are not likely to pose a risk to human health or the environment, while the remaining polymers still must be individually evaluated. The categories of polymers that are not likely to pose risks are exempted from the full PMN process.[63]

The EPA's polymer exemption was first instituted in 1984 and was later broadened in 1995. The 1985 exemption has some legacy application, but the 1995 polymer exemption is currently in effect for all polymers made or imported since May 30, 1995.

1. Current Polymer Exemption

The polymer exemption was originally promulgated so that the EPA could concentrate its premanufacture review efforts on substances that are more likely than the exempted polymers to pose a risk to human health or the environment. During the course of many years of reviewing PMNs for polymers, the EPA generated internal guidelines for identifying polymers that do not pose significant risks. In 1993 the EPA proposed incorporating the internal guidelines it had developed to further expand the types of polymers that do

---

61. 40 C.F.R. § 720.36(g).
62. 51 Fed. Reg. 15096, 15098 (Apr. 22, 1986). This final rule adds in the preamble that pesticidal intent is demonstrated when the manufacturer files an Experimental Use Permit under the Federal Insecticide, Fungicide, and Rodenticide Act. 7 U.S.C. §136. However, if there are both pesticidal and non-pesticidal uses for the R&D substance then the requirements of the R&D exemption must be followed.
63. 40 C.F.R. § 723.250.

not need a full PMN review.[64] These guidelines are now embodied in the current polymer exemption.

There is a pending rulemaking to require certain classes of polymers with perfluorinated units—polymers in which fluorine atoms are substituted for the hydrogen atoms that are present in many polymers—to go through the PMN process. The proposed rule would make the polymer exemption unavailable for these polymers because, as the EPA explained in its proposed rule, the EPA could not assume that all such polymers are risk-free.[65] The EPA cited "liver, developmental, and reproductive toxicity at very low exposure levels" as well as data that indicates that some perfluorinated polymers may be carcinogens. These generalizations have been criticized by the chemical industry.[66]

The polymer exemption is an exemption from the premanufacture notice requirements and not an exemption from all of the many programs under the Toxic Substances Control Act. An exempt polymer is subject to all of the other TSCA programs, including (but not limited to) the substantial risk reporting in § 8(e) of the statute,[67] Significant New Use Rules, import certifications, and export notifications.

2. Eligibility Requirements

The regulations spell out a detailed set of conditions a polymer must meet in order to be exempt from the PMN process.[68] The conditions are that the substance must meet the definition of a polymer, it must not be specifically excluded, it must meet specific chemical criteria, and the entity manufacturing or importing the substance must file reports and keep records. Some of these conditions overlap.

The first condition for the polymer exemption is that the substance must meet the definition of a "polymer" stated in the exemption, which is not the same as a chemist's definition of a polymer. This regulatory definition is also not the same as the definition the EPA uses for Inventory purposes, and is just a small subset of that much broader definition.[69] To keep all of the different

---

64. 58 Fed. Reg. 7679, 7680 (Feb. 8, 1993).
65. 71 Fed. Reg. 11484 (Mar. 7, 2006). As of the Fall 2009 Semiannual Regulatory Agenda, the EPA intended to finalize this proposed rule in early 2010. Regulatory Plan and Semiannual Regulatory Agenda, EPA-230-Z-09-002, 99-100 (Fall 2009), *available at* http://www.epa.gov/lawsregs/documents/regagendabook-fall09.pdf.
66. See comments submitted in EPA Docket OPPT-2002-0051, *available at* http://www.regulations.gov. For more detail on perfluorinated polymers, *see* EPA's enforcement action concerning PFOA in Chapter 7, Reporting and Recordkeeping.
67. EPA, Office of Toxic Substances, TSCA Section 8(e) Reporting Guide, 5 (June 1991) [hereinafter 1991 Reporting Guide].
68. 40 C.F.R. § 723.250.
69. Compare the broader definition given in the Toxic Substances Control Act Inventory Representation For Polymeric Substances, section I A.

definitions straight, the definition used in the polymer exemption will be referred to as the "exemption definition of polymer". The exemption definition of polymer is given in § 723.50 (b) as:

> *Polymer* means a chemical substance consisting of molecules characterized by the sequence of one or more types of monomer units and comprising a simple weight majority of molecules containing at least 3 monomer units which are covalently bound to at least one other monomer unit or other reactant and which consists of less than a simple weight majority of molecules of the same molecular weight. Such molecules must be distributed over a range of molecular weights wherein differences in the molecular weight are primarily attributable to differences in the number of monomer units. In the context of this definition, sequence means that the monomer units under consideration are covalently bound to one another and form a continuous string within the molecule, uninterrupted by units other than monomer units.

In simpler terms, this exemption definition of polymer means that a polymer must have a backbone of one or more types of basic building blocks, or monomers, which are chemically bound to each other. The backbone must have at least three monomer units and either a fourth monomer unit or a functional group.[70] If the polymer were to be weighed, at least half the weight would be from molecules with three or more building blocks in the backbone plus one more monomer or functional group. Again weighing the polymer, no more than half of the molecules can be identical—that is, there must be some variation in the length of the chemical backbone. The weight differences must be mostly caused by different backbone lengths, and not by different chemical groups attached to the backbone.[71]

Many chemicals that a chemist would consider to be polymers do not meet this exemption definition of polymer. For example, enzymes are polymers made of amino acid monomers, but they do not meet the exemption definition of a polymer because all of the enzyme molecules will have the same chain length and molecular weight.[72] The EPA explained its logic in a Q&A:

> Q: Are proteins (enzymes) produced by biotechnology techniques considered a polymer—i.e. a polymer of 20 amino acids?
>
> A: Proteins whether or not produced by biotechnology techniques are not considered polymers. The reason being, proteins can be assigned a specific

---

70. *See* Polymer Exemption Guidance Manual, (June 1997) [hereinafter Polymer Exemption Guidance Manual], *available at* http://www.epa.gov/oppt/newchems/pubs/polyguid.pdf.
71. The definition as set forth in the regulation governs the exemption.
72. *See* Polymer Exemption Guidance Manual, 7.

molecular structure and molecular formula. Polymers are characterized by an indefinite number of repeating monomeric units.[73]

a. Exclusions—Polymers That Must Be on the Inventory

The second condition for the polymer exemption is that the substance cannot be specifically excluded. In practical terms, this means that once a person determines that the substance meets the definition of "polymer," he or she must also check the list of exclusions to be certain that the substance is not excluded from the polymer exemption. If the substance is excluded, then no one can manufacture or import it without going through the PMN process. There are five types of polymers that are excluded. These are polymers that are cationic or expected to be cationic in the environment; polymers with elements outside of specified ranges; polymers that degrade, decompose, or depolymerize; polymers made from substances that are not on the Inventory and are not otherwise exempt from Inventory listing; and heavy polymers that absorb water.

Cationic polymers were excluded because the EPA was concerned about their ecotoxicity.[74] Cationic polymers are defined in the regulations as:

> *Cationic polymer* means a polymer that contains a net positively charged atom(s) or associated groups of atoms covalently linked to its polymer molecule.[75]

Examples of cationic polymers include polymers with phosphonium, sulfonium, and ammonium groups.[76] Polymers that are reasonably anticipated to become cationic in the natural aquatic environment, such as in rivers and streams, are also excluded, and this includes polymers with amine or isocyanate groups.[77]

Cationic polymers must go through the PMN process, with two exceptions.[78] The first exception is for solid polymers that are not dissolved or dispersed in water, and are only used in the solid phase. Ion exchange materials are examples of these cationic solid polymers that do qualify for the polymer exemption. The second exception is for polymers that are large compared to the number of cationic groups. If the combined functional group weight of

---

73. TSCA Questions and Answers from the October, 1990 EPA-Industry Living with TSCA Workshop, 7 question 21 (Oct. 1992) [hereinafter Living with TSCA Q&A].
74. 60 Fed. Reg. 16316 (Mar. 29, 1995).
75. 40 C.F.R. § 723.250(b).
76. *See* Polymer Exemption Guidance Manual, 8.
77. *Id.*
78. 40 C.F.R. § 723.250(d)(1).

the cationic groups in the polymer is five thousand daltons[79] or more then the polymer qualifies for the polymer exemption and does not need to go through the PMN process. Another way of expressing this is that if there is no more than one cationic group for every five thousand protons and neutrons in the atoms that comprise the polymer, then the cationic polymer has a low "cationic density" and qualifies for the polymer exemption so anyone can manufacture or import it without going through the PMN process.

Polymers that have elements outside of ranges in 40 C.F.R. § 723.250(d)(2) are excluded from the polymer exemption, and anyone who is going to manufacture them or import them must file a PMN if they are not already on the Inventory. This exclusion requires that a polymer that qualifies for the polymer exemption must:

- have at least two elements from among carbon, hydrogen, nitrogen, oxygen, silicon, and sulfur as an integral[80] part of its composition, and
- have only the following as the integral part of its composition (except as impurities):
  - carbon, hydrogen, nitrogen, oxygen, silicon, and sulfur;
  - the monatomic counterions Na—, Mg—^{2}, Al—^{3}, K—, Ca—^{2}, Cl—, Br—, or I—;
  - fluorine, chlorine, bromine, and iodine covalently bound to carbon; and
  - lithium, boron, phosphorus, titanium, manganese, iron, nickel, copper, zinc, tin, and zirconium, provided that these elements cannot be present in combination as 0.20 weight percent or more.

79. The unit of molecular weight is the dalton. The molecular weight of a substance is roughly calculated by adding up the number of protons and neutrons (ignoring relatively light electrons for this explanation). Carbon-12 is the standard for measuring daltons. Carbon-12 has 6 protons and 6 neutrons and a molecular weight of 12 daltons. If there were a hypothetical molecule with 417 Carbon-12 atoms, it would have a molecular weight of 5004. If one cationic group were added to this hypothetical molecule, the equivalent weight of the functional group would exceed 5000 and it would not be disqualified from the polymer exemption simply because it is a cationic polymer.

80. "Integral" is not defined in the regulations, but the EPA did suggest what it means by integral when it said:

> In addition to the six elements listed above, only certain other elements are permitted either as counterions or as an integral part of the polymer. These additional elements are as follows: fluorine, chlorine, bromine and iodine (F, Cl, Br and I) when covalently bonded to carbon, and the monatomic counterions chloride, bromide, and iodide (Cl-, Br- and I-). Polymer Exemption Guidance Manual, 9.

So, counterions are not an "integral" part of a polymer.

No other elements can be present, so, for example, a polymer may not have any boron, any fluoride ions, or more than 0.20 weight percent of lithium as an integral part of its composition and still qualify for the polymer exemption.

Polymers that degrade, decompose, or depolymerize are excluded from the polymer exemption. A polymer is excluded if the polymer is designed to degrade, decompose, or depolymerize or if it can reasonably be anticipated to degrade, decompose, or depolymerize even if it is not designed to do so. Degradation, decomposition, or depolymerization includes any process that breaks the polymer down to smaller substances.[81] For example, degradation may occur by "oxidation, hydrolysis, attack by solvents, heat, light, or microbial action."[82] The EPA recognized that most polymers degrade to some extent over time, and added that normal degradation in landfills and by weathering is not the type of degradation that would remove a polymer from the polymer exemption.[83] However, substantial biological degradation in a waste treatment system would disqualify a polymer from the polymer exemption,[84] presumably because of the environmental distribution that would probably be the result. Any polymer that degrades, decomposes, or depolymerizes except by weathering or in a landfill must go through the PMN process before it can be manufactured in the United States or imported.

Even if a polymer does degrade, it can still qualify for the polymer exemption if the manufacturer can restrict the uses to those where degradation will not take place. The EPA addressed an example of a polymer that has two uses; in one use it breaks down in water, but in the other use it is incorporated into a solid article that is not expected to break down. The EPA said that if the manufacturer can ensure that the polymer is only used as part of an article that is not expected to break down, then the polymer will qualify for the polymer exemption.[85] As a practical matter, if the manufacturer is distributing the polymer to other end users, it is probably relatively more burdensome to enter into and enforce contracts restricting the use of the polymer than it would be to file a PMN. Filing a PMN certainly exposes the manufacturer to less risk of violating the TSCA regulations.

Polymers made from substances that are not on the Inventory or subject to an exemption from Inventory listing are excluded from the polymer

---

81. 40 C.F.R. § 723.250 (d)(3).
82. *Id.*
83. The EPA gave a subjective definition:

> [t]he restriction refers to polymers that undergo considerable degradation, under normally anticipated conditions of use or disposal, and in a reasonable length of time. Polymer Exemption Guidance Manual, 38.

84. Polymer Exemption Guidance Manual, 37.
85. *Id.* at 38.

exemption, unless the non-Inventory starting material is either charged to the reaction vessel or incorporated in the resulting polymer at two weight percent or less and the manufacture takes place outside of the United States.[86] This is a corollary of the "two percent rule," which simply stated permits a person to disregard any reactant that is either charged to the reaction vessel or incorporated into the resulting polymer at two percent or less by weight.[87] Note that a substance generally cannot be distributed in commerce or used as a reactant if it is not on the Inventory, and so a substance that is not on the Inventory can only be used as a reactant if the reaction takes place outside of the United States, or if the substance is excluded from the Inventory requirement, or if the substance is formed as a non-isolated intermediate.[88] Reactants that are not on the Inventory and are not the subject of an exemption from PMN requirements may be used to form a polymer that qualifies for the polymer exclusion only if they are charged or incorporated at two percent or less by weight. If a polymer is made from a substance that is not on the Inventory, or that is not exempt from Inventory requirements, and is charged or incorporated into the resulting polymer at more than two percent by weight, then the resulting polymer must go through the PMN process before it is imported into the United States.[89] If a starting material does not have to be on the Inventory, then a polymer made from that starting material still qualifies for the polymer exemption.[90] Examples of materials that do not have to be on the Inventory are nonisolated intermediates, polymers subject to the polymer exemption, and drugs regulated under the Federal Food, Drug, and Cosmetics Act.[91]

A prepolymer is a partially polymerized material that is further polymerized later in a manufacturing process. A prepolymer that is on the Inventory can be used to make an exempt polymer even if the prepolymer incorporates a monomer that is not on the Inventory.[92]

If a manufacturer or importer needs to know if any of the monomers to be used in excess of two percent are on the confidential Inventory, it can submit a bona fide notice of intent to manufacture to the EPA.[93] The EPA will respond and tell the submitter if the monomer is on the confidential Inventory. The EPA will not respond to a submitter that does not intend to manufacture or

86. 60 Fed. Reg. 16316 (Mar. 29, 1995).
87. *See* Chapter 3, The Inventory. Note that the polymer exemption for polyesters does not disregard starting materials that are charged or present at less than two percent. Polymer Exemption Guidance Manual, 43 (question 37).
88. *See* 60 Fed. Reg. 16316 (Mar. 29, 1995).
89. Draft PMN Q&A, 1-21–1-22, question 102-7.
90. Polymer Exemption Guidance Manual, 18.
91. 21 U.S.C. §§ 301–399.
92. Draft PMN Q&A, 2-13, question 208-6.
93. *Id.* at 1-21–1-22, question 102-7. *See* the discussion of bona fide letters in this chapter.

import the monomer, and as a result there is no means to find out if a monomer is on the confidential Inventory if the submitter only intends to import the resulting polymer. In that case, the importer has three alternatives. It can search the public Inventory, and if the polymer is not listed it can submit a bona fide notice to import the polymer to determine if it is on the confidential Inventory. If the polymer itself is not on the Inventory, the prospective importer has no alternative to filing a PMN or LoREX or LVE exemption; it cannot take advantage of the polymer exemption.[94]

The EPA was concerned that incompletely reacted monomers or other reactants may present risks to human health or the environment; and so the only way it could ensure the safety of a polymer was to ensure that the starting materials are on the Inventory.[95]

The final exclusion from the polymer exemption is for high molecular weight polymers that absorb water. If the average molecular weight of the polymer is ten thousand or more, and the polymer is capable of absorbing its own weight of water, then it does not qualify for the polymer exemption and the polymer must go through the PMN process before it is manufactured or imported into the United States. The EPA had reviewed a study revealing an increase in lung tumors caused by exposure to a super absorbent polymer of the type used in disposable diapers and paper towels, and concluded that it could not exclude this class of large, water absorbing polymers.[96]

b. Criteria

Once a polymer has met the polymer exemption definition of polymer, and is not specifically excluded from the polymer exemption, it still must meet one of the three criteria contained in the regulations[97] to qualify for the polymer exemption.

Polymers meet the first criterion if they have a number average molecular weight[98] greater than or equal to one thousand daltons and less than ten thousand daltons, have a range of lighter and shorter molecules within specified limits, and meet limits on the reactive functional groups that can be present.[99] This criterion is sometimes referred to as the (e)(1) exemption because it is in subsection (e)(1) of the regulation.

To explain the range of shorter polymer molecules that can be present to meet this first criterion, it is helpful to consider how polymers are

94. *Id., see also* Draft PMN Q&A, 1-56, question 119-3.
95. *See* 60 Fed. Reg. 16316 (Mar. 29, 1995).
96. *See id.*
97. 40 C.F.R. § 723.250(e).
98. Number average molecular weight is defined as "the arithmetic average (mean) of the molecular weight of all molecules in a polymer." 40 C.F.R. § 723.250(b).
99. 40 C.F.R. § 723.250(e)(1).

typically manufactured. When most polymers are made, the end product will be a mixture of molecules with a range of molecular weights and chain lengths, depending on how many repeating units of monomers have been incorporated into the polymer chain. The polymer will be a mixture of relatively longer and heavier molecules with more monomers and relatively shorter and lighter molecules with fewer monomers in the backbone. To meet the first criterion, the resulting polymer cannot have a high percentage of short polymers, called oligomers. Oligomers are defined in the regulation as polymers that are made of only a few repeating monomer units, for example two, three, or four units.[100] Polymers that qualify for the first criterion must have less than 10 percent of oligomers with a molecular weight below five hundred, and less than 25 percent of oligomers with a molecular weight below one thousand daltons. The reason that the EPA was concerned about shorter and lighter molecules is because those molecules are more likely to be absorbed by living organisms and pose a potential health risk.[101]

Because the EPA was concerned about low molecular weight molecules, unreacted starting materials count towards the 10 and 25 percent limits. The preamble to the final regulation states that "[u]nder the final rule, companies are free to manufacture any exempted polymer with any residual reactant content desired, as long as the percentages of low MW species do not exceed the levels specified in the exemption criteria."[102]

Reactive functional groups are groups of atoms that are part of the polymer and are intended or anticipated to undergo chemical reactions.[103] The EPA divided all the possible reactive functional groups into three categories: low-concern, moderate-concern, and high-concern. Reactive functional groups from all of these categories can be present in a polymer that qualifies for the exemption criteria, but each of these categories has different restrictions. There are many functional groups that are not *reactive* functional groups, for example, nitro groups that are not specially activated, and esters and ethers. There are no limitations on the non-reactive functional groups that can be present in a polymer that qualifies for the polymer exemption.[104]

---

100. 40 C.F.R. § 723.250(b).
101. 60 Fed. Reg. 16316 (Mar. 29, 1995).
102. *Id.* at preamble. Note that this is not fully consistent with the language of the regulation, which is limited to low molecular weight oligomers. It would be prudent to follow the interpretation in the preamble to the rule because it is more restrictive, and not rely on the rule as actually written.
103. "Reactive functional group" is:

> an atom or associated group of atoms in a chemical substance that is intended or can reasonably be anticipated to undergo further chemical reaction. 40 C.F.R. § 723.250(b).

104. Polymer Exemption Guidance Manual, 41.

The low-concern reactive functional groups can be present on an exempt polymer in any amount. The list of low-concern reactive functional groups is limited to:

- carboxylic acid groups;
- aliphatic hydroxyl groups;
- unconjugated olefinic groups that are considered "ordinary," i.e., not specially activated either by being part of a larger functional group, such as a vinyl ether, or by other activating influences, e.g., a strongly electron-withdrawing sulfone group with which the olefinic groups interact;
- butenedioic acid groups;
- those conjugated olefinic groups contained in naturally-occurring fats, oils, and carboxylic acids;
- blocked isocyanates, including ketoxime-blocked isocyanates;
- thiols;
- unconjugated nitrile groups; and
- halogens, except that reactive halogen-containing groups such as benzylic or allylic halides cannot be included.

The EPA noted that there are several classes of organic polymers that are included in the polymer exemption because they only have these low-concern reactive functional groups. The Polymer Exemption Guidance Manual says:

> In addition, carboxylic esters, ethers, amides, urethanes, and sulfones are implicitly permitted because polyesters, polyethers, polyamides, polyurethanes, and polysulfones are among the types of polymers allowed under the exemption, as long as these functional groups have not been modified to enhance their reactivity. One such group that would not be allowed is the dinitrophenyl ester of a carboxylic acid, which is far more reactive due to the activating functionality.[105]

The moderate-concern reactive functional groups can be present in an exempt polymer, but only if the polymer has a combined total functional group equivalent weight greater than or equal to one thousand, that is, provided that there are at least one thousand daltons of molecular weight in

105. Polymer Exemption Guidance Manual, 11.

the polymer molecule for each moderate-concern reactive group.[106] These moderate-concern reactive functional groups are:

- acid halides;
- acid anhydrides;
- aldehydes;
- hemiacetals;
- methylolamides;
- methylolamines;
- methyloureas;
- alkoxysilanes with alkoxy greater than C2-alkoxysilanes;
- allyl ethers;
- conjugated olefins (except those in naturally-occurring fats, oils, and carboxylic acids, which are in the low-concern group);
- cyanates;
- epoxides;
- imines; and
- unsubstituted positions ortho or para to phenolic hydroxyl.

All other reactive functional groups are high-concern. A polymer with any high-concern reactive functional group can only meet this first exemption criterion if the combined reactive group equivalent weight, including the moderate-concern groups listed above, is greater than or equal to five thousand.[107]

The EPA restricted the reactive functional groups because it was concerned that they could react with living tissues or chemicals in the body, and permitted only those reactive functional groups that generally do not react with living tissue.[108]

The second criterion that a polymer may meet to qualify for the polymer exemption is sometimes referred to as the (e)(2) exemption because it is in subsection (e)(2) of the regulation.[109] This second criterion applies to polymers with a larger molecular weight and relatively few short chain molecules. There are no restrictions on the functional group that these polymers may have. The polymer must have a number average molecular weight great than ten thousand daltons, have less than 2 percent oligomers below a molecular weight of five hundred daltons, and less than 5 percent oligomers below a

106. The low-concern functional groups are not taken into account in calculating the reactive group equivalent weight. *See* Polymer Exemption Guidance Manual, 12.

107. *Id.*

108. 60 Fed. Reg. 16316 (Mar. 29, 1995).

109. 40 C.F.R. § 723.250(e)(2).

molecular weight of one thousand. These polymers must meet the definition of a polymer,[110] and must not fall within any of the exclusions.

The third and final criterion that a polymer may meet to qualify for the polymer exemption is if it is a polyester. The regulations define a polymer as a polyester if its "molecules contain at least two carboxylic acid ester linkages, at least one of which links internal monomer units together."[111] Only polyesters made from a list of specific reactants can qualify for the polymer exemption.[112] Even a small amount—less than 2 percent—of a reactant that is not on the list will disqualify a polyester from meeting this criterion.[113] Not all of the listed reactants were on the Inventory as of the 1997 publication of the Polymer Exemption Guidance Manual,[114] or the 2005 Draft Questions & Answers for the New Chemicals Program,[115] so it is important to check the Inventory before manufacturing these polymers in the United States. The Polymer Exemption Guidance Manual says that the listed reactants that are not on the Inventory may be used outside of the United States, and the imported polymer will meet the exemption criterion for polyesters.[116] However, the preamble to the final rule says that the agency did not include some reactants on the list of permissible reactants because they were not on the Inventory.[117] In the case of a conflict between a preamble and a guidance, courts will weigh the preamble more heavily because it has gone through the notice and comment process.

3. Recordkeeping and Reporting

While a company is evaluating whether a polymer qualifies for the polymer exemption, the company must follow the rules for the R&D exemption from premanufacure notice requirements if it has not filed a PMN and an NOC

110. Very high molecular weight polymers with extensive cross-linking will meet the requirement in the definition of "polymer" that it consist "of less than a simple weight majority of molecules of the same molecular weight" unless the polymer is formed into only one gigantic molecule. Otherwise, the size of the molecule is limited by the size of the bead, pellet, droplet, or flake that is formed. Polymer Exemption Guidance Manual, 36, question 3.
111. 40 C.F.R. § 723.250(b).
112. *See* 40 C.F.R. § 723.250(e)(3) for the full list of permissible reactants.
113. Polymer Exemption Guidance Manual, 43 (question 37).
114. Polymer Exemption Guidance Manual, 12.
115. Draft PMN Q&A, 2-12–2-13, question 208-4.
116. *Id.* at 46.
117. 60 Fed. Reg. 16316, 16324 (Mar. 29, 1995).

for the polymer.[118] The R&D exemption has its own set of recordkeeping requirements.[119]

Once a company has done enough research to conclude that a polymer it manufactures falls within the polymer exemption, it must follow the recordkeeping and reporting requirements set out in the polymer exemption.[120]

The reporting requirements in the polymer exemption require each manufacturer and importer to mail a report to the EPA by January 31 of each year providing information on each polymer that it has manufactured or imported for the first time during the previous calendar year. A company may submit a report for each plant site or one consolidated report for the entire company, but should not duplicate information if it submits one report for each plant site.[121] The report must include the following information:

- the manufacturer or importer's name and address and the name and address of a person to contact for technical details; and
- the number of polymers falling under the polymer exemption that the company submitting the report first manufactured or imported during the previous calendar year.

The EPA uses these letters to determine what plants to audit for compliance with the polymer exemption, and to track how often companies rely on the polymer exemption.[122]

If the exempt polymer also meets the requirements of the R&D exemption, then a manufacturer or importer can rely on the R&D exemption and not file the annual notifications that would otherwise be due.[123]

In addition to submitting information to the EPA, the manufacturer or importer must keep records of all the polymers it has made or imported in reliance on the polymer exemption. The manufacturer or importer must

---

118. The preamble to the final polymer exemption rule says:

> Manufacturers are expected to follow the provisions of the exemption for research and development (R&D) activities during the period of evaluation of eligibility of a substance under the exemption criteria prior to actual manufacture under the exemption provisions. Such R&D activities will be subject to the R&D procedural and recordkeeping provisions in the PMN rule at 40 C.F.R. § 720.36 and § 720.78, respectively.

60 Fed. Reg 16316, 16324 (Mar. 29, 1995); *see also*, Polymer Exemption Guidance Manual, 48, question 60.

119. *See* the R&D discussion in this chapter.
120. 40 C.F.R. § 723.250(f).
121. 60 Fed. Reg. 16316, 16325 (Mar. 29, 1995).
122. Draft PMN Q&A, 3-12, question 304-1.
123. *Id.* at 3-13, question 304-4.

maintain the following data for five years from the date of first manufacture or import of each exempt polymer:

- for each reactant used in manufacture of the polymer, the chemical identity, to the extent the manufacturer knows or can reasonably ascertain it, including the chemical name and CAS number or EPA Accession number;[124]
- a representative structural diagram of the exempt polymer;
- information demonstrating that the polymer is not excluded from the polymer exemption;
- production and import volumes for the first three years of manufacture or import;
- records of the first date of manufacture or import; and
- analytical data[125] demonstrating that the exempt polymer meets one of the criteria for the exemption; if analytical data is not available and not necessary then theoretical data may be substituted.[126]

It is important to keep records of each exempt polymer. To do that, a manufacturer that changes its formulations must determine how the two percent rule is applied to define when it has made a distinct polymer.

In addition, the manufacturer or importer must create and maintain a certification stating that the polymer is made for a commercial use other than R&D, that it meets the regulatory definition of a polymer, that it is not excluded by any of the exclusions to the polymer exemption, and that it meets one of the criteria for the exemption. The certification must also state that the certification itself is truthful.[127]

If the EPA requests any of the information kept under this rule, the manufacturer or importer must submit it within 15 working days. Confidential business information may be bracketed or underlined and stamped "CONFIDENTIAL" and the EPA will handle it as CBI.[128]

4. Superseded Polymer Exemption

The polymer exemption had originally grown out of a petition filed by the Chemical Manufacturer's Association (now called the American Chemistry

124. The EPA did not require use of the Chemical Abstracts naming system for exempt polymers, but encourages its use for recordkeeping.
125. Examples of analytical methods are given in the regulations and in the Polymer Exemption Guidance Manual.
126. 40 C.F.R. § 723.250(j).
127. 40 C.F.R. § 723.250(h). The EPA does not provide a form for this certification.
128. 40 C.F.R. § 723.250(n).

Council).[129] Section 5(h) of TSCA permits any person to petition the EPA for an exemption from the PMN rules if "the manufacture, processing, distribution in commerce, use, and disposal of such substance" does not present any unreasonable risk of injury to health or the environment."[130]

As originally promulgated in 1985 there was a requirement to file a "limited premanufacture notice" 21 days before manufacturing an exempt polymer.[131] If the EPA did not take any action in response to the limited premanufacture notice, the new polymer was added to the Inventory as soon as the manufacturer filed an NOC. As a result, there are polymers that qualified for the old polymer exemption on the Inventory. There is no longer any requirement to file a limited premanufacture notice.

The presence of exempt polymers on the Inventory is the main continuing relevance of the old polymer exemption. However, a company that did file a limited premanufacture notice under the old rule has the option of following the new rules or following the old rule and placing the substance on the Inventory.[132]

There is a very important caveat concerning polymers that were listed on the Inventory as a result of the superseded polymer exemption. The Inventory listings can be very misleading. The company that submitted the limited PMN will typically have listed composition limits for unreacted monomers and low molecular weight species, among other things, and these composition limits are restrictions on the Inventory listed polymer. If a polymer does not meet these composition limits it is not on the Inventory. Unfortunately, these limits are not disclosed in the Inventory listing. As a result, a manufacturer or importer who wants to rely on such an Inventory listing will need to contact the EPA to determine what the composition limits are. Polymers that were placed on the Inventory as a result of the superseded polymer exemption will be flagged on the Inventory with a Y2 for polyesters and a Y1 for other exempt polymers,[133] so there is at least a way to know when more investigation is required to determine the parameters of the Inventory listing.

---

129. 46 Fed. Reg. 54688 (Nov. 3, 1981).

130. The EPA promulgated the original polymer exemption rule under TSCA § 5(h)(4), which provides in full:

> The Administrator may, upon application and by rule, exempt the manufacturer of any new chemical substance from all or part of the requirements of this section if the Administrator determines that the manufacture, processing, distribution in commerce, use, or disposal of such chemical substance, or that any combination of such activities, will not present an unreasonable risk of injury to health or the environment. A rule promulgated under this paragraph (and any substantive amendment to, or repeal of, such a rule) shall be promulgated in accordance with paragraphs (2) and (3) of section 2605(c) of this title.

131. For the superseded requirement, see 49 Fed. Reg. 46066, 46088 (Nov. 21, 1984).

132. 40 C.F.R. § 723.250(i).

133. Draft PMN Q&A, 1-56–1-57, question 119-5.

Polymers containing less than 32 percent carbon, biopolymers, and polymers made from reactants containing halogen atoms or cyano groups had been excluded from the polymer exemption as promulgated in 1984. These exclusions were not retained in the 1994 amendment and polymers with less than 32% carbon, biopolymers and polymers made from reactants containing halogen atoms, or cyano groups can now qualify for the polymer exemption.

5. Practical Implications

It is always worthwhile analyzing whether it makes more sense to rely on the polymer exemption or file a PMN. The answer will depend on the specific polymer, and how likely it is that the manufacturer or importer will change the process or tweak the polymer to enhance its properties.

The main advantage of filing a PMN is that the polymer will ultimately be listed on the Inventory. Once the polymer is on the Inventory, the two percent rule gives considerable latitude to make changes in the polymer. So long as the changed polymer corresponds to the representation of the original polymer on the Inventory, the changed polymer may be made or imported without assembling the data required to substantiate the changed polymer's qualification for the polymer exemption. Another advantage is that the manufacturer or importer will not need to file annual reports.

An additional advantage of filing a PMN is that the risk of error may be minimized. For example, there are many analytical determinations that must be made to substantiate the polymer exemption. Suppose a manufacturer finds out years after starting commercial production of a polymer that the analyses it relied on to support the polymer exemption were wrong and the polymer does not qualify for the polymer exemption because it has too much unreacted oligomer. That manufacturer will have to stop producing the polymer because it is illegal to produce a substance unless it is either on the Inventory or qualified for an exemption. The manufacturer will have to quarantine its stocks of the polymer because it is also illegal to use a substance that was produced in violation of the premanufacture notification regulations.[134] If the manufacturer had gone through the PMN process, then it would have been able to continue making the polymer because the Inventory representation does not include limits on the amount of unreacted oligmer in the resulting polymer.

In its Draft Questions & Answers for the New Chemicals Program the EPA confirms that this type of analytical error would result in a PMN violation. It suggests that if some batches do not meet the requirements for the polymer exemption then either more testing or "another strategy" would be required to assure compliance.[135]

---

134. TSCA § 15.
135. Draft PMN Q&A, 3-13, question 304-3.

A disadvantage of filing a PMN is that any other manufacturer or importer may make or import the polymer without going through the time consuming PMN process, and in essence may take a free ride on the work done to shepherd the chemical through the PMN process. Even if the substance is listed on the confidential Inventory, anyone who has actual plans to manufacture or import the chemical may submit a request to the EPA to search the confidential Inventory to see if the substance is listed there.[136]

6. Violations and Enforcement

Administrative penalties for violation of the polymer exemption are assessed in accordance with the § 5 Enforcement Response Policy (§ 5 ERP).[137] The EPA has the authority to seek injunctions and seize products that were made in violation of the terms of the exemption,[138] but typically considers civil enforcement actions to be sufficient to compel compliance.[139]

Under the § 5 ERP, polymer exemption violations can be penalized as PMN violations, which can quickly lead to significant penalties.[140]

D. Chemicals Formed When Other Substances Are Used or Exposed

Chemicals formed when other chemicals are stored or exposed to the elements, or on end use of a chemical, mixture or article[141] are exempt from PMN notification requirements,[142] which provide:

> The following substances are not subject to the notification requirements of this part:
>
> ....

---

136. *See* Chapter 3, The Inventory.
137. Amended TSCA § 5 Enforcement Response Policy [hereinafter § 5 ERP] as amended and restated (June 8, 1989) and further amended in Memorandum from John J. Neylan, Director, Policy and Grants Division, Office of Compliance Monitoring, to Michael J. Walker, Enforcement Counsel, Toxics Litigation Division, (July 1, 1993), *available through* http://cfpub.epa.gov/compliance/resources/policies/civil/tsca/.
138. TSCA §§ 7, 17.
139. § 5 ERP, 3–4.
140. § 5 ERP, 12. For a discussion of the TSCA enforcement policies, *see* Chapter 14, Penalties and Enforcement. For a discussion of the penalties applicable to PMN violations, *see* Chapter 4, Premanufacture Notifications.
141. *See* Chapter 2, TSCA's Scope.
142. 40 C.F.R. § 720.30.

(h) The chemical substances described below: (Although they are manufactured for commercial purposes under the Act, they are not manufactured for distribution in commerce as chemical substances per se and have no commercial purpose separate from the substance, mixture, or article of which they are a part.)

....

(3) Any chemical substance which results from a chemical reaction that occurs incidental to exposure of another chemical substance, mixture, or article to environmental factors such as air, moisture, microbial organisms, or sunlight.

(4) Any chemical substance which results from a chemical reaction that occurs incidental to storage or disposal of another chemical substance, mixture, or article.

(5) Any chemical substance which results from a chemical reaction that occurs upon end use of another chemical substance, mixture, or article such as an adhesive, paint, miscellaneous cleanser or other housekeeping product, fuel additive, water softening and treatment agent, photographic film, battery, match, or safety flare, and which is not itself manufactured or imported for distribution in commerce or for use as an intermediate.

(6) Any chemical substance which results from a chemical reaction that occurs upon use of curable plastic or rubber molding compounds, inks, drying oils, metal finishing compounds, adhesives, or paints, or any other chemical substance formed during the manufacture of an article destined for the marketplace without further chemical change of the chemical substance except for those chemical changes that occur as described elsewhere in this paragraph.

(7) Any chemical substance which results from a chemical reaction that occurs when (i) a stabilizer, colorant, odorant, antioxidant, filler, solvent, carrier, surfactant, plasticizer, corrosion inhibitor, antifoamer or defoamer, dispersant, precipitation inhibitor, binder, emulsifier, deemulsifier, dewatering agent, agglomerating agent, adhesion promoter, flow modifier, pH neutralizer, sequesterant, coagulant, flocculant, fire retardant, lubricant, chelating agent, or quality control reagent functions as intented, or (ii) a chemical substance, which is intended solely to impart a specific physiochemical characteristic, functions as intended.

Generalizing about these exemptions, (h)(3) exempts chemicals formed when substances on the Inventory are exposed to the elements, (h)(4) exempts chemicals formed when substances on the Inventory react in storage or after they are disposed of, (h)(5) exempts chemicals formed when commercial products or articles are used, (h)(6) exempts chemicals formed from using products that are used to make articles, and (h)(7) exempts chemicals formed when chemicals are used that modify the properties of another substance.

These are oversimplifications, and there is significant overlap between these exemptions.

1. Chemicals Formed on Exposure—the (h)(3) Exemption

Chemicals formed incidental to exposure to the environment are not subject to PMN regulations and do not have to be on the Inventory. The word "incidental" in the regulations indicates that the exposure cannot be a part of the manufacturing process because when "incidental" is used in the TSCA regulations it generally means that there was no intentional act. For example, it would appear that if a chemical were deliberately exposed to sunlight as the last step of a manufacturing process, and the resulting chemical is the chemical with commercial value, then the final exposure step could not be considered "incidental."

2. Chemicals Formed on Storage or Disposal—the (h)(4) Exemption

The (h)(4) exemption addresses chemicals formed incidental to storage or disposal. Like the (h)(3) exemption, the (h)(4) exemption uses the word "incidental" to modify the exempt chemicals, and presumably excludes chemicals that are formed intentionally during the disposal process.

The definition of "manufacture or import for commercial purposes" makes clear that chemicals formed during disposal are made for commercial purposes.[143] It also clarifies that these substances may be impurities or byproducts. Note that substances that are required to be on the Inventory but which have not been put on the Inventory may still be disposed of without violating TSCA,[144] provided the disposal does not violate a chemical-specific rule or order.

3. Chemicals Formed on End Use—the (h)(5) Exemption

An example of a substance exempted by the (h)(5) exemption is the chemical reaction product that is formed when paint dries. That same chemical would be subject to PMN regulations if it were intentionally made as a commercial product for distribution as a chemical product or an intermediate, but not when it is formed as a result of the use of paint. If the paint is applied to an article, then the chemicals formed on use of the paint are also exempt from the premanufacture notification requirements under the (h)(6) exemption.

Chemicals formed when an article is used are also exempt from PMN requirements. The EPA gives as an example the combustion products formed

---

143. 40. C.F.R. § 720.3(r).

144. TSCA § 15.

when a candle is burned. Because a candle is an article, and its end use involves burning, the combustion products are exempt from the premanufacture notification requirements.[145] Again, those same substances may be subject to premanufacture notification requirements if they are made for distribution as a product or intermediate under other circumstances. One commenter questioned the EPA about fragrances that are in candles, and whether they are considered to be released on end use of the candle.[146] If the fragrance is incorporated into the candle for release it must be on the Inventory. Typically fragrances are not formed on end use of a candle and would not qualify for the (h)(5) exemption.

The term "end use" is not defined, and neither is the term "use." The common sense and dictionary definitions have to be used in the absence of a regulatory definition.

Salts generally have to be listed on the Inventory even if the acid form of the same chemical is on the Inventory. In the limited circumstance when a salt that is not on the Inventory is formed upon end use of another substance, mixture or article, or when an additive functions as intended, it may be exempt from premanufacture notification requirements under the (h)(5), (h)(6), or (h)(7) exemption.[147]

4. Chemicals Formed on Manufacture of an Article—the (h)(6) Exemption

The (h)(6) exemption applies to substances formed during the manufacture of an article.[148] The article must be intended for commercial distribution,[149] and must not undergo any other chemical reactions before it is distributed, except for reactions to form chemicals that are exempt from PMN requirements.

For example, dyes or fire retardants that are applied to fabrics must be on the Inventory if they are made in or imported into the United States. But if those dyes or fire retardants chemically react with the fabrics, the reaction products are exempt from PMN requirements.[150] The theory is that the

145. Draft PMN Q&A, 2-9, question 207-4.
146. Letter from John DiFazio, Assistant General Counsel, Consumer Specialty Products Association, to Office of Pollution Prevention and Toxics Document Control Office, EPA (Mar. 15, 2004), *available through* www.regulations.gov in Docket OPPT-2003-0055.
147. Draft PMN Q&A, 2-25, question 218-3 (noting that other exemptions such as the ones in 40 C.F.R. § 720.30(h)(6) and (h)(7) could also exempt a salt that is not on the Inventory from the premanufacture notification requirements).
148. *See* Chapter 2, TSCA's Scope.
149. The regulation says "destined for the marketplace" (40 C.F.R. § 720.30(h)(6)), which logically must require distribution.
150. Draft PMN Q&A, 2-10, question 207-7.

reaction products are not made for distribution "as a chemical substance *per se* and have no commercial purpose separate from the mixture or article of which they may be a part".[151] In plainer terms, the reaction product may well be the chemical that imparts color or fire resistance, but it is not distributed in commerce as a commercial chemical on its own in isolation from the article on which it is formed.

If that reaction product were manufactured in or imported into the United States and sold as a dye or a fire retardant, it would need to be on the Inventory. If the chemical were made outside the United States and incorporated into an article before importation into the United States then it would not need to be on the Inventory because chemicals imported as part of and incorporated into articles are exempt.[152]

The EPA implied in draft guidance that a chemical manufactured under this exemption cannot be further reacted or used as a starting material without filing a PMN, although that appears to be an overstatement.[153]

Another example of a substance exempt from premanufacture notification under this section is a chemical that may be formed when fibers are made. If the fibers are used in a way that depends wholly or partially on their shape or design, and they do not undergo any chemical changes on end use except those chemical changes that have no commercial purpose apart from the item that they form a part of, then the fibers are articles.[154] If new chemical substances are formed when a fiber that is an article is made from an existing chemical, those new chemical substances are exempt from the premanufacture notification requirements because of the (h)(6) exemption.

5. Chemicals Formed When Property Modifiers Are Used—the (h)(7) Exemption

This exemption applies when chemicals that are used only to modify the properties of another material functions as intended. The regulation lists specific products that qualify for this exemption when they are used and also grants an exemption when any substance that is "intended solely to impart a specific physiochemical characteristic, functions as intended."

This exemption engendered considerable confusion, and the EPA sent a clarification letter to many members of the regulated community in 1994

---

151. *Id.*

152. *Id.*

153. *Id.* at 1-65–1-66, question 125-1. This may be read to imply that a substance formed during the manufacture of an article may not be further reacted unless it is on the Inventory. However, this Q&A is ambiguous and could be read to say that the reaction product must be on the Inventory.

154. *Id.* at 2-9–2-10, question 207-6.

from Joseph Carra, Deputy Director of the Office of Pollution Prevention and Toxics (the Carra Letter).[155] The Carra Letter said, with respect to the (h)(7) exemption and its counterpart in the Inventory regulations:

> The kinds of substances listed in these provisions are frequently used to improve reaction conditions in chemical manufacturing processes in order to increase the yield of the desired product, to reduce undesirable impurities or byproducts, to ensure the optimal performance of a commercial product, or to make the commercial product easier or safer to handle by customers.

The Carra Letter added that a substance must meet all three of these qualifications to be eligible for the (h)(7) exemption:

1. The substance is formed from a chemical reaction that involves the use of a chemical substance of the type described under 40 C.F.R. 710.4(d)(7) or 720.30(h)(7);
2. The substance does not function to provide one or more primary properties that would determine the use of the product or product mixture distributed in commerce, even though it may impart certain physicochemical characteristics to the product or product mixture of which it is a part; and
3. The substance is not itself the one intended for distribution in commerce as a chemical substance per se. Although it may be a component of the product, product mixture, or formulation actually distributed in commerce, it has no commercial purpose separate from the product, product mixture, or formulation of which it is a component.

These same three criteria were reiterated in the EPA's draft Q&A.[156]

The Carra Letter addressed a particularly vexing example of a polymer salt in inks. Insoluble polymer acids are converted to soluble amine salts of the polymer by pH neutralization when certain inks are made. The salts are made during the formulation of the ink, and other ink formulation ingredients are present. EPA concluded that the polymer salts do not contribute a primary property of the commercial ink although they do impart physicochemical properties to the ink. They are not the product intended for distribution in commerce, and they have no commercial purpose outside of the ink formulation in which they are formed. As a result of these conclusions, these polymer salts are not required to be on the Inventory and entities that make or import them as part of an ink product are not subject to the PMN regulations. In contrast, if they were manufactured or imported as polymer salts for

155. Letter from Joseph S. Carra, Deputy Director, Office of Pollution Prevention and Toxics, EPA, to redacted (June 29, 1994).
156. Draft PMN Q&A, 2-23–2-24, question 218-1.

distribution on their own, outside of a product that they modify, then a manufacturer or importer would be subject to Inventory and PMN requirements. The question of polymer salts had earlier been brought up in the more nuanced context of polymer salts formed by addition of amines or ammonium hydroxide to make polymers soluble. The amine or ammonia is lost when the ink cures, and in this sense the salts are transient.[157]

The Carra Letter went on to address the implications of making a yarn treatment product before it is added to the yarn to which it will provide antistatic properties. If a salt form of antistatic agent is made by pH neutralization of an acid precursor during the formulation process of making the yarn treatment product, then the salt does provide a primary purpose of the yarn treatment product, and it is not exempt from the Inventory and PMN regulations. This is the case even if other yarn treatment ingredients are present in the formulation when the acid precursor is neutralized. The distinction between this example and the polymer salt example is that the polymer salts were made as part of the ink formulation and do not contribute a primary performance characteristic of ink, but in this example the acid is made as part of a product that is intended only as a yarn treatment and it does contribute one of the primary performance characteristics of the yarn treatment product.

Industry members asked the EPA more questions in light of the Carra Letter, and the EPA issued further clarifications. One of these clarifications[158] gave three additional examples of how to apply the (h)(7) exemption. In the first, the questioner posited that the sodium, potassium, and ammonium salts of trisulfonic acid are listed on the Inventory. Aqueous solutions of all three salts are blended, resulting in a new shade of dye. The questioner pointed out that there are a total of 81 different salts that could be formed by the exchange of ions, and asked whether they must all be on the Inventory. The EPA replied that the free exchange of ions in solution does not result in new chemicals that must be on the Inventory. Spray drying would not result in new chemicals that must be on the Inventory because the questioner was not isolating individual salts.

In the second example, a dyestuff manufacturer presented a question in which a salt presumed to be the sodium salt of trisulfonic acid is less soluble than the potassium or mixed sodium-potassium salt. The questioner used potassium carbonate to dissolve the sodium salt and produce a higher concentration solution. The questioner believed that the chromaphore was the sulfonate anion, and not the salt, and asked whether the eight possible salts

157. Letter from Charles L. Elkins, Director, Offices of Toxic Substances, EPA to James E. Remsen of National Association of Printing Ink Manufacturers, Inc. (Mar. 27, 1990).

158. Letter from Mary E. Cushmac, Chief, Policy and Administrative Section, New Chemicals Branch, to Fred H. Parry of Hoechst Celanese Corporation (Aug. 12, 1994).

must be on the Inventory. The EPA responded that "the trisulfonic acid is not capable of functioning as a dyestuff until it is converted to the soluble salt." As a result, the new salts "provide the primary function which determines the use of the dyestuff" and they are not exempt from Inventory listing or PMN rules. Once they are on the Inventory they can also be isolated and sold as chemicals on their own.

In the third example, a polyacrylic acid type thickener is pH neutralized to form a salt, and the salt is subsequently added to a pigment dispersion to thicken it. The EPA noted that the salt is formed as a thickening agent in a product that is only a thickening agent, and the salt provides the primary property of the thickening agent. Therefore it is not exempt from Inventory and PMN rules. If the salt were formed during the formulation of the pigment it would be exempt because it would not provide a primary property of the pigment, and the salt does not function separately from the pigment product.

One of the specific products that qualifies for this exemption is a flow modifier. If a flow modifier is added to a product, it will typically undergo chemical reactions that will change the characteristics of the product. If the flow modifier is distributed as a separate chemical substance, it must be on the Inventory because it is either manufactured or imported for a commercial purpose. However the substances that form when the flow modifier is put into the product and change the physical properties of the product are exempt from the premanufacture notification requirements.[159]

Although the regulation itself says that chemicals formed when a pH neutralizer functions as intended, the EPA has turned this on its head in guidance. The EPA's guidance says that a pH neutralizer brings a solution to neutral or close to neutral, and includes bringing a solution from pH 14 (extremely basic) to pH 7 (neither basic nor acidic) is pH neutralization. The EPA added that "[t]his change in pH will usually result in a substantial change in the chemical species present and contribute to the function of the chemical. The new chemicals resulting from the pH neutralizing reaction are subject to PMN reporting requirements."[160] In contrast "pH adjustment," which is not a term used in the regulations, means "fine tuning" the pH of a solution according to the guidance. If an acid with a pH of 3 is altered so that it has a pH of 2 then this is "adjustment" and any new chemical substance would be exempt from premanufacture notification under the (h)(7) exemption, according to the EPA's guidance.[161] Making a solution a stronger acid or a stronger base is the opposite of neutralization, and it is hard to see how

159. Draft PMN Q&A, 2-7–2-8, question 206-1.

160. *Id.* at 2-23, question 217-2.

161. *Id.* at 2-23.

that could be exempted under the phrase "pH neutralizer" that is used in the regulation.[162]

As always, it is prudent to take a conservative approach when guidance is contrary to a regulation. "Adjusting" the pH of a solution by making it a stronger acid or a stronger base is not exempted by the language of the regulation, and neutralizing a solution is not exempted by the guidance. In this case, the more conservative approach is not to rely on this exemption for pH changes of any kind unless the EPA considers the specific fact pattern and makes a determination on the applicability of the exemption in writing. The EPA suggests contacting a Prenotice Coordinator if there is any ambiguity in applying the guidance.

Note that there may be defenses for failure to comply with a guidance when the guidance is directly at odds with regulations adopted after notice and comment.

In another Q&A in the same guidance, the EPA said that if a polymer "is deliberately converted to a water-absorbing polymer by neutralization, that conversion constitutes manufacture for commercial purposes as a chemical substance, rather than processing. … The resulting neutralized substances would also not be excluded from reporting under 720.30(h)(7)."[163] This is consistent with the requirement that the excluded substance cannot provide a primary property that determines the use of the resulting product.

E. Chemicals Made or Imported Solely for Export, Impurities, and Nonisolated Intermediates

Each of these categories of substances is exempt from the PMN requirements. Each category is also exempt from additional TSCA programs and for that reason each is addressed in Chapter 2, TSCA's Scope.

III. Exemptions Requiring Prior Notice to the EPA

In addition to the self-executing exemptions from the PMN requirements discussed in this chapter, § 5(h)[164] of TSCA gives EPA the authority to

162. Many of these same points were made in comments to the draft guidance. Letter from Mark Herwig, Manager, CMP Programs, General Electric Corporate Environmental Programs to Office of Pollution Prevention and Toxics Document Control Office, EPA (Mar. 15, 2004); Letter from Glen J. Barrett, Senior Health Scientist, American Petroleum Institute to Office of Pollution Prevention and Toxics, EPA (Mar. 8, 2004), both *available through* http://regulations.gov in Docket OPPT-2003-0055.
163. Draft PMN Q&A, 2-24–2-25, question 218-2.
164. 15 U.S.C. § 2604(h).

approve requests to exempt from those requirements chemical substances that do not "present any unreasonable risk of injury to health or the environment," whether such chemical substance will be used for test marketing, as permitted by the statute itself subject to EPA imposed restrictions, or such other purposes as allowed by EPA by rule. This standard of "unreasonable risk of injury to health or the environment" that governs the statutory authority to grant TMEs, LVEs and LoREX exemptions appears nine times in the TSCA statute. No definition of what constitutes unreasonable risk is contained in TSCA, although considerable efforts have been expended to provide guidance. In promulgating the expanded LVE and the new LoREX exemption, EPA determined that those exemptions would not create such a risk by considering (i) the safeguards built into the rules, (ii) the low production volume and the low release/exposures involved, (iii) the benefits to industry and the public provided by the new substances, and (iv) the benefits to the public by EPA's enhanced ability to focus its resources on reviewing greater volume chemicals and higher risk uses.[165]

EPA has established procedures under this statutory authority that allow expedited approvals[166] for chemical substances used for test marketing, chemical substances produced in low volumes, and chemical substances with low environmental release and human exposures. Chemical substances permitted to be manufactured, processed, or imported under these provisions are not subject to the requirements of filing an NOC and do not become listed on the TSCA Inventory, but are subject to various other TSCA restrictions, such as the obligation to record adverse reactions,[167] the obligation to inform the EPA about substantial risk information,[168] the obligation to make export notifications,[169] and the obligation to make import certifications.[170] For chemical substances that are eligible for these exemptions, each company needs to evaluate the benefits of these exemptions in light of its business practices to determine whether those benefits outweigh the attendant restrictions. Because the substances subject to a TME, LVE, or LoREX are not listed on the Inventory, these exemptions only confer benefits on the company that

165. 60 Fed. Reg. 16336, 16345 (Mar. 29, 1995).

166. § 26(c) of TSCA allows the EPA to take action with respect to any category of chemical substances if TSCA authorizes such action with respect to an individual chemical that is part of that chemical category.

167. TSCA § 8(c); 15 U.S.C. § 2625(c).

168. TSCA § 8(e); 15 U.S.C. § 2607(e).

169. TSCA § 12(b); 15 U.S.C. § 2611(b). It is unlikely that a substance subject to a TME, LVE, or LoREX exemption would be subject to a test rule to trigger these export notification requirements. The TME is time limited, so it is likely such an exemption would expire prior to the issuance of any test rule, and with respect to chemicals marketed under an LVE or LoREX exemption, the EPA retains significant authority to revoke those exemptions, which is a quicker route to imposing restrictions than rulemaking.

170. TSCA § 13; 15 U.S.C. § 2612.

files for the exemption, which might be considered a distinct competitive advantage.

A. Test Marketing Exemption

TSCA § 5(h)(1)[171] authorizes EPA to exempt from PMN and SNURs chemical substances that will be used for test marketing purposes. Unlike the other exemptions discussed *infra* requiring EPA prior approval, the holder of a TME has a limited time to conduct the test marketing. TME chemicals undergo a shortened 45 day review period and are not subject to user fees.

1. Eligibility Requirements

To be eligible to apply for a TME, a manufacturer must plan to distribute in commerce a predetermined amount of a chemical substance, to a defined number of potential customers, in a predetermined timeframe, for the purpose of exploring market viability prior to the broader distribution of that chemical substance.[172]

2. Exemption Application

Manufacturers must submit an application at least 45 days before beginning manufacture of the chemical substance for test marketing that contains the following information:[173]

- "[a]ll existing data regarding health and environmental effects, including physical/chemical properties or, in the absence of such data, a discussion of toxicity based on structure-activity relationships (SAR) and relevant data on chemical analogues;"[174]
- the maximum amount of the chemical to be manufactured;

---

171. 15 U.S.C. § 2606(h)(1).
172. 40 C.F.R. § 720.3(gg).
173. 40 C.F.R. § 720.38.
174. Unlike with PMN, LVE, and LoREX exemption filings, there is no requirement in the regulations to update such information during the TME review period. However, it would seem prudent to do so. Remember also that information that rises to substantial risk level information must be submitted under TSCA § 8(e). Arguably information submitted voluntarily to update a TME exemption submission would not satisfy the TSCA § 8(e) requirement since the information would not be submitted pursuant to a mandatory reporting requirement. For a discussion of the § (8)e reporting requirements, *see* Chapter 7, Reporting and Recordkeeping.

- the maximum number of people who may be given the chemical during test marketing;
- the maximum number of people who may be exposed to the chemical as a result of test marketing, including information regarding duration and route of such exposures;
- a description of the test marketing activity, including how such activity can be distinguished from full scale commercial production and research and development, and how long the test marketing will last; and
- a sanitized copy of the application if the manufacturer is claiming any of the submitted information confidential.[175]

EPA must publish a notice in the Federal Register both when it receives an application for a TME and when that application has been granted or denied.[176] The review period for a TME is 45 days.[177] However, unlike with PMN, LoREX, and LVE filings, EPA takes the position that the manufacturer cannot begin to manufacture at the end of the review period unless EPA has made an affirmative finding that the test marketing will not present any unreasonable risk of injury to health or the environment.[178]

The regulations do not impose on TME applicants the requirement to use the PMN form, as is specifically required by regulation for both the LVE and LoREX exemptions. TMEs are specifically excused from those notification requirements.[179] The regulation governing use of the PMN form says it is only applicable to companies required to submit a notice.[180] The EPA, however, in some of its literature[181] and through the EPA TSCA hotline, does tell submitters to use that form. In other older literature, EPA takes the opposite position.[182] The EPA prenotice submission office does concede that there is no statutory authority to require submitters to submit notices using the PMN form and that it is not required to be used, but does suggest that the use of the

175. 40 C.F.R. § 720.80(b)(2).

176. 15 U.S.C. § 2604(h)(6).

177. *Id.*

178. 48 Fed. Reg. 21721, 21725 (May 13, 1983); EPA Draft Instruction Manual for Reporting Under the TSCA § 5 New Chemicals Program, 6–7 (2003) [hereinafter PMN Instruction Manual], *available through* http://www.epa.gov/oppt/newchems/.

179. 40 C.F.R. § 720.30(d) states that chemicals that are distributed in commerce pursuant to a TME under 40 C.F.R. § 720.38 are not subject to the PMN notification requirements. *See also*, PMN Instruction Manual, 21–22.

180. 40 C.F.R. § 720.40(a).

181. Draft PMN Q&A, 3-5, question 302-2.

182. Chemical Bulletin Exemptions, 10, A.3. EPA states that while the application need not be in any specific form, the submitter must make a demonstration, to EPA's satisfaction, that the test marketing will not create any unreasonable risk.

form helps to expedite the review process.[183] While there is no statutory authority to require use of the PMN form, as a practical matter companies should not unduly antagonize the EPA by insisting on using an alternative. Note that using the TME form requires filers to certify compliance with PMN regulations that are not otherwise applicable to TMEs, such as submission or descriptions of all data known or reasonably ascertainable by the submitter.

3. Continuing Obligations

Most likely because TMEs are time limited, the regulations do not list a host of substantial continuing obligations, as they do for chemicals produced under the LVE or LoREX exemptions. It seems clear that anyone manufacturing and distributing in commerce any chemical under a TME must adhere to the statements in the information presented to the EPA in the application for the TME, as well as to any other restrictions imposed by the EPA. However, the regulations specify only that records must be maintained for five years from the final date of manufacture documenting the information submitted in the TME application and compliance with any restrictions imposed by EPA when granting the TME.[184] There is no procedure established for notifying customers of restrictions on the use of the chemical or for dealing with customers who use the chemical in ways other than specified in the TME. EPA had originally proposed a processor notification rule, but withdrew that requirement in light of arguments from industry that manufacturers who distribute chemicals for test marketing purposes know how people will use those chemicals because this knowledge is needed to make sure the manufacturer is in compliance with the TME.[185] EPA does take the position that if a manufacturer learns that any of its customers is using the chemical for purposes other than as designated in the TME, the manufacturer must stop distribution of the chemical to that customer.[186] However, there is no prohibition in the regulations against a processor continuing to use TME materials after the TME period expires. Unless specifically required in the approval of the TME, there is no continuing obligation to submit new information about the chemical after the granting of the TME. Information that rises to the level of significant risk information under TSCA § 8(e) would have to be reported pursuant to that reporting obligation. EPA did not reserve the right to revoke

---

183. Telephone Interview with David Shutz, Prenotice Coordinator, EPA (Dec. 23, 2008). Mr. Shutz noted that the EPA material referred to above (Draft PMN Q&A, 3-5, question 302-2) might need to be revised to make clear the PMN form is not required. *See also* 73 Fed. Reg 78261, 78266 (Dec. 22, 2008), the proposed rule dealing with electronic filings of PMNs, noting that applications for TMEs are not required to be on the PMN form.

184. 40 C.F.R. § 723.78(c).

185. 48 Fed. Reg. 21722, 21727 (May 13, 1983).

186. *Id.*

the TME either, but this might be of little practical application, since TMEs are time limited.

4. Practical Implications

Since the exemption's introduction at the beginning of the TSCA program, 767 TME applications were filed through July 14, 2008. As a comparison, in the same time frame, 35,229 PMNs were filed,[187] or about 45 times as many PMNs were filed as TMEs. Using the TME route potentially allows for a 45 day quicker introduction of a chemical to market.[188] Neither the statute nor the regulations prohibit the simultaneous submission of a TME and PMN, but EPA advises submitters that unless they can prove genuine test marketing will take place, the application will be denied.[189] EPA has said that unless the submitter can clearly distinguish between test marketing and full scale commercial activities its policy is not to accept PMNs on TME substances until ninety days before the TME's expiration date.[190] Under EPA's Sustainable Futures[191] program for expedited PMNs, EPA makes an exception to its policy for qualified filers, who are explicitly authorized to file TMEs and PMNs simultaneously to obtain the benefits of the shorter TME review period. While not expressly required, it would be prudent to notify recipients of chemicals that are being sent for test marketing purposes that the materials are being test marketed pursuant to a TME, and of any restrictions imposed in the TME approval.

A person who has received a test marketing exemption for a significant new use is exempted from compliance with the SNUR, unless the SNUR specifically overrides this general rule.[192]

Companies must consider whether they can suitably adapt their work processes to allow them to consistently meet the restrictions of the TME. They should also consider whether or not their customer base, direct and indirect, will also be able to consistently meet these obligations. Because test marketing is usually done over a short time period, the ability to comply with the requirements of the TME should be easily manageable.

---

187. E-mail from Anna Coutlakis, member, New Chemicals Prenotice Branch, EPA, to Miriam V. Gold, Attorney at Law (Jan. 9. 2009, 14:22:09 EST) (on file with author).
188. *See* Chapter 4, Premanufacture Notifications.
189. Chemical Bulletin Exemptions, 11 (Nov. 1986).
190. 67 Fed. Reg, 76282, 76285 (Dec. 11, 2002).
191. *See* http://www.epa.gov/oppt/sf/.
192. 40 C.F.R. § 721.45(a). For the test marketing exemption to apply to SNURs, a company that is subject to a SNUR must be able to file a test marketing exemption to avoid the restrictions in the SNUR. *See* the discussion *infra* concerning the application of the LVE, LoREX, and polymer exemptions to SNURs.

B. Low Volume Exemption

EPA promulgated the initial LVE rule in 1985 in response to petitions from several industry trade groups.[193] That initial rule exempted chemical substances that would be produced or imported in volumes up to and including one thousand kilograms a year from the full PMN requirements, subject to certain restrictions. Based on its experiences with the LVE, EPA issued an amendment to the LVE rules in 1995, increasing the amount of production or importation up to and including ten thousand kilograms a year, subject to certain restrictions. LVE chemicals undergo a shortened thirty day review period and are not subject to user fees.

1. Eligibility Requirements

To be eligible to apply for an LVE, a manufacturer or importer (hereinafter manufacturer[194]) must be willing to limit its production or importation to ten thousand kilograms or less a year.[195] For these purposes, a year is defined as every twelve month period following the end of the LVE's initial review period.[196] The manufacturer must have a good faith intention to manufacture the chemical substance for commercial purposes within one year after the end of the LVE's initial review period.[197] A chemical is not eligible for an LVE if it, or any likely metabolites, environmental transformation products or byproducts, or any impurities therein could cause serious acute, chronic, or environmental effects under expected conditions of manufacturing, processing, distribution, use, or disposal.[198] In addition, a chemical may not be eligible for an LVE if EPA cannot determine that the total aggregate production volume, including from other previously granted LVEs, will not present an unreasonable risk to health or the environment.[199] Should this be the case, EPA will request the prior exemption holder to certify that it has begun production or will begin production within one year after termination of the

193. 50 Fed. Reg. 16477 (Apr. 26, 1985).
194. This usage is consistent with the statute generally, which defines "manufacture" as "to import into the customs territory of the United States ..., produce, or manufacture". TSCA § 3(7).
195. 60 Fed. Reg. 16336, 16347 (Mar. 29, 1995), 40 C.F.R. § 723.50(c)(1). The original LVE exemption was for substances manufactured in the amount of 1000 kilograms or less. That rule became effective on Aug. 26, 1985. 50 Fed. Reg. 16477 (Apr. 26, 1985). Exemptions granted under the superseded rule remain effective, but any modification of the terms of such an exemption must be made under the revised rule. 60 Fed. Reg. 16336, 16337 (Mar. 29, 1995).
196. 60 Fed. Reg. 16336, 16337 (Mar. 29, 1995).
197. *Id.* at 16348 (Mar. 29, 1995); 40 C.F.R. § 723.50(e)(2)(xi)(D).
198. 60 Fed. Reg. 16336, 16347 (Mar. 29, 1995); 40 C.F.R. § 723.50(d).
199. 40 C.F.R. § 723.50(f)(1).

review period. If the exemption holder does not make such a certification within 21 days of receipt of EPA's notice, EPA will issue a notice of ineligibility to the first exemption holder.[200]

Entities that were granted LVEs prior to May 26, 1995 under the original LVE regulations are allowed to continue to produce those chemicals subject to the regulations then in effect and any other requirements imposed in the LVE itself. Those original regulations allowed for the production of only one thousand kilograms per year. Manufacturers wishing to amend such exemptions must file a new exemption notice, meeting the requirements set forth below.[201]

2. Exemption Application

Manufacturers must submit a notice of intent to manufacture thirty days before beginning commercial manufacture of the chemical substance, using the same form as would be used for PMNs,[202] and containing the following information:[203]

- manufacturer identity;
- chemical identity;
- impurities;
- synonyms or trade names;
- byproducts;
- production volume (manufacturers can put in a production volume lower than 10,000 kilograms and the EPA will do its risk assessment based on that lower level, but the manufacturer will be limited to annual production of this lower level);
- intended categories of use;
- for manufacturer controlled sites, identity of such sites, process descriptions, and information on worker exposures and environmental releases;
- for non-manufacturer controlled sites, processing and use operation descriptions, estimated number of such sites, and information on worker exposures and environmental releases, if such information is known or readily available to the manufacturer (otherwise EPA will apply its own, more conservative estimates to account for uncertainties);
- type of notice, i.e., for an LVE the first page should say "TSCA section 5(h)4 exemption notice pursuant to paragraph (c)(1), (this is a preprinted checkbox on the PMN form itself);

200. 40 C.F.R § 723.50(f)(2).
201. 40 C.F.R. § 723.50(m).
202. *See* Chapter 14, Premanufacture Notifications.
203. 40 C.F.R. § 723.50(e)(2).

- test data in the possession or control of the submitter pertaining to the health or environmental effects of the chemical;[204]
- PMN certifications plus specific ones tailored to the exemption; and
- a sanitized copy of the notice if the manufacturer is claiming any of the submitted information confidential.[205]

The review period for an LVE exemption ends thirty days after receipt of the notice by the TSCA Document Control Officer.[206] EPA will acknowledge the receipt of the notice and will indicate in that letter the date the review period begins.[207] If EPA has taken no action during the thirty day review period, the manufacturer may begin to manufacturer the new chemical substance at the end of that review period.[208] If EPA determines that the chemical substance is ineligible for an LVE, EPA will notify the manufacturer.[209] The manufacturer may at any time during the review period request a suspension of the review period to address any unresolved issues,[210] on its own volition or at the request of the EPA.[211]

3. Continuing Obligations

A manufacturer producing a substance subject to an LVE has substantial continuing compliance obligations. The manufacturer is required to submit to EPA any test data or other information indicating that the chemical substance may not qualify for the LVE within 15 working days of receipt of such information.[212] Submitting data or information under this mandatory requirement may fulfill obligations to submit reports under TSCA § 8(e).[213] The manufacturer cannot change the uses described in the original exemption notice or the human exposure and environmental release controls

---

204. If a submitter obtains possession, knowledge, or control of new information relevant to the chemical substance, the submitter must submit that information within ten days of receipt, but no later than five days before the end of the review period. If the new information becomes available during the last five days of the notice review period, the submitter must immediately inform its EPA contact by telephone. 40 C.F.R. § 723.50(i). This obligation is similar to the obligation imposed on a submitter of a PMN, which is discussed in Chapter 4, Premanufacture Notifications.
205. 40 C.F.R. § 723.50(l).
206. 40 C.F.R. § 723.50(g)(1).
207. 40 C.F.R. § 723.50(e)(1).
208. 40 C.F.R. § 723.50(g)(2).
209. 40 C.F.R. § 723.50(h)(1).
210. 40 C.F.R. § 723.50(g)(1).
211. *See* discussion on EPA requests to extend the PMN review period in Chapter 4, Premanufacture Notifications.
212. 40 C.F.R. § 723.50(i).
213. *See* Chapter 7, Reporting and Recordkeeping.

described therein.[214] If the manufacturer listed a specific physical form of the chemical in the notice, it can only change that form to another form that will not result in increased human exposures or increased environmental releases.[215] The annual production volume cannot exceed the lesser of ten thousand kilograms per year or the production amount, if any, that the manufacturer indicated on the LVE notice.[216] The manufacturing site cannot be changed, except subject to certain conditions as noted below. Should the manufacturer want to make any of these changes (to form, use, human exposure and environmental release controls, production volume in excess of the amount noted on the LVE notice, or site), the manufacturer must submit a new exemption notice.[217] The new notice need not contain all of the information previously submitted, but must contain the following:

- identity of the new chemical substance;
- manufacturer's name and name and contact information of a technical contact;
- location of the new site, new worker protection or environmental release controls and new use information, as applicable; and
- original EPA designated exemption number and a new certification by the manufacturer.[218]

A manufacturer can change the site of manufacturer without making a new exemption notice only if two conditions are met. The first condition deals with human exposure. The magnitude, frequency, and duration of human exposure at the new site must be equal to or less than it was at the old site.[219] To meet this condition the manufacturer must maintain records demonstrating that the technology employed in the new manufacturing site is basically the same technology it employed at the original site, so that there is not an appreciable difference in worker exposures.[220] With respect to use of a different technology, the manufacturer must demonstrate that the new technology actually decreases worker exposure levels because of improvements in that area.[221] The second condition for changing the site of manufacture deals with environmental releases. Either the chemical substance cannot be released to surface waters or to waste streams, or surface water concentrations must be maintained at or below one part per billion, or some other concentration

---

214. 40 C.F.R. § 723.50(j)(1).
215. 40 C.F.R. § 723.50(j)(2).
216. 40 C.F.R. § 723.50(j)(3).
217. 40 C.F.R. § 723.50(j)(4).
218. 40 C.F.R. § 723.50(j)(5).
219. 40 C.F.R. § 723.50(j)(6)(i)(A).
220. 60 Fed. Reg. 16336, 16340 (Mar. 29, 1995).
221. *Id.*

level approved by the EPA.[222] EPA will provide manufacturers with the water concentration of concern used by EPA in conducting its risk assessment.[223] The manufacturer can meet the water release conditions by calculating the surface water concentrations using the method described at 40 C.F.R. § 721.90 and § 721.91 and maintaining records of the calculations.[224]

EPA must be notified of the manufacturing site change within thirty days after beginning manufacture. The notification must contain:

- the manufacturer's name and name and contact information of a technical contact at the new site;
- street address of the new site;
- original EPA designated exemption number;
- the date on which manufacture began at the new site;
- any claim of confidentiality;
- a statement by the manufacturer that the notification is an amendment to the original exemption application; and
- an original signature of an authorized official. The notification may be submitted on EPA form 7710-56 "Notice of Commencement of Manufacture."[225]

As noted below, the manufacturer must keep copies of records that support the statements made in the notice, including calculations made.

Some of the more significant requirements of the LVE deal with notifications to customers about LVE restrictions and the obligations of the manufacturer in the event it learns a customer in not adhering to those restrictions. Manufacturers must notify processors and industrial users that the chemical can be used only for the particular uses and under the controls specified in the exemption.[226] Notification can be made by labeling, letter, or any other method that adequately communicates the restrictions.[227] If the manufacturer learns that a direct or indirect customer is not complying with the applicable restrictions, the manufacturer must cease selling the chemical to the customer or supplier of the customer unless it has notified the customer in writing of the customer's failure to conform to the restrictions within five working days of receiving such information and the customer has responded in writing, within fifteen working days of such notice of noncompliance, that it is aware of the restrictions applicable to the LVE and will comply

222. 40 C.F.R. § 723.50(j)(6)(i)(B).
223. 60 Fed. Reg. 16336, 16340 (Mar. 29, 1995).
224. *Id.*
225. 40 C.F.R. § 723.50(j)(6)(ii).
226. 40 C.F.R. § 723.50(k)(1).
227. *Id.*

with them.[228] If after receiving such an assurance, the manufacturer again learns that the customer is not complying with the restrictions, the manufacturer must stop supplying the chemical to that customer and must report the compliance failure to EPA within 15 days of obtaining such knowledge.[229] EPA will notify the manufacturer within thirty days of receipt of such notice whether and under what conditions it can resume selling the chemical to the customer.[230]

Records are required to be kept for five years after the date of last manufacture at either the manufacturing site or the site of importation to demonstrate compliance with the terms of the LVE. Not all records need to be kept for the duration of production plus five years. For example, manufacturing records need only be kept for five years from the date of manufacture. However records pertaining to the LVE application itself and information submitted subsequently should be kept for the full period, because violations of the provisions dealing with submittal of the application itself or subsequent studies can be considered continuing violations. Records should include documents that indicate compliance with the following sections of the regulations:

- section (c), annual production or importation volumes;
- section (e), compliance with the information provided by the manufacturer in the exemption notice;
- section (f), with respect to exemption holders that have certified that manufacture began within one year after the expiration of the review period;
- section (h), with respect to chemical substances that EPA determines after the review period are ineligible;
- section (i), with respect to any additional information about the chemical substance submitted to EPA;
- section (j), with respect to any changes in manufacturing site, use, human exposure and environmental release controls and manufacturing; and
- section (k), customer notification procedures.[231]

---

228. 40 C.F.R. § 723.50(k)(3).
229. 40 C.F.R. § 723.50(k)(4).
230. *Id.* This process is very similar to the process required for noncompliance with significant new use rules. *See, e.g.* 40 C.F.R. § 721.5(d) and Chapter 12, Significant New Use Rules.
231. 40 C.F.R. § 723.50(n). These recordkeeping requirements were inadvertently dropped out of the rules in a technical correction made by the EPA at 60 Fed. Reg. 34462 (July 3, 1995). They were reinstated by the EPA four years later at 64 Fed. Reg. 31987 (June 15, 1999). It is unclear whether or not a manufacturer who relied on the first technical correction and did not maintain records during the four year gap period could be found in violation of the now reinstated recordkeeping requirements. The prudent course would be for any manufacturer in that situation to attempt, to the extent possible, to reassemble that documentation for the information submitted in the application and for information submitted subsequent to the

EPA has the right to inspect and copy such records at reasonable times.[232] The manufacturer must also send copies of such records to EPA within 15 working days of receipt of any such request by EPA.[233]

4. LVE Revocation

EPA has the right to revoke the exemption at any time if it makes a determination that the chemical does not meet the requirements of the LVE.[234] EPA will notify the manufacturer of its preliminary determination, possibly based on new information,[235] that the chemical was not eligible for an LVE, and will give the manufacturer an opportunity to challenge the EPA's preliminary determination or to explain its good faith efforts to comply with the terms of the exemption.[236] New information that the substance was not eligible for an LVE could include new data indicating that the substance had significant risk potential.[237] The manufacturer has 15 days to reply, and will be able to continue to manufacture the chemical during this time period and until notified by the EPA of its final determination.[238] However, manufacturers not manufacturing or otherwise using the substance at the time of the EPA notification cannot begin such manufacture or other use until EPA makes its final determination.[239] If EPA finds that the chemical does not meet the terms of the LVE, and that the manufacturer did not act with due diligence and good faith to meet such requirements, the manufacture will have to stop all production, distribution, or use of the chemical within seven days of such notification.[240] If EPA finds that the chemical does not meet the terms of the LVE, but that the manufacturer did act with due diligence and good faith to meet such requirements, the manufacturer can continue to manufacture the chemical if it files a PMN within 15 days of the notification by the EPA that the chemical did not meet the terms of the LVE. Such manufacture or other use can continue during the PMN review period unless EPA takes action under TSCA § 5(e) or § 5(f).[241]

During the nine years between the promulgation of the original LVE exemption in 1985 and the revised LVE regulations in 1995, EPA had never

---

application grant. Production records for that gap period would already be beyond the statute of limitations.

232. 40 C.F.R. § 723.50(n)(3).
233. 40 C.F.R. § 723.50(n)(4).
234. 40 C.F.R. § 723.50(h)(2)(i)(A).
235. 50 Fed, Reg. 16477, 16481 (Apr. 26, 1985).
236. 40 C.F.R. § 723.50(h)(2)(i)(B).
237. 50 Fed. Reg., 16477, 16481–16482 (Apr. 26 1985).
238. 40 C.F.R. § 723.50(h)(ii).
239. 40 C.F.R. § 723.50(h)(2)(i)(B).
240. 40 C.F.R. § 723.50(h)(2)(v).
241. 40 C.F.R. § 723.50(h)(2)(vi).

used the post-review period revocation mechanism.[242] EPA has advised that since the implementation of the LVE program, it has revoked only one LVE.[243]

5. Practical Implications

LVEs have proven to be very popular vehicles to get new chemical substances into commerce. Since the exemption's introduction in mid 1985, 9524 LVEs were filed through July 14, 2008. This number does not include LVE modifications. As a comparison, since the introduction of PMNs in 1979, 35,229 PMNs were filed through July 14, 2008,[244] or almost four times as many PMNs were filed as LVEs in seven fewer years. Using the LVE route potentially allows for a two month quicker introduction of a chemical to market[245] and does not allow competitors to use the substance without filing their own LVE or PMN. EPA does not allow the simultaneous submission of an LVE and PMN. The regulations do not specifically prohibit the submission of a PMN immediately after the expiration of the LVE review period, and in fact there could be some advantages to doing this in terms of ongoing record-keeping. But, by making an LVE notice, the submitter is attesting that it intends to manufacture at a volume of ten thousand kilograms or less a year. EPA has said it considers submission of a PMN for a greater production volume to be a contrary statement of intent, but the same company may submit a PMN for the same chemical nine months after approval of the LVE.[246] Despite the EPA's warning that it will closely scrutinize a company's good faith intent in filing an LVE, there is no inconsistency in filing a subsequent PMN for ten thousand kilograms or less.

Companies must consider whether they can suitably adapt their work processes to allow them to consistently meet the restrictions of the LVE. They should also consider whether or not their customer base, direct and indirect, will also be able to consistently meet these obligations. Companies that deal with small volume chemicals on a regular basis likely will be better positioned to manage these compliance obligations than companies that deal predominately with large volume, less restricted, chemical substances. Companies should also have a plan in place to deal with revocations, because in the event the EPA finds that the chemical was not eligible for an LVE and the company did not exercise due diligence and good faith in meeting the LVE

242. 60 Fed. Reg. 16336, 16340 (Mar. 29, 1995).
243. Telephone interview with Anna Coutlakis, member, New Chemicals Prenotice Branch, EPA (Jan. 9. 2009).
244. E-mail from Anna Coutlakis, member, EPA New Chemicals Prenotice Branch, EPA, to Miriam V. Gold, Attorney at Law (Jan. 9. 2009, 14:22:09 EST) (on file with author).
245. *See* Chapter 4, Premanufacture Notifications.
246. Draft PMN Q&A, 3-9, question 303-7.

requirements, the company will have only seven days from the date of notification in which to stop all production, distribution, or use of the chemical. While it is not clear what constitutes "due diligence and good faith" for these purposes, it would seem that having an effective environmental, health, and safety system in place would be sufficient.

C. Low Release and Exposure Exemption—LoREX

When EPA updated the LVE regulations in 1995, it added a new exemption for chemicals with low environmental releases and low human exposures during their life cycles as part of its overall pollution prevention strategy.[247] The principal focus of the LoREX exemption was on release and exposure, not on toxicity.[248] The rationale for the exemption was to encourage companies to develop manufacturing, processing, use, and disposal techniques that minimize exposures from chemicals to people and the environment.[249] LoREX chemicals undergo a shortened thirty day review period and are not subject to user fees.

1. Eligibility Requirements

To be eligible to apply for a LoREX exemption, a manufacturer must meet stringent exposure and environmental release requirements. Eligibility does not depend on production quantity.[250]

With respect to consumers and the general public, there are four limitations imposed during the lifecycle of the chemical substance.[251] First, there can be no dermal exposure. Second, there can be no inhalation exposure, except for permitted limited exposures from incineration. For ambient air releases from incineration, releases cannot exceed one microgram per cubic meter maximum annual average concentration, calculated using the following formula:

(kilogram/day of release after treatment) X (number of release days per year) X (9.68 x 10^{-6}) micrograms per cubic meter.[252]

Third, there cannot be exposure in drinking water greater than one milligram per year, which generally equates to an ambient surface water concentration below one part per billion, unless EPA approves a higher surface water concentration based on information submitted to it in the exemption notice.

247. 60 Fed. Reg. 16336, 16337 (Mar. 29, 1995).
248. *Id.*
249. *Id.*
250. PMN Instruction Manual, 8-9.
251. 40 C.F.R. § 723.50(c)(2)(i).
252. 40 C.F.R. § 723.50(c)(2)(iv).

To apply for a higher surface water concentration a submitter must demonstrate, based either on the chemical substance that is the subject of the exemption notice or a close structural analogue, that the higher surface water concentration will not present an unreasonable risk of injury to aquatic species or human health.[253] While EPA will assume that compliance with the one part per billion water concentration will equate to compliance with the one milligram per year exposure in drinking water, EPA does reserve the right to require lower surface water concentrations when concerns for serious chronic effects are raised or under conditions where actual water drinking exposures are likely to significantly exceed the one milligram per year level.[254] Fourth, there can be no releases to the land, to groundwater, or to a landfill unless the manufacturer has demonstrated in the exemption notice that the chemical has negligible groundwater migration potential.[255] To prove migration potential is negligible, the exemption notice must be accompanied by data on the biodegradation and leeching potential of the substance or a close analogue, data on the physical and chemical properties of the chemical, or other data that clearly establishes significant releases to the groundwater will not occur.[256] Test data recommended by the EPA include an inherent biodegradability in soil test,[257] an anaerobic biodegradability of organic chemicals test,[258] and either a sediment and soil adsorption isotherm test[259] or a soil thin layer chromatography test.[260,261] EPA encourages submitters to discuss the testing criteria with the TSCA Prenotice Coordinator before beginning testing.

With respect to workers, there can be no dermal or inhalation exposure during the lifecycle of the chemical substance. Dermal and inhalation exposure controls used in accordance with applicable EPA guidance can be used to satisfy these workplace exposure requirements.[262] For example, for dermal exposures, EPA believes that the requirements of TSCA § 5(e) consent orders and SNURs generally provide adequate dermal exposure controls.[263] These controls include use of chemical protective equipment and chemical protective clothing.[264] With respect to occupational inhalation exposure controls, the manufacturer should identify the operations where such exposures

253. 40 C.F.R. § 723.50(c)(2)(iii).
254. 60 Fed. Reg. 16336, 16338 (Mar. 29, 1995).
255. 40 C.F.R. § 723.50(c)(2)(v).
256. 60 Fed. Reg. 16336, 16338 (Mar. 29, 1995).
257. 40 C.F.R. § 796.3400.
258. 40 C.F.R. § 796.3140.
259. 40 C.F.R. § 796.2750.
260. 40 C.F.R. § 796.2700.
261. 60 Fed. Reg. 16336, 16338 (Mar. 29, 1995).
262. 40 C.F.R. § 713.50(c)(2)(ii).
263. For a discussion of these types of controls, *see, e.g.*, Chapter 12, Significant New Use Rules.
264. 60 Fed. Reg. 16336, 16341 (Mar. 29, 1995).

are likely to occur, assess the magnitude, frequency, and duration of potential exposure, assess the effectiveness of controls and select the control(s) that will provide appropriate protection.[265] EPA recommends the submitter comply with the requirements of TSCA § 5(e) consent orders and SNURS to demonstrate control of exposures. These requirements stipulate the use of respiratory protection in accordance with National Institute of Occupational Safety and Health regulations at 29 C.F.R. § 1910.134.[266]

A chemical is not eligible for a LoREX exemption if it, or any likely metabolites, environmental transformation products or byproducts, or any impurities therein could cause serious acute, chronic, or environmental effects under expected conditions of manufacturing, processing, distribution, distribution, use, or disposal.[267] However, unlike the situation when someone holds a prior LVE for the same chemical substance, there is no issue with the granting of additional LoREX exemptions for the same chemical substance to multiple applicants. This is because LoREX exemptions are based on exposure and not on volume, so there should be no argument that total aggregate production volume, including from other previously granted LoREX exemptions, will present an unreasonable risk to health or the environment.

2. Exemption Application

Manufacturers must submit a notice of intent to manufacture thirty days before beginning commercial manufacture of the chemical substance, using the same form as would be used for PMNs,[268] and containing the following information:[269]

- manufacturer identity;
- chemical identity;
- impurities;
- synonyms or trade names;
- byproducts;
- estimated maximum production volume during the first year of production and the estimated maximum amount to be manufactured during each twelve month period in the first three years of production;
- intended categories of use;

---

265. *Id.*
266. *Id.* at 16342.
267. 60 Fed. Reg. 16336, 16347 (Mar. 29, 1995); 40 C.F.R. § 723.50(d).
268. *See* Chapter 4, Premanufacture Notifications.
269. 40 C.F.R. § 723.50(e)(2).

- for manufacturer controlled sites, identity of such sites, process descriptions, and information on worker exposures and environmental releases;
- for non-manufacturer controlled sites, processing and use operation descriptions, estimated number of such sites, and information on worker exposures and environmental releases;
- type of notice, i.e., for a LoREX exemption, the first page should say "TSCA section 5(h)4 exemption notice pursuant to paragraph (c)(2)" (this is a preprinted checkbox on the PMN form itself);
- test data in the possession or control of the submitter pertaining to the health or environmental effects of the chemical;[270]
- PMN certifications plus specific ones tailored to the exemption; and
- a sanitized copy of the notice if the manufacturer is claiming any of the submitted information confidential.[271]

Note that the PMN form contains some boxes that can be checked to indicate an agreement to manufacture the LoREX material at less than a binding volume, which would be in addition to the estimates that the regulations require. This box should not be checked, since there is no benefit to agreeing to a binding volume because the restrictions that accompany a LoREX are based on exposure. Such an agreement would only create an additional hurdle for a manufacturer should it seek to increase its volume at any time.

The review period for a LoREX exemption ends thirty days after receipt of the notice by the TSCA Document Control Officer.[272] EPA will acknowledge the receipt of the notice and will indicate in that letter the date the review period begins.[273] If EPA has taken no action during the thirty day review period, the manufacturer may begin to manufacture the new chemical substance at the end of that review period.[274] If EPA determines that the chemical substance is ineligible for a LoREX exemption, EPA will notify the manufacturer.[275] The manufacturer may at any time during the review

270. If a submitter obtains possession, knowledge, or control of new information relevant to the chemical substance, the submitter must submit that information within ten days of receipt, but no later than five days before the end of the review period. If the new information becomes available during the last five days of the notice review period, the submitter must immediately inform its EPA contact by telephone. 40 C.F.R. § 723.50(i). This obligation is similar to the obligation imposed on a submitter of a PMN, which is discussed in Chapter 4, Premanufacture Notifications.
271. 40 C.F.R. § 723.50(l).
272. 40 C.F.R. § 723.50(g)(1).
273. 40 C.F.R. § 723.50(e)(1).
274. 40 C.F.R. § 723.50(g)(2).
275. 40 C.F.R. § 723.50(h)(1).

period request a suspension of the review period to address any unresolved issues.[276]

3. Continuing Obligations

A manufacturer producing a substance subject to a LoREX exemption has substantial continuing compliance obligations. The manufacturer is required to submit to EPA any test data or other information indicating that the chemical substance may not qualify for the LoREX exemption within 15 working days of receipt of such information.[277] Submitting data or information under this mandatory requirement may fulfill obligations to submit reports under TSCA § 8(e).[278] The manufacturer cannot change the uses described in the original exemption notice or the human exposure and environmental release controls described therein.[279] If the manufacturer listed a specific physical form of the chemical in the notice, it can only change that form to another form that will not result in an increased human exposures or increased environmental releases.[280] The manufacturing site cannot be changed, except subject to certain conditions as noted below. Should the manufacturer want to make any of these changes (to form, use, human exposure, and environmental release controls), the manufacturer must submit a new exemption notice.[281] The new notice need not contain all of the information previously submitted, but must contain the following:

- identity of the new chemical substance;
- manufacturer's name and name and contact information of a technical contact;
- location of the new site, new worker protection or environmental release controls and new use information, as applicable; and
- original EPA designated exemption number and a new certification by the manufacturer.[282]

A manufacturer can change the site of manufacture without making a new exemption notice only if two conditions are met. The first condition deals with human exposure. The magnitude, frequency, and duration of human exposure at the new site must be equal to or less than it was at the old site.[283]

---

276. 40 C.F.R. § 723.50(g)(1).
277. 40 C.F.R. § 723.50(i).
278. *See* Chapter 7, Reporting and Recordkeeping.
279. 40 C.F.R. § 723.50(j)(1).
280. 40 C.F.R. § 723.50(j)(2).
281. 40 C.F.R. § 723.50(j)(4).
282. 40 C.F.R. § 723.50(j)(5).
283. 40 C.F.R. § 723.50(j)(6)(i)(A).

To meet this condition the manufacturer must maintain records demonstrating that the technology employed in the new manufacturing site is basically the same technology it employed at the original site, so that there is not an appreciable difference in worker exposures.[284] With respect to use of a different technology, the manufacturer must demonstrate that the new technology actually decreases worker exposure levels because of improvements in that area.[285] The second condition for changing the site of manufacture deals with environmental releases. Either the chemical substance cannot be released to surface waters or to waste streams, or surface water concentrations must be maintained at or below one part per billion, or some other concentration level approved by the EPA.[286] EPA will provide manufacturers with the water concentration of concern used by EPA in conducting its risk assessment.[287] The manufacturer can meet the water release conditions by calculating the surface water concentrations using the method described at 40 C.F.R. § 721.90 and § 721.91 and maintaining records of the calculations.[288]

EPA must be notified of the manufacturing site change within thirty days after beginning manufacturer. The notification must contain:

- the manufacturer's name and name and contact information of a technical contact at the new site;
- street address of the new site;
- original EPA designated exemption number;
- the date on which manufacture began at the new site;
- any claim of confidentiality;
- a statement by the manufacturer that the notification is an amendment to the original exemption application; and
- an original signature of an authorized official. The notification may be submitted on the NOC, EPA form 7710-56.[289]

As noted below, the manufacturer must keep copies of records that support the statements made in the notice, including calculations made.

Some of the more significant requirements of the LoREX exemption deal with notifications to customers about product restrictions and the obligations of the manufacturer in the event it learns a customer is not adhering to those restrictions. Manufacturers must notify processors and industrial users that the chemical can be used only for the particular uses and under the

---

284. 60 Fed. Reg. 16336, 16340 (Mar. 29, 1995).
285. *Id.*
286. 40 C.F.R. § 723.50(j)(6)(i)(B).
287. 60 Fed. Reg. 16336, 16340 (Mar. 29, 1995).
288. *Id.*
289. 40 C.F.R. § 723.50(j)(6)(ii).

controls specified in the exemption.[290] Notification can be made by letter, labeling, or any other method that adequately communicates the restrictions.[291] Prior to distributing the chemical to anyone the manufacturer must also obtain a written agreement that the recipient will not further distribute the chemical until it has been reacted, incorporated into an article, or otherwise put into a physical form or state in which environmental releases and human exposures above the eligibility criteria for the LoREX exemption will not occur.[292] If the manufacturer learns that a direct or indirect customer is not complying with the applicable restrictions, the manufacturer must cease selling the chemical to the customer or supplier of the customer unless it has notified the customer in writing of the customer's failure to conform to the restrictions within five working days of receiving such information and the customer has responded in writing, within fifteen working days of such notice of noncompliance, that it is aware of the restrictions applicable to the LoREX exemption and will comply with them.[293] If after receiving such an assurance, the manufacturer again learns that the customer is not complying with the restrictions, the manufacturer must stop supplying the chemical to that customer and must report the compliance failure to EPA within fifteen days of obtaining such knowledge.[294] EPA will notify the manufacturer within thirty days of receipt of such notice whether and under what conditions it can resume selling the chemical to the customer.[295]

Records are required to be kept for five years from the date of final manufacture at either the manufacturing site or the site of importation to demonstrate compliance with the terms of the LoREX. Not all records need to be kept for the duration of production plus five years. For example, manufacturing records need only be kept for five years from the date of manufacture. However records pertaining to the LoREX application itself and information submitted subsequently should be kept for the full period, because violations of the provisions dealing with submittal of the application itself or subsequent studies can be considered continuing violations. Records should include documents that indicate compliance with the following sections of the regulations:

- section (c), annual production or importation volumes;
- section (e), compliance with the information provided by the manufacturer in the exemption notice;

---

290. 40 C.F.R. § 723.50(k)(1).
291. 40 C.F.R. § 723.50(k)(1).
292. 40 C.F.R. § 723.50(k)(2).
293. 40 C.F.R. § 723.50(k)(3).
294. 40 C.F.R. § 723.50(k)(4).
295. *Id.* This process is very similar to the process required for noncompliance with significant new use rules. *See, e.g.*, 40 C.F.R. § 721.5(d) and Chapter 12, Significant New Use Rules.

- section (f), with respect to exemption holders that have certified that manufacture began within one year after the expiration of the review period;
- section (h), with respect to chemical substances that EPA determines after the review period are ineligible;
- section (i), with respect to any additional information about the chemical substance submitted to EPA;
- section (j), with respect to any changes in manufacturing site, use, human exposure and environmental release controls and manufacturing; and
- section (k), customer notification procedures.[296]

EPA has the right to inspect and copy such records at reasonable times.[297] The manufacturer must also send copies of such records to EPA within 15 working days of receipt of any request by EPA.[298]

4. LoREX Revocation

EPA has the right to revoke the exemption at any time if it makes a determination that the chemical does not meet the requirements of the LoREX exemption.[299] EPA will notify the manufacturer of its preliminary determination, possibly based on new information,[300] that the chemical was not eligible for an exemption and give the manufacturer an opportunity to challenge the EPA's preliminary determination or to explain its good faith efforts to comply with the terms of the exemption.[301] New information that the substance was not eligible for a LoREX exemption could include new data indicating that the substance had significant risk potential.[302] The manufacturer has 15 days to reply, and will be able to continue to manufacture the chemical during this

296. 40 C.F.R. § 723.50(n). These recordkeeping requirements were inadvertently dropped out of the rules in a technical correction made by the EPA at 60 Fed. Reg. 34462 (July 3, 1995). They were reinstated by the EPA four years later at 64 Fed. Reg. 31987 (June 15, 1999). It is unclear whether or not a manufacture who relied on the first technical correction and did not maintain records during the four year gap period could be found in violation of the now reinstated recordkeeping requirements. The prudent course would be for any manufacturer in that situation to attempt, to the extent possible, to reassemble that documentation for the information submitted in the application and for information submitted subsequent to the application grant. Production records for that gap period would already be beyond the statute of limitations.
297. 40 C.F.R. § 723.50(n)(3).
298. 40 C.F.R. § 723.50(n)(4).
299. 40 C.F.R. § 723.50(h)(2)(i)(A).
300. 50 Fed, Reg. 16477, 16481 (Apr. 26, 1985).
301. 40 C.F.R. § 723.50(h)(2)(i)(B).
302. 50 Fed. Reg., 16477, 16481–16482 (Apr. 26 1985).

time period and until notified by the EPA of its final determination.[303] However, manufacturers not manufacturing or otherwise using the substance at the time of the EPA notification cannot begin such manufacture or other use until EPA makes its final determination.[304] If EPA finds that the chemical does not meet the terms of the LoREX exemption, and that the manufacturer did not act with due diligence and good faith to meet such requirements, the manufacture will have to stop all production, distribution, or use of the chemical within seven days of such notification.[305] If EPA finds that the chemical does not meet the terms of the LoREX exemption, but that the manufacturer did act with due diligence and good faith to meet such requirements, the manufacturer can continue to manufacture the chemical if it files a PMN within 15 days of the notification by the EPA that the chemical did not meet the terms of the exemption. Such manufacture or other use can continue during the PMN review period unless EPA takes action under TSCA sections 5(e) or 5(f).[306] EPA has advised that since the implementation of the LoREX program in 1995, it has not revoked any LoREX exemptions.[307]

5. Practical Implications

EPA had envisioned that manufacturers, especially those whose new chemical was likely to require a TSCA §5(e) Consent Order, would prefer to propose and agree to restrictions and avoid the lengthy § 5(e) approval process. The LoREX eligibility requirements are similar to requirements often imposed through a §5(e) Consent Order.[308] Despite EPA's view that the LoREX exemption would prove to be an effective substitute to regulation under section § 5(e), industry has not utilized this exemption. Since the exemption's introduction in mid 1995, only 37 LoREX exemption notices were filed through July 14, 2008.[309] This number does not include LoREX modifications, to the extent there were any. As a comparison, since the introduction of PMNs in 1979, 1421 TSCA § 5(e) consent orders were concluded through July 14, 2008.[310] Using the LoREX exemption route potentially allows for a two month quicker introduction of a chemical to market.[311] LoREX exemptions

---

303. 40 C.F.R. § 723.50(h)(ii).
304. 40 C.F.R. § 723.50(h)(2)(i)(B).
305. 40 C.F.R. § 723.50(h)(2)(v).
306. 40 C.F.R. § 723.50(h)(2)(vi).
307. Telephone interview with Anna Coutlakis, member, New Chemicals Prenotice Branch, EPA (Jan. 9. 2009).
308. 60 Fed. Reg. 16336, 16337 (Mar. 29, 1995).
309. E-mail from Anna Coutlakis, member, New Chemicals Prenotice Branch, EPA, to Miriam V. Gold, Attorney at Law (Jan. 9. 2009, 14:22:09 EST) (on file with author).
310. *Id.*
311. *See* Chapter 4, Premanufacture Notifications.

are most frequently used for dangerous, site limited chemicals, such as intermediates.[312]

Companies must consider whether they can suitably adapt their work processes to allow them to consistently meet the restrictions of the LoREX exemption. They should also consider whether or not their customer base, direct and indirect, will also be able to consistently meet these obligations. Companies that deal with chemicals subject to § 5(e) Consent Orders or SNURS on a regular basis likely will be better positioned to manage these compliance obligations than companies that deal predominately with unrestricted chemicals on the TSCA inventory. Companies should also have a plan in place to deal with revocations, because in the event the EPA finds that the chemical was not eligible for a LoREX exemption and the company did not exercise due diligence and good faith in meeting the LoREX exemption requirements, the company will have only seven days from the date of notification in which to stop all production, distribution, or use of the chemical. While it is not clear what constitutes "due diligence and good faith" for these purposes, it would seem that having an effective environmental, health, and safety system in place would be sufficient.

D. The Polaroid Exemption for Instant Film and Peel-apart Film

In 1982 the EPA granted an exemption from the PMN process for chemicals used to make or process instant photo and peel-apart film articles.[313] This is often referred to as the Polaroid exemption, because Polaroid made instant film and filed a petition with the EPA to establish this exemption under TSCA § 5(h)(4).[314] It is of limited continuing importance since Polaroid discontinued making instant film and instant film cameras in 2008.[315] Fujifilm is one of the last suppliers of this type of film in the United States.[316] As early as 1997 the EPA characterized the Polaroid exemption as "rarely used."[317]

In summary, the Polaroid exemption applies to sealed articles that contain all of the chemicals required to manufacture and develop instant film. Manufacturers may start manufacturing or importing these films immediately on filing a notice with the EPA, but must file a PMN and wait for the

---

312. Telephone Interview with David Shutz, Prenotice Coordinator, EPA (Dec. 23, 2008).
313. 40 C.F.R. § 723.175.
314. 47 Fed. Reg. 24308 (June 4, 1982).
315. http://www.polaroid.com/ifilm/en/index.html.
316. *See, e.g.*, http://www.fujifilmusa.com/products/professional_photography/film/fujifilm_instant_films/pack_holder/index.html.
317. Chemistry Assistance Manual for Premanufacture Notification Submitters, EPA 744-R-97-003, 118 (1997) *available at* http://www.epa.gov/oppt/newchems/pubs/chem-pmn/.

PMN review period to expire before they can distribute the film in commerce. The substance is not added to the Inventory and a new PMN is required if any person plans on making or importing the substance for any purpose outside the scope of the exemption.[318] The exemption requires special handling to control exposures. It also has strict recordkeeping requirements.

318. 47 Fed. Reg. 24308, 24316 (June 4, 1982).

CHAPTER

6

Microorganisms

I. Introduction

Microorganisms are "chemical substances" subject to the Toxic Substances Control Act (TSCA)[1] requirements and rules. While it seems counterintuitive to think of living organisms as chemicals, the United States Environmental Protection Agency (EPA) has taken this position since the inception of TSCA. In one of the first regulations issued under TSCA, the EPA explained that certain microorganisms made in or imported into the United States must be reported for listing as chemical substances (the list is referred to as the Inventory.)[2] The EPA received a comment during the rulemaking process that: "[c]ommercial biological preparations such as yeasts, bacteria, and fungi should not be considered 'chemical substances' under TSCA." The EPA responded: "[t]he Administrator disagrees with this comment. The term chemical substance is defined to mean 'any organic or inorganic substance of a particular molecular identity including any combination ... occurring in nature.' This definition does not exclude life forms which may be manufactured for commercial purposes and nothing in the legislative history would suggest otherwise."[3]

At least some members of the regulated community followed this interpretation and reported the microorganisms that EPA said were required to be reported for the initial Inventory. According to the EPA, 192 microorganisms were reported for the initial Inventory.[4] Most if not all of the initially reported microorganisms would not be required to be on the Inventory under current policies.[5]

The EPA has asserted that it has authority to apply TSCA to transgenic plants and animals, although it has not yet done so.[6]

Current regulations subject microorganisms to TSCA, and all microorganisms that are not intergeneric are already on the Inventory.[7] Intergeneric microorganisms, which must be on the Inventory before they are made or imported, are microorganisms that are the result of genetic manipulation and

1. 15 U.S.C. §§ 2601–2695d.
2. This regulation was issued in connection with compiling the initial TSCA Inventory. For background on the Inventory, see Chapter 3, The Inventory.
3. 42 Fed. Reg. 64572, 64584–85, comment 30 (Dec. 23, 1977).
4. Identification of Microorganisms Currently Listed on the TSCA Chemical Substance Inventory (Aug. 31, 1994).
5. *Id.*
6. EPA, Microbial Products Of Biotechnology Final Regulation Under The Toxic Substances Control Act A Summary of The Public's Comments And The Agency's Response, 12–13 (Mar. 26, 1997) [hereinafter Microbial Comments], available at http://www.epa.gov/oppt/biotech/pubs/pdf/c006.pdf. EPA is considering whether or not to regulate transgenic plants and animals. Regulatory Plan and Semiannual Regulatory Agenda, EPA-230-Z-09-002, 111–112 (Fall 2009).
7. 40 C.F.R. § 725.8(b).

incorporate genetic material from at least two different genera of microorganisms. The actual regulatory definition is a bit more cumbersome, and defines an intergeneric microorganism as "a microorganism that is formed by the deliberate combination of genetic material originally isolated from organisms of different taxonomic genera."[8] The definition includes microorganisms that contain "a mobile genetic element which was first identified in a microorganism in a genus different from the recipient microorganism," but does not include microorganisms that contain "introduced genetic material consisting of only well-characterized, non-coding regulatory regions from another genus."

The TSCA microorganism regulations create a premanufacture review mechanism to put microorganisms on the TSCA Inventory that is very similar to the premanufacture notifications (PMNs) used for traditional chemicals. Under the microorganism regulations, any person who plans to make or import a new intergeneric microorganism must file a microbial commercial activity notice (MCAN) ninety days before commencing manufacture or importation. Any person that intends to make, import, or process an existing microorganism for a significant new use must also file an MCAN ninety days in advance of doing so. The entire structure of the traditional chemical regulatory process is restated in the microorganism regulations, from the premanufacture filings to research and development (R&D) exemptions, to a form of significant new use notifications. A review of the other chapters of this book discussing the foregoing topics for traditional chemical substances will assist anyone in dealing with these topics with respect to microorganisms. This chapter is designed to introduce the requirements exclusively applicable to microorganisms and provide a guide to available resources.

The microorganism regulations introduce the concept of TSCA experimental release applications (TERAs), which has no parallel in the traditional chemistry regulations. Although R&D exemptions are available for microorganisms, a microorganism may not be released into the environment under an R&D exemption. Before a microorganism that is not on the Inventory is released into the environment, the manufacturer or importer must file either an MCAN or a TERA. The advantage of a TERA is that it is an expedited application. A TERA can only be used for an R&D substance.

Although the regulations governing microorganisms focus on MCANs and TERAs, the principle that microorganisms are chemical substances has greater implications. This interpretation subjects microorganisms to all of the TSCA programs, including recording allegations of significant adverse

8. 40 C.F.R. § 725.3.

reactions under § 8(c), substantial risk reporting under § 8(e),[9] export notifications under § 12 and import certifications under § 13,[10] to name a few.[11]

The history of microorganism regulation under TSCA illustrates how slow the regulatory process can be. Although the EPA had stated in 1977 that microorganisms were subject to TSCA, it first issued a proposed policy statement in 1984 under a coordinated framework developed by many different governmental agencies. In 1986 the EPA issued an interpretation confirming that intergeneric microorganisms are chemical substances, and in 1994 the EPA issued proposed regulations. It was not until 1997 that the TSCA rules governing microorganisms were finalized.[12] During this time the question of how to regulate microorganisms was the subject of active and lively debate.

II. Microbial Commercial Activity Notice

The EPA receives very few MCANs each year. In 2007 it received three MCANs covering eight microorganisms, and just one TERA.[13] Only 43 intergeneric microorganisms have been added to the Inventory through the MCAN process.[14] In contrast, in the 18 months covering 2007 and the first half of 2008, 1071 PMNs and 630 applications for low volume exemptions from the PMN requirements were filed.[15]

The statutory basis for the requirement to file an MCAN is in TSCA § 5(a),[16] which provides that with limited exceptions, no person may:

> (A) manufacture a new chemical substance on or after the 30th day after the date on which the Administrator first publishes the list required by section 2607(b) of this title [the TSCA Inventory], or
> (B) manufacture or process any chemical substance for a use which the Administrator has determined, in accordance with paragraph (2), is a significant new use,

9. *See* Chapter 7, Reporting and Recordkeeping.
10. 40 C.F.R. § 725.920.
11. *See* Chapter 8, Exports and Imports. Microorganisms were specifically exempted from the 2006 Inventory Update Rule. *See* Chapter 3, The Inventory.
12. 62 Fed. Reg. 17910 (Apr. 11, 1997), *available at* http://frwebgate3.access.gpo.gov/cgi-bin/PDFgate.cgi?WAISdocID=15508723970+0+2+0&WAISaction=retrieve.
13. http://www.epa.gov/oppt/ar/2007-2009/reviewnewchem/newbiotech.htm.
14. Data *available at* http://www.epa.gov/biotech_rule/pubs/submain.htm.
15. http://www.epa.gov/oppt/ar/2007-2009/reviewnewchem/index.htm.
16. 15 U.S.C. § 2604(a)(1). The requirements of TSCA § 5 are addressed in Chapter 3, The Inventory, Chapter 4, Premanufacture Notifications, Chapter 5, PMN Exclusions and Exemptions and Chapter 12, Significant New Use Rules.

> unless such person submits to the Administrator, at least 90 days before such manufacture or processing, a notice, in accordance with subsection (d) of this section, of such person's intention to manufacture or process such substance and such person complies with any applicable requirement of subsection (b) of this section.

Because "manufacture" is defined to include importing in TSCA § 3, importers are also subject to these statutory requirements.

Manufacturers and importers of new intergeneric microorganisms must file an MCAN ninety days before commencing those activities. There are exemptions set out in the regulations, and these are for contained activities (Tier I and Tier II exemptions discussed infra),[17] test marketing,[18] use of small quantities for R&D[19] and microorganisms made or imported for export only.[20] The test marketing exemption and R&D exemption are based on the exemptions for traditional chemical substances. The exemption for contained activities is unique to microorganisms.

There are several exemptions from the MCAN requirements for microorganisms made or imported solely for research and development. If there is no intentional testing outside of a structure the microorganism is exempt if another federal agency requires compliance with National Institutes of Health Guidelines,[21] or if the research and development is performed under the supervision of a technically qualified individual and there are controls in place to contain or inactivate the microorganisms and involved individuals are notified of certain specified health risks.[22]

Research and development on certain microorganisms listed in the regulations may be conducted outside of a structure if a manufacturer or importer has the work supervised by a technically qualified person and certifies to the EPA in advance that it has notified state and local authorities and is in compliance with specific requirements which vary by the listed microorganism.[23]

Microorganisms that qualify for a Tier I exemption are exempt from the MCAN requirements. Tier I applies when the recipient organism is one of ten specifically listed microorganisms[24] and if it is the recipient of specific types

17. 40 C.F.R. § 725.1.
18. 40 C.F.R. §§ 725.1, 725.110 and 725.300. Only one test marketing exemption has been approved for a microorganism. *See* http://www.epa.gov/biotech_rule/pubs/submain.htm.
19. 40 C.F.R. §§ 725.1, 725.100, 725.110 and 725.200.
20. 40 C.F.R. § 725.8(c)(3).
21. 40 C.F.R. § 725.232. The National Institutes of Health Guidelines are the Guidelines for Research Involving Recombinant DNA Molecules (July 5, 1994).
22. 40 C.F.R. § 725.234.
23. 40 C.F.R. § 725.238.
24. Microbial Comments, 40.

of genetic material from another organism and does not contain any listed genetic sequences.[25] To qualify for this exemption, the manufacturer or importer must have specified physical containment and controls in place, including having a structure that is "designed and operated to contain the new microorganisms," building access control, personal safety and hygiene procedures, and procedures to inactivate the microorganisms in wastes and exhaust gases,[26] must submit a certification to the EPA ten days before manufacture or import of the microorganism, and must maintain records.[27]

The Tier II exemption is an expedited, 45 day review for certain microorganisms.[28] Microorganisms qualify for a Tier II exemption if the recipient organism is one of the same ten that qualify for the Tier I exemption, and has only the types of added genetic material permitted for the Tier I exemption.[29] There must be some containment and physical controls, but they do not need to reach the level of the containment and physical controls for a Tier I exemption; the regulations require only that they be "adequate."[30] A Tier II exemption request must be submitted at least 45 days before the first manufacture or import.[31] EPA may approve the request with or without conditions, and it may deny the request. If EPA denies the request the submitter may submit an MCAN.

In addition, any microorganisms that are exempt from the statutory definition of chemical substances are exempt from all the TSCA requirements, and these include

- mixtures that include microorganisms, although the component intergeneric microorganisms and chemicals are chemical substances;[32]
- pesticides "when manufactured, processed, or distributed in commerce for use as a pesticide";
- tobacco and tobacco products;
- source material, special nuclear material or byproduct material as defined in the Atomic Energy Act of 1954;[33]
- firearms, shells and cartridges; and
- any "food, food additive, drug, cosmetic, or device" as defined in § 201 of the Federal Food, Drug, and Cosmetic Act (FFDCA),[34]

25. 40 C.F.R. §§ 725.400 and 725.424.
26. 40 C.F.R. § 725.422.
27. 40 C.F.R. § 725.424.
28. Microbial Comments, 40.
29. 40 C.F.R. § 725.428.
30. *Id.*
31. 40 C.F.R. § 725.450.
32. 40 C.F.R. § 725.8(c)(2).
33. 42 U.S.C. § 2011–2297.
34. 21 U.S.C. § 301–399.

"when manufactured, processed, or distributed in commerce for use as a food, food additive, drug, cosmetic or device."[35]

The elements of the PMN process that are carried over to microorganism MCANs include:

- requirements to submit health and safety and other information with the MCAN;[36]
- joint submissions with suppliers claiming information as confidential;[37]
- the obligation to submit new information during the ninety day MCAN review period;[38]
- confidentiality claims and confidential listing on the Inventory;[39]
- the ability to submit a letter confirming a bona fide intent to manufacture, import or process a microorganism, to determine if it is already listed on the confidential Inventory;[40]
- recordkeeping requirements;[41]
- exemptions under TSCA § 5(h)(4) if the microorganism "will not present an unreasonable risk of injury to health or the environment";[42]
- the requirement to file a Notice of Commencement within thirty days of the first manufacture or import;[43] and
- the requirement to file an MCAN for a significant new use of a microorganism.[44]

Microorganisms are added to the Inventory after the ninety day MCAN review period expires and the filer submits a Notice of Commencement of manufacture or importation.[45]

III. TSCA Experimental Release Application

Instead of filing an MCAN, a person who intends to make or import a new intergeneric microorganism for research and development purposes, but

35. TSCA § 3(2); 15 U.S.C § 2602(2). *See also* Microbial Comments, 13.
36. 40 C.F.R. §§ 725.25, 725.150, 725.155, and 725.160.
37. 40 C.F.R. § 725.25(e).
38. 40 C.F.R. § 725.36.
39. 40 C.F.R. §725.80. and 725.85.
40. 40 C.F.R. § 725.15.
41. 40 C.F.R. § 725.65.
42. 40 C.F.R. § 725.190.
43. 40 C.F.R. § 725.67.
44. 40 C.F.R. § 725.900.
45. 40 C.F.R. § 725.1(d).

either does not meet the criteria for an exemption, or chooses not to follow the exemption mandates, may submit a TERA. A TERA enables the filer to perform specific research and development steps, but does not authorize the filer to proceed beyond the research and development stage. A TERA does not culminate in Inventory listing of the microorganism; if the filer wishes to proceed beyond research and development it must file an MCAN.[46]

In 2007 the EPA received just one TERA.[47] Since the inception of the microorganism rules in 1997 a total of only 46 TERAs have been approved.[48]

A TERA must be filed at least sixty days before the research and development begins.[49] The EPA will either approve the TERA, with or without imposing conditions, or reject it. A TERA must include details of the planned R&D; information on confinement, mitigation, and emergency termination;[50] and health and environmental effects data in the submitter's possession or control.[51] The EPA has sixty days to review a TERA, but the submitter may not proceed without written authorization from the EPA.[52]

IV. Enforcement

Because the microorganism regulations were issued under TSCA § 5, the Enforcement Response Policy (ERP) for § 5 applies to any violation of the microorganism rules governing MCANs and TERAs. Violations of the substantial risk reporting provisions of TSCA and the import and export regulations would be penalized under the ERP for §§ 8, 12 and 13. Similarly, each type of violation would be penalized under the corresponding ERP applicable to traditional chemicals.

No reported decisions have been found concerning violations of TSCA relating to microorganisms.

---

46. 40 C.F.R. § 725.1(c) and (d).
47. http://www.epa.gov/oppt/ar/2007-2009/reviewnewchem/newbiotech.htm.
48. Data available through http://www.epa.gov/biotech_rule/pubs/submain.htm.
49. 40 C.F.R. § 725.250.
50. 40 C.F.R. § 725.255.
51. 40 C.F.R. § 725.260.
52. 40 C.F.R. § 725.270.

CHAPTER
7

Reporting and Recordkeeping

I. Introduction

In the Toxic Substances Control Act (TSCA)[1] Congress made a finding that "adequate data should be developed with respect to the effect of chemical substances and mixtures on health and the environment."[2] When it drafted the reporting and recordkeeping requirements in TSCA § 8, Congress implemented that finding by establishing reporting and recordkeeping requirements applicable to manufacturers, importers, processors, and distributors.

The provisions of TSCA § 8 require reporting information to the United States Environmental Protection Agency (EPA) about production of chemicals, studies showing significant adverse effects, and health and safety studies. They also require maintaining records of allegations of significant adverse effects. The major recordkeeping and reporting requirements in TSCA § 8 are:

- TSCA § 8(a) authorizes EPA to promulgate rules requiring manufacturers and importers of certain chemical substances and mixtures to maintain records and submit reports of production volumes, distribution, use, and human exposure under the Preliminary Assessment Information Rule (PAIR) and Inventory Update Reporting (IUR) Rule;
- TSCA § 8(c) requires that any person who manufactures, processes, or distributes in commerce any chemical substance or mixture maintain records of "significant adverse reactions to health or the environment;" the recordkeeping obligation extends to mere allegations made without formal proof or regard for evidence;
- TSCA § 8(d) authorizes EPA to promulgate rules requiring manufacturers, importers, and processors to submit lists of health and safety studies in their possession, known to them, or initiated on specific chemicals substances; and
- TSCA § 8(e) requires that any person who manufactures, processes, or distributes in commerce a chemical substance or mixture immediately inform the EPA of information that reasonably supports the conclusion that such substance or mixture presents a substantial risk of injury to health or the environment.

TSCA § 8(b) requires the EPA to keep the TSCA Inventory of existing chemicals because it directs EPA to "compile, keep current, and publish a list of each chemical substance which is manufactured or processed in the United States." This mandate is one of the central features of TSCA.[3]

1. 15 U.S.C. §§ 2601–2695d.
2. TSCA § 2(b)(1); 15 U.S.C. § 2601(b)(1).
3. *See* Chapter 3, The Inventory.

There are numerous other recordkeeping and reporting requirements in addition to the requirements in TSCA § 8. For example, the asbestos program[4] has extensive recordkeeping requirements, as does the lead program.[5] As another example, chemical manufacturers and importers have reporting and recordkeeping requirements in connection with the Premanufacture Notice (PMN) program.[6] Many of these other reporting and recordkeeping requirements concern health and safety characteristics of chemicals, and it would be a mistake to refer to the TSCA § 8 programs as the only programs requiring recordkeeping and reporting of information, including health and safety data. The common element among the TSCA § 8 programs is that they require reporting and recordkeeping without regard to other statutory authorizations, that is, the reporting and recordkeeping requirements of this section are not a prerequisite to obtaining statutory authorization to undertake some new activity. If a manufacturer, importer, or processor has the required information in its possession, it must report it to the EPA and keep the required records even if it is not seeking to expand its use of the subject chemical.

In practice, the mechanisms of TSCA § 8 can inform the EPA about the lifecycle of chemical substances and their health and environmental effects. Such information is used by EPA in other programs for risk assessment purposes, data gap identification, and to monitor ongoing activities. Data collection under § 8 most often occurs at the early stages of regulatory decision making. The agency is generally quite protective of its information collection program, ensuring through civil enforcement that complete and accurate information is provided by the regulated community.[7]

As with all TSCA compliance strategies, training, broadly provided throughout an organization and reinforced on a periodic basis, is essential. In addition, the development of internal systems to identify information that is germane to TSCA § 8 requirements and to channel that information to those with expertise to manage the information appropriately, is key to achieving and maintaining compliance.

---

4. *See* Chapter 16, Asbestos.
5. *See* Chapter 18, Lead.
6. Premanufacture Notices are required under TSCA § 5 before manufacturing or importing a new chemical substance. *See* Chapter 4, Premanufacture Notifications.
7. EPA's policy in assessing penalties for violation of TSCA § 8 reporting is set forth in EPA, Toxic and Pesticides Enforcement Division, Office of Regulatory Enforcement, Office of Enforcement and Compliance Assurance, Amended TSCA Enforcement Response Policy, 5 (revised Mar. 31, 1999) [hereinafter Reporting Rule ERP], *available through* http://cfpub.epa.gov/compliance/resources/policies/civil/tsca/

II. TSCA § 8(a) Reports

Pursuant to TSCA § 8(a), EPA may promulgate rules requiring companies to maintain records and to submit reports on their chemical manufacturing, importing, and processing activities. The Agency has exercised that authority in two significant rulemakings, the PAIR and the IUR, as well as in several rules that apply only to specific chemicals or chemical groups.[8]

A. The Preliminary Assessment Information Rule—PAIR

Under PAIR, manufacturers and importers of listed chemical substances are required to report a standard set of data to the EPA. The data set includes items such as the quantities manufactured or imported, whether the chemical is used on site or distributed, how much is released to the environment, and purposes to which customers put the chemical. The required data is listed on the PAIR Form, and use of the EPA's form is mandatory.[9]

The information to be included on the form is intended to gather very preliminary exposure data to permit the Agency to assess testing priorities.[10] When promulgated in 1980, PAIR was intended by EPA to be the first of a series of progressively more detailed reporting rules under TSCA § 8(a) to establish a comprehensive assessment of chemical substances.[11]

A separate PAIR form must be completed for each chemical and each site where a listed chemical substance or mixture is manufactured or imported in quantities of five hundred kilograms (eleven hundred pounds) or more, unless an exemption applies.[12]

PAIR regulations anticipate the automatic inclusion of chemicals designated on a list called the Priority Testing List issued by the Interagency Testing Committee (ITC). EPA has taken the position that it can require reporting for these chemicals upon issuing a final rule in the Federal Register, and that providing notice and an opportunity to comment on additions to the list of chemicals for PAIR reporting is unnecessary.[13]

---

8. Chapter 3, The Inventory.
9. 40 C.F.R. § 712.28(a). The PAIR form is EPA Form No. 7710–35, Manufacturer's Report Preliminary Assessment Information, *available at* http://www.epa.gov/oppt/chemtest/pubs/pairform.pdf.
10. *See* 45 Fed. Reg. 26992 (June 22, 1982). As stated by the Agency, "the information collected under this rule will answer a critical need for basic data that can be used in setting priorities for testing chemicals and for assessing risks associated with chemicals." *Id.*
11. *See* 45 Fed. Reg. 13646 (Feb. 29, 1980).
12. 40 C.F.R. §§ 712.25, 712.28(a).
13. 71 Fed. Reg. 47122, 47123 (Aug. 16, 2006); 66 Fed. Reg. 38955, 38956 (July 26, 2001).

1. Persons Covered/Exemptions

At the time a chemical substance is listed for PAIR reporting through publication in the Federal Register, each manufacturer and importer of the chemical substance for commercial purposes in bulk form must report information from the complete corporate fiscal year preceding the listing.[14] There are several significant exemptions.[15] These are:

- a research and development exemption for anyone who manufactured or imported the chemical substances during the reporting period solely for scientific experimentation, analysis, or research;
- a small production/import exemption for anyone who during the reporting period manufactured or imported less than five hundred kilograms (eleven hundred pounds) of the chemical substance at a single plant site;
- a small manufacturer/importer exemption for anyone who qualifies as a small manufacturer or importer, defined as entities with total annual sales below $30,000,000 for all sites owned or controlled by the foreign or domestic parent company and with total production of the listed chemical substance at a single plant site below 45,400 kilograms (100,000 pounds) for the reporting period, however, chemicals can be marked with an asterisk in the PAIR regulations and then this exemption is inapplicable;
- byproducts;
- non-isolated intermediates; and
- impurities.

Processors generally are not subject to PAIR reporting as the Agency believes that its data needs regarding processor activities may be met by information reported by manufacturers and importers.

2. Chemicals Subject to PAIR Reporting/Lists and Reporting Periods

Chemical substances, mixtures, or in some instances, categories of substances, that have been or are subject to PAIR reporting are identified in 40 C.F.R. § 712.30. The list is expanded in two ways. Chemicals identified by the ITC in its biannual recommendations of chemicals for priority testing under TSCA § 4 are required to be added to the PAIR list.[16] In addition to reacting to ITC recommendation or designation of priority testing chemicals, EPA may

14. 40 C.F.R. § 712.20.
15. 40 C.F.R. § 712.25.
16. 40 C.F.R. § 712.30(c).

separately designate chemicals as subject to PAIR.[17] The EPA did not issue any PAIR rules between August 2006 and October 2009.[18]

Importers are required only to report on listed chemicals imported "in bulk form." This is defined as the importation of a chemical substance in any quantity, in cans, bottles, drums, barrels, packages, tanks, bags, or other containers used for purposes of transportation or containment, if the chemical substance has an end use or commercial purpose separate from the container.[19] Importers in bulk need not report on listed chemicals in mixtures or articles, as those terms are defined in TSCA. Nevertheless, the Agency requires that "importers ... report chemical substances imported in bulk in any grade of purity, in aqueous solution, or containing additives (such as stabilizers or other chemicals) to maintain the integrity or physical form of the substance."[20]

3. Information to Be Reported/Form and Instructions

Manufacturers and importers subject to PAIR reporting must complete and submit a two page PAIR Form for each chemical at each site at which a listed chemical was manufactured or imported, although the reporting company may decide whether to have headquarters or each plant site complete and submit the forms.[21] The report must be submitted by the date specified in the regulation for the particular chemical.[22] The information submitted must cover the respondent's latest complete corporate fiscal year as of the effective date of the rulemaking listing the chemical substance.[23] There is no continuing obligation to report or update information submitted.

Part A of the PAIR Form solicits information regarding plant site activities, including total quantities manufactured or imported of a chemical substance, routine quantities lost through emissions or waste, whether processes are enclosed, controlled, or open, and details regarding use of the chemical substance on site and possible worker exposure. Part B of the PAIR Form seeks information regarding the use and processing of the chemical substance by downstream customers, including consumer and industrial markets, quantities produced for export, market names, and nature of processes

17. 40 C.F.R. § 712.30(b).
18. 71 Fed. Reg. 47122 (Aug. 16, 2006). The authors' search did not reveal subsequent rules.
19. 40 C.F.R. § 712.3.
20. 47 Fed. Reg. 26992 (June 22, 1982). *See also* 40 C.F.R. § 712.5(c), requiring that chemical substances in any grade of purity, in aqueous solutions and those containing an additive to maintain integrity or physical form must be reported as the chemical substance and not as mixtures.
21. 40 C.F.R. § 712.30(d).
22. 40 C.F.R. § 712.30.
23. 40 C.F.R. § 712.30(a)(2).

(i.e., controlled or open). The regulations only require submission of readily obtainable information concerning downstream customers.[24]

In reporting information, the respondent is required to provide numbers that represent its best estimate based on readily available data. Exact numbers, therefore, are not required and EPA's assessment has been that permitting estimates to be reported will provide data sufficient for the purposes of the rule and make reporting easier. In some areas, such as the estimate of manufacturing losses, the respondent is required to specify the estimated accuracy of the quantities reported. Concerning the accuracy of reporting customer activities, the Form requires estimates of quantities by customer use only within a +/—50 percent accuracy. Where a respondent cannot report within +/—5 percent, or where a secrecy agreement with a customer forecloses disclosure, the respondent may report "unknown."

The technical accuracy of the report, and if a claim is made, the confidentiality of information, must be certified by the respondent. As is common in TSCA reporting, a technical contact familiar with the information submitted must be identified.

B. Other Chemical Specific Rules

There are several data gathering rules that were initially issued during the 1980s on a chemical specific basis instead of as PAIR rules, and which have continuing viability. They require submission of data by manufacturers or importers, or people who intend to manufacture or import 11-aminoundecanoic acid, p-tert-butylbenzoic acid, p-tert-butyltoluene, p-tert-butylbenzaldehyde, chlorinated naphthalenes, chlorinated terphenyl, phosphonic acid [1,2-ethanediyl-bis[nitrilobis-(methylene)]], tetrakis—or its salts, hexachloronorbornadiene, hexafluoropropylene oxide, or 4,4′-methylenebis(2-chloroaniline).[25] Some of the rules require submission of notices on specified uses of the substances, and some require submission of data, including full or partial PMNs. Any person who intends to manufacture or import one of these substances must notify the EPA in accordance with the specific rule.

C. Comprehensive Assessment Information Rule—CAIR

EPA's Comprehensive Assessment Information Rule (CAIR) adopted by Final Rule in 1988[26] was intended to standardize TSCA § 8(a) rules by

24. 40 C.F.R. § 712.2.
25. These rules are collected in 40 C.F.R. § 704.
26. *See* 53 Fed. Reg. 51698 (Dec. 22, 1988).

providing a set of uniform questions for EPA and other agencies to use in assembling specific reporting requirements, and establishing uniform reporting and recordkeeping provisions. Following the Agency's first use of CAIR in 1989, an industry challenge resulted in a stay of the effectiveness of the regulation pending EPA amendments. Although amendments were proposed in 1993, they were never finalized and the Agency has stated that it "does not anticipate taking action for some time as it reassesses its TSCA information needs."[27] In 1995, the CAIR rule was formally withdrawn by the Agency and deleted from the Code of Federal Regulations.[28]

D. Practical Implications

There are several different ways to ensure compliance with the requirements of § 8(a), depending on the organization and its technical sophistication. Nevertheless, one critical and overriding aspect of managing compliance with § 8(a) is to ensure receipt in a timely fashion of rules promulgated pursuant to § 8(a). The "manual," yet simplest, way of doing this is to assign someone to monitor the Federal Register to see if chemicals manufactured or imported by the company show up on the PAIR list. This responsibility is typically assigned to someone in the regulatory department, or someone who has obligations for regulatory compliance, in addition to other responsibilities. The electronic way of doing this is to license software that maintains and updates lists of these chemicals on a regular real time basis and that can be connected to production data bases to look for matches. Whether manual or automatic, a system to ensure companies are made aware of additions to the PAIR list is mandatory for manufacturers and importers.

It is almost too obvious to state that companies should be aware of chemical substances that they manufacture or import, but in fact this is often not the case, and is where a compliance problem arises. The regulatory requirements are typically published by chemical name and Chemical Abstracts Service (CAS) Number, whereas in many companies trade names are more commonly used when tracking chemicals. The Material Safety Data Sheet (MSDS)[29] system most often is the easiest place to determine whether a product or an isolated intermediate contains a component that is subject to regulation. With respect to imports, they should be cleared by a regulatory review prior to importation not only for general TSCA compliance, but also to ascertain whether or not there are any TSCA reporting requirements under TSCA

27. 60 Fed. Reg. 31917 (June 19, 1995).

28. *See Id.*

29. *See* the Hazard Communication Standard regulations at 29 C.F.R. § 1910.1200, issued under the Occupational Safety and Health Act, for a discussion of Material Safety Data Sheets.

§ 8(a). Once an import is cleared, regulatory personnel should ensure that the import, by component, is maintained on a list or database that can be cross checked when new regulations are published. With respect to imports that are claimed confidential, companies should have an ongoing procedure to obtain Inventory and compliance certifications from the supplier to determine if there are components subject to TSCA § 8(a) reporting. The certification process is more likely to be effective in providing relevant information to the importer if the importer provides a list of regulated substances to check against, as opposed to asking for a blanket certification.

Once it is established that a product that is either imported into or made in the United States contains a regulated component, the information required by the PAIR rule must be assembled. To complete Part A of the PAIR Form, data must be gathered from the import and manufacturing functions. To complete Part B of the form, data must be gathered from marketing and sales functions that have access to information concerning downstream uses.

III. TSCA § 8(c) Recordkeeping—Allegations of Significant Adverse Reactions

TSCA § 8(c) requires that any person who manufactures, processes, or distributes in commerce any chemical substance or mixture must maintain records of "significant adverse reactions" to health and the environment. Such allegations do not have to be disclosed or reported to EPA unless the Agency requests them. Allegations made by employees, i.e., those allegations that relate to occupational exposure, must be maintained for thirty years. All other allegations must be maintained for five years.

The statute provides:

> Any person who manufactures, processes, or distributes in commerce any chemical substance or mixture shall maintain records of significant adverse reactions to health or the environment, as determined by the Administrator by rule, alleged to have been caused by the substance or mixture. ... Records required to be maintained under this subsection shall include records of consumer allegations of personal injury or harm to health, reports of occupational disease or injury, and reports or complaints of injury to the environment submitted to the manufacturer, processor, or distributor in commerce from any source.[30]

---

30. TSCA § 8(c).

The recordkeeping obligation of TSCA § 8(c) provides a means to identify previously unknown chemical hazards by revealing patterns of adverse effects that might otherwise go undetected.[31]

A. Persons Subject/Exemptions

Manufacturers, importers, and some processors and distributors are subject to TSCA § 8(c). The statutory language broadly applies TSCA § 8(c) to all manufacturers, processors, and distributors of a chemical substance, and importers are also included because the term "manufacture" is defined in the TSCA statute to include "import."[32] EPA's regulations implementing this subsection create several exemptions to the statute's broad scope of coverage. Distributors who do not also manufacture or process the chemical substances are defined as "sole distributors" and are exempt.[33] Retailers are also exempt provided that they distribute to ultimate customers that are not commercial entities and provided that they do not also manufacture or process the subject chemicals.[34]

The regulations do not explicitly exempt some of the activities that are considered processing under other TSCA programs, but the effect of the regulations is to exempt all processors other than those who repackage or make mixtures. The 8(c) regulations state that they apply to processors if "(i) the person processes chemical substances to produce mixtures (including solutions[35]), or (ii) the person repackages chemical substances or mixtures."[36] This excludes processors who use chemicals without processing them, and processors who prepare chemicals for distribution as part of an article.[37] However, these activities, which do not trigger TSCA § 8(c) obligations, are considered to be processing for the purpose of other TSCA regulations; use as an intermediate is defined as processing in the test rule regulations promulgated under TSCA § 4, and preparation of a substance for distribution as part of an article is defined as processing in TSCA § 3 (10).[38] In its preamble to the final rule, the EPA acknowledged that it was excluding processors who prepare a substance as part of an article, and noted that if it did not have such an

31. 48 Fed. Reg. 38178 (Aug. 22, 1983).
32. TSCA § 3(7).
33. 40 C.F.R. § 717.7(c).
34. 40 C.F.R. §§ 717.3(h) and 717.7(d).
35. 50 Fed. Reg. 46766, 46768 (Nov. 13, 1985).
36. 40 C.F.R. § 717.5(b).
37. While there may not be TSCA obligations to record such allegations, other statutes may mandate recording and reporting.
38. *See* Chapter 2, TSCA's Scope.

exclusion even shoemakers who apply dye to shoes would be within the scope of the 8(c) rule.[39]

A manufacturer or importer must keep records under TSCA § 8(c) if it owns or controls 50 percent or more of the voting stock or equity, or otherwise has the power to control the management and policies, of any site that makes or imports the relevant substance.[40] In this regard, the manufacture or import of a chemical substance at any site directly owned or controlled by the corporate entity or indirectly by a controlled subsidiary suffices to subject the entirety of that entity to the TSCA § 8(c) rule and the obligation to maintain records for that substance. In guidance interpreting the rule, the EPA said that if a company owns two subsidiaries, one of which manufactures a substance and the other of which processes it, the company is required to comply with the TSCA § 8(c) rules as a manufacturer, and must collect any allegations received by its processing subsidiary.[41]

EPA states in guidance that allegations received by a foreign subsidiary of a U.S. parent company are considered to be received by the U.S. parent company, and must be recorded.[42] The regulations do not impose a similar requirement on processors.

With regard to U.S. subsidiaries of foreign parents, the recordkeeping obligation does not extend to the foreign parent and the EPA cannot require the foreign parent to keep records. However, when a foreign subsidiary of a U.S parent receives allegations, the EPA considers the allegation to have been received by the U.S. parent company, and the U.S. parent is responsible for recording allegations arising from the foreign subsidiary.[43]

A manufacturer, or certain activities of a manufacturer, are exempt from TSCA § 8(c) if the sole means of manufacture of a chemical substance involves mining or other extractive functions.[44] Extractive functions include mining ores, extracting petroleum or natural gas, quarrying non-metallic minerals, mine or otherwise extracting coal, or separating gases from the atmosphere. Note, however, that the exemption applies only to the initial extractive process. Further processing or refinement is considered manufacturing subject to this rule.[45]

---

39. 48 Fed. Reg. 38178, 38183 (Aug. 22, 1983).
40. 40 C.F.R. § 717.5(a). In the case of a company that is owned equally by two other companies, both have obligations to direct the EPA to recordable information. 50 Fed. Reg. 46766, 46768 (Nov. 13, 1985).
41. EPA, TSCA Section 8(c) Final Rule Questions and Answers, 2 (Nov. 1983) [hereinafter 1983 8(c) QA].
42. EPA, Office of Toxic Substances, Questions and Answers Concerning the TSCA Section 8(c) Rule, 20 (July 1984). [hereinafter 1984 8(c) QA].
43. 1984 8(c) QA, 20.
44. 40 C.F.R. § 717.7(a)(1).
45. As an example, EPA responded to a question by stating that smelting is a form of manufacturing. 1983 8(c) QA, 9.

In addition, a person who uses a substance is exempt from TSCA § 8(c) recordkeeping if the allegation concerns:

- "[c]hemical substances that result from chemical reactions that occur incidental to exposure of another chemical substance, mixture or article to environmental factors such as air, moisture, microbial organisms, or sunlight;"
- "[c]hemical substances that result from chemical reactions that occur incidental to storage or disposal or other chemical substances, mixtures or articles;"
- "[c]hemical substances that result from chemical reactions that occur upon end use of other chemical substances, mixtures, or articles such as adhesives, paints, miscellaneous cleaners or other housekeeping products, fuel additives, water softening and treatment agents, photographic film, batteries, matches, or safety flares, and that are not themselves manufactured or imported for distribution in commerce for use as chemical intermediates;"
- "[c]hemical substances that result from chemical reactions that occur upon the use of curable plastic or rubber molding compounds, inks, drying oils, metal finishing compounds, adhesives, or paints, or other chemical substance formed during the manufacture of an article destined for the marketplace without further chemical change of the chemical substance; and"
- "[c]hemical substances that result from chemical reactions that occur when (A) a stabilizer, colorant, odorant, antioxidant, filler, solvent, carrier, surfactant, plasticizer, corrosion inhibitor, antifoamer or defoamer, dispersant, precipitation-inhibitor, binder, emulsifier, deemulsifier, dewatering agent, agglomerating agent, adhesion promoter, flow modifier, pH adjuster, sequestrant, coagulant, flocculent, fire retardant, lubricant, chelating agent, or quality control reagent functions as intended, or (B) a chemical substance which is intended solely to impart a specific physiochemical characteristic, functions as intended."[46]

Such chemical specific exemptions were adopted consistent with EPA's view that simply using a chemical substance does not render a person subject to TSCA § 8(c).[47] However, the person who manufactures or imports the chemical that is used and undergoes further incidental reaction is responsible for recordkeeping under TSCA § 8(c). The regulations make this clear when they state that manufacturers and importers must keep records of

---

46. 40 C.F.R. § 717.7(a)(2). These exemptions from the TSCA § 8(c) regulations are also exemptions from the Premanufacture Notice regulations in TSCA § 5, with very minor changes.
47. 1983 8(c) QA, 4.

"[a]ny allegation identifying a substance produced coincidentally during processing, use, storage or disposal of a chemical substance it manufactures."[48] This language in the regulations was intended to clarify that the rule's obligations fall primarily on those "responsible for making and distributing chemical products in U.S. commerce"[49] instead of exempting incidentally produced chemicals entirely.[50]

Companies that engage in covered manufacturing, importing, or processing must keep records that are received by their distribution subsidiaries. For example, a gasoline manufacturer must record allegations received by its subsidiary that owns retail gas stations.[51]

There are no exemptions for small manufacturers, importers, or processors.[52] There are also no exemptions for research and development substances.[53]

B. Chemicals Covered

The recordkeeping obligations under TSCA § 8(c) generally apply to all chemical substances regulated under TSCA provided they are not produced by an exempt process or person. This is in contrast to TSCA § 8(a), which is limited to chemicals identified by EPA and listed in a rulemaking.

The chemicals that are excluded from the definition of "chemical substance" are also excluded from the provisions of TSCA § 8(c). These include pesticides, tobacco, nuclear material, firearms, foods, drugs, cosmetics, and medical devices.[54] All effluents, emissions, and discharges from manufacturing and processing facilities, including pharmaceutical and pesticide manufacturers,[55] are subject to TSCA and otherwise qualifying allegations concerning them must be recorded.[56]

A company is not responsible for keeping allegations concerning a chemical substance it does not manufacture, import, or process.

---

48. 40 C.F.R. § 717.5(a)(2)(iv).
49. 50 Fed. Reg. 46766, 46767 (Nov. 13, 1985).
50. *Id.* at 46769.
51. 1983 8(c) QA, 6-7; 1984 8(c) QA, 20.
52. 1984 8(c) QA, 6.
53. *Id.* at 39, 41.
54. *See* Chapter 2, TSCA's Scope for a discussion of the exclusions from the definition of "chemical substance."
55. 1984 8(c) QA, 38.
56. 40 C.F.R. § 717.5.

C. Allegations Subject to Recordkeeping

Persons subject to TSCA § 8(c) must record and maintain allegations of significant adverse health or environmental effects.[57] Allegations may be nothing more than an assertion without supporting facts or proof, and are recordable even if the results of an investigation reveal that that party making the allegation could not have been exposed. Allegations subject to recordkeeping include those submitted in writing and signed by the alleger, and those that are made orally. In the case of an oral allegation, the company either must transcribe the allegation into a written form for recordkeeping, or it must inform the alleger that such allegation may be subject to recordkeeping requirements and request that the alleger submit such allegation to the company in writing and signed.[58] If the alleger fails to respond to a company request that an oral request be made in writing, no further action is necessary. An allegation subject to recording and recordkeeping may be made by any person on that person's own behalf, or on behalf of others.[59]

An "allegation" is defined as "a statement, made without formal proof or regard for evidence, that a chemical substance or mixture has caused a significant adverse reaction to health or the environment."[60] In turn, the phrase "significant adverse reactions" is defined as "reactions that may indicate a substantial impairment of normal activities, or long-lasting or irreversible damage to health or the environment."[61]

The allegation must identify one or more of the following as the cause of an adverse effect:

- a specific substance;
- a mixture or article in which a specific substance is contained;
- a specific company process or operation; or
- an effluent, emission, or other discharge from a manufacturing, processing or distribution site.[62]

Common sources of § 8(c) allegations are worker compensation claims, lawsuits, complaints by neighbors, employee or union complaints, and communications with medical staff. They may arise as well in plant community activities, product stewardship, and customer communications.

57. 40 C.F.R. § 717.10.
58. 40 C.F.R. § 717.10(b)(1).
59. 40 C.F.R. § 717.10(c).
60. 40 C.F.R. § 717.3(a).
61. 40 C.F.R. § 717.3(i).
62. 40 C.F.R. § 717.10(b)(2).

The regulations set forth several examples of significant adverse effects to human health or the environment, including:

- "[l]ong-lasting or irreversible damage to human health such as cancer or birth defects;"
- "[p]artial or complete impairment of bodily functions, such as reproductive disorders, neurological disorders or blood disorders;"
- "impairment of normal activities experienced by all or most of the persons exposed at one time;"
- "impairment of normal activities which is experienced each time an individual is exposed;"
- "[g]radual or sudden changes in the composition of animal or plant life, including fungal or microbial organisms, in an area;"
- "[a]bnormal number of deaths of organisms (e.g., fish kills);"
- "[r]eduction of the reproductive success or the vigor of a species;"
- "[r]eduction in agricultural productivity, whether crops or livestock;"
- "[a]lterations in the behavior or distribution of a species; and"
- "[l]ong lasting or irreversible contamination of components of the physical environment, especially in the case of ground water, and surface water and soil resources that have limited self-cleansing capability."[63]

The above is not an exhaustive list.

Companies are not required to record significant adverse reactions that are "known human effects," defined as commonly recognized human health effects of a particular substance or mixture as described in scientific articles or publication abstracts in standard reference sources or the firm's product labeling or MSDS. This exemption, however, does not apply if the effect was significantly more severe than previously described, was manifested after a significantly shorter exposure period or lower exposure level, or was manifested by an exposure route different from that described.[64] As an illustration, the EPA gave a hypothetical of a worker who writes that when working with chemical X he has experienced tingling fingers and nausea at exposure levels that do not exceed twenty parts per million (ppm). Although the reported reaction is a "known human effect," because the literature documents the effect solely at the higher exposure level of 100 ppm, the allegation of significant adverse effect at the much lower exposure level is recordable.[65]

Significant adverse environmental reactions are not recordable if the reaction can be directly attributable to an accidental spill or other accidental

63. 40 C.F.R. § 717.12.

64. 40 C.F.R. § 717.12(b); 40 C.F.R. § 717.3(c).

65. 48 Fed. Reg. 38178, 38181 (Aug. 22, 1983). The initial 1983 rulemaking contains this and other useful hypothetical illustrations illustrating TSCA § 8(c) recordkeeping requirements.

discharge, emission exceeding permitted limits, or other incident of environmental contamination that has been reported to the federal government.[66]

D. Recordkeeping Requirements

The essence of TSCA § 8(c) is recordkeeping and a firm subject to the requirements of this rule is required to establish and maintain records of significant adverse reactions alleged to have been caused by chemical substances or mixtures manufactured or processed by the firm. All records are to be maintained together[67] at the firm's headquarters or any such other appropriate location central to the firm's chemical operations.[68]

The following information must be readily accessible as the allegation record:

- "[t]he original allegation as received;"
- "[a]n abstract of the allegation and other pertinent information as follows:
  - [t]he name and address of the plant site that received the allegation;
  - [t]he date the allegation was received at that site;
  - [t]he implicated substance, mixture, article, company process or operation, or site discharge;
  - [a] description of the alleger (e.g., company employee, individual consumer, plant neighbor). If the allegation involves a health effect, the sex and year of birth of the individual, if ascertainable;
  - [a] description of the alleged health effect(s). The description must relate how the effect(s) became known and the route of exposure, if explained in the allegation;
  - [a] description of the nature of the alleged environmental effect(s), identifying the affected plant and/or animal species, or contaminated portion of the physical environment; and
  - [t]he results of any self-initiated investigation with respect to an allegation."

As early as 1984 the EPA anticipated privacy concerns in allegations that are made during medical examinations. The EPA said that "when reporting is

---

66. 40 C.F.R. § 717.12(d).
67. 1984 8(c) QA, 20.
68. 40 C.F.R. § 717.15(a). EPA said in 1984 that keeping 8(c) records in a computerized database does not satisfy recordkeeping requirements, and the original or microfiche copy must be retained. 1984 8(c) QA, 16. However, the statement that a microfiche copy is acceptable appears to open the possibility of retaining a scanned copy on a computer system in lieu of keeping paper copies or originals.

required the alleger's identity will most likely not be part of the abstract of the allegation that would be reported to EPA."[69] This statement gives companies enough flexibility to withhold information to protect personal privacy consistent with more recently enacted laws.

The results of any self initiated investigation about the allegation must be included, although EPA expressly acknowledges that it does not require, recommend, or even encourage that such investigation take place. The EPA does encourage companies to tell the person making the allegation how the allegation was resolved.[70]

If other reports and records are required by any other law, such as the Occupational Safety and Health Act, those reports and records must be retained with the TSCA § 8(c) record. The rule further specifies that allegation must be filed in a manner such that records are retrievable according to chemical identity, mixture identity, article identity, company process or operation, or site effluent, emission, or other discharge.[71]

Records of significant adverse reaction to the health of employees must be retained for a period of thirty years from the date such reaction was first reported to or known by the person maintaining such records.[72] An allegation made to a chemical manufacturer A from firm B regarding an employment related exposure at firm B must be maintained by the manufacturer A for thirty years.

All other allegations, i.e., not related to occupational exposure, must be retained for five years.[73]

If a firm ceases to do business, the successor is required to receive and keep all the TSCA § 8(c) records of the predecessor. If there is no successor to a firm that has ceased to do business, the firm is required to transmit the records to EPA.[74]

E. Inspections and Reporting

EPA may request TSCA § 8(c) records at inspection. Generally, it will do so to determine whether a company possesses an awareness of its recordkeeping obligations and to assess the quality of the company's system to ensure allegations are forwarded to its central location for recordkeeping.

In addition, EPA may request submission of TSCA § 8(c) records by notice in the Federal Register. In such instances, the reporting period will be

---

69. 1984 8(c) QA, 4, 15.
70. *Id.* at 18.
71. 40 C.F.R. § 717.15(c).
72. 40 C.F.R. § 717.15(d).
73. *Id.*
74. 40 C.F.R. § 717.15(e).

specified in the notice but in no case will such reporting period be less than 45 days from the effective date of the notice. The Agency rarely has exercised its authority to request submission through notice in the Federal Register. It did so in 1987 when it requested records and reports regarding significant adverse reactions to chlorendic acid (CAS No. 115-28-6) and chlorendic anhydride (CAS No. 115-27-5)[75] and again in 1988 with regard to a number of chemical substances within the categories of tri(alkyl/alkoxy)phosphates and diisocyanates.[76]

A person required to submit copies of TSCA § 8(c) records may request that all or a part of the information be treated as business confidential. If no claim is made at the time the records are submitted to EPA, the records will be placed in an open file available to the public without further notice. To make a claim of confidentiality, two versions of each document must be submitted. One copy must be complete with information claimed confidential marked "confidential," "proprietary," or "trade secret" and accompanied with a brief statement of the basis of such claim. The second version must be complete except with the claimed confidential information redacted.[77]

F. Practical Implications

Even if there were no TSCA requirement to record allegations of significant adverse effects, there is a business value in maintaining a robust system to track, investigate, and analyze these allegations. Recording adverse effects makes it easier to recognize when a pattern is established. Tracing the root cause of any pattern may provide useful information for improving MSDSs, labels, personal protective equipment, waste disposal practices, and effluent controls, and in turn these actions may prevent or minimize product liability and workers' compensation claims.

Additionally, if there are classes of chemistry about which there tend to be more allegations than others, this might be information of value to company research efforts. To the extent the sources of problems can be identified and removed from new products, the more attractive those new products will be.

Procedures should be put in place to ensure that recordable information reaches the appropriate people who are responsible for maintaining 8(c) records. Lawyers may receive allegations in tort complaints,[78] nurses may receive oral allegations during examinations and while providing first aid, sales representatives may receive allegations during sales visits, and customer

75. 52 Fed. Reg. 48321 (Dec. 21, 1987).
76. 53 Fed. Reg. 1408 (Jan. 19, 1988).
77. 40 C.F.R. § 717.19.
78. 1984 8(c) QA, 23.

service people may receive allegations in the guise of complaints about product performance. All these are potential sources of allegations that products, raw materials, intermediates, impurities, wastes, or processes may cause adverse effects to humans or the environment. Once these sources are identified, each employee in a position likely to get this type of information must be trained to recognize 8(c) information and to transmit that information to the person responsible for recording the allegations. From an operational perspective it is better to train employees to route all allegations to the person designated by the company to keep § 8(c) records than to try to train people on all of the nuances of recording.

A recordable allegation, or a pattern of recordable allegations may rise to the level of "reasonable support for the conclusion that a substance poses a substantial risk to health or the environment," which must be submitted to the EPA under TSCA § 8(e).[79] Therefore, each time an allegation is recorded the prior allegations should be reviewed to determine if a pattern of recordable allegations has been established, and the pattern should be reviewed for 8(e) reportability.

Employees who make allegations subject to recording may not be retaliated against for having done so.[80]

IV. TSCA § 8(d) Health and Safety Data Reporting

TSCA § 8(d) requires the EPA to promulgate rules requiring manufacturers, importers, processors, and distributors to submit lists and copies of unpublished health and safety studies on specified chemicals or mixtures. Those studies must be listed or submitted if they were conducted or initiated by or for the manufacturer, importer, processor, or distributor, known to such person, or reasonably ascertainable by such person. The intent of the regulations is to give EPA information to determine the need to issue test rules under TSCA § 4, restrictions on use under TSCA § 5, or prohibitions on the manufacture, use or distribution pursuant to TSCA § 6 on the basis that the chemical substance or mixture presents an unreasonable risk of harm to human health or the environment.

The obligations under TSCA § 8(d) are not self implementing; they are triggered only when the EPA promulgates a rule identifying chemicals and then the regulated industry must list or submit studies on those chemicals.

79. 50 Fed. Reg. 46766, 46768–69 (Nov. 13, 1985).
80. TSCA § 23; 1984 8(c) QA, 23.

In this regard the obligation to submit information to the EPA is similar to TSCA § 8(a) rules.

A. Persons Subject/Exemptions

The reporting obligations of TSCA § 8(d) apply to manufacturers, including importers, who fall within the North American Industry Classification System (NAICS) subsector 325 (chemical manufacturing and allied products) or Industry Group 32411 (petroleum refineries) to the extent such manufacturer or importer:

- in the ten years preceding the rulemaking listing the chemical substance or mixture, either proposed to manufacture or import, or had manufactured or imported the substance or mixture, including as a known byproduct; or
- as of the effective date on which the chemical substance or mixture is listed, proposed to manufacture or import or are manufacturing or importing the listed substance or mixture; or
- after the effective date on which the chemical substance or mixture is listed, propose to manufacture or import the listed substance or mixture during the reporting period.[81]

Processors are not otherwise subject to the reporting requirements of TSCA § 8(d) unless EPA states specifically that processors should report in a Federal Register notice or rule promulgation.[82]

TSCA § 8(d) is retroactive in its application such that a company that manufactured or imported a listed substances anytime within the ten years preceding the rulemaking listing the chemical must report.

B. Chemicals Covered

Chemical substances and mixture subject to TSCA § 8(d) reporting are identified in the Federal Register.[83] Chemicals that are designated or recommended for testing by the ITC may be added to the rule through immediate

81. 40 C.F.R. § 716.5. In 1998, EPA narrowed the scope of persons subject to TSCA § 8(d) reporting to generally exclude processors as part of regulatory reform, concluding that narrowing the scope of persons covered would have but a negligible impact on the type and comprehensiveness of information submitted. 63 Fed. Reg. 15765 (Apr. 1, 1998).

82. *Id.*

83. 40 C.F.R. § 716.120.

final rulemaking (up to fifty chemicals per year). Non-ITC chemicals can be added to the § 8(d) rule through notice and comment rulemaking.[84]

Once a chemical substance or mixture is added to the rule, the reporting period typically terminates sixty days after the effective date of the listing.[85]

Importers who bring chemicals into the United States as part of articles are subject to TSCA § 8(d) reporting rules. The 8(d) rules apply to "importers"[86] and the definition of "importer" includes any person who brings a chemical substance into the U.S. as part of a mixture or an article.[87] The EPA's call for health and safety data on lead in children's toys[88] is an example of an § 8(d) rule that clearly is intended to include importers of chemical substances in articles. In the preamble to that rule, the EPA said:

> The import of children's products that contain lead or lead compounds constitutes the manufacture of lead or lead compounds under TSCA. EPA believes importers of such products are the entities most likely to have the type of health and safety studies EPA is seeking.[89]

Manufacturers and importers of research and development chemicals are subject to § 8(d) rules.[90]

C. Information to Be Reported

Pursuant to the 1998 amendments to its rule, EPA will specify the types of health and safety data requested in its rulemaking as well as the chemical grade and purity of the chemical substance for which reporting is required.[91] If the manufacturer or importer possesses a copy of a study, it must submit it. If the manufacturer or importer has knowledge of a study but not a copy, it must identify the study in a list submitted to EPA.[92] The Agency has defined "health and safety study" broadly to include:

> any study of any effect of a chemical substance or mixture on health or the environment or on both, including underlying data and epidemiological studies,

---

84. 40 C.F.R. § 716.105.
85. 40 C.F.R. § 716.65.
86. 40 C.F.R. § 716.5.
87. 40 C.F.R. § 716.3.
88. 40 C.F.R. § 716.21(a)(8).
89. 73 Fed. Reg. 5109, 5110–11 (Jan. 29, 2008).
90. Dow Chemical Co. v. EPA, 605 F.2d 673 (3rd Cir. 1979).
91. 40 C.F.R. § 716.20(b)(5); 63 Fed. Reg. 15765, 15766 (Apr. 1, 1998).
92. 40 C.F.R. § 716.30.

studies of occupational exposure to a chemical substance or mixture, and any test performed under TSCA.[93]

A health and safety study may comprise information that is obtained as a result of a formal, disciplined study, and also information relating to the effects of a chemical substance or mixture on health or the environment. Specific examples provided by EPA include:

- "[l]ong-and short-term tests of mutagenicity, carcinogenicity, or teratogenicity; data on behavioral disorders; dermatoxicity; pharmacological effects; mammalian absorption, distribution, metabolism, and excretion; cumulative, additive, and synergistic effects; and acute, subchronic, and chronic effects;"
- "[t]ests for ecological or other environmental effects on invertebrates, fish, or other animals, and plants, including: Acute toxicity tests, chronic toxicity tests, critical life-stage tests, behavioral tests, algal growth tests, seed germination tests, plant growth or damage tests, microbial function tests, bioconcentration or bioaccumulation tests, and model ecosystem (microcosm) studies;"
- "[a]ssessments of human and environmental exposure, including workplace exposure, and impacts of a particular chemical substance or mixture on the environment, including surveys, tests, and studies of: Biological, photochemical, and chemical degradation; structure/activity relationships; air, water and soil transport; biomagnification and bioconcentration; and chemical and physical properties ...; and"
- "[m]onitoring data, when they have been aggregated and analyzed to measure the exposure of humans or the environment to a chemical substance or mixture."[94]

EPA's position is that all unpublished health and safety studies are reportable, regardless of the objectives of developing the data.[95]

EPA identifies a number of exemptions from the § 8(d) reporting requirements. These include:

- "studies which have been published in the scientific literature";
- studies previously submitted to EPA pursuant to TSCA § 8(e), TSCA § 4, with premanufacture or significant new use notices, or submitted "for your information" in support of EPA's TSCA Existing Chemicals Program;

93. 40 C.F.R. § 716.3.
94. *Id.*
95. EPA, Question and Answer Summary, EPA Seminar on Industry Obligations under TSCA, 13 (June 10, 1986).

- studies conducted or initiated by or for another person who will report under TSCA § 8(d);
- for mixtures that are known to contain a listed chemical substance, studies of acute toxicity, eye and skin irritation, dermal sensitization, and physical and chemical properties;
- for mixtures that are known to contain a listed chemical substance, analyzed aggregations of monitoring data acquired for more than five years preceding the date the substance was listed;
- analyzed aggregations of monitoring data on mixtures when the monitoring data are not analyzed to determine the exposure or concentration level of the substance or mixture listed;
- studies on a chemical present only as an impurity, unless EPA directs otherwise;
- "studies on chemical substances or listed mixtures previously submitted by trade associations."[96]

In conducting a search of records, EPA has indicated that a person required to report may limit such search to records in the location(s) where the required information is typically kept with inquiry to those employees who are responsible for keeping such records or advising on the health and safety aspects of chemicals. Persons are not required to search for reportable information dated prior to January 1, 1977, the effective data of TSCA, unless specifically directed to do so.[97]

D. The Reporting Period

Once a substance is listed for TSCA § 8(d) reporting, existing studies are required to be reported within sixty days.[98] The ITC will review the submitted information to assess whether test data are sufficient or whether a recommendation for testing should be made. If a study is initiated within the sixty day period, notification to EPA of study initiation must be provided.[99] Upon completion of such an initiated study, the study must be submitted to the Agency within thirty days, regardless of the expiration of the initial sixty day reporting period.[100]

---

96. 40 C.F.R. § 716.20.
97. 40 C.F.R. § 716.25.
98. 40 C.F.R. § 716.65.
99. 40 C.F.R. § 716.60(b)(1).
100. 40 C.F.R. § 716.65.

E. Guidance/Management Practices

Compliance with TSCA § 8(d) is generally achieved and maintained in the same manner as TSCA §§ 8(a) and 8(c). An integral part of compliance will be to designate someone, typically in the regulatory department, to review the Federal Register on a regular basis to determine whether chemicals substances designated for TSCA § 8(d) reporting give rise to any obligations. As discussed above, this can be done using either manual or electronic systems.

A somewhat unique compliance dilemma posed by TSCA § 8(d) is that its reporting obligations are triggered not only by chemical substances or mixtures that may be currently manufactured and imported, but also those that were manufactured or imported any time in the ten years preceding the listing of the chemical substance or mixture. Generally, this information is maintained by regulatory compliance personnel, particularly those involved in OSHA hazard communication program compliance and MSDS generation.

EPA has directed that a search of records for studies may be limited "to records in the location(s) where the required information is typically kept, and to records kept by [those] who [are] responsible for keeping such record or advising the period on the health and environmental effects of chemicals."[101] This will include personnel in any corporate regulatory/toxicology department, environmental services department (regarding environment studies), plant safety, health and environmental personnel (regarding potential monitoring and industrial hygiene data), and additionally, sales and marketing, on the basis that such employees may have knowledge of studies in the possession of customers and suppliers. As with any endeavor to satisfy a regulatory information demand, the internal request disseminated among appropriate company employees for reportable information, and each employee response to such internal request, should be documented and preserved.

V. TSCA § 8(e) Substantial Risk Reporting

TSCA § 8(e) requires reporting to the EPA within thirty calendar days if people who make, import, process, or distribute chemical substances in the United States learn that those chemicals substances may pose a substantial risk of injury to health or the environment.

TSCA § 8(e) is unique and often problematic in practice because the statute is self implementing and does not require that EPA issue regulations effectuating the statutory intent. EPA has interpreted the statute only through

101. 40 C.F.R. § 716.25.

a series of formal and informal guidances published in the Federal Register, in Agency speeches, and in letters to the regulated industry. Although the Agency denies that its guidances have changed over time, they have certainly matured and addressed more and more specific fact patterns over the thirty years of TSCA's existence. In order to fully grasp the EPA's view of the substantial risk reporting requirements it is necessary to trace the history of these evolving pronouncements, a task that must be undertaken without the benefit of detailed regulations issued pursuant to notice and comment.[102]

TSCA § 8(e) is also unique among the requirements of § 8 because it requires reporting without any published notice from the EPA that reporting is required for a specific chemical. As a result, companies must have procedures in place so that reportable information is channeled to people who are responsible for reporting that information to the EPA in the required time frames, and that this is done on a continuous basis and not just when the EPA has published a notice that reporting is required. In contrast, under the remaining reporting programs in TSCA § 8, information must be submitted to the EPA triggered by an EPA rule and not triggered solely by generation of the data.

A. The Statutory Language

Section 8(e) of TSCA states in full:

> Notice to Administrator of substantial risks
>
> Any person who manufactures, processes, or distributes in commerce a chemical substance or mixture and who obtains information which reasonably supports the conclusion that such substance or mixture presents a substantial risk of injury to health or the environment shall immediately inform the Administrator of such information unless such person has actual knowledge that the Administrator has been adequately informed of such information.

The TSCA § 8(e) reporting requirement is considered by EPA to be one of the most important health and safety data reporting provisions under TSCA and has been characterized by the Agency as "an 'early warning' mechanism for keeping the Agency and others apprised of new found serious chemical hazards and/or exposures."[103] Section 8(e) is broad in scope and requires the exercise of judgment in determining the reportability of information within a

102. The Administrative Procedure Act, 5 U.S.C. § 500, requires notice to the affected public and an opportunity for the public to comment before regulations are promulgated.
103. EPA, Office of Toxic Substances, TSCA Section 8(e) Reporting Guide, 2 (June 1991) [hereinafter 1991 8(e) Guide].

narrow timeframe, no later than the thirtieth calendar day after the date such information is obtained.[104]

In general, most submissions made to EPA under TSCA § 8(e) contain toxicity data gathered during testing of commercial or research and development chemicals. However, certain types of information on exposure and environmental effects and release must also be reported.

B. EPA's Interpretative Guidances

EPA has issued numerous guidances that provide insight into the types of studies that it wants reported and generally explain the EPA's interpretation of the requirements of TSCA § 8(e). It is important to keep in mind that these are only guidances; they are not laws or regulations and they are open to revision. That means, in EPA's words, that guidance it issues "does not impose any binding requirements upon either the regulated community or the Agency" and the guidance is not "determinative" of future positions the Agency may take.[105] However, the EPA will assess penalties for failure to comply with its interpretation of the law. As a result, a decision not to report when the guidances state a study is reportable should be made only when scientifically justified and with advice of counsel.

On the other hand, where the guidances relax the statutory obligation to report, a company that does not report does so at peril of violating the statute because the guidances are not binding interpretations of the statute.[106]

The most current comprehensive guidance is the EPA's 2003 Notification of Substantial Risk; Policy Clarification and Reporting Guidance, published in the Federal Register on June 3, 2003[107] (the 2003 Reporting Guidance) and corrected in a Federal Register notice on January 12, 2005.[108] The 2003 Reporting Guidance restated and amended a seminal 1978 guidance[109] that the EPA had issued early in the history of TSCA, which is now largely supplanted except for questions and answers that were in the 1978 guidance

---

104. While the statutory language requires reporting "immediately," the EPA has determined that this requirement is met if the information is submitted within thirty days. 68 Fed. Reg. 33129 (June 3, 2003).

105. 68 Fed. Reg. 33129, 33130–31 (June 3, 2003). *See also*, EPA, Frequent Questions, September 2006, A.5 [hereinafter 2006 Frequent Questions], *available at* http://www.epa.gov/opptintr/tsca8e/pubs/frequentlyaskedquestionsfaqs.htm. EPA has taken the position that it is authorized to issue binding regulations but has chosen not to do so. 68 Fed. Reg. 33129, 33130 (June 3, 2003).

106. *See* the discussion, *infra*, of In Re MTBE Products Liability Litigation, 559 F. Supp. 424 (S.D.N.Y. 2008).

107. 68 Fed. Reg. 33129 (June 3, 2003).

108. 70 Fed. Reg. 2162 (Jan 12, 2005).

109. 43 Fed. Reg. 11110 (Mar. 16, 1978).

which still retain some viability. EPA also maintains a "Frequent Questions" page on its Web site[110] where it provides questions and answers. These more recent guidances reflect the EPA's current interpretations, although older guidances cover more topics and are valuable in elucidating reporting issues so long as they are not contradicted by the more recent guidances. The primary guidances are:

- 43 Fed. Reg. 11110, Toxic Substances Control Act Statement of Interpretation and Enforcement Policy; Notification of Substantial Risk (Mar. 16, 1978) (the 1978 Statement of Interpretation), now largely superseded;
- EPA, Office of Toxic Substances, Section 8(e) Reporting Guide (June 1991) (1991 8(e) Guide), still in effect;
- Letter from Victor Kimm, Deputy Assistant Administrator, Office of Prevention, Pesticides, and Toxic Substances, EPA, to Robert M. Sussman (April 2, 1992) (the Kimm Letter), still in effect;
- 68 Fed. Reg. 33129, TSCA Section 8(e); Notification of Substantial Risk; Policy Clarification and Reporting Guidance (June 3, 2003) (the 2003 Reporting Guidance), which supplanted the 1978 Statement of Interpretation and changed the deadlines for submittals, reinstated guidance on environmental effects, and added to the categories of information that do not need to be reported;
- EPA, Comment And Response Document For Revised Policy Statement Of Section 8(e) of TSCA, OPPT-2002-0067-0002 (Feb. 20, 2003) (the 8(e) Comment Document), giving public comments on the development of the 2003 Reporting Guide and the EPA's responses to those comments; and
- EPA, Frequent Questions, January 2005 and September 2006.[111]

In the context of TSCA § 8(e), all interpretations other than the bare language of the statute itself and the relatively rare court holdings are derived from these EPA guidances.

Several of these guidances had their genesis in the EPA's Compliance Audit Program (CAP), which was a voluntary self audit program announced

---

110. http://www.epa.gov/oppt/tsca8e/pubs/frequentlyaskedquestionsfaqs.html.

111. The EPA formerly published status reports giving the EPA's conclusions about the resportability of each 8(e) report it received. These status reports are still available but have been supplanted by more up to date guidances in a more accessible format.

by the EPA in 1991[112] and terminated in 1996.[113] EPA had asserted that industry was not in compliance with TSCA § 8(e), and therefore offered an opportunity to come into compliance with a cap on companies' potential liability. Members of the regulated industry countered that if they were out of compliance it was because the EPA was issuing revised guidance and the EPA had not consistently applied the principles it had articulated. To put an end to any confusion, the EPA issued new guidance in connection with the CAP, including the 1991 8(e) Guide and the Kimm Letter. During the CAP, the EPA suspended portions of the 1978 Statement of Interpretation concerning environmental contamination and effects because of all of the complaints it received about the difficulty of applying the 1978 Statement of Interpretation as written. It was not until 2003 when the EPA issued its 2003 Reporting Guidance that the EPA finalized guidance on environmental contamination and effects and completed the guidances it had promised during the course of the CAP.

The CAP has very little continuing significance other than being the source of so much guidance on § 8(e) interpretation.

EPA posts 8(e) reports it receives on its Web site, which are very useful for benchmarking, as well as for obtaining information about specific chemicals, though they are not very useful for guidance because they are merely industry interpretations.[114] The EPA has also posted searchable summaries of 8(e) submissions in the Toxic Substances Control Act Test Submissions (TSCATS) database.[115]

C. Persons Subject to Reporting

The TSCA § 8(e) reporting obligation applies to any "person" engaged in the manufacture, import, processing, or distribution in commerce of the chemical substance at issue. The term "person" is defined by the Agency to include natural persons, business entities (a firm, corporation, sole proprietorship, joint venture, partnership, or association), any State or political subdivision

---

112. 56 Fed. Reg. 4128 (Feb. 1, 1991). This Federal Register notice includes the terms of the registration agreement that CAP participants were required to sign. The registration agreement was modified by 56 Fed. Reg. 19514 (Apr. 26, 1991) and by 56 Fed. Reg. 28458 (June 20, 1991), *available at* http://www.epa.gov/oppt/tsca8e/pubs/rguide03.html.
113. TSCA Section 8(e); Notification of Substantial Risk; Policy Clarification and Reporting Guidance, 68 Fed. Reg. 33129, 33131 (June 3, 2003) [hereinafter 2003 Reporting Guidance].
114. The EPA posts 8(e) reports at http://www.epa.gov/opptintr/tsca8e/pubs/8eandfyisubmissions.htm.
115. The TSCATS database is accessible through the EPA Web site, *available at* http://www.epa.gov/opptintr/tsca8e/pubs/basicinformation.htm.

of a State, and any department or agency of the federal government.[116] "Persons" are subject to the requirements of TSCA § 8(e) only to the extent they are engaged in activities involving manufacture, importation, processing, and distribution of chemicals substances or mixtures under the jurisdiction of TSCA when they receive reportable information. A corollary is that trade associations, laboratories, and consultants generally are not obligated to report, although information is sometimes reported by these types of businesses on a "for your information" or "FYI" basis.[117] Another corollary is that a company that has stopped manufacturing, importing, processing, and distributing a chemical is not required to report new substantial risk information.[118]

There is no *de minimis* exemption for manufacturing, importing, processing, or distributing small amounts of a chemical, nor is there an exemption for small businesses.[119]

Officers and employees of a company who are capable of appreciating the significance of possible substantial risk information are also individually subject to the requirements of TSCA § 8(e) and retain potential liability. EPA has stated that companies may relieve their individual officers and employees of personal responsibility for reporting substantial risk information directly to EPA by adopting and implementing a policy and procedure for employee submission and company processing of substantial risk information.[120] Although it is important to put procedures in place to implement the reporting obligation, the EPA does not have authority to relieve individuals of their obligations to comply with the statute. Third parties who may bring citizens' suits to compel compliance with TSCA and other governmental agencies that may prosecute TSCA violations criminally are not bound by the EPA's guidance saying that individuals will be relieved of their TSCA obligations. At most, the EPA's guidance sets forth the circumstances in which the EPA will exercise its discretion not to seek penalties from individuals for TSCA § 8(e) violations. As expressed in EPA's 2003 Reporting Guidance, qualifying procedures must:

- "specify the information that officers and employees must submit;"
- "indicate how such submissions are to be prepared and the company official to whom they are to be submitted;"
- "note the federal penalties for failing to report; and"

116. 1991 8(e) Guide, 4.
117. *See infra* regarding FYI submissions.
118. 1991 8(e) Guide, 4–5.
119. *Id.* at 4–5.
120. The EPA does not have the authority to absolve individuals of criminal liability, but this is a valuable statement of the EPA's intent to exercise discretion in civil enforcements and in referrals to the Department of Justice for criminal prosecution.

- "provide a mechanism for promptly advising officers and employees is writing of the company's disposition of the report, including whether or not the report was submitted to EPA (and if not reported, informing employees of their right to report to EPA, as protected by TSCA section 23)."[121]

While the Agency's concern was to address the potential personal liability of individuals within a company, a company is otherwise well advised to adopt and implement procedures that ensure that substantial risk information is identified and managed appropriately, if for no other reason than to minimize its own potential liability.

D. Chemicals Covered

TSCA § 8(e) applies to all chemical substances or mixtures under TSCA jurisdiction and manufactured, processed, or distributed in commerce. Chemicals not under TSCA jurisdiction, and therefore not covered by TSCA § 8(e) reporting obligations include firearms, shells and cartridges, and:

- any pesticide (as defined in the Federal Insecticide, Fungicide, and Rodenticide Act (FIFRA)[122] when manufactured, processed, or distributed in commerce for use as a pesticide;
- tobacco or any tobacco product;
- any source material, special nuclear material or byproduct material(as such terms are defined in the Atomic Energy Act of 1954 (AEA)[123] and regulations issued under such Act; and
- any food, food additive, drug, cosmetic, or device (as such terms are defined in Section 201 of the Federal Food, Drug, and Cosmetic Act (FFDCA)[124] when manufactured, processed or distributed in commerce for use as a food, food additive, drug, cosmetic, or device.[125]

To address the potential overlap of TSCA and FIFRA in the development of pesticides, EPA takes the position that a chemical substance that is in the process of research and development as a pesticide is subject to TSCA and potential § 8(e) reporting until the manufacturer or importer demonstrates the intent to produce the pesticide by submitting an application for an experimental

121. 2003 Reporting Guidance, 33137.
122. 7 U.S.C. § 136.
123. 42 U.S.C. §§ 2001–2297.
124. 21 U.S.C. §§ 301–399.
125. TSCA § 3 (citations omitted).

use permit (EUP) or registration under FIFRA.[126] Note that under FIFRA the EPA asserts jurisdiction over potential pesticides long before filing an EUP, and that can cause some significant questions about under which statute to report.

TSCA § 8(f) clarifies that only commercial manufacture or processing comes within the scope of § 8, and so chemicals manufactured, imported, or processed for purely academic purposes are not subject to reporting under TSCA § 8(e).[127] A person does not have a reporting obligation for chemicals that are "used" and not otherwise manufactured, imported, processed, or distributed. In this context, "used" means used as a chemical processing aid, catalyst, or reaction solvent. People who "use" paints and coatings are subject to 8(e) reporting.[128]

Qualifying studies on all of the following types of chemicals must be reported, even though some of them are exempt from other TSCA requirements:

- articles;
- byproducts;
- catalysts;
- chemicals distributed in commerce;
- chemicals manufactured solely for export;
- commercial substances;
- chemicals that have uses as food, food additives, drugs, cosmetics, or devices (FDA uses) and non-FDA uses;
- imported chemicals;
- impurities;
- intermediates (including non-isolated intermediates as well as pesticide intermediates);
- manufactured chemicals;
- substances exempt from PMN requirements because they have a low volume exemption or a low environmental release and human exposure exemption (LoREX);
- microorganisms that are TSCA covered and products made from them;
- mixtures of chemicals;

126. EPA, Comment And Response Document For Revised Policy Statement Of Section 8(e) Of TSCA, OPPT-2002-0067-0002, 5 (Feb. 20, 2003) [hereinafter 8(e) Comment Document].
127. *See* Chapter 5, PMN Exclusions and Exemptions for a discussion of purely academic research and development in the context of the research and development exemption to the PMN rules.
128. 8(e) Comment Document, 6.

- nanoscale materials and engineered nanoscale materials, some of which do not require PMNs because the bulk form of the substance is on the TSCA Inventory;
- chemicals developed as pesticides, up until the time an EUP is filed;
- pesticide intermediates, inerts, impurities, and byproducts;
- chemicals that have both pesticidal use and non-pesticidal use;
- emissions from pesticide and pharmaceutical manufacturing facilities;[129]
- polymers (including polymers covered by the Polymer Exemption);[130]
- processed chemicals (processing includes repackaging); and
- R&D chemicals, including laboratory reagents.[131,132]

It is a common misconception that chemical substances or mixtures exempt from TSCA § 5 requirements are wholly outside the purview of TSCA on a statutory basis. This is not so and this misconception presents a dangerous risk of non-compliance.

It is also important to note that it is not uncommon for a chemical substance to have a use that is both within and without TSCA's jurisdiction depending on the markets into which the chemical substance is sold. For example, a chemical substance sold for cosmetic application alone would be outside TSCA jurisdiction and toxicity data generated in relation to the substance would not be subject to potential TSCA § 8(e) reporting. If the same chemical substance is also sold for industrial application then it is subject to TSCA and reporting of substantial risk information is mandatory. One must keep in mind as well that markets do not remain static. The toxicity data concerning a chemical substance that was not submitted last month on the basis that the sole application of the substance was as a cosmetic may become "immediately" reportable this month when the substance is sold into a different application.

There are numerous other possible situations in which a company can obtain information that is not reportable solely because the subject chemical is not subject to TSCA. For example, a report concerning a chemical that is

129. *Id.* at 4–5.

130. *See* Chapter 5, PMN Exclusions and Exemptions, for a discussion of the Polymer Exemption, which is an exemption from the PMN requirements of TSCA § 5.

131. The Court in *Dow Chemical Co. v. EPA*, 605 F.2d 673 (3rd Cir. 1979) found that the processing, import, or manufacture of small quantities of chemicals for research and development purposes was a commercial purpose and was therefore within the scope of § 8 of TSCA; the 8(e) Comment Document, 34, lists the citations for EPA's assertions that research and development materials are subject to TSCA § 8(e) reporting.

132. Although the EPA has said that independent laboratories are not responsible for 8(e) reporting, that is not the case if the laboratory processes chemicals, and most laboratories do process chemicals. *See* 2006 Frequent Questions, A.7.

not present in the United States would not need to be submitted, and a report concerning a chemical that is solely used as a drug is not reportable. However, if that chemical is subsequently imported into the United States or used for a purpose that is within the TSCA definition of "chemical substance" then the preexisting substantial risk information must be reported.

Because the penalties continue to accumulate on a daily basis, it is sometimes prudent to submit 8(e) information even if the product is not currently being sold for a TSCA use. If there is a likelihood that the substance will become subject to TSCA, many companies choose to report the information under TSCA § 8(e) to avoid the very difficult management procedures that would be required to track when such exempt substances become subject to the TSCA § 8(e) reporting requirement. There is no penalty for reporting something that does not need to be reported.

E. Information That Must Be Reported

TSCA § 8(e) requires the submission of information "which reasonably supports the conclusion that [a] substance or mixture presents a substantial risk of injury to health or the environment." The reporting obligation extends to information that does not conclusively demonstrate that a substantial risk exists; rather reportable information need merely "reasonably support" a conclusion of substantial risk. Reporting usually requires judgment calls about whether the information rises to a reportable level. Although the EPA discourages over reporting and "file dumps,"[133] it is prudent to report in cases of uncertainty because of the consequences that follow from a failure to report.

Many companies will try to use the Agency guidance as providing a "bright line" as to information that must be reported under TSCA § 8(e), although there are no "bright line" standards to apply across the board. This is particularly so with regard to toxicity data.

Preliminary data must be reported, and the time to report starts to run as soon as a person capable of appreciating the significance of the information receives it.[134] There is no flexibility to wait until the final study is fully completed and reviewed. For example, evidence of reportable increases in benign tumors is often found in interim sacrifices during long term studies, and these increases are reportable before the long term study is finalized.[135]

---

133. Letter from Victor Kimm, Deputy Assistant Administrator, Office of Prevention, Pesticides, and Toxic Substances, EPA, to Robert M. Sussman, 2 (April 2, 1992) [hereinafter Kimm Letter].

134. 2006 Frequent Questions, A.16.

135. *Id.* at A.1.

In general, whether information is reportable under TSCA § 8(e) depends upon the seriousness of the adverse effect, and the fact or probability of the effect's occurrence, which is directly related to the fact or probability of exposure. As explained by EPA:

> In determining TSCA Section 8(e)—applicability/reportability, these two criteria should be weighted differently depending upon the seriousness of the effect or the extent of the exposure, i.e., the more serious the effect, the less heavily one should weigh actual or potential exposure, and vice versa. For example, in cases, where serious effects such as birth defects or cancer (as evidenced by benign and/or malignant tumors) are observed, the mere fact that the implicated chemical is in commerce (including chemicals at the research and development stage) constitutes sufficient evidence of exposure to submit the new-found toxicity data.[136]

Whether the risk is a reasonable risk to take is not a factor in whether the effect is reportable.[137]

Sources of potentially reportable information include traditional laboratory and field studies that are designed and controlled. These include in vivo experiments, in vitro experiments, epidemiological studies, and environmental monitoring studies. Undesigned and uncontrolled studies may also generate reportable results. These include any observations that yield a pattern of effects, or a single observation of "cancer, birth defects, mutation, death, or serious incapacitation in a human" attributable to one or more chemicals. These can come from medical surveys, clinical studies, reports from consumers or workers, or one time observations.[138]

1. Human Health Effects

Whether or not effects that chemical substances may produce in humans are reportable requires analyzing the severity of the effect and the likelihood or extent of exposure. As the effects become more severe, less consideration is given to the extent of exposure, and severe effects are reportable even in the absence of potential exposure. A severe effect observed in humans, obtained directly by observation or indirectly through epidemiology studies or medical surveys is always reportable. Because the effect is observed or reported in humans, there is no question regarding exposure to people. Similarly, for severe effects, if the subject chemical is in commerce then that is presumed to

136. 1991 8(e) Guide, 3.
137. 2006 Frequent Questions, A.1.
138. 2003 Reporting Guidance, 33139.

be sufficient evidence of the potential for exposure to warrant reporting.[139] These severe effects include "cancer, mutation, birth defects or toxic effects resulting in death, or serious prolonged incapacitation, including the loss of a normal bodily function resulting in relatively serious impairment of normal activities."[140]

Less severe effects observed in humans are reportable if there is a potential for wider exposure, although there is no hard and fast test for determining when the balance tips in favor of reportablity.[141]

Substantial risk information may be generated in animal and in vitro as well as human studies. Animal or in vitro studies may provide evidence of potential human health effects. Serious risks observed in any test subject are reportable without regard to the extent of potential exposure. As stated by the Agency in the 1991 Reporting Guide:

> TSCA Section 8(e) requires the timely submission of evidence from animal studies that implicates the tested chemical as causing serious toxicological effects (e.g., cancer, neurotoxicity, birth defects). A decision to report the observance of such serious toxicological effects should not hinge in any way on a judgment of either the actual or potential exposure to the chemical or a judgment about the degree of relevancy of the findings to an overall assessment of human risk. In other words, the decision to report under Section 8(e) in such cases should be based simply on the observance of the serious toxicological effects.[142]

a. Carcinogenicity

Evidence of cancer in people or test animals must be reported with very little consideration given to potential exposure. The mere fact that the subject chemical is in commerce is sufficient potential exposure to warrant reporting.[143]

b. Mutagenicity

Serious in vivo genotoxicological effects are reportable under TSCA § 8(e). These include gene and chromosome mutations.[144] A single positive in vivo test should be reported. In vitro effects must be considered more carefully

---

139. 2006 Frequent Questions, A.16.
140. *Id.* at A.23, 2003 Reporting Guidance and 1978 Statement of Interpretation.
141. 2006 Frequent Questions, A.23.
142. 1991 8(e) Guide, 26.
143. *Id.* at 3.
144. *Id.* at 28–29.

for reporting. A single instance of mutagenicity in an in vitro study is not reportable without more evidence of a substantial risk. That evidence can be supplied by a positive result that exceeds the positive control. A single strong positive result for a chemical that people are widely exposed to or that is produced in significant volumes should also be reported. Multiple positive in vitro tests should be reported, although the EPA's guidance does not require reporting for research and development substances, it may be difficult to track when R&D substances are commercialized and so these studies should be reported if there is any possibility the substance will be commercialized.[145]

c. Acute Toxicity

The reportability of acute toxicity results in animals requires balancing the severity of the effect against the likelihood of exposure. Results showing that the subject chemical is highly toxic should be reported without considering potential exposure; exposure should be taken into consideration in determining whether to report moderate toxicity, and results showing low toxicity should not be reported even if there is exposure. The EPA provided the following numerical ranges for reporting high, moderate, and low exposure:

- oral LD50 <50 mg/kg is highly toxic; report without considering exposure;
- oral LD50 =50-500 mg/kg is moderately toxic; consider exposure in determining reportability;
- oral LD50 >500 mg/kg is low toxicity; not reportable;
- dermal LD50 <200 mg/kg is highly toxic; report without considering exposure;
- dermal LD50 >200-2,000 mg/kg is moderately toxic; consider exposure in determining reportability;
- dermal LD50 >2,000 mg/kg is low toxicity; not reportable;
- inhalation LC50 (4-hr.) <200 ppm (<2 mg/l) is highly toxic; report without considering exposure;
- inhalation LC50 (4-hr.) >200-5,000 ppm is moderately toxic; consider exposure in determining reportability; and
- inhalation LC50 (4-hr.) >5,000 ppm (>50mg/l) is low toxicity; not reportable;
- LD50 is the dose that is lethal to 50 percent of the test animals; LC50 is the concentration that is lethal to 50 percent of the test animals.[146]

---

145. Kimm Letter, enclosure, 5–6.
146. 2006 Frequent Questions, A.22.

Sensitization and irritation observed during acute toxicity studies may also be reportable.[147]

d. Neurotoxicity

Neurotoxic effects can be observed in both acute and longer term studies. Signs and symptoms of severe neurotoxic effects include:

- convulsions;
- paralysis;
- paresis;
- paresthesia;
- lethargy;
- tail elevation;
- twitching;
- reflex changes;
- spasticity;
- fasciculation;
- anesthesia;
- limb splay;
- flaccidity;
- hyperactivity;
- rigidity;
- coma;
- gait abnormalities;
- tremor;
- hypersensitivity
- ataxia;
- excess salivation
- circling
- urinary incontinence;
- rearing;
- behavioral change
- narcosis;
- abnormal pupil size;
- loss of pain response;
- twitching; and
- catatonia.[148]

---

147. *Id.*
148. Kimm Letter, enclosure, 4.

Companies should consult the labs that performed the studies if there is any doubt about how they used these terms.[149]

These observations are reportable except if the animal is dying (moribund).[150] If these observations are made in dying animals that also show other reportable adverse effects then the EPA guidance suggests including them in the 8(e) submission.[151] If these effects are seen in dying animals but are the same as known effects of structurally similar chemicals, then the observation may be biologically significant even though the animal was dying. In that case the effects seen in dying animals are reportable.[152]

Transient effects are not reportable unless there is additional evidence that would indicate a substantial risk.[153]

e. Subacute or Chronic Toxicity

A range of adverse effects can be observed during the course of subacute, chronic, and repeated dose studies. Symptoms of toxicological effects described above for acute studies may be observed in these longer term studies, and are reportable if they are severe or if the balance of severity and exposure warrants reporting. Gross or histopathological examination may also reveal significant adverse effects. If gross examination shows liver or kidney weight change of less than or equal to 10 percent of total body weight then the results are not reportable without additional indicia of significant adverse effects. The EPA did not give detailed guidance on weight changes in other organs.[154]

Statistically or biologically significant changes in clinical or enzyme chemistry (e.g., neurotoxic esterase inhibition, cholinesterase inhibition, or peroxisome proliferation) are reportable.[155] Statistically or biologically significant oncogenic effects, reproductive/developmental effects, neurotoxicological effects, or organ specific or organ-system specific effects should be also be reported without factoring in the level of exposure.[156]

One basic problem in applying the EPA's guidances has been that studies that determine the no observed effect level (NOEL) of a substance always result in some observed effect as a result of the study chemical. The EPA addressed this problem in the Kimm Letter by advising results are not generally

149. *Id.*
150. 2006 Frequent Questions, A.21.
151. *Id.*
152. Kimm Letter, enclosure, 4.
153. *Id.*
154. 2006 Frequent Questions, A.20.
155. Kimm Letter, enclosure, 6.
156. *Id.* at 8.

reportable if they are based on "general, non-specific" changes in the test animals that show a:

- NOEL ≥200 mg/kg/day in an oral study of ≤4 weeks or an equivalent dose in an inhalation study of ≤4 weeks; or
- NOEL ≥400 mg/kg/day in a dermal study of ≤4 weeks; or
- NOEL ≥100 mg/kg/day in an oral study of ≤3 months or an equivalent dose in an inhalation study of ≤3 months; or
- NOEL ≥200 mg/kg/day in a dermal study of ≤3 months; or
- NOEL ≥50 mg/kg/day in an oral study of ≥3 months or an equivalent dose in an inhalation study of ≥3 months; or
- NOEL ≥100 mg/kg/day in a dermal study of ≥3 months.[157]

If the NOELs are lower than these values, the reports should be considered for reporting even if they are based on general, non-specific effects, taking into account the severity of the effect, whether there was a dose response, and other factors that support a finding of a substantial risk.

f. Skin/Eye Irritation and Sensitization

Skin and eye irritation studies are not generally reportable if the test substance is expected to be an irritant because its pH is less than three (a strong acid) or greater than eleven (a strong base), or if the test substance has particles that are rough. Reportability depends on the severity of the observed response, and unexpectedly severe responses may be reportable. Reportability also depends on the potential for exposure. If there is a low potential for exposure because the substance is a research and development chemical, will be used only in low concentrations, or will be used in a closed system, the studies generally are not reportable unless workers will be exposed anyway.[158]

Sensitization is a systemic response, and studies showing strong sensitization should be reported without regard to potential exposure. Less severe effects can be balanced against the potential exposure. EPA has said that moderate sensitization is not immediately reportable if observed in chemicals that have a low potential exposure because they are research and development chemicals, or they will be used in low concentrations, or they will be used in a closed system. However, EPA recommends reevaluating the reporting decision if the chemical is later used in a different manner with a greater potential for exposure. In practice it is difficult to track chemicals and

157. *Id.* at 8–9.
158. *Id.* at 2.

reevaluate them, and companies may decide to report at the research and development stage to avoid inadvertently failing to report later.

The EPA guidance does not address how to evaluate sensitization studies using the local lymph node assay (LLNA) which is a relatively new test. The results of an LLNA are reported in terms of the concentration of the test substance that will produce a stimulation index value of three in the test animal, and this is called the EC3. Until the EPA has taken a position on reportability of LLNA results, it would be prudent to adopt a somewhat conservative approach although that may result in over reporting. The checklist in Chapter 20, Practice Tools, incorporates a conservative approach of reporting all LLNA results with an EC3 of less than 50 percent, based on benchmarking against the sensitization studies that have been reported to the EPA under § 8(e).

g. Benign Tumors

Benign tumors are reportable when "either statistically or biologically significant increases over controls are observed." They may become malignant, and they may pose serious health effects themselves.[159]

h. Reproductive or Developmental Toxicity

Teratogenic effects observed during studies of reproductive or developmental toxicity are reportable, and so are other adverse effects on the developing organism and the test animals' reproductive systems.

Although liver and kidney weight changes are not generally reportable if they are less than 10 percent of body weight, this rule does not apply to developmental toxicity studies, and liver and kidney weight changes are reportable if observed in these studies.[160]

These effects are reportable even if they are reversible, and whether they are observed prenatally or postnatally.[161] Reproductive or developmental toxicity is reportable whether or not there is maternal toxicity. Similarly, maternal toxicity observed during a reproductive or developmental toxicity study is reportable in the absence of reproductive or developmental toxicity.[162]

---

159. 2006 Frequent Questions, A.17.
160. *Id.* at A.20.
161. *Id.* at A.19.
162. *Id.* at A.18.

i. Previously Unknown Exposure

In 2006 the EPA said in guidance that reports of previously unknown human exposure to a chemical known or suspected to cause serious adverse effects must be reported:

> The discovery of previously unknown and significant human exposure to a chemical, when combined with knowledge that the subject chemical is recognized or suspected as being capable of causing serious adverse health effects (e.g., cancer, birth defects, neurotoxicity), provides a sufficient basis to require the reporting of the new-found exposure data to EPA under section 8(e).[163]

The EPA also said in the same guidance that previously unknown and unsuspected distribution of a chemical in commercial products is reportable if the chemical is known to cause serious adverse effects.[164] Many types of studies could be reportable under this guidance. The EPA suggested in the questions leading to these responses that a study would be reportable if it demonstrated "absorption of lead following oral or dermal exposure to a particular type of article for [sic] which it was not previously known that such absorption could occur." Other examples include studies that show the presence in blood of chemicals that are suspected to cause adverse effects, indoor air monitoring results that show higher than expected levels of contaminants, and studies showing drinking water contamination by chemicals suspected of causing adverse effects.[165]

Discovery of previously unknown presence of a hazardous or toxic chemical in a product is reportable if widespread or significant exposure is substantially likely to occur and presents a substantial risk of injury to health or the environment.[166] The substance's toxicity, its concentration in the product, potential exposures, and the product's lifecycle should all be taken into consideration in determining reportability. The EPA advises that if the product is in commerce, exposure can be presumed for extremely toxic substances.

2. Environmental Effects

The EPA's position on reportability of environmental effects has undergone two upheavals. The EPA's original guidance about environmental effects in

---

163. *Id.* at A.25.
164. *Id.* at A.27.
165. *See infra* discussion of the EPA's 8(e) enforcement action against DuPont for an example of EPA allegations concerning failure to report the discovery of substances in human blood suspected of causing adverse effects.
166. 2006 Frequent Questions, A.26.

the 1978 Statement of Interpretation generated some confusion among the regulated industry.[167] As a result, in 1991 during the 8(e) CAP, EPA suspended the portions of the 1978 Statement of Interpretation addressing environmental effects until it could develop refined § 8(e) reporting guidance on the subject.[168] Although the EPA gave some very basic guidance that environmental effects were reportable, for the next 12 years regulated entities had no detailed guidance on what the EPA expected to be reported. That detailed guidance was provided in the 2003 Reporting Guidance, which includes several fairly clear statements of when environmental effects must be reported.

Although the 2003 Reporting Guidance is clear, users must be careful to consider exactly which category of environmental effect they are evaluating. Non-emergency situations of environmental contamination are broken into the discovery of the following categories of effects: widespread and previously unsuspected distribution in environmental media; bioaccumulation; adverse effects; changes in species' interrelationships; and facile transformation or degradation to a chemical having an unacceptable risk. Emergency incidents of environmental contamination are a separate category of reportable environmental effects. Each category of environmental effect has a unique set of criteria to weigh in determining reportability. A common mistake is to apply criteria that are only applicable to one category, such as widespread distribution in environmental media, to other categories where they are inapplicable.

a. Non-emergency Situations of Environmental Contamination

All of the types of non-emergency environmental reports that must be submitted to the EPA under TSCA § 8(e) involve the discovery of adverse effects associated with chemicals that are known to be in the environment, or the discovery that chemicals known to have adverse effects are present in the environment.

i. Widespread Distribution

The discovery that chemicals that are known to have adverse effects are widespread in environmental media is reportable under § 8(e). There must be more to a study than simply finding a substance associated with a substantial risk in the environment before the study becomes reportable. The distribution in the environment must have been not only unknown but also unsuspected and previously considered unlikely,[169] and there must also be a

167. At this point the differences between the 2003 Reporting Guidance and the 1978 Statement of Interpretation with respect to environmental effects are only of academic interest.

168. *See* 56 Fed. Reg. 49478 (Sept. 30, 1991).

169. 2006 Frequent Questions, A.27.

substantial likelihood that organisms will be exposed or that such exposure has already occurred.[170] There is no requirement that an actual adverse effect be observed before reporting under this prong of the environmental effect guidance.[171]

The EPA has said that companies should consider a range of factors in determining if distribution is widespread, including the amount of contamination, as well as the extent and the pattern of contamination.[172]

The presence of substances in the environment below benchmark levels of concern established by the EPA will not be considered to be widespread. Examples of these benchmark levels of concern are Maximum Contaminant Levels established for drinking water, Ambient Water Quality Criteria established for receiving bodies of water, and Reference Doses or Concentrations. Environmental concentrations below these values are generally not reportable, and concentrations above these levels are generally sufficient to trigger reporting so long as the subject chemical is associated with substantial risks. Similarly, concentrations above Toxicity Characteristic Limits established under the Resource Conservation and Recovery Act may be reportable.[173] When permits, orders, and regulations such as Department of Transportation regulations concerning pipeline releases[174] establish thresholds above which chemical concentrations must be reported or some other action must be taken, there is a presumption that lower concentrations are not reportable under TSCA § 8(e).[175] That presumption can be overcome and reporting may be merited if additional evidence, such as information that the substance is more toxic than expected, points to greater risk.

If a company establishes internal levels of concern for a substance that are lower than any levels set by an agency, it should report studies as if the internal level were the applicable ones.[176]

Even if a benchmark is exceeded, a study is not subject to TSCA § 8(e) reporting unless the environmental distribution is extensive. The EPA gave examples in its 2006 Frequent Questions, and said that a spill of thousands of pounds of a toxic chemical that migrates to groundwater and may result in drinking water contamination is reportable. However a relatively small spill that was cleaned up before it could result in "substantial distribution to the environment" would not be reportable.[177] Applying this same logic, the EPA

---

170. 2003 Reporting Guidance, 33138.
171. 8(e) Comment Document, 18.
172. *Id.* at 14.
173. 2003 Reporting Guidance, 33138.
174. 2006 Frequent Questions, A.29. The Department of Transportation regulations concerning pipeline releases are at 49 C.F.R. Parts 191–195.
175. 2006 Frequent Questions, A.28.
176. *See infra* the discussion of the PFOA settlement.
177. 2006 Frequent Questions, A.27.

said that field tests conducted on pesticides in the research and development stage are not typically considered to have resulted in widespread distribution of the test substance in the environment. However, if another type of reportable observation is made, such as the presence of human health effects, the field test results may be reportable.[178]

New information concerning site specific but still widespread contamination can be reportable. For example, although polychlorinated biphenyls (PCBs) are known to be widespread environmental contaminants, discovery of PCBs at a specific site should be evaluated for reporting.[179]

The presence of chemicals in permitted landfills and other disposal facilities does not require 8(e) reporting.

Environmental media include soil, water, and air, as well as indoor air and commercial products.[180] However, the pattern of potential exposure should be evaluated when determining whether a contaminant in a commercial product is widespread. The EPA has said that if a constituent is tightly bound in a plastic product there would be minimal exposure and reporting would not be required. Any constituent that is listed on an MSDS would not be previously unsuspected and would not trigger a reporting obligation.[181]

Workplace exposures are reportable under this prong of the 2003 Reporting Guidance if there is a sudden release of a large quantity of a chemical, but known workplace exposures are not reportable.[182]

ii. Bioaccumulation

If there is a known adverse effect associated with a chemical, and there is also a potential for widespread exposure, then new information indicating pronounced bioaccumulation is reportable. Bioaccumulation in fish beyond five thousand times water concentration, or an n-octanol/water partition coefficient of greater than twenty-five thousand are measures and indications of pronounced bioaccumulation.[183]

iii. Adverse Effects

If an adverse effect that was not previously known is observed in connection with a chemical that is known to have bioaccumulated "to a pronounced degree" or known to be widespread in environmental media, that result must be reported.[184] It is not the fact of bioaccumulation that is reportable under

178. 8(e) Comment Document, 5.
179. 2006 Frequent Questions, A.32
180. *Id.* at A.27.
181. 8(e) Comment Document, 14–15.
182. *Id.* at 15.
183. 2003 Reporting Guidance, 33138.
184. *Id.*

this prong of 8(e), and it is not the fact of widespread distribution. It is the previously unknown adverse effect that is reportable.

The 2006 Frequent Questions include the following parameters describing when data on acute and chronic toxicity in aquatic organisms must be reported:

- concern level high for Acute LC50 or EC50 (mg/L) <1 or Chronic EC50 (mg/L) <0.1; consider exposure when determining reportablity;
- concern level moderate for Acute LC50 or EC50 (mg/L) 1-100 or Chronic EC50 (mg/L) 0.1-10; consider exposure when determining reportablity;
- concern level low for Acute LC50 or EC50 (mg/L) >100 or Chronic EC50 (mg/L) >10; not reportable; and
- concern level low for Acute LC50 or EC50 (mg/L) no effects at saturation, or Chronic EC50 (mg/L) no effects at saturation; not reportable.

LC50 is the lethal concentration in 50 percent of organisms, and EC50 is the concentration at which 50 percent of organisms show effects such as those adversely affecting reproductive performance or loss of mobility. [185]

iv. Changes in Species' Interrelationships

An observation of a change in species' interrelationships is reportable under TSCA § 8(e).[186] The EPA said "changes in population behavior, growth, survival, etc. that in turn affect other species' behavior, growth, or survival, should be reported." Examples of reportable information include eutrophication, which is when water bodies have too high a concentration of nutrients and some organisms grow excessively, and interference with biochemical cycles.

v. Facile Transformation

A study that shows that a chemical that has bioaccumulated or is widespread in the environment and is capable of easily breaking down into one or more chemicals associated with known risks is reportable.[187] The text of the 2003 Guidance does not require that a chemical be widespread in the environment or that it has bioaccumulated before facile transformation to a chemical with known risks is reportable. Logically, if the chemical were not in the environment the fact of facile transformation would not be related to an environmental effect, however.

185. 2006 Frequent Questions, A.24.
186. 2003 Reporting Guide, 33138.
187. *Id.*

b. Emergency Incidents of Environmental Contamination

The 2003 Reporting Guidance requires reporting emergency incidents of environmental contamination. Those incidents are defined as:

> [a]ny environmental contamination by a chemical substance or mixture to which any of the above adverse effects has been ascribed and which because of the pattern, extent, and amount of contamination (1) seriously threatens humans with cancer, birth defects, mutation, death or serious or prolonged incapacitation, or (2) seriously threatens non-human organisms with large-scale or ecologically significant population destruction.

The EPA said that similar criteria for other species have not been developed and data should be evaluated on a case by case basis. However, companies are reporting data on other environmental species, and conservative assumptions are made in the checklists for reporting in Chapter 20, Practice Tools.

F. Information That Is Not Reportable

The statutory language of TSCA § 8(e) relieves a person from the obligation to report substantial risk information if "such person has actual knowledge that the Administrator has been adequately informed of such information."[188] It is prudent to interpret that exception quite literally; regulated companies should report under TSCA § 8(e) unless they have proof that the EPA has received or will receive the same reports.

At least one court has refused to give any weight to the EPA's many statements in guidances that reporting information to states satisfies an obligation to report under TSCA § 8(e). In *In Re MTBE Products Liability Litigation*,[189] the Court concluded that guidances that are at odds with the statutory language of TSCA § 8(e) are not entitled to any deference. The statute only permits a person to avoid reporting substantial risk information if that person has "actual knowledge that the Administrator has been adequately informed of such information." Therefore, the Court found that the portions of the 2003 Reporting Guidance and the 2006 Frequent Questions were simply wrong when they said that reporting substantial risk information to a state meets a person's 8(e) obligations.

---

188. TSCA § 8(e).
189. 559 F. Supp. 424 (S.D.N.Y. 2008).

The *MTBE* Court analyzed the EPA's guidances under the principal enunciated by the United States Supreme Court in *Chevron U.S.A. Inc. v. Natural Resources Defense Council, Inc.*[190] *Chevron* held that courts should defer to agencies for interpretations of the statutes they administer if the statutes are silent or ambiguous about a point. The Court in *MBTE* found that the deference discussed in *Chevron* does not apply to the 2003 Reporting Guidance or the 2006 Frequent Questions because Congress did not delegate authority to the EPA to make rules under TSCA § 8(e), and the guidances were not rules, as the EPA has explicitly stated. In addition, the statute is clear that a report must be submitted unless the EPA administrator has been informed of the substantial risk information, and the EPA guidances simply ignored the statutory requirement.

MTBE was a citizens' suit under TSCA § 20 seeking to compel oil companies to report certain information concerning methyl tertiary butyl ether under TSCA § 8(e). As the *MTBE* case makes clear, people bringing citizens' suits are not bound by EPA guidance that purports to relax strict compliance with the statutory language. Similarly, there is no reason why any other federal agency would be compelled to interpret TSCA the way the EPA does in the guidances.[191]

EPA guidances do provide an indication of when EPA will exercise its discretion not to seek administrative penalties for failure to report substantial risk information that has been or will be reported to another agency. The guidances concerning when the EPA considers itself to be adequately informed of substantial risk information reported to any agency other than the EPA are relevant only to that extent. The statements in the guidances therefore fall into two categories. The first category includes statements that retain some viability after *MTBE* because they describe when a study that has been reported to the EPA has been reported to the EPA in a manner that adequately informs the EPA of the results. The second category includes the statements that the EPA has made that at best indicate when the EPA will exercise enforcement discretion but do not preclude anyone from relying on the stricter statutory obligation.

The first category includes the following descriptions in the 2003 Reporting Guidance of situations when substantial risk information does not need to be reported under TSCA § 8(e) because the EPA has already been adequately informed:

- emergency incidents of environmental contamination that are immediately reported to the EPA under a statutory program administered by the EPA;[192]

190. 467 U.S. 837 (1984).
191. For example, there is no reason why a conspiracy charge could not be predicated on a failure to report substantial risk information to the EPA even if the information had been reported to a state agency. *See infra W.R. Grace.*
192. The statutes administered by the EPA are listed at http://www.epa.gov/lawsregs/laws/index.html.

- site specific emergency incidents of environmental contamination that are reported to the EPA subject to an immediate reporting requirement under any federal statute;
- reports of non-emergency widespread distribution in environmental media that are required to be reported to the EPA under a statute administered by the EPA within ninety days;
- site specific incidents of widespread distribution that are reported to the EPA subject to an immediate reporting requirement under any federal statute;
- all other types of otherwise reportable information concerning environmental effects that are required to be reported to the EPA pursuant to a statute administered by the EPA within thirty days; and
- EPA studies.[193]

In the Frequent Questions, the EPA gave the following examples, among others, of incidents that do not need to be reported under TSCA § 8(e) if they are properly reported to the EPA under other statutes:

- "[r]eports of releases of reportable quantities (RQs) of CERCLA §102(a) hazardous substances (reportable under 40 CFR part 302); and"
- "[r]eports of spills to navigable waters or adjoining shorelines of oil in quantities that may be harmful to public health or welfare, or to the environment, under the Clean Water Act and Oil Pollution Act (reportable under 40 CFR Part 110 for oil discharges and 40 CFR § 116 for hazardous substances discharges)."[194]

As an example of applying these guidances, FIFRA § 6(a)(2) has a reporting obligation that is analogous to the reporting obligation under TSCA § 8(e) for chemicals used in pesticides. Pesticides themselves are not subject to TSCA, but there are many chemicals used in pesticide formulations that are not pesticides. If a pesticide manufacturer studies chemicals such as inerts or safteners before they are formulated into the final pesticide product, they may obtain substantial risk information that is subject to both FIFRA § 6(a)(2) and TSCA § 8(e). In this case, the pesticide manufacturer will satisfy its TSCA obligations by reporting the information to EPA pursuant to FIFRA § 6(a)(2).

Both the low volume exemption (LVE) and the LoREX exemption have mandatory requirements to submit to the EPA test data which indicates that the substance may not qualify for the exemption.[195] Such test data must be submitted within 15 working days. Therefore, a submittal made under this

---

193. 2003 Reporting Guidance, 33139.
194. 2006 Frequent Questions, A.8.
195. 40 C.F.R. § 723.50(i).

requirement of the LVE and LoREX exemptions will satisfy the obligation to submit a § 8(e) report.

The second category of statements in EPA guidances is inconsistent with the statute itself, and therefore does not survive scrutiny after the *MTBE* case. These are the statements to the effect that the statutory obligation to report substantial risk information to the EPA is satisfied if the information is:

- in a publicly available draft or final publication from any Federal agency other than the EPA;
- developed by a Federal agency other than the EPA as a result of a toxicological testing or study program, or site evaluation for chemical contamination, if EPA is participating in the design, review or evaluation of testing or sampling plans or resulting data;
- in electronic or paper copies of scientific publications, including bibliographic databases;
- in scientific databases;
- in news publications, including print, radio, or television reports in the United States;
- in proceedings of a scientific conference in the United States so long as information is captured by transcripts, abstracts, or other records and is cited in a database, publication, or Federal agency report within ninety days after the person subject to reporting obtains information from the conference;[196]
- an emergency incident of environmental contamination that is immediately reported to a state with an EPA delegated or authorized program;[197]
- an environmental emergency that is reported immediately to state or local emergency response committees (SERCs and LERCs respectively);[198]
- a site specific emergency incident of environmental contamination that is reported subject to an immediate reporting requirement under any federal statute to an agency other than the EPA;
- an emergency incident of environmental contamination if the information is developed in connection with a State or Federally authorized remediation program;
- an emergency incident of environmental contamination if it relates to a site controlled by another person who has a reporting obligation under TSCA § 8(e);
- a non-emergency showing of widespread distribution in environmental media if information is required to be reported to an agency other than

196. 2003 Reporting Guidance, 33139.
197. *Id.*; 2006 Frequent Questions, A.8.
198. 2006 Frequent Questions, A.13.

the EPA under a statute administered by the EPA, or to a state with an EPA delegated or authorized program, within ninety days;

- widespread contamination if the information is developed in connection with a State or Federally authorized remediation program;
- a site specific incident of widespread distribution that is reported to any agency other than the EPA subject to an immediate reporting requirement under any federal statute;
- widespread distribution relating to a site controlled by another person who has a reporting obligation under TSCA § 8(e); and
- all other types of otherwise reportable information concerning environmental effects if it is required to be reported to any agency other than the EPA pursuant to a statute administered by the EPA, or to a state with an EPA delegated or authorized program within thirty days.[199]

In its Frequent Questions, the EPA gives the following examples, which do not survive scrutiny under *MTBE*, of incidents that do not need to be reported under TSCA § 8(e):

- "[r]eports of incidents involving hazardous materials regulated by the Department of Transportation under the Hazardous Materials Transportation Act (reportable under 49 CFR part 171 for the transportation of hazardous materials, 49 CFR part 191 for natural gas and other gases transported by pipeline, and 49 CFR 195 for liquids transported by pipeline);"[200] and
- information that is submitted to a state or federal remediation program (other than through the EPA) even if the remediation is voluntary so long as it is conducted with the knowledge of the state, under a program authorized by the state.[201]

As the Court in *MTBE* noted, if a person can demonstrate that the EPA was actually informed of substantial risk information that was submitted to a different agency, then the TSCA § 8(e) reporting obligations would be satisfied. However, the person claiming to have satisfied TSCA § 8(e) bears the burden of proving that the EPA was adequately informed of the substantial risk information, and for this reason also, relying on the EPA guidances that purport to permit reporting to another agency is not prudent.

The EPA considers itself adequately informed of significant risk information if it has previously received information that a new study merely corroborates. It is important to note that information that is not strictly

199. 2003 Reporting Guidance, 33139.
200. 2006 Frequent Questions, A.28.
201. *Id.* at A.9.

corroborative, but which identifies a serious toxic effect at lower dose than previously observed, or which confirms a serious effect that was previously only suspected, must be reported under TSCA § 8(e). To be corroborative a study must duplicate the "route of exposure, dose, species, strain, sex, time to onset of effect, nature and severity of the effect."[202] Information that only corroborates known information, such as the presence of a chemical known to have serious effects within the range of known concentrations in human tissue, is not reportable. EPA has said that "chemical blood levels and other biological monitoring data recorded in the NHANES (National Health and Nutrition Examination Survey) data base, is not reportable."[203]

Information concerning chemical substances that are not manufactured in, imported into, processed in, or distributed in the United States is not reportable. Emergency incidents of environmental contamination and widespread distribution that occur outside of the United States are not reportable unless there is a substantial likelihood that contamination will result in the United States.

G. How to Submit

1. When Submittals Are Due

Substantial risk information that must be reported to EPA must be submitted "immediately," a term that has no statutory definition in TSCA. In its 2003 Reporting Guidance, EPA stated that "a person has 'immediately informed' the Administrator if human health information is received by the EPA not later than the thirtieth calendar day after the date the person obtained such information."[204] The EPA has said it is not sufficient for the submittal to be postmarked within thirty days, and it is up to the submitter to ensure that the EPA receives it within the required time frame.[205] Emergency incidents of environmental contamination must be reported to the EPA by telephone as soon as the person has knowledge of the incident. That could be on the order of minutes or hours,[206] but it would be difficult to argue that waiting a full day is contemplated. If the information is required to be, and has been, reported under another statute administered by EPA, such as CERCLA, the TSCA § 8(e) report is unnecessary. Any supplementary information must also be reported immediately.

---

202. 2003 Reporting Guidance, 33139.
203. 2006 Frequent Questions, A.2.
204. 2003 Reporting Guide, 33138.
205. 8(e) Comment Document, 4.
206. *Id.* at 21.

The reporting clock starts when any officer or employee of the business who is capable of appreciating the significance of the information first comes into possession of the information.[207] If a "prudent person similarly situated could reasonably be expected" to have or know the information then the person and the company will be deemed to have it; that is, ignorance is not a complete excuse for failure to submit information under TSCA § 8(e).

To be in possession does not require having a written copy of the information. Knowledge of substantial risk information can be acquired through personal conversations, presentations, and telephone calls.

The possession of reportable information in a foreign affiliate corporation outside the jurisdiction of U.S. law becomes reportable by the U.S. affiliate corporation once that information is shared with the affiliate, verbally or in writing. This is because the U.S. affiliate comes into possession of the information. However, if the U.S. affiliate is not a manufacturer, importer, distributor in commerce, or processor of the chemical substance or mixture at issue, it would then have no reporting obligation. In other words, an entity does not become a manufacturer, importer, distributor in commerce, or processor solely because a foreign affiliate or subsidiary engages in one of those activities. This is in contrast to the TSCA § 8(c) obligation of a manufacturer to record and maintain allegations of significant adverse reactions.

A trap for the unwary may arise when substantial risk information is generated by a foreign affiliate, other than a majority owned or controlled subsidiary. The mere possession of such information by the foreign entity will not trigger a reporting obligation in the United States in the absence of any other factors. However, if the foreign entity has an agreement with the domestic company giving the domestic company rights to foreign generated data, the EPA could argue that this type of agreement gives the domestic company "control" of the data. Data sharing agreements are typically entered into to share research costs and allocate costs and profits internationally for tax purposes. Although it is important to determine if such an agreement is in effect, it has become common for U.S. companies to routinely submit reportable information generated by foreign affiliates notwithstanding the fact that there is in some instances no legal obligation to do so.

A similar issue can occur in a corporate acquisition or merger. Toxicity data in the possession of an acquired foreign entity may come within the possession of a U.S. acquirer by virtue of a corporate stock or asset transaction thus triggering an obligation to immediately report substantial risk information concerning a chemical substance or mixture that the U.S. parent or affiliate manufactures, imports, or distributes in commerce.

Section 8(e) reportable information may arise in a wide variety of settings, including draft, interim, or final written reports or verbal reports that involve

207. 2003 Reporting Guidance, 33137.

observations, data, and conclusions from human or animal studies or events, environmental studies or events (including chemical monitoring studies), or emergency incidents of environmental contamination.

2. Cover Letters

The EPA has adopted a standard cover sheet for 8(e) submittals, but its use is purely voluntary and most companies simply write a cover letter. The cover sheet is called a TSCA Health & Safety Study Cover Sheet,[208] and was designed to collect information under TSCA §§ 4, 8(d), 8(e) and the Voluntary Children's Chemical Evaluation Program (VCCEP)[209] and was intended to provide a transition to electronic reporting although electronic reporting has not been implemented for 8(e) reporting.[210]

It is easier for the EPA to track submissions if there is a separate submission for each chemical, instead of consolidating multiple reports in one submission.[211] In practice, most submittals are for only one chemical.[212]

If a company that has signed a TSCA § 5(e) order needs to submits an 8(e) report on the subject substance, it should first check to determine whether the (5)e order has any impact on the 8(e) report. For example, most 5(e) orders require the company to identify the 5(e) order and the PMN number in a cover letter.

The statutory reporting obligation is satisfied by "informing" the Administrator of substantial risk information. The information solicited by the EPA's cover sheet is all that must be submitted to initially meet that statutory requirement. Many companies chose to submit the full studies that they have received as part of their initial submittal. If the EPA requests the full studies and backup data, those must be submitted.

3. "FYI" Submissions

Entities that either do not have a reporting obligation, such as trade associations, and companies that have concluded that their information does not rise to the level of substantial risk information can report studies to the EPA on a "for your information" basis. Reporting information on an FYI basis does not technically satisfy that entity's reporting obligation. As a result, companies should be careful to report on an FYI basis only when they are

---

208. TSCA Health & Safety Study Cover Sheet is *available through* http://www. regulations.gov in Docket No. EPA-HQ-OPPT-2006-0499.
209. *See* Chapter 10, Voluntary Initiatives.
210. 72 Fed. Reg. 18993 (Apr. 16, 2007).
211. 2006 Frequent Questions, A.6.
212. *See* the EPA's list of 8(e) Notices and FYI Submissions at http://www.epa.gov/opptintr/tsca8e/pubs/8eandfyisubmissions.htm.

clearly not obligated to report information but still want to bring it to the EPA's attention. For example, a company that has ceased all activities relating to a chemical may learn substantial risk information, which should only be reported as an FYI submission.

4. Practical Implications of Submitting 8(e) Studies

As soon as there is sufficient evidence to conclude that a study shows a substantial risk, product stewardship principles come into play. Depending on the procedures in place at each company and the significance of the observed effect, product stewardship could require warnings on product labels and MSDSs, notification to customers and implementing workplace safety precautions.

TSCA § 8(e) reports are made public, and if the fact that a company is investigating a specific chemical could reveal trade secrets, certain information in the submittal can be marked as confidential.

H. Confidentiality

A person may claim that some or all of the information submitted to EPA pursuant to TSCA § 8(e) is Confidential Business Information (CBI). CBI is subject to the statutory confidentiality provisions of TSCA § 14.[213]

However, although many companies claim CBI for large portions of 8(e) submittals, TSCA § 14(b) provides that health and safety studies on chemicals that have been offered for distribution in commerce are not confidential under TSCA. EPA has said it will not keep confidential the results of these studies, or the chemical identities of the test substances.[214] Although in practice the EPA has abided by claims that submissions contained CBI, on January 21, 2010 it issued a policy stating that as a general practice it will reveal the names of chemicals that are the subject of 8(e) reports if the chemicals are on the publicly available version of the Inventory.[215] When 8(e) reports are submitted with a claim of confidentiality for the chemical identity of a substance on the nonconfidential Inventory, the EPA will write to the submitter and state that it has found that the chemical identity is not entitled to CBI treatment. The submitter may appeal that determination.

Manufacturing processes and the percentages of substances in formulations can be claimed as CBI, and if necessary to protect the confidentiality of such information the EPA will not release the chemical identity under the

213. 40 C.F.R. Part 2.
214. 2003 Reporting Guidance, 33140.
215. 75 Fed. Reg. 3462 (Jan. 21, 2010).

January 2010 policy.[216] The Company's identity can also be claimed as confidential to avoid revealing that the Company is performing research and development on a substance or that the Company is manufacturing or importing a chemical substance.

To submit CBI under TSCA § 8(e), two copies of the written information must be provided. The first copy should be complete with all CBI clearly identified by boxing, circling, or underlining. All such pages containing CBI must be stamped "CONFIDENTIAL." The second copy should have all CBI removed. This second copy will be available in EPA's public files.

Any person who submits CBI to EPA in the context of a substantial risk report will be required to complete a detailed questionnaire in support of the claim of confidentiality. Unlike with many confidentiality claims where substantiation is only required when there is a Freedom of Information Act request, claims of confidentiality for information in 8(e) reports must be submitted with the 8(e) report.[217]

VI. Enforcement

EPA has indicated that it will not take enforcement actions against individuals related to their exercise of personal responsibility for reporting under TSCA § 8(e) if their employers implement compliance policies and procedures to ensure reporting of substantial risk information.[218] In order to provide that protection to officers and employees, companies must have a policy and procedure for channeling substantial risk information to the person responsible for reporting that information directly to EPA, and a procedure for company processing of substantial risk information.[219]

The enforcement response policy applicable to § 8 is entitled The Enforcement Response Policy for Reporting and Recordkeeping Rules and Requirements for TSCA Sections 8, 12, and 13 (the Reporting Rule ERP).[220] As discussed in connection with imports and exports, which uses the same

---

216. *Id.* at 3463.
217. 2003 Reporting Guidance, 33140.
218. Individuals who have reporting responsibility under the corporate policy and procedure do not benefit from this EPA policy.
219. A model policy and procedure designed to meet the minimum requirements for qualifying for the EPA policy is located in Chapter 20, Practice Tools. The EPA does not have the authority to absolve individuals of criminal liability or liability for violation of the clear language of the statute, but the guidances provide a valuable statement of the EPA's intent to exercise discretion in civil enforcements and referrals to the Department of Justice for criminal prosecution.
220. EPA, Toxic and Pesticides Enforcement Division, Office of Regulatory Enforcement, Office of Enforcement and Compliance Assurance (revised Mar. 31, 1999) [hereinafter Reporting

ERP,[221] the EPA may seek civil penalties, refer a violation for criminal penalties under TSCA § 16, seek to enjoin a violation, issue a Notice of Noncompliance if the violation was minor, or a combination of these.

Like all of the ERPs, the Reporting Rule ERP calls for determining the nature, circumstances, extent, and gravity of the violation to determine the gravity based penalty.[222] Each individual component is given a score, and a penalty is calculated based on a matrix. The penalty is then adjusted up or down based on factors such as history of prior violations, culpability, ability to pay, and such other matters as justice may require. The nature of all Reporting Rule violations is hazard assessment. The circumstances reflect the possibility that harm will result from the violation, whereas the extent of a violation depends on the extent of the potential harm.

The original maximum penalties in the Reporting Rule ERP must be increased by a factor of 1.5 for violations occurring after January 13, 2009 because the penalties applicable to all environmental violations have been increased.[223]A failure to report under §§ 8(a), (d) and (e), and failure to make records under TSCA § 8(c) are all Circumstance Level 1. Violations are assessed for only one day for failure to report emergency incidents of environmental contamination under TSCA § 8(e) and for failure to record allegations under TSCA § 8(c). Failures to report all other 8(e) information, and failures to report under §§ 8(a) and (d) are assessed penalties for each day that the violation continues.[224]

A failure to maintain records other than allegations of substantial risk, and a failure to report a study under § 8(d) that the manufacturer knows of but does not possess are both circumstance Level 2 violations, and penalties are assessed for one day of violation.[225]

It is a circumstance Level 3 violation to fail to maintain 8(c) records (as opposed to a failure to create the record in the first place) in the manner required by the regulations governing allegations of adverse effects, and a one day penalty may be assessed. If EPA asks for missing information under §§ 8(a) PAIR, 8(d) or 8(e) and it is not provided, the circumstance is Level 3 and the penalties apply per day of violation.[226]

Late 8(e) reports are circumstance Level 4 and the EPA imposes penalties for each day that the report is late.

Rule ERP], *available through* http://cfpub.epa.gov/compliance/resources/policies/civil/tsca/

221. *See* Chapter 8, Exports and Imports.
222. *See* Chapter 14, Penalties and Enforcement.
223. For details on penalty increases and how to calculate the applicable penalties based on the penalties recited in the Reporting Rule ERP, *see* Chapter 5, Penalties and Enforcement.
224. Reporting Rule ERP, 9.
225. *Id.* at 10.
226. *Id.*

Minor violations are circumstance Level 6, and these include sending a report to the wrong EPA office and not identifying the report as being submitted under TSCA § 8, and sending a report to the wrong EPA office after receiving a prior notice of noncompliance for the same type of report. The Reporting Rule ERP calls for imposing one day penalties for these violations.[227]

The extent of a reporting violation will be classified as major if it is a violation of §§ 8(c), (d), or (e) and directly interferes with the EPA's response to imminent hazards, unreasonable risks, or substantial endangerment to health or the environment. Violations of §§ 8(d) or (e) that involve human data, and violations of § 8(e) involving emergency incidents of environmental contamination, and all of the Level 6 violations described above, are classified as major extent.[228]

The extent of a violation is significant if it is a violation of §§ 8(d) or (e) involving anything other than human data, emergency incidents of environmental contamination, physical chemical properties, or environmental fate data. A violation is also significant in extent if it is a Level 1, 2, 3, or 4 violation of a PAIR rule, a chemical specific 8(a) rule, or any 8(c) violation that is not categorized as major extent.

Failure to submit physical chemical or environmental fate data under § 8(d) is minor in extent.[229]

The penalty matrix in the Reporting Rule ERP recites maximum penalties of $25,000 per day for Level 1, major violations that occurred prior to January 30, 1997. The maximum is now $37,500 for violations after January 12, 2009.[230] Failure to file an 8(e) report involving human data is an example of a Level 1, Major violation.

Although penalties can mount up very quickly, in some instances the per day penalties are capped. For example, the per day penalties for violations of § 8(e) are capped at one daily penalty plus only one more daily penalty for each thirty days of violation; in calculating the penalty for all days after the first day, the total number of days of violation is divided by thirty. Violation of a chemical specific 8(a) rule is capped at one day plus one more day per year (divide the total number of days after the first one by 360), and violation of all other penalties is capped at the first day plus two more per year (divide the total number of days after the first one by 180).

A second type of cap comes into play for violations of § 8(a) chemical specific rules, PAIR, and § 8(c). All of these will be penalized for a maximum

---

227. *Id.*

228. *Id.* at 11.

229. *Id.* at 12.

230. Interim penalty increases were made, and for a full discussion of the penalties in effect for violations over time, *see* Chapter 14, Penalties and Enforcement.

of one year's penalties. There is no maximum cap for § 8(e), and the cap for violations of § 8(d) vary according to the extent of the violation.

The Reporting Rule ERP states that the EPA may impose penalties for each chemical involved in the violation, and for each effect that was not reported under § 8(e).[231]

Once the gravity based penalty is calculated, it can be adjusted for voluntary self reporting, voluntary self reporting within one month, the violator's attitude, the violator's ability to pay, the effect the penalty will have on the violator's ability to do business, any history of prior such violations the violator may have, the violator's degree of culpability, and "such other matters as justice may require."

Perhaps the most publicized enforcement action under TSCA § 8 was the EPA's 2004 action against DuPont concerning perfluorooctanoic acid (PFOA), which DuPont settled in 2005. PFOA is a processing aid in the manufacture of flouropolymers, including Teflon® coatings. Under the terms of the settlement, DuPont agreed to pay $10,250,000 to the EPA and perform two supplemental environmental projects (SEPs). The first SEP was biodegradation testing of products made with certain fluorinated chemicals called fluorotelomers, and the estimated cost of that SEP was $5,000,000. The second SEP involved chemistry resources for junior high schools and high schools in Wood County, West Virginia, and it was estimated to cost $1,250,000.

The EPA had alleged in two complaints that DuPont learned in 1981 that PFOA could potentially cause birth defects in rats, and the same year DuPont studied PFOA in the blood of pregnant workers and obtained results showing that PFOA was present in workers' blood and could cross the placenta of pregnant women. The complaint states that the following year, DuPont submitted a study under TSCA § 8(e) indicating that PFOA could cross rat placentas, but did not submit the human data. In 2000, DuPont produced the study to opposing counsel in a toxic tort action, but did not submit it to the EPA. Opposing counsel then submitted the study to the EPA, which is presumably what precipitated the enforcement action.

The complaints also alleged that in 1991 DuPont set an internal guideline of one part per million for safe exposure to PFOA in drinking water. During the 1980s DuPont had collected information showing the presence of PFOA in drinking water above the level it had set. EPA also alleged that DuPont violated the Resource Recovery and Conservation Act (RCRA) because it did not submit the information it had concerning PFOA's ability to move across human placentas, in response to a request for toxicological information about PFOA under a RCRA corrective action permit. According to the Consent

231. Reporting Rule ERP, 12–13.

Agreement and Final Order entered in the Environmental Appeals Board,[232] there were several more instances of late or non-reporting. DuPont denied all the allegations.

There are several important lessons from this enforcement proceeding. First, substantial risk information can be a powerful tool to toxic tort plaintiffs if the company has not submitted it to the EPA. Second, internal levels of concern should be treated as if they were agency established benchmarks setting levels of concern for environmental contaminants. Third, whenever a document is reviewed in the context of production for litigation, it should be reevaluated for reporting under TSCA § 8(e) and the obligation to trigger a review will fall on litigation counsel who may not have familiarity with TSCA.

In *U.S. v W.R. Grace*,[233] the United States charged the defendants with criminal conspiracy to defraud the government. The government did not charge the defendants with TSCA violations for failure to submit reports under TSCA § 8(e), but it did charge that failing to submit timely 8(e) reports was an act in furtherance of the alleged conspiracy. W.R. Grace was ultimately acquitted, but this case is an illustration of how alleged TSCA violations could be penalized much more severely under statutes other than TSCA.

---

232. In the Matter of E.I. du Pont de Nemours and Company, Docket Nos. TSCA–HQ-2004-0016, RCRA–HQ-2004-0016, and TSCA–HQ-2005-5001 (Dec. 21, 2005, amended Jan. 8, 2009), *available through* http://www.epa.gov.

233. 455 F. Supp.2d 1156 (Mont. 2006).

CHAPTER 8

Exports and Imports

I. Regulation of Exports

Unlike most sections of the Toxic Substances Control Act (TSCA),[1] which deal with protecting the health of people and the environment of the United States, § 12(b) is intended to inform foreign governments of hazards that may be associated with a chemical substance or mixture so that those governments may devise whatever constraints, if any, they deem appropriate to protect their own residents and environment.[2] The Export Notification rule implemented under § 12(b) has been modified over the years to conform the domestic export notification program to international norms, to the extent permitted under applicable law.[3]

A. Scope of Coverage of Export Notifications

Section 12(b) of TSCA requires exporters to notify the United States Environmental Protection Agency (EPA) before, or on the date of, export of certain chemical substances or mixtures. The covered chemical substances are those (i) for which data are required under § 4 or § 5(b), (ii) for which an order has been issued under § 5, (iii) for which a rule has been proposed or issued under § 5 or § 6, or (iv) with respect to which an action is pending, or relief has been granted under § 5 or § 7.[4] A significant new use rule is a rule under § 5 and chemicals that are the subject of proposed or issued significant new use rules are subject to the § 12(b) notification requirements.[5]

The export rule requires export notification for Polychlorinated Biphenyls (PCBs) or PCB articles, for any purpose other than disposal, except where the PCBs are present in a concentration of less than of equal to fifty parts per million by weight or volume.[6] All other exports of articles are exempt from the notification requirements, unless specifically required by the content of § 5, § 6, or § 7 actions.[7] For example, a rule proposed on lead and zinc fishing

1. 15 U.S.C. §§ 2601–2695d.
2. 45 Fed. Reg. 82844 (Dec. 16, 1980).
3. EPA announced that the United States intended to participate in an international information sharing program sponsored by the United Nations called the Prior Informed Consent Program. 57 Fed. Reg. 58390 (Dec. 9, 1992).
4. 40 C.F.R. § 707.60.
5. 40 C.F.R. § 721.20.
6. 40 C.F.R. § 707.60(c)(3) & (4). This *de minimis* exception for PCBs was added to the rule in the amendments announced in 71 Fed. Reg. 66234 (Nov. 14, 2006). *See* the discussion later in this section on the inclusion of *de minimis* levels for export notifications for an explanation of the rationale for this amendment.
7. 40 C.F.R. § 707.60(b).

sinkers did specifically require export notifications for these articles.[8] Exporters who are granted exemptions from regulatory prohibitions to exportation under § 5 or § 6 must also file export notifications.[9]

If the EPA action that prompts the notice is a proposed rule, the export notification requirement begins only thirty days after publication of the proposal in the Federal Register.[10]

To obtain a list of the chemical substances subject to export notification, exporters can check the "Current List of Chemical Substances Subject to TSCA Section 12(b) Export Notification Requirements."[11] The list contains the date it was last updated. Exporters can also purchase or license commercial software packages that tend to be updated more frequently, are more user friendly, and can electronically search the exporters' databases for the chemical substances subject to actual and proposed rules, orders or consent decrees.

The regulatory actions that trigger export notifications do not sunset, except for § 4 test rules. Therefore, all chemicals for which export notifications are required, except those chemicals that require export notifications only because they are subject to a promulgated § 4 test rule, continue to require export notifications in perpetuity, or until they are withdrawn. Test rules expire, however they may be in effect for as long as ten years.[12] EPA publishes a list of "Sunset Dates/Status for Chemicals Subject to Section 4 Actions."[13] This list contains the date it was last updated. Keep in mind that a notification that a § 4 chemical has sunset does not necessarily mean that an export notice is no longer required. That chemical may also be the subject of another TSCA action triggering export notice requirements, so the exporter still needs to conduct due diligence. EPA is developing a

---

8. 59 Fed. Reg. 11122, 11142 (Mar. 9, 1994). EPA has indicated it is re-evaluating this proposed rule. Regulatory Plan and Semiannual Regulatory Agenda, EPA-230-Z-09-002, 194 (Fall 2009) [hereinafter Fall 2009 Regulatory Agenda], *available at* http://www.epa.gov/lawsregs/documents/regagendabook-fall09.pdf.
9. 40 C.F.R. § 707.60(e).
10. 40 C.F.R. § 707.65(b).
11. *Available at* http://www.epa.gov/oppt/import-export/pubs/12blist.pdf. EPA includes a disclaimer with this list, which provides that the list contained on its Web site is a service to the regulated community and is not intended to be relied on in lieu of relevant Federal Register documents, orders, or the Code of Federal Regulations.
12. 58 Fed. Reg. 40238, 40239 (July 27, 1993). Test rules continue in effect through the end of the period when companies can claim reimbursement for use of the data they developed under the test rule.
13. *Available at* http://www.epa.gov/oppt/chemtest/pubs/sunsettable.html. EPA includes a disclaimer with this list, which provides that the list contained on its Web site is a service to the regulated community and is not intended to be relied on in lieu of relevant Federal Register documents, orders or the Code of Federal Regulations.

Web-based database[14] of every chemical regulated under TSCA. It is too early to know how accurate and up to date that tool will eventually be.

When the export notification rule was first published, there was no *de minimis* level below which chemical substances in mixtures would be exempt from the export notification requirements. EPA said that it could not determine a universal safe level because some substances remained toxic in very small quantities.[15] Subsequently, in the 2006 amendments to the export rule, EPA did include a *de minimis* amount below which no export notice would be required. In explaining the rationale for the change, EPA made clear that the change was "not an indication that EPA has determined that chemicals are generally not toxic at lesser concentrations."[16] Instead, EPA explained the change as a "reflection of the circumstances under which EPA believes foreign governments want to receive information regarding chemicals imported into their countries."[17]

For this aspect of TSCA, instead of looking at domestic needs, EPA considered internationally developed norms. First, EPA considered the Globally Harmonized System of Classification and Labeling of Chemicals (GHS),[18] an internationally developed tool for chemical hazard communication. One of the goals of GHS labeling is to facilitate international trade in chemicals whose hazards have been assessed based on internationally agreed upon criteria. Just like TSCA § 12(b), GHS is used to communicate information on chemicals to foreign governments. Consistent with the GHS, EPA determined that no notification would be required for chemicals where such chemical is present in a concentration of less than 1 percent by weight or volume,[19] with two exceptions. The first exception is that export notifications must be made for known or potential human carcinogens if the chemical is present in a concentration of 0.1 percent or more, by weight or volume.[20] EPA's regulations define a carcinogen based both on domestic as well as international classifications.[21] The second exception arises in connection with

14. http://iaspub.epa.gov/sor_internet/registry/substreg/home/overview/home.do.
15. 45 Fed. Reg. 82844, 82845 (Dec. 16, 1980).
16. 71 Fed. Reg. 66234, 66238 (Nov. 14, 2006).
17. *Id.*
18. Globally Harmonized System of Classification and Labeling of Chemicals, adopted by the United Nations Economic and Social Council (July 2003).
19. 40 C.F.R. § 707.60 (c)(1).
20. 40 C.F.R. § 707.60(c)(2).
21. Carcinogen is defined based the latest edition of the of the Report on Carcinogens issued by the U.S. Dept. of Health and Human Services, Public Health Service, National Toxicology Program and the latest editions of the Monographs and Supplements on the Evaluation of Carcinogenic Risks to Humans issued by the World health Organization International Agency for Research on Cancer, Lyons, France. Alpha-naphthylamine (CAS No. 134-32-7) and 4-nitrobiphenyl (CAS No. 92-93-3) are specially called out as being within the definition.

the export of PCBs, which require an export notification when exported in a concentration of greater than fifty parts per million.[22] EPA determined this different *de minimis* concentration level for PCBs after considering the treatment of PCBs under international treaties, such as the Stockholm Convention and the Basel Convention on the Control of Transboundary Movements of Hazardous Wastes and their Disposal.[23] So, there now exist three different *de minimis* levels, 1 percent, 0.1 percent and fifty parts per million, depending on what is being exported.

The export notification requirement applies to a TSCA regulated chemical substance, and is not dependent on its end use. For those export notifications required because the EPA has restricted certain end uses, export notification must be given to EPA without regard to the actual intended use. For example, if the EPA restricts use under § 5 to permit only the manufacture of an article, notification of export must still be given even if the foreign purchaser intends to make other use of the chemical substance.[24]

Chemical substances, mixtures, or articles containing substances or mixtures manufactured, processed or distributed in commerce solely for export and labeled "for export only" are generally exempt from the provisions of TSCA.[25] This exemption does not apply (i) to § 8 reporting and recordkeeping requirements, (ii) if the EPA determines that the chemical substance, mixtures or article will present an unreasonable risk of injury to health or the environment in the United States,[26] or (iii) if the EPA determines it requires testing to make the determination in sub provision (ii) above.[27] An export notice will also not be required for chemicals denied entry into the United States that are being returned to the country of origin, unless a TSCA § 5, § 6, or § 7 rule or order applies to the chemical.[28]

In at least one respect, the EPA's statements about when export notifications are mandatory are inconsistent with a court's statements. EPA has said that the § 12(b) notification requirements apply not only to persons who sign a final testing consent agreement under § 4 or a consent order under § 5, but also to any other person who intends to export any substance covered by those agreements or orders.[29] The EPA often enters into Enforceable Consent Orders (ECAs) rather than carrying out the burdensome rulemaking process

---

22. 40 C.F.R. § 707.60(c)(3).
23. 71 Fed. Reg. 66234, 66238 (Nov. 14, 2006).
24. 45 Fed. Reg. 82844, 82845 (Dec. 16, 1980).
25. TSCA § 12(a)(1).
26. The only chemicals in this category are PCBs, asbestos, certain metal working fluids, and hexavalent chromium. *See* Chapter 11, Bans and Restrictions.
27. TSCA § 12(a).
28. 48 Fed. Reg. 34734, 34738 (Aug. 1, 1983).
29. 40 C.F.R. § 60(a)(11).

required for § 4 test rules.[30] Consistent with this interpretation, EPA puts into its Federal Register notices announcing voluntarily entered into ECAs that "EPA's ECA regulations require that each ECA contain a statement that manufacturers or processors signing the ECA, as well as any other person, shall comply with export notification requirements in TSCA section 12(b)."[31] At least one court has taken issue with this assertion by the EPA as relates to ECAs requiring testing. In *NRDC v. EPA*,[32] the Natural Resources Defense Council and the AFL-CIO sued EPA, alleging that EPA had failed to meet its statutory obligations because, among other things, it did not issue test rules for chemicals designated by the Interagency Testing Committee.[33] The Court held that EPA violated TSCA by negotiating consent agreements instead of issuing § 4 test rules. The Court further noted the other TSCA provisions that are triggered by the issuance of a test rule, and found that these provisions, including the export notification requirements of § 12(b), would not be triggered by a voluntary agreement.[34] Compliance with agency interpretations is always the best course of action at the outset, but companies should be aware of possible defense arguments in the event they find themselves the subject of enforcement proceedings in this type of situation.

B. Content and Timing of Export Notifications

The exporter must submit a notification of export or of intent to export a regulated chemical substance or mixture. For purposes of § 12(b), exporter is defined as "the person who, as the principal party in interest in the export transaction, has the power and responsibility for determining and controlling the sending of the chemical substance or mixture to a destination out of the customs territory of the United States."[35]

The export notification must be postmarked on the earlier of (i) within seven days of forming the intent to export or (ii) the date of the export. The notice of intent must be based on a definite contractual obligation, or an intra-company agreement, to export the chemical.[36] A nonspecific intention to export based on past business practices or a general expectation of continued demand for a substance does not trigger a notice.[37] The EPA gave several examples at an industry meeting of how this might work in practice.

30. *See* Chapter 9, Test Rules.
31. *See, e.g.*, 70 Fed. Reg. 39624, 39627 (July 8, 2005).
32. 595 F. Supp. 1255 (S.D.N.Y 1984).
33. *Id.* at 1261.
34. *Id.*
35. 40 C.F.R. § 707.63(b).
36. 40 C.F.R. § 707.65(a)(3).
37. 45 Fed. Reg. 82844, 82845 (Dec. 16, 1980).

It explained that if acceptance of the order constituted the formation of the contract, notification must be made within the earlier to occur of seven days after contract acceptance, or export.[38] If fulfillment of the order constituted the formation of the contract, notification must be made within the earlier to occur of seven days of fulfilling the order or export.[39]

While no particular form is required, the notice must be in a writing, marked "Section 12(b) Notice," and must contain:

- name of the regulated chemical, as it appears in the triggering action. If a category is regulated, the category and the name of the individual regulated chemical in that category must both be included. The name should be the name that appears in Volume 1 of the EPA Chemical Substance Inventory, or its supplements;
- name and address of exporter;
- country or countries of import;
- date or dates of export or intended export; and
- triggering section of TSCA.

Information about several substances going to several countries may be combined into one notice to EPA.[40] The notice should be sent to EPA by mail or delivered by hand or courier. The mail address is: Document Control Office (7407M), Office of Pollution Prevention and Toxics (OPPT), Environmental Protection Agency, 1200 Pennsylvania Ave., NW., Washington, DC 20460–0001 (Attention: TSCA Section 12(b) Notice). For hand delivery, the address is: OPPT Document Control Office (DCO), EPA East, Rm. 6428, Environmental Protection Agency, 1201 Constitution Ave., NW., Washington, DC (Attention: TSCA Section 12(b) Notice).[41] EPA is required to send notification to the country of import within five working days after receipt of an export notice.[42] The EPA notice identifies the regulated substance, summarizes the regulatory action taken or the availability of data, designates an EPA official for contact, and includes a copy of the pertinent Federal Register notice.[43]

Since the promulgation of the first export rule, EPA has reduced the required frequency for submitting export notifications. In its original export rule,[44] EPA imposed the same annual filing requirements without regard to

---

38. EPA, TSCA Questions and Answers from the October, 1990 EPA-Industry Living with TSCA Workshop, question 43 (Oct. 1992) [hereinafter Living with TSCA Q&A].
39. *Id.* at question 43.
40. 45 Fed. Reg. 82844, 82846 (Dec. 16, 1980).
41. 40 C.F.R. § 707.65(c).
42. 40 C.F.R.§ 707.70(a).
43. 40 C.F.R.§ 707.70(b).
44. 45 Fed. Reg. 82844 (Dec. 16, 1980).

which section of TSCA triggered the requirement. In a subsequent amendment,[45] EPA reduced the annual requirement for § 4 chemical substances to a requirement of only one notice for the first shipment to a particular country. The purpose of this change was to distinguish for foreign governments those substances for which EPA did not have sufficient data on a particular chemical to make a fully informed decision from those which EPA had determined to be of concern, and to better align itself with international practices.[46] And, in the 2006 amendments EPA further reduced the requirement for annual notifications in deference to the desires of foreign countries as evidenced in international treaties.

Currently, an annual export notice for a particular country is only required when the triggering event for the notice is an action under § 5(f), § 6 or § 7.[47] Those three sections deal with unreasonable risks and imminent hazards, and there are relatively few situations that result in actions under those sections. If the notice is triggered by any other section of TSCA (§ 5(e), § 5(a)(2), § 4 or § 5(b)) the exporter must give the notice only for the first export or intended export of that substance to a particular country.[48] If an exporter made an export notification for a chemical to a country prior to January 16, 2007, that notice would count as the one time required notification for that particular substance to that particular country for the listed triggering action. This provision allows exporters who had given notice of exports prior to the rule change to benefit from such prior export notifications. Each exporter has an obligation to make the export notification, even if it knows that another exporter has made a notification for the same chemical to the same country.[49] When acquiring other companies, acquirers should consider making export notifications for new exports in the name of the acquirer, even if the selling party had previously made the required notifications.[50]

The change away from predominately annual notifications per country per substance has three consequences. First, with respect to chemicals that are the subject of more than one triggering event, exporters are required to notify EPA with respect to each triggering event to which the chemical is or becomes subject even if they previously notified EPA about the export of that chemical to that country as a result of an earlier triggering event.[51] This means that if an exporter made a notice under one triggering section before another

---

45. 58 Fed. Reg. 40238 (July 27, 1993).
46. *Id.* at 40239.
47. 40.C.F.R. § 707.65(a)(2)(i).
48. 40 C.F.R. § 707.65(a)(2)(ii).
49. 71 Fed. Reg. 66234, 66241 (Nov. 14, 2006). EPA explained, in response to a comment, that § 12(b) refers to "any person" who exports or intends to export, meaning clearly that the notification requirement pertains to each exporter.
50. *See* Chapter 15, Acquisitions and Divestitures.
51. 71 Fed. Reg. 66234, 66239 (Nov. 14, 2006).

triggering section was implicated, the exporter must make a new export notification as a result of the additional triggering action at the time of its next export. When notifications were done on an annual basis by country, this requirement may have been easier to track. The second implication of the change is on records retention policies. While there is a general requirement under TSCA, unless otherwise specified, that records be maintained for five years from the date of the applicable action, since the exporter would have to prove compliance with the requirement at the time of first export, export notifications should be maintained for five years beyond the date the exporter stops doing business in the particular substance instead of just five years from the date of first export. The third implication is that the export notification requirements under TSCA are now more closely aligned with the United Nations Prior Informed Consent (PIC) program, in which EPA had announced it was participating in 1992.[52] Under PIC, participating exporting countries provide notice to participating importing countries prior to exporting a chemical which has been banned or severely restricted in the country of export. Exporting countries are not permitted to export chemicals against the wishes of the importing countries.[53] However, EPA does not have the general authority under TSCA to prevent the export of chemicals in conformance to the wishes of an importing country.[54]

The country of import, as required in the § 12(b) notification, means the country of destination. "The country of destination is defined as the country where the goods are to be consumed, further processed, or manufactured, as known to the shipper at the time of exportation. If the shipper does not know the country of ultimate destination, the shipment is credited to the last country to which the exporter knows the merchanidise will be shipped."[55]

C. Confidentiality

Confidentiality comes up in three very distinct ways in complying with the export notice rules. In some instances, the exporter will not know the composition of the materials to be exported because the supplier has claimed the composition as confidential. In those cases the exporter will need to obtain a certification from the supplier saying whether export notifications are required.

In some cases, the exporter will know the exact chemical identity of the substance to be exported, but will not know whether that substance is subject

---

52. 57 Fed. Reg. 58390 (Dec. 9, 1992).
53. 58 Fed. Reg. 40238, 40239 (July 27, 1993).
54. *Id.* at 40240.
55. 45 Fed. Reg. 82844, 82846 (Dec. 16, 1980).

to an export notification requirement because the EPA is required to treat the chemical identity of the substance that requires export notifications as confidential. As noted above, if a substance is subject to a proposed or issued significant new use rule (SNUR) then anyone who intends to export that substance must file an export notice. Some SNURS only list the generic chemical family name of the substance subject to the rule.[56] This situation arises when the original manufacturer or importer claimed that the exact chemical identity was confidential when it filed a premanufacture notice prior to the first import or manufacture of the substance. Because the substance identity is confidential, the EPA cannot publish the identity of the substance subject to the SNUR. If the SNUR only lists the generic chemical family name of the substance subject to the rule then an exporter will not know whether the chemical it intends to export is subject to an export notification requirement simply by consulting the Federal Register or a list of SNURs that have been proposed or promulgated. Those sources will not have the Chemical Abstract Service (CAS) Number or exact chemical identity of the substances subject to the SNUR.

Manufacturers, importers, and processors of the substance to be exported can ask the EPA whether the substance is subject to a SNUR. The mechanism for asking the EPA is called a bona fide notice of intent to manufacture, import, or process a substance.[57] If the prospective exporter is not the manufacturer or importer and does not itself process the substance to be exported, there is no formal mechanism to ask the EPA whether the substance to be exported is subject to a SNUR. However, the exporter should ask the manufacturer or importer if the substance is subject to a SNUR. The manufacturer or importer can submit a bona fide notice to the EPA and it is responsible for knowing if the substance is subject to a SNUR or it will be at risk of violating the SNUR rules.

If the exporter is exporting a substance and wants to assert a confidentiality claim concerning any of the information that must be submitted as part of the § 12(b) notice, it can claim confidentiality by marking the specific information on each page with a label such as "confidential business information," "proprietary," or "trade secret."[58] The EPA will still disclose the information in its notices to foreign governments, but a claim of confidentiality will stop the EPA from disclosing the information to other parties, except in accordance with the procedures of TSCA § 14 and 40 C.F.R. Part 2.[59] If the exporter fails to assert a claim of confidentiality with the export notice, EPA may make

56. *See* Chapter 12, Significant New Use Rules.

57. 40 C.F.R. § 721.11. *See* Chapter 12, Significant New Use Rules.

58. 40 C.F.R. § 707.75(a) and (b).

59. 40 C.F.R. § 707.75(c).

the information public without further notice.[60] If the EPA receives a Freedom of Information Act request for information claimed confidential in a § 12(b) notice, the claim of confidentiality will have to be substantiated. EPA advises that the following questions will be among those that will need to be answered to substantiate such a claim:[61]

1 Do you assert that disclosing the information you have claimed confidential should substantially harm your competitive position? If so, what are those harmful effects, and why should they be regarded as substantial? What is the causal relationship between disclosure and the harmful effect?
2 If you have previously exported this chemical in any form to the destination country, what precautions did you take to protect the information you now claim as confidential from disclosure?
3 To what extent has it been, or will it be, revealed to others that this chemical will be exported by you to the destination country? What precautions have you taken regarding undesired disclosure of the information you have claimed confidential?
4 Has EPA, another Federal Agency, or a Federal court made any determinations regarding the confidentiality of any item you have claimed confidential? If so, please attach copies.
5 How long should confidential treatment be given the information you have claimed confidential?
6 If you have claimed exporter identity plus any other item of information confidential, and EPA keeps exporter identity confidential, how would disclosing the other information you claimed confidential substantially harm your competitive position?
7 If you have claimed more than one item of information confidential, and EPA keeps one item confidential, how would disclosing the other information you claimed confidential substantially harm your competitive position?

It would be prudent to prepare answers to these questions at the time of making the claim of confidentiality, even though substantiation is not required to be submitted with the claim itself.

---

60. 40 C.F.R. § 707.75(d).

61. 45 Fed. Reg. 84844, 82849 (Dec. 16, 1980). These questions were spelled out by the EPA in the original export rule, but are not intended to limit EPA's ability to request more substantiation. These questions are somewhat more limited than the questions EPA requires for substantiation in connection with the premanufacture notification (PMN) rule, which can be found at 40 C.F.R. § 720.85(b)(3)(iv), and which could be useful to consult.

D. Ensuring Compliance with Export Notification Requirements

Understanding the export notification requirements is only the first step in putting together systems and procedures to ensure compliance. How to do this depends on the nature of each particular exporter's business, how often and what types of products are exported, and the exporter's internal business systems and work processes. Each company must design a compliance with export notification program around these factors, eliminating the possibility of a one size fits all program. Companies might want to consider the elements set forth below in deciding how best to manage compliance with TSCA export notification requirements.

1. Match Products to Controlled Chemical Substances

The initial task is to understand the nature of what the company sells and how it enters a new product into its internal business system. Does the company sell articles? If so, it will first need to determine if the article contains a chemical substance or mixture which has a separate end use from the article and will be released or removed from the article. If it does not contain such substances or mixtures, the article is not subject to TSCA § 12(b), except if it contains PCBs in a concentration of more than fifty parts per million or except if it contains substances that are specifically restricted in articles in § 5, § 6 or § 7 actions.[62,63] What is the master repository of products by chemical composition at the company? Typically, the Material Safety Data Sheet (MSDS) database is the master repository of products by chemical composition, but an alternative could exist. The master repository must be updated each time there is a change in the composition of the product, such as because of a process change or a reengineering of the product. The employees who are involved with making any such potential changes need to understand their responsibility to keep the master repository current. Procedures should be written that control how those changes are made, documented and communicated.

The next step is to have a mechanism for checking the chemical substances in the master repository against the list of chemicals subject to § 12(b). As noted above, there are a variety of sources of such lists, such as the one

62. 40 C.F.R. § 707.60(b) and (d).
63. *See, e.g.*, 59 Fed. Reg. 11122, 11142 (Mar. 9, 1994). This proposed ban on small lead and zinc sinkers explicitly requires export notifications. *See* EPA's Current List of Chemical Substances Subject to TSCA Section 12(b) Export Notification Requirements (Oct. 10, 2009), *available at* http://www.epa.gov/oppt/import-export/pubs/12blist.pdf. EPA has indicated it is re-evaluating this proposed rule. Fall 2009 Regulatory Agenda, 104.

maintained by the EPA on its Web site or proprietary databases. If exporting chemical substances or mixtures is an important part of the company's business, the responsibility for monitoring the federal register to catch additions to the export list before they are included on the EPA Web site or a licensed proprietary database should be assigned to a regulatory specialist on an ongoing basis. Finally, a product list containing substances subject to the notification requirements because one or more of their components are subject to § 12(b) should be created and maintained. The list should contain product name, regulated chemical component, section of TSCA responsible for triggering the § 12(b) requirement, and an identification of the applicable requirement (annual notice or one time notice). The list should also have a column for history of notifications, setting forth the triggering section that was the subject of the notification, the country of export and the date of the notification. The EPA Web site should periodically be reviewed for § 4 test rules that have sunset and this information should be verified and then incorporated into the list. This list could be maintained in hard copy or electronically, but it should always have a last revision date for document control purposes. An alternative to having such a list would be to insert the elements of the list into an existing database, such as the master repository. Most often the person responsible for creating and updating this list is a regulatory specialist.

2. Export Processing

Once the information is compiled, the next step is to make sure that the people who are responsible in the company for exports, including through the mails or courier services, perform their functions consistently with the requirements for export notifications. As always, the best way to do this depends on what the company does and how it does it. For companies that seldom export, training the export specialist, or having a written procedure requiring the export specialist to check the product list manually each time she makes an export may be sufficient. Someone in the organization, either the regulatory specialist or the export specialist, must enter onto the list the history of notifications made for each chemical substance. A copy of the notification must also be maintained in accordance with appropriate record retention requirements for at least five years after the most recent export of the substance to the same country.

If the company frequently exports many different products containing chemical substances subject to the export notification requirements, a manual check will likely not be the optimal way to ensure compliance. A preferable approach would be to insert flags in the company's enterprise resource planning system, its order processing system, or its export system that alert the export specialist that a particular product being exported is subject to an export requirement. The export specialist can be trained to pass this information on to the regulatory specialist, who will handle the notification process. Or, the export specialist can be trained to do the process herself. The process consists of reviewing the export list of regulated products to determine what the requirement for the product is, checking the product export history, and sending the notification, which must be postmarked within seven days of forming the intent to export or on the date of the export, whichever is earlier. Another alternative would be to have a highly automated system, where the export system is connected to the master repository database, in which the export list resides, and every time an order is entered for export, the export system checks the master repository database and automatically triggers a report to the export specialist telling her the requirement and the notification history, and providing an appropriate notification form. In making the notification, remember that most systems are likely to operate based on product name, but that the notification needs to be made based on the name of the regulated chemical substance.

3. Sample Notification Form

While there is no required format for a § 12(b) export notification, the following sample notification contains all the required elements:

[Date] Via Mail, Return Receipt Requested[64]

Document Control Office (7407M)
Office of Pollution Prevention and Toxics
Environmental Protection Agency
1200 Pennsylvania Avenue NW
Washington, DC 20460-0001
Attention TSCA Section 12(b) Notice

Subject: TSCA § 12(b) Notification of Export

Dear Document Control Officer:

Name and CASRN of Regulated Chemical:
[insert, name, e.g., Benzene, 1,1'-oxybis[2,3,4,5,6-pentbromo- (CASRN 1163-19-5)]

64. If the export notice is hand delivered, it should be addressed to OPPT Document Control Office (DCO), EPA East, Rm. 6428, Environmental Protection Agency, 1201 Constitution Ave., NW., Washington, DC (Attention: TSCA Section 12(b) Notice).

TSCA Section to which Chemical is Subject:
[insert, e.g., 4(a)]

Company Address, Telephone Number:
[Insert name, address and phone number of company making the export]

Country or Countries of Import:
[insert, e.g., Australia]

Date of Export or Intended Export:
[insert, e.g., 7/11/09]

We appreciate your assistance in recording this notification. Should you need additional information or assistance concerning this report, please call the undersigned at telephone number (Insert phone number of company contact).

Very truly yours,
(Insert company name)

By:____________________

Title:__________________

---

4. Notification Retention Requirements

While there is no specific recordkeeping requirement under TSCA § 12(b), TSCA generally requires that records be kept for five years.[65] However for notifications that are one time only, likely those notifications should be kept for at least five years after the most recent export of the same substance to the same country to be able to prove that the required § 12(b) notice was made for the first export. If the first notice cannot be located, it would be prudent to file again before the next export of the same substance to the same country.

E. Mercury Export Ban

In 2008, Congress amended TSCA § 12(b) by passing the Mercury Export Ban of 2008,[66] which prohibits the export of elemental mercury effective

---

65. *See, e.g.*, 40 C.F.R. § 720.78, re: PMN requirements and 40 C.F.R. § 717.15 re: records of significant adverse reactions. In *3M Co, v. Browner*, 17 F.3d 1453 (D.C. Cir. 1994), the court established a five year statute of limitations in a TSCA civil penalty action.
66. Pub. L. No. 110-414, § 1, 122 Stat. 4341 (2008). Codified at 15 U.S.C. §§ 5(f) and 11(c).

January 1, 2013.[67] That Act requires EPA to report to Congress within one year of the date of the Act on mercuric chloride, mercurous chloride or calomel, mercuric oxide, and other mercury compounds, if any, that are currently used in significant quantities in products or processes.[68] The Act also allows petitions for an essential use exemption from the ban for a specified use at an identified foreign facility for up to three years and up to ten metric tons of elemental mercury, if EPA makes required findings.[69] EPA has announced that it intends to file a notice of proposed rule making in early 2011 to establish the standards and procedures regarding essential use exemptions.[70]

II. Regulation of Imports

Customs regulations require that every shipment of chemicals into the United States must be accompanied by a certification that the shipment is subject to TSCA and in compliance with TSCA, or a certification that the shipment is not subject to TSCA.[71] These regulations are based on § 13 of TSCA, which mandate that the Secretary of the Treasury refuse entry into the customs territory of the United States, as defined in the Harmonized Tariff Schedule (HTS), of any chemical substance, mixture, or article containing a chemical substance or mixture if such entry (i) fails to comply with any TSCA rule in effect or (ii) is offered for entry in violation of (a) TSCA §§ 5, 6, or subchapter IV (governing lead), (b) a rule or order under TSCA §§ 5, 6, or subchapter IV or (c) an order issued in a civil action brought under TSCA §§ 5 or 7, or subchapter IV.[72] The term customs territory of the United States as used in the HTS includes the fifty States, the District of Columbia, and Puerto Rico.[73] Section 13 also sets forth procedural and other requirements in connection with an entry refusal,[74] and authorizes the Secretary of the Treasury, after consultation with the Administrator of the EPA, to issue rules to administer these requirements.[75] The operative sections of the Code of Federal Regulations (C.F.R.) dealing with imports are those noted above issued by Customs. The C.F.R. section setting out the EPA's statements about

67. TSCA § 12(c)(1).
68. TSCA § 12(c)(3)(A). The statute sets forth the requirements of the report to be made to Congress.
69. *Id.* The statute sets forth the required findings that need to be made by EPA.
70. Fall 2009 Regulatory Agenda, 105.
71. 19 C.F.R. § 12.121.
72. TSCA § 13(a)(1).
73. Harmonized Tariff Schedule of the United States, 3 (2008) (Rev. 1).
74. TSCA § 13(a)(2).
75. TSCA § 13(b).

importation under TSCA are the EPA's policy, and not regulations, because the EPA does not have rulemaking authority under the statute.[76]

A. Importer Defined

The requirements of § 13 apply to an importer, as that term is defined in the Customs regulations. The Customs regulations state:

> Importer means the person primarily liable for the payment of any duties on the merchandise, or an authorized agent acting on his behalf. The importer may be:
> (1) The consignee, or
> (2) The importer of record, or
> (3) The actual owner of the merchandise, if an actual owner's declaration and superseding bond has been filed in accordance with 12 C.F.R. § 141.20, or
> (4) The transferee of the merchandise, if the right to withdraw merchandise in a bonded warehouse has been transferred in accordance with subpart C of 19 C.F.R. § 144.[77]

Under the definition of importer, a variety of different entities can sign the import certification. This flexibility was intended to minimize disruption in the importation process, by allowing the person who normally acts as the importer for customs transactions to sign the certification statement, as well as others.[78] The importer of record can be a foreign company so long as there is a U.S. resident who is authorized to accept service of process in the state or territory where the port of entry is located.[79] The authorized resident must file a bond having a corporation as surety to secure payment of any increased or additional duties that may be found to be due.[80] The importer may be the person primarily liable for payment of duties or one of its agents. In some cases, a domestic purchaser may cause the importation and handle the entire entry process itself, while in other cases it may use a broker or other agent.[81] The importer who signs the certification statement need not be the most

76. 48 Fed. Reg. 55462 (Dec. 13, 1983); 40 C.F.R. § 707.20(a).
77. 19 C.F.R. § 101.1.
78. 48 Fed. Reg. 34734, 34735 (Aug. 1, 1983).
79. *But see*, Living with TSCA Q&A, question 44, advising that a U.S. company that imports directly from another U.S. company's foreign plant is the importer of record.
80. EPA, Toxic Substances Control Act: A Guide for Chemical Importers/Exporters, EPA 560/1-91-001, Office of Toxic Substances, EPA, question 31 (Apr. 1991) [hereinafter 1991 Guide].
81. 48 Fed. Reg. 55462, 55463 (Dec. 13, 1983).

knowledgeable person, as long as the importer is assured that the shipment meets the TSCA requirements.[82]

B. Import Shipment Certifications[83]

1. Individual Shipment Certifications

The importer itself, or its authorized agent, must fulfill the TSCA certification requirement by filing either a positive certification if the chemical shipment is subject to TSCA and is in compliance with applicable TSCA requirements or a negative certification if the chemical shipment is not subject to TSCA. The Customs Regulations[84] specify the exact language that must be used to make the applicable certification:

> **Positive Certification.** I certify that all chemical substances in this shipment comply with all applicable rules or orders under TSCA and that I am not offering a chemical substance for entry in violation of TSCA or any applicable rule or order thereunder.

> **Negative Certification.** I certify that all chemical substances in this shipment are not subject to TSCA.

The appropriate certification must be filed with the director of the port of entry before release of the shipment and must appear as a typed or stamped legend, except when subject to a blanket certification as discussed below, on (i) an appropriate entry document or commercial invoice or on an attachment to that entry document or invoice or (ii) in the event of a release for an immediate delivery, on the commercial invoice or an attachment to that invoice.[85]

82. 48 Fed. Reg. 34734, 34735 (Aug. 1, 1983).
83. Import Certifications are kept by the Customs Service. Copies of certifications are only forwarded to EPA when Customs suspects a violation. Living with TSCA Q&A, question 48.
84. 19 C.F.R. § 12.121(a)(1).
85. 19 C.F.R. § 12.121(a)(2)(i).

The certification statements may be signed using an authorized facsimile signature.[86] For those entries or entry summaries processed electronically, the applicable certification will be in the form of a Certification Code transmitted as part of the Automated Broker Interface (ABI) transmission.[87] CAS Numbers are not necessary for each chemical covered by certification. However, the presence of CAS Numbers helps to expedite proper verification.[88]

2. Blanket Certifications

Subject to the approval of the port director, an importer may use a "blanket" certification to cover multiple shipments of the same product during a one-year period beginning with the date of approval.[89] In approving the use of a blanket certification, the port director will consider the reliability of the importer and the customs broker used by the importer.[90] Due diligence should be conducted on customs brokers to establish reliability before engaging a customs broker. A blanket certification must be filed with the port director on the letterhead of the certifying firm; must list the products covered by name, harmonized tariff schedule, and subheading number; must identify the foreign supplier by name and address; and must be signed by an authorized person.[91] Importers authorized to use blanket certifications must also include a statement on each commercial invoice or entry document referring to the blanket certification and incorporating it by reference. Such statement need not be signed.[92] Certifications need to be filed with each district where importations are anticipated.[93]

EPA has provided a format for blanket certifications and related invoice statements that can be used by importers who use the blanket certification approach:[94]

Positive Blanket Certification

To: District Director
U. S. Customs Service
City, State, Zip Code

---

86. 19 C.F.R. § 12.121(c).
87. 1991 Guide, question 14.
88. *Id.* at question 16.
89. 19 C.F.R. § 12.121(a)(2)(ii).
90. *Id.*
91. *Id.*
92. *Id.*
93. 1991 Guide, question 20.
94. *Id.* at 22–24.

CERTIFICATE

The undersigned, as an authorized agent of (insert name of importer], hereby certifies that all chemical substances in all shipments of products (s) listed herein and imported from suppliers listed below, namely:

PRODUCTS
(list name and HTS item number)

SUPPLIERS
(list name and address)

comply with all applicable rules or orders under TSCA, and (insert name of importer) is not offering a chemical substance for entry in violation of TSCA or any applicable rule or order thereunder.

Dated this ____ day of ____20_.

____
(Authorized signature)

____
(Title)

Blanket Negative Certification

To: District Director
U. S. Customs Service
City, State, Zip Code

CERTIFICATE

The undersigned, as an authorized officer or agent of (insert name of importer), hereby certifies that all chemical substances in all shipments of product(s) listed herein and imported from suppliers listed below, namely:

PRODUCTS
(list name and HTS item number)

SUPPLIERS
(list name and address)

are not subject to TSCA.

Dated this ___ day of ________, 20__.

____
(Authorized signature)

____
(Title)

Form of Statement on Each Commercial Invoice or on Entry Document for Complying Products

Importation of the products described above are subject to certification on file with the District Director in respect of compliance with TSCA executed by (insert name of importer) on (insert date of the applicable blanket positive certification), the terms of which, including the fact of its execution are incorporated herein by reference.

Form of Statement on Each Commercial Invoice or on Entry Document for Products Not subject to TSCA

Importation of the products described above are subject to certification on file with the District Director indicating that they are not subject to TSCA executed by (insert name of importer) on (insert date of the applicable blanket negative certification), the terms of which, including the fact of its execution are incorporated herein by reference.

---

3. Certifications for Chemical Substances Imported by Mail

While substances that are imported through the mail, or by courier services such as Federal Express or United Parcel Service, may not be examined by Customs as a practical matter, certification is also required for such shipments.[95] Recognizing the difficulty the import requirement poses for importers for these types of shipments, especially with respect to unsolicited samples, EPA has developed a system of post importation certification. Foreign suppliers should be advised to include the necessary information with the shipment, which the importer can then use to prepare the post importation certification. This certificate should be sent to U.S. E.P.A., M7405, 1200 Pennsylvania Avenue, N.W., Attn: TSCA § 13 Coordinator, Chemical Control Division, Washington, DC.[96] The addressee can elect to separate the samples, accept one, sign and submit the post importation certificate for that sample, and reject the other. The addressee remains responsible for the cost of returning or disposing of the rejected sample.[97]

To reduce the administrative burden to importers and the EPA, EPA also established a blanket certification procedure that importers can use for repeat shipments of small quantities of chemical substances imported through the mails. The importer must file a § 13 import certification with EPA the first time the chemical substance is imported by mail. With this certification, the importer must include a statement of its intent to use a blanket certification for future shipments of the chemical substance. The importer must submit an annual report to EPA, postmarked by January 31 of the following year, for each chemical substance that is imported under a blanket certification, identifying each shipment. The annual report should be sent to the same address as noted in the prior paragraph.[98]

C. Products Subject to Positive Certification

Products subject to positive certification are chemical substances, mixtures, or articles containing a chemical substance or mixture as those terms are defined under TSCA, which are either on the TSCA Inventory, or are not on the TSCA Inventory but are being imported in compliance with TSCA. A chemical substance is any organic or inorganic substance of a particular molecular identity including (i) any combination of such substances

---

95. *Id.* at 6. Compliance Guide For the Chemical Import Requirements of the Toxic Substances Control Act (EPA 305-B-08-001), Office of Enforcement and Compliance Assurance, EPA, 5 (June 2008) [2008 Guide], *available at* http://www.epa.gov/compliance/resources/publications/monitoring/tsca/importguidejune2008.pdf.
96. 1991 Guide, question 55. The address of EPA since then has changed, and the new address is noted in this text.
97. 1991 Guide, question 56. *See also*, Living with TSCA Q&A, question 20.
98. 13 TSCA Chemicals-In-Progress Bulletin, No. 1, 7 (Apr. 1992). EPA is no longer publishing the Chemicals-In-Progress Bulletin series.

occurring in whole or in part as a result of a chemical reaction or occurring in nature and (ii) any element or uncombined radical (except as exempted).[99] The term chemical substance also includes microorganisms.[100] The EPA has determined that the following are chemical substances, and not articles:[101] aluminum oxide, bauxite, bismuth, coal, crude oil, crushed stone, gasoline, liquefied petroleum gas, lysine (unless imported for use as a food additive), natural gas, oxalic acid, peat moss (except as peat pots, which are articles), pitch, potassium sorbates (unless imported for use as a food additive) and tetraethyl lead. Chemical substances subject to TSCA, but meeting the requirements for exemption from premanufacturing notification requirements, must also have positive certifications.[102] These are chemical substances imported solely for research and development,[103] for test marketing,[104] under a low volume/low release/low exposure exemption,[105] or qualifying for the polymer exemption.[106]

Wastes are chemical substances subject to TSCA, and each import of waste into the country requires a positive certification,[107] even if the wastes are accompanied by a manifest as required under the Resource Conservation and Recovery Act[108] or consist entirely of byproducts, which are not subject to the premanufacturing notification requirements.[109]

A mixture is any combination of two or more chemical substances if the combination does not occur in nature and is not, in whole or in part, the result of chemical reaction; except that such term does not include any combination which occurs, in whole or in part, as a result of a chemical reaction if none of the chemical substances comprising the mixture is a new chemical substance and if the combination could have been manufactured for commercial purposes without a chemical reaction at the time the chemical substances comprising the combination were combined.[110] Each chemical substance in the mixture, other than impurities, must be identified. The import certification applies only to chemical substances intentionally present

---

99. TSCA § 3(2)(A). Exemptions are set out in § 3(2)(B) and are discussed in Chapter 5, PMN Exclusions and Exemptions.
100. 2008 Guide, 2.
101. 1991 Guide, 15.
102. 48 Fed. Reg. 55462, 55463 (Dec. 13, 1983).
103. 40 C.F.R. § 720.36; *see also* EPA, Question and Answer Summary, EPA Seminar on Industry Obligations Under TSCA, 10 (May 5, 1987); and EPA, 1989 TSCA Industry Seminar Questions & Answers, question number 17.
104. 40 C.F.R. § 720.38.
105. 40 C.F.R. § 723.50.
106. 40 C.F.R. § 723.250.
107. 1991 Guide, question 69.
108. *Id.* at question 71.
109. *Id.* at question 70.
110. TSCA § 3(8). *See* Chapter 2, TSCA's Scope.

in the import.[111] For example, impurities and byproducts with no separate commercial purpose[112] do not need import certifications unless they are PCBs.[113]

The import certification regulation currently exempts imported articles themselves,[114] but chemical substances and mixtures in an article that are intended to be removed or released from the article, and have an end use or commercial purpose separate from the article of which they are a part, are subject to import certification requirements.[115] An example of a chemical substance or mixture that is intended to be released from the article and has a separate end use than the article would be ink in pens. Conversely, transformer fluids in transformers, lighter fluids in cigarette lighters, and crankcase oil in automobiles are not intended to be removed from the articles of which they are a part and have no commercial purpose separate and apart from these articles, and so would not need import certificates. Those same chemical substances, if imported in drums, cans, or other containers, are subject to import certification requirements.[116]

If a chemical substance is being imported for both a TSCA purpose, as noted above, and a non-TSCA purpose, as discussed below, the importer must identify to Customs the quantity of the chemical substance being imported subject to TSCA, and the quantity being imported not subject to TSCA. The importer must file both a positive certification for the quantity subject to TSCA and a negative certification for the quantity not subject to TSCA.[117]

D. Products Subject to Negative Certification or to No Certification

Some products excluded from the definition of chemical substance in § 3(2)(B) require a negative certification. These include pesticides, as defined by the Federal Insecticide, Fungicide, and Rodenticide Act (FIFRA); food, food additives, drugs, drug intermediates, cosmetics, cosmetic intermediates, or devices subject to the Federal Food, Drug, and Cosmetic Act (FFDCA); nuclear source materials, special nuclear materials or nuclear by-product materials; and firearms and ammunition. While a guide for importers and exporters published by EPA in 1991 (1991 Guide)[118] made a distinction in

111. 48 Fed. Reg. 55462, 55463 (Dec. 13, 1983).
112. 48 Fed. Reg. 34734, 34737 (Aug. 1, 1983).
113. 1991 Guide, questions 66, 67 & 68.
114. 2008 Guide at 2.
115. 42 Fed. Reg. 64572 (Dec. 23, 1977).
116. *Id.* at 64583. For additional examples, *see also*, Living with TSCA Q&A, question 4.
117. 1991 Guide, question 38.
118. 1991 Guide.

certification requirements between FIFRA regulated products and FFDCA regulated products depending on whether those products are accompanied by EPA Form 3450-1 or FDA Import Form FD 701, respectively,[119] the final rule issued by the Customs Service[120] made no such distinction and mandates use of a negative certification in either case. In a response to commentators suggesting such a distinction based on the 1991 Guide, and contrary to the position of EPA, Customs notes that "this approach (requiring no certification if the FIFRA or FFDCA products are accompanied by FIFRA or FFDCA forms) would not appreciably reduce the regulatory burden on importers"[121] and is not being adopted. However, the Compliance Guide for Chemical Import Requirements of the Toxic Substances Control Act (2008 Guide)[122] published approximately eight years after the rule issued by the Customs Service contained a chart advising importers that a negative TSCA certification is required "unless the shipment is clearly identified as being a pesticide or other chemical not subject to TSCA [...the shipment is accompanied by FDA Form FD701 or EPA (FIFRA) Form 3540-1]."[123] It is clear under TSCA that EPA must defer to the Treasury Department (Customs) to issue implementing rules under § 13.[124] What is less clear is whether or not Customs has the authority under TSCA to require any actions, such as negative certifications, as to items that are not chemical substances as defined under TSCA. In the checklist at the end of the 2008 Guide, EPA makes clear that an importer "may certify" that such a shipment is not subject to TSCA.[125] The prudent course of action would be to make negative import certifications under these circumstances.

The only products listed in § 3(2)(B) for which Customs and EPA agree that certifications are not required are tobacco or tobacco products and articles.[126] The term article is not defined under the TSCA statute itself, but is defined under regulations promulgated by the Customs Service and the EPA. Article means a manufactured item which:

(1) (i) Is formed to a specific shape or design during manufacture,
  (ii) Has end use functions dependent in whole or in part upon its shape or design during the end use, and

119. *Id.* at question 22. This is consistent with EPA's position, as was expressed earlier in EPA, Question and Answer Summary, EPA Seminar on Industry Obligations under TSCA, OTS Existing Chemicals Program, Question 23 (May 5, 1987).
120. 65 Fed. Reg. 10701, 10703 (Feb. 29, 2000).
121. *Id.*
122. 2008 Guide.
123. *Id.* at 8.
124. TSCA§ 13(b). Customs and Border Protection is now within the Department of Homeland Security.
125. 2008 Guide, 22.
126. 1991 Guide, question 22.

(iii) Has either no change of chemical composition during its end use or only those changes of composition which have no commercial purpose separate from that of the article and that may occur as described below; except that fluids and particles are not considered articles regardless of shape or design.

(2) The allowable changes of composition, noted above, are those which result from a chemical reaction that occurs upon the end use of other chemical substances, mixtures or articles such as adhesives, paints, additives, water softening and treatment agents, photographic films, batteries, matches, and safety flares in which the chemical substance manufactured upon end use of the article is not itself manufactured for distribution in commerce or for use as an intermediate.[127]

Not all importation onto soil governed by the United States requires import certifications. The Customs Territory of the United States is limited to the fifty states, the District of Columbia, and Puerto Rico. Therefore, TSCA does not regulate imports into Guam and other U.S. protectorates.[128] In addition, certification is not required for chemicals imported under entry for transportation and exportation, such as a product being transported through the United States from Canada to Mexico[129] or for importation into a Foreign Trade Zone.[130] However, if the substance is later withdrawn from the Foreign Trade Zone for use in the United States, a certification would be required at that time.[131]

If an importer imports a product for a use not governed by TSCA, and finds that the contemplated sale does not occur, the importer may later sell the product for a TSCA use, so long as the product complies with TSCA (for example, the chemical is on the TSCA Inventory, or qualifies for an exemption from the PMN requirements) and the substance is not further regulated under §§ 5, 6, or 7 of TSCA in a way that would preclude the intended use.[132] The importer should take care to preserve any records which support the position that the original intended use of the product was not covered by TSCA because a change in use subsequent to importation, and inconsistent with the importation certification, can constitute a violation under TSCA.[133]

---

127. 19 C.F.R. § 12.120(a). Article is also defined under TSCA regulations at 40 C.F.R. §§ 704.3, 710.2(e) and 720.3(3).
128. *See* Chapter 2, TSCA's Scope.
129. 1991 Guide, question 57.
130. *Id.* at question 63.
131. *Id.*
132. *Id.* at question 44.
133. *Id.* at question 39.

E. Import for Export Only

As noted in the discussion of exports above, chemical substances, mixtures, or articles containing such substances or mixtures manufactured, processed, or distributed in commerce solely for export and labeled as for export only are generally exempt from the provisions of TSCA.[134] This exemption does not apply to § 12(b) export notification requirements, to § 8 reporting and recordkeeping requirements, or to chemical substances, mixtures, or articles that the EPA determines will present an unreasonable risk of injury to health or the environment in the United States.[135] This statutory exemption includes importation of chemical substances solely for export because the word "manufacture" is defined to include importation.[136] A chemical substance that will be relabeled or processed and will not be used in the United States may be imported solely for export.[137]

While the statutory exemption noted above clearly excludes the requirement of making an import certification for chemical substances imported for export only, EPA has taken the position that the requirements of § 13 do apply to chemical substances imported for export only.[138] Although there are very good arguments based on the statute itself that these requirements cannot be enforced in the context of import for export only, it seems prudent to make import certifications in this situation.

F. Basis of Certification

The EPA expects that the importer[139] will makes its certification as to whether each chemical substance being imported complies with TSCA §§ 5, 6, and 7, or is not subject thereto, based upon its own actual knowledge.[140] Prior to importation, due diligence should be conducted to determine the identity of each chemical substance that is part of the imported product and the TSCA Inventory should be checked to ensure that all the chemical substances in question are in fact on the Inventory. Due diligence would include a review of the MSDS, product literature, and label for the product, as well as requesting

---

134. TSCA § 12(a)(1).
135. TSCA § 12(a).
136. TSCA § 3(7).
137. Living with TSCA Q&A, question 22. *See* Chapter 2, TSCA's Scope.
138. *Id.* "...§ 13 (import certification) rules are applicable." 2008 Guide at 23.
139. EPA recognizes that neither it nor Customs has any authority under TSCA or any other law to place TSCA requirements directly on the foreign exporter, and so has put the onus for compliance on the importer. 45 Fed. Reg. 79730 (Dec. 1, 1980). The foreign shipper cannot sign the import certification. Living with TSCA Q&A, question 45.
140. 40 C.F.R. § 707.20(c)(iii).

verification from the foreign supplier of the components by CAS Number. In the event that the foreign supplier claims the chemical identity of the product to be imported confidential, an importer might consider relying on the warranty or certification from the foreign supplier.[141] However, since the EPA will still look to the importer if the certification is incorrect,[142] importers should document good faith efforts to comply with the certification requirements by asking for the information directly from the supplier, and by reviewing the MSDS, labels and product literature. The greater the effort an importer makes to learn the identities of the chemical substances and their TSCA compliance, the greater the chances that the EPA may obviate or mitigate the assessment of a civil penalty if the certification is later determined to be incorrect.[143] If an importer decides to rely on the warranty of the foreign supplier, it might want to add to that warranty an indemnification from the foreign supplier against all losses and penalties arising in connection with a breach of that warranty. Losses to the importer could be quite large because, for example, if the substance turns out not to be on the TSCA Inventory, the inability of the importer to supply customers could result in breaches of many contracts, and damages for such breaches. The following language could be considered, and should be adapted to the particular circumstances:

> Supplier represents and warrants that all the chemical substances in [product] are on the TSCA Inventory. Supplier shall indemnify and hold harmless purchaser and its customers of [product[144]], and their respective officers, directors and employees against from all losses, liabilities, claims, damages, fines, penalties and expenses, including reasonable legal fees and expenses, incurred by purchaser and its customers resulting from a breach of the foregoing representation and warranty. This provision shall survive termination of the supplier-purchaser relationship.

Make sure that the foreign supplier has assets in the United States, which could be used to satisfy any judgment obtained for breach of the warranty.

An alternative to relying on the supplier's warranty is to ask EPA to search the Inventory, including the confidential portion, by establishing a "bona fide intent to import" the chemical substance.[145] The requirements to establish a bona fide intent to import a chemical substance are the same as the requirements

141. 1991 Guide, question 27.
142. Ultimate liability for compliance always rests with the importer. Living with TSCA Q&A, question 45.
143. 40 C.F.R. § 707.20(c)(iii).
144. As written, this provision would apply to an importer who resells product. In the event that the importer uses the imported product in its manufacture, substitute for "product" the following: "finished products containing [product]."
145. 40 C.F.R. § 720.25.

for checking the confidential portion of the Inventory prior to submission of a PMN.[146] EPA will allow a bifurcated request, in which the foreign supplier gives EPA directly any required information that the foreign supplier claims as confidential, and the other nonconfidential required information is provided by the importer. EPA will process this request as soon as it has received the complete information from both the importer and the foreign supplier.[147]

In addition to verifying that the chemical substance is on the TSCA Inventory, the importer must also determine whether the chemical substance is subject to (i) a SNUR under TSCA § 5(a)(2); or (ii) rules prohibiting or limiting importation, processing or distribution under TSCA §§ 5(e), 5(f), or 6; or (iii) a judicial order under TSCA § 7.[148] For an importation of any chemical substance subject to any of these rules or orders, the importer must ensure that it can comply with the relevant rules and orders in order to sign the positive TSCA certification. In addition to searching the Federal Register and lists maintained by EPA, importers can purchase or license commercial software packages that tend to be updated more frequently, are more user friendly, and can electronically search the exporters' databases for the chemical substances subject to actual and proposed rules, orders or consent decrees. As mentioned above, EPA is also developing a Web-based database[149] of every chemical regulated under TSCA. It is too early to know how accurate and up to date that tool will eventually be.

G. Additional TSCA Requirements Applicable to Importers

Because the term "manufacture" in defined in TSCA to include "import," anyone who imports chemical substances is subject to all the requirements of TSCA. Brief summaries[150] of those requirements, which are more fully discussed in other sections of this book, are set forth below. Prior to importation, the importer should ascertain which of these requirements apply to the product to be imported and put in place procedures or systems to facilitate compliance. This is especially important for importers that do not typically deal with TSCA. While most of these requirements will arise upon or after importation, be aware that there may be § 4 or § 8 rules which require notification to EPA prior to, or on the date of, importation of

---

146. These requirements are discussed in Chapter 3, The Inventory.

147. 40 C.F.R. § 720.45(a)(4).

148. 48 Fed. Reg. 55462, 55463 (Dec. 13, 1983).

149. http://iaspub.epa.gov/sor_internet/registry/substreg/home/overview/home.do.

150. *See* 2008 Guide at 8–10.

a specified chemical.[151] That notification must be made before the positive import certification can be made.[152]

Under § 4, EPA has the authority to require importers to conduct testing on the health and environmental effects of chemical substances and mixtures. Test rules continue for a period of five years from the date the data from all required tests have been submitted or an amount of time equal to that which was required to develop the test data, whichever is longer. In terms of conducting required testing, importers are treated the same as domestic manufacturers.

Section 8 authorizes EPA to require importers to keep certain records and to report certain information to the EPA. The relevant sections are:

- § 8(a), Inventory Update Rule;
- § 8(a), Preliminary Assessment Information Reporting Rule;
- § 8(a), Chemical Specific Record Keeping and Reporting Rules;
- § 8(c), Allegations of Significant Adverse Reactions Recordkeeping and Reporting Rule;
- § 8(d), Unpublished Health and Safety Data Reporting Rule; and
- § 8(e), Substantial Risk Information Reporting Requirement.

Section 12(b) of TSCA requires exporters of chemical substances to notify the EPA of shipments of chemical substances for which data are required under TSCA §§ 4 or 5(b), an order has been issued under TSCA § 5, a proposed or final rule has been issued under TSCA §§ 5 or 6, or an action is pending or relief has been granted under TSCA §§ 5 or 7.

H. Ensuring Compliance with Import Certification Requirements

Understanding the import certification requirements is only the first step in putting together systems and procedures to ensure compliance. How to do this depends on the nature of the each particular importer's business, how often and what types of products are imported and the importer's internal business systems and work processes. Each company must design a compliance with import certification program around these factors, eliminating the possibility of a one size fits all program. Companies might want to consider the elements set forth below in deciding how best to manage compliance with TSCA import certification requirements.

---

151. *See, e.g.*, 40 C.F.R. § 790.45(d)(1).

152. 48 Fed. Reg. 55462 (Dec. 13, 1983).

1. General Importation Arrangements

The first step in establishing TSCA compliance procedures is to gain an understanding of the volume of the company's imports, the types of products being imported, and the ports through which products are, or will be, imported. Customs brokers should be interviewed, even if only to know with whom the company might be dealing in the case of detained shipments. If the company will be importing a repeat volume of shipments of certain chemicals, whether subject to TSCA, FIFRA, or the FFDCA, through a port or ports, determine whether the port director accepts blanket certifications. Understand how imports are handled by the company, what is done internally and what the customs brokers manage, what type of systems are in place to process imports, and the details of how imports are handled on a day to day basis. To ensure compliance, the company should mandate that employees import only through the company-sanctioned process, and not directly themselves. Sometimes employees receive imports directly through the mail or a courier service, often unsolicited. Make sure employees understand their obligations to inform the import specialist in such cases so that post importation certifications can be made.

2. Determining Type of Certification Required, if Any

A process needs to be established requiring the import specialist to notify the regulatory specialist prior to accepting any import shipment of a new chemical substance, including any article containing a chemical substance or mixture with a separate end use that will be released from the article. The information should come before the shipment arrives at the port of entry, and should be accompanied by a description of the product's use, chemical identity, and its components. A determination needs to be made as to whether the product is for a use regulated under FIFRA, FFDCA, or TSCA. If the product is regulated by TSCA, a further determination needs to be made as to whether it is exempt from the PMN requirements, and if it is not, whether it is on the TSCA Inventory.

To determine whether the product is on the TSCA Inventory, check the nonconfidential portion of the Inventory, or, if it is on the confidential Inventory, submit a "bona fide intent to import" to the EPA or request a warranty and indemnification from the foreign supplier. Determine whether a product subject to TSCA is subject to (i) a SNUR under TSCA § 5(a)(2), (ii) rules prohibiting or limiting importation, processing or distribution under TSCA §§ 5(e), 5(f), or 6 or (iii) a judicial order under TSCA § 7.[153]

---

153. *Id.* at 55463 (Dec. 13 1983).

For this information, check with the supplier, EPA lists, Federal Register notices or a commercial data base.

Once a product has been imported, it should be entered into the company's import system, either as a commercial product or a research and development sample, designating which type of certification is required, and whether it is subject to TSCA but exempt from the PMN requirements. While the same positive certification applies whether or not the product is required to be on the Inventory, make sure the company's systems distinguish between products that can be imported for commercial purposes and products that cannot. This is important for ensuring compliance with the PMN requirements.

3. Documentation and Certification Retention Requirements

The required language for the different types of certifications is set out earlier in this chapter. While there is no specific recordkeeping requirement under TSCA § 12(b), TSCA generally requires that records be kept for five years.[154] For TSCA[155] purposes, TSCA import certifications should be kept for five years and any documents used in determining the compliance of the substance with TSCA (such as supplier certification letters, MSDS and the like) for five years from the date of last import of the product, since the company will be relying on those documents the entire time it imports the product, not just the first time.

III. Enforcement

While EPA has the authority to prosecute importers and exporters for failure to comply with the requirements of TSCA §12 and §13, the Customs Service has the concurrent jurisdiction to detain inbound shipments not in compliance with § 13. The Court in *ALM v. U.S. E.P.A.*[156] upheld these co-existing, independent enforcement mechanisms, explaining that Customs may not be able to identify every non-complying shipment at the port because of the large volume of imports and the inefficiency and inconvenience of physical searches of every import by Customs Service officials. Depriving EPA of the

---

154. *See, e.g.*, 40 C.F.R. § 720.78, re: PMN requirements and 40 C.F.R. § 717.15 re: records of significant adverse reactions. In *3M Co, v. Browner*, 17 F.3d 1453 (D.C. Cir. 1994), the court established a five year statute of limitations in a TSCA civil penalty action.

155. For customs, tax, or other reasons, an importer may need to keep additional documentation for other time periods.

156. 974 F.2d 380 (3rd Cir. 1992).

right to enforcement would allow violating importers to escape civil penalties, a result that the court found contrary to TSCA's purpose.

A. EPA Enforcement

The enforcement response policy applicable to §§ 12 and 13 is entitled The Enforcement Response Policy for Reporting and Recordkeeping Rules and Requirements for TSCA Sections 8, 12 and 13 (the Reporting Rule ERP).[157] Under this policy, the EPA may seek civil penalties, refer a violation for criminal penalties under TSCA § 16, seek to enjoin a violation, issue a Notice of Noncompliance if the violation was minor, or a combination of these.[158]

Like all of the ERPs,[159] the Reporting Rule ERP calls for determining the nature, circumstances, extent, and gravity of the violation to determine the gravity based penalty. Each individual component is given a score, based on a matrix. The penalty is then adjusted up or down based on factors such as a history of prior violations, culpability, ability to pay, and such other matters as justice may require.[160] The nature of all Reporting Rule violations is hazard assessment.[161] The circumstances reflect the possibility that harm will result from the violation[162] while the extent of a violation depends on the extent of the potential harm.[163] All § 12(b) export notification violations are level 4 circumstances, which is a one day violation[164] and significant extent.[165] Section 13 import certification violations are level 6 if they involve a negative or no certification and the chemical is otherwise in compliance with TSCA, which is a one day penalty[166] and significant extent.[167] Section 13 violations that involve a negative, positive, or no certification when the substance is in violation of §§ 5, 6, or 7 have the same circumstance level and the same extent level as the underlying §§ 5, 6, or 7 violation and are per day violations.[168]

---

157. EPA, Toxic and Pesticides Enforcement Division, Office of Regulatory Enforcement, Office of Enforcement and Compliance Assurance (revised Mar. 31, 1999) [hereinafter Reporting Rule ERP], *available* through http://cfpub.epa.gov/compliance/resources/policies/civil/tsca/.
158. *Id.* at 2.
159. For a complete discussion on how ERPs operate, *see* Chapter 14, Penalties and Enforcement.
160. Reporting Rule ERP, 6.
161. *Id.* at 5.
162. *Id.* at 9.
163. *Id.* at 11.
164. *Id.* at 10.
165. *Id.* at 24.
166. *Id.* at 10.
167. *Id.* at 24.
168. *Id.* at 11.

The penalty for a variable § 13 violation is capped at the amount of a Circumstance Level 3, Significant Extent violation, per count.[169] It is important to note that § 12 and § 13 penalties are in addition to penalties for the underlying violation. For example, if a substance was imported with a positive certification, but should have been on the TSCA Inventory and was not, the EPA may impose both penalties for the incorrect certification and for the violation of the Inventory requirements.

At the time the matrix was drafted, for violations after January 30, 1997 the one day § 12(b) penalty was $6600, the one day § 13 penalty was $1430, and the variable § 13 penalty was capped at $11,000 per count. Pursuant to the Debt Collection Improvement Act of 1996, EPA is required to increase penalties at least every four years to ensure that inflation does not erode the deterrent effect of the penalties. The penalty for a particular violation depends on the date of the violation, so the Code of Federal Regulations should be consulted to determine the appropriate penalty.[170]

TSCA § 12(b) violations are assessed per chemical per country, either per year if the notification requirement is an annual one, or only for the first required export per country if the notification requirement is not an annual requirement.[171] Except for the variable violation, § 13 violations are assessed one violation per chemical per day, regardless of the number of shipments or the number of ports through which a chemical enters on the same day. In the Reporting Rule ERP, EPA gives several examples of how to determine the number of violations based on the number of shipments. For example, it explains that if the same chemical is imported on the same day to one or more ports in three separate shipments, there is one violation. If the same chemical is imported once a week over a period of five weeks, there are five separate violations, one for each day in which there was an import. If six different chemicals are imported in six separate shipments on the same day, six separate violations would be assessed, one for each chemical in a different shipment. However, if two or more chemicals are imported on the same day in only one shipment, then only one violation would be assessed.[172]

Gravity based penalties can be reduced based on the Reporting ERP up to 50 percent for self-reporting within thirty days, and another 15 percent for

---

169. *Id.*
170. 40 C.F.R. Part 19. Penalty increases are announced in the Federal Register. 69 Fed. Reg. 7121 (Feb. 13, 2004); 73 Fed. Reg. 75340 (Dec. 11, 2008). *See* Chapter 14, Penalties and Enforcement, for a discussion of relevant dates and how to calculate the applicable maximum penalties for the relevant time periods.
171. At the time this policy was published, more TSCA § 12(b) triggering events required annual export notification. Based on changes to the export notification requirements, it would seem, logically, that the failure to make the notification, whenever that is required, is the violation.
172. Reporting Rule ERP, 27.

attitude and more for taking all steps to mitigate the violation,[173] but in no event can the gravity based penalty be less than the economic benefit to the violator.[174] The gravity based penalties can be increased for prior violations and poor attitude.

If the violations of the import or export regulations were discovered and reported to the EPA in compliance with the EPA's Audit Policy, complete or 75 percent penalty mitigation may be available.[175]

A. Customs Enforcement

1. Detention Procedures

The director of the port of entry, or port of arrival, must detain shipments of chemical substances, mixtures or articles, at the importer's risk and expense:

> 1 [w]henever the Administrator [of the EPA] has reasonable grounds to believe that the shipment is not in compliance with TSCA and notifies the port director to detain the shipment;
> 2 [w]henever the port director has reasonable grounds to believe that the shipment is not in compliance with TSCA; or
> 3 [w]henever the importer fails to certify compliance with TSCA.[176]

When the port director detains a shipment, it is required to give prompt notice to the EPA and the importer. The notice must specify the reasons for the detention.[177] The port director can only hold a detained shipment in its custody for 48 hours. After that time, the port director must turn the shipment over to the EPA for storage or disposal, unless the importer has posted a bond.

2. Post-detention Options

The port director can release a detained shipment upon posting of a bond if the port director has reasonable grounds to believe that the shipment may be brought into compliance or when he deems that the procedures for the

---

173. *Id.* at 15–16.
174. *Id.* at 16.
175. *See* Chapter 14, Penalties and Enforcement.
176. 19 C.F.R. § 12.122(b).
177. 19 C.F.R. § 12.122(c).

issuance of bonds[178] have been satisfied. Chemical substances, mixtures, or articles released under bond must be held intact and cannot be used or otherwise disposed of until the EPA makes a final determination as to whether the shipment should be refused entry.[179]

If the port director detains a shipment, the importer may submit written documentation to the EPA, with a copy to the port director, within twenty days from the date of notice of detention, to demonstrate why the shipment should not be detained. The EPA has ten days to make a determination to allow or deny entry from the date of receipt of the importer's documentation. If the importer makes no submission, the EPA must make a determination to allow or deny entry within thirty days from the notice of detention.[180] In either case, the EPA must notify the importer and the port director of its determination.

If the EPA finds that shipment is not in compliance, the port director will refuse delivery to the importer, stating the basis for such refusal, or if the shipment had been released on bond, demand redelivery, giving the reasons for such demand. If the shipment is not received back within thirty days from the date of the redelivery notice, the port director will assess liquidated damages in the full amount of the bond.[181]

The importer can bring the shipment into compliance with TSCA or export the shipment within the first to occur of (i) ninety days of notice of detention or (ii) thirty days of demand for redelivery. If the importer decides to export the shipment, it must file an export notice if the goods are not being returned to the country of origin and a TSCA § 5, § 6, or § 7 rule or order applies to the chemical substance.[182] If the importer decides to abandon the shipment, the importer must present a written notice of intention to abandon to the port director and the EPA, which notice serves as a waiver of any right to export the shipment. Regardless of abandonment, the importer remains liable for any expense incurred in the storage and disposal of the shipment.[183]

---

178. 19 C.F.R. § 141.66. A bond on Customs Form 301, containing the bond conditions set forth in 19 C.F.R. § 113.62 or 19 C.F.R. § 113.69, as appropriate, may be given for the production of any required document, which is not available at the time of entry.
179. 19 C.F.R. § 12.123(b).
180. 19 C.F.R. § 12.123(a).
181. 19 C.F.R. § 12.123(c).
182. 48 Fed. Reg. 34734, 34738 (Aug. 1, 1983).
183. 19 C.F.R. § 12.126.

CHAPTER

9

Test Rules

I. Objectives of Legislation

In the late 1970s when Congress was drafting the Toxic Substances Control Act (TSCA),[1] there were major gaps in the national system for regulating chemicals. Chemicals were introduced into commerce without any mechanism for reviewing their effects, with the sole exceptions of pesticides, drugs, and food additives.[2] Neither the United States Environmental Protection Agency (EPA) nor industry had thorough health effects data on the vast majority of chemicals in homes, offices, and products, and no agency had the authority to assess and regulate chemical hazards comprehensively.

A primary objective of Congress in passing TSCA was to require industry to test new and existing chemicals.[3] Congress' concern was not limited to chemicals that were suspected of posing health or environmental risks—it was also concerned about the chemicals to which people were exposed every day, even if there was no particular reason to suspect a health or environmental risk. As a result, Congress said that either the possibility of risk, or the widespread exposure to chemicals, could trigger a testing requirement.

Section 4 of TSCA spells out the mechanism for requiring industry to study the existing chemicals that are already on the market and in the environment. To date over two hundred chemicals have been subject to test rules, either through administrative rulemaking or through voluntary consent orders.[4]

Because TSCA was one of the last major environmental statutes to be enacted by Congress, many people at the time believed that TSCA was only needed to fill the gaps in the other programs. The EPA's Fall 2009 Semiannual Regulatory Agenda refers to plans it had to use TSCA in connection with other statutes,[5] including an effort that began in 1996 to issue § 4 test rules to gather information on Hazardous Air Pollutants to support the Clean Air Act.

---

1. 15 U.S.C. § 2601–2695d.
2. S. Rep. No. 94-698 at 3 (1976).
3. *Id.* at 2.
4. Calculated from Sunset Dates of Chemicals Subject to Final TSCA Section 4 and Related 12(b) Actions, September 1, 2009, *available at* http://www.epa.gov/oppt/chemtest/pubs/sunsettable.html. This total does not include studies performed pursuant to the voluntary initiatives such as the High Production Volume challenge, but does include HPV chemicals that were not voluntarily studied and were later the subject of test rules. *See* Chapter 10, Voluntary Initiatives, for a discussion of the HPV and other voluntary programs.
5. The Regulatory Agenda is published each spring and fall, and sets out the regulations the EPA is in the process of developing or plans to develop in the long term. Regulatory Plan and Semiannual Regulatory Agenda, EPA-230-Z-09-002, (Fall 2009) [hereinafter Fall 2009 Regulatory Agenda], *available at* http://www.epa.gov/lawsregs/documents/regagendabook-fall09.pdf.

However, the EPA is withdrawing those plans because, among other things, it is reassessing how to prioritize actions on existing chemicals.[6]

Nevertheless, it is the strict and inhibiting administrative burden placed on the EPA when requiring testing under § 4 that is often identified as a failing of TSCA. Unlike the Federal Insecticide, Fungicide, and Rodenticide Act (FIFRA), for example, which presumes a pesticide is unsafe unless the manufacturer proves otherwise, TSCA presumes safety unless EPA can establish otherwise.[7] Indeed, EPA until recently pursued testing most aggressively outside of the rulemaking process through voluntary initiatives such as the High Production Volume Testing Initiative and the Nanoscale Materials Stewardship Program.[8]

Section 4 of TSCA permits the EPA to require manufacturers and processors of chemicals that are already in production to test the chemicals they make and process. There are threshold determinations that the EPA must make before it can issue a test rule, and these deal with the risk that may be posed by the chemical, the extent of exposure to the chemical, and whether there is a genuine need for new data.[9] The testing requirement of § 4 looks mandatory on the surface—the EPA must require testing if the statutory preconditions are met. Of course, however, the EPA is afforded substantial deference when deciding if the preconditions are met.

Congress created the Interagency Testing Committee (ITC) to come up with a list of priority chemicals for § 4 testing.[10]

Testing can be very expensive, and Congress anticipated industry's concern about fair cost-sharing. The statute therefore required EPA to issue rules for cost-sharing.[11] EPA complied and issued rules requiring a company that is exempted from testing to reimburse other companies that conduct the testing.[12]

Logically, Congress would have wanted the EPA to take action if the test results show a risk, and so the statute requires EPA to initiate action under other sections of TSCA to prevent or reduce the risk, unless it determines that the risk is reasonable.[13]

6. Fall 2009 Regulatory Agenda, 108-109.
7. *See* F. Powell, Law and the Environment, 328 (1997).
8. *See* Chapter 10, Voluntary Initiatives for a discussion of the High Production Volume Challenge Program, and *see* Chapter 2, TSCA's Scope for a discussion of nanomaterials.
9. TSCA § 4(a).
10. TSCA § 4(e).
11. TSCA § 4(c).
12. *See* 40 C.F.R. Part 791.
13. TSCA § 4(f).

II. Threshold Requirements for Issuing Test Rules

TSCA § 4(a) requires the EPA to issue rules requiring testing a chemical or mixture if either of two alternate sets of threshold requirements are met. The first set of threshold requirements focuses on the potential risk presented by the chemical and the second set focuses on potential exposure to the chemical.

The risk-based requirements in § 4(a)(1)(A), or "A" findings, require testing if the EPA finds that the manufacture, distribution, processing, use, or disposal of a chemical substance or mixture may present an unreasonable risk of injury to health or the environment.

The exposure-based requirements in § 4(a)(1)(B), or "B" findings, require testing if the EPA finds that: (i) the chemical substance will be produced in substantial quantities and it is, or is expected to, be in the environment in substantial quantities; or (ii) there is or may be significant human exposure. In either case, the EPA must also find two additional elements present before requiring testing: (i) there is insufficient data on the chemical to determine or predict the effects of the chemical on health or the environment; and (ii) testing is necessary to develop data to determine or predict its effects on health or the environment.[14] And, in the case of a mixture, the EPA must find that it is not more efficient to test the components of the mixture than to test the mixture itself.[15]

A. Who Must Perform Testing

Once a test rule is promulgated, the statute imposes the testing obligation on manufacturers, importers and processors, and entities that intend to manufacture, import, or process a chemical or mixture.[16] However, there are significant limitations on who can be required to perform testing. A manufacturer or importer cannot be required to test effects of processing, and a processor cannot be required to test effects of manufacturing or importing.[17]

---

14. *See* TSCA § 4(a)(1)(A)(ii), (iii) and TSCA § 4(a)(1)(B)(ii)–(iii).
15. TSCA § 4(a)(2).
16. TSCA § 4(b)(3)(B).
17. A manufacturer or entity that intends to manufacture a chemical or mixture can be required to test that chemical or mixture only if the EPA makes a finding that there is not already enough data on the effects of *manufacturing*, distribution, use, or disposal on health or the environment. TSCA §4(b)(3)(B)(i). Similarly, a processor or prospective processor can be required to test that chemical or mixture only if the EPA makes a finding that there is not enough data on the effects of *processing*, distribution, use, or disposal on health or the environment. TSCA § 4(b)(3)(B)(ii).

Manufacturers, importers, and processors can be required to test for the effects of distribution in commerce, use, or disposal.[18]

Manufacturers and importers of chemical substances present as byproducts or impurities can be made subject to test rules on a case by case basis.[19] Manufacturers and processors may work cooperatively, or they may hire another entity to conduct the testing.[20]

Manufacturers, importers, and processors of less than five hundred kilograms (eleven hundred pounds) annually, and manufacturers and importers solely for research and development, are subject to test rules. However, EPA will first look to manufacturers or importers of larger quantities for compliance with test rules. EPA will publish a Federal Register notice requiring these entities to conduct testing if they are the only entities that can be required to perform the testing, or if no larger quantity manufacturer or importer submits a letter of intent to conduct testing.[21]

B. Contents of Test Rules

Once the EPA finds that the threshold requirements are present, it must issue a test rule that identifies the chemical or mixture and the test standards, and the due date for submitting testing results on existing chemicals.[22] The test rule may require submission of preliminary data before the testing is complete.[23]

The EPA must consider the cost of the testing protocols and whether laboratory facilities will be available.[24] Every year, the EPA must review the test protocols and revise them if necessary. The EPA can only require workplace epidemiology studies if it confers with the National Institute for Occupational Safety and Health.[25]

The EPA has a broad range of effects and chemical characteristics for which it can require testing, limited only by the requirement that the effects

18. *See, e.g.*, the EPA's final test rule for diethylene glycol butyl ether, 53 Fed. Reg. 5932 (Feb. 26, 1988).
19. 63 Fed. Reg. 19694 (Apr. 21, 1998).
20. TSCA § 4(b)(3)(A).
21. 40 C.F.R. § 790.42; 63 Fed. Reg. 19694 (April 21, 1998). Note, however, that this HAP rule is only applicable to manufacturers of 25,000 pounds or more of any HAP per year.
22. TSCA § 4(b).
23. TSCA § 4(b)(1).
24. *Id.* The EPA sporadically polls testing labs to determine if there is sufficient capacity to perform tests required under TSCA. *See* EPA Census of TSCA Testing Laboratories, Final Report (Oct. 10, 1996).
25. TSCA § 4(b)(2)(A).

or characteristics may present an unreasonable risk of injury to health or the environment.[26]

Test rules expire at the end of the reimbursement period. The reimbursement period[27] is at least five years after the last non-duplicative test has been submitted to the EPA. In addition to being published in the Federal Register, the EPA has posted on the Internet a more easily accessible list of all of test rules promulgated so far for which a sunset date has been calculated.[28]

C. Exemption from Test Rules

A manufacturer or processor may apply to the EPA for an exemption from a test rule.[29] A manufacturer or processor subject to a test rule may submit a request for exemption from any or all of the required tests if it can show that the EPA has already received and adopted a proposed study plan for the testing, the chemical substance at issue is equivalent to a test substance or mixture for which the required data is being submitted, or the submission of the required test data would be duplicative.[30] An applicant for an exemption must submit a sworn statement agreeing to reimburse entities who actually generated the required data.[31]

Anyone subject to a test rule has an obligation, from the date the test rule becomes effective until the end of the reimbursement period, to either test or to obtain an exemption and pay reimbursement. The reimbursement period is that period that begins with the submission to the EPA of data from the last non-duplicative test to be completed under a test rule and ends after an amount of time equal to that required to develop the data or after five years, whichever is later.[32]

The data reimbursement regulations only take effect when private efforts to jointly agree on reimbursement cannot be reached. When this occurs, the EPA is required to issue a reimbursement order requiring that exempt parties provide "fair and equitable reimbursement" to those who incurred the costs.[33]

The reimbursement procedures provide for the opportunity for a hearing before the American Arbitration Association, publication in the Federal Register of the request for a hearing, and the appointment of a hearing officer

26. TSCA § 4(b)(1).
27. Reimbursement periods are discussed *infra*.
28. Sunset Dates of Chemicals Subject to Final TSCA Section 4 and Related 12(b) Actions (Sept. 1, 2009), *available at* http://www.epa.gov/oppt/chemtest/pubs/sunsettable.html.
29. *See* TSCA § 4(c).
30. 40 C.F.R. Part 970, Subpart E—Exemptions from Test Rules.
31. 40 C.F.R. § 790.99.
32. 40 C.F.R. § 791.3(h).
33. TSCA § 4(c)(3).

to order a fair and equitable reimbursement. The order may be based upon production volume levels pursuant to a formula set forth in the data reimbursement regulation, but this is not obligatory. The hearing officer's final order is reviewable in federal court.[34]

D. Hazardous Air Pollutants

EPA had taken steps to issue a test rule on hazardous air pollutants (HAPs).[35] This program found its genesis in the initial purpose of the TSCA legislation. There are data gaps in understanding HAPs and the Clean Air Act requires filling those data gaps to add or delete chemicals from the statutory list of HAPs in § 112 of the Clean Air Act. Several manufacturers entered into enforceable consent agreements governing testing of HAPs.[36] EPA has announced that it is withdrawing the 1996 proposed test rule because the developed record does not address more recent scientific advances, among other reasons.[37] It has said it will reassess how to better address potential concerns with these HAPs in the context of its enhanced chemical management program.[38]

E. Use of Test Results

Whenever the EPA receives test data it publishes a notice in the Federal Register and makes the nonconfidential portions of the data available to the public.[39]

If the test data indicates that there may be a reasonable basis to conclude that the chemical presents "a significant risk of serious or widespread harm to human beings from cancer, gene mutation or birth defects," the EPA has one hundred eighty days to initiate an action under §§ 5, 6, or 7 of TSCA to prevent or reduce the risk, or publish a statement in the Federal Register explaining its conclusion that the risk is not unreasonable.[40] The Administrator may extend the time by no more than ninety days.[41] The standards embodied in this section are consistent with the objectives of the drafters—before the EPA must take

34. 40 C.F.R. Part 791.
35. The EPA's proposed rule is at 61 Fed. Reg. 33177 (June 26, 1996), amended at 62 Fed. Reg. 67465 (Dec. 24, 1997) and amended again at 63 Fed. Reg. 19694 (Apr. 21, 1998).
36. 65 Fed. Reg. 37550 (June 15, 2000); 62 Fed. Reg. 2607 (Jan. 17, 1997).
37. Fall 2009 Regulatory Agenda, 108-109.
38. *Id.*
39. TSCA § 4(f).
40. *Id.*
41. *Id.*

action, it must have evidence that the risk is fairly high, but it only needs to have an indication that there may be a reasonable basis that the risk is present.

F. Export Notification

Once a test rule issues, any exporter of the chemical subject to that rule must file a notice of export under § 12(b).[42] Generally, the requirement to file notices of export terminates when the test rule sunsets.[43] However, the requirement to file notices of export for dioxins and dibenzofurans terminates only if all the required data has been submitted and there are no positive test results.[44]

G. The Interagency Testing Committee

The ITC was formed pursuant to TSCA § 4(e), which established a committee to make recommendations to the EPA for prioritizing chemicals for testing.[45] The ITC meets every other month, and each May and November publishes a report listing its recommendations for testing.[46] In its reports, the ITC lists chemicals that it "recommends" considering for § 4 test rules, and those it "designates" for § 4 test rules, and this combined list of chemicals is called the Priority Testing List.[47]

---

42. 40 C.F.R. § 707.60 requires export notifications if "[d]ata are required under section 4 ..."; *see* Chapter 8, Exports and Imports.
43. *Id.*
44. 40 C.F.R. § 707.72.
45. The ITC is composed of sixteen members from a wide array of governmental organizations that may benefit from developing test data. Eight members are required by statute, including the Council on Environmental Quality, the Department of Commerce's National Institute of Standards & Technology or National Oceanographic and Atmospheric Administration, the Environmental Protection Agency, the National Cancer Institute, the National Institute of Environmental Health Sciences, the National Institute for Occupational Safety and Health, the National Science Foundation, and the Department of Labor's Occupational Safety and Health Administration. TSCA §4 (e)(2)(A). The ITC has eight additional liaison members from such varied agencies as the Agency for Toxic Substances and Disease Registry, the Consumer Product Safety Commission, and the Department of Agriculture. *See* the 48th Report of the ITC. This extensive representation supports the concept that TSCA § 4 was envisioned as a mechanism to obtain test data for other agencies. *See* http://www.epa.gov/opptintr/itc/.
46. *See generally* the ITC reports *available through* http://www.epa.gov/opptintr/itc.
47. *Id.*

The statute sets out the ITC's responsibilities for prioritizing chemical substances for testing in detail.[48]

Every six months the ITC must update the Priority Testing List, and give its reasons for any revisions it makes. The EPA must publish the Priority Testing List in the Federal Register when it receives it from the ITC. Within one year of the date the ITC designates a chemical on the Priority Testing List, the EPA must either initiate a § 4 rulemaking, or publish a notice in the Federal Register explaining why it has not done so.[49] The EPA does not have any deadlines for acting on chemicals recommended for consideration on the Priority Testing List.[50]

The EPA can decide not to initiate a § 4 rulemaking on a designated chemical only if it finds that the statutory preconditions are not met, or if it has entered into a binding consent agreement.[51]

Other TSCA information gathering requirements are triggered by a chemical's appearance on the Priority Testing List. The Preliminary Assessment Information Reporting (PAIR) regulations[52] mandate that EPA require manufacturers and importers to submit PAIR information on chemicals that the ITC recommends for consideration.[53] The PAIR rule requires a quick and dirty collection of readily obtainable information on a chemical's use and properties.[54] Similarly, the § 8(d) health and safety study regulations require

48. Chief among the ITC's responsibilities is the obligation to prepare a list of chemicals and mixtures, individually or in groups, prioritized in the order in which the ITC recommends testing. The ITC must consider all the factors relevant to determining the testing priority of a chemical, including the quantities manufactured, the quantities in the environment, the number of people who may be exposed in the workplace and the extent of their exposure, the extent of exposure to the general public, if the chemical is closely related to another chemical known to present an unreasonable risk, the available risk data, if testing will lead to useful risk data, and if facilities and personnel are available for conducting the tests. By statute, the total number of chemicals and mixtures designated for testing at any one time cannot exceed fifty. TSCA § 4(e).
49. Publishing an Advance Notice of Proposed Rulemaking (ANPR) is sufficient to initiate a § 4 rulemaking, but the EPA should not use an ANPR to unreasonably delay agency action. *See NRDC v. EPA*, 595 F.Supp. 1255 (S.D.N.Y. 1984).
50. 40 C.F.R. § 790.20(b)(2). Once the EPA receives ITC's list of chemicals that are "recommended-with-intent-to-designate" it also conducts a preliminary investigation into possible testing needs. It holds a public "focus meeting" to gather information about the subject chemical, evaluates 8(a) and 8(d) submissions, and reaches preliminary conclusions about the testing to be performed. At that point, EPA holds a second public meeting to review its preliminary conclusions. 40 C.F.R. §790.22.
51. 40 C.F.R. § 790.20(b)(1)(ii).
52. *See* Chapter 7, Reporting and Recordkeeping.
53. 40 C.F.R. § 712(b); *see also* 40 C.F.R. § 790.22(a)(2). Chemicals will be added to the PAIR rule if the ITC has recommended them but has not designated them within 12 months after recommending them. 40 C.F.R. § 712.1(b).
54. The regulations limit the number of chemicals added to the PAIR rule because they have been designated and recommenced by the ITC to fifty in any one year. 40 C.F.R. § 712.1(b).

the EPA to mandate the submission of studies under § 8(d) for all chemicals added to the Priority Testing List.[55]

The ITC uses the information gathered from many sources, including PAIR and § 8(d) submissions to reevaluate its recommendations for further testing and determine if recommendations should be upgraded to designations.[56]

As a practical matter, the EPA takes a very long time to promulgate a test rule. For example, the EPA issued a test rule covering 34 chemicals that the Occupational Safety and Health Administration (OSHA) was concerned about because of skin absorption.[57] That rule was effective May 26, 2004. However, OSHA had first sent a list of chemicals to the ITC in 1991, with a request that the ITC review the data available concerning skin absorption. The ITC first designated 84 of those chemicals in 1993. The EPA issued PAIR and TSCA § 8(d) rules in 1993, 1994, and 1995, and subsequently entered into a voluntary enforceable consent agreement for testing one chemical. EPA proposed the test rule in 1999 and finalized it five years later.

One side effect of the glacial pace of issuing test rules has been to give industry an added opportunity to be heard before issuance. Not only can a company follow the lists of designated and recommended chemicals by reading the ITC reports, companies are often given an opportunity to voluntarily submit data even before the ITC recommends a chemical for consideration.

Although thorough information gathering is a worthwhile objective, it does have the effect of delaying test rule issuance.

H. Interpretations and Guidance

1. Meaning of "Unreasonable Risk"

TSCA § 4(a)(1)(A) requires the EPA to promulgate a test rule if the agency makes an "A" finding that a chemical or mixture "may present an unreasonable risk of injury to health."

A finding of chemical risk is a function of two factors: (i) human exposure and (ii) the toxicity of the substance. Judicial review of agency test rules premised on "unreasonable risk" has focused particularly on the extent of human exposure to a toxic chemical and so has sought to draw the line between testing based on simple speculation as to risk, on the one hand, and scientific uncertainty when risk is not merely illusory, on the other.

---

55. 40 C.F.R. § 761.105(b); *see also* 40 C.F.R. § 790.22(a)(2) (recommended chemicals only).
56. 58 Fed. Reg. 43608, 43610 (July 23, 2003). *See also* 40 C.F.R. § 790.20(a).
57. 69 Fed. Reg. 22402 (Apr. 26, 2004).

To date, both the Third and the D.C. Circuits have issued rulings on test rules based on "A" findings. In *Ausimont v. EPA*,[58] a test rule issued for fluoroalkenes was challenged by manufacturers on the grounds that "before issuing a test rule, EPA must demonstrate that humans are actually exposed to the chemicals to such a degree that serious harm could result if the substances are toxic."[59] Upholding the EPA's rule, the Court concluded that the statutory phrase "may present" allows the EPA "to act when an existing possibility of harm raises reasonable and legitimate cause for concern." The EPA may not issue a test rule "based on little more than scientific curiosity."[60]

In *Chemical Manufacturers Association v. EPA*,[61] the court examined a challenge to EPA's test rule for ethylhexanoic acid (EHA), a chemical substance consumed in the manufacturing process and thus causing no exposure to consumers, but which the EPA asserted workers were exposed to. The rule required a ninety day subchronic toxicity test, a developmental toxicity test, and a pharmacokinetics test. The D.C. Circuit identified two primary issues: (i) whether EPA must produce direct evidence of human exposure rebutting industry evidence casting doubt on such exposure and (ii) whether a test rule may issue where exposure to any individual is likely to be a rare, brief event. In addressing the first issue, the court concluded that "it is reasonable for EPA to rely on inferences in issuing a § 4 test rule, so long as all the evidence—including the industry evidence—indicates a more-than-theoretical probability of exposure."[62] Turning to the nature of probable exposures, the court observed that the EPA had concluded that even one time exposure to EHA may be sufficient to harm a developing fetus. The court found that it "should not substitute its judgment" for that of the EPA on the issue of whether occasional exposure to a developmental toxicant can ever merit a test rule.[63] "So long as there is a more-than-theoretical probability that the toxic substance in rare or single doses presents an 'unreasonable risk of injury to health,' the statutory standard is met whatever the infrequency of exposure."[64]

In summary, because exposure is a component of "unreasonable risk," the EPA must establish some probability of exposure. However, the EPA may demonstrate such exposure indirectly through circumstantial evidence.

58. 838 F.2d 93 (3d Cir. 1988).
59. *Id.* at 95.
60. *Id.* at 97.
61. 859 F.2d 977 (D.C. Cir. 1988).
62. *Id.* at 989.
63. *Id.* at 990.
64. *Id.* at 991.

2. Meaning of "Substantial Quantities" or "Substantial Human Exposure"

As distinct from the "unreasonable risk" standard of § 4(a)(1)(A), under § 4(a)(1)(B) EPA must issue a test rule if it makes a "B" finding that a chemical substance is produced in substantial quantities and (i) it is, or is expected to, enter the environment or (ii) there is or may be significant human exposure. Unlike in an "A" finding, there is no risk-based criterion to satisfy in a "B" finding. However, as with the phrase "unreasonable risk," the terms "substantial" and "significant" are not defined in the statute, nor are they elucidated in any way in the legislative history of TSCA. Yet, they have been the subject of litigation.

In *Chemical Manufacturers Association v. EPA*,[65] a challenge was brought regarding a test rule issued for cumene, which at the time was one of the top fifty chemicals produced in the United States at approximately 3.3 billion pounds annually. In November 1984, the ITC recommended that cumene be considered for testing for health effects. In late November 1985, the EPA responded to the ITC recommendation by issuing its proposed test rule based initially on an "A" finding of "significant risk" and also a "B" finding, that cumene was produced in substantial quantities and that there was substantial environmental release with the potential for substantial human exposure. However, when EPA published its final rule in 1988, it relied solely on its "B" finding.

In evaluating industry's challenge, the court observed that

> TSCA contains no definition of "substantial," nor does its legislative history. And the legislative history does not in any other respect lend any specific support to CMA's position. In these circumstances, Congress is deemed to have implicitly delegated to the EPA the power to define or interpret "substantial," and we will sustain the agency's interpretation as long as it is rational and consistent with the statutory scheme and legislative history.[66]

Notwithstanding such substantial deference, "an agency must cogently explain why it has exercised its discretion in a given manner" and "must offer a 'rational connection between the facts found and the choice made.'"[67] Unable to determine "on what basis or in light of what criteria the EPA concluded either that the quantities of cumene found to enter the environment ... were 'substantial' or that the human exposure potential resulting therefrom was 'substantial,'" the court remanded the case to EPA "to articulate the

---

65. 899 F.2d 344 (5th Cir. 1990).
66. *Id.* at 354.
67. *Id.* at 358.

standards or criteria on the basis of which it found the quantities of cumene entering the environment ... to be 'substantial' and the human exposure potentially resulting to be 'substantial.'"[68]

In direct response to the remand, in 1991 EPA proposed and in 1993 it issued its TSCA Section 4(a)(1)(B) Statement of Policy.[69] This policy statement identified the triggers EPA will use to determine: (i) "substantial" production; (ii) "substantial" release; and (iii) "substantial" and "significant" human exposure. The policy sets a threshold of one million pounds per year for findings of "substantial production." According to EPA, this "narrows" the universe of chemicals potentially subject to TSCA § 4 testing under a "B" finding to eleven percent of the TSCA Inventory.[70]

If the criterion for "substantial production" is met, then the Agency must make at least one of three additional findings under TSCA § 4(a)(1)(B)(i) before testing is required. The first is that the substance enters, or may be reasonably anticipated to enter, the environment in "substantial quantities." In the policy the Agency articulated a standard of one million pounds per year release or release of 10 percent or more of total production volume, whichever is lower.[71] The policy says EPA will find "substantial" human exposure in connection with a "B" finding when one thousand workers, ten thousand consumers or one-hundred thousand members of the general population are exposed. The different numeric values for worker, consumer, and general population exposures are intended "to reflect the inherent differences in the probable exposure scenarios for particular categories of individuals."[72] Thus, "workers are generally exposed on a more routine or direct basis than consumers, and consumers are generally exposed on a more routine or direct basis than the general public."[73]

Finally, EPA concluded that it had insufficient experience to generically define criteria in making a finding of "significant" human exposure. Rather, EPA the declared "[a] finding of 'significant' exposure will generally be made on a case-by-case basis, taking into consideration, among other factors, the manner of use, substance specific physical properties, concentration levels, and the duration and frequency of the exposure to the substance."[74]

In contrast to the plaintiffs in *Chemical Manufacturers Association v. EPA*, the plaintiffs in *Physicians Comm. for Responsible Med. v. Johnson*,[75] were seeking an order compelling the EPA to issue test rules for High Production

---

68. *Id.* at 359.
69. 58 Fed. Reg. 28736 (May 14, 1993).
70. *Id.* at 28739.
71. *Id.* at 28740.
72. *Id.* at 28742.
73. *Id.*
74. *Id.* at 28744.
75. 436 F.3d 326 (2d Cir. 2006).

Volume (HPV) chemicals. The plaintiffs contended that the EPA had made de facto "B" findings when it initiated a voluntary testing program for HPV chemicals.[76] In fact, the EPA conceded that it had found that HPV chemicals were made in substantial quantities and that there was insufficient data and testing was needed to determine the effects of the chemicals. However, the Court found that the EPA had not made findings of substantial release or substantial exposure, and therefore was not required to issue test rules for HPV substances.

3. Enforceable Consent Agreements and Voluntary Testing Agreements

The EPA often enters into enforceable consent agreements (ECAs) and voluntary testing agreements rather than carry out the burdensome rulemaking process required for § 4 test rules. In fact, the EPA has detailed regulations for how to go about negotiating a consent agreement.

EPA recently negotiated two ECAs governing testing of fluoropolymers and fluorotelomers. EPA's focus was perfluorooctanoic acid (PFOA), which is used in making fluoropolymers and is a breakdown product of fluorotelomers. EPA was concerned that PFOA is persistent in the environment, is found in human blood, and has developmental effects in laboratory animals.[77] The two ECAs require laboratory scale incineration testing of the subject chemicals.[78] These ECAs issued much faster than a test rule would have, just three years after EPA began a priority review of PFOA.

EPA's practice of entering into consent agreements seems obviously flawed. The EPA has said that it has implied authority to enter into consent agreements[79] but it is far from clear that EPA really has that authority. In *NRDC v. EPA*,[80] the Court held that the EPA violated TSCA by negotiating consent agreements instead of issuing § 4 test rules.[81] As a practical matter,

---

76. *See* Chapter 10, Voluntary Initiatives.
77. *See* http://www.epa.gov/oppt/pfoa/pubs/pfoainfo.html#pfos.
78. 70 Fed. Reg. 39624 (July 8, 2005) (announcement of fluorotelomer incineration ECA) and Fed. Reg. 39630 July 8, 2005) (announcement of fluoropolymer incineration ECA).
79. 40 C.F.R. § 790.1(b).
80. 595 F.Supp.1255 (S.D.N.Y. 1984).
81. That litigation was brought by the Natural Resources Defense Council and the AFL-CIO alleging that EPA failed to meet its statutory obligations because, among other things, it did not issue test rules for chemicals designated by the ITC. 595 F. Supp. at 1259 (S.D.N.Y. 1984). The EPA said in the *NRDC* case that it had not found that the preconditions were met, but the Court, in rather strong language, said:

> EPA's negotiation and acceptance of voluntary testing agreements by the manufacturers obviously reflects EPA's belief that additional data concerning the chemicals in question needs to be developed. The absence of a formal finding of testing necessity cannot hide

this conclusion leaves industry free to take advantage of EPA's regulations on consent agreements, even though those who enter into consent agreements must be aware of their vulnerability to challenge and the possibility of subsequent test rules.

4. The Regulations on Consent Agreements

In partial reaction to the NRDC ruling, the regulations governing voluntary consent agreements specify that failure to comply with a consent agreement is a "prohibited act" in violation of § 15, with the explicit intent that this regulation can be used to subject entities that violate a consent agreement to civil and criminal penalties.[82] Similarly, the regulations state that violation of a consent agreement is a "violation of this Act" under TSCA § 20(a)(1) and can subject an entity to citizen suits.[83] Consent agreements must contain a statement that the manufacturer or processor agrees that violations are "prohibited acts" that will trigger TSCA § 15's enforcement provisions.[84]

The EPA does not need to find that any of the preconditions to issuance of a § 4 rule exist before entering into a consent order. When the EPA determines that a consent agreement could be feasible, it publishes a notice in the Federal Register asking industry to participate.[85]

EPA's evident de facto findings of such a necessity. It is the substance not the form of agency action that is relevant upon review.

The Court catalogued the other TSCA provisions that are triggered by the issuance of a test rule, and found that these would not be triggered by a voluntary agreement. Chief among them are:

- section 5(a) & (b)—requiring submission to EPA of test data prior to new manufacture of chemicals subject to test rule;
- section 8(a)(3)(A)—requiring record-keeping and imposing reporting requirements on small quantity manufacturers of test rule chemicals;
- section 12(b)—requiring notice to foreign governments where substances are being exported of test rule data availability;
- section 14(a)(1)—imposing sanctions for noncompliance with testing programs; and
- section 19(a)(1)(A)—authorizing judicial review of testing rules.

The Court found that there simply could be no substitute for rulemaking. After this decision, it seems quite clear that the EPA is not entitled to rely on consent agreements, and must proceed to formal rulemaking to obtain § 4 test data.

82. 40 C.F.R. § 790.65(b) and (c).
83. 40 C.F.R. § 790.65(d).
84. 40 C.F.R. § 790.60(a)(13). In the preamble to the Interim Final Rule still in effect, the EPA stated that it is a "fundamental principle" that "parties who voluntarily accept their requirements waive their right to challenge the legal justification for those requirements." 51 Fed. Reg. 23076 (June 30, 1986). However, this requirement seems to be based on the practical obstacles of *NRDC v. EPA* instead of a philosophical preference.
85. As an example of a request for industry participation, *see* 68 Fed. Reg. 18626 (Apr. 16, 2003).

Consent orders are published in the Federal Register.[86] To date, industry has agreed to test for health and environmental effects, chemical fate, and perform exposure monitoring for about one hundred chemical substances and one mixture.

5. Compliance and Procedures

There are relatively few daily operations that directly relate to TSCA § 4. When a test rule is issued for a substance made or processed by a company, that test rule will have unique requirements and will likely be managed on a case-by-case basis. However, there are several activities that should be part of a set of procedures implementing test rule requirements. These are:

- keeping track of § 4 test rules to ensure compliance for chemicals already used in manufacturing or processing; this can be accomplished by a regulatory specialist in one of many ways:
    - manual daily review of the Federal Register;
    - subscription to http://www.regulations.gov free Federal Register daily e-mail, which sends out the Federal Register table of contents;
    - subscription to a fee-based service such as CHEMTOX® or Ariel™ databases, that lists substances subject to regulatory requirements, including test rules, and can be cross-referenced to a material safety data sheet (MSDS) database; and/or
    - all of these options require a regulatory affairs specialist to maintain a list of chemicals manufactured or processed by the company; this can be accomplished using a centralized MSDS system;
- product managers should access the list of § 4 substances before bringing a new raw material into a production process or changing a production process to manufacture a new chemical substance; again, this can be accomplished in one of many ways:
    - checking the fee-based services;
    - querying the regulatory affairs specialist;
    - directly maintaining lists of § 4 substances; or
    - in the case of a new product, checking for § 4 substances can be done during the process of preparing an MSDS;
- purchasing managers should access the list of § 4 substances before importing a new chemical into the United States. Some of the alternatives for accomplishing this are set out in the previous bullet;
- whoever is responsible for tracking new test rules and ECAs should inform people involved in exporting chemical substances when a test rule or ECA issues (or sunsets) for a substance in a product made or

86. 40 C.F.R. §§ 799.5000 and 799.5025.

processed by the company. The person responsible for exports must track those products and either submit export notifications under § 12(b) or provide information on intended exports to the person responsible for submitting the export notifications. This can be accomplished in a variety of ways, including:
  - through a software program that can cross check test rules against orders taken for chemical shipments; or
  - by the person responsible for exports, either manually, by contacting a regulatory affairs specialist, or by using a software program;
- ideally, a mechanism should be in place to track test rule sunsets and ensure that export notifications are not submitted after the test rule expires, but this is only to avoid unnecessary paperwork and is not required to ensure compliance with TSCA requirements.

It is worth watching daily Federal Registers that report on issuance of the ITC's Priority Testing List to see what chemicals may ultimately be subject to a § 4 Test Rule. It certainly is preferable to submit data voluntarily than to be subject to a PAIR or 8(d) rule, with their associated penalties for violation.

It is beneficial to have a mechanism in place to spot Federal Register notices announcing EPA's willingness to negotiate a consent agreement. Even if a company does not intend to participate in testing, it may have an interest in following the development of the consent agreement because those companies that will perform the testing may seek reimbursement.

III. Enforcement

EPA has issued an Enforcement Response Policy (ERP) for § 4 violations that follows the basic format of all its TSCA ERPs.[87] Each type of violation is categorized by its nature, extent, and circumstances and then a monetary penalty is calculated and upwards and downwards adjustment factors are determined. All § 4 violations are assigned a "nature" of hazard assessment violations. EPA assigns higher penalties to violations involving studies of longer duration simply because they will disrupt the EPA's schedule more significantly.

Violations such as falsifying data, failure to test, failure to complete testing, failure to adhere to test standards, or modifying standards in a way that seriously impairs the EPA's ability to evaluate the test substance merit the highest penalties. Other violations that the EPA penalizes include late

87. EPA, Enforcement Response Policy for TSCA §4 Test Rules, (May 28, 1986), *available at* http://www.epa.gov/compliance/resources/policies/civil/tsca/tscasec4ruleserp-052886.pdf.

submission of a completed study, failure to adhere to test standards or modifying standards, and starting a study late even if it is completed on time.

A matrix in the ERP supplies the gravity based penalties for each combination of nature, circumstances, and extent. However, the penalties applicable to violations that occurred in 2006, 2007, and 2008 must be increased by a factor of 1.3, and the penalties applicable to 2009 violations that occurred after January 12, 2009 must be increased by a factor of 1.5. These increased penalties are required by the Civil Penalties Inflation Adjustment Act of 1990, 28 U.S.C. 2461, as amended by the Debt Collection Improvement Act of 1996, 31 U.S.C. 3701, which required each federal agency to adjust its maximum penalties to maintain a deterrent effect in the face of inflation. As required by that legislation, EPA increased the daily maximum penalties to $27,500 effective after January 30, 1997 and again to $32,500 effective March 15, 2004, and again to $37,500 effective January 12, 2009. The Debt Collection Improvement Act requires penalty adjustments every four years and so another increase should be forthcoming in 2013.

The Audit Policy should be consulted to determine if a complete or 75 percent mitigation of penalties is available.[88]

In calculating penalties, it is important to keep in mind the sunset provisions of § 4 test rules. When a violation of § 4 arises, the export notification requirements of § 12(b) may also have been violated if the product was exported. After the sunset date of a test rule, the export notification requirement also terminates. As a practical matter, this means that if the test rule expired in 2005, there can be no export notification penalties imposed for an export in 2006.

---

88. *See* Chapter 14, Penalties and Enforcement, for a complete discussion of the Audit Policy and the mitigating factors applicable to all the TSCA ERPs.

CHAPTER 10

Voluntary Initiatives

I. Background of Voluntary Initiatives

In the late 1990s, three paradigm shifts converged to cause the United States Environmental Protection Agency (EPA) to move away from command and control toward a more collaborative approach with its historic antagonists to achieve the Toxic Substances Control Act (TSCA) policy goal that "adequate data...be developed with respect to the effect of chemical substances and mixtures on health and the environment...[by] those who manufacture ... [and] ... process such chemical substances and mixtures ...."[1]

The first of these new paradigms was the recognition that notwithstanding the clear policy goal of TSCA, its legal structure was self-defeating.[2] Government reports had concluded repeatedly that EPA was too slow in gathering the testing data needed to understand the risk posed to the public so as to be able to deal with that risk effectively.[3] Judicial review under heightened scrutiny is one reason that the TSCA process is lengthy and underused.[4] Throughout its history, the ambiguities and complexities of the law encouraged chemical manufacturers to challenge chemical testing rules, with consequent delays.[5] Public interest groups similarly have used the judicial system to try to either force EPA to fulfill its obligations under TSCA or to strengthen perceived weaknesses of new regulations issued by EPA.[6]

The second paradigm shift was the growing acceptance by the chemical industry of an increasing responsibility to ensure the safety of its products and operations and to make visible to the public its progress on safety. The chemical industry, through its trade group the Chemical Manufacturers

---

1. TSCA§2(b)(1), 15 U.S.C. § 2601.
2. Environmental Defense Fund, Toxic Ignorance: The Continuing Absence of Basic Health Testing for Top-Selling Chemicals in the United States, 24 (1997) [hereinafter Toxic Ignorance], *available at* http://www.edf.org/documents/243_toxicignorance.pdf.
3. *See, e.g.*, U.S. Gen. Accounting Office, Toxic Substances: EPA's Chemical Testing Program Has Not Yet Resolved Safety Concerns, GAO/RCED-91-136, (June 19, 1991); U.S. Gen. Accounting Office, Toxic Substances: Status of EPA's Reviews of Chemicals Under the Chemical Testing Program, GAO/RCED -92-31FS (Oct. 31, 1991); U.S. Gen. Accounting Office, Toxic Substances Control Act: EPA's Limited Progress in Regulating Toxic Chemicals, GAO/T/RCED-94-212 (May 17, 1994).
4. John. S. Applegate, *The Perils of Unreasonable Risk: Information, Regulatory Policy, and Toxic Substances Control*, 91 Colum. L.Rev. 261, 325 (Mar. 1991).
5. *See* Shell Chemical v. EPA, 826 F.2d 295 (5th Cir. 1987); Ausimont U.S.A., Co. v. EPA, 838 F.2d 93 (3d Cir. 1988); Chemical Manufacturers v. EPA, 859 F.2d 977 (D.C. Cir. 1988).
6. *See, e.g.*, Helstosky v. EPA, No. 01-1069, 2001 WL 799950 (D.C. Cir. 2001), in which PETA challenged EPA's issuance of final test guidelines.

Association, in 1988 adopted Responsible Care®[7] in the wake of disasters like Bhopal and Love Canal to counter strong and rising public opinion that it was not an industry to be trusted, or even one to be allowed to remain onshore. Since the inception of Responsible Care®, the industry began, though sometimes begrudgingly, to work together with its former adversaries, the governmental regulators and the environmentalists, to find and resolve areas of mutual interest.[8]

The third paradigm shift was the rising access to, and expectations created by, the Internet. No longer could there be any secrets about either what chemicals were being made in, or transported through, the neighborhood, or found in foods or articles of everyday use, and the risks, known or perceived, from those chemicals. The Congress had planted the seeds for this shift, perhaps without full understanding of its implications, with the enactment of the Toxic Release Inventory in 1986.[9] The public was interested in disclosure and now had the means to ensure easy access. For the first time, the simple fact of having to report releases to the public changed industrial behavior, and command-and-control regulation was not the motivating factor in achieving environmental benefits.

On April 21, 1998, Earth Day, consistent with these trends, Vice President Al Gore announced a Chemical Right-to-Know Initiative (ChemRTK) to expand public access to information about releases of chemicals to the environment. [10] This overarching program was to have three distinct components: a program to develop a base set of health effects data for chemicals manufactured or imported in quantities exceeding one millions pounds a year,[11] a program to generate additional health effects testing for chemicals to which

---

7. The Chemical Manufacturers Association was renamed the American Chemistry Council in 2000. All members of the American Chemistry Council must adhere to the Responsible Care Codes of Management Practices and report to the Council on their implementation. The Codes were intended to cover every aspect of chemical operations. Responsible Care© is described at http://www.americanchemistry.com/s_responsiblecare/sec.asp?CID=1298&DID=4841.
8. ACC stated that the industry group "has welcomed the high level of cooperation between all parties involved to produce an effective agreement ... [on] HPV chemicals. The framework is an improvement over normal "command and control" regulatory approaches and is a possible model for future cooperative regulatory efforts. It is also a further demonstration of the industry's commitment to product stewardship and Responsible Care." Chemical Manufacturer Association, Special Alert, Attachment 1, 4 (Oct. 8, 1998).
9. Statistics on emissions of the chemicals that were required to be disclosed under the Toxic Release Inventory, from 1988 to 2007, show that releases decreased by 47.5 percent. 2007 TRI Public Data Release Data Charts and Tables, Section B, at B-5, *available at* http://www.epa.gov/tri/tridata/tri07/pdr/SectionB.pdf.
10. Background on this initiative is *available at* http://www.epa.gov/hpv/pubs/general/rtkfaqs.htm#What%20CRTK.
11. This is known at the High Production Volume (HPV) Challenge.

children might be disproportionately exposed,[12] and an expansion of emissions reporting for chemicals that persist in the environment, known as persistent, bioaccumulative toxins (PBTs).

II. High Production Volume Challenge Program

The High Production Volume (HPV) Challenge Program originated as a response to a report released by the Environmental Defense Fund (EDF) in 1997, *Toxic Ignorance*, that found that basic health effects data was lacking or not publicly available for most HPV chemicals.[13] An HPV chemical is one that is imported into, or manufactured in, the United States in volumes in excess of one million pounds per year. Using publicly available data, EDF analyzed a sample of one hundred HPV chemicals and concluded that only 29 percent of the HPV chemicals in the United States met a minimum data requirement for health hazard screening.[14] That initial research was followed by a study by EPA that concluded that of the 2863 organic HPV chemicals studied, no basic toxicity information was publicly available for 43 percent of the high volume chemicals manufactured domestically and that a full set of basic toxicity information was available for only 7 percent of those chemicals.[15] The industry organization, the Chemical Manufacturers Association (now known as the American Chemistry Council, or ACC) issued a report as well. It found that 47 percent of the one hundred HPV chemicals it reviewed had full SIDS health data sets, confirming the premise that basic toxicity testing data was not publicly available for a great majority of the approximately twenty-eight hundred industrial chemicals manufactured, imported, or processed in the United States in volumes in excess of one million pounds a year.[16] While each of the studies had different quantitative findings, the consistent theme in all of them was that significant basic data was absent on

12. This is known as the Voluntary Children's Chemical Evaluation Program (VCCEP).
13. Toxic Ignorance, 7.
14. *Id.* at 15. The study looked only for health screening data as established by the Organization for Economic Development's (OECD) Screening Information Data Set (SIDS), and not at the full SIDS set.
15. EPA, Office of Pollution Prevention and Toxics, Chemical Hazard Data: What Do We Really Know About the Safety of High Production Volume Chemicals? 2 (Apr. 1998), *available at* http://www.epa.gov/hpv/pubs/general/hazchem.pdf
16. American Chemistry Council, Public Accountability of SIDS-Related Testing Data for U.S. High Production Volume Chemicals (June 12, 1998). Copies of this report are available from ACC by calling 301-617-7824 and requesting report number 610336 and through http://www.regulations.gov by searching for documents EPA-HQ-OPPT-2005-0033-0101 and EPA-HQ-OPPT-2005-0033-0102.

chemicals produced and used in large quantities in the United States, contributing to the lack of risk assessments on potential hazards.

A. The Voluntary Program

In October 1998, ACC, EPA and EDF issued a joint press release unveiling a framework for voluntary industry testing of HPV chemicals. On December 26, 2000 EPA published a Notice in the Federal Register entitled Data Collection and Development on High Production Volume (HPV) Chemicals, setting forth the requirements of the voluntary program and summarizing the progress of the voluntary program to date.[17]

1. Program Mechanics

The information required to be provided by sponsors of chemicals was derived from a battery of tests agreed upon by the international community as appropriate for screening high volume chemicals for toxicity, commonly referenced as the Organization for Economic Cooperation and Development (OECD) Screening Information Data Set (SIDS) minimum base set.[18] Initially EPA identified chemicals as being HPV based on the reporting for the 1990 Inventory Update Rule (IUR). Subsequently, EPA issued a guidance for removing a chemical from this list.[19] EPA also considered any HPV chemicals managed in the foreign counterpart programs, the OECD HPV SIDS Program or in the International Council of Chemical Associations (ICCA) HPV program to be sponsored and not subject to TSCA § 4 rulemaking unless those commitments were not met.[20] Data is not publicly available on the EPA Web site for the chemicals sponsored indirectly through the international programs.[21]

---

17. 65 Fed. Reg. 81686 (Dec. 26, 2000).
18. Six basic toxicity endpoints have been adopted by the OECD as the minimum required for SIDS: acute toxicity; repeat dose toxicity; developmental and reproductive toxicity; mutagenicity (gene mutation and chromosomal aberration/damage essays); ecotoxicity (studies in fish, invertebrates, and algae); and environmental fate (including physical/chemical properties: melting point, boiling point, vapor pressure, *n* –octanol/water partition coefficient, hydrolysis, transport/distribution, and biodegradation).
19. Removal of a chemical from the HPV list required evidence that the chemical was no longer being produced by any company or group of companies at a total aggregate volume of one million pounds or greater and the chemical was not likely to become an HPV chemical in the future. The claim had to be verifiable based on business plans, past production patterns, and credible trends in the market.
20. 65 Fed. Reg. 81686, 81692 (Dec. 26, 2000).
21. EPA, Office of Pollution Prevention and Toxics, Status and Future Directions of the High Production Volume Challenge Program, EPA 743-R-04-001, 9-10 (Nov. 2004), *available at* http://www.epa.gov/hpv/pubs/general/hpvstatr.htm.

The voluntary program, as announced, was to have three elements: a fixed timetable and a fixed list of chemicals; continuous public access to status and results;[22] and international sharing of testing responsibility.[23] To participate in the voluntary HPV program, companies had to volunteer to sponsor a chemical, either alone or in combination with others. Companies were asked to submit a commitment letter by December 1, 1999, listing the HPV chemicals to be sponsored, including those in categories, by Chemical Abstract Service (CAS) Numbers and chemical names, the year the evaluation would be started for each and the year test plans would be submitted.[24] The next step was to submit test plans with robust summaries of existing studies and proposals as to tests needed to complete the SIDS testing requirements as promised in the commitment letter.[25] The EPA notice set out the required testing end points and referred participating companies to an OECD publication for more definitive guidance.[26] To allow for public participation, sponsoring companies were asked to not implement test plans until after one-hundred and twenty days of the posting of a test plan.[27] The final step in the program was for the sponsoring companies to submit robust summaries of the completed studies for posting on the HPV portion of the EPA's Web site.[28] The OECD guidance document on the requirements of completing a robust summary appears on the EPA's Web site.[29] EPA defined a robust summary as a document that sets out "technical information necessary to adequately describe an experiment or study and includes the objectives, methods, results, and conclusions of the full study report, which can either be an experiment or … an estimation or prediction method."[30]

In an effort to minimize duplicative testing and unnecessary use of test animals, EPA agreed to consider accepting data from existing studies that were not conducted in accordance with appropriate OECD test guidelines, EPA test guidelines, or Good Laboratory Practice Standards, if the data were

---

22. Data is *available at* http://www.epa.gov/HPV/hpvis/index.html. There is also a list of new additions to data at http://www.epa.gov/HPV/whatsnew.htm. The latter includes an e-mail notification sign-up to receive updates.
23. 65 Fed. Reg. 81686, 81693 (Dec. 26, 2000).
24. *Id.* at 81694.
25. *Id.*
26. *Id.*
27. *Id.* at 81694–5. The document referenced in the Federal Register Notice as providing definitive guidance was the third edition of the Screening Information Data Set Manual of the OECD Programme on the Co-operative Investigation of High Production Volume Chemicals (July 1997).
28. 65 Fed. Reg. 81686, 81694 (Dec. 26, 2000).
29. OECD, Guidance for Developing Robust Summaries for SIDS Dossiers (Document number ENV/JM/EXCH(99), 13 (Oct.8 1999), *available at* http://www.epa.gov/chemrtk/pubs/general/robsumgd.htm.
30. 71 Fed. Reg. 13708, 13719 (Mar. 16, 2006).

demonstrated to be otherwise scientifically valid.[31] In addition, EPA allowed for certain endpoints not to be tested if, given the totality of what is known about a chemical, there was sufficient existing data consistent with the EPA's guidance on determining the data adequacy.[32]

In response to industry's concerns that searching for preexisting data to meet the requirements of the HPV challenge program might expose companies to liability for failure to submit substantial risk information as required under TSCA § 8(e), EPA advised participants that for the purposes of the HPV voluntary program it would consider information contained in an expanded list of databases as having been known to EPA within the meaning of § 8(e).[33] In addition, EPA advised that any other potential liability for § 8(e) violations would be limited according to the terms of the Registration Agreement for TSCA § 8(e) Compliance Audit Program.[34] Chemicals tested in accordance with the voluntary program are not subject to a test rule, thereby eliminating imposition of an automatic TSCA §12(b) export requirement.

Reference materials and program status can be found at the EPA's Web site.[35] While the HPV program is at this stage fully mature, these materials may be of some value in understanding how future voluntary initiatives might be structured.

2. Program Results

The three parties that cooperated to create the framework for the HPV Challenge Program have each reviewed the results and have come to somewhat different conclusions.[36] Just as they had viewed the data that gave rise to the program initially through different lenses, they have made their assessments of the results of the program through those different lenses. Sometimes they reach their conclusions based on different sets of facts; sometimes they

---

31. 65 Fed. Reg. 81686, 81690 (Dec. 26, 2000).
32. *Id.*
33. Letter from Susan H. Wayland, Deputy Assistant Administrator, EPA. (Oct. 14, 1999) [hereinafter Wayland Letter], *available at* http://www.epa.gov/HPV/pubs/general/ceoltr2.htm.
34. *Id.* For a discussion of the § 8(e) Compliance Audit Program, *see* Chapter 7, Reporting and Recordkeeping.
35. http://www.epa.gov/hpv/index.htm.
36. EPA, Office of Pollution Prevention and Toxics, Status and Future Directions of the High Production Volume Challenge Program, EPA 743-R-04-001, (Nov. 2004), *available at* http://www.epa.gov/hpv/pubs/general/hpvstatr.htm. Environmental Defense, High Hopes, Low Marks A Final Report Card On The High Production Volume Chemical Challenge (2007), *available at* http://www.edf.org/documents/6653_HighHopesLowMarks.pdf. American Chemistry Council, High Production Volume (HPV) Challenge Program: A Landmark Program Making More Health and Environmental Data Publicly Available Than Ever Before (Dec. 4, 2007).

interpret the same set of facts differently. All of the original parties agree that the program has resulted in making more health and safety data on large volume chemicals publicly available at a faster speed than ever before. Approximately twenty-two hundred chemicals were sponsored, of which fourteen hundred were sponsored directly under the HPV Challenge Program and eight hundred and sixty were sponsored indirectly through the ICCA HPV Initiative.[37] In addition to individual company sponsors, at least one hundred consortia worked together on sponsorship commitments.[38]

All of the original parties agreed that there were issues with bringing online the technical resources to implement the program and that certain timetables were delayed. Each recognized that EPA had not yet implemented test rules dealing with most of the orphan chemicals, but they characterized the reasons for this lack of action differently. The true value of the program can only be evaluated years from now, when an assessment can be made as to whether or not the generation and collection of the screening data led to a minimization of the risks from chemical production and use and greater safety for people and the environment.

The EPA has begun the process of integrating the results from the HPV Challenge into its enhanced existing chemicals management program.[39] The enhanced chemicals management program was announced in September 2009. With respect to HPV chemicals, its main elements are development of action plans for specific chemicals, four of which were made public for HPV chemicals in January 2010;[40] preparing hazard characterizations for HPV chemicals; and issuing significant new use rules.[41]

B. Orphan Chemicals

While the responses to the voluntary HPV program were substantial, there were nevertheless chemicals that no one sponsored, and those chemicals are often referred to as orphan chemicals. As of EPA's most recent update on its Web site, from 2006, 267 chemicals fell into this category.[42] Data

---

37. http://www.epa.gov/chemrtk/pubs/general/basicinfo.htm. The HPV Challenge Program had twenty-eight hundred chemicals on its list at one time. 71 Fed. Reg. 13708, 13709 (Mar. 16, 2006).
38. http://www.epa.gov/chemrtk/pubs/general/basicinfo.htm. A list of sponsors is *available at* http://www.epa.gov/chemrtk/pubs/update/spncomp.htm.
39. http://www.epa.gov/hpv/index.htm.
40. *See* Chapter 11, Bans and Restrictions.
41. http://www.epa.gov/oppt/existingchemicals/pubs/enhanchems.html#newreg.
42. The list of orphan chemicals is revised periodically and is *available at* http://www.epa.gov/hpv/pubs/general/hpvunspn.pdf.

for most of these chemicals were being obtained through a combination of TSCA § 4 test rules,[43] TSCA § 8(a) Preliminary Assessment and Information Reporting (PAIR) rules,[44] and TSCA § 8(d) Health and Safety Data Reporting (HaSDR) rules.[45] Test rules require that designated tests be conducted on specified chemicals, PAIR rules require producers and importers to submit existing data on production or importation volumes, end uses, and exposures, and HaSDR rules require producers and importers to submit copies and lists of existing unpublished health and safety studies.

1. Test Rules

The first HPV test rule was issued on March 16, 2006,[46] more than five years after its announcement as a proposed rule and for only 17 of the originally proposed 37 chemicals.[47] The time lag between proposal and issuance of the final rule was due to the difficulty EPA has meeting the statutory requirements for issuing test rules.[48] It found that the 17 chemicals were produced in substantial quantities, meaning quantities in excess of one million pounds, based on IUR data.[49] EPA determined that there was broad exposure to workers from these widely used industrial chemicals. Each was identified by the National Occupational Exposure Survey as having a total worker exposure in excess of one thousand workers, demonstrating that there was or might be substantial human exposure to them.[50] EPA further determined that there was insufficient data to determine or predict their health and environmental effects by searching for data on the SIDS endpoints, which were mostly lacking.[51] Because of the broad exposures and the lack of available data, EPA concluded that testing was needed to develop data to allow it to determine whether these chemicals presented an unreasonable risk to human health and the environment.[52] This first rule was subsequently amended later

---

43. For a discussion of TSCA § 4 test rules, *see* Chapter 9, Test Rules.
44. For a discussion of TSCA § 8(a) PAIR rules, *see* Chapter 7, Reporting and Recordkeeping.
45. For a discussion of TSCA § 8(d) HaSDR rules, *see* Chapter 7, Reporting and Recordkeeping.
46. 71 Fed. Reg. 13708 (Mar. 16, 2006).
47. Of the originally proposed 37 chemicals, 11 were being sponsored in the voluntary HPV Challenge Program and SIDS program, 2 were being sponsored in the ICCA HPV Initiative, and 7 were removed from the list based on 2002 IUR data because they were imported or manufactured in volumes lower than the one million pound threshold. 71 Fed. Reg. 13708, 13720 (Mar. 16, 2006).
48. For a discussion of the requirements of issuing TSCA test rules and the difficulties EPA has experienced in this area, see Chapter 9, Test Rules.
49. 71 Fed. Reg. 13708, 13713 (Mar. 16, 2006).
50. *Id.*
51. *Id.*
52. *Id.*

in the year to delete one substance, coke oven light oil, because the finding that there was substantial worker exposure to this substance proved to be incorrect based on new data provided by the industry.[53]

This test rule, for the most part, incorporated the criteria established under the voluntary program and used similar program mechanics. The rule established the same potential endpoints for testing[54] and allowed the consideration of testing not done in accordance with the specified guidelines if in fact such studies were otherwise scientifically valid, including structure-activity relationship information and category approaches.[55] Unlike the voluntary program, however, the rule mandated that testing be completed within 13 months of the effective date of the rule. Further, the rule did not expand databases for the purposes of TSCA § 8(e) compliance and did not limit penalty assessment. Finally, chemicals subject to a test rule are also subject to the export notification requirements of TSCA § 12(b).[56]

For the purposes of testing, EPA established two tiers of companies: Tier 1 companies, which are initially responsible to comply, and Tier 2 companies, which will have a secondary obligation. Tier 1 companies are companies that are not Tier 2 companies and manufacture or intend to manufacture an HPV chemical subject to the test rule.[57] Tier 2 includes those companies who manufacture or intend to manufacture a test rule substance solely as one or more of the following: byproduct; impurity; naturally occurring substance; nonisolated intermediate; component of a Class 2 substance; in amounts of less than eleven hundred pounds annually; in small quantities for research and development; or those who process or intend to process a test rule substance, as all of those terms are defined in TSCA or its implementing regulations.[58]

Tier 1 companies are required to submit a notice of intent to test, or an exemption request if they believe another company or a consortium will be conducting the testing.[59] Unlike in the voluntary HPV Challenge Program, Tier 1 companies that receive an exemption and Tier 2 companies must reimburse those companies that conduct the testing. Most companies subject to a test rule agree privately on data compensation.[60] If the parties do not agree, they are subject to the data reimbursement rules under TSCA § 4(c), which

53. 71 Fed. Reg. 71058, 71060 (Dec. 8, 2006).
54. 71 Fed. Reg. 13708, 13709 (Mar. 16, 2006).
55. *Id.* at 13713.
56. 40 C.F.R. 707.60(a)(1). For a discussion of export notification requirements, *see* Chapter 8, Exports and Imports.
57. 71 Fed. Reg. 13708, 13730 (Mar. 16, 2006).
58. *Id.*
59. *Id.* at 13718.
60. *Id.* at 13719.

allow for a hearing with the American Arbitration Association in front of a hearing officer.[61]

On July 24, 2008, EPA issued a proposed test rule for the second group of 19 HPV chemical substances.[62] The proposed rule has basically the same substance as the first test rule on HPV chemical substances. It also requests additional testing on several SIDS endpoints for five chemicals in the first HPV test rule because EPA, after evaluation, determined the existing data and experience were not sufficient to predict the effect of those substances on health or the environment.[63] EPA has said that the issuance of a test rule on a substance does not preclude it from requiring additional testing, if a need for such testing becomes clear. EPA expects to finalize the second test rule in 2010 and propose subsequent test rules for additional orphan chemicals.[64]

2. Reporting Rules

EPA issued two reporting rules on August 16, 2006, a PAIR under TSCA § 8(a)[65] and a HaSDR under TSCA § 8(d),[66] each for 243 HPV Challenge Program orphan chemicals[67] recommended by the Interagency Testing Committee (ITC) to EPA for priority testing consideration. The ITC was established under TSCA § 4(e) to recommend chemicals and chemical mixtures to EPA for consideration for priority testing. The ITC added certain orphan chemicals to the Priority Testing List in its 55th and 56th ITC Reports, as subsequently amended. EPA does not have authority to remove a chemical from the Priority Testing List once it has been put on the list by the ITC.[68] EPA must make those chemicals subject to PAIR and HaSDR reporting requirements, unless requested not to do so by the ITC. Under the PAIR, manufacturers, including importers, of the chemicals listed in the rule were required to submit a one-time report on general production/importation volume, end use, and exposure-related information using the PAIR Form.[69] Under the HaSDR, certain past, current, and proposed manufacturers, importers, and processors, if specified, were required to submit to EPA copies

61. *Id.*
62. 73 Fed. Reg. 43314 (July 24, 2008).
63. *Id.* at 43322.
64. Regulatory Plan and Semiannual Regulatory Agenda, EPA-230-Z-09-002, 97 (Fall 2009) [hereinafter Fall 2009 Regulatory Agenda], *available at* http://www.epa.gov/lawsregs/documents/regagendabook-fall09.pdf.spring09.pdf.
65. 71 Fed. Reg. 47122 (Aug. 16, 2006).
66. *Id.* at 47130.
67. *Id.* at 47123.
68. *Id.*
69. The PAIR form is entitled Manufacturer's Report-Preliminary Assessment Information (EPA Form No. 7710–35). *See* 40 C.F.R. 712.28.

and lists of unpublished health and safety studies on the designated chemicals they manufacture, import, or process.[70]

Consistent with its emphasis on obtaining as much information as possible in a voluntary manner, the rule set forth a new commitment policy that allowed companies to voluntarily sponsor any of these chemicals under the HPV Challenge Program[71] and have them deleted from these rules. The following month EPA announced the withdrawal of 22 chemicals for which it received commitments of sponsorship to the voluntary HPV Challenge Program.[72] Further, consistent with the original intention of the HPV Challenge Program not to duplicate international testing programs, EPA deleted four chemicals from the rules that were being sponsored under the OECD HPV SIDS Program and/or the ICCA HPV Initiative.[73] Lastly, EPA removed seven chemicals that were documented to no longer be within the definition of HPV.[74] EPA noted that the determinations made for the removal of the 33 chemicals fell within the definition of good cause required by law to allow EPA to take such action.[75] The following spring EPA removed two more chemicals from the rules because they were also part of the voluntary HPV Challenge Program,[76] leaving a total of 208 chemicals subject to the PAIR and HaSDR reporting rules issued in 2006.

III. Voluntary Children's Chemical Evaluation Program

A component of EPA's Chemical Right-to-Know Initiative,[77] the Voluntary Children's Chemical Evaluation Program (VCCEP)[78] was intended to encourage the development of information about the health effects, exposures and risks of industrial chemicals to children. While the VCCEP is a voluntary program that focuses on the development of data and assessments, as with the HPV program, EPA indicated that it would consider whether a test rule

70. For a discussion of the types of studies required to be submitted, *see* 71 Fed. Reg. 47130, 47132 (Aug. 16, 2006).
71. 71 Fed. Reg. 47122, 47124 (Aug. 16, 2006). The new commitment policy was subsequently amended and is *available at* http://www.epa.gov/HPV/pubs/general/hpvpolcy2.htm.
72. 71 Fed. Reg. 57439, 57442 (Sept. 29, 2006).
73. *Id.*
74. *Id.*
75. *Id.*
76. 72 Fed. Reg. 21119, 21121 (Apr. 30, 2007).
77. In its Chemical Right-to-Know initiative, the EPA committed to "review and report on what new testing may be needed to assess the special impact chemicals may have on children." 65 Fed. Reg. 81700, 81701 (Dec. 26, 2000).
78. Materials on the VCCEP are *available at* http://www.epa.gov/oppt/vccep/index.html.

under TSCA Section 4 was appropriate for chemicals not sponsored in the VCCEP.[79]

EPA developed the VCCEP using a stakeholder involvement process. EPA envisioned running the VCCEP as a pilot, to be evaluated to determine whether, and if so what, modifications could be made to make the VCCEP run more efficiently.[80] At the outset, EPA believed that the VCCEP presented a unique opportunity for diverse stakeholders to "demonstrate that they can jointly manage, participate in, and generate results in an in-depth hazard, exposure, and risk assessment program."[81] Further, EPA established the program as one that might have broader applications in the future, beyond VCCEP itself, such as a vehicle to follow up on chemicals of concern identified through the HPV program.[82]

A. Program Mechanics

1. Selection of Chemicals for VCCEP

By design, the VCCEP focused on chemicals "found to be present as contaminants in: human tissues or fluids (e.g., adipose tissues, blood, breast milk, breath); food and water children may eat and drink; and air children may breathe...."[83] Using those criteria, EPA reviewed a number of biomonitoring and environmental databases[84] and then deleted from its initial screen chemicals not produced in or imported into the United States, chemicals being phased out under the Montreal Protocol,[85] and chemicals being adequately managed by other ongoing programs.[86] This resulted in over one hundred fifty chemicals assembled as a working list of candidate chemicals for VCCEP.[87]

---

79. 65 Fed. Reg. 81700, 81701 (Dec. 26, 2000).
80. *Id.* at 81714.
81. *Id.* at 81715.
82. *Id.*
83. *Id.* at 81701.
84. There was an exception to the selection process that identified three polybrominated diphenyl ethers without relying on the use of databases. This class of chemicals was found to be increasing in concentration in human breast milk in a Swedish study. 65 Fed. Reg. 81700, 81701 (Dec. 26, 2000).
85. The Montreal Protocol participants agreed to phase out ozone-depleting chemicals. Documents concerning the Montreal Protocol are gathered at http://www.epa.gov/history/topics/montreal/index.htm.
86. 65 Fed. Reg. 81700, 81701 (Dec. 26, 2000).
87. A list of these chemicals may be found in USEPA, Methodology for Selecting Chemicals for the Voluntary Children's Chemical Evaluation Program Pilot. 65 Fed. Reg. 81700, 81701 (Dec. 26, 2000).

For the VCCEP Pilot Program, EPA further culled the VCCEP chemical candidates to identify 23 chemicals[88] for which it sought sponsorship. A primary factor considered in selecting chemicals for the VCCEP Pilot Program was the presumed availability of hazard data from such sources as the OECD SIDS Program and commitments in the HPV Challenge Program during the early years.

2. Submission Collection Tiers

Unlike the HPV Voluntary Challenge Program, VCCEP has three potential data collection tiers, with Tiers 2 and 3 each requiring successively higher testing requirements if determined to be necessary following evaluation by an EPA third-party peer consultant contractor. In addition to the submission of data for each tier, four types of assessments are required for each stage of the VCCEP: a hazard assessment, an exposure assessment, a risk assessment, and a data needs assessment.[89] The data needs assessment is not required in Tier 1 and Tier 2.

To be resource efficient, the initial tier, Tier 1, required testing endpoints that are consistent with the testing required under the HPV Challenge Program. EPA advised the sponsors to consider doing upper level testing in the first instance instead of repeating the screening studies that were being developed for the HPV chemicals.[90] The full battery of potential tests over the three tiers includes acute studies (oral, dermal, or inhalation); ninety-day rodent feeding studies; oncogenicity studies in two species of rodents; prenatal developmental toxicity studies in rodents and nonrodents; two-generation reproduction study in rodents; general metabolism study in rodents, mutagenicity studies; acute and subchronic neurotoxicity in rats; immunotoxicity study in rodents; and developmental neurotoxicity study in rodents.[91]

After each submission in a tier, EPA requests a third-party contractor to convene a group of scientists and relevant experts from various stakeholder groups to discuss whether the potential hazards, exposures, and risks to children have been adequately evaluated and to provide input on the hazard and exposure data needs.[92] The third-party contractor then provides a report to the EPA, which EPA reviews along with the original sponsor submission.[93] The entire peer consultation process, including meetings and deliberations, is open to the public. Members of the public also have an opportunity to

---

88. These chemicals are listed at 65 Fed. Reg. 81700, 81704 (Dec. 26, 2000).
89. 65 Fed. Reg. 81700, 81710 (Dec. 26, 2000).
90. *Id.* at 81706.
91. *Id.* at 81702.
92. *Id.* at 81712.
93. *Id.*

provide oral or written comments at such meetings.[94] Once the peer consultation process is concluded, EPA will review the original submission and the report of the third-party contractor to determine any additional data needs.[95]

3. Sponsor Commitments

Individual chemical companies and consortia can commit to sponsor a chemical or chemicals on a tier basis. Because of the voluntary nature of the VCCEP, EPA acknowledged outright that sponsors make voluntary commitments that are not enforceable contracts.[96] Sponsors can withdraw from commitments at any time. The only authority EPA has to impose testing requirements is to promulgate a TSCA § 4 test rule. Sponsors were asked to send EPA a commitment letter to sponsor chemicals for Tier 1 between January 25, 2001 and June 25, 2001. The letter needed to identify the chemical by name and CAS Number, and to contain a commitment to start developing the Tier 1 hazard and exposure data within six months after the end of the sign-up period, that is by December 25, 2001. Sponsors could delay the start year for developing the data to be consistent with commitments made to the HPV Challenge Program. Similarly, companies and consortia could forward the same type of commitment letter to sponsor a chemical for Tier 2 and Tier 3. Those commitments would be due within four months of the issuance of EPA's data needs assessment for the respective tier.[97] Twenty of the twenty-three chemicals were sponsored by thirty-five companies and ten consortia; three chemicals remain unsponsored.[98]

EPA has announced that is negotiating an enforceable consent agreement to obtain biodegradation and environmental fate testing for decabromodiphenyl ether. EPA had requested this information under the VCCEP, but had not received any commitment to conduct the testing.[99]

B. Program Evaluation

As part of the initial announcement of the VCCEP pilot in 2000, EPA had stated it would evaluate the pilot three and six years after its start to determine

94. *Id.* at 81713.
95. *Id.* at 81714.
96. *Id.* at 81715.
97. *Id.*
98. 71 Fed. Reg. 67121, 67122 (Nov. 20, 2006).
99. Fall 2009 Regulatory Agenda, 97. This is one of the chemicals for which EPA has issued an action plan; *see* the discussion of the Polybrominated Diphenyl Ethers (PBDEs) Action Plan in Chapter 11, Bans and Restrictions.

whether, and what, modifications could be made to the program run more efficiently. Because the pilot had not generated enough activity at the three-year mark, EPA conducted its first evaluation at the five-year mark, midway into the program. EPA announced its request for comments on the implementation of VCCEP in 2006.[100] In that announcement, EPA summarized the results of the program as of August 2006:[101]

- sponsor commitments were received for twenty chemicals for Tier 1 by the six month deadline;
- chemical assessments were submitted for 12 chemicals for Tier 1 and all of those assessments were made available on the VCCEP Web site within one month of receipt by EPA;
- twelve chemical assessments had gone through the Peer Consultation Process, and the Peer Consultation meetings were held within an average of 2.4 months of receipt of the chemical assessment;
- peer consultation reports were available for twelve chemicals, and reports were issued within an average 4.1 months after the Peer Consultation meetings;
- EPA issued Data Needs Decisions on six chemicals, finding that three had Tier 2 data needs and that three did not;
- one chemical received a sponsor commitment to provide Tier 2 information; and
- EPA was informed that two chemicals will not receive sponsor commitment to provide Tier 2 information.

In response to its request for comments, EPA received 138 comments from 11 organizations. Those comments are summarized in an interim report.[102] Based on these comments, and its own review of the pilot, EPA announced some proposed modest changes, dealing primarily with timeliness and efficiency issues, to the VCCEP.[103]

To deal with comments that the chemicals initially selected were a particularly well-studied group for which little additional assessment was needed, EPA proposed selecting future chemicals for the program that are identified as being of special concern and needing hazard and exposure data relevant to characterizing risks to children.[104] Those identifications were supposed to be

---

100. 71 Fed. Reg. 67121 (Nov. 20, 2006).
101. Results are summarized at 71 Fed. Reg. 67121, 67123 (Nov. 20, 2006).
102. EPA, Office of Pollution Prevention and Toxics, Chemical Information and Testing Branch, Compiled by Eastern Research Group, Inc. Interim VCCEP Evaluation, Summary of Comments on the VCCEP Pilot Program, (Mar. 18, 2007), *available at* http://www.epa.gov/oppt/vccep/pubs/summaryrpt.pdf.
103. 73 Fed. Reg. 36512 (June 27, 2008).
104. *Id.* at 36513.

made primarily using the Chemical Assessment and Management Program (ChAMP), which was established by the EPA to address trilateral cooperation between the United States, Canada, and Mexico. However, ChAMP has been withdrawn by the current administration so it is unclear how and whether this process will proceed, if at all. Proposed changes to the assessment approach include establishing due dates for sponsor submissions and peer consultations, including for responding to follow-up actions.[105] EPA would also indicate when it believes it is reasonable to combine Tiers 2 and 3 into a single tier to resolve potential chemical risks.[106] The other proposed modifications deal with enhancing the effectiveness of the peer consultation process. Sponsors would take on more responsibility earlier in this process. They would be responsible for contracting with, and paying, the third party consultant to manage the process.[107] The sponsor would develop revised assessments that address issues raised in the peer consultation meeting report and make them publicly available within ninety days of the issuance of the report.[108] EPA would then use the sponsor revised assessments and the meeting report to issue its Data Needs Decision within ninety days of receipt of the revised assessment.[109]

IV. Nanoscale Materials Stewardship Program

The EPA implemented a voluntary program to collect data on nanomaterials.[110] In January of 2008 EPA announced the Nanoscale Materials Stewardship Program (NMSP) to encourage voluntary submissions on the risks posed by nanomaterials and management practices.[111] EPA divided the NMSP into two phases. The first phase, which was called the basic program, called for submission of known and reasonably ascertainable data on such topics as "material characterization, hazard, use, potential exposures, and risk management practices."[112] The nonbinding deadline for those submissions was in July 2008, although as of January 2009 only 29 companies had submitted information and seven more had agreed to but had not yet done so.

---

105. *Id.*
106. *Id.*
107. *Id.*
108. *Id.*
109. *Id.*
110. *See* Chapter 2, TSCA's Scope for a discussion of the status of nonmaterial under TSCA.
111. 73 Fed. Reg. 4861 (Jan. 28, 2008).
112. *Id.* at 4863.

In January 2009 EPA issued an interim assessment of the NMSP.[113] It called the basic phase of the program a success, although it did not receive enough information to determine the molecular identity of many of the nanoscale materials that were the subject of the submissions. The EPA noted that it received 123 submissions on 58 different chemicals. Because there is no inventory of nanoscale materials EPA devoted considerable effort to estimating how many commercial nanomaterials are currently made in order to determine if there was a gap between the number of commercial nanomaterials and the number of commercial nanomaterials that were the subject of NMSP reporting. It estimated that NMSP participants reported on only approximately one-third of the chemicals from which commercially available nanomaterials are made, and only approximately one-tenth of the commercially available nanomaterials, which may be composed of multiple chemicals.[114]

The second phase of the NMSP is an in-depth program, scheduled to be concluded by January 2010. Participants agreed to sponsor new studies that may address physical characteristics, health and environmental effects, fate and transport, monitoring or estimating exposures or releases, and an evaluation of engineering controls and personal protective equipment. As of April 2009 only five companies committed to conduct new studies.[115] This indicates that the NMSP will not significantly fill the data gaps that currently prevent a full understanding of the risks posed by nanomaterials.

V. Shifting Winds

EPA had begun its Chemical Assessment and Management Program (ChAMP) in 2007[116] to implement broader international commitments to ensure the safety of existing chemicals. Over the last several years, EPA expanded the horizon of ChAMP to potentially include voluntary challenge programs for wider categories of chemicals and chemicals present in the

113. EPA, Nanoscale Materials Stewardship Program Interim Report, 3 (Jan., 2009)[hereinafter NMSP Interim Report] *available through* http://www.epa.gov/oppt/nano/.
114. NMSP Interim Report, 18.
115. EPA, Nanoscale Materials Stewardship Program *available through* http://www.epa.gov/oppt/nano/.
116. ChAMP was created initially to implement commitments made at the Security and Prosperity Partnership of North America Leaders Summit, in Montebello, Canada, in August 2007. The United States agreed to complete screening-level chemical prioritizations and initiate action as appropriate on an estimated 6,750 chemicals, including HPV chemicals and chemicals produced or imported in quantities of twenty-five thousand pounds or more. Background on the ChAMP program is *available at* http://www.epa.gov/champ/pubs/basic.html.

United States in lower quantities. While these programs had not yet reached any critical mass, the underlying assumption was that much of this work might be done in a cooperative way with industry, mirroring the HPV and VCCEP initiatives. ChAMP has now been superseded by a new enhanced chemical management program currently being rolled out by the EPA.[117] EPA has announced that while its priority is the passage of a more effective chemical management statute, it will work more actively with the tools available to it under TSCA (§§ 4, 5, 6, and 8) to require information needed to understand the risks posed by chemicals, to develop chemical action plans for high risk chemicals, and to regulate those risks.[118] It is likely that this new emphasis on a more regulatory and less voluntary approach will be accompanied by a greater emphasis on enforcement.

117. *See* http://www.epa.gov/oppt/existingchemicals/pubs/enhanchems.html.

118. *Id.*

CHAPTER

11

Bans and Restrictions

I. Introduction to Types of Restrictions

Much of the Toxic Substances Control Act (TSCA)[1] is directed toward regulation of new chemicals and uses, through premanufacture notifications (PMNs) or Significant New Use Rules (SNURs), or the development of test data for existing chemicals. TSCA § 6,[2] in contrast, presents the legal framework for the United States Environmental Protection Agency (EPA) to prohibit, limit, or impose other conditions on the manufacture, processing, distribution, or use of existing chemicals. With the exception of polychlorinated biphenyls (PCBs) and elemental mercury, the use of which Congress itself restricted under TSCA § 6(e) and § 6(f) respectively, the statutory authority under TSCA § 6(a) to regulate existing chemicals is severely restricted. In taking action to regulate an existing chemical, the EPA must justify its action with substantial evidence on the record that the chemical substance "presents or may present an unreasonable risk" and that its action is the "least burdensome regulation sufficient to regulate the substance at issue." There have been few rulemakings by the Agency meeting these standards.

The heavy burden that the statute places on the EPA before the EPA can regulate a chemical because it poses an unreasonable risk has led many people to criticize TSCA as unworkable. For example, Representative Bobby L. Rush opened a hearing on TSCA reauthorization on February 26, 2009 by noting that a statute that does not support a ban of asbestos needs to be overhauled. He said:

> Furthermore, once EPA has made a determination that a chemical poses a health and environmental hazard, they have been unable to act on this determination. Section 6 of TSCA provides EPA with broad authority to regulate and ban chemicals but the burden of proof for action has been so high that banning a chemical is virtually impossible, and I think most Americans would be very surprised to learn that asbestos, a known carcinogen that kills 8,000 Americans each and every year, has not been banned by the EPA under TSCA because the courts have ruled that EPA did not meet its evidentiary burden of proving that asbestos is an "unreasonable risk to the public." If TSCA is incapable of providing EPA with the regulatory tools to ban asbestos, then the statutes seem to be in dire need of serious repair, and I want to make it clear that reexamining TSCA is not only good for the public health but it is also good for business.[3]

1. 15 U.S.C. §§ 2601–2695d.
2. 15 U.S.C. § 2605.
3. Hearings on Revisiting the Toxic Substances Control Act of 1976, before the Subcomm. on Commerce, Trade, and Consumer Protection, 111th Cong. 4 (testimony of Bobby Rush),

Notwithstanding the obstacles, EPA announced in 2009 that it was prepared to begin the process of issuing restrictions under § 6 for a small group of chemicals that may meet the statutory standards.[4]

A. Regulatory Action to Address a Finding of Unreasonable Risk

Under TSCA § 6(a), "if the Administrator finds that there is a reasonable basis to conclude that the manufacture, processing, distribution in commerce, use or disposal of a chemical substance or mixture … presents … an unreasonable risk of injury to health or the environment," the EPA Administrator is required to initiate rulemaking to take one or a combination of the following actions:

- prohibiting the manufacture, processing, or distribution of the substance or mixture, or limiting the amount that may be manufactured, processed, or distributed;
- prohibiting the manufacture, processing, or distribution of the substance or mixture for particular uses or in excess of certain concentrations;
- requiring that the substance or mixture or any article containing it be marked with or accompanied by clear and adequate warnings and instructions;
- requiring that manufacturers and processors make and retain records or monitor or conduct tests which are reasonable and necessary to assure compliance;
- prohibiting or otherwise regulating any commercial use of the substance or mixture;
- prohibiting or otherwise regulating any disposal of the substance or mixture;
- requiring that manufacturers or processors give notice of any unreasonable risk of injury to distributors, other persons in possession of the substance, or the public; and
- requiring that the manufacturer or processor replace or repurchase the substance or mixture.[5]

---

preliminary transcript *available at* http://energycommerce.house.gov/Press_111/20090226/transcript_20090226_ct.pdf.

4. *See* Existing Chemicals Action Plans, *available at* http://www.epa.gov/oppt/existingchemicals/pubs/ecactionpln.html, and discussion *infra*.
5. TSCA § 6(a).

All chemicals subject to rules under TSCA § 6 are also subject to the export notification requirements of TSCA § 12, so there is no need for a ban or restriction to explicitly require export notifications.[6]

Before promulgating any rule under TSCA § 6(a), EPA must consider and publish a statement with respect to:

- the effects of the substance or mixture on health and the magnitude of the exposure of people;
- the effects of the substance or mixture on the environment and the magnitude of the environmental exposure;
- the benefits of using the substance or mixture and the availability of substitutes; and
- the reasonably ascertainable economic consequences of a restriction, taking into account the effect on the economy, small business, technological innovation, the environment, and public health.[7]

The Agency is specifically required by the statute to use "the least burdensome requirements" to protect adequately against a risk of injury to health or the environment.[8] Further, if EPA finds that the risk of injury to health or the environment could be eliminated or reduced to a sufficient extent by actions taken under another federal law or laws administered in whole or in part by EPA, such as the Clean Water Act[9] or the Clean Air Act,[10] the Agency may not issue rules under TSCA § 6(a) unless it determines "that it is in the public interest to protect against such risk" under TSCA § 6.[11] Under TSCA's judicial review provisions, a reviewing court is required to set aside rulemaking under TSCA § 6(a) if a "rule is not supported by substantial evidence in the rulemaking record … taken as a whole."[12]

Hazardous substances are often inadvertently made because a manufacturing process is contaminated or because the manufacturing parameters are not adequately controlled. TSCA § 6(b) gives the Agency authority to review quality control procedures and require revisions "to the extent necessary" to remedy the inadequacy of existing procedures.

---

6. *See*, Chapter 8, Exports and Imports. Note that there are *de minimis* levels in the export requirements but the *de minimis* exemptions under the export rules do not apply to PCBs.
7. TSCA § 6(c)(1).
8. TSCA § 6(a).
9. 33 U.S.C. § 1251.
10. 42 U.S.C. § 7401.
11. TSCA § 6(a).
12. TSCA § 19(c)(1)(B)(i).

1. Procedures for Rulemaking

When acting to prohibit or restrict the manufacture, processing, distribution, or use of a chemical substance or mixture under TSCA § 6(a), the Agency must comply with the rulemaking standard set forth in the Administrative Procedures Act.[13] This requires the publication of a notice of proposed rulemaking in the Federal Register, an opportunity for interested persons to comment, and publication of the final rule not less than thirty days before its effective data.[14]

Given the statutory requirements imposed on EPA by TSCA § 6(a) to support any rulemaking with "substantial evidence in the rulemaking record" regarding unreasonable risk, economic effects, and assessment of potentially less burdensome alternatives, the Agency has promulgated supplementary rulemaking procedures.[15] The procedure to promulgate a rule to restrict a chemical begins with the publication in the Federal Register of a draft "finding that there is a reasonable basis to conclude that the manufacture, processing, distribution in commerce, use or disposal of the chemical substance(s) or mixture(s) at issue, or any combination of such activities, presents or will present an unreasonable risk of injury to health or the environment."[16] The process includes:

- proposed regulation;
- requests to participate in informal hearing;
- comments;
- informal hearing;
- legislative hearing;
- requests for cross-examination;
- ruling on cross-examination requests;
- cross-examination; and
- reply to comments.[17]

2. Corrosion Proof Fittings and the Asbestos Rule

Most of the EPA's rules banning uses of asbestos under TSCA § 6(a) were overturned in *Corrosion Proof Fittings v. EPA*.[18] As mentioned above, EPA's inability to ban such a notoriously hazardous substance is often used as an

13. 5 U.S.C. § 553.
14. *See* 5 U.S.C. § 553; TSCA § 6(c).
15. 40 C.F.R. Part 750.
16. 40 C.F. R. § 750.2(b).
17. 40 C.F.R. Part 750, Subpart A, Appendix A.
18. Corrosion Proof Fittings v. EPA, 947 F.2d 1201 (5th Cir. 1991).

example of the deficiencies in the TSCA statute in general.[19] It took ten years of regulatory proceedings and effort before the EPA promulgated a final rule under TSCA § 6(a) prohibiting the manufacture, importation, processing, and distribution in commerce of most asbestos-containing products.[20] Based on a conclusion that asbestos is a potential carcinogen at all levels of exposure, regardless of type of asbestos or size of the fiber, the rule imposed a three-stage ban of most commercial uses of asbestos. In 1991 the Circuit Court in *Corrosion Proof Fittings* held that the rule was unlawful in almost all respects.[21] The Court found that the EPA failed to support the rule with substantial evidence. Observing that "Congress did not enact TSCA as a zero-risk statute," the Court's analysis demonstrates the high bar TSCA § 6(a) sets for the Agency when seeking to regulate existing chemicals.

The Court held that the EPA must promulgate the least burdensome regulation that adequately protects the environment. By banning most uses of asbestos, the Court opined that the EPA had chosen the most burdensome possible restrictions. To meet the statutory requirements, the EPA must evaluate each of the less burdensome restrictions and determine the costs and benefits associated with them, and the EPA had not performed that analysis. The Court concluded that the EPA had also not met its burden of showing that asbestos poses an "unreasonable risk" to human health or the environment. In particular, the EPA had not balanced the costs and benefits of its proposed restrictions, and therefore could not have made a determination about the reasonableness of the risks posed by asbestos. Because of these shortcomings, the Court vacated the EPA's rule and remanded it to the EPA. The Court clarified its opinion and stated that products could be banned if they had once been manufactured, imported, or processed but such activities had stopped as of July 12, 1989, which was the date the regulations were issued.[22] The Court had explained that products that are not in commerce do not pose a risk, but a risk would be present if they were reintroduced into commerce and so the EPA was justified in banning them.

On remand, the EPA found that there were six categories of asbestos containing products that were not manufactured, imported, or processed as of July 12, 1989.[23] They are:

- flooring felt (paper felt containing asbestos);
- commercial paper (a paper product containing asbestos that is used as insulation or as a muffler);

---

19. *See* the Preliminary transcript of House of Representatives Hearing on "Revisiting the Toxic Substances Control Act of 1976," *available at* http://energycommerce.house.gov/Press_111/20090226/transcript_20090226_ct.pdf.
20. *See* 54 Fed. Reg. 29460 (July 12, 1989).
21. Corrosion Proof Fittings v. EPA, 947 F.2d 1201 (5th Cir. 1991).
22. *Id.* at 1230.
23. 59 Fed. Reg. 33208 (June 28, 1994).

- corrugated paper (a corrugated paper containing asbestos);
- rollboard (two sheets of asbestos paper laminated together);
- specialty paper (paper containing asbestos that is used as a filter or cooling tower fill); and
- all other uses of asbestos that are new after July 12, 1989.

Asbestos cannot be put to any use that was not commercial on July 12, 1989.[24] All stock that was on hand as of the dates of the bans, which went into effect in the 1990s, had to be labeled as asbestos with a note that they could not be distributed in commerce.[25] Any person subject to a ban had six months after it went into effect to dispose of the banned asbestos products.[26]

II. Regulation of PCBs under TSCA § 6(e)

Of the myriad of chemical substances regulated under TSCA, PCBs are subject to unique treatment. Indeed, upon enactment of TSCA, Congress prohibited the manufacture, processing, distribution, and use of PCBs in any manner other than a "totally enclosed manner," subject to exceptions that may be issued by EPA if it finds that such exception would not result in "an unreasonable risk of injury to health or the environment."[27] These restrictions were unique because at the time TSCA was passed it did not single out any other chemical for a ban in this manner.

PCBs describe a group of over two hundred structurally-related chemical compounds, or congeners. Each congener has two benzene rings and a range of chlorine atoms. Colorless crystals in pure form, commercial PCB products are liquids because the melting point is depressed when PCBs are mixed; PCBs are practically insoluble in water and soluble in oils and organic solvents.

PCBs were first manufactured commercially in 1929. Because of the insulating capacity and flame retardant nature of PCBs, they were widely used as coolants and lubricants in transformers and electrical equipment. PCBs were also commonly used in the formulation of a great variety of common products such as plastics, paints and varnishes, pesticides, carbonless copy paper, adhesives, sealants, newsprint, fluorescent light ballasts, and

---

24. 40 C.F.R. §§ 763.165, 763.167 and 763.169. The EPA may grant exemptions under 40 C.F.R. § 763.173.
25. 40 C.F.R. § 763.171.
26. 40 C.F.R. § 763.169.
27. TSCA § 6(e).

caulking compounds.[28] An estimated 99 percent of PCBs manufactured for use by U.S. industry was made by the Monsanto Chemical Company under the trademark Aroclor.[29] As the use of electricity became widespread through the twentieth century, electrical equipment suppliers such as General Electric and Westinghouse became major users of PCBs. Manufacture ceased in the United States in 1977. It is estimated that 1.1 billion pounds of PCBs were produced prior to the cessation of manufacture.[30]

PCBs are persistent in the environment and tend to accumulate in living creatures and to then enter the food chain where they concentrate. Widespread distribution of PCBs in soil and water was first determined in the 1960s. Acute exposure to high concentrations of PCBs causes a persistent form of acne called chlorine-acne or chloracne. Based on sufficient evidence of carcinogenicity in experimental animals, the EPA,[31] the International Agency for Research on Cancer,[32] and the National Toxicology Program[33] have all classified some PCBs as possibly causing cancer in humans.[34]

While PCBs are regulated under the Clean Water Act,[35] the Comprehensive Environmental Response, Compensation, and Liability Act (Superfund or

28. http://www.epa.gov/epawaste/hazard/tsd/pcbs/pubs/about.htm; William P. Kucewicz, Public Health Implications Of Polychlorinated Biphenyls (PCBs) In The Environment, A Position Paper of the American Council of Science and Health, 9 (2005) *available at* http://www.acsh.org/publications/pubID.1030/pub_detail.asp [hereinafter PCB Position Paper].
29. Under Monsanto's Aroclor nomenclature system, each Aroclor is assigned a four digit number. The last two digits indicate the approximate percentage weight of chlorine in the product, and the first two digits indicate the type of material as follows: 12—chlorinated biphenyls; 25—blend of chlorinated biphenyls and chlorinated terphenyls (75:25); 44—blend of chlorinated biphenyls and chlorinated terphenyls (60:40); and 54—chlorinated terphenyls.
30. PCB Position Paper, 9.
31. *See* http://www.epa.gov/iris/subst/0294.htm.
32. *See* http://monographs.iarc.fr/ENG/Classification/crthalllist.php.
33. *See* http://ntp.niehs.nih.gov/ntp/roc/eleventh/profiles/s149pcb.pdf.
34. The adverse health effects of chronic exposure to PCBs remain a matter of some debate. The EPA has concluded that "PCBs have been demonstrated to cause a variety of adverse health effects. PCBs have been shown to cause cancer in animals. PCBs have also been shown to cause a number of serious non-cancer health effects in animals, including effects on the immune system, reproductive system, nervous system, endocrine system and other health effects. Studies in humans provide supportive evidence for potential carcinogenic and non-carcinogenic effects of PCBs." http://www.epa.gov/epawaste/hazard/tsd/pcbs/pubs/effects.htm. However, the American Council on Science and Health maintains: "No conclusive evidence exists to support the position that background levels in the general population, or even the much higher levels that occurred among some occupational groups, have resulted in carcinogenic or other chronic adverse health effects. In humans, the only effects correlated with chronic or high-level PCB exposure are skin and eye irritation. These effects, however, have not been observed in populations exposed to PCBs through fish consumption or from other environmental sources." PCB Position Paper, 39.
35. 33 U.S.C. §1251.

CERCLA),[36] the Federal Insecticide, Fungicide, and Rodenticide Act,[37] the Resource Conservation and Recovery Act,[38] the Safe Drinking Water Act,[39] the Hazardous Materials Transportation Act,[40] and the Federal Food, Drug, and Cosmetic Act,[41] TSCA by far establishes the most comprehensive legislative and regulatory scheme governing the lifecycle of PCBs.

A. The Statutory Prohibition on Manufacture, Processing, and Distribution of PCBs

In enacting § 6(e) of TSCA, Congress established a framework addressing the disposal of PCBs, the phase-out of PCB manufacture, importation, processing and distribution, and limitation in the use of PCBs. Specifically, § 6(e) provides that:

- within six months of the effective date of TSCA (Jan. 1, 1977), EPA was required to prescribe methods to dispose of PCBs and to require that PCB containers be marked with appropriate warnings;
- as of January 1, 1978, PCBs could be manufactured, processed, distributed, and used only in a "totally enclosed manner;"
- as of January 1, 1979, all manufacture of PCBs was prohibited; and
- as of June 1, 1979, all processing and distribution of PCBs in commerce were prohibited.

These broad statutory prohibitions are subject to limited exceptions that may be created by the EPA. Section 6(e)(2)(B) of TSCA allows EPA to authorize by rule the continued use of PCBs in a non-totally enclosed manner if the EPA finds that no unreasonable risk of injury to health or the environment would result.[42] Section 6(e)(3)(B) also permits the Administrator to grant case-by-case exemptions to the statutory prohibitions on manufacturing, processing, and distribution. Such an exemption, which may be granted for one year, subject to additional terms and conditions, may be made upon a finding that (i) an unreasonable risk of injury to health or the environment would not result and (ii) good faith efforts have been made to develop a

36. 42 U.S.C. §9601.
37. 7 U.S.C. §136.
38. 42 U.S.C. §6901.
39. 42 U.S.C. §300f.
40. 49 U.S.C. § 5101.
41. 21 U.S.C. § 301.
42. 15 U.S.C. § 2605(e)(2)(B).

substitute chemical substance for the PCBs which itself does not pose a risk of injury to health or the environment.[43]

In § 6(e) of TSCA, therefore, Congress created a statutory presumption that PCBs pose an unreasonable risk of injury to human health and the environment, placing upon EPA the burden to establish that any regulatory exception to the statutory ban on manufacture, processing, and distribution would not cause unreasonable risk.

B. The Regulatory Scheme

EPA's PCB control program codifies prohibited and authorized uses of PCBs, establishes marking and labeling requirements, and sets forth storage, disposal, and recordkeeping requirements.[44] The Agency's PCB program has been the subject of numerous regulatory actions, a number of legal challenges, and many enforcement proceedings.

1. Regulation of PCBs at the 50 ppm Level

TSCA's ban on the manufacture, processing, and distribution of PCBs applies to all PCB concentrations in any mixture or medium. Therefore, an important first act by the EPA in implementing its PCB control program was to establish a regulatory cutoff point based on the concentration of PCBs. Because enormous amounts of PCBs were used in the past with little control on disposal practices, PCBs are widely dispersed and found worldwide at low concentrations.[45] As explained by EPA:

> Because PCBs are now so pervasive, the effect of not having a cut-off concentration would be to extend the prohibitions and other requirements of § 6(e) of TSCA to almost all human activity. Many foods, such as fish and milk, as well as the human body often contain detectable concentrations of PCBs.[46]

In a 1978 rulemaking, the Agency initially established a 500 part per million (ppm) regulatory cutoff in order to regulate disposal of most PCBs.[47] This was followed by another final rule in 1979, with the effective date of July 2, 1979, which lowered the 500 ppm cutoff point to 50 ppm, with the

43. 15 U.S.C. § 2605(e)(3)(B).
44. 40 C.F.R. Part 761.
45. 44 Fed. Reg. 31514, 31516 (May 31, 1979).
46. *Id.*
47. 43 Fed. Reg. 7150 (Feb. 17, 1978).

exception of waste oil as a sealant, coating, or dust control, the use of which was prohibited if the waste oil contained any detectable concentration of PCB.[48] In support of the 50 ppm regulatory limit, the Agency contended that lowering the cutoff limit to 10 ppm would "provide an additional degree of environmental protection but would have a grossly disproportionate effect on the economic impact and would have a serious technological impact on the organic chemicals industry."[49] EPA believed that the 50 ppm standard protects human health and the environment and is not overly burdensome."[50] In *Environmental Defense Fund v. EPA*,[51] the Court of Appeals for the District of Columbia struck down the 50 ppm standard on the grounds that the Agency had failed to provide substantial evidence that the cutoff "provides adequate protection for human health and the environment."[52] The Court found:

> It is ... troubling that the Administrator apparently is not aware of the amount of PCBs excluded from regulation by the fifty ppm or other possible cutoffs. Particularly because the Administrator has found that any exposure to PCBs may have adverse effects, the Administrator's flat exclusion of some industrial sources of contamination must undergo careful scrutiny. While some cutoff may be appropriate, we note that the Administrator did not explain why the regulation could not be designed expressly to exclude ambient sources, thus directly fulfilling congressional intent, rather than achieve that goal indirectly with a cutoff, thereby partly contravening congressional intent. Thus, a desire to exclude ambient sources of contamination, without more, cannot support the regulatory cutoff.[53]

The court subsequently granted a joint motion by EPA and the Environmental Defense Fund for a stay of its mandate striking down the 50 ppm regulatory cutoff for 18 months, after which any party could request that the mandate issue.[54] The EPA reacted by issuing rules that incorporated the 50 ppm cutoff, and the court lifted its stay in 1984.[55]

Materials with concentrations of PCBs below 50 ppm generally are not regulated under TSCA.[56] Instances where use, disposal, or distribution is

---

48. 44 Fed. Reg. 31514 (May 31, 1979).
49. *Id.* at 31516.
50. *Id.*
51. 636 F.2d 1267 (D.C. Cir. 1980).
52. *Id.* at 1284.
53. *Id.* at 1282.
54. 46 Fed. Reg. 27615 (May 20, 1981).
55. 53 Fed. Reg. 24206 (June 27, 1988).
56. *See, e.g.*, 40 C.F.R. § 761.1.

prohibited or regulated at concentrations less than 50 ppm include, among others:

- the use of waste oil that contains any detectable concentration of PCB as a sealant, coating, or dust control agent;
- the marketing and burning of used oil at any quantifiable level of PCBs;
- retrofilled transformers, unless they are tested to confirm PCB concentrations less than 50 ppm;[57]
- the open burning of PCBs, other than otherwise allowed under Part 761;[58]
- PCBs at 3 parts per billion (ppb) or greater discharged to a treatment works or to navigable waters, unless the discharge is in accordance with a PCB discharge limit included in a NPDES permit;
- PCBs less than 50 ppm where such lower concentration results from dilution intended to avoid regulation;[59]
- PCBs in detergent bars leaving the manufacturing site or imported into the United States at concentrations equal to or greater than 5 ppm;[60]
- PCB remediation waste at any concentration if resulting from a spill or release of PCBs greater than or equal to 50 ppm after July 2, 1979, or ≥ 500 ppm after April 19, 1978 but prior to July 2, 1979;[61] and
- remediation wastes which are at any concentration of PCBs if the PCBs are from a source not authorized under Part 761.

2. PCB Terminology

The Agency's regulation of PCBs is highly dependent on characterization of the type and use of PCB-containing materials in dictating prohibited and authorized activities involving PCBs, marking requirements, storage and disposal requirements, recordkeeping, and exemptions. This is particularly so regarding concentration of PCBs, as the 50 ppm regulatory threshold is commonly incorporated within regulatory definitions. A basic understanding of regulatory defined terms is therefore necessary.

a. Definition of PCBs and the Discounting Factor

PCBs are defined as "any chemical substance that is limited to the biphenyl molecule that has been chlorinated to varying degrees or any combination of

57. *See, e.g.*, 40 C.F.R. § 761.30(a)(1)(B).
58. 40 C.F.R. § 761.50(a).
59. 40 C.F.R. § 761.1(b)(5).
60. 40 C.F.R. § 761.3 (excluded manufacturing process condition).
61. 40 C.F.R. § 761.50(b)(3)(ii).

substances which contains such substance. ..."[62] As is apparent from this definition, PCBs are a family of compounds consisting of two benzene rings (biphenyl) and one to ten chlorine atoms. There are 209 specific PCB family members (congeners), each of which is unique in respect to the position of the chlorine atom on the PCB molecule.

The toxicity of PCBs is dependent on the toxicity of the individual PCB congeners present within the mixture. In partial recognition of the distinguishing characteristics of monochlorinated and dichlorinated biphenyls, in a 1984 rulemaking[63] the Agency modified the PCB definition to "discount" inadvertently generated monochlorinated biphenyls by a factor of 50 and dichlorinated biphenyls by a factor of 5 when determining the total quantity of PCBs.[64] Thus, for example, and as illustrated by the Agency:

> [A]ssume a product is analyzed and found to have a PCB concentration of 510 ppm PCBs. After further analysis it is determined that the product contains 10 ppm of decachlorinated biphenyl and 500 of monochlorinated biphenyl. Since the discounting factor for monochlorinated biphenyl is 50, this product, for purposes of this regulation, contains only 10 ppm of monochlorinated biphenyl (500 ppm monochlorinated biphenyl ÷ 50 discounting factor = 10 ppm PCBs). This product would be found in compliance since, for purposes of this regulation, it would be considered to contain only 20 ppm PCBs (10 ppm attributed to monochlorinated biphenyl and 10 ppm attributed to decachlorinated biphenyl).[65]

The discounting factors apply to all activities involving *inadvertently generated* monochlorinated and dichlorinated PCBs. Intentionally generated lesser chlorinated PCBs are not subject to the discount factors.[66]

The phrase "inadvertently generated" is not specifically defined but is likewise an operative phrase in the exemptions granted to "excluded manufacturing processes" and "excluded PCB products" discussed below. Monochlorinated and dichlorinated PCBs generated as byproducts or impurities in a manufacturing process or ambient PCBs are clearly "inadvertently generated." Conversely, EPA has made clear that "the discounting factors for monochlorinated and dichlorinated biphenyls are not to be used in quantifying ... recycled PCBs," because such PCBs were "intentionally generated PCBs" in the raw materials being recycled.[67] While unclear, it is reasonable

---

62. 40 C.F.R. § 761.3.
63. 49 Fed. Reg. 28172 (July 10, 1984).
64. 40 C.F.R. § 761.3.
65. 49 Fed. Reg. 28172, 28179 (July 10, 1984).
66. *Id.*
67. *Id.* at 28175.

to conclude that "inadvertently generated" relates to the intention of the manufacturer or generator at the time the less chlorinated PCBs were created—rather than the generation or placement of extant PCBs in the media at issue. Thus, with regard to soils impacted by a PCB spill, the discount factor would apply to lesser chlorinated PCBs only if (i) the source of the PCBs was known and (ii) it could be concluded that the PCBs were "inadvertently generated" in their initial manufacturing process.

b. Excluded Manufacturing Processes, Excluded PCB Products, and Recycled PCBs

Paralleling § 6(e), the regulations provide that "no persons may use any PCB, or any PCB Item regardless of concentration, in any manner other than in a totally enclosed manner within the United States unless authorized."[68] Exceptions to the authorization requirement are provided for excluded manufacturing processes and excluded PCB products.

Following lengthy negotiation and effort to develop consensus, in 1984 the Agency exempted from the authorization requirement the manufacture of chemicals in processes that inadvertently generate PCBs if certain conditions were met. Excluded manufacturing processes are those processes in which quantities of PCBs are inadvertently generated, provided: (i) the concentration of inadvertently generated PCBs in manufactured or imported products have an annual average of less than 25 ppm with a 50 ppm maximum; (ii) the concentration of PCBs in detergent bars is less than 5 ppm; (iii) the release of PCBs from the manufacturing process to ambient air is less than 10 ppm; (iv) the amount of PCBs in wastewater is less than 100 microgram per liter; and (v) disposal of any other process wastes from the manufacturing process above 50 ppm are managed according to the storage and disposal requirements of Part 761, subpart D.[69]

Excluded PCB products, i.e., products that contain PCBs but which may be manufactured, used, and distributed in commerce, are defined as PCB materials with concentrations less than 50 ppm.[70] This exclusion, adopted in 1988,[71] was based on a finding by the Agency "that activities involving products containing less than 50 ppm PCBs generally do not present an unreasonable risk of injury to human health or the environment" and that "the incremental risks associated with the ... use of products with PCBs levels up to 50 ppm are outweighed by the tremendous costs that would be incurred

---

68. 40 C.F.R. § 761.20(a). The EPA's initial categorization of certain uses as totally enclosed was successfully challenged in *Environmental Defense Fund v. EPA*.
69. 40 C.F.R. § 761.3.
70. *Id.*
71. *See* 53 Fed. Reg. 24206 (June 27, 1988).

by banning the further processing, distribution in commerce, and use of PCBs at these levels."[72] Examples of excluded PCB products include but are not limited to:

- "non-Aroclor inadvertently generated PCBs as a byproduct or impurity resulting from a chemical manufacturing process;"
- products contaminated with Aroclor or other PCB materials from historic PCB uses (e.g., investment casting waxes);
- recycled fluids and/or equipment contaminated during use involving the products described above (including heat transfer and hydraulic fluids and equipment and other electrical equipment components); and
- used oils, provided (i) the source of the used oils was legally manufactured, processed, distributed, or used before October 1, 1984 or pursuant to an authorization granted by EPA and (ii) the resulting PCB concentration (i.e., below 50 ppm) is not a result of dilution, or leaks and spills of PCBs in concentrations greater than 50 ppm.[73]

The authorization exemption for recycled PCBs is limited to those PCBs that appear in the processing of paper products or asphalt roofing materials. Such processes must also ensure that there is no detectable concentration of PCBs in asphalt roofing materials leaving the processing site, or in the case of paper recycling, that the concentration of PCBs in paper products leaving the site has an annual average concentration of PCBs of less than 25 ppm with a 50 ppm maximum.[74] As noted above, the discounting factors for monochlorinated and dichlorinated biphenyls are not used in quantifying the recycled PCBs.[75]

It is important to note that while anyone who engages in excluded manufacturing processes or processes, distributes in commerce, or uses excluded PCB products or recycled PCBs may do so without a specific EPA authorization, there are nonetheless certification and reporting obligations.[76]

72. *Id.* at 24208.
73. 40 C.F.R. § 761.3.
74. *Id.* Additional conditions limit releases of PCBs from an emission point source to less than 10 ppm and limit the PCB concentration in wastewaters to 3 microgram per liter, about 3 ppb.
75. 49 Fed. Reg. 28172, 28175 (July 10, 1984).
76. *See* 40 C.F.R. § 761.185.

c. "PCB Bulk Product Waste," "PCB-Contaminated," "PCB Transformer," and Other Regulatory PCB Nomenclature

The following materials incorporate the 50 ppm regulatory standard as a matter of definition. Therefore, such items generally are subject to regulation only if the concentration of PCBs is equal to or greater than 50 ppm:

- PCB bulk product waste is "waste derived from manufactured products containing PCBs in a non-liquid state, at any concentration where the concentration at the time of designation for disposal was ≥ 50 ppm PCBs." PCB bulk product waste includes, but is not limited to, debris from the demolition of man-made structures manufactured, coated, or serviced with PCBs, PCB wastes from the shredding of automobiles, househole appliances, plastics wastes, and fluorescent light ballasts containing PCBs in the potting material;[77]
- PCB-Contaminated is any non-liquid material containing PCBs at concentrations ≥50 ppm but <500 ppm; a liquid material containing PCBs at concentrations ≥ 50 ppm but <500 ppm or where insufficient liquid material is available for analysis, a non-porous surface having a surface concentration of >10 micrograms/100 cm^2 but <100 micrograms/100 cm^2.[78] The term "PCB-Contaminated Electrical Equipment" is defined in a similar fashion.
- PCB remediation waste includes environmental media, certain sewage sludges, and debris from buildings and man-made structures resulting from the spill, leakage, or unauthorized disposal of PCBs. The concentration criteria applicable to PCB remediation waste differs as to the date of release and, in some instances, the PCB concentration of the source. Generally, spills of PCB liquids containing <50 ppm are not remediation wastes, unless the release is from a source not authorized for use.[79]
- PCB sewage sludge includes sewage sludge as defined in 40 C.F.R. § 503.9(w), i.e., the solid, semi-solid, or liquid residue generated during the treatment of domestic sewage in a treatment works, and which contains ≥50 ppm PCBs, as measured on a dry weight basis.[80]

Other materials are defined for regulation at higher concentration levels, notably PCB Transformers, defined as transformers containing ≥500 ppm PCBs,

77. 40 C.F.R. § 761.3.
78. *Id.*
79. *Id.* PCB remediation wastes are discussed *infra.*
80. *Id.*

and PCB Capacitors, defined as any capacitor containing ≥500 ppm PCBs.[81] PCB Transformers and PCB capacitors that have concentrations below the ≥500 ppm criteria are not unregulated; rather they fall within the category of materials defined as "PCB-contaminated" or "PCB contaminated equipment."

C. Prohibitions and Authorized PCB Activities

1. "Totally Enclosed Manner"

The regulations reiterate the statutory ban on the manufacture, processing, distribution in commerce, or use of PCBs in other than a "totally enclosed manner," a phrase defined by EPA as "any manner that will ensure no exposure of human beings or the environment to any concentration of PCBs."[82] Examples of activities that are determined to be "totally enclosed" include the following:

> [D]istribution in commerce of intact, non-leaking electrical equipment such as transformers (including transformers used in railway locomotives and self propelled cars), capacitors, electromagnets, voltage regulators, switches (including sectionalizers and motor starters), circuit breakers, reclosers, and cables that contain PCBs at any concentration and processing and distribution in commerce of PCB Equipment containing an intact, non-leaking PCB Capacitor.[83]

If an activity is not conducted in a "totally enclosed manner," it must be authorized or must qualify for an exemption, with the exception of the use, processing, and distribution of "excluded PCB products," "excluded manufacturing processes," recycled PCBs, and certain uses of sewage sludge containing PCBs.

---

81. *Id.*
82. 40 C.F.R. Part 761, Subpart B. The present regulatory definition is a revision of an earlier Agency characterization of "totally enclosed manner" as "any manner that will ensure that any exposure of human beings or the environment to any concentration of PCBs will be insignificant; that is, not measurable or detectable by any scientifically acceptable analytical method." In a 1984 rulemaking, the qualifier of "significant/insignificant" exposure was removed. *See* 49 Fed. Reg. 44634, 44636 (Nov. 8, 1984).
83. 40 C.F.R. § 761.20.

2. Authorizations

Those specified "non-totally enclosed" PCB activities that have been authorized include:

- use in and servicing of transformers (other than railroad transformers);[84]
- use in and servicing of railroad transformers;[85]
- use in mining equipment;[86]
- use in heat transfer systems;[87]
- use in hydraulic systems;[88]
- use in carbonless copy paper;[89]
- use in and servicing of electromagnets, switches, and voltage regulators;[90]
- use and reuse of PCBs in natural gas pipeline systems, use and reuse of PCB-contaminated natural gas pipe;[91]
- research and development;[92]
- use in scientific instruments;[93]
- use in capacitors;[94]
- use in and servicing of circuit breakers, reclosers, and cable;[95]
- continued use of porous surface contaminated with PCBs regulated for disposal by spills of liquid PCBs;[96]
- use in and servicing of rectifiers;[97]
- use of PCBs in air compressor systems;[98]
- use of PCBs in other gas or liquid transmission systems;[99] and
- use of decontaminated materials.[100]

In many instances, the use authorization provides that PCBs may only be used in such equipment at concentrations less than 50 ppm and that servicing

84. 40 C.F.R. § 761.30(a).
85. 40 C.F.R. § 761.30(b).
86. 40 C.F.R. § 761.30(c).
87. 40 C.F.R. § 761.30(d).
88. 40 C.F.R. § 761.30(e).
89. 40 C.F.R. § 761.30(f).
90. 40 C.F.R. § 761.30(h).
91. 40 C.F.R. § 761.30(i).
92. 40 C.F.R. § 761.30(j).
93. 40 C.F.R. § 761.30(k).
94. 40 C.F.R. § 761.30(l).
95. 40 C.F.R. § 761.30(m).
96. 40 C.F.R. § 761.30(p).
97. 40 C.F.R. § 761.30(r).
98. 40 C.F.R. § 761.30(s).
99. 40 C.F.R. § 761.30(t).
100. 40 C.F.R. § 761.30(u).

of the equipment may be done only with fluids containing less than 50 ppm. This applies to use in mining equipment, heat transfer systems, and hydraulic systems. In other applications, including transformers, electromagnets, switches and voltage regulators, circuit breakers and rectifiers, the use authorizations permit the continued use of PCBs at any concentration for the remainder of the useful life of the equipment.

a. Transformers

In its 1982 rulemaking granting the use authorization for transformers, EPA observed that:

> [t]ransformers are used extensively by electric utilities and other industries to transmit and distribute electric power efficiently. The use of PCBs in transformers has resulted in the dielectric fluid of some transformers containing between 60 and 70 percent PCBs by design. The transformers designed to contain mineral oil dielectric fluid have been contaminated with PCBs during past servicing and manufacturing activities.
>
> EPA estimates that there are 39,600 PCB Transformers designed to contain PCBs in use in the electric utility industry and approximately 91,600 in all other applications. EPA also estimates that there are over 20 million mineral oil transformers in use in the electric utility industry and 5 million in all other applications.[101]

Concluding that authorization to use PCBs in transformers for the remainder of the useful life of the transformer does not present an unreasonable risk, the Agency found, among other things, that if it failed to grant the authorization, the cost to the public and industry would be in the billions of dollars, primarily as a result of the disruption of electrical service.[102]

Although the use of PCBs in transformers generally is authorized regardless of PCB concentration, the regulatory scheme setting forth use, servicing, storage, registration, and disposal conditions distinguishes between transformers that contain greater than or equal to 500 ppm PCBs, defined as "PCB Transformers," and those transformers that contain greater than or equal to 50 ppm but less than 500 ppm, transformers that fall within the definition of "PCB-Contaminated Electrical Equipment." Broadly, the regulatory conditions on the use and servicing of PCB Transformers cover certain use prohibitions, requirements concerning registration, inspection, marking, and servicing of PCB containing dielectric fluids.

---

101. 47 Fed. Reg. 37342, 37345 (Aug. 25, 1982).
102. *Id.* at 37346.

In assessing the widespread use of PCB Transformers in the early 1980s, the Agency estimated that approximately ten thousand such transformers were used on the premises of food and feed facilities.[103] In response, EPA phased out the use of PCB Transformers that pose an exposure risk to food or feed, concluding with an absolute prohibition after October 1, 1985.[104] Restrictions apply as well to the use of PCB Transformers in or near commercial buildings. As of October 1, 1990, the use of network PCB Transformers with secondary voltages greater than or equal to 480 volts, including 480/277 volt systems was prohibited. Lower secondary voltage radial PCB Transformers in or near commercial buildings that did not have electrical protection to avoid transformer ruptures caused by high current faults were to be removed from service in 1991.[105]

As of December 1998, all PCB Transformers were to be registered with the EPA, National Program Chemical Division.[106] Registration with the EPA is now required in lieu of an earlier regulatory requirement to register PCB Transformers with the local fire department.[107] Registration is made on EPA Form 7720-12,[108] and should be submitted by certified mail, return receipt requested. As of December 1985, all PCB Transformers in or near commercial buildings were to be registered with all building owners within thirty meters of the transformer.[109]

Visual inspection of each PCB Transformer must be conducted at least once every three months. If a leak is discovered, the transformer must be repaired or replaced; cleanup of the released PCBs must commence within 48 hours. If the PCB Transformer is involved in a fire-related incident—any incident in which heat and/or pressure causes a transformer rupture—the National Response Center (NRC) must be notified immediately at 1-800-424-8802. Records of inspection and maintenance history must be maintained for life of the transformer until three years after disposal.[110]

All PCB Transformers and transformer locations are to be marked with the designated large PCB Mark.[111]

---

103. *Id.* at 37349.
104. 40 C.F.R. § 761.30(a)(i).
105. *Id.*
106. *Id.* at 761.30(a)(vi).
107. *See* 63 Fed. Reg. 35384, 35392 (June 29, 1998).
108. The Transformer Registration form is *available at* http://www.epa.gov/epawaste/hazard/tsd/pcbs/pubs/772012.pdf.
109. 40 C.F.R. § 761.30(a)(vii).
110. 40 C.F.R. § 761.30(a)(ix)–(xiii).
111. 40 C.F.R. § 761.45.

PCB Transformers may be serviced (including topping off) with dielectric fluid at any PCB concentration. Any PCBs removed during servicing must be captured and either reused or disposed of.[112]

b. Porous Surfaces

Porous surfaces, such as concrete, may be used after contamination with spills of liquid PCBs at concentrations greater than or equal to 50 ppm for the remainder of the useful life of the surface and subsurface material if certain spill response actions are taken. These include: removal of the source of PCB contamination; if the surface is accessible, washing and rinsing of the surface; coating of the surface to prevent release of residual PCBs or otherwise rendering the surface inaccessible; and marking to designate the presence of PCBs.[113]

3. Exemptions

Section 6(e)(3)(B) of TSCA provides that any person may petition the Administrator for an exemption from the prohibition against the manufacture, processing, and distribution in commerce of PCBs. The Administrator may by rule grant an exemption if the Administrator finds that "(i) an unreasonable risk of injury to health or the environment would not result, and (ii) good faith efforts have been made to develop a chemical substance which does not present an unreasonable risk of injury to health or the environment and which may be substituted for such polychlorinated biphenyl."[114] The maximum length of any exemption is one year. In limited circumstances, such as the manufacture, importation, processing, and distribution of PCBs for the purpose of R&D, the Agency has granted class exemptions which may be renewed from year to year by means of a properly and timely filed renewal request, or in some instances automatically as long as there is no increase in the amount of PCBs to be processed and distributed, imported, manufactured, or exported.[115]

All exemptions must be evaluated using the formal notice and comment rulemaking procedures.[116]

---

112. 40 C.F.R. § 761.30(a)(2).
113. 40 C.F.R. § 761.30(p).
114. TSCA § 6(e)(3)(B).
115. 40 C.F.R. § 761.80(i).
116. 40 C.F.R. Part 750, Subparts B and C. The exemptions that have been granted by the Agency are listed at 40 C.F.R. § 761.80.

D. Marking of PCBs and PCB Items

Generally, all electrical equipment with PCBs greater than or equal to 50 ppm, and containers in which PCB equipment may be placed, must bear a warning label that will last as long as the PCB Article, PCB Equipment, or PCB Container. The label must bear letters on white or yellow background; the size of the mark is to be at least six inches on each side. Where this mark is specified but the PCB item is too small to accommodate its size, a smaller mark is specified. [117]

These regulations require marking PCB Transformers, but do not clearly state who is responsible for making sure they are marked. In *In the Matter of Nello Santacroce & Dominic Fanelli d/b/a Gilroy Associates*,[118] the Environmental Appeals Board concluded that only owners and operators of PCB Transformers have an obligation to mark them. A person who owns property that has a PCB Transformer on it is not liable for failure to mark it if that person does not own or operate it.

The location of PCB Transformers and PCB Large Low Voltage Capacitors must be marked in addition to marking the equipment itself, by marking the vault door, machinery room door, fence, hallway, pole, or means of access.[119]

E. Storage and Disposal

EPA has promulgated detailed rules regarding storage of PCB Articles[120] that are intended for reuse, as well as well as PCB wastes stored pending ultimate disposal. The regulations governing disposal of PCB wastes specify disposal method based on type and character of PCB waste at issue.

1. Storage for Reuse

A PCB Article may be stored for reuse indefinitely in a facility constructed to meet the following criteria: (i) the roof and walls are adequate to prevent rain

---

117. The smaller mark is one inch by two inches. 40 C.F.R. § 761.45.
118. EAB Appeal No. 92-6 (1993), *available at* http://www.epa.gov/eab/disk3/nello.pdf.
119. 40 C.F.R. § 761.40(j)–(k).
120. "PCB Articles" are defined as "any manufactured article, other than a PCB Container, that contains PCBs and whose surface(s) has been in direct contact with PCBs. 'PCB Article' includes capacitors, transformers, electric motors, pumps, pipes and any other manufactured item (1) which is formed to a specific shape or design during manufacture, (2) which has end use function(s) dependent in whole or in part upon its shape or design during end use, and (3) which has no change of chemical composition during its end use or only those changes of composition which have no commercial purpose separate from that of the PCB Article." 40 C.F.R. § 761.3.

water from reaching the stored materials; (ii) the floor has continuous six-inch high curbing and provides containment volume equal to at least two times the internal volume of the largest PCB Article or PCB Container in storage; (iii) there are no drains, valves, or openings that would permit escape of liquids; (iv) the floors and curbing must be constructed of Portland cement, concrete, or a continuous, smooth, non-porous surface; and (v) it must not be in a one-hundred-year flood plain.[121] PCB Articles may also be stored indefinitely in units permitted under the Resource Recovery and Conservation Act (RCRA).[122]

If a storage facility does not meet the preceding requirements, storage for reuse is limited to five years. Marking requirements and recordkeeping apply to such PCB Articles stored for reuse.

2. Storage and Disposal of PCB Wastes

Although the term "PCB waste" is not well-defined,[123] the regulations specifically define the storage and disposal requirements for eight categories of PCB containing materials either removed from authorized use or resulting from spills or releases.[124] These include:

- PCB liquids removed from use;
- PCB Items removed from use;
- PCB remediation waste;
- PCB bulk product waste;
- PCB household waste;
- PCB research and development waste;
- PCB/Radioactive waste; and
- PCB-contaminated porous surfaces.[125]

a. Storage for Disposal

The storage for disposal requirements[126] apply to PCBs wastes at concentrations of 50 ppm or greater and PCB Items with PCB concentrations of 50 ppm or greater.

Generally, storage pending disposal is limited to one year from the date the material was determined to be a PCB waste, typically the date on which

---

121. 40 C.F.R. §§ 761.35(c) and 761.65(b).
122. 42 U.S.C. §6901.
123. 40 C.F.R. § 761.3 defines "PCB wastes" in a circular fashion as "those PCBs and PCB Items that are subject to the disposal requirements of subpart D [of Part 761]."
124. *See* 40 C.F.R. § 761.50(b).
125. 40 C.F.R. § 761.50(b)(1)–(8).
126. 40 C.F.R. § 761.65.

the item is removed from service when there is no intent to reuse it. A one-year extension to the storage limitation may be obtained upon demonstration to the EPA that "continuing attempts to dispose of or secure disposal for [the] waste within the one year time limit have been unsuccessful."[127] Additional extensions of the storage limitation may be obtained if the requester supplies specific justification for the additional extension and indicates what measures it is taking to secure disposal.

b. Disposal of PCB Wastes

A summary of the disposal methods of common PCB wastes is provided in Table 11.1. Because this is only a summary the pertinent regulations should be consulted for more detailed requirements.

Table 11.1 Bans and Restrictions

Waste Type	*Disposal Method(s)*
PCB Liquids	
• if ≥50 ppm	incinerator, consistent with 761.70
• if ≥50 ppm <500 ppm, and	
o if mineral oil dielectric fluid, or	may be disposed of in a high efficiency boiler pursuant to 761.71(a)
o other PCB liquids	may be disposed of in a high efficiency boiler pursuant to 761.71(b)
• if PCB liquids ≤500 ppm from incidental sources, such as precipitation, condensation, leachate, or load separation and are associated with PCB Articles or non-liquid PCB wastes	in a chemical waste landfill
PCB Articles	
• Transformers	incineration or in a chemical waste landfill if all free flowing liquid is removed, the transformer is filled with solvent and allowed to stand for 18 hours, and then the solvent is removed

127. 40 C.F.R. § 761.65(a)(2).

Waste Type	*Disposal Method(s)*
• Capacitors	PCB Small Capacitors may be disposed of as municipal solid waste, unless the owner is a manufacturer of PCB Equipment PCB large High or Low Voltage Capacitors ≥500 ppm PCBs must be disposed of via incineration
• PCB hydraulic machines containing ≥50 ppm PCBs and in which all free flowing liquid has been removed	decontamination pursuant to 761.79, in a licensed municipal solid waste landfill, scrap metal recovery oven, or smelter operation
• PCB-Contaminated Electrical Equipment	removal of all free-flowing liquids and decontamination, disposal in a licensed municipal landfill, scrap metal recovery, or chemical waste landfill
PCB Remediation Wastes	
• Bulk PCB remediation waste (soils, sediments, dredged materials, mud, PCB sewage sludge, industrial sludge, debris)	unless sampled, such waste shall be assumed to contain ≥50 ppm PCBs and the waste must be dewatered and disposed of in a RCRA permitted landfill; sampled PCB remediation waste <50 ppm may be disposed of at a state-permitted or registered municipal solid waste facility, a RCRA permitted facility, or a PCB disposal facility
• Cleanup wastes (e.g. personal protective equipment waste, cleaning solvents, abrasives, and equipment)	some materials may be reused after decontamination pursuant to 761.79; non-liquid cleaning materials and PPE may be disposed of at a state-permitted or registered municipal solid waste facility, a RCRA permitted facility, or a PCB disposal facility
PCB Bulk Product Waste	*performance-based requirements*—TSCA incinerator, chemical waste landfill, RCRA permitted disposal facility if the material is plastic, such as plastic insulation from wire or cable; radio, television and computer casing, disposal in a solid waste landfill *alternative "risk-based" disposal*—may be approved by the Administrator upon application
PCB Household Wastes	may be managed in a facility permitted, licensed or registered by a State to manage municipal or industrial solid or a facility approved to dispose of PCB bulk product waste

Waste Type	*Disposal Method(s)*
PCB Wastes Generated from R&D or PCB Chemical Analysis Activities	liquid wastes, including rinse solvents, as a PCB Liquid, *supra*, or as approved by the Administrator; non-liquid waste, as non-liquid cleaning materials and PPE, *supra*

F. Remediation of PCBs and the PCB Spill Cleanup Policy

Depending on the date of the release and nature of contaminated media, EPA provides several cleanup and disposal options. Any party may proceed to clean up any PCB remediation waste based on the concentration of PCBs found, and may do so either: (i) as a self-implementing on-site cleanup and disposal; (ii) consistent with performance-based disposal standards; or (iii) pursuant to a risk-based cleanup and disposal approval received from the Administration.[128] In addition, and with regard to a more limited class of PCB spills and releases, a party may proceed with cleanup and disposal under the EPA's PCB Spill Cleanup Policy.[129]

PCB cleanups are overseen by the EPA's Office of Solid Waste and Emergency Response (OSWER), which handles cleanups in general, and not by the Office of Prevention, Pesticides, and Toxic Substances, which is the office that implements most of the TSCA programs. In addition to PCB cleanups, OSWER implements the TSCA regulations concerning PCB disposal, storage, processing, and distribution for disposal.[130] Which office handles which function is detailed in two memoranda issued by the EPA.[131]

1. Self-implementing Cleanup and Disposal

The self-implementing cleanup procedure is intended for "moderately-sized" sites[132] "where there should be low residual environmental impact from the

128. 40 C.F.R. § 761.61.
129. 40 C.F.R. Part 761 Subpart G.
130. 72 Fed. Reg. 57235, 57237 (Oct. 9, 2007).
131. Memorandum from Susan Parker Bodine and James Guilliford, Administration of PCB Program, EPA (Mar. 6, 2008), *available at* http://www.epa.gov/epawaste/hazard/tsd/pcbs/pubs/delmemo.pdf, and Memorandum from Susan Parker Bodine, Re-Delegation of OSWER's Management of the Disposal and Cleanup of Polychlorinated Biphenyls (PCBs) (Feb. 11, 2008), *available at* http://www.epa.gov/epawaste/hazard/tsd/pcbs/pubs/redelmemo.pdf.
132. EPA has described a "moderately-sized site" as encompassing approximately one acre. EPA, January 2009 Version, Revisions to the PCB Q and A Manual, 77 (Jan. 2009) [hereinafter PCB Q&A Manual]. This manual is updated periodically and the most recent updates are *available at* http://www.epa.gov/epawaste/hazard/tsd/pcbs/pubs/guidance.htm#QandA.

remedial activities." This procedure may not be used to clean up surface or groundwater, marine or freshwater sediments, sewers or sewer treatment systems, any private or public drinking water sources or distribution systems, grazing lands, or vegetable gardens.[133] Prior to the commencement of cleanup activities, a site characterization must be conducted to assess the nature of the contamination and its location across the site.[134]

Thirty days before the commencement of cleanup activities, notification in writing of the intended remediation must be provided to the EPA Regional Administrator. The notice must include information regarding the nature of the contamination, including the kinds of materials contaminated, a summary of the procedures used to sample contaminated and adjacent areas, and a table or cleanup site map showing PCB concentrations measured in all pre-cleanup sampling. It must also include topographic maps and sample locations, and a proposed cleanup plan for the site. The notice must also include a written certification signed by the owner of the property that all sample and analytical plans and procedures are on file at the location designated in the certificate and available for EPA inspection.[135] If EPA does not respond to the notice within thirty days, the cleanup may proceed without a written response from EPA.

The cleanup levels applicable in a self-implemented cleanup depend upon the category of remediation waste, i.e., bulk PCB remediation waste, non-porous surfaces, porous surfaces, and liquids, whether the location of the waste is a "high occupancy area" or "low occupancy area," and whether an engineered control, such as a cap, is installed. For bulk remediation materials, such as soils and sediments, EPA allows self-implementing cleanup levels of 1 ppm in high occupancy areas and 25 ppm in low occupancy areas.[136]

2. Performance-based Disposal Option

The PCB regulations include requirements for disposal of remediation wastes generated in cleanups that are not conducted under the self-implementation option.[137] Liquid PCB remediation wastes are to be

---

133. 40 C.F.R. § 761.61(a)(1).
134. 40 C.F.R. Part 761, Subpart N.
135. 40 C.F.R. § 761.61(a)(3). While notification is required, "EPA has determined that a self-implementing cleanup conducted in accordance with 761.61(a) will not pose an unreasonable risk, so individual approvals are not required. The pre-cleanup notification is intended to assure EPA that the person in charge of the cleanup or the owner of the site understands the self-implementing requirements and that the contamination at the site can effectively be cleaned through the self-implementing process." PCB Q&A Manual, 80.
136. 40 C.F.R. § 761.61(a)(4).
137. 40 C.F.R. § 761.61(b).

disposed of consistent with the disposal requirement for PCB Liquids, which primarily require incineration. Non-liquid PCB remediation waste is to be disposed of in a high temperature TSCA incinerator, an approved chemical waste landfill, or other approved facility. Material dredged from waters of the United States containing less than 50 ppm PCBs may be managed in accordance with a permit issued under the Clean Water Act or issued by the Army Corps of Engineers under of the Marine Protection, Research, and Sanctuaries Act.[138]

3. Risk-based Disposal Option

Any persons wishing to sample, cleanup, or dispose of PCB remediation waste in a manner other than pursuant to the self-implementation procedure or the performance-based option must apply in writing to the EPA Regional Administrator in the region where the cleanup activities will take place, or to the Director of the Office of Resource Conservation and Recovery, should the application involve more than one site in multiple regions. EPA will issue a written decision on each application, approving the application if it finds that the proposed method will not pose an unreasonable risk of injury to health or the environment.[139]

4. The PCB Spill Cleanup Policy

In a 1987 rulemaking, EPA promulgated its so-called PCB Spill Cleanup Policy.[140] The Policy applies to spills of PCBs at concentrations greater than or equal to 50 ppm that occurred after May 4, 1987. The PCB Spill Cleanup Policy is driven by the release of PCBs at greater than or equal to 50 ppm, without regard to the concentration of PCBs in the contaminated media. As noted above, an incentive to remediate a spill or release of PCBs, and to initiate a cleanup under the PCB Spill Cleanup Policy, is provided by the fact that such spill or release is "unauthorized disposal" subjecting a party to civil and perhaps criminal penalties. As stated by EPA:

> The PCB Spill Cleanup Policy provides a presumption against enforcement penalties for the unauthorized disposal of the original spill, in exchange for quick and effective cleanup of the spill. If the waste resulting from the spill were regulated for disposal at its as-found concentration (as is PCB remediation waste), there would no disincentive for owners of PCBs to dilute them to less

---

138. *Id.*
139. 40 C.F.R. § 761.61(c).
140. 40 C.F.R. Part 761, Subpart G; 52 Fed. Reg. 10688 (Apr. 2, 1987).

> regulated or unregulated levels by spilling. Under §761.61, to create an incentive to clean up old spills, PCB remediation waste can be cleaned up at its as-found concentration. However, to provide a disincentive to "disposing" of the original source material by spilling it, a penalty for the original generation of the waste is possible. The potential penalty is not associated with the cleanup requirements.[141]

Thus, although a spill of material containing 50 ppm or more PCBs is considered improper disposal, compliance with the Spill Cleanup Policy states EPA's willingness to create "a presumption against enforcement action for penalties and the need for further cleanup under TSCA."[142] EPA therefore designed the Spill Cleanup Policy to effectuate quick and effective cleanup of "fresh" spills that have little time to migrate from the spill site or otherwise migrate. As defined by the Agency, a "fresh" spill is one that is less than 72 hours old.[143]

Several types of higher risk spills are excluded from the scope of the PCB Spill Cleanup Policy and must be addressed in accordance with site-specific requirements established by the EPA regional offices. These include: spills resulting in direct contamination of surface waters; spills that result in direct contamination of sewers and sewage treatment systems; spills impacting private or public drinking water sources; spills that contaminate animal grazing lands; and spills that contaminate vegetable gardens.[144]

a. Reporting Requirements

Under CERCLA § 103, all spills involving one pound or more by weight of PCBs within a twenty-four hour period must be reported to the National Response Center. Additionally, under the PCB Spill Cleanup Policy, where a spill directly contaminates surface water, sewers, drinking water supplies, grazing lands, or vegetable gardens, the responsible party must notify the EPA regional office in the shortest time possible, but in no case later than 24 hours after discovery, and must proceed with cleanup. If a spill exceeds ten pounds of PCBs by weight but does not directly contaminate any of the media referenced above, the responsible party must notify the EPA regional office and proceed to decontaminate the spill area in accordance with this PCB Spill Cleanup Policy in the shortest time possible after discovery, but in no case

---

141. PCB Q&A Manual, 73–74.
142. 40 C.F.R. § 761.135(a).
143. *Id.* at 74.
144. 40 C.F.R. § 761.120(d).

later than 24 hours after discovery.[145] In summary, the reporting obligations are as follows:

- for spills of ≥1 lb by weight PCBs within a 24-hour period, report immediately to NRC at 1(800) 424-8802;
- for spills ≥1 lb by weight PCBs and directly contaminating surface water, sewer, drinking water supplies, grazing lands, or vegetable gardens, report immediately to NRC at 1(800) 424-8802 (if release ≥1 lb within a 24-hour period) and EPA Regional Office in shortest time possible after discovery but in no case later than 24 hours after discovery;
- for spills ≤10 lbs by weight PCBs with no impact to surface water, sewer, drinking water supplies, grazing lands, or vegetable gardens, report immediately to NRC at 1(800) 424-8802 (if within a 24-hour period), only (no reporting to EPA required); and
- for spills >10 lbs by weight PCBs, report immediately to NRC at 1(800) 424-8802 (if release ≥1 lbs within a 24 hour period) and to EPA Regional Office (irrespective of duration of release) in shortest time possible after discovery but in no case later than 24 hours after discovery.

b. Requirements for Spill Cleanups

The method of cleaning up PCB spills varies depending on whether the spill has a low concentration of PCBs below 500 ppm and no more than one pound PCBs by weight[146] or a high concentration of 500 or more ppm or PCB quantities greater than one pound.[147] In both cases, response to the spill must commence quickly. The decontamination requirements relating to cleanup of small quantities of low concentration PCB "must be completed within forty eight hours after the responsible party was notified or became aware of the spill."[148] With regard to high-concentration PCB spills, or low-concentration spills greater than one pound PCBs by weight, the cleanup must be commenced "as quickly as possible and within no more than twenty four hours, or within forty eight hours for PCB Transformers, after the responsible party was notified or became aware of the spill," unless delayed by weather or other circumstance outside the control of the responsible party. [149] The occurrence of a spill on a weekend or overtime costs are not acceptable reasons to delay response.

145. 40 C.F.R. § 761.125(a)(1).
146. 40 C.F.R. § 761.125(b).
147. 40 C.F.R. § 761.125(c).
148. 40 C.F.R. § 761.125(b)(1)(iii).
149. 40 C.F.R. § 761.125(c)(1).

Following cleanup, the responsible party must document the cleanup with records identifying the source of the spill, the estimated date and time of spill occurrence, the date and time cleanup was completed and description of cleanup/decontamination activities, and pre- and post-cleanup sampling. A certification statement is also to be signed by the responsible party stating that the cleanup requirements have been met and that the information contained in the records is true to the best of his/her knowledge.

5. Transfer of Contaminated Real Property

The EPA had interpreted the ban on transferring PCBs to prohibit transferring PCB contaminated real property if the contamination occurred after the ban went into effect in 1978. The EPA had required the owners of PCB contaminated sites to clean up the sites and receive EPA's approval of the cleanup before the sites could be sold. In 2003 the EPA reversed its position and opined that the earlier interpretation was not compelled by the statute.[150] The EPA's reversal was based on two policy considerations, first, that a transfer would not affect the status quo of the PCB contamination and therefore would not increase risks posed by the PCBs, and second, that a prohibition on transfer unless a site is cleaned up could thwart the purchase of an ongoing business, resulting in loss of jobs.

This new interpretation is merely a policy statement. Because it was not promulgated as a regulation the EPA and courts are free to disagree with the conclusions in this policy interpretation.

G. Import and Export of PCBs for Disposal

The importation of PCBs is "manufacturing"[151] for purposes of TSCA and the PCB regulations. Therefore, the statutory prohibition on manufacture of PCBs absent an authorization or exemption applies equally to the importation of PCBs. Additionally, no person may import PCBs or PCB Items for disposal without an exemption.[152]

Similarly, no person may export PCBs or PCB Items for disposal with the exception of PCBs and PCB Items at concentrations less than 50 ppm, which

---

150. Robert E. Fabricant, Interpretive Statement on Change in Ownership of Real Property Contaminated with PCBs (Aug. 14, 2003), *available at* http://www.epa.gov/epawaste/hazard/tsd/pcbs/pubs/distincom.pdf.

151. "Manufacture" is defined as meaning "to produce, manufacture, or import into the customs territory of the United States." 40 C.F.R. § 761.3.

152. 40 C.F.R. § 761.93(a).

may be exported for disposal. If the concentration of PCBs is unknown, the material must be treated as if it contains greater than or equal to 50 ppm.[153]

H. Notification of PCB Waste Activity, Manifests, Records, and Reports

1. Notifications and Manifesting PCB Waste

Similar to the hazardous waste activity notification requirements in RCRA, with limited exceptions, the generator, transporter, commercial storer, and disposer of PCB waste[154] must have provided prior notice of such activity to EPA on EPA Form 7710-53[155] and have received an EPA identification number. For each generator storing PCB waste, a separate notification must be submitted to EPA for each PCB storage facility; each such facility will be issued a unique identification number by EPA. If the facility already has received a RCRA generator identification, it is the practice of EPA to use the same number for purposes of PCB waste activity.

Generators who store PCB wastes on a temporary basis for up to 30 days from the date of their removal from service in a manner consistent with regulation[156] are exempt from the requirement to provide prior notice of PCB waste activity and to file EPA Form 7710-53. In such instances the generator is deemed to have received the identification number "40 C.F.R. PART 761" for use on manifests.[157] This exemption is limited to temporary storage of:

- non-leaking PCB Articles and PCB Equipment;
- leaking PCB Articles and PCB Equipment if the items are placed in a non-leaking PCB Container containing sorbant materials;
- PCB Containers containing non-liquid PCBs such as contaminated soil, rags, and debris; and
- PCB Containers containing liquid PCBs at concentrations ≥50 ppm, provided a Spill Prevention, Control, and Countermeasure Plan has been prepared for the temporary storage area.

---

153. 40 C.F.R. § 761.97.
154. "PCB waste" is defined as "those PCBs and PCB Items that are subject to the disposal requirements of subpart D [of Part 761]." 40 C.F.R. § 761.3. Therefore, PCBs that are not regulated for disposal, e.g., non-liquid bulk waste or debris from the demolition of buildings containing PCB concentrations less than 50 ppm, are not subject to the notification and manifesting requirements.
155. The form is *available at* http://www.epa.gov/epawaste/hazard/tsd/pcbs/pubs/771053.pdf.
156. 40 C.F.R. § 761.65(c)(1)–(6).
157. 40 C.F.R. § 761.205.

All PCB Items in such temporary storage must be checked for leaks at least once every 30 days. Containers used for the storage of liquid or non-liquid PCB waste must meet the requirements set forth in the DOT Hazardous Materials Regulations,[158] unless such PCB wastes are at concentrations of less than 20 ppm or there is less than one pound of PCBs regardless of concentration.[159]

While a generator of PCB waste engaged in the temporary storage described above need not obtain a unique PCB waste activity identification number, it is recommended by EPA that the generator do so nonetheless. There are three reasons for obtaining a number: (i) there is no charge or fee associated with obtaining a unique identification number, (ii) the generator can take advantage of one-year storage, assuming compliance with the storage facility requirements,[160] and (iii) there have been instances reported where PCB disposal facilities have rejected PCB wastes otherwise correctly manifested under the generic identification number "40 C.F.R. Part 761."

Also similar to RCRA, a generator may not offer PCB wastes to transporters, disposers, or commercial storage facilities who have not received an EPA PCB waste activity identification number.[161]

A generator who transfers control of PCB wastes by transporting, or offering for transport by his own vehicle or by a vehicle owned by another, is required to prepare a manifest on EPA Form 8700-22,[162] or if the State to which the shipment is manifested specifies a manifest form and requires its use, then the shipment must be manifested on that form.

When the generator uses a third party to transport the PCB waste to a commercial storage facility or disposer, the generator must confirm by telephone or other means of confirmation that the commercial storage facility or disposer actually received the manifested waste. If the generator does not receive the hand-signed return manifest within 35 days after the independent transporter received the PCB waste, the generator must contact the disposer or commercial storage facility to determine whether the PCB waste has actually been received. If the generator has not received the hand-signed return manifest within ten days of the call to the independent transporter, the generator is required to file an exception report to EPA.[163] The signed return manifest from the commercial storage facility or disposer must be retained by the generator for three years.[164]

---

158. 40 C.F.R. Parts 171 through 180.
159. 40 C.F.R. § 761.65(c).
160. 40 C.F.R. § 761.65(b).
161. 40 C.F.R. § 761.65(c).
162. EPA's manifest form 8700-22 is available only from an entity approved by EPA to distribute copies. *See* http://www.epa.gov/osw/hazard/transportation/manifest/index.htm.
163. 40 C.F.R. § 761.208(a)(4).
164. 40 C.F.R. § 761.209.

2. Records

Each owner or operator of a facility, other than a commercial storage facility or disposer of PCB waste, using or storing at any one time at least 45 kilograms (99.4 pounds) of PCBs contained in PCB Containers, or one or more PCB Transformers, or fifty or more PCB Large High or Low Voltage Capacitors is required to develop and maintain at the facility annual records and an annual document log. The annual document log and annual records must be maintained for at least three years after the facility ceases to use or store PCBs and PCB Items at the triggering quantity.

Annual records are to include: all signed manifests generated by the facility during the calendar year; all certificates of disposal; and records of inspection and cleanups performed. The annual document log is to include: the name, address, and EPA identification number of the facility; the unique manifest number of every manifest generated by the facility; for bulk PCB waste, its weight in kilograms, and date it was first removed from service for disposal, placed into transport, received for disposal; the serial number, if available, for each transformer and capacitor in service; unique number designations for PCB Containers with description of the PCB materials within the containers; quantification of the total number of PCB Transformers, large High or Low Voltage PCB Capacitors; the total weight in kilograms of PCBs in service; and records of each telephone call, or other means of verification agreed upon by the parties, made to each designated commercial storer or designated disposer to confirm receipt of PCB waste.[165]

Specific recordkeeping requirements are also identified for disposers and commercial storage facilities of PCB waste,[166] incineration facilities,[167] chemical waste landfill facilities,[168] and high efficiency boiler facilities.[169]

III. Mercury Federal Agency Ban

Congress directly imposed restrictions on distribution of mercury when it enacted the Mercury Export Ban of 2008,[170] which added a new TSCA § 6(f) banning the sale, distribution, or transfer of elemental mercury by

165. 40 C.F.R. § 761.180(a).
166. 40 C.F.R. § 761.180(b).
167. 40 C.F.R. § 761.180(c).
168. 40 C.F.R. § 761.180(d).
169. 40 C.F.R. § 761.180(e).
170. Pub. L. No. 110-414, § 1, 122 Stat. 4341 (2008). Codified at 15 U.S.C. §§ 5(f) and 11(c). This law also amended TSCA § 12 to prohibit the export of elemental mercury effective January 1, 2013. *See* Chapter 8, Exports and Imports.

federal agencies.[171] Federal agencies may not "convey, sell or distribute" elemental mercury under its jurisdiction. This is subject to only two exceptions; agencies may transfer mercury to effectuate the ban, and agencies may transfer and lease coal.

IV. CFCs

Chlorofluorocarbons (CFCs) had been banned under TSCA for use in most aerosols,[172] but this ban was removed from the TSCA regulations in 1995. The TSCA regulations were no longer necessary because the use of these chemicals as propellants was subsequently banned under the Clean Air Act.

V. Hexavalent Chromium

Under the authority of TSCA § 6, EPA banned distribution in commerce of hexavalent chromium-based water treatment chemicals for use in comfort cooling towers.[173] Hexavalent chromium is a form of chromium that the EPA has classified as a carcinogen.[174] Comfort cooling towers are defined to be "towers that are dedicated exclusively to and are an integral part of heating, ventilation, and air conditioning or refrigeration systems."[175] It is still permissible to distribute hexavalent chromium-based water treatment chemicals for use in cooling systems that are not comfort cooling towers, but the chemicals must then be labeled in accordance with the regulations.[176] Distributors must submit a report to EPA notifying it that they are distributors, and they must update the report to reflect any changes in their status.[177] The regulations impose recordkeeping requirements on distributors.[178]

In contrast to the asbestos ban that was largely overturned in *Corrosion Proof Fittings*, the ban on distributing hexavalent chromium was much more narrowly targeted and was supported by extensive analysis of the alternative products available for use, and a detailed cost analysis.[179]

---

171. The export provisions of the Mercury Export Ban are codified at TSCA § 12(c)(1) and discussed in Chapter 8, Exports and Imports.
172. 40 C.F.R. Part 762.
173. 40 C.F.R. § 749.68(e).
174. 55 Fed. Reg. 222, 229 (Jan. 3, 1990).
175. 40 C.F.R. § 749.68(d)(4).
176. 40 C.F.R. § 749.68(g).
177. 40 C.F.R. § 749.68(i).
178. 40 C.F.R. § 749.68(h).
179. 55 Fed. Reg. 222 (Jan. 3, 1990).

VI. Metalworking Fluids

EPA also banned certain uses of metalworking fluids under TSCA § 6. These chemicals were restricted based on the EPA's conclusion that the unrestricted distribution and use of them in conjunction with other chemicals in metalworking fluids will present an unreasonable risk of injury.[180] The restricted chemicals are:

- the triethanolamine salt of tricarboxylic acid described in PMN P-83–1005;
- the form of tricarboxylic acid described in PMN P-83-1062;
- the triethanolamine salt of a substituted organic acid described in PMN P-84–310; and
- mixed mono and diamides of an organic acid described in PMN P-84–529.

Any person producing a product that could be used as metalworking fluid, or using a metalworking fluid, that includes the triethanolamine salt of tricarboxylic acid described in PMN P-83–1005, is prohibited from adding any nitrosating agent to the metalworking fluid or product.[181] Anyone distributing this substance in either a metalworking fluid or a product that can be used as a metalworking fluid must send a copy of the regulations to the recipient, use a label specified in the regulations, and send a letter to the recipient explaining the restrictions and containing statements specified in the regulations.[182]

Any person who distributes the form of tricarboxylic acid described in PMN P-83-1062 in a form in which it could be combined with water and triethanolamine to form P-83–1005, must send a letter to the recipient enclosing the regulations, explaining the restrictions, and containing statements specified in the regulations.[183]

Because the exact chemical identities of these substances are confidential, manufacturers and importers may submit a bona fide request to the EPA to determine if the substances they make or import are subject to these restrictions.[184] For the same reason, no processor, distributor, or user of these substances will be in violation of the regulations unless they also manufacture

---

180. 49 Fed. Reg. 2762, 2763 (Jan. 23, 1984).
181. 40 C.F.R. § 747.200(c).
182. 40 C.F.R. § 747.200(d).
183. 40 C.F.R. § 747.200(d)(3).
184. 40 C.F.R. § 747.200(e). *See* the discussion of bona fide requests in Chapter 3, The Inventory.

or import the substance, or unless they have received a letter described above summarizing the regulations.[185]

There are exemptions for research and development, impurities and articles, and substances made or imported for export only.[186]

Use of the triethanolamine salt of a substituted organic acid described in PMN P-84–310 and mixed mono and diamides of an organic acid described in PMN P-84–529 were also restricted under TSCA § 6 because EPA found that each of these substances posed "virtually identical" health risks to those which prompted EPA to regulate P-83-1005 and P-83-1062.[187] The use restrictions, labeling, warning, exemptions, and procedural requirements are the same as for the triethanolamine salt of tricarboxylic acid described in PMN P-83–1005.[188]

VII. Chemicals Under Evaluation

EPA announced in late 2009 that it is evaluating several chemicals with a view to restricting their use under § 6. This is part of the Agency's initiative to strengthen its chemical management programs using existing statutory authority.[189] The EPA identified chemicals based on factors such as toxicity, production volume, consumer exposure, and whether biomonitoring reveals their presence in human blood. EPA issued action plans for further regulatory review of the following categories of chemicals:

- phthalates, which are primarily used as plasticizers;
- perfluorinated chemicals (PFCs), which have many uses including for non-stick cookware, breathable fabrics, and oil, stain, and water repellants;
- polybrominated diphenyl ethers, which are primarily used as flame retardants; and
- short-chain chlorinated paraffins, which are used in many applications including in lubricants and coolants, as plasticizers, and as flame retardants; and other chlorinated paraffins.

185. 40 C.F.R. § 747.200(e).
186. 40 C.F.R. § 747.200(f).
187. 49 Fed. Reg. 24658, 24659 (June 14, 1984) and 49 Fed. Reg. 36846, 36847 (Sept. 20, 1984), respectively.
188. 40 C.F.R. §§ 747.195 and 747.115.
189. *See* Existing Chemicals Action Plans, *available at* http://www.epa.gov/oppt/existingchemicals/pubs/ecactionpln.html.

Each action plan includes an overview of each chemical, a description of its toxicity, the planned restrictions, and the factors supporting those restrictions. The EPA said it has also begun preparing action plans for benzidine dyes and pigments, and Bisphenol A.[190]

The action plan for pthalates[191] identifies eight pthalates that are candidates for further rulemaking: dibutyl phthalate, diisobutyl phthalate, butyl benzyl phthalate, di-n-pentyl phthalate, di(2-ethylhexyl) phthalate, di-n-octyl phthalate, diisononyl phthalate, and diisodecyl phthalate. EPA intends to begin the process to issue findings that these pthalates present "or may present an unreasonable risk of injury to health or the environment" pursuant to TSCA § 5(b)(4)(A) and "presents or will present an unreasonable risk" pursuant to TSCA § 6(a). By 2012 EPA expects to have enough information to determine if these merit further restrictions or bans under TSCA § 6. EPA will consider issuing a Significant New Use Rule (SNUR) for di-n-pentyl phthalate.[192] The perfluorinated chemicals that are the subject of the action plan for PFCs include perfluoroalkyl sulfonates (PFAS) and perfluoroalkyl carboxylates (PFAC), both of which are chemical families.[193] PFAS includes perfluorooctane sulfonic acid, and PFAC includes perfluorooctanoic acid (PFOA).[194] EPA intends to propose actions to restrict PFAS and PFAC, although the action plan does not give specific actions other than evaluating whether the facts would support a TSCA § 6(a) finding that these substances present "or will present an unreasonable risk."[195]

The polybrominated diphenyl ethers action plan[196] outlines proposed actions to issue a SNUR for the use of two chemicals in this class, pentabromodiphenyl ether and octabromodiphenyl ether, in articles. With respect to a third chemical in this class, decabromodiphenyl ether, EPA intends to begin rulemaking processes to issue (i) a SNUR for its use in articles, (ii) a test rule, and (iii) a rule under TSCA § 5(b)(4) to designate it as a chemical that "presents or may present an unreasonable risk of injury to human health or

---

190. *Id.*

191. EPA, Pthalates Action Plan (Dec. 30, 2009), *available through* http://www.epa.gov/oppt/existingchemicals/pubs/actionplans/phthalates.html.

192. *Id.* at 11.

193. EPA, Long-Chain Perfluorinated Chemicals (PFCs) Action Plan (Dec. 30, 2009)[hereinafter Action Plan PFCs], *available through* http://www.epa.gov/oppt/existingchemicals/pubs/actionplans/pfcs.html.

194. See Chapter 7, Reporting and Recordkeeping for a discussion of enforcement of reporting requirements concerning PFOA. There have been three SNURs issued for PFAS. Action Plan PFCs, 1.

195. Action Plan PFCs, 20.

196. EPA, Polybrominated Diphenyl Ethers (PBDEs) Action Plan, (Dec. 30, 2009), *available through* http://www.epa.gov/oppt/existingchemicals/pubs/actionplans/pbde.html.

the environment." [197] It also plans to develop alternatives to decabromodiphenyl ether, which some companies have agreed to phase out.[198]

The EPA notes in the action plan for chlorinated paraffins that some of the chemicals in this class that are currently manufactured in or imported into the United States are not on the Inventory,[199] and their manufacturers and importers must submit premanufacture notifications (PMNs).[200] Section 5(e) orders may result from the PMN process for those chemicals. EPA is considering issuing a finding under TSCA § 6(a) that short-chain chlorinated paraffins present "or will present an unreasonable risk," and is also considering bans or restrictions under § 6.[201]

VII. Enforcement

A. PCB Penalty Policy

The EPA issued a Polychlorinated Biphenyls (PCB) Penalty Policy[202] (PCB Penalty Policy) that follows the basic format and approach of the TSCA Civil Penalty Policy, which the EPA published in 1980.[203] The PCB Penalty Policy categorizes all violations according to their nature, extent, and circumstances in order to determine a gravity based penalty. Then the gravity based penalty is adjusted upwards for factors such as prior history of violations, and downwards for factors such as cooperation with EPA and prompt self-reporting.

All violations of the PCB regulations are classified as "chemical control" violations because they affect the release of PCBs into the environment.[204]

The extent of PCB violations depends on whether they relate to storage, marking, manifesting, inspection, recordkeeping, and other violations that do not involve PCB disposal, or whether they relate to disposal of PCBs. The extent of non-disposal violations is based on the total weight of the PCBs involved. The weight is adjusted to take concentration into account. Violations are minor if they involve less than 1200 kilograms or 220 gallons of PCBs, or

---

197. *Id.* at 1.
198. *Id.* at 13.
199. *See* Chapter 3, The Inventory.
200. EPA, Short-Chain Chlorinated Paraffins (SCCPs) and Other Chlorinated Paraffins Action Plan, 8 (Dec. 30, 2009), *available through* http://www.epa.gov/oppt/existingchemicals/pubs/actionplans/sccps.html
201. *Id.* at 8.
202. EPA, Polychlorinated Biphenyls (PCB) Penalty Policy (Apr. 9, 1990) [hereinafter PCB Penalty Policy] *available through* http://cfpub.epa.gov/compliance/resources/policies/civil/tsca/. *See* Chapter 14, Penalties and Enforcement.
203. 45 Fed. Reg. 59770 (Sept. 10, 1980).
204. PCB Penalty Policy, 2.

fewer than 50 large capacitors, 15 fifty-five gallon drums of solids, or 5 drained transformers. Significant violations are those that are greater than minor violations but less than 6000 kilograms or 1100 gallons of PCBs, or fewer than 250 large capacitors, 75 fifty-five gallon drums of solids, or 25 drained transformers. Any quantities in excess of the cutoffs for significant violations are major in extent.[205]

Violations involving PCB disposal are treated as more serious, and the penalties are based on the cost of cleanup and proper disposal of the PCBs. The extent of violations are minor if they involve disposal of less than 25 kilograms or 5 gallons of PCBs or less than 625 square feet of a non-porous surface, 60 square feet of soil, 20 square feet of a porous surface, or 60 cubic feet of other materials. The extent is significant if the quantities exceed the minor category but are less than 125 kilograms or 25 gallons of PCBs or less than 3125 square feet of a non-porous surface, 300 square feet of soil, 100 square feet of a porous surface, or 300 cubic feet of other materials. Quantities in excess of these limits result in a violation of major extent.[206] All spills into water or ditches or drains leading to water, or into food or feed are categorized as major because of the potential harm.[207]

The quantities of PCBs involved in a violation are reduced based on the concentration of PCBs involved. However, these concentration adjustments are not based on determining the total pounds of PCBs. The reduction is 50 percent for PCB concentrations of 0 to 49 ppm, 30 percent for concentrations of 50 to 499 ppm, and no reductions at 500 ppm.[208] No concentration adjustment is granted if the violation involved dispersion of any detectable levels of PCBs when they are put to a dispersed use, such as use for dust control, for heat recovery, or as a sealant or coating. If the violation is due to a failure to test the concentration of PCBs then no concentration adjustment is available. The concentration adjustment is also unavailable if the PCBs are measured by the square foot, cubic foot, or number of items, or if the PCBs were diluted in violation of the regulations.[209]

The third factor in determining the gravity based penalty is the circumstance, which is a term that connotes the likelihood of harm to human health or the environment. Violations are categorized into six circumstance levels, with level one being the most severe. Level one and level two violations are considered high range violations. Level one violations include: uncontrolled discharges, manufacturing or importing PCBs in violation of the regulations, unauthorized incidental PCB generation, failure to comply with

205. PCB Penalty Policy, 4–5.
206. PCB Penalty Policy, 5–7.
207. PCB Penalty Policy, 7–8.
208. PCB Penalty Policy, 8.
209. PCB Penalty Policy, 8–9.

the requirements to manifest PCBs or major errors in manifesting, and failure to permit an EPA inspector to enter a facility if the EPA has reason to believe that the facility removed PCBs before an inspector could gain entry. Level two violations include processing or distributing PCBs without an exemption or in violation of a condition of an exemption, unauthorized use of PCBs or use in violation of a condition of an authorization, including failing to register transformers,[210] storing combustible liquids near a transformer, failure to report a fire, or failure to inspect PCB Transformers or keep records of inspections. Failure to mark PCB items in a way that clearly advertises the presence of PCBs, and storage of PCBs in areas where they could be released into the environment are also level two violations.[211]

Levels three and four are medium range violations. Level three violations include disposal facilities', transporters', and storage facilities' failure to keep records or major recordkeeping lapses, leaks in PCB Articles where the PCBs did not migrate beyond the outside surface of the article, and failure to submit an annual report or an exception report in connection with manifesting. Level four violations include failure to completely comply with transformer registration requirements if basic information has been provided concerning transformer locations, failure to remove combustible materials other than combustible liquids and incomplete inspections or records of inspections. Storage violations such as having small cracks in floors or curbing, failing to conduct all required inspections if a significant portion of the required inspections were conducted, storage for longer than one year and failure to date PCB Items in storage are all level four violations. Manufacturers', processors', and users' failure to completely comply with recordkeeping requirements are also level four violations.[212]

Levels five and six are low range violations. Level five violations include violations of marking requirements so long as some of the requirements have been followed. Level six violations include occasional omission of data on records and manifests, and failure to label small capacitors, fluorescent light ballasts, or large low voltage capacitors as "no PCBs."[213]

A matrix in the PCB Penalty Policy supplies the gravity based penalties for each combination of nature, circumstances, and extent. However, the penalties applicable to violations that occurred in 2006, 2007, and 2008 must be increased by a factor of 1.3, and the penalties applicable to 2009 violations that occurred after January 12, 2009 must be increased by a factor of 1.5. These increased penalties are required by the Civil Penalties Inflation

---

210. While the PCB Penalty Policy refers at page 10 to registration with the local fire department, that requirement is no longer in effect.
211. PCB Penalty Policy, 9–11.
212. PCB Penalty Policy, 11–12.
213. PCB Penalty Policy, 12.

Adjustment Act of 1990,[214] as amended by the Debt Collection Improvement Act of 1996,[215] which required each federal agency to adjust its maximum penalties to maintain a deterrent effect in the face of inflation. As required by that legislation, EPA increased the daily maximum penalties to $27,500 effective after January 30, 1997[216] and again to $32,500 effective March 15, 2004,[217] and again to $37,500 effective January 12, 2009.[218] The Debt Collection Improvement Act requires penalty adjustments every four years and so another increase should be forthcoming in 2013.

The EPA will assess penalties for each separate violation of each PCB requirement. However, if an entity does not conduct inspections and as a result does not maintain records of inspections it will only be penalized for failing to conduct the inspection because the two violations are not independent. The EPA limited the penalty for missing quarterly inspections to four inspections or $250,000, whichever is less. It also limited the number of violations for missing annual reports or inspections to one each for the prior three years, and a cap of one total for earlier violations.[219]

Many PCB violations continue for a period of time, and the EPA will either penalize those based on the total amount of PCB involved, or by multiplying the gravity based penalty times the number of days of violation.

As is the case with all of the enforcement response policies for TSCA violations, the PCB Penalty Policy calls for adjusting the gravity based penalty up or down based on the violator's degree of culpability, history of prior violations, ability to pay, [220] attitude, self-reporting, timeliness of self-reporting, and economic benefit to the violator of not complying with the applicable regulations. In addition, the PCB Penalty Policy permits the EPA to assess the violator for the EPA's costs of cleaning up any PCBs.[221]

The Audit Policy should be consulted to determine if a complete or 75 percent mitigation of penalties is available.[222]

214. 28 U.S.C. § 2461.
215. 31 U.S.C. § 3701.
216. 61 Fed. Reg. 69360 (Dec. 31, 1996).
217. 69 Fed. Reg. 7121 (Feb. 13, 2004).
218. 73 Fed. Reg. 75340 (Dec. 11, 2008); 74 Fed. Reg. 626 (Jan. 7, 2009).
219. PCB Penalty Policy, 13.
220. *See* In re Ray Birnbaum Scrap Yard, TSCA Appeal No. 92-5 (EAB, 1994), where the Environmental Appeals Board upheld a reduction for a proposed PCB violation to $1700 from $16,236. Decision *available at* http://www.epa.gov/eab/disk5/raybirn.pdf.
221. PCB Penalty Policy, 15–19.
222. *See* Chapter 14, Penalties and Enforcement, for a complete discussion of the Audit Policy and the mitigating factors applicable to all the TSCA ERPs.

B. Enforcement Actions and Inspections

The EPA has had a very active enforcement program for PCB violations. It also actively enforces the PCB regulations through civil penalty proceedings.

In fiscal year 2008 it inspected 112 facilities for PCB compliance.[223] The EPA published a PCB Inspection Manual[224] describing the inspection process for inspectors who are reviewing PCB compliance at facilities.[225] It contains detailed summaries of all of the PCB regulations and has charts of the specific requirements applicable to PCB incinerators, chemical waste landfills, high efficiency boilers, and scrap metal recovery ovens and smelters.

---

223. EPA Office of Compliance, National Enforcement Trends (NETS) Report, G-1b (May 2009), *available through* http://www.epa.gov/compliance/data/results/nets.html#numbers.

224. PCB Inspection Manual, EPA-305-X-04-003, (Aug. 2004), *available at* http://epa.gov/oecaerth/resources/publications/monitoring/tsca/manuals/pcbinspect/index.html.

225. *See also* Chapter 14, Penalties and Enforcement.

CHAPTER

12

Significant New Use Rules

I. Introduction to Significant New Use Rules—SNURs

The Toxic Substances Control Act (TSCA)[1] gives the United States Environmental Protection Agency (EPA) the authority to designate a new use of a chemical substance as a "significant new use," and anyone who manufactures, imports, or processes[2] a chemical for such a use must file a notice ninety days before starting that activity. The advance notification program for "significant new uses" is very similar procedurally to the Premanufacture Notice (PMN) program for putting chemical substances on the TSCA Inventory.[3] TSCA § 5 says in part:

> (1) Except as provided in subsection (h), no person may—
>
> ***
>
> (B) manufacture or process any chemical substance for a use which the Administrator has determined, in accordance with paragraph (2), is a significant new use,
>
> unless such person submits to the Administrator, at least 90 days before such manufacture or processing, a notice, in accordance with subsection (d), of such person's intention to manufacture or process such substance and such person complies with any applicable requirement of subsection (b).
>
> (2) A determination by the Administrator that a use of a chemical substance is a significant new use with respect to which notification is required under paragraph (1) shall be made by a rule promulgated after a consideration of all relevant factors, including—
>
> (A) the projected volume of manufacturing and processing of a chemical substance,
>
> (B) the extent to which a use changes the type or form of exposure of human beings or the environment to a chemical substance,
>
> (C) the extent to which a use increases the magnitude and duration of exposure of human beings or the environment to a chemical substance, and
>
> (D) the reasonably anticipated manner and methods of manufacturing, processing, distribution in commerce, and disposal of a chemical substance.[4]

---

1. 15 U.S.C. §§ 2601-2695d.
2. *See* Chapter 4, Premanufacture Notifications, for a discussion of what constitutes processing.
3. *See* Chapter 4, Premanufacture Notifications.
4. TSCA § (5)(a).

Like the PMN process, the significant new use notification process enables the EPA to evaluate the risks that may be presented by a new use of a substance and gives the EPA an opportunity to gather risk data and regulate the use if it may present unreasonable risks.

The advance notice that must be filed before engaging in any significant new use is called a Significant New Use Notice (SNUN).[5] When the EPA designates a use as a significant new use, it promulgates a Significant New Use Rule (SNUR) and publishes a notice in the Federal Register.[6] There were 912 SNURs as of November 2009, covering at least thirteen hundred individual chemicals.[7] Only manufacturers, importers, and processors are required to file SNUNs.

"Significant new uses" under the statute are specific ways of making, importing, processing, using, or disposing of a chemical that may present greater risks than the uses already engaged in with that chemical. Significant new uses can be anything that could expose people or the environment to a risk, and can be as diverse as using the substance other than as an intermediate, using it without personal protective equipment, or using it in a way that could result in releases to water.

The statutory standards for issuing a SNUR are quite flexible. The statute does not require EPA to make specific findings, and only requires that the EPA consider "all relevant factors" including volume, how use changes exposure, and handling methods, as set out in the excerpt of the statute quoted above. However, the SNUR regulations impose much more stringent requirements on the EPA before it can issue a SNUR.

Under the SNUR regulations, the EPA either must make findings that justify issuance of an order under TSCA § 5(e),[8] or must determine that new uses may result in significant changes in human exposure or environmental releases, or that there is a concern about the health or environmental effects of the substance.[9] The findings necessary for issuance of a § 5(e) consent order are that there is insufficient information to evaluate the effects of the substance on health and the environment. The EPA must also find that either (i) without sufficient information to permit an evaluation of the substance's effects on health and the environment, there may be an unreasonable risk to health or the environment, or (ii) the substance will be produced in substantial

---

5. The acronyms SNUR and SNUN are pronounced as if they were words instead of reading out the letters.
6. Most SNURs are in 40 C.F.R. Part 721 but one SNUR for a microorganism is at 40 C.F. R. § 725.1075.
7. Reported by the EPA as of September 30, 2004 in its New Chemicals Program Summary of Accomplishments *available at* http://www.epa.gov/oppt/newchems/pubs/accomplishments.htm.
8. 40 C.F.R. § 721.160.
9. 40 C.F.R. § 721.170(a).

quantities and (x) the substance enters the environment or may be reasonably anticipated to enter the environment in substantial quantities, or (y) there is or may be significant or substantial human exposure to the substance.[10]

The findings necessary for issuance of a SNUR in the absence of an order under TSCA § 5(e) are that new uses may result in significant changes in human exposure or environmental releases, or that there is a concern about the substance's health or environmental effects.[11] Significant new uses can only be uses that have not been identified in the PMN as the uses for the substance.[12] The findings relating to a concern about health or environmental effects include that the substance or its metabolites may be a carcinogen or cause acutely toxic effects, serious chronic or acute effects, or developmentally toxic effects, as shown by specified types of test data or comparison to analogous substances. The EPA could also find that the substance or its impurities or byproducts may cause significant adverse environmental effects under reasonably anticipated conditions.

An example of a significant new use is the use described in the SNUR for potassium N,N-bis (hydroxyethyl) cocoamine oxide phosphate, and potassium N,N-bis (hydroxyethyl) tallowamine oxide phosphate.[13] The SNUR for these two chemicals says that any use "in a consumer product at concentrations greater than five percent by weight" is a significant new use for which a SNUN is required. These two chemicals were the subject of PMNs which described them as surfactants for industrial cleaning products, but said that they could possibly be used in consumer cleaning products and personal care products. Test data showed that these two chemicals were strong irritants at high concentrations, but at lower concentrations they were at most only mild irritants. The EPA remained concerned that exposure to concentrations above 5 percent could pose risks, and that was sufficient to justify issuance of the SNUR for consumer uses at higher concentrations.[14]

In practical effect, a SNUR is a regulatory restriction on use of a substance. The vast majority of companies avoid engaging in the significant new uses detailed in SNURs, and do not have to file SNUNs. In 2002 the EPA estimated that SNURS had been issued on over nine hundred chemicals over time, but very few people decided to engage in the new use and so fewer than 25 SNUNs had been filed.[15]

Many SNURs set a limit on the amount of the substance that can be made or processed, and if a company wants to make or process greater amounts it

10. TSCA § 5(e).
11. 40 C.F.R. § 721.170(a).
12. 40 C.F.R. § 721.170(c).
13. 40 C.F. R. § 721.8100.
14. 49 Fed. Reg. 35011, 35014-15 (Sept. 5, 1984).
15. 67 Fed. Reg. 12879, 12881 (Mar. 20, 2002).

will have to perform toxicology tests and evaluate safe handling methods before the EPA will permit it to exceed the limit set in the SNUR. In the example above of the SNUR designating use in concentrations greater than 5 percent in consumer products as a significant new use, the EPA would have required testing before making or processing such a product. The EPA almost always requires test data before a company can engage in a significant new use. The test data will typically either point to the appropriate precautions or demonstrate that no precautions are necessary.

SNUNs are submitted on the PMN form. After a submitter files a SNUN it must wait ninety days for EPA comment before engaging in the significant new use, but that ninety-day review period may be extended or suspended.[16]

The EPA is required to publish a notice in the Federal Register every time it receives a SNUN[17] but has not done so.[18]

II. Practical Implications

Processors must be careful to find out if substances they are purchasing from outside vendors are subject to a SNUR. Manufacturers must inform purchasers of their chemicals if there is a SNUR in effect, and most will make a notation on the Material Safety Data Sheet (MSDS) for the subject chemical. However, some SNURs have specific requirements for MSDS contents.

III. When and How SNURs Are Issued

SNURs are issued for substances that are either on the TSCA Inventory,[19] or for which a PMN has been filed.[20] The EPA can restrict the uses that the PMN submitter engages in by entering into a consent order under TSCA § 5(e) with that entity. However, a § 5(e) consent order is only binding on the one entity that signs it with the EPA. In order to make the restrictions in the § 5(e) consent order binding on all of the regulated industry, the EPA must

16. 40 C.F.R. § 721.25.
17. TSCA § 5(d)(2).
18. In response to a request under the Freedom of Information Act made December 11, 2008, the EPA was not able to identify any publication in the Federal Register reporting the receipt of a SNUN.
19. *See* Chapter 3, The Inventory.
20. *See generally* 40 C.F.R. §§ 721.160 and 721.170.

promulgate a SNUR.[21] EPA issues SNURs for most substances that are subject to a 5(e) order.[22] These are often referred to as "5(e) SNURs."

If the 5(e) consent order prohibits manufacture or import of the substance, no SNUR will be needed because the substance will not be put on the Inventory and it cannot be made or imported without notifying the EPA through the PMN process. If the EPA determines that no SNUR is necessary even though it has entered into a 5(e) consent order, it must publish a notice in the Federal Register explaining its reasoning.[23]

The EPA can also promulgate a SNUR for a substance that is not the subject of a 5(e) consent order, but in those cases the EPA must make a finding that new uses may result in significant changes in human exposure or environmental releases, or that there is a concern about the substance's health or environmental effects.[24] These are referred to as "non-5(e) SNURs." Historically non-5(e) SNURs could not be issued to designate significant new uses as uses without worker protection or hazard communications but that is no longer the case.[25] Non-5(e) SNURs are issued when the uses described in a PMN do not warrant restrictions, but other uses could present risks to human health or the environment.[26]

All of the definitions in the premanufacture notification regulations apply to SNURs.[27]

There are three procedures that the EPA can use to issue SNURs. These are direct final rulemaking, interim final rulemaking, and notice and comment rulemaking.[28] In direct final rulemaking, the EPA issues a SNUR as a final rule, without providing any other notice to the regulated community, other than to the PMN filer, that it intends to promulgate a SNUR. The SNUR will become effective sixty days after its publication in the Federal Register, unless someone submits a written notice within thirty days after the SNUR is published in the Federal Register that the commenter intends to file adverse or critical comments. The written notice need only identify the SNUR and say that the author will file adverse or critical comments. Then the EPA will withdraw the SNUR and publish the withdrawal in the Federal Register. The EPA will propose the SNUR as a proposed rule, and establish a thirty-day period

---

21. EPA's Draft Questions & Answers for the New Chemicals Program, 1-61-62, question 123-1 (undated) [hereinafter Draft PMN Q&A] *available at* http://www.epa.gov/oppt/newchems/pubs/qanda-newchems.pdf.
22. 40 C.F.R. § 721.160(a).
23. 40 C.F.R. § 721.160(a)(2). An example of a Federal Register notice explaining why no SNUR was issued after entry into a § 5(e) consent order is 72 Fed. Reg. 14681 (Mar. 29, 2007).
24. 40 C.F.R. § 721.170(a).
25. Draft PMN Q&A, 1-62-63, question 123-2.
26. Draft PMN Q&A, 1-64, question 123-7.
27. 40 C.F.R. § 721.3.
28. 40 C.F.R. § 721.160(c).

for public comments on the SNUR. EPA must then consider any comments it receives and determine whether or not a SNUR is warranted. If the EPA decides that the SNUR is warranted, it will issue a final rule and publish the final rule in the Federal Register. This procedure is considered expedited because often no comments are submitted and so it is a shortcut around the traditional notice and comment rulemaking.

In notice and comment rulemaking, which is an option for promulgating SNURs, the EPA issues a proposed SNUR in the Federal Register, and announces a thirty-day period during which anyone can submit comments on the proposal. The EPA must consider any comments it receives and may issue a final rule if it determines that a SNUR is warranted.

If the EPA chooses to issue an interim final rule, it will be effective immediately upon publication in the Federal Register, but it will expire after one hundred and eighty days if the EPA receives written comments and does not respond to those comments by promulgating a final SNUR within that one hundred and eighty-day period. Comments may be submitted during the first thirty days after publication of the interim final rule. The EPA said it will issue interim final rules when it believes that someone will engage in the significant new use before a SNUR could be effective under direct final rulemaking or notice and comment rulemaking.

IV. How to Determine if a SNUR Exists

Before manufacturing, importing, or processing any chemical, it is important to determine if a SNUR exists, and a company must have procedures in place to search for new SNURs that are issued for chemicals the company is already using. If the company knows the identity of the chemical it plans to make, import, or process, then the first step is to look for the chemical on the Inventory, where substances subject to a SNUR are marked with an "S."[29] SNURS are also listed in the SNUR regulations in the Code of Federal Regulations.[30] The EPA's Substance Registry Service is another good source of information about the programs and regulations that govern specific chemicals,[31] and there are also commercially available databases that flag

29. Draft PMN Q&A, 1-64, question Q 123-8.
30. SNURs are listed in 40 C.F.R. Part 721. One SNUR for a microorganism is listed in Part 725, at 40 C.F.R. § 725.1075.
31. The Substance Registry Service is *available at* http://iaspub.epa.gov/sor_internet/registry/substreg/home/overview/home.do. *See* Chapter 20, Practice Tools for information on using the Substance Registry Service Web site.

SNUR chemicals. All new SNURs are published in the daily Federal Register and it is relatively easy to check the Federal Register every day on line.[32]

Trade secrets greatly complicate SNUR compliance. Many times a supplier of a chemical will not disclose the names of all the chemicals in a product, and that makes it impossible to look for SNURs in the regulations or in commercial databases. The procedures for determining if a SNUR exists in this situation will be addressed later in this chapter.

Trade secrets create even more conceptual and practical problems when the EPA does not list the chemical identity of substances that are subject to SNURs. As strange as it may be, many SNURs only identify the generic family that the subject chemical belongs to because the manufacturer or importer who filed a PMN on that substance has claimed the chemical identity as Confidential Business Information. As a result, the EPA has promulgated rules that apply to specific chemicals, but the EPA will not publish the names of the specific chemicals that are subject to the rules. The SNURs that do not disclose the name of the chemicals that they apply to are really only public notices that more investigation is required before making, importing, or processing chemicals in that generic class of substances.

V. How to Determine if a SNUR on a Substance Identified by Generic Name Is Applicable

If a manufacturer, importer, or processor plans on handling a chemical that is in one of the generic categories listed in the SNUR regulations, it may ask the EPA whether the chemical is subject to a SNUR.[33] The manufacturer, importer, or processor has to submit a request detailing its bona fide intent to manufacture, import, or process the substance, and this is commonly referred to as a bona fide request or letter. The EPA only has to respond if it concludes that the submitter actually has a bona fide intent to make, import, or process the chemical for a commercial purpose. Because of confidentiality concerns, the EPA will not respond to requests under the Freedom of Information Act.[34]

The bona fide request must include the chemical identity of the substance, a description of the research and development activities that have been conducted to date, the purpose for which the submitter intends to manufacture, import, or process the substance, and an elemental analysis of the substance. The bona fide request must also include either an X-ray diffraction pattern of

---

32. *See* Chapter 20, Practice Tools.
33. 40 C.F.R. § 721.11.
34. 5 U.S.C. § 552.

an inorganic substance, a mass spectrum of an organic substance, or an infrared spectrum; however if those do not identify the substance with certainty then additional analytical data must be submitted to conclusively establish the chemical substance's identity. The submitter must sign a written statement that the manufacture, importation or processing is for commercial purposes. The SNUR regulations[35] define "process for commercial purposes" as:

> the preparation of a chemical substance or mixture containing the chemical substance, after manufacture of the substance, for distribution in commerce with the purpose of obtaining an immediate or eventual commercial advantage for the processor. Processing of any amount of a chemical substance or mixture containing the chemical substance is included in this definition.

The regulations do not define "manufacture for commercial purposes" or "import for commercial purposes" but this definition implies that any processing, manufacture, or importation for distribution in pursuit of a commercial advantage will be sufficient for bona fide requests.

A prospective importer or processor may not know the identity of the substance it is purchasing from another source because the manufacturer is claiming the identity as a trade secret. In that case, the prospective importer or purchaser must have the manufacturer directly supply the EPA with the information needed for a bona fide request.[36]

If the EPA agrees that the submitter has a bona fide intent to manufacture, import, or process a substance subject to a SNUR, it will notify the submitter if the chemical is subject to a SNUR and what section of the Code of Federal Regulations is relevant. The EPA is supposed to respond to a complete bona fide request within thirty days,[37] but it is prudent to allow much more time for a response.

VI. How to Read a SNUR

Reading and understanding a SNUR can be quite difficult. SNURs typically look like a string of code, and they have to be interpreted by teasing apart the cross-references. The regulations contain a set of standard significant new uses, and each specific SNUR may cross-reference one or more of the standard significant new uses instead of describing each significant new use in each SNUR. In some cases, SNURs even cross-reference portions of other SNURs.

---

35. 40 C.F.R. 721.3.
36. 40 C.F.R. 721.11(c).
37. 40 C.F.R. § 721.11(g).

The significant new uses that are described in SNURs can be confusing because they are not "uses" in the sense that people expect. They are often methods of handling the SNUR substance; one common significant new use is handling the SNUR substance without a respirator. If the EPA wants to know if anyone plans on handling the SNUR substance without a respirator it will issue a SNUR requiring a notice before anyone can handle that substance without a respirator. That has the effect of requiring people to use respirators because that is usually much easier than filing a SNUN.

An example of a SNUR is the one for octanoic acid, hydrazide, in § 721.5385. That SNUR says in full:

> (a) Chemical substance and significant new uses subject to reporting. (1) The chemical substance identified as octanoic acid, hydrazide (PMN P-92–1086) is subject to reporting under this section for the significant new uses described in paragraph (a)(2) of this section.
> (2) The significant new uses are: (i) Protection in the workplace. Requirements as specified in §721.63 (a)(1), (a)(3), (a)(4), (a)(5)(iv), (a)(5)(v), (a)(5)(vi), (a)(5)(vii), (a)(6)(ii), (b) (concentration set at 0.1 percent), and (c).
> (ii) Hazard communication program. Requirements as specified in §721.72 (a), (b), (c), (d), (e) (concentration set at 0.1 percent), (f), (g)(1)(i), (g)(1)(ii), (g)(1)(vii), (g)(2)(i), (g)(2)(ii), (g)(2)(iii), (g)(2)(iv), (g)(2)(v), (g)(3)(ii), (g)(4)(i), and (g)(5).
> (iii) Industrial, commercial, and consumer activities. Requirements as specified in §721.80(q).
> (iv) Disposal. Requirements as specified in §721.85 (a)(1) and (b)(1).
> (b) Specific requirements. The provisions of subpart A of this part apply to this section except as modified by this paragraph.
> (1) Recordkeeping. Recordkeeping requirements as specified in §721.125 (a) through (j) are applicable to manufacturers, importers, and processors of this substance.
> (2) Limitations or revocation of certain notification requirements. The provisions of §721.185 apply to this section.
> (3) Determining whether a specific use is subject to this section. The provisions of §721.1725(b)(1) apply to this section.

Subsection (a) identifies the substance that is subject to the SNUR, and states that each of the uses that are cross-referenced in the remainder of the subsection is a significant new use. PMN P-92–1086 is the number assigned to the PMN that was filed by the original PMN submitter.

Subsection (a)(2) cross-references the significant new uses relating to workplace protection. It uses the word "requirements" to identify the significant new uses, although the significant new uses are not themselves "requirements" in the traditional sense of the word. The first cross-reference is to

§721.63(a)(1), which states that it would be a significant new use to manufacture, import, or process a SNUR substance without having a program requiring anyone who may be dermally exposed to wear personal protective equipment to prevent dermal exposure. Therefore, use of octanoic acid, hydrazide without personal protective equipment to prevent dermal exposure would be a significant new use.

The cross-reference to §721.63(a)(3) adds that it would be a significant new use to manufacture, import, or process a substance without demonstrating that the personal protective equipment used provides an impervious barrier to prevent dermal exposure under normal and expected working conditions. It adds that the only acceptable demonstrations that the personal protective equipment is impervious to the SNUR substance, in combination with other chemicals in the work area, are specific types of testing, or an evaluation of the manufacturer's specifications or a sample of the materials used in the personal protective equipment. Therefore, anyone who intends to manufacture, import, or process octanoic acid, hydrazide must be able to demonstrate either through testing or evaluation of specifications or a sample, that the personal protective equipment to be used is impervious to the SNUR substance. If the prospective manufacturer, importer, or processor cannot make that demonstration, it must submit a SNUN at least ninety days prior to engaging in that activity.

The remaining cross-references in this SNUR, and in SNURs in general, can all be parsed by the same method of reviewing the cross-referenced provisions. Some SNURs do identify significant new uses that are not part of the standardized set, such as the limitation on use in consumer products at concentrations above 5 percent, in the example given earlier in this chapter.[38] Those should be self-explanatory, but if they are not, any ambiguities can usually be resolved by consulting the Federal Register notices for the dates the SNUR was proposal and promulgated, because these give the rationale for issuing the particular SNUR.

VII. Bona Fide Letters to Determine a Confidential Manufacturing Limit

Not infrequently a SNUR will provide that it is a significant new use to manufacture or import the SNUR substance in excess of an undisclosed quantity limitation. The published SNUR cross-references a consent order issued under TSCA § 5(e) that the entity that filed the PMN on the SNUR substance has agreed to. The quantity limitation in the consent order is often confidential

38. The SNUR in that example is at 40 C.F. R. § 721.8100.

and not freely accessible to the public. That is the case with the SNUR for octanoic acid, hydrazide set out above. It provides that it is a significant new use to use the SNUR substance "as specified in §721.80(q)." Section 721.80(q) in turn says: "Aggregate manufacture and importation volume for any use greater than that allowed by the section 5(e) consent order referenced in subpart E of this part for the substance" is a significant new use of the substance. Therefore, it is a significant new use of octanoic acid, hydrazide to manufacture or import it in excess of a quantity that is a secret. Note that the consent order is only referenced in the SNUR by way of a cross-reference to § 721.80(q).

All manufacturers, importers, and processors of substances subject to secret significant new uses have a heavy burden to ensure that they are in compliance with the SNUR. There is a process for submitting a bona fide intent to manufacture, import, or process the chemical substance in order to determine if the proposed use is a significant new use, and then the EPA will reveal the significant new use of that substance. Going back to the octanoic acid, hydrazide example, any prospective manufacturer or importer must find out what the quantity limitation is, or risk violating the SNUR by manufacturing or importing a quantity that is classified as a significant new use. The easiest way to do this is to consult the company that entered into the § 5(e) consent order if the name of the company is public information. If the secret quantity limitation cannot be obtained that way, the prospective manufacturer or importer has no choice other than to submit a bona fide letter to the EPA.

To make SNURs such as the one applicable to octanoic acid, hydrazide even more difficult to interpret, the procedure describing the bona fide letter is in another SNUR instead of one of the subparts of the SNUR regulations that have general applicability. The reference in the octanoic acid, hydrazide SNUR to determining if a use of the substance is a significant new use by following the provisions of 40 C.F.R. § 721.1725(b)(1) is in fact a reference to the bona fide letter procedure set out in the SNUR for benzoic acid, 3,3′-methylenebis [6 amino-, di-2-propenyl ester].[39]

The procedure described in § 721.1725(b)(1) states that a bona fide letter to determine whether a proposed use is a significant new use must include all of the information required for a bona fide letter to determine if a substance is subject to a SNUR.[40] These requirements include the chemical identity of the substance, a description of the research and development activities that have been conducted to date, the purpose for which the submitter intends to

---

39. 40 C.F.R. § 721.1725(b)(1).
40. 40 C.F.R. § 721.1725(b)(1)(ii)(A). This section refers to the requirements of § 721.6, but this is an error because the requirements of a bona fide letter to determine if a substance is subject to a SNUR are located ate 40 C.F.R. § 721.11.

manufacture, import, or process the substance and an elemental analysis of the substance, and either an X-ray diffraction pattern of an inorganic substance, a mass spectrum of an organic substance, or an infrared spectrum; however if those do not identify the substance with certainty then additional analytical data must be submitted to conclusively establish the chemical substance's identity. The submitter must sign a written statement that the manufacture, importation, or processing is for commercial purposes. In addition, if the purpose of the bona fide letter is to determine the parameters of a confidential SNUR, the submitter must describe the specific use intended for the substance.[41]

If the EPA concludes that the submitter of the bona fide letter does have a bona fide intent to manufacture, import, or process the substance, the EPA will tell the submitter if its proposed use is subject to a SNUR. If the proposed use is not subject to a SNUR, the EPA will tell the submitter what uses are significant new uses.[42] Notwithstanding EPA's statement in the cross-referenced SNUR that it will inform the submitter of a bona fide letter of the significant new uses, the EPA has said otherwise in at least one SNUR preamble. In that preamble,[43] the EPA said that it will only reveal whether the intended manufacturing volume that the submitter of a bona fide letter says it intends to make is more or less than the confidential volume that qualifies the manufacture as a significant new use. If the submitter's volume is less, the EPA will not reveal the trigger volume. In that case the submitter must submit another bona fide letter if it later intends to increase its manufacturing volume. The practical implication is that a submitter should give the EPA the maximum potential volume it may make in the initial bona fide letter, or it will risk having to make a series of bona fide requests.

There is a thirty-day time limit in the cross-referenced SNUR for EPA's response, but it is likely that a response will take longer and submitters should plan accordingly and consider filing a SNUN to determine if the use is a significant new use.

VIII. Standardized Set of Significant New Uses

Part B of the SNUR regulations[44] is a listing of standardized significant new uses. These significant new uses apply to a particular chemical only if they are cross-referenced in the SNUR for that chemical.[45] The standardized

41. 40 C.F.R. § 721.1725(b)(1)(ii)(B).
42. 40 C.F.R. § 721.1725(b)(1)(iv).
43. 68 Fed. Reg. 15061, 15077 (Mar. 28, 2003).
44. 40 C.F.R § 721.50.
45. 54 Fed. Reg. 31298 (July 27, 1989).

significant new uses include uses without workplace protections, uses without hazard communications, uses for industrial, commercial, and consumer activities, methods of disposal and releases to water.

The standardized set of significant new uses appears on its surface to set out requirements for handling a SNUR substance. In effect, they are requirements because most manufacturers, importers, and processors of SNUR substances would rather follow the requirements of the SNUR than file a SNUN if at all possible. However, looking at the standardized set of significant new uses from a different, more literal, perspective, they are only a list of handling procedures, and if anyone handles SNUR substances any other way, they will be engaging in a significant new use.

Many of the standardized significant new uses refer to activities undertaken by an "employer." "Employer" is defined as "any manufacturer, importer, processor, or user of chemical substances or mixtures"[46] and does not literally mean an entity that has people on its payroll. The term "employer" is misleading in the SNUR context and will not be used in this discussion. To the extent that the standardized SNURs seem to impose obligations on "users" of substances, it is important to keep in mind that people who use substances, but do not manufacture, import, or process those substances do not have any obligation to file a SNUN for a significant new use.[47]

The following summaries of the standardized significant new uses relating to workplace protection are intended to give an overview of the significant new uses, but the language of the regulation should be consulted in each instance to answer specific questions about their interpretation and application.

A. Significant New Use if Used Without Workplace Protection

If a SNUR cross-references a subsection of 40 C.F.R. § 721.63 then it will be a significant new use to manufacture, import, or process the SNUR substance without a program to establish workplace protections. Each subsection specifies a different workplace protection practice. Manufacturers, importers, and processors must evaluate their work areas and determine who is reasonably likely to be exposed to the SNUR substance. Workplace practices and engineering controls can be a factor in determining who is reasonably likely to be exposed.[48]

---

46. 40 C.F.R. § 721.3.
47. TSCA § 5(a)(1)(B) requires only that manufacturers, importers and processors file SNUNs.
48. 54 Fed. Reg. 31298, 31300 (July 27, 1989).

§ 721.63(a)(1): It is a significant new use to manufacture, import, or process the substance without having a program requiring anyone who is reasonably likely to be exposed through the skin to wear personal protective equipment to prevent dermal exposure.

§ 721.63(a)(2)(i): It is a significant new use to manufacture, import, or process the substance without having a program requiring anyone who is reasonably likely to be exposed to wear gloves.

§ 721.63(a)(2)(ii): It is a significant new use to manufacture, import, or process the substance without having a program requiring anyone who is reasonably likely to be exposed to wear full body chemical protective clothing.

§ 721.63(a)(2)(iii): It is a significant new use to manufacture, import, or process the substance without having a program requiring anyone who is reasonably likely to be exposed to wear chemical goggles or equivalent eye protection.

§ 721.63(a)(2)(iv): It is a significant new use to manufacture, import, or process the substance without having a program requiring anyone who is reasonably likely to be exposed to wear clothing covering the arms, legs and torso. This subsection does not require that the clothing be tested for imperviousness.

§ 721.63(a)(3): It is a significant new use to manufacture, import, or process the substance for a use by a manufacturer, importer, processor, or user who does not have a program to demonstrate that each item of personal protective equipment provides a an impervious barrier to prevent dermal exposure. Note that users do not need to file SNURs. The demonstration should address the actual work conditions, and not just the SNUR substance in isolation. It should also address equipment wear, such as tears, punctures, and abrasions.[49] This demonstration may be made by:

§ 721.63(a)(3)(i): Testing involving subjecting the personal protective equipment to the expected exposure conditions and substances or

§ 721.63(a)(3)(ii): Evaluating the specifications of the personal protective equipment or the materials used in the personal protective equipment.

§ 721.63(a)(4): It is a significant new use to manufacture, import, or process the substance without having a program to provide a

49. *Id.*

respirator to anyone who may be exposed by inhaling the substance. It is a significant new use if they do not in fact wear the respirator. The respirator must be approved by the National Institute of Occupational Health and Safety (NIOSH).

§ 721.63(a)(5)(i) through (xv)

These subsections list specific types of respirators that may be used to satisfy the requirements of § 721.63(a)(4) to have a program to require use of respirators. If the required respirator is not used, the use is a significant new use. NIOSH maintains a search tool to find certified respirators on its website.[50]

§ 721.63(a)(6): It is a significant new use to manufacture, import, or process the substance without having a program to provide a respirator in the case of an inhalation exposure or other personal protective equipment in the case of dermal exposure, to anyone who is reasonably likely to be exposed to substance in any of six forms. It is a significant new use if they do not in fact wear the respirator or personal protective equipment. If one or more of the following subsections are listed in the SNUR, the forms of the substance that must be protected against are:

§ 721.63(a)(6)(i): Dust.
§ 721.63(a)(6)((ii): Mist.
§ 721.63(a)(6)(iii): Fume.
§ 721.63(a)(6)(iv): Smoke.
§ 721.63(a)(6)(v): Vapor.
§ 721.63(a)(6)(vi) Gas.

§ 721.63(b): This subsection does not give a significant new use, but instead creates concentration-based exemption from the requirement to file a SNUN if the personal protective equipment specified in § 721.63 is not used. If the SNUR cross-references this subsection and provides a concentration value then substances present in the work place at a concentration lower than or equal to the concentration specified in the SNUR are exempt from filing a SNUN. If the substance becomes concentrated during use or processing and exceeds the specified concentration, then the exception does not apply if the manufacturer, importer or processor has reason to know that.

§ 721.63(c): This subsection describes what a distributor must do if it learns that another entity may be engaging in a significant

50. http://www2a.cdc.gov/drds/cel/cel_form_code.asp.

new use by failing to have a program to protect workers from exposure dermally or by inhalation. It is slightly less restrictive than the procedures that are binding on all companies that distribute substances that are subject to a SNUR.[51] It adds that if a distributor of a substance learns that a recipient is doing anything inconsistent with a program requiring personal protective equipment under a SNUR, the distributor must assume that the recipient is engaging in a significant new use. The distributor must follow the procedures applicable to all distributors that learn that a recipient of a SNUR substance is engaging in a significant new use without filing a SNUN. In summary, those procedures require the distributor to notify the recipient and the EPA that the recipient is engaging in a significant new use, and stop shipments unless the recipient agrees not to engage in a significant new use. However, this subsection permits the distributor to avoid notifying the EPA and possibly ceasing shipments if it can document all of the following:

- The distributor has notified the recipient that the recipient is engaging in an activity that is inconsistent with a personal protective equipment program set forth in a SNUR, and the distributor is aware of the lapse. In other words, the recipient is likely engaging in a significant new use. The distributor must submit that notice within 15 working days of the date it has knowledge of the activity.
- The recipient provides a written assurance that the recipient has implemented a personal protective equipment program and will take appropriate measures to avoid activities that are inconsistent with it. The distributor must receive this written assurance within 15 days of its original notice to the recipient.
- If the distributor receives information after the written statement of assurance, to the effect that the recipient is engaging in activities that are inconsistent with the personal protective equipment program, then the distributor must follow the stricter procedures in 40 C.F.R. § 721(d) including notifying the EPA and possibly stopping further shipments.

51. 40 C.F.R. § 721.5(d).

B. Significant New Use if Used Without a Hazard Communication Program

If a SNUR cross-references a subsection of 40 C.F.R. § 721.72 then it will be a significant new use to manufacture, import, or process the SNUR substance unless the manufacturers, importers, processors, and users have a hazard communication program to warn about the risks that the substance poses. This group of significant new uses builds on a system of hazard communication established by the Occupational Health and Safety Administration (OSHA). OSHA has promulgated Hazard Communication Standards[52] that require employers to assess hazards posed by the chemicals they make or import and provide hazard information on labels and in MSDSs. Employers and processors of chemicals that pose hazards must make the labels and MSDSs available in the work place and train their employees in safe handling procedures.

These standardized significant new uses do not adopt all of the OSHA requirements exactly, and a manufacturer, importer, or processor should not assume that they are complying with OSHA requirements by complying with SNUR requirements. For example, there is no TSCA requirement to reveal a trade secret chemical identity to a physician or nurse during a medical emergency,[53] yet OSHA does have that requirement.[54] The OSHA regulations also define "employer" radically differently than the TSCA regulations. Under the OSHA hazard communication standard, an "employer" is someone other than a government that has employees,[55] while the SNUR regulations define "employer" as a manufacturer, importer, processor, or user of a chemical substance, as discussed above.[56]

Each subsection of 40 C.F.R. § 721.72 specifies a different hazard communication method. As before, the following summaries of the standardized significant new uses relating to hazard communication are intended to give an overview of the significant new uses, but the language of the regulation should be consulted to answer specific questions about their interpretation.

§ 721.72: It is a significant new use to manufacture, import or process the substance unless each manufacturer, importer, processor, or user has a hazard communication program. Note that users do not need to file SNURs.

---

52. 29 C.F.R. § 1910.1200; additional background on the OSHA hazard communication standard is *available at* http://www.osha.gov/SLTC/hazardcommunications/.
53. 54 Fed. Reg. 31298, 31299 (July 27, 1989).
54. 29 C.F.R. § 1910.1020(f)(3).
55. 29 C.F.R. § 1910.2(d).
56. 40 C.F.R. § 721.3.

§ 721.72(a): It is a significant new use to manufacture, import, or process the substance unless each manufacturer, importer, processor or user has a *written* hazard communication program that describes how labels, MSDSs, and other warnings will be implemented in accordance with the applicable SNUR. The written program must be available to all employees, contractors and their representatives. An existing OSHA hazard communication program is sufficient if it meets all the requirements of this subsection. The program must include:

§ 721.72(a)(1): A list of all SNUR substances in the work area, which must be kept in the work area and use the same chemical name as the MSDS for that substance.

§ 721.72(a)(2): How the manufacturer, importer, processor, or user will inform employees of the chemical hazards involved in activities such as cleaning reactors and the substances that are in unlabeled pipes.

§ 721.72(a)(3): How the manufacturer, importer, processor, or user will inform contractors that the SNUR substance is in the work place, and if they are reasonably likely to be exposed to the substance they must be informed about the restrictions on significant new uses.

§ 721.72(b)(1): It is a significant new use to manufacture, import, or process the substance unless each manufacturer, importer, processor, or user ensures that each container is labeled.

§ 721.72(b)(1)(i): It is a significant new use to manufacture, import, or process the substance unless each manufacturer, importer, processor, or user ensures that each container label has at a minimum:

§ 721.72(b)(1)(i)(A): A statement of the health hazards posed by the SNUR substance and appropriate precautions. The precautions in the SNUR or identified by the manufacturer, importer, processor, or user must be set forth.

§ 721.72(b)(1)(i)(B): The common name of the substance.

§ 721.72(b)(1)(i)(C): A statement of the environmental hazards posed by the SNUR substance and appropriate precautions. The precautions in the SNUR or identified by the manufacturer, importer, processor, or user must be set forth.

§ 721.72(b)(1)(i)(D): A statement of the exposure pathways and the appropriate precautions. The precautions in the SNUR or identified by the manufacturer, importer, processor or user must be set forth.

§ 721.72(b)(1)(ii): A manufacturer, importer, processor, or user may use signs or other written materials such as placards or operating procedures instead of labels on stationary process containers. The written materials must identify the containers that hold the SNUR substance and convey the information that would be required of a label. The written materials must be in the work area during working hours. Use of these methods of communication will not cause the use to be a significant new use.

§ 721.72(b)(1)(iii): No labels are required for portable containers that are to be used immediately by the person who transfers the SNUR substance from a labeled container. Absence of a label on such a portable container will not cause the use to be a significant new use.

§ 721.72(b)(1)(iv): Manufacturers, importers, processors, and users may not remove labels on containers of the SNUR substance that they receive from other entities unless they immediately relabel the container with the required information. Removal of a label without immediately relabelling is a significant new use.

§ 721.72(b)(2): Manufacturers, importers, processors, and users must label containers of the SNUR substance that they distribute with at least the following information. Failure to so label is a significant new use.

§ 721.72(b)(2)(i)(A): A statement of the health hazards posed by the SNUR substance, the health precautions in the SNUR or identified by the manufacturer, importer, processor, or user, the common name of the substance, a statement of the environmental hazards posed by the SNUR substance, the environmental precautions in the SNUR or identified by the manufacturer, importer, processor, a statement of the exposure pathways and the exposure precautions in the SNUR or identified by the manufacturer, importer, processor, or user.

§ 721.72(b)(2)(i)(B): The name and address of the manufacturer or person who can give additional information concerning the hazards posed by the SNUR substance and appropriate emergency procedures.

§ 721.72(b)(2)(ii): The label cannot conflict with the label required by the Hazardous Materials Transportation Act[57] and implementing regulations.

57. 18 U.S.C § 1801.

§ 721.72(b)(3): The label or other communication must be legible and prominent or else the use will be a significant new use.

§ 721.72(b)(4): The label or other communication must be in English or else the use will be a significant new use, but the information may be repeated in other languages.

§ 721.72(b)(5): If the label or other notice is applied to a mixture containing two or more SNUR substances, or one SNUR substance together with another substance that requires a warning under the OSHA Hazard Communication Standard, then this subsection applies. The manufacturer, importer, processor, or user of such a mixture may set forth the most protective forms of control measures. If there is any variation from the control measures specified in the SNURs, the manufacturer, importer, processor, or user must ask the EPA for a determination of equivalency before stating those control measures on the label or other communication. The procedure for obtaining a determination of equivalency is set forth in 40 C.F.R. § 721.30.

§ 721.72(c)(1): It is a significant new use to manufacture, import or process the substance unless each manufacturer, importer, processor, or user obtains or prepares MSDSs for the SNUR substance.

§ 721.72(c)(2): It is a significant new use to manufacture, import or process the substance unless each manufacturer, importer, processor, or user obtains or prepares MSDSs for the SNUR substance containing at least the following information:

§ 721.72(c)(2)(i): The name used on the label; the chemical and common name if they are not confidential, and the generic chemical name if the specific chemical name is confidential.

§ 721.72(c)(2)(ii): Physical characteristics of the substance such as vapor pressure and flash point, that the manufacturer, importer, processor, or user knows.

§ 721.72(c)(2)(iii): Physical hazards of the substance including potential for fire, explosion, and reactivity, that the manufacturer, importer, processor, or user knows.

§ 721.72(c)(2)(iv): Potential human health and environmental hazards set out in the applicable SNUR.

§ 721.72(c)(2)(v): Signs and symptoms of exposure and medical conditions that are expected to be aggravated by exposure, that the manufacturer, importer, processor, or user knows.

§ 721.72(c)(2)(vi): The primary routes of exposure to the substance.

§ 721.72(c)(2)(vii): Precautions to control worker exposure and environmental release that are set out in the applicable SNUR, or alternative control measures approved by the EPA.[58]

§ 721.72(c)(2)(viii): Generally applicable precautions for safe handling and use of the substance, including hygiene, protections during equipment repair and maintenance, and spill and leak response, that the manufacturer, importer, processor or user knows.

§ 721.72(c)(2)(ix): Generally applicable control measures such as engineering controls, work practices, or personal protective equipment, that the manufacturer, importer, processor or user knows.

§ 721.72(c)(2)(x): Emergency first aid procedures, that the manufacturer, importer, processor, or user knows.

§ 721.72(c)(2)(xi): The date the MSDS was prepared or last revised.

§ 721.72(c)(2)(xii): The name, address, and telephone number of a person who can give hazard evaluation and emergency procedures for the substance.

§ 721.72(c)(3): If there is no information concerning one of the categories of information required to be on the MSDS, the MSDS must state that no relevant information was found, instead of leaving a blank space or omitting the category entirely.

§ 721.72(c)(4): The manufacturer, importer, processor or user may prepare one MSDS to cover multiple mixtures that have similar compositions.

§ 721.72(c)(5): If the manufacturer, importer, processor, or user learns significant new information on the hazards posed by the substance or protections from hazards posed by the substance, it must update the MSDS within three months. If the substance is not currently manufactured, imported, processed, or used by that person, it must update the MSDS before reintroducing the substance.

§ 721.72(c)(6): The manufacturer, importer, processor, or user must send the MSDS with the first shipment to any recipient, and again with or before the first shipment after the MSDS is revised.

---

58. Alternative control measures are permitted by 40 C.F.R § 721.30.

§ 721.72(c)(7): The manufacturer, importer, processor, or user must keep the MSDS in the workplace, accessible to employees when they are in their work areas.

§ 721.72(c)(8): The manufacturer, importer, processor, or user may keep the MSDS in any form, so long as it is in the workplace, and readily accessible to employees when they are in their work areas. The MSDS may cover groups of substances.

§ 721.72(c)(9): The MSDS must be in English but may be repeated in other languages.

§ 721.72(d): It is a significant new use to manufacture, import, or process the substance unless each manufacturer, importer, processor, or user provides information and training to its employees concerning the SNUR substance. The information and training must take place when each employee is first assigned to a work area that has the SNUR substance and whenever the SNUR substance is introduced into a work area for the first time.

§ 721.72(d)(1): It is a significant new use to manufacture, import, or process the substance unless each manufacturer, importer, processor, or user provides information and training to its employees concerning the SNUR substance. The information and training must take place when each employee is first assigned to a work area that has the SNUR substance and whenever the SNUR substance is introduced into a work area for the first time. The information must include:

§ 721.72(d)(1)(i): The hazard communication requirements for the SNUR substance.

§ 721.72(d)(1)(ii): The operations in the work area where the SNUR substance is present.

§ 721.72(d)(1)(iii): Where the written hazard communications program is kept and how to access it, including the list of SNUR substances and the MSDSs.

§ 721.72(d)(2): It is a significant new use to manufacture, import, or process the substance unless each manufacturer, importer, processor, or user provides information and training to its employees concerning the SNUR substance. The information and training must take place when each employee is first assigned to a work area that has the SNUR substance and whenever the SNUR substance is introduced into a work area for the first time. The training must include:

§ 721.72(d)(2)(i): Methods to detect the presence or release of the SNUR substance.

§ 721.72(d)(2)(ii): The potential human health and environmental hazards specified in the SNUR.

§ 721.72(d)(2)(iii): Steps employees can take to protect themselves and the environment from the SNUR substance, including procedures the manufacturer, importer, processor, or user has implemented to prevent exposure to the SNUR substance, and other measures required by the SNUR. If the EPA has approved alternative control measures those may be substituted.[59]

§ 721.72(d)(2)(iv): The requirements of the hazard communication program implemented by the manufacturer, importer, processor, or user, including an explanation of the labeling system and the MSDS and instruction on obtaining and using hazard information.

§ 721.72(e): If this subsection is cross-referenced in a SNUR, the SNUR will give a concentration, as in the SNUR for octanoic acid, hydrazide discussed earlier in this chapter. If the SNUR substance is present in the workplace only as a mixture, and its concentration does not exceed the concentration in the SNUR, there is no requirement to file a SNUN before using the substance. If the manufacturer, importer, processor, or user has reason to believe that the SNUR substance becomes more concentrated then this exemption does not apply.

§ 721.72(f): A manufacturer, importer, processor, or user of the substance does not need to implement a separate procedure to address the hazard communication provisions of the SNUR so long as they are fully addressed by programs that have already been implemented. This subsection is cross-referenced in virtually all SNURs that require a hazard communication program. EPA explained that this is intended to avoid unnecessary duplication of effort.[60]

§ 721.72(g): If this subsection is cross-referenced in a SNUR, a manufacturer, importer, processor, or user of the substance must include the specific statements and warnings described in the SNUR on each label and MSDS, or the manufacturer, importer, or processor will be engaging in a significant new use. The label and MSDS may include additional statements, but they cannot change the meaning of the specified statements. The standardized statements include

---

59. *Id.*

60. 54 Fed. Reg. 31298, 31302 (July 27, 1989).

human health warnings and precautions, and environmental warnings and precautions. SNURs often specify additional statements in the text of the SNUR.

§ 721.72(g)(1): This subsection lists the standardized human health hazard statements, which are.

§ 721.72(g)(1)(i): This substance may cause skin irritation.

§ 721.72(g)(1)(ii): This substance may cause respiratory complications.

§ 721.72(g)(1)(iii): This substance may cause central nervous system effects.

§ 721.72(g)(1)(iv): This substance may cause internal organ effects.

§ 721.72(g)(1)(v): This substance may cause birth defects.

§ 721.72(g)(1)(vi): This substance may cause reproductive effects.

§ 721.72(g)(1)(vii): This substance may cause cancer.

§ 721.72(g)(1)(viii): This substance may cause immune system effects.

§ 721.72(g)(1)(ix): This substance may cause developmental effects.

§ 721.72(g)(2): This subsection lists the standardized human health hazard precautionary statements which are below. The precautionary statements are:

§ 721.72(g)(2)(i): When using this substance avoid skin contact.

§ 721.72(g)(2)(ii): When using this substance avoid breathing substance.

§ 721.72(g)(2)(iii): When using this substance avoid ingestion.

§ 721.72(g)(2)(iv): When using this substance use respiratory protection.

§ 721.72(g)(2)(v): When using this substance use skin protection.

§ 721.72(g)(3): This subsection lists the standardized environmental hazard statements, which are:

§ 721.72(g)(3)(i): This substance may be toxic to fish.

§ 721.72(g)(3)(ii): This substance may be toxic to aquatic organisms.

§ 721.72(g)(4): This subsection lists the standardized environmental hazard precautionary statements. The precautionary statements are:

§ 721.72(g)(4)(i): Notice to users: disposal restrictions apply.

§ 721.72(g)(4)(ii): Notice to users: spill clean-up restrictions apply.

§ 721.72(g)(4)(iii): Notice to users: do not release to water.

§ 721.72(g)(5): If this subsection is cross-referenced in the SNUR, then each "human health or environmental hazard precautionary statement" must be followed by the words "See MSDS for details." Almost every SNUR that requires a precautionary statement also requires this statement. The wording of this subsection is ambiguous, and it is unclear whether the intent was to require these statements for "human health hazard statements" in subsection (g)(1), or "environmental hazard precautionary statements" in subsection (g)(3).

§ 721.72(h)(1): If this subsection is cross-referenced in the SNUR, then the specific statement identified in the subsections below must be included on labels for the SNUR substance, in addition to all other required statements. Additional statements may be included so long as they do not alter the meaning of the required statements. The statements called for in this subsection are classified as precautionary, human health hazard, human health precautionary, environmental hazard, and environmental hazard precautionary.

§ 721.72(h)(1)(i): This subsection lists the standardized precautionary statements. The precautionary statements are:

§ 721.72(h)(1)(i)(A): The health effects of this chemical substance have not been determined.

§ 721.72(h)(1)(i)(B): When using this substance, use skin protection.

§ 721.72(h)(1)(i)(C): Use respiratory protection when there is a reasonable likelihood of exposure in the work area from dust, mist, or smoke from spray application.

§ 721.72(h)(1)(i)(D): Chemicals similar in structure to this substance have been found to cause cancer in laboratory animals.

§ 721.72(h)(1)(ii): This subsection lists the standardized human health hazard statements. The statements are:

§ 721.72(h)(1)(ii)(A): This substance may cause skin irritation.

§ 721.72(h)(1)(ii)(B): This substance may cause respiratory complications.

§ 721.72(h)(1)(ii)(C): This substance may cause central nervous system effects.

§ 721.72(h)(1)(ii)(D): This substance may cause internal organ effects.

§ 721.72(h)(1)(ii)(E): This substance may cause birth defects.

§ 721.72(h)(1)(ii)(F): This substance may cause reproductive effects.

§ 721.72(h)(1)(ii)(G): This substance may cause cancer.

§ 721.72(h)(1)(ii)(H): This substance may cause immune system effects.

§ 721.72(h)(1)(ii)(I): This substance may cause developmental effects.

§ 721.72(h)(1)(iii): This subsection lists the standardized human health hazard precautionary statements. The statements are:

§ 721.72(h)(1)(iii)(A): When using this substance avoid skin contact.

§ 721.72(h)(1)(iii)(B): When using this substance avoid breathing substance.

§ 721.72(h)(1)(iii)(C): When using this substance avoid ingestion.

§ 721.72(h)(1)(iii)(D): When using this substance use respiratory protection.

§ 721.72(h)(1)(iii)(E): When using this substance use skin protection.

§ 721.72(h)(1)(iv): This subsection lists the standardized environmental hazard statements. The statements are:

§ 721.72(h)(1)(iv)(A): This substance may be toxic to fish.

§ 721.72(h)(1)(iv)(B): This substance may be toxic to aquatic organisms.

§ 721.72(h)(1)(v): This subsection lists the standardized environmental hazard precautionary statements. The statements are:

§ 721.72(h)(1)(v)(A): Notice to users: disposal restrictions apply.

§ 721.72(h)(1)(v)(B): Notice to users: spill clean-up restrictions apply.

§ 721.72(h)(1)(v)(C): Notice to users: do not release to water.

§ 721.72(h)(1)(vi): If this subsection is cross-referenced in a SNUR, it requires the human health and precautionary statements on labels to add "See MSDS for details." The wording of this subsection is ambiguous, and it is unclear whether the intent was to require these statements for "environmental hazard statements" in subsection (h)(1)(iv).

§ 721.72(h)(2): If this subsection is cross-referenced in the SNUR, then the specific statement identified in the subsections below must be included on MSDSs for the SNUR substance, in addition to all other required statements. Additional statements may be included so long as they do not alter the meaning of the required statements.

§ 721.72(h)(2)(i): This subsection lists the standardized precautionary statements. The precautionary statements are:

§ 721.72(h)(2)(i)(A): The health effects of this chemical substance have not been determined.

§ 721.72(h)(2)(i)(B): When using this substance, use skin protection.

§ 721.72(h)(2)(i)(C): Use respiratory protection when there is a reasonable likelihood of exposure in the work area from dust, mist, or smoke from spray application.

§ 721.72(h)(2)(i)(D): Chemicals similar in structure to this substance have been found to cause cancer in laboratory animals.

§ 721.72(h)(2)(ii): This subsection lists the standardized human health hazard statements. The statements are:

§ 721.72(h)(2)(ii)(A): This substance may cause skin irritation.

§ 721.72(h)(2)(ii)(B): This substance may cause respiratory complications.

§ 721.72(h)(2)(ii)(C): This substance may cause central nervous system effects.

§ 721.72(h)(2)(ii)(D): This substance may cause internal organ effects.

§ 721.72(h)(2)(ii)(E): This substance may cause birth defects.

§ 721.72(h)(2)(ii)(F): This substance may cause reproductive effects.

§ 721.72(h)(2)(ii)(G): This substance may cause cancer.

§ 721.72(h)(2)(ii)(H): This substance may cause immune system effects.

§ 721.72(h)(2)(ii)(I): This substance may cause developmental effects.

§ 721.72(h)(2)(iii): This subsection lists the standardized human health hazard precautionary statements. The statements are:

§ 721.72(h)(2)(iii)(A): When using this substance avoid skin contact.

§ 721.72(h)(2)(iii)(B): When using this substance avoid breathing substance.

§ 721.72(h)(2)(iii)(C): When using this substance avoid ingestion.

§ 721.72(h)(2)(iii)(D): When using this substance use respiratory protection.

§ 721.72(h)(2)(iii)(E): When using this substance use skin protection.

§ 721.72(h)(2)(iv): This subsection lists the standardized environmental hazard statements. The statements are:

§ 721.72(h)(2)(iv)(A): This substance may be toxic to fish.

§ 721.72(h)(2)(iv)(B): This substance may be toxic to aquatic organisms.

§ 721.72(h)(2)(v): This subsection lists the standardized environmental hazard precautionary statements. The statements are:

§ 721.72(h)(2)(v)(A): Notice to users: disposal restrictions apply.

§ 721.72(h)(2)(v)(B): Notice to users: spill clean-up restrictions apply.

§ 721.72(h)(2)(v)(C): Notice to users: do not release to water.

C. Significant New Uses Involving Industrial, Commercial, and Consumer Activities

There is an exemption from the SNUR rules for manufacturing solely for export.[61] This exemption makes interpreting SNURs that classify manufacturing methods as significant new uses very difficult to interpret if the SNUR material is manufactured for export only. Logically, if manufacturing a substance in an open container or without personal protective equipment is a significant new use, but the substance is manufactured for export only, then the SNUR rules should not apply. However, it is inconceivable that the

61. 40 C.F.R. § 721.45(g). *See also* the discussion of manufacturing for export only in Chapter 2, TSCA's Scope.

exemption for manufacturing for export only was intended to apply this broadly and defeat controls meant for protection of human health and the environment. There is one standardized significant new use for "[a]ny manner or method of manufacture (excluding import) of the substance associated with any use," and this is the only standardized significant new use that the EPA has specifically said is inapplicable when the substance is manufactured for export only.[62]

Many of the terms used in the industrial, commercial and consumer significant new uses are defined in the SNUR regulations,[63] and the defined terms are italicized in this discussion. The standardized significant new uses in this section of the regulations are:

§ 721.80(a): Use in *non-enclosed processes.* A non-enclosed process is defined as "any equipment system (such as an open-top reactor, storage tank, or mixing vessel) in which a chemical substance is manufactured, processed, or otherwise used where significant direct contact of the bulk chemical substance and the workplace air may occur."[64]

§ 721.80(b): Manufacture in *non-enclosed processes. See* § 721.80(a) above for the definition of "non-enclosed process."

§ 721.80(c): Processing in *non-enclosed processes. See* § 721.80(a) above for the definition of "non-enclosed process."

§ 721.80(d): Use beyond the *site* of manufacture or import. Site is defined as "a contiguous property unit. Property divided only by a public right-of-way is one site. There may be more than one manufacturing plant on a single site."[65]

§ 721.80(e): Processing beyond the *site* of manufacture or import. *See* § 721.80(d) above for the definition of "site."

§ 721.80(f): Any manufacturing of the substance in the United States, although importing is not a significant new use. When this subsection was originally proposed, EPA said it intended to use this standardized significant new use if the PMN were submitted by an importer, but manufacture in the United States would increase potential exposure and releases.[66]

§ 721.80(g): Use other than as an intermediate.

§ 721.80(h): Use other than as a *site-limited intermediate.* Site-limited intermediate is defined as "an intermediate manufactured, processed, and used only within a site and not distributed in

62. 54 Fed. Reg. 31298, 31302 (July 27, 1989).
63. The definitions peculiar to the SNUR regulations are in 40 C.F.R. § 721.3.
64. 40 C.F.R. § 721.3.
65. *Id.*
66. 52 Fed. Reg. 15594, 15607 (Apr. 29, 1987).

commerce other than as an impurity or for disposal. Imported intermediates cannot be 'site-limited.'"[67]

§ 721.80(i): Use as an intermediate if the concentration in a product intended for distribution exceeds the concentration specified in the SNUR for that substance.

§ 721.80(j): Use in any way that is not described in the PMN specified in the SNUR for that substance.

§ 721.80(k): Use in any way that is not described in the TSCA § 5(e) consent order specified in the SNUR for that substance.

§ 721.80(l): *Non-industrial use.* Non-industrial use is defined as "use other than at a facility where chemical substances or mixtures are manufactured, imported, or processed."[68]

§ 721.80(m): *Commercial use.* Commercial use is defined as "the use of a chemical substance or any mixture containing the chemical substance in a commercial enterprise providing saleable goods or a service to consumers (e.g., a commercial dry cleaning establishment or painting contractor)."[69] This is a very narrow definition of "commercial" because the Commerce Clause of the U.S. Constitution extends to many other activities that are deemed commercial.

§ 721.80(n): Non-commercial use.

§ 721.80(o): Use in a *consumer product.* A consumer product is defined as "a chemical substance that is directly, or as part of a mixture, sold or made available to consumers for their use in or around a permanent or temporary household or residence, in or around a school, or in recreation."[70]

§ 721.80(p): Manufacture plus import in total in a volume greater than the volume specified in the SNUR for that substance. Note that there is no limit on the number of companies that can take advantage of manufacturing the substance up to the volume limit. For example, if a SNUR says that manufacturing more than 10,000 kilograms is a significant new use, then each of ten (or more) companies can manufacture 9,999 kilograms without notifying the EPA by filing a SNUN. This type of SNUR, which sets volume limits, really does not limit the total amount of the SNUR substance distributed in commerce or into the environment, but only limits the amount of the substance that each manufacturer or importer can introduce into commerce

67. 40 C.F.R. § 721.3.
68. *Id.*
69. *Id.*
70. *Id.*

without submitting a SNUN. In contrast, the EPA will not grant a Low Volume Exemption if there is a possibility that the 10,000 kilogram per year threshold for a Low Volume Exemption will be exceeded if there are multiple exemption holders.[71]

§ 721.80(q): Manufacture plus import in total in a volume greater than the volume specified in the TSCA § 5(e) consent order for that substance. *See* the note above concerning the volume limits in § 721.80(p).

§ 721.80(r): Manufacture plus import in total in a volume greater than the volume specified in the SNUR for that substance, unless the manufacturer or importer submits results of health or environmental effects studies that are conducted in accordance with the SNUR for that substance. *See* the note above concerning the volume limits in § 721.80(p).

§ 721.80(s): Manufacture plus import in total in an annual volume greater than the volume specified in the SNUR for that substance. *See* the note above concerning the volume limits in § 721.80(p).

§ 721.80(t): Manufacture plus import in total in an annual volume greater than the volume specified in the TSCA § 5(e) consent order for that substance. *See* the note above concerning the volume limits in § 721.80(p).

§ 721.80(u): Manufacture plus import in total in an annual volume greater than the volume specified in the SNUR for that substance, unless the manufacturer or importer submits results of health or environmental effects studies that are conducted in accordance with the SNUR for that substance. *See* the note above concerning the volume limits in § 721.80(p).

§ 721.80(v): Use in the form of:
§ 721.80(v) (1) A powder.
§ 721.80(v) (2) A solid.
§ 721.80(v) (3) A liquid.
§ 721.80(v) (4) A gas.

§ 721.80(w) Any manner or method of manufacture of the substance in the following form associated with any use:
§ 721.80(w)(1) A powder.
§ 721.80(w)(2) A solid.
§ 721.80(w)(3) A liquid.
§ 721.80(w)(4) A gas.

---

71. *See* Chapter 5, PMN Exclusions and Exemptions.

§ 721.80(x) Any manner or method of processing of the substance in the following form associated with any use:
§ 721.80(x)(1) A powder.
§ 721.80(x)(2) A solid.
§ 721.80(x)(3) A liquid.
§ 721.80(x)(4) A gas.

§ 721.80(y) Use involving an application method that generates:
§ 721.80(y)(1) A vapor, mist, or aerosol.
§ 721.80(y)(2) A dust.

D. Significant New Uses Involving Disposal

The SNUR regulations list standardized significant new uses relating to disposal of SNUR substances. For three of the four categories of significant new uses in this section, if a method of disposal is cross-referenced, it is the *only* method of disposal that will *not* be a significant new use. All other methods of disposal will be significant new uses. These significant new uses do not authorize the forms of disposal specified if they conflict with any federal, state or local waste disposal requirements.

A special caveat is required for interpreting §§ 721.85(a) and 721.85(b). Both use tortured language to restrict disposal of process streams. When these rules were originally proposed, the proposed definition of "process stream" encompassed the stream from manufacturing and the stream from processing. The proposed definition was "all reasonably anticipated transfer, flow, or disposal of a chemical substance, regardless of physical state or concentration, through all intended operations of manufacturing or processing, including the cleaning of equipment."[72] Therefore, § 721.85(a), which addressed the process stream from manufacturing or use, would have created a significant new use for disposal of the stream from manufacturing or use. However, before the regulations were actually promulgated, the EPA changed the definition of "process stream" to exclude manufacturing, and added a new definition of "manufacturing stream" which excludes processing.[73] "Process stream" is now limited to "all reasonably anticipated transfer, flow, or disposal of a chemical substance, regardless of physical state or concentration, through all intended operations of processing, including the cleaning of equipment."[74] "Manufacturing stream" is defined as "all reasonably anticipated transfer, flow, or disposal of a chemical substance, regardless of physical

72. 52 Fed. Reg. 15594, 15617 (Apr. 29, 1987).
73. 54 Fed. Reg. 31298, 31302 (July 27, 1989).
74. 40 C.F.R. § 721.3.

state or concentration, through all intended operations of manufacture, including the cleaning of equipment."[75] The significant new uses in §§ 721.85(a) and 721.85(b) were not updated to differentiate between process streams and manufacturing streams when the definitions were changed. As a result, § 721.85(a) is ambiguous as written because there is no "process stream" associated with manufacturing a substance. It is prudent to interpret § 721.85(a) as it was originally intended, to apply to manufacturing streams, although in the context of an enforcement action it may be possible to argue that it does not provide notice of the intended significant new use.

§ 721.85(a) Disposal of a process stream associated with any use of the SNUR substance, or disposal of the process stream associated with any manner or method of manufacturing the SNUR substance, unless the disposal is by the listed method. *See* the discussion above concerning interpreting the term "process stream" in the context of this subsection. This section is ambiguous, but a reasonable interpretation is that it applies to disposal of a stream generated from manufacturing or use but not to disposal of a stream generated from processing the SNUR substance.

§ 721.85(a)(1) Incineration.
§ 721.85(a)(2) Landfilling.
§ 721.85(a)(3) Deep well injection.

§ 721.85(b) Disposal of a process stream associated with any use of the SNUR substance, or disposal of the process stream associated with any manner or method of processing the SNUR substance, unless the disposal is by the listed method. See the discussion above concerning interpreting the term "process stream" in the context of this subsection. This section is ambiguous, but a reasonable interpretation is that it applies to disposal of a stream generated from processing or use but not to disposal of a stream generated from manufacturing the SNUR substance.

§ 721.85(b)(1) Incineration.
§ 721.85(b)(2) Landfilling.
§ 721.85(b)(3) Deep well injection.

§ 721.85(c) Disposal of a use stream associated with any use of the SNUR substance, unless the disposal is by the listed method. "Use stream" is defined as "all reasonably anticipated transfer, flow, or disposal of a chemical substance, regardless of physical state or concentration, through all intended operations

75. *Id.*

of industrial, commercial, or consumer use."[76] "Use" is not defined. Note that this subsection does not apply to processing streams, manufacturing streams, processing or manufacturing.

§ 721.85(c)(1) Incineration.

§ 721.85(c)(2) Landfilling.

§ 721.85(c)(3) Deep well injection.

§ 721.85(d) If this subsection is cross-referenced in a SNUR, then all disposal of the SNUR substance is a significant new use, if the disposal is associated with any use of the substance, or any manufacture or processing of it.

E. Significant New Uses Involving Release to Water

Section 721.90 of the SNUR regulations lists the standardized significant new uses relating to release of SNUR substances to water. If a SNUR cross-references a subsection relating to release to water, it is a significant new use to engage in that activity.

§ 721.90(a) Any predictable or purposeful release of a manufacturing stream associated with any use of the substance is a significant new use if it is listed below and cross-referenced in a SNUR. "Manufacturing stream" is defined as "all reasonably anticipated transfer, flow, or disposal of a chemical substance, regardless of physical state or concentration, through all intended operations of manufacture, including the cleaning of equipment."[77] Note this subsection does not apply to processing.

§ 721.90(a)(1) Into the waters of the United States.

§ 721.90(a)(2) Into the waters of the United States, unless one of the following treatment technologies cross-referenced in the SNUR is implemented. If part of the treatment is performed by a publicly owned treatment works, the discharger can perform the other treatment steps.

§ 721.90(a)(2)(i) Chemical precipitation and settling.

§ 721.90(a)(2)(ii) Biological treatment (activated sludge or equivalent) plus clarification.

§ 721.90(a)(2)(iii) Steam stripping.

§ 721.90(a)(2)(iv) Resin or activated carbon adsorption.

§ 721.90(a)(2)(v) Chemical destruction or conversion.

§ 721.90(a)(2)(vi) Primary wastewater treatment.

---

76. *Id.*

77. *Id.*

§ 721.90(a)(3) Into the waters of the United States unless there is primary and secondary wastewater treatment, as defined in the regulations implementing the Clean Water Act.[78]

§ 721.90(a)(4) Into the waters of the United States if the following formula yields a estimate for surface water concentration in excess of the number specified in the SNUR:

$$\frac{\text{number of kilograms/day/site released}}{\text{receiving stream flow (million liters/day)}} \times 1000 = \text{N parts per billion}$$

§ 721.91 provides detailed instructions for carrying out this computation. A manufacturer may request permission from the EPA to use direct measurement or alternate calculations, but the EPA has ninety days to respond to a request.

§ 721.90(b) Any predictable or purposeful release of a process stream containing the SNUR substance associated with any use of the substance is a significant new use if it is listed below and cross-referenced in a SNUR. "Process stream" is defined as "all reasonably anticipated transfer, flow, or disposal of a chemical substance, regardless of physical state or concentration, through all intended operations of processing, including the cleaning of equipment."[79] Note that this subsection does not apply to manufacturing, and unlike the SNUR in the previous subsection of the regulations, this subsection categorizes uses as significant new uses only if the SNUR substance is part of the released stream.

§ 721.90(b)(1) into the waters of the United States.

§ 721.90(b)(2) Into the waters of the United States, unless one of the following treatment technologies cross-referenced in the SNUR is implemented. If part of the treatment is performed by a publicly owned treatment works, the discharger can perform the other treatment steps.

§ 721.90(b)(2)(i) Chemical precipitation and settling.

§ 721.90(b)(2)(ii) Biological treatment (activated sludge or equivalent) plus clarification.

§ 721.90(b)(2)(iii) Steam stripping.

§ 721.90(b)(2)(iv) Resin or activated carbon adsorption.

§ 721.90(b)(2)(v) Chemical destruction or conversion.

§ 721.90(b)(2)(vi) Primary wastewater treatment.

---

78. The Clean Water Act is 33 U.S.C. §1251 and the implementing regulation referred to is 40 C.F.R. Part 133.

79. 40 C.F.R. § 721.3.

§ 721.90(b)(3) Into the waters of the United States unless there is primary and secondary wastewater treatment, as defined in the regulations implementing the Clean Water Act.

§ 721.90(b)(4) Into the waters of the United States if the following formula yields a estimate for surface water concentration in excess of the number specified in the SNUR:

$$\frac{\text{number of kilograms/day/site released}}{\text{receiving stream flow (million liters/day)}} \times 1000 = \text{N parts per billion}$$

§ 721.91 provides detailed instructions for carrying out this computation. A manufacturer may request permission from the EPA to use direct measurement or alternate calculations, but the EPA has ninety days to respond to a request.

§ 721.90(c) Any predictable or purposeful release of a use stream containing the SNUR substance associated with any use of the substance is a significant new use if it is listed below and cross-referenced in a SNUR. "Use stream" is defined as "all reasonably anticipated transfer, flow, or disposal of a chemical substance, regardless of physical state or concentration, through all intended operations of industrial, commercial, or consumer use."[80] Note that this subsection does not apply to manufacturing or processing, and this subsection categorizes uses as significant new uses only if the SNUR substance is part of the released stream.

§ 721.90(c)(1) Into the waters of the United States.

§ 721.90(c)(2) Into the waters of the United States, unless one of the following treatment technologies cross-referenced in the SNUR is implemented. If part of the treatment is performed by a publicly owned treatment works, the discharger can perform the other treatment steps.

§ 721.90(c)(2)(i) Chemical precipitation and settling.

§ 721.90(c)(2)(ii) Biological treatment (activated sludge or equivalent) plus clarification.

§ 721.90(c)(2)(iii) Steam stripping.

§ 721.90(c)(2)(iv) Resin or activated carbon adsorption.

§ 721.90(c)(2)(v) Chemical destruction or conversion.

§ 721.90(c)(2)(vi) Primary wastewater treatment.

§ 721.90(c)(3) Into the waters of the United States unless there is primary and secondary wastewater treatment, as defined in the regulations implementing the Clean Water Act.

80. *Id.*

§ 721.90(c)(4) Into the waters of the United States if the following formula yields a estimate for surface water concentration in excess of the number specified in the SNUR:

$$\frac{\text{number of kilograms/day/site released}}{\text{receiving stream flow (million liters/day)}} \times 1000 = \text{N parts per billion}$$

§ 721.91 provides detailed instructions for carrying out this computation. A manufacturer may request permission from the EPA to use direct measurement or alternate calculations, but the EPA has ninety days to respond to a request.

IX. Alternative Controls

EPA has established a procedure to allow use of alternative control measures instead of some of the control measures specified in SNURS. This was necessary because in some instances a SNUR's reliance on respirators may conflict with the Occupational Safety and Health Administration's preference for engineering controls, which would be an alternative control measure.[81] If these alternative control measures are implemented the use will not be a significant new use. EPA will entertain applications from manufacturers, importers or processors who propose alternatives to measures to control worker exposure or environmental releases.[82] Applicants must submit a request to EPA for a determination of equivalency to:

Document Control Office (DCO) (7407M)
Office of Pollution Prevention and Toxics (OPPT)
Environmental Protection Agency
1200 Pennsylvania Ave., NW.
Washington, DC 20460–0001
ATTN: SNUR Equivalency Determination

The request for a determination of equivalency must include the submitter's name, the chemical identity of the SNUR substance, a citation to the SNUR in the Code of Federal Regulations, a detailed description of the planned use, specifications of the alternative worker exposure or environmental release control measure, an analysis justifying why the alternative provides substantially the same degree of protection as the control measure specified in the SNUR, and all previously unsubmitted test data on the SNUR

---

81. 53 Fed. Reg. 28354, 28356 (July 27, 1988).
82. 40 C.F.R. § 721.30.

substance that would be required for filing a new PMN.[83] The test data that is required for a PMN is discussed earlier in this book, and requires submitting all of the test data in the submitter's possession or control and all other data concerning the health and environmental effects of the substance that are known to or reasonably ascertainable by the submitter.[84]

EPA has proposed electronic filing regulations and if these go into effect then requests for determinations of equivalency filed after the effective date must be made using the ePMN software, and may be filed on paper, through CD, DVD, or EPA's Central Data Exchange (CDX) for one year after the effective date of the new rules, and thereafter must be submitted via CD, DVD, or CDX for the next year, and then only through CDX.[85]

The regulations require EPA to review requests for determinations of equivalency within forty five days, and mail determinations back to the submitter. The submitter can only begin to manufacture, import or process for a use involving the alternative control measures if the EPA determines that the alternative control measures provide substantially the same degree of protection as the SNUR controls. Any deviation from the terms of the EPA's approval will be a significant new use.

Several of the standardized significant new uses expressly contemplate alternative control measures, subject to approval by the EPA. For example, if a mixture has two or more SNUR substances in it, the label must include the most protective measures, but the label may include alternative control measures if the EPA has provided a determination of equivalency.[86]

Several SNURS also reference the procedure for a determination of equivalency. For example, the SNUR for 2-thiazolidinone[87] specifies types of respirators that must be used in the workplace, but adds that a new chemical exposure limit (NCEL) of 0.7 milligrams per cubic meter as an eight-hour time-weighted average may be used as an alternative if the manufacturer, importer, or processor submits an application for a determination of equivalency and it is approved by the EPA. This NCEL was approved for the original PMN submitter in the form of a consent order under TSCA § 5(e), but 5(e) consent orders are only binding on the signatory, and so the EPA used this process to make the NCEL binding on other entities.

83. 40 C.F.R. § 721.30(b).
84. *Id.*
85. 73 Fed. Reg. 78261, 78273 (Dec. 22, 2008).
86. 40 C.F.R. § 721.721.72(b)(5).
87. 40 C.F.R. § 721.10002.

X. Entities That Must File Significant New Use Notices—SNUNs

SNURs apply to every company or person that plans to manufacture, import, or process a chemical subject to a SNUR and engage in the significant new use themselves[88] or distribute the substance in commerce.[89]

Each manufacturer, importer, or processor must file its own SNUN, even if another company has filed one and the review period has elapsed. EPA will permit companies to file SNUNs jointly so that they can commence using the substance at the same time. For example, a manufacturer and several of its customers that process a SNUR substance may file one SNUR jointly. If the EPA changes a SNUR based on information it receives from a company that filed a SNUN, it may amend the SNUR so that other companies will not have to file a SNUN based on a use that the EPA determines not to pose an unreasonable risk.[90]

If a significant new use relates to import, the principal importer of a substance subject to a SNUR is required to file a SNUN.[91] The "principal importer" is defined as the "first importer who, knowing that a chemical substance will be imported for a significant new use rather than manufactured in the United States, specifies the chemical substance and the amount to be imported."[92] The definition adds that "[o]nly persons who are incorporated, licensed, or doing business in the United States may be principal importers."

The principal importer is the person who specifies the product and the amount to be imported, although the principal importer may not know the chemical identity of the product. If the foreign supplier does not reveal the identity of the substance to the importer, the foreign supplier can tell the EPA directly and provide information for a bona fide letter, and preserve its trade secrets. A principal importer must know that the product will be imported instead of produced domestically. If no one company meets all these criteria the importer should contact the EPA's Prenotice Coordinator to determine who should file the SNUN.[93]

It seems from the definition of "principal importer" that the principal importer must know that the substance will be used for a significant new use

88. 40 C.F.R. § 721.5(a)(1).
89. 40 C.F.R. § 721.5(a)(2).
90. http://www.epa.gov/opptintr/newchems/pubs/snun.htm.
91. 40 C.F.R. § 721.5(e).
92. 40 C.F.R. § 721.3.
93. 48 Fed. Reg. 21722, 21726–27 (May 13, 1983); this Federal Register notice promulgated the PMN rule, but its discussion of principal importers is made applicable to SNURs by 49 Fed. Reg. 35011, 35012 (Sept. 5, 1984).

before there is an obligation to file a SNUN. However, the preamble in the Federal Register does not discuss any such requirement,[94] and indeed such a requirement would be inconsistent with the obligations imposed on manufacturers and processors to determine whether their substances are subject to SNURs. Entities that meet all of the other elements of the definition of "principal importer" should take affirmative steps to determine if there is an applicable SNUR.

In some cases the manufacturer, importer, or processor will not use a SNUR substance for a significant new use, but will distribute the substance to another entity that will engage in the significant new use. For convenience, we will refer to such a manufacturer, importer, or processor as a "distributor" in this subchapter. Distributors are required to file SNUNs under some circumstances even though they are not themselves engaging in a significant new use. There is a presumption that a distributor intends the significant new use to take place even if it does not know what the recipients will do with a SNUR substance.[95] A distributor does not have to file a SNUN if it can overcome that presumption by proving that it has informed the recipient of the significant new uses and the Code of Federal Regulation section where the SNUR is located. Alternatively, if the distributor can document that the recipient knows what the significant new uses are and the Code of Federal Regulations citation for the SNUR, or that the recipient is not able to engage in a significant new use, then the distributor does not need to file a SNUN.[96] "[A]ny person who purchases or otherwise obtains a chemical substance directly from a person who manufactures, imports, or processes the substance" meets the definition of "recipient" in the SNUR regulations.[97]

A distributor cannot ignore clear evidence that a recipient is not complying with the SNUR even if the distributor can document that the recipient knew about the SNUR. The distributor has the burden of filing a SNUN if it "has knowledge" when it distributes the substance to a recipient that the recipient intends to engage in a significant new use without filing a SNUN.[98] A company has the requisite knowledge when an employee who, because of that person's position or responsibility in the company should know abut the SNUR, becomes aware that the recipient is engaging in the significant new use.[99] If it later learns that a recipient is using a SNUR substance for a significant new use and the recipient has not filed a SNUN, the distributor must

94. 49 Fed. Reg. 35011, 35012 (Sept. 5, 1984).
95. *Id.*
96. 40 C.F.R. § 721.5(a)(2).
97. 40 C.F.R. § 721.3.
98. 40 C.F.R. § 721.5(b).
99. 53 Fed. Reg. 28354, 28356 (July 27, 1988).

stop all shipments of the SNUR substance to that recipient and must file a SNUN itself unless it can document each of the following:[100]

- the distributor has notified the recipient and the EPA Office of Enforcement and Compliance Assurance that the recipient is engaging in a significant new use without filing a SNUN. The distributor must submit that notice within fifteen working days of the date it has knowledge of the violation;
- the recipient has responded within fifteen days of receiving the notice and provided a written assurance that the recipient is aware of the SNUR and will not engage in a significant new use of the SNUR chemical; and
- the distributor has given the EPA Office of Enforcement and Compliance Assurance a copy of the recipient's written assurance.

If the EPA does not agree with recipient's statement that it is not engaging in a significant new use, then the EPA can notify the distributor and the distributor must immediately stop all distribution to the recipient. Distribution can only resume once either the distributor or recipient files a SNUN and the ninety-day review period elapses.

If the distributor has knowledge that the recipient is engaging in a significant new use even after receiving a contrary statement of assurance from the recipient, then the distributor must immediately stop all distribution of the substance to the recipient. The distributor must also notify the EPA Office of Enforcement and Compliance Assurance immediately, and may not resume distribution to that recipient until the distributor or recipient files a SNUN and the ninety-day review period has elapsed, or the EPA notifies the distributor that it may resume distribution to that recipient.[101] The regulation is written broadly, and appears to require a distributor to immediately stop all shipments to a particular recipient even if the first written statement of assurance related to a different substance. Once a recipient supplies a false statement of assurance the distributor is not entitled to trust the recipient concerning any SNUR if it has knowledge that the recipient is engaging in a significant new use without filing a SNUN.

The EPA said that this process was designed to avoid business disruptions unless there was a violation of the SNUR rules. This should not provide any comfort to distributors because the EPA may take enforcement action directly against a recipient.[102] Distributors should avoid putting themselves in the position of having to report one of their customers to the EPA by making sure that such a drastic step is unnecessary.

A processor that can document that it does not know the identity of the chemicals it obtains and does not know that a SNUR is in effect cannot

100. 40 C.F.R. § 721.5(d).
101. *Id.*
102. 53 Fed. Reg. 28354, 28355 (July 27, 1988).

possibly comply with the SNUR and the regulations recognize that and excuse the recipient from the obligation to file a SNUN.[103] Manufacturers and importers cannot take advantage of this provision. Processors still need to take steps to attempt to get the necessary information because of the requirement to document their state of knowledge. An early Federal Register preamble suggests options for documentation, including letters from suppliers stating that the substance is not subject to a SNUR, EPA responses to bona fide letters, or analytical evidence proving that the substance cannot be a SNUR substance.[104]

XI. Exemptions from SNUR Requirements

Many of the exemptions from PMN requirements are applicable to SNURs, but because SNURs cover processors the SNUR rules are adapted to cover processing when required. A person who has received a test marketing exemption for a significant new use[105] or has been granted an exemption under TSCA § 5(h)(5)[106] is exempt from SNUR requirements. A person who manufactures, imports, or processes a SNUR substance solely for research and development[107] or as an impurity[108] or as a byproduct that is burned as a fuel, disposed of as waste, or from which other substances are extracted for commercial purposes[109] is exempt from SNUR requirements. An importer or processor who imports or processes the substance as part of an article is exempt from the SNUR requirements, but a manufacturer of an article is not.[110] A person who manufactures, imports, or processes a SNUR substance solely for export is exempt from filing a SNUN so long as the substance is labeled as

---

103. 40 C.F.R. § 721.5(c). This exception from the requirement to file a SNUN only applies to processors. Manufacturers and importers have an obligation to identify their chemicals and determine if SNURs apply.
104. 49 Fed. Reg. 35011, 35012 (Sept. 5, 1984). The language of the applicable regulation has been changed since the date of this Federal Register notice and as a result the EPA's statements in the preamble may not be binding on the EPA.
105. 40 C.F.R. § 721.45(a). For the test marketing exemption to apply to SNURs, a company that is subject to a SNUR must be able to file a test marketing exemption to avoid the restrictions in the SNUR. See the discussion *infra* concerning the application of the LVE, LoREX and polymer exemptions to SNURs.
106. This rarely used provision of the TSCA statute provides that the EPA may grant exemptions from the PMN and SNUN requirements for:

> any chemical substance (A) which exists temporarily as a result of a chemical reaction in the manufacturing or processing of a mixture or another chemical substance, and (B) to which there is no, and will not be, human or environmental exposure.

107. 40 C.F.R. § 721.45(b).
108. 40 C.F.R. § 721.45(d).
109. 40 C.F.R. § 721.45(e). These activities must be done by a public or private organization.
110. 40 C.F.R. § 721.45(f).

intended for export when it is distributed[111] and is not a substance that the EPA has found will present an unreasonable risk of injury by issuing a rule under TSCA § 6 or an order under TSCA § 5(f).

The SNUR rules also contain two unique exemptions peculiar to the nature of SNURs. The first exemption is necessary because of the statutory requirement that a significant new use must be "new." The EPA has interpreted this to mean that it must be new as of the date that the SNUR was first proposed. Otherwise, anyone could prevent a use from being "new" if they engaged in that use before the SNUR became effective, and then there would be no statutory basis for issuing a SNUR.[112] If a person wants to manufacture, import, or process a substance that is the subject of a proposed SNUR after it has been proposed but before the SNUR has become effective, that person can submit a SNUN. The EPA calls this an "advance compliance" exemption. The EPA will give that person written notice of compliance if the EPA cannot make a finding that the proposed use will present an unreasonable risk of injury to health or the environment, or if the EPA and the person enter into a consent order under TSCA § 5(e). The 5(e) consent order will be effective when the SNUR is effective.[113] The submitter does not need to wait for the ninety-day SNUR review period to elapse before manufacturing, importing, or processing the SNUR substance, but if the SNUR becomes effective before the EPA issues a notice of compliance then the submitter must stop its activities until the ninety-day review period elapses. Of course, there is no binding legal requirement to file a SNUN until the SNUR becomes effective, but the advantage of the advance compliance exemption is that once the SNUR is effective the submitter can continue to engage in its prior practice so long as the EPA has completed its review process.

The second unique exemption applies to people who are operating under the terms of a § 5(e) consent order.[114] Most § 5(e) consent orders specify that they terminate when a SNUR issues, but if there are inconsistent terms that survive the promulgation of a SNUR then any person who entered into the 5(e) consent order is exempt from SNUR compliance so long as that person is complying with the 5(e) consent order.[115]

---

111. 40 C.F.R. § 721.45(g); *see also* TSCA § 12 (a)(1)(b). Logically it is difficult to see why this should exempt manufacturers, processors and users from workplace protection and hazard communication requirements.
112. *See generally*, 53 Fed. Reg. 28354, 28356 (July 27, 1988); 55 Fed. Reg. 45994, 45995 (Oct. 31, 1990); *but see*, 69 Fed. Reg. 70404 (Dec. 6, 2004) where the EPA explained that all uses of the SNUR substance would be significant new uses because the only existing manufacturer was discontinuing manufacture of the substance, and therefore "new uses" had been engaged in prior to the SNUR proposal.
113. 40 C.F.R. § 721.45(h).
114. 40 C.F.R. § 721.45(i).
115. 53 Fed. Reg. 28354, 28357 (July 27, 1988).

Several of the exemptions from the PMN requirements do not apply on their face to SNURs because they state they are exemptions from "certain of the premanufacture notice requirements of section 5(a)(1)(A) of the Toxic Substances Control Act," and that is a reference to the premanufacture notification program only. The SNUR program is authorized in TSCA § 5(a)(1)(B). The exemptions that incorporate this reference to PMNs and not SNURs are the polymer exemption,[116] low volume exemption, LoREX,[117] and the instant photo and peel-apart film exemption.[118] The practical effect of not having these exemptions apply to the SNUR program is that companies cannot file for or rely on one of these exemptions to avoid the restrictions in a SNUR.

A SNUR should not issue for a use already exempted under one of these exemptions because the use would not be "new."

XII. R&D Exemption for SNURs

R&D substances are exempt from SNURs.[119] Even before the SNURs were amended to specifically include the R&D exemption, the EPA took the position that the R&D rule was applicable to anyone who manufactured, imported, or processed a substance for a significant new use.[120]

The R&D exemption from SNUR requirements is different from the PMN R&D exemption in several respects. The most significant difference is that SNURs apply to noncommercial research laboratories, which are otherwise exempt from the PMN requirements. The SNUR regulations do not have any counterpart to the PMN regulations at 40 C.F.R. § 720.30(i) which exempts noncommercial research conducted in laboratories by "academic, government, or independent not-for-profit research organizations (e.g., universities, colleges, teaching hospitals, and research institutes)."

While the EPA intended the two R&D exemptions to be substantively the same, it did make some changes to accommodate the differences between the PMN program and the SNUR program.[121] SNURs apply to processors as well as manufacturers and importer of substances, and so the SNUR R&D exemption also covers processing.

116. TSCA § 723.250(a).
117. TSCA § 723.50(a).
118. TSCA § 723.175(a).
119. 40 C.F.R. § 721.47(a)(1). The statutes provides in § 5(h)(3) that R&D substances are exempt from SNURs.
120. 51 Fed. Reg. 10596 (Apr. 22, 1986).
121. 53 Fed. Reg. 28354, 28356 (July 27, 1988).

An R&D substance that is the subject of a SNUR must be disposed of consistent with the SNUR; if the SNUR puts restrictions on disposal the R&D processor is not exempt from those restrictions.[122] Similarly, any further use of the R&D substance must be consistent with the SNUR restrictions.[123] For example, if the SNUR prohibits incorporating the R&D substance into an article unless the processor files a SNUN, then the processor cannot incorporate the substance into an article without violating the R&D exemption rules. As a result there is no blanket authorization to distribute surplus R&D material if it is an impurity or part of an article. The R&D regulations must be followed even if the purpose of the R&D is to evaluate the substance for its pesticidal properties.

All other requirements of the R&D exemption from the PMN program[124] apply to SNURs.

XIII. Filing a SNUN

Anyone who plans to manufacture, import, or process a substance for a significant new use subject to a SNUR must file a SNUN at least ninety days before the planned activity.[125] The fee for filing a SNUN is $2,500, except that businesses with less than $40 million in annual sales have a reduced fee of $100.[126] No manufacturing, importation, or processing of the substance for the significant new use can take place until the EPA has had ninety days to review the SNUN, or until any extensions or suspensions of the review period have elapsed.[127] SNUNs are filed on the PMN form and all the requirements and considerations applicable to PMNs apply to SNUNs including data submission requirements.[128] The EPA follows the same procedures for reviewing SNUNs as it does for PMNs.[129]

SNUNs should be submitted to:

U.S. Environmental Protection Agency
OPPT Document Control Office (7407M)
1200 Pennsylvania Ave., NW
Washington, DC 20460

122. 40 C.F.R. § 721.47(d)(1).
123. 40 C.F.R. § 721.47(d)(2).
124. *See* Chapter 4, Premanufacture Notifications.
125. 40 C.F.R. § 721.25(a).
126. Draft PMN Q&A, 1-37, question 108-6.
127. 40 C.F.R. § 721.25(d).
128. 40 C.F.R. § 721.25(a); 53 Fed. Reg. 28354, 28354 (July 27, 1988).
129. 40 C.F.R. § 721.25(c).

They should be accompanied by a cover letter giving the citation in the Code of Federal Regulations to the SNUR, and a description of the significant new use that the submitter intends to engage in.[130]

Two or more companies can file one SNUN together if they are both obligated to file a SNUN. All the companies that file the SNUN must sign the certification portion of the PMN form. Each remains individually responsible for searching for relevant information in its possession or control or reasonably ascertainable by it.[131]

During the ninety-day review period after a SNUN is filed, the EPA may take action to "prohibit or limit the manufacture, processing, distribution in commerce, use, or disposal" of the SNUN substance. If it does not take any action to restrict activities concerning the SNUN substance it should explain why in a notice published in the Federal Register,[132] although a search of the Federal Register did not reveal any such publications.

The EPA may recommend testing in a SNUR, but the recommended tests are not mandatory. The downside to deciding not to perform the recommended testing is that without test results the EPA is more likely to issue an order restricting use of the substance under TSCA § 5(e).[133]

A. Recordkeeping Requirements

All records in a SNUN must be retained for five years from the date of submission, according to the regulations.[134] As a practical matter, this is likely to be inadequate, and the complete SNUN file should be retained for five years after the last day on which the SNUR substance was used for a significant new use or distributed to others. The manufacturer, importer or processor has the burden of proving compliance with a SNUR, and should keep records of its compliance so it can defend an enforcement action. Since the statute of limitations for TSCA enforcement is five years,[135] it is important to maintain records for five years after the relevant activity has been discontinued.

Additional recordkeeping requirements may be imposed as part of a SNUR.[136] A standardized set of recordkeeping requirements for SNUR substances is set forth in the regulations.[137] The following standardized

130. http://www.epa.gov/opptintr/newchems/pubs/snun.htm.
131. 40 C.F.R. § 721.25(b).
132. TSCA § 5(g).
133. 63 Fed. Reg. 44562, 44572 (Aug. 20, 1998).
134. 40 C.F.R. § 721.40.
135. 3M Co. v. Browner, 17 F. 3d 1453 (D.C. Cir. 1994).
136. 40 C.F.R. § 721.100.
137. 40 C.F.R. § 721.125.

recordkeeping requirements only apply if they are cross-referenced in a SNUR for a particular chemical substance.[138]

§ 721.125(a) Records documenting the manufacturing and import volume and dates of manufacturing and import.

§ 721.125(b) Records documenting the volume of the substance purchased by processors, names and addresses of suppliers, and dates of purchase.

§ 721.125(c) Records documenting the names and addresses of all people or entities who receive the substance directly from the manufacturer, importer, or processor, the date of each sale or transfer and the quantity transferred on each date.

§ 721.125(d) Records documenting the establishment of a program for personal protective equipment under § 721.63.

§ 721.125(e) Records documenting the determination that chemical protective equipment is impervious to the SNUR substance, as required under § 721.63.

§ 721.125(f) Records documenting the establishment and implementation of a hazard communication program under § 721.72.

§ 721.125(g) Copies of labels described in § 721.72(b).

§ 721.125(h) Copies of MSDSs described in § 721.72(b).

§ 721.125(i) Records documenting compliance with applicable industrial, commercial and consumer use limitations under § 721.80.

§ 721.125(j) Records documenting compliance with disposal restrictions program under § 721.85. These records must include the method of disposal, location of disposal sites, dates of disposal, and volume disposed of. If the estimated disposal volume is not known, then alternative records must be kept that demonstrate a program to comply with the SNUR's disposal requirements.

§ 721.125(k) Records documenting establishment and implementation of procedures that ensure compliance with discharge to water limitations under § 721.90.

Entities that are complying with the requirements for avoiding a determination that their use is a significant new use should comply with these requirements to prove that they are not required to file a SNUN.

---

138. 54 Fed. Reg. 31298 (July 27, 1989).

XIV. Exporting a SNUR Substance

If a chemical substance is the subject of a SNUR or a proposed SNUR, then anyone who intends to export it must submit a notice of export under TSCA § 12(b).[139]

It is important to watch the Federal Register regularly to determine if any substance that will be exported is the subject of a proposed SNUR. It is not sufficient to check the list of SNURS in the Code of Federal Regulations, because that only lists SNURS that have been issued.

XV. Enforcement

Violation of a SNUR carries the same range of civil and criminal penalties as violation of a PMN. The EPA may seek an injunction or seize substances made in violation of a SNUR.[140]

Administrative penalties for violating a SNUR are assessed according to the Section 5 Enforcement Response Policy (§ 5 ERP).[141] Under the § 5 ERP, violations are categorized as chemical control, control-associated data-gathering, or hazard assessment violations. Violations are also categorized by their "circumstance," which is a measure of how likely the violation is to cause harm. Circumstance level 1 is the most likely to cause harm, and level 6 is the least likely to cause harm. Finally, the violation is categorized by "extent," which is a surrogate for the volume of a substance that was involved in the violation.[142]

Violation of the warning and supervision conditions for an R&D exemption is a chemical control violation[143] and penalties are assessed on a per-day basis[144] Violation of the recordkeeping condition for an R&D exemption is a control-associated data-gathering violation,[145] and penalties are assessed on a one-time basis.[146] Failure to file a SNUN is a hazard assessment violation.

---

139. 40 C.F.R. § 721.20. *See* the discussion of substances for export only, *supra*.
140. TSCA §§ 7, 17; 40 C.F.R. § 721.35.
141. Amended TSCA § 5 Enforcement Response Policy as amended and restated (June 8, 1989) and further amended in Memorandum from John J. Neylan, Director, Policy and Grants Division, Office of Compliance Monitoring, to Michael J. Walker, Enforcement Counsel, Toxics Litigation Division, (July 1, 1993) [hereinafter § 5 ERP], *available through* http://cfpub.epa.gov/compliance/resources/policies/civil/tsca/
142. *See* Chapter 14, Penalties and Enforcement.
143. § 5 ERP, 7.
144. *Id.* at 26.
145. *Id.* at 7.
146. *Id.* at 26.

Commercial use of a substance produced in violation of a SNUR is also a hazard assessment violation.[147] Failure to submit a SNUN for a significant new use is a circumstance level 1 violation if the substance was distributed to others, and is a circumstance level 2 violation if the substance was not distributed to others.[148] In both cases the penalties will be assessed per day of violation. Withholding information or submitting false information in a SNUN is also circumstance level 1, and is assessed per day of violation. Recordkeeping violations are level 4, provided that the missing records can be produced within five days of a request by EPA. Recordkeeping violations are level 3 if the records cannot be produced within five days of a request by EPA. In either case, they are assessed as one-day violations.[149] Commercial use violations may be assessed.[150]

The § 5 ERP gives an example of a penalty calculation for failure to file a SNUN:[151]

> A company produced a chemical substance regulated by a SNUR, for a significant new use as defined by the SNUR, without submitting a Significant New Use Notice to EPA. The substance was incorporated into a consumer use product. The company produced the chemical 9 times, with 3,000 pounds produced on each occasion. EPA discovered the violation. The company is charged with a failure to submit a Significant New Use Notice, level 1, major, per-day.
>
> 9 x $25,000 = $225,000

The maximum daily penalty was $25,000 when this example was written, but it is now $37,500 per day, and so the penalty for this example must be adjusted to account for the periodic increases in the maximum penalty.

XVI. Current Issues

EPA has begun to use SNURs to control the use and handling of nanomaterials. Based on the statements the EPA made in promulgating nanomaterial SNURs it appears likely that it will issue SNURs for many new nanomaterials based on their particle size alone. In November 2008 EPA issued a direct final SNUR covering two nanoparticles.[152] EPA also issued two direct final SNURs on carbon nanotubes but later withdrew them because it received a notice

147. *Id.* at 7.
148. *Id.* at 9.
149. *Id.* at 10.
150. *See* Chapter 14, Penalties and Enforcement.
151. § 5 ERP, Appendix 1, Example 5.
152. 73 Fed. Reg. 65743, 65751–52 (Nov. 5, 2008).

that adverse comments would be submitted.[153] EPA has since reproposed them.[154] Exactly how EPA would address the potential health risks posed by nanoparticles was the subject of intense speculation in the years leading up to these SNURs. SNURs are the logical means for controlling the risks that may be posed by nanomaterials in general, but the administrative burden of regulating nanomaterials chemical-by-chemical could be overwhelming and the EPA said it would not issue a SNUR that is generally applicable to all nanoparticles without regard to their chemical composition.

One of the two nanoparticles that was the subject of the November 2008 SNUR is a siloxane modified silica nanoparticle, and the other is a siloxane modified alumina nanoparticle. EPA explained in the SNUR that it was concerned about dermal and inhalation exposures for new uses that were not described in the PMNs filed for those substances. It suggested that a ninety-day inhalation toxicity test would help characterize the human health effects for each substance. The SNURs for these two substances say that it would be a significant new use to use either substance without specified personal protective equipment, for any use other than the uses specified in the PMNs for those substances, and to manufacture, process or use them in powder form. The preamble to the SNUR says that the PMNs do not claim confidentiality for use of these substances as additives, but the PMN for one of these substance clearly limits the kind of additive for which it was intended, but everything except the word "additive" is claimed as confidential.[155] Therefore, any other entity that intends to manufacture, import, or process any nanoparticles described by the generic names for these substances should submit a bona fide letter to determine their exact chemical compositions and the specifics of what uses are significant new uses.

The two proposed SNURs for nanotubes also said that it would be a significant new use to use them without appropriate personal protective equipment to protect workers from inhalation risks. These risks are posed without regard to the exact chemical composition of the nanomaterials, and therefore more SNURs will likely be issued for nanomaterials.

153. 74 Fed. Reg. 29982, 29991 (June 24, 2009); 74 Fed. Reg. 42177 (Aug. 21, 2009).

154. 74 Fed. Reg. 57430 (Nov. 6, 2009).

155. PMN P-05-673 is available in the docket for the SNUR, and through http://www.regulations.gov in Docket EPA–HQ–OPPT–2008–0251.

CHAPTER 13

Compliance Programs

I. The Landscape

In the last twenty-five years there has been a major shift toward greater accountability for corporations and their directors and officers for violations of law, whether in the areas of environment, antitrust, securities, or others. New theories of liability have been created, and prosecutors have received greater power to punish corporate offenders. Corporate officers and other employees can no longer expect only a small fine or probation for regulatory violations.

In addition to this increase in penalties to promote deterrence, the Government added to its crime fighting tool kit incentives to organizations to maintain internal mechanisms for preventing and detecting crime. The oldest of these programs was the Department of Defense Voluntary Disclosure Program, which was initiated in 1986.[1] It was not so much an amnesty or immunity program, but rather a means for defense contractors to bring to light potential civil or criminal fraud. Since that time there has been a proliferation of corporate compliance program models, both government and industry sponsored, all attempting to encourage corporations to police themselves. The Government, recognizing its limited resources to fight crime, has enlisted corporate America in this effort.[2]

In the environmental field, the United States Environmental Protection Agency (EPA) established its Incentives for Self-Policing: Discovery, Disclosure, Correction and Prevention of Violations (Audit Policy).[3] It permits complete mitigation of civil penalties if the violator complies with all of its requirements, one of which is discovery of the violation through either an audit or application of a compliance management system.

Many companies have responded to government incentives by establishing their own programs to manage compliance and bring potential violations to light. It is impractical to establish a different compliance program for each environmental law to which the company is subject. The task in establishing and maintaining a Toxic Substances Control Act (TSCA)[4] compliance program is to understand the various governmental and industry[5] sponsored

---

1. *See* Letter from William H. Taft, IV, Deputy Secretary of Defense, to defense contractors, outlining the elements of the program (July 24, 1986).
2. *See, e.g.*, U.S. Department of Health and Human Services, Office of Inspector General, Voluntary Disclosure Program Guidelines (June 9, 1995); U.S. Department of Defense, Office of Inspector General, Voluntary Disclosure Program (May 5, 1989).
3. 65 Fed. Reg. 19618 (Apr. 11, 2000) [hereinafter Audit Policy]. *See* Chapter 14, Penalties and Enforcement.
4. 15 U.S.C. §§ 2601–2695d.
5. Failure to incorporate and follow applicable industry practice or government regulatory standards weighs against a finding of an effective compliance program. *See* United States Sentencing Guidelines Manual, Appendix C, amendment 422, effective November 1, 1991, *available*

corporate compliance programs that might be applicable to an organization and to design a program so that it achieves the optimal benefits from these overlapping—yet, not quite the same—programs. In addition, the program as designed must fit the company's culture and business operations, and be flexible enough to accommodate other legal requirements applicable to the company.

Effective compliance standards and procedures are more than a general statement of the company's intention to follow the law and any adverse consequences to employees who violate the law. Establishing such standards and procedures requires an understanding of how the business operates, how the law works, and how each element of the particular law impacts a specific operation of the business. It is not enough to tell an export specialist that all exports must be made in compliance with TSCA. The export specialist must be told specifically what he or she must do to ensure that all imports are made in compliance with TSCA.

The most effective procedures are written with the active participation of the employees who will follow the procedures. A compliance person, who may believe that a certain method of operation is preferable when it is not practical, should not write such procedures in isolation from the employees who will operate under the procedures.

This chapter will discuss Government policy and guidance documents (policies) on compliance programs directly applicable to TSCA. To be able to seek maximum mitigation of penalties or leniency, a compliance program must meet the mandated elements of these policies.[6] This chapter will also discuss the general concept of management systems, an approach initially sponsored by nongovernmental organizations but now endorsed by the EPA.[7] It will then offer a practical approach to establishing a compliance program flexible enough to incorporate almost all the requirements applicable to most companies. While no one off-the-shelf system can work for all companies, the approach outlined can be applied universally, to companies big and

---

through http://www.ussc.gov, and Supplement to Appendix C, amendment 673, effective November 1, 2004 [hereinafter collectively Guidelines Manual], *available at* http://www.ussc.gov/2004guid/APPC-2004SUPP.pdf.

6. There are additional requirements imposed in these policies, which are beyond the scope of this chapter. Additional elements include requirements such as voluntary disclosure or full cooperation with government officials. Whether or not to comply with these additional requirements is the type of judgment which can only be made on a case-by-case basis, after consultation between management and legal counsel, and an analysis of all the consequences flowing from the particular situation.

7. EPA, Position Statement of Environmental Management Systems (May 15, 2002, reissued Dec. 13, 2005) [hereinafter EMS Statement], *available at* http://www.epa.gov/ems/position/position.htm. In the EMS Statement, EPA endorsed the use of Environmental Management Systems and promised to lead by example by developing and using EMSs in government facilities.

small, in industries simple and complex. The resulting integrated compliance management system will be as different from anyone else's as the company in which it resides is from other companies. Only compliance systems tailored to a particular company can be effective in that company.

II. Government Policies Encouraging Compliance Programs

Since the advent of the Department of Defense Voluntary Disclosure Policy noted above, the federal government has been actively pursuing different courses to motivate compliance. Some of the programs have been established by the various federal agencies to encourage violators of the laws that they administer to discover and disclose violations of those laws at the Agency level. Other policies deal with whether or not the government will criminally prosecute those companies that violate the law. And, yet others deal with rewarding companies for compliance efforts during the sentencing phase.

A. The Organizational Sentencing Guidelines

1. Legal Framework of the Organizational Sentencing Guidelines

The Organizational Sentencing Guidelines (OSG) were a result of the Sentencing Reform Act of 1984 (Reform Act),[8] which became effective on November 1, 1987.[9] One goal of the Reform Act was to create a uniform system of sentencing in federal courts by limiting the discretion previously enjoyed by the courts. By eliminating parole, it sought to ensure that defendants would serve most of any court imposed sentence. The Reform Act provided for the establishment of a permanent Sentencing Commission (USSC) and gave specific directives to the USSC as to the content of the guidelines envisioned by the Congress. The USSC established a range of factors that the court can consider in determining sentences and statutory maximums and minimums for sentences, by category of offense committed.

The USSC is an independent agency in the judicial branch of the United States Government. It promulgates sentencing guidelines and policy

8. Sentencing Reform Act of 1984, Title II of the Comprehensive Crime Control Act of 1984,18 U.S.C. § 3551and 28 U.S.C. § 991.

9. The Supreme Court upheld the establishment of the United States Sentencing Commission against claims that it violated the doctrine of separation of powers and excessively delegated Congress's legislative authority. Mistretta v. United States, 448 U.S. 361 (1989).

statements for federal courts,[10] periodically reviews and revises previously promulgated guidelines,[11] and submits guideline amendments to the Congress not later than the first day of May of each year.[12] The initial work of the USSC primarily dealt with offenses by individuals.[13]

On November 1, 1991, after having completed the initial guidelines for individuals, the USSC issued the initial OSG, which were later revised in 2004.[14] The OSG initially substantially reduced the wide discretion allowed judges when sentencing corporate wrongdoers. The OSG established a systematic scheme for sentencing, allowing the judge no discretion to sentence outside of the qualitative minimum and maximum range. In 2005, the Supreme Court ruled that the Sixth Amendment right to a jury trial required federal sentencing guidelines be advisory, not mandatory.[15] While many judges still adhere to the guidelines, "early indications suggest that judges are using their discretion to give longer white collar sentences.... But in some cases, judges have handed down much lower sentences than would have been required ...just a few years ago."[16] Since the guidelines are still effective in some fashion, it is helpful to understand how they operate. Sentences are computed based on culpability scores. One of the two criteria[17] the Court may use to reduce the culpability score of the defendant is the existence of an "effective program to prevent and detect violations of law."[18] The OSG make clear that failure to prevent or detect the violation, by itself, does not mean the program was not effective. The OSG are often cited as the reason companies must have compliance programs.

The USSC and its publications are a valuable source for developing some basic understanding of the OSG.[19] There are very few judicial opinions relating to the OSG. More than 90 percent of organizational cases settle because companies generally prefer to obtain certainty and closure rather than to risk the expense and uncertainty of continued litigation.[20] As one commentator noted, "Company counsel will search in vain for decided cases on this subject; thus far there are no reported cases interpreting what is meant

10. 28 U.S.C. § 994(a).
11. 28 U.S.C. § 994(o).
12. 28 U.S.C. § 994(p).
13. The Sentencing Guidelines for individuals were submitted to Congress in 1987 and became effective that year.
14. *See* Guidelines Manual.
15. United States v. Booker, 543 U.S. 220 (2005).
16. Amir Efrati, *Looser Rules on Sentencing Stir Concerns About Equity*, Wall St. J., Nov. 5, 2009.
17. A defendant may also get credit for one of the following in calculating the Culpability Score: self-reporting (minus five points), cooperation (minus two points), and acceptance of responsibility (minus one point). Guidelines Manual, § 8C2.5(g).
18. An effective program can result in a reduction of three points in the Culpability Score. Guidelines Manual, § 8C2.5(f).
19. *See* http://www.ussc.gov.
20. Paula DeSio, *Fundamentals of Organizational Compliance*, (April 2001).

by an 'effective' program."[21] Recognizing the lack of specific guidance for what constitutes an effective program, the USSC convened a high-level advisory group (the Group) to review the OSG after ten years in practice and asked the Group to put particular emphasis on the criteria for an effective compliance program.[22] In its testimony, the Group noted the need to make sure there were no more "paper programs"[23] and recommended that the structure of the guidelines be changed to move the requirements of a compliance program from an application note into a separate guideline of the OSG, which would give the program elements more visibility and allow for more specific commentary on the elements of such a program.[24] These changes were made effective on November 1, 2004.[25]

2. Elements of an Effective OSG Compliance Program[26]

(a). Standards and procedures to prevent and detect criminal conduct must be established. Standards include standards and internal controls that are "reasonably capable of reducing the likelihood of criminal conduct." While the notes to the OSG do not specify that the compliance standards and procedures must be in any particular format or in writing, the more complex the requirements, or the more requirements that govern any particular business process, the more likely those requirements will need to be in writing to be effective. In general, a larger organization will need to institute formal, written procedures and standards. In some organizations, even smaller ones, only what is written down and measured actually gets accomplished.[27] If operating procedures are contained in written documents, compliance procedures should be as well. The procedures should be in a writing that can be easily understood by those who must follow it. If employees do not speak English well, consideration should be given to translating procedures into a language spoken by company personnel.

Often companies have compliance programs that are law-specific (e.g., antitrust compliance, securities law compliance, customs law compliance).

---

21. Kirk S. Jordon and Joseph E. Murphy, *Compliance Programs: What the Government Really Wants*, 14 ACCA Docket, 10 (1996).
22. Presentation of the Ad Hoc Advisory Group on the Organizational Sentencing Guidelines, United States Sentencing Commission, 9 (Oct, 7, 2003) [hereinafter Ad Hoc OSG], *available at* http://www.ussc.gov/qfsearch/SearchServlet?&query=DeSio&bbindex=DocRoot&starthit=26&lang=&encoding=UTF8&url=http%3A%2F%2Fwww.ussc.gov%2Fpublicat%2Fcloning.PDF.
23. Ad Hoc OSG, 15.
24. *Id.* at 18–19.
25. Guidelines Manual.
26. *Id.* at § 8B2.1(b). The headings to subsections (a) through (g) are summaries of the guidelines. These topics originally appeared in § 8A1.2, Application Note 3(k), with a somewhat different emphasis, prior to the November, 2004 amendments.
27. Guidance Manual, § 8B2.1 Application Note 1.

In the environmental area, the compliance manuals tend to follow the architecture of the media-specific federal environmental laws: a section or manual on the Clean Air Act of 1970, a section or manual on the Federal Water Pollution Act of 1972, a section or manual on TSCA, etc. However, business operations are neither law-specific nor media-specific. One business operation may involve compliance with many different legal requirements under different laws. To be an effective procedure, the procedure must ensure that the person who is expected to follow the laws is given the tools to meet the legal requirements.

Procedures should also incorporate industry practices, and not only governmentally imposed requirements.[28] Failure to incorporate applicable industry practices can lead to a finding of an ineffective compliance program.[29]

Expert internal or external resources must be made available to employees to help make these determinations. The compliance program should contain an organizational chart, informing employees about who is responsible for each compliance task and to whom they can turn for guidance. Job descriptions should include compliance responsibilities.

(b). The highest level governing authority of the organization (generally the Board of Directors or its functional equivalent) must have oversight of the program. Specific high level individual(s) must be assigned overall responsibility for the program. Specific individual(s) must be delegated operational responsibility and given access to the governing authority as well as the high level person in charge, and must be given adequate resources and authority to implement the program.

The OSG define high-level personnel of the organization as "individuals who have substantial control over the organization or who have a substantial role in the making of policy.... includ[ing] a director; an executive officer; an individual in charge of a major business or functional unit...; and an individual with a substantial ownership interest."[30]

The goal of this criterion is to ensure that a top-level executive in the organization is held specifically accountable for this activity and that the Board, or a subcommittee of the Board, exercise supervision over the program. The Board, or its subcommittee, must receive at least an annual presentation on the implementation and effectiveness of the program.[31] It is axiomatic that unless management visibly supports a program, that program will wither on the vine. Employees can easily tell if management is truly behind the program, or is just paying lip service. Company senior executives need to

---

28. *Id.* at Application Note 2(A).
29. *Id.* at Application Note 2(B).
30. *Id.* at § 8A1.2, Application Note 3(b).
31. *Id.* at § 8B2.1, Application Note 3.

make the program their own, to participate in training programs, to refer to the program in presentations, and to generally be viewed as being committed.

The larger the organization, the more technical the requirements, the more likely it will be that the high-level executive responsible for compliance will delegate many of the operational functions to staff. The Compliance Officer is the person responsible for ensuring that a program appropriate to the organization is established and functions as intended. The Compliance Officer should have a direct line to the CEO and Board of Directors on these activities. The Compliance Officer is sometimes the General Counsel; sometimes the Compliance Officer is not in the office of the General Counsel and independently reports to the President or Chief Executive Officer.

(c). The organization should use reasonable efforts not to give authority to exercise a substantial measure of discretion on its behalf to personnel it knew, or should have known, have committed illegal activities or engaged in conduct inconsistent with a compliance and ethics program.

Obviously, employees suspected of engaging in illegal or improper activities should not be put in such positions, if such conduct is related to the "specific responsibilities the individual is ... to be assigned."[32]

The requirement of "due diligence" suggests that the company would be prudent to conduct pre-employment background investigations of all applicants, especially of those to whom it would assign compliance responsibilities. Background checks of applicants must be done in conformance with applicable federal and state laws, which impose certain limitations. One way to conduct these checks is to hire a responsible third party in this field.

(d). The organization must take reasonable steps to effectively communicate its standards and procedures to all employees and other agents, as appropriate, by conducting training programs and by disseminating information that explains in a practical manner what is required.

Procedures and manuals, however well written, that exist somewhere on a shelf or a Web site are not sufficient. The company must actively and routinely disseminate the compliance program, by using any combination of means that would be effective in the company's culture. Training programs come in a variety of media. Newsletters, periodic e-mails, posters, and seminars are common. Seminars can be given by in-house staff, by external experts, online, or by any combination of these. Sometimes it is most effective to send an individual to a specialized program by an outside provider, especially when a legal responsibility pertains to only one or a few employees. What is

32. *Id.* at Application Note 4. The concern here is that someone not be denied employment or promotion because of past activities in violation of other federal, state, or local laws, if such past activities are not relevant to the current position.

most important in training is that the program is tailored to the individual's responsibilities. Many training programs indiscriminately launched in companies require all employees to participate. In TSCA training, someone responsible for imports and exports is not likely to benefit from a long training on process changes; someone responsible for production is not likely to benefit from a long training on imports and exports. While short overviews of the entire statutory scheme might be generally helpful, too much detail in an area that is not job related can overload employees. Training that specifically tells people what they need to do, is repeated in operating procedures, and is reinforced on the job, is training that is likely to impact behavior.

Interesting videos and graphics keep people's attention. Case studies, requiring people to participate in providing solutions, tend to have better retention rates than lectures, which provide a summary of the law and the penalties associated with noncompliance.

Training programs should be done on a regular basis. They need not be long; they need not use the latest technology. They need only to be related to the work of the employee and repeated on a regular basis. In smaller companies, training programs can consist of informal staff meetings.[33] Ensure that all employees required to attend do so, take attendance, and maintain the attendance records.

Note that the program is not only to be designed for employees' use, but also for agents, as appropriate. The term "agent" is defined to include "any individual, including a director, an officer, an employee, or an independent contractor, authorized to act on behalf of the organization."[34] This means that the company's program must be designed in such a way as to ensure that third-party contractors performing activities with TSCA responsibilities are in fact capable of performing those activities in compliance with TSCA.

(e). The organization must take reasonable steps to achieve compliance with its program, including utilizing monitoring and auditing systems to detect criminal conduct, evaluating program effectiveness periodically, and having in place and publicizing a reporting system whereby employees and other agents can report or seek guidance about criminal conduct without fear of retribution.

Auditing and monitoring are ways of determining whether the program actually works in preventing and detecting violations. There are many different methods that can be used to do audits. TSCA audits can be done on a stand-alone basis, or as part of a broader facilities audit; on a regularly scheduled basis or randomly; or by internal or external resources. Audits should be

33. Guidance Manual, § 8B2.1 Application Note 2(C)(iii).

34. *Id.* at § 8A1.2, Application Note 3(d).

designed to focus on high-sensitivity areas in a way that minimizes the disruption to the operating unit or department being audited, while maximizing the reach of the auditors. Audits must not only find areas of noncompliance; they should have a follow-up system that ensures that the immediate issue is addressed and that the compliance system is reviewed and corrected as needed to prevent future noncompliances.

To evaluate a program's effectiveness, management should look at both noncompliances and near-misses. Too many near-misses will result in a noncompliance—it is just a matter of time. Near-misses can include calls to the hotline about particular conduct, even if the conduct was not technically a violation of a law or a standard. Program elements have to be continually assessed to optimize effectiveness.

Many companies have hotlines or help lines employees can call to report potential noncompliances. The nomenclature notwithstanding, either of these can be an effective vehicle to allow employees to report situations they believe may be violations of law or situations that make them uncomfortable. While employees should be given the option of making these calls anonymously, employers are better able to follow up and give feedback on calls when the identity of the caller is known. Often, the legal or human resources department monitors these calls in-house. There are also external services that can be retained to staff a company hotline.

Another technique sometimes also used in very large organizations is the ombudsman. The ombudsman is empowered to hear employee disclosures of suspected violations of law, ethics, or company policy, to investigate those disclosures, and to recommend remedial actions.

(f). The standards must be consistently enforced through appropriate incentives to promote compliance and appropriate disciplinary measures to deter engaging in criminal conduct or failing to take steps to prevent or to detect an offense.

To be effective, employees found to have violated the law must face disciplinary action. All employees must be treated consistently, which means that the level of the violation must dictate the disciplinary action. How to discipline an employee who is found to have knowingly violated the law is less of a challenge than dealing with an employee who made an error, or a situation where it is not clear where the problem resides. Interestingly, this element deals with discipline for an individual who failed to detect the violation, perhaps a manager who did not affectively supervise or did not make it clear to employees that compliance is an integral part of the job. This criterion also suggests that appropriate incentives to perform in accordance with the program should also be included, but gives no guidance as to what such incentives might be.

No action should be taken with respect to employee discipline or incentives without a clear understanding of the applicable employment laws.

(g). The organization must take reasonable corrective actions to address an offense that is detected and to prevent further similar offenses, including revising its compliance program. Responding appropriately to a violation may include making restitution for the violation, punishing the violator, and revising the compliance program itself to prevent any further such noncompliances. The first sub-element, of taking reasonable steps in response to a problem can only be determined on a case-by-case basis, depending on the offense in question. The last sub-element is often referred to as continuous improvement, and is one of the most important elements of management systems. While not a factor in whether a compliance program is effective in reventing and detecting violations of law, the failure to timely self-report an offense may jeopardize the ability of the organization to receive a three-point deduction from its culpability score when sentencing is being determined.[35]

3. Additional General Concepts Applicable to Effective Programs

The seven elements discussed above are the minimum requirements to prove that an organization has exercised due diligence to prevent and detect criminal conduct and has promoted an organizational culture that encourages ethical conduct and compliance with laws. The Guidelines contain one further general factor that should inform the design of all elements of the program, which is that the organization periodically conduct risk assessments as to the possibility of criminal conduct so as to optimize its ability to focus its resources where most needed.[36] This section on risk assessment responds to the mandate in the Sarbanes-Oxley Act of 2002[37] that required the USSC to review and amend the OSG to ensure that the guidelines "are sufficient to deter and punish organizational criminal misconduct."[38]

The commentary provides three areas that should be part of such an assessment:

- the nature and seriousness of any potential criminal conduct that could occur;

35. *Id.* at § 8C2.5(f).
36. *Id.* at § 8B2.1(c).
37. 15 U.S.C. 7201.
38. Guidance Manual, § 8B2.1 Application Note 6.

- the likelihood that criminal conduct might occur, given the nature of the organization's businesses; and
- the prior history of the organization with respect to compliance matters.

B. Department of Justice Voluntary Disclosure Policy for Environmental Violations

On July 19, 1991 the Department of Justice (DOJ) released a guidance memorandum entitled Factors in Decisions on Criminal Prosecutions for Environmental Violations in the Context of Significant Voluntary Compliance or Disclosure Efforts by the Violator (DOJ Disclosure Policy).[39] This Policy is not mandatory, and is intended only as internal guidance to DOJ attorneys. It explains the current general practice of the DOJ in making criminal prosecutorial and other decisions.[40] The DOJ Disclosure Policy assumes sufficient evidence of criminal conduct to prosecute effectively, but seeks to ensure that such prosecutions do not create a disincentive to or undermine the goal of encouraging critical self-auditing, self-policing, and voluntary disclosure. It is a leniency policy, which establishes factors the prosecutor can consider in deciding whether and as to what offence to charge a party in an environmental criminal case. Design of a TSCA compliance program must carefully address these factors, the successful adoption of which can result not in a reduced penalty, but in a decision not to prosecute in the first instance. Most of these factors are similar to those found in the OSG and the other governmental and industry programs discussed in this chapter.

The DOJ Disclosure Policy sets forth the factors[41] to be considered in determining whether the company had a comprehensive compliance program.[42]

1. "Was there a strong institutional policy to comply with all environmental requirements?"

---

39. U.S. Department of Justice, Factors in Decisions on Criminal Prosecutions for Environmental Violations in the Context of Significant Voluntary Compliance or Disclosure Efforts by the Violator (Jul. 19, 1991) [hereinafter DOJ Disclosure Policy], *available through* http://www.usdoj.gov/enrd/Current_topics.html.
40. The guidance makes clear that it is not intended to be relied upon to create a right or benefit, substantive or procedural, for any third party. It is provided to guide the effective use of limited enforcement resources. *Id.* at § IV.
41. Other elements to be considered are: whether the company voluntarily disclosed the violation, whether the company cooperated fully with the government, whether there was pervasive noncompliance (many or high level employees involved), whether there was an effective disciplinary system in place, and whether there were complete and prompt efforts to lessen any environmental harm that occurred. *Id.* at § IIA, B, & D.
42. The headings to Subsections 1 through 8 are taken directly from the DOJ Disclosure Policy.

This factor suggests that the company must be visibly on record as requiring compliance with all environmental requirements. A policy on environmental compliance should be easily accessible and known to all employees. The DOJ Disclosure Policy offers an example of a company that had a compliance program, but made no effort to disseminate its content, impress upon employees its significance, train its employees in its application, or oversee its implementation. The DOJ Disclosure Policy gives no credit for such a program, finding that the company did not demonstrate good faith in terms of its compliance efforts.[43]

2. "Had safeguards beyond those required by existing law been developed and implemented to prevent noncompliance from occurring?"

This factor makes it clear that establishing a program that looks to do the minimum possible will probably not be satisfactory. Requiring employees to follow the law is part of the cost of doing business and a company needs to show more to justify leniency.

3. "Were there regular procedures, including internal or external compliance and management audits, to evaluate, detect, prevent, and remedy circumstances like those that led to the noncompliance?"

This factor suggests implementing some of the elements often associated with environmental management systems, such as looking beyond the immediate issue to do root cause analysis to prevent the occurrence of noncompliances.

4. "Were there procedures and safeguards to ensure the integrity of any audit conducted?"

This factor resembles that of the OSG with respect to audits that are reasonably designed to detect criminal activity, and explicitly adds the extra notion of integrity of the audit. The DOJ Disclosure Policy offers an example of a company that conducts an audit only after an employee has threatened to report a violation to federal authorities. The audit is focused on the particular alleged violation, ignoring the possibility that the violation may be indicative of other unlawful activities. The company fails to bolster its compliance efforts even after discovery of the violation. The DOJ Disclosure Policy, considering all the factors in the hypothetical, finds that the only potentially positive action is the "so-called" audit, but discounts the audit because it was so narrowly focused and was undertaken only to head off a possible criminal investigation.[44]

5. "Did the audit evaluate all sources of pollution (*i.e.*, all media), including the possibility of cross-media transfers of pollutants?"

This factors adds an interesting element, that of looking across media specific laws and regulations to have a broader and arguably more effective audit.

43. DOJ Disclosure Policy, § III, Example 2.

44. *Id.* at § III, Example 2.

The concept of looking across specific laws and regulations to the underlying operations of the business is the preferable way to structure a compliance system. Because TSCA is not specific to any one environmental medium, a thorough and well-designed TSCA audit should look at all the environmental media. For example, the EPA can use TSCA to regulate the release to water of a specific chemical, or its presence as breathable particles in the workplace, or its method of disposal.[45] In those circumstances an audit should investigate all of the pertinent media.

6. "Were the auditor's recommendations implemented in a timely fashion?"

This factor seems to go somewhat further than that in the OSG, which speaks to remedying the violation at issue and taking steps to prevent its recurrence. An auditor's recommendation can go beyond responding to a discovered violation, and may instead deal with improvements to a compliance program before the occurrence of a violation, to prevent the violation from occurring in the first instance.

Timely correction of noncompliance is an important factor. In another example, the DOJ Disclosure Policy discusses a hypothetical Company G, which does an audit, finds a problem, and begins to gradually correct the violations. The DOJ Disclosure Policy reports that Company G could have received some consideration for its efforts, but its failure to disclose and the slowness of its remedial work militate against it receiving a substantial degree of leniency.[46]

7. "Were adequate resources committed to the auditing program and to implementing its recommendations?"

This factor is a direct statement of the need to commit adequate resources to both the original compliance plan and to continuously improving it.

8. "Was environmental compliance a standard by which employee and corporate departmental performance was judged?"

This factor makes clear that all relevant employees and departments need to be evaluated on environmental compliance. Unless people are held accountable for this metric, it is surely not going to get the same attention as other performance metrics.

C. Federal Prosecution of Corporations

Another source that needs to be considered in developing a compliance plan is that portion of the United States Attorneys' Manual (the Manual) dealing

45. The EPA can regulate handling of a chemical through promulgation of a Significant New Use Rule pursuant to TSCA § 5. *See* Chapter 12, Significant New Use Rules; 40 C.F.R. Part 721. The EPA can also regulate environmental releases and exposure through TSCA § 6. *See* Chapter 11, Bans and Restrictions.
46. DOJ Disclosure Policy, § III, Other examples, para. 5.

with the federal prosecution of corporations, and more particularly with implementing compliance programs.[47] That Manual is broader than the DOJ Voluntary Disclosure Policy discussed above in that it deals generally with charging corporations for any crimes, not only for environmental crimes. The chapter dealing with the federal prosecution of corporations had its genesis in a series of documents. The first was issued on June 16, 1999 by the Deputy Attorney General of the DOJ and is often referred to as the Holder Memo. [48] The Holder Memo was replaced by the Thompson Memo in 2003,[49] which considerably stiffened the guidelines to focus on corporate fraud prosecutions in the aftermath of Enron and related corporate failures. The third in the series, the McNulty Memo in 2006,[50] replaced the Thompson Memo, in response to concerns that the privilege waiver provisions in the Thompson Memo were eroding corporate clients' right to confidentiality and negatively affecting corporate compliance efforts. On August 28, 2008,[51] the DOJ announced that it was withdrawing the McNulty Memo, revising its guidelines in certain respects, and putting them into the Manual. The Manual is now the repository of the guidelines, as they now exist.

The Manual provides guidance as to what factors should generally inform a prosecutor in making the decision whether and with what offence to charge a party in a criminal case. During all of the iterations, the existence and effectiveness of a corporation's compliance plan remained one of the elements the DOJ considers in determining how to resolve a potential criminal case by means other than an indictment. The Manual makes clear that "[i]n making a decision to charge a corporation, the prosecutor generally has wide latitude in determining when, whom, how, and even whether to prosecute for violations of Federal criminal law."[52] Just as with the DOJ Voluntary Disclosure Policy, the Manual makes clear that the factors are only guidelines, are not determinative of outcome, and need not be considered in every case. Nevertheless, design of a TSCA compliance program should carefully address

---

47. The relevant portion of the United States Attorneys' Manual is *available at* http://www.usdoj.gov/usao/eousa/foia_reading_room/usam/title9/28mcrm.htm.
48. Memorandum by Eric H. Holder to All Component Heads and United States Attorneys, Bringing Criminal Charges Against Corporations, and attachment, "Federal Prosecution of Corporations" (June 16, 1999).
49. Memorandum by Larry D. Thompson to All Component Heads and United States Attorneys, Principles of Federal Prosecution of Business Organizations (Jan. 20, 2003).
50. Memorandum by Paul J. McNulty to All Component Heads and United States Attorneys, Principles of Federal Prosecution of Business Organizations (Dec. 12, 2006).
51. *See* DOJ Press Release, *available at* http://www.usdoj.gov/opa/pr/2008/August/08-odag-757.html.
52. U.S. Department of Justice, United States Attorneys' Manual, Title 9, Chapter 9-28.000, Principles of Federal Prosecution of Business Organizations, 4 [hereinafter Manual], *available at* http://www.usdoj.gov/usao/eousa/foia_reading_room/usam/title9/28mcrm.htm.

these factors, the successful adoption of which can result not in a reduced penalty, but in a decision not to prosecute in the first instance.

The Manual recognizes that no compliance program can ever prevent all criminal activity, and recommends two critical factors be considered in making an evaluation of the Compliance Program: Is the program "adequately designed for maximum effectiveness in preventing and detecting wrong doing" and does "management ...enforce the program or (does it) tacitly encourage or pressure employees to engage in misconduct?"[53]

While the Manual does not set out any precise formulations, it does list three fundamental questions that a prosecutor should ask: "Is the ... program well designed? Is the program being applied earnestly and in good faith? Does the ... program work?"[54] To answer these questions, the Manual suggests a series of considerations,[55] some of which will be familiar from the other programs discussed above:

- comprehensiveness of the compliance program;
- extent and pervasiveness of the criminal conduct;
- number and level of the corporate employees involved;
- seriousness, duration, and frequency of the misconduct;
- remedial actions taken by the corporation, including restitution, disciplinary action, and revisions to corporate compliance programs;
- promptness of any disclosure of wrongdoing to the government;
- adequacy of corporate governance mechanisms that could effectively detect and deter corporate wrongdoing;
- sufficiency of resources provided to audit, document, analyze, and utilize the results of the corporation's compliance efforts;
- adequacy of informing and convincing employees about the compliance program and the corporation's commitment to it; and
- adequacy of design of compliance program to detect the particular types of misconduct most likely to occur in a particular corporation's line of business.

How the factors in the DOJ Disclosure Policy or the Manual actually influence prosecutorial discretion is difficult to evaluate. Press releases of the Department of Justice or the local U.S. Attorney's office announcing decisions to prosecute big companies "rarely indicate, even tangentially, that the company's compliance program has in fact been evaluated and virtually never what the results of any such evaluation were."[56]

53. *Id.* at 15.
54. *Id.*
55. The list of considerations is taken directly from the Manual, 15–16.
56. William B. Lytton and Winthrop M. Swenson, "*The Effective Answer to Corporate Misconduct: Public Sector Encouragement of Private Sector Compliance Programs*," ACCA Docket 20, no. 10, 53 (2002).

D. EPA Audit Policy

On April 11, 2000 the EPA issued its Audit Policy.[57] The Audit Policy, which superseded an earlier 1995 Audit Policy,[58] made some minor revisions and clarifications, but maintained the basic structure and terms of the earlier document. In addition to providing for reductions of up to 100 percent of gravity based penalties[59] that represent that part of the potential fine in excess of the economic benefit to the violator for compliance with the Audit Policy, EPA will generally elect not to recommend criminal prosecution by DOJ for a disclosing violator that meets most of the conditions of the Policy. The ultimate prosecutorial decision resides with the DOJ, which will refer to the DOJ Voluntary Disclosure Policy and the Manual for guidance.[60] Because there are some deviations in these various documents, all must be considered in establishing the Company's TSCA compliance policy. The Audit Policy[61] has a nine-point list of criteria that the EPA will consider in mitigating penalties.[62] One of those nine points deals with compliance management systems, and contains a valuable discussion of the elements of interest to the EPA. It sets forth the following elements that should be in a Compliance Management System:[63]

- Compliance policies, standards and procedures that identify how employees and agents are to meet [legal] requirements...;
- Assignment of overall responsibility for over[sight]...and assignment of specific responsibility for assuring compliance at each facility...;
- Mechanisms for systematically assuring that compliance policies, standards and procedures are being carried out, including auditing ... periodic evaluation ... and a means ... to report violations ... without fear of retaliation;

---

57. 65 Fed. Reg. 19617 (Apr. 11, 2000).
58. 60 Fed. Reg. 66706 (Dec. 22, 1995).
59. For TSCA violations, gravity based penalties are the penalties that the EPA calculates applying a series of policies on penalties applicable to the various types of regulatory violations. These policies are the EPA's Enforcement Response Policies. For an in-depth discussion of the Enforcement Response Policies, *see* Chapter 14, Penalties and Enforcement.
60. 65 Fed. Reg. 19620 (Apr. 11, 2000).
61. In the original 1995 Audit Policy, EPA used the term "due diligence" instead of Compliance Management System. The change in nomenclature was less a substantive change than a change to be more in conformance with language used by industry and by regulators to refer to a systematic management plan or systematic efforts to achieve and maintain compliance. 65 Fed. Reg. 19620, 19625 (Apr. 11, 2000).
62. For a discussion of the application of the Audit Policy as a whole, *see* Chapter 14, Penalties and Enforcement.
63. The list of elements is taken directly from the Audit Policy, 65 Fed. Reg. 19618, 19625 (Apr. 11, 2000).

- Efforts to communicate effectively ... standards and procedures to all employees and other agents;
- Appropriate incentives to managers and employees ... including consistent enforcement through appropriate disciplinary mechanisms; and
- Procedures for the prompt and appropriate correction of any violations, and any necessary modifications to the ... compliance management system to prevent future violations.

Most EPA Regional offices apply these criteria strictly, and ask probing questions of companies seeking to take advantage of the Audit Policy benefits. In at least one instance the EPA seriously questioned whether a compliance management system could qualify because it did not require feedback to a person who initiated a request for a change to confirm that the change had been made properly. The requirement of a feedback loop is not explicitly stated in the Audit Policy, but is necessitated by it.[64]

In revising its earlier 1995 Audit Policy, in addition to using its experience over the past five years administering the initial program, EPA cooperated closely with the DOJ, the states, public interest groups, and the regulated community.[65] The consultations between groups on determining the content of compliance programs are useful to the regulated community in that the required elements of programs are becoming much more uniform. As the discussion has shown, the various governmental authorities have harmonized most of their requirements over time.

III. Management Systems

A variety of organizations around the world have devised model management systems.[66] Management systems are usually designed to be dedicated to environmental considerations, or to business processes of the company. The original management systems, even those dedicated to the environmental systems, were not compliance-focused. However, a TSCA compliance

64. *See, e.g.*, for precedents on feedback loops in TSCA guidance, the EPA § 8(e) Policy, which has the effect of saying that the EPA will not seek penalties from individuals if their employers have compliance procedures requiring feedback to anyone who proposes reporting "significant risk" information to the EPA. 63 Fed. Reg. 33129, 33137 (June 3, 2003).

65. 65 Fed. Reg. 19618 (Apr. 11, 2000).

66. In addition to ISO 14001, other well known environmental management systems include: Responsible Care©, adopted by the American Chemistry Council (formerly known as the Chemical Manufacturers Association) in 1988, Eco-Management Auditing Scheme (EMAS), adopted by the Council of the European Community in 1993, and Environmental Standard BS 7750, adopted by the United Kingdom in 1994.

program can be integrated easily into these systems, or any other business management system, giving it more relevance to the organization.

A. International Organization for Standardization

One of the earliest of the nongovernmental organizations to popularize the concept of management systems, and perhaps the largest such organization, is the International Organization for Standardization (ISO). Established in 1947, ISO develops common standards to promote the international exchange of goods and services and the worldwide development of intellectual, scientific, technological, and economic activity.[67] In 1987, ISO began publishing generic management system standards for use in any business or organization. These initial generic standards, known as the ISO 9000 series, were widely adopted by the marketplace, and adherence became a requirement of doing business in some sectors. Customers viewed use of the standard almost as a guaranty that suppliers certified to ISO 9000 would deliver the same product or service each and every time. ISO revised this first series of quality standards in 2000, with the publication of ISO 9001:2000. In the charter to that revision, ISO specifically stated that the 9001:2000 standard can be used "to assess the organization's ability to meet customer, *regulatory* and the organization's own requirements" (emphasis added).

The popularity of the original ISO 9000 series led to the development and publication in 1996 of ISO 14001, an environmental management system (EMS) standard[68] that can be used to minimize the effects of a company's activities on the environment. There is some movement among professionals in the international standards area toward a closer alignment of these two standards to create a more efficient and effective auditing program. ISO has said it has no plans to merge the two standards, but it does have an ongoing technical collaboration to achieve a high degree of compatibility between the two systems to make it easy to implement them side-by-side, or as an integrated management system. This collaboration addresses such issues as common terminology and structure of the standards.[69]

---

67. *See* http://www.iso.org/iso/home.htm for background information on ISO.
68. *See* Roger Strelow and Norman A. Varney Jr., *"A Radically Different Environmental Standard,"* ACCA Docket 14, no. 3, 12–26 (1996).
69. http://www.iso.org/iso/iso_catalogue/management_standards/iso_9000_iso_14000/compatibility.htm. ISO says that one of its biggest achievement in this regard is the development of a joint auditing standard for quality and environmental management systems.

Both of these ISO management systems use the Plan, Do, Check, Act methodology. This common methodology is sometimes referred to as a continuous improvement cycle. Its steps are:

- planning, which is the initial stage of the project, where requirements of various stakeholders are identified, and objectives and processes to meet those requirements are established;
- doing, which is the implementation of the procedures established in the planning stage;
- checking, which is monitoring or auditing, and requires reviewing the system designed to ensure that the system is accomplishing the stated objectives and that management is aware of any deviations and communicates the results of its reviews to employees; and
- acting, which is taking the corrective actions needed to eliminate the cause of nonconformances or violations in order to prevent reoccurrence.

B. EPA National Enforcement Investigations Center

The work of the EPA National Enforcement Investigations Center (NEIC), conducting civil multimedia compliance investigations, has increasingly involved identifying causes of noncompliance. NEIC determined that the root causes could, in many cases, be traced to inadequate EMSs. In response to this finding, NEIC developed key elements for a compliance-focused EMS (CFEMS) to be incorporated into settlement agreements with organizations that violated environmental regulations.[70] In reviewing the NEIC protocol, remember that this protocol was developed in response to violations, and may not be appropriate in all respects for all organizations. Nevertheless, this protocol may be imposed on any company if it does not develop a compliance program which is effective in the first instance. NEIC advises that the elements it developed should be incorporated into an overall EMS using the "plan, do, check, and act" model. "Consequently, the CFEMS…is intended to supplement, not replace, EMS models developed by voluntary consensus standards bodies, such as ISO 14001…."[71] The goals of the CFEMS are to improve the organization's compliance with environmental law and to

70. EPA, Office of Enforcement and Compliance Assurance, Office of Criminal Enforcement, Forensics and Training, Compliance-Focused Environmental Management System—Enforcement Agreement Guidance, EPA-330/9-97-002, as revised through June 2005 [hereinafter NEIC CFEMS] *available at* http://www.epa.gov/Compliance/resources/policies/NEIC/cfems_05.pdf.

71. *Id.* at 1.

improve the organization's environmental performance.[72] Not surprisingly, given that the goals of the CFEMS link compliance with good environmental citizenship, the key elements of the program blend both aspects into one coherent program.

The NEIC CFEMS describes 12 key elements:[73]

- statement of management's commitment to compliance with law, continuous improvement in environmental performance and adequate resourcing;
- description of the organization of the EMS, which job functions have which specific roles, responsibilities, and authorities, and how communications of issues and information flow throughout the organization;
- specification of accountabilities and responsibilities for managers, on-site service providers and contractors (personnel), and description of incentives to perform and consequences for failing to perform in accordance with EMS requirements;
- description of processes for identifying, interpreting and communicating requirements of CFEMS to personnel and of processes to ensure communication with regulatory agencies about requirements and compliance;
- identification of operations which need to be controlled for environmental protection and to meet legal requirements, including: measurements and monitoring, process for identifying where documented procedures are needed to prevent violations or pollutant releases and for developing the procedures, the self-assessment system for supervisors and trained staff, and the process of obtaining environmental inputs into relevant business decisions;
- description of requirements for a corrective action system: procedures for investigations, remedial actions, root cause analysis, tracking and effectiveness verification of corrective and preventive actions, and verification of such procedures as well as procedures for internal and external reporting of potential violations and release incidents;
- identification training requirements: who, how, and what, and the process of documenting training;
- description of how environmental planning will be integrated into organizational decision making and how written targets and objectives are established and tracked;

---

72. NEIC credits the following sources: EMS assessment protocols developed by Deloitte and Touche LLP for the Global Environmental Management Initiative (1992); ISO 14001 "EMS – Specification with guidance for use" (1996); National Sanitation Foundation EMS standards (NSF 110-1995); EPA memo entitled Final EPA Policy on the Inclusion of Environmental Auditing Provisions in Enforcement Settlements (Nov. 11, 1986); and the 1995 EPA Audit Policy." *Id.* at 2.
73. The elements are stated in the EPA NEIC CFEMS.

- identification of documentation: records supporting the EMS, who maintains them, how and where, protocols for responding to inquiries and document control procedures, and the data management systems for internal waste tracking, environmental data and hazardous waste determinations;
- description of the company's program for preventing, reducing, recycling, reusing and minimizing waste and emissions, including procedures to encourage material substitutions, as well as mechanisms for identifying candidate materials and for tracking progress;
- description of continuous improvement activities, including evaluations, external audits, management reviews and communications of the above; and
- description of outreach to the community on the environmental aspects of the company's operations and general environmental awareness.

IV. Company-specific Program Development

The major objective of having a compliance program is to ensure compliance with the law. It is also good business, because complying with the law allows the company to stay in business and to operate as a good corporate citizen. The government provides ample disincentives to violating the law, including civil and criminal penalties. Government incentives for implementing an EMS are helpful to companies who inadvertently get into trouble and should certainly be considered in designing a TSCA compliance program.

A. Status Quo Assessment

A thorough assessment of the company should be undertaken before designing a TSCA compliance program to determine the most effective structure. That assessment includes determining what programs are in existence for the company, the details of the company's work flow, and how TSCA may be relevant to the work flow and job functions at the company. As mentioned above, there is no pre-packaged EMS that will apply to each company because each company will have its own unique businesses and cultures.

1. Overall Assessment

The first series of questions to ask are about the narrow specifics of what compliance or compliance-like programs already exist, including:

- Does the company already have an existing compliance program or programs for TSCA or other legal requirements?

- What is the scope of the existing program—TSCA compliance, environmental law compliance, or law compliance? Note that compliance programs developed for other purposes, such as human resources and tax accounting, may have valuable statements concerning an overarching policy of compliance with laws.
- What are the elements of the programs already in place? Do employees know about the programs?
- Does the company have a management system in place?
- Do employees believe that the program is "real," or that it is just a paper program with no teeth?

If there is any uncertainty about the fact or breadth of an existing program, a short survey of all, or a randomly chosen group of, employees, on-site service providers, and contractors may provide some relevant and useful information. The survey can also be used to help management understand if the existing program is a dynamic one that has successfully survived mergers, acquisitions, divestitures, and reductions in force.

The next series of inquiries should be directed to the company's areas of business and operations:

- Where does the company operate? Domestically or internationally?
- Does the company operate in heavily regulated business areas?
- Does the company manufacture, formulate, or use chemicals?
- Has the Company, or any predecessors, been investigated for violations of law?
- Has the industry in which the company operates been investigated for violations of law on a somewhat regular basis?
- Has the company recently acquired another company, in the same or different business areas?
- Is environmental compliance a critical part of the company's compliance picture?

The key job here is to understand what other laws apply to the company and which of those laws, based on the company's operations, could create the largest risk in the event of noncompliance. While this book deals only with TSCA compliance, understanding the full scope of these other issues is important in determining how best to position and structure a TSCA compliance program.

The last general series of inquiries is about the culture of the company. There is no one factor more important in designing a TSCA compliance program than having a good understanding of the company's culture:

- How do things generally get done in the company?
- How are resources allocated?

- Is the company systematic in its approach or ad hoc?
- Are work processes documented or more seat of the pants?
- Is root cause analysis used to solve business problems, or is each problem dealt with independently?
- Is the company technology savvy or paper based?
- Is the company proactive or reactive?
- Is the culture one of teams or individuals? Volunteers? Or "it's not in my job description?"
- Is the company hierarchical or collegial?
- Is it managed domestically or from outside the United States?

All of these questions, and more, need to be addressed before beginning to design or improve a TSCA compliance program. While some cultures are more amenable to compliance programs than others, the task is to design the program to maximize its effectiveness in the culture that exists. Culture change is another topic that takes lots of time and effort. It is always best to start by recognizing what exists.

2. TSCA Requirements Matrix by Function

Once an analysis of the situation in the company has been completed, from an overall compliance, operations, and culture perspective, the specific TSCA requirements that impact the company's work need to be identified. TSCA is unique among environmental statutes in that it is neither media nor operations specific. TSCA regulations can span an entire company, starting with research and development, through manufacturing, formulation, procurement, importing, exporting, sales, and disposal. No other environmental statute has so broad a range. This broad range makes compliance with TSCA more of a challenge. Many functions across a company need to be involved in complying with the myriad regulations and guidances issued under the law.

The table below summarizes the TSCA requirements that must be considered and what functions in the organization are most likely to be involved in ensuring TSCA compliance by specific requirement. Some functions are specifically impacted in complying with the law, such as imports or exports. Other functions, such as information technology, should be thought of more as important participants in achieving compliance. They can enable the impacted function to get it right or to get it wrong. All of these functions need to be involved in the creation of the TSCA compliance program, or in integrating TSCA compliance into other existing programs. Every company will deal with these functions differently, whether in-house or using external vendors.

TSCA Requirements Matrix by Function

	Company Functions								
TSCA $ Requirement	*R&D*	*Regulatory*	*Sales Mkting*	*Production*	*Customer Service*	*Import Export*	*Shipping*	*Legal **	*IT*
4: Testing existing chemicals that may present risks	✓	✓							
5: PMNs	✓	✓		✓					
5: New chemicals	✓	✓		✓					
5(a): SNUR	✓	✓	✓	✓	✓	✓	✓		✓
5(e)e: Consent decree	✓	✓	✓	✓	✓	✓	✓	✓	✓
5(h): PMN exceptions		✓		✓					
6: Reg of existing chemicals		✓	✓				✓		✓
6(a): PMN chemicals	✓	✓	✓	✓					
6(e): PCBs		✓							
8(a): PAIR		✓							
8(b): Inventory	✓	✓		✓					
8(c): SigAdverse Reactions		✓	✓	✓	✓		✓	✓	

	Company Functions								
TSCA § Requirement	*R&D*	*Regulatory*	*Sales Mkting*	*Production*	*Customer Service*	*Import Export*	*Shipping*	*Legal**	*IT*
8(d): Studies		✓							
8(e): Substantial Risk		✓	✓	✓					
12(b): Export notification		✓	✓			✓	✓		✓
13: CBI Designation		✓						✓	
21: Citizens' Petitions				✓				✓	
27: Test Methods		✓							
Title II: Asbestos		✓							
Title III: Radon		✓							
Title IV: Lead		✓							

* Because the authors are lawyers, we exercised restraint in listing the topics in which lawyers should be involved, but fundamentally believe that counsel can contribute significantly to each of the elements of a compliance program.

B. Compliance Program Implementation

Once the assessments are made as to what is required, what the Company has and what the Company needs, the next questions are whether to integrate TSCA compliance with other compliance programs, whether to integrate compliance into a management system, and if so, which management system to use. The authors propose establishing a fully integrated system so that compliance is indistinguishable from the operations of the business. Such a program will be more robust and use fewer resources than a traditional stand-alone compliance program.[74] The discussion in this section uses a process that could achieve a fully integrated compliance and management system, but could be used more selectively to achieve basic compliance. The decision as to how to go forward is left with management and those designing and implementing the system. How much emphasis any company should put on the elements described below is a function of the company culture and the particular situation of the company. Achieving effectiveness requires more than lockstep adherence to a program. In the final analysis, achieving compliance is part of the culture and ethics of the organization. The structure of the program is an important facilitation device.

1. Management Support

Perhaps the most important element of any program is ensuring management support. All of the government and industry programs noted above talk to the need for top-level or executive commitment to compliance. Without visible management support, it is virtually impossible to have a robust compliance program.[75] Anyone who has ever worked in a company understands the importance of obtaining management support for any initiative or program. Without such support, implementing and maintaining the program will be a task like that of Sisyphus, pushing a big boulder up a steep hill. The work of getting and staying there may be so substantial as to erode any possibility of effectiveness.

Selling compliance is not much different than selling a product or a service. How to sell a program depends on the style of the salesperson, the culture

---

74. For a discussion by the authors on the merits of integrating environmental, health and safety compliance into the operations of the business, using ISO 9001:2000 as the management system into which to integrate, *see* Jean Warshaw and Miriam V. Gold, *Bringing Down the Green Wall: Integrating EHS Compliance into the Business*, ACCA Docket 20, no. 4, 24–40 (2002).

75. When one of the authors, Miriam V. Gold, was teaching law students about compliance programs, she went so far as to recommend to the class of aspiring lawyers that they should have a clear understanding about their prospective employer's commitment to this area before accepting a position to avoid signing up for what could be a career-ending opportunity.

of the organization, and the way different audiences view the issues. The key is flexibility. The marketing has to be done in a way to ensure the message will be heard and understood. Selling to management is different than selling to rank-and-file employees. The first sale is usually to management. Depending on what resonates most in the management culture, the program can be sold either through its benefits, through the potential costs of not having a program, the personal liabilities attendant on violations, or any combination.

Perhaps most importantly, a robust compliance program helps to institutionalize integrity. There is tremendous psychic value in doing the right thing. Especially in this time of corporate implosions due to integrity lapses, management is more likely to be attuned to the need to reinforce the notion of doing the right thing. Shareholders, employees, customers—likely all stakeholders—would want to be associated with a company which has as part of its fabric good governance principles, part of which includes compliance. Good compliance systems help to enhance and preserve corporate reputation, something that is now viewed as a prerequisite to prosperity.

If the company or industry has been involved in any government actions or private litigation involving allegations of wrongdoing, management would understand the benefits of avoiding the costs, both in expenses and in management time, dealing with those types of situations. The savings from these types of activities could easily fund a top-level program.[76] The subject matter of the wrongdoing may vary, but the process of dealing with a noncompliance issue cuts across the substantive issues.

What is sometimes not as well understood is how a compliance program can help to leverage competitive advantage. Ensuring compliance requires a sophisticated understanding of business work processes. Reviewing those processes from a compliance perspective can result in more efficient and more productive processes, streamlining how work moves along in the organization. Understanding how products move from customer order to export shipment of the goods is necessary to ensure compliance with the export provisions of TSCA. Regulations are best met by complying with standard operating procedures, decreasing the variability of the work. Trends discovered in reviews of compliance systems, especially those with a management system focus, can be of great help in identifying external forces that impact the services or products of the business, or those of the competition, allowing the company to have first mover advantage.

---

76. For an example of how significant penalties can be in high profile matters, DuPont recently agreed to settle alleged violations of the substantial risk reporting requirements of TSCA § 8 by paying a penalty of $10,250,000 to the EPA and performing two environmentally beneficial supplemental environmental projects estimated to cost a total of $6,250,000. This was a controversial enforcement proceeding and many industry members contended that the EPA had applied its guidances inconsistently, but it remains a vivid example of the costs of involvement in an enforcement proceeding. *See* Chapter 7, Reporting and Recordkeeping.

The internal assessments and external audits that are part of all management programs allow executives an up-front view of how an organization is running, and an opportunity to control critical issues. In most organizations, potential issues do not percolate up to management until the issues have moved further along, limiting the ability of management to deal with them early and easily. Management reviews, which take place on a regular schedule, avoid the tension between the need to point out a developing issue and the desire to assume the issue will self-resolve.

As mentioned earlier, compliance can be easily folded into other existing or developing programs, eliminating some of the cost and efforts of a duplicate program. Whether a company uses ISO or is trying to achieve Six Sigma,[77] compliance can be slotted right in, giving even more support to the company's activities. If the company later shifts its initiatives, the compliance program will just have to move along in the same direction. Compliance programs must be dynamic anyway.

Good domestic compliance programs help in laying the groundwork for a company to globalize. Since all countries have somewhat different legal requirements, putting in place and using a robust system on a domestic level is a prerequisite of getting it right when the company expands to a different legal and cultural scheme. TSCA has foreign equivalents. Most share some common goals, but operate in different ways. Knowing how to deal with TSCA controls certainly is an asset in dealing with the controls of product regulatory schemes of other countries.

The flip side of the benefits that accrue to companies with robust compliance programs is the costs of not having one. One big concern is the "big case." Penalties for TSCA violations can be quite large.[78] Penalties do not only impose monetary obligations on corporations, they can include individual liability[79] and jail terms. With the renewed emphasis on management accountability as a result of the recent corporate scandals, it appears likely that the government will renew its determination to go up the corporate ladder to find those responsible for the actions.[80] A picture of the "perp walk" in practice is worth a thousand words.

---

77. Much has been written about Six Sigma implementation at Allied Signal and General Electric Corporation. General Electric Corporation explains Six Sigma in basic terms on its Web site at http://www.ge.com/en/company/companyinfo/quality/whatis.htm. Companies often go through different initiatives such as the "quality process" touted by Malcolm Baldridge. Implementing a compliance system in connection with such initiatives is one way to integrate compliance at very little marginal cost.
78. For a more complete discussion of penalties, *see* Chapter 14, Penalties and Enforcement.
79. While many companies indemnify employees for misconduct arising from mere negligence, most companies are unlikely to indemnify an employee for allegations of criminal wrongdoing and may even be prohibited from doing so under state law.
80. For a discussion of theories of corporate liability, *see* Chapter 14, Penalties and Enforcement.

A perception of impropriety is enough by itself to result in negative publicity and trial by the press. No executive wants to be involved in a media circus. Typically, vindications of wrongdoers appear buried somewhere in the news, appearing long after the reader has lost all interest in the problem. Careers can be seriously adversely impacted, even by association. In addition, there is always the fear of being left behind. If other companies, customers, suppliers, and competitors are embarking on upgraded compliance systems, benchmarking studies will soon note that trend, leaving those not involved in this activity behind. No executive wants to be left behind.

The policy statement on TSCA compliance can either be part of a general overall compliance with law statement, which then mentions TSCA as one of the many laws governing the conduct of the company, or compliance with environmental law policy, again mentioning TSCA in the text, or a specific compliance with TSCA section. The template chosen should be one that fits with how each company conducts its business. Another option to combine all of the different templates is to use hyperlinks in policy statements, a general policy statement then cascading down to more specific policy statements. However done, the policy statement on law compliance should be easily accessible to employees. An employee should not have to click through dozens of screens in pursuit, or comb the shelves of a basement library to find it. The policy statement, in and of itself, is just a statement of intention. Policy statements are not self-executing.

A high-level champion is someone of sufficient rank to have the attention and respect of the Chief Executive Officer and Board of Directors. For the purpose of compliance, that person should have a direct line to the CEO and Board. The champion must also be someone who will be perceived by the employee population as having sufficient support, integrity, and personal power to make difficult calls, while at the same time being accessible to, and empathetic with, employees. Sometimes the Compliance Officer is the General Counsel; sometimes another high-level technically trained employee; sometimes the head of human resources. The personal characteristics of the person and the strong belief of that person in the importance of the function are as, if not more, important than professional background. This is not a job for the weak of spirit, the noncommitted, or someone who has been passed over and is counting the months toward retirement. And, of course, there should be no hint at all that the person had any propensity to engage in illegal, or unethical, activities.

Resource commitment is much more than providing for a budget or the hiring of one or several people to do the work. Lawyers or regulatory people who are experts in TSCA are needed to provide input on TSCA's requirements. Alone, they are inadequate to get the program on track or to keep the program on track. Depending on how broadly TSCA cuts across a company's operations, parts of other functions also have to be tapped to be part of the resource commitment. The TSCA Requirements Matrix by Function, above, gives some indication of the type of functions that must contribute to the development and maintenance of the TSCA compliance program. Human resources and employee relations, as well as others, could also be added to those functions. In a highly automated organization, the IT professionals must be involved in ensuring that TSCA required controls are inserted and maintained in the company's computer systems. The Human Resources Department is an important asset when developing performance management systems, or incentive or other reward systems, which include TSCA compliance. Employee relations can be tapped to prepare an internal advertising campaign to employees on the importance of compliance, and to keep the message alive in more subtle ways.

Another formal activity management must perform is that of management review of the program on a regularly scheduled basis. Executives are very busy people, with lots of diverse and time-consuming activities. If the senior management team and the Board take the time personally to review a company program, employees know that management is serious. Management review might consist of a summary review of the findings of assessments, audits, and preventive and corrective actions. A schedule of planned activities, such as trainings, assessments, and audits, should also be presented to management. Some companies do a rolling review at each management meeting, with an annual review for the Board. Like all other elements of compliance programs, management review should be done in a way and in a time frame that matches the organization. Senior management reviews should be done at least annually. A company with a history of TSCA compliance problems, or in an industry with TSCA compliance issues, might want to do more frequent management reviews.

Senior members of management need to be perceived as personally committed, as well as actually to be personally committed. There is a difference between the two and both matter. Visibility of the commitment is almost as important as the commitment itself. A member of management could be present at compliance training sessions, if done in person, or may appear on tape on an electronic training program. Executives might make a habit of referring to compliance on a regular basis, in subtle ways. Many opportunities exist in the work place: a thank you to an operator who raised an issue or suggested a preventive action, a sentence in a presentation stressing goals that no corners should be cut when it comes to compliance, a quick appearance at a working meeting of a compliance team. Knowledge of this type of informal participation spreads like wildfire and can be the difference between a program that is well-designed and struggling, and one that is effective. Executives cannot be expected to be aware of all the opportunities—the coordinators of the program need to be the people to find and make those opportunities available to management.

2. Organizational Infrastructure

The TSCA compliance program benefits from whatever support is available in the organizational structure. To the extent that there are structures within the company that can be adapted to support TSCA compliance, they should be exploited for that purpose. Some common infrastructure areas are: organizational charts, job descriptions, performance management systems, and new hire orientation.

People in the organization with the primary TSCA compliance functions should have those functions clearly stated on the organizational charts of the company. The executive with compliance responsibilities should certainly be designated as the Compliance Officer, or the TSCA Compliance Officer, as the case may be. In large organizations, there will likely be dedicated personnel, who can be designated. In smaller organizations, employees with specific TSCA designated positions might have other responsibilities. For example, the Research Manager might also be the TSCA coordinator. While being sensitive to the fact that organizational charts have limited capacity for text, it is helpful to have the TSCA responsibility listed on the chart as well as the designation of Research Manager. This signals to the organization that there is someone who is responsible for these functions to whom to go for assistance. Lawyers typically have broader responsibilities in-house than just TSCA, and are usually designated as the Environmental Counsel or Environmental, Health & Safety Counsel. Such a designation would suffice. Clearly, a one-person in-house legal department would not have such specificity.

Job descriptions should be prepared that accurately describe the roles and responsibilities of employees with TSCA compliance responsibilities. Again, the larger the organization, the more likely there will be employees dedicated to this task. But, those are not the only employees with TSCA responsibilities. Job descriptions of employees in import, export, research, production—virtually all employees whose operations are impacted by TSCA—should all have a segment on the TSCA responsibilities. This exercise can be done in conjunction with the development of TSCA compliance procedures, discussed below. Employees cannot comply with a law unless they are aware that their operations are impacted by that law and how they are impacted.[81]

Once the job descriptions are completed, the next infrastructure item is performance management. Employees should be evaluated in their performance

81. From a timing perspective, it might be preferable to develop the TSCA compliant procedures first, and then to use that information in revising job descriptions to include affirmative TSCA compliance responsibilities. In this regard, TSCA compliance is different from antitrust compliance, in that antitrust prohibits many activities, such as conspiring with competitors to raise price, instead of requiring companies to affirmatively act in a certain manner, such as only making and selling products on the TSCA Inventory.

reviews on TSCA compliance. While credit should not be given for simply fulfilling basic compliance responsibilities, perhaps there should be some positive feedback for making suggestions that improve compliance or for adapting work processes to facilitate compliance. Of course, there needs to be a consequence for not complying, or for not giving compliance the respect it warrants. The company's disciplinary policy should make clear that the company will penalize employees for not complying with the law, including up to termination of employment.

The final infrastructure activity involving the Human Resources Department is new employee orientation. Typically, in the first several days or weeks on the job, new employees have some type of orientation, whether it just involves filling out benefit and tax forms, or more comprehensive new employee training. New employee orientation should have an introduction to compliance with law, and should mention TSCA. That introduction, in the case of a company that just has a fill out the forms orientation, can be as simple as handing the employee a Compliance with Law policy statement, or a short reference to where company policies are located. If the company has a fuller orientation program, TSCA compliance should be included as appropriate to the program and the job responsibilities of the new employee. The orientation program is not likely to accomplish sufficiently detailed TSCA training, but rather to set the tone.[82]

3. Employee Reporting Mechanisms

To ensure that employees have a place to go if they suspect that a violation of TSCA has occurred, or may occur, a reporting mechanism should be put in place. The best method for obtaining employee input on potential legal or ethical lapses is for employees to feel comfortable enough to be able to discuss these types of issues with a supervisor, or another organizational resource, such as a human resources manager or a member of the legal department. Unfortunately, employees do not always have that level of comfort. Sometimes the supervisor is part of the problem, or is perceived to be part of the problem, or the employee is not sufficiently well acquainted with the other possible avenues of reporting the problem in the organization.

There are a number of reporting mechanisms that should be considered. In larger organizations, there may be the possibility of dedicated staff, one or more people whose job it is to assist employees with ethical or legal dilemmas,

---

82. In some organizations, Compliance with Law training is done on a schedule such that new employees are not always trained on the first day of work. Having some reference to TSCA Compliance and other compliance in the new employee orientation would serve as a bridge between the time the employee first comes to work and the actual in-depth training. Of course, a shorter bridge is preferable to a longer one.

in what might be referred to as the office of the ombudsman. More commonly, companies have hotlines or help lines, which employees can call, including anonymously if they choose to do so. A senior person in the human resources department, the compliance department, or the legal department often staffs the hotlines or help lines. Additionally, there are external services, which can be retained to serve as a hotline or help line.

There are several key features needed to ensure that the reporting mechanism selected will accomplish its purpose of surfacing problems before they spin out of control. The mechanism should be publicized from time to time to ensure that employees are aware of it. The mechanism should be user-friendly and responsive. If an employee needs to search for a phone number, dial into a phone that is repeatedly busy or just rings off the hook, chances are that the employee will not make the call. Making a help line call is likely to be a difficult decision for an employee. Make sure that someone is there to take that call. If a voice mailbox answers the call, someone needs to respond to the caller quickly, probably within a one-day period, if even just to acknowledge the call. The company must assure the employee there will be no retaliation for invoking the reporting mechanism. The literature or training sessions discussing the reporting mechanism should make the company's policy on non-retaliation clear, and the company should be diligent in ensuring the enforcement of that policy. Employees should be advised that reporting a violation that implicates the reporting employee may not result in complete amnesty, but may be considered a mitigating factor. While it might be attractive to give full amnesty to an employee who turns himself or herself in,[83] the OSG and other governmental policies may make that impractical in criminal matters. Have a feedback loop in the reporting mechanism, notifying the employee who made the allegation as to the outcome of the investigation, assuming the allegation was not made anonymously. If the investigation and corrective actions that are likely to result from the investigation will take a long time, consider making interim notifications as well.

If a lawyer answers the help line, he or she must take those calls in conformance with the ethics rules of the jurisdiction in which the lawyer is licensed to practice or in which the lawyer is giving the advice. These rules create a tension between the rights of the company to insist that its employees report any violations and the ethics requirements imposed on company counsel. The New York State Bar Association issued an opinion[84] on this topic, which posed the question of whether an in-house attorney may "participate in a 'compliance

83. The government gives this benefit to companies in some of its leniency policies, such as the U. S. Department of Justice, Corporate Leniency Policy (Aug. 10, 1993).

84. New York State Bar Association, Committee on Professional Ethics, Opinion 650 (June 30, 1993), available at http://www.nysba.org/AM/Template.cfm?Section=Ethics_Opinions&TEMPLATE=/CM/ContentDisplay.cfm&CONTENTID=18737.

with law' program under which employees are required to report illegal or unethical behavior?" The opinion approved such participation subject to certain qualifications. When it appears that there might be a conflict between the corporation and the employee making the call, the lawyer should determine if the employee is represented by independent counsel, and if so, should advise the employee that he or she would be happy to deal directly with the employee's counsel. If the employee is not represented by independent counsel, which is more likely at this juncture, the opinion stated that reading the following script to the employee would be adequate to advise the employee:

> I want to caution you that I am an attorney for the Company and not for you or other employees. Therefore, while I can record your complaint, I cannot and will not give you legal advice, and you should not understand our conversation to consist of such advice. I do advise you to seek your own counsel, however, as your interests and the Company's may differ. Having said this, I would be happy to listen to your complaint.[85]

The threshold of what constitutes a conflict of interest or an adverse interest in this type of situation is not high, requiring the lawyer to be sensitive to this quandary of trying to elicit information so that the corporation can be served while at the same time not behaving unethically. Crossing the line can result, among other things, in the lawyer being prevented from continuing to represent the company on the particular matter and in the privilege with respect to the conversation belonging to the employee, not to the corporation.

A lawyer may be tempted to go beyond the scripted warning when an employee is a colleague. Often an environmental lawyer will personally know the individual calling a help line, and departing from the script may be inevitable, but should only be done with a full understanding of the implications.

4. Procedure Development Process

The heart of the compliance program is the procedures or systems that connect the legal requirements imposed by TSCA with the actual operations of the business and the jobs of individual employees. The more clearly an employee understands what he or she must do to complete the job in compliance with TSCA, the more likely it will be that the employee will not violate

---

85. This statement should be modified to explicitly deal with the issues of confidentiality and privilege. Consider adding: "I will try to keep your identity confidential, but cannot guaranty that. Information you give me may be subject to the attorney-client privilege, but that privilege belongs to the company, my client, and not to you. This means that the company can determine whether and with whom to share the information."

the law. It is not usually sufficient to train an employee on the requirements of TSCA once a year, or once in several years, and expect that employee to be able to connect the legal requirement to the job. Making these connections would be challenging enough if the employee only needed to comply with TSCA when doing the task, but more likely than not an employee who must comply with TSCA must also comply with other laws as well.

To the extent feasible, embedding TSCA requirements in an existing business system, or if none exists, in any written instructions for particular job functions, is the preferred method. Having separate compliance manuals or systems for job functions is less desirable in that it requires employees to take another step, such as looking up a requirement in another manual or checking another system. Requiring employees to check with specialized expert personnel before performing a regulated task, especially one that must be performed on a frequent basis, creates a tension between getting the job done quickly and getting the job done in compliance with TSCA.

One way of thinking about how to handle TSCA requirements is depicted in these four different approaches to a compliance integration scheme:

- ad hoc—when a compliance issue is recognized, the employee calls upon a specialist;
- procedure—the procedure points to a designated specialist to be involved when a compliance issue surfaces;
- procedure—the procedure gives a person whose job is impacted the tools to respond to the situation; and
- automated—operations managed by computerized system designed and maintained with the input of specialists.

A TSCA compliance program will likely have a mix of these four approaches. The goal is to create a program that matches the needs and resources of the company as closely as possible. In a technologically savvy company with a host of TSCA compliance issues, such as a chemical company, the compliance program should be as automated as possible. The function of the specialist, an attorney or regulatory specialist with TSCA responsibility or both, will vary depending on the approach. For example, if using a highly automated system, the specialist will be responsible for ensuring that the content of the computer systems is up-to-date in terms of new regulatory requirements and new operations or company products.

Using the information developed in the status quo assessment, the company is able to drill down to modify or prepare procedures for actual business processes[86] that are impacted by TSCA requirements. The task is to make

86. *See* Chapter 20, Practice Tools for an explanation of how a procedure might be constructed and a number of model procedures for specific business processes. These models are included

sure that every element of TSCA that governs the work place is taken into consideration. There are at least two different routes along which to proceed, and chances are both will be used to some degree. One route is to review each documented business process in the company and identify those for which there are TSCA implications. In a company with a good business process system, this approach might be preferred as the assumption will likely be that all business processes have been mapped out accurately and documented. After completing this exercise with the documented business processes, consider whether there are any TSCA requirements for which there were no documented business processes, and whether that is because the process doesn't exist at the company or was just not documented. It might be that a company does not need to deal with the export requirements of TSCA because the company makes no exports. The other approach would be to start with the TSCA requirements, and work from those requirements to likely business processes. This is more challenging to do, but might be the only option in a company that does not have fully documented work processes.

Another decision that needs to be made is whether to work sequentially through all the business processes and the business operations or whether to do all of these at one time, under the auspices of a steering committee. In part, this decision will be driven by the amount of resources available to get the job done. Either approach will work, and there are as many good arguments for doing everything simultaneously as there are for working sequentially. Sequentially is less resource intensive and does allow for adjustments in approach as new ways of working are learned.

To demonstrate the concept, consider the seemingly simple requirement of TSCA that only chemicals on the TSCA Inventory, or that are exempt[87] from the requirements of being on the TSCA Inventory, can be manufactured, processed, used in, or imported into, the United States. If a chemical is not otherwise exempt from the TSCA Inventory requirements, and is not on the TSCA Inventory, a premanufacture notification[88] must be filed prior to introducing it into commerce. The task here is to identify those business processes in the company where new chemicals can enter the company, and then decide how best to control those entry points to ensure no new chemicals are

---

to provide some guidance in preparing procedures that integrate TSCA compliance, but are not intended to substitute for doing the work contemplated in this section, analyzing the specific operations, and preparing procedures that reflect the actual operations of a specific company. The model procedures follow an ISO type format.

87. At the time TSCA was enacted, the goal of Congress was to regulate only those chemicals which were not already subject to other regulations. Accordingly, chemicals already subject to FIFRA and the FFDCA are not subject to TSCA. In addition, TSCA itself provides for some limited exemptions, subject to certain restrictions, such as for chemicals solely for research and development or chemicals for test marketing.

88. *See* Chapter 4, Premanufacture Notifications.

being introduced without a TSCA review. The questions that should be asked include the following: Who decides on what new raw materials will be used in production? Who decides what suppliers are qualified to supply a new raw material? Who can select a new raw material supplier? Who can approve a change to an existing raw material supplier's manufacturing site or manufacturing process? Who can select a toll or custom manufacturer? Who can make a process change in manufacturing? Who is involved in production planning? Who can determine whether a product should be imported or sourced locally? Who can purchase raw materials for the laboratories? Who imports raw materials or products? Who is involved in new product development? Who in new product development determines whether and when a new chemical will be produced? Who is involved in process development? Who in process develop determines whether and when a new process will be introduced into a domestic manufacturing facility? Are any of these business processes documented?

If there are any documented procedures governing these business processes, the employees who were involved in producing those documented procedures should be brought together, process by process, with any additional people who might be of assistance, such as lawyers, regulatory specialists, shipping, and logistics personnel and information technology professionals. For example, one TSCA control for a new raw material vendor may be to require a TSCA sign-off as a condition of input into the company's enterprise resource system (ERP) or billing system. Such a sign-off might require some new code, to be written by an information technology professional for the ERP, and the acquiescence of the logistics department to modify the entry input process.

Procedures should be written or modified only with the active participation of those who will implement the procedures. The procedures need to be designed so as to be able to be implemented. A lawyer, or regulatory specialist, may believe that a certain method of operating is preferable from a compliance perspective, but that method may be totally impractical from an operations perspective. Employees are not likely to carry out a procedure that makes their tasks extremely difficult. While getting a group of people to come to a consensus and document that consensus may be a challenge, responding to the authorities as to why those employees failed to follow the procedure is likely a greater challenge.

One of the most difficult decisions that needs to be made for every work process is to define when the persons or operating teams with the authority to make the operating decisions needs to seek expert advice or when they can be trained to make the TSCA compliance decision themselves. Reasonable people can differ. The goal should be to supportively delegate as much responsibility for TSCA compliance as possible. Given the right tools, employees charged with these responsibilities will likely rise to the occasion. Retaining the responsibility to have all of these decisions made by specialists often results in work process blockages as operations people wait in line to get their questions answered, creating the incentive to skip getting the right answer altogether.

Effective delegation is not a line in a procedure that requires the operator to "act in compliance with all applicable laws." In the example discussed above about whether a new chemical has entered the company when making a manufacturing process change, the procedure may have a checklist which allows the employee making the manufacturing process change to decide whether the change made requires seeking expert advice. That checklist might inquire as to whether the proposed change does any of the following:

- Introduce a new raw material, vendor or vendor site?
- Result in a new chemical substance as the end product of the manufacturing process as determined by qualitative analysis?
- Result in a new byproduct or impurity that imparts valuable properties to the resulting product?
- Involve a polymer that will have a different proportion of monomers, reactive solvents, chain transfer agents, cross-linking agents, bases, or free radical initiators incorporated into the polymer after the proposed change is implemented?
- Involve removing an intermediate from equipment in which it is manufactured, if the intermediate was not normally removed from the equipment in which it was manufactured prior to the change?
- Involve making changes to the product specifications?
- Result in a change in production site, or remove or add regulated equipment?

If the answer to any of the above questions is yes, consult the Regulatory Affairs Specialist before proceeding with the proposed change. If the answer to all of the above questions is no, please proceed to the next step in the Process Change Procedure.

Good document practice requires that procedures be dated and reviewed on a predetermined frequency to ensure that the procedures still reflect the workplace. How often to review a procedure depends on the particular procedure and how static or fluid the company is. A three-year cycle is likely a good rule of thumb. Of course, when there are changes in TSCA or in regulations, guidance, or case law, review the impacted procedures right away to ensure that as written they still ensure compliance, or to make whatever modifications are needed.

5. Training

When the compliance procedures are finished, the company will have a record of how TSCA impacts the operations, which functions in the company are involved, and how each function is involved. The next step is to design training programs. The company must actively and routinely disseminate the compliance program, by using any combination of means that would be effective in the company's culture. Considerations include media type, content, and training logistics. The key is to design training that ensures employees are aware of the program, understand its significance, and are sufficiently familiar with the contents to apply the legal requirements correctly in carrying out their jobs. Nothing is worse than training employees who cannot even remember attending the training!

Training programs can be delivered in a variety of media. Newsletters, periodic e-mails, posters, and seminars are common. Seminars can be given in person by in-house staff or by external experts. Sometimes it is most effective to send an individual to a specialized program by an outside provider, especially when a legal responsibility pertains to only one or a few employees. This type of seminar is especially valuable for the internal regulatory specialist to keep abreast of new developments and best practices in the TSCA compliance field.

In large or geographically dispersed companies, where it is logistically impractical or uneconomical to conduct in-person training, computer-based training can be a cost-effective alternative. Web-based programs can be developed in-house, or purchased packaged online programs can be customized. It is essential to be wary, however, of using generic training programs that may summarize the law well, but demonstrate no relationship to the company's operations and potential TSCA issues.

Regardless of the mode of delivery, it is important to make the programs interesting. Employees pay more attention if the training involves problems such as those actually encountered in their workplace. Case studies, requiring people to participate in providing solutions, tend to have better retention rates than lectures, which provide a summary of the law and the penalties associated with noncompliance. Interspersing videos and graphics also tends to keep trainees' attention better than plain PowerPoint presentations or lectures. The people in the communications, public relations, or training department are likely to be expert at understanding how to adapt programs to the target audience. The message should always be the same. Consistency counts. Delivery can and should vary.

Effective training is tailored to an individual's responsibilities. Many TSCA training programs are generic, summarizing all the provisions of TSCA and detailing in particular the penalties for noncompliance. Someone responsible for purchasing raw materials is not likely to benefit from a long training on imports and exports; someone responsible for imports and exports is not likely to benefit from a long training on the intricacies of the test rules. While a short overview of the statutory scheme might be generally helpful, too much detail in an area that is not job-related can turn employees off. Training that specifically tells people what they need to do, is repeated in operating procedures, and is reinforced by the job, is training that is likely to impact behavior.

One suitable training method is to use the procedures already developed as the basis for the training. Not only should employees be told how to operate under the procedure, such as how to execute an export, but also the rationale behind the procedure, including what TSCA requires, why, and the penalties for noncompliance. It would be useful to include in this training the requirements of any other applicable laws or regulations.[89] Training focused on what is actually done in the workplace tends to be brief and to the point, and thus likely to be remembered. The time-consuming task is in the design of the training as opposed to its implementation.[90]

Another complementary approach to training might be more of the issue-spotting type. Some TSCA requirements are not susceptible to being wholly procedurized. For example, no procedure can predict all of the instances when a customer complaint rises to the level of an allegation of a significant adverse effect that must be recorded under TSCA § 8(c). However, the procedures governing what to do with such information once it is recognized as potentially recordable can readily be incorporated into a procedure. The company may be too small to have developed written procedures or may not be able to include TSCA compliance in whatever operating procedures do exist. The process of designing issue-spotting training is similar to the process of designing procedures. The program should be designed by determining in which functions specific TSCA issues are likely to occur and then preparing training programs that emphasize those issues to the target audience. The training program might be prepared in components, with an overall summary introduction and specific sections for specific functions. The goal of the training is not so much to tell employees how to handle the TSCA requirement as it is to alert employees that there might be a TSCA requirement and to designate a resource to whom to go for assistance in that event.

In designing a training program, it is important to consider having senior management be part of the training. A different member of senior management can personally appear to introduce training programs on a rotating or an as-available basis, or a video or DVD of an executive can be played before in-person training sessions. A senior executive can also appear on online training.

If there are personnel who do not speak English as a primary language, it is worth considering having the training given in multiple languages.

---

89. While this book is specifically about TSCA compliance, training should be designed to cover as many different laws as are relevant to the operations as are possible. Obviously different groups of experts will be involved in working on different aspects, but the more integrated the approach overall, the more efficient and effective it will be.

90. *See* Chapter 20, Practice Tools for an example of a TSCA training program.

Lastly, when designing the content, it is worthwhile to insert an element of fun into the training. Training is a serious matter; TSCA compliance is a serious subject. But serious does not necessarily mean boring. Offering small prizes, such as company logo items or lunch passes, to employees who ask questions or offer insights on case studies, and other such options are useful for keeping employees' attention.

Logistics are often the difference between success and failure. People must attend, or participate in, the training for it to be effective. Training should be mandatory. Participation in training can be reinforced in the performance management system. But the program should not rely just on a "stick" approach. It should be easy to participate as well. Training programs should be scheduled as far in advance as possible. Then, reminders should be sent from time to time as the date approaches. Busy people sometimes forget or over schedule. Training should also be accessible. Accessibility may be an issue with people who regularly work off-site, such as sales personnel or telemarketers. Incorporating TSCA training sessions into other scheduled meetings, like sales meetings, should be considered. This may involve some lobbying, but it is economical as well. While online training may offer certain conveniences, it must be accessible using the information technology systems used by employees. If employees need access from remote locations from which they will be dialing in, it is important to make sure the information technology people review the potential online programs to ensure that they are suitable from a technological perspective.

Training programs must be done on a regular basis. A multiyear strategic plan for what will be done when, where, and how is recommended. Training does not need to be long or formal. If using procedure based training, do training each time you modify the procedure. Depending on the modification, training can be as little as a brief e-mail explaining the changes to those impacted, and a request to read the new procedure. Whenever an employee takes a new position, that employee should be trained on the applicable procedures. A supervisor can do training, so long as the supervisor has the proper tools. In addition to these specific times to do training, it is useful to consider connecting the training cycle to the procedure review cycle.

For TSCA training that is not connected to the procedure review cycle, such as issue-spotting training, it is worth considering requiring supervisors to have a section in each employee's annual objectives on required training for the year, including TSCA training. Training need not be done on an annual basis. Frequency is not the same as effectiveness. Depending on the industry, the company's TSCA issues, the company's TSCA compliance track record, and the company's employee retention rate, a two- or three-year training cycle might be adequate. For areas in which the company is experiencing more difficulty, the company should consider reviewing the training module and procedures and repeating that training on a more frequent basis.

Attendance should be taken at training programs to ensure all employees required to attend do so, and the attendance records should be maintained. Some companies keep a signed copy of a training record in an employee's personnel file. Other companies use an electronic tracking system, which allows anyone with access, such as a supervisor, to review the records easily. Many online training providers provide tracking systems in addition to content. The company should be able to demonstrate that an employee received periodic and substantively appropriate TSCA training.

6. Goals and Incentives

Management uses goals and objectives to signal to employees what it considers important, i.e., the high-priority items. Often, these goals are connected to incentives to motivate the desired behavior. Goals and incentives may be designed on an individual employee basis, departmental basis, or company-wide basis, depending on the aim sought to be accomplished. Often company-wide goals cascade down through the organization, identifying with more particularity the requirements each employee needs to meet to accomplish the goal.

Compliance goals and incentives in companies are often of the negative sort, such as penalties for failures to comply with legal requirements. This is not surprising in that compliance failures can lead to serious penalties for the company. But, just as the government, in its policies of the last decade, began to use a carrot approach as well as a stick approach with companies, companies should in turn also use a carrot approach with employees.

Goals and incentives need to be designed with great care, to ensure that they do not have unintended consequences. For example, a goal of not violating TSCA, or 100 percent legal compliance, may have the unintended consequence of encouraging employees not to detect and report violations, which would be entirely counter to the principles of a compliance program. These types of issues need to be considered with great care.

With this caveat in mind, realistic and compliance-oriented goals can and should be set. Goals need to be measurable—what does achievement look like? Process-oriented goals work effectively. If a company is just embarking on establishing a TSCA compliance program, putting in place some or all of the elements of the program can be the goal for the year. In a company with good operating procedures, one goal which would involve many employees could be: "Identifying all company business processes which have TSCA implications, and establishing teams to consider and integrate those TSCA impacts into existing operating procedures and to develop procedures where there are none existing." Another goal along these lines might be directed to the information technology professionals: "Modify the existing export program to ensure conformance with TSCA §12(b) requirements."

To the extent possible, goals that facilitate TSCA compliance but reach beyond compliance to the objectives of other parts of the organization should also be considered. Consider the use of metrics, such as the amount of time it takes to prepare a Premanufacture Notice (PMN) for a new substance, or how many PMNs go through the EPA without the need for a consent decree. Both of these goals not only facilitate TSCA compliance, but also support new product development by reducing time to market, a perennial industry favorite, and by eliminating suspect chemicals from new products.

If systemic areas that need improvement are discovered through auditing or a compliance system, consider developing goals around the improvements of those areas. Streamlining the TSCA compliance system in measurable ways could be an appropriate goal for a more mature system.

Like the compliance system itself, goals should be dynamic, changing to meet the challenges of the workplace.

7. Auditing

As discussed above, audits are a critical part of an EMS. The objective of any audit is to determine if systems and processes are in place to enable the facility to conduct its business in conformance with the applicable laws. The audits may be systems audits, which focus on the procedures that are in place, without specifically looking for violations that may have occurred as a result of any lapse in the procedures, or they can be compliance audits, which typically follow the paper trails of specific transactions, and are designed at least in part to uncover regulatory violations. Systems audits can be preferable if the purpose of the audit is to ensure that the compliance program as a whole is set up correctly. Compliance audits can be preferable if the purpose of the audit is to monitor whether the programs are being followed. Both have a place in EMS implementation.

Audits can be performed by outside service providers, or by in-house teams made up of people with the appropriate expertise. For example, a TSCA audit team conducting an audit in a manufacturing facility may have a production manager from a facility other than the one being audited, a TSCA Coordinator, and an export specialist. If a lawyer participates in an audit, he or she may be faced with the same issues presented by answering hotline calls, and may need to caution individuals that the company lawyer does not represent individuals.

There is often a level of stress in any facility about to be audited because employees are naturally concerned that some lapse, or worse, on their part will be discovered. Companies should reassure employees that audits are not witch hunts, and will be conducted in an impartial and fair manner, with a continual improvement focus. Nonetheless, if violations are discovered during the audit, they could be grounds for termination or discipline depending on the circumstances, and statements about an upcoming audit should not mask this fact.

Before designing the audit protocol, it is important to determine the purpose of the audit. For example, an audit of compliance with export notification requirements will have a different group of functions involved than an audit of how a laboratory manages compliance with the research and development exemption to the PMN requirements.

The TSCA Requirements Matrix by Function, earlier in this chapter, is a starting place for designing the audit protocol. Using export notifications as an example again, the matrix shows that people in regulatory, sales and marketing, import/export, shipping, and information technology functions are all likely to have responsibilities relevant to export notification compliance. A systems audit will require delving into each of the functions these people perform, preparing a flow chart showing how information flows from each person to the next, charting how the ultimate notification is generated and how the records of having submitted the notification are kept. The Exporting Commercial Shipments procedure given in Chapter 20, Practice Tools, or a version customized for the company being audited, lists a set of steps that could be audited against.

Some lawyers advocate having audits set up as reports to the lawyer seeking legal advice on the law and legal strategies for managing the audit findings. The audits could be shielded from discovery under the attorney-client privilege if the audit is properly framed. However, it is generally not worth the effort to have a lawyer control the audit process for several reasons. The presence of lawyers in the process heightens employees' concerns about the purpose to which the audit findings will be put, and may result in less free discussions. In most cases, if there is a violation, the EPA's Audit Policy may result in a complete mitigation of penalties for any violation that is discovered, and as a result the findings will be communicated to the EPA even if they are not turned over to the EPA in the form of an audit report. Finally, the attorney-client privilege does not shield the underlying facts from discovery; only the form of the communication between a lawyer and a client is privileged.

The integrity of an audit depends on how the audit is commissioned within the organization and what happens to the audit findings. Who receives the audit results is an important consideration. If the head of production is the person commissioning and receiving the audit results, he or she may be tempted to try to influence the drafting of the final audit to avoid finding fault with production procedures. As a result, an audit report should be commissioned by and given to a person whose position in the corporation is independent of institutional biases.

How the audit is handled after the auditors deliver their report is also a factor in assessing its integrity. The audit findings should not be changed after they are prepared. If a person whose activities have been audited has a rebuttal to an audit finding, that rebuttal should be added to the audit report, either in the body or as an appendix. Not only does that allow a reviewer to track the thought processes behind the response, it allows the reviewer to understand the initial findings themselves. This practice should generally also be followed by lawyers who review the audits; even if they disagree with the interpretation of a requirement cited by an auditor, lawyers should add their comments to the audit rather than changing the audit conclusions. This is often accomplished by incorporating a chart of audit findings, with spaces for further post-audit comments.

Audits frequently unearth issues that must be addressed. The timetable for responding to these issues by making changes to current practice is another element of the integrity of the audit. Too long a time period makes a mockery of the audit process.

Finally, the method chosen for responding to an audit finding can be an element of the audit's integrity. If there is a choice between making a systemic change that will address the root cause of the circumstances that gave rise to an adverse audit finding or taking some action on the order of orally advising line operators to change how they handle a certain chemical, then the more systemic change is preferable.

8. Corrective Actions

Every compliance program should have an enhanced tracking feature, such as a corrective action system. This component will not only track all required corrective actions to completion, but also have the ability to group issues to spot and analyze trends, to facilitate root cause analysis, and to design systemic fixes to the program. For example, correcting a violation of the export requirements of TSCA § 12(b) is not the same as understanding why the violation occurred and fixing the system or procedure to prevent a reoccurrence of the violation. The goal is of course to understand any developing trends and data before the violation occurs to prevent it in the first instance. If each problem is viewed in an isolated way, the ability to understand the potential for failure is reduced.

The corrective action system should be the repository for all follow up actions required in the compliance program. The source for corrective actions, which need to be tracked, might include the following:

- department self-assessments;
- internal, external, or EPA audits;
- EPA or internal investigations;
- complaints from employees, agents, customers, consumers, community members, or end users;
- ideas for improvements from suppliers, employees, agents, customers, consumers, community members, or end users;

- spills, exposures, or releases;
- lawsuits; and
- violations of law and potential violations of law.

A departmental self-assessment might result in findings for improvements in the compliance program as well as findings of actual violations of law or procedure. The findings should be documented and a plan of action established, including what would need to be done, by whom, and by when. That action plan would then be monitored to ensure that the actions were actually accomplished in a timely way. Once the action plan is completed, a final step for the corrective action would be to establish a timeframe by which to ensure that the corrective action was actually effective. Completion and effectiveness are not necessarily the same concept. In the example above of the TSCA §12(b) violation, which might have been discovered during a departmental self-assessment, the corrective action might be completed when a notice of export or a self-disclosure report is filed with the EPA. Resolving this action alone may or may not be effective in preventing reoccurrences of the problem. If the problem was caused because the employee responsible for filing the export notices was on vacation, the same violation might occur the next time that employee is on vacation and an export notification has to be filed. A more complete remedy might be to change the system to automatically prevent exports if the operator does not remove "12(b) notice required" flag, or more simply, to prepare written instructions, including when such notices are required and how to prepare and file them, for whomever is covering the export desk when the export specialist is on vacation.

9. Management Review

Management review is the review by management at different levels of the effectiveness of the compliance program. At the departmental level, management might be involved in a monthly or quarterly review of corrective action items for its department to ensure that all actions stay on track. At the more senior level, management review might consist of an annual overall review of the functioning of the compliance program. This would include schedules of last year's and next year's training sessions and audits, operations and findings of the corrective action systems, company-wide trend analysis, personnel, budgets, target setting, and accomplishments, and the like. Focusing senior management's attention on all of the attributes of the compliance program on at least an annual basis ensures that the program is not only properly designed, but that it is being implemented as designed. No one wants to make a presentation to senior management demonstrating that corrective actions are being completed late on a regular basis, or that auditor findings are being routinely ignored. And, as noted previously, management review is an important element not only because it ensures that the program is properly resourced and effective, but also because it serves as an indication to the employees of the importance of the compliance program. Furthermore, it fulfills some of the requirements of the governmental leniency programs.

10. Recordkeeping

TSCA requires that certain records be kept for specified periods of time. In addition to those records that are required to be kept, it should be considered whether there are other records that will be voluntarily kept and for how long. There is a five-year statute of limitations for actions by the EPA for TSCA violations, but in many cases records should be maintained for much longer. For example, records demonstrating that a substance qualifies for an exemption from the PMN requirements should be maintained for five years after the substance is no longer manufactured or imported, and not just five years from the date the records were created. Recordkeeping requirements for each TSCA program are discussed in connection with those programs.

Beyond the regulatory requirements and the statute of limitations, there is a fair amount of debate about the pros and cons of keeping records that are not required to be kept and for what period of time. One school of thought recommends that records should be kept indefinitely as a way to demonstrate proper action. Keeping records indefinitely is expensive. Paper records require large climate-controlled storage areas. Electronic records are expensive to decipher once the technology ceases to be in popular use.[91] As a practical matter, even if a company could afford to keep those volumes of records, the costs of sorting through and finding what is needed when it is needed could be astronomical, especially in a litigation context. The better approach is to consider document retention periods for TSCA records on a type-of-record approach, as a company should for all other records as part of the company's record retention program. For example, audit reports, though not legally required to be retained, should be kept for at least the period of time needed to document that all findings were reviewed, corrected, and found to be effective, but there is no requirement to keep them longer.

11. Community Outreach

Community outreach is more a feature of an environmental management system than of a traditional compliance system. To the extent that operations could potentially impact the company's surrounding community from a TSCA

---

91. Just think how hard it is to find a record player for vinyl albums.

perspective, such as on-site spills that could reach beyond the company's fence line, it is worthwhile to consider establishing some type of community outreach program that allows the company to be a good neighbor. In the event of any problems with the community, TSCA-related or otherwise, the time invested in being a good neighbor would certainly be of value.

CHAPTER

14

Penalties and Enforcement

I. Statutory Basis for Enforcement

The Toxic Substances Control Act (TSCA)[1] was passed into law in 1976, the heyday of command-and-control environmental legislation supported by severe penalties for violations. In line with this approach, Congress gave the United States Environmental Protection Agency (EPA) and the courts many tools to enforce the statute's provisions.

The enforcement provisions of TSCA are broad and provide authority to enjoin violations, impose staggering penalties, and seize chemicals, as well as require manufacturers to recall or repurchase chemicals they have sold. These enforcement powers are set out in TSCA §§ 7, 15, 16, and 17.

In addition, citizens can bring private enforcement actions under TSCA § 20, and can petition the EPA to issue, amend, or repeal a rule or order under § 21.

TSCA is a strict liability statute, which means that evidence that someone intended or tried to comply does not excuse a violation[2] except in the context of criminal penalties.

II. EPA Enforcement Statistics

In the nine years spanning EPA fiscal years 2001 through 2009, inclusive, EPA issued 1786 complaints and proposed orders for TSCA violations. Violations of rules concerning lead paint (818 actions), polychlorinated biphenyls (PCBs) (383 actions) and asbestos in schools (226 actions) accounted for the vast majority of enforcement actions. Of the remaining 359 complaints and proposed orders, 41 were primarily for violations of the premanufacture notification and significant new use rules of TSCA § 5, 98 were for violations of the reporting and recordkeeping rules in TSCA § 8, and 36 were for violations of the import and export rules of TSCA §§ 12 and 13. The rest of the actions related to other TSCA programs, including lead paint certification, test rules, and asbestos contractor accreditation.[3]

These statistics demonstrate that the PCB, lead, and asbestos programs have been more heavily policed than the programs relating to industrial chemicals. By their nature, the PCB, lead, and asbestos programs are

1. 15 U.S.C. § 2601–2695d.
2. *See, e.g.*, In the Matter of Troy Chemical Corp., Docket No. II-TSCA-8(a)-98-0101, (OALJ Oct. 14, 1999), *available at* http://www.epa.gov/oalj/orders/troy2.htm.
3. Enforcement data compiled from the EPA's Compliance Information System database available through the EPA Enforcement & Compliance History Online (ECHO) at http://www.epa-echo.gov/echo/compliance_report_icis.html.

Table 14.1 EPA Enforcement Statistics
Complaints and Proposed Orders Issued
Totals and Selected Programs

Note: The total of all TSCA complaints and proposed orders is shown under the heading "All TSCA Programs"
The numbers for other programs listed are subsets of "All TSCA Programs."

Year	*All TSCA Programs*	*PMNs and § 5*	*PCBs and § 6*	*Reporting and § 8*	*Export § 12*	*Import § 13*	*Lead Subchapter IV*	*Asbestos in Schools § 203*
2001	169	4	59	12	11	4	15	19
2002	185	10	52	15	3	2	39	4
2003	254	1	40	17	3	0	126	25
2004	269	12	37	20	0	2	159	26
2005	184	3	36	9	1	1	102	25
2006	186	3	43	8	3	0	98	28
2007	204	3	44	9	2	0	95	46
2008	209	3	44	5	2	0	119	30
2009	126	2	28	3	1	1	65	23
Totals	1786	41	383	98	26	10	818	226

Table compiled from data obtained through http://www.epa-echo.gov/echo/compliance_report_icis.html
Years are EPA fiscal years, which run from October 1 through September 30. Fiscal year 2010 is October 1, 2009 through September 30, 2010.

easier to inspect. For example, if an electrical transformer is not labeled to show that it contains PCBs, that lapse will be evident to an inspector. In contrast, if a manufacturer incorrectly identifies a chemical and believes that a premanufacture notification has been filed for that chemical, that lapse will probably only be detected by a skilled chemist.

As a practical matter, the PCB, lead, and asbestos violations are the "low hanging fruit" for EPA inspectors looking for violations. On the other hand, these same violations are the ones most easily addressed by the regulated community, and lapses may demonstrate a systematic failure to have effective compliance programs.

III. Law

A. What Constitutes a Violation of TSCA

Section 15 of TSCA, entitled "Prohibited Acts," enumerates the acts that violate TSCA. It says, somewhat obviously, that a violation of any reporting obligation,[4] any test rule,[5] or any other requirement of §§ 4 or 5[6] is a violation. Similarly, it is a TSCA violation to fail to maintain required records or allow the EPA to inspect a facility. It adds a very critical dimension to the list of violations by stating that *using* a substance that was manufactured in violation of TSCA is itself a violation of TSCA. The most significant language is that "it shall be unlawful for any person to ... (2) use for commercial purposes a chemical substance or mixture which such person knew or had reason to know was manufactured, processed, or distributed in commerce in violation of" the § 5 and premanufacture notification (PMN) rules, a ban or restriction under TSCA §§ 6 or 7, or a rule or order under those sections.

The practical effect of prohibiting use of a substance that was manufactured, processed, or distributed in violation of TSCA is that as soon as anyone has reason to know a substance was manufactured, processed, or distributed in violation of TSCA, he or she should immediately quarantine the substance. Failure to quarantine the substance could inadvertently lead to its use, which

4. *See* Chapter 3, The Inventory on reporting obligations under the Inventory Update Rule under TSCA § 8, Chapter 4, Premanufacture Notifications, on reporting obligations under TSCA § 5, Chapter 7, Reporting and Recordkeeping, on TSCA's reporting requirements under § 8, and Chapter 8, Exports and Imports, on reporting obligations under TSCA §§ 12 and 13.
5. *See* Chapter 9, Test Rules, on TSCA § 4.
6. *See* Chapter 4, Premanufacture Notifications, on TSCA § 5.

is a separate violation from the initial improper manufacture.[7] The EPA has authority to impose separate penalties for commercial use. EPA's data shows that it issued twenty complaints or proposed orders for commercial use violations during fiscal years 2001 through 2009.[8]

"Manufacture" is defined circularly as "to import," "produce," or "manufacture."[9] Even though this definition is less than useful, practitioners do not have significant difficulty applying it. People use the common sense meaning of manufacture to include making and synthesizing chemical substances or mixtures. It is important to remember that "manufacture" includes importation into the customs territory of the United States,[10] and so a chemical that is imported into theUnited States in violation of §§ 5, 6, or 7 cannot be legally used in the United States under § 15. Section 15 does not prohibit use or processing of a chemical substance that was imported in violation of the import certification requirements of § 13, and so it is arguably legal to use a chemical that was imported without a required import certification (although failure to certify is a TSCA violation).

The activities that violate § 15 include:

- violating any rule or order issued under § 4;
- violating any § 5 requirement, or any rule or order issued under § 5, for example, an order under § 5(e) or the premanufacture notification requirements;
- using for commercial purposes a chemical substance or mixture with knowledge or reason to know that it was manufactured, imported, processed, or distributed in violation of § 5 or a rule or order under § 5;
- violating any § 6 requirement, or any rule or order issued under § 6, for example, those restricting use and disposal of PCB items;
- using for commercial purposes a chemical substance or mixture with knowledge or reason to know that it was manufactured, imported, processed, or distributed in violation of § 6 or a rule or order under § 6;
- failure to establish or maintain records required by § 8 or a rule issued under § 8;

---

7. Quarantining also shows that the company has taken all steps reasonably necessary to mitigate the violation, which can help to reduce penalties, as discussed in connection with the EPA's Enforcement Response Policies and Audit Policies, *infra*.
8. Data compiled from http://www.epa-echo.gov/echo/compliance_report_icis.html. However, it is not clear from the case reports for the listed actions whether each of these twenty enforcement actions contained allegations of commercial use.
9. TSCA § 3(7).
10. Section 3 of TSCA defines "manufacture" to include "import into the customs territory of the United States (as defined in general note 2 of the Harmonized Tariff Schedule of the United States)." "Customs Territory of the United States" as used in General note 2 of the Harmonized Tariff refers to only the States, The District of Columbia and Puerto Rico.

- failure to permit entry or inspection;
- failure to establish or maintain records required by § 12 or a rule issued under § 12, for example, an export notification;
- failure to establish or maintain records required by § 13 or a rule issued under § 13, for example, an import certification; and
- violating any requirement of Subchapter II, concerning asbestos, or any order issued under Subchapter II.

There appear to be a few gaps in § 15's prohibitions. It does not prohibit violation of an order under TSCA § 7's provisions, which include seizure and recall of imminently hazardous substances. The effect of this is that a violation of an order under § 7, which must be a court order as opposed to an order of the EPA, can only be penalized by the court and not by the EPA, because § 16 only gives the EPA authority to penalize violations of § 15. The activities that are not prohibited by § 15, but are prohibited by other applicable authorities include:

- using for commercial purposes a chemical substance or mixture if a § 4 test rule requirement for that chemical substance or mixture was violated;
- violation of a court order under § 7;
- manufacture, importing, processing, or using for commercial purposes a chemical substance or mixture if a § 8 requirement for that chemical substance or mixture was violated;
- failure to comply with a subpoena issued under § 11, but note that failure to comply with a court order enforcing a subpoena may be contempt;
- the act of exporting the chemical substance or mixture subject to an export notification requirement does not violate § 15; it is only the failure to establish or maintain records that violates § 15; and
- using for commercial purposes a chemical substance or mixture, which chemical substance or mixture was imported in violation of an import certification requirement for that chemical substance or mixture, although the substance is subject to seizure under § 17.

B. Civil and Criminal Enforcement

As of 2009 the maximum daily civil penalty for all TSCA violations, except those dealing with certain asbestos violations, is $37,500. Section 16 of TSCA provides that a person who violates TSCA is liable for penalties of up to $25,000 per day for each violation.[11] However, after TSCA was enacted

---

11. 15 U.S.C. § 2615(a).

Congress passed the Civil Penalties Inflation Adjustment Act of 1990,[12] which required each federal agency to adjust its maximum penalties to maintain a deterrent effect in the face of inflation. As required by that legislation, EPA increased the daily maximum penalties to $27,500 effective after January 30, 1997,[13] and again to $32,500 effective March 15, 2004,[14] and again to $37,500 effective January 12, 2009.[15] The Debt Collection Improvement Act requires penalty adjustments every four years and so another increase should be forthcoming in 2013. When calculating penalties it is important to use the maximum penalty that was in effect at the time of the violation.[16]

Penalties for violations of some provisions of TSCA's asbestos program are lower than the penalties for the other programs. The statute as originally enacted provided for maximum penalties of $5,000[17] for local education agencies that failed to conduct inspections in accordance with the regulatory requirements, failed to develop a management plan, violated the worker protection regulations, or submitted false reports. The same maximum penalties applied to contractors who failed to get proper accreditation. This maximum was raised for local education agencies to $5,500 starting January 31, 1997, to $6,500 starting March 16, 2004, and to $7,500 starting January 13, 2009. Because of technical errors in promulgating the regulations, penalties applicable to contractors who failed to get proper asbestos accreditation are slightly different. The maximum for contractors was raised to $5,500 starting March 16, 2004, and to $7,500 starting January 13, 2009.[18]

The statute requires a hearing under the Administrative Procedure Act[19] if the company or person that the EPA proposes to penalize asks for one. The EPA must give fifteen days notice of the right to request a hearing before it issues a final order. The EPA has promulgated Consolidated Rules of Practice for civil penalty assessments[20] that is a procedure manual for all civil TSCA penalty assessments. The Consolidated Rules of Practice governs hearings and appeals to the EPA's Environmental Appeals Board.

Once the EPA issues an order after a hearing, the losing party can appeal to the Federal Circuit Court for the District of Columbia, or any other Circuit

---

12. 28 U.S.C. § 2461, as amended by the Debt Collection Improvement Act of 1996, 31 U.S.C. § 3701.
13. 61 Fed. Reg. 69360 (Dec. 31, 1996).
14. 69 Fed. Reg. 7121 (Feb. 13, 2004).
15. 73 Fed. Reg. 75340 (Dec. 11, 2008); 74 Fed. Reg. 626 (Jan. 7, 2009).
16. 73 Fed. Reg. 75340, 75345 (Dec. 11, 2008).
17. 15 U.S.C. § 2647.
18. 73 Fed. Reg. 75340, 75341, 75345 (Dec. 11, 2008).
19. 5 U.S.C. §§ 500 – 596. It mandates uniform procedures among the various executive agencies for rulemaking, hearings, agency adjudications and administrative appeals.
20. 40 C.F.R. Part 22; Consolidated Rules of Practice Governing the Administrative Assessment of Civil Penalties, 64 Fed. Reg. 40138 (July 23, 1999).

Court where that person lives or transacts business. The appeal must be filed within thirty days of the date of the order.[21]

The statute itself requires the EPA to take various factors into account in establishing a penalty. These are the "nature, circumstances, extent, and gravity of the violation or violations and, with respect to the violator, ability to pay, effect on ability to continue to do business, any history of prior such violations, the degree of culpability, and such other matters as justice may require."[22] This list of factors is the subject of detailed discussion in the Enforcement Response Policies, *infra*.

Section 16(b) imposes criminal penalties, which may be collected or imposed in addition to civil penalties. Any person who violates § 15, or its counterpart § 409 prohibiting violation of the lead reduction provisions of TSCA, can be fined up to $25,000 per day of violation or up to one year in prison. To be criminal under this section, a violation must be knowing or willful. A prosecutor can prove the knowing or willful standard was met if the defendant deliberately avoids learning the truth. In *United States v. Pacific Hide & Fur Depot*,[23] the Circuit Court reversed a conviction because the prosecution had not introduced proof that the defendant deliberately avoided learning the nature of the substances he was dealing with and therefore knowing or willful conduct could not be inferred.

The EPA maintains a database of thirty indictments under TSCA since 1983,[24] twenty-six of which involved PCBs, two of which involved asbestos, and two of which involved lead. There have been indictments under other TSCA provisions, including the reporting and recordkeeping requirements of TSCA § 8.[25]

Note that only violations of §15 are potentially criminal. Therefore, using a chemical that was imported without a proper import certification under § 13 is not criminal, although willful failure to prepare the import certification is criminal.

---

21. TSCA § 16(a)(3).
22. TSCA § 15(2)(B).
23. 768 F.2d 1096 (9th Cir. 1985).
24. The EPA's criminal indictments under TSCA are *available through* http://cfpub.epa.gov/compliance/criminal_prosecution/index.cfm.
25. For example, W.R. Grace was indicted for withholding information that allegedly should have been reported under TSCA § 8(e), but this case did not appear in the EPA database. *See* http://www.epa.gov/compliance/resources/newsletters/cleanup/cleanup19s.pdf. W.R. Grace was acquitted in 2009. *See* David S. Hilzenrath and Carrie Johnson, *W.R. Grace Acquitted In Mont. Asbestos Case*, Washington Post, May 9, 2009, *available at* http://www.washingtonpost.com/wp-dyn/content/article/2009/05/08/AR2009050803632.html.

C. Specific Enforcement and Seizure

Section 17 gives federal district courts jurisdiction over actions to enjoin violations of §§ 15, 5, and 6 of TSCA and to compel any action required by TSCA. It also gives the district courts jurisdiction over actions for injunctive relief against any person who manufactures, imports, or processes a chemical substance manufactured in violation of §§ 5 or 6, or product manufactured in violation of the lead requirements of TSCA. If the substance or product was distributed in commerce, an injunction under this section can include requirements for the manufacturer, importer, or processor to notify its customers and the public of the risks, and recall, replace, or repurchase the substance or product.

Any chemical substance or mixture, or any article containing them, or any product governed by TSCA's lead provisions, that was manufactured or imported in violation of TSCA is subject to seizure pursuant to § 17 (b). This includes chemicals that were imported in violation of the import certification requirements of § 13. The statute provides that seizure "proceedings shall conform as nearly as possible to proceedings in rem in admiralty."

In contrast to § 7, § 17 does not require a chemical to pose an imminent hazard before § 17 can be applied. EPA has stated that it will not seek § 17's broad remedies unless it is apparent that monetary penalties will not compel compliance. For example, it will seek to enjoin a violation or seize a chemical in cases involving outright refusal to comply or a history of repeat violations.[26]

The District Court in *U.S. v. Commonwealth Edison*[27] found that § 17 supported the EPA's causes of action to restrain various violations of TSCA. It went on to note that there may be situations that present a threat of harm that cannot be remedied by compliance with existing regulation. In these cases § 17 is inadequate to address the threat presented and § 7's methods for addressing imminent hazards serve as a complement to § 7.

D. Imminent Hazard Seizure and Injunctions

Section 7 of TSCA gives the EPA authority to sue to seize imminently hazardous chemical substances, and seek injunctive relief against any person who

26. *See* TSCA § 5 Enforcement Response Policy as amended and restated (June 8, 1989) and further amended in Memorandum from John J. Neylan, Director, Policy and Grants Division, Office of Compliance Monitoring, to Michael J. Walker, Enforcement Counsel, Toxics Litigation Division, 5 (July 1, 1993) [hereinafter § 5 ERP], *available through* http://cfpub.epa.gov/compliance/resources/policies/civil/tsca/.
27. 620 F. Supp. 1404 (N.D. Ill, 1985).

manufactures, imports, processes, distributes, uses, or disposes of imminently hazardous chemical substances, alone or as part of a mixture or article. The EPA rarely relies on § 7.[28]

The EPA has an extremely high burden to meet to prove that a chemical substance is imminently hazardous, and this may explain why § 7 is used so infrequently. An "imminently hazardous chemical substance or mixture" is defined, for this section only, as:

> For the purposes of subsection (a) of this section, the term "imminently hazardous chemical substance or mixture" means a chemical substance or mixture which presents an imminent and unreasonable risk of serious or widespread injury to health or the environment. Such a risk to health or the environment shall be considered imminent if it is shown that the manufacture, processing, distribution in commerce, use, or disposal of the chemical substance or mixture, or that any combination of such activities, is likely to result in such injury to health or the environment before a final rule under section 2605 of this title can protect against such risk.[29]

Section 7 can only be invoked through litigation. The EPA must bring suit to seize or enjoin use of an imminently hazardous substance unless it has promulgated a rule that is immediately effective under TSCA § 6 prohibiting or imposing limits on the use or manufacture of a chemical. The District Court noted in *U.S. v. Commonwealth Edison* that the "government presumptively establishes that the regulatory scheme is incomplete" when it sues under § 7 instead of § 17.[30]

A district court has authority to issue any temporary or permanent injunction necessary to protect human health or the environment from unreasonable risks associated with an imminently hazardous chemical substance. Among other things, the court may order a manufacturer, processor, or distributor to notify its customers and the public of the risks, and recall, replace, or repurchase the substance.

EPA may bring suit in the Federal District Court in Washington, D.C. or anywhere the defendant lives, is present, or does business. The EPA may serve the defendant anywhere in the United States that it can find the defendant. The EPA may issue subpoenas under § 7 (c)(1)(C), although it has broader subpoena-issuing powers under § 11(c).[31]

---

28. In *U.S. v. Commonwealth Edison*, 620 F. Supp. 1404 (N.D. Ill. 1985), the EPA sued Commonwealth Edison to require it to identify where PCBs had been spilled, investigate the extent of the spill, notify property owners and clean up the sites. The Court found that the EPA properly invoked TSCA § 7, although the EPA had already promulgated PCB regulations.
29. TSCA § 7(f).
30. 620 F.Supp. at 1411.
31. *See infra*.

E. Whistleblower Protection

TSCA § 23 protects whistleblowers from retaliation from their employers in limited circumstances. Employers may not fire or discriminate against whistleblowers who start or testify in any proceeding under TSCA or assist in any actions that further TSCA's purpose.[32] Actions that are purely internal to a company and do not involve reporting to a governmental agency are not protected by the statute. An employee's remedy for retaliation is to file a complaint with the Secretary of Labor within thirty days of the employer's action. The Secretary of Labor may order reinstatement and damages including back pay and compensatory damages.[33] This protection is not available to employees who deliberately caused the violation in the first place.[34]

TSCA is not unique in having a whistleblower protection. At least seven other environmental statutes, including the Comprehensive Environmental Response, Compensation and Liability Act (CERCLA),[35] the Solid Waste Disposal Act (SWDA),[36] the Federal Water Pollution Control Act (FWPCA),[37] the Energy Reorganization Act of 1974 (ERA)[38], the Safe Drinking Water Act (SDWA)[39] and the Clean Air Act (CAA)[40] have similar provisions.[41]

IV. EPA Enforcement Policies and Procedures

The EPA established policies and procedures for calculating the amount of civil penalties for TSCA violations. It maintains a series of Enforcement Response Policies (ERPs) covering each of the sections of the TSCA statute and describing in great detail how the EPA used a multitude of factors to determine the severity of each type of violation and what the appropriate monetary penalty should be.

The ERPs only come into play once the EPA has learned of a violation, either through self-reporting, an EPA inspection, or a whistleblower. To encourage companies to self-report potential violations, the EPA issued its Incentives for Self-Policing: Discovery, Disclosure, Correction, and Prevention

32. TSCA § 23(a); 15 U.S.C. § 2622(a).
33. TSCA § 23(b).
34. TSCA § 23(c).
35. 42 U.S.C. § 9610.
36. 42 U.S.C. § 7001.
37. 33 U.S.C. § 1367.
38. 42 U.S.C. § 5851.
39. 42 U.S.C. § 300j-9.
40. 42 U.S.C. § 7622.
41. Anderson v. U.S. Dept. Of Labor, 422 F.3d 1155 (10th Cir. 2005).

of Violations (Audit Policy),[42] which offers the possibility of completely mitigating the penalties under the ERPs if the violator has self-reported and meets the many other prerequisites in the Audit Policy.

Most companies begin their analysis of the potential ramifications that could follow a TSCA violation by determining if they meet the Audit Policy criteria for complete penalty mitigation. If they do meet all of the criteria, then the dollar value of the potential penalties that they have avoided becomes an academic question. However, the Audit Policy assumes familiarity with some of the terms in the ERPs, and so it is helpful to discuss the ERPs first. The ERPs are also important if the Audit Policy only provides a reduction in penalty, instead of complete penalty mitigation.

A. EPA's Enforcement Response Policies

The EPA adopted ERPs for each of the major TSCA provisions. There is an ERP that applies to violations of § 4 test rules[43] as well as one that applies to the Good Laboratory Practice rules established under § 4,[44] one for §§ 8, 12 and 13 adverse effect reporting and imports and exports,[45] one for § 5 including the premanufacture notification rules,[46] one for PCBs,[47] two for lead,[48] and one for asbestos.[49,50]

---

42. 65 Fed. Reg. 19618 (Apr. 11, 2000) [hereinafter Audit Policy].
43. EPA, Office of Compliance Monitoring, Office of Pesticides and Toxic Substances, Enforcement Response Policy for Test Rules Under Section 4 of the Toxic Substances Control Act (May 28, 1986).
44. EPA, Office of Compliance Monitoring, Office of Pesticides and Toxic Substances, TSCA Good Laboratory Practices Regulations Enforcement Response Policy (Apr. 9, 1985).
45. EPA, Toxic and Pesticides Enforcement Division, Office of Regulatory Enforcement, Office of Enforcement and Compliance Assurance, The Enforcement Response Policy For Reporting And Recordkeeping Rules And Requirements for TSCA Sections 8, 12 and 13 (Mar. 1, 1999) [hereinafter Reporting Rule ERP].
46. Amended TSCA § 5 Enforcement Response Policy as amended and restated (June 8, 1989) and further amended in Memorandum from John J. Neylan, Director, Policy and Grants Division, Office of Compliance Monitoring, to Michael J. Walker, Enforcement Counsel, Toxics Litigation Division, (July 1, 1993) [hereinafter § 5 ERP].
47. EPA, Polychlorinated Biphenyls (PCB) Penalty Policy (Apr. 9, 1990).
48. Memorandum from Jesse Baskerville, Director, Toxics and Pesticides Enforcement Division, Office of Regulatory Enforcement, EPA, Interim Guidance for Enforcing the TSCA § 402 Abatement Rule "Firm and Lead Abatement Professional Certification Requirements" (Mar. 8, 2000); and EPA, Office of Enforcement and Compliance Assurance, Office of Civil Enforcement, Waste and Chemical Enforcement Division, Section 1018 – Disclosure Rule Enforcement Response and Penalty Policy (Dec. 2007).
49. Interim Final Enforcement Response Policy for the Asbestos Hazard Emergency Response Act (Jan. 31, 1989).
50. All the ERPs are *available through* http://cfpub.epa.gov/compliance/resources/policies/civil/tsca/.

ERPs do not have the force of law, and they were never promulgated as regulations. They are merely the Agency's guidance for how it will calculate penalties. They are not binding on courts that review agency penalty determinations on appeal and the EPA Office of Administrative Law and Environmental Appeals Board considers them to be no more than benchmarks to take into account in establishing penalties. *In the Matter of GCA Chemical Corporation*.[51] They are important because the EPA follows them to the letter when initially calculating penalties, and often insists that it has no discretion to vary from them. In most cases they provide an upper limit on the penalties a company will face for a particular violation.[52]

The ERPs are important to read through as soon as a company suspects a violation, because they discuss situations in which multiple regulatory provisions are typically violated, and it is often critical to assess whether the EPA can impose penalties for multiple violations. It is also important to make a preliminary judgment about the range of possible penalties so that management can make informed decisions about how to manage the potential violation.

All of the ERPs follow the format and approach of the TSCA Civil Penalty Policy, which the EPA published in 1980.[53] Each begins by determining "gravity based penalties," which are the presumptive penalties for each possible type of violation. Then they apply adjustment factors to increase or reduce the gravity based penalties based on circumstances specific to each company.

The gravity based penalties take the seriousness of the violation into account by using three of the factors specified in § 16 (a)(2)(B) of the TSCA statute for assessing penalties. These three factors are "nature," "circumstance," and "extent." The EPA's interpretation of these three factors has little to do with their dictionary meanings, but the ERPs are easy to follow to calculate a dollar value for virtually any type of violation. Each of them uses "nature," "circumstances," and "extent" to create a matrix showing dollar penalties for each type of violation.

The "nature" of a violation depends on how the violation prevents the EPA from performing its information gathering or regulatory functions under TSCA.[54] The ERPs classify these functions as "chemical control," "control-associated data gathering," or "hazard assessment." Chemical control violations are violations of use and handling restrictions on particular chemical substances. Chemical control violations are only applicable when the EPA

51. Docket No: TSCA-4-2000-0130, 8 (OALJ June 18, 2002).

52. If a respondent requests a hearing to contest a penalty, the EPA can seek to amend its complaint to claim higher penalties if the facts warrant that. 64 Fed. Reg. 40138, 40153 (July 23, 1999).

53. 45 Fed. Reg. 59770 (Sept. 10, 1980).

54. *See, e.g.*, § 5 ERP, 20.

has already imposed restrictions on the use and handling of specific chemicals. Penalties are highest for this category because the Agency has already determined that these substances require further regulation. In the context of § 5, these restrictions can be imposed pursuant to a Significant New Use Rule, a consent order under § 5(e) or a unilateral order issued by the EPA under § 5(f). Hazard assessment violations occur when the company has not reported information that it should have reported to the EPA, or has not filed required notices. The EPA does not have enough information to determine if the chemical substance poses risks or not, and therefore has assigned a medium level of monetary penalties. Commercial use of a chemical manufactured or imported in violation of TSCA will also be categorized as a hazard assessment violation. All recordkeeping and reporting violations under §§ 8, 12, and 13 are categorized as hazard assessment violations.[55] Control-associated data gathering violations are violations of recordkeeping requirements, generally in situations in which the data should have been retained internally and not automatically reported to the EPA. The penalties for this category are the lightest.

The "circumstance" of a violation is derived from the harm that either could have occurred or actually did occur as a result of the violation. In the context of a violation of § 5's premanufacture notification requirements, it does not matter whether actual harm occurred—higher penalties will be assessed whenever the EPA would have regulated a chemical substance as if it had a higher potential to harm human health or the environment. "Circumstance" is based on the potential to cause harm, not whether actual harm occurred and so a violator cannot argue successfully that the "circumstance" should be reduced based on lack of real harm. *All Regions Chemical Labs, Inc. v. EPA*.[56]

The ERPs correlate "extent" of a violation with the volume of the substance involved in the violation. Each of the ERPs subcategorizes extent in terms of "major," "significant," and "minor." Minor extent violations receive lower monetary penalties than significant and major extent violations. The volumes associated with each extent level decrease going from chemical control violations to hazard assessment to control-associated data gathering violations. For example, under the § 5 ERP, a chemical control violation is reduced from the significant category to the minor category if the volume involved is lower than 250 pounds. For a hazard assessment violation, this trigger is set at 750 pounds, and for a control associated data gathering violation this trigger is set at 1000 pounds.

Only the actual pounds of a chemical substance are measured to determine extent. If a chemical is in a mixture or article, only the portion of the

55. *See* the Reporting Rule ERP.
56. 932 F.2d 73 (1st Cir. 1991).

mixture or article that is the subject chemical is counted, and not the entire mass of the mixture or article.

The dollar values assigned to the gravity based penalties in the ERPs must be recalculated because, as discussed *supra*, the EPA has increased the daily maximum penalties several times, most recently effective as of January 12, 2009.[57]

The EPA has further categorized violations as one-day or per-day violations. The per-day violations can easily add up to millions of dollars because each day of violation can be penalized separately. The ERPs specify which types of violations are per-day and which are one-day. Generally, penalties for violations relating to manufacturing are based on the volume of each batch made. The date of the violation is the date the batch is completed. The EPA will assess per-day violations when there is an imminent hazard, or when there was an intent to disregard TSCA.

The ERPs apply the remaining factors specified in § 16 to adjust the gravity based penalty. These factors are "ability to pay, effect on ability to do business, any history of prior such violations, the degree of culpability, and such other matters as justice may require." Much gets shoehorned into the last category of "such other factors as justice may require."

The most significant penalty mitigations come from self-reporting. The ERPs provide for an automatic 25 percent penalty reduction based on self-reporting, and another 25 percent reduction for self-reporting within thirty days of when a company has reason to believe that there may be a potential violation. To qualify for these reductions, a company must self-report before it has notice of any upcoming inspection, and must not be subject to a mandatory disclosure requirement. The violation must not have been previously reported to the EPA, for example by a whistleblower. For an Inventory violation, the date that a company has reason to believe that there may be a violation is the date that the company knows that a chemical substance it is manufacturing, importing or distributing is not on the public version of the TSCA Inventory.[58]

---

57. 73 Fed. Reg. 75340 (Dec. 11, 2008); 74 Fed. Reg. 626 (Jan. 7, 2009). If the ERP based the gravity based penalties on a maximum penalty of $25,000, then each gravity based penalty for a violation after January 13, 2009 must be increased by the ratio of the maximum in effect at the time of the violation to the maximum in effect when the § 5 ERP was written. That ratio is $37,500 divided by $25,000, or 1.5. For example, if the applicable ERP was based on a maximum penalty of $25,000 and the ERP leads to a calculation of a $15,000 gravity based penalty, then the penalty for that same violation occurring after January 12, 2009 would be $22,500. For violations between January 31, 1997 and March 15, 2004, the gravity based penalties must be increased by $27,500/$25,000, or a factor of 1.1. For violations between March 16, 2004 and January 12, 2009 the gravity based penalties must be increased by $32,500/$25,000, or a factor of 1.3. These ratios do not apply to violations of the asbestos requirements of TSCA.
58. § 5 ERP, 18.

The EPA will either allow a deduction from the gravity based penalty for environmentally beneficial expenditures needed to ameliorate the violation or a 15 percent reduction for taking all steps reasonably requested or expected by the EPA to respond to the violation. Industry generally relies on the more assured 15 percent penalty reduction alternative. The most common type of action that qualifies for the 15 percent penalty reduction is quarantining a substance that may have been manufactured or imported in violation of the premanufacture notification requirements of § 5. Depending on the size of the penalty and cost of mitigating the effects of the violation, different alternative reductions will be more favorable. In some circumstances where a substance has been completely used and there is no mitigation possible, the EPA may allow the 15 percent penalty reduction.

The EPA may increase or decrease the penalty by another 15 percent based on the violator's attitude. The EPA has the discretion to lower or increase penalties because of attitude. Companies can present evidence that they reacted responsibly in detecting and responding to the potential violation. Companies should point to any effort to mitigate a violation by quarantining the substance involved, notifying customers that they should not use or process the substance, and cooperating with the EPA after self-reporting or the EPA's discovery of a violation because these are all factors in obtaining the penalty reduction for attitude. On the other hand, failing to cooperate with the EPA or continuing to distribute or use the subject substance could backfire in the form of a penalty enhancement.

The EPA will also take prior violations into account in determining a penalty. Under the ERPs, the EPA will not increase a penalty for a self-reported violation because of prior violations. The EPA will only increase a penalty under an ERP for prior violations if the violation for which it is calculating the penalty is not self-reported. In contrast, if a company has a history of TSCA violations it may not qualify for the penalty reductions under Audit Policy, and should consider self-reporting under the applicable ERP.

The EPA can also reduce a penalty by up to 25 percent if the violation can reasonably be considered out of the violator's control. The § 5 ERP gives an example of an importer who relies on an incorrect certification from the supplier that the chemical is on the Inventory, when in fact it is not, provided also that the importer knew only the trade name of the chemical substance and not the chemical identity. Presumably if the importer knew the chemical identity it should have checked the Inventory itself.[59]

59. *Id.* at 19.

B. Penalty Assessments

Each EPA Region, as well as EPA Headquarters, can assess a penalty for a TSCA violation. The EPA will typically exercise considerable discretion in reducing negotiated penalties. The Consolidated Rules of Practice[60] governs civil penalty assessments, and requires that each Region have a Regional Judicial Officer who is a lawyer and conducts hearings and may have authority to approve settlements.[61]

1. Negotiating a Penalty

In almost all circumstances, a company will have notice of a violation before the EPA files a complaint seeking an administrative penalty. If the EPA discovered the violation during an inspection, then the inspector may give his or her findings to the company before a complaint is filed, and if the violation is self-reported the company will clearly know in advance of a formal complaint.

In either case, the company should take the opportunity to negotiate a penalty before the EPA files a complaint. The EPA usually issues a press release when it files significant complaints, but if there is a simultaneous settlement the EPA will include the amount of the settlement in its press release. Because EPA's complaints usually seek large penalties for TSCA violations, its press releases often imply that companies are major environmental scofflaws. A company can avoid this inference by negotiating a more realistic penalty that is publicized in the EPA's initial press release.[62]

The Consolidated Rules of Procedure confirms that a penalty proceeding can be commenced and settled simultaneously.[63] Many people take advantage of this option, as demonstrated by the consent agreements posted on the Environmental Appeals Board Web site that say that they were simultaneously commenced and concluded.[64]

---

60. 22 C.F.R. Part 22.
61. 22 C.F.R. § 22.4(b).
62. *See, e.g.*, press release "EPA Finds PCB-Containing Equipment for Sale Without Proper Identification on eBay" (Oct. 2, 2009), which announces the monetary settlement value and not the penalties that could have been sought in an administrative complaint, *available at* http://yosemite.epa.gov/opa/admpress.nsf/ab2d81eb088f4a7e85257359003f5339/b29b37a0ec602b9e852576430065c303!OpenDocument.
63. 22 C.F.R. § 22.13(b).
64. *See, e.g.*, In the Matter of Fujifilm Manufacturing U.S.A., Inc. Docket No. TSCA-HQ-2008-5029 (Oct. 20, 2008), *available through* http://yosemite.epa.gov/oa/EAB_Web_Docket.nsf/Unpublished~Final~Orders?OpenView.

The EPA has a policy supporting the use of alternative dispute resolution in resolving enforcement cases.[65]

a. Supplemental Environmental Projects

In the context of a settlement, the EPA may allow most of a penalty to be offset by a Supplemental Environmental Project (SEP), which is a project that a company entering into a settlement can perform to benefit the environment. EPA guidances impose numerous conditions on performing a SEP, but it is always worth exploring whether a SEP can be used to offset penalties.[66] There are no promulgated regulations on SEPs, and so permitting a SEP is solely within the EPA's discretion.

In fiscal year 2008, the EPA accepted SEPs worth $39,000,000[67] demonstrating that SEPs play a very important role in reducing cash penalties and diverting penalty money to environmentally beneficial projects.

A SEP can offset up to 75 percent of a penalty, but the penalty cannot be decreased below the economic benefit of noncompliance plus 10 percent of the gravity based penalty.[68] Usually no more than 80 percent of the value of the SEP can be used to offset the cash penalty payment.[69] For example, if a SEP costs $200,000 and the gravity based penalty is $100,000, up to 80% of the SEP costs, or $160,000 could have been used to offset a higher penalty, but the offset for a penalty of $100,000 cannot ordinarily exceed $75,000.

The EPA has established several parameters for a SEP.[70] The SEP must have some relationship, or nexus, to the violation, the company must not have a preexisting legal obligation to perform the project, and the SEP cannot merely be a charitable donation.[71] The SEP cannot be a project that the company would likely be required to do because of any other reason, including another enforcement proceeding. The EPA will only negotiate a SEP as part of a settling a civil penalty proceeding. While the SEP policy states that the EPA must have begun an enforcement proceeding, it will negotiate SEPs after receiving a self-report of a violation, but before it has taken any

---

65. 65 Fed. Reg. 81858 (Dec. 27, 2000), *available at* http://www.epa.gov/adr/epaadrpolicyfinal.pdf.
66. EPA, Supplemental Environmental Projects Policy (effective May 1, 1998) [hereinafter SEP Policy], *available at* http://www.epa.gov/compliance/resources/policies/civil/seps/fnlsup-hermn-mem.pdf.
67. *See* http://www.epa.gov/compliance/resources/reports/endofyear/eoy2008/2008enfcrossmediahighlights.html#cat 3.
68. SEP Policy, 14.
69. *Id.* at 16.
70. *Id. See also*, the EPA's brochure entitled Supplemental Environmental Projects, EPA 300-B-00-007, (July 2000).
71. *Id.*

administrative action.[72] The EPA will negotiate the details of the SEP during the settlement discussions, and may seek an active role in defining the project. For this reason, it cannot be a project the company has already begun.[73]

The requirement that the SEP have a nexus to the violation has often been used to reject SEPs for TSCA violations. The EPA's SEP policy states that a nexus is present only if:

- the project is designed to reduce the likelihood that similar violations will occur in the future;
- the project reduces the adverse impact to public health or the environment to which the violation at issue contributes; or
- the project reduces the overall risk to public health or the environment potentially affected by the violation at issue.

If the violation is failure to file export notifications under § 12(b) of TSCA, for example, that violation is so far removed from actual environmental impact that it is difficult to perform a capital project that can be even vaguely related. Old statistics on the SEPs that EPA has permitted show that it has allowed a lower ratio of SEP expenditures to dollar of penalty for TSCA violations than for violations of most other environmental statutes.[74] However, that should not stop a company from trying to implement a project that will benefit the local community instead of simply paying the EPA.

If a company has a preexisting legal obligation to perform a project, such as installing pollution control equipment to meet a permit requirement, then it cannot qualify as a SEP. However, if a company has a deadline two or more years in the future, and does not obtain any other benefits from early compliance, then meeting the deadline early can be a SEP.[75]

The EPA has eight categories of SEPs that it will accept, concluding with the catchall "other."[76] These categories are:

- public health, benefiting the population put at risk by the violation;
- pollution prevention;
- pollution reduction;
- environmental restoration and protection of the affected ecosystem;

---

72. *Id.*
73. *Id.*
74. Protecting the Public and the Environment Through Innovative Approaches; Fiscal Year 2001 Enforcement and Compliance Assurance Accomplishments, EPA300-R-02-010, p.72. For example, the value of SEPs for TSCA violations was only about 20 percent of the value of administrative penalties. For EPCRA, the SEPs were valued about the same as the penalties, and for the Clean Air Act, SEPs were valued at over eight times the administrative penalties. The only program for with a lower SEP to administrative penalty ratio is FIFRA.
75. SEP Policy.
76. *Id.*

- emergency planning and preparedness, available only for violations of emergency planning, spill or release requirements;
- assessments and audits, limited to compliance audits conducted by small businesses or small communities, and pollution prevention or environmental quality assessments;
- environmental compliance promotion, which is providing training or technical support to other members of the regulated community; and
- other, provided EPA headquarters approves.

For example, S.C. Johnson entered into an administrative settlement for allegedly violating the Federal Insecticide, Fungicide, and Rodenticide Act by selling an asthma product containing an unregistered pesticide. EPA agreed that it could fund an asthma foundation to purchase and operate a mobile asthma clinic[77] as a SEP.

The EPA has developed a model SEP Consent Agreement governing the conduct of a SEP.[78]

There are disadvantages to SEPs:

- they take time and effort to negotiate;
- usually a company will spend more money on a penalty plus SEP than it would on a paying the penalty alone;
- settlement agreements involving SEPs will have stipulated penalties for failure to complete the SEP; and
- a company that publicizes its SEP will be required to state that it was undertaken in the context of an enforcement proceeding.

On the positive side, SEPs funnel money and beneficial projects to the company's community and are a productive way to ensure that penalty money is used for environmental improvements.

b. Economic Benefit

The EPA will not reduce a penalty below the value of the money saved by not complying with TSCA. The EPA's economic benefit model is referred to as BEN.[79]

Using the BEN model can lead to rather high economic benefits from noncompliance. For example, if a company has failed to install $1,000,000 of pollution control equipment for 72 months, and that equipment would have

---

77. Protecting the Public and the Environment Through Innovative Approaches; Fiscal Year 2001 Enforcement and Compliance Assurance Accomplishments, EPA300-R-02-010, p.49.
78. Model Supplemental Environmental Project Consent Agreement and Order, 1999, *available at* http://www.epa.gov/compliance/resources/policies/civil/seps/sepcafo.pdf.
79. The BEN model is *available at* http://www.epa.gov/compliance/civil/econmodels/#ben.

cost $10,000 per year to operate, then the BEN model yields an economic benefit of $605,000.[80]

c. Audits

As part of a negotiated settlement, the EPA is often receptive to incorporating provisions for an audit into the settlement agreement. The EPA will permit the company to report any suspected violations and receive either no penalty or a stipulated penalty that is more favorable than otherwise obtainable.[81]

The EPA also negotiates auditing agreements with companies in the absence of a settlement agreement.

d. Ability to Pay

If a company cannot pay the adjusted gravity based penalty and remain in business, the penalty may be reduced to keep the company viable. The EPA puts financial information from the company into a model called ABEL to determine the appropriate penalty in these situations. There are analogous models called INDIPAY and MUNIPAY for assessing individuals' and municipalities' ability to pay.[82]

An example of how the EPA applied the ABEL model to reduce a gravity based penalty from $2,571,267 to $300,000 based on ability to pay is provided in *In the Matter of MarChem Corporation.*[83]

2. Complaints

One of the first things to do when a company receives an administrative complaint is to carefully review it to determine if it is legally adequate. The questions to ask include:

- Does the act complained of really violate TSCA?
- Is the penalty calculated correctly in accordance with an Enforcement Response Policy?
- What defenses does the company have?

---

80. Bill S. Forcade and Elizabeth D. Anderson, *How to Minimize Civil Penalties In Environmental Enforcement*, 30 ENVTL. L. REP. 11031 (2000).

81. *See, e.g.*, In the Matter of Ashland, Inc., TSCA-HQ-2007-5013 (EAB Aug. 16, 2007), *available through* http://yosemite.epa.gov/oa/EAB_Web_Docket.nsf/Unpublished~Final~Orders?OpenView. This Consent Agreement is a useful model of an agreement requiring a compliance audit.

82. ABEL, INDIPAY and MUNIPAY are accessible through the EPA Web site at http://www.epa.gov/compliance/civil/econmodels/#ben.

83. TSCA-HQ-2007-5008 (EAB Oct. 5, 2007), *available through* http://yosemite.epa.gov/oa/EAB_Web_Docket.nsf/Unpublished~Final~Orders?OpenView.

The Consolidated Rules of Practice recites the elements that must be in a TSCA complaint.[84] These include a reference to § 16's civil penalty authority, a reference to the statutory and regulatory provisions that were allegedly violated, the factual basis for the allegations, and the relief and monetary penalty sought. The complaint must provide notice of the respondent's right to a hearing, specify if the Administrative Procedure Act applies (which it does), and be accompanied by a copy of the Consolidated Rules of Practice.

In instances in which either a State or the Federal government could commence an enforcement action, recent guidelines from the National Association of Attorneys General and the United States Department of Justice Environment and Natural Resources Division describe the cooperation between the two entities.[85]

3. Defenses

This section will focus on defenses that may be generally applicable to enforcement proceedings, and not defenses that are specific to a particular type of violation. The defenses that are specific to a particular type of violation are usually related to a failure of proof that the statutory elements of a violation were met. Those defenses are based on a careful reading of the regulations and statute, and the best place to start to determine what defenses are available to a specific allegation is the regulations and statute proscribing the alleged behavior.

a. Statute of Limitations

EPA cannot recover civil penalties for any violation that occurred more than five years before the EPA commenced an administrative penalty proceeding. Although the EPA routinely sought penalties for violations more than five years old, this issue was finally resolved in *3M v. Browner*,[86] which held that a federal catch-all statute of limitations applied to TSCA penalty proceedings.

b. Estoppel

Equitable estoppel is a defense that may preclude the imposition of penalties, although it will not preclude injunctive relief. Applying equitable estoppel, if a company has relied on advice from the EPA about how to comply with its

---

84. 22 C.F.R. §22.14(a).

85. National Association of Attorneys General and Department of Justice, Environment & Natural Resources Division, Guidelines for Joint State/Federal Civil Environmental Enforcement Litigation (Mar. 2003), *available at* http://www.justice.gov/enrd/ENRDFiles/Guidelines-for-joint-state-federal-civil-environmental-enforcement-litigation.pdf.

86. 17 F.3d 1453 (D.C. Cir. 1994).

regulations, the EPA may be estopped from penalizing it. Estoppel does not permit noncompliance, and a court may issue an injunction even if the violation was due to EPA's actions.[87] In *In the Matter of Troy Chemical Corp.*,[88] an Administrative Law Judge denied the EPA's motion for accelerated judgment because Troy asserted that it relied on statements made by the EPA that led it to misconstrue the time periods for Inventory Update Rule reporting.

c. The Paperwork Reduction Act

The Paperwork Reduction Act[89] requires each agency, including the EPA, to obtain approval from the Office of Management and Budget (OMB) before collecting information from ten or more members of the public. The OMB issues a confirmation, referred to as an OMB control number, for each approval it grants. The EPA cannot penalize any person for failing to respond to a request for information unless the EPA's request for information (i) has a valid OMB control number and (ii) states that no response is required unless there is a valid OMB control number.[90] OMB approvals are valid for only three years.

If the EPA does not comply with these requirements of the Paperwork Reduction Act, a respondent can raise the noncompliance as a complete defense to a penalty proceeding.[91] As a result, a respondent in a penalty proceeding charged with failing to prepare records or submit information to the EPA should check to be certain that the EPA obtained a valid OMB control number for the information request, and published the required notice with the call for information. The EPA cannot impose a penalty if it did not comply with the Paperwork Reduction Act.[92]

d. Jurisdiction

It is axiomatic that the EPA must have jurisdiction over any entity that it seeks to bring an enforcement action against. For example, the EPA has said it cannot enforce the import certification requirements against a

---

87. The EPA maintains a TSCA hotline, which is currently staffed by a third party vendor. It is not likely that equitable estoppel would apply to advice from the hotline. If the vendor's employees send copies of EPA documents, then those documents could give rise to an equitable estoppel.
88. Docket No. II-TSCA-8(a)-98-0101 (OAL Oct. 14, 1999).
89. 44 U.S.C. § 3501.
90. 44 U.S.C. § 3512, *see also* Center For Safety v. National Hwy Traf., 244 *F.3d 144* (D.C. Cir. 2001).
91. 44 U.S.C. § 3512.
92. *See* In re Lazarus, 7 E.A.B. 318 (EAB 1997).

foreign shipper, and has only the U.S. importer to look to in an enforcement action.[93]

e. Invalidity of an Order

In one relatively narrow context, the EPA has said that the invalidity of an order may not be raised as a defense in an enforcement proceeding for violating the order. It remains to be seen whether EPA will take this position in other contexts. EPA said the validity of the order itself can only be challenged by pre-enforcement judicial review.[94]

The EPA announced this interpretation in a Federal Register notice addressing the Endocrine Disrupter Screening Program. The EPA was addressing enforcement of orders requiring testing of chemicals for their hormone mimicking activities, and stated that the only way to challenge the order itself would be to seek judicial review of the initial issuance of the order. Under the Endocrine Disrupter Screening Program orders are issued under the Federal Food, Drug, and Cosmetics Act,[95] but the enforcement proceeding is the same as TSCA § 16. Orders will be issued directly to the companies subject to them, and so the order recipients should have actual knowledge of the issuance of the order. This is in contrast to a TSCA § 4 test rule, which is announced to the regulated community in the Federal Register. However, the EPA did not limit its statement about the non-reviewability of the content of orders to orders about which the recipients have actual knowledge. Instead, the EPA generalized and said that TSCA § 16 limits the issues that may be raised in an enforcement proceeding to whether there was a violation of an applicable order.[96]

4. Consent Agreements

Any agreement that the EPA and an alleged violator enter into must be memorialized in a consent agreement.[97] Typically, the EPA will prepare the first draft of the consent decree and then provide it to the respondent for review.

The company, which is the respondent in a penalty proceeding, must agree to the following elements in a consent decree: (i) that the tribunal has jurisdiction over it; (ii) either that the respondent admits the facts recited in the complaint, or neither admits nor denies them; (iii) that it consents to the

93. TSCA Questions and Answers from the October, 1990 EPA-Industry Living with TSCA Workshop, question 46 (Oct. 1992).
94. 74 Fed. Reg. 17560, 17576 (Apr. 15, 2009).
95. 21 U.S.C. § 301–399.
96. *Id.*
97. 40 C.F.R. § 2218(b)(2).

penalties agreed to, and any other agreed-upon terms and conditions such as corrective action; and (iv) that it waives its right to appeal or contest any allegations.[98] While the EPA has form consent agreements that it uses, a company is free to negotiate all of the terms the EPA proposes.

The EPA can issue a combined complaint and consent agreement in one document. A combined complaint and consent agreement is advantageous to a respondent because any trade press coverage or EPA press release may include the settlement amount instead of the typically much larger proposed penalty.

5. Appeals to the Office of Administrative Law and Environmental Review Board

Companies that request a hearing on the EPA's penalty assessments will have the hearing in the EPA Office of Administrative Law. Administrative Law Judges (ALJs) in the Office of Administrative Law are EPA employees.

ALJs are not obligated to follow the applicable penalty policy in determining the appropriate penalty,[99] and will reevaluate the penalty using the ERP as a guidepost. In many instances they find that the ERP produced the appropriate penalty. But in cases where the ERP has resulted in a penalty that is disproportionate to the violation, or to other penalties that other violators have had to pay, the ALJ will reduce it. See, for example, *In the Matter of AE Associates, Inc.*,[100] where the ALJ decreased the EPA's penalty of $5,500 for asbestos violations to $500, finding that the penalty policy did not differentiate enough between violations of different seriousness. A good discussion of the range of factors that the ALJ may consider, and the ALJ's disdain for rote application of the ERP, is found in *In the Matter of GCA Chemical Corporation* (*GCA*).[101] In *GCA*, the ALJ found that the penalty policy for Inventory Update Rule violations imposed an identical penalty in every case, without regard to the particular circumstances, and reduced the EPA's proposed penalty of $37,400 to $6,600 because of the mitigating circumstances.

Decisions of the Office of Administrative Law may be appealed to the Environmental Appeals Board (EAB). The EAB's Practice Manual[102] provides guidance on its procedures and requirements.

---

98. *Id.*
99. In re DIC Americas, Inc., TSCA -II-8(a)-90-0109 (Dec. 30, 1993), TSCA Appeal No. 94-2 6 E.A.D. 184, (Sept. 27, 1995).
100. Docket No. II-TSCA-1-99-0262 (OALJ Nov. 30, 2001).
101. Docket No: TSCA-4-2000-0130 (OALJ June 18, 2002).
102. The Environmental Appeals Board Practice Manual (June 2004) [hereinafter EAB Practice Manual], *available at* http://yosemite.epa.gov/oa/EAB_Web_Docket.nsf/General+Information/Environmental+Appeals+Board+Guidance+Documents?OpenDocument.

The Environmental Appeals Board is a panel of four EPA lawyers who hear appeals of penalty determinations. The EAB usually forms three-member panels to hear cases. It reviews hearing officers' decisions to determine if they are supported by a preponderance of the evidence, and usually gives deference to the fact-finder's factual conclusions.[103]

6. Appeals to the Circuit Court

Determinations of the EAB can be appealed to the District Court in Washington, D.C. or any other district in which the respondent resides or transacts business.[104] The District Court will only review the EAB's decision to determine if it was arbitrary and capricious. *Rogers Corp. v. E.P.A.*[105]

C. EPA's Audit Policy

1. Introduction

EPA established its Audit Policy to encourage companies to self-report and self-correct TSCA violations.[106] It states the EPA's policy of forgiving any penalties it could assess, or forgiving 75 percent of the penalties, if a self-reporting company meets its prerequisite conditions. Over thirty-five hundred different entities had resolved violations by using the Audit Policy through mid-2008.[107]

The Audit Policy is based on the recognition that the government does not have the resources to uncover every environmental violation, and needs the help of the regulated community. To work towards the EPA's goal of universal compliance, the Audit Policy encourages companies to discover their own violations, report them to the EPA, correct the immediate violation, and make systematic changes to its practices to prevent the violation from occurring again. The Audit Policy generally functions quite well to meet these objectives, because it significantly rewards companies that meet the Audit Policy goals.

It is important to keep in mind that the Audit Policy is simply a policy, and its application rests in the discretion of the agency. It does not have the force

---

103. EAB Practice Manual, 20.
104. Administrative Procedure Act, 5 U.S.C. § 704; TSCA § 16(a).
105. 275 F.3d 1096 (D.C. Cir. 2002).
106. 65 Fed. Reg. 19618 (Apr. 11, 2000) [hereinafter Audit Policy]. The Audit Policy supplanted an earlier version published in 1995 in the Federal Register at 60 Fed. Reg. 66706 (Dec. 22, 1995). The 1995 policy is no longer pertinent, except for the historical development of amnesty policies in general.
107. 73 Fed. Reg. 44991, 44994 (Aug. 1, 2008).

of law because it was not promulgated as a regulation, and it is unlikely that a company could sue to require the EPA to comply with the Audit Policy. The Audit Policy explicitly states that it is not intended to create any enforceable rights.[108] When self-reporting under the Audit Policy, management should be told that obtaining the benefits of the Audit Policy is not assured, although to date the EPA has applied the policy fairly consistently.[109]

In 2008 the EPA issued a policy tailored for acquisitions.[110] New owners can get a "clean start" at facilities they have just acquired if they audit within nine months of the closing or enter into an audit agreement with the EPA and agree to an audit plan. If the new owner audits without an audit agreement, all potential violations must be disclosed to the EPA within 21 days of discovery, or 45 days after the closing, whichever is later. New owners must promptly correct any violation, and must comply with the remaining audit policy conditions. In return, the EPA will not assess penalties against the new owner for the period before the closing, and will not assess penalties for the economic benefit of noncompliance for the period before the closing provided that the new owner corrects the violation within 60 days of discovering it, or any longer period to which the EPA agrees. New owners will be assessed for the economic benefit of any operation and maintenance activities that they did not perform because of the violation. EPA will also permit pre-closing due diligence to qualify as an audit, although it does not meet the Audit Policy definition of a systematic discovery because it is a one-time occurrence.[111]

Sellers do not get any relief under the targeted policy, and the EPA specifically stated that it may pursue sellers for penalties in appropriate circumstances.[112]

2. Complete Penalty Mitigation

The Audit Policy offers complete mitigation of the possible penalties for a violation of environmental laws if nine conditions are met:

- systematic discovery of the violation through an environmental audit or a compliance management system;
- voluntary discovery;
- prompt disclosure;

---

108. 65 Fed. Reg. 19618, 19627.
109. The EPA Office of Regulatory Enforcement issued an Audit Policy Interpretive Guidance (Jan. 1997) and Audit Policy Frequently Asked Questions (2007), *available through* http://www.epa.gov/compliance/incentives/auditing/auditpolicy.html.
110. 73 Fed. Reg. 44991 (Aug. 1, 2008).
111. *Id.* at 44999-50.
112. *Id.* at 45004.

- discovery and disclosure independent of government or third-party plaintiff;
- correction and remediation;
- prevent recurrence;
- no repeat violations;
- other violations excluded; and
- cooperation.

These labels are not self-explanatory, and each requires further discussion.

1. Systematic Discovery of the Violation Through an Environmental Audit or a Compliance Management System

To meet this criterion, a company must have discovered the potential violation through either an environmental audit or through application of a compliance management system.[113] While the Audit Policy describes compliance management systems in detail, its definition of "audit" is fairly cursory.

The Audit Policy definition of environmental audit is as follows:

> "Environmental Audit" is a systematic, documented, periodic and objective review by regulated entities of facility operations and practices related to meeting environmental requirements.[114]

The Audit Policy leaves a lot of room to argue that a fairly informal internal review constitutes an audit, so long as there is a systematic approach, records of the audit data, analysis, findings, and recommendations, some schedule for conducting audits, and provided that the auditors are not the same people whose functions are being audited.

There are many circumstances in which it is not possible to argue that a violation was found during an audit. For example, if a toxicologist receives a study of adverse effects of a chemical and realizes that the chemical tested is not described correctly, that could lead to the further realization that the company has been using an incorrect Chemical Abstract Services (CAS) Number for the chemical. If the correct CAS Number is not listed on the TSCA Inventory, then the company may have violated the PMN requirements of TSCA § 5.[115] This discovery would not be in the context of an audit because it was not made during a systematic review of company operations. Similarly, no spontaneous discovery of a potential violation outside of the

113. *See*, Chapter 13, Compliance Programs.
114. Audit Policy, 19625.
115. *See* Chapter 4, Premanufacture Notifications.

context of a systematic review of company operations could meet the Audit Policy criteria for an audit.

Even a thorough, systematic review would not qualify as an audit if it were not documented. This emphasizes the importance of well-considered and well-planned audits.

In contrast to its relative silence on what constitutes an audit, the EPA detailed its concept of a compliance management system that meets the Audit Policy requirements. Such a system must have six elements, designed to motivate employees to "prevent, detect and correct violations:"[116]

- [c]ompliance policies, standards and procedures that identify how employees and agents are to meet [legal] requirements…;
- [a]ssignment of overall responsibility for over[sight]…and assignment of specific responsibility for assuring compliance at each facility…;
- [m]echanisms for systematically assuring that compliance policies, standards and procedures are being carried out, including …auditing… periodic evaluation…and a means …to report violations…without fear of retaliation;
- [e]fforts to communicate effectively…standards and procedures to all employees and other agents;
- [a]ppropriate incentives to managers and employees…including consistent enforcement through appropriate disciplinary mechanisms; and
- [p]rocedures for the prompt and appropriate correction of any violations, and any necessary modifications to the…compliance management system to prevent future violations.[117]

When a company claims the benefits of the Audit Policy, the EPA will generally seek proof that it has all of these elements in place. It will ask for copies of compliance policies, and scrutinize them for what they say about compliance with the requirements that were violated in the matter at issue. If those policies are not specific enough to identify the people or job functions responsible for compliance, the EPA may seek other materials such as organization charts or job descriptions. The EPA will ask for a copy of any audit policy or a description of the company's audit practices, as well as its statement to employees that they will not suffer any adverse consequences from reporting violations. The EPA will also ask about training programs that employees attend and the company's incentives to encourage compliance. Finally, the EPA will want to know what steps the company took to correct or mitigate the subject violation and prevent future violations.

116. Audit Policy, 19621.
117. *Id.* at 19625.

2. Voluntary Discovery

By "voluntary discovery" the EPA means that the company discovered the potential violation through its own initiative, and not through monitoring or auditing required by a permit, consent decree, regulation, order, or other compulsory obligation.[118] As an example, the Audit Policy specifies that a violation found during an audit that is required by a consent decree or settlement agreement is not voluntarily discovered. However, to encourage companies to adopt environmental management systems, if a consent decree or settlement agreement requires implementation of an environmental management system, violations discovered during an audit that is part of the environmental management system are considered to have been discovered voluntarily.

If an audit was begun voluntarily and later embodied in a settlement agreement, then the Audit Policy may still be applied to mitigate penalties.[119]

There are no regulatory requirements to self-report TSCA violations.[120]

3. Prompt Disclosure

Prompt disclosure of a TSCA violation means only one thing in the Audit Policy: self-reporting within twenty-one days of discovering the potential violation, or the following business day if the twenty-first day is on a weekend or Federal holiday.[121]

The twenty-one day period for self-reporting begins to run when any employee, contractor, or agent "has an objectively reasonable basis for believing that a violation has, or may have, occurred."[122] An "objectively reasonable basis" for belief is measured by a "prudent person" standard, and is based on what a prudent person with the same information would have concluded.[123] As a result, the twenty-one day period begins to run when a person who is prudent would have enough information to reasonably conclude that there may have been a violation.

This standard does not allow time for confirming that a violation has in fact occurred, and often puts companies in a quandary when deciding whether or not to self-report. If the company self-reports before it is reasonably certain there has been a violation, then it runs the risk of creating a tempest

---

118. *Id.* at 19621.
119. EPA, Office of Regulatory Enforcement, Audit Policy Interpretive Guidance, EC-G-2002-149, 2 (Jan. 1997) [hereinafter Audit Interpretive Guide], *available through* http://www.epa.gov/compliance/incentives/auditing/auditpolicy.html.
120. *See* discussion, *infra*.
121. *Id.* at 19621.
122. *Id.*
123. *Id.*

when there is no violation. If it waits to confirm a violation, it runs the risk that the EPA will determine that the self-report was not timely. If the self-report is not timely, then the company cannot get any benefit from the Audit Policy.[124]

The Audit Policy addresses acquisitions, but the EPA has issued a subsequent policy applicable to acquisitions, discussed *supra*.

4. Discovery and Disclosure Independent of Government or Third-Party Plaintiff

Independent discovery and disclosure is shorthand for discovery and disclosure through a company's own initiative, and not in a race to prevent imminent discovery by the EPA or an adversary in litigation. In this respect, it complements the element of initiative in "voluntary discovery," which refers to finding a problem that was not unearthed during a compulsory analysis.

The types of imminent discovery that preclude application of the Audit Policy are an EPA civil investigation that has already begun, a third-party formal or informal complaint or notice of intent to sue,[125] a whistleblower report, or any other event that makes governmental discovery imminent.[126] If the company does not know about a civil investigation that has already begun, the EPA may still mitigate penalties under the Audit Policy.[127]

The EPA recognized that a company with multiple facilities may operate those facilities independently of each other, and that an audit at one facility will not reach another commonly owned facility. Therefore, a company with multiple facilities can take advantage of Audit Policy penalty mitigation for violations at facilities where discovery of the potential violation is not imminent.[128] The EPA did not allude to the fact that it audits facility-by-facility, especially when commonly owned facilities are in different EPA Regions, but that provides an additional justification for encouraging companies to come forward to report violations at other of its facilities, even if the EPA is actively auditing one of those facilities.

The Audit Policy encourages companies to enter into multi-facility corporate auditing agreements to avoid some of the problems that can arise when audits are performed serially at several facilities. For example, a company that is conducting a multi-facility audit could be partially precluded from obtaining Audit Policy relief if any of its facilities is inspected by EPA prior to

124. The ERPs require self-reporting within thirty days, instead of the Audit Policy's twenty-one days, and so some benefits under the ERPs may still be available if the Audit Policy deadline has elapsed.

125. *See*, Citizens' Suits, *infra*.

126. Audit Policy, 19622.

127. *Id.* at 19626.

128. *Id.* at 19622.

completion of the internal audit. As another example, unless a company enters into a prior agreement governing the conduct of an audit and subsequent self-reporting, it is possible that one systematic error could be uncovered that applies to multiple facilities. This could require a company to report audit findings for facilities although the on-site audit has not even commenced for that facility. The EPA has stated that if it can infer from one self-report that other violations have occurred, then the inferred violations must be reported within the initial self-reporting period, or the inferred violations will not be promptly disclosed.[129] The EPA is open to resolving all these potential problems through an agreement before a company begins its audit.[130]

5. Correction and Remediation

To meet the Audit Policy criterion of correction and remediation, a company must correct any harm that it caused by the potential violation.[131] In the TSCA context, this could mean taking actions such as quarantining a chemical substance that it manufactured in violation of the premanufacture notification requirements of § 5, or recalling waste that was shipped to a disposal facility in violation of a Significant New Use Rule under § 5.[132] The company must also certify in writing that it has corrected the violation.

The company must correct the violation as soon as possible, but in any event no later than sixty days after it discovered the violation, which could be as soon as thirty-nine days after self-reporting. The EPA may specify a shorter time for correction. If a correction will take more than sixty days to implement, the EPA may exercise discretion to permit that if the company notifies the EPA within the sixty-day period.[133] As a practical matter, the company will probably be in contact with the EPA after making the self-report, and will discuss informally how long a correction will take.

The EPA has the discretion to require a company to enter into a consent order or decree requiring compliance or remediation as a condition to obtaining Audit Policy relief.[134]

6. Prevent Recurrence

The Audit Policy does not say much about what a company must do to prevent recurrence of the violation, other than that it may need to improve its auditing program or compliance management system.

---

129. Audit Interpretive Guide, 3.
130. *See* EPA's Audit Policy Update, Volume 4, No. 2 (Dec. 1999) EPA 300-N-99-020.
131. Audit Policy, 19622.
132. *See* Chapter 4, Premanufacture Notifications.
133. Audit Policy, 19622.
134. *Id.* at, 19626.

7. No Repeat Violations

A company that has been notified by the EPA or a third-party of the same type of violation, or a closely related one, at the same facility in the past three years cannot qualify for Audit Policy penalty mitigation.[135] If the EPA or a state has mitigated a penalty then that constitutes a prior violation, because in that case the company had an opportunity to correct the underlying cause of the violation.[136] If the company has multiple facilities, it cannot receive Audit Policy penalty mitigation if any of its facilities had a pattern of the same type of violation, or closely related ones, in the past five years.

The time periods are measured from the time the company received notice from the EPA or a third-party of the first violation. The notice could be a notice of violation or warning letter.[137] The subsequent violation is within the three- or five-year period if it actually occurred within three or five years of the date the company received notice of the first violation.[138]

8. Other Violations Excluded

"Other" violations are violations that preclude application of the Audit Policy because of their seriousness. If there is serious environmental harm from the violation, or if the violation may result in substantial endangerment to public health or the environment, then no penalty relief is available under the Audit Policy. Similarly, no penalty relief is available under the Audit Policy if the violation is a violation of a consent agreement or any order or plea agreement, or any cleanup agreement, on the theory that penalty relief would vitiate any incentive to comply in the first place.[139]

9. Cooperation

The criterion of cooperation requires that the company that self-reports cooperate with the EPA's efforts to determine if the Audit Policy applies.[140] Since any company that self-reports will want to prove that the Audit Policy applies, there is very little reason not to cooperate. However, the Audit Policy recognizes that a company may try to withhold information that would

---

135. *Id.* at, 19622.
136. *Id.* at 19623.
137. Audit Interpretive Guide, 9.
138. Audit Interpretive Guide, 8.
139. Audit Policy, 19623. This limitation seems inconsistent with the penalty relief available for violations of law, because arguably penalty relief vitiates the incentive to comply with laws also. However, the EPA noted in the Audit Policy that this prohibition had not been applied as of the date the Audit Policy was issued. Audit Policy, 19623.
140. Audit Policy, 19623.

reflect negatively on its application for Audit Policy penalty mitigation, and requires companies to be fully forthcoming.

The EPA reserves the right to ask for copies of audit reports, and for extensive information if the violation is criminal, including documentation and employee interviews.[141]

3. 75 Percent Penalty Mitigation

The Audit Policy offers 75 percent penalty mitigation for companies that self-report but do not meet the criterion of discovering the violation through an audit or the application of a compliance management system. Depending on the circumstances, substantially equivalent penalty mitigation may be possible through applying the incentives in the ERPs, without expending the resources necessary to prove compliance with the remaining eight Audit Policy criteria. When considering self-reporting in a circumstance that only qualifies for 75 percent reduction under the Audit Policy, it could be useful to do the arithmetic to compare the penalty for a self-reported violation under the Audit Policy or under the applicable ERP, although the EPA intended that a 75 percent or greater penalty reduction would only be available if the Audit Policy criteria are met.[142]

Any penalty remaining after application of the Audit Policy can be further reduced by the amount of a SEP.[143] The SEP cannot be one that is required to meet the Audit Policy criteria; for example, it cannot be institution of a compliance management system if that is necessary to prevent future violations under the sixth criterion of the Audit Policy.[144]

4. Limits on Penalty Mitigation

The EPA will not reduce a penalty below the economic benefit the self-reporting company realized by cutting corners and causing the violation in the first place. The EPA does not want to give a competitive advantage to violators while it gives an economic advantage for self-reporting.[145]

5. Additional Audit Policy Incentives

The EPA touts its policy of not referring potential criminal activity for prosecution if a company otherwise complies with the Audit Policy.

141. *Id.*
142. Audit Interpretive Guide, 10.
143. *Id.*
144. *Id.*
145. Audit Policy, 19620.

However, there are significant limits that a company should be aware of, even if it qualifies for 100 percent penalty mitigation. The Audit Policy does not give complete assurances that EPA will not refer a matter to the Justice Department, or that the Justice Department will not prosecute if it concludes that there was a crime. At most, it states the EPA's policy to generally not refer companies that self-report potential criminal violations to the Justice Department for prosecution, provided the company acted in good faith and has a systematic approach to preventing further violations.[146] The policy reiterates that "conscious disregard of or willful blindness to" the law will be prosecuted.[147] The EPA's policy does not extend to individuals whose actions are potentially criminal, or other business entities that may have participated in a criminal act.[148] This leaves a company that uncovers a potentially criminal violation at risk for prosecution of itself, its employees, and its affiliates after self-reporting.

The EPA's Audit Policy Interpretive Guidance[149] gives an example that is an important reminder of the limits of the Audit Policy. According to the Interpretive Guidance, Chiquita Brands International self-reported a criminal violation committed by its subsidiary, John Morrell and Company. While the government chose not to prosecute Chiquita Brands International, it did prosecute and convict John Morrell and Company and several corporate officials for conspiracy and Clean Water Act (CWA) felonies.[150]

A further caution comes from the fact that the EPA provides recommendations not to prosecute to the Department of Justice or United States Attorneys' Office,[151] which are not bound by the EPA recommendation.

The EPA also offers the incentive of not routinely asking for copies of a company's audit reports, provided the EPA learned of the potential violation through self-reporting.[152]

D. EPA's Small Business Compliance Policy

The EPA has a more lenient self-reporting policy for small businesses and small governments, designed to encourage those entities to become more environmentally conscious and to ask for assistance when they need it.

146. *Id.* at 19618–19619.
147. *Id.* at 19619.
148. *Id.* at 19620.
149. Audit Interpretive Guide, 38.
150. That self-report was made under a prior Audit Policy version, but the changes made in the current version would not have affected the results in that matter.
151. Audit Policy, 19624.
152. *Id.* at 19620.

The Small Business Compliance Policy[153] defines small businesses and small governments as those that have one hundred or fewer people working for it.[154] The EPA will waive 100 percent of a small business' penalty, but retains the right to seek the full amount of any significant benefit the business obtained from its violation. There are also provisions for waiving penalties if the small business cannot pay.[155]

Small businesses may also qualify for the Audit Policy's penalty mitigation, but because the standards in the Small Business Compliance Policy are so much easier to meet, there are only limited situations in which a small business would opt to prove the higher standards in the Audit Policy. These situations are when a violation involves criminal activity, because in that case a company can receive penalty mitigation under the Audit Policy, but cannot receive penalty mitigation under the Small Business Compliance Policy.[156] Similarly, if a small business has two or more unrelated environmental violations in the prior five years, it would not qualify for penalty mitigation under the Small Business Compliance Policy but it could qualify for mitigation under the Audit Policy. In both of these circumstances a small business should try to meet the Audit Policy requirements.

EPA may choose to address multi-facility violations through a combination of the Audit Policy and the Small Business Compliance Policy.[157]

The principal elements to meet to get the benefits of the Small Business Compliance Policy are voluntary discovery, prompt disclosure, expeditious correction, no relevant history of violations, no serious harm, and no criminal activities. Each of these is described below.

Any action that results in voluntary discovery of a potential violation may qualify the small business for penalty relief under the Small Business Policy.[158] The company must discover the potential violation before it has a state or federal inspection. The discovery cannot be a result of testing or monitoring

---

153. *See* the Small Business Compliance Policy, 65 Fed. Reg. 19629 (Apr. 11, 2001) effective March 11, 2000, *available through* http://www.epa.gov/compliance/incentives/smallbusiness/index.html. This policy implements § 223 of the Small Business Regulatory Enforcement Act of 1996, 5 U.S.C. §§ 601.

154. *Id.* at 11. The EPA calculates the one hundred people by adding employees and "contract employees."

155. *Id.* at 15–16.

156. *Id.* at 4. It may be inadvisable for a small business to self-report potentially criminal activities under the Audit Policy, because the EPA's policy of not making criminal referrals gives very limited benefits. *See* the discussion of the Audit Policy, *supra.*

157. *Id.* at 4–5.

158. *Id.* at 1, 5. There is an inconsistent statement at page 4 of the Small Business Policy, to the effect that "The Small Business Policy applies only to violations discovered through audits and during government sponsored on-site compliance assistance activities." However, that appears to be contrary to the intent of the Small Business Policy.

required by a permit or other compulsory obligation.[159] It cannot have been previously brought to light by an inspector, whistleblower, or citizen's suit.[160]

The potential violation must be disclosed in writing within 21 days of when a company officer, director, employee, or agent "learns facts" that "reasonably lead him or her to believe that a violation may exist."[161] The small business must correct the violation within ninety days, if possible, and if it will take more than ninety days, the business must submit a compliance schedule. The EPA may incorporate that schedule into a compliance order. If the small business needs to institute pollution prevention measures, it may take up to three hundred and sixty days from discovery to implement them.[162] If the violation is not remedied in these time periods, the EPA may seek full penalties against the tardy small business.[163]

A small business cannot obtain relief under the Small Business Policy if it has received a warning letter, notice of violation, field citation, citizen suit complaint, or any other enforcement action for the same violation within the prior three years. It is also barred from relief if it received penalty mitigation under the Small Business Policy (or a State or Tribal analog) for the same or similar violation in the past three years, or if it has been the subject of two enforcement actions for any environmental violation in the past five years.[164]

Violations that cause actual serious environmental harm, or pose an imminent and substantial endangerment, to human health, safety, or the environment cannot be processed under the Small Business Policy.[165]

E. EPA Inspections

EPA altered its TSCA compliance inspection priorities over the last five years. In fiscal year 2005 there were 1611 TSCA inspections, of which 1191 involved the core chemical regulatory programs and 420 of which were focused on lead, asbestos, and PCBs. In contrast, in fiscal year 2008 there were 1441 TSCA inspections, of which only 56 were for the core regulatory programs,

159. *Id.* at 12.
160. *Id.* at 15.
161. *Id.* at 13.
162. *Id.* at 14.
163. *Id.* at 17.
164. *Id.* at 14–15.
165. *Id.* at 15.

and 1381 focused on lead, asbestos, and PCBs. The remaining four inspections in 2008 related to Good Laboratory Procedures.[166]

TSCA §11 grants the EPA broad authority to conduct inspections. The EPA may inspect any premises where chemical substances, articles, or lead products that have been or are intended to be distributed in commerce may be found. This includes manufacturing facilities, trucks, ships, warehouses, and any other place these items are present. The EPA can inspect anything that relates to whether the substances, articles, or lead products are subject to TSCA, and whether they are in compliance with TSCA. This includes, among other things, production records, processing procedures, operating procedures, order records, tolling agreements, records of significant adverse reactions, and many other types of records. By statute, an inspection must be reasonably prompt, be conducted at reasonable times and within reasonable limits, and be conducted in a reasonable manner.

Before the EPA can conduct an inspection, it must give the owner, operator, or person in charge written notice of the inspection. If the EPA wants access to financial, sales, pricing, personnel, or research data, the statute requires EPA to describe that information in the written notice. However, the EPA may inspect research data in connection with an inspection of compliance with a § 4 test rule or to determine compliance with the adverse effect reporting provisions of § 8.

The inspector must give his or her credentials before conducting any inspection.

Section 11 also gives the EPA authority to issue subpoenas for testimony, documents, and things. These subpoenas can only be enforced by a district court, on penalty of contempt.[167] The EPA has inherent authority to seek a judicial subpoena, in addition or as an alternative to § 11 administrative subpoenas.[168]

In *EPA v. Alyeska Pipeline Service Co.*,[169] the Ninth Circuit stated that a TSCA subpoena must meet three criteria before a Court will enforce it:

- the agency must have authority to conduct an investigation;
- the agency must have followed any required procedural steps; and
- the evidence the agency seeks must be relevant and material to the investigation.

If the EPA can prove these three criteria are met, a court will enforce the subpoena unless it is overly broad or burdensome.

---

166. National Enforcement Trends, FY 2004–FY 2008 Federal Inspections and Evaluations *available at* http://www.epa.gov/compliance/resources/reports/nets/nets-g1-inspections5year.pdf.
167. EPA v. Alyeska Pipeline Service Co., 836 F.2d 443 (9th Cir. 1988).
168. Boliden Metech, Inc., v. U.S., 695 F. Supp 77 (R.I. 1988).
169. 836 F.2d 443, 446 (9th Cir. 1988).

The EPA also has authority to obtain a warrant from a district court to conduct an inspection. U.S. v. M/V Sanctuary.[170]

1. EPA's Policies

The EPA has a Multi-Media Investigation Manual (Multi-Media Manual)[171] that is a guide for investigators on conducting an inspection and a useful reference for industry. The Multi-Media Manual is geared to inspections of compliance with multiple statutes, but gives information on how the TSCA portion of such an inspection will be conducted. The Multi-Media Manual echoes the statutory admonitions, including the requirement to conduct inspections at reasonable hours.

The Multi-Media Manual lists the documents that the EPA has that an inspector should review before conducting the inspection. Not all of the documents are relevant to TSCA, but the following are:

- process and wastewater flow charts;
- prior inspection reports;
- enforcement documents, including:
  - consent decrees;
  - notices of noncompliance;
  - notices of violations;
  - responses to the enforcement documents;
- reports submitted to the EPA; and
- production levels.

2. Responding to an Inspection

As soon as anyone has notice of an impending inspection, they should gather the materials the inspectors will want to review, and make sure everyone at the facility knows how to respond to the investigators. While some of the following pointers are quite basic, it is important to convey the fundamental concepts to the people who will be interfacing with the inspector:

Do:

- be courteous to the inspector;
- identify and gather any requested documents in advance and produce all of them regardless of whether they reveal a violation;

---

170. 540 F.3d 295 (4th Cir. 2008).

171. EPA, Office of Enforcement, Multi-Media Investigation Manual, EPA-330/9-89-003-R (Mar. 1992) [hereinafter Multi-Media Manual], *available through* http://www.epa.gov/compliance/resources/publications/civil/programs/.

- make sure there are legal grounds for the inspector to enter, and that there are no legal grounds for denying entry;
- request an opening conference to determine what the inspector is looking for;
- ask for the inspector's credentials if they are not offered;
- have one person assigned to accompany the inspector while on the premises at all times;
- answer the inspector's questions fully and honestly;
- plan a site tour for the inspector;
- ask for split samples if the inspector takes samples;
- assert business confidentiality when appropriate;
- make copies of instant and digital photographs, and request copies of photographs to be developed later;
- request a closing conference;
- get a receipt for all items taken or copied by the inspector; and
- ask for a copy of the inspector's final report.

Do not:

- refuse entry without legal grounds;
- hide requested documents; or
- volunteer information that is not requested.

The notice of inspection may limit the inspection to one TSCA program. For example, the inspection could be limited to compliance with § 8(e) requirements to submit notices of significant risk information, it could be directed to the premanufacture notification requirements of § 5, or it could cover all TSCA requirements. The letter will typically specify the kinds of documentation that the inspectors will want to inspect. It is advisable to review these materials in advance to see exactly what the inspector will see, and avoid the element of surprise if there is a violation on the face of a document. It will often be possible to refute any inference of a violation, and all the arguments should be marshaled at this point. For example, if the inspection notice states that all notices of export under § 12(b) should be assembled, and a quick review shows that some letters were not submitted until after the export may have taken place, it may be possible to gather documentation showing that the exports occurred later than expected and the notices were indeed timely.

It is potentially criminal to deny the inspector entry. Section 16 criminalizes violations of § 15, and § 15 prohibits refusing to permit an inspection. Even without the threat of criminal prosecution, a responsible corporate citizen should cooperate with any legally mandated inspection.

In general, staff should be fully responsive and honest with the inspectors. Many people at the facility will not be accustomed to being interviewed, and they should be prepared with the types of questions the inspectors may ask. In particular, it is important that all staff members understand the company policies and any compliance management system that is in place. If they cannot respond to questions about policies or compliance management systems, their lack of knowledge could be used as evidence that the policy or system is ineffective, or worse, not really in place.

Staff should cooperate with the inspectors, but they should not volunteer any information that is not specifically requested. Sometimes, in an effort to be cooperative, people will volunteer evidence of previously undetected violations, and this should be avoided. For example, if the inspector uncovers evidence that a particular Notice of Commencement[172] was filed late and explains the issue to the plant employees, it is very tempting to respond that the same thing had happened before without adverse consequences. Everyone should also understand that if they volunteer unsolicited information it will not place the facility in a better position than if the inspector discovers it for him or herself. The EPA will treat any violations that it learns of during an inspection as if it were discovered by the inspector, even if employees consider them to be voluntarily disclosed, and the EPA will not grant any penalty reductions for self-disclosure. The best course of action is to evaluate self-reporting additional violations that the inspector did not discover after the inspection has concluded.

If an environmental manager accompanies the inspector throughout the facility, he or she can perform several functions that will improve the inspection progress. The manager can reassure employees that they should be answering the inspector's questions, keep track of photographs that the inspector has taken, and make lists of information that the inspector requests. The manager will also be in a very good position to report to management how the inspection went and what violations the inspector may have discovered that must be corrected.

The following documents may be requested by the inspector, depending on the scope of the inspection:

- records of prior enforcement proceedings;
- documents showing eligibility for exemptions or exclusions, for example, R&D exemptions, polymer exemptions, classification by the Federal Food, Drug, and Cosmetic Act as a food, drug, or cosmetic, etc.;
- company policies on auditing and TSCA compliance;
- company compliance management systems;
- any inventory maintained by the company listing the chemical substances it makes, imports or processes;

---

172. *See* Chapter 4, Premanufacture Notifications on the premanufacture notification and notice of commencement requirements under TSCA § 5.

- test data;
- PMN submissions;
- standard operating procedures for manufacturing, or process flow sheets;
- production records;
- importation records;
- § 5(e) and § 5(f) orders;
- low volume exemptions;
- test marketing exemptions;
- PCB inventory, use, and handling records;
- PCB labels, manifests, inspection logs, clean-up reports;
- files containing § 8(c) allegations of adverse effects;
- § 8(e) reports of significant adverse effects;
- § 8(e) compliance policy, if any has been implemented;
- Inventory Update Rule reports;
- PAIR reports;
- studies on chemicals listed under § 8(d);
- manufacturing records showing products and volumes manufactured or imported;
- order-taking records;
- export and shipping records;
- export notifications; and
- import certifications and shipping records.[173]

On the day that the inspection begins, the inspector will conduct an opening conference, which is his or her opportunity to explain the purpose of the inspection and seek cooperation. The company can and should ask to see the inspector's credentials. EPA inspectors should comply with company safety rules, including attending an orientation before entry into the plant, if that is required of all visitors to the areas the inspectors will enter.

The company and the inspector can set the ground rules for the inspection. The inspector should review the written notice of inspection with the company.[174] The inspector should also give the company a TSCA Inspection Confidentiality Notice, outlining the company's right to claim that certain information is confidential business information (CBI).[175] The inspector and the company should agree on procedures for copying documents and taking pictures. If the inspector wants to take pictures, he or she should respect the confidentiality of those pictures. If the photographs must be sent to a

173. *See* Multi-Media Manual, 71.
174. *Id.* at 66.
175. *Id.*

third-party for developing, the developer must have TSCA CBI clearance.[176] The inspector should permit the company to mark the pictures as CBI, although this may only be possible with instant pictures. The inspector should also permit the company to make copies of any pictures.

TSCA does not specifically give inspectors the authority to take samples, but the statute does give authority to inspect all things that bear on TSCA compliance. Therefore, rather than reject a request to take a sample, the better practice would be to allow sampling if the EPA agrees to leave a split sample with the company.

The EPA may ask for a general site tour, to orient themselves to the particular operations at the facility. This is a legitimate part of an inspection and the company should be prepared to conduct the inspectors around the facility and answer basic questions about the manufacturing processes.

The inspection itself will consist of interviews with employees and document review. The Multi-Media Manual lists the objectives of inspections for each of the major programs under TSCA. PCB marking is a particularly easy target for an inspector, and most inspectors will inspect any PCB equipment at the facility and note violations.

There should be a closing conference, but it is not usually very informative. The purpose is to discuss preliminary findings from the inspection, but very often the written inspection report or follow-up enforcement action will contain allegations that the inspectors did not discuss during the closing conference. Perhaps one reason for this phenomenon is that the Multi-Media Manual states that "the less certain the team leader is about a specific violation or issue, the more reason not to discuss it at the closing conference."[177] The EPA may leave a list of additional documents that it needs to review, and the facility may agree to mail copies to the EPA. The EPA will provide a signed receipt for all items, pictures, and copies it has taken, and will leave a list of items and documents that the facility claims to contain CBI. Finally, the inspector should be willing to discuss when the final report is likely to be ready, and whether the EPA will mail copies to the facility. The EPA usually does not agree to automatically send a copy of the final report, and the company may have to make a Freedom of Information Act request for it.

After the inspection, the inspector drafts a report, circulates it within the EPA, and then finalizes it. This final report is the basis for any follow-up enforcement activity.[178]

Even before the facility receives a copy of the final report, it should immediately correct any violations that it learned of during the inspection, even if the inspector did not note the violations. There are many reasons to correct

176. Multi-Media Manual, 27.
177. *Id.* at 33.
178. *Id.* at 86.

any violations, the most important of which is to be in compliance with the law. The other benefits are that immediate correction should qualify the company for reduced penalties, and may avoid imposition of continuing penalties for violations that are calculated on a daily basis.

V. Self-Reporting Violations to the EPA

A company can only qualify for penalty reductions from self-reporting a violation to the EPA under the Audit Policy, an ERP, or the Small Business Compliance Policy if the EPA has not already scheduled an inspection or discovered the violation itself.

A. No Obligation to Self-Report

There is no statutory requirement to self-report potential violations of TSCA. However, if a company opts not to self-report, it cannot just continue to violate the law. It must stop that activity. In this respect TSCA is different from many other environmental programs that routinely require companies to self-report permit violations.[179] Note, however, that consent agreements may impose self-reporting obligations, and all such obligations must be complied with. Similarly, other statutes and regulations may require self-reporting.

B. Advantages of Self-Reporting

There are many advantages to self-reporting, which explains why many companies routinely self-report violations even though there is no requirement in TSCA to do so. The two primary advantages that motivate most companies to self-report are that it is a good way to come into compliance and that the penalties are much lower for a self-reported violation than for a violation that the EPA discovers. Another advantage is that management can use a self-reported violation to emphasize to employees and to regulators its commitment to compliance and demonstrate that the company will take all steps necessary to come into compliance.

The EPA often assists a company that self-reports in ways that would not be possible if it does not learn of the violation. If a company learns that a chemical it has manufactured for distribution in commerce is not on the

---

179. For example, permits for industrial discharges to local water treatment works require disclosing violations to prevent harm to the biological treatment systems.

Inventory, it is a further—potentially criminal—violation of TSCA to sell that chemical. The company should immediately quarantine any remaining stock of that chemical. The company likely will have to let customers know that it is no longer able to sell the product, and once the company tells a customer, the chances of EPA discovering the violation increase. The EPA often works with a company that self-reports this type of problem by giving the company permission to use the quarantined supply once the chemical is listed on the Inventory. The EPA recognizes that the company would otherwise be faced with disposing of the quarantined supply, which would violate the EPA goal of minimizing waste.[180] Similarly, the EPA can give a company permission to use a batch even if there was an upset that required isolating an intermediate that is not on the Inventory.[181]

C. Disadvantages of Self-Reporting

The primary disadvantage of self-reporting is that a company may pay a penalty for a violation that the EPA would never discover on its own. Even if the Audit Policy applies to reduce the penalties to zero, the company will have to spend considerable time in making the report and justifying complete penalty mitigation. Another disadvantage is that a self-reported violation will count as a "prior violation" that may increase the penalty assessed on a future violation.

D. Procedure for Self-Reporting

There is no required procedure for self-reporting under the Enforcement Response Policies. However, a written self-report is critical for the company's proof of compliance with the self-reporting requirements. If a self-report is faxed to the EPA, a company should keep a printout of the transmission confirmation from the fax machine to show that the fax was indeed sent. If the self-report is sent by Federal Express or Express Mail, the company should get a delivery confirmation and keep it in the file together with the self-report. An oral report should be confirmed in writing. These items are proof of the

---

180. An example of a Consent Agreement authorizing use of materials that EPA found to have been imported in violation of TSCA is *In the Matter of Fujifilm Manufacturing, U.S.A., Inc.*, Docket No. TSCA-HQ-2008-5029 (Oct. 20, 2008), *available at* http://yosemite.epa.gov/OA/EAB_WEB_Docket.nsf/Verity%20View/8C0AF2008B545D9F852574EF00637CB6/$File/Consent%20Agreement%20...1.pdf.

181. *See* Chapter 4, Premanufacture Notifications, for a discussion of TSCA's Inventory requirements and the issues involving isolated intermediates.

timeliness of the self-report, which is important for the additional 25 percent penalty reduction under the ERPs for self-reporting within thirty days.

Many companies seem to be reluctant to telephone the EPA before filing a self-report, perhaps out of a concern that the EPA will take advantage of prior notice of the violation. This should not be a concern. Telephoning the EPA in advance to establish a personal rapport can be very helpful in the penalty assessment process. Having a personal contact will also be helpful if there are further questions about the self-report or if the company wants to elaborate on its position later. The self-reporting letter should be ready to send at the time of the initial phone call to the EPA so that the letter can follow the call.

To identify the correct person to whom the letter should be addressed, the EPA regional office should be called to ask the name of the person who handles self-reported violations under the ERP applicable to the TSCA provision that has potentially been violated.

In contrast to the ERPs, the Audit Policy requires that a self-report be in writing.[182] It is still advisable to telephone the EPA and tell them about an upcoming self-report under the Audit Policy. EPA Headquarters and each Region have each identified one person as the person to whom self-reports under the Audit Policy should be addressed. Call the EPA for the name of that person or check the EPA Web site.[183] If the company has facilities in more than one EPA Region and the potential violation relates to more than one Region, the self-report should be made to headquarters in Washington, D.C.

The letter should not concede that there has been a violation. The Audit Policy requires a company that is self-reporting to specify the violation that it is reporting but it is acceptable to report that a violation may have occurred, instead of confirming that one has definitely occurred.[184] While the company may have concluded at this point that there has been a violation, it should leave open the possibility that it will discover further facts that show that its actions were in compliance with TSCA. The letter should explain what the potential violation is, how and when the company discovered it, and what it has done or intends to do to mitigate the effects of the violation. The letter should make a case that the company qualifies for further fifteen 15 percent penalty reductions for taking all steps reasonably expected to mitigate the violation and for a good attitude. The self-report letter should explain how the company has met each of the criteria for penalty mitigation under the Audit Policy. If there is no time to detail how each of the criteria are met before the 21-day self-reporting deadline passes, a letter can be submitted as soon as possible. The EPA will then send a routine follow-up letter seeking

182. Audit Policy, 19621.

183. The EPA lists the names of the Audit Policy contacts at http://www.epa.gov/compliance/incentives/auditing/auditdisclose.html.

184. Audit Interpretive Guide, 4.

more information if the initial letter does not include all of the necessary information.[185] This follow-up letter is a useful guide to the comprehensive information to include in a self-report.

The oral and written self-disclosures should claim confidentiality for any CBI. The EPA has a policy on disclosure of information submitted under the Audit Policy which says that generally the EPA will presume that a self-report contains CBI and will not consider releasing self-reports to third-parties under the Freedom of Information Act until the self-report is finally resolved, provided the self-reporter made a claim of CBI that the EPA has not rejected.[186] After the parties have finally resolved a self-report, the EPA will make a determination about whether or not the self-report contains information that is properly classified as CBI and will release or withhold it accordingly.

After receiving a self-report, the EPA has five years from the date of each self-reported violation to issue a complaint assessing a penalty. The five-year statute of limitations begins to run on the date of the violation, and not on the date of the self-report.[187] While no one should expect this to happen, there have been occasions when the EPA has not issued a complaint for a penalty assessment before the statute of limitations has expired on all of the violations disclosed in a self-report.

VI. Private Enforcement Options

When enacting TSCA, Congress expanded the precedents of other environmental laws encouraging private participation in enforcing the law. Congress had first introduced the notion of enforcement by private parties of environmental legislation when it enacted the first environmental citizens' suit provisions in the 1970 Amendments to the Clean Air Act (CAA)[188] to remedy a perceived failure of the government to enforce the original CAA statute.[189]

Prior to the 1970 CAA Amendments, private individuals could sue to enforce some non-environmental laws for their own personal benefit, such as by commencing treble damage suits under the antitrust laws or stockholder

---

185. The follow up letter is *available through* http://www.epa.gov/compliance/incentives/auditing/auditdisclose.html.

186. Memorandum from Steven A. Herman entitled Confidentiality of Information Received Under Agency's Self-Disclosure Policy (undated), *available through* http://www.epa.gov/compliance/incentives/auditing/auditsupinfo.html.

187. *See* 3M Co. v. Browner, 17 F.3d 1453 (DC Cir. 1994).

188. Clean Air Act § 304, 42 U.S.C. § 7604.

189. Robert B. June, *Citizen Suits: The Structure of Standing Requirements for Citizen Suits and the Scope of Congressional Power*, 24 Envtl. L. 761, 764 (1994).

derivative suits under the securities laws.[190] The new environmental provisions authorized the public to act as "private attorneys general" who would enforce the law for public benefit, rather than for personal compensation.[191] While citizens' suit provisions are now standard in environmental legislation,[192] Congress intensely debated the initial introduction of this concept into the CAA. It decided to strike the balance between citizen participation in environmental enforcement and citizen interference with governmental enforcement[193] by granting citizens the right to sue, subject to certain constraints. Congress implemented a citizens' suit provision in TSCA § 20, and furthered the concept of public involvement when it adopted TSCA § 21,[194] which allows any person to petition EPA to initiate a rulemaking under specified sections of TSCA. Parties have the option of using either or both mechanisms to seek relief, so long as they meet the requirements of the sections selected.

A. Citizens' Suits

In passing § 20 of TSCA, Congress built on the success of the "private attorney general" concept embodied in the CAA and other statutes that predated TSCA, and reaffirmed that individuals could play an important role in enforcing environmental legislation by bringing suit to protect the public interest if the Administrator of the EPA was lax in carrying out his duties under the Act.[195]

1. Procedures

Section 20 of TSCA allows any person to bring a civil action in a U.S. federal district court against any person, including the United States and any other governmental instrumentality or agency to the extent permitted by the eleventh amendment to the Constitution, to restrain violations of TSCA or any rule issued under §§ 4, 5 or 6, or an order under § 5, or against the Administrator of the EPA to compel the performance of any non-discretionary act or duty.[196]

---

190. Kerry D. Florio, *Attorneys' Fees in Environmental Citizen Suits: Should Prevailing Defendants Recover?* 27 B.C. Envtl. Aff. L. Rev. 707, 709 (2000).
191. *Id.* at 709.
192. *Id.* at 799 n.20, for a list of references to other statutes with similar provisions.
193. *Id.* at 711.
194. The provision was analogous to the citizens' petition provisions contained in the Consumer Product Safety Act, which became effective in October, 1975. 122 Cong. Rec. 27,160 (1976).
195. H. R. 94-1341, 56 and S. R. 94-698, 28.
196. TSCA § 20(a).

Prior to commencing suit, the plaintiff must give the Administrator, and any person who is alleged to have violated the law, at least sixty days notice of intent to sue. The plaintiff need only give ten days notice of intent to sue for failure of the Administrator to take action to respond to an imminent hazard under § 7.[197] Trial courts and the appellate courts have the authority to award reasonable attorneys' fees and expert fees and court costs, as appropriate.[198]

The timeline for giving notice to sue cannot be ignored. In *Basel Action Network v. Maritime Administration*, the court rejected the plaintiffs' claim that they could file an action within the sixty-day notice period, or cure the failure to wait sixty days by filing an amended complaint.[199] The court explained that the sixty-day waiting period could not be waived and had to be strictly construed because the government had waived sovereign immunity.[200] The court further noted that the rationale behind the sixty-day waiting period was to give the violator or the governmental agency the opportunity to achieve compliance.[201]

2. Remedies

While EPA may seek broad forms of mandatory injunctive relief under TSCA, private plaintiffs can only seek a restraint of ongoing violations.[202] Additionally, private plaintiffs cannot enforce the penalty provisions as a method for recovering compensatory damages.[203]

The courts have interpreted the citizens' suit provisions of TSCA using the plain language of the statute, the legislative history, and by reference to similar provisions in other environmental statutes to find that citizens are not entitled to compensatory damages.[204] In *Adams v. Republic Steel Corp.*, the court, finding that there were no cases discussing whether compensatory damages were available under TSCA, looked at the legislative history of TSCA and determined that § 20 was modeled after similar provisions in other environmental legislation. The court then looked to cases interpreting similar language in the CWA[205] and concluded that the United States Supreme Court decision in *Middlesex Cty. Sewerage Auth. v. Sea Clammers*,[206] holding that

197. TSCA § 20(b).
198. TSCA § 20(c).
199. Basel Action Network v. Maritime Admin., 370 F. Supp. 2d 57, 76 (D.D.C. 2005).
200. *Id.*
201. *Id* at 77.
202. Brewer v. Ravan, 680 F. Supp. 1176, 1183–84 (M.D.Tenn. 1988).
203. *Id.* at 1184.
204. Adams v. Republic Steel Corp., 621 F. Supp. 370, 376 (W.D. Tenn. 1985).
205. 33 U.S.C. § 1365 (1988).
206. Middlesex Cty. Sewerage Auth. v. Sea Clammers, 453 U.S. 1 (1981).

compensatory damages are not available under the CWA, was determinative for TSCA as well.[207]

Sipes v. Russell also stands for the proposition that private plaintiffs are not entitled to compensatory damages and can only seek injunctive relief.[208] In this case, plaintiff mother leased residential property from defendant lessor, which did not disclose the existence of lead-based paint in the home. Within eight months of taking possession of the property, plaintiff son had toxic levels of lead in his system, causing severe and permanent injuries. Plaintiffs sought compensatory damages as a statutory penalty under TSCA. The court noted that on its face the statute permits only the United States to impose fines and penalties on TSCA violators.[209]

A citizens' suit under § 20 can only be brought to remedy an existing violation, whether it is continuous or intermittent. In *Gwaltney of SmithField, LTD, v. Chesapeake Bay Foundation, Inc. et al.*,[210] the Supreme Court reviewed differences of opinions in three circuits. While the case dealt with the interpretation of the CWA's citizen suits provisions,[211] Congress used the same language in TSCA as it did in the CWA. In fact, in concluding that Congress meant what the language of the CWA said, the Court made note that TSCA and several other environmental statutes used the same exact language for the same reasons.[212]

In *In Re MTBE Products Liability Litigation*,[213] a citizens' suit under TSCA § 20 seeking to compel oil companies to report certain information concerning MTBE under TSCA § 8(e), the Court concluded that EPA guidances that are at odds with the statutory language of TSCA are not entitled to any deference. The *MTBE* Court analyzed the EPA's guidances under the principal enunciated by the Supreme Court in *Chevron U.S.A. Inc. v. Natural Resources Defense Council, Inc.*[214] *Chevron* held that courts should defer to agencies for interpretations of the statutes they administer if the statutes are silent or ambiguous about a point. The Court in *MBTE* found that the deference discussed in *Chevron* did not apply to the several EPA guidances in question because Congress did not delegate authority to the EPA to make rules under TSCA § 8(e), and the guidances were not rules. In addition, TSCA was clear that a report must be submitted unless the EPA administrator has been

207. Adams v. Republic Steel Corp., 621 F. Supp. 370, 376 (W.D. Tenn. 1985).
208. Sipes v. Russell, 89 F. Supp. 2d 1199, 1205 (D.Kan. 2000).
209. *Id.*
210. 484 U.S. 49 (S. Ct. 1987).
211. 33 U.S.C. § 1365(a).
212. 484 U.S. 49, 57 (S. Ct. 1987).
213. 559 F. Supp. 424 (S.D.N.Y. 2008).
214. 467 U.S. 837 (1984).

informed of the substantial risk information, and the EPA guidances simply ignored the statutory requirement.

As the *MTBE* case makes clear, people bringing citizens' suits are not bound by EPA guidance that purports to relax strict compliance with the statutory language. Similarly, there is no reason why any other federal agency would be compelled to interpret TSCA the way the EPA does in the guidances.[215]

B. Citizens' Petitions

Section 21 of TSCA allows any person to petition the EPA to initiate a proceeding for the issuance, amendment, or repeal of a rule under §§ 4, 6, or 8 or an order under §§ 5(e) or 6(b)(2).[216] Unlike § 20, which can only be used to review nondiscretionary acts, § 21 can be used to require the EPA to review discretionary acts as well as nondiscretionary acts.[217] Environmental groups have recently been successful in bringing citizen's petitions to change the lead rules.[218]

1. Procedures

The EPA may, but is not required to, hold a public hearing or conduct an investigation to determine whether or not a petition should be granted.[219] The EPA has ninety days to either grant or deny the petition. If the petition is granted, the EPA must promptly initiate the appropriate action; if the petition is denied, the EPA must publish the reasons for the denial in the Federal Register.[220] Within sixty days of denial of a petition by the Administrator, or in the event of no action, within sixty days following the expiration of the ninety-day period in which the EPA is required to act on the petition, the petitioner may start an action in a U.S. district court to compel the EPA to initiate the requested action.[221]

---

215. For example, there is no reason why a conspiracy charge could not be predicated on a failure to report substantial risk information to the EPA even if the information had been reported to a state agency.
216. TSCA § 21(a).
217. NRDC v. USEPA, 595 F. Supp 1255, n. 5 (S.D.N.Y. 1984).
218. *See* http://www.epa.gov/oppt/chemtest/pubs/petitions.html, and Chapter 18, Lead.
219. TSCA § 21(b)(2).
220. TSCA § 21(b)(3).
221. TSCA § 21(b)(4).

2. Preparing a Citizens' Petition

After receiving twenty-seven petitions, only six of which were granted, EPA issued a Guidance for Petitioning the Environmental Protection Agency under Section 21 of the Toxic Substances Control Act (the Guidance) to help petitioners satisfy the criteria so that EPA could more easily respond.[222] The Guidance provides general requirements for all petitions and special considerations depending on the section of the statute that is the basis of the petition, as follows:

- name, address, phone number, and contact person and for an organization, the nature of its purpose and membership;
- a description of the relief requested, the applicable section of TSCA, and how the action requested would address the problem presented;
- a description of the problem sufficient to help the EPA make a finding of "unreasonable risk,"[223] which might include the following information about the chemical or chemicals of concern:
  - the nature and severity of harm to humans or the environment;
  - exposure data on the actual or potential release to the environment or actual or potential contact with humans;
  - extent of the harm presented or potentially presented; and
  - possible methods by which the risk could be reduced, the degree of risk reduction that could be achieved, the costs of risk reduction methods, and the impacts of any regulation on the economy, small businesses and other affected entities; and
- a discussion of why TSCA is the most appropriate way to regulate the risk presented, explaining:
  - why TSCA is preferable to other Federal statutes to deal with the risk;
  - actions that are being or could be taken by State and local authorities to provide the desired relief; and
  - why Federal controls would be more effective than State or local controls.[224]

---

222. 50 Fed. Reg. 46825, 46826 (Nov. 13, 1985).
223. "The term unreasonable risk is not defined in the statute, but … Congress intended EPA to balance the benefits derived from risk reduction against the social and economic costs incurred, taking into account such factors as the extent and magnitude of risk imposed; the societal consequences of removing or restricting use of products; availability and potential hazards of substitutes; and impacts on industry, employment, and international trade." 50 Fed. Reg. 45825, 46826 (Nov. 13, 1985).
224. 50 Fed. Reg. 46825, 46827 (Nov. 13, 1985).

In addition to the general information noted above, EPA recommended particular information be included based upon the provision of the statute upon which relief is being sought. Petitions seeking to initiate a test rule under § 4 should provide data to demonstrate:

- the chemical may pose an unreasonable risk of harm to health or the environment, or will be produced in substantial quantities that may result in significant human exposure or environmental release;
- insufficient data exist about the effects of the chemical to reach a reasonable assessment of the impacts of its commercial production; and
- testing is needed to develop such data.

The petition must also explain how the data developed from the test rule will help resolve the problem identified in the petition.[225]

Petitions seeking to initiate an order under § 5(e) prohibiting or limiting the manufacture, processing, distribution in commerce, use, or disposal of a new chemical should provide data to demonstrate:

- the information available to EPA is insufficient to permit a reasoned evaluation of the health and environmental effects of a chemical;
- the chemical may present an unreasonable risk of injury to health or the environment, or the chemical will be produced in substantial quantities that may result in significant human exposure or substantial environmental releases; and
- how the requested order will provide the desired relief.[226]

Petitions seeking to initiate an order under § 6(b)(2) requiring a description of, and if necessary changes to, a company's quality control procedures, should provide information to demonstrate a reasonable basis to conclude that the chemical is produced in a manner which unintentionally causes an unreasonable risk.[227]

Petitions seeking to initiate a rule under § 8 requiring gathering, retaining, and reporting information concerning various factors relating to potential hazards posed by the production and use of chemical substances and mixtures, should provide information to demonstrate the benefits to be derived from such a rule.[228]

---

225. *Id.* Note that these are the questions the EPA must answer before issuing a test rule under TSCA § 4.
226. 50 Fed. Reg. 46825, 46827 (Nov. 13, 1985).
227. *Id.*
228. *Id.*

3. Citizens' Petitions Practice under TSCA

Notwithstanding the concerns of Congress about the potential for increased workload for EPA and the courts,[229] from the passage of the Act until 2000 approximately "fifty § 21 petitions had been submitted to EPA, most of which have been denied. These petitions have been submitted by industry, environmental groups, and private citizens."[230] Some examples of these actions are: (a) the denial of a petition submitted to initiate a proceeding for the issuance of a rule to prohibit the manufacture and distribution of nitrilotriacetic acid (NTA), based on the finding that projected levels of exposure of the general population from the use of NTA in laundry detergents would be generally low, the associated risks to human health would also be low, and the Agency needed to deal with higher priority problems;[231] (b) the denial of a petition requesting the ban of the manufacture, distribution, possession, or use of alphachloroacetophenone (CN) for use in tear gas thermal grenades or foggers, based on the finding there was no evidence that the risks associated with the proper use of CN outweighed the benefits;[232] (c) the denial of a petition seeking amendment of the PCB rule, based on the finding that the proper clarification could be accomplished without amending the rules;[233] (d) the denial of a petition seeking amendment of the definition of PCB in the PCB rules, finding that such amendment would conflict with the Congressional requirement in § 6(e) of TSCA to eliminate all PCBs from the environment;[234] and, (e) the denial of a petition to initiate a rulemaking to amend and broaden the definition of generator under the PCB rules, on the basis that the amendment is unnecessary and would not result in greater protection to health or the environment because the existing regulations provide equivalent and adequate protection against unreasonable risk.[235]

A Freedom of Information Act request by the authors dated July 17, 2009 resulted in a list from EPA of approximately fifty petitions from the enactment of TSCA through January 28, 2001. There was no indication in the response why the list ended at the beginning of 2001. A search in the EPA's Federal Register documents collection returned notices of approximately ten more petitions filed from 2001 to 2008. Two more were filed through August 2009.[236] Until the EPA granted two petitions relating to lead in

229. 122 Cong. Rec. at 27160 (1976).
230. Lynn Bergeson, TSCA: Toxic Substances Control Act 108 (American Bar Association, 2000).
231. 45 Fed. Reg. 72778 (Nov. 3, 1980).
232. 47 Fed. Reg. 333 (Jan. 5, 1982).
233. 47 Fed. Reg. 2379 (Jan. 15, 1982).
234. 52 Fed. Reg. 25068 (July 2, 1987).
235. 59 Fed. Reg. 43582–43583 (Aug. 24, 1994).
236. *See* http://www.epa.gov/oppt/chemtest/pubs/petitions.html.

mid-2009,[237] EPA seemed no more willing to grant petitioners the relief they sought in those later petitions than they had in the earlier petitions. However, the failure to obtain the relief requested in the petition did not necessarily mean that no action was taken by the EPA.

Another outcome of a petition may be to have the EPA take some action other than the one sought in the petition. For example, the Cystic Fibrosis Foundation petitioned the EPA in 2001 for a rulemaking banning the use of a group of bacteria, Burkholderia Cepacia Complex, or Bcc, because Bcc can cause severe infections in people with cystic fibrosis. The EPA determined that there were no existing commercial uses of Bcc, and therefore the more appropriate restriction would be issuance of a Significant New Use Rule (SNUR).[238] The SNUR was published on June 13, 2003[239] and made effective on August 12, 2003, approximately two and a half years after the filing of the petition.[240]

More recently, the Sierra Club and several other organizations petitioned the EPA to initiate rulemaking under TSCA § 6(a) to adopt the California Air Resources Board (CARB) standard to protect the public, including victims of disasters such as Hurricane Katrina, from the dangers of formaldehyde emissions from composite wood products.[241] EPA denied the specific request to initiate rulemaking to adopt the CARB standard nationwide because of the "significant differences in the legal standards applicable to the California Health and Safety Code ...and TSCA section 6, and the insufficiency of the information available to EPA."[242] While denying the specific request, EPA did decide to "investigate whether and what type of regulatory or other action might be appropriate to protect against risks posed by formaldehyde emitted from pressed wood products."[243] EPA published an advance notice of proposed rulemaking and stakeholder meeting schedule[244] and the launch of a field study.[245] EPA has announced that at the conclusion of its work, it will determine whether it should take action, either under TSCA or through other

---

237. *Id.*
238. The petition was filed on August 2, 2001 and reported at 66 Fed. Reg. 56105 (Nov. 6, 2001). The SNUR was proposed in 2002, at 67 Fed. Reg. 1179 (Jan. 9, 2002).
239. 68 Fed. Reg. (June 13, 2003).
240. 40 C.F.R. § 725.1075.
241. Petition from Carl Pope, Sierra Club and others, to Stephen Johnson, Administrator, U.S. EPA (Mar. 20, 2008), *available at* http://www.epa.gov/oppt/chemtest/pubs/petition3.pdf. 73 Fed. Reg. 22369 (Apr. 25, 2008).
242. 73 Fed. Reg. 36504, 36506 (June 27, 2008).
243. *Id.* at 36507.
244. 73 Fed. Reg. 73620 (Dec. 3, 2008)
245. 73 Fed. Reg. 79083 (Dec. 24, 2008).

unspecified approaches.[246] EPA has a web page devoted to its efforts on this topic.[247]

4. Legal Standard of Review of Citizens' Petitions

The type of action requested in a petition determines the legal standard for review. If the petition sought to initiate a proceeding for the issuance of a rule under § 4 or an order under § 5(e), the petitioner has to demonstrate, in a *de novo* proceeding, by a preponderance of the evidence, that (a) the information available to the EPA is insufficient to permit a reasoned evaluation of the health and environmental effects of the chemical substance and (b) in the absence of such information, (i) the substance may present an unreasonable risk to health or the environment, or (ii) the substance will be produced in substantial quantities and it enters or may reasonably enter the environment in substantial quantities, or (iii) there is or may be significant human exposure.[248]

If the petition sought to initiate a proceeding for the issuance of a rule under §§ 6 or 7 or an order under § 6(b)(2), the petitioner has to demonstrate, in a *de novo* proceeding, by a preponderance of the evidence, that there is a reasonable basis to conclude that the issuance of such a rule or order is necessary to protect health or the environment against an unreasonable risk of injury to health or the environment.[249] In any case, the court can only order the EPA to initiate the action requested by the petitioner. Additionally, the court can evaluate whether the EPA has prioritized the use of its available resources to address the greatest risks, and if the court determines that the risks addressed by the petitioner are lesser than those being addressed by the EPA, the court may permit the EPA to defer initiating the action requested by the petitioner.[250] A court's review considers the same factors as the Guidance.

In contrast to the detailed description of the *de novo* review set forth above for denials of petitions to issue new rules, TSCA provides no description of the type of review available for denials of petitions to amend or repeal existing rules. Absent a statutory command to use a particular standard of review, the review available to an aggrieved petitioner is the arbitrary and capricious standard of review prescribed by the Administrative Procedure Act.[251] The legislative history suggests that appeals by petitioners from the denial of

246. Regulatory Plan and Semiannual Regulatory Agenda, EPA-230-Z-09-002, 107 (Fall 2009), *available at* http://www.epa.gov/lawsregs/documents/regagendabook-fall09.pdf.

247. http://www.epa.gov/oppt/chemtest/formaldehyde/index.html.

248. TSCA § 21(b)(4).

249. *Id.*

250. *Id.*

251. Walker v. EPA, 802 F. Supp 1568, 1574 (S.D.Tex. 1992).

petitions for amendment or repeal of rules or orders would be considered under a different standard than the denials of petitions to initiate rules and were covered by the judicial review standard set forth in § 19. Congress wanted to avoid subjecting the EPA to "constant petitions challenging rules or orders for which adequate judicial review is provided under section 19 …, if the Administrator denies a petition to amend or repeal an action under section 4, 5(e), 6 or 8, the conference substitute permits review of such denial only under the Administrative Procedure Act."[252,253]

C. Interplay between Private Enforcement Options Under TSCA

A person can opt to initiate a petition under § 21 or to bring an action dealing with the same issues under § 20. These two channels of seeking relief are not mutually exclusive. In *NRDC v. USEPA*,[254] the court found that a person may sue under § 20 even if that person could also bring a petition under § 21. In that case, plaintiffs had brought a citizen's suit under § 20 alleging that EPA failed to fulfill its obligations to give priority consideration to a list of chemicals recommended for such consideration by the Interagency Testing Committee. EPA sought dismissal of the action on the grounds, among others, that the plaintiff's only recourse, or at least its first recourse, was to file a petition to initiate a proceeding under § 21. Quoting the plain language of the statute,[255] the court found that the plaintiffs had the option of proceeding under either section, or both sections, as it decided.[256]

It is not uncommon for activists to proceed on both fronts with respect to issues of interest. For example, challenges to the voluntary High Production Volume (HPV) Challenge Program were initiated under both § 20 and § 21. On December 27, 1999,[257] People for the Ethical Treatment of Animals (PETA) on its own behalf and on behalf of four other organizations, including Physicians Committee for Responsible Medicine, filed a citizens' petition

252. H. R. No. 94-1679, 98 (same as S. R. No. 94-1302). The Administrative Procedure Act is codified at 5 U.S.C. § 500. It mandates uniform procedures among the various executive agencies for rulemaking, hearings, agency adjudications and administrative appeals. These requirements are designed to ensure that administrative agencies act within their constitutional scope, and that procedures are uniform from agency to agency.
253. For an excellent discussion on the interpretation of the standards of judicial review under TSCA §§ 20 and 21, *see* Environmental Defense Fund v. Reilly, 909 F.2d 1497, 1501–1509 (D.C. Cir. 1990).
254. 595 F. Supp. 1255 (S.D.N.Y. 1984).
255. TSCA § 21(b)(5) says: "The remedies under this section shall be in addition to, and not in lieu of, other remedies provided by law.
256. NRDC v. USEPA, 595 F. Supp. 1255, 1260 n. 5 (S.D.N.Y. 1984).
257. 65 Fed. Reg. 2164 (Jan. 13, 2000).

requesting that EPA issue a TSCA § 8(a) Preliminary Assessment Information Rule[258] and a Heath and Safety Data Reporting rule under TSCA § 8(d).[259] While agreeing with the petition's underlying premise that both relevant existing positive data that indicate an effect and negative data that do not indicate an effect should be considered and made publicly available before any further screening level hazard testing is undertaken under the HPV Challenge Program or associated test rules,[260] EPA nevertheless denied the petition, finding that there was no need for such a rule to protect health or the environment against an unreasonable risk of injury, the standard required under the law.[261]

While probably not required to do so under its guidance, EPA addressed the petitioners' argument that the requested rules were necessary to fulfill the objectives of the HPV Challenge Program. EPA indicated first that the HPV Challenge Program was intended to maximize the use of existing data. It explained that participants in the program had been advised to use existing data and had indicated a willingness to do so, and that EPA was working with other bodies, both domestically and internationally, to ensure scientific acceptability of alternative test methods. The requirement that companies allow one hundred and twenty days between the posting and implementation of test plans allowed anyone having relevant test data to submit the data. The collaborative nature of the HPV Challenge Program encouraged the formation of consortia to share data on a global basis.[262]

EPA further noted that the requested regulations would substantially duplicate data that the HPV Challenge Program participants already had an incentive to provide, in contravention of TSCA § 8(a)(2). While unsponsored chemicals may be included in TSCA § 4 test rules, there was no requirement to promulgate a rule under TSCA § 8 prior to initiating a rulemaking under TSCA § 4. Anyone with data would have a strong incentive to submit that data to EPA during the rulemaking period.[263]

The final point made by EPA in denying the petition was that the requested regulations would be a less effective and efficient means to gather existing screening level hazard data than the HPV Challenge Program. The success of the HPV Challenge Program, EPA argued, was due to its voluntary, as opposed to regulatory attributes: less resource intensive (e.g., robust

---

258. For a discussion of PAIR rules under TSCA § 8(a), see Chapter 7, Reporting and Recordkeeping.

259. For a discussion of Health and Safety Data Reporting rules under TSCA § 8(d), see Chapter 7, Reporting and Recordkeeping.

260. For a discussion of the HPV Challenge Program and associated test rules, *see* Chapter 10, Voluntary Initiatives.

261. 65 Fed. Reg. 18097 (Apr. 6, 2000).

262. *Id.* at 18098–99.

263. *Id.* at 18099.

summaries prepared by submitters in standard, electronic, format), less adversarial, information submitted and publicly available sooner, and more effective interactive stakeholder input.[264]

Petitioners sued, seeking the court's *de novo* review of their petition to initiate rulemaking under § 8 of TSCA.[265] The court granted defendant's motion for summary judgment, ruling the plaintiffs failed to produce evidence that the risk posed to health or the environment was unreasonable or that the rules sought were needed to protect against such a risk. Plaintiffs had only produced evidence of specific risks associated with some of the chemicals out of the 2800 chemicals in the HPV program, while seeking rules pertaining to the entire set of HPV chemicals.[266]

---

264. *Id.* at 18101.
265. PETA v. Whitman, 00-D-1090 (D. Colo. Jan. 8, 2002).
266. *Id.* at 4–5.

CHAPTER

15

Acquisitions and Divestitures

I. Audit Policy as Applied to New Owners

The United States Environmental Protection Agency (EPA) has offered some comfort to buyers that discover violations during due diligence or a post-Closing[1] audit of newly acquired facilities. The EPA issued an Interim Approach to Applying the Audit Policy[2] to New Owners (Interim Approach)[3] because the generally applicable Audit Policy had some disincentives for new owners to self-report. The Interim Approach is intended to leverage the EPA's "ability to make effective use of scarce government resources"[4] "to encourage owners of newly acquired facilities to undertake a comprehensive examination of and improvements to a facility's environmental compliance and its compliance management systems."[5] Under the Interim Approach, an acquiring entity that was not responsible for compliance at the acquired facility, did not cause and could not have prevented the violation, did not own the largest share of the acquired entity before the Closing, and did not have a corporate parent in common with the acquired entity has greater flexibility to obtain penalty relief.[6] These preconditions mean that corporate spin-offs and operators who become owner/operators, among others, cannot qualify for Interim Approach treatment.

Both the Audit Policy and the Interim Approach permit penalty mitigation for all environmental statutes, including the Toxic Substances Control Act (TSCA).[7]

Acquiring entities can claim Audit Policy benefits for nine months after the Closing. For nine months, they can self-report to the EPA within the later to occur of 45 days after the Closing or 21 days of discovering a violation that occurred before the Closing, and can obtain Audit Policy treatment even if the discovery was not in the context of a periodic audit.[8] The EPA will also allow the acquiring entity to enter into an audit agreement with the EPA any time during the first nine months after the Closing, and that audit agreement will permit the company to self-report on a schedule that is more relaxed than 21 days after each violation is discovered.[9]

---

1. Closing as used in this chapter means the date on which the acquisition became effective and the business was transferred from the seller to the buyer.
2. The Audit Policy was announced in the Federal Register at 65 Fed. Reg. 19618 (Apr. 11, 2000). *See* Chapter 14, Penalties and Enforcement.
3. 73 Fed. Reg. 44991 (Aug. 1, 2008). It is called an interim approach because the EPA considers it a work in progress.
4. 73 Fed. Reg. 44991, 44992 (Aug. 1, 2008).
5. *Id.* at 44993.
6. *Id.* at 44995.
7. 15 U.S.C. § 2601–2695d.
8. *Id.* at 44996.
9. *Id.*

The Interim Approach waives all penalties from activities that predate the Closing, including economic benefits of the noncompliance, if its terms are met. However, the new owner may be penalized for the economic benefit of noncompliance starting at the date of the Closing. If the economic benefit was due to failure to make a necessary capital expenditure, or due to a competitive advantage from noncompliance, the new owner will have sixty days or another timeframe subject to EPA approval from the date of discovering the violation to remedy it before it will be charged for those types of economic benefit.[10]

The EPA tailored the application of the Audit Policy to encourage its greater use in the acquisition context. Five[11] of the Audit Policy's preconditions were modified in the Interim Approach, though some of these changes had been previously implemented. In the context of an acquisition the EPA has not imposed a requirement that the audit be periodic and systematic to be eligible for total gravity based penalty mitigation. The EPA gave new owners an extended period after the Closing to self-report. The acquired entity's history of violations will not prevent the acquiring entity from obtaining mitigation. And, finally, the EPA made clear that the element of cooperation included providing such information as needed to support the assertion that the entity claiming relief is a "new owner."[12]

However, there are still major questions to be answered under the Interim Approach. While EPA has said that its goal is to use a common-sense approach and eliminate the analysis of corporate history and the terms of the transaction in determining who is a "new owner" eligible for Interim Approach relief, it is easy to imagine that the implementation of such a user-friendly method will not be so easily achieved.

II. Buyer's Investigation[13]

Most companies conduct a general review of the TSCA status of a seller's products and processes, as part of environmental due diligence. At a minimum, TSCA due diligence gives the buyer a feel for the seller's basic attitude about TSCA compliance. If the seller has meticulous records and the TSCA status of all of its chemicals appears to be accurate then it is more likely that TSCA compliance is assured. On the other hand, if the seller has haphazard

10. *Id.* at 44998.
11. The fifth precondition that was changed deals with voluntary discoveries, and that is not relevant in the context of TSCA acquisition investigations.
12. 73 Fed. Reg. 44991, 44999–45004.
13. For the purpose of this section, the term buyer's investigation includes both due diligence and auditing.

records and has not thoroughly analyzed the chemistry of the products it is making then it is much more likely that the buyer will discover problems long after the acquisition, with the potential attendant production interruptions and penalties that can follow. This due diligence also can give the buyer some insight into developing regulatory issues with the seller's product line and sites. Reports of allegations of significant adverse reactions under § 8(c), reports of substantial risk information under § 8(e), § 5(e) consent orders and Significant New Use Rules (SNURs) can provide valuable information regarding the likely risks of using the chemical substances that are part of the transaction.

The buyer has a number of choices to make as to what TSCA issues to review before the Closing as part of due diligence, and which to delay until a post-Closing audit, either directly following the Closing under the Interim Approach, or even later under the Audit Policy. There is no quick answer as to what issues should be considered in what order. Those issues that might impact the buyer's ability to conduct the business in the manner in which it envisions should probably be addressed earlier rather than later. In part, making this assessment is a function of the importance of TSCA to the business being acquired, the knowledge base of the buyer, and the amount of time and resources available to the buyer. Given the havoc surrounding any such transaction, it is reasonable to expect that not all areas will receive a thorough review at the outset.

Systematic problems discovered pre-Closing can possibly be addressed before the Closing by the seller, whereas problems discovered after the Closing will likely need to be addressed by the buyer. Who pays for the resolution of the problem may well be different than who operationally addresses the problem, because that liability can be allocated in the acquisition agreement between the parties. Buyers can also mitigate damages arising in connection with violations they find either before or after Closing by self-reporting under the Interim Approach; violations found once the Interim Approach is no longer applicable might also qualify for complete mitigation under the Audit Policy or partial mitigation under an applicable Enforcement Response Policy. As with any TSCA violation, there is always the risk of business disruption. For example, if a buyer discovers an Inventory violation under § 5 of TSCA long after the Closing, it could be faced with having to cease manufacturing the product until it is put on the Inventory and extensive penalties calculated on the volume of the chemical that it made.[14] Once the buyer has reason to know that it is making a chemical that is not on the Inventory, continuing to manufacture it will most likely be a criminal violation.[15]

---

14. *See* Chapter 14, Penalties and Enforcement.
15. *Id.*

While potential liabilities can be allocated in the acquisition agreement, the goal of TSCA due diligence should be to identify the practices that could lead to ongoing violations and disrupt the buyer's business or expose it to significant penalties, and not to open every file to ensure all past actions were perfect. There will almost inevitably be some relatively minor violations without continuing impact on the operations.

A. Questions to Ask and Documents to Review

The table set out below includes TSCA-related questions that should be investigated by the buyer, either before or after the Closing. These questions may require further inquiry whenever a response indicates a need for more in-depth information. The table is more comprehensive than short due diligence time schedules may permit and some triage may be inevitable. It is also directed to the purchase of a chemical business because that type of transaction will have the most TSCA implications. However, other users of industrial chemicals, such as chip manufacturers that use polymers, electronics companies that use degreasers, and textile mills that use dyes and polymers, all rely on chemicals and all have some TSCA compliance obligations to consider in acquisitions and divestitures. Those companies that use chemicals rather than manufacturing them can use the table as a starting point for tailoring due diligence to their business. Those companies should start with the more general question of determining the nature of their TSCA obligations, if any.

The responses to these questions not only provide information about compliance and emerging regulatory trends that might impact the business, but also can be helpful in assessing how best to integrate TSCA compliance for the newly acquired business into the buyer's systems after the acquisition, if the acquired business will not be operated on a stand-alone basis.

Table 15.1 Buyer's Investigation*

	Question/Documents to Review	*Purpose of Question*
	General questions	
1	Have there been TSCA audits, either internally or by the EPA?	Reviewing audit reports is a good way to determine the strengths and weaknesses of a TSCA compliance program. If there are audit reports, what steps were taken to address adverse findings? The absence of audits may provide advance warning that there is no systematic compliance program.

	Question/Documents to Review	*Purpose of Question*
2	Have there been any TSCA enforcement proceedings or penalty assessments in the past five years?	This also is a good way to determine the strengths and weaknesses of a TSCA compliance program. The resolution of an audit may be relevant to the buyer—for example, if further audits were required as part of the resolution of an alleged violation, have those audits been completed and have any penalties on violations discovered during the audit been paid?
3	Are there TSCA compliance policies?	Well documented and soundly thought out compliance management systems and policies indicate a thorough TSCA compliance approach.
	§ 4	
4	Are any substances that the seller manufactures or processes subject to § 4 test rules?	The buyer should understand the costs that will be incurred in conducting any such required, but not yet completed, testing. Test rules will also give rise to an export notification requirement, and the buyer should follow up to determine if such notifications were required and have been made.
	§ 5	
5	Has the seller filed PMNs?	It is important to know how the business described the chemistry of its products. Where possible, it is helpful to obtain copies of the PMNs. If there are PMNs in the ninety-day review period, the buyer cannot make the substance until the seller files an NOC, or the buyer files a new PMN and then an NOC.
6	Has the EPA issued a Test Marketing Exemption (TME) for any of the seller's products?	If the EPA has not issued a TME for a chemical substance that is being test-marketed, but is not on the Inventory, the seller may be in violation of TSCA, and the buyer may be at risk for penalties and business disruptions if it continues manufacturing that product. Note that the EPA does not transfer TMEs, but such exemptions are in any event time-limited and of short duration.

Question/Documents to Review	Purpose of Question
7 Has the EPA issued a Low Volume Exemption (LVE) for any of the seller's products? a. If so, have customer notifications been made? b. Are the terms of the exemption being complied with?	If the EPA has not issued an LVE for a chemical substance that is being manufactured, but is not on the Inventory, the seller may be in violation of TSCA, and the buyer may be at risk for penalties and business disruptions if it continues manufacturing that product. Only one party to the transaction can rely on the LVE being available to it. The EPA may grant LVEs to multiple parties, but only if the cumulative volume is sufficiently low.
8 Has the EPA issued a Low Release and Exposure (LoREX) exemption for any of the seller's products? a. If so, have customer notifications been made? b. Are agreements with customers available?	If the EPA has not issued a LoREX exemption for a chemical substance that is being manufactured, but is not on the Inventory, the seller may be in violation of TSCA, and the buyer may be at risk for penalties and business disruptions if it continues manufacturing that product.
9 Is the seller relying on a Research & Development (R&D) exemption? a. If so, have the requirements of the R&D exemption been met? b. Are R&D letters to recipients of the substance available?	If the seller is not in compliance with the requirements of the R&D exemption then the substance must be on the Inventory or the seller will be in violation of TSCA, and the buyer may be at risk for penalties and business disruptions if it continues manufacturing that product. A more detailed due diligence will include a review of laboratory operations to determine if substances that are the subject of R&D activities are handled in accordance with the R&D exemption.
10 Is the seller relying on a polymer exemption? a. If so, is the polymer eligible for the exemption? b. Is the required annual report available for review? c. Are the required records available for review?	If the seller is not in compliance with a polymer exemption the substance must be on the Inventory or the seller will be in violation of TSCA, and the buyer may be at risk for penalties and business disruptions if it continues manufacturing that product.

	Question/Documents to Review	*Purpose of Question*
11	Are there § 5(e) consent orders applicable to any substances made, processed, disposed of, or purchased?	Each § 5(e) order will, to some extent, need to be reviewed because each one will contain a unique set of requirements for handling the subject material. Section 5(e) orders trigger export notification requirements.
12	Are there SNURs applicable to any substances made, processed, disposed of, or purchased?	Each SNUR will, to some extent, need to be reviewed because each one will contain a unique set of requirements for handling the subject material. SNURs trigger export notification requirements.
13	Review all products, raw materials, substances that are processed, and isolated intermediates; are they on the Inventory, and if not, why not? Review MSDSs for those substances. Review assurances from suppliers that their materials are listed on the Inventory.	Although not mandatory under TSCA, many chemical manufacturers list the TSCA status of their products on the MSDSs. If the seller adopted this practice, then the MSDS can be a valuable resource for assessing TSCA compliance, although it is not a substitute for confirming the chemistry and the Inventory status. A technically skilled person should review production chemistry and confirm that the reaction products are as represented. Alternatively, and probably more costly, the products could be chemically analyzed.
	§ 6	
14	Is there a PCB Inventory?	An inventory of PCB equipment must be maintained.
15	Have there been PCB spills? a. What was the concentration of PCBs? b. How were the PCBs cleaned up? c. Where are records of the clean up?	The PCB Spill Cleanup Policy has very specific requirements for cleaning up a PCB spill. Technically any PCB spill is a TSCA violation, and the EPA has said it will not penalize companies that adhere to the PCB Spill Cleanup Policy. Therefore, a buyer should ensure that the Spill Cleanup Policy was complied with, or seek to obtain indemnities from the seller. The buyer may also have cleanup obligations itself if the spill was not properly cleaned up.

Question/Documents to Review	Purpose of Question
16 Are there PCB Transformers or Capacitors? a. Where are they? b. Are they in use? c. If not in use, when did storage begin? d. Are they labeled?	
§ 8	
17 Are any of the substances identified in response to item 13 above subject to § 8(d)?	If any substances are on the list of § 8(d) chemicals, then follow-up should be done concerning the procedures for submitting studies.
18 Review the latest Inventory Update submission.	This will include production information, and will give the buyer a good sense of where imported substances are brought into the United States.
19 Has the seller submitted reports pursuant to § 8(e)?	Section 8(e) noncompliance can be a source of significant penalties, and the seller's compliance status and systems for compliance should be examined generally. These reports should be reviewed substantively to determine if the substances involved are likely to be restricted by regulation.
20 Does the seller have records of allegations of significant adverse reactions under § 8(c)?	These should be reviewed to determine if the substances involved could be restricted by regulation.
§§ 12 and 13	
21 What chemicals are exported, and how are export notifications tracked and managed?	If there are exports, then the seller's compliance with export notification requirements should be evaluated.
22 What chemicals are imported, and how are import certifications managed?	If there are imports, then the seller's compliance with import certification requirements should be evaluated.

* *See* SOCMA's Toxic Substances Control Act Manual and Checklists (Dec. 1, 1995).

B. Documents to Copy

A buyer may have many reasons to review or refer back to TSCA files relating to substances it will be manufacturing, importing, processing, or distributing after the Closing. If the purchase is of the entire business, including all offices, files, and employees, the relevant documents will just be part of the transaction. If the purchase is of a business line, a division, or some other portion of a business, the buyer might have to specify what documents it needs as part of the transaction. Often companies agree in the acquisition document to cooperate with one another in sharing of files, for certain purposes, though a buyer might prefer to have certain documents in its possession and control. The following documents are all part of the TSCA history that the buyer might want to have in its possession after Closing.

General

1. Audit reports and follow-up documentation of how the seller addressed any deficiencies. These will enable the buyer to institute corrective action to address deficiencies.
2. Documentation of enforcement proceedings and their dispositions. Resulting Consent Orders may impose continuing obligations on the successor.
3. Compliance policies.

TSCA § 4

4. Records relating to test rules and cost-sharing. The buyer may be the successor to cost-sharing agreements.

TSCA § 5

5. All Premanufacture Notices (PMNs) and Notices of Commencement (NOCs) that the seller filed. The buyer may find, even many years down the road, that a substance is incorrectly listed on the Inventory. If that is due to one of several specified types of errors in a PMN filed by the seller, the buyer may be able to correct the Inventory listing, and the PMN is important in making the correction. In addition, the buyer may not be able to locate an NOC for a substance that was the subject of a PMN filed by the seller. The EPA has taken the position that a PMN cannot be transferred, so either the NOC must be located or the buyer must file a new PMN. Obtaining a copy of an NOC or PMN from the EPA becomes more involved when information in those forms is confidential business information.

6. Records documenting compliance with all exemptions from PMN requirements that the seller relied upon. The buyer will need to apply for a new Test Marketing Exemption (TME) because the EPA does not consider TMEs to be transferable. The parties can assign Low Volume Exemptions (LVEs), Low Release and Exposure (LoREX) exemptions, and polymer exemptions, but must have the documentation to be able to comply.
7. All 5(e) Consent Orders, SNURs, and Significant New Use Notifications (SNUNs) relating to the acquired business. The buyer will need to establish or continue a compliance system to meet the order's or rule's obligations

TSCA § 6

8. PCB Inventory and required submittals to the EPA. The buyer will need to maintain the PCB Inventory.

TSCA § 8

9. Studies on § 8(d) substances.
10. Production and importation records needed for IUR updates. Depending on the timing and form of the acquisition, the buyer may be required to report on manufacture and importation prior to the Closing.
11. Section 8(e) reports and § 8(c) records.

TSCA § 12

12. Section 12(b) export notifications. A new corporate entity cannot rely on the export notifications filed by the seller, and should file new ones in connection with its first exports to each destination country, either once or annually, as required.

III. Seller's Pre-Sale Analysis

Before putting a business on the market for sale, sellers typically conduct some type of analysis as part of the packaging of the business, including pricing, marketing, and creating a document room for buyers to use in conducting due diligence. Seller's due diligence is a means of (i) planning how to separate the business to be sold from the remaining businesses, if applicable; (ii) expediting the sale by preparing for the buyer's inevitable questions;

(iii) identifying compliance problems so it can decide how to deal with them; and (iv) pricing in problems that will not be addressed before the Closing. A review of TSCA issues may be a part of that analysis. The role of TSCA in that analysis depends in part on how important compliance with TSCA is to the conduct of the business. Note that EPA has not given the seller the same additional incentives to conduct a pre-Closing audit as it has given to the buyer to conduct a post-Closing audit in the Interim Approach.

Depending on the nature of the seller and the structure of the transaction, TSCA seller-side due diligence can take different forms. If the seller ceases to exist as a result of the transaction, it will not have residual liability concerns because it will no longer exist.[16] This occurs when a company is merged into the buyer and the buyer is the only entity that continues in existence after the merger. It also occurs when an entire company, as opposed to a subsidiary of a larger entity, is sold in a stock transaction. Such sellers still need to perform some diligence to determine whether there will be any major impact on the sale price from TSCA noncompliance and to be able to respond to a buyer's due diligence questions.

If the seller will remain in business after the divestiture of the business, it might be required to indemnify the buyer for pre-Closing liabilities and should attempt to quantify these liabilities.

A. Questions to Ask and Documents to Review

The seller should consider in advance how it will respond to any violation it discovers during due diligence. Even if the scope of the pre-Closing review is limited, there is always the possibility that a violation will be found during such a review. There are advantages as well as disadvantages to self-reporting to the EPA any violations discovered. One of the main advantages of such self-disclosure is the potential for waiver of 50 percent or more of the penalties that the EPA would impose under the Enforcement Response Policies applicable to TSCA, or a waiver of 75 percent of the gravity based penalties under the EPA's Audit Policy.[17] The EPA's Incentives for Self-Policing: Discovery, Disclosure, Correction and Prevention of Violations,[18]

---

16. There can be situations in which individual employees or shareholders of corporations retain some liabilities, and in those situations the sellers' reasons for conducting due diligence are the same as any other seller that is continuing in operation. For example, individuals may have liability for failing to report under TSCA § 8(e), although individuals are rarely if ever penalized in their individual capacities. Or major shareholders can be asked to personally indemnify the new owners for certain pre-Closing liabilities.
17. *See* Chapter 14, Penalties and Enforcement for a discussion of the Audit Policy and the Enforcement Response Policies.
18. 65 Fed. Reg. 19618 (Apr. 11, 2000).

known as the Audit Policy, allows 75 percent penalty waivers so long as its requirements are met.[19] The Audit Policy does not offer 100 percent penalty waivers unless the violation was discovered as part of a periodic audit,[20] and unique audits such as those done for pre-Closing review are rarely periodic. With this in mind, the seller should make sure that any pre-Closing activities it intends to conduct that may expose a violation of TSCA are set up in advance to maximize the ability to meet the requirements of the various EPA penalty mitigation policies. Sellers should also be mindful that TSCA § 16 makes it a crime to knowingly or willfully violate TSCA, so a seller must react quickly to correct continuing violations it discovers to avoid criminal risks.

There are disadvantages to self-reporting as well, including the possibility that the EPA will not agree that the Audit Policy conditions have been met and will not significantly reduce penalties. The seller may not know the EPA's response until long after the Closing.

The table set out below includes TSCA-related questions that should be considered by the seller as part of its pre-Sale activities. These questions may require further inquiry whenever a response indicates a need for more in-depth information. The table is more comprehensive than short due diligence time schedules may permit and some triage may be inevitable. It is also directed to the sale of a chemical business because that type of transaction will have the most TSCA implications. However, other users of industrial chemicals, such as chip manufacturers that use polymers, electronics companies that use degreasers, and textile mills that use dyes and polymers, all rely on chemicals and all have some TSCA compliance obligations to consider in acquisitions and divestitures. Those companies that use chemicals rather than manufacturing them can use the table as a starting point for tailoring due diligence to their businesses. Those companies should start with the more general question of what is the nature of their TSCA obligations, if any.

If there are any liabilities imposed on the seller by virtue of any of the items noted in the above checklist, those liabilities may pass to the buyer on Closing, depending on the structure of the transaction. More importantly, however, from a buyer's perspective, if the violations continue in the course of operations of the business, the buyer will be violating TSCA from the first day after the Closing.

---

19. The EPA has enforcement policies applicable to the different types of violations possible under TSCA. Each of these enforcement policies contains provisions on mitigating penalties. The seller should consult the relevant enforcement policy in the event that it does not qualify for relief under the Audit Policy. *See* Chapter 14, Penalties and Enforcement for a discussion of the EPA's enforcement policies.
20. 65 Fed. Reg. 19618, 19625 (Apr. 11, 2000). Complete penalty waivers are also available if the violation was discovered as part of the application of a compliance management system, but that will rarely be applicable in the context of a pre-divestiture audit.

Table 15.2 Seller's Analysis*

	Question/Documents to Review	*Purpose of Question*
	General questions	
1	Have there been TSCA audits, either internally or by the EPA?	Reviewing audit and inspection reports is a good way to identify potential liabilities. Were adverse findings adequately remedied?
2	Have there been any TSCA enforcement proceedings or penalty assessments in the past five years?	The resolution of the proceedings may be relevant to the buyer—for example, if further audits were required as part of the resolution of an alleged violation, have those audits been completed and have any penalties on violations discovered during the audit been paid?
3	Are there TSCA compliance policies and procedures?	This will indicate to a purchaser that the seller was knowledgeable about its obligations, addressed them, and will make the purchaser more comfortable with this part of due diligence. Well-documented and soundly thought-out compliance management systems and policies can support a claim for penalty mitigation under the Audit Policy if violations are discovered during due diligence if the seller chooses to self-report.
	§ 4	
4	Are any substances that the business manufactures, imports, or processes subject to § 4 test rules?Will those substances continue to be manufactured, imported, or processed by another business unit of the seller's after the Closing?	The seller will need to know if another business unit that it retains will continue to manufacture, import, or process the substance after the Closing to determine how the costs should be allocated. If both parties will continue making, importing, selling, or processing the chemical, they should contractually allocate testing costs. The seller should gather any testing agreements and records of costs incurred in testing.
	§ 5	
5	Has the business filed a Notice of Commencement (NOC) for each substance for which it filed a premanufacture notification (PMN)?	The EPA takes the position that a purchaser cannot manufacture or import a substance until the seller files a NOC. The seller should determine if it will accelerate any existing manufacturing or importation plans to enable it to file an NOC before the anticipated Closing date. If the seller expects that it will continue to manufacture the PMN substance after the Closing, then it will be able to file the NOC after the Closing.

	Question/Documents to Review	Purpose of Question
6	Has the EPA issued a Test Marketing Exemption (TME) for any of the seller's products?	If the EPA has not issued a TME for a chemical substance that is being test marketed, but is not on the Inventory, the seller may be in violation of TSCA. The EPA does not permit transfer of TMEs. Because TMEs are time-limited and are of short duration, the seller should consider whether to wait until after any such exemptions have expired before Closing, or should just conclude its test marketing and eliminate any issue.
7	Has the EPA issued a Low Volume Exemption (LVE) for any of the seller's products? a. If so, have customer notifications been made? b. Are the terms of the exemption being complied with?	If the EPA has not issued an LVE for a chemical substance that is being manufactured, but is not on the Inventory, the seller may be in violation of TSCA. Only one party to the transaction can rely on the LVE being available to it. The EPA may grant LVEs to multiple parties, but only if the cumulative volume is sufficiently low.
8	Has the EPA issued an exemption for certain chemicals with Low Release and Exposure (LoREX) for any of the seller's products? a. If so, have customer notifications been made? b. Are agreements with customers available?	If the EPA has not issued a LoREX exemption for a chemical substance that is being manufactured, but is not on the Inventory, the seller may be in violation of TSCA.
9	Is the seller relying on a Research & Development (R&D) exemption? a. If so, have the requirements of the R&D exemption been met? b. If so, are R&D letters to any recipient of the substance available?	If the seller is not in compliance with the requirements of the R&D exemption then the substance must be on the Inventory or the seller may be in violation of TSCA. A more detailed due diligence will include a review of laboratory operations to determine if substances subject to R&D activities are handled in accordance with the R&D exemption.

Question/Documents to Review	*Purpose of Question*
10 Is the seller relying on a polymer exemption? a. If so, is the polymer eligible for the exemption? b. Is the required annual report available for review? c. Are the required records available for review?	If the seller is not in compliance with a polymer exemption the substance must be on the Inventory or the seller may be in violation of TSCA.
11 Are there consent orders under TSCA § 5(e) applicable to any substances made, imported, processed, disposed of, or purchased?	Each § 5(e) order will need to be reviewed because each one will contain a unique set of requirements for handling the subject material. Section 5(e) consent orders trigger export notification requirements.
12 Are there SNURs applicable to any substances made, processed, disposed of, or purchased?	Each SNUR will need to be reviewed because each one will contain a unique set of requirements for handling the subject material. SNURs trigger export notification requirements.
13 Review all products, raw materials, substances that are processed, and isolated intermediates; are they on the Inventory, and if not, why not? Review assurances from suppliers that their materials are listed on the Inventory.	This provides a way to ensure that the substances required to be on the Inventory are correctly listed. A person who is familiar with the production chemistry should review it and confirm that the reaction products are as represented.
§ 6	
14 Is there a PCB Inventory?	An inventory of PCB equipment must be maintained.
15 Have there been PCB spills? a. What was the concentration of PCBs? b. How were the PCBs cleaned up? c. Where are records of the clean up?	The PCB Spill Cleanup Policy has very specific requirements for cleaning up a PCB spill. Technically any PCB spill is a TSCA violation, and the EPA has said it will not penalize companies that adhere to the PCB Spill Cleanup Policy.
16 Are there PCB Transformers or Capacitors? a. Where are they? b. Are they in use? c. If not in use, when did storage begin? d. Are they labeled?	

Question/Documents to Review		Purpose of Question
	§ 8	
17	Are any of the substances identified in response to item 13 above subject to Section 8(d)?	The seller should confirm its compliance with the § 8(d) reporting requirements.
18	Has the business submitted reports pursuant to § 8(e)?	§ 8(e) can be a source of significant penalties. The seller should confirm its compliance.
	§§ 12 and 13	
19	What chemicals are exported, and how are export notifications tracked and managed?	If there are exports, then the business' compliance with export notification requirements should be evaluated. Monetary penalties for systematic noncompliance can be significant, and the parties can contractually allocate liability for pre-Closing violations. The parties can also negotiate whether to provide a warranty that the procedures in place at the time of the Closing are in compliance with export notification requirements.
20	What chemicals are imported, and how are import certifications managed?	If there are imports, then the business' compliance with import certification requirements should be evaluated. Monetary penalties for systematic noncompliance can be significant, and the parties can contractually allocate liability for pre-Closing violations. The parties can also negotiate whether to provide a warranty that the procedures in place at the time of the Closing are in compliance with import notification requirements.
	Wrap-up general questions	
21	Could any of the results of the TSCA due diligence adversely affect the value of the business for the purchaser? Are there actions the seller can take to minimize any adverse impact?	The seller should consider self-reporting violations it may have found and whether self-reporting would enhance its position in the transaction.

**See* SOCMA's Toxic Substances Control Act Manual and Checklists (Dec. 1, 1995).

B. Documents to Retain

A seller needs to keep documents after the Closing to address any liabilities it may retain. In those circumstances the most important documents to retain are those that explain why it took certain actions that may be questioned in the future. Even if a seller is not retaining any TSCA liabilities, it should consider keeping compliance records for the period of survival of any TSCA compliance warranties and indemnifications, should a conflict later develop with the buyer. Sometimes these documents are instead transferred to the buyer, and a provision is put in the acquisition contract that allows the seller access to such documents for a period of time.

A seller that is divesting a business line must determine if there is any overlap between the business to be divested and its remaining business. If there are substances that the divested business will manufacture that are also to be manufactured by the seller after the Closing, the seller should be sure to retain copies of all of the regulatory files for those substances.

There are TSCA implications if both companies manufacture the same substances after the Closing. These arise in the context of substances that are subject to substance-specific orders, rules, or exceptions from other TSCA requirements. When a substance is the subject of a consent order under § 5(e),[21] that consent order will generally only be binding on the original signatory. However, the seller will have the option of transferring the consent order to the buyer or retaining it. In either case, the seller should retain a copy of the file that includes the § 5(e) order and its history because it will be manufacturing that substance and will need to have on hand the history of the restrictions on its use. A seller should be particularly careful to retain the confidential version of any § 5(e) consent orders that have confidential terms cross-referenced in a SNUR.[22] SNURS often cross-reference confidential terms from § 5(e) consent orders, and it can be cumbersome to obtain those confidential terms from the EPA.

Similarly, when a substance is the subject of an LVE or LoREX exemption from the premanufacture notification requirements of TSCA § 5,[23] the EPA will allow the exemption to be transferred to the buyer, but if the seller will continue to manufacture the substance it may not want to transfer it. Even if the seller does choose to transfer the exemption to the buyer, it will have

---

21. The EPA may require a company that has filed a PMN to enter into a consent order governing handling of a substance if the EPA suspects it may pose a threat to health or the environment. These orders are issued under § 5(e) of TSCA. More recent § 5(e) consent orders terminate when the EPA issues a SNUR, but older § 5(e) consent orders remain in effect and binding on the original signatory.
22. *See* Chapter 12, Significant New Use Rules.
23. *See* Chapter 5, PMN Exclusions and Exemptions for a discussion of these exemptions from the premanufacture notice requirements.

amassed information in the pertinent files that will be important to provide if it files a PMN to enable it to manufacture the substance. It should clearly retain the pertinent documents.

IV. Transfer Requirements

There are no binding rules or definitive guidances that inform the regulated community as to the effects of transfers of ownership on parties' obligations under § 5, and how to best manage those effects. EPA recognizes this, and has announced that it is considering adopting a rule:

- "to provide a clear procedural mechanism to address such transfers;"
- "to require the transferee to specifically assume all of the legal obligations associated with the transferred right to manufacture; and"
- "to provide notice to the Agency of a proposed transfer thereby allowing the Agency to engage in more meaningful compliance monitoring."[24]

The EPA has announced its intention to issue a proposed notice of rulemaking on this topic at the end of 2010.[25]

Until the EPA issues its proposed rule, a company engaged in such a business transaction must look at other sources to decide how to manage these issues. The EPA has taken the position that when it approves an exemption from the PMN requirements of TSCA § 5, that approval is unique to the company that sought the exemption, and must be formally transferred if a buyer is to have the benefit of it. The EPA also takes the position that the same entity that filed the PMN must file the NOC to put the substance on the Inventory. The EPA based its logic on TSCA § 5(a)(1) and on the regulations:

> Section 5(a)(1) of TSCA states that "**no person**" may manufacture a new chemical substance, nor manufacture or process any chemical substance for a significant new use, unless "**such person**" submits to EPA at least 90 days before such manufacturing or processing, a PMN or SNUN notice. "Person" is defined by 40 CFR 720.3(x) to include "any natural person, firm, company, corporation, joint-venture, partnership, sole proprietorship, association, or any other business entity, any state or political subdivision thereof, any municipality, any interstate body, and any department, agency or instrumentality of the Federal Government.[26]

---

24. Regulatory Plan and Semiannual Regulatory Agenda, EPA-230-Z-09-002, 107 (Fall 2009), *available at* http://www.epa.gov/lawsregs/documents/regagendabook-fall09.pdf.
25. *Id.*
26. http://www.epa.gov/oppt/newchems/pubs/succesor.htm.

As a result of the EPA interpretations, a buyer must file transfer notices with the EPA if it wants to continue to rely on its predecessor's LVE, LoREX exemption, or older polymer exemption that required EPA approval. A buyer must also notify the EPA if it is assuming the responsibilities of the seller under a § 5(e) consent order. Buyers and sellers must also determine how they will manage any PMN that has not yet resulted in placing a substance on the Inventory. A purchaser will need to file a new SNUN if its use of a SNUR substance is a significant new use.

There are several possible ways to overcome the potential problems posed by EPA's position that a buyer cannot file the NOC if the seller filed the PMN. The seller can agree to supply the product for the buyer after the Closing, and then the seller could legitimately file the NOC and place the substance on the Inventory.[27] The buyer can also file a PMN as quickly as possible, so that it can be in a position to manufacture the substance as soon as EPA approves.

EPA has taken the position on its Web site that TMEs[28] are not transferable and therefore has not provided a form to transfer a TME. The EPA justified its position on the basis that TMEs are of relatively short duration.

The EPA has created a collection of forms to use to notify it when a § 5(e) consent order, an LVE, a LoREX exemption or a polymer exemption granted before May 30, 1995 is transferred from a manufacturer to its successor.

Prior to May 30, 1995 a polymer exemption required EPA approval, and if the successor company wants to rely on a polymer exemption that was explicitly approved, instead of relying on the current automatic exemptions, then it will have to file a successor transfer form. A successor should review an older polymer exemption to determine if it confers any advantages not available under the current automatic exemption. The current polymer exemption requires entities that rely on it to file a report by January 31 of each year providing information on each polymer that it has manufactured or imported for the first time during the previous calendar year.[29] To be prudent, successor companies should include in that report all of the polymers that it has made for the first time instead of relying on the reports filed by the predecessor company.

None of these successor transfer notices should be required if the transaction is structured as a stock transfer as a matter of corporate law. In that situation, the new entity is by operation of law the successor to the corporation that obtained the exemption from the PMN requirements and should be entitled to continue to rely on the exemption. However, the EPA states on its

27. The supply arrangement cannot be an exclusive tolling arrangement. *See* 40 C.F.R. § 720.22 (a)(2).

28. Test Market Exemptions are governed by 40 C.F.R. § 720.38.

29. *See* Chapter 5, PMN Exclusions and Exemptions.

Web site that mergers will trigger successor transfer notices, and implies that mergers will trigger a requirement for the surviving company to file a new PMN if the company that merges into it did not file an NOC at the time of the merger, and it is always prudent to follow EPA guidance.[30]

In all other cases, where the seller and buyer agree to transfer a § 5(e) consent order, an LVE, a LoREX exemption or an older polymer exemption, the parties should use the forms provided by the EPA for that purpose.[31] Most recent § 5(e) consent orders have provisions for notifying the EPA of a transfer and have forms included as an attachment.[32] Each of these forms contemplates that they will be filed after the Closing, because they each begin:

> Effective on ________________, the Company did sell or otherwise transfer to ________________________________ ("Successor in Interest") the rights and liabilities associated with manufacture of the above-referenced chemical substance, which was the subject of a …

Most recent § 5(e) consent orders also specify requirements for transfer of the rights and obligations of the order.[33] They explicitly state that the order cannot be transferred before the signatory files an NOC. In order to qualify as a successor, the buyer must acquire the full interest of the seller to make the subject chemical. The buyer must be incorporated, licensed, or doing business in the United States.[34] The model consent orders require the seller to send copies of the consent order and the transfer form to the buyer by registered mail on or before the Closing date. The seller must then send the EPA the completed transfer notice by registered mail within ten days of the Closing. After the Closing, the buyer must keep a copy of what the EPA refers to as the "Transfer Document," at all locations where the § 5(e) substance is manufactured or imported.

---

30. There is sound basis for disputing this because the merged entity is the successor to the pre-merger entities by operation of law. While the EPA may not be on sound legal footing to insist on a successor transfer notice or new PMN in such a circumstance, it is prudent to comply. If there will be a name change, that could flag questions about compliance with the successor transfer positions the EPA has taken. If the post-merger company is self-reporting past violations of the acquired business under the Interim Approach, and relying on its lack of control of the acquired business prior to the Closing to explain waiting for the closing to self-report, then it may be faced with taking inconsistent positions with the EPA if it does not file successor transfer forms.
31. These forms are *available at* http://www.epa.gov/oppt/newchems/pubs/succesor.htm.
32. *See* the model § 5(e) consent orders *available at* http://www.epa.gov/opptintr/newchems/pubs/boilerpl.htm.
33. *Id.*
34. This is a requirement of all entities that submit a PMN. *See* 40 C.F.R. § 720.22(3).

V. PCB-contaminated Sites

For many years, the EPA took the position that real property that is contaminated with polychlorinated biphenyls (PCBs) could not be sold unless the site was remediated. The EPA changed its interpretation in 2003 to permit the sale of PCB-contaminated real estate.[35]

The EPA's earlier interpretation had relied on the statutory prohibition on distributing PCBs in commerce.[36] The EPA's revised policy is not founded on any statutory analysis other than an assertion that the earlier conclusion is not compelled by the statute, and instead relies on the policy objective of not imposing barriers to economic redevelopment of real property and the recognition that its prior policy may have delayed cleanups.

VI. Contractual Allocations of Rights, Obligations, and Liabilities

Contracts for the purchase and sale of businesses broadly address the same basic questions. All parties need to know in detail what is being transferred or merged, for what price, in what condition, and what happens if the business or assets are not in the promised condition. In addition, the parties need to consider what operational responsibilities each will have to the other after the Closing, if any, such as supply or service obligations. TSCA requirements may play a role in dealing with some of these issues.

A. Representations and Warranties

The condition of the assets or business is addressed in representations and warranties. With respect to TSCA, the seller usually makes two warranties: that the business is operating in compliance with TSCA, except as otherwise set forth in a schedule, and that the seller is making available to the buyer all of the information that it has relating to TSCA compliance. These two warranties have two purposes. First, they help the parties understand the issues and manage the parties' expectations. Second, they provide the basis for remedies in case they prove to be inaccurate.

---

35. Memorandum from Robert E. Fabricant and Susan B. Hazen, Interpretive Statement on Change in Ownership of Real Property Contaminated With PCBs (Aug. 14, 2003), *available at* http://www.epa.gov/epawaste/hazard/tsd/pcbs/pubs/distincom.pdf.

36. TSCA § 6(e).

1. Compliance with Law

The warranty that the business and assets are being operated in conformity with regulatory requirements is often entitled Compliance with Law, and potentially has three levels. First, is that the business as a whole is generally in compliance with law; second is that the business is in compliance with environmental laws generally; and third, that the business is in compliance with TSCA. While buyers want these warranties to survive for at least the five-year statute of limitations, sellers are unlikely to agree to such a long time period.

A fairly typical Compliance with Law representation by the seller that states that it is in material compliance with environmental laws follows:

Except as described in [Schedule X], the business to be purchased and Seller as it relates to the business to be purchased, are in material compliance, and to the best of Seller's knowledge there exists no alleged noncompliance, with all applicable statutes, orders, rules, and regulations promulgated by governmental authorities (foreign or domestic) relating in any respect to the [business to be purchased], including without limitation those relating to health, safety, and the environment, including without limitation, environmental laws, statutes, orders, rules, and regulations relating to discharge, spill, or release of any material including but not limited to hazardous materials, contamination of air, soil, ground water, or the environment, handling, storage, transportation, and disposal of any material. Except as described in [Schedule X], the [business to be purchased] and Seller have received no notice of alleged violation of or noncompliance with any such statute, order, rule, or regulation or to the best of their knowledge, know of any reasonable basis therefore.

"Environmental law" should be specifically defined to include TSCA because not everyone perceives it as an environmental law.

There are many variations on this clause that are informed by the specifics of the particular transaction. Both transactional lawyers and environmental lawyers should be involved in drafting a clause or clauses that reflect the circumstances in the involved transaction.

Many foreign jurisdictions have Inventory listing laws that are analogs of the TSCA Inventory requirements. The seller will want to limit such compliance warranties to jurisdictions in which the seller has already been manufacturing or selling the products. The seller is not likely to agree to include in the warranty countries to which it did not sell products, but to which the buyer would like to expand its operations.

2. Availability of Information

The buyer will also want a warranty in the contract confirming that seller has made available to it all the materials needed to review TSCA compliance. The following template can be tailored for that purpose:

> Seller has delivered to Buyer all of the following documentation:
>
> (a) copies of material safety data sheets for all products, product components, raw materials, and intermediates purchased, manufactured, used, or sold in connection with the business, and all wastes treated, stored, or disposed of as a result of manufacture of the products (collectively, the Materials);
> (b) the composition, together with an enumeration of the components, and any by-products or impurities by percentage concentration, for each product;
> (c) copies of all worker health and safety claims, allegations, complaints, and studies or summaries thereof, in the possession or control of seller or known to seller, relating to persons employed by seller or third parties in connection with the operations of the business or the care, use, handling, storage, transportation, or disposal of the Materials;
> (d) copies of all epidemiological studies or surveys conducted or held by seller or others (including but not limited to any governmental entity), in the possession or control of seller or known to seller, relating to exposure to any of the Materials;
> (e) schedules listing the types of toxicological studies performed by or for seller or others, on any of the Materials, and copies of all reports of such studies in the possession or control of seller, or reasonably available to seller;
> (f) written documentation of any material facts known to Seller that:
>   (i) indicate the presence of any occupational illness in the work force of the business;
>   (ii) indicate that any of the Materials cause any illness; or
>   (iii) relate to any other condition which may form the basis for the assessment of a significant liability relating to worker health or safety or product liability in connection with the business, not otherwise disclosed pursuant to this Agreement;
> (g) copies of files relating to returns of Materials and customer claims, allegations, and complaints, whether made under warranties or otherwise, during the past four (4) years; and
> (h) a complete and accurate written description of, and copies of any files relating to, any claims, allegations or complaints in the possession or control of seller or known to seller, that were made by any person, whether or not employed by seller, alleging that the products, production

activities, or conditions at the facilities resulted in any adverse effect on humans or the environment, nuisance or pollution.

B. Indemnities

Acquisition agreements typically contain indemnification provisions that deal with breaches of the warranties, or general indemnification provisions relating to liabilities that resulted from the conduct of the business before and after the Closing. Those indemnification provisions should cover TSCA matters in the same manner as other issues. Special areas to consider for TSCA would be whether or not the indemnifications should include or exclude (i) penalties assessed by the EPA for TSCA violations and (ii) losses resulting from business interruptions caused by TSCA violations, such as if a product or a constituent of a product is not on the TSCA Inventory and cannot be manufactured and sold. Often, indemnification provisions exclude consequential damages, and such a business loss would likely be considered a consequential damage. EPA, in the Interim Approach, addresses the possibility that some indemnification provisions might specifically try to exclude penalties resulting from self-disclosures by buyers, stating: "If sellers were to include 'no tell' clauses in their transaction or indemnity agreements, such clauses may well be voidable as contrary to public policy."[37]

Limits on the extent of any money available for indemnifiable claims can include an overall negotiated cap on damages available under the indemnification provisions and a deductible or basket that must be satisfied by the buyer before it can assert a claim for indemnity. Once a cap limit has been reached, a buyer cannot make a claim against the seller for even the most egregious TSCA violation.[38] TSCA personnel and environmental lawyers should review the applicable clauses because they will likely be the people involved in making any available TSCA claims, and they need to be mindful of the time and other requirements of making those claims.

VII. Post-Closing Obligations

Obligations of the parties to one another can be set forth in either the post-Closing covenants in the acquisition agreement or in separate ancillary

37. 73 Fed. Reg. 44991, 45004 (Aug. 1, 2008).

38. However, the buyer may be able to persuade the EPA to seek penalties directly from the seller.

agreements, such as service agreements. Examples of post-Closing obligations might include how to share the costs of testing under a § 4 test rule on a substance that both the buyer and the seller will continue to manufacture, the seller's obligation to produce the first commercial quantity of a substance and to file an NOC, or the provision of transitional TSCA services to the buyer for a period of time.

VIII. Business Integration

After the acquisition is completed, the buyer may want to rationalize its operations to minimize costs. For example, if the buyer will make any changes to the manufacturing processes, either by moving manufacturing lines from one plant to another or by altering existing processes, then the changed or relocated processes need to be carefully reviewed for TSCA compliance. If the newly-acquired product lines use a chemical subject to a SNUR or § 5(e) consent order, then facilities to which those product lines are relocated must be able to meet the requirements imposed by the SNUR or § 5(e) consent order.

Both the buyer and seller need to consider adjustments to their compliance programs to reflect the new status quo. The seller will have to re-assign TSCA compliance tasks if employees who were integral to TSCA compliance have left the company. The seller may need to file PMNs if it transferred LVEs or LoREX exemptions to the buyer and plans to make the pertinent substance in the future. The buyer will have to decide whether it will operate the new business as a stand-alone fully integrated business or whether some of the functions will be transferred to corporate staff. In making these determinations, the buyer will have to consider all of the TSCA requirements to ensure that the responsibilities for those are appropriately transferred along with any supporting files or software programs, such as § 8(c) records of allegations and § 12(b) export notification systems. This is easier to do when the people with the responsibility for these obligations in the selling company are transferred with the business to the buying company. Sometimes, especially in situations where TSCA is not integrated into the business systems, buyers neglect to include its requirements when transferring operations. The buyer might need to make § 12(b) export notifications if any of the acquired chemicals are subject to this provision, because if it is a different entity than the seller, it cannot rely on prior notifications made by the seller and must very quickly gear up to file export notifications on all of the chemicals it will be newly exporting after the Closing. This requirement will be fact-dependent; in the case of a merger of two companies the surviving entity can take the position that is the same entity that previously filed the export notifications, but in the case of an asset sale or purchase of a business unit it most likely can not.

Depending on the international structure of the acquiring corporation, the acquired business may need to change its practices and search the records of any new foreign parent company when it gathers information in response to a rule under TSCA § 8(d) or when it submits prior studies as part of a premanufacture notification under TSCA § 5.[39]

After an acquisition, the combined company may have a larger collection of toxicity data and substantial risk information. If that is the case, the company must ensure that it complies with TSCA § 8(e) by immediately reporting substantial risk information that becomes reportable as a result of the acquisition. For example, if the acquired company had significant risk information about Chemical A, but did not make or import Chemical A, it would not have had a reporting obligation. However, if the acquiring company makes Chemical A, as of the Closing it will have reportable data and must submit a TSCA § 8(e) report to the EPA. Prompt reporting will decrease the potential penalties that could accrue over time for the new owner.

39. *See* Chapter 7, Reporting and Recordkeeping and Chapter 4, Premanufacture Notifications. *See also*, EPA, TSCA Questions and Answers from the October, 1990 EPA-Industry Living with TSCA Workshop, question 39 (Oct. 1992).

CHAPTER

16

Asbestos Hazard Emergency Response Act

I. Asbestos, a Short History

As discussed in the earlier chapters of this book, in the initially enacted version of the Toxic Substances Control Act (TSCA)[1] Congress required the United States Environmental Protection Agency (EPA) to promulgate regulations to control the import, manufacture, and processing of chemical substances. In the Asbestos Hazard Emergency Response Act[2] (hereinafter sometimes referred to as the Act or the AHERA), which amended TSCA, Congress switched its focus to the remediation of existing school buildings with asbestos containing materials. This shift toward remediation and toward educational facilities has continued to varying degrees in the enactment of the subsequent chapters of TSCA.[3]

Asbestos is a substance that poses a risk of lung cancer, asbestosis, and mesothelioma.[4] Asbestosis is a serious, progressive, long-term, non-cancer disease caused by inhaling asbestos fibers that irritate lung tissues. The resultant scarring makes it difficult for oxygen to get into the blood. Symptoms include shortness of breath and a dry, crackling sound in the lungs.[5] Mesothelioma is a rare form of cancer found in the thin lining of the lung, chest, abdomen, and heart.[6] The largest number of deaths from exposure to asbestos is caused by lung cancer. Symptoms include coughing, shortness of breath, persistent chest pains, hoarseness, and anemia.[7] Asbestos is classified by the EPA as a Class A known human carcinogen in its Integrated Risk Management System.[8] The latency period for these diseases can be as long as twenty or thirty years.

Asbestos is a mineral fiber. There are several types of asbestos fibers, some of which are more harmful than others. Long known for its heat resistant properties and high tensile strength, asbestos was added to many different types of products to provide strength, heat insulation, and fire resistance. It could be found in products as varied as steam pipes, boilers, furnace ducts, floor tiles, vinyl sheet flooring, adhesives, cement sheet, millboard, paper insulation, door gaskets, soundproofing, patching and joint compounds, roofing, shingles, siding, artificial ashes and embers, fireproof gloves, stove-top

1. 15 U.S.C. §§ 2601–2695d.
2. Asbestos Hazard Emergency Response Act, Pub. L. 94-469, title II §201, as added Pub. L. 99-519, §2, (1986), 100 Stat. 2970, as amended.
3. *See, e.g.*, Chapter 17, Indoor Radon Abatement Act and Chapter 19, Healthy High-Performance Schools Act.
4. http://www.epa.gov/oppt/asebstos/pubs/ashome.html.
5. http://www.epa.gov/oppt/asbestos/pubs/help.html#info.
6. *Id.*
7. *Id.*
8. http://www.epa.gov/NCEA/iris/subst/0371.htm.

pads, ironing board covers, hairdryers, automobile brake pads, linings, clutch facings, and gaskets.[9]

The only way to determine if a material contains asbestos is to have it tested and analyzed by qualified professionals. In addition to requiring technical expertise to test for asbestos, when samples are incorrectly taken there may be an increased health risk if fibers are released.[10] Asbestos materials that are intact and in good condition generally do not pose a health risk. The potential for an asbestos containing material (ACM) to release harmful fibers depends primarily on its condition. Dry material that can be crumbled by hand pressure, often referred to as "friable ACM," is more likely to release fibers, particularly when damaged.[11] Materials considered "nonfriable ACM," such as vinyl-asbestos floor tile, can also release harmful fibers when sanded, sawed, or otherwise disturbed.[12]

The health hazards of asbestos have long been recognized. There is evidence asbestos manufacturers were aware of the health threats it posed as early as the 1930s.[13] Despite the growing knowledge of asbestos' hazard, production and use of the mineral continued until the EPA began restricting its use in 1973.[14] In the 1980s, asbestos litigation began to clog court dockets around the country. Asbestos is regulated by a number of different federal agencies in different venues.[15] EPA tried to ban most uses of asbestos using its authority under TSCA § 6 authority, but was rebuffed by the courts.[16]

EPA began to identify schools as a potential source of asbestos hazards in the 1970s, and it began a technical assistance program in 1979 to encourage

---

9. http://www.epa.gov/oppt/asbestos/pubs/ashome.html.
10. http://www.epa.gov/asbestos/pubs/ashome.html#identify.
11. EPA, Office of Pollution Prevention and Toxics, The ABCs of Asbestos in Schools, 4 (2003) [hereinafter Asbestos ABC], *available at* http://www.epa.gov/asbestos/pubs/abcsfinal.pdf.
12. Asbestos ABC, 6.
13. James C. Stanley, Note, *Asbestos in Schools: The Asbestos Hazard Emergency Response Act and School Asbestos Litigation*, 42 Vand. L. Rev. 1685, 1690 n.28 (1987).
14. *Id.* at n.29 (1987).
15. At the federal level, handling of asbestos is covered by a variety of regulatory schemes. *See* 42 U.S.C.§ 7413 (Clean Air Act) air-pollution controls; 15 U.S.C. § 2641 (Asbestos Hazard Emergency Response Act), governing removal of asbestos from schools; 30 C.F.R. § 71.702 (Mine Safety and Health Administration), regulating mineworkers' exposure to asbestos dust; 40 C.F.R. § 763.80 (EPA regulations implementing AHERA); 40 C.F.R. § 763.120 (EPA workplace safety rules regulating asbestos in state and local public buildings); 29 C.F.R. § 1910.1001 (Occupational Safety and Health Administration), rules regulating occupational exposure to asbestos in a variety of industries); 29 C.F.R. § 926.1101, rules regulating occupational exposure to asbestos in the construction industry. State regulation of asbestos is also pervasive.
16. Corrosion Proof Fittings v. EPA, 947 F.2d 1201 (Oct. 18, 1991), *clarified*, 947 F.2d 1201 (Nov. 15, 1991). This case is discussed in Chapter 11, Bans and Restrictions.

schools to voluntarily identify and correct hazards.[17,18] Because its technical assistance program was not generating sufficient response from the educational community, EPA, under TSCA § 6(a)(3), issued a regulation in May of 1982[19] requiring public and private elementary and secondary schools to inspect their buildings for asbestos-containing materials, notify employees, parents, and teachers of any findings and provide employees with instructions on how to reduce exposures.[20] When reviewing the results of the rule, the United States General Accounting Office (GAO) found that the rule created a serious dilemma for school officials by requiring inspections and notifications, but not specifying when asbestos was hazardous enough to warrant abatement.[21] The GAO further found that the lack of definitive federal criteria resulted in states and localities using different criteria in arriving at their decisions, with some school officials overreacting and unnecessarily spending money or underreacting and continuing to expose school occupants to hazardous asbestos conditions.[22]

II. Requirements of the Act and Implementing Regulations

Citing the deficiencies in the then-current asbestos in schools programs,[23] Congress enacted the Act in 1986 to establish uniform regulations that require inspections of, and response actions for, ACM[24] in public and private elementary and secondary schools, as well as schools operated by the Department

17. *Review of Federal Efforts to Reduce Asbestos Hazards in Schools: Hearing Before the House Subcomm. on Commerce, Transportation and Tourism of the H. Comm. on Energy and Commerce*, 1 (Sept. 26, 1984) (Statement for the Record by Hugh J. Wessinger, Senior Associate Director Resources, Community, and Economic Development Division, U.S. Gen. Accounting Office) [hereinafter Wessinger Statement].
18. In the first law dedicated to the issues of asbestos in schools, the Asbestos School Hazard Detection and Control Act of 1980, Congress authorized the Department of Education to provide grants to schools to detect and abate asbestos hazards.
19. 47 Fed. Reg. 23360 (May 27, 1982).
20. *Id.*
21. Wessinger Statement, p. 2.
22. Wessinger Statement p. 3.
23. TSCA § 201 cites the findings of Congress in enacting the legislation. Congress found that (i) the EPA rule on inspection and notice of asbestos included neither standards for proper identification of ACM nor a requirement that response work be carried out in a safe and complete way; (ii) there was no uniform program for accrediting asbestos workers and that schools were not required to use accredited personnel; and (iii) the existing technical guidance was insufficient. 15 U.S.C.§ 2641(a).
24. "ACM when referring to school buildings means any material or product which contains more than 1 percent asbestos." 40 C.F.R. § 763.83.

of Defense for its dependents. Any obligation imposed on a governor of a state under the Act must be carried out by the Secretary of State with respect to any school operated by the Department of State for its dependents.[25] The Secretary of State is required to perform the same functions for its overseas schools, to the extent feasible and consistent with national security.[26] EPA issued the regulations required under the Act on October 30, 1987.[27] Former manufacturers of asbestos quickly brought an action to challenge the regulation for failing to fulfill AHERA's mandates, but the Court of Appeals held that the "regulations represent a reasonable interpretation of AHERA's less than pellucid demands."[28]

Each local education agency (LEA)[29] is required to develop an asbestos management plan and to make that plan available to the public. The LEA must designate a person to implement all its responsibilities under the Act and must ensure that person is properly trained.[30] The LEA can delegate its duties under the Act, but it remains responsible for their performance.[31] Only accredited personnel can be used. Schools can elect to establish a maintenance program to abate any hazard if ACM is merely damaged or subject to potential damage, but must perform abatement if there is actual or potential significant damage. Procedures for ensuring the protection and education of workers and building occupants must be established, and for the transportation and disposal of asbestos-containing waste.

A. Inspections

To establish a baseline for further asbestos management activities, LEAs were required, by October 12, 1988, to inspect all school buildings they use to identify locations of friable and nonfriable asbestos containing building

25. 15 U.S.C.§ 2643(l)(1).
26. 15 U.S.C.§ 2643(l)(2).
27. 52 Fed. Reg. 41826 (Oct. 30, 1987). EPA reasoned that the issuance of the rule fell within the statutory time requirement because the EPA Administrator had signed the rule on October 17, 1987, which was "within 360 days after October 22, 1986," as required by 15 U.S.C. § 2643(a).
28. Safe Buildings Alliance v. EPA, 846 F.2d 79, 85 (D.C.Cir. 1988).
29. The Act defines a "local educational agency" as: "(A) any LEA as defined in § 14101 of the Elementary and Secondary Education Act of 1965, (B) the owner of any private, nonprofit elementary or secondary school building, and (C) the governing authority of any school operated under the defense dependents' education system…." 15 U.S.C. § 2641(7).
30. 40 C.F.R. § 763.84(g). For a list of the designated person's responsibilities see http://yosemite.epa.gov/R10/OWCM.NSF/d14dabb756dc1fb3882565000062f164/aa29f684c418f87588256508007d6372!OpenDocument.
31. 40 C.F.R. § 763.80(a).

materials (ACBM).[32,33] Buildings acquired or leased after that date have to be inspected prior to use as a school building, except those used for emergency situations are to be inspected within thirty days after beginning such use.[34] Inspections must be made by an accredited inspector,[35] who must:[36]

- visually inspect the area to identify the locations of all suspected ACBM;
- touch all suspected ACBM to determine whether it is friable;
- identify all homogeneous areas of friable suspected ACBM and all homogeneous areas of nonfriable suspected ACBM;
- assume that some or all of the homogeneous areas are ACM, and, for each homogeneous area that is not assumed to be ACM, collect bulk samples and submit them for analysis;
- assess friable material in areas where samples are collected, friable material in areas that are assumed to be ACBM, and friable ACBM identified during a previous inspection; and
- record and submit the following items to the LEA designate for inclusion in the management plan within thirty days of the inspection:
  - an inspection report containing date of inspection, signature of inspector(s), state of accreditation(s), and if applicable, accreditation number(s);
  - an inventory of the locations of the homogeneous areas where samples were collected, exact location where each bulk sample was collected, dates of sampling, homogeneous areas where friable suspected ACBM was assumed to be ACM, and homogeneous areas where nonfriable suspected ACBM was assumed to be ACM;
  - a description of how the sampling locations were selected, the name, signature of each accredited inspector who collected the samples, state of accreditation, and, if applicable, accreditation number;
  - a list of whether the homogeneous areas identified above are surfacing material, thermal system insulation,[37] or miscellaneous material; and

32. "Asbestos-containing building material (ACBM) means surfacing ACM, thermal system insulation ACM, or miscellaneous ACM that is found in or on interior structural members or other parts of a school building." 40 C.F.R. § 763.83.
33. 40 C.F.R. § 763.85(a)(1).
34. 40 C.F.R. § 763.85(a)(2).
35. 40 C.F.R. § 763.85(a)(3).
36. 40 C.F.R. § 763.85(a)(4).
37. "Thermal system insulation that has retained its structural integrity and that has an undamaged protective jacket or wrap that prevents fiber release shall be treated as nonfriable and therefore is subject only to periodic surveillance and preventive measures as necessary." 40 C.F.R. § 763.85(c).

- assessments made of friable material, the name and signature of each accredited inspector making the assessment, state of accreditation, and if applicable, accreditation number.

There are five types of exclusions from these initial inspection requirements, the first four of which are based on inspections conducted prior to December 14, 1987. First, LEAs do not have to conduct an inspection in specific areas of schools where ACBM has already been identified. Second, if previous sampling done in substantial compliance with the rule indicated that no ACM was present, no inspection needs to be done. Third, LEAs do not have to inspect specific areas where records indicate all ACM was removed. Fourth, states holding a waiver from the inspection requirements of the rule can grant exclusions to schools that had performed inspections in substantial compliance with the rule. And fifth, for schools built after October 12, 1988, LEAs can receive an inspection exclusion if the architect or project engineer responsible for the construction, or an accredited inspector, signs a statement that no ACBM was specified as a building material in any construction document for the building, or, to the best of that person's knowledge, no ACBM was used as a building material in the building.[38] Evidence of reliance on of any of these exclusions must be contained in the management plan.[39] If ACBM is subsequently found in an area that has been excluded from the initial inspection requirement, the LEA has one hundred and eighty days to come into conformance with these requirements.[40]

B. Reinspections

LEAs must reinspect all friable and nonfriable known or assumed ACBM in each school building at least once every three years.[41] Reinspections must be made by an accredited inspector,[42] who must:[43]

- visually reinspect and reassess the condition of all friable known or assumed ACBM;
- visually inspect material that was previously considered nonfriable ACBM and touch the material to determine whether it has become friable since the last inspection;

38. 52 Fed. Reg. 41826, 41831 (Oct. 30, 1987).
39. 40 C.F.R. § 763.99.
40. 40 C.F.R. § 763.99(c).
41. 40 C.F.R. § 763.85(b)
42. 40 C.F.R. § 763.85(b)(2).
43. 40 C.F.R. § 763.85(b)(3).

- identify any homogeneous areas with material that has become friable since the last inspection;
- for each homogeneous area of newly friable material that is already assumed to be ACBM, bulk samples may be collected and submitted for analysis;
- assess the condition of the newly friable material in areas where samples are collected, and newly friable materials in areas that are assumed to be ACBM;
- reassess the condition of friable known or assumed ACBM previously identified; and
- record and submit to the LEA designate for inclusion in the management plan within thirty days of the inspection the following:
  - an inspection report containing date of inspection, signature of the person making the reinspection, state of accreditation(s), and if applicable, accreditation number(s), and any changes in the condition of known or assumed ACBM;
  - an inventory of exact locations where samples were collected during the reinspection, description of the manner used to determine sampling locations and the name, signature, state of accreditation, and if applicable, accreditation number, of each accredited inspector who collected the samples; and
  - any assessments or reassessments made of friable material and the name, signature, state of accreditation, and if applicable, accreditation number, of the accredited inspector making the assessments.

C. Periodic Surveillance

In addition to the reinspection required once every three years, each LEA must survey each building it uses as a school that contains ACBM or is assumed to contain ACBM at least once every six months after a management plan is in effect.[44] The person conducting the survey must visually inspect all areas that are identified in the management plan as ACBM or assumed ACBM and submit a signed report to the LEA designate containing the date of the surveillance and any changes in the condition of the materials for inclusion in the management report.[45]

---

44. 40 C.F.R. § 763.92(b)(1).
45. 40 C.F.R. § 763.92(b)(2).

D. Sampling, Analysis, and Assessment

In response to criticisms that EPA's early efforts to deal with the asbestos issues in schools were too vague to give LEAs sufficient guidance, Congress mandated in the Act that specific standards be set for the proper identification and assessment of ACM.[46] LEAs have the option of assuming that suspected ACBM is ACM. If the LEA chooses not to do so, it must hire an accredited inspector to collect samples for analysis. Sufficient samples must be taken, in a statistically valid manner, as set forth in the rule, to make the determination;[47] the samples must be submitted to an accredited laboratory[48] for analysis. The accreditation program is now run by the National Institute of Standards and Technology, the successor to the National Bureau of Standards, and a list of laboratories accredited to perform polarized light microscopy (PLM) analysis can be found at http://ts.nist.gov/Standards/scopes/plmtm.htm. A homogeneous area is not classified as containing ACM only if the results of all required samples demonstrate asbestos in amounts of 1 percent or less.[49] If any one sample shows asbestos is present in an amount greater than 1 percent, the area will be considered as containing ACM.[50] The name and address of the laboratory performing the analysis, the date of analysis, and the name and signature of the person performing the analysis must be submitted to the LEA designate within thirty days of the analysis for inclusion into the management plan.[51]

The assessment procedure set out in the rule requires the inspector to classify ACBM, whether confirmed or assumed to be ACM, after each inspection and reinspection,[52] into the broad categories set out in the rule and to explain the basis of each such assessment.[53] The seven categories are damaged or

46. 15 U.S.C.§ 2641(a)(1).
47. 40 C.F.R. § 763.86.
48. The rule had allowed LEAs to use laboratories that received interim accreditation for polarized light microscopy (PLM) analysis under the EPA Interim Asbestos Bulk Sample Analysis Quality Assurance Program until the National Bureau of Standards (NBS) PLM Program became operational and laboratories accredited through that program were available. 40 C.F.R. § 763.87(a).
49. 40 C.F.R. § 763.87(c)(1).
50. 40 C.F.R. § 763.87(c)(2).
51. 40 C.F.R. § 763.87(d).
52. The inspector must also use this same procedure with respect to any ACBM identified in prior inspections that were the basis for qualifying for the exclusions noted in 40. C.F.R. § 763.99 and 40 C.F.R. § 763.88(a)(1).
53. 40 C.F.R. § 763.88(b).

significantly damaged thermal system insulation ACM,[54] damaged friable surfacing ACM,[55] significantly damaged friable surfacing ACM,[56] damaged or significantly damaged friable miscellaneous ACM,[57] ACBM with potential

---

54. The regulation provides:

> Damaged or significantly damaged thermal system insulation ACM means thermal system insulation ACM on pipes, boilers, tanks, ducts, and other thermal system insulation equipment where the insulation has lost its structural integrity, or its covering, in whole or in part, is crushed, water-stained, gouged, punctured, missing, or not intact such that it is not able to contain fibers. Damage may be further illustrated by occasional punctures, gouges or other signs of physical injury to ACM; occasional water damage on the protective coverings/jackets; or exposed ACM ends or joints. Asbestos debris originating from the ACBM in question may also indicate damage.

40 C.F.R. § 763.83.

55. The regulation provides:

> Damaged friable surfacing ACM means friable surfacing ACM which has deteriorated or sustained physical injury such that the internal structure (cohesion) of the material is inadequate or which has delaminated such that its bond to the substrate (adhesion) is inadequate, or which, for any other reason, lacks fiber cohesion or adhesion qualities. Such damage or deterioration may be illustrated by the separation of ACM into layers; separation of ACM from the substrate; flaking, blistering, or crumbling of the ACM surface; water damage; significant or repeated water stains, scrapes, gouges, mars or other signs of physical injury on the ACM. Asbestos debris originating from the ACBM in question may also indicate damage.

Id.

56. "Significantly damaged friable surfacing ACM means damaged friable surfacing ACM in a functional space where the damage is extensive and severe." *Id.*

57. The regulation provides:

> Damaged friable miscellaneous ACM means friable miscellaneous ACM which has deteriorated or sustained physical injury such that the internal structure (cohesion) of the material is inadequate or, if applicable, which has delaminated such that its bond to the substrate (adhesion) is inadequate or which for any other reason lacks fiber cohesion or adhesion qualities. Such damage or deterioration may be illustrated by the separation of ACM into layers; separation of ACM from the substrate; flaking, blistering, or crumbling of the ACM surface; water damage; significant or repeated water stains, scrapes, gouges, mars or other signs of physical injury on the ACM. Asbestos debris originating from the ACBM in question may also indicate damage.

Id. "Significantly damaged friable surfacing ACM means damaged friable surfacing ACM in a functional space where the damage is extensive and severe." *Id.*

for damage,[58] ACBM with potential for significant damage[59] and any remaining friable ACBM or friable suspected ACBM.[60]

Factors that can be considered by the inspector in making these classifications include the location and amount of damage,[61] condition (type, severity, and extent of damage),[62] accessibility,[63] potential for disturbance,[64] known or suspected causes of damage,[65] and preventive measures that might eliminate the reasonable likelihood of damage.[66] The inspector needs to provide a signed and dated assessment, containing the state of accreditation, and if applicable, accreditation number, to the LEA designate for inclusion in the management plan within thirty days of the assessment.[67]

The LEA must hire a person accredited to develop management plans, who on the basis of the reports of inspection, reinspection and assessment, and other activities he deems prudent, will recommend appropriate response actions. That person must submit a dated and signed recommendation, containing the state of accreditation, and, if applicable, accreditation number, to the LEA designate for inclusion in the management plan.[68]

---

58. The applicable regulation provides:

    Potential damage means circumstances in which:
    (1) Friable ACBM is in an area regularly used by building occupants, including maintenance personnel, in the course of their normal activities.
    (2) There are indications that there is a reasonable likelihood that the material or its covering will become damaged, deteriorated, or delaminated due to factors such as changes in building use, changes in operations and maintenance practices, changes in occupancy, or recurrent damage.

    Id.
59. Potential significant damage means circumstances in which:

    (1) Friable ACBM is in an area regularly used by building occupants, including maintenance personnel, in the course of their normal activities.
    (2) There are indications that there is a reasonable likelihood that the material or its covering will become significantly damaged, deteriorated, or delaminated due to factors such as changes in building use, changes in operations and maintenance practices, changes in occupancy, or recurrent damage.
    (3) The material is subject to major or continuing disturbance, due to factors including, but not limited to, accessibility or, under certain circumstances, vibration or air erosion *Id.*
60. "Friable when referring to material in a school building means that the material, when dry, may be crumbled, pulverized, or reduced to powder by hand pressure, and includes previously nonfriable material after such previously nonfriable material becomes damaged to the extent that when dry it may be crumbled, pulverized, or reduced to powder by hand pressure." *Id.*
61. 40 C.F.R. § 763.88(c)(1).
62. 40 C.F.R. § 763.88(c)(2).
63. 40 C.F.R. § 763.88(c)(3).
64. 40 C.F.R. § 763.88(c)(4).
65. 40 C.F.R. § 763.88(c)(5).
66. 40 C.F.R. § 763.88(c)(6).
67. 40 C.F.R. § 763.88(a)(2).
68. 40. C.F.R. § 763.88(d).

E. Response Actions

Specific response actions are specified for the different possible categories of ACBM. The five major response actions specified in the rule are operations and maintenance,[69] repair, encapsulation, enclosure, and removal.[70] The LEA can select the least burdensome options among the various approved response actions so long as the response actions selected are sufficient to protect human

Table 16.1 ACBM Response Actions

ACBM Category	*Response Action**
Damaged or Sufficiently Damaged Thermal System Insulation	Repair the damaged area or remove the damaged material if repair is not possible. Maintain all thermal system insulation ACM and its covering in an intact state and undamaged condition.
Damaged Friable Surfacing ACM or Damaged Friable Miscellaneous ACM	Encapsulate, enclose, remove, or repair the damaged material.
Significantly Damaged Friable Surfacing ACM or Significantly Damaged Friable Miscellaneous ACM	Unless not necessary, immediately isolate the functional space and restrict access. Remove the material or enclose or encapsulate.
Friable Surfacing ACM, Thermal System Insulation ACM, or Friable Miscellaneous ACM, any one of which has a Potential for Damage	Implement an operations and maintenance program.
Friable Surfacing ACM, Thermal System Insulation ACM, or Friable Miscellaneous ACM, any one of which has a Potential for Significant Damage	Implement an operations and maintenance program. Institute preventative measures to eliminate reasonable likelihood that ACM or its covering will become significantly damaged, deteriorated, or delaminated. If preventive measures cannot be effectively implemented, remove the materials unless other response actions would be effective. Immediately isolate the area and restrict access, unless not necessary.

*Response Actions are set forth in 40 C.F.R. §§ 763.90(b)–(f).

69. 40 C.F.R. § 763.91.
70. 40 C.F.R. § 763.90.

health and the environment.[71] The LEA always has the option of removing ACBM from a school building at any time.[72]

Response actions other than small-scale short-duration (SSSD)[73] repairs must be designed and conducted by accredited personnel[74] and must be carried out as mandated by applicable worker protection and work practice laws.[75] Some require cleaning before initiation of the response action.[76] Upon completion of any response action to remove, encapsulate, or enclose ACBM, except for SSSD repairs, the area must be visually inspected[77] and air samples collected and analyzed by an accredited laboratory[78] using a specified method. The accreditation program is now run by the National Institute of Standards and Technology, and a list of laboratories accredited to perform

---

71. 40 C.F.R. § 763.90(a).
72. *Id.*
73. "Small-scale, short-duration activities (SSSD)" are tasks such as, but not limited to:

    a. Removal of asbestos-containing insulation on pipes.
    b. Removal of small quantities of asbestos-containing insulation on beams or above ceilings.
    c. Replacement of an asbestos-containing gasket on a valve.
    d. Installation or removal of a small section of drywall.
    e. Installation of electrical conduits through or proximate to asbestos-containing materials.

    SSSD can be further defined by the following considerations:

    f. Removal of small quantities of ACM only if required in the performance of another maintenance activity not intended as asbestos abatement.
    g. Removal of asbestos-containing thermal system insulation not to exceed amounts greater than those which can be contained in a single glove bag.
    h. Minor repairs to damaged thermal system insulation which do not require removal.
    i. Repairs to a piece of asbestos-containing wallboard.
    j. Repairs, involving encapsulation, enclosure, or removal, to small amounts of friable ACM only if required in the performance of emergency or routine maintenance activity and not intended solely as asbestos abatement. Such work may not exceed amounts greater than those which can be contained in a single prefabricated mini-enclosure. Such an enclosure shall conform spatially and geometrically to the localized work area, in order to perform its intended containment function.

    40 C.F.R. 763, Subpart E, Appendix C, Model Accreditation Plan, A.8.
74. 40 C.F.R. § 763.90(g).
75. Worker protection and work practice requirements under the following rules must be followed: 29 C.F.R. 1926.58 (Occupational Safety and Health Administration asbestos worker protection standards for construction), 40 C.F.R. Part 763, subpart G (EPA asbestos worker protection standards for public employees), and 40 C.F.R. Part 61, subpart M (National Emission Standards for Hazardous Air Pollutants—Asbestos). 40 C.F.R. § 763.90(h).
76. 40 C.F.R. § 763.91(c) establishes the requirements for an initial cleaning and requires the accredited management planner hired by the LEA to recommend whether additional cleaning is needed, and if so, the methods and frequency of such cleaning.
77. 40 C.F.R. § 763.90(i)(1).
78. 40 C.F. R. § 763.90(i)(2).

the transmission electron microscopy (TEM) can be found at http://ts.nist.gov/Standards/scopes/temtm.htm. The technical requirements for considering the response action complete are set out in the rule.[79]

An operations and maintenance program response that might disturb friable ACBM must be designed and implemented by accredited personnel[80] and requires the implementation of the procedures set forth below to protect building occupants:

- restrict access to only those people necessary to perform the maintenance project;[81]
- post signs;[82]
- shut off or temporarily modify the air-handling system and restrict other sources of air movement;[83]
- use work practices or other controls to inhibit the spread of any released fibers;[84]
- clean all fixtures or other components in the immediate work area;[85] and
- put the asbestos debris and other cleaning materials in a sealed, leak-tight container.[86]

In the event of a minor fiber release episode, which is defined as the falling or dislodging of three square or linear feet or less of friable ACBM,[87] the procedures require the responders to thoroughly saturate the debris using wet methods,[88] clean the area,[89] put the asbestos debris in a sealed, leak-tight container,[90] and repair, seal, or encapsulate the damaged ACM or immediately implement the appropriate response action set forth in the chart of response actions earlier in this section.[91] In the event of a major friable release episode, which is defined as the falling or dislodging of more than three

79. *See* 40 C.F.R. § 763.90(i)(3), (4), (5) and (6) for measurement requirements using TEM and alternatively, phase contrast microscopy (PCM).
80. 40 C.F.R. § 763.91(e). This requirement of accredited personnel does not apply to SSSD activities.
81. 40 C.F.R. § 763.91(d)(1).
82. 40 C.F.R. § 763.91(d)(2).
83. 40 C.F.R. § 763.91(d)(3).
84. 40 C.F.R. § 763.91(d)(4).
85. 40 C.F.R. § 763.91(d)(5).
86. 40 C.F.R. § 763.91(d)(6).
87. 40 C.F.R. § 763.91(f).
88. 40 C.F.R. § 763.91(f)(1)(i).
89. 40 C.F.R. § 763.91(f)(1)(ii). This section refers to the cleaning methods described in (e), but the cleaning methods are actually described in (c).
90. 40 C.F.R. § 763.91(f)(1)(iii).
91. 40 C.F.R. § 763.91(f)(1)(iv).

square or linear feet of friable ACBM,[92] the responders must restrict access to only those personnel needed to complete the action and post signs[93] and shut off or modify the air-handling system to prevent the distribution of fibers to other areas in the building.[94] The response action for any major fiber release episode must be designed and implemented by accredited personnel.[95]

F. Transportation and Disposal

EPA has not promulgated regulations under the Act for the transportation and disposal of asbestos containing waste material as required by TSCA § 203(h).[96] TSCA § 204(f) mandates that if the EPA failed to issue such regulations, transportation and disposal must be done in accordance with the EPA's most current version of its Asbestos Waste Management Guidance.[97] Transportation covers all activities from receipt of the containerized asbestos waste at the generation site until it has been unloaded at the disposal site. No visible emissions to the outside air are permitted during waste transport, and the rules suggest additional safeguards to ensure that this standard is met for both the transporter and the waste disposal site.

G. Training and Labeling

While members of LEA maintenance and custodial staff do not have to be accredited, they must be trained to work in a building that contains ACBM, whether or not they are required to work with ACBM.[98] The training must be completed before the start of operations and maintenance activities pursuant to a management plan or sixty days after the start of employment for new employees, must be at least two hours long, and must include information about the following:[99]

- asbestos, its various uses and forms;[100]
- health effects associated with asbestos exposure;[101]

---

92. 40 C.F.R. § 763.91(f)(2).
93. 40 C.F.R. § 763.91(f)(2)(i).
94. 40 C.F.R. § 763.91(f)(2)(ii).
95. 40 C.F.R. § 763.91(f)(2)(iii).
96. 15 U.S.C. § 2643(h).
97. 40 C.F.R. Part 763, Subpart E, Appendix D. Regulations governing the transport of asbestos containing waste regulated by the National Emission Standard for Hazardous Air Pollutants (NESHAP) under the Clean Air Act were issued by the Department of Transportation (DOT). Both the NESHAP and DOT rules must be followed.
98. 40 C.F.R. § 763.92(a)(1).
99. *Id.*
100. 40 C.F.R. § 763.92(a)(1)(i).
101. 40 C.F.R. § 763.92(a)(1)(ii).

- locations of ACBM in each school building in which they work;[102]
- recognition of damage, deterioration, and delamination of ACBM;[103] and
- name and telephone number of the LEA designate and the availability and location of the management plan.[104]

Members of the staff who conduct any activities that will result in the disturbance of ACBM must receive an additional 14 hours of training,[105] which must include:

- descriptions of the proper methods of handling ACBM;[106]
- information on the use of respiratory protection as contained in the EPA/NIOSH Guide to Respiratory Protection for the Asbestos Abatement Industry,[107] and other personal protection measures;[108]
- requirements of 40 C.F.R. § 763.92 and § 763.91, Appendices A, C, and D of subpart E, 40 C.F.R. part 763, subpart G, and in 40 C.F.R. Part 61, subpart M, and OSHA regulations contained in 29 C.F.R. § 1926.58;[109] and
- hands-on training in the use of respiratory protection, other personal protection measures, and good work practices.[110]

Maintenance and custodial staff who have attended EPA-approved asbestos training or received equivalent training for operations and maintenance activities and periodic surveillance activities involving asbestos are considered to have met this additional training requirement.[111]

A warning label must be attached next to any friable and nonfriable ACBM and suspected ACBM assumed to be ACM located in routine maintenance areas, such as boiler rooms, at each school building, including friable ACBM that was responded to by a means other than removal and ACBM for which no response action was taken.[112] The labels, which must be prominently displayed and readily visible, must say:

---

102. 40 C.F.R. § 763.92(a)(1)(iii).
103. 40 C.F.R. § 763.92(a)(1)(iv).
104. 40 C.F.R. § 763.92(a)(1)(v).
105. 40 C.F.R. § 763.92(a)(2).
106. 40 C.F.R. § 763.92(a)(2)(i).
107. EPA Number 560/OPPTS–86–001 (Sept. 1986).
108. 40 C.F.R. § 763.92(a)(2)(ii).
109. 40 C.F.R. § 763.92(a)(2)(iii).
110. 40 C.F.R. § 763.92(a)(2)(iv).
111. 40 C.F.R. § 763.92(a)(3).
112. 40 C.F.R. § 763.95(a).

CAUTION: ASBESTOS. HAZARDOUS. DO NOT DISTURB WITHOUT PROPER TRAINING AND EQUIPMENT.[113]

H. Management Plans

The rule requires the development and maintenance of an asbestos management plan to be the repository of all of the mandated information and actions. A complete and updated plan for each school must be kept in the LEA's administrative office and must be freely available for inspection by representatives of EPA, the state, and the general public.[114] Each school must keep a copy of the complete and updated management plan for that school and must similarly make it available, including to workers, before any work begins in any area of a school building.[115] After submitting the management plan to the governor as required under the rule and at least once each school year, the LEA must notify in writing parent, teacher, and employee organizations about the availability of management plans, and must include in the management plan a description of the steps taken to notify such organizations, and a dated copy of the notification.[116]

The management plan for each school was initially required to be developed on or before October 12, 1988 and to be submitted to an agency designated by the governor of the state in which the LEA is located.[117] If an LEA wants to use a building as a school after October 12, 1988, the LEA must submit a management plan for the school to the agency designated by the governor prior to its use as a school.[118] Governors of each state have ninety days to review a management plan, after which the LEA must implement the plan if it has not been disapproved.[119] The plan must be maintained and kept current by the LEA with ongoing operations and maintenance, periodic surveillance, inspection, reinspection, and response action activities.[120] The management plan must include:

- the name and address of each school building and whether the school building contains friable ACBM, nonfriable ACBM, and friable and nonfriable suspected ACBM assumed to be ACM;[121]

---

113. 40 C.F.R. §§ 763.95(b)) and (c).
114. 40 C.F.R. §§ 763.93(g)(1) and (2).
115. 40 C.F.R. § 763.93(g)(3).
116. 40 C.F.R. § 763.93(g)(4).
117. 40 C.F.R. § 763.93(a)(1).
118. 40 C.F.R. §§ 763.93(a)(2) and((3).
119. 40 C.F.R. § 763.93(b).
120. 40 C.F.R. § 763.93(d).
121. 40 C.F.R. § 763.93(e)(1).

- for each inspection conducted before December 14, 1987:[122]
  - the inspection date;
  - a blueprint, diagram, or written description that identifies each location and approximate square or linear footage of any homogeneous or sampling area where material was sampled for ACM, and, if possible, the exact locations where bulk samples were collected, and the dates of collection;
  - analyses of any bulk samples, dates of analyses, and any other laboratory reports pertaining to the analyses;
  - a description of any response actions or preventive measures taken to reduce asbestos exposure, including, if possible, the names and addresses of all contractors involved, start and completion dates of the work, and results of any air samples analyzed during and upon completion of the work; and
  - a description of required assessments of material that was identified before December 14, 1987 as friable ACBM or friable suspected ACBM assumed to be ACM, and the name, signature, state of accreditation, and if applicable, accreditation number of each accredited person making the assessments;
- for all other inspections and reinspections:[123]
  - the inspection or reinspection date, name, signature, state of accreditation and, if applicable, accreditation number of each accredited inspector performing the inspection or reinspection;
  - a blueprint, diagram, or written description that identifies clearly each location and approximate square or linear footage of homogeneous areas where material was sampled for ACM, the exact location where each bulk sample was collected, date of collection, homogeneous areas where friable suspected ACBM is assumed to be ACM, and where nonfriable suspected ACBM is assumed to be ACM;
  - a description of the manner used to determine sampling locations, and name, signature of each accredited inspector collecting samples, the state of accreditation, and if applicable, accreditation number;
  - analyses of any bulk samples collected and analyzed, the name and address of any laboratory doing the analysis, a statement that the laboratory meets the applicable requirements of accreditation, the date of analysis, and the name and signature of the person performing the analysis; and

122. 40 C.F.R. § 763.93(e)(2).
123. 40 C.F.R. § 763.93(e)(3).

  - a description of required assessments of all ACBM and suspected ACBM assumed to be ACM, and the name, signature, state of accreditation, and if applicable, accreditation number of each accredited person making the assessments;
- the name, address, and telephone number of the LEA designate, and the course name, dates, and hours of training taken by that person to carry out the duties;[124]
- recommendations made to the LEA about response actions, the name, signature, state of accreditation of each person making the recommendations, and if applicable, accreditation number;[125]
- detailed descriptions of preventive measures and response actions to be taken, including methods to be used, for any friable ACBM, the locations where such measures and action will be taken, reasons for selecting the response action or preventive measure, and a schedule for beginning and completing each preventive measure and response action;[126]
- with respect to the person or persons who inspected for ACBM and who will design or carry out response actions with respect to the ACBM, except for operations and maintenance, one of the following statements:[127]
  - if the state has adopted a contractor accreditation program, a statement that the person(s) is accredited under such plan; or
  - a statement that the LEA used, or will use, persons who have been accredited by another state that has adopted a contractor accreditation plan or is accredited by an EPA-approved course under the Act;
- a detailed description in the form of a blueprint, diagram, or writing of any ACBM or suspected ACBM assumed to be ACM which remains in the school once response actions are undertaken, which description must be updated as response actions are completed;[128]
- plans for reinspection, operations, and maintenance activities, and for periodic surveillance, description of the recommendation made by the management planner regarding additional cleaning as part of an operations and maintenance program, and the response of the LEA to that recommendation;[129]
- a description of steps taken to inform workers and building occupants, or their legal guardians, about inspections, reinspections, response

124. 40 C.F.R. § 763.93(e)(4).
125. 40 C.F.R. § 763.93(e)(5).
126. 40 C.F.R. § 763.93(e)(6).
127. 40 C.F.R. § 763.93(e)(7).
128. 40 C.F.R. § 763.93(e)(8).
129. 40 C.F.R. § 763.93(e)(9).

actions, and post-response action activities, including periodic reinspection and surveillance activities that are planned or in progress;[130]

- an evaluation of the resources needed to complete response actions successfully and carry out reinspection, operations and maintenance activities, periodic surveillance, and training;[131]
- with respect to each consultant who contributed to the management plan, the name of the consultant and one of the following statements:[132]
  - if the state has adopted a contractor accreditation plan, a statement that the consultant is accredited under such plan; or
  - a statement that the contractor is accredited by another state which has adopted a contractor accreditation plan, or is accredited by an EPA-approved course developed under the Act;
- an LEA may require a statement in the plan signed by an accredited management plan developer that he or she has prepared or assisted in the preparation of such plan or has reviewed such plan, and that such plan is in compliance with the rule; such statement may not be signed by a person who, in addition to preparing or assisting in preparing the management plan, also implements, or will implement, the management plan;[133]
- records required under the rule must be maintained as part of the management plan;[134] and
- the management plan must contain a statement, signed by the LEA designate, which certifies that the responsibilities of the LEA as specified in the rule have been, or will be, met.[135]

I. Recordkeeping

The rule sets out detailed provisions about the types of records that must be kept as part of the management plan in a centralized location in the administrative office of both the school and the LEA. For each homogeneous area where all ACBM has been removed, records must be retained for three years after the next required reinspection.[136]

For each preventive measure and response action taken for friable and nonfriable ACBM or suspected ACBM assumed to be ACM, records must

---

130. 40 C.F.R. § 763.93(e)(10).
131. 40 C.F.R. § 763.93(e)(11).
132. 40 C.F.R. § 763.93(e)(12).
133. 40 C.F.R. § 763.93(f).
134. 40 C.F.R. § 763.93(h).
135. 40 C.F.R. § 763.93(i).
136. 40 C.F.R. § 763.94(a).

include a detailed description of what was done, including methods used, where it was done, why it was done, start and completion dates, names and addresses of all contractors involved, states of accreditation and accreditation numbers, and if ACBM was removed, the name and location of storage or disposal site of the ACM.[137] Additionally, the records must include the name and signature of any person collecting any air sample at the completion of certain response actions, where and when the samples were collected, name and address of the laboratory analyzing the samples, and with respect to the analysis, the date, results, method, name, and signature of the person performing the analysis, and a statement that the laboratory meets the applicable requirements.[138]

Records of required training must include the person's name, job title, date, location, and number of hours completed.[139] For each periodic surveillance, records must include the name of each person performing the surveillance, the date of the surveillance, and any changes in the conditions of the materials.[140] For each cleaning, records must include the name of each person performing the cleaning, the date of such cleaning, the locations cleaned, and the methods used to perform such cleaning.[141] For operations and maintenance activities performed disturbing friable ACBM, records of procedures to protect building occupants must include the name of each person performing the activity, the start and completion dates, where the activity occurred, a description of the activity including preventive measures used, and if ACBM is removed, the name and location of storage or disposal site of the ACM.[142]

For each major asbestos operations and maintenance activity disturbing friable ACBM, other than SSSD, that is performed, records must include the name and signature, state of accreditation, and if applicable, accreditation number of each person performing the activity, start and completion dates, where it occurred, what occurred, including preventive measures used, and if ACBM is removed, the name and location of the storage or disposal site of the ACM.[143] For each fiber release episode, records must include the date and location of the episode, the method of repair, preventive measures or response action taken, the name of each person performing the work, and if ACBM is removed, the name and location of storage or disposal site of the ACM.[144]

---

137. 40 C.F.R. § 763.94(b)(1).
138. 40 C.F.R. § 763.94(b)(2).
139. 40 C.F.R. § 763.94(c).
140. 40 C.F.R. § 763.94(d).
141. 40 C.F.R. § 763.94(e).
142. 40 C.F.R. § 763.94(f).
143. 40 C.F.R. § 763.94(g).
144. 40 C.F.R. § 763.94(h).

J. Waiver and Delegation to States[145]

The governor of any state can request a waiver from the federal asbestos program if the state is implementing a program that is more stringent.[146] At this time 11 states have received waivers for their programs.[147] The waiver request must include:

- state provisions or proposed provisions for which the request is made;[148]
- state agency that will be responsible for implementing the requirements for which a waiver is requested, the names, job titles, and phone numbers of responsible officials in that agency, and if more than one agency will be responsible, a description of the functions to be performed by each agency, how the program will be coordinated by the lead agency, and the names, job titles, and phone numbers of responsible officials in the agencies;[149]
- detailed rationale, with supporting papers, as to why the state asbestos program provisions for which the request is made are at least as stringent as the federal requirements;[150]
- any special situations, problems, and needs pertaining to the waiver request and how the State intends to handle them;[151]
- resources the State intends to devote to the provisions relating to the waiver request;[152]
- specific or enabling State laws and regulations relating to the request, including provisions for assessing criminal and/or civil penalties;[153] and
- assurance the lead agency or other cooperating agencies have the legal authority necessary to carry out the requirements relating to the request.[154]

---

145. The rule sets out an Asbestos Model Accreditation Plan for the states at Part 763, Subpart E, Appendix C.
146. 40 C.F.R. § 763.98(a)(1).
147. The states operating their own programs under the waiver provisions of AHERA are: Connecticut, Colorado, Louisiana, Massachusetts, Maine, Oklahoma, Rhode Island, Texas, Utah, Illinois, and Kentucky. E-mail from Tom Simons, Fibers and Organics Branch, National Program Chemicals Division, Office of Pollution Prevention and Toxics to Miriam V. Gold (Feb. 20, 2009, 11:12 am EST) (on file with author).
148. 40 C.F.R. § 763.98(b)(1).
149. 40 C.F.R. § 763.98(b)(2).
150. 40 C.F.R. § 763.98(b)(3).
151. 40 C.F.R. § 763.98(b)(4).
152. 40 C.F.R. § 763.98(b)(5).
153. 40 C.F.R. § 763.98(b)(6).
154. 40 C.F.R. § 763.98(b)(7).

EPA has thirty days to determine if the waiver request is complete[155]and then thirty additional days to publish the request in the Federal Register for comment.[156] If any objection is filed during the comment period, EPA must schedule a public hearing.[157] The criteria to be used by EPA in deciding whether or not to accept the state waiver shall include a determination that the state has the legal authority to implement its own program,[158] that the program is at least as stringent as the federal program,[159] that the state has adequate enforcement mechanisms,[160] that the lead agency and any cooperating agencies have adequate qualified personnel,[161] that the State will devote adequate resources,[162] and that the State gives satisfactory assurances when requested by EPA that necessary steps will be taken within a reasonable time to conform with applicable criteria.[163]

EPA has thirty days after the close of the comment period or following a public hearing, whichever is applicable, to publish its decision and its rationale as to the waiver request in the Federal Register.[164] Substantial modifications to approved state programs must be submitted to the EPA.[165] Annual reports must be submitted to the Regional EPA Office containing a summary of the state's program activities during the last reporting period, including enforcement actions taken, changes in the implementation of the program during the last reporting period, and any other information that EPA may request.[166]

EPA has substantial oversight over state programs, including the ability to make unannounced visits to LEAs[167] and to require conferences when it feels a state program is deficient.[168] If a state does not correct deficiencies, EPA can rescind the waiver.[169]

155. 40 C.F.R. § 763.98(c)(1).
156. 40 C.F.R. § 763.98(c)(2).
157. 40 C.F.R. § 763.98(c)(3).
158. 40 C.F.R. § 763.98(d)(1).
159. 40 C.F.R. § 763.98(d)(2).
160. 40 C.F.R. § 763.98(d)(3).
161. 40 C.F.R. § 763.98(d)(4).
162. 40 C.F.R. § 763.98(d)(5).
163. 40 C.F.R. § 763.98(d)(6).
164. 40 C.F.R. § 763.98(e).
165. 40 C.F.R. § 763.98(f).
166. 40 C.F.R. § 763.98(g).
167. 40 C.F.R. § 763.98(h).
168. 40 C.F.R. § 763.98(i).
169. 40 C.F.R. § 763.98(j).

K. Miscellaneous Provisions

The Act contained a number of miscellaneous provisions to support the goal of effective and responsible asbestos management. The Act reserved to the EPA or the governor of the state the authority to take emergency action in the event that the LEA does not respond to an imminent and substantial threat to health or the environment posed by airborne asbestos or the condition of friable ACM in a school building.[170] The Act made clear that it was not intended to preempt any other state or federal law,[171] to influence the disposition of any civil action,[172] or to preclude any court from awarding damages associated with the abatement of ACM.[173] No federal cause of action is created by the Act.[174] States have the ability to establish additional liabilities or more stringent requirements for schools within its borders.[175]

EPA was required to conduct a study of the availability of liability insurance prior to October 1, 1990[176] and to conduct a study of ACM in public buildings and commercial buildings prior to October 22, 1987.[177] The Act created whistleblower protections for people who provide information relating to a potential violation of its provisions and delegated responsibility for conducting reviews of any such allegations to the Secretary of Labor.[178] An asbestos ombudsman position was created to deal with complaints and grievances submitted by anyone with respect to the provisions of the Act.[179]

III. Enforcement

The EPA enforces AHERA through civil penalties and referrals for criminal prosecution, and citizens can bring suit through the citizens' petition provisions of TSCA. EPA has consistently brought civil enforcement proceedings against schools and owners of school buildings, and has recently turned its enforcement attention to charter schools that may be unfamiliar with AHERA's requirements. In an enforcement announced September 30, 2008, the EPA fined six Arizona charter schools that EPA said did not have any

170. 15 U.S.C. § 2648.
171. 15 U.S.C. § 2649(a).
172. 15 U.S.C. § 2649(e).
173. 15 U.S.C. § 2649(b).
174. 15 U.S.C. § 2649(d).
175. 15 U.S.C. § 2649(c).
176. 15 U.S.C.§ 2650.
177. 15 U.S.C.§ 2653.
178. 15 U.S.C.§ 2651.
179. 15 U.S.C.§ 2652.

ACM in their buildings but failed to establish management plans in compliance with AHERA.[180] The EPA resolved several other enforcement proceedings against charter schools in 2008 and 2009.[181]

A. Civil Penalty System

The Act[182] provides a two-tier penalty system for AHERA violations. The lower tier carries maximum daily penalties of $7,500 for violations as of January 13, 2009, which is one-fifth of the penalties for other TSCA violations.[183] That tier is reserved for enumerated violations by LEAs, and contractors who fail to obtain accreditation. The higher tier carries maximum daily penalties as of January 13, 2009 of $37,500, and applies the penalty provisions in TSCA § 16[184] to all other asbestos-related TSCA violations. The statute also provides for citizens' suits, citizens' petitions, and injunctive relief.

The Act directs the EPA to consider schools' primary educational objective when assessing penalties, and requires the EPA to consider the ability of the LEA to continue to provide educational services, the culpability of the LEA, its ability to pay, and the significance of the violations.

The EPA took these mandates into account when it issued its enforcement response policy for AHERA (the AHERA ERP) in 1989,[185] as amended.[186]

---

180. Press Release, EPA, EPA fines six Arizona charter school operators for asbestos violations. Schools failed to have inspections completed and asbestos management plans (Sept. 30 2008), *available at* http://yosemite.epa.gov/opa/admpress.nsf/d0cf6618525a9efb852573590 03fb69d/5725995f34568986852574d4006653e6!OpenDocument&Highlight=2,asbestos.

181. *See* charter school enforcements reported in EPA press releases *available at* http://yosemite.epa.gov/opa/admpress.nsf/d0cf6618525a9efb85257359003fb69d/1aba19eead2104b285257 544005fcb6a!OpenDocument&Highlight=2,asbestos,school (Arizona school in 2009), http://yosemite.epa.gov/opa/admpress.nsf/d0cf6618525a9efb85257359003fb69d/9c6f0c65 793297628525749d0052fbe7!OpenDocument&Highlight=2,asbestos (Delaware school in 2008), http://yosemite.epa.gov/opa/admpress.nsf/d0cf6618525a9efb85257359003fb69d/17 e8e9294369176c8525749d0050def3!OpenDocument&Highlight=2,asbestos (Philadelphia school in 2008), http://yosemite.epa.gov/opa/admpress.nsf/d0cf6618525a9efb85257359003 fb69d/17e8e9294369176c8525749d0050def3!OpenDocument&Highlight=2,asbestos (additional Arizona schools in 2008), and http://yosemite.epa.gov/opa/admpress.nsf/ d0cf6618525a9efb85257359003fb69d/e3ffe72bbae144e98525732f007278b0!OpenDocument &Highlight=2,asbestos (Tucson schools in 2007).

182. 15 U.S.C. § 2647.

183. 73 Fed. Reg. 75340, 75341, 75345 (Dec. 11, 2008).

184. *See* Chapter 14, Penalties and Enforcement.

185. EPA, Interim Final Enforcement Response Policy for the Asbestos Hazard Emergency Response Act (Jan. 31, 1989) [hereinafter AHERA ERP].

186. Memorandum from Jesse Baskerville, Director, Toxics and Pesticides Enforcement Division, Office of Regulatory Enforcement, EPA, Revision of the AHERA Enforcement Response Policy: Civil Penalties for Failure to Conduct Reinspections (Aug. 4, 1998); EPA, Toxics and Pesticides Enforcement Division, Office of Regulatory Enforcement, Enforcement Response

Under the AHERA ERP no penalties are assessed against LEAs for first time violations if they are relatively low level violations. Instead, Notices of Noncompliance, which do not carry penalties, are issued for these first time violations. Civil complaints can be issued if the LEA does not comply with a Notice of Noncompliance. For example, in *In the Matter of Rose & Alex Pilibos*,[187] the EPA Region issued a default order penalizing the owners of a private school building because they had allegedly not submitted a management plan in accordance with the Notice of Noncompliance issued to them, and they did not respond to the EPA's complaint. Civil complaints may also be issued for subsequent violations and more serious first violations.[188] The 1998 AHERA ERP amendments authorize penalties for first time violations if the LEA fails to inspect or reinspect using accredited contractors.

1. Lower Tier Penalties

The lower tier of penalties is used for designated violations by an LEA and by contractors. The LEA violations that qualify for the lower tier are:

- failure to conduct an inspection to determine if ACM is present in a school pursuant to the regulations;
- knowingly submitting false information to the governor regarding an inspection or an inspection statement;
- failure to develop a management plan; and
- failure to comply with the worker protection requirements in TSCA § 56.[189]

The AHERA ERP interprets the failure to conduct ACM inspections pursuant to the regulations to include all aspects of regulatory compliance, including using accredited individuals and laboratories, and bulk sample

---

Policy for the Asbestos Model Accreditation Plan (MAP) Addendum to the AHERA ERP (Mar. 9, 1998); Memorandum from John J. Neylan III, Director, Policy and Grants Division, Office of Compliance Monitoring, EPA, Unaccredited Supervisor/Worker Violations Under the AHERA Interim Final Enforcement Response Policy (Jan. 19, 1990); and Memorandum from John J. Neylan III, Director, Policy and Grants Division, Office of Compliance Monitoring, EPA, Changes Relating to Accreditation Violations/Penalty Amounts Resulting from ASHAA Reauthorization/Amendment (Jan. 27, 1992).

187. Docket No. TSCA-09-91-0011 (Region 9 Regional Judicial Officer, 1991).

188. AHERA ERP, 3.

189. The statute also imposes a lower tier penalty on false statements to a governor in connection with a request to defer the deadline for submitting a management plan, but the statute only permitted deferrals until May 9, 1989 and the statute of limitations on such violations has long passed.

analysis requirements.[190] Failing to develop a management plan includes failure to prepare the plan in accordance with the regulations, using an unaccredited person to prepare the plan, missing any required elements, failing to submit it to the state, failure to make the public aware of its availability, and failure to actually make it publicly available.[191] In contrast to the expansive interpretation of these two provisions, submitting false information only includes information that is actually submitted, and does not include willfully withholding information.[192]

Private non-profit schools are accorded the lower tier penalties even though they do not meet the statutory definition of a LEA.[193] Employees of LEAs do not qualify for the lower tier penalties, but the ERP excuses them from penalties for first-time violations that are not egregious or willful.[194]

The existence of lower tier penalties and Notices of Noncompliance does not mean that the potential penalties are necessarily *de minimis*. The EPA announced in 2004 that it had found widespread violations in five schools in Puerto Rico, including one incident in which a teacher and students removed two thousand square feet of asbestos containing vinyl floor tiles without using any protective equipment. The Commonwealth of Puerto Rico entered into a settlement requiring it to spend $5,600,000 to identify and correct AHERA violations, and the Puerto Rico Department of Education agreed to inspect all schools and come into compliance with AHERA, including preparing and updating asbestos management plans.[195] Other school systems have agreed to significant expenditures also, including Newark, New Jersey ($2,250,000)[196] and Yonkers, New York ($131,000).[197]

---

190. AHERA ERP, 8.

191. *Id.* at 9.

192. *Id.* at 8.

193. *Id.* at 21.

194. *Id.* at 20.

195. *See* Press Release, EPA, *EPA* Settlement Will Bring Puerto Rico Schools into Compliance with Asbestos Regulations (Feb, 27, 2004), *available at* http://yosemite.epa.gov/opa/admpress.nsf/d0cf6618525a9efb85257359003fb69d/4de889020a76933585257147006e4e93!OpenDocument&Highlight=2,asbestos; EPA, Office of Regulatory Enforcement, Enforcement Alert, vol. 7, no. 1 (Sept 2004), *available at* www.epa.gov/compliance/resources/newsletters/civil/enfalert/aheraalert0721.pdf. *See also*, Charles G. Garlow, *Asbestos—The Long-Lived Mineral*, 19 NAT. RESOURCES & ENV'T, 36 (Spring 2005).

196. Press Release, EPA, EPA Settlement Will Bring Newark Schools into Compliance With Asbestos Regulations (Jan. 1, 2005), *available at* http://yosemite.epa.gov/opa/admpress.nsf/cafbebb41895f4a9852572a000657b5c/cb1b852a19abe3f1852570d10053d046!OpenDocument.

197. Press Release, EPA, EPA Settlement Will Bring Yonkers Schools into Compliance with Asbestos Regulations (Dec. 3, 2004), *available at* http://yosemite.epa.gov/opa/admpress.nsf/cafbebb41895f4a9852572a000657b5c/036e9fc4b845c1b88525711f00633816!OpenDocument.

Contractors who fail to obtain proper accreditation are also subject to lower tier penalties if they inspect for ACM or design, conduct or employ individuals to conduct response actions for friable ACM in a school, public, or commercial building. Contractors who are federal employees do not qualify for these lower tier penalties.[198] The lower tier penalties for contractors were enacted in 1990 by the Asbestos School Hazard Abatement Reauthorization Act of 1989, which amended AHERA.[199] This amendment postdates and supersedes discussions in the preamble to the final AHERA rule[200] and in the AHERA ERP that say that only LEAs are eligible for the lower tier penalties.

All of the enforcement response policies follow the basic framework of establishing a gravity based penalty that can be adjusted upward or downward based on the facts of the violation. The gravity based penalty is determined by analyzing criteria referred to as the nature, circumstances, and extent of the violation.[201] The AHERA ERP follows this same framework for lower tier violations and assigns a nature, circumstance, and extent to each violation and then uses a matrix to determine the gravity based penalty. Under the AHERA ERP all LEA violations have the same nature, and as a result the nature is not relevant for determining potential penalties.[202] There are six circumstance levels, and levels 1 and 2 carry the highest potential penalties because they are reserved for violations that are likely to cause harm. These are the violations causing the greatest exposure to school children and workers. Levels 3 and 4 are reserved for violations with a significant chance of harm, and levels 5 and 6 are reserved for violations with a small chance of causing harm.[203] The extent of a violation increases with increasing potential harm, and so greater quantities of asbestos result in higher extent categories. Violations are classified as major if the total amount of ACM cannot be determined or if they involve more than three thousand square feet or one thousand linear feet of ACM. Significant violations involve more than one hundred and sixty square feet or two hundred and sixty linear feet of ACM, but less than the triggers for major extent violations, and minor violations involve less than or equal to one hundred and sixty square feet or two hundred and sixty linear feet of ACM.[204]

---

198. 15 U.S.C.§ 2647.
199. Public Law No: 101-637 (1990).
200. 52 Fed. Reg. 41826, 41842-43 (Oct. 30, 1987).
201. Nature, circumstances, and extent are attributes that are common to each enforcement response policy. For a detailed discussion of these attributes, *see* Chapter 14, Penalties and Enforcement.
202. AHERA ERP, 12.
203. *Id.*
204. AHERA ERP, 12–13.

The EPA can seek multiple violations for the same event. For example, it can penalize both the LEA and a contractor for the same violation. However, if there are multiple violations at one school, penalties against the LEA are capped at $5,000 per day[205] plus an inflation adjustment.

The gravity based penalties can be adjusted downward by 25 percent if the LEA acted prudently and responsibly but did not know about its AHERA obligations.[206] The gravity based penalties can be adjusted downward by another 25 percent if the LEA did not have control over the violations.[207] Downward adjustments of 15 percent are also available for cooperative attitude.[208] Voluntary self-reporting qualifies the LEA for a 25 percent reduction and voluntary self-reporting within thirty days of learning of the violation qualifies for another 25 percent reduction, for a total reduction of 50 percent for prompt self-reporting.[209] Complete penalty mitigation is available when the LEA can document that it made reasonable efforts to hire third parties who are in compliance with the AHERA requirements.[210]

Upward adjustments may be made for prior violations, unless the LEA self-reported the violation under consideration. A 15 percent upward adjustment may be made for an uncooperative attitude.[211]

All penalties assessed against LEAs are to be spent by the LEA on AHERA compliance. Commentators have noted that this vitiates the deterrent aspects of a penalty because the LEA can use the penalty money.[212] If the LEA does not spend at least the amount of the penalty, the unspent funds go to the Asbestos Trust Fund.[213]

The Act provided for maximum penalties of $5,000 when it was enacted. This maximum was raised for educational agencies to $5,500 starting January 31, 1997, to $6,500 starting March 16, 2004 and to $7,500 starting January 13, 2009. Because of technical errors in promulgating the regulations, the date ranges for penalties applicable to contractors who failed to get proper asbestos accreditation are slightly different. The maximum for contractors was raised to $5,500 starting March 16, 2004, and to $7,500 starting January 13, 2009.[214]

205. *Id.* at 10.
206. *Id.* at 13.
207. *Id.* at 14.
208. *Id.* at 14, 15.
209. *Id.* at 15.
210. *Id.* at 7, 14.
211. *Id.* at 14, 15.
212. Charles G. Garlow, *Asbestos—The Long-Lived Mineral*, 19 Nat. Resources & Env't, 36, 40 (Spring, 2005).
213. AHERA ERP, 16. For an example of an order requiring the penalty to be spent on compliance and the balance paid to the trust fund, *see* In the Matter of Rose & Alex Pilibos, Docket No. TSCA-09-91-0011 (Region 9 Regional Judicial Officer, 1991).
214. 73 Fed. Reg. 75340, 75341, 75345 (Dec. 11 2008).

2. Higher Tier Penalties

AHERA violations in general are violations of TSCA § 15, which provides in part that it is unlawful to "fail or refuse to comply with … any requirement of subchapter II of this chapter or any rule promulgated or order issued under subchapter II of this chapter." All violations of TSCA § 15 are subject to the current per day maximum penalty of $37,500.[215] Exceptions are that a LEA is not liable for these higher tier penalties under any circumstances,[216] and certain violations by contractors are penalized at the lower tier.

The AHERA ERP states that higher tier penalties are generally capped at the maximum penalty for each school building, no matter how many separate violations occurred at that building.[217] At least one reported order considers each separate structure at a school to be a separate building, including a track storage shed, a snack bar, a pool pump house, and a water well pump house.[218] If the violation is egregious the EPA reserves the right to exceed this cap.[219] If the violator was not performing asbestos remediation and had no reason to know asbestos was present, a waiver of penalties may be appropriate if that person agrees to obtain AHERA training.[220]

All higher tier penalties are in the same category for the nature of the violation, and so the nature can be disregarded when calculating the gravity based penalties. The AHERA ERP classifies each violation into *sui generis* circumstance levels and extent categories. Both upward and downward adjustments may be made, consistent with the adjustments available to LEAs.

Any violator can also qualify for complete penalty mitigation under the Audit Policy if it meets its requirements.[221]

B. Injunctions, Citizens' Suits, and Criminal Enforcement

The EPA can seek injunctions under AHERA if a violation poses an imminent and substantial endangerment to human health or the environment.[222]

Most of the enforcement options available for non-asbestos violations are also available for asbestos violations. For example, TSCA § 16 authorizes the

215. The statutory provision for these penalties is TSCA § 16, and the penalty increases were promulgated in 73 Fed. Reg. 75340, 75341, 75345 (Dec. 11 2008).
216. TSCA § 48(b).
217. AHERA ERP, 16.
218. In The Matter of Louis W. Alves and Associates, Inc., Docket No. TSCA-09-93-0009, 2 (Region 9 Judicial Officer, 1994).
219. AHERA ERP, 18.
220. *Id.* at 19–20.
221. 65 Fed. Reg. 19618 (Apr. 11, 2000). *See* Chapter 14, Penalties and Enforcement.
222. TSCA § 208.

EPA to seek injunctions to compel compliance with AHERA even if there is no substantial endangerment, and offers a much broader basis for obtaining an injunction than the AHERA provisions. Knowing or willful AHERA violations can lead to criminal prosecution.

Anyone can file a citizen complaint if there is ACM in a school building, and the EPA or state must investigate and respond.[223] Citizens' petitions seeking issuance, amendment, or repeal of AHERA regulations may be brought under AHERA[224] or under the citizens' petition provisions of TSCA § 20.[225]

C. Inspections and Audits

The EPA conducts inspections of LEAs and contractors to determine if they are in compliance with the AHERA requirements. EPA Region 10 found these violations most often when it conducted inspections:

- failure to designate a person to ensure the AHERA requirements are implemented;
- failure to inform workers or the building occupants at least once a year about inspections, response actions, and post-response action activities that are planned or are in progress;
- failure to notify parent, teacher, or employee organizations about the Management Plan's availability once a year;
- failure to conduct or document the six-month asbestos periodic surveillance on all of its buildings;
- failure to provide appropriate training for its maintenance and/or custodial staff;
- failure to post asbestos warning labels in routine maintenance areas (boiler rooms);
- failure to maintain complete records on removals/repairs on materials containing asbestos, asbestos fiber releases, and/or maintenance and operations activities, including lack of information on whether the laboratory used for analyzing the samples is accredited, accreditations of people conducting the activities, how the activities were performed, etc.; and
- failure to conduct the three-year reinspection.[226]

223. TSCA § 48(d).
224. TSCA § 48(e).
225. *See* Chapter 14, Penalties and Enforcement.
226. EPA Region 10, AHERA News—Jan. 1998, no. 10.

The EPA has prepared an audit protocol for use by LEAs and contractors that want to perform self-audits covering asbestos and AHERA compliance.[227]

D. State Enforcement

States that have implemented their own asbestos regulations can independently enforce them. State regulations must be at least as stringent as AHERA, and therefore an AHERA violation also will be a state violation. For example, the Washington State Department of Labor and Industries penalized a consultant for violating AHERA and the Washington Industrial Safety and Health Act[228] in *Prezant Assocs. v. Labor & Indus.* [229] In that case, an asbestos consultant agreed that it would comply with both the Washington Administrative Code and AHERA in conducting an asbestos inspection at a university.[230] The Washington Court of Appeals affirmed a penalty imposed by the Department of Labor and Industries, noting that the contractor had not followed AHERA's requirements, and consequently had violated the Washington laws as well.

227. Protocol for Conducting Environmental Compliance Audits of Facilities with PCBs, Asbestos, and Lead-based Paint Regulated under TSCA, EPA 300-B-00-004, (Mar. 2000), *available through* http://cfpub.epa.gov/compliance/resources/policies/incentives/auditing/.
228. Wash. Rev. Code § 49.17.010.
229. 165 P.3d 12 (2007).
230. This case did not discuss the possibility of a breach of contract action for failure to comply with AHERA, but suggests that such an action may be possible where a consultant agrees to be bound by the procedural requirements of AHERA.

CHAPTER 17

Indoor Radon Abatement Act

I. Radon, a Short History

As discussed in the earlier chapters of this book, in the initially enacted version of the Toxic Substances Control Act (TSCA)[1] Congress required the United States Environmental Protection Agency (EPA) to promulgate regulations to control the import, manufacture, and processing of chemical substances. In the Indoor Radon Abatement Act (hereinafter sometimes referred to as the Act or the IRAA),[2] which amended TSCA, Congress created an alternative to the traditional regulatory framework. The IRAA envisioned that the EPA would play a very different role in minimizing the health risks from indoor radon. EPA was positioned as a developer of technical and educational information and a manager of grant programs, all intended to educate the public and to promote the creation of solutions at the state level in response to citizen awareness campaigns.

As a result of EPA's role under the IRAA, the radon programs that EPA administers are all advisory, and while EPA is a valuable source of information on radon measurement, control, and mitigation, none of its programs are mandatory. Some of the states have used the information developed under the IRAA to develop mandatory programs, which are briefly outlined at the end of this chapter.

Radon is a substance that poses a threat of lung cancer. It is produced when radium, a naturally occurring substance, breaks down. Radium is present in a variety of substances, including soil and rock. When those substances are used in building materials, radon gas can be emitted into the indoor air. Radon can also enter the indoor air from adjacent soil or rock.[3] Radon is odorless, colorless, and tasteless. Testing is the only way to determine whether or not a home contains radon.[4]

Public awareness of the health risks from radon was very regionalized and focused on local issues. Health problems associated with radon began to occur in western states with uranium mining in the 1950s and 1960s, when a high incidence of lung cancer was detected among uranium miners.[5] The impacted states, together with the federal government, developed programs to assist those living near uranium mines or mill tailings sites.[6]

---

1. 15 U.S.C. §§ 2601–2695d.
2. Indoor Radon Abatement Act, Pub. L. 94-469, title III §301, as added Pub. L. 100-551, §1(a), (1988), 102 Stat. 2755, as amended.
3. United States General Accounting Office Report, Indoor Air Pollution: An Emerging Health Problem, CED-80-111, 4 (Sept. 24, 1980) [hereinafter Emerging Health Problem].
4. EPA, Home Buyer's and Seller's Guide to Radon, 402-K-06-093, 1, (Nov. 2006), *available at* http://www.epa.gov/radon/pubs/hmbyguid.html.
5. EPA and Conference of Radiation Control Directors, Office of Radiation Program, Summary of State Radon Programs, 7 (Aug. 1987) [hereinafter State Summary].
6. *Id.* Congress enacted the Uranium Mill Tailings Radiation Control Act, 42 U.S.C. § 7901 (1978) to deal with the health and environmental risks that could emanate from

Mining played a role in the development of radon programs in Florida as well. Elevated radon levels were found in homes built on reclaimed phosphate mining sites, and those homes were investigated in the 1970s.[7]

As early as 1980, the United States General Accounting Office (GAO) had issued a report to Congress[8] highlighting the then developing problem of indoor air quality in general. The report found that most air pollution cleanup activity had been focused on the outdoor air, while indoor air pollution in the nonworkplace could constitute a potentially more serious threat, given where people spend their time.[9] One of the more harmful substances identified in the report was radon. In addition to highlighting the issues, the GAO concluded that because no one federal agency had responsibility for indoor air quality in the nonworkplace, federal actions to deal with this problem had been piecemeal and could possibly exacerbate the problem.[10] The GAO report singled out the United States Department of Energy's efforts to conserve energy by making buildings more air tight as having the unintended consequence of keeping radon from being vented to the outside and dissipated.[11] The report concluded with the recommendation to amend the Clean Air Act to give EPA the authority to deal with the emerging issue of indoor air pollution outside of the workplace.[12] This was not done.

The topic came to national attention in late 1984. A nuclear power plant worker was found to be highly radioactive and his exposure was traced back to his home in Pennsylvania, where radon concentrations were as high as one hundred and thirty times the federal occupational exposure standard for underground uranium mines. The home was located on a geological formation, called the Reading Prong, which is in New Jersey, New York, and Pennsylvania.[13] Similarly high levels were found in other homes.[14]

---

uranium mill processing sites in ten states and to develop a future licensing program for such sites.

7. State Summary, 9.
8. Emerging Health Problem.
9. *Id.* at 1. In support of its argument, the GAO cited a Council on Environmental Quality report that estimated that more than $213 billion would be spent from 1977 through 1986 in pursuit of clean outdoor air.
10. *Id.* at 11. The GAO summarized the situation by quoting from a then recent Office of Technology Assessment (OTA) report that concluded that "the Federal government does not appear to have recognized the significance of indoor air quality as a potential health problem …"
11. *Id.* at 16.
12. *Id.* at 22.
13. United States General Accounting Office Report, Air Pollution: Hazards of Indoor Radon Could Pose a National Health Problem, GAO/RCED-86-170, 10 (June 30, 1986) [hereinafter National Health Problem].
14. *Id.*

The GAO revisited this topic again at the request of the Pennsylvania Congressional Delegation.[15] The GAO noted the lack of reliable data, but cited the EPA's conclusion that radon poses a threat of lung cancer at very low levels and that there is no safe level of exposure.[16] The GAO further noted the work being done in this area by EPA, other federal agencies, and the states[17] and concluded that on the federal level, there was sufficient statutory authority to do research and provide technical assistance, but not to regulate.[18] GAO concluded its report with basically the same recommendation it had made six years earlier, that Congress designate EPA as the federal agency responsible for federal radon efforts. It recommended amending the Clean Air Act or enacting or amending other legislation.[19]

At about the same time, the media was writing about the risks associated with indoor radon pollution and quoting federal warnings that radon in homes could cause five thousand to twenty thousand lung cancer deaths a year. An article in the New York Times asserted:

> All the experts agree that, even according to the lowest estimates of risk, radon poses one of the nation's worst environmental threats, imperiling hundreds of thousands of households at least. Even those who believe that Federal officials have overstated radon's deadliness assert that the naturally formed radioactive gas is responsible for 10,000 of the nation's 130,000 annual lung cancer deaths.[20]

II. Requirements of the Act

Congress enacted the Indoor Radon Abatement Act of 1988 and set a national goal that indoor air be as free from radon as the outside air. The Act provided incentives for states to establish radon programs, conduct surveys, and develop information on the public health hazard of radon, and directed the EPA to support those programs by developing information, standards, and

15. *Id.*
16. *Id.* at 19.
17. *Id.* at 36–41.
18. *Id.* at 44–47.
19. *Id.* at 49.
20. Erik Eckholm, *Radon: Threat is Real, But Scientists Argue Over its Severity*, N.Y. Times, Sept. 2, 1986, *available at* http://query.nytimes.com/gst/fullpage.html?res=9A0DE5D71E3EF931A3575AC0A960948260&sec=health&spon=&pagewanted=1#.

testing programs.[21] At the time of passage of the Act, fewer than half of the states had a radon reduction program in place.[22]

Because radon is a naturally occurring substance and the health concerns it presents are not directly caused by human intervention, the federal government could not easily propose the standard regulatory framework to deal with the evolving radon issues. Since industry had not generally caused the problem of heath risks from indoor radon, there was no industry or industry group that could be expected to remediate the problem at its own expense. No one had put radon, or a substance containing radon, into homes, schools, and other buildings. Unlike the preceding titles of TSCA, which mandated the EPA to regulate the culpable industries, this new amendment to TSCA mandated EPA to develop and provide information and expertise to the public and the states. The alternative of the federal government regulating the behavior of individual homeowners in this respect was not one that Congress had the will or the resources to implement.

A. EPA Citizen's Guide

The Act required EPA to publish by June 1, 1989 an updated version of its 1986 document entitled A Citizen's Guide to Radon (the Citizen's Guide), and to periodically revise the document as needed.[23] The updated guide was to include (i) a description by action levels of the health risks associated with different levels of radiation exposure[24] broken out for sensitive populations[25] and for people engaged in potentially risk-increasing behavior,[26] (ii) the costs and technological feasibility of reducing radon concentrations in existing and new buildings,[27] (iii) the relationship between various testing techniques and between measurements based on such and the action levels described,[28] and (iv) outdoor radon levels country wide.[29]

In January of 2009, EPA published its most recent version of the Citizen's Guide.[30] In sixteen easy-to-read pages, the Guide explains the sources of

21. Press Release, EPA, Indoor Radon Abatement Act of 1988 (Oct. 28, 1988).
22. 134 Cong. Rec. 15263 (daily ed. Oct. 7, 1988) (statement of Sen. Chafee) [hereinafter Chafee Statement].
23. 15 U.S.C. § 2663 (a)(1).
24. *Id.*
25. 15 U.S.C. § 2663 (a)(2)(A).
26. 15 U.S.C. § 2663 (a)(2)(B).
27. 15 U.S.C. § 2663 (a)(2)(C).
28. 15 U.S.C. § 2663 (a)(2)(D).
29. 15 U.S.C. § 2663 (a)(2)(E).
30. EPA, A Citizen's Guide to Radon: The Guide to Protecting Yourself and Your Family from Radon, 402/K-09/001 (Revised January 2009) [hereinafter Citizen's Guide], *available at* http://www.epa.gov/radon/pubs/.

radon, how testing can be done, and how levels of radon can be reduced. It contains lists of state and federal resources to implement its suggestions. In the Guide, EPA states its current estimate that about twenty-one thousand annual lung cancer deaths are radon-related and that those who smoke are at higher risk.[31] The Guide also cites the Surgeon General, who warned, in a health advisory:

> Indoor radon is the second-leading cause of lung cancer in the United States and breathing it over prolonged periods can present a significant health risk to families all over the country. It's important to know that this threat is completely preventable. Radon can be detected with a simple test and fixed through well-established venting techniques.[32]

B. Model Construction Standards and Techniques

The Act also required EPA to work with organizations involved in establishing national building construction standards and techniques and to solicit public comments to develop model construction standards and techniques for controlling radon levels in new buildings.[33] The Act further required EPA to work to ensure that the model standards and techniques so developed were adopted by the appropriate private and governmental entities.[34]

The EPA issued Model Standards and Techniques for the Control of Radon in New Residential Buildings in 1994.[35] The publication was intended to serve as a model for jurisdictions developing building codes or standards applicable to their radon control requirements,[36] primarily for one- and two-family homes and other residential buildings of three stories or less.[37] There is no requirement in the Act that new homes meet any specific radon level or that private home owners must test their homes.[38] Consistent with its limited authority under the Act, the EPA was careful to point out in several sections that the Model Standards were not intended to supersede radon resistant

---

31. *Id.* at 16.
32. *Id.* quoting the Surgeon General Health Advisory (Jan. 2005).
33. 15 U.S.C. § 2665.
34. *Id.*
35. EPA, Air and Radiation, Model Standards and Techniques for the Control of Radon in New Residential Buildings, EPA 402-R-94-009 (Mar. 1994) [hereinafter Model Standards], *available at* www.epa.gov/radon/pubs/newconst.html.
36. *Id.* at 2.
37. *Id.* at 8, Section 6.0.
38. EPA, Office of Air and Radiation, Building Radon Out: A Step-by-Step Guide on How to Build Radon-Resistant Homes, 402-K-01-004 (Apr. 2001) [Building Radon Out], *available at* http://www.epa.gov/radon/pubs/index.html.

construction standards[39] and were not the only acceptable way of reducing radon in new construction.[40] While the publication itself envisioned future editions would be prepared with additional experience,[41] the EPA, on its Web site,[42] notes that the publication is not being updated but should continue to be useful as a reference.

C. Technical Assistance to States for Radon Programs

The Act required the EPA, or any other federal agency or department it might designate, to provide technical assistance to the states.[43] The Act listed a host of activities that would fulfill this requirement, such as:[44] establishing a clearinghouse of radon related information; operating a voluntary proficiency program for rating the effectiveness of radon measurement devices, radon mitigation devices and entities, and people offering such services;[45] design and implementation of training seminars; publication of information materials about health risks and mitigation methods; operating cooperative projects with the states, including home evaluation programs targeted at homes of low-income people; demonstrating radon mitigation methods, again targeting such demonstrations to homes of low-income people; establishing a national database of radon levels organized by state; developing radon measurement and mitigation techniques that would be suitable for use in buildings housing child care facilities; and providing relevant professional organizations information on technology and methods of radon assessment and mitigation.[46] At the request of a state, EPA could provide further assistance, such as designing and implementing radon surveys, public information and education programs, programs to control radon in homes, methods of measuring and mitigating radon in buildings that house child care facilities, and assessing mitigation alternatives in unusual structures.[47]

Congress legislated funds for the various mandates, including $1,500,000 to initially establish the proficiency rating program and seminars,[48] but it required that those programs establish fees for private users to make the programs self-funding.[49] Congress further legislated $3,000,000 for each of three

39. Model Standards, 2, Section 1.0.6.
40. *Id.* at 3, Section 2.0.4.
41. *Id.* at 2.
42. http://www.epa.gov/radon/pubs/newconst.html.
43. 15 U.S.C. § 2665 (a).
44. 15 U.S.C. § 2663 (a)(1)–(8).
45. The proficiency testing program was required to be put into place by October 28, 1989. 15 U.S.C. § 2663 (a)(2).
46. 15 U.S.C. § 2665 (c).
47. 15 U.S.C. § 2665 (b).
48. 15 U.S.C. § 2665 (d)(1).
49. 15 U.S.C. § 2665 (d)(2).

successive fiscal years beginning in 1989 for the other provisions of §§ 303 Citizen's Guide, 304 Model Construction Standards and Techniques and 305 Technical Assistance.

While EPA was only granted specific authorization and responsibility in the Act to establish a Radon Measurement Proficiency (RMP) Program, EPA had already established a radon action program in 1985 and an RMP Program in 1986 to help homeowners obtain accurate radon measurements. In October of 1989, the GAO published a report of its findings that radon measurements were uncertain because testing devices varied in capability and consistency and homeowners did not always follow EPA's recommended testing procedures.[50] In testimony before subcommittees of the House and the Senate the following year, EPA recommended that Congress provide EPA authority to (i) make the RMP Program mandatory, (ii) establish mandatory quality assurance requirements and controls on measurement companies, and (iii) develop guidelines on the nature of state programs and levels of control needed at the state level to ensure radon measurements are accurate.[51]

To deal with the issues presented by the GAO, Congress amended[52] § 305 of TSCA. The amendment required the EPA to conduct research to develop, test, and evaluate radon and radon progeny measurement methods and protocols,[53] and to study the feasibility of establishing a mandatory proficiency program,[54] which would include the recommendations of the GAO report.[55] Congress also required EPA to establish additional user fees to fund the research of measurement methods and protocols for the fiscal years 1991, 1992, 1993, 1994, and 1995.[56]

---

50. United States General Accounting Office, Report to the Chairman, Comm. on Science, Space, and Technology, House of Representatives, Air Pollution Uncertainty Exists in Radon Measurements, GAO/RCED-90-25, 1 (Oct. 1989).
51. *Improvements Needed in the Environmental Protection Agency's Testing Programs for Radon Testimony: Hearing Before the H. Subcomm. on Natural Resources, Agriculture Research, and Environment, Comm. on Science, Space and Technology*, GAO/T-RCED-90-54, 1 (May, 16, 1990) (Statement for the Record by Richard L. Hembra, Director, Environmental Protection Issues Resources, Community, and Economic Development Division, EPA).
52. Omnibus Budget Reconciliation Act of 1990, Pub. L. 101-508, § 10202, 104 Stat. 1388, 381–382 (1990).
53. 15 U.S.C. § 2665(d)(5).
54. 15 U.S.C. § 2665(d)(6).
55. The study, with EPA's recommendations, was due to Congress by Mar. 1, 1991. 15 U.S.C. § 2665(d)(6). That report was never concluded. Telephone interview with Philip Jalbert, Radon Team Leader, EPA Indoor Environment Division (Sept. 19, 2008) [hereinafter Jalbert Interview].
56. 15 U.S.C. § 2665(d)(7).

As required by the Act, EPA issued a proposed regulation in 1990[57] dealing with user fees. The final rule, effective April 18, 1994,[58] established user fees for one year for the National Radon Measurement Program and the National Radon Contractor Proficiency Program. State and local governments were specifically exempted from the fee requirements.[59] EPA intended to recoup the costs of the programs, culminating in complete private funding in the fifth year.[60] The rule issued in 1995 established the fee schedule for 1995,[61] which was almost unchanged due to reduced costs of the programs, and for the following three years.[62]

EPA began to publicly explore privatizing the RMP in a public workshop in May 1996.[63] The Agency reasoned that since the implementation of the RMP a decade before (i) the radon services industry had matured sufficiently to make direct EPA involvement in proficiency determinations no longer necessary, (ii) approximately half the states had stronger radon public health and consumer protection activities, and (iii) the private sector might be able to operate the program cost effectively.[64] After a public stakeholder process, EPA subsequently closed the RMP program in October of 1998.[65] In response to requests, EPA officially recognized two private sector organizations, The National Radon Safety Board and The National Environmental Health Association's National Radon Proficiency Program,[66] as having programs equivalent to the EPA National Radon Proficiency Program. The recognition of equivalency was valid from March 30, 2001 to December 31, 2002.[67]

D. Grant Assistance to States for Radon Programs

In furtherance of its goals to eliminate the hazards posed by indoor radon, Congress authorized up to $10,000,000 for grant assistance to the states for

57. 55 Fed. Reg. 50492 (Dec. 16, 1990).
58. 59 Fed. Reg. 13166 (Mar. 18, 1994).
59. *Id.* at 13176.
60. *Id.*
61. 60 Fed. Reg. 41813, 41814 (Aug. 14, 1995).
62. *Id.* at 41815.
63. 61 Fed. Reg. 19277 (May 1, 1996).
64. *Id.* at 19278.
65. www.epa.gov/radon/radontest.html.
66. *Id.*
67. Letter from Mary T. Smith, Director Indoor Environments Division, Office of Air and Radiation, EPA, Mr. Larry L. Marcum, J.D., M.P.A., Manager, Research and Development, Radon Program Manager, National Environmental Health Association, National Radon Proficiency Program (Mar. 30, 2001) (on file with the EPA) and Letter from Mary T. Smith, Director Indoor Environments Division, Office of Air and Radiation, EPA to Ms. Nancy Bredhoff, President, National Radon Safety Board (Mar. 30, 2001) (on file with the EPA).

radon programs for each of fiscal years 1989, 1990, and 1991.[68] While this authorization has expired, new appropriations have been granted annually at the request of EPA.[69] The Act delineated some of the requirements of an application for a grant[70] and mandated that preference in the grant process be given to states that have made reasonable efforts to ensure the adoption of the Model Construction Standards and Techniques.[71] Activities eligible for grants were: surveys of radon levels; development of information and educational materials about assessment, mitigation, and control techniques; programs to control radon in buildings; purchase of radon measurement equipment or devices; purchase and maintenance of analytical equipment; costs of EPA approved training programs, and general overhead and administration; development of data storage and management system; radon mitigation methods and technologies demonstrations; and toll-free radon hotlines.[72] In the event that applications for grants exceeded the money authorized, EPA was required to set priorities based, among other things, on (i) the seriousness and extent of the contamination problem, (ii) the potential for the project to reduce radon levels, and (iii) the potential for development of innovative radon assessment techniques and mitigation measures of program management approaches.[73]

Grants were not to exceed 75 percent of the program costs for the first year of the grant, 60 percent in the second year and 50 percent in the third year.[74] States were allowed to share grant money with local governments for certain designated activities, i.e., development of public information and education materials, implementation of radon control programs, and costs of EPA-approved training programs.[75] There were also several limitations as to how the grant money could be used, such as limiting the percentage that could be spent on administrative costs.[76] As a condition of funding, states had to agree to provide the EPA with all radon-related information generated using grant funds[77] and to provide to the public a list of firms that received a passing grade under the EPA proficiency rating program.[78] EPA was charged with the responsibility of making the same list available to the public in states that did

---

68. 15 U.S.C. § 2666(j)(1).
69. EPA, State and Tribal Indoor Radon Grants Program Guidance and Handbook, 1 (Jan. 2005), *available at* http://www.epa.gov/radon/sirgprogram.html.
70. 15 U.S.C. § 2666(b).
71. 15 U.S.C. § 2666(d).
72. 15 U.S.C. § 2666(c).
73. 15 U.S.C. § 2666(e).
74. 15 U.S.C. § 2666(f).
75. 15 U.S.C. § 2666(g).
76. 15 U.S.C. § 2666(l).
77. 15 U.S.C. § 2666(h)(2).
78. 15 U.S.C. § 2666(h)(3).

not receive such grants, unless the state assumed responsibility for so doing.[79]

While the Act did not explicitly specify that grants were available to Indian Tribes, EPA reasoned that Congress clearly intended the Act to have nationwide coverage[80] and did not intend to omit tribal lands.[81] Accordingly, EPA formally added Indian Tribes and Intertribal Consortia to the list of parties eligible for grants under TSCA.[82] To prove its eligibility for a grant, the Tribe or each member of the Consortium would have to demonstrate that it is recognized by the Secretary of the Interior, has an existing robust government with authority to implement the grant's activities and is reasonably expected to be able to administer the grant program.[83]

E. Radon in Schools

The Act required EPA to determine the extent of radon contamination in schools by state.[84] EPA was to give the list of high risk areas within each state to the agency designated by the state governor and to provide guidance regarding the risks of high levels of radon, testing information, and radon reduction methods. [85] EPA was required to make available testing devices and the use of EPA laboratories, or to recommend other laboratories to evaluate the results of the testing.[86] EPA was also tasked to select high-risk schools in which to conduct diagnostic and remedial work, for the dual purposes of reducing radon in the selected schools and developing technology and expertise to share with the states and local educational agencies.[87] Congress authorized a total of $1,500,000 to implement these provisions[88] and requested EPA to provide Congress with a report of its activities in the schools by October 1, 1989.[89]

EPA issued its report to Congress on radon in schools in October 1993.[90] The report provided the results of the mandated National School Radon

---

79. *Id.*
80. 66 Fed. Reg. 3781, 3791 (Jan. 16, 2001).
81. *Id.* at 3792.
82. *Id.* at 3796.
83. *Id.* at 3792.
84. 15 U.S.C. § 2667(a)(4).
85. 15 U.S.C. § 2667(a)(5)(A).
86. 15 U.S.C. § 2667(a)(5)(B).
87. 15 U.S.C. § 2667(a)(6).
88. 15 U.S.C. § 2667(b).
89. 15 U.S.C. § 2667(a)(7).
90. EPA, Office of Radiation and Indoor Air, National School Radon Survey, Report to Congress (Oct. 1993) [hereinafter School Survey].

Survey, which had been initiated during the 1990–1991 school year.[91] The survey was required by two pieces of legislation, § 307 of the IRAA and § 118(k) of the Superfund Amendments and Reauthorization Act of 1986[92] to determine the extent of radon contamination in school buildings.[93] The survey was designed to include approximately twelve hundred public schools nationwide.[94] One thousand and seventy-two schools received short-term radiation detectors to be placed in ground floor rooms only; one hundred and twenty-five schools received both short-term and long-term detectors to be placed in all rooms, regardless of location.[95] Pursuant to the legislation, EPA did not have the right to enter the schools and relied instead on voluntary participation.[96] Participation rates were 77.1 percent and 80 percent, respectively.[97]

EPA concluded from the survey that the country had a radon exposure problem in its schools. While there was some correlation between schools with high radon levels and areas of the country with high radon levels, fully 10 percent of schools with elevated radon levels were located in areas with low potential for radon. Based on these findings, EPA confirmed its recommendation that all schools should test for radon.[98]

F. Regional Radon Training Centers

Congress authorized $1,000,000 per year for fiscal years 1989, 1990, and 1991[99] for the EPA to make grants to institutions of higher learning[100] that proposed to establish regional radon training centers to develop information and provide training on radon risks, methods of measurement, and mitigation.[101] Criteria to be used by EPA in making these grants included: how well the grant would promote the development of information and the implementation of training programs; the expertise of the applicant in radon measurement,

---

91. School Survey, 2.
92. Superfund Amendments and Reauthorization Act of 1986, 42 U.S.C. § 7401.
93. EPA first studied radon in schools in Fairfax, Virginia in 1988. The results of that study were used to develop EPA, Radon Measurements in Schools—An Interim Report, Report No. 520/1/89-010.
94. School Survey, 5.
95. *Id.* at 7.
96. *Id.* at 5.
97. *Id.* at 9.
98. *Id.* at 15. For purposes of this study, EPA considered screening measurements equal to or in excess of the action level of 4 pCi/L to be elevated. However, there has not been any safe level of radon exposure established.
99. 15 U.S.C. § 2668(f).
100. 15 U.S.C. § 2668(a).
101. 15 U.S.C. § 2668(b).

mitigation, training, and information development and dissemination; the severity of the radon problem in the area; and the geographic area of the proposed center.[102] Four regional training centers were established:[103] Eastern Regional Training Center,[104] Southern Regional Training Center,[105] Midwest Universities Radon Consortium,[106] and the Western Regional Radon Training Center.[107] These regional centers continue to work with EPA but are now self-supporting.[108]

G. Study of Radon in Federal Buildings

Congress required that each Federal department or agency that owned a Federal building conduct a study,[109] using specified EPA documents for study design,[110] to determine the extent of radon contamination in each such building. EPA was to provide technical guidance to its sister agencies and to have final approval authority over study designs submitted to the EPA.[111] The other federal agencies and departments were to report the results of their studies to EPA by June 1, 1990[112] and EPA was to report to Congress on the results of all of the studies that it collected by October 1, 1990.[113]

EPA issued the required report to Congress in October of 1992.[114] Twenty-two federal agencies reported radon testing results.[115] Twenty-three agencies did not report radon testing results to EPA and claimed various exemptions from the statutory requirements.[116] The reported results indicated that 95.9 percent of the measurements for the buildings tested had no results at or

102. 15 U.S.C. § 2669(d).
103. http://www.epa.gov/iaq/rrtcs.html#srrtc.
104. http://www.cpe.rutgers.edu/programs/radon.html.
105. http://eng.auburn.edu/distance-learning/ce/live/srrtc/index.html.
106. http://cce.umn.edu/CCE-Main/Radon-Courses-for-Professionals/.
107. http://www.wrrtc.net/ .
108. Jalbert Interview.
109. 15 U.S.C. § 2669(a).
110. 15 U.S.C. § 2669(c).
111. *Id.*
112. 15 U.S.C. § 2669(e).
113. 15 U.S.C. § 2669(f).
114. EPA, Office of Radiation Programs, Radon in Federal Buildings, A Report to Congress on the Results of Federal Agency Surveys (Oct. 1992) [hereinafter Federal Buildings].
115. The Agencies reporting were: the Departments of Agriculture, Army, Energy, Interior, Navy, Air Force, Commerce, Health and Human Services, Labor, State, Treasury and Transportation and the Environmental Protection Agency, General Services Administration, National Aeronautics and Space Administration, Smithsonian Institution, U.S. Information Agency, Federal Reserve System, Government Printing Office, National Security Agency and the Tennessee Valley Authority. Federal Buildings, 1-1.
116. *Id.* at 1–2. A list of those not reporting and the rationale therefore can be found at 3–79.

above the action level of 4 picocuries per liter (pCi/L).[117] While there is no designated level at which exposure to radon has been determined to be safe, the action level is the standard measurement used to determine if there is a problem requiring further review. Despite some data integrity issues identified by the General Accounting Office in reviewing the actions of the participating Federal Agencies,[118] EPA opined that the large number of measurements made by the agencies was sufficient to adequately represent the radon distribution in the tested buildings.[119] EPA summarized the status of ongoing activities by the agencies: (i) some were still doing initial tests and some were doing follow up testing to confirm high levels found during screening; (ii) some with large landholdings using a phased approach to testing; (iii) seven were engaging in mitigation activities; (iv) four were not requiring any mitigation due to low levels; (v) four were considering mitigation plans; and (vi) seven were not communicating plans as of report date.[120]

III. Summary of State Radon Legislation

The Act did not envision the implementation of a robust regulatory framework at the federal level. The Act was designed to enable the federal government, under the auspices of the EPA, to provide the states with sufficient assistance so that the states could tackle what was perceived to be a local issue in need of local solutions. In fact, the Senate bill was given the working name of the State Radon Program Development Act of 1988,[121] before it was enacted and formally named the Indoor Radon Abatement Act. As Senator Chafee, a sponsor of the legislation, stated:

> The irony of the situation is that this health hazard does have workable solutions. Testing for radon is easy and relatively inexpensive .... Likewise, remedial action techniques ... do not usually carry costs. And yet, fewer than 25 States have any kind of radon-reduction programs in place. To start getting these solutions in place, we need legislation to provide guidance, information, and assistance.
>
> This measure will do just that. It gives the States a chance to tackle this problem with full Federal backing. In fact, this bill provides over $40 million to address the problem of radon gas. It will help us learn more about radon and what we can do to protect ourselves.[122]

---

117. *Id.* at 1–3, Table 1-1.
118. *Id.* at 3-1–3-2.
119. *Id.* at 3-2.
120. *Id.* at 2–7.
121. S. 744, 100th Cong. § 2 (as passed by Senate, Oct. 7, 1988).
122. Chafee Statement.

A. State Programs in Existence Before Indoor Radon Abatement Act

The most complete report on the status of state programs before the passage of the Act reviews information in place as of July 1, 1987,[123] more than a full year before enactment. The report acknowledged that changes in the scope of the state programs were happening very quickly at that time due to the development of more data,[124] but that the basic analysis of the report would nevertheless be useful in providing a baseline of the situation at one point in time. The report further noted the expectation that there would be great variations in state programs due to particular local characteristics, such as the nature of the terrain, the existence of geological or measurement data indicating potential problems, technical uncertainties, differing financial capabilities, and different institutional structures.[125]

EPA categorized all of the activity in the states into one of four wide levels of development, based on the information available to it at the time. While all of the states had some type of program, most of those programs were not the result of specific legislation directed at indoor radon issues.[126]

The first grouping was Level 1, Information Program, which consisted of seven states.[127] These states were not managing radon issues, but were disseminating EPA information to homeowners upon request.[128] They did not perceive the need to create a program and had neither a mandate nor resources to do so.[129]

The biggest grouping, Level 2, Formative Program, consisted of 24 states.[130] These states were starting to address the issue, but were not conducting extensive testing. They were doing some limited testing, generally screening or follow up. They disseminated EPA information upon request, and some were developing state-specific materials. Several were considering conducting extensive surveys.[131] Level 2 states acknowledged the possibility of a radon problem.

---

123. State Summary.
124. *Id.* at 2.
125. *Id.* at 1–2.
126. *Id.* at 18–19, Table 3, Legislative Initiatives.
127. The states at Level 1 were: Arkansas, Hawaii, Louisiana, Mississippi, Nevada, South Dakota, and Texas. *Id.* at 13, Table 1, Current Level of State Radon Program Development.
128. *Id.* at 10.
129. *Id.* at 16.
130. The States at Level 2 were: Alaska, Arizona, California, Delaware, Georgia, Idaho, Iowa, Massachusetts, Minnesota, Missouri, Montana, Nebraska, New Hampshire, New Mexico, North Carolina, North Dakota, Ohio, Oklahoma, Oregon, South Carolina, Utah, Vermont, Washington, and West Virginia. *Id.* at 13, Table 1, Current Level of State Radon Program Development.
131. *Id.* at 10.

They had one or a portion of one person working on radon issues, as well as some limited funding.[132]

The 14 states[133] at Level 3, Developing Program, were conducting extensive testing and state wide surveys. These states were actively disseminating EPA information. Some were performing measurements and were participating in EPA's State Radon Survey Program.[134] They also had one or more people dedicated to radon issues and some limited funding. Many also had formed task forces to address these issues.[135]

The five states[136] at Level 4, Operational Program, all had reasonably confirmed radon problems. All had funding for radon programs.[137] Three of the states had funding in excess of $4 million each. All had small staffs assigned.[138] All worked with task forces and all had sponsored several thousand tests. Extensive information and training programs were operating. At least fifty homes in each state were conducting private radon prevention or mitigation.[139] These states also provided free or low-cost radon detectors to homeowners.[140]

In the aggregate, $20,000,000 dollars and 119 full time employees were allocated specifically to radon in all of the states.[141] The states of New Jersey, New York, and Pennsylvania were responsible for 88.5 percent of the monies and 55.1 percent of the personnel.[142]

B. Current Status of State Radon Programs

Currently approximately forty states have legislation dealing with radon,[143] the majority of which require disclosure of known radon levels, along with levels of other contaminants in connection with the sale of a home. No states

---

132. *Id.* at 16.
133. The States at Level 3 were: Alabama, Colorado, Connecticut, Illinois, Indiana, Kansas, Kentucky, Maryland, Michigan, Rhode Island, Tennessee, Virginia, Wisconsin, and Wyoming. *Id.* at 13, Table 1, Current Level of State Radon Program Development.
134. *Id.* at 10.
135. *Id.* at 17.
136. The states at Level 4 were: Florida, Maine, New Jersey, New York, and Pennsylvania. *Id.* at 13, Table 1, Current Level of State Radon Program Development.
137. *Id.* at 11.
138. *Id.* at 17.
139. *Id.* at 11.
140. *Id.* at 27.
141. *Id.* at 17.
142. *Id.* at 20.
143. The information contained in this section was derived primarily from compilations of existing state legislation found at http://www.ncsl.org/programs/environ/envHealth/radonstats07.htm and at http://www.eli.org/Program_Areas/iaq_databases.cfm.

currently require the testing of private homes for radon.[144] Almost half of the states have laws establishing requirements for radon testing and mitigation companies. Six states[145] require radon testing in schools, and two of those states[146] require mitigation if radon levels are found to be excessive. Eight states[147] require radon testing in child care centers, and three of those states[148] require mitigation if radon levels are found to be excessive. New Hampshire requires testing in state buildings and mitigation if radon levels in those buildings are found to be excessive. Three states[149] require that new school construction be radon-resistant and five states[150] require that new homes be radon resistant. As of July 2008,[151] about fifty bills dealing with radon had been introduced in recent state legislative sessions in 17 states. Approximately twenty-four of those bills dealt with disclosure in homes, schools, childcare facilities, and public buildings; seven dealt with licensing and certification of radon professionals; five dealt with construction standards; fourteen dealt with a variety of miscellaneous issues, such as tax credits; and one, in Illinois, required that sellers of residential property have the property tested for radon and radon progeny by a licensed radon contractor and furnish a prospective buyer with the test results.

IV. Indoor Radon Air Abatement Effectiveness

Measuring the efficiency and effectiveness of the Act is beyond the scope of this book, other than to point the reader to some discussions on this topic. One could argue that one measure of the success of this legislation in stimulating local solutions to the problem of indoor radon contamination might include the review of state-level programs, as noted above, before the enactment of the Act and more recently. A more meaningful approach would no doubt look at any developing trends in the number of deaths per population from radon induced lung cancer over the approximately twenty years since the enactment of the Act. And, since it takes many years to develop lung cancer from radon exposure, the most important criteria might at this time involve the number of

144. As of Dec. 2008.
145. Colorado, Connecticut, Florida, Rhode Island, Virginia, and West Virginia.
146. Rhode Island and West Virginia.
147. Connecticut, Florida, Idaho, Iowa, Maryland, Michigan, New Jersey, and Rhode Island.
148. Idaho, Maryland, and Michigan.
149. Connecticut, New Jersey, and Rhode Island.
150. New Jersey, Michigan, Minnesota, Washington, and Maine.
151. This information was derived from a compilation of pending state legislation at http://www.ncsl.org/print/environ/radonlegis07.pdf.

existing and new homes, schools, day care, and other facilities that have been mitigated or otherwise have been built with radon resistant construction.

The United States Office of Management and Budgets periodically reviews federal programs to measure how well the government is spending tax payer dollars. In a review for fiscal year 2005,[152] it gave the EPA's Indoor Air Quality Program, which includes radon programs, a rating of moderately effective, the middle category for programs that are performing. The Program was given the following scores for the noted element assessments: Program Purpose & Design, 80 percent; Strategic Planning, 75 percent; Program Management, 89 percent; and Program Results/Accountability, 60 percent. The assessment cited three primary shortcomings: (i) EPA needed more authority to meets its risk reduction goals; (ii) there was no independent evaluation as to whether the meeting of annual program goals would improve human health; and (iii) EPA budget requests should make clear the impact of funding on performance.

In the article, *The U.S. Radon Problem, Policy, Program and Industry: Achievements, Challenges and Strategies*,[153] the author provides a less positive review of the success of the Act over the last twenty years. He points out that more homes have been added to the housing inventory with excess levels of radiation than have been mitigated, that funding and activity in this area has decreased since the early 1990s, and that rental units, which disproportionately house low-income populations, have seen no significant radon risk reduction.[154]

---

152. http://www.whitehouse.gov/omb/expectmore/detail/10004374.2005.html.

153. W.J. Angell, *The U.S. Radon Problem, Policy, Program and Industry: Achievements, Challenges and Strategies*, Radiation Protection Dosimetry 1–6 (2008).

154. *Id.* at 1.

CHAPTER 18

Lead

I. Introduction to Lead Regulation

Lead is a metallic element that occurs in nature. It is a notorious poison and exposure to lead reduces children's IQs.[1] Lead exposure also causes an array of other health effects, including "neurotoxicity, developmental delays, hypertension, impaired hearing acuity, impaired hemoglobin synthesis, and male reproductive impairment."[2]

There is no conclusive proof that lead and lead compounds cause cancer in humans, according to the United States Department of Health and Human Service's (DHHS) Agency for Toxic Substances and Disease Registry, although the United States Environmental Protection Agency (EPA) has classified lead as a probable carcinogen and the DHHS has classified lead and lead compounds as reasonably anticipated to be human carcinogens, based on animal tests and limited human studies.[3]

Children are particularly vulnerable to lead's effects because children often put their hands in their mouths, and if they have touched dust from deteriorating lead paint they will ingest lead.[4] Children also absorb more of the lead to which they are exposed, and because their neurological systems are still developing the exposures are particularly detrimental.[5] No safe levels of lead exposure have been established for children.[6]

Lead does not degrade in the environment. The EPA has described lead as persistent and "virtually indestructible."[7]

Exposure to lead has been a health problem for centuries, and may even have contributed to the fall of Rome.[8] Ancient Romans drank wine sweetened with a grape syrup that was made in lead pots, and a single teaspoon of this syrup was enough to cause chronic poisoning.[9]

Lead has been increasingly regulated as its risks have become understood. The Consumer Product Safety Commission banned lead in paint manufactured after February 1978,[10] but significant risks are still presented by peeling or

---

1. United States Department Of Health and Human Services Public Health Service, Agency for Toxic Substances and Disease Registry, Toxicological Profile for Lead, 23 [hereinafter Lead Tox Profile], *available at* http://www.atsdr.cdc.gov/toxprofiles/tp13.pdf.
2. Integrated Risk Information System information on lead and lead compounds, *available at* http://www.epa.gov/NCEA/iris/subst/0277.htm.
3. Lead Tox Profile, 9, 24.
4. 73 Fed. Reg. 216992, 21693 (Apr. 22, 2008).
5. Lead Tox Profile, 24–25.
6. *Id.* at 10.
7. 73 Fed. Reg. 216992, 21693 (Apr. 22, 2008).
8. John Noble Wilford, *Roman Empire's Fall Is Linked With Gout and Lead Poisoning*, N.Y. Times, Mar. 17, 1983, *available at* http://query.nytimes.com/gst/fullpage.html?sec=health&res=9403E0D71539F934A25750C0A965948260&scp=2&sq=ancient%20rome%20lead&st=cse.
9. *Id.*
10. 16 C.F.R. Part 1303. *See also* United States Consumer Product Safety Commission Staff Recommendations For Identifying And Controlling Lead Paint On Public Playground

flaking paint in homes that were built before the ban went into effect.[11] Historically, lead was used as an additive for gasoline, but that use was banned starting in 1996, although it is still permissible in fuel for off-road vehicles and airplanes.[12] Lead was used in drinking water pipes and solder until the Safe Drinking Water Act set lower limits for lead in these items in 1998.

Lead still has many current uses, and its primary industrial use is in batteries.[13] After that, its most common use is in ammunition.[14]

In part because some U.S. regulations are media-specific and some are directed only to particular activities, lead is regulated under a host of different programs. Lead disposal is regulated under the Resource Conservation and Recovery Act,[15] some releases into the environment are regulated under the Emergency Planning & Community Right-to-Know Act,[16] lead is prohibited in drinking water pipes under the Safe Drinking Water Act[17] and there is a maximum airborne concentration under the Clean Air Act.[18] Workplace concentrations of lead in the air are regulated under the Occupational Safety and Health Act,[19] and the United States Food and Drug Administration prohibits using lead foil for wine bottles and lead solder for food cans.

II. TSCA Lead Programs

The restrictions on lead under the Toxic Substances Control Act (TSCA)[20] are just a small portion of the universe of lead regulation. This chapter is limited to an introduction to the TSCA lead programs, all of which focus on lead paint, the hazards inherent in removing lead paint, hazards from deteriorated lead paint, and renovations where lead paint is present.

There are two primary TSCA lead programs, the Renovation, Repair, and Painting Rule and the Disclosure Rule.[21] Both were authorized by The Residential Lead-Based Paint Hazard Reduction Act of 1992,[22] codified as

---

Equipment, Executive Summary *available at* http://www.cpsc.gov/CPSCPUB/PUBS/lead/6005.html.

11. Lead Tox Profile, 19.
12. *Id.* at 2.
13. *Id.* at 19, 294.
14. *Id.* at 2.
15. 42 U.S.C. § 6901 (1976).
16. 42 U.S.C. § 11001 (1986).
17. 42 U.S.C. § 300f (1974); *see also* the regulations at 40 C.F.R. § 141.43.
18. The National Ambient Air Quality Standard, or NAAQS, for lead is 1.5 micrograms per cubic meter. 40 C.F.R. § 50.12.
19. 29 U.S.C. § 651; regulations are at 29 C.F.R. § 1910.1025.
20. 15 U.S.C. §§ 2601–2695d.
21. 40 C.F.R. § 745.100.
22. 42 U.S.C. § 4852d. *See* 61 Fed. Reg. 90604 (Mar. 6, 1996).

TSCA § 402. The Renovation, Repair, and Painting Rule addresses activities relating to renovation in certain buildings that may have lead contamination and lead paint. It requires notification to owners, tenants, and occupants of buildings about the hazards and control of lead-based paint prior to renovations, requires certification for anyone performing the renovations, and specifies work practice standards for inspections and renovations. The Disclosure Rule was jointly issued by the EPA and the Department of Housing and Urban Development (HUD) and it requires disclosure of known lead paint and lead hazards when certain residential property is sold or leased. A third TSCA lead program in Subpart L of the regulations is primarily addressed to training programs and certification of lead contractors. None of the TSCA rules mandate removing lead paint, although states are free to promulgate laws requiring lead paint removal.[23]

III. The Renovation, Repair, and Painting Rule

In June of 2008 EPA finalized a new regulation requiring notifications, training, and certifications in connection with renovating target housing and child-occupied facilities.[24] It was implemented in phases and must be complied with fully by April 22, 2010.[25] Predecessors of this rule have been in effect since 1996,[26] but the new regulation expands the certification and training requirements as well as the information that must be posted and distributed in connection with renovations. It has several components, including a requirement to distribute an updated EPA pamphlet on renovating when lead paint is present, safe work practices, recordkeeping, and certification of firms and renovators.

A. Scope of Rule

The Renovation, Repair, and Painting Rule applies to both residential housing and some types of nonresidential buildings.[27] The regulations apply to all "target housing" and "child-occupied facilities." "Target housing" is residential

23. 73 Fed. Reg. 21692, 21701 (Apr. 22, 2008).
24. 40 C.F.R. Subpart E.
25. 40 C.F.R. § 745.80.
26. 61 Fed. Reg. 45778 (Aug. 29, 1996).
27. The Renovation, Repair, and Painting Rule is in the regulations under the title "Residential Property Renovation," and all of the TSCA lead regulations are in Part 745 of 40 C.F.R, which is entitled "Lead-Based Paint Poisoning Prevention In Certain Residential Structures." These titles are misleading because the rule covers many nonresidential structures.

and is defined in the statute as housing built prior to 1978, excluding units without separate bedrooms and excluding housing for the elderly or disabled so long as no child younger than six years old lives there.[28] However, a "child-occupied facility," does not need to be a residence and includes most day care facilities, preschools, and kindergartens as well as other businesses such as some hospitals and camps. It is defined as any building or part of a building (i) that was built before 1978, (ii) which any individual child visits at least two days per week for at least three hours each visit, (iii) which that same child visits for at least six hours per week,[29] (iv) which that same child visits at least sixty hours per year, and (v) provided the child is under six years old.[30] The rule does not apply to work performed in common areas such as hallways if the child only passes through them, or to outdoor spaces. However, the rule does apply to common areas such as restrooms that children routinely use, and to the exterior sides of any portion of the building that meets the definition of a child-occupied facility.[31]

There are two separate, inconsistent, definitions of "child-occupied facility" in the TSCA lead regulations. It is important to note that the presence of six-year-old children does not bring a facility within the scope of the definition of "child-occupied facility" in the Renovation, Repair, and Painting Rule in Subpart E,[32] but six year olds do bring a facility within the definition of "child-occupied facility" in the older certification and training rule in the Lead Based Paint Activities Rule in Subpart L.[33] This inconsistency is carried throughout the rest of the regulations, and six-year-olds do not trigger the Renovation, Repair, and Painting Rule in Subpart E in general, but they do trigger the regulations in Subpart L. This is a significant source of potential confusion in light of the fact that both Subparts E and L require certification for individuals and firms performing specified work in child-occupied facilities. Care should be taken to determine which definition of "child-occupied facility" applies.

There are several exceptions to the Renovation, Repair, and Painting Rule. It does not apply at all to abatement projects designed to permanently eliminate all hazards caused by lead paint.[34] Minor repairs and maintenance are exempt if all the work done within a thirty-day span does not disturb more than six square feet of interior paint in any room, or twenty square feet of

---

28. TSCA § 401; 15 U.S.C. § 2681. The Secretary of Housing and Urban Development can designate an earlier cutoff date if a state banned lead paint before 1978.
29. This element of the definition is subsumed in the requirement that there be at least two visits per week of three hours duration each.
30. 40 C.F.R. § 745.83.
31. *Id.*
32. *Id.* referring to children "under 6 years of age."
33. 40 C.F.R. § 745.223, referring to children "6 years of age or under."
34. 40 C.F.R. § 745.82, 745.83 (definition of "renovation").

exterior paint. To qualify as a minor repair, the work cannot include window replacements or demolition of painted surfaces and cannot employ specified practices.[35] Work that is not done for compensation does not have to be done in accordance with the rules.[36] Renovation is exempt if the renovator obtains a copy of a written determination by a certified inspector or risk assessor that the renovation will not affect paint or other any other surface coatings that has lead in excess of one milligram per square centimeter or in excess of 0.5 percent by weight.[37] The renovation is also exempt if a certified renovator properly uses a test kit that the EPA has formally recognized, provided that the renovation will not affect paint or any other surface coating that has lead in excess of one milligram per square centimeter or in excess of 0.5 percent by weight.[38] The EPA posts the recognized test kits on its Web site.[39]

The requirement to distribute informational pamphlets does not apply to emergency renovations.[40] Certain emergencies are exempt from the requirements to post warning signs, contain waste, handle waste in accordance with the regulations, and use trained and certified personnel, but only to the extent necessary to respond to the emergency.[41] There is no emergency exemption from the requirements to clean using trained and certified renovators, or to verify the cleaning and keep records. There is an exemption from the training requirements and work practice standards for renovations in target housing

---

35. *See* the definitions of "minor repair and maintenance activities" and "renovation" in 40 C.F.R. § 745.83. The prohibited practices are using a heat gun on lead-based paint at 1100 degrees or above, and open-flame burning or torching. In addition, use of machines that remove paint by sanding, grinding, power planing, needle gun, abrasive blasting, or sandblasting disqualify the repair from being minor unless a HEPA exhaust control is used. 40 C.F.R. § §745.85(a)(3).
36. 40 C.F.R. § 745.82(a).
37. 40 C.F.R. § 745.82(a)(1).
38. 40 C.F.R. § 745.82(a)(2). The renovator must test each component that will be affected by the renovation. "Component" is defined in 40 C.F.R. § 745.83 as a design or structural element or fixture. Each component is distinguished from the other components by form, function, and location. For example, crown moldings, fireplaces and hand rails are all components. To qualify for the exemption, although the renovator must test each component affected by the renovation, if the components make up a structure such as the stair treads and risers of the same staircase, the renovator only needs to test one of the components. The renovator must test all of the components if they appear to have been repainted or refinished separately.
39. Recognized test kits must meet the criteria in 40 C.F.R. 745.88, which include enhanced requirements in effect as of Sept. 1, 2010. The recognized test kits are posted at http://www.epa.gov/lead/pubs/kits.htm.
40. 40 C.F.R. § 745.82(b). For this purpose only, emergency renovations are unplanned renovations in response to a sudden an unexpected event that presents a safety or health hazard. Interim controls to respond to elevated blood lead levels in children who live in the premises are also emergency responses that provide an exemption from the rules.
41. *Id.* Emergency renovations that are unplanned renovations in response to a sudden and unexpected event that presents a safety or health hazard qualify for this exemption. Interim controls to respond to elevated blood levels in children do not qualify for this exemption.

if the owner signs a statement that the building to be renovated is the owner's residence, the owner is not the parent, legal guardian, or foster parent of any children under six, no pregnant women live there, the residence is not a child-occupied facility, and the owner acknowledges that the work practices mandated by the regulations will not be required.[42] In October 2009 the EPA proposed eliminating this exemption.[43]

EPA announced that it intends to extend the renovation regulations to public buildings built before 1978 and to commercial buildings that are not child-occupied. Final action on such a rule is expected in 2013.[44]

B. Certification and Training

Contractor certification and training rules were first put into effect in 1998. Those initial rules required lead paint professionals to be certified and trained and imposed an accreditation program for training programs, individual certifications for renovators, and specific work practice standards.[45]

The Renovation, Repair, and Painting Rule, as of April 22, 2010, modifies the preexisting rule to allow only certified firms to perform or advertise that they can perform renovations or dust sampling in housing and child-occupied facilities built before 1978. All such renovations and dust sampling must be performed by certified firms and certified or trained individuals, and at least one certified individual must be assigned to each renovation.[46] The preexisting training and certification requirements extended only to lead inspection, risk assessment, and abatement. Individuals become certified as renovators and dust sampling technicians by attending approved courses run by the EPA or authorized states and tribes.[47] EPA-approved providers can only grant certifications for the federal programs, and only providers approved by state and tribal programs can grant certifications for those authorized state and tribal programs.[48] The EPA may revoke certifications it grants for specified causes.[49]

---

42. 40 C.F.R. § 745.82(c). The regulations also require a statement that the owner is not the informal caretaker of a child under six who sleeps at the residence most nights. However, this would be a subcategory of child-occupied facilities.
43. 74 Fed. Reg. 55506 (Oct. 28, 2009).
44. Regulatory Plan and Semiannual Regulatory Agenda, EPA-230-Z-09-002, 95 (Fall 2009) [hereinafter Fall 2009 Regulatory Agenda], *available at* http://www.epa.gov/lawsregs/documents/regagendabook-fall09.pdf.
45. *See* http://epa.gov/lead/pubs/leadcert.htm.
46. 40 C.F.R. §§ 745.81(a)(2) and (3) and 40 C.F.R. 745.89.
47. 40 C.F.R. § 745.90.
48. State and tribal authorization is discussed *infra*.
49. 40 C.F.R. § 745.91.

As of June 2008, all training programs that offer certification as a renovator or dust sampling technician had to be accredited by the EPA.[50]

Congress mandated that the EPA collect fees from EPA accredited training programs and certified contractors[51] to cover the EPA's "costs of administering and enforcing the standards and requirements applicable to lead-based paint training programs and contractors."[52]

C. Distributing Informational Pamphlets Before Renovating—the Pre-Renovation Education Rule

Section 406 of TSCA[53] required the EPA to publish a pamphlet concerning, among other things, the risks of renovating when lead paint is present, and to promulgate regulations requiring contractors to provide a copy of the pamphlet to owners and occupants of target housing. The EPA has revised its original pamphlet and rule, referred to as the Pre-Renovation Education Rule, in its 2008 Renovation, Repair, and Painting Final Rule.[54] The revised pamphlet, which is required to be used after December 2008, is *Renovate Right: Important Lead Hazard Information for Families, Child Care Providers and Schools (*Renovate Right).[55]

All renovators or firms in states or tribes that do not have authorized programs[56] must give owners and occupants a copy of the Renovate Right pamphlet. State or tribal programs take precedence over the Federal program upon authorization, and states or tribes may design their own informational pamphlet. Renovators must give the Renovate Right pamphlet to owners and at least one adult resident of target housing no more than sixty days before starting renovations in a living area.[57] If the owner lives in the home to be renovated no one else needs to be given the pamphlet. The renovator must get a signed acknowledgement from the owner that he or she received the pamphlet, or the renovator must get a certificate of mailing at least seven days before the renovation begins. If the owner does not live in the home, then the renovator must get a written acknowledgement from an adult occupant that

50. 40 C.F.R. § 745.81(a)(1).
51. TSCA § 402; 15 U.S.C. § 2682(a)(3).
52. 74 Fed. Reg. 11863 (Mar. 20, 2009). The fees are set out at 40 C.F.R. §§ 745.92 and 745.238.
53. 15 U.S.C. § 2686.
54. 73 Fed. Reg. 21692 (Apr. 22, 2008).
55. 40 C.F.R. § 745.81(b). This requirement went into effect on December 22, 2008. 40 C.F.R. § 745.81(b). The Renovate Right pamphlet is EPA document EPA-740-F-08-002.
56. The EPA publishes a list of authorized states and tribes at http://www.epa.gov/lead/pubs/traincert.htm. However, each state and tribal program should be individually consulted to determine which programs it is authorized to administer.
57. 40 C.F.R. § 745.85(a).

he or she received the pamphlet. If the occupant does not give a written acknowledgment the renovator may certify delivery,[58] or obtain a certificate of mailing at least seven days before beginning the renovation.[59]

If the renovation is in a common area of a multiple dwelling, the renovator must provide the Renovate Right pamphlet to the owner and get the same acknowledgement or certificate of mailing as required for renovations in living areas. However, the renovator must also give each affected unit notice of the work to be performed and make the Renovate Right pamphlet available. The renovator may satisfy this requirement by giving each affected unit a written notice describing the planned renovations and where they are, the start and end dates and the fact that the Renovate Right pamphlet is available. If the scope of the work or the dates change, the renovator must distribute up-to-date information to the owner and occupants in advance of any changes. The renovator must give a copy of the pamphlet to each occupant who requests one. Alternatively, instead of notifying each tenant in writing, the renovator can post signs where occupants of affected units will see them during the renovations, and post a copy of the pamphlet or describe how to get a copy. Again, the renovator must give a copy of the pamphlet to each occupant who requests one.[60]

A renovator must keep records of its efforts to notify all occupants of the renovations and to provide them with the Renovate Right pamphlet for three years after completion of the renovation.[61]

Similar requirements govern notifications in child-occupied facilities.[62] No more than sixty days before starting renovations, the renovator must give the building owner the Renovate Right pamphlet and either get a written acknowledgment or a certificate of mailing. If the building is not owned by the child-occupied facility, an adult representative of the child-occupied facility must also be given the pamphlet. The renovator must get a written acknowledgment from the representative, or obtain a certificate of mailing or certify that it delivered the pamphlet to the facility but was unsuccessful in

---

58. The regulations require the certification of delivery to an adult occupant to specify:

> the address of the unit undergoing renovation, the date and method of delivery of the pamphlet, names of the persons delivering the pamphlet, reason for lack of acknowledgment (e.g., occupant refuses to sign, no adult occupant available), the signature of a representative of the firm performing the renovation, and the date of signature.

40 C.F.R. § 745.84(a)(2)(i).

59. The EPA has attached to the Renovate Right pamphlet sample pre-renovation forms to use before and after the renovation rules come fully into effect. The Renovate Right pamphlet is *available at* http://www.epa.gov/lead/pubs/renovaterightbrochure.pdf.

60. 40 C.F.R. § 745.84(b)(2).

61. 40 C.F.R. § 745.86.

62. 40 C.F.R. § 745.84(c).

obtaining the acknowledgment.[63] Parents and guardians of children using the facility must also receive the Renovate Right pamphlet and information about the nature and locations of the renovations and the start and end dates, sixty days before the work begins.[64] The renovator must follow the similar distribution or posting procedures as required for work in multiple dwellings.[65]

The notification requirements leave open issues that will have to be resolved in practice. For example, if a guardian has received a copy of the pamphlet but the parent cannot be reached, is the renovator in violation?

D. Work Practice Standards

Starting April 22, 2010 all renovations in target housing and child-occupied facilities must be performed in accordance with the work practice standards for lead.[66] The work practice standards are a common sense set of practices designed to minimize exposure to dusts that may be contaminated with lead, and to ensure a thorough cleaning of the worksite when the renovation is complete. Renovators must post signs warning people to stay out of the work area.[67] The work area must be contained so that no dust or debris can escape.[68] If work is done inside buildings, then all furniture and other objects must be removed or wrapped in impermeable materials or plastic sheeting and sealed, and all ducts, doors, and windows must also be sealed with impermeable materials so that no dust or debris can escape and all floors must be covered with impermeable material.[69] If work is done outside buildings, all doors and windows within twenty feet of the work must be closed; if there are doors in the work area they must be covered with impermeable materials so that dust and debris can not pass through; and ground must be covered with impermeable material for at least ten feet beyond the renovations if possible, and more if needed to catch debris.[70]

---

63. The certification must include the same information as the certification for delivery to occupants of target housing. *See* 40 C.F.R. § 745.84(c)(1)(ii)(A).
64. The preamble to the regulations state that only parents of children under six must receive these materials. 73 Fed. Reg. 21692, 21702-03 (Apr. 22, 2008). The regulations do not address the requirements in hospital and pediatric rehabilitation settings, but the facility administrator cannot share patient names under HIPAA, the Health Insurance Portability and Accountability Act, Pub. L. 104-191 (1996). Presumably the facility administrator can provide the notifications.
65. 40 C.F.R. § 745.84(c)(2).
66. 40 C.F.R. § 745.81(a)(4).
67. 40 C.F.R. § 745.85(a)(1).
68. 40 C.F.R. § 745.85(a)(2).
69. 40 C.F.R. § 745.85(a)(2)(i).
70. 40 C.F.R. § 745.85(a)(2)(ii).

Practices that could disburse lead are prohibited. These include open flame burning or torching, and using a heat gun if it is 1100 degrees or hotter. Sanding, planing, and other practices that create dust are prohibited unless a HEPA filter is used to collect the dust.[71]

The regulations are designed to minimize lead poisoning from waste materials. Waste must be contained, and any chute used must be covered. At the end of each work day, waste must be contained or placed behind a barrier that prevents release of the waste and prevents access to the waste. Renovation waste must be contained while it is transported off-site.[72]

Very thorough cleaning is required when each renovation is complete.[73] All paint chips and debris must be collected and sealed in a heavy-duty bag. The impermeable sheeting that was used must be misted and folded with the dirty side inward, and either taped shut or sealed in heavy-duty bags and disposed of. If the renovation was inside a building, then the renovator must clean all objects and surfaces. The walls must be cleaned with damp cloths or a HEPA vacuum, and all other surfaces and objects must be cleaned with a HEPA vacuum. All surfaces that are not carpeted or upholstered must be wiped with a damp cloth. All uncarpeted floors must be mopped and the rinse water must be kept separate from the wash water. At the end of the cleaning, a certified renovator must inspect to see if there is any dust debris or residue, and if there is the area must be re-cleaned and re-inspected.

After the cleaning passes this visual inspection, a certified renovator must damp wipe each windowsill in the work area and compare the cloth to a cleaning verification card. The regulations define a cleaning verification card as a card developed and distributed or approved by the EPA to compare against wet and dry disposable cleaning cloths to determine if the cleaning was properly done.[74] If the cleaning was not thorough, the windowsill must be re-cleaned and re-inspected. If the cleaning still is not adequate, the renovator must wait at least one hour for the windowsill to dry and wipe it with a dry cloth to finish the cleaning. Floors and countertops must be cleaned following a similar procedure. The warning signs can be removed after the cleaning verification procedure is complete.

A certified renovator must visually verify the cleanup in any external areas, including the ground and any exterior windowsills. Alternatively, if the owner or any law requires dust clearance sampling, that can substitute for the visual inspection. The renovator must re-clean if any dust or debris remains.[75]

71. 40 C.F.R. § 745.85(a)(3).
72. 40 C.F.R. § 745.85(a)(4).
73. 40 C.F.R. § 745.85(a)(5).
74. 40 C.F.R. § 745.83.
75. 40 C.F.R. § 745.85.

E. Recordkeeping and Reporting

The Renovation, Repair, and Painting Rule requires renovators to create certifications and keep records that demonstrate compliance with the each detail of the renovation rules for three years, or longer if required by another law.[76] In practice it is important to retain compliance documents for longer, and the exact length of time depends on the state in which the renovator operates. In most jurisdictions the statute of limitations for a tort action brought by a person who was a child at the time of an injury can be extended beyond the time that would have been allowed for an adult to bring a tort action.[77] In any event records should be maintained for the five years of the TSCA statute of limitations.[78]

IV. The Disclosure Rule—Disclosure of Known Lead on Sale or Rental of Target Housing

TSCA regulations require sellers and landlords to disclose the presence of lead-based paint and lead hazards in target housing.[79] These regulations, usually referred to as the "Disclosure Rule," were jointly issued by the EPA and HUD, pursuant to a mandate in Section 1018 of Title X of the Residential Lead-Based Paint Hazard Reduction Act of 1992.[80] The only affirmative act the Disclosure Rule requires is disclosure; TSCA does not require landlords and sellers to conduct any lead abatement projects.[81] As the EPA said in the enforcement response policy for the Disclosure Rule, "[t]he purpose of the Disclosure Rule is to ensure that individuals and families receive the information necessary *to protect themselves* and their families from lead-based paint and/or lead-based paint hazards."[82] Because the Disclosure Rule does not require any reduction of lead in homes, it has been criticized as a weak response to a national crisis.[83] On the other hand, the cost of removing lead

76. 40 C.F.R. § 745.86(a) and (b).
77. *See, e.g.*, New York Civil Practice Law and Rules 208.
78. 3M Co. v. Browner, 17 F.3d 1453 (D.C. Cir. 1994).
79. 40 C.F.R. § 745.100.
80. 42 U.S.C. § 4852d. *See* 61 Fed. Reg. 90604 (Mar. 6, 1996).
81. 40 C.F.R. § 745.107(a). Lead programs under other statutes do require lead abatement; for example, federal agencies and purchasers of certain federal property are required to abate lead under Title X of the Residential Lead-Based Paint Hazard Reduction Act of 1992. 66 Fed. Reg. 1206 (Jan. 5, 2001).
82. Section 1018—Disclosure Rule Enforcement Response and Penalty Policy, Dec. 2007, 5 (emphasis added).
83. Christopher P. Daignault, *Comment: Tomorrow's Unleaded Children: Child Care Facilities, Lead Paint And The Law*, 18 J. Contemp. Health L. & Pol'y 197, 218 (Winter, 2001).

in a building can exceed the value of the building, and if rules required removing lead in residences where children live, the consequence could be landlords' refusal to rent to families with children.[84]

Real estate agents are responsible for ensuring compliance with the regulations, including telling lessors and sellers about their obligations. Real estate agents are not liable if they have informed the owner or lessor of the disclosure obligations, but the seller or lessor did not tell the agent about known lead paint or lead paint hazards.[85]

The Disclosure Rule applies nationwide, including in states and tribes with authorized lead programs.[86] It also applies to the federal government when it sells or leases property. It does not apply to foreclosure sales, leases of housing that has been certified to be lead free, short-term leases of one hundred days or less that have no possibility of renewal or extension, and renewals of existing leases when all required information has been disclosed and is still current.[87]

Sellers and landlords of target housing must disclose to prospective purchasers or tenants details of any lead-based paint or lead-based paint hazards of which they are aware. They must give the prospective purchasers and tenants records of any lead testing, and a copy of the EPA/HUD pamphlet entitled "Protect Your Family From Lead in Your Home"[88] or another pamphlet that has EPA approval.[89] Prospective purchasers and tenants must receive the disclosure and a warning before the contract or lease becomes binding, and purchasers must be given ten days to conduct a risk assessment or inspection.[90]

The contract for sale of target housing must include this warning:

> Every purchaser of any interest in residential real property on which a residential dwelling was built prior to 1978 is notified that such property may present exposure to lead from lead-based paint that may place young children at risk of developing lead poisoning. Lead poisoning in young children may produce permanent neurological damage, including learning disabilities, reduced intelligence quotient, behavioral problems, and impaired memory. Lead poisoning also poses a particular risk to pregnant women. The seller of any interest in residential real property is required to provide the buyer with any information on lead-based paint hazards from risk assessments or inspections in the seller's

84. Stephanie P. Brown, Federal Lead-Based Paint Enforcement Bench Book, 2009, 5, *available at* http://www.healthyhomestraining.org/LSWP/NCHH_Federal_LBP_Benchbook_1-23-09.pdf.
85. 40 C.F.R. § 745.115.
86. 40 C.F.R. § 745.101.
87. *Id.*
88. EPA #747-K-94-001.
89. 40 C.F.R. § 745.107(a).
90. 40 C.F.R. § 745.100.

> possession and notify the buyer of any known lead-based paint hazards. A risk assessment or inspection for possible lead-based paint hazards is recommended prior to purchase.[91]

Contracts must also disclose details of the known lead paint and lead paint hazards and list the reports that were provided to the buyer. The buyer must acknowledge receipt of the required information and pamphlet, and the opportunity to conduct an inspection or risk assessment or written waiver of that opportunity.[92]

If an agent was involved in the sale, the contract must state that the agent is aware of the obligation to ensure compliance with the Disclosure Rule and inform the seller of the seller's obligations. The seller, buyer, and agent must certify their statements concerning lead.[93]

Landlords must give similar warnings, and leases must contain similar statements and disclosures, except that lessees are not afforded an opportunity to conduct a risk assessment or inspection.

Contracts and leases must be retained for three years, but as is the case with other TSCA programs, the statute of limitations may be significantly longer and documents should be retained until the longest statute of limitations runs.

V. Lead-Based Paint Activities

Part L of the TSCA lead regulations predates the Renovation, Repair, and Painting Rule and the Disclosure Rule, although it has elements of both of those newer rules. It contains detailed work practices for lead-based paint activities, and an equally detailed program for accrediting and training contractors who perform "lead-based paint activities" and renovations.[94] Broadly, these regulations require careful work practices and training and certification for all contractors who perform renovations or inspections, remove or encapsulate lead in target housing and child-occupied facilities.

"Lead-based paint activities" are defined as inspection, risk assessment or abatement in target housing or child-occupied facilities. "Inspection" is defined in turn as "a surface-by-surface investigation to determine the presence of lead-based paint and the provision of a report explaining the results of the investigation;" "risk assessment" is defined as an on-site investigation

---

91. 40 C.F.R. § 745.113.
92. *Id.*
93. *Id.*
94. 40 C.F.R. § 745.220.

into lead-based paint hazards, coupled with a report on the hazards and options for reducing them. "Abatement" is defined as "measures designed to permanently eliminate lead-based paint hazards," from the inception of the project through testing to determine if any lead remains at the work site.[95] Lead-based paint activities do not include interim controls.[96]

The lead-based paint activities rule only applies in states and to Indian Tribes that do not have authorized state or tribal programs, except that the Federal Government must comply even if there is an authorized state or tribal program. These rules do not apply to people who do work on residences they own, unless people outside their own immediate families live there during the work, or unless a child living in the building has elevated blood lead levels, in which case the rules do apply.[97]

Under the lead-based paint activities rule, only certified individuals and firms may conduct lead-based paint activities.[98] Individuals may become certified by attending an accredited course and meeting additional requirements that vary according to the specific activity the person is certified to do.[99] Individuals must be recertified every three years if they took a course and had a hands-on assessment, or every five years if they took a course and a proficiency test.[100] Firms may be certified also, and certified firms may only employ certified individuals to conduct lead-based paint activities. All training programs must be accredited by the EPA before training can be offered to certify inspectors, risk assessors, supervisors, project designers, abatement workers, or for refresher courses.[101] The certification requirements of the lead-based paint activities rule predate the renovation rule and cover activities that are not included in the renovation rule, such as abatement and encapsulation of lead paint.

There are work practice standards that must be employed in all lead-based paint activity.[102] For example, for inspections, the regulations detail the minimum requirements including where to select paint samples to test, how to sample, how to test, what records to keep, and reports that must be prepared.

---

95. The definitions are in 40 C.F.R. § 745.223. In October 2009 the EPA said that it intends to lower the concentration of lead necessary for a determination that paint is lead-based paint. *See* http://www.epa.gov/oppt/chemtest/pubs/petitions.html.
96. 66 Fed. Reg. 1206, 1207 (Jan. 5, 2001).
97. 40 C.F.R. § 745.220(b).
98. 40 C.F.R. § 745.233.
99. 40 C.F.R. § 745.226.
100. 40 C.F.R. § 745.226(e).
101. Detailed rules for course accreditation are in 40 C.F.R. § 745.225.
102. 40 C.F.R. § 745.227.

VI. Dangerous Levels of Lead—The Lead Rule

Section 403 of TSCA[103] required the EPA to issue regulations to identify levels of lead in paint, dust, and contaminated soil that would result in adverse human health effects. EPA issued those regulations in 2001, establishing numerical thresholds above which dust and contaminated soil are considered hazards.[104] Three trade associations challenged the Lead Rule's numerical thresholds because the rule takes into account all sources of lead in dust and soil, even if the lead did not originate from lead paint. The trade associations argued that the statute focuses on lead-based paint and not all sources of lead. The court found the Lead Rule to be a permissible construction of the statute in *National Multi Housing Council V. U.S.E.P.A.*[105] In August 2009 the National Center for Healthy Housing and other groups petitioned the EPA to lower the thresholds for classifying lead in dust and contaminated soil as hazardous. EPA responded in October 2009 that it would begin the rulemaking process.[106]

VII. State and Tribal Programs

Most states have their own lead programs which have been authorized by the EPA and supplant the lead-based paint activities rule in subpart L.[107] States and tribes may seek authorization under the Renovation, Repair, and Painting Rule in addition to the lead-based paint activities rule of Subpart L. Section 404 of TSCA[108] requires state programs to be at least as protective as the TSCA program before the EPA can authorize them. In those jurisdictions where the state or tribal program has not been authorized by EPA, both the federal and state or tribal programs will be in effect. States and Tribes may become authorized by the EPA to administer and enforce the renovation

103. 15 U.S.C. § 2683.

104. 66 Fed. Reg. 1206 (Jan. 5, 2001); 40 C.F.R. § 745.65.

105. 292 F.3d 232 (D.C. Cir. 2002).

106. The petition and response are *available at* http://www.epa.gov/oppt/chemtest/pubs/petitions.html.

107. The States with authorized lead programs as of 2009 are Alabama, Arkansas, California, Colorado, Connecticut, Delaware, Georgia, Hawaii, Illinois, Indiana, Iowa, Kansas, Kentucky, Louisiana, Maine, Maryland, Massachusetts, Minnesota, Michigan, Mississippi, Missouri, Nebraska, New Hampshire, New Jersey, North Carolina, North Dakota, Ohio, Oklahoma, Oregon, Pennsylvania, Rhode Island, Tennessee, Texas, Utah, Vermont, Virginia, Washington, West Virginia, and Wisconsin. In addition, the Cherokee Nation and the Lower Sioux and Upper Sioux have authorized programs, as have the District of Columbia and Puerto Rico. http://www.epa.gov/lead/pubs/traincert.htm.

108. 15 U.S.C. § 2684.

rules (in 40 C.F.R. § 745.80-.91) or just the pre-renovation education provisions (in 40 C.F.R. § 745.84), or the training, certification, accreditation and work practice rules (in 40 C.F.R. § 745.225, .226 and .227),[109] and therefore it is critical to check to see if the federal rules apply for particular programs.[110] The state or tribe must submit detailed descriptions of their proposed program together with a comparison of the proposed program with the federal program to demonstrate that the state or tribal program is at least as stringent.[111]

The States and Tribes may not administer and enforce the Disclosure Rule, although they may have separate related laws that they enforce in parallel with federal enforcement of the Disclosure Rule.

VIII. Lead in Children's Products and Fishing Sinkers

As the result of a lawsuit brought by the Sierra Club,[112] the EPA issued a rule under TSCA § 8(d) concerning lead and lead compounds. Under this rule, entities that manufacturer or import consumer products intended for children, and who also manufacture or import lead or lead compounds, were required to submit unpublished health and safety data to the EPA.[113] The rule did not apply to manufacturers or importers of children's jewelry containing lead because lead in children's jewelry had already been regulated by the Consumer Product Safety Commission. The EPA later clarified that the rule only applied to products for children that also contained lead or lead products.[114] As is the case with all TSCA § 8(d) rules requiring submission of unpublished health and safety data, that rule was only in effect for a limited period of time.

EPA has proposed TSCA rules dating back to 1994 banning certain small lead and zinc fishing sinkers, but those rules have never been finalized.[115] The only continuing relevance of the proposed rule is that exporters must notify

109. 40 C.F.R. § 745.320.

110. 73 Fed. Reg. 21692, 21747 (Apr. 22, 2008).

111. 40 C.F.R. § 745.324.

112. Sierra Club v. Johnson, C 06-5641 PJH (ND CA) Settlement Agreement (Apr. 13, 2007), *available at* http://www.sierraclub.org/environmentallaw/lawsuits/docs/2007-04-12-EPASierraIKESettlement.pdf.

113. 40 C.F.R. § 716.21(a)(8). *See also* 73 Fed. Reg. 5109 (Jan. 29, 2008).

114. The clarification that the products intended for children must contain lead or lead products for the rule to be applicable is found in an e-mail from Mike Mattheisen of the EPA to James Votaw of WilmerHale, EPA-HQ-OPPT-2007-0487-0016 (Feb. 28,2008), *available through* http://www.regulations.gov.

115. 59 Fed. Reg. 11122 (Mar. 9, 1994).

the EPA before exporting lead or zinc sinkers that are one inch or less in any dimension.[116] EPA announced in its Semiannual Regulatory Agenda in 2009 that it intended to withdraw the 1994 proposal,[117] but modified that stance in the Fall 2009 Regulatory Agenda to say that it will reevaluate the 1994 proposal.[118]

The Sierra Club and other organizations petitioned the EPA in 2009 under TSCA § 21 to prohibit the manufacture and use of lead wheel weights. The EPA granted the petition in August, and said it will propose regulations.[119]

IX. Enforcement

Of all the TSCA programs, the lead programs are the most actively enforced. About half of all the TSCA-related complaints and proposed orders that the EPA issued in fiscal years 2001 through 2009 were for lead violations.[120] Section 409 of TSCA subjects all violations of the TSCA lead program to the civil and criminal penalties in TSCA § 16. The current maximum daily penalty for a TSCA violation after January 12, 2009 is $37,500.[121] The maximum penalty is scheduled for review and possible increase to keep up with inflation in 2012 and every four years after that.[122]

The EPA may conduct inspections at any renovation in target housing or child-occupied facilities to ensure compliance, and has the authority under TSCA § 11 to issue subpoenas.[123]

A. Renovation, Repair, and Painting Rule Enforcement

States and Tribes with authorized programs enforce their own programs. EPA has stated that it reserves the right to enforce the Renovation, Repair, and Painting Rule in states that have their own authorized programs.

---

116. The restrictions were proposed under TSCA § 6, and all substances for which rules are proposed under TSCA § 6 are subject to export notification requirements under TSCA § 12(b). *See* Chapter 11, Bans and Restrictions and Chapter 8, Exports and Imports.
117. EPA's Semiannual Regulatory Agenda, 99, EPA-230-Z-09-001 (Spring 2009), *available through* http://www.epa.gov/lawsregs/search/regagenda.html.
118. Fall 2009 Regulatory Agenda 104.
119. The § 21 petition and the EPA's response are *available at* http://www.epa.gov/oppt/chemtest/pubs/petitions.html.
120. *See* Chapter 14, Penalties and Enforcement, Table 1.
121. 73 Fed. Reg. 75340 (Dec. 11, 2008).
122. *Id.* at 75341; *see* Chapter 14, Penalties and Enforcement.
123. 40 C.F.R. § 745.87.

This practice of bringing federal enforcement proceedings where the state has an authorized program is called "overfiling."[124]

In enforcement proceedings, and when the enforcement agency seeks a subpoena, the regulations state that there is a presumption that all renovations in target housing and child-occupied facilities have lead paint present.[125]

The EPA has not developed an enforcement response policy specifically for the Renovation, Repair, and Painting Rule or the Pre-Renovation Education Rule. In *In the Matter of Millennium Quests, Inc.*,[126] the Regional Judicial Hearing Officer relied on the enforcement response policy for PCBs in the absence of an enforcement response policy that was directly applicable to the Pre-Renovation Education Rule.

B. Disclosure Rule Enforcement

The Disclosure Rule can be enforced by either the EPA or HUD. In an unusual twist, the elements of a violation and the potential penalties vary depending on which agency brings the enforcement proceeding.[127] HUD can seek an injunction against any violation, but it can only bring a proceeding for a monetary penalty if the violator knowingly violated the regulations.[128] In contrast, the EPA does not need to prove that a violation was knowing and can penalize unintentional violations.[129] The statutory limit for violations of the TSCA Disclosure Rule was originally set at $10,000 but was raised incrementally to $16,000 for violations after January 12, 2009.[130] Finally, an injured lessee or purchaser has a private right of action for treble damages plus attorneys' fees under the Residential Lead-Based Paint Hazard Reduction Act[131] but not under TSCA.[132]

The enforcement response policy for the TSCA Disclosure Rule is entitled Section 1018—Disclosure Rule Enforcement Response and Penalty Policy (December 2007) (the Disclosure Rule ERP). Under this policy, the EPA may seek civil penalties, refer a violation for criminal penalties under TSCA § 16,

---

124. 68 Fed. Reg. 27557, 27558 (May 20, 2003).
125. 40 C.F.R. 745.87(e).
126. Docket No.: TSCA-03-2005-0261, Region III (Jan. 1, 2009), *available at* http://yosemite.epa.gov/OA/EAB_WEB_Docket.nsf/ce9f7f898b59eae28525707a00631c97/ce7d9f02b07e62dd85257536006b322d!OpenDocument.
127. Claude E. Walker, *Lead-Based Paint Real Estate Notification and Disclosure Rule*, 8 Buff. Envt'l. L.J. 65, 73 (Fall, 2000).
128. 42 U.S.C. § 4852d(b)(1) and (2).
129. 42 U.S.C. § 4852d(b)(5).
130. 73 Fed. Reg. 75340, 75345 (Dec. 11 2008). The penalties were increased to $11,000 for violations that occurred from Jan. 30, 1997 through Jan. 12, 2009.
131. 42 U.S.C. § 4852d(b)(3) and (4).
132. Cudjoe Ex Rel. Cudjoe v. Dept. of V. A., 426 F.3d 241, 248 (3d Cir. 2005).

seek to enjoin a violation, issue a Notice of Noncompliance if the violation was minor, or a combination of these.[133]

Like all of the ERPs, the Disclosure Rule ERP calls for determining the nature, extent, and gravity of the violation to determine the gravity based penalty, which is then adjusted up or down based on factors such as cooperation and history of violations. The nature of all Disclosure Rule violations is hazard assessment. The circumstances depend on how much the violation prevented evaluation of the existing information. The extent of a violation depends on whether there are children younger than six, at least six but younger then eighteen, or pregnant women in the target housing.[134]

The Disclosure Rule ERP contains a penalty matrix, showing the penalties applicable for each combination of circumstances and extent. Because the nature is the same for all Disclosure Rule violations the penalties do not vary based on nature.[135] The matrix was drafted when the maximum penalty was $11,000, and so the penalties should be multiplied by a factor equal to the maximum penalty in effect at the time of the violation divided by $11,000.

The EPA can seek the economic benefit the violator achieved from noncompliance, if the adjusted gravity based penalty is not a deterrent to future violations.[136]

Penalties can be reduced to just 5 percent of the gravity based penalty if the violator proves that there was no lead in the target housing at the time of the violation. The penalties can be reduced by 50 percent if there was no interior lead paint, up to 40 percent if a major potential source of lead was removed prior to the violation, and up to 25 percent if the were no lead paint hazards, even if there was lead paint.[137]

Because the Disclosure Rule has overlapping requirements, a separate penalty can be imposed for violation of each of them. In *In the Matter of John P. Vidiksis*[138] the administrative law judge imposed penalties of $97,545 for 69 violations stemming from 34 lease transactions, and one sale transaction. *In the Matter of Rod Bruner and Century 21 Country North*[139] illustrates how proposed penalties can become a significant deterrent. In that case, the EPA

---

133. Disclosure Rule ERP, 8–9.

134. *Id.* at 11–13.

135. *Id.* at 30.

136. *Id.* at 14.

137. *Id.* at 21–22.

138. TSCA-03-2005-0266, ALJ, (Oct. 10, 2007) *affirmed* 14 E.A.D.__(Apr. 22, 2009), *available at* http://www.epa.gov/oalj/orders/vidiksis-id-101007.pdf. *See also* In the Matter of Apartment Investment and Management Company, Docket No. TSCA HQ-2002-0003 (EAB Jan. 15, 2002), *available at* http://www.epa.gov/compliance/resources/decrees/civil/rlphra/aimcoca.pdf.

139. EPA Region 5, Docket No. TSCA-05-2003-0009, Judicial Hearing Officer Order (May 19, 2003), *available at* http://www.epa.gov/compliance/resources/rjos/bruner-century21-ord.pdf.

proposed penalties of $34,100 for the following alleged violations stemming from the sale of a $69,000 house:

- "failure to provide a U.S. EPA approved lead information pamphlet" as required by 40 C.F.R. § 745.107(a)(1);
- "failure to allow the purchaser a ten-day period to conduct a risk assessment or lead inspection" as required by 40 C.F.R. § 745.110(a);
- "failure to include as an attachment to the sales contract a lead warning statement" as required by 40 C.F.R. § 745.113(a)(1);
- "failure to include as an attachment to the sales contract all records or reports available to the seller regarding lead-based paint and/or lead based paint hazards in the house or a statement that no such reports existed" as required by 40 C.F.R. § 745.113(a)(3);
- "failure to include as an attachment to the sales contract a statement from the purchaser acknowledging receipt of the information" as required by 40 C.F.R. § 745.113(a)(4); and
- "failure to include as an attachment to the sales contract an acknowledgment signed by the seller, the agents and the purchaser that their statements are accurate to the best of their knowledge, along with the dates of their signatures" as required by 40 C.F.R. § 745.113(a)(7).[140]

The Bruner proceeding was reportedly settled for $8,525,[141] which was a significant portion of the selling price of the home at issue.

The EPA has brought numerous Disclosure Rule enforcement proceedings.[142] In the context of settlements the EPA has negotiated lead paint abatement,[143] although it does not have authority to mandate abatement under TSCA.

---

140. *Id.* at 4-5.

141. EPA Region 5 Office of Regional Counsel 2004 Enforcement Action Summaries, 7; see also Enforcement and Compliance History Online *available at* http://www.epa-echo.gov/cgi-bin/get1cReport.cgi?tool=echo&IDNumber=110015752014.

142. *See, e.g.*, In Re Harpoon Partnership, EAB TSCA Appeal No. 04-02 (2005), *available at* http://www.epa.gov/eab/disk11/harpoon.pdf; In the Matter of Wesley A. Brown, TSCA-7-2000-0029, Region VII (Oct. 26, 2000), *available at* http://www.epa.gov/compliance/resources/rjos/brownwa-rpt.pdf.

143. U.S. v. A & M Properties, Inc., Case Number 08-11814 (E.D. Mich. July 24, 2008) (granting motion to enter consent decree); In the Matter of Apartment Investment and Management Company, Docket No. TSCA HQ-2002-0003 (EAB Jan. 15, 2002), *available at* http://www.epa.gov/compliance/resources/decrees/civil/rlphra/aimcoca.pdf.

CHAPTER

19

Healthy High-Performance Schools Act

I. Context of the Act

As discussed in the earlier chapters of this book, in the initially enacted version of the Toxic Substances Control Act (TSCA)[1] Congress required the United States Environmental Protection Agency (EPA) to promulgate regulations to control the import, manufacture, and processing of chemical substances. In the Healthy High-Performance Schools Act (hereinafter sometimes referred to as the Act or HHPS),[2] which amended TSCA, Congress again used the alternative to the traditional regulatory framework that it had employed to minimize health risks from indoor radon contamination.[3] The HHPS envisioned that the EPA would play a role somewhat similar to the one it had with respect to radon to create a healthy school environment for all children. EPA was positioned as a developer of technical and educational information and a manager of grant programs, to encourage states, local governments, and school systems to build green schools. EPA was directed to coordinate its work with other agencies also responsible for various aspects of creating healthy schools, such as the United States Department of Education (DE) and the United States Department of Health and Human Services (DHHS).

As a result of EPA's role under the HHPS, the programs that EPA administers are all advisory, and while EPA is a valuable source of information on environmental health programs and school site selection criteria, none of its programs are mandatory. Some states and localities have used the information developed by the EPA and its sister agencies prior to the implementation of HHPS to develop mandatory programs. Because the Act is relatively new, and the activities required by EPA are still in their infancy, it is too early to determine the likely success HHPS will have in reaching its goals.

The HHPS was a minor provision in the Energy Independence and Security Act of 2007 (EISA),[4] and did not receive much comment. Neither the press release issued by the White House[5] outlining the provisions of the newly enacted EISA, nor the NEW YORK TIMES article[6] summarizing the legislation contained any references to the provisions of the HHPS. EISA dealt with much more contentious and publicly debated issues, such as increasing the supply of alternative fuel sources by setting (i) a mandatory renewable fuel standard requiring fuel producers to use at least 36 billion gallons of biofuel

---

1. 15 U.S.C. §§ 2601–2695d.
2. Health High-Performance Schools Act, Pub. L. 94-469, title III §301, as added Dec. 19, 2007, Pub. L. 110-140, Title IV, Subtitle E, § 461(a), 121 Stat. 1640.
3. *See* Chapter 17, Indoor Radon Abatement Act.
4. Energy Independence and Security Act of 2007, Pub. L. 110–14, 121 Stat. 1801 (2007).
5. Press Release, Office of the Press Secretary, White House, President Bush Signs Energy Bill To Improve Fuel Economy And Reduce Oil Dependence (Dec. 17. 2007).
6. John M. Broder, *House, 314-100, Passes Broad Energy Bill; Bush Plans to Sign It*, N.Y. TIMES, Dec. 19, 2007.

in 2022 and (ii) a national fuel economy standard of 35 miles per gallon by 2020. The EISA also addressed improvements in energy efficiency in lighting and appliances, requirements for Federal agency energy efficiency and renewable energy use, and established an Office of High-Performance Green Buildings in the United States General Services Administration (GSA), which office is to play a role in disseminating information developed by EPA under HHPS.

Interestingly, Congress had initially promoted the concept of healthy high-performance school buildings in the No Child Left Behind Act of 2001,[7] in which it required DE to conduct a study to determine the characteristics of unhealthy public school buildings and the impact of such buildings on students.[8] It also established a grant program, to be administered by the DE in consultation with the Department of Energy (DOE) and EPA, for the purpose of developing healthy, high-performance school building projects that significantly reduce energy usage in school buildings, meet federal and state health and safety codes, and support healthful, energy efficient, and environmentally sound practices.[9]

How TSCA became home to a program dealing with healthy high-performance schools is not clear. TSCA had originally been enacted more than thirty years earlier to force manufacturers and processors of chemical substances to develop data about the effects of such substances on health and the environment and to give the EPA the authority to regulate and control the research, manufacture, and processing of such chemical substances. For the most part, those who were to be regulated by TSCA would be part of private industry. The first amendment to TSCA, the Asbestos Hazard Emergency Response Act,[10] introduced to TSCA the problems of exposure to asbestos-containing materials in public schools. The second amendment to TSCA, the Indoor Radon Abatement Act,[11] while dealing more broadly with the issue of exposure to radon indoors, did add one section[12] in that amendment mandating the EPA to conduct a study of exposure to indoor radon in the schools. Since then, and dealing with other mandates as well, EPA has developed many tools and information sources to assist schools. For example, EPA

7. No Child Left Behind Act of 2001, Pub. L. 107-110, 20 U.S.C. § 6301.

8. *Id.* at § 5414.

9. *Id.* at § 5583.

10. Asbestos Hazard Emergency Response, Pub. L. 94-469, title II, § 201, as added Pub. L. 99-519, § 2 (Oct. 22, 1986) 100 Stat. 2970. *See* Chapter 16, Asbestos Hazard Emergency Response Act.

11. Indoor Radon Abatement Act, Pub. L. 94-469, title III, § 301, as added Pub. L 100-551, § 1(a) (Oct. 28, 1988) 102 Stat. 2755. *See* Chapter 17, Indoor Radon Abatement Act.

12. TSCA § 307.

developed the Indoor Air Quality (IAQ) Tools for Schools Program[13] to reduce exposures to indoor environmental contaminants in schools, including radon and asbestos, through the adoption of indoor air quality management practices. The IAQ Tools for Schools Program is a comprehensive resource to help schools identify, correct, and prevent indoor air quality problems. HHPS encourages the further dissemination and use of this, and other similar, tools.

II. Requirements of the Act

Congress enacted the Healthy High-Performance Schools Act to ensure that all children would be able to attend schools that are free of harmful substances, are energy efficient, and can accommodate children with disabilities and special needs. The Act provided grants for assistance to the states and directed EPA, in conjunction with DE and the DHHS, to establish model guidelines for siting of school facilities and for environmental health programs for schools.

The Act is ambiguous about whether EPA's authority under this Act is limited in time. One possible interpretation is that it will expire December 19, 2012, five years after the date of enactment.[14] The ambiguity arises because this sunset provision is located in the discussion of EPA's authority to make grants, in § 501, which uses the word "section" instead of title, when discussing the time limitation. Support for the alternative reading, that the sunset provision applies to the entire title, is found in § 503,[15] which requires EPA to submit an annual report to Congress on "all activities carried out in this title, until the expiration of authority"[16] as described in the sunset provision.

A. Grants for Healthy School Environments

The Act allowed,[17] but did not require, EPA in conjunction with DE, to make grants to the states (i) to provide technical assistance to schools to use existing EPA tools to address environmental issues and (ii) to develop and implement environmental health programs that include standards for building

13. Information about the Indoor Air Quality (IAQ") Tools for Schools Program is *available at* http://www.epa.gov/iaq/schools/actionkit.html.
14. 15 U.S.C. § 2695(b).
15. 15 U.S.C. § 2695b(a).
16. *Id.*
17. TSCA § 501(a) provides that the EPA "**may** provide grants to States…." (emphasis added) By its plain language the Act does not require the making of such grants. 15 U.S.C.S. § 2695(a).

design, construction, and renovation, as well as identification and resolution of ongoing environmental problems in school facilities.[18]

One of the existing EPA programs specifically referenced in this section of the Act is the Tools for Schools Program. The Indoor Air Quality Tools for Schools (IAQ TfS) kit was first issued in 1996 and was most recently revised in 2009.[19] The kit contains an action plan to improve indoor air quality at little or no cost using existing in-house staff. EPA, in a cover letter to school administrators introducing the revised IAQ TfS kit, summarized the progress of this initiative since the publication of the original IAQ TfS kit, as follows:

> 13.5 million students, staff, and faculty in 25,000 schools throughout the United States are experiencing good IAQ in accordance with EPA guidelines. Approximately 54 percent of these schools have reported improved workplace satisfaction, 33 percent reported a decrease in asthma episodes, 29 percent reported fewer visits to the school nurse or health office, and 27 percent reported an increase in attendance.[20]

Topics addressed in the kit include mold, radon, secondhand smoke, asthma, portable classrooms, basic measurement equipment, hiring professional assistance, codes and regulations, and integrated pest management, as well as other typical indoor air pollutants and pollutants from motor vehicles and equipment. The program uses checklists for different job functions, e.g., facilities managers, teachers, nurses, food service workers, videos and awards programs, and fact sheets on major issues.

The other program mentioned in this section of Act is The Healthy School Environments Assessment Tool (HealthySEATv2).[21] It was adapted from a database tool originally developed by the Los Angeles Unified School District to conduct self-assessment inspections in its approximately nine hundred school facilities and substantially modified by EPA to make it widely available to the more than fourteen thousand school districts nationwide. It is free software that can be customized and helps school districts evaluate and manage their school facilities for key environmental, safety, and health issues. EPA has also included critical elements of all of its regulatory and voluntary

18. *Id.*

19. The Indoor Air Quality Tools for Schools (IAQ TfS) kit, EPA Document Number 402-K-07-008 (hard copy) or 402-C-05-001 (CD-ROM), portions of which are *available at* http://www.epa.gov/iaq/schools/actionkit.html. The entire kit can be ordered free of charge from EPA's National Service Center for Environmental Publications (NSCEP): at P.O. Box 42419, Cincinnati, OH, 45242-0419, Phone: 1-800-490-9198, Fax: (301) 604-3408, or e-mail at nscep@bps-lmit.com.

20. www.epa.gov/iaq/schools/pdfs/kit/coverletter.pdf. Undated letter from The U.S. EPA Indoor Air Quality Tools for Schools Team to School Official.

21. http://www.epa.gov/schools/healthyseat/basicinformation.html.

programs for schools, as well as Web links to more detailed information. EPA emphasizes in its literature that districts that choose to use the software will have no reporting requirements and no obligation to use the checklist provided. Topics addressed by HealthySEATv2 include chemical management, construction and renovation, energy efficiency, hazardous materials, hazardous waste, health, safety and injury prevention, indoor air quality, moisture/mold control, non-hazardous waste, outdoor air pollution, pest control/integrated pest management, portable/relocatable classrooms, ultra-violet radiation, and water (drinking, waste, storm, and efficiency).

B. Model Guidelines for Siting of School Facilities

EPA, in consultation with DE and HHS, was required to issue voluntary school site selection guidelines by June 19, 2009, 18 months after the enactment of the Act.[22] Those guidelines must take into account children's special vulnerability to hazardous substances or pollution exposure where the potential for contamination exists; available transportation modes in the area; energy efficiency; and the potential to use the school as an emergency shelter.[23] EPA has convened a special Task Group, composed of diverse constituents, to provide initial input to EPA on the content of the draft guideline document. EPA expected that the Task Group would complete its work in December, 2009.[24] As of this writing, the guidelines were not yet available.

Several years before the enactment of HHPS, EPA had released a report[25] dealing with some of the issues mentioned in the section on siting of school facilities. EPA recognized that the need to accommodate substantial new student enrollment would require the building or renovation of thousands of school buildings and that the decisions inherent in those activities would have important implications—educational, environmental, economic, and fiscal.[26] One goal of the study was to develop literature on how school location and design impacted school travel trends.[27] Not surprisingly, the study found that siting schools close to students, in walkable neighborhoods, reduced traffic and vehicular emissions of concern by approximately 15 percent,[28] produced a 13 percent increase in walking and biking,[29] and

---

22. 15 U.S.C. § 2695a.
23. *Id.*
24. http://www.epa.gov/schools/siting.html.
25. EPA, Travel and Environmental Implications of School Siting, EPA 231-R-03-004 (Oct. 2003) [hereinafter School Siting], *available at* http://www.epa.gov/smartgrowth/school_travel.htm.
26. *Id.* at 2.
27. *Id.* at 3.
28. *Id.* at 26.
29. *Id.*

achieved a better learning environment with higher student achievement and other health benefits.[30]

Building on this study and other publicly available research, EPA issued a request for proposals (RFP)[31] to, among other things:

- identify and summarize widely used policies and practices that may be a barrier to implementing environmentally responsible smart growth school siting and design solutions;
- identify and summarize school siting and design strategies that have broad applicability and can provide localities and states with the flexibility to overcome these barriers (including new schools and opportunities to re-use or renovate existing schools). These strategies should lead to superior environmental outcomes, meet education goals, and meet other state/local goals (e.g., schools as centers of communities, student physical activity and health goals, reducing stress on transportation systems, meeting fiscal requirements, efficient use of tax dollars); and
- identify, analyze and document existing policies and practices at the state level or on a state-wide basis that influence school siting and design.[32]

Grants under this RFP were to be issued in the fall of 2007 and results are expected in the fall of 2012.

Though not mentioned as a resource in the siting section of the HHPS, DE has released energy design guidelines for school facilities, by climate and location.[33] How all of these governmental resources, and ongoing private work in this field, will inform the voluntary siting guidelines to be issued by EPA will not be evident until those guidelines are issued.

An early assessment by one commentator has concluded that the lack of specific guidance by Congress and the voluntary nature of the guidelines to be proposed are not adequate to build environmentally appropriate schools in an effective manner.[34] The author reviewed the case study of the Vista Learning Center Project undertaken by the Los Angeles Unified School District, which was to be built on an abandoned oil field saturated with toxins.[35] Because of the failure to undertake a full-scale environmental assessment, that school was built on land acquired 24 years before the opening date,

---

30. *Id.* at 5.
31. Request for Grant Proposals, EPA-OPEI-0704: Reducing the Environmental and Health Impacts of School Siting.
32. *Id.*
33. *Available at* http://www1.eere.energy.gov/buildings/energysmartschools/design_guides.html.
34. Sandra Sutak, *Green Schools, Brown Fields: School Siting Legislation Provides a Weak Foundation*, 21 Tul. Envtl. L.J. 427 (2008).
35. *Id.* at 428.

and was slated to be opened 12 years after the breaking of ground at a cost in excess of $300,000,000 as of 2007.[36] After a further review of existing state legislation in this area, the author concludes[37] that a better model for federal involvement in school siting decisions would be the approach taken in The Asbestos Hazard Emergency Response Act (AHERA).[38] AHERA combines a traditional regulatory framework with EPA oversight, mandated procedures, and enforcement.

A fifty-state survey conducted several years before the enactment of the HHPS found that there was a real need for action to prevent the construction of schools on land where children could be exposed to hazardous substances.[39] The report found:

> Twenty (20) states have no policies of any kind affecting the siting of schools in relation to environmental hazards.... Fourteen (14) states have policies that prohibit outright the siting of schools on or near sources of pollution or other hazards that pose a risk to children's safety... Twenty-one (21) states have school siting policies that direct or suggest school siting officials "avoid" siting schools on or near specified man-made or natural environmental hazards.... Twenty-three (24) [sic] states have no policies that require sponsors of new school projects to investigate or assess environmental hazards at potential school sites....[40]

C. Public Outreach

EPA is required to submit annual reports to Congress of its activities under this Act until its authority expires on December 19, 2012.[41] The Federal Director, a position created under the EISA[42] to create a high-performance green buildings clearinghouse,[43] is required to ensure that the clearinghouse receives information from the EPA on the exposure of children to environmental hazards in school buildings, and makes that information available to the public.[44] Several other federal agencies already had preexisting Web sites providing good resources in this area. EPA maintains a site called "Your one-stop

---

36. *Id.*
37. *Id.* at 442–447.
38. TSCA Title II, discussed in Chapter 16, Asbestos Hazard Emergency Response Act.
39. Rhode Island Legal Services (RILS), Not in My Schoolyard: Avoiding Environmental Hazards at School Through Improved School Site Selection Policies, A Report to the U.S. Environmental Protection Agency (2006), *available at* http://stage.nylpi.org/pub/School_Siting_Final.pdf.
40. RILS at 3–4.
41. 15 U.S.C. § 2695b(a).
42. 42 U.S.C. § 17092(a).
43. 42 U.S.C. § 17083(1).
44. 15 U.S.C. § 2695b.

location for information and links to school environmental health issues."[45] DE maintains the National Clearinghouse for Educational Facilities, which includes several sections dealing with healthy high-performance schools.[46] And DOE maintains a Web site that deals with energy-smart schools.[47] What the GSA clearinghouse required by EISA will add to the mix is yet to be seen.

D. Environmental Health Program

Congress seemed to confer on EPA the lead role for developing voluntary guidelines for states to use to customize and implement an environmental health program. The elements of an environmental health program are quite broad and go beyond the mandate one would expect for the EPA. However, EPA is directed to consult with DE, DHHS and "other relevant agencies"[48] in issuing such guidelines.

Congress enunciated four areas of concern to be addressed in developing the voluntary guidelines. First, the legislation makes clear that the EPA is to look at findings under all relevant federal laws that deal with school facilities relating to health, safety, productivity, and disabilities or special needs, not only those pursuant to the HHPS and the EISA.[49] Secondly, EPA is required to take into account studies using the high-performance green building measurement tools identified in the EISA.[50] This requirement may be a way of managing the issue of data integrity in the studies that are to inform the guidelines. The third requirement is a list of more specific topics that might impact school facilities: environmental issues (such as lead, asbestos, radon, elemental mercury emissions, pollutant emissions), natural lighting, ventilation, heating, cooling, moisture control, mold, maintenance, cleaning, pest control activities, acoustics and any other issues dealing with the health, comfort, productivity, and performance of those in school buildings.[51] The final area of concern set out is the special vulnerability of low-income and minority children to exposures from contaminants, hazardous substances, and emissions.[52]

45. http://cfpub.epa.gov/schools/index.cfm.
46. http://www.edfacilities.org/rl/healthy_schools.cfm.
47. http://www1.eere.energy.gov/buildings/energysmartschools/.
48. 15 U.S.C. § 2695c(a).
49. 15 U.S.C. § 2695c(a)(1).
50. 15 U.S.C. § 2695c(a)(2).
51. 15 U.S.C. § 2695c(a)(3).
52. 15 U.S.C. § 2695c(a)(7).

The guidelines are to provide technical assistance regarding siting, design, management, and operation of school facilities[53] and to assist the states and the public to better understand and improve the environmental health of children.[54] They are also to be collaborative with federally funded pediatric health centers in conducting environmental investigations at school sites.[55]

The public information clearinghouse established under the EISA is required to disseminate information that the EPA provides in the annual report mentioned in § 503(a) as well as any other information provided by the EPA on the exposure of children to environmental hazards in school facilities.[56]

E. Authorization of Appropriations

Congress authorized to be appropriated $1,000,000 for fiscal year 2009, and $1,500,000 for each of fiscal years 2010 through 2013.[57]

53. 15 U.S.C. § 2695c(a)(4).
54. 15 U.S.C. § 2695c(a)(6).
55. 15 U.S.C. §2695c(a)(5).
56. 15 U.S.C. § 2695c(b). The obligation to disseminate information on the exposure of children to environmental hazards is the same here as in TSCA § 503(b). The only difference is that in this section the obligation is not limited to the Federal Director, but also includes the Commercial Director established under EISA.
57. This section on appropriations appears to be the last section in HHPS, given the amended Table of Contents for TSCA provided in the EISA (TSCA § 505(b)). However § 462 of the EISA, which directly follows this amended Table of Contents, is entitled "Study on Indoor Environmental Quality in Schools," a topic that would seem to fit within the language and the goals of the HHPS, but was not included by Congress.

CHAPTER

20

Practice Tools

I. Chapter Resources

A. Chapter 2 TSCA's Scope Resources

On CD:

- 42 Fed. Reg. 64572 (Dec. 23, 1977) Inventory Reporting Requirements *42 FR 64572 Inventory 12-23-77*
- 51 Fed. Reg. 15096 (April 22, 1986) Toxic Substances; Revisions of Premanufacture Notification Regulations; Final Rule *51 FR 15096 PMN Revisions 4-22-86*
- 73 Fed. Reg. 2854 (Jan. 16, 2008) Proposed Clarification for Chemical Identification Describing Activated Phosphors for TSCA Inventory Purposes *73 FR 2854 Phosphors 1-16-08*
- 73 Fed. Reg. 64946 (Oct. 31, 2008) Toxic Substances Control Act Inventory Status of Carbon Nanotubes *73 FR 64946 Nanotubes 10-31-08*
- 74 Fed. Reg. 57430 (Nov. 6, 2009) Proposed Significant New Use Rules on Certain Chemical Substances *74 FR 57430 Nano SNURs 11-6-09*
- E-mail from David E. Giamporcaro, Industry and Small Business Liaison, EPA, Clarification of Applicability of Significant New Use Rules to Listserv (July 28, 2009) *Clarification of nanotube SNURs 7 28 09*
- EPA's Draft Questions & Answers for the New Chemicals Program (undated) PMN Q&A *Draft PMN Q&A*
- EPA, Office of Toxic Substances, 1989 TSCA Industry Seminar Questions & Answers (undated) *Industry Seminar Q&A 1989*
- In The Matter Of Concord Trading Corporation, Docket No. TSCA-94-H-19 (EPA Office of Administrative Law Judges July 24, 1997) *Concord Trading 7-24-97*
- Letter from Edwin F. Tinsworth, Acting Director of Office of Toxic Substances, EPA, to Geraldine V. Cox, Chemical Manufacturers Association, captioned "Nonisolated Intermediate Definition" (undated) *Tinsworth Letter*
- Letter from Tracy C. Williamson, Ph.D., Chief, Industrial Chemistry Branch, EPA, to Michael P. Walls, American Chemistry Council (May 28, 2008) *Williamson Letter*
- Nanoscale Materials Stewardship Program Interim Report (Jan. 2009) *NMSP Interim Rep 1-09*
- Question and Answer Summary, EPA Seminar on Industry Obligations under TSCA (June 10, 1986) OTS Existing Chemicals Program (July 28, 1986) *Industry Obligations Q&A 1986*
- Semiannual Regulatory Agenda, EPA-230-Z-109-001 (Spring 2009) *Spring 2009 Semiannual Reg A*

- Regulatory Plan and Semiannual Regulatory Agenda, EPA-230-Z-09-002, 111-112 (Fall 2009) *Semiannual Reg Agenda Fall 2009*
- The Phosphor Letters, including Memorandum from Linda Travers, Director, Information Management Division, EPA to Charles Elkins, Director, Office of Toxic Substances, EPA, TSCA Reportability of Doped Semiconductors (Undated); Letter from Dr. Vincent DeCarlo, EPA to Carmen Venezia of Sylvania (Oct. 12, 1979); Letter from Henry Lau, EPA, to Robert Kovalak of General Electric (Mar. 5, 1982) *Phosphor Letters*
- TSCA Inventory Status of Nanoscale Substances—General Approach (Jan. 23, 2008) *Nano Inventory Status 1-23-08*
- TSCA Questions and Answers from the October, 1990 EPA-Industry Living with TSCA Workshop (Oct.1992) *Living with TSCA Q&A 1990*
- Toxic Substances Control Act Inventory Representation For Chemical Substances Of Unknown Or Variable Composition, Complex Reaction Products And Biological Materials: UVCB Substances *UVCB Substances*
- Toxic Substances Control Act Inventory Representation For Combinations of Two Or More Substances: Complex Reaction Products *Complex Reaction Products*
- Toxic Substances Control Act Inventory Representation For Products Containing Two Or More Substances: Formulated And Statutory Mixtures *Formulated & Statutory Mixtures*

On Internet:

- EPA's Draft Questions & Answers for the New Chemicals Program (undated), *available at http://www.epa.gov/oppt/newchems/pubs/qanda-newchems.pdf*
- In The Matter Of Concord Trading Corporation, Docket No. TSCA-94-H-19. (EPA Office of Administrative Law Judges July 24, 1997), *available at http://www.epa.gov/oalj/orders/cconcord.htm*
- Nanoscale Materials Stewardship Program Interim Report (Jan. 2009), *available at http://www.epa.gov/oppt/nano/nmsp-interim-report-final.pdf*
- Semiannual Regulatory Agenda, EPA-230-Z-109-001 (Spring 2009), *available at http://www.epa.gov/lawsregs/documents/regagendabook-spring09.pdf*
- The Project on Emerging Nanotechnologies' nanomaterial consumer product inventory, *available at http://www.nanotechproject.org/inventories/consumer/*
- Toxic Substances Control Act Inventory Representation For Products Containing Two Or More Substances: Formulated And Statutory Mixtures, *available through http://www.epa.gov/oppt/newchems/pubs/guideman.htm*

- TSCA Inventory Status of Nanoscale Substances—General Approach (Jan. 23, 2008), *available at http://www.epa.gov/oppt/nano/nmsp-inventorypaper2008.pdf*
- TSCA Nanoscale Materials Inventory Paper: Public Comments with EPA Responses, EPA-HQ-OPPT-2004-0122-0098(Dec. 20, 2007), *available at www.regulations.gov* in Docket ID: EPA-HQ-OPPT-2004-0122

B. Chapter 3 The Inventory Resources

On CD:

- 42 Fed. Reg. 64572 (Dec. 23, 1977) Inventory Reporting Requirements *42 FR 64572 Inventory 12-23-77*
- 43 Fed. Reg. 9254 (Mar. 6, 1978) Inventory Reporting Regulations Supplemental Clarification and Notice of Meetings *43 FR 9254 Inventory Clarify 3-6-78*
- 45 Fed. Reg. 50544 (Jul. 29, 1980) Availability of TSCA Revised Inventory (addressing corrections) *45 FR 50544 Inventory 7-29-80*
- 51 Fed. Reg. 21438 (June 12, 1986) Partial Updating of TSCA Inventory Data Base; Production and Site Reports; Final Rule *51 FR 21438 IUR 6-12-86*
- 54 Fed. Reg. 27174 (June 28, 1989) Polymers Manufactured Using Free-Radical Initiators; Clarification of Reporting Requirements *54 FR 27174 Free Radicals 6-28-89*
- 59 Fed. Reg. 53461 (Oct. 24, 1994) TSCA Inventory; Notice of Intent to Remove 38 Reported Chemical Substances from the TSCA Inventory *59 FR 53461 Inv Removals 10-24-94*
- 60 Fed. Reg. 16298 (Mar. 29, 1995) Premanufacture Notification; Revisions of Premanufacture Notification Regulations; Final Rule *60 FR 16298 PMN Revisions 3-29-95*
- 60 Fed. Reg. 16316 (Mar. 29, 1995) Premanufacture Notification Exemptions; Revisions of Exemptions for Polymers; Final Rule *60 FR 16316 Polymer Exempt 3-29-95*
- 60 Fed. Reg. 33201 (June 27, 1995) TSCA Chemical Substance Inventory Removal of 36 Incorrectly Reported Chemical Substances from the TSCA Inventory *60 FR 33201 Inv Removals 6-27-95*
- 70 Fed. Reg. 75059 (Dec. 19, 2005) TSCA Inventory Update Reporting Revisions *70 FR 75059 IUR 12-19-05*
- EPA, The TSCA Inventory, Submitting Successful Corrections, (undated) *Corrections*
- Enforcement Response Policy for Reporting and Recordkeeping Rules and Requirements for TSCA Sections 8, 12 and 13 *Reporting Rule ERP*

- EPA's Draft Questions & Answers for the New Chemicals Program (undated) PMN Q&A *Draft PMN Q&A*
- Polymer Exemption Guidance Manual EPA 744-B-97-001(June 1997) *Polymer Exemption Guidance Manual*
- Toxic Substances Control Act Inventory Representation For Certain Chemical Substances Containing Varying Carbon Chain Lengths (Alkyl Ranges Using The CX-Y Notation) *Alkyl Ranges*
- Toxic Substances Control Act Inventory Representation For Chemical Substances Of Unknown Or Variable Composition, Complex Reaction Products And Biological Materials: UVCB Substances *UVCB Substances*
- Toxic Substances Control Act Inventory Representation For Combinations of Two Or More Substances: Complex Reaction Products *Complex Reaction Products*
- Toxic Substances Control Act Inventory Representation For Polymeric Substances *Polymeric Substances*
- Toxic Substances Control Act Inventory Representation For Products Containing Two Or More Substances: Formulated And Statutory Mixtures *Formulated & Statutory Mixtures*

On Internet:

- Enforcement Response Policy for Reporting and Recordkeeping Rules and Requirements for TSCA Sections 8, 12 and 13, *available at http://www.epa.gov/compliance/resources/policies/civil/tsca/erp8_12r.pdf*
- In Re Dic Americas, Inc., TSCA Appeal No. 94-2, Final Decision and Order, Environmental Appeals Board (Sept. 27, 1995), *available at http://www.epa.gov/eab/disk9/dicameri.pdf*
- Instructions for Reporting for the 2006 Partial Updating of the TSCA Chemical Inventory Fred Arnold, EPA Economics, Exposure and Technology Division, Office of Pollution Prevention and Toxics, Aaron Osborne, ERG (undated), *available at http://www.epa.gov/oppt/iur/pubs/spring_2006_iur_training.pdf*
- IUR case studies, slides and Q&As are *available through http://www.epa.gov/oppt/iur/*
- Kanto consent agreement Consent Agreement, TSCA-HQ-2007-5011. Environmental Appeals Board (Entered Oct. 5, 2007), *available at http://yosemite.epa.gov/OA/EAB_WEB_Docket.nsf/Verity%20View/DB6DDB340C1359E88525737000445303/$File/cafo…200000000.pdf*
- Pertinent sections of the regulations in the Code of Federal Regulations are *available at http://ecfr.gpoaccess.gov/cgi/t/text/text-idx?sid=6b48a819a970c79bdd997d8291f7f120&c=ecfr&tpl=/ecfrbrowse/Title40/40cfrv30_02.tpl*

- The Polymer Exemption Guidance Manual EPA 744-B-97-001 (June 1997), *available through http://www.epa.gov/oppt/newchems/pubs/guideman.htm*
- The public Inventory can be partially accessed without charge at the EPA's Substance Registry Service at *http://iaspub.epa.gov/sor_internet/registry/substreg/home/overview/home.do*
- Toxic Substances Control Act Inventory Representation For Certain Chemical Substances Containing Varying Carbon Chain Lengths (Alkyl Ranges Using The CX-Y Notation), *available through http://www.epa.gov/opptintr/newchems/pubs/guideman.htm*
- Toxic Substances Control Act Inventory Representation For Chemical Substances Of Unknown or Variable Composition, Complex Reaction Products And Biological Materials: UVCB Substances, *available through http://www.epa.gov/opptintr/newchems/pubs/guideman.htm*
- Toxic Substances Control Act Inventory Representation For Combinations Of Two Or More Substances: Complex Reaction Products, *available through http://www.epa.gov/opptintr/newchems/pubs/guideman.htm*
- Toxic Substances Control Act Inventory Representation For Polymeric Substances can be accessed through *http://www.epa.gov/opptintr/newchems/pubs/guideman.htm*
- Toxic Substances Control Act Inventory Representation For Products Containing Two Or More Substances: Formulated And Statutory Mixtures, *available through http://www.epa.gov/opptintr/newchems/pubs/guideman.htm*
- U.S. Environmental Protection Agency, Office of Pollution Prevention and Toxics, Correcting IUR Submissions, *available at http://www.epa.gov/oppt/iur/pubs/guidance/correctingsubs.html.* For more information, see also *http://www.epa.gov/oppt/iur/index.html*

Procedures on CD:

- Model Procedure Template *Procedure Model*
- Procedure Number CORP. 17, Process or Design Change Review *Procedure Process Change*
- Procedure Number CORP. 19, Control of Nonconforming Commercial Product *Procedure Nonconf Product*
- Procedure Number CORP. 20, Assessment of New Suppliers *Procedure New Suppliers*
- Procedure Number CORP. 26, New Product Development *Procedure New Products*

C. Chapter 4 Premanufacture Notifications Resources

On CD:

- 42 Fed. Reg. 64572 (Dec. 23, 1977) Inventory Reporting Requirements *42 FR 64572 Inventory 12-23-77*
- 48 Fed. Reg. 21722 (May 13, 1983) Premanufacture Notification; Premanufacture Notice Requirements and Review Procedures *48 FR 21722 PMNs 5-13-83*
- 51 Fed. Reg. 15096 (Apr. 22, 1986) Toxic Substances; Revisions of Premanufacture Notification Regulations *51 FR 15096 PMN Revisions 4-22-86*
- 60 Fed. Reg. 16298 (Mar. 29, 1995) Premanufacture Notification; Revisions of Premanufacture Notification Regulations; Final Rule *60 FR 16298 PMN Revisions 3-29-95*
- 65 Fed. Reg. 19618 (Apr. 11, 2000) Incentives for Self-Policing: Discovery, Disclosure, Correction and Prevention of Violations *65 FR 16298 Audit Policy 4-11-00*
- 67 Fed. Reg. 76282 (Dec. 11, 2002) Sustainable Futures—Voluntary Pilot Project Under the TSCA New Chemicals Program; Notice *67 FR 76282 Sustainable 12-11-02*
- 73 Fed. Reg. 20921 (Apr. 17, 2008) Security and Prosperity Partnership; Notice of Public Meeting *73 FR 20921 Security Prosperity 4-17-08*
- 73 Fed. Reg. 44991 (Aug. 1, 2008) Interim Approach to Applying the Audit Policy to New Owners *73 FR 44991 Audit New Owners 8-1-08*
- 73 Fed. Reg. 78261 (Dec. 22, 2008) TSCA Section 5 Premanufacture and Significant New Use Notification Electronic Reporting; Revisions to Notification Regulations *73 FR 78261 PMN efiling 12-22-08*
- 75 Fed. Reg. 773 (Jan. 6, 2010) TSCA Section 5 Premanufacture and Significant New Use Notification Electronic Reporting; Revisions to Notification Regulations 75 FR 773 ePMNs 1-6-10
- Chemical Processing Under TSCA (1992)
  - *Chemical Processing part 1*
  - *Chemical Processing part 2*
  - *Chemical Processing part 3*
  - *Chemical Processing part 4*
  - *Chemical Processing part 5*
- Chemistry Assistance Manual for Premanufacture Notification Submitters, EPA 744-R-97-003 (1997)
  - *Chemistry Assistance Manual Intro*
  - *Chemistry Assistance Manual Ch 1*
  - *Chemistry Assistance Manual Ch 2*
  - *Chemistry Assistance Manual Ch 3*

    - *Chemistry Assistance Manual App*
    - *Chemistry Assistance Manual Index*
- EPA Draft Instruction Manual for Reporting under the TSCA § 5 New Chemicals Program (2003) *PMN Instruction Manual*
- EPA's Draft Questions & Answers for the New Chemicals Program (undated) PMN Q&A *Draft PMN Q&A*
- In The Matter of E. I. DuPont De Nemours & Co. Docket No. TSCA-III-731 (ALJ 1998) *DuPont ALJ 1998*
- Risk-Based Ecotoxicity model 5(e) order (Sept. 2004) *5 e Order Ecotoxicity*
- Sustainable Futures training introduction slides (Sustainable Futures intro and background and Sustainable Futures mechanism) *Sustainable Futures Slides*
- The NOC form *NOC form*
- The PMN form
    - *PMN e-Form*
    - *PMN paper form part 1*
    - *PMN paper form part 2*
- § 5 ERP amended and restated on June 8, 1989 *§ 5 ERP 1989*
- § 5 ERP amended by the Memorandum from John J. Neylan, Director, Policy and Grants Division, Office of Compliance Monitoring, to Michael J. Walker, Enforcement Counsel, Toxics Litigation Division, dated July 1, 1993 *§ 5 ERP 1993 amend*

On Internet:

- 40 C.F.R Part 720 is *available at http://ecfr.gpoaccess.gov/cgi/t/text/text-idx?c=ecfr&sid=a8476d2942e8f03d060b8c378e451cf6&rgn=div5&view=text&node=40:30.0.1.1.9&idno=40 and through http://www.gpoaccess.gov*
- Chemistry Assistance Manual for Premanufacture Notification Submitters, 105, EPA 744-R-97-003 (1997), *available at http://www.epa.gov/oppt/newchems/pubs/chem-pmn/*
- Summary of EPA's HPV Chemical Hazard Data Availability Study, *available at http://www.epa.gov/HPV/pubs/general/hazchem.htm*
- Information on initiating a test rule for orphan HPV chemicals, *available at http://www.epa.gov/hpvis/index.html*
- EPA Draft Instruction Manual for Reporting under the TSCA § 5 New Chemicals Program (2003) *available at http://www.epa.gov/oppt/newchems/*
- EPA's Draft Questions & Answers for the New Chemicals Program (undated) *available at http://www.epa.gov/oppt/newchems/pubs/qanda-newchems.pdf*

- EPA overheads entitled "Thought Starter: Resetting the TSCA Chemical Inventory?" (May 13, 2008), *available at http://www.epa.gov/CHAMP/pubs/inventoryreset.pdf*
- The EPA Web site with contact information for the Prenotice Coordinators is *http://www.epa.gov/oppt/newchems/pubs/roster.htm*
- The PMN form can be downloaded from *https://cdx.epa.gov/ssl/pmn/download.asp* and *http://www.epa.gov/opptintr/newchems/pubs/pmnpart1.pdf* and *http://www.epa.gov/opptintr/newchems/pubs/pmnpart2.pdf*
- The CDX system is described at http://www.epa.gov/cdx/index.htm
- The CAS Web site is *http://www.cas.org*
- In The Matter of E. I. Dupont De Nemours & Co. Docket No. TSCA-III-731 (ALJ 1998), *available at http://www.epa.gov/oalj/orders/denemour.htm*
- ALJ decisions are *available at http://www.epa.gov/oalj/orders.htm*
- The chemical categories are described together with their hazards and recommended testing at *http://www.epa.gov/oppt/newchems/pubs/cat02.htm*
- Production and exposure triggers for § 5(e) orders are *available at http://www.epa.gov/oppt/newchems/pubs/cat02.htm*
- EPA's Sustainable Futures Web site is *http://www.epa.gov/oppt/sf/*
- Sustainable Futures training introduction slides are *available at http://www.epa.gov/oppt/sf/presentations/sf/sfintro1.pdf*
- Excerpts from the OPPT Accomplishments Report (Jan. 2007 - June 2008), *available at http://www.epa.gov/oppt/ar/2007-2008/working/sustainable.htm*
- Model TSCA § 5(e) orders *available through http://www.epa.gov/opptintr/newchems/pubs/boilerpl.htm*
- The NOC form is *available at http://www.epa.gov/opptintr/newchems/pubs/filenoc.htm*
- § 5 ERP amended and restated (June 8, 1989) and further amended by in the Memorandum from John J. Neylan, Director, Policy and Grants Division, Office of Compliance Monitoring, to Michael J. Walker, Enforcement Counsel, Toxics Litigation Division (July 1, 1993), *available through http://cfpub.epa.gov/compliance/resources/policies/civil/tsca/*
- In the Matter of Fujifilm Manufacturing, U.S.A., Inc., Docket No. TSCA-HQ-2008-5029 (Oct. 20, 2008), *available through http://yosemite.epa.gov/oa/EAB_Web_Docket.nsf/Unpublished~Final~Orders?OpenView*
- In the Matter of Ashland, Inc., EAB Order in Docket Number TSCA-HQ-2007-5013 (Aug. 16, 2007), *available through http://yosemite.epa.gov/oa/EAB_Web_Docket.nsf/Unpublished~Final~Orders?OpenView*

Procedures on CD:

- Model Procedure Template *Procedure Model*
- Procedure Number CORP. 17, Process or Design Change Review *Procedure Process Change*
- Procedure Number CORP. 19, Control of Nonconforming Commercial Product *Procedure Nonconf Product*
- Procedure Number CORP. 20, Assessment of New Suppliers *Procedure New Suppliers*
- Procedure Number CORP. 26, New Product Development *Procedure New Products*
- Procedure Number Reg. Aff. 2, Premanufacture Notifications and Notices of Commencement *Procedure PMNs NOCs*
- Model Bona Fide Request for Inventory Listing *Procedure Bona Fide Letter*

D. Chapter 5 PMN Exclusions and Exemptions Resources

On CD:

- 46 Fed. Reg. 54688 (Nov. 3, 1981) Premanufacture Notification; Receipt of Petition Requesting Commencement of Exemption Rulemaking Proceedings *46 FR 54688 PMN Exemptions 11-3-81*
- 48 Fed. Reg. 21722 (May 13, 1983) Premanufacture Notification; Premanufacture Notice Requirements and Review Procedures *48 FR 21722 PMNs 5-13-83*
- 49 Fed. Reg. 46066 (Nov. 21, 1984) Premanufacture Notification Exemptions; Exemptions for Polymers *49 FR 46066 Polymer Exempt 11-21-84*
- 49 Fed. Reg. 50201 (Dec. 27, 1984) Premanufacture Notification; Proposed Revisions of Regulation *49 FR 46066 R&D 12-27-84*
- 50 Fed. Reg. 16477 (Apr. 26, 1985) Premanufacture Notification Exemption; Exemption for Chemical Substances Manufactured in Quantities of 1,000 Kg or Less Per Year *50 FR 16477 LVE 4-26-85*
- 51 Fed. Reg. 15096 (Apr. 22, 1986) Toxic Substances; Revisions of Premanufacture Notification Regulations *51 FR 15096 PMN Revisions 4-22-86*
- 58 Fed. Reg. 7661 (Feb. 8, 1993) Premanufacture Notification; Revisions of Premanufacture Notification Regulations; Proposed Rule *58 FR 7661 PMNs 2-8-93*
- 58 Fed. Reg. 7679 (Feb. 8, 1993) Premanufacture Notification Exemptions; Revisions of Exemptions for Polymers; Proposed Rule *58 FR 7679 Polymer Exempt 2-8-93*

- 60 Fed. Reg. 16316 (Mar. 29, 1995) Premanufacture Notification Exemptions; Revisions of Exemptions for Polymers; Final Rule *60 FR 16316 Polymer Exempt 3029-95*
- 60 Fed. Reg. 16336 (Mar. 29, 1995) Premanufacture Notification Exemption; Revision of Exemption for Chemical Substances Manufactured in Small Quantities; Low Release and Exposure Exemption; Final Rule *60 FR 16336 LVE LoREX 3-29-95*
- 64 Fed. Reg. 31987 (June 15, 1999) Recordkeeping Requirements for Low Volume Exemption and Low Release and Exposure Exemption; Technical Correction *64 FR 31987 LoREX 6-15-99*
- 67 Fed. Reg. 76282 (Dec. 11, 2002) Sustainable Futures—Voluntary Pilot Project Under the TSCA New Chemicals Program; Notice *67 FR 76282 Sustainable 12-11-02*
- 75 Fed. Reg. 4295 (Jan. 27, 2010) Premanufacture Notification Exemption for Polymers; Amendment of Polymer Exemption Rule to Exclude Certain Perfluorinated Polymers *75 FR 4295 Polymer Exempt 1-27-10*
- Amended TSCA Section 5 Enforcement Response Policy (Jan. 8, 1989) *Sect 5 ERP Amend 1-8-89*, as further amended by memorandum from John J. Neylan, III, Director, Policy and Grants Division, Office of Compliance Monitoring, Amendment to the TSCA Section 5 Enforcement Response Policy—Penalty Limit For Untimely Submissions (July 1, 1993) *Sect 5 ERP Amend 7-1-93*
- EPA Draft Instruction Manual for Reporting Under The TSCA § 5 New Chemicals Program (2003) *PMN Instruction Manual*
- EPA's Draft Questions & Answers for the New Chemicals Program (undated) *Draft PMN Q&A*
- Letter from Charles L. Elkins, Director, Offices of Toxic Substances, EPA to James E. Remsen of National Association of Printing Ink Manufacturers, Inc. (Mar. 27, 1990) in collection of *h 7 Letters*
- Letter from Joseph S. Carra, Deputy Director, Office of Pollution Prevention and Toxics, EPA, to redacted (June 29, 1994) in collection of *h 7 Letters*
- Letter from Mary E. Cushmac, Chief, Policy and Administrative Section, New Chemicals Branch, to Fred H. Parry of Hoechst Celanese Corporation (Aug. 12, 1994) in collection of *h 7 Letters*
- Toxic Substances Control Act Inventory Representation For Polymeric Substances *Polymeric Substances*
- TSCA Questions and Answers, October, 1992, From the October, 1990 EPA-Industry Living with TSCA Workshop *Living with TSCA Q&A 1990*
- TSCA Section 8(e) Reporting Guide, June 1991 *8e Reporting Guide 6-91*

On Internet:

- 40 C.F.R Part 720 is *available at http://ecfr.gpoaccess.gov/cgi/t/text/text-idx?c=ecfr&sid=a8476d2942e8f03d060b8c378e451cf6&rgn=div5&view=text&node=40:30.0.1.1.9&idno=40* and through *http://www.gpoaccess.gov*
- EPA, Draft Questions & Answers for the New Chemicals Program (undated), [hereinafter Draft PMN Q&A], *available at http://www.epa.gov/oppt/newchems/pubs/qanda-newchems.pdf*
- Polymer Exemption Guidance Manual, June 1997 is *available at http://www.epa.gov/oppt/newchems/pubs/polyguid.pdf*

Procedures on CD:

- Model Procedure Template *Procedure Model*
- Procedure Number Reg. Aff. 3, Procedure for the Test Marketing Exemption from PMN and SNUR Requirements*Procedure TME*
- Procedure Number Reg. Aff. 4, Procedure for LVE and LoREX Exemptions from PMN Requirements *Procedure LVE LoREX*
- Procedure Number Lab. 11, Qualifying for the R&D Exemption at Laboratories *Procedure R&D Labs*
- Procedure Number Lab. 5, Sampling R&D Substances to Third Parties *Procedure Sampling*
- Procedure Number Pilot Plant 11, Qualifying for the R&D Exemption at Pilot Plants *Procedure R&D Pilot Plants*

E. Chapter 6 Microorganisms Resources

On CD:

- 62 Fed. Reg. 17910 (Apr. 11, 1997) Microbial Products of Biotechnology; Final Regulation Under the Toxic Substances Control Act; Final Rule *62 FR 17910 Microorgs 4-11-97*
- EPA, Microbial Products Of Biotechnology Final Regulation Under The Toxic Substances Control Act A Summary of The Public's Comments And The Agency's Response (Mar. 26, 1997) *Microbial Comments 3-26-97*
- Identification of Microorganisms Currently Listed on the TSCA Chemical Substance Inventory (Aug. 31, 1994) *Microorg Listing 8-31-94*

On Internet:

- EPA, Microbial Products Of Biotechnology Final Regulation Under The Toxic Substances Control Act A Summary of The Public's Comments And The Agency's Response, *available at http://www.epa.gov/oppt/biotech/pubs/pdf/c006.pdf*
- Identification of Microorganisms Currently Listed on the TSCA Chemical Substance Inventory (Aug. 31, 1994), *available at http://www.epa.gov/biotech_rule/pubs/pdf/listing.pdf*

F. Chapter 7 Reporting and Recordkeeping Resources

On CD:

- 43 Fed. Reg. 11110 (Mar. 16, 1978) Statement of Interpretation and Enforcement Policy; Notification of Substantial Risk *43 FR 11110 8e Interpretation 3-16-78*
- 68 Fed. Reg. 33129 (June 3, 2003) TSCA Section 8(e); Notification of Substantial Risk; Policy Clarification and Reporting Guidance *68 FR 33129 8e Clarification 6-3-09*
- 70 Fed. Reg. 2162 (Jan. 12, 2005) TSCA Section 8(e) Reporting Guidance; Correction, Clarification of Applicability, and Announcement Regarding the Issuance Questions and Answers *70 FR 2162 8e Clarification 1-12-05*
- 75 Fed. Reg. 3462 (Jan. 21, 2010) Claims of Confidentiality of Certain Chemical Identities Submitted under Section 8(e) of the Toxic Substances Control Act *75 FR 3462 8e Confidential 1-21-10*
- EPA, Frequent Questions, January 2005 and September 2006 *8e Frequent Questions 11-26-09*
- EPA, Comment And Response Document For Revised Policy Statement Of Section 8(e) of TSCA, OPPT-2002-0067-0002 (Feb. 20, 2003) *8e Comments 2-20-03*
- EPA, Office of Toxic Substances, Section 8(e) Reporting Guide (June 1991) *8e Reporting Guide 6-91*
- EPA, TSCA Section 8(c) Final Rule Questions and Answers, 2 (Nov. 1983) *8(c) QA 11-83*
- Letter from Susan H. Wayland, Deputy Assistant Administrator, EPQ, to multiple recipients, concerning HPV and 8(e) reporting (Oct. 14, 1999) *Wayland HPV Letter 10-14-99*
- Letter from Victor Kimm, Deputy Assistant Administrator, Office of Prevention, Pesticides, and Toxic Substances, EPA, to Robert M. Sussman (April 2, 1992) *8e Kimm Letter 4-2-92*

- Toxic and Pesticides Enforcement Division, Office of Regulatory Enforcement, Office of Enforcement and Compliance Assurance, EPA., Revised March 31, 1999, Effective June 1, 1999 Reporting Rule ERP
- TSCA Health & Safety Study Cover Sheet (both pdf and Word versions) *8e cover sheet pdf 8e cover sheet Word*
- Questions and Answers Concerning the TSCA Section 8(c) Rule, Questions Received at: Seminar on Toxic Substances Control Act Section 8(c) Recordkeeping and Reporting Allegations of Adverse Reactions November 10, 1983 (July 1984) *8c QA 7-84*

On Internet:

- § 8(e) submittals made since mid-2004 are posted on the EPA Web site at http://www.epa.gov/opptintr/tsca8e/pubs/8eandfyisubmissions.html. The EPA posts the 8(e) submittals in pdf format
- Frequent Questions, January 2005 and September 2006 is *available at* http://www.epa.gov/opptintr/tsca8e/pubs/frequentlyaskedquestionsfaqs.htm
- TSCA Health & Safety Study Cover Sheet, *available through www.regulations.gov* in Docket No. EPA-HQ-OPPT-2006-0499

Procedures on CD:

- Model Procedure Template *Procedure Model*
- Introduction to the TSCA § 8(e) Reporting Checklists *Procedure Reporting Checklists*

Accompanying Checklists:

- Environmental 8e Checklist Enviro:
  - Checklist to Determine Whether Non-Emergency Incidents of Contamination are Reportable Under Section V (b)(1) of EPA's 2003 Policy Statement
  - Checklist to Determine Whether Previously Unknown Bioaccumulation or Presence in Organisms is Reportable Based on Section V(b)(2) of EPA's 2003 Policy Statement
  - Checklist to Determine Whether Previously Unknown Environmental Effects are Reportable Based on Section V(b)(3) (4) and (5) of EPA's 2003 Policy Statement
  - Checklist to Determine Whether Emergency Incidents of Environmental Contamination are Reportable Under TSCA 8(e) Based on Section V(c) of EPA's 2003 Policy Statement
- Checklist to Determine Whether a Multigeneration Reproduction or Reproductive/Developmental Study is 8(e) Reportable *8e Checklist Multirep and Repdev*

- Checklist to Determine Whether a Sensitization Study is 8(e) Reportable *8e Checklist Sensitizn*
- Checklist to Determine Whether a LD50/LC50 Test is 8(e) Reportable *8e Checklist LD LC50*
- Subacute/Subchronic/Chronic studies *8e Checklist Subacute:*
  - Checklist to Determine Whether a Subacute/Subchronic/Chronic Study is 8(e) Reportable
- Checklist to Determine Whether A Study Exhibits Neurotoxic Effects
- Checklist to Determine Whether Skin or Eye Irritation/Corrosivity Study is 8(e) Reportable *8e Checklist SkinEye*

G. Chapter 8 Exports and Imports Resources

On CD:

- 42 Fed. Reg. 64572 (Dec. 23, 1977) Inventory Reporting Requirements *42 FR 64572 Inventory 12-23-77*
- 45 Fed. Reg. 79730 (Dec. 1, 1980) Special Classes of Merchandise *45 FR 79730 Customs 12-1-80*
- 45 Fed. Reg. 82844 (Dec. 16, 1980) Chemical Imports and Exports; Notification of Export *45 FR 82844 Exports 12-16-80*
- 48 Fed. Reg. 34734 (Aug. 1, 1983) Customs Regulations Amendments Relating to Special Classes of Merchandise *48 FR 34734 Customs 8-1-83*
- 48 Fed. Reg. 55462 (Dec. 13, 1983) Chemical Imports and Exports; General Import Requirements and Restrictions Policy for Import of Chemical Substances *48 FR 55462 Imports 12-13-83*
- 57 Fed. Reg. 58390 (Dec. 9, 1992) Prior Informed Consent Information-Sharing Program; Notice of Participation *57 FR 58390 PIC 12-9-92*
- 58 Fed. Reg. 40238 (Jul. 27, 1993) Export Notification Requirement; Change to Reporting Requirements *58 FR 40238 Export Changes 7-27-93*
- 65 Fed. Reg. 10701 (Feb. 29, 2000) Importation of Chemicals Subject to the Toxic Substances Control Act *65 FR 10701 Customs Imports 2-29-00*
- 71 Fed. Reg. 66234 (Nov. 14, 2006) Export Notification; Change to Reporting Requirements *71 FR 66234 Exports 11-14-06*
- 1989 TSCA Industry Seminar Questions & Answers *Industry Seminar Q&A 1989*
- Compliance Guide For the Chemical Import Requirements of the Toxic Substances Control Act (EPA 305-B-08-001), U.S. EPA, Office of Enforcement and Compliance Assurance (June 2008) *Import Compliance Guide 6-08*

- EPA, Office of Enforcement & Compliance Assurance EPA 305-8-99-001 Introduction to the Chemical Import Requirements of the Toxic Substances Control Act (June 1999) *Import Introduction 7-99*
- Question and Answer Summary, EPA Seminar on Industry Obligations Under TSCA, OTS Existing Chemicals Division (May 5, 1987) *Industry Obligations QA 5-87*
- The Enforcement Response Policy for Reporting and Recordkeeping Rules and Requirements for TSCA Sections 8, 12 and 13, Toxic and Pesticides Enforcement Division, Office of Regulatory Enforcement, Office of Enforcement and Compliance Assurance, U.S. E.P.A., Revised March 31, 1999, Effective June 1, 1999 *Reporting Rule ERP*
- TSCA Questions and Answers, October 1992 From the October, 1990 EPA-Industry Living with TSCA Workshop *Living with TSCA Q&A 1990*
- Toxic Substances Control Act: A Guide for Chemical Importers/ Exporters (EPA 560/1-91-001), U.S. EPA, Office of Toxic Substances (Apr. 1991) *Import Export Guide 4-91*

On Internet:

- Current List of Chemical Substances Subject to TSCA Section 12(b) Export Notification Requirements, *available at http://www.epa.gov/oppt/import-export/pubs/12blist.pdf*
- Current List of Sunset Dates/Status for Chemicals Subject to Section 4 Actions, *available at http://www.epa.gov/oppt/chemtest/pubs/sunsettable.html*
- EPA web based data base of every chemical regulated under TSCA, *available at http://iaspub.epa.gov/sor_internet/registry/substreg/home/overview/home.do*
- Compliance Guide For the Chemical Import Requirements of the Toxic Substances Control Act (EPA 305-B-08-001), U.S. EPA, Office of Enforcement and Compliance Assurance (June 2008), *available at http://www.epa.gov/compliance/resources/publications/monitoring/tsca/importguidejune2008.pdf*

Procedures on CD:

- Model Procedure Template *Procedure Model*
- Procedure Number International Operations 6, Importing Chemical Substances *Procedure Imports*
- Procedure Number International Operations 7, Exporting Commercial Shipments *Procedure Exports*

H. Chapter 9 Test Rules Resources

On CD:

- 58 Fed. Reg. 28736 (May 14, 1993), TSCA Section 4(a)(1)(B) Final Statement of Policy; Criteria for evaluating Substantial Production, Substantial Release, and Substantial or Significant Human Exposure *58 FR 28736 Test Rules 5-14-93*
- Enforcement Response Policy for Test Rules Under Section 4 of the Toxic Substances Control Act (May 28, 1986) *Sect 4 Test Rule ERP*
- TSCA Good Laboratory Practices Regulations Enforcement Response Policy (Apr. 9, 1985) *Sect 4 GLP ERP*

On Internet:

- Enforcement Response Policy for Test Rules Under Section 4 of the Toxic Substances Control Act (May 28, 1986), *available at http://www.epa.gov/compliance/resources/policies/civil/tsca/tscasec4ruleserp-052886.pdf*
- Interagency Testing Committee reports are *available through http://www.epa.gov/opptintr/itc*
- Regulations governing test rules are *available through http://www.epa.gov/oppt/chemtest/pubs/790_799.html*
- Semiannual Regulatory Agenda, EPA-230-Z-109-001 (Spring 2009), *available at http://www.epa.gov/lawsregs/documents/regagendabook-spring09.pdf*
- Regulatory Plan and Semiannual Regulatory Agenda, EPA-230-Z-09-002, 111-112 (Fall 2009), *available at http://www.epa.gov/lawsregs/documents/regagendabook-fall09.pdf*
- Sunset Dates of Chemicals Subject to Final TSCA Section 4 and Related 12(b) Actions, (Sept. 1, 2009) *available at* http://www.epa.gov/oppt/chemtest/pubs/sunsettable.html
- Fluoropolymer and fluorotelomer testing information and information on enforceable consent agreements concerning them is available on the EPA Web site at http://www.epa.gov/oppt/pfoa/pubs/pfoainfo.html#pfos

I. Chapter 10 Voluntary Initiatives Resources

On CD:

- 65 Fed. Reg. 81658 (Dec. 26, 2000) Testing of Certain High Production Volume Chemicals *65 FR 81658 HPV Test Rule Proposal 12-26-00*

- 65 Fed. Reg. 81686 (Dec. 26, 2000) Data Collection and Development on Certain High Production Volume (HPV) Chemicals *65 FR 81686 HPV 12-26-00*
- 65 Fed. Reg. 81700 (Dec. 26, 2000) Voluntary Children's Chemical Evaluation Program *65 FR 81700 VCCEP 12-26-00*
- 71 Fed. Reg. 13708 (Mar. 16, 2006) Testing of Certain High Production Volume Chemicals *71 FR 13708 HPV Test Rule 3-16-06*
- 71 Fed. Reg. 47122 (Aug. 16, 2006) Preliminary Assessment Information Reporting; Addition of Certain Chemicals *71 FR 47122 HPV PAIR 8-16 06*
- 71 Fed. Reg. 47130 (Aug. 16, 2006) Health and Safety Data Reporting; Addition of Certain Chemicals *71 FR 47130 HPV 8d 8-16-00*
- 71 Fed. Reg. 57439 (Sept. 29, 2006) Withdrawal of Certain Chemical Substances from Preliminary Assessment Information Reporting and Health and Safety Data Reporting Rules *71 FR 57439 HPV 9-29-06*
- 71 Fed. Reg. 67121 (Nov. 20, 2006) Implementation of the Pilot Voluntary Children's Chemical Evaluation Program; Request for Comment *71 FR 67121 VCCEP 11-20-06*
- 72 Fed. Reg. 21119 (Apr. 30, 2007) Removal of Two Chemical Substances from Preliminary Assessment Information Reporting and Health and Safety Data Reporting Rules *72 FR 21119 HPV 4-30-07*
- 73 Fed. Reg. 4861 (Jan. 28, 2008) Nanoscale Materials Stewardship Program *73 FR 4861 Nano Stewardship 1-28-08*
- 73 Fed. Reg. 36512 (June 27, 2008) Modification of the Voluntary Children's Chemical Evaluation Program; Notice of Public Meeting *73 FR 36512 VCCEP mods 6-27-08*
- 73 Fed. Reg. 43314 (July 24, 2008) Testing of Certain High Production Volume Chemicals; Second Group of Chemicals; Proposed Rule *73 FR 43314 HPV Test Rule 6-24-08*

On Internet:

- Chemical Right to Know Initiative background information is *available at* Background on this initiative is *available at http://www.epa.gov/hpv/pubs/general/rtkfaqs.htm#What%20CRTK*
- Environmental Defense Fund, Toxic Ignorance: The Continuing Absence of Basic Health Testing for Top-Selling Chemicals in the United States (1997), *available at http://www.edf.org/documents/243_toxicignorance.pdf.*
- Environmental Defense, High Hopes, Low Marks A Final Report Card On The High Production Volume Chemical Challenge, (2007), *available at http://www.edf.org/documents/6653_HighHopesLowMarks.pdf*

- EPA homepage for the High Production Volume program is *http://www.epa.gov/hpv/index.htm*
- EPA, Nanoscale Materials Stewardship Program, *available through http://www.epa.gov/oppt/nano/stewardship.htm*
- EPA, Nanoscale Materials Stewardship Program Interim Report (Jan., 2009), *available through http://www.epa.gov/oppt/nano/*
- EPA, Office of Pollution Prevention and Toxics, Chemical Hazard Data: What Do We Really Know About the Safety of High Production Volume Chemicals? (Apr. 1998), *available at http://www.epa.gov/hpv/pubs/general/hazchem.pdf*
- EPA, Office of Pollution Prevention and Toxics, Status and Future Directions of the High Production Volume Challenge Program, EPA 743-R-04-001, 9-10 (Nov. 2004) *available at http://www.epa.gov/hpv/pubs/general/hpvstatr.htm*
- EPA Toxic Release Inventory data is *available through http://www.epa.gov/tri/tridata*
- High Production Volume Chemicals data is available from the EPA system at *http://www.epa.gov/HPV/hpvis/index.html.* There is also a list of new additions to that data at *http://www.epa.gov/HPV/whatsnew.htm*
- Interim VCCEP Evaluation, Summary of Comments On the VCCEP Pilot Program, U.S. Environmental Protection Agency, Office of Pollution Prevention and Toxics, Chemical Information and Testing Branch, Compiled by Eastern Research Group, Inc. (Mar. 18, 2007), *available at http://www.epa.gov/oppt/vccep/pubs/summaryrpt.pdf*
- Letter October 14, 1999 from Susan H. Wayland, Deputy Assistant Administrator, U.S. E.P.A. (Oct. 14, 1999), *available at http://www.epa.gov/HPV/pubs/general/ceoltr2.htm*
- Montreal Protocol documents, concerning the phase out of ozone depleting chemicals are *available at http://www.epa.gov/history/topics/montreal/index.htm*
- OECD, Guidance for Developing Robust Summaries for SIDS Dossiers (Document number ENV/JM/EXCH(99), Oct.8 1999), *available at http://www.epa.gov/chemrtk/pubs/general/robsumgd.htm*
- Orphan chemicals list for the HPV Challenge Program is revised periodically and is *available at http://www.epa.gov/hpv/pubs/general/hpvunspn.pdf*
- Responsible Care© is described at *http://www.americanchemistry.com/s_responsiblecare/sec.asp?CID=1298&DID=4841*
- Voluntary Children's Chemical Evaluation Program ("VCCEP") materials are *available at http://www.epa.gov/oppt/vccep/index.html*

J. Chapter 11 Bans and Restrictions Resources

On CD:

- 43 Fed. Reg. 7150 (Feb. 17, 1978) Polychlorinated Biphenyls (PCB's) *43 FR 7150 PCBs 2-17-78*
- 44 Fed. Reg. 31514 (May 31, 1979) Polychlorinated Biphenyls (PCBs) Manufacturing, Processing, Distribution in Commerce, and Use Prohibitions *44 FR 31514 PCB limits 5-31-79*
- 72 Fed. Reg. 57235 (Oct. 9, 2007) Transfer of Polychlorinated Biphenyl Cleanup and Disposal Program from the Office of Prevention, Pesticides and Toxic Substances to the Office of Solid Waste and Emergency Response *72 FR 57235 PCB management 10-9-07*
- EPA, January 2009 Version, Revisions to the PCB Q and A Manual (Jan. 2009) *PCB Q&A Manual 1-09* Check for updates at *http://www.epa.gov/epawaste/hazard/tsd/pcbs/pubs/guidance.htm#QandA*
- EPA, Long-Chain Perfluorinated Chemicals (PFCs) Action Plan (Dec. 30, 2009) *Action Plan PFCs 12-30-09*
- EPA, Polybrominated Diphenyl Ethers (PBDEs) Action Plan, (Dec. 30, 2009) *Action Plan PBDEs 12-30-09*
- EPA, Pthalates Action Plan (Dec. 30, 2009) *Action Plan Phtalates 12-30-09*
- EPA, Short-Chain Chlorinated Paraffins (SCCPs) and Other Chlorinated Paraffins Action Plan, 8 (Dec. 30, 2009) *Action Plan Paraffins 12-30-09*
- EPA, TSCA Assistance Office and Exposure Evaluation Division, Office of Toxic Substances, The PCB Regulations Under TSCA: Over 100 Questions and Answers to Help You Meet These Requirements 740R83101 (Aug. 1983) *PCB Q&A 11-83*
- Memorandum from Susan Parker Bodine and James Guilliford, Administration of PCB Program, EPA (Mar. 6, 2008) *PCB management memo 3-6-08*
- Memorandum from Susan Parker Bodine, Re-Delegation of OSWER's Management of the Disposal and Cleanup of Polychlorinated Biphenyls (PCBs) (Feb. 11, 2008) *PCB management memo 2-11-08*
- PCB Inspection Manual, EPA-305-X-04-003, (Aug. 2004) *PCB Instruction Man 8-04*
- Polychlorinated Biphenyls (PCB) Penalty Policy (Apr. 9, 1990) *PCB Penalty Policy 4-9-90*
- Robert E. Fabricant, Interpretive Statement on Change in Ownership of Real Property Contaminated with PCBs (Aug. 14, 2003) *PCB change in ownership 8-14-03*

On Internet:

- EPA homepage for PCBs is at *http://www.epa.gov/epawaste/hazard/tsd/pcbs/index.htm*
- EPA Office of Compliance, National Enforcement Trends (NETS) Report (May 2009), G-1b, *available through http://www.epa.gov/compliance/data/results/nets.html#numbers*
- EPA, Long-Chain Perfluorinated Chemicals (PFCs) Action Plan (Dec. 30, 2009) *available through http://www.epa.gov/oppt/existingchemicals/pubs/actionplans/pfcs.html*
- EPA, Polybrominated Diphenyl Ethers (PBDEs) Action Plan, (Dec. 30, 2009), available through http://www.epa.gov/oppt/existingchemicals/pubs/actionplans/pbde.html
- EPA, Pthalates Action Plan (Dec. 30, 2009), *available through http://www.epa.gov/oppt/existingchemicals/pubs/actionplans/phthalates.htm*l
- EPA, Short-Chain Chlorinated Paraffins (SCCPs) and Other Chlorinated Paraffins Action Plan, 8 (Dec. 30, 2009), *available through http://www.epa.gov/oppt/existingchemicals/pubs/actionplans/sccps.html*
- EPA Web site with PCB guidance materials is at *http://www.epa.gov/epawaste/hazard/tsd/pcbs/pubs/guidance.htm#QandA*
- In re Ray Birnbaum Scrap Yard, TSCA Appeal No. 92-5 (EAB, 1994), *available at http://www.epa.gov/eab/disk5/raybirn.pdf*
- In the Matter of Nello Santacroce & Dominic Fanelli d/b/a Gilroy Associates, EAB Appeal No. 92-6 (1993), *available at http://www.epa.gov/eab/disk3/nello.pdf*
- Notification of PCB Activity, EPA Form 7710-53, used to notify the EPA of disposal activities, *available at http://www.epa.gov/epawaste/hazard/tsd/pcbs/pubs/771053.pdf*
- PCB Transformer Registration Form, EPA form 7720-12, *available at http://www.epa.gov/epawaste/hazard/tsd/pcbs/pubs/772012.pdf*
- Polychlorinated Biphenyls (PCB) Penalty Policy, *available through http://cfpub.epa.gov/compliance/resources/policies/civil/tsca/*
- William P. Kucewicz, Public Health Implications Of Polychlorinated Biphenyls (PCBs) In The Environment, A Position Paper of the American Council of Science and Health, 2005, *available at http://www.acsh.org/publications/pubID.1030/pub_detail.asp*

K. Chapter 12 Significant New Use Rules Resources

On CD

- 48 Fed. Reg. 21722 (May 13, 1983) Premanufacture Notification; Premanufacture Notice Requirements and Review Procedures *48 FR 21722 PMNs 5-13-83*
- 49 Fed. Reg. 35011 (Sept. 5, 1984) Significant New Uses of Chemical Substances; Certain Chemicals *49 FR 35011 SNURS 9-5-84*
- 52 Fed. Reg. 15594 (Apr. 29, 1987) Significant New Uses of Chemical Substances; General Provisions for New Chemical Follow-Up *52 FR 15594 SNURs 4-29-87*
- 53 Fed. Reg. 28354 (July 27, 1988) Significant New Use Rules; Amendments to General Provisions *53 FR 28354 SNURs 7-27-88*
- 54 Fed. Reg. 31298 (July 27, 1989) Significant New Use Rules; General Provisions for New Chemical Follow-Up *54 FR 31298 SNURs 7-27-89*
- 73 Fed. Reg. 65743 (Nov. 5, 2008) Significant New Use Rules on Certain Chemical Substances *73 FR 65743 Nano SNUR 11-5-08*
- 73 Fed. Reg. 78261 (Dec. 22, 2008) TSCA Section 5 Premanufacture and Significant New Use Notification Electronic Reporting; Revisions to Notification Regulations *73 FR 78261 PMN efiling 12-22-08*
- Amended TSCA Section 5 Enforcement Response Policy (Jan. 8, 1989) *Sect 5 ERP Amend 1-8-89*, as further amended by memorandum from John J. Neylan, III, Director, Policy and Grants Division, Office of Compliance Monitoring, Amendment to the TSCA Section 5 Enforcement Response Policy—Penalty Limit For Untimely Submissions (July 1, 1993) *Sect 5 ERP Amend 7-1-93*

On Internet:

- EPA's Questions and Answers for the New Chemicals Program, undated draft available on the EPA Web site through *http://www.epa.gov/oppt/newchems/pubs/guideman.htm*
- The EPA's Substance Registry Service is on the EPA Web site at *http://iaspub.epa.gov/sor_internet/registry/substreg/home/overview/home.do*

Procedures on CD:

- Model Procedure Template *Procedure Model*
- Procedure Number Reg. Aff. 3, Procedures for PMN and SNUR Exemptions Needing EPA Approvals: The Test Marketing Exemption *Procedure TME*
- Procedure Number Lab. 5, Sampling R&D Substances to Third Parties *Procedure Sampling*
- Model Bona Fide Request for Inventory Listing *Procedure Bona Fide Letter*

L. Chapter 13 Compliance Programs Resources

On CD:

- 65 Fed. Reg. 19618 (Apr. 11, 2000) Incentives for Self-Policing: Discovery, Disclosure, Correction and Prevention of Violations *65 FR 19618 Audit Policy 4-11-00*

On Internet:

- United States Sentencing Guidelines Manual, Appendix C, amendment 422, effective November 1, 1991, *available at http://www.ussc.gov* and Supplement to Appendix C, amendment 673, effective November 1, 2004, *available at http://www.ussc.gov/2004guid/APPC-2004SUPP.pdf*
- EPA, Position Statement of Environmental Management Systems (May 15, 2002, reissued Dec. 13, 2005), *available at http://www.epa.gov/ems/position/position.htm*
- United States Sentencing Commission publications, general information *available at http://www.ussc.gov*, with specific information about the Organizational Sentencing Guidelines *available at http://www.ussc.gov/orgguide.htm*
- U.S. Department of Justice, Factors in Decisions on Criminal Prosecutions for Environmental Violations in the Context of Significant Voluntary Compliance or Disclosure Efforts by the Violator (Jul. 19, 1991), *available through http://www.usdoj.gov/enrd/Current_topics.html*
- United States Attorneys' Manual, Federal Prosecution of Business Organizations, *available at http://www.usdoj.gov/usao/eousa/foia_reading_room/usam/title9/28mcrm.htm.*
- International Standards Organization publications, background information *available at http://www.iso.org/iso/home.htm*, with specific information about the quality management standard and the environmental management standard *available at http://www.iso.org/iso/iso_catalogue/management_standards/iso_9000_iso_14000.htm*
- EPA, Office of Enforcement and Compliance Assurance, Office of Criminal Enforcement, Forensics and Training, Compliance-Focused Environmental Management System—Enforcement Agreement Guidance, EPA-330/9-97-002, as revised through June 2005, *available at www.epa.gov/compliance/resources/publications/incentives/ems/*
- New York State Bar Association, Committee on Professional Ethics, Opinion 650 (June 30, 1993), *available at http://www.nysba.org/AM/Template.cfm?Section=Ethics_Opinions&TEMPLATE=/CM/ContentDisplay.cfm&CONTENTID=18737*

M. Chapter 14 Penalties and Enforcement Resources

On CD:

- 45 Fed. Reg. 59770 (Sept. 10, 1980) Guidelines for the Assessment of Civil Penalties under Section 16 of the Toxic Substances Control Act; PCB Penalty Policy *45 FR 59770 1980 Penalty Policy 9-10-80*
- 61 Fed. Reg. 69360 (Dec. 31, 1996) Civil Monetary Penalty Inflation Adjustment Rule *61 FR 69360 Penalty Adjust 12-31-96*
- 64 Fed. Reg. 40138 (July 23, 1999) Consolidated Rules of Practice Governing the Administrative Assessment of Civil Penalties, Issuance of Compliance or Corrective Action Orders, and the Revocation, Termination or Suspension of Permits *64 FR 40138 Rules of Practice 7-23-99*
- 65 Fed. Reg. 19618 (Apr. 11, 2000) Incentives for Self-Policing: Discovery, Disclosure, Correction and Prevention of Violations *65 FR 19618 Audit Policy 4 11 00*
- 65 Fed. Reg. 81858 (Dec. 27, 2000) Policy on Alternative Dispute Resolution *65 FR 81858 ADR Policy 12-27-00*
- 69 Fed. Reg. 7121 (Feb. 13, 2004) Civil Monetary Penalty Inflation Adjustment Rule *69 FR 7121 Penalty Adjust 2-13-04*
- 73 Fed. Reg. 44991 (Aug. 1, 2008) Interim Approach to Applying the Audit Policy to New Owners *73 FR 44991 Audit New Owners 8-1-08*
- 73 Fed. Reg. 75340 (Dec. 11, 2008) Civil Monetary Penalty Inflation Adjustment Rule *73 FR 75340 Penalty Adjust 12-11-08*
- 74 Fed. Reg. 626 (Jan. 7, 2009) Civil Monetary Penalty Inflation Adjustment Rule *74 FR 626 Penalty Adjust 1-7-09*
- Amended TSCA Section 5 Enforcement Response Policy (Jan. 8, 1989) *Sect 5 ERP Amend 1-8-89*, as further amended by memorandum from John J. Neylan, III, Director, Policy and Grants Division, Office of Compliance Monitoring, Amendment to the TSCA Section 5 Enforcement Response Policy—Penalty Limit For Untimely Submissions (July 1, 1993) *Sect 5 ERP Amend 7-1-93*
- Enforcement Response Policy for Test Rules Under Section 4 of the Toxic Substances Control Act (May 28, 1986) *Sect 4 Test Rule ERP*
- EPA, Office of Compliance Monitoring, Office of Pesticides and Toxic Substances, Interim Final Enforcement Response Policy for the Asbestos Hazard Emergency Response Act (Jan. 31, 1989) AHERA ERP 1-31-89 as amended by Memorandum from Jesse Baskerville, Director, Toxics and Pesticides Enforcement Division, Office of Regulatory Enforcement, EPA, Revision of the AHERA Enforcement Response Policy: Civil Penalties for Failure to Conduct Reinspections (Aug. 4, 1998) *AHERA ERP Amend 8-4-89*

- EPA, Office of Enforcement, Multi-Media Investigation Manual, EPA-330/9-89-003-R (Mar. 1992) *Multi-Media Manual*
- EPA, Office of Regulatory Enforcement, Audit Policy Interpretive Guidance, EC-G-2002-149 (Jan. 1997) *Audit Interp Guide*
- EPA, Office of Enforcement and Compliance Assurance, Office of Civil Enforcement, Waste and Chemical Enforcement Division, Section 1018—Disclosure Rule Enforcement Response and Penalty Policy (Dec. 2007) *Lead Disclosure ERP 12-07*
- In re DIC Americas, Inc., TSCA Appeal No. 94-2 6 E.A.D. 184, (Sept. 27, 1995) *Dic Americas 9-27-95*
- In the Matter of Troy Chemical Corp., Docket No. II-TSCA-8(a)-98-0101 (OAL Oct. 14, 1999) *Troy Chemical 10-14-99*
- Memorandum from Jesse Baskerville, Director, Toxics and Pesticides Enforcement Division, Office of Regulatory Enforcement, EPA, Interim Guidance for Enforcing the TSCA § 402 Abatement Rule "Firm and Lead Abatement Professional Certification Requirements" (Mar. 8, 2000) *Lead ERP Memo 3-8-00*
- Model Supplemental Environmental Project Consent Agreement and Order, (1999) *SEP CAFO 1-99*
- Polychlorinated Biphenyls (PCB) Penalty Policy (Apr. 9, 1990) *PCB Penalty Policy 4-9-90*
- Supplemental Environmental Projects Policy, effective May 1, 1998 (Apr. 10, 1998) *SEP Policy 4-10-98*
- The Enforcement Response Policy For Reporting And Recordkeeping Rules And Requirements for TSCA Sections 8, 12 and 13 (Mar. 31, 1999) *Reporting Rule ERP*
- The Environmental Appeals Board Practice Manual (June 2004) *EAB Manual 6-04*
- TSCA Good Laboratory Practices Regulations Enforcement Response Policy (Apr. 9, 1985) *Sect 4 GLP ERP*

On Internet:

- Audit Policy Frequently Asked Questions (2007), *available through http://www.epa.gov/compliance/incentives/auditing/auditpolicy.html*
- EPA Audit Policy contacts are *available through http://www.epa.gov/compliance/incentives/auditing/auditdisclose.html*
- EPA's BEN model for calculating the economic benefit of a violation, for the purpose of determining a minimum administrative penalty, *available through http://www.epa.gov/compliance/civil/econmodels/#ben*
- EPA Enforcement Response Policies are *available through http://cfpub.epa.gov/compliance/resources/policies/civil/tsca/*

- EPA enforcement statistics from the Integrated Compliance Information System are *available through http://www.epa-echo.gov/echo/compliance_report_icis.html*
- EPA, Office of Regulatory Enforcement, Audit Policy Interpretive Guidance, EC-G-2002-149 (Jan. 1997), *available through http://www.epa.gov/compliance/incentives/auditing/auditpolicy.html*
- EPA, Office of Enforcement, Multi-Media Investigation Manual, EPA-330/9-89-003-R (Mar. 1992), *available at http://www.epa.gov/compliance/resources/publications/civil/programs/*
- Decisions and orders from the EPA Office of Administrative Law Judges are *available at http://www.epa.gov/aljhomep/orders.htm*
- Decisions from the EPA Environmental Appeals Board are *available at http://www.epa.gov/boarddec/*
- In the Matter of Troy Chemical Corp., Docket No. II-TSCA-8(a)-98-0101, (Oct. 14, 1999), *available at http://www.epa.gov/oalj/orders/troy2.htmhttp://www.epa.gov/oalj/orders/troy2.htm*
- In re DIC Americas, Inc., TSCA-II-8(a)-90-0109 (Dec. 30, 1993), TSCA Appeal No. 94-2 6 E.A.D. 184, (Sept. 27, 1995), *available at http://www.epa.gov/eab/disk9/dicameri.pdf*
- Supplemental Environmental Project information and guidance is *available through http://cfpub.epa.gov/compliance/resources/policies/civil/seps/*
- The Environmental Appeals Board Practice Manual, June 2004, *available at http://yosemite.epa.gov/oa/EAB_Web_Docket.nsf/General+Information/Environmental+Appeals+Board+Guidance+Documents?OpenDocument.*
- TSCA enforcement actions are sometimes announced by the EPA in press releases available through http://yosemite.epa.gov/opa/admpress.nsf/Press%20Releases%20-%20Pesticides%20and%20Toxic%20Chemicals!OpenView

N. Chapter 15 Acquisitions and Divestitures Resources

On CD:

- 65 Fed. Reg. 19618 (Apr. 11, 2000) Incentives for Self-Policing: Discovery, Disclosure, Correction and Prevention of Violations *65 FR 19618 Audit Policy 4-11-00*
- 73 Fed. Reg. 44991 (Aug. 1, 2008) Interim Approach to Applying the Audit Policy to New Owners *73 FR 44991 Audit New Owners 8-1-08*
- Successor transfer forms for:
    - TSCA § 5(e) consent orders *Successor Trans 5e Order*
    - Low Volume Exemptions before May 30, 1995 *Successor Trans LVE pre May 95*

  - Low Volume Exemptions after May 30, 1995 *Successor Trans LVE post May 95*
  - Low Release and Exposure Exemptions (LoREX) *Successor Trans LoREX*
- Polymer Exemptions before May 30, 1995 *Successor Trans polymer pre May 95*
- Memorandum from Robert E. Fabricant and Susan B. Hazen, "Interpretive Statement on Change in Ownership of Real Property Contaminated With PCBs" (Aug. 14, 2003) *PCB Property Transfer 8-14-03*

On Internet

- Successor transfer forms for transferring LVEs, LoREX, 5(e) consent orders and polymer exemptions dated before May 30, 1995 are available on the EPA Web site through *http://www.epa.gov/oppt/newchems/pubs/succesor.htm*
- Model TSCA § 5(e) consent orders are available on the EPA Web site through *http://www.epa.gov/opptintr/newchems/pubs/boilerpl.htm*
- Memorandum from Robert E. Fabricant and Susan B. Hazen, "Interpretive Statement on Change in Ownership of Real Property Contaminated With PCBs" (Aug. 14, 2003), available on the EPA Web site at *http://www.epa.gov/epawaste/hazard/tsd/pcbs/pubs/distincom.pdf*

O. Chapter 16 Asbestos Hazard Emergency Response Act Resources

On CD:

- 52 Fed. Reg. 41826 (Oct. 30, 1987) Asbestos-Containing Materials in Schools *52 FR 41826 ACM 10-30-87*
- 73 Fed. Reg. 75340 (Dec. 11, 2008) Civil Monetary Penalty Inflation Adjustment Rule *73 FR 75340 Penalty Adjust 12-11-08*
- 74 Fed. Reg. 626 (Jan. 7, 2009) Civil Monetary Penalty Inflation Adjustment Rule *74 FR 626 Penalty Adjust 1-7-09*
- EPA, Office of Compliance Monitoring, Office of Pesticides and Toxic Substances, Interim Final Enforcement Response Policy for the Asbestos Hazard Emergency Response Act (Jan. 31, 1989) AHERA ERP 1-31-89 as amended by Memorandum from Jesse Baskerville, Director, Toxics and Pesticides Enforcement Division, Office of Regulatory Enforcement, EPA, Revision of the AHERA Enforcement Response Policy: Civil Penalties for Failure to Conduct Reinspections (Aug. 4, 1998) *AHERA ERP Amend 8-4-89*

- Collection of AHERA Enforcement Response Policy *AHERA ERP Updates*:
  - EPA, Toxics and Pesticides Enforcement Division, Office of Regulatory Enforcement, Enforcement Response Policy for the Asbestos Model Accreditation Plan (MAP) Addendum to the AHERA ERP (Mar. 9, 1998);
  - Memorandum from John J. Neylan III, Director, Policy and Grants Division, Office of Compliance Monitoring, EPA, Unaccredited Supervisor/Worker Violations Under the AHERA Interim Final Enforcement Response Policy (Jan. 19, 1990); and
  - Memorandum from John J. Neylan III, Director, Policy and Grants Division, Office of Compliance Monitoring, EPA, Changes Relating to Accreditation Violations/Penalty Amounts Resulting from ASHAA Reauthorization/Amendment (Jan. 27, 1992)

On Internet:

- List of laboratories accredited by the National Institute of Standards and Technology, the successor to the National Bureau of Standards, to perform polarized light microscopy (PLM) analysis is *available at http://ts.nist.gov/Standards/scopes/plmtm.htm*
- List of laboratories accredited by the National Institute of Standards and Technology, the successor to the National Bureau of Standards, to perform the transmission electron microscopy ("TEM") is *available at http://ts.nist.gov/Standards/scopes/temtm*
- The EPA Web site on asbestos is *available at http://www.epa.gov/oppt/asbestos/index.html*

P. Chapter 17 Indoor Radon Abatement Act Resources

On CD:

- 59 Fed. Reg. 13166 (Mar. 18, 1994) User Fees for Radon Proficiency Programs *59 FR 131 User Fees 3-18-94*
- 60 Fed. Reg. 41813 (Aug. 14, 1995) User Fees for Radon Proficiency Programs *60 FR 41813 User Fees 8-14-95*
- 66 Fed. Reg. 3782 (Jan. 16, 2001) Environmental Program Grants for Tribes *66 FR 3782 Grants 1-16-01*

On Internet:

- The EPA Web site on radon is available at http://www.epa.gov/radon/. This is a good source for information, including many of the publications noted in the chapter

- Information about the four regional radon training centers established by the EPA to develop information and provide training on radon risks, methods of measurement and mitigation is *available at* follows: Eastern Regional Training Center at *http://www.cpe.rutgers.edu/programs/radon.html*; Southern Regional Training Center at *http://eng.auburn.edu/distance-learning/ce/live/srrtc/index.html*; Midwest Universities Radon Consortium at *http://cce.umn.edu/CCE-Main/Radon-Courses-for-Professionals/*, and the Western Regional Radon Training Center at *http://www.wrrtc.net/*
- Information about existing state legislation can be found at the Web site of the National Conference of State Legislators at *http://www.ncsl.org/programs/environ/envHealth/radonstats07.htm* and at the Web site of the Environmental Law Institute at *http://www.eli.org/Program_Areas/iaq_databases.cfm*
- Information about pending state legislation can be found on the Web site of the National Conference of State Legislators at *http://www.ncsl.org/print/environ/radonlegis07.pdf*
- EPA, A Citizen's Guide to Radon: The Guide to Protecting Yourself and Your Family from Radon, 402-K-07-009 (Revised May 2007), *available at www.epa.gov/radon/pubs/citguide.html*

Q. Chapter 18 Lead Resources

On CD:

- 61 Fed. Reg. 90604 (Mar. 6, 1996), Lead; Requirements for Disclosure of Known Lead-Based Paint and/or Lead-Based Paint Hazards in Housing; Final Rule *61 FR 90604 Lead Paint 3-6-96*
- 73 Fed. Reg. 5109 (Jan. 29, 2008) Health and Safety Data Reporting; Addition of Certain Chemicals *73 FR 5109 Lead 8d 1-29-09*
- 73 Fed. Reg. 21692 (Apr. 22, 2008) Lead; Renovation, Repair, and Painting Program; Lead Hazard Information Pamphlet; Notice of Availability; Final Rule *73 FR 21692 Lead Renovation 4-22-08*
- 73 Fed. Reg. 75340 (Dec. 11, 2008) Civil Monetary Penalty Inflation Adjustment Rule *73 FR 75340 Penalty Adjust 12-11-08*
- 74 Fed. Reg. 626 (Jan. 7, 2009) Civil Monetary Penalty Inflation Adjustment Rule *74 FR 626 Penalty Adjust 1-7-09*
- EPA, Office of Enforcement and Compliance Assurance, Office of Civil Enforcement, Waste and Chemical Enforcement Division, Section 1018—Disclosure Rule Enforcement Response and Penalty Policy (Dec. 2007) *Lead Disclosure ERP 12-07*
- Lead; Renovation, Repair, and Painting Program Response To Public Comments (Apr. 2008) (public comments on the Renovation rule and EPA responses) *Lead Renovation Comments 4-08*

- Memorandum from Jesse Baskerville, Director, Toxics and Pesticides Enforcement Division, Office of Regulatory Enforcement, EPA, Interim Guidance for Enforcing the TSCA § 402 Abatement Rule "Firm and Lead Abatement Professional Certification Requirements" (Mar. 8, 2000) *Lead ERP Memo 3-8-00*
- Renovate Right: Important Lead Hazard Information for Families, Child Care Providers and Schools, EPA document EPA-740-F-08-002 (Mar. 2008) *Renovate Right 3-08*

On Internet:

- EPA's lead home page is *http://www.epa.gov/lead/index.html*
- The Lead pre-renovation form is available at *http://www.epa.gov/lead/pubs/pre-renovationform.pdf*
- TSCA lead regulations in 40 C.F.R Part 745 are *available at http://ecfr.gpoaccess.gov/cgi/t/text/text-idx?c=ecfr&sid=55c9bcd1578a073849c0d225df10c1fb&rgn=div5&view=text&node=40:30.0.1.1.13&idno=40*
- The Residential Lead-Based Paint Hazard Reduction Act of 1992, including Section 1018, is *available at http://www.epa.gov/lead/pubs/titleten.html*

R. Chapter 19 Health High-Performance Schools Resources

On Internet:

- DOE maintains a Web site that deals with energy smart schools at *http://www1.eere.energy.gov/buildings/energysmartschools/*
- EPA maintains a site which it calls "Your one-stop location for information and links to school environmental health issues," at *http://cfpub.epa.gov/schools/index.cfm*
- EPA, Travel and Environmental Implications of School Siting, EPA 231-R-03-004 (Oct. 2003), *available at http://www.epa.gov/smartgrowth/school_travel.htm*
- Information about the EPA Indoor Air Quality ("IAQ") Tools for Schools Program is *available at http://www.epa.gov/iaq/schools*
- Information about the EPA The Healthy School Environments Assessment Tool ("HealthySEATv2") is *available at http://www.epa.gov/schools/healthyseat/basicinformation.html*
- Rhode Island Legal Services (RILS), Not in My Schoolyard: Avoiding Environmental Hazards at School Through Improved School Site Selection Policies, A Report to the U.S. Environmental Protection Agency (2006), *available at http://stage.nylpi.org/pub/School_Siting_Final.pdf*

- The National Clearinghouse for Educational Facilities posted several resources for dealing with healthy high performance schools at *http://www.edfacilities.org/rl/healthy_schools.cfm*

S. Chapter 20 Section VI Supplementary Research Resources

On Internet:

- TSCA hotline:
  Telephone: (202) 554-1404
  E-mail: tsca-hotline@epa.gov
  Requests for documents can be faxed to: (202) 554-5603
  Online contact form: http://www.epa.gov/oppt/import-export/contact.html
- EPA Docket Center:
  Telephone: (202) 566-0280
  E-mail: oppt.ncic@epa.gov
  Fax: (202) 566-9744
  Mailing Address:
  U.S. Environmental Protection Agency
  EPA Docket Center
  Pollution Prevention and Toxics Docket, Mail Code 28221T
  1200 Pennsylvania Avenue, NW
  Washington, DC 20460
- Substance Registry Service, an Internet based registry of chemicals that are regulated under any EPA program, *available at http://iaspub.epa.gov/sor_internet/registry/substreg/home/overview/home.do*
- Semiannual Regulatory agendas, *available at http://www.epa.gov/regulations/search/regagenda.html.*
- Federal Register notices:
  - EPA has a selective collection of Federal Register notices relating to TSCA that are older than September 1994 on its Web site at: *http://www.epa.gov/fedrgstr/EPA-TOX/pre1994/hisindex.htm.*
  - Federal Register notices from 1994 to the present are also available in either html or pdf format through the United States Government Printing Office, *available through http://www.gpoaccess.gov/fr/index.html.*
  - Federal Depository Libraries, *available through http://www.gpoaccess.gov/fr/index.html.*
  - HeinOnline has full images of all Federal Register notices starting with Volume 1 in 1936 *available through http://www.heinonline.org.*

    - The Government Printing Office sends out a daily e-mail with the table of contents for that day's Federal Register, registration *available through http://listserv.access.gpo.gov/.*
- Updates on rulemaking dockets *available through http://www.regulations.gov.*
- TSCA regulations *available through http://www.gpoaccess.gov, and http://ecfr.gpoaccess.gov/cgi/t/text/text-idx?c=ecfr&tpl=%2Findex.tpl.*
- HeinOnline posts the Code of Federal Regulations, *available through http://www.heinonline.org.*

II. Procedures

A. Model Procedure Template

The model procedures contained in this section can form the basis of an integrated TSCA compliance program. If your company has a system in place, such as ISO 9000, you should follow the design used by your company to the extent possible. Under each heading in the template below, we explain how the sections of the template could be used. In the model procedures themselves, we provide in italics explanations of the procedures and some common choices. To be truly effective, the procedures need to be adapted to fit your company, in terms of organization, business systems, style, and culture. There is no one size fits all possibility.

1. Procedure Number

The numbering system can be used to provide information to the user as to the scope of the procedure: a) whether corporate-wide or specific to a job function or b) relationship to groupings of work processes. It should take into consideration how the company is organized, such as whether there are separate business units, whether the company is centralized or decentralized, the number of locations, and operating units. In the models presented here, for the sake of simplicity, we are assuming a centralized organization with one headquarters location and one operating site. The procedure numbers will indicate whether the procedure is for use of the entire company, a single site, or a particular job function. Procedures beginning with the designation CORP. are company-wide procedures. The CORP. designation will be followed by a number. A site-specific procedure would be designated by the site name, followed by a number. A department-specific procedure would be designated by the department name, followed by a number. For example, CORP.5 would be a procedure applicable to the entire corporation; SITE.5 would be a procedure applicable to the operating site; and RA.5 would be a procedure applicable to the Regulatory Affairs Department. The regulatory function is named Regulatory Affairs in these procedures but should be conformed to the name used in your particular company.

If possible, it is useful to group procedures under work processes, so that each procedure dealing with a particular work process has the same initial number, such as 5, followed by a random site or department number. For example, CORP. 26 would deal with the company's new product development process. Each department involved in that work process would designate its operating procedures for new product development by department name, by the number 26, and by random number. For example, each Research Department procedure involved in new product development would begin RE.26.

Corporate-wide procedures would be high level, more generally outlining requirements. Department procedures would be more specific, getting into the detail of work processes, what function has what responsibility, and how that responsibility will be carried out.

2. Procedure Name

Each procedure should have a plain English name, sufficient to indicate the content of the procedure to someone reviewing an index. In the model procedures, we explain the legal requirements behind each procedure in this section in italics.

a. Key Objective

The procedure should summarize the main objective or objectives of the procedure. The legal requirement is often ancillary to the business requirement in an integrated procedure. For example, a procedure dealing with how to export products might have the objective of exporting products in a timely, accurate, and cost-effective manner. The export would of course have to meet legal requirements, but that may not necessarily be the key objective of the procedure.

b. Applicable References

Insert in this section the relevant sections of the law, any guidance documents, and any other company procedures that are related to this procedure. If a list of external requirements (laws, industry requirements) is provided, someone can easily determine which external requirements are being addressed and which are not. So, for our purposes, references to the applicable sections of TSCA might be included in each procedure. Similarly, some procedures may make reference to the Responsible Care Codes of the American Chemistry Council, where the procedure goes further than the absolute minimum legal requirement.

In some companies, there is a general master procedure for each work process, which addresses the work to be done by function, and leaves to each of the involved functions the task to develop specific functional procedures to implement the master procedure. This cross-reference check allows someone new to the particular work process to understand how all of the parts of the company come together to make the action taken place. Related procedures could also be listed if knowledge of such procedures would enhance understanding of the work process. The design used should follow the design used by the company for its business process system. Likely related or implementing procedures are sometimes noted in the commentary in italics next to the particular step in the model procedure.

c. Document History

REVISION NO. DATE AUTHOR RATIONALE

Most management systems recommend that a history be kept of revisions to procedures and forms. This history helps in understanding why and when changes were made. Revision numbers also help users ensure that they are not using superseded procedures. Procedural changes can be a result of many things, including changed legal requirements, corrective actions, audit findings, reorganizations, or transformations of the underlying business operations.

d. Procedure

The actual procedure should be a series of actions, by department or specific job functions, which need to be undertaken to implement the work process. In a less complex organization, all of the steps needed to implement a work process, with sufficient detail, might be contained in one procedure; in a more complex organization, there might be cascading procedures, with growing levels of detail. It is important to document the steps that are critical to ensure that the process happens correctly. If it doesn't matter how something is done, don't bother documenting it. The description of the steps should be done by the people who are involved in the activity.

B. Procedure Number CORP. 17, Process or Design Change Review*

As discussed in The Inventory Chapter, § 5 of the Toxic Substances Control Act (TSCA) requires that all chemicals manufactured, processed, or used in the United States must be on a comprehensive list of chemicals maintained by the United States Environmental Protection Agency pursuant to § 8(b) of TSCA, called the TSCA Inventory. Changes to processes, including changing raw materials, solvents, or the method of manufacture could result in the formation of a new chemical not on the TSCA Inventory. Employees must understand what constitutes a process change and where such process changes may occur in the company's operations. With that information in hand, the company is able to make certain those changes are adequately reviewed from a TSCA perspective. This procedure deals with the management of a process change that might have an impact on TSCA compliance, arising in a number of identified company work processes. Procedure Number CORP. 20, Assessment of New Suppliers, gives an example of how various functions at a company might interact to assess a new supplier, including the potential TSCA impact. Procedure Number Corp. 19, Control of Nonconforming Commercial Product, gives a similar example, but omits the particulars of how the functions at any specific company might deal with nonconforming product manufactured. A company should review its work processes and procedures to see in which of them this Procedure Number CORP. 17 should be incorporated; this is advisable because of the possibility of a process change triggering TSCA. The checklist at the end of this procedure gives some examples of where TSCA impacts might arise. Possible work processes would include dealing with nonconforming raw materials or nonconforming work in progress, product specification changes, changes to manufacturing site, and recalls.

1. Key Objective

This document describes the procedure for ensuring that process changes made in the manufacture, use, or processing of commercial products, or changes in the design of commercial products, are in compliance with all applicable regulations.

2. Applicable References

TSCA § 5.
TSCA§ 8(b).

---

* *Procedures may include steps that are not required by TSCA but are suggested business practices.*

(Add all other regulatory schemes relevant to the Company's products, such as FIFRA, FFDCA, or any foreign equivalents, and incorporate them into this procedure).

Procedures governing assessment of new suppliers, evaluations of raw materials, supplier audits, TSCA premanufacturing notification, waste management, and preparation of specifications, labels, and MSDSs.

3. Document History

REVISION	DATE	AUTHOR	RATIONALE
0.	2010	THE TOXIC SUBSTANCES CONTROL ACT: A PRACTICAL GUIDE[1]	
1.			

4. Procedure

Step 1. All process or design changes in commercial products are considered by a business team assigned to that product.

Step 2. The assigned business team will designate a team review member (the Liaison) who is responsible for seeking regulatory input in advance of any process or design changes to commercial products. The Liaison, with the assistance of the team, must answer the questions in the attached "**Regulatory Affairs Checklist for Proposed Changes.**" If the answer to any of the questions in the proposed checklist is in the affirmative, the liaison must notify the Manager of Regulatory Compliance (MRC) of this development and ensure that the proposed change is not implemented until cleared by the MRC.

Step 3. The MRC must evaluate each proposed change to determine whether a new chemical substance required to be on the TSCA Inventory, or any other chemical inventories on which the product is listed, will be formed by the process change. The MRC must also evaluate whether a chemical substance subject to a Significant New Use Rule (SNUR) or any other restriction will be formed by or handled differently as a result of the process change. The Liaison must provide the MRC with information needed to complete such evaluation.

Step 4. If a new chemical substance required to be on the TSCA Inventory or any other relevant chemical inventory will be formed, the MRC shall inform the Liaison of this requirement and shall advise the Liaison whether any exemptions are possible and the terms of such exemptions, and if no exemptions are possible, the cost and time frame required to put such chemical substance on the TSCA *(and other)* Inventory. The MRC shall inform the

---

1. MIRIAM V. GOLD & JEAN WARSHAW, THE TOXIC SUBSTANCES CONTROL ACT: A PRACTICAL GUIDE (OXFORD UNIVERSITY PRESS 2010).

Liaison of any restrictions or applicable SNURs and the cost and time required for compliance.

Step 5. The MRC shall also determine whether any other changes are required (such as hazard information, MSDS/label changes, packaging changes). The MRC shall advise the Liaison of any other potential regulatory impacts resulting from the process or design change. The Liaison shall prepare to marshal the necessary resources to implement the needed change.

Step 6. The Liaison shall report the TSCA and other regulatory impacts, if any, to the team evaluating the change. The team shall decide whether to abandon the process change, attempt to modify the change, or seek to have the new chemical substance put on the TSCA Inventory and any other Inventories. If the team determines to proceed, it must notify the MRC who will proceed to address the regulatory impacts of such change.

6. Regulatory Affairs Checklist of Proposed Changes

Does the Proposed Change:

A. Introduce a new raw material, vendor, or vendor site?
B. Result in a new chemical substance either in the manufacturing process or as the end product of the manufacturing process as determined by qualitative analysis?
C. Result in a new byproduct or impurity that imparts valuable properties to the resulting product?
D. Involve a polymer that will have a different proportion of monomers, reactive solvents, chain transfer agents, cross-linking agents, bases, or free radical initiators charged to the reaction vessel or incorporated into the polymer after the proposed change is implemented?
E. Involve removing an intermediate from equipment in which it is manufactured, if the intermediate was not normally removed from the equipment in which it was manufactured prior to the change?
F. Involve making changes to the product specifications?
G. Result in a change in production site, or remove or add regulated equipment?
H. Involve a chemical subject to a Significant New Use Rule?

If the answer to any of the above questions is "YES," consult the MRC.

C. Procedure Number CORP. 19, Control of Nonconforming Commercial Product*

As discussed in The Inventory Chapter, § 5 of the Toxic Substances Control Act (TSCA) requires that all chemicals manufactured, processed, or used in the United States must be on a comprehensive list of chemicals maintained by the United States Environmental Protection Agency pursuant to § 8(b) of TSCA, called the TSCA Inventory. When commercial product is not manufactured according to specifications, that nonconforming product could be, or could contain, a chemical substance not on the TSCA Inventory, which would limit the ability to sell the product "as is" or to rework it. This procedure deals with how to assess the TSCA implications of the management of manufactured nonconforming commercial product.

1. Key Objective

This procedure describes the method for controlling the disposition of manufactured nonconforming commercial product.

2. Applicable References

TSCA § 5
TSCA § 8(b)
(Add all other regulatory schemes relevant to the Company's products, such as FIFRA, FFDCA or any foreign equivalents)
Procedures governing preparation of specifications, labels, and MSDS, and the management of waste.

3. Document History

REVISION	DATE	AUTHOR	RATIONALE
0.	2010	THE TOXIC SUBSTANCES CONTROL ACT: A PRACTICAL GUIDE[1]	
1.			

4. Procedure

Step 1. The management of nonconforming commercial product is considered by a business team assigned to that product. *Indicate which functions in*

---

* *Procedures may include steps that are not required by TSCA but are suggested business practices.*

1. MIRIAM V. GOLD & JEAN WARSHAW, THE TOXIC SUBSTANCES CONTROL ACT: A PRACTICAL GUIDE (OXFORD UNIVERSITY PRESS 2010).

the company would be involved in this process, such as manufacturing, logistics, warehouse, product manager, business manager etc.

Step 2. *Indicate the responsibilities of each function assigned to the team with respect to the management of the disposition of nonconforming final product, and add steps to specify the sequence of actions by such functions and/or the team. Possible dispositions might include discarding the material as waste, reworking the material, or selling it "as is." Nonconforming commercial product can be discovered at the site of manufacture, at a warehouse, or anywhere on the distribution chain, including at a customer location.*

Step 3. The assigned business team will determine how the nonconforming product was made. With respect to such manufacturing, the team must answer the questions in the attached "**Regulatory Affairs Checklist for Nonconforming Commercial Product.**" If the answer to any of the questions in the checklist is in the affirmative, the team will designate a team review member (the Liaison), who is responsible for seeking regulatory input.

Step 4. The assigned business team will determine what the likely possibilities are for the disposition of the nonconforming final product, including selling it "as is" or reworking it. With respect to any such proposed action, the team must answer the questions in the attached "**Regulatory Affairs Checklist for Nonconforming Commercial Product.**" If the answer to any of the questions in the proposed checklist is in the affirmative, the team will designate a team review member (the Liaison), who is responsible for seeking regulatory input in advance of taking any such action from the Manager of Regulatory Compliance (MRC). The Liaison must ensure that the proposed change is not implemented until cleared by the MRC.

Step 5. The MRC must evaluate each completed and prospective action to determine whether a new chemical substance required to be on the TSCA Inventory was formed during the manufacture of the nonconforming commercial product, is in the nonconforming commercial product, or will result from the reworking of the nonconforming commercial product. The MRC must also evaluate whether a chemical substance subject to a Significant New Use Rule (SNUR) or any other restriction is a component of the nonconforming product. The Liaison must provide the MRC with information needed to complete such evaluation.

Step 6. If a new chemical substance not on the TSCA Inventory will be formed by rework, the MRC shall advise the Liaison as to whether any exemptions from Inventory requirements are applicable and the terms of such exemptions. If no exemptions are applicable, the MRC will inform the Liaison of the approximate cost and time frame required to put such chemical substance on the TSCA Inventory.[2] If a new chemical substance not on the TSCA Inventory was formed during the manufacture of the nonconforming commercial product, the MRC shall inform the Liaison of this, and if the Liaison wants to make a disposition other than treating the final commercial product as waste, the MRC shall also inform the Legal Department, which will recommend a course of action to deal with the potential noncompliance.[3] The MRC shall inform the Liaison of any SNURs or other restrictions on constituents of the nonconforming product and the cost and time required for compliance.

Step 7. The MRC shall also determine whether any other changes are required (such as hazard information, MSDS/label changes, packaging changes). The MRC shall advise the Liaison of any other potential regulatory impacts resulting from the proposed course of action.

Step 8. The Liaison shall report the TSCA and other regulatory impacts, if any, to the team evaluating how to manage the nonconforming commercial product. The team shall decide which course of action to take. The team must notify the MRC, who will proceed to address the regulatory impacts of the intended course of action. If the team decides to dispose of the nonconforming commercial product as waste, it will advise the Waste Management Specialist who will make all arrangements to dispose of the nonconforming commercial product as waste, taking into account any restrictions imposed by Significant New Use Rules.

6. Regulatory Affairs Checklist for Nonconforming Commercial Product:

Did the manufacture of nonconforming commercial product, or does the proposed disposition:

A. Result in a new chemical substance either during the manufacturing process or as the end product of the manufacturing process as determined by qualitative analysis?

---

2. It is highly unlikely that a company will want to take the time and trouble to put a substance on the Inventory to be able to dispose of nonconforming commercial product in a way other than waste, but we leave this option here for consideration in the event that the product was produced in very large quantities or was very expensive.
3. Section 15 of TSCA prohibits "use for commercial purposes" of any substance if "such person knew or had reason to know" it was manufactured in violation of the Premanufacture Notification requirements. 15 U.S.C. § 2614. Therefore any substance not on the TSCA Inventory should be quarantined until its disposition is determined. Similarly a substance that was made with an isolated intermediate that is not on the Inventory cannot be used for a commercial purpose even if that end product is on the Inventory.

B. Result in a new byproduct or impurity that imparts valuable properties to the resulting product?
C. Involve a polymer that will have a different proportion of monomers, reactive solvents, chain transfer agents, cross-linking agents, bases, or free radical initiators charged to the reaction vessel or incorporated into the polymer after the proposed change is implemented?
D. Involve removing an intermediate from equipment in which it is manufactured, if the intermediate was not normally removed from the equipment in which it was manufactured prior to the change?
E. Involve making changes to the product specifications?
F. Involve a chemical subject to a Significant New Use Rule?

If the answer to any of the above questions is "YES," consult the MRC.

D. Procedure Number CORP. 20, Assessment of New Suppliers*

As discussed in The Inventory Chapter, § 5 of the Toxic Substances Control Act (TSCA) requires that all chemicals manufactured, processed, or used in the United States must be on a comprehensive list of chemicals maintained by the United States Environmental Protection Agency pursuant to § 8(b)of TSCA, called the TSCA Inventory. Before purchasing a chemical from a new supplier, the company needs to ascertain that the chemical is on the TSCA Inventory. While obtaining a certification of TSCA compliance from the supplier may be helpful, the best method is to ensure that the new supplier's material is in fact on the TSCA Inventory. The assessment to be made for new suppliers could be part of a general process change assessment. The important issue is to understand where process changes may occur in the company's processes, and to make certain those changes are adequately reviewed from a TSCA perspective. This procedure illustrates how a company might assess a new supplier and how the potential TSCA impact might be evaluated. Naming and responsibilities of functions will vary company by company.

1. Key Objective

This document describes the process for approving new suppliers of chemicals.

2. Applicable References

TSCA § 5
TSCA § 8(b)
Procedures governing process changes, evaluations of raw materials, preparation of specifications, and supplier audits.

3. Document History

REVISION	DATE	AUTHOR	RATIONALE
0.	2010	THE TOXIC SUBSTANCES CONTROL ACT: A PRACTICAL GUIDE[1]	
1.			

---

* *Procedures may include steps that are not required by TSCA but are suggested business practices.*

1. Miriam V. Gold & Jean Warshaw, The Toxic Substances Control Act: A Practical Guide (Oxford University Press 2010).

4. Procedure

Step 1. Anyone needing to obtain either a new raw material or a new source of supply of a raw material (the Requestor) notifies the Senior Buyer that a new raw material or a new raw material supplier is required, and the reason for such request.

Step 2. The Senior Buyer is responsible for identifying a potential new supplier candidate. The Senior Buyer notifies the candidate supplier of the company's interest and negotiates a tentative supply price, in consultation with the affected business unit. The Senior Buyer apprises the candidate supplier of the need for a raw material approval evaluation.

Step 3. The Senior Buyer requests the candidate supplier provide a commercially produced representative sample of the new raw material to the appropriate Technical Support Representative (TSR) in the production facility where the raw material will be used.

Step 4. The TSR is responsible for having the representative sample analyzed. This analysis may include the preparation of laboratory batches of the final product. A Laboratory Raw Material Evaluation Form must be completed by those conducting the analysis and distributed to the Marketing Representative, TSR, Operations Manager, Quality Coordinator, Senior Buyer, and EHS Manager. *(This last designated function ensures that any new raw material entering the production facility is acceptable in terms of the facility's operating permits).* If the raw material fails to meet all applicable requirements, the Senior Buyer is responsible for notifying the candidate supplier. The Senior Buyer can decide to work with the candidate supplier to understand whether the deficiencies can be corrected, or whether to seek out another candidate supplier.

Step 5. If the raw material meets all applicable requirements, the TSR is responsible for obtaining approval from the positions noted in Step 4, and for having the new supplier's chemicals evaluated in accordance with CORP. 17 Process or Design Change Review (*CORP. 17 should be the master process change procedure which requires evaluation of TSCA status of chemicals before they are used, among other things. The Manager of Regulatory Compliance is part of the process change evaluation team, as needed)* prior to the scheduling a plant evaluation of the new raw materials with the Operations Manager.

Step 6. The Operations Manager is responsible for conducting a plant evaluation in compliance with PP.20.3. *(PP.20.3 should be a subsidiary procedure to be implemented at a lower level of the corporate hierarchy. It governs the conduct of plant evaluations of materials and processes, taking into consideration issues like scheduling, dealing with final product produced, process safety and so on. Such a procedure should be developed in accordance with the user's* *plants and capabilities.)* Once the plant evaluation is completed, the TSR completes and distributes Plant Raw Material Evaluation Form to all the parties in Step 4.

Step 7. If the raw material fails to meet plant evaluation criteria, the Senior Buyer notifies the candidate supplier. The Senior Buyer can decide to work with the candidate supplier to understand whether the deficiencies can be corrected, or to seek out another candidate supplier.

Step 8. If the candidate raw material is approved, the Quality Coordinator is responsible for preparing Raw Material Specifications in accordance with CORP. 22 and for inserting those specifications in the approved raw material data base. *(CORP. 22 should address how raw material specifications must be written and approved.)*

Step 9. If the candidate raw material is approved and the supplier is a new supplier, the EHS Manager is responsible for notifying the Responsible Care Supplier Audit Team of the need for a new supplier audit as required in PP.20.4. *(PP.20.4 should include the protocol for the conduct of a new supplier audit. The audit involves a review of the supplier's operations for operational capability, compliance with legal requirements, and Responsible Care© Codes. The audit report may decline use of the supplier, accept the supplier, or accept the Supplier subject to designated corrective actions.)*

Step 10. The Senior Buyer is responsible for informing the supplier and completing negotiations for a supply contract for the raw material meeting the Raw Material Specifications. The Senior Buyer will present the Legal Department Supply Contract Form to the supplier for signature. A lawyer in the Legal Department must approve any deviations from the referenced form. The Senior Buyer will obtain the signature of the authorized company representative once the contract is agreed to by both parties.

Step 11. Upon receipt of all the approvals noted in this procedure, including the execution of a supply contract, the supplier is added to the list of approved suppliers for the specific raw material.

Step 12. The Operations Manager must quarantine any product produced in the production facility using a new raw material until approved for use by the Marketing Representative and, if required by contract[s], by the customer[s].

E. Procedure Number CORP. 26, New Product Development*

As discussed in The Inventory Chapter, § 5 of the Toxic Substances Control Act (TSCA) requires that all chemicals manufactured, processed, or used in the United States must be on a comprehensive list of chemicals maintained by the United States Environmental Protection Agency pursuant to § 8(b) of TSCA, called the TSCA Inventory. New products and the production processes for manufacturing new products could result in the formation of new chemicals and intermediates not on the TSCA Inventory. New products and new intermediates may also be subject to Significant New Use Rules (SNURs) and other product restrictions under TSCA. The company must make certain new products and the processes for making them are adequately reviewed from a TSCA perspective. This procedure deals with the process steps for manufacturing or importing a new product that might have an impact on TSCA compliance.

Most companies have several identified stages that new products go through, from initial research and development through full commercialization. Each company should adapt these procedures to conform to the new product development stages that they have identified. This procedure is designed to carry the TSCA review through this process, using as an example a multi-staged new product development scheme with the following Phases:

- *Initial R&D planning—Phase 1*
- *Product candidate synthesis and testing—Phase 2*
- *Promotion of product candidate—Phase 3*
- *Product safety, efficacy, and market research—Phase 4*
- *Promotion to commercialization—Phase 5*
- *Commercialization—Phase 6.*

There are different TSCA considerations at each stage.

1. Key Objective

This document describes the procedure for ensuring that new products are developed efficiently, with full consideration of regulatory obligations and risks, and meet customer requirements.

2. Applicable References

TSCA § 5
TSCA § 8(b)

---

* *Procedures may include steps that are not required by TSCA but are suggested business practices.*

(Add all other regulatory schemes relevant to the Company's products, such as FIFRA, FFDCA, or any foreign equivalents, and incorporate them into this procedure).

Procedures governing assessment of new suppliers, evaluations of raw materials, supplier audits, TSCA premanufacture notification and exemptions, and preparation of specifications, labels, and MSDSs.

3. Document History

REVISION	DATE	AUTHOR	RATIONALE
0.	THE TOXIC SUBSTANCES CONTROL ACT: A PRACTICAL GUIDE[1]		
1.			

4. Procedure

Step 1. Phase 1 Initial R&D Planning

Phase 1 is the project planning stage. In Phase 1 a list of approved projects is developed and a team is selected that is responsible to develop the product following the New Product Development Process. Any employee of the business, alone or with colleagues, can submit ideas to the New Product Development Committee (NPDC).

A. Phase 1 Project Proposal Format

Project proposals should contain the following elements:

1. Objective or Goal
2. Market Justification
3. Technical Justification
4. State of the Art/Competition
5. Technical Requirements
6. Timing Considerations
7. Estimate of Resources from
    a. Research
    b. Development

8. Health, Safety, and Environmental Considerations (including Responsible Care® if the company is a signatory)

---

1. MIRIAM V. GOLD & JEAN WARSHAW, THE TOXIC SUBSTANCES CONTROL ACT: A PRACTICAL GUIDE (OXFORD UNIVERSITY PRESS 2010).

B. Phase 1 Organization and Responsibilities of the New Product Development Committee (NPDC)

1. The Vice-President of Research chairs the NPDC.
2. Committee members include Research Managers, Directors of New Business Development, Director of Production, and the Manager of Regulatory Compliance (MRC).

   The NPDC is responsible for collecting and assessing Project Proposals. It reviews potential Project Proposals with the submitters against strategic business objectives, and develops a list of potential Project Proposals. The list of potential Project Proposals is reviewed with the Company Management Committee and a final list of Project Proposals is developed for implementation.

   The NPDC is responsible for monitoring the implementation of the Product Proposals through Phase 5 promotion. The activities of the NPDC are reviewed at a minimum of once a year by the Company Management Committee. During Phase 3, the NPDC must seek approval of the Research and Development Committee to promote candidate substances to Phase 4. During Phase 5, the NPDC must seek approval of the Company Management Committee to promote candidate substances to Phase 6. Activities of Phase 6 are the joint responsibility of the Resource Managers and appropriate Business Center Sponsor, and should be monitored by the appropriate Business Unit or Units.

Step 2. Phase 2 Product Candidate Synthesis And Testing

The Company Management Committee will designate a team leader for every Project Proposal, and the various functions and units will assign appropriate staff to each Project Team. The Project Team is responsible for conducting the activities set out in Phases 2 through 5, in accordance with the steps set out in the procedure.

Phase 2 activities constitute initial product candidate synthesis and testing. Project Team activities include:

A. Phase 2 Research: The Laboratory Director will ensure compliance with Procedure Number Lab. 11, Qualifying for the R&D Exemption at Laboratories.

The Research Representative will ensure the synthesis of product candidates, and will ensure collection and recordkeeping of the following data:

1. Structure
2. Molecular Formula
3. Characterization method and appropriate analytical references, when applicable

4. Chemist
5. Color
6. Form
7. Quantity Submitted
8. Date Prepared
9. Index Formula
10. Notebook number, when applicable
11. Disposal methods and environmental releases

Whether a calibrated or uncalibrated method was used will be recorded next to any physical data/analytical data. Uncalibrated measurements are used only for preliminary determinations and not for specification of product characteristics.

The analytical team is responsible for the analytical definition and method development to characterize the product candidate to meet toxicological testing requirements.

Upon verification of the chemical identity of the product candidate, the Research Representative shall inform the MRC who will determine if the substance is on the TSCA Inventory or subject to a SNUR.

B. Phase 2 Development: The Development Representative will ensure the screening of product candidates. External evaluation by selected customers (technical partners) may be initiated to obtain early performance feedback, especially in areas where the company is unable to perform the key tests necessary, or to obtain early validation of company test results. In Phase 2 there is no commitment to commercialization. The Director of Marketing of the Business Unit responsible for the experimental product area must approve in writing sampling an R&D substance outside of the company and shall ensure compliance with Procedure Number Lab. 5, Sampling R&D Substances to Third-Parties. If sampling is to a destination outside of the United States, the Director of Marketing shall inform the MRC who shall determine if the substance is subject to the export notification requirements of TSCA § 12(b).

The Application Laboratory Representative on the team is responsible for providing the following data:

1. Application data to meet the performance criteria of the product profile, which may consist of customer-specific tests
2. Analysis of opportunities in other business units
3. Sampling to internal resources

C. Phase 2 Patent: A designated team representative will review literature and patents relevant to team activity, and will ensure collection and recordation of the following data:

1. Is the compound or composition patented?
2. Do other organizations hold patents on the candidate?
3. Are U.S. patents or foreign counterparts applied for, or is an invention report on file with the corporate patent department?

The inventor will prepare an Invention Report for consideration by the corporate patent department. The Invention Report should contain at least the following elements:

1. Subject of the Invention—a general description of the invention
2. General Embodiment—specific or generic compound structures or blends involved, when applicable
3. Preferred Embodiments—preferred structures or blends, when applicable
4. Prior Art

D. Phase 2 Safety: Toxicology testing as necessary.

The toxicological and environmental issues for Phase 3 product candidate promotion are dependent upon the site of manufacture, product form, final end-use, and ultimate method of disposal. The Team Leader, along with a representative of the Regulatory Affairs Department, will ensure that the appropriate issues have been addressed and summarize the results in the Product Candidate Dossier for each product candidate that will be submitted for promotion to Phase 3.

E. Phase 2 Marketing: The Marketing Representative will update the product profile as necessary.

The Marketing Representative on the team is responsible for providing the following data and activity concerning promotion of a Phase 2:

Marketing plan that contains the minimum of the following elements:

1. Strategic Benefits
2. Market Trends
3. Competitive Advantages
4. Financial Benefit Forecast
5. Promotional Plan based on internal data and customer feedback

The Marketing Representative will establish provisional product specifications with appropriate Process Development and Production representatives.

Upon completion of Phase 2 activities for a product candidate, the Team Leader must complete a Phase 2 Activity Checklist.

Copies of the Promotion Certificate and Checklist are kept by the Team Leader and upon promotion to Phase 3 are filed in the Phase 3 Promotion Dossier.

Phase 2 Activity Checklist

Activity	Date Completed	Initials
Structure		
Verification		
Patent		
Performance		
Validation		
Safety		
Marketing		
Process		
Development		
Representative		
Sample Preparation		
Toxicology		
Analytical		
Validation		

Step 3. Phase 3 Transition from Phase 2 to Phase 4

After the NPDC reviews the Phase 2 product dossier, it arranges a meeting with the R&D Committee and the project team to review and assess the Product Candidate Dossier to ensure that activities required to take place to assess promotion to Phase 4 have occurred, that the candidate meets strategic business objectives, and that there are no obvious health, safety, environmental, or regulatory considerations that will derail commercialization of the product candidate. The R&D Committee will ask for any needed follow-up and will either approve promotion to Phase 4 outright or conditionally, or will reject promotion. In any case, the rationale for its actions will be explained to the Company Management Committee during the next scheduled NPDC review by the Company Management Committee. Upon promotion of a candidate, a copy of the Product Candidate Dossier will be sent to the Director of Process Development by the team leader. The R&D Committee approval of a product candidate in Phase 3 is documented by the signatures on the Phase 3 promotion certificate. One copy of the Phase 3 Product Candidate Dossier will be maintained by the Research Department Records Coordinator and one copy will be forwarded to the Director of Process Development.

The Phase 3 Product Candidate Dossier will document Phase 1 through 2 Activities.

The Phase 3 Promotion Certificate consists of the following format:

Phase 3 Promotion Certificate

Compound ____________ Phase 1 and Phase 2 activities have been reviewed by the NPDC, which recommended to the R&D Committee the promotion of the candidates to Phase 4. Such promotion was approved by the R&D Committee on ____________, and the candidate compounds were promoted to Phase 4 in the New Product Development Process.

Team Leader____________________

Sponsor ________________________

Vice-President of Research ___________________________

Step 4. Phase 4 Product Safety, Efficacy, And Market Research

In Phase 4, a representative sample is prepared that is suitable for toxicological assessments and appropriate analytical methods development. The quantity of sample and testing required are determined by the MRC, after consultation with the appropriate toxicologist.

Upon promotion to Phase 4, all quality critical data is reviewed and if required, re-measured with calibrated instruments. This new document is stamped "Product Dossier Copy."

A. Phase 4 Intellectual Property

The team continues to monitor the patent status of the product candidate and support actions by the patent department to either obtain a patent from the United States Patent and Trademark Office or possibly strengthen the existing cases.

B. Phase 4 Regulatory

The team, in conjunction with a representative of the Regulatory Affairs Department, addresses any appropriate toxicological/Responsible Care® issues required. The MRC shall advise the Product Team as early as possible during Phase 4 whether any imported raw materials, isolated intermediates manufactured during the production process, or the candidate product itself must be the subject of a premanufacture notice (PMN) prior to commercialization of the candidate product. If so, the Product Team shall establish a timeline for gathering information required for submission of a PMN and for filing the PMN at least ninety days prior to anticipated commercial manufacture of the candidate product. If the MRC concludes that the PMN review period is likely to exceed ninety days, or that the candidate product is likely to be the subject of an order restricting any aspect of its use or handling, the MRC shall bring such facts to the attention of the Product Team and the team shall plan accordingly. Any PMN shall be applied for in accordance with Procedure Number Reg. Aff. 2, Premanufacture Notifications and Notices of Commencement. The team will also review any SNURs and product restrictions identified by the Manager, Product Registration and Compliance and plan for managing the product candidate in accordance with SNUR requirements and product restrictions.

C. Phase 4 Marketing

The Marketing Representative on the team is responsible for defining at a minimum of the following elements:

1. Market demand forecast, short and long term
2. Pricing
3. Financial benefit, profitability
4. Finalized product specification

The Marketing Representative is responsible for finalizing product specifications and sampling of the product candidate to other business centers. The Marketing Representative is responsible for ensuring that notifications of health risks associated with the chemical accompany any sampling; the MRC shall provide assistance as requested.

D. Phase 4 Product Development

The Application Laboratory Representative on the team will perform the following activities:

1. Application evaluation of pilot samples
2. Further application development testing as required
3. Further customer sampling for design verification

E. Phase 4 Process Development

The Process Development Team Representative will perform the following activities:

1. Process definition, summarized in Chemical Development quarterly and interim/final reports
2. Analytical procedures definition
3. Environmental evaluation
4. Safety evaluation

5. Pilot Plant demonstration, if required. All pilot plant activities involving the candidate product shall be in conformance with Procedure Number Pilot Plant 11, Qualifying for the R&D Exemption at Pilot Plants if the candidate is not on the TSCA Inventory or if it is subject to a SNUR.

Documentation supporting these activities are collected in the Product Files and finalized in the Process Release and/or Technology Package.

F. Phase 4 Analytical

Analytical Methods Development occurs as required to meet Marketing, Development, and Product Safety Needs.

The team leader ascertains that all Phase 4 activities take place prior to commencement of Phase 5. A Phase 4 activity check list is completed.

Phase 4 Activity Checklist

Activity	Date Completed	Initials
Patent		
Regulatory/Product Safety		
Marketing		
Product Development		
Process Development		
Analytical		

Step 5. Promotion from Phase 4 to Phase 6

Prior to promotion to Phase 6, a Phase 5 Product Candidate Dossier is completed. Promotion to Phase 6 requires approval by the NPDC after Phase 4 activities are complete. A review for promotion to Phase 6 is initiated by the request of the Project Team Leader to the Vice-President of Research, who puts this proposal request on the agenda of the Company Management Committee. The Company Management Committee can approve the promotional outright or conditionally, or reject it.

The Phase 5 Product Candidate Dossier will consist of a notebook containing a minimum of the following elements:

Index and Title
Section 0 Activity Checklist and Phase 5 Promotion Certificate
Section 1 Product Profile
Section 2 Provisional Product Information
Section 3 Customer Feedback Evaluation

Section 4 Market Introduction Plan
Section 5 Cost Estimate
Section 6 Patent Status
Section 7 Process Development
Section 8 Production—Production Plan
Section 9 Analytical
Section 10 Product Safety and Regulatory
Section 11 Phase Guideline Exceptions

Phase 5 Promotion Certificate

Phase 5 Promotion Certificate

Compound __________ Phase 4 Activities have been reviewed by the Project Team, and recommended for promotion to Phase 6 by the NPDC to the Company Management Committee. The Company Management Committee approved promotion to Phase 6 in the Product Development Scheme on ________________.
Company President: ____________________________________
Vice-President of Business Unit: ____________________________
Vice-President of Research: ________________________________
Vice-President of Production: ______________________________
Vice-President of Regulatory Affairs:_________________________

Copies of the Phase 5 Product Dossier will be forwarded to and filed by the Research Records Coordinator and Director of Process Development.

Step 6. Phase 6 Commercialization.
Upon promotion to Phase 6, the project team is disbanded and the responsibility for Phase 6 activities rests jointly with the Director of the appropriate Business Center and the Resource Manager.

The MRC shall inform the Director of the appropriate Business Center and the Resource Manager when the PMN review period has expired for each isolated intermediate in the production process and each constituent of the product, if they are subject to the PMN process. The product may be manufactured only after the PMN review period has expired for each such substance.

The Production Manager shall inform the MRC immediately upon completion of manufacture of the first batch of product made for commercial use other than research and development. The MRC shall file a Notice of Commencement with the United States Environmental Protection Agency in accordance with Procedure Number Reg. Aff. 2 Premanufacture Notifications and Notices of Commencement.

F. Procedure Number Reg. Aff. 2, Premanufacture Notifications and Notices of Commencement*

As discussed in the Premanufacture Notifications Chapter, § 5(a) of the Toxic Substances Control Act (TSCA) requires manufacturers and importers of chemical substances to notify the United States Environmental Protection Agency (EPA) at least ninety days in advance of manufacturing or importing a new chemical substance that is not on the TSCA Inventory. The notification is made on a form called the Premanufacture Notice (PMN). If the EPA does not take any affirmative steps to restrict manufacturing, importing, processing, or any other aspect of handling the chemical substance, the PMN filer is free to commence manufacture or import at the expiration of that ninety-day period. Within thirty days of the first manufacture or importation the PMN filer must submit a Notice of Commencement (NOC). After the NOC is filed, the EPA automatically puts the chemical substance on the TSCA Inventory and then anyone is free to manufacture or import it, subject to any Significant New Use Rule (SNUR) that the EPA may promulgate.

The statute and regulations exclude numerous substances from the definition of "chemical substance" and these excluded substances are not subject to the PMN requirements and are not the subject of this Procedure.

Additional substances qualify for exemptions from the PMN requirements. The EPA's PMN form is also used for certain exemption applications and other notifications. The exemption applications that must use the PMN form are the Low Volume Exemption and Low Release and Exposure Exemption. Use of the PMN form is optional for applying for a Test Marketing Exemption.

The PMN form is also used for Significant New Use Notices (SNUNs), and for so-called "mock PMNs," which are submissions in the context of enforcement proceedings. Note that requirements for the SNUNs are not the same as for PMNs., and are addressed in Procedure Number Reg. Aff. 7, Procedure for SNUNs.

This Procedure does not apply to research and development substances that are made, imported, or handled solely by laboratories or facilities in compliance with either Procedure Number Lab. 11, Qualifying for the R&D Exemption at Laboratories or Procedure Number Pilot Plant 11, Qualifying for the R&D Exemption at Pilot Plants.

This Procedure is limited to PMNs directed towards Inventory listing of the subject chemicals, and mock PMNs.

* *Procedures include steps that are not required by TSCA but are suggested business practices.*

1. Key Objective

This document describes the procedure required to list a chemical substance on the TSCA Inventory, and for submitting mock PMNs. The steps include gathering information to submit a PMN, filling out the PMN form, and continuing to update information during the EPA's ninety-day review period. It also describes the procedure for notifying the EPA when the PMN filer commences manufacture or import of the PMN substance.

2. Applicable References

TSCA § 5(a)
40 C.F.R. Part 720
Procedure Number Lab. 5, Sampling R&D Substances to Third Parties
Procedure Number Lab. 11, Qualifying for the R&D Exemption at Laboratories
Procedure Number Pilot Plant 11, Qualifying for the R&D Exemption at Pilot Plants
Procedure Number Reg. Aff. 3, Procedure for the Test Marketing Exemption from PMN and SNUR Requirements
Procedure Number Reg. Aff. 4, Procedure for LVE and LoREX Exemptions from PMN Requirements
Procedure Number Reg. Aff. 7, Procedure for SNUNs
Procedure Number Reg. Aff. 8, Procedure for SNURs

3. Document History

REVISION	DATE	AUTHOR	RATIONALE
0.	2010	THE TOXIC SUBSTANCES CONTROL ACT: A PRACTICAL GUIDE[1]	
1.			

4. Procedure

Step 1. The Manager of Regulatory Compliance (MRC) shall maintain a list of all chemicals manufactured or imported by the Company. Such list shall include the TSCA Inventory and SNUR status of each chemical. *(For mock PMNs, begin with Step 7.)*

Step 2. Each Product Manager, Director of Marketing of any Business Unit, Production Manager, and any other person who intends to manufacture or

1. MIRIAM V. GOLD & JEAN WARSHAW, THE TOXIC SUBSTANCES CONTROL ACT: A PRACTICAL GUIDE (OXFORD UNIVERSITY PRESS 2010).

import a chemical substance shall consult the list of chemicals manufactured or imported by the Company. If the chemical is not on that list, or is on the list without a notation that it is on the TSCA Inventory, such person shall notify the MRC in writing. If the chemical is on the list with a notation that it is subject to a Significant New Use Rule, see Procedure Number Reg. Aff. 8, Significant New Use Rules.

Step 3. The MRC shall search the publicly available TSCA Inventory and determine if the chemical substance is listed. If the substance is not on the publicly available TSCA Inventory, the MRC shall determine based on the chemistry of the substance and the generic chemical names on the confidential Inventory whether it is possible that the substance is on the confidential Inventory. If it may be on the confidential Inventory, the MRC shall confer with the requester and decide if it is appropriate to submit a bona fide letter to request confirmation from the EPA about the Inventory status of the substance.

Step 4. The MRC shall determine based on the chemistry of the substance whether the substance is subject to a publicly available SNUR *(possible only if the substance is on the public Inventory)* or whether the substance may be subject to a confidential SNUR. If it may be subject to a confidential SNUR, the MRC shall confer with the requester and decide if it is appropriate to submit a bona fide letter to request confirmation from the EPA about the SNUR status of the substance. If the substance is or may be subject to a SNUR, see Procedure Number Reg. Aff. 8, Significant New Use Rules.

Step 5. If the substance is not on the Inventory, the MRC shall determine if the substance is excluded from the definition of "chemical substance" because it is a pesticide, a food, a nuclear material, or any other substance excluded from TSCA's scope. The MRC shall also determine if the substance is eligible for an exemption from the PMN requirements because it is to be made for test marketing, in low volumes, is an exempt polymer, or any other type of substance eligible for an exemption. If the substance is excluded or qualifies for an exemption, no PMN is required; see Procedure Number Reg. Aff. 3, Procedure for the Test Marketing Exemption from PMN and SNUR Requirements, Procedure Number Reg. Aff. 4, Procedure for LVE and LoREX Exemptions from PMN Requirements.

Step 6. The MRC shall respond in writing to the requester advising of the Inventory and SNUR status of the substance and any other restrictions or requirements associated with the subject chemical substance. The MRC shall inform the requester if the substance is in a chemical category, or will be produced on a scale, or result in exposures that will likely trigger an order under TSCA § 5(e), or is potentially subject to any other restrictions or requirements. If the substance is not on the public or confidential Inventory and is not excluded or eligible for an exemption from the PMN requirements, the MRC, the Product Manager, the Director of Marketing of the applicable

Business Unit, and the Production Manager, as applicable, shall confer and determine whether the business plans justify the time and expense of filing a PMN. As part of this analysis, they shall consider the time and costs of negotiating a TSCA § 5(e) consent order if the substance is in a chemical category for which consent orders are likely, the tests likely to be required under a consent order, and the costs of complying with any applicable restriction or requirement. Regulatory compliance and ecotoxicity experts, whether in-house or consultants, should be involved in evaluating data available for structurally similar substances, and the costs of this evaluation should be considered in advance. If the business considerations preclude filing a PMN, no manufacture or importation of the substance may be undertaken.

Step 7. If the decision in Step 6 is to proceed with filing a PMN, or if the PMN filing is for a mock PMN, the MRC shall gather information sufficient to describe the substance's chemical identity, physicochemical properties, manufacturing, processing, and use information, test data, other data, and optional pollution prevention information. The MRC shall determine if the PMN substance is in a category of chemicals subject to a Test Rule under TSCA § 4, and if it is, the MRC shall assemble all tests required by the Test Rule and submit them with the PMN. The MRC shall request information from the Product Manager, Production Manager, suppliers in the case of PMN substances to be imported, suppliers and manufacturers of precursors and in-house or external chemists as necessary, to conclusively determine the chemical identity of the PMN substance. The MRC shall collect all information required by the PMN form that similarly situated people and companies would be expected to know. The MRC shall also obtain all information requested by the PMN form that is in the company's possession or control, and shall seek information in at least the following places:

- the Company's files, including files maintained by:
  - its employees who do research, development, test marketing, or commercial marketing of the PMN substance;
  - its employees who are reasonably likely to have relevant data;
  - its agents who do research, development, test marketing, or commercial marketing of the PMN substance (agents are working under contract or other special arrangements with the Company);
- these entities, if they are associated with the Company in the research, development, test marketing, or commercial marketing of the PMN substance:
  - corporate subsidiary companies;
  - corporate parent companies;
  - partnerships in which the Company is a general partner and limited liability companies (LLCs) in which the Company has a majority interest; and

- all companies in which a parent company owns or controls 50 percent or more of the voting stock or LLC membership interests;
- all partnerships in which a parent company is a general partner, and LLCs in which the parent company has a majority interest; and
- all entities that stand in one of the described relationships with a covered subsidiary, partnership or parent of the Company.

The MRC shall inform each such person and entity of the obligation to submit updates, further studies, and data results during the EPA's review of the PMN.

Step 8. The MRC shall confer with the Legal Department to determine the identity of all entities described in Step 7.

Step 9. The MRC shall retain copies of requests to all entities and people listed in Step 7, follow-up communications until responses are received, and all responses.

Step 10. The Product Manager shall coordinate with any suppliers who are not willing to divulge to the PMN filer proprietary or trade secret information necessary to establish the chemical identity of the PMN substance. Such suppliers may submit a joint PMN or may file a letter of support with the EPA.

Step 11. The MRC shall contact an EPA Prenotice Coordinator prior to filing the PMN if the PMN is a consolidated PMN or an intermediate PMN.

Step 12. The MRC shall prepare a draft of the PMN form and circulate it to the Product Manager, Director of Marketing of the relevant Business Unit, Production Manager, and any other internal stakeholder, with a request to review it for accuracy and identify all information that is Confidential Business Information (CBI). If any information is CBI, the MRC shall prepare a "sanitized" PMN with the CBI information redacted. The MRC shall inform each reviewer and internal stakeholder of the obligation to submit new pertinent information and changed information on the PMN form to the EPA during the PMN review period, including changes of projected production volumes, places of manufacture, changed exposure scenarios, and all other changes to information on the PMN form. At this point, filers of mock PMNs should skip Step 13, sign and submit the PMN as set forth in Step 14, skip Steps 15 through 19, and conclude with Step 20.

Step 13. Once all reviewers have commented on the draft PMN, the MRC shall assign a TS-number to the PMN, and shall submit the required filing fee, with the TS-number, to the EPA.

Step 14. The MRC shall finalize the PMN, ensuring that all information is accurate and complete, and shall sign the certifications. The MRC shall submit the original plus two duplicate copies of the PMN, plus one copy of any sanitized PMN to the EPA, if filing on paper.

Step 15. Once the EPA informs the company that the PMN is complete, the MRC shall enter the date of complete filing in a master calendar system, together with the anticipated expiration of the ninety-day PMN review period.

Step 16. If the MRC receives updated status reports on ongoing studies, further test or study results, or any changes to the information submitted on the PMN form, the MRC shall submit such information to the EPA within ten days of receipt by any person at the company, but not later than five days before the end of the PMN review period. The MRC shall telephone the EPA if such information is received within five days of the end of the PMN review period.

Step 17. If the EPA takes any actions to restrict manufacture, importation, or use of the PMN substance the MRC shall inform all potentially affected stakeholders and determine the appropriate course of action, which may include negotiating a consent order or abandoning the PMN process.

Step 18. If the EPA does not take any actions to restrict manufacture, importation, or use of the PMN substance during the ninety-day PMN review period, the MRC shall inform all interested persons that the substance may be manufactured or imported, provided that they shall notify the MRC immediately upon completion of the first production or importation.

Step 19. Within thirty days of completion of the first production or importation of the PMN substance for a purpose that is not excluded or exempted from the PMN requirements, the MRC shall file a Notice of Commencement (NOC) with the EPA, using the EPA NOC form.

Step 20. The MRC shall archive one complete set of documents relating to the PMN, including the records of all locations searched for pertinent information, all tests and studies submitted with or described in the PMN, the completed PMN form as submitted, and all correspondence with the EPA concerning the PMN. The MRC shall document in the file all studies and test data that were not submitted or described in the PMN that were reviewed, with the rationale for not submitting or describing them. The complete set shall be retained in the corporate archives for five years after the company ceases to manufacture or import the PMN substance.

G. Procedure Number Reg. Aff. 3, Procedure for the Test Marketing Exemption from PMN and SNUR Requirements*

As discussed in the PMN Exclusions and Exemptions Chapter, § 5(a) of the Toxic Substances Control Act (TSCA) requires manufacturers and importers of chemical substances to notify the Environmental Protection Agency (EPA) at least ninety days in advance of manufacturing or importing a new chemical substance that is not on the TSCA Inventory, or ninety days in advance of manufacturing, importing, or processing a chemical substance subject to a Significant New Use Rule (SNUR). However, there are numerous exemptions from these requirements to file a PMN or Significant New Use Notification (SNUN).

This Procedure applies to the Test Marketing Exemption (TME) from the PMN and SNUR rules. Use of the PMN form to apply for the TME is optional but encouraged and this Procedure assumes use of the PMN form for that purpose.[1]

The statute and regulations exclude numerous substances from the definition of "chemical substance" and these excluded substances are not subject to the PMN or SNUR requirements and are not the subject of this Procedure.

This Procedure does not apply to research and development substances that are made, imported, or handled solely by laboratories or facilities in compliance with either Procedure Number Pilot Plant 11, Qualifying for the R&D Exemption at Pilot Plants, or Procedure Number Lab. 11, Qualifying for the R&D Exemption at Laboratories.

1. Key Objective

This document describes the procedure required to submit an application to the EPA to exempt a chemical substance from the requirements of the PMN and SNUR rules because the substance will be manufactured or imported for test marketing purposes only. The steps include gathering information to submit the application using the PMN form, and post-approval steps to comply with the exemption requirements.

This procedure should be followed when the Manager of Regulatory Compliance (MRC) has determined that a substance (a) that any person in the Company intends to manufacture or import is not on the TSCA Inventory, or that a substance that any person intends to manufacture, import, or process is subject to a SNUR, and (b) may qualify for a TME exemption from the PMN and SNUR requirements.

---

* *Procedures include steps that are not required by TSCA but are suggested business practices.*

1. Note that signing the PMN form requires signing a certification that the form is complete and includes all test data in the applicant's possession or control and a description of all other data known to or reasonably ascertainable by the applicant. This certification would not be required if the application were submitted in letter format.

2. Applicable References

TSCA § 5(a)
TSCA § 5(h)
40 C.F.R. § 720.38
40 C.F.R. Part 720
40 C.F.R. Part 721
Procedure Number Reg. Aff. 2, Premanufacture Notifications and Notices of Commencement
Procedure Number Pilot Plant 11, Qualifying for the R&D Exemption at Pilot Plants
Procedure Number Lab. 11, Qualifying for the R&D Exemption at Laboratories

3. Document History

REVISION	DATE	AUTHOR	RATIONALE
0.	2010	THE TOXIC SUBSTANCES CONTROL ACT: A PRACTICAL GUIDE[2]	
1.			

4. Procedure

Step 1. The MRC shall determine if the substance is excluded from the definition of "chemical substances" that are subject to the PMN and SNUR rules. If the substance is excluded, see the Procedure applicable to compliance with the specific exclusion.

Step 2. The MRC, the Product Manager, the Director of Marketing of the applicable Business Unit, and the Production Manager, as applicable, shall confer and determine whether the business plans justify the time and expense of filing a TME application, and complying with any applicable restriction or requirement. If they do not, no manufacture or importation of the substance may be undertaken without compliance with the PMN and SNUR rules. (Note that if the PMN form is used the effort and expense of gathering information for a TME or PMN is the same, while there are no user fees applicable to TME applications.)

Step 3. If the decision in Step 2 is to proceed with filing an application for a TME, the MRC shall gather information sufficient to describe the substance's chemical identity, physicochemical properties, manufacturing, processing and use information, test data, other data, and optional pollution prevention

---

2. MIRIAM V. GOLD & JEAN WARSHAW, THE TOXIC SUBSTANCES CONTROL ACT: A PRACTICAL GUIDE (OXFORD UNIVERSITY PRESS 2010).

information. The MRC shall request information from the Product Manager, Production Manager, suppliers in the case of TME substances to be imported, suppliers and manufacturers of precursors and in-house or external chemists as necessary to conclusively determine the chemical identity of the TME substance. The MRC shall collect all information required by the PMN form that similarly situated people and companies would be expected to know. The MRC shall also obtain all information requested by the PMN form that is in the company's possession or control, and shall seek information in at least the following places:

a. the Company's files, including files maintained by:
   i. its employees who do research, development, test marketing, or commercial marketing of the TME substance;
   ii. its employees who are reasonably likely to have relevant data;
   iii. its agents who do research, development, test marketing, or commercial marketing of the TME substance (agents are working under contract or other special arrangements with the submitter);
b. corporate subsidiary companies if the subsidiaries are associated with the Company in the research, development, test marketing, or commercial marketing of the TME substance;
c. corporate parent companies if the parent companies are associated with the Company in the research, development, test marketing, or commercial marketing of the TME substance;
d. partnerships in which the Company is a general partner and limited liability companies (LLCs) in which the Company has a majority interest, if the partnerships or LLCs are associated with the Company in the research, development, test marketing, or commercial marketing of the TME substance;
e. all companies in which a parent company owns or controls 50 percent or more of the voting stock or LLC membership interests, if those companies are associated with the Company in the research, development, test marketing, or commercial marketing of the TME substance;
f. all partnerships in which a parent company is a general partner, and LLCs in which the parent company has a majority interest, if the partnerships or LLCs are associated with the Company in the research, development, test marketing, or commercial marketing of the TME substance; and
g. all entities that stand in one of the described relationships with a covered subsidiary, partnership or parent of the Company, provided they are involved in the research, development, test marketing, or commercial marketing of the TME substance.

Step 4. The MRC shall confer with the Legal Department to determine the identity of all entities described in Step 3.

Step 5. The MRC shall retain copies of requests to all entities and people listed in Step 3, follow-up communications until responses are received, and all responses.

Step 6. The Product Manager shall coordinate with any suppliers who are not willing to divulge to the Company proprietary or trade secret information necessary to establish the chemical identity of the TME substance. Such suppliers may submit a joint PMN form or may file a letter of support with the EPA.

Step 7. The MRC shall prepare a draft of the PMN form and circulate it to the Product Manager, Director of Marketing of the relevant Business Unit, Production Manager, and any other internal stakeholder, with a request to review it for accuracy and identify all information that is Confidential Business Information (CBI). If any information is CBI, the MRC shall prepare a "sanitized" PMN form with the CBI information redacted. The MRC shall inform each reviewer and internal stakeholder of the obligation to submit new pertinent information and changed information on the PMN form to the EPA during the TME review period, including changes of projected production volumes, places of manufacture, changed exposure scenarios, and all other changes to information on the PMN form.

Step 8. The MRC shall finalize the PMN form, ensuring that all information is accurate and complete, and shall sign the certifications. The MRC shall submit the original PMN form plus one copy of any sanitized PMN form to the EPA, if filing on paper.

Step 9. Once the EPA informs the company that the PMN form is complete, the MRC shall enter the date of complete filing in a master calendar system, together with the anticipated expiration of the 45-day TME review period.

Step 10. If the MRC receives updated status reports on ongoing studies, further test or study results, or any changes to the information submitted on the PMN form, the MRC shall submit such information to the EPA within ten days of receipt by any person at the Company, but not later than five days before the end of the TME review period. The MRC shall telephone the EPA if such information is received within five days of the end of the TME review period.

Step 11. Upon receipt of EPA's written approval of the TME, the MRC shall send a summary of the requirements of the exemption, designating the responsible parties in the organization, to the following people, as appropriate, depending on the nature of the restrictions:

a. Manager, EHS in the plants that will manufacture the chemical—responsible for implementing any restrictions dealing with human exposure and environmental releases in the manufacturing plant;

b. Production Manager—responsible for ensuring compliance with any volume restrictions and for ensuring that no changes take place in the site of manufacture or in the technology used for manufacture;
c. Manager, Importation—responsible for ensuring compliance with any volume restrictions of a chemical that will be imported;
d. Manager, Marketing—responsible generally for communications with customers as to restrictions on the chemical, and for ensuring that sales staff is knowledgeable about any restrictions that will impact customer use. He is responsible for:
    i. sending a letter to customers of the TME substance informing customers of the TME restrictions. This information can be included with the customer letter explaining the test marketing program;
    ii. sending a list of customers notified pursuant to this Procedure to Manager, Customer Service, and ensuring that the list is kept up to date; and
    iii. informing sales and marketing personnel of the restrictions on the chemicals, and of advising such personnel to promptly notify Manager, Marketing and MRC if they become aware that a customer is not complying with any restrictions.
e. Manager, Customer Service—responsible for maintaining the list of approved customers, as received from Manager, Marketing, for TME chemicals, and for working with IT support to implement computer controls in the business processing system so that the chemicals can only be shipped to the designated approved customers;
f. Manager, Information Technology, Business Processing Systems—responsible for ensuring that controls are established in the business processing system so that only designated customers can receive subject chemical; and
g. MSDS/Label Specialist—responsible for ensuring that restrictions regarding the handling and use of the subject chemical are inputted into the chemical MSDS and inserted on the label, as appropriate.

Step 12. No changes can be made to the importation, production, distribution, and EHS plans for the chemical without notification to, and approval of, the MRC:

a. should any manager want to make a change, that manager will notify the MRC of the nature of the proposed change and the benefits of the proposed change;
b. the MRC, with the assistance of an appropriate team, will determine whether such a change can be made in accordance with the exemption restrictions and the regulations, the costs of making such a change, and whether the implementation of such a change will require either notification to the EPA or pre-approval from the EPA; and

c. the MRC will present the determination of the team to the Manager, Marketing, who will decide whether or not to go forward with the change.

Step 13. Any Company employee that becomes aware that a direct or indirect customer is using a chemical subject to a TME in violation of any of the restrictions in the approved TME must notify the Manager, Marketing, and the MRC:

a. the Manager, Marketing, will notify Manager, Customer Service, and Manager, Information Technology, Business Processing Systems, that the customer's name is to be deleted from the list of customers to whom the chemical can be distributed;
b. the Manager, Customer Service, and the Manager, Information Technology, Business Processing will immediately delete the customer name from approved recipients of the TME substance;
c. the Manager, Customer Service, will ensure that any orders in progress to such customer are canceled, and will advise the Manager, Marketing, of all such canceled orders; and
d. the Manager, Marketing, will manage all customer communications arising in connection with any nonpermitted use.

Step 14. The MRC shall archive one complete set of documents relating to the TME application, including:

a. the records of all locations searched for pertinent information,
b. all tests and studies submitted with or described in the PMN form;
c. all tests and studies reviewed but not submitted with or described in the PMN form, with reasons for not submitting or describing them;
d. the completed PMN form as submitted and all correspondence with the EPA concerning the TME;
e. all records supporting the exemption notice, including projected manufacturing and importation volumes; and
f. all correspondence between noncompliant customers and the company.

The complete set shall be retained in the corporate archives for five years after the Company ceases to manufacture or import the TME substance in reliance on the TME.

H. Procedure Number Reg. Aff. 4, Procedure for LVE and LoREX Exemptions from PMN Requirements*

As discussed in the PMN Exclusions and Exemptions Chapter, § 5(a) of the Toxic Substances Control Act (TSCA) requires manufacturers and importers of chemical substances to notify the Environmental Protection Agency (EPA) at least ninety days in advance of manufacturing or importing a new chemical substance that is not on the TSCA Inventory. However, there are numerous exemptions from this requirement to file a PMN.

This Procedure applies to the low volume exemption (LVE) and to the low release and exposure (LoREX) exemption from the rules. Use of the PMN form to apply for LVEs and LoREX exemptions is mandatory.

The statute and regulations exclude numerous substances from the definition of "chemical substance" and these excluded substances are not subject to the PMN requirements and are not the subject of this Procedure.

This Procedure does not apply to research and development substances that are made, imported, or handled solely by laboratories or facilities in compliance with either Procedure Number Pilot Plant. 11, Qualifying for the R&D Exemption at Pilot Plants, or Procedure Number Lab. 11, Qualifying for the R&D Exemption at Laboratories. Note that LVEs and LoREX exemptions are not exemptions from Significant New Use Rules.

1. Key Objective

This document describes the procedure required to submit an application to the EPA to exempt a chemical substance from the requirements of the PMN rules because the substance will be manufactured or imported in annual quantities of less than ten thousand kilograms or has low environmental releases and low human exposure. The steps include gathering information to submit the application using the PMN form, and post-application steps to comply with the exemption requirements.

This procedure should be followed when the Manager of Regulatory Compliance (MRC) has determined that a substance that any person in the Company intends to manufacture or import is not on the TSCA Inventory, and may qualify for a LVE or LoREX exemption from the PMN requirements.

2. Applicable References

TSCA § 5(a)
TSCA § 5(h)

---

* *Procedures include steps that are not required by TSCA but are suggested business practices.*

40 C.F.R. Part 720
40 C.F.R. § 723.50
Procedure Number Reg. Aff. 2, Premanufacture Notifications and Notices of Commencement
Procedure Number Pilot Plant 11, Qualifying for the R&D Exemption at Pilot Plants
Procedure Number Lab. 11, Qualifying for the R&D Exemption at Laboratories

3. Document History

REVISION	DATE	AUTHOR	RATIONALE
0.	2010	THE TOXIC SUBSTANCES CONTROL ACT: A PRACTICAL GUIDE[1]	
1.			

4. Procedure

Step 1. The MRC shall determine if the substance is excluded from the definition of "chemical substances" that are subject to the PMN rules. If the substance is excluded, see the Procedure applicable to compliance with the specific exclusion.

Step 2. The MRC, the Product Manager, the Director of Marketing of the applicable Business Unit, and the Production Manager, as applicable, shall confer and determine whether the business plans justify the time and expense of filing an LVE or LoREX application, and complying with any applicable restriction or requirement. If they do not, no manufacture or importation of the substance may be undertaken without compliance with the PMN rules. (Note that because LVE and LoREX applications use the PMN form the effort and expense of gathering information for any of these is the same, while there are no user fees applicable to LVEs and LoREX applications.)

Step 3. If the decision in Step 2 is to proceed with filing an application for an LVE or LoREX exemption, the MRC shall gather information sufficient to describe the substance's chemical identity, physicochemical properties, manufacturing, processing and use information, test data, other data, and optional pollution prevention information. The MRC shall request information from the Product Manager, Production Manager, suppliers in the case of LVE or LoREX substances to be imported, suppliers and manufacturers of precursors and in-house or external chemists as necessary to conclusively determine

1. MIRIAM V. GOLD & JEAN WARSHAW, THE TOXIC SUBSTANCES CONTROL ACT: A PRACTICAL GUIDE (OXFORD UNIVERSITY PRESS 2010).

the chemical identity of the LVE or LoREX substance. The MRC shall collect all information required by the PMN form that similarly situated people and companies would be expected to know. The MRC shall also obtain all information requested by the PMN form that is in the company's possession or control, and shall seek information in at least the following places:

a. the Company's files, including files maintained by:
   i. its employees who do research, development, test marketing, or commercial marketing of the LVE or LoREX substance;
   ii. its employees who are reasonably likely to have relevant data;
   iii. its agents who do research, development, test marketing, or commercial marketing of the LVE or LoREX substance (agents are working under contract or other special arrangements with the Company);
b. corporate subsidiary companies if the subsidiaries are associated with the Company in the research, development, test marketing, or commercial marketing of the LVE or LoREX substance;
c. corporate parent companies if the parent companies are associated with the Company in the research, development, test marketing, or commercial marketing of the LVE or LoREX substance;
d. partnerships in which the submitter is a general partner and limited liability companies (LLCs) in which the Company has a majority interest, if the partnerships or LLCs are associated with the Company in the research, development, test marketing, or commercial marketing of the LVE or LoREX substance;
e. all companies in which a parent company owns or controls 50 percent or more of the voting stock or LLC membership interests, if those companies are associated with the Company in the research, development, test marketing, or commercial marketing of the LVE or LoREX substance;
f. all partnerships in which a parent company is a general partner, and LLCs in which the parent company has a majority interest, if the partnerships or LLCs are associated with the Company in the research, development, test marketing, or commercial marketing of the LVE or LoREX substance; and
g. all entities that stand in one of the described relationships with a covered subsidiary, partnership, or parent of the Company, provided they are involved in the research, development, test marketing, or commercial marketing of the LVE or LoREX substance.

Step 4. The MRC shall confer with the Legal Department to determine the identity of all entities described in Step 3.

Step 5. The MRC shall retain copies of requests to all entities and people listed in Step 3, follow-up communications until responses are received, and all responses.

Step 6. The Product Manager shall coordinate with any suppliers who are not willing to divulge to the Company proprietary or trade secret information necessary to establish the chemical identity of the LVE or LoREX substance. Such suppliers may submit a joint PMN form or may file a letter of support with the EPA.

Step 7. The MRC shall prepare a draft of the PMN form and circulate it to the Product Manager, Director of Marketing of the relevant Business Unit, Production Manager, and any other internal stakeholder, with a request to review it for accuracy and identify all information that is Confidential Business Information (CBI). If any information is CBI, the MRC shall prepare a "sanitized" PMN form with the CBI information redacted. The MRC shall inform each reviewer and internal stakeholder of the requirement to submit new pertinent information and changed information on the PMN form to the EPA during the LVE or LoREX review period and after approval of the exemption, including changes of projected production volumes, places of manufacture, changed exposure scenarios, and all other changes to information on the PMN form.

Step 8. The MRC shall finalize the PMN form, ensuring that all information is accurate and complete, and shall sign the certifications. The MRC shall submit the original PMN form plus one copy of any sanitized PMN form to the EPA, if filing on paper.

Step 9. Once the EPA informs the company that the PMN form is complete, the MRC shall enter the date of complete filing in a master calendar system, together with the anticipated expiration of the thirty-day LVE or LoREX review period.

Step 10. If the MRC receives updated status reports on ongoing studies, further test or study results, or any changes to the information submitted on the PMN form, the MRC shall submit such information to the EPA within ten days of receipt by any person at the Company, but not later than five days before the end of the LVE or LoREX review period. The Manager of Regulatory Compliance shall telephone the EPA if such information is received within five days of the end of the LVE or LoREX review period.

Step 11. Upon expiration of the LVE or LoREX review period, if the EPA has not taken any affirmative steps to deny the exemption application, the MRC shall inform all stakeholders of the expiration of the LVE or LoREX review period without EPA objection, and consequent regulatory authorization to rely on the exemption. The MRC shall send a summary of the requirements of the exemption, designating the responsible parties in the organization, to the following people, as appropriate, depending on the nature of the restrictions:

a. Manager, EHS in the plants that will manufacture the chemical—responsible for implementing any restrictions dealing with human exposure and environmental releases in the manufacturing plant;

b. Production Manager—responsible for ensuring compliance with any volume restrictions and for ensuring that no changes take place in the site of manufacture or in the technology used for manufacture;
c. Manager, Importation—responsible for ensuring compliance with any volume restrictions of a chemical that will be imported;
d. Manager, Marketing—responsible generally for communications with customers as to restrictions on the chemical, and for ensuring that sales staff is knowledgeable about any restrictions that will impact customer use:
   i. with respect to LoREX exemption substances, is responsible for ensuring that customers for the LoREX substance receive, sign, and return an agreement that they will not further distribute the substance until it has been reacted, incorporated into an article, or otherwise put into a physical form or state in which environmental releases and human exposures above the designated levels will not occur;
   ii. with respect to LoREX exemption substances, is responsible for sending a list of customers notified pursuant this Procedure to Manager, Customer Service, and ensuring that the list is kept up-to-date; and
   iii. is responsible for informing sales and marketing personnel of the restrictions on the chemicals, and of advising such personnel to promptly notify Manager, Marketing and MRC if they become aware that a customer is not complying with any restrictions.
e. Manager, Customer Service—responsible for maintaining the list of approved customers, as received from Manager, Marketing for LoREX chemicals, and for working with IT support to implement computer controls in the business processing system so that the chemicals can only be shipped to the designated approved customers;
f. Manager, Information Technology, Business Processing Systems—responsible for ensuring that controls are established in the business processing system so that only designated customers can receive subject chemicals;
g. MSDS/Label Specialist—responsible for ensuring that restrictions regarding the handling and use of the subject chemical are inputted into the chemical MSDS and inserted on the label, as appropriate; and
h. Manager, Toxicology—responsible for reviewing any new data or information about the chemical substance to determine whether it indicates that the substance may not qualify for the LoREX or LVE exemption;
   i. such information shall be forwarded within ten working days to the MRC, with a recommendation as to whether that information is required to be sent to EPA as part of the Company's continuing obligations; and

ii. if required to be submitted to the EPA, the MRC will send any such data or information to the EPA within 15 working days of receipt by the Company of the data or information.

Step 12. No changes can be made to the importation, production, distribution, and EHS plans for the chemical without notification to, and approval of, the MRC:

a. should any manager want to make a change, that manager will notify the MRC of the nature of the proposed change and the benefits of the proposed change;
b. the MRC, with the assistance of an appropriate team, will determine whether such a change can be made in accordance with the exemption restrictions and the regulations, the costs of making such a change, and whether the implementation of such a change will require either notification to the EPA or pre-approval from the EPA; and
c. the MRC will present the determination of the team to the Manager, Marketing, who will decide whether or not to go forward with the change.

Step 13. If a change to the site of manufacture is internally approved:

a. with respect to human exposures:
   i. if the technology to be employed at the new site is the same as that used at the existing site, the MRC and the Manager, EHS, shall determine whether the magnitude, frequency, and duration of human exposure at the new site is equal to or less than that at the old site; or
   ii. if the technology to be employed at the new site differs from the technology used at the existing site, the MRC and the Manager, EHS, shall determine whether the magnitude, frequency, and duration of human exposure at the new site is less than that at the old site;
b. with respect to environmental releases, the MRC and the Manager, EHS, shall determine if the chemical substance will not be released at the new site to surface waters or to waste streams, or that surface water concentrations will be maintained at or below 1 part per billion, or some other concentration level approved by EPA. They shall make these determinations using the methods set forth in the regulations;
c. if the calculations made pursuant to Steps 13a and 13b allow for a site change, the MRC shall notify all stakeholders involved in implementing the site change about the restrictions applicable to the new site, with internal notifications as specified in Step 11 above.

d. Within thirty days after beginning manufacturing at the new site, the MRC shall submit to the EPA notification of site change using the EPA's PMN form. The notification must contain:
   i. the Company name and name and contact information of a technical contact at the new site;
   ii. street address of the new site;
   iii. original EPA-designated exemption number;
   iv. date on which manufacture began at new site;
   v. claims of confidentiality, if any;
   vi. statement by the Company that the notification is an amendment to the original exemption application; and
   vii. an original signature of an authorized official.

Copies of all records supporting the site change notification, including exposure determinations and environmental release calculations, shall be maintained in the file with the original exemption application.

Step 14. If a change to the uses or physical form, human exposure, or environmental release controls, production volume in excess of any binding amount noted on the exemption notice, or manufacturing site that does not meet the requirements in Step 13 above is internally approved, the MRC must file a new exemption notice.

a. The new exemption notice must contain the following:
   i. identity of the chemical substance;
   ii. the Company name and name and contact information of a technical contact; location of new site, new worker protection, or environmental release controls and new use information, as applicable; and
   iii. original EPA designated exemption number and a new certification.
a. No changes can be made until the exemption notice is approved or the time for approval has passed.
b. Once the exemption notice has been approved, or the time for approval has lapsed, the MRC must make the internal notifications as specified in Step 11 above.

Copies of all records supporting the new exemption notice, including exposure determinations and environmental release calculations, shall be maintained in the file with the original exemption application.

Step 15. Any company employee that becomes aware that a direct or indirect customer is using a chemical subject to an LVE or LoREX exemption in violation of any of the restrictions in the LVE or LoREX exemption must notify the Manager, Marketing, and the MRC.

a. The Manager, Marketing, must notify the customer in writing, within five working days of receipt of such information, about the nonpermitted uses and request that the customer acknowledge that it is aware of the restrictions and will comply with them;
b. if the Manager, Marketing, receives a written reply from the customer within 15 working days with such assurances, the Company does not have to discontinue distribution to such customer;
c. if the Manager, Marketing does not receive such an assurance within the 15-working-day time period, the Company must then immediately discontinue distribution to such customer;
d. the Manager, Marketing, will notify Manager, Customer Service, and Manager, Information Technology, Business Processing Systems, that the customer's name is to be deleted from the list of customers to whom the chemical can be distributed;
e. the Manager, Customer Service, and the Manager, Information Technology, Business Processing, will immediately delete the customer name;
f. the Manager, Customer Service, will ensure that any orders in progress to such customer are canceled, and will advise the Manager, Marketing, of all such canceled orders;
g. the Manager, Marketing, will manage all customer communications arising in connection with any nonpermitted use; and
h. if after receiving the assurances noted in (ii) above, the Company again learns that the customer is not complying with the restrictions,
    i. the Company must immediately stop distributing the chemical to that customer;
    ii. the Manager, Marketing, will notify Manager, Customer Service, and Manager, Information Technology, Business Processing Systems, that the customer's name is to be deleted from the list of customers to whom the chemical can be distributed;
    iii. the Manager, Customer Service, and the Manager, Information Technology, Business Processing, will immediately delete the customer name;
    iv. the Manager, Customer Service, will ensure that any orders in progress to such customer are canceled, and will advise the Manager, Marketing, of all such canceled orders; and
    v. the MRC must inform the EPA of this compliance failure within 15 days of obtaining knowledge of such compliance failure.

Step 16. The MRC shall archive one complete set of documents relating to the LVE or LoREX application, including:

a. the records of all locations searched for pertinent information,
b. all tests and studies submitted with or described in the PMN form;

c. all tests and studies reviewed but not submitted with or described in the PMN form, with reasons for not submitting or describing them;
d. the completed PMN form as submitted and all correspondence with the EPA concerning the LVE or LoREX exemption;
e. all records supporting the exemption notice, including projected manufacturing and importation volumes; and
f. all correspondence between noncompliant customers and the company.

The complete set shall be retained in the corporate archives for five years after the company ceases to manufacture or import the LVE or LoREX substance in reliance on the LVE or LoREX exemption.

I. Procedure Number Reg. Aff. 25, TSCA § 8(e) and 8(c) Compliance*

As discussed in Chapter 7, Reporting and Recordkeeping, § 8(e) of the Toxic Substances Control Act (TSCA) requires that any person who imports, manufactures, processes, or distributes chemical substances or mixtures in the United States and who obtains information generated in the United States or in another country that reasonably supports a conclusion that a chemical substance or mixture may present a substantial risk of injury to human health or the environment must immediately report such information to the United States Environmental Protection Agency (EPA), unless the person knows that EPA has already been adequately informed. The information must be submitted to the Agency within thirty calendar days of the individual or business obtaining the information. For information to be reportable under § 8(e), it does not need to establish conclusively that a risk exists and does not need to provide evidence that the substance is hazardous to human health or the environment under actual conditions of use and exposure. The information may relate to actual instances of serious human health or environmental injury caused by the chemical or mixture or to observations that are early indications of such effects. Incidents of environmental contamination may also be reportable under TSCA § 8(e) and should be reviewed under this procedure in order to determine its immediate reportability as soon as the Company has knowledge of the incident.

TSCA § 8(c) requires that any person who imports, manufactures, processes, or distributes in commerce any chemical substance or mixture maintain records of "significant adverse reactions to health or the environment." The recordkeeping obligation extends to mere allegations made without formal proof or regard for evidence. The requirements apply to both written and oral information and to individuals as well as businesses. Research and development (R&D) compounds, intermediates (except pharmaceutical intermediates), by-products, and impurities are not exempt from the requirements.

Once information relating to adverse effects or reactions is collected, from whatever source, the information must be reviewed to see whether it is an allegation of a significant adverse effect that under § 8(c) must be maintained in the company's files, usually referred to as recordable, or if it is a report of a significant adverse that must be reported to the EPA under § 8(e). Feedback must be given to the employee raising an allegation of significant risk under § 8(e).

EPA has said it will not enforce TSCA 8(e) obligations against individuals if their employers have adopted and implemented a policy and procedure for employee submission and company processing of substantial risk information.

---

* *Procedures may include steps that are not required by TSCA but are suggested business practices.*

This procedure applies to the Company and its subsidiaries.

This procedure is applicable to chemical substances and mixtures as defined in TSCA § 3(2).

1. Key Objective

This document describes the procedure to:

- assure that potential substantial risk information is expeditiously and consistently reviewed across the Company and reported, as appropriate, to EPA within thirty calendar days of when the Company first obtained the information or recorded;
- provide a corporate mechanism through which the Company's employees and officers may discharge their individual obligations to report substantial risk information to the EPA under TSCA § 8(e); and
- provide a mechanism for recording allegations of substantial adverse effects.

2. Applicable References

TSCA§ 8(e)
TSCA § 8(c)

- 43 Fed. Reg. 11110, Toxic Substances Control Act Statement of Interpretation and Enforcement Policy; Notification of Substantial Risk (March 16, 1978) (1978 Statement of Interpretation);
- EPA, TSCA Section 8(e) Reporting Guide (June 1991);
- Letter from Victor Kimm, USEPA, to Robert M. Sussman (April 2, 1992);
- Comment And Response Document For Revised Policy Statement Of Section 8(e) OF TSCA, OPPT-2002-0067-0002 (February 20, 2003);
- 68 Fed. Reg. 33129, TSCA Section 8(e); Notification of Substantial Risk; Policy Clarification and Reporting Guidance (June 3, 2003) (2003 Reporting Guidance);
- EPA, Frequent Questions, January 2005 and September 2006; and
- TSCA § 8(e) Reporting Checklists attached to this Procedure.

(Add all other regulatory schemes relevant to the Company's recording or reporting of adverse effects, such as, e.g. FIFRA, FFDCA, OSHA, or any foreign equivalents, and incorporate them into this procedure.)

Procedures governing functions that may be the first to obtain information concerning significant adverse effects, such as health services, litigation, and customer relations.

3. Document History

REVISION	DATE	AUTHOR	RATIONALE
0.	2010	THE TOXIC SUBSTANCES CONTROL ACT: A PRACTICAL GUIDE[1]	
1.			

4. Procedure

Step 1. INITIAL ESCALATION

All employees shall evaluate risk information on an ongoing basis and report all potential substantial risk information and allegations of adverse effects to one of the functions designated below, or directly to the Company's TSCA Coordinator, within one business day. Emergency incidents of environmental contamination must be reported as soon as possible. Upon doing so, the employee fully discharges his or her reporting obligation under § 8(e) under EPA policy.

The designated functions are:

(a) **Nurse** for injuries or complaints about adverse effects experienced by Company employees (*companies should require employees to report any work-related injuries to a medical office, if there is one, or to some other designated function, to address Workers' Compensation issues. The medical office or the Workers' Compensation coordinator should have a procedure in place to investigate the bona fides of the report and to take any needed corrective actions*);

(b) **Customer Complaint System** for information or allegations concerning adverse effects experienced by a customer or its employees (*most companies will have a system for managing customer complaints; a comment from a customer that a product caused an effect such as a rash should be entered into the system and reviewed as an allegation of an adverse effect*);

(c) **Director of Toxicology** for toxicity or ecotoxicity studies;

(d) **Litigation Counsel** for claims or allegations made in litigations (*most companies with in-house counsel require that any lawsuits be managed by counsel; allegations in a lawsuit regarding adverse effects of a product should be reviewed as an allegation of an adverse effect*);

---

1. MIRIAM V. GOLD & JEAN WARSHAW, THE TOXIC SUBSTANCES CONTROL ACT: A PRACTICAL GUIDE (OXFORD UNIVERSITY PRESS 2010).

(e) **Production Site Environmental Affairs Department, EHS Coordinator** for environmental issues and contamination from, allegations relating to, or adverse effects observed following spills occurring at a Facility (*production sites should have systems to monitor issues which occur during production);*

(f) **Transportation Manager** for contamination from, allegations relating to, or adverse effects observed following spills during the transport of materials outside of any Company facility (*companies should have systems to manage issues which occur in transporting goods*);

(g) **Warehouse Manager** for contamination from, allegations relating to, or adverse effects observed following spills at any Company or publicly owned warehouses (*companies should have systems to manage issues which occur during warehousing); and*

(h) **Manager of Regulatory Compliance** (MRC) for all other information or allegations concerning adverse effects, including emergency incidents of environmental contamination, and adverse effects experienced by neighbors, the community or visitors, and all other information from other Divisions or sources. All such information from sources outside the United States must be reported to the MRC when a U.S. employee is informed of it.

In some instances, employees may obtain substantial risk information before the substance is subject to TSCA. For example, the substance may be a pesticide that is exempt from TSCA, or the substance may not be present in the United States. If the substance becomes subject to TSCA because it is used for a non-pesticidal purpose, or because it is imported into the United States, such information becomes reportable. Therefore, all such information shall be provided to a person in one of the designated functions or the TSCA Coordinator within one business day whether or not the person who obtained that information believes that the substance is subject to TSCA. Upon doing so, the employee fully discharges his or her reporting obligation under § 8(e) under EPA policy.

All people in the designated functions listed above who receive potential substantial risk information or allegations of adverse effects shall immediately inform the TSCA Coordinator.

Step 2. Information Gathering

The TSCA Coordinator shall assemble all information needed to evaluate potential substantial risk information for reporting under TSCA § 8(e). If reporting is directly addressed in the Reporting Checklists attached to this Procedure the TSCA Coordinator shall determine if reporting is required.

The TSCA Coordinator shall determine if allegations of adverse effects must be recorded and maintained in Company files under TSCA § 8(c).

Step 3. Formation of an 8(e) Committee

The TSCA Coordinator (or designee) shall convene an 8(e) Committee if reporting is not directly addressed in the Reporting Checklists to evaluate possible substantial risk information and decide whether such information should be reported to EPA under TSCA § 8(e). The 8(e) Committee consists of the TSCA Coordinator and other people with relevant expertise, including, for example the Manager of Regulatory Affairs, a toxicologist, business representative, and such other personnel as may be advisable on a case-by-case basis as determined by the TSCA Coordinator. The TSCA Coordinator (or designee) is the Chairperson of the 8(e) Committee. Legal counsel shall advise the 8(e) Committee but shall not vote, and if legal counsel is not available the 8(e) Committee shall proceed without counsel. In the case of emergency incidents of environmental contamination, the TSCA Coordinator shall determine if the incident has been reported to the National Response Center, and if it has not then further consideration of reporting under TSCA § 8(e) is required and the TSCA Coordinator shall proceed to Step 5's follow through requirement.

Step 4. 8(e) Committee Review and Decision Making

The 8(e) Committee shall meet by the twenty-fifth day after substantial risk information has been obtained. The 8(e) Committee meets in person or remotely to evaluate possible substantial risk information and decides by consensus whether the information should be reported to EPA under § 8(e). However, if all members of the 8(e) Committee agree based on information circulated to them prior to a scheduled meeting that the information clearly warrants § 8(e) reporting, the 8(e) Committee does not have an obligation to meet and the TSCA Coordinator shall proceed with Step 5. (*Large companies may establish a regular schedule of meetings every three weeks.*)

Step 5. 8(e) Committee Decision Follow Through

After the 8(e) Committee reaches a decision on whether the information should be reported to the EPA under § 8(e), the TSCA Coordinator shall:

1) inform management of the relevant business about the reporting decision within three days;
2) inform the Corporate Vice President of Environment, Health & Safety about the reporting decision within three days;
3) inform in writing the employee who first obtained the possible substantial risk information of the Company's reporting decision within three days, and if the Company decision was not to report, the written notification to the employee shall include the information set forth in Step 6;
4) determine within five days whether the Business Unit considers any information in a § 8(e) notice to be Confidential Business Information (CBI);

5) prepare, sign, and submit a § 8(e) letter directly to EPA within thirty calendar days of obtaining substantial risk information, together with copies with CBI deleted, if required, and serve as liaison with EPA for such § 8(e) notices;
6) provide EPA with substantiation of CBI claims;
7) maintain corporate records related to 8(e) Committee decisions using the pertinent Reporting Checklist from those attached to this Procedure, and maintain copies of all § 8(e) submissions to EPA; completed copies of such Reporting Checklists and submissions must be kept by the Company as long as the subject chemical is manufactured, imported, processed, or distributed by the Company; and
8) maintain centralized corporate records related to allegations of substantial adverse effects for thirty years in the case of allegations by employees and for the six years after the chemical is last manufactured, imported, or processed by the Company in the case of all other allegations, and periodically review the centralized records to determine if a pattern of allegations should be referred to the 8(e) Committee for consideration as substantial risk information.

Step 6. Employee Right to Appeal and Report Directly to EPA
If the employee who first obtained the possible substantial risk information or any member of the 8(e) Committee disagrees with a decision to refrain from reporting possible substantial risk information, he or she may appeal within three days to the management of the relevant business and, if desired, to the Company Board of Directors, which will make the final reporting decision on behalf of the Company before the thirty-day reporting period has elapsed. All Company employees and officers shall have the right to report the information directly to the EPA if he or she disagrees with the Company's decision not to report it. The Company will not take any retaliatory actions against the employee if he or she decides to report the information directly to EPA. If the employee elects to submit the information directly to the EPA, the employee shall inform the TSCA Coordinator, who shall assure that CBI is submitted to the EPA in a manner that will not jeopardize its confidentiality.

Step 7. Employee and Officer Awareness
The TSCA Coordinator shall ensure that each employee and officer is aware of this Procedure and their obligations under this Procedure. The TSCA Coordinator shall:

1) publicize this Procedure within the Company to ensure expeditious processing of possible substantial risk information and allegations of significant adverse effects, and periodically advise employees and officers of their obligation to report possible substantial risk information and allegations of substantial adverse effects to the TSCA Coordinator;

2) publicize the penalties for failure to comply with TSCA § 8(e), including civil penalties not to exceed $37,500 per day for each violation,[2] and criminal penalties upon conviction, of fines, imprisonment for not more than one year, or both; and
3) establish a core training program to explain the purpose of TSCA § 8(e) and § 8(c) and the Company reporting procedure. This training program will include the type of information to be reported, who within the Company to report to, the civil and criminal penalties for failing to report, and the employee's right to report the information to EPA himself or herself.

Attachments:
Introduction to the TSCA § 8(e) Reporting Checklists
TSCA § 8(e) Reporting Checklists

2. The maximum penalty of $37,500 went into effect January 12, 2009, and is scheduled for another increase in 2013.

1. Introduction to the TSCA § 8(e) Reporting Checklists*

Greatly simplified, § 8(e) of the TSCA statute requires any person who learns that certain chemical substances may pose a substantial risk of injury to health or the environment to report that information to the EPA. These checklists were designed to help determine what information needs to be reported. This introduction gives background on § 8(e) reporting, discusses the information that does not have to be reported, and discusses some aspects of how to submit reports. It does not cover every topic related to TSCA § 8(e), and is only intended as a handy reference.

EPA has issued numerous guidances that provide insight into the types of studies that it wants reported. It is important to keep in mind that these are only *guidances*, they are not laws or regulations and they are open to interpretation. That means, in EPA's words, that guidance it issues "does not impose any binding requirements upon either the regulated community or the Agency."[3] However, guidance is the Agency's interpretation of the statute itself, and the statute is binding law. The EPA will assess penalties for failure to comply with its interpretation of the law. As a result, deviations from the EPA's guidance may be made, but should be made only when scientifically justified. Deviations from the checklists may also be made when they are justified, in consultation with the Director of Toxicology, because the checklists incorporate some conservative interpretations of the EPA guidance. On the other hand, there is no penalty for overreporting, and in case of genuine doubt studies should be reported.

These checklists are intended to be living documents, and should be modified as new interpretations of TSCA appear. To make a modification, contact the Director of Toxicology.

The statutory language of TSCA § 8(e) says in full:

> **(e) Notice to Administrator of substantial risks**
>
> **Any person who manufactures, processes, or distributes in commerce a chemical substance or mixture and who obtains information which reasonably supports the conclusion that such substance or mixture presents a substantial risk of injury to health or the environment shall immediately inform the Administrator of such information unless such person has actual knowledge that the Administrator has been adequately informed of such information.**

---

* *Procedures may include steps that are not required by TSCA but are suggested business practices.*

3. 68 Fed. Reg. 33129, 33130 (June 3, 2003).

This introduction covers the following topics:

- Who has a reporting obligation?
- Chemicals that are subject to TSCA § 8(e) reporting
- Chemicals that are *not* subject to TSCA § 8(e) reporting
- Reportability of studies on low exposure substances
- Types of information that are reportable
- Types of information that are *not* reportable
- When is the report due?
- Confidentiality claims

a. Who has a reporting obligation?

The company has an obligation to report substantial risk information to the EPA for chemicals that it manufactures, imports, processes, or distributes in commerce in the United States.

In addition, every individual who can appreciate the significance of substantial risk information has a reporting obligation under the statute. EPA has said it will exercise discretion not to penalize individual employees, except for "officials" who have authority to implement § 8(e) reporting, for violations of this personal responsibility if their corporate employers establish procedures for § 8(e) reporting.

b. Chemicals that are subject to TSCA § 8(e) reporting

TSCA has a complex set of exemptions from its many requirements, but few of these exemptions apply to § 8(e) reporting. For example, R&D chemicals are not subject to premanufacture notification requirements, but an adverse effect demonstrated by an R&D chemical must be reported under § 8(e). Qualifying studies on all of the following types of chemicals must be reported, even though some of them are exempt from other TSCA requirements:

- commercial substances
- R&D chemicals
- chemicals manufactured solely for export
- catalysts
- byproducts
- impurities
- microorganisms
- nanoscale materials and engineered nanoscale materials
- chemicals developed as pesticides, up until the time an experimental use permit (EUP) is filed
- pesticide intermediates, inerts, impurities, and byproducts
- chemicals that have both pesticidal use and non-pesticidal use

- chemicals that have uses as food, food additives, drugs, cosmetics, or devices (FDA uses) and non-FDA uses
- chemicals the company imports
- chemicals the company manufactures
- chemicals the company processes (processing includes repackaging)
- mixtures of chemicals

c. Chemicals that are *not* subject to TSCA § 8(e) reporting

Section 8(e) reporting is only required for chemicals that are within the TSCA definition of "chemical substances." Chemicals that are not "chemical substances" and are not subject to § 8(e) reporting include:

- pesticides, as defined in FIFRA, when manufactured, processed, or distributed in commerce for use as a pesticide.[4]
- tobacco or tobacco products
- nuclear materials, as defined in the Atomic Energy Act
- firearms, shells, and cartridges
- food, food additives, drugs, cosmetics, or devices as defined in the Federal Food, Drug, and Cosmetic Act, when manufactured, processed, or distributed in commerce for use as a food, food additive, drug, cosmetic, or device
- chemicals that the Company does not manufacture, import, or process (processing includes repackaging)

Chemicals that are not present in the United States are commonly understood to be outside of TSCA's scope. As a result, reporting is not required unless the chemical has been in the United States.

Note that chemicals that have some uses that are covered by TSCA and some that are covered by FIFRA or the FFDCA are subject to TSCA § 8(e) reporting when manufactured for undifferentiated purposes and when used for TSCA-covered purposes.

---

4. Under TSCA guidances, intermediates, inerts, impurities, and contaminants are not pesticides. FIFRA recognizes that substances can be pesticides when no EUP is filed; FIFRA requires reporting on inerts, impurities, contaminants, metabolites, and degradates. The TSCA guidances appear to overreach the statutory definition, but as a matter of ongoing practice the TSCA guidances should be applied, with the understanding they may not be enforceable.

d. Reportability of studies on low-exposure substances

In many cases, the EPA guidances permit balancing the risk presented by a chemical substance against the potential exposure to the substance. As a result, a study showing a high risk may be reportable even if the substance is not commercial, and a study on a commercial product may be reportable although only a slight effect was observed. Because of the difficulty of tracking when an R&D substance becomes commercial, the Company will, as a general matter, report all studies as if the test chemical is already commercialized.

The checklists can be modified on a case-by-case basis with the understanding that a study that has not been reported because the test substance is not commercial should be reviewed for reportability once the substance becomes commercial.

e. Types of information that are reportable

Any information that "*reasonably supports* the conclusion that such substance or mixture presents a substantial risk of injury to health or the environment" is reportable, and reporting is required well before you have the luxury of reaching a scientific conclusion. Therefore, all of these sources may yield information that is reportable:

- study results
- preliminary results of incomplete studies
- information learned in discussions with overseas colleagues
- medical and health surveys

People in many job functions may receive potentially reportable significant risk information. Some examples include:

- health care professionals may observe sensitization, irritation, neurological effects, tumors, and other adverse effects
- environmental remediation specialists may obtain reports of environmental contamination or bioaccumulation
- toxicologists may receive reports of animal studies showing ataxia, lethargy, or other reportable effects
- plant managers may learn of spills into the environment
- customer relations personnel may receive complaints of rashes, nauseating odors, and other human health effects.

f. Types of information that are *not* reportable

Information is not reportable if you know that the EPA already has the information. While the EPA has said in guidance that some information that has been or will be reported to other agencies is not reportable under TSCA § 8(e), this Company has chosen to report all information unless we know that the EPA has already received it. This position is in keeping with the statutory language.

Corroborative information is not reportable, but to be corroborative the information must substantially duplicate or confirm a prior result. The route of exposure, dose, species, strain, and sex of the test animal, time to onset of effect, nature, and severity of the effect must be the same. Similarly, a well-recognized and well-established serious adverse effect need not be reported. However, observations of known effects during an emergency incident of environmental contamination may be reportable.

Reports of non-emergency environmental contamination that were reviewed prior to the EPA's June 3, 2003 guidance do not need to be reported unless someone reviews them because of new information, and the new information together with the preexisting report meet the criteria for reporting this type of information.

An environmental effect does not need to be reported under TSCA § 8(e) if it is:

- A non-emergency incident of environmental contamination
  - that must be reported within ninety days to EPA pursuant to a statute administered by EPA
  - that must be reported to the EPA in connection with an authorized site remediation program
  - outside of the United States if it is not likely to result in contamination in the United States
- an emergency incident of environmental contamination
  - that must be reported to the EPA immediately pursuant to a statute administered by EPA
  - that must be reported the EPA in connection with an authorized site remediation program
  - outside of the United States if it is not likely to result in contamination in the United States
- all other environmental substantial risk information
  - that must be reported to the EPA within thirty days pursuant to a statute administered by EPA

g. When is the report due?

In every case except an emergency incident of environmental contamination, TSCA § 8(e) reporting is due no later than the thirtieth calendar day after anyone at the Company receives reportable information.

Emergency incidents of environmental contamination must be reported immediately to the National Response Center, (800) 424–8802, and the EPA.

Note that the National Response Center is operated by the Coast Guard, and as a result notifying the National Response Center does not meet the statutory requirement unless you know that the report has been submitted to the EPA.

The clock on the thirty-day time period starts when a person employed by the Company who is capable of appreciating the significance of the risk information first comes into possession of information that "reasonably supports" a conclusion that there is a substantial risk. Many people in addition to toxicologists are capable of appreciating the significance of risk information, and the clock starts whenever such a person sees a study. The clock can begin ticking well before there is a scientific conclusion that a substantial risk is present. Under this standard, preliminary results of studies are reportable.

h. Confidentiality Claims

The EPA will maintain trade secrets as confidential information if the § 8(e) submission states that it contains Confidential Business Information (CBI), and if a redacted, or "sanitized" copy is supplied to the EPA for public view.

Health and safety studies on chemicals that have been offered for distribution in commerce are not confidential under TSCA § 14(b), and EPA has said it will not keep confidential the results of these studies, or the chemical identities of the test substances. From the extent of CBI claims in § 8(e) submittals it is apparent that many companies must be submitting such information and claiming confidentiality. However, manufacturing processes and formulations can be claimed as confidential. The Company's identity can also be claimed as confidential to avoid revealing that the Company is performing R&D on a substance or that the Company is manufacturing or importing a chemical substance.

Study Title:	______	*Business Unit:*	______
Chemical/Product Name:	______		
Laboratory:	______		
Chemical No.:	______		
Study Date:	______	*Study No.:*	______

Checklist to Determine Whether Non-Emergency Incidents of Environmental Contamination are Reportable Under Section V(b)(1) of EPA's 2003 Policy Statement

Note: the newly obtained information deals with contamination, not adverse effects

		YES	NO
1.	Chemical was found widespread in environmental media (air, indoor air, soil, water, commercial products) and there is a substantial likelihood of exposure to people or organisms. • If yes, specify the environmental media: ______	☐	☐
2.	Chemical was PREVIOUSLY UNSUSPECTED of being in the environmental media.	☐	☐
3.	Information exists that reasonably supports a known serious non-trivial health effect or serious environmental effect for the chemical. • If yes, specify briefly: ______	☐	☐
4.	Concentrations of the chemical are equal to or greater than "benchmark levels" such as reference dose, MCL, drinking water standard, permit level, *or lower internal company guideline* (can *assume* no substantial risk below these levels). • If yes, specify briefly: ______	☐	☐
5.	Decision: 8(e) reportable If "yes," submit: summary only: ______ report & summary ______	☐	☐

Note to Reviewer

- If the answers to all questions 1, 2, 3, AND 4 are "yes" the information is section 8(e) reportable in US.
- Evaluate reporting in Canada under CEPA § 70.
- See introduction to checklists to determine 8(e) reportability if other mandatory reporting requirement exists.
- If not reportable because substance is used as a pesticide, drug, or food additive, evaluate for reporting under FIFRA or FFDCA.

Signature of Reviewer: ______________________ Date ____/____/____

Study Title:	__________	*Segment:*	__________
Chemical/Product Name:	__________		
Laboratory:	__________		
FAT No./TK No./Other No.:	__________		
Study Date:	__________	*Study No.:*	__________

Checklist to Determine Whether Previously Unknown Bioaccumulation or Presence in Organisms is Reportable Based on Section V(b)(2) of EPA's 2003 Policy Statement

Note: the newly obtained information deals with bioaccumulation or biomonitoring, not adverse effects

		YES	NO
1.	Chemical has a bioconcentration factor greater than 500.	☐	☐
2.	Chemical has a log P of greater than 4.0 and less than or equal to 7.0.	☐	☐
3.	Biomonitoring shows presence of substance in humans or other organisms.	☐	☐
4.	Biomonitoring, bioconcentration factor or log P in questions 1 or 2 is NOT known to EPA.	☐	☐
5.	The chemical is known to have a non-trivial adverse effect • If yes, specify: __________	☐	☐
6.	The chemical has the potential for widespread exposure. • If yes, specify: __________	☐	☐
7.	Decision: 8(e) reportable If "yes" submit: summary only: _____ report & summary _____	☐	☐

Note to Reviewer

- If the answers to any question 1, 2, or 3 is "yes" and the answer to all questions 4, 5, AND 6 are "yes" the information is section 8(e) reportable in the US and, if applicable, in Canada under CEPA § 70.
- See introduction to checklists to determine 8(e) reportability if other mandatory reporting requirement exists.
- If not reportable because substance is a pesticide, drug, or food additive, evaluate for reporting under FIFRA or FFDCA.

Exposure status – describe:

- Current application (e.g., industrial, commercial, consumer, FIFRA only, FFDCA only)
____

Signature of Reviewer: __________ Date ___ / ___ / ___

Study Title: ______________________ *Segment:* ______________
Chemical/Product Name: ______________________
Laboratory: ______________________
FAT No./TK No./Other No.: ______________________
Study Date: ______________________ *Study No.:* ______________

Checklist to Determine Whether Previously Unknown Environmental Effects are Reportable Based on Section V(b)(3) (4) and (5) of EPA's 2003 Policy Statement

Note: the newly obtained information deals with adverse environmental effects

			YES	NO
1.	The chemical was found to have a non-trivial adverse effect.		☐	☐
	• Check all applicable information:			
	Aquatic:	Acute LC50 (96 hr) fish or Acute EC50 (48 hr) invertebrates—less than or equal to 1 mg/l (1 ppm) (without regard to exposure potential).	☐	☐
		Chronic LC50 fish or Acute EC50 invertebrates—less than or equal to 0.1 mg/l (.1 ppm) (without regard to exposure potential).	☐	☐
		Acute LC50 (96 hr) fish or Acute EC50 (48 hr) invertebrates – between 1-100 mg/l (1-100 ppm) AND the substance is intended to be used commercially in an application with a likelihood of exposure.	☐	☐
		Chronic LC50 fish or Acute EC50 invertebrates between 0.1–10 mg/l (.1–10 ppm) AND the substance is intended to be used commercially in an application with a likelihood of exposure.	☐	☐
	Other:	LC50 or EC50 concentrations for non-mammalian species, less than or equal to concentrations equivalent to those above for reporting without regard to exposure potential.	☐	☐
		LC50 or EC50 concentrations for non-mammalian species in a range equivalent to those above for reporting only if there is an exposure potential AND the substance is intended to be used commercially in an application with a likelihood of exposure.	☐	☐
		Invertebrate or vertebrate study found significant adverse changes.	☐	☐
	Other studies (consult Acute, Subacute/Chronic/Subchronic, and other checklists for adverse effect reporting) • describe briefly: ______________________________		☐	☐
2.	The non-trivial adverse effect is NOT known to EPA.		☐	☐

3.	The chemical is known to have bioaccumulated to a pronounced degree, or to be widespread in environmental media. • If yes, specify: ____________________	☐	☐
4.	Ecologically significant changes in species' interrelationships are observed, (e.g., excessive stimulation of primary producers, or interference with critical biochemical cycles)	☐	☐
5.	Facile transformation or degradation to a chemical having a substantial risk.	☐	☐
6.	Decision: 8(e) reportable If "yes, "submit: summary only: ________ report & summary ________	☐	☐

Note to Reviewer

- If the answers to any subpart of question 1 is "yes" and the answer to either question 2 or 3 is "yes" the information is section 8(e) reportable in US and, if applicable, in Canada under CEPA § 70.
- If the answers to either question 4 or 5 is "yes" the information is section 8(e) reportable
- See introduction to checklists to determine 8(e) reportability if other mandatory reporting requirement exists.
- If not reportable because substance is a pesticide, drug, or food additive, evaluate for reporting under FIFRA or FFDCA.

Exposure status – describe:

- Current application (e.g., industrial, commercial, consumer, FIFRA only, FFDCA only) ____________________

Signature of Reviewer: ____________________________ Date ____/____/____

Study Title:	______________	*Segment:*	______________
Chemical/Product Name:	______________		
Laboratory:	______________		
FAT No./TK No./Other No.:	______________		
Study Date:	______________	*Study No.:*	______________

Checklist to Determine Whether Emergency Incidents of Environmental Contamination are Reportable Under TSCA 8(e) Based on Section V(c) of EPA's 2003 Policy Statement

		YES	NO
1.	The chemical was found to have contaminated the environment.	☐	☐
2.	The chemical has a known non-trivial adverse effect.		
3.	The pattern, extent and concentration of contamination seriously threaten humans with cancer, birth defects, mutation, death, or serious or prolonged incapacitation, or seriously threaten non-human organisms with large-scale or ecologically significant population destruction.	☐	☐
5.	Decision: 8(e) reportable If "yes, "submit: summary only: ________ report & summary ____________	☐	☐

Note to Reviewer

- If the answer to ALL of questions 1, 2, and 3 are "yes" the information is 8(e) reportable. Immediate notification to the National Response Center [(800) 424–8802 or (202) 267–2675] may be required.
- Evaluate for reporting in Canada under CEPA § 70.
- See introduction to checklists to determine 8(e) reportability if other mandatory reporting requirements exist.
- If not reportable because substance is a pesticide, drug, or food additive, evaluate for reporting under FIFRA or FFDCA.

Signature of Reviewer: ______________________ Date ____/____/____________

Study Title: ______________________ *Business Unit:* ______________
Chemical/Product Name: ______________________
Laboratory: ______________________
Chemical No.: ______________________
Study Date: ______________________ *Study No.:* ______________

Checklist to Determine Whether a Multigeneration Reproduction or Reproductive/Developmental Study is 8(e) Reportable

		Yes	*No*	*Not Applic.*
1.	The study revealed statistically or biologically significant tetratogenic embryotoxic or fetotoxic findings, e.g., embryolethality, embryotoxicity, fetotoxicity, malformations, variations, spontaneous abortion, etc. (without regard to level of maternal toxicity).	☐	☐	☐
2.	Statistically or biologically significant reductions in birth weights were recorded.	☐	☐	☐
3.	Statistically or biologically significant reductions in fertility or gestational changes were recorded.	☐	☐	☐
4.	Statistically or biologically significant developmental effects were recorded. • If yes, specify effects: ______________________ ______________________	☐	☐	☐
5.	Statistically or biologically significant gross pathological and/or histopathological change(s) or rare malformations for the species/strain used were recorded. • If yes, specify changes: ______________________ ______________________	☐	☐	☐
6.	Clinical and/or behavioral signs and symptoms of neurotoxicity were recorded (see checklist for neurotoxicity).	☐	☐	☐
7.	Study is reportable based on criteria on Subacute/Subchronic/Chronic Study checklist.	☐	☐	☐
8.	Decision: 8(e) reportable: If "yes" submit: summary only ______ report & summary ______	☐	☐	

Note to Reviewer:

- If the answer to any question is "yes" the study IS 8(e) reportable in the US and, if applicable, in Canada under CEPA § 70.
- If not reportable because substance is a pesticide, drug, or food additive, evaluate for reporting under FIFRA or FFDCA.

Exposure status – describe:

- Current application (e.g. industrial, commercial, consumer, FIFRA only, FFDCA only)
  ____

Signature of Reviewer: ______________________ Date ___/___/___

Study Title: ______________________ *Business Unit:* ______________
Chemical/Product Name: ______________________
Laboratory: ______________________
Chemical No.: ______________________
Study Date: ______________________ *Study No.:* ______________

Checklist to Determine Whether a Sensitization Study is 8(e) Reportable

Test method (check one): Buehler ☐ Maximization ☐
Other (specify) ☐ ______________ LLNA ☐

		Yes	*No*	*Not Applic.*
1.	Treatment-related mortalities occurred indicative of extreme toxicity were observed.	☐	☐	☐
2.	Clinical and behavioral signs and symptoms of neurotoxicity were recorded (see checklist for neurotoxicity).	☐	☐	☐
3.	Unexpected and serious clinical and gross necropsy results were recorded. • If yes, briefly indicate the signs and symptoms recorded: ______________________________	☐	☐	☐
4.	In Local Lymph Node Assay, a 3-fold or greater increase in incorporation of ^{3}HTdR compared with controls was seen.	☐	☐	☐
5.	The chemical was found to be a sensitizer in animals in Buehler or Maximization tests (greater than 20% were sensitized) or in LLNA (EC3<50%).	☐	☐	☐
6.	If the test substance is intended to be used in an application with a likelihood of widespread human exposure and it was found to be a sensitizer in animals (greater than 0% were sensitized or in LLNA incorporated radioactive material is 3 times higher than the control value) the study is reportable in Canada.	☐	☐	☐
7.	Decision: 8(e) reportable: If "yes" submit: summary only ________ report & summary ________	☐	☐	

Note to Reviewer

- If the answer 1, 2, 3, 4, OR 5 is "yes" the study IS 8(e) reportable in US and, if applicable, in Canada under CEPA § 70.
- If the answer to 6 is "yes" the study IS reportable under CEPA § 70 in Canada, if applicable.
- If not reportable because substance is a pesticide, drug, or food additive, evaluate for reporting under FIFRA or FFDCA.

Exposure status – describe:

- Current application (e.g., industrial, commercial, consumer, FIFRA only, FFDCA only) ______________

Signature of Reviewer: ______________________ Date ___/___/___

Study Title:	________________	*Business Unit:*	________________
Chemical/Product Name:	________________		
Laboratory:	________________		
Chemical No.:	________________		
Study Date:	________________	*Study No.:*	________________

Checklist to Determine Whether a LD50/LC50 Test is 8(e) Reportable

		Yes	*No*	*Not Applic.*
1.	a. Oral LD50 value is less than or equal to 50 mg/kg.	☐	☐	☐
	b. Dermal LD50 value is less than or equal to 200 mg/kg.	☐	☐	☐
	c. Inhalation LC50 (4-hr.) is less than or equal to 200 ppm (2 mg/l).	☐	☐	☐
2.	Clinical and/or behavioral signs and symptoms of neurotoxicity were recorded (see checklist for neurotoxicity).	☐	☐	☐
3.	Decision: 8(e) reportable: If "yes" submit: summary only ________ report & summary ________	☐	☐	

Note to Reviewer:

- If any answer to any part of question 1 is "yes" OR the answer to question 2 is "yes" the study is reportable under 8(e) in US and, if applicable, in Canada under CEPA § 70.
- If not reportable because substance is a pesticide, drug, or food additive, evaluate for reporting under FIFRA or FFDCA.
- For non-mammalian species see the checklists for environmental effects.

Exposure status – describe:

- Current application (e.g., industrial, commercial, consumer, FIFRA only, FFDCA only) ________________

Signature of Reviewer: ________________ Date ____/____/____

Study Title: ______________________ *Business Unit:* ______________
Chemical/Product Name: ______________________
Laboratory: ______________________
Chemical No.: ______________________
Study Date: ______________________ *Study No.:* ______________

Checklist to Determine Whether a Subacute/Subchronic/Chronic Study is 8(e) Reportable

		Yes	*No*	*Not Applic.*
1.	Clinical and/or behavioral signs and symptoms of neurotoxicity were recorded (see checklist for neurotoxicity).	☐	☐	☐
2.	Statistically or biologically significant gross pathological and/or histopathological and/or reproductive/developmental change(s), including benign or malignant tumors, was (were) recorded. • If yes, specify changes: ______________________ ______________________	☐	☐	☐
3.	Statistically or biologically significant organ weight change(s) was (were) recorded, either in conjunction with blood chemistry changes or alone if organ weight changes are severe. • If yes, specify: ______________________ ______________________	☐	☐	☐
4.	Statistically or biologically significant changes in clinical or enzyme chemistry (e.g., neurotoxic esterase inhibition, cholinesterase inhibition, peroxisome proliferation) were recorded. • If yes, specify changes: ______________________ ______________________	☐	☐	☐
5.	NOELs for general, nonspecific effects were recorded at or below EPA thresholds of concern: (a) 200 mg/kg for oral and inhalation studies and 400 for a dermal study of four weeks or less; b) 100 for oral and inhalation studies and 200 for a dermal study of between four weeks and three months; c) 50 for oral and inhalation studies and 100 for a dermal study of more than three months.	☐	☐	☐
6.	Only general, non-specific effects were observed and NOELs were at levels above EPA thresholds of concern (see question 5 for the thresholds) without other information assisting interpretation.	☐	☐	☐
7.	Decision 8(e) reportable: If "yes" submit: summary only ________ report & summary ________	☐	☐	

Note to reviewer:

- If the answer to any questions 1, 2, 3, 4, OR 5 is "yes" the study IS 8(e) reportable in US and, if applicable, in Canada under CEPA § 70.
- If the answer to question 6 is "yes" the study IS NOT 8(e) reportable.
- If not reportable because substance is a pesticide, drug, or food additive, evaluate for reporting under FIFRA or FFDCA.

Exposure status – describe:

- Current application (e.g., industrial, commercial, consumer, FIFRA only, FFDCA only) ______________

Signature of Reviewer: ______________________ Date ____/____/____

Study Title: ____________________ *Business Unit:* ____________
Chemical/Product Name: ____________________
Laboratory: ____________________
Chemical No.: ____________________
Study Date: ____________________ *Study No.:* ____________

Checklist to Determine Whether A Study Exhibits Neurotoxic Effects

		Yes	*No*	*Not Applic.*
1.	Signs and symptoms of neurotoxicity were recorded. Signs and symptoms of neurotoxicity include abnormal pupil size, anesthesia, ataxia, behavioral change, catatonia, circling, coma, convulsions, excess salivation, fasciculation, flaccidity, gait abnormalities, hyperactivity, hypersensitivity, lethargy, limb splay, loss of pain response, narcosis, paralysis, paresis, paresthesia, rearing, reflex changes, rigidity, spasticity, tail elevation, tremor, twitching, urinary incontinence, etc. • If yes, specify the signs and symptoms recorded: ____________________ ____________________	☐	☐	☐
2.	Signs and symptoms of neurotoxicity were found to be sustained or intermittent and not merely transient.	☐	☐	☐
3.	Signs and symptoms of neurotoxicity were biologically or statistically significant.	☐	☐	☐
4.	Signs and symptoms indicative of neurotoxicity occurred in non-moribund animals.	☐	☐	☐
5.	Signs and symptoms of neurotoxicity occurred in moribund animals AND the chemical is structurally related to a chemical that has known neurotoxicological effects. • If yes, specify: ____________________ ____________________	☐	☐	☐
6.	Decision 8(e) reportable: If "yes" submit: summary only ________ report & summary ________	☐	☐	

Note to reviewer:

- If the answer to ALL questions 1, 2, 3, AND 4 are "yes" then the study IS 8(e) reportable in US and, if applicable, in Canada under CEPA 70.
- If the answer to both questions 1 and 5 are "yes" the study IS 8(e) reportable.
- If not reportable because substance is a pesticide, drug, or food additive, evaluate for reporting under FIFRA or FFDCA.

Exposure status – describe:

- Current application (e.g., industrial, commercial, consumer, FIFRA only, FFDCA only)
  ____

Signature of Reviewer: ____________________ Date ____/____/____

Study Title: ______________________ *Business Unit:* ______________
Chemical/Product Name: ______________________
Laboratory: ______________________
Chemical No.: ______________________
Study Date: ______________________ *Study No.:* ______________

Checklist to Determine Whether Skin or Eye Irritation/Corrosivity Study is 8(e) Reportable

1. Type (check one): skin irritation ☐ eye irritation ☐ skin corrosivity ☐

		Yes	*No*	*Not Applic.*
2.	Clinical and/or behavioral signs and symptoms of neurotoxicity were recorded (see checklist for neurotoxicity).	☐	☐	☐
3.	Unexpected serious clinical and/or gross necropsy results were recorded.	☐	☐	☐

- If yes, briefly indicate the signs and symptoms recorded:
  ____
  ____
  ____
  ____

4.	Severe irritation or corrosivity in eye or on skin was recorded at $3.0 < pH < 11.0$ and was NOT expected based on chemical structure or chemical family.	☐	☐	☐

NOTE: NOT 8(e) reportable if $pH < 3.0$ or $pH > 11$.

5. Decision: 8(e) reportable: ☐ ☐
If "yes" submit: summary only ________ report & summary ________

Note to Reviewer
- If the answer to any question 2, 3, or 4 is "yes" the study IS 8(e) reportable in US and, if applicable, in Canada under CEPA § 70.
- If not reportable because substance is a pesticide, drug, or food additive, evaluate for reporting under FIFRA or FFDCA.

Exposure status – describe:
- Current application (e.g., industrial, commercial, consumer, FIFRA only, FFDCA only) ______________

Signature of Reviewer: ______________________ Date ___/___/______

J. Procedure Number International Operations 1, Importing Chemical Substances*

1. Key Objective

This document describes the process involved in importing chemicals, including samples, finished goods, raw materials, intermediates and non-commercial products from worldwide sources, including affiliated companies and third-party suppliers.

2. Applicable References

TSCA § 13

(Add all other regulatory schemes relevant to the export of the Company's products)

Procedures governing shipment changes, carrier selection, product database updates and carrier selection, preparation of blanket TSCA certifications, and selection of customs brokers.

3. Document History

REVISION	DATE	AUTHOR	RATIONALE
0.	2010	THE TOXIC SUBSTANCES CONTROL ACT: A PRACTICAL GUIDE[1]	
1.			

4. Procedure

Step1. All imports of chemicals must be done through the company's International Operations function.

Step2. Every morning, the International Trade Specialist (ITS) does a download from Purchasing System and the Incoming Sample Tracking System to the Import Management System (IMS). *(Every company will have different automated or manual systems from which to pull notifications of imported products or chemicals. All these systems ideally should feed into one central system to control the import function).*

Step3. Upon receipt of invoices and/or shipment information, the ITS establishes an entry file for the particular shipment. The ITS records appropriate

---

* *Note: Procedures may include steps that are not required by TSCA but are suggested business practices.*

1. MIRIAM V. GOLD & JEAN WARSHAW, THE TOXIC SUBSTANCES CONTROL ACT: A PRACTICAL GUIDE (OXFORD UNIVERSITY PRESS 2010).

information to prioritize the clearance of the imported goods based upon shipment arrival and/or business needs. As original foreign supplier invoices are received, copies are distributed to the Accounting Department, the Senior Buyer (for purchases), and/or sample requestor (for inbound samples).

Step 4. The ITS reviews the import transaction record to determine Customs entry requirements and dutiable and non-dutiable charges.

Step 5. The ITS obtains and sends chemical identity or composition to the Manager, Product Compliance (MPC) for those chemicals for which there is no blanket TSCA certification on file for the current year or for which other regulatory classification is needed. The MPC provides product regulatory data such as TSCA certifications, harmonized tariff system (HTS) numbers, transportation classifications, and ascertains whether or not the shipment is in connection with a cleared Premanufacturing Notification.

Step 6. The ITS provides the information collected in Step 5 to the designated Customhouse Broker (CHB).

Step 7. For a commercial shipment in connection with a cleared Premanufacturing Notification, the ITS shall provide all requested data and documentation to the MRC to support preparation of the Notice of Commencement.

Step 8. The MPC shall also determine if the presence of the subject chemical in the United States will trigger a chemical specific reporting requirement, and if so will gather and submit the required information as required under *(insert relevant procedure reference such as the procedure for compliance with TSCA substantial risk reporting)*. The MRC will update the product database to reflect this information.

Step 9. The ITS shall not allow importation of any chemical for which the MPC does not provide a TSCA certification, and shall direct its return to the supplier.

Step 10. The ITS creates, reviews, enters, updates, and maintains product, invoice, and shipment data in IMS. Upon creation of an invoice and shipment record the ITS will verify the IMS calculated entered value prior to printing required entry documents.

Step 11. The ITS selects inland carrier based on policy or instructions from the Senior Logistics Manager. Analyst. The ITS advises CHB accordingly.

Step 12. The ITS distributes, as needed, the following documents:

TO: CHB at port of entry:

- Proforma Invoice and/or Foreign Supplier Invoice
- Shipment Recap Sheet

- Transportation Document
- Broker's Letter of Instruction

TO: Senior Logistics Manager and U.S. receiving locations:

- U.S. Weight List
- Broker's Letter of Instruction

Step 13. The ITS ensures that the CHB fulfills these responsibilities:

a) Submitting the entry package to U.S. Customs Service for clearance.
b) Surrendering necessary documentation to secure other governmental agency releases.
c) Preparing the delivery order/inland bill of lading according to ITS instructions.
d) Notifying the ITS and designated domestic carrier of the release date and arrange for the timely delivery/pickup of required paperwork by the domestic carrier.
e) Transmitting entry data to the ITS.

Step 14. The ITS verifies Customs duties owed and requests duty check from the Accounting Department unless paid by Automated Clearing House (ACH). Duty Checks are sent to the CHB for submission to U.S. Customs within the time frame set by regulations.

Step 15. The ITS reconciles shipment problems and communicates import issues to appropriate parties. Potential changes that could occur include but are not limited to:

a) Upon notification by the Shipper of delayed shipment, product, or quantity variance the ITS would notify either the Senior Buyer, who would then notify the receiving warehouse and any other interested parties, or the Sample Requestor, who would then notify any other interested parties.
b) Upon notification by the warehouse discrepancies the ITS would notify the Supplier and other interested parties and ensure appropriate corrective action is taken.

Step 16. The ITS audits and approves for payment broker and carrier invoices and forwards verified and coded invoices to Accounts Payable for payment.

Step 17. The ITS verifies U.S. Customs liquidation notices to determine if increases are justified, refunds due or protest should be filed. The ITS consults with International Trade Counsel on these issues.

Step 18. The MRC reviews blanket certifications annually, during the month of December, and prepares re-certifications as appropriate.

Step 19. The ITS maintains required documentation in entry files according to the Company's record retention policy. TSCA certifications shall be maintained for five years.

K. Procedure Number International Operations 2, Exporting Commercial Shipments*

As discussed in Chapter 8, Exports and Imports, § 12(b) of the Toxic Substances Control Act (TSCA) requires exporters to notify the Environmental Protection Agency (EPA) before exporting chemicals for which data are required under §§ 4 or 5(b), an order has been issued under § 5, a rule has been proposed or issued under section §§ 5 or 6, or an action is pending or relief has been granted under §§ 5 or 7. For exports to be in compliance with § 12(b), the Company needs to ensure that the people who are in a position to develop the information showing which products contain chemicals subject to these TSCA provisions make that information available to the employees exporting the products in a timely manner. In addition, while not the subject of this book, exports are subject to a number of other export control rules administered by different agencies, such as the Department of Commerce, the Department of State, and the Treasury Department. There are automated programs available that can be purchased or licensed to deal with these requirements. This procedure is written to indicate some areas where the process is connected to a third-party database that screens the data for compliance and other areas in which the process is done in a more manual fashion.

1. Key Objective

This document describes the procedure used by International Operations to export commercial shipments.

2. Applicable References

TSCA § 12(b)

(Add all other regulatory schemes relevant to the export of the Company's products, such as export control regulations administered by the Department of Commerce, the Department of State, and/or the Treasury Department.)

Procedures governing shipment changes, carrier selection, product database updates and carrier selection.

3. Document History

REVISION	DATE	AUTHOR	RATIONALE
0.	2010	THE TOXIC SUBSTANCES CONTROL ACT: A PRACTICAL GUIDE[1]	
1.			

---

* *Procedures may include steps that are not required by TSCA but are sug-gested business practices.*

1. MIRIAM V. GOLD & JEAN WARSHAW, THE TOXIC SUBSTANCES CONTROL ACT: A PRACTICAL GUIDE (OXFORD UNIVERSITY PRESS 2010).

4. Procedure

Step 1. Each morning, the Export Specialist (ES) downloads orders from the Order Processing System to the Export System. At the same time the order is downloaded into the Export System, the data is simultaneously added to the same fields in other export documents. *(In this case, the Company's Export System is connected to a third-party vendor site which screens the shipment for parties to whom exports cannot be made under current regulations).*

Step 2. The ES reviews the order for accuracy, completeness, and special customer requirements.

Step 3. The ES obtains the following information from the Product Database: country of origin, export restrictions, if any, on the product, and hazardous materials designation. *(There should be a procedure which details who is responsible for keeping these fields current in the Product Database, and how those updates are made and controlled).*

Step 4. In the event there are restrictions on the export of the product, the ES requests guidance from the International Trade Counsel, who will assist in obtaining the required license.

Step 5. If the product is being exported to a particular destination for the first time in the calendar year, the ES checks the Product Database to determine if the product requires an annual TSCA § 12(b) export notice to the particular destination, or if the product requires a one-time TSCA § 12(b) notification to the particular destination, and if such notification has already been made. If the appropriate notification has not already been made, the ES informs the Manager of Regulatory Compliance(MRC). The MRC shall make all required notifications within seven days of receipt of an order in the Order Processing System, but no later than the date of export. (*Another alternative might be to have form letters for this purpose available to the ES to use to make the notifications within the required time frame, and to send a copy of the notification to the MRC for retention.) (There should be a procedure which demonstrates how the MRC reviews new and existing products for § 12(b) designation, how this field is kept current in the Product Database, and how the§ 12(b) notifications are made and retained.)*

Step 6. If the product is designated as containing hazardous materials on the Product Database, the ES obtains guidance from the MRC as to shipping instructions. Prior to shipment, the ES must notify the applicable warehouse of these requirements by email.

Step 7. The ES prepares and transmits the following documents:

a) Prepares the Warehouse Release and Packing List (P/L), adding to them the batch numbers and Export Marks.

b) Sends the Warehouse Release form to the shipping warehouse as an authorization to ship. In addition, for ocean shipments, the warehouse must wait for the Dock Receipt (D/R) from either the freight forwarder or International Operations.
c) A copy of the P/L is sent to the freight forwarder requesting booking for ocean freight. If the customer uses his own forwarder it makes the booking.
d) For ocean or air shipment the required documents are sent to the freight forwarder who prepares the ocean Bill of Lading or airway bill (AWB). The forwarder then distributes the necessary documents to the customer, carrier, and required regulatory agencies. Copies of the completed documents are returned to the ES.
e) An invoice and packing list is sent to the customer's freight forwarder when used in lieu of the Company freight forwarder. The freight is delivered, to a domestic location, in accordance with instructions from this forwarder.

Step 8. The ES distributes copies of the commercial invoice to the following internal departments:

a) Accounts Payable
b) Credit Department
c) Customer Service
d) Order File
e) Duty Drawback Administrator

(If the Company has a central document management system, the distribution of copies would likely not be needed.)

L. Procedure Number Lab. 11, Qualifying for the R&D Exemption at Laboratories*

As discussed in the PMN Exclusions and Exemptions Chapter, § 5(h)3 of the Toxic Substances Control Act (TSCA) exempts from TSCA §§ 5(a) and (b) (the PMN and Significant New Use rules, respectively) small quantities of chemicals if used solely for research and development (R&D) purposes under specified circumstances. TSCA's PMN rules apply to manufacturers and importers; the Significant New Use Rules apply to processors as well as manufacturers and importers.

Much more stringent requirements are imposed on facilities that do not meet ***all*** *of the following conditions:*

- *exposure to the chemical substances is controlled through the implementation of prudent laboratory practices for handling chemical substances of unknown toxicity;*
- *it is a contained research facility;*
- *relatively small quantities of chemical substances are used on a nonproduction basis; and*
- *activities involve the use of containers for reactions, transfers, and other handling of substances designed to be easily manipulated by a single individual.*

This Procedure applies only to laboratories that do meet all these conditions.

Facilities that do not meet all the conditions above must follow Procedure Number Pilot Plant 11, Qualifying for the R&D Exemption at Pilot Plants.

If R&D substances are sampled to third-parties, see Procedure Number Lab. 5, Sampling R&D Substances to Third Parties.

1. Key Objective

This document describes the procedure for laboratories to manufacture, import, or process research and development compounds in compliance with the TSCA exemption for research and development substances.

2. Applicable References

TSCA § 5(h)3
40 C.F.R. § 720.36 (exemption from PMN requirements)
40 C.F.R. § 720.78(b) (recordkeeping for the R&D exemption)
40 C.F.R. § 721.47 (exemption from SNUR requirements)

Procedures governing MSDSs, Labels, Shipping, Import/Export, Sampling Experimental Compounds to Third Parties.

---

* *Procedures include steps that are not required by TSCA but are suggested business practices.*

3. Document History

REVISION	DATE	AUTHOR	RATIONALE
0.	2010	THE TOXIC SUBSTANCES CONTROL ACT: A PRACTICAL GUIDE[1]	
1.			

4. Procedure

Step 1. The Laboratory Director shall establish prudent laboratory practices for handling chemical substances of unknown toxicity, requiring all R&D substances to be made and used by or directly under the supervision of a technically qualified individual. The Laboratory Director shall establish procedures for compliance with those practices, and shall identify the individuals responsible for specific tasks under those procedures. The Laboratory Director shall ensure that no amount of the R&D substance is processed, distributed, or used for any commercial purpose other than R&D unless it is distributed only as an impurity or part of an article or in accordance with any SNUR that may be applicable.

Step 2. Each Research Scientist who is responsible for R&D activities shall monitor the use of all laboratory substances, including all reagents, controls and products, and shall ensure that none are manufactured, imported, or used in excess of the amounts necessary for R&D purposes.

Step 3. Prior to disposal or commercial use of any R&D substances that remain after the conclusion of R&D activities, the Research Scientist shall inform the Manager of Regulatory Compliance of the identity of the substance to be disposed of or used. The Manager of Regulatory Compliance shall inform the Research Scientist of all SNUR restrictions on disposal or use of the R&D substance. The Research Scientist shall ensure that all of the R&D substance that remains after the conclusion of R&D activities is disposed of or used in accordance with all SNUR restrictions.

Step 4. The Research Scientist shall keep records of the following in accordance with the Company's Record Retention Program, but not for less than five years from the conclusion of R&D using an R&D substance:

- if more than one hundred kilograms of the R&D substance is manufactured or imported in any one year, what the substance is, the production volume, and how the R&D substance was disposed of;
- compliance with SNUR restrictions on disposal or use of R&D substances after the conclusion of R&D, if applicable; and

1. MIRIAM V. GOLD & JEAN WARSHAW, THE TOXIC SUBSTANCES CONTROL ACT: A PRACTICAL GUIDE (OXFORD UNIVERSITY PRESS 2010).

- copies of or citations to the records reviewed to evaluate whether the R&D substance poses a health risk, if applicable because of sampling to another facility.

Step 5. The Laboratory Director shall keep documentation of all prudent laboratory practices that were instituted, in accordance with the Company's Record Retention Program, but not for less than five years from the conclusion of R&D on the experimental product.

Step 6. The Manager of Regulatory Compliance and the Research Scientist shall keep copies of all health risk notifications and records of how the notifications were disseminated, if applicable, because of sampling to another facility, in accordance with the Company's Record Retention Program, but not for less than five years from the conclusion of R&D on the experimental product.

M. Procedure Number Lab. 5 Sampling R&D Substances to Third-Parties*

As discussed in the PMN Exclusions and Exemptions Chapter, § 5(h)3 of the Toxic Substances Control Act (TSCA) exempts from TSCA §§ 5(a) and (b) (the PMN and Significant New Use rules, respectively) small quantities of new chemicals or chemicals subject to a Significant New Use Rule (SNUR), if used solely for research and development (R&D) purposes under specified circumstances. R&D substances are often sampled for outside testing to laboratories or to customers. If the product is not on the TSCA Inventory, or is the subject of a SNUR, the R&D substance must be sampled in a way that meets the TSCA exemption requirements for research and development samples. TSCA's PMN rules apply to manufacturers and importers; SNURs apply to processors as well as manufacturers and importers.

1. Key Objective

This document describes the procedure for sampling experimental compounds to third-parties, such as customers, contract laboratories, and engineering firms in compliance with the TSCA exemption for research and development substances.

2. Applicable References

TSCA § 5(h)3
40 C.F.R. § 720.36 (exemption from PMN requirements)
40 C.F.R. § 720.78(b) (recordkeeping for the R&D exemption)
40 C.F.R. § 721.47 (exemption from SNUR requirements)
Procedures governing MSDSs, Labels, Shipping, Import/Export

3. Document History

REVISION	DATE	AUTHOR	RATIONALE
0.	2010	THE TOXIC SUBSTANCES CONTROL ACT: A PRACTICAL GUIDE[1]	
1.			

---

* *Procedures include steps that are not required by TSCA but are suggested business practices.*

1. Miriam V. Gold & Jean Warshaw, The Toxic Substances Control Act: A Practical Guide (Oxford University Press 2010).

4. Procedure

Step 1. The Director of Marketing of the Business Unit (Dir. Marketing) responsible for the experimental product area must approve, in writing, sampling an R&D substance outside of the company. Requests should be made to the Dir. Marketing in writing, specifying to whom the sample will be sent, the rationale for the sampling, and the amount of the sample requested to be sent.

Step 2. The Dir. Marketing should consult with the other business centers in the company in reaching a decision as to whether or not to approve a request to sample an experimental product.

Step 3. Once the Dir. Marketing approves the request to sample, implementation of the request shall be delegated by the Dir. Marketing to a Marketing Representative (Market Rep.). The Market Rep. shall check the MSDS/label database for an approved MSDS and label for the experimental sample. If an MSDS and label are available, the Market Rep. shall print out a label and an MSDS, and proceed to Step 5.

Step 4. If an MSDS and label are not available in the MSDS/label database, the Market Rep. shall advise the Manager of Regulatory Compliance (MRC), and the MSDS Specialist. The MSDS Specialist shall prepare an MSDS and label for the experimental product.

Step 5. The MRC shall review the components of the R&D Substance to determine whether they are listed on the TSCA Inventory, and other inventories, or are subject to a SNUR, and whether the R&D substance is subject to any TSCA export notification requirements, and the transportation classifications. If the TSCA Inventory and SNUR status of the R&D substance is not readily available, the MRC shall proceed on the assumption that the substance is not on the Inventory and/or is subject to a SNUR because of its generic category. The MRC shall advise the Market Rep. and the MSDS Specialist of the determinations, and shall update the product database with any new information. The MRC shall advise the Shipping Department whether export notifications are required for export of the experimental substance. *(Regulatory information about the experimental product is entered in the product database, which feeds the MSDS/label database, by the MRC. The MSDS Specialist prepares the new MSDS and label in accordance with the procedure for making MSDS and labels.)* If the experimental substance is on the TSCA Inventory and is not subject or potentially subject to a SNUR, no further action is required under this Procedure. Consult the Patent Department for any required secrecy or non-analysis agreement and the Shipping and Export Procedures for shipping and export requirements.

Step 6. The Market Rep. shall contact the Patent Department to determine if a secrecy or non-analysis agreement is necessary. If the receiving entity is a laboratory, and the experimental substance is not on the TSCA Inventory or is subject to a SNUR, the Market Rep. shall send the receiving entity an appropriately completed copy of Attachment 1 to this Procedure, TSCA R&D Exemption Letter—First Alternative, Sampling to Laboratories. If the receiving entity countersigns and returns the TSCA R&D Exemption Letter—First Alternative, Sampling to Laboratories without changes, proceed to Step 9.

Step 7. If the receiving entity is not a laboratory or does not countersign the TSCA R&D Exemption Letter—First Alternative, Sampling to Laboratories without changes, go to Procedure Number Pilot Plant 11, Qualifying for the R&D Exemption at Pilot Plants. Appropriate personnel together with the MRC shall follow the Steps 1, 2, and 5 of Procedure Number Pilot Plant 11, Qualifying for the R&D Exemption at Pilot Plants to evaluate any health risk posed by the experimental product. If the MRC determines that the R&D substance poses any risks, and therefore written risk notifications of health risks are required, the MRC shall prepare written notifications to be given to the recipient facility. The MRC and the Research Scientist must retain copies of the written risk notifications and records of how the notifications were disseminated. The MRC shall provide to the Market Rep. copies of or citations to the records that were reviewed to evaluate whether the R&D substance poses a health risk.

Step 8. If the receiving entity (i) is not a laboratory or (ii) makes any changes to the TSCA R&D Exemption Letter—First Alternative, Sampling to Laboratories, or (iii) does not countersign the TSCA R&D Exemption Letter—First Alternative, Sampling to Laboratories, the Market Rep. shall include any health risk notification prepared by the MRC in Step 7, in a TSCA R&D Exemption Letter—Second Alternative, Sampling to Pilot Plants and Certain Laboratories, which is Attachment 2 to this Procedure. The Market Rep. shall send the TSCA R&D Exemption Letter—Second Alternative to the intended recipient and obtain a countersigned copy prior to sending the sample. No samples may be shipped until the TSCA R&D Exemption Letter is received back with a signature from a responsible individual at the recipient facility. The Market Rep. must give the MRC and the Research Scientist copies of all TSCA R&D Exemption Letters that are sent and received.

Step 9. For shipments within the United States, the Market Rep. must complete the Sample Shipping Form and bring the form and the sample to the Shipping Department for shipment to the third-party. As required in the Shipping Form checklist, the Market Rep. must append a cover letter, the MSDS, label, and, for samples subject to a SNUR or not listed on the TSCA Inventory, the completed TSCA R&D Exemption Letter with the recipient's signature. As appropriate, the cover letter should describe the identity, type, and quantity of sample enclosed, and the intended application. When a sample is identified by code (e.g., in non-analysis agreements), then the appropriate code should be used in place of the product's identification.

Step 10. For shipments outside of the United States, in addition to the above requirements, the Market Rep. must notify International Operations and comply with Import/Export procedures. *(The export procedure will deal with the actual steps to export samples as well as other legal requirements, e.g., export control laws).*

Step 11. The Shipping Department will prepare the shipment, either for domestic or international destination, in accordance with information received from the MRC.

Step 12. The Market Rep. must distribute documentation as follows:

- complete copies of documentation shall be maintained by the Research Scientist responsible for the R&D substance;
- copies of or citations to the records that the MRC reviewed to evaluate whether the R&D substance poses a health risk shall be maintained by the MRC and the Research Scientist;
- a copy of the fully executed TSCA R&D Exemption Letter shall be maintained by Marketing Department in a customer file and by the Research Scientist;
- an executed original of secrecy or non-analysis agreement shall be maintained by the Patent Department; and
- a copy of TSCA R&D Exemption Letter shall be maintained by the Regulatory Affairs Department and the Research Scientist

Step 13. All records shall be maintained in accordance with the Company's Record Retention Program, but not for less than five years from the conclusion of all R&D on the subject substance.

Sampling Experimental Compounds to Third Parties

Attachment 1

TSCA R&D Exemption Letter—First Alternative

Sampling to Laboratories

All instructions in italics should be deleted for the final letter.
Put on Company Letterhead
Enclose a duplicate copy of this letter
Do not send sample until a countersigned copy of this letter is received back from the addressee

[Date]

[Recipient's name and address]

Re: Notice Concerning Shipment of Research & Development Product

Dear ____:

[Company name] will be sending you a sample of *[identify R&D substance]*. This substance is a research and development product that is [not listed on the Toxic Substances Control Act Inventory] [or] [subject to a Significant New Use Rule issued under the Toxic Substances Control Act [*give citation of the SNUR*]. You may use this product only for research and development as required by the TSCA regulations found at 40 C.F.R. § 720.36 or § 721.47.

Handle this substance with care. Because it is an R&D substance, we do not have complete information about the risks inherent in its use and handling. Please consult the enclosed MSDS and the product label for risk information, keeping in mind that not all of the risks that may be presented are known. *[Include any limited health and safety information you may have and note that the data is not exhaustive.]* The relevant regulations only permit us to send you this sample if:

- you will use the R&D sample only in relatively small quantities for research and development and not for production (*if there is a SNUR that may apply, add: disposal or use of material remaining after R&D activities must be in accordance with any applicable Significant New Use Rule*);
- you will only use the R&D sample in a contained research laboratory;
- your activities involve the use of containers for reactions, transfers, and other handling of substances designed to be easily manipulated by a single individual; and
- you will limit exposure to the R&D sample by implementing prudent laboratory practices described in the TSCA regulations at 40 C.F.R.

§ 720.36 or § 721.47 for handling chemical substances of unknown toxicity.

Please contact us if you have any questions concerning the use of this substance under the Toxic Substances Control Act.

[Not mandatory, but good practice to add any patent and confidentiality provisions as appropriate after consultation with the Patent Department.]

Please confirm that you meet these conditions by signing the enclosed copy of this letter and returning it to me. Once I have your signature on the enclosed copy I will send you the R&D sample.

Very truly yours,

[name]

Confirmed:

[Recipient Company]

By: ____________________

Date: ____________________

Attachment 2

TSCA R&D Exemption Letter—Second Alternative
For Sampling to Pilot Plants and Certain Laboratories

All instructions in italics should be deleted for the final letter.
Put on Company Letterhead
Enclose a duplicate copy of this letter
Do not send sample until a countersigned copy of this letter is received back from the addressee

[Date]

[Recipient's name and address]

Re: Notice Concerning Shipment of Research & Development Product

Dear ____:

[Company name] will be sending you a sample of *[identify R&D substance]*. This substance is a research and development product that is [not listed on the Toxic Substances Control Act Inventory] [or] [subject to a Significant New Use Rule issued under the Toxic Substances Control Act]. You may use this product only for research and development as described in the TSCA regulations found at 40 C.F.R. § 720.36 or § 721.47.

Handle this substance with care. Because it is an R&D substance, we do not have complete information about the risks inherent in its use and handling. Please consult the enclosed MSDS and the product label for risk information, keeping in mind that not all of the risks that may be presented are known. *[Describe any health risk information that is not on the MSDS and label.]*

Please contact us if you have any questions concerning the use of this substance under the Toxic Substances Control Act. *[If there is a SNUR that may apply, add: disposal or use of material remaining after R&D activities must be in accordance with any applicable Significant New Use Rule.]*

[Not mandatory, but good practice to add:] Please confirm that you will use this substance for R&D in compliance with the TSCA R&D exemption by signing the enclosed copy of this letter and returning it to me. Once I have your signature on the enclosed copy I will send you the R&D sample.

[Not mandatory, but good practice to add any patent and confidentiality provisions as appropriate after consultation with the Patent Department; if added, obtain recipient's signature before sampling.]

Very truly yours,

[name]

Confirmed:

[Recipient Company]

By: ___________________

Date: ___________________

N. Procedure Number Pilot Plant 11, Qualifying for the R&D Exemption at Pilot Plants*

As discussed in the PMN Exclusions and Exemptions Chapter, § 5(h)3 of the Toxic Substances Control Act (TSCA) exempts from TSCA §§ 5(a) and (b) (the PMN and Significant New Use rules, respectively) small quantities of chemicals if used solely for research and development (R&D) purposes under specified circumstances. TSCA's PMN rules apply to manufacturers and importers; the Significant New Use Rules (SNURs) apply to processors as well as manufacturers and importers.

This Procedure applies to pilot plants that manufacture or import new chemicals that are not on the TSCA Inventory, or that manufacture, import, or process chemicals subject to SNURs.

It covers manufacture of the substance by the pilot plant, and use of substances manufactured at other facilities. This Procedure also applies to certain laboratories that are required to evaluate the risks associated with R&D substances to qualify for the R&D exemption from the PMN and SNUR requirements.[1]

Facilities that do meet all the conditions above may follow Procedure Number Lab. 11, Qualifying for the R&D Exemption at Laboratories.

If R&D substances are sampled to third-parties, see Procedure Number Lab. 5, Sampling R&D Substances to Third-Parties.

1. Key Objective

This document describes the procedure for pilot plants to manufacture, import, or process research and development compounds in compliance with the TSCA exemptions for research and development substances.

2. Applicable References

TSCA § 5(h)3
40 C.F.R. § 720.36 (exemption from PMN requirements)

---

* *Procedures include steps that are not required by TSCA but are suggested business practices.*

1. *Laboratories that are required to evaluate risks associated with R&D chemicals to qualify for the R&D exemption from the PMN and SNUR requirements are those that do not meet all of the following conditions:*
    - *exposure to the chemical substances is controlled through the implementation of prudent laboratory practices for handling chemical substances of unknown toxicity;*
    - *it is a contained research facility;*
    - *relatively small quantities of chemical substances are used on a nonproduction basis; and*
    - *activities involve the use of containers for reactions, transfers, and other handling of substances designed to be easily manipulated by a single individual*

40 C.F.R. § 720.78(b) (recordkeeping for the R&D exemption)
40 C.F.R. § 721.47 (exemption from SNUR requirements)
Procedures governing MSDSs, Labels, Shipping, Import/Export, Sampling Experimental Compounds to Third-Parties.

3. Document History

REVISION DATE AUTHOR RATIONALE
0. 2010 The Toxic Substances Control Act: A Practical Guide[2]
1.

4. Procedure

Step 1. The Pilot Plant Director shall obtain the following information from suppliers of substances used in the pilot plant, or from the Product Manager or Manager of Regulatory Compliance (MRC) for all developmental products to be made in the pilot plant:

- chemical identity information including chemical name and CAS number;
- the MSDS and any product label;
- whether the substance is on the TSCA Inventory;
- whether the substance is subject to a SNUR or restricted by any other law;
- if the substance is brought into the pilot plant, information in the supplier's possession or control concerning significant adverse reactions reasonably associated with exposure to the substance;
- if the substance is to be made by the pilot plant, information in possession or control of the companies that own and operate the pilot plant, including data in the possession of research partners and agents wherever located, concerning significant adverse reactions reasonably associated with exposure to the substance;
- health and environmental effects data and data concerning significant adverse reactions reasonably associated with exposure to the substance, in the possession or control of the companies that own and operate the pilot plant, including data in the possession of research partners and agents wherever located;
- information supplied by importers or suppliers of the substance; and
- information on health effects from any EPA rule or order under a TSCA § 4 Test Rule, a TSCA § 5 order, or a TSCA § 6 product restriction.

---

2. Miriam V. Gold & Jean Warshaw, The Toxic Substances Control Act: A Practical Guide (Oxford University Press 2010).

The Pilot Plant Director shall not permit any substance to be made or used in the pilot plant without the specified information.

Step 2. The Pilot Plant Director shall provide copies of all information collected in Step 1 to the MRC, who shall evaluate health and environmental risk data concerning the R&D substance and update the MSDS and product label if appropriate. *(Regulatory information about the experimental product is entered in the product database, which feeds the MSDS/label database, by the MRC. The MSDS Specialist prepares the new MSDS and label in accordance with the procedure for making MSDS and labels.)*

Step 3. The Pilot Plant Director shall establish procedures requiring all R&D substances to be used by or directly under the supervision of a technically qualified individual. The Pilot Plant Director shall ensure that no amount of any R&D substance that is not on the TSCA Inventory or that is subject to a SNUR is processed, distributed, or used for any commercial purpose other than R&D unless it is distributed only as an impurity or part of an article or in accordance with any SNUR that may be applicable.

Step 4. Each Pilot Plant Supervisor who is responsible for R&D activities shall monitor the use of all R&D substances, including all reagents, controls, and products, and shall ensure that none that are not on the TSCA Inventory or subject to a SNUR are manufactured, imported or used in excess of the amounts necessary for R&D purposes.

Step 5. If the MRC determines that the R&D substance may pose any risks, and therefore written notifications of health risks are required,[3] the MRC shall prepare an appropriate written notification of the risks that may be associated with the R&D substance. The notification shall be designed to adequately inform all people who may potentially be exposed to the R&D substance. Such notification may be by a container label, conspicuous notices where exposure may occur, written notification to each person potentially exposed, or any other notification system. The MRC shall update the MSDS and label as appropriate. The MRC shall provide the notification to the Pilot Plant Director. The Pilot Plant Director shall use the notifications prepared by the MRC to inform all company employees and all people to whom it directly distributes the R&D substance, who are engaged in experimentation, research, or analysis on the R&D substance, of the risks that may be associated with the R&D substance. The Pilot Plant Director shall provide the notifications to all people involved in the manufacture, processing, use, transport, storage, and disposal of the R&D substance.

---

3. Required only for substances that are not on the TSCA Inventory or that are subject to a SNUR, but advisable for all R&D substances.

Step 6. The MRC and the Pilot Plant Director must retain copies of all health risk notifications and records of how the notifications were disseminated, in accordance with the Company's Record Retention Program, but not for less than five years from the conclusion of R&D on the experimental product.

Step 7. The MRC shall inform the Pilot Plant Director of all SNUR restrictions on disposal or use of the R&D substance. The Pilot Plant Director shall establish procedures to ensure that all of the R&D substance that remains after the conclusion of R&D activities is disposed of or used in accordance with all SNUR restrictions.

Step 8. The Pilot Plant Director shall keep records of the following in accordance with the Company's Record Retention Program, but not for less than five years from the conclusion of R&D using an R&D substance:

- if more than 100 kilograms of the R&D substance is manufactured or imported in any one year, what the substance is, the production volume, and how the R&D substance was disposed of;
- compliance with SNUR restrictions on disposal or use of R&D substances after the conclusion of R&D, if applicable; and
- copies of or citations to the records reviewed to evaluate whether the R&D substance poses a health risk.

III. Model Bona Fide Request for Inventory Listing

All instructions in italics should be deleted for the final letter.

Put on submitter's letterhead.

Insert date.

Document Control Office (DCO) (7407M)
Office of Pollution Prevention and Toxics (OPPT)
Environmental Protection Agency
1200 Pennsylvania Ave., NW.
Washington, DC 20460–0001

ATTN: Inventory Bona Fide Submissions

Re: Bona fide intent to manufacture or import a chemical substance

Dear Sir or Madam:

[Company name] plans to use a chemical substance for commercial purposes that is not listed by specific chemical name in the public portion of the Inventory. We are therefore submitting this bona fide request in accordance with 40 C.F.R. § 720.25 to determine if this substance is in included on the confidential Inventory.

We are providing the following information required by 40 C.F.R. § 720.25:

- The specific chemical identity of the substance we intend to use is *[see attachment to this letter to determine how to best describe the chemical substance]. [If an importer cannot provide the chemical identity information because it is claimed confidential by its foreign manufacturer or supplier, use the best description available in the preceding sentence and insert the following:]* Our foreign supplier *[insert name of foreign supplier]* considers the information requested as to chemical identity as confidential and will supply it directly to EPA. *[If a manufacturer cannot provide chemical identity information because the new chemical substance is manufactured using a reactant that has a specific chemical identity claimed as confidential by its supplier, the notice must contain chemical identity information that is as complete as known by the manufacturer and then insert the following:]* The supplier of the confidential reactant *[insert name of supplier]* considers the information requested as to chemical identity confidential and will supply it directly to EPA.
- We began conducting research and development related to this substance in *[insert year]*. The research and development activities conducted to

date *[describe, including the general types of research and development activities such as synthesis, substance isolation/purification, formulating, product development, process development, end-use application, toxicity testing, etc. Also indicate whether any pilot plant or production-scale plant evaluations have been conducted involving the manufacture or processing of the substance]. [If an importer is unable to provide this information from the foreign manufacturer or supplier, indicate instead how long and in what country or countries the substance has been in commercial use and whether the importer believes that the substance has already been used commercially, in any country, for the same purpose or application that the importer is intending.]*

- The major intended application or use of the substance or *[describe]*.
- Enclosed is *[an infrared spectrum of the substance, or alternative spectra or other data which identify the substance if infrared analysis is not suitable for the substance or does not yield a reasonable amount of structural information. When using alternative spectra or instrumental analysis, submit a spectrum or instrumental readout for the substance]. [If an importer cannot provide the chemical identity information because it is claimed confidential by its foreign manufacturer or supplier, use the best description available in the preceding sentence and insert the following:]* Our foreign supplier *[insert name of foreign supplier]* considers the information requested as to chemical identity as confidential and will supply it directly to EPA. *[If a manufacturer cannot provide chemical identity information because the new chemical substance is manufactured using a reactant that has a specific chemical identity claimed as confidential by its supplier, the notice must contain chemical identity information that is as complete as known by the manufacturer and then insert the following:]* The supplier of the confidential reactant *[insert name of supplier]* considers the information requested as to chemical identity confidential and will supply it directly to EPA.
- We intend to submit a Premanufacture Notice (PMN) around *[insert month and date]* for this substance if EPA informs us that the substance is not on the Inventory.
- Most likely we will manufacture or process the substance at the facility we control at *[insert the address of the facility][For an imported substance, only provide this information if the importer will be processing the substance and delete the word manufacture; otherwise delete this bullet point]*.
- We intend to manufacture this substance in United States for non-exempt commercial purposes, probably using *[insert a description of the most probable manufacturing process that would be used]. [Delete this bullet point if the chemical substance is not going to be manufactured domestically]*.

- As an importer, we intend to most likely process or use the substance for *[describe the commercial purpose]. [If the substance is not expected to be processed or used at any facility under your control, delete the first sentence and substitute instead:]* The substance will not be processed or used at any facility under our control. As far as we know, or can reasonably ascertain, the substance will be processed or used at sites controlled by others *[describe how] [If you do not know how this substance will be processed or used at sites controlled by others, delete the prior sentence and substitute:]* We do not know and cannot reasonably ascertain how this substance will be processed or used at sites controlled by others. *[Delete this bullet point if the substance is not going to be imported].*

[Company name] intends to manufacture or import the chemical substance identified in this notice, *[insert chemical name],* for commercial purposes.

If you have any questions, please contact me at *[insert phone and email contact information].*

Very truly yours,

[insert Company name]

By:________________________

Name:________________________

Title:________________________

Attachment

Instructions for Determining Chemical Identity

(a)(1) The specific chemical identity of the substance that the person intends to manufacture or import, which includes the following:

(i) The currently correct Chemical Abstracts (CA) name for the substance, based on the Ninth Collective Index (9CI) of CA nomenclature rules and conventions, and consistent with listings for similar substances in the Inventory. For each substance having a chemical composition that can be represented by a specific, complete chemical structure diagram (a Class 1 substance), a CA Index Name must be provided. For each chemical substance that cannot be fully represented by a complete, specific chemical structure diagram (a Class 2 substance), or if the substance is a polymer, a CA Index Name or CA Preferred Name must be provided (whichever is appropriate based on CA 9CI nomenclature rules and conventions). In addition, for a Class 2 substance, the notice must identify the immediate chemical precursors and reactants by specific chemical name and Chemical Abstracts Service Registry Number (CASRN), if the number is available. Trade names or generic names of chemical precursors or reactants are not acceptable as substitutes for specific chemical names.

(ii) The currently correct CASRN for the substance if a CASRN already exists for the substance.

(iii) For a Class 1 substance and for any Class 2 substance for which a definite molecular formula is known or reasonably ascertainable, the correct molecular formula.

(iv) For a Class 1 substance, a complete, correct chemical structure diagram; for a Class 2 substance or polymer, a correct representative or partial chemical structure diagram, as complete as can be known, if one can be reasonably ascertained.

(2) For a polymer, the submitter must also report the following:

(i) The specific chemical name and CASRN, if the number is available, of each monomer and other reactant used, at any weight percent, to manufacture the polymer. Trade names or generic names of chemical reactants or monomers are not acceptable as substitutes for specific chemical names.

(ii) The typical percent by weight of each monomer and other reactant in the polymer (weight of the monomer or other reactant expressed as a percentage of the weight of the polymeric chemical substance manufactured), and the maximum residual amount of each monomer present in the polymer.

(iii) For monomers and other reactants used at 2 weight percent or less (based on the dry weight of the polymer manufactured), indicate on the PMN form any such monomers and other reactants that should be included as part of the polymer description on the Inventory, where the weight percent is based on either (A) the weight of monomer or other reactant actually charged to the reaction vessel, or (B) the minimum weight of monomer or other reactant required in theory to account for the actual weight of monomer or other reactant molecules or fragments chemically incorporated (chemically combined) in the polymeric substance manufactured.

(iv) For a determination that 2 weight percent or less of a monomer or other reactant is incorporated (chemically combined) in a polymeric substance manufactured, as specified in paragraphs (a)(2)(iii)(B) of this section, analytical data or appropriate theoretical calculations (if it can be documented that analytical measurement is not feasible or not necessary) to support this determination must be maintained at the site of manufacture or import of the polymer.

(v) Measured or estimated values of the minimum number-average molecular weight of the polymer and the amount of low molecular weight species below 500 and below 1,000 molecular weight, with a description of how the measured or estimated values were obtained.

(3) The person must use one of the following two methods to develop or obtain the specified chemical identity information reported under paragraphs (a) (1) and (2) of this section and must identify the method used in the notice:

(i) *Method 1.* Obtain the correct chemical identity information required by paragraphs (a) (1) and (2) of this section directly from the Chemical Abstracts Service (CAS), specifically from the CAS Registry Services Inventory Expert Service, prior to submitting a notice to EPA. A copy of the chemical identification report obtained from CAS must be submitted with the notice.

(ii) *Method 2.* Obtain the correct chemical identity information required by paragraphs (a) (1) and (2) from any source. The notice will be incomplete according to §720.65(c)(1)(vi) if the person uses Method 2 and any chemical identity information is determined to be incorrect by EPA.

IV. Sample TSCA Awareness Training Program

Miriam V. Gold & Jean Warshaw, The Toxic Substances Control Act: A Practical Guide

(Oxford University Press 2010)

Notes on sample training program

- This set of slides is a suggestion for building a program
- Introduction should be by highest level management available in person or by the CEO by Internet or video
- Delete slides that are less relevant to specific audience
- Go into relevant areas in more depth
- Workshop on last slides are to evaluate the compliance system in place—small breakout groups with presentations to entire group will facilitate enhancements to the system as needed; consult Chapter 13, Compliance, "TSCA Requirements Matrix by Function" to select processes appropriate to the group being trained
- Designed as a one-hour lecture with 25 minutes of workshops and 20 minutes of presentations by workshop groups

Introduction
• Company commitment • Company compliance with law policy • Individual responsibility for compliance • Describe any company ombudsman, help line programs, or other employee reporting mechanisms

TSCA Overview

- Dates back to 1976
- Designed to allow the EPA to collect information and use it to regulate chemicals
- Little information existed about the vast quantity of chemicals other than drugs or pesticides
- TSCA gathers information to support air, water, and waste programs
- TSCA imposed the first requirements for manufacturers and importers to submit (sometimes develop) health and environmental information

Major Programs
• Inventory and Premanufacture Notifications • Significant New Uses • Microorganisms • Testing • Product restriction, e.g., PCBs • Adverse effects reporting • Recording allegations of effects • Import certifications and export reporting

Scope

- Explain what the company does that is covered by TSCA—e.g., chemical distributor
- TSCA applies to "manufacturers," "processors," "distributors," and "users" of "chemical substances"
- "Manufacture" is defined as:

"To import into the customs territory of the United States,… produce or manufacture." § 3(7)

Scope

• "Process" includes
  ◦ formulation
  ◦ preparing as part of an article
  ◦ repackaging
• Explain if the company is a processor

Scope

- "Distribute in commerce" is defined as:
  - selling in commerce
  - introduction into commerce
  - holding after introduction into commerce
- "Use" is not defined
- Explain if the company is a distributor or user of chemicals

What is a "Chemical Substance"?

- Chemicals of a "particular molecular identity"
- TSCA definition excludes:
  - mixtures
  - pesticides
  - tobacco or tobacco products
  - nuclear materials
  - firearms, shells, and cartridges
  - food, food additives, drugs, cosmetics, or devices
- Exclusions apply to every TSCA program

The TSCA Inventory

- All chemical substances are either *NEW, EXISTING,* or excluded from TSCA
- *EXISTING* Chemicals are on the TSCA Inventory
- The Premanufacture Notice rules prohibit:
  - manufacturing or importing a NEW chemical
  - UNLESS a Premanufacture Notice (PMN) is filed 90 days in advance

Significant New Uses
• SNUR rules prohibit manufacturing, importing, or processing a chemical already on the Inventory for a significant new use • UNLESS a Significant New Use Notice is filed 90 days prior to manufacturing, importing, or processing for that significant new use • A Significant New Use is any use that the EPA has determined may present concerns, and that no one had engaged in before

Nonisolated Intermediates

- Nonisolated intermediates do not have to be on the Inventory
- A nonisolated intermediate is any intermediate that is manufactured and consumed without intentional removal from enclosed equipment in which it is manufactured
- An intermediate is deemed isolated if it is stored in a reaction vessel after manufacture; this is a question of intent, not length of storage time
- A quality control sample is not deemed isolated

Note: use this slide if the company performs chemical synthesis

Process Changes

- TSCA may be implicated if a change in the U.S. or outside of the U.S.:
  - introduces a new raw material or new supplier
  - results in a new chemical as the end product
  - changes the sequence of adding raw materials
  - changes the reaction temperature
  - results in a new byproduct or impurity that imparts valuable properties to the resulting product
  - involves a chemical subject to a SNUR

Process Changes

- TSCA may be implicated if a change in the U.S.:
  - involves removing an intermediate from the equipment in which it is manufactured, if the intermediate was not removed from the equipment in which it was manufactured prior to the change
  - involves storing a nonisolated intermediate

PCBs

- Generally, PCBs cannot be manufactured, processed, or distributed
- Inadvertent manufacture of unintentional impurities is not prohibited, if regulations are followed
- For inadvertently generated PCBs, there are reporting and document retention requirements in the regulations

Note: delete this slide if not likely to manufacture PCBs inadvertently, but mention concept in case of future generation

PCB Items

- PCB Capacitor or Transformer means any capacitor or transformer that contains ≥ 500 ppm PCB
- Can only use if totally enclosed
- Must register PCB Transformers
- Must inspect periodically
- Must start cleaning up a leak in 48 hours
- Marking requirements
- Must comply with disposal or decontamination requirements

Note: use this slide if there are capacitors or transformers in the facility and facility managers are attending

The PMN Process
• Information gathering • Estimates of production volume, use, exposure, and fate • All test data and other data on health and environmental effects • Update data during the PMN period • A U.S. company must search for relevant data from affiliates • Can file consolidated PMNs for similar chemicals • Cannot manufacture or import until the end of the 90 day PMN review period

PMN Exemptions

- R&D
- Polymer exemption
- Low Volume Exemption
- Low Release and Exposure—LoREX
- These are not exemptions from reporting and recordkeeping requirements
- These are not exemptions from every TSCA program

Note: this slide is not a comprehensive list of exemptions—list the ones pertinent to specific company

Export Notifications

- First export to a particular country in any calendar year for certain chemicals; or
- First export to a particular country for certain other chemicals
- Requirements sunset if they are based on expired test rules
- No exemption for R&D substances, impurities, or byproducts
- Exemptions: manufacture for export; *de minimis* exemption for chemicals < 1%

Note: use this and next slide if attendees are in an import or export function

Import Certifications Importers must certify:

- Positive certification that a shipment is subject to TSCA and complies with TSCA, or
- Negative certification that a shipment is not subject to TSCA
- These must be filed at the port of entry
- Blanket certifications are valid for one year
- Articles are not covered, but chemicals that are intended to be released or removed from articles require import certifications

Substantial Risk Reporting § 8(e)
• Any person who manufactures, imports, processes, or distributes a chemical substance in commerce must report within 30 days any information that reasonably supports the conclusion that the chemical substance presents a substantial risk of injury to health or the environment • No regulations, just guidances • Must *currently* manufacture, import, process, or distribute to have a reporting obligation • Substantial risk information comes from: spills, toxicity studies, conferences, REACH dossiers, etc.

Records of Significant Adverse Reactions

Keep records of oral or written allegations—§ 8(c)—that:

- Implicate a chemical substance by naming:
    - the chemical
    - a mixture that contains the chemical
    - an article that contains the chemical
    - a process or operation in which the chemical is used
    - a manufacturing discharge
- Records must be maintained in a central location
- Allegations of significant adverse reactions come from: customer and neighbor complaints, litigations, OSHA recordables, employee complaints to health services, etc.

Additional Resources

- List and hand out company policies on:
  - compliance with law and environmental compliance
  - section 8(e) procedure
  - company-specific TSCA procedures
  - explain where TSCA information is kept in the company
  - identify in-house TSCA expertise
  - www.epa.gov TSCA information sites

Workshop—for Production Managers

How does information flow within the company to collect and route data on:

- Premanufacture Notifications?
- Managing isolated intermediates?
- Process changes?
- Managing PCBs?
- Adverse effects reporting?
- Inventory Update?
- How are new restrictions conveyed to the people who need to act on them?
- Is there sufficient awareness?
- Does information reach the correct people?

Workshop—for Import/Export Function

How does information flow within the company to collect and route data on:

- Import certifications?
- Export reporting?
- How are new restrictions conveyed to the people who need to act on them?
- Is there sufficient awareness?
- Does information reach the correct people?

Workshop—for Lab Personnel

How does information flow within the company to collect and route data on:

- PMN exemptions?
- R&D exemption?
- Significant New Use Notifications?
- Disposal restrictions in Significant New Use Rules?
- Adverse effects reporting?
- Sampling to third-parties?
- How are new restrictions conveyed to the people who need to act on them?
- Is there sufficient awareness?
- Does information reach the correct people?

Workshop—for Customer Service
How does information flow within the company to collect and route data on: • Significant New Use Notifications? • Consent decrees? • Adverse effects reporting? • How are new restrictions conveyed to the people who need to act on them? • Is there sufficient awareness? • Does information reach the correct people?

V. Confidentiality

The United States Environmental Protection Agency (EPA) has promulgated regulations under the Toxic Substances Control Act (TSCA)[1] to protect from disclosure to third-parties confidential business information (CBI) submitted to the Agency. The statutory provision requiring EPA to create protections for CBI is TSCA § 14.[2] TSCA § 14 defines the nature of the CBI that should be maintained in confidence by reference to the Freedom of Information Act, which in turn protects information from disclosure if it consists of "trade secrets and commercial or financial information obtained from a person and privileged or confidential."[3] Examples of information considered CBI under TSCA include chemical formulas, material inputs identification, process information, chemical substance identities, company names, site locations, and volumes of substances manufactured, imported, or processed. The EPA may make public any information claimed as CBI in health and safety studies on substances or mixtures that have been offered for commercial sale or for which testing is required under § 4[4] or for which notification is required under § 5.[5] However, EPA cannot disclose process information or information about the proportion of chemical substances in a mixture.[6]

The protection EPA has traditionally afforded to information companies claim as confidential has recently come under increasing scrutiny. The Kid-Safe Chemicals Act,[7] which has not been enacted as of this writing, would substantially toughen the requirements for making CBI claims. It calls for all CBI claims to be made in writing with a justification for the claims and a certification from the submitter's chief executive officer that the information has not been made public at the time the claim is made.[8] The EPA's principles for TSCA reform[9] also express a desire to restrict CBI claims. Those principles call for substantiation of CBI claims at the time they are made, and for a prohibition on claiming health and safety data as CBI. Although § 14 of the TSCA statute does not prohibit EPA from disclosing health and safety data that is designated as CBI, until recently the EPA did not rely on this

---

1. 15 U.S.C. §§ 2601-2659d.
2. 15 U.S.C. § 2613.
3. 5 U.S.C. § 552(b)(4).
4. *See* Chapter 9, Test Rules.
5. TSCA § 14(b)(1); *see* Chapter 4, Premanufacture Notification.
6. TSCA § 14(b)(1).
7. Kid-Safe Chemicals Act of 2008, H.R. 6100, S. 3040, 110th Congress.
8. Kid-Safe Chemicals Act of 2008, § 513, *available at* http://www.govtrack.us/congress/billtext.xpd?bill=s110-3040.
9. Essential Principles for Reform of Chemicals Management Legislation, (Sept. 30, 2009), *available at* http://www.epa.gov/oppt/existingchemicals/pubs/principles.pdf

exemption to reject claims of CBI in health and safety studies. In January 2010 the EPA announced a new general practice of making findings that the chemical identities of the subjects of health and safety studies submitted under TSCA § 8(e) are not CBI if those chemicals are listed on the public version of the TSCA Inventory.[10] EPA must notify the submitter of the CBI before it releases CBI, except when the disclosure is: to officers or employees of the United States in connection with their official duties for the protection of health or the environment or law enforcement purposes; to contractors working for the United States on TSCA programs; or when relevant to a proceeding under TSCA, but disclosures in the context of proceedings must be made in such a manner as to preserve confidentiality to the extent practical.[11]

While the rules vary somewhat on what information must be submitted to support a claim of confidentiality and when such information must be submitted, basically all the rules governing CBI under specific TSCA programs require proof by the party claiming confidentiality that it has maintained the CBI in confidence and that the disclosure of the CBI would be competitively harmful.

EPA sets outs examples of questions that are illustrative of what it might require to support a claim of confidentiality, but they are not intended to be exhaustive and the EPA can certainly require more evidence. For example, for confidential information submitted in a report of substantial risk information under TSCA § 8(e) the questions are:

1. Is your company asserting this confidential business information (CBI) claim on its own behalf? If the answer is no, please provide company name, address and telephone number of entity asserting claim.
2. For what period do you assert your claim(s) of confidentiality? If the claim is to extend until a certain event or point in time, please indicate that event or time period. Explain why such information should remain confidential until such point.
3. Has the information that you are claiming as confidential been disclosed to any other governmental agency, or to this Agency at any other time? Identify the Agency to which the information was disclosed and provide the date and circumstances of the same. Was the disclosure accompanied by a claim of confidentiality? If yes, attach a copy of said document reflecting the confidentiality agreement [*sic*].
4. Briefly describe any physical or procedural restrictions within your company relating to the use and storage of the information you are claiming CBI.

---

10. 75 Fed. Reg. 3462 (Jan. 21, 2010).
11. TSCA § 14(a).

5. If anyone outside your company has access to any of the information claimed CBI, are they restricted by confidentiality agreement(s). If so, explain the content of the agreement(s).
6. Does the information claimed as confidential appear or is it referred to in any of the following:
   a. Advertising or promotional material for the chemical substance or the resulting and product;
   b. Material safety data sheets or other similar materials (such as technical data sheets) for the substance or resulting end product (include copies of this information as it appears when accompanying the substance and/or product at the time of transfer or sale);
   c. Professional or trade publications; or
   d. Any other media or publications available to the public or to your competitors.If you answered yes to any of the above, indicate where the information appears, include copies, and explain why it should nonetheless be treated as confidential.
7. Has EPA, another federal agency, or court made any confidentiality determination regarding information associated with this substance? If so, provide copies of such determinations.
8. Describe the substantial harmful effects that would result to your competitive position if the CBI information is made available to the public? In your answer, explain the causal relationship between disclosure and any resulting substantial harmful effects. Consider in your answer such constraints as capital and marketing cost, specialized technical expertise, or unusual processes and your competitors [*sic*] access to your customers. Address each piece of information claimed CBI separately.
9. Has the substance been patented in the U.S. or elsewhere? Is a patent for the substance currently pending?
10. Is this substance/product commercially available and if so, for how long has it been available on the commercial market?
    a. a. [*sic*] If on the commercial market, are your competitors aware that the substance is commercially available in the U.S.?
    b. b. [*sic*] If not already commercially available, describe what stage of research and development (R&D) the substance is in, and estimate bow soon a market will be established.
    c. c. [*sic*] What is the substance used for and what type of product(s) does it appear in.
11. Describe whether a competitor could employ reverse engineering to identically recreate the substance?
12. Do you assert that disclosure of this information you are claiming CBI would reveal:
    a. a [*sic*] confidential processes used in manufacturing the substance;
    b. b [*sic*] if a mixture, the actual portions of the substance in the mixture; or

c. c [*sic*] information unrelated to the effects of the substance on human health or the environment?If your answer to any of the above questions is yes, explain how such information would be revealed.

13. Provide the Chemical Abstract Service Registry Number for the product, if known. Is your company applying for a CAS number now or in the near future? If you have applied for a CAS number, include a copy of the contract with CAS.
14. Is the substance or any information claimed CBI the subject of FIFRA regulation or reporting? If so, explain.[12]

CBI claims must be made at the time the CBI is submitted, and the information required to be submitted must be presented in two separate documents, one with the CBI redacted (often referred to as a "sanitized" copy). The sanitized copy will be made available to the public. In many cases, the copy with CBI included should be submitted to the Agency separately, either to a different address or in a different envelope to ensure that it is not inadvertently put in a public file. For the most part, substantiation need not accompany the claim of CBI.[13] Even if the substantiation is not required at the time the claim is made, as a practical matter, it makes sense for the submitter to consider what substantiation it will be prepared to offer should the EPA ask for such substantiation, and to thoroughly consider the claim before asserting it.

VI. Supplementary Research Sources

This section describes how to obtain TSCA-related information from the EPA and other government offices and public databases. The listing of subscription based and public databases is not exhaustive.

12. http://www.epa.gov/opptintr/tsca8e/pubs/confidentialbusinessinformation.html. Note that this list of questions has been expanded since it was included in the June 1991 TSCA Section 8(e) Reporting Guide.
13. Notices of Commencement of manufacture or import are an exception, and the substantiation must be submitted with any notice that claims CBI status for information on the form. 40 C.F.R. § 720.102(c)(2). For reports of significant risk information submitted under TSCA § 8(e), the EPA guidance does not make substantiation mandatory at the time CBI is submitted because it says that the "submitter should substantiate any CBI claims." 68 Fed. Reg. 33129, 33140 (June 3, 2002).

A. Information from the EPA

1. TSCA Hotline

The EPA maintains a TSCA hotline, formally known as the TSCA Assistance Information Service ("TAIS"), which is staffed by an outsourced service provider. The hotline provides basic information about TSCA, and contacts to EPA personnel who can provide more in-depth background. The hotline is a good resource for specific documents, and can fax or mail documents on request. The contact information for the TSCA hotline is:

Telephone: (202) 554-1404
E-mail: tsca-hotline@epa.gov
Requests for documents can be faxed to: (202) 554-5603
Online contact form: http://www.epa.gov/oppt/import-export/contact.html

EPA established the TAIS in 1977 pursuant to § 26(d) of TSCA, which states:

> (d) ASSISTANCE OFFICE.—The Administrator shall establish in the Environmental Protection Agency an identifiable office to provide technical and other nonfinancial assistance to manufacturers and processors of chemical substances and mixtures respecting the requirements of this Act applicable to such manufacturers and processors, the policy of the Agency respecting the application of such requirements to such manufacturers and processors, and the means and methods by which such manufacturers and processors may comply with such requirements.

The EPA is migrating its information assistance program from the TSCA Hotline to an Internet-based set of frequently asked questions, or FAQs. Those FAQs are on the EPA Web site at http://toxics.custhelp.com. There are plans to have a more limited call center with a reduced number of people to answer questions. The limited call center will attempt to answer complex questions or questions that are not addressed by the FAQs.[14]

2. EPA Docket Center

Documents filed with the EPA, and documents relevant to rulemaking, are collected at the EPA Docket Center. Most TSCA information should be available through http://www.regulations.gov, discussed below, but some, such as

---

14. Contract between EPA and ABVI Goodwill Industries of Greater Rochester, effective August 1, 2008, EP-W-08-050, 2-2.

Toxic Release Inventory filings, can be accessed by contacting the EPA Docket Center by one of the following means:

Telephone: (202) 566-0280
E-mail: oppt.ncic@epa.gov
Fax: (202) 566-9744
Mailing Address:
U.S. Environmental Protection Agency
EPA Docket Center
Pollution Prevention and Toxics Docket, Mail Code 28221T
1200 Pennsylvania Avenue, NW
Washington, DC 20460

3. Substance Registry Service

The EPA maintains an Internet based registry of all chemicals that are regulated under any EPA program, at http://iaspub.epa.gov/sor_internet/registry/substreg/home/overview/home.do. There are many ways to search the Substance Registry Services to find data concerning specific chemicals. To find chemicals regulated under various TSCA provisions, follow these steps:

1. go to http://iaspub.epa.gov/sor_internet/registry/substreg/home/overview/home.do;
2. click on the tab at the top that says "Search & Retrieve;"
3. click on the link that says "Search by List;"
4. in the box that asks for "List Name" type in TSCA;
5. a list of TSCA programs will appear, and select the program for which information is sought;
6. click on "search" at the bottom of the page.

The resulting list will be generated, and can be exported in several formats, including as am Excel spreadsheet.

For example, by selecting typing in "TSCA" in the box in step 4, and selecting "TSCA 4 Tests (358[15])—Testing of Existing Chemicals" in step 5, the program will retrieve all the chemicals subject to a TSCA § 4 test rule. That list can be exported and saved. By clicking on the name of any chemical in the resulting list, additional information concerning that chemical and its regulatory status will appear in a pop up box.

The EPA put the entire Inventory online and it can be accessed through http://www.epa.gov/opptintr/newchems/pubs/invntory.htm#files. The Inventory

---

15. The number in the parenthetical will change as the number of subject chemicals increases.

status of specific chemicals can also be investigated through the Substance Registry Service. This is not a definitive listing, and may not be fully up-to-date. If a chemical shows up on the Substance Registry Service as being on the Inventory, that is most likely sufficient to conclude that the chemical is on the Inventory. However, if a substance is not on the Substance Registry Service, it could be because it is described differently than the chemical name that is being searched for, or it could be because the identity of the substance is Confidential Business Information. Confidential Business Information is not included in the registry.

4. Semiannual Regulatory Agendas

EPA publishes a semiannual regulatory agenda every spring and fall, setting out all of the rules that it expects to promulgate and the status of each rule-making proceeding. These are available at http://www.epa.gov/regulations/search/regagenda.html. The semiannual regulatory agenda is a valuable tool for following the EPA's plans for the TSCA programs. A good way to search through it is to download the pdf file and search for the acronym "TSCA" or any other program such as "Inventory Update Rule".

5. Freedom of Information Act Requests

Under the Freedom of Information Act (FOIA) 5 U.S.C. § 552, the federal government must release information, data and documents to the public, unless there is an exemption. The EPA may charge for copies of documents and has a procedure for requesting that the fees be waived. There are several ways to make a FOIA request to the EPA. These include:

1. writing to EPA headquarters in Washington, D.C. at National Freedom of Information Officer, U.S. Environmental Protection Agency, 1200 Pennsylvania Avenue, NW (2822T), Washington, DC 20460;
2. writing to one of the EPA Regions at the address given in 40 C.F.R. § 2.101
3. E-mailing EPA headquarters at hq.foia@epa.gov;
4. E-mailing one of the EPA Regions at rXfoia@epa.gov, where X is the number of the region, so the address for Region 2 is r2foia@epa.gov as an example; and
5. submitting an online request at http://www.epa.gov/foia/make_a_request.html.

The authors recommend a written request using the U.S. Mail.

Companies often seek competitive data on other businesses through FOIA requests.

6. Specific TSCA Programs

EPA maintains Web pages with links to regulations, guidance documents, forms, and additional resources for each of the major TSCA programs. Most of these Web pages are listed at http://www.epa.gov/opptintr/index.html, which is the home page of the EPA Office of Pollution Prevention and Toxics.

B. Federal Register Notices and Code of Federal Regulations

1. Federal Register Notices

The EPA publishes Federal Register notices when it receives PMNs, NOCs, and citizen's suits. It also publishes Federal Register notices when it issues proposed rules, final rules, and some guidances. Final rules are then published in the Code of Federal Regulations. In addition to setting out the language of the proposed or final rules, Federal Register notices contain a discussion and interpretations of the rules. These discussions, called preambles, are critical to a full understanding of most regulations. Therefore, the Federal Register notices published with the proposed and final rules are important to consult.

The best way to keep informed about materials that the EPA publishes in the Federal Register on an ongoing basis is to subscribe to the daily table of contents (described below) and look for EPA actions, or subscribe to a private service that fills that function. All of the federal agencies are listed in the daily table of contents, in alphabetical order.

HeinOnline is the only comprehensive and easy to use source the authors know of for historical Federal Register notices. HeinOnline is a subscription service available through its Web site at http://www.heinonline.org. It has full images of all Federal Register notices starting with Volume 1 in 1936. It also has a searchable text version of the Federal Register notices. Most other databases only have Federal Register notices back as far as 1994. Many of the Federal Register notices on the accompanying CD are used with the permission of HeinOnline.

The EPA has selected Federal Register notices available on its Web site, but the complete set only goes back as far as 1994, which is not particularly useful when researching regulations that date back to TSCA's inception in 1976. EPA has a selective collection of Federal Register notices relating to TSCA that are older than September 1994 on its Web site at: http://www.epa.gov/fedrgstr/EPA-TOX/pre1994/hisindex.htm

Federal Register notices from 1994 to the present are also available in either html or pdf format through the United States Government Printing Office's Web site at http://www.gpoaccess.gov/fr/index.html. The authors recommend downloading any documents of interest because the materials available through this site change.

Federal Register notices are available at Federal Depository Libraries throughout the United States. For a current list of these libraries, check the Government Printing Office Web site at http://www.gpoaccess.gov/fr/index.html. Note that some of these repository libraries maintain their collections on mircrofiche, which is unwieldy to use.

LexisNexis® and Westlaw® research services also have Federal Register notices in their subscription-based databases, but neither of them maintains a complete collection. The Lexis database goes back to July 1, 1980 and therefore does not have some of the critical early TSCA notices.

2. Daily Federal Register Table of Contents

The Government Printing Office sends out a daily e-mail with the table of contents for that day's Federal Register. To subscribe to the daily e-mail follow these steps:

1. go to http://listserv.access.gpo.gov/;
2. click on the link that says "Online mailing list archives";
3. click on the link that says "FEDREGTOC-L";
4. click on the link that says "Join or leave the list (or change settings)";
5. fill out the form that appears to register for the daily e-mail; and
6. the GPO will send a confirming e-mail and registration requires clicking on the link in that e-mail.

3. Updates on Rulemaking Dockets

After receiving notice of a proposed rule, rule, guidance, or other Federal Register notice, subscriptions are available to e-mail notifications when the EPA docket for that topic is updated. The Docket Number for each agency action appears in each Federal Register notice relating to that action.

As an example of how to receive updates on EPA actions, the Interim Audit Policy for new owners of facilities was announced at 73 Fed. Reg. 44990 (Aug. 1, 2008). Searching for the word "docket" in that Federal Register notice shows that the action is in Docket ID No. EPA–HQ– OECA–2007–0291. To sign up for daily, weekly, or monthly updates on the Audit Policy as it applies to acquisitions, follow these steps:

1. go to http://www.regulations.gov;
2. in the box that that is entitled "Enter Keyword or ID:" type in EPA–HQ–OECA–2007–0291, and click on the "search" icon directly beneath that;
3. a list of documents in that docket will appear, and on the right of the screen there will be a column of icons that say "open docket folder"—click on any of those icons;

4. near the top of the page that opens there will be a link that says "Sign Up for E-mail Alerts"—click on that link;
5. a pop-up screen will appear asking for an e-mail address and how often updates should be sent when new documents are added to the docket; and
6. regulations.gov will send a confirming e-mail and registration requires clicking on the link in that e-mail.

Comments on proposed rules and other materials published in the Federal Register with an invitation to comment are in the applicable docket on http://www.regulations.gov. The initial publication will have the docket number, and a search under that docket number will show all the submittals.

C. TSCA Statute

The best way to access up-to-date versions of the TSCA statute is to use LexisNexis or Westlaw or another well-maintained database. The versions that the EPA links to are not always current, and the General Printing Office's online version at http://www.gpoaccess.gov/uscode/index.html can be out of date.

D. TSCA Regulations

Several sources make the TSCA regulations available, and these include:

1. the Government Printing Office, which has links to the current regulations at http://www.gpoaccess.gov. TSCA regulations are in Title 40, §§ 700-799;
2. the Government Printing Office also has an eCFR system at http://ecfr.gpoaccess.gov/cgi/t/text/text-idx?c=ecfr&tpl=%2Findex.tpl which is significantly easier to use than http://www.gpoaccess.gov;
3. HeinOnline is a subscription based service that posts the Code of Federal Regulations on its Web site at http://www.heinonline.org; and
4. LexisNexis and Westlaw also post the Code of Federal Regulations.

1. Miscellaneous

The New York Times and other newspapers have free[16] archive search functions. These are useful for reading news reports relevant to toxic substances,

16. The New York Times has said it will charge for online access starting in early 2011. Richard Pérez-Peña, *The Times to Charge for Online Access*, N.Y. Times, Mar. 17, 1983, *available at*

such as historical information on Love Canal or Bhopal. The NEW YORK TIMES' Web site is http://www.nytimes.com, and the search function appears under the banner headline. LexisNexis is also a good source of newspaper articles on a subscription basis.

2. Revision Tracking

Many of the EPA's guidance documents are undated. Absent version numbers or dates, the best way to track document versions is by reviewing the metadata attached to the documents.

As an example of how to use metadata to get document dates, the current version of the EPA's Questions & Answers for the New Chemicals Program is undated, and the EPA's Web site does not refer to version numbers, but the pdf document has useful data buried in it. If it is opened using Adobe® Reader®, the "File" pulldown menu will have a tab called "Properties," and the document dates will be revealed by clicking on the tab labeled "Properties."

---

http://mediadecoder.blogs.nytimes.com/2010/01/20/the-times-to-charge-for-online-access/?scp=2&sq=to%20charge%20for%20articles&st=cse.

VII. Toxic Substances Control Act Statute

15 U.S.C. §§ 2601 - 2695

SUBCHAPTER I - CONTROL OF TOXIC SUBSTANCES

Sec.	
2601. (TSCA § 2)	Findings, policy, and intent.
2602. (TSCA § 3)	Definitions.
2603. (TSCA § 4)	Testing of chemical substances and mixtures.
2604. (TSCA § 5)	Manufacturing and processing notices.
2605. (TSCA § 6)	Regulation of hazardous chemical substances and mixtures.
2606. (TSCA § 7)	Imminent hazards.
2607. (TSCA § 8)	Reporting and retention of information.
2608. (TSCA § 9)	Relationship to other Federal laws.
2609. (TSCA § 10)	Research, development, collection, dissemination, and utilization of data.
2610. (TSCA § 11)	Inspections and subpoenas.
2611. (TSCA § 12)	Exports.
2612. (TSCA § 13)	Entry into customs territory of the United States.
2613. (TSCA § 14)	Disclosure of data.
2614. (TSCA § 15)	Prohibited acts.
2615. (TSCA § 16)	Penalties.
2616. (TSCA § 17)	Specific enforcement and seizure.
2617. (TSCA § 18)	Preemption.
2618. (TSCA § 19)	Judicial review.
2619. (TSCA § 20)	Citizens' civil actions.
2620. (TSCA § 21)	Citizens' petitions.
2621. (TSCA § 22)	National defense waiver.
2622. (TSCA § 23)	Employee protection.
2623. (TSCA § 24)	Employment effects.
2624. (TSCA § 25)	Studies.
2625. (TSCA § 26)	Administration.
2626. (TSCA § 27)	Development and evaluation of test methods.
2627. (TSCA § 28)	State programs.
2628. (TSCA § 29)	Authorization of appropriations.
2629. (TSCA § 30)	Annual report.

SUBCHAPTER II - ASBESTOS HAZARD EMERGENCY RESPONSE

2641. (TSCA § 201)	Congressional findings and purpose.
2642. (TSCA § 202)	Definitions.
2643. (TSCA § 203)	EPA regulations.

(TSCA § 2)

Sec. 2601. Findings, policy, and intent

(a) Findings

The Congress finds that –

(1) human beings and the environment are being exposed each year to a large number of chemical substances and mixtures;

(2) among the many chemical substances and mixtures which are constantly being developed and produced, there are some whose manufacture, processing, distribution in commerce, use, or disposal may present an unreasonable risk of injury to health or the environment; and

(3) the effective regulation of interstate commerce in such chemical substances and mixtures also necessitates the regulation of intrastate commerce in such chemical substances and mixtures.

(b) Policy

It is the policy of the United States that –

(1) adequate data should be developed with respect to the effect of chemical substances and mixtures on health and the environment and that the development of such data should be the responsibility of those who manufacture and those who process such chemical substances and mixtures;

(2) adequate authority should exist to regulate chemical substances and mixtures which present an unreasonable risk of injury to health or the environment, and to take action with respect to chemical substances and mixtures which are imminent hazards; and

(3) authority over chemical substances and mixtures should be exercised in such a manner as not to impede unduly or create unnecessary economic

barriers to technological innovation while fulfilling the primary purpose of this chapter to assure that such innovation and commerce in such chemical substances and mixtures do not present an unreasonable risk of injury to health or the environment.

(c) Intent of Congress

It is the intent of Congress that the Administrator shall carry out this chapter in a reasonable and prudent manner, and that the Administrator shall consider the environmental, economic, and social impact of any action the Administrator takes or proposes to take under this chapter.

(TSCA § 3)

Sec. 2602. Definitions

As used in this chapter:

(1) the[1] term "Administrator" means the Administrator of the Environmental Protection Agency.

(2) (A) Except as provided in subparagraph (B), the term "chemical substance" means any organic or inorganic substance of a particular molecular identity, including –

(i) any combination of such substances occurring in whole or in part as a result of a chemical reaction or occurring in nature and

(ii) any element or uncombined radical.

(B) Such term does not include –

(i) any mixture,

(ii) any pesticide (as defined in the Federal Insecticide, Fungicide, and Rodenticide Act [7 U.S.C. 136 et seq.]) when manufactured, processed, or distributed in commerce for use as a pesticide,

(iii) tobacco or any tobacco product,

(iv) any source material, special nuclear material, or byproduct material (as such terms are defined in the Atomic Energy Act of 1954 [42 U.S.C. 2011 et seq.] and regulations issued under such Act),

(v) any article the sale of which is subject to the tax imposed by section 4181 of the Internal Revenue Code of 1986 [26 U.S.C. 4181] (determined without regard to any exemptions from such

---

1. So in original. Probably should be capitalized.

tax provided by section 4182 or 4221 or any other provision of such Code), and

(vi) any food, food additive, drug, cosmetic, or device (as such terms are defined in section 201 of the Federal Food, Drug, and Cosmetic Act [21 U.S.C. 321]) when manufactured, processed, or distributed in commerce for use as a food, food additive, drug, cosmetic, or device.

The term "food" as used in clause (vi) of this subparagraph includes poultry and poultry products (as defined in sections 4(e) and 4(f) of the Poultry Products Inspection Act [21 U.S.C. 453(e) and (f)]), meat and meat food products (as defined insection 1(j) of the Federal Meat Inspection Act [21 U.S.C. 601(j)]), and eggs and egg products (as defined in section 4 of the Egg Products Inspection Act [21 U.S.C. 1033]).

(3) The term "commerce" means trade, traffic, transportation, or other commerce (A) between a place in a State and any place outside of such State, or (B) which affects trade, traffic, transportation, or commerce described in clause (A).

(4) The terms "distribute in commerce" and "distribution in commerce" when used to describe an action taken with respect to a chemical substance or mixture or article containing a substance or mixture mean to sell, or the sale of, the substance, mixture, or article in commerce; to introduce or deliver for introduction into commerce, or the introduction or delivery for introduction into commerce of, the substance, mixture, or article; or to hold, or the holding of, the substance, mixture, or article after its introduction into commerce.

(5) The term "environment" includes water, air, and land and the interrelationship which exists among and between water, air, and land and all living things.

(6) The term "health and safety study" means any study of any effect of a chemical substance or mixture on health or the environment or on both, including underlying data and epidemiological studies, studies of occupational exposure to a chemical substance or mixture, toxicological, clinical, and ecological studies of a chemical substance or mixture, and any test performed pursuant to this chapter.

(7) The term "manufacture" means to import into the customs territory of the United States (as defined in general note 2 of the Harmonized Tariff Schedule of the United States), produce, or manufacture.

(8) The term "mixture" means any combination of two or more chemical substances if the combination does not occur in nature and is not, in whole

or in part, the result of a chemical reaction; except that such term does include any combination which occurs, in whole or in part, as a result of a chemical reaction if none of the chemical substances comprising the combination is a new chemical substance and if the combination could have been manufactured for commercial purposes without a chemical reaction at the time the chemical substances comprising the combination were combined.

(9) The term "new chemical substance" means any chemical substance which is not included in the chemical substance list compiled and published under section 2607(b) of this title.

(10) The term "process" means the preparation of a chemical substance or mixture, after its manufacture, for distribution in commerce–

(A) in the same form or physical state as, or in a different form or physical state from, that in which it was received by the person so preparing such substance or mixture, or (B) as part of an article containing the chemical substance or mixture.

(11) The term "processor" means any person who processes a chemical substance or mixture.

(12) The term "standards for the development of test data" means a prescription of –

(A) the –

(i) health and environmental effects, and

(ii) information relating to toxicity, persistence, and other characteristics which affect health and the environment, for which test data for a chemical substance or mixture are to be developed and any analysis that is to be performed on such data, and

(B) to the extent necessary to assure that data respecting such effects and characteristics are reliable and adequate–

(i) the manner in which such data are to be developed,

(ii) the specification of any test protocol or methodology to be employed in the development of such data, and

(iii) such other requirements as are necessary to provide such assurance.

(13) The term "State" means any State of the United States, the District of Columbia, the Commonwealth of Puerto Rico, the Virgin Islands, Guam, the Canal Zone, American Samoa, the Northern Mariana Islands, or any other territory or possession of the United States.

(14) The term "United States", when used in the geographic sense, means all of the States.

(TSCA § 4)

Sec. 2603. Testing of chemical substances and mixtures

(a) Testing requirements

If the Administrator finds that–

(1) (A) (i) the manufacture, distribution in commerce, processing, use, or disposal of a chemical substance or mixture, or that any combination of such activities, may present an unreasonable risk of injury to health or the environment,

(ii) there are insufficient data and experience upon which the effects of such manufacture, distribution in commerce, processing, use, or disposal of such substance or mixture or of any combination of such activities on health or the environment can reasonably be determined or predicted, and

(iii) testing of such substance or mixture with respect to such effects is necessary to develop such data; or

(B) (i) a chemical substance or mixture is or will be produced in substantial quantities, and (I) it enters or may reasonably be anticipated to enter the environment in substantial quantities or (II) there is or may be significant or substantial human exposure to such substance or mixture,

(ii) there are insufficient data and experience upon which the effects of the manufacture, distribution in commerce, processing, use, or disposal of such substance or mixture or of any combination of such activities on health or the environment can reasonably be determined or predicted, and

(iii) testing of such substance or mixture with respect to such effects is necessary to develop such data; and

(2) in the case of a mixture, the effects which the mixture's manufacture, distribution in commerce, processing, use, or disposal or any combination of such activities may have on health or the environment may not be reasonably and more efficiently determined or predicted by testing the chemical substances which comprise the mixture; the Administrator shall by rule require that testing be conducted on such substance or mixture to develop data with respect to the health and environmental effects for which there is an insufficiency of data and experience and which are relevant to a determination that the manufacture, distribution in commerce, processing, use, or disposal of such substance or mixture, or that any combination of such activities, does or does not present an unreasonable risk of injury to health or the environment.

(b) Testing requirement rule

(1) A rule under subsection (a) of this section shall include–

(A) identification of the chemical substance or mixture for which testing is required under the rule,

(B) standards for the development of test data for such substance or mixture, and

(C) with respect to chemical substances which are not new chemical substances and to mixtures, a specification of the period (which period may not be of unreasonable duration) within which the persons required to conduct the testing shall submit to the Administrator data developed in accordance with the standards referred to in subparagraph (B).

In determining the standards and period to be included, pursuant to subparagraphs (B) and (C), in a rule under subsection (a) of this section, the Administrator's considerations shall include the relative costs of the various test protocols and methodologies which may be required under the rule and the reasonably foreseeable availability of the facilities and personnel needed to perform the testing required under the rule. Any such rule may require the submission to the Administrator of preliminary data during the period prescribed under subparagraph (C).

(2) (A) The health and environmental effects for which standards for the development of test data may be prescribed include carcinogenesis, mutagenesis, teratogenesis, behavioral disorders, cumulative or synergistic effects, and any other effect which may present an unreasonable risk of injury to health or the environment. The characteristics of chemical substances and mixtures for which such standards may be prescribed include persistence, acute toxicity, subacute toxicity, chronic toxicity, and any other characteristic which may present such a risk. The methodologies that may be prescribed in such standards include epidemiologic studies, serial or hierarchical tests, in vitro tests, and whole animal tests, except that before prescribing epidemiologic studies of employees, the Administrator shall consult with the Director of the National Institute for Occupational Safety and Health.

(B) From time to time, but not less than once each 12 months, the Administrator shall review the adequacy of the standards for development of data prescribed in rules under subsection (a) of this section and shall, if necessary, institute proceedings to make appropriate revisions of such standards.

(3) (A) A rule under subsection (a) of this section respecting a chemical substance or mixture shall require the persons described in subparagraph (B) to conduct tests and submit data to the Administrator on such

substance or mixture, except that the Administrator may permit two or more of such persons to designate one such person or a qualified third party to conduct such tests and submit such data on behalf of the persons making the designation.

(B) The following persons shall be required to conduct tests and submit data on a chemical substance or mixture subject to a rule under subsection (a) of this section:

(i) Each person who manufactures or intends to manufacture such substance or mixture if the Administrator makes a finding described in subsection (a)(1)(A)(ii) or (a)(1)(B)(ii) of this section with respect to the manufacture of such substance or mixture.

(ii) Each person who processes or intends to process such substance or mixture if the Administrator makes a finding described in subsection (a)(1)(A)(ii) or (a)(1)(B)(ii) of this section with respect to the processing of such substance or mixture.

(iii) Each person who manufactures or processes or intends to manufacture or process such substance or mixture if the Administrator makes a finding described in subsection (a)(1)(A)(ii) or (a)(1)(B)(ii) of this section with respect to the distribution in commerce, use, or disposal of such substance or mixture.

(4) Any rule under subsection (a) of this section requiring the testing of and submission of data for a particular chemical substance or mixture shall expire at the end of the reimbursement period (as defined in subsection (c)(3)(B) of this section) which is applicable to test data for such substance or mixture unless the Administrator repeals the rule before such date; and a rule under subsection (a) of this section requiring the testing of and submission of data for a category of chemical substances or mixtures shall expire with respect to a chemical substance or mixture included in the category at the end of the reimbursement period (as so defined) which is applicable to test data for such substance or mixture unless the Administrator before such date repeals the application of the rule to such substance or mixture or repeals the rule.

(5) Rules issued under subsection (a) of this section (and any substantive amendment thereto or repeal thereof) shall be promulgated pursuant to section 553 of title 5 except that (A) the Administrator shall give interested persons an opportunity for the oral presentation of data, views, or arguments, in addition to an opportunity to make written submissions; (B) a transcript shall be made of any oral presentation; and (C) the Administrator shall make and publish with the rule the findings described in paragraph (1)(A) or (1)(B) of subsection (a) of this section and, in the case of a rule respecting a mixture, the finding described in paragraph (2) of such subsection.

(c) Exemption

(1) Any person required by a rule under subsection (a) of this section to conduct tests and submit data on a chemical substance or mixture may apply to the Administrator (in such form and manner as the Administrator shall prescribe) for an exemption from such requirement.

(2) If, upon receipt of an application under paragraph (1), the Administrator determines that–

(A) the chemical substance or mixture with respect to which such application was submitted is equivalent to a chemical substance or mixture for which data has been submitted to the Administrator in accordance with a rule under subsection (a) of this section or for which data is being developed pursuant to such a rule, and (B) submission of data by the applicant on such substance or mixture would be duplicative of data which has been submitted to the Administrator in accordance with such rule or which is being developed pursuant to such rule, the Administrator shall exempt, in accordance with paragraph (3) or (4), the applicant from conducting tests and submitting data on such substance or mixture under the rule with respect to which such application was submitted.

(3) (A) If the exemption under paragraph (2) of any person from the requirement to conduct tests and submit test data on a chemical substance or mixture is granted on the basis of the existence of previously submitted test data and if such exemption is granted during the reimbursement period for such test data (as prescribed by subparagraph (B)), then (unless such person and the persons referred to in clauses (i) and (ii) agree on the amount and method of reimbursement) the Administrator shall order the person granted the exemption to provide fair and equitable reimbursement (in an amount determined under rules of the Administrator)–

(i) to the person who previously submitted such test data, for a portion of the costs incurred by such person in complying with the requirement to submit such data, and

(ii) to any other person who has been required under this subparagraph to contribute with respect to such costs, for a portion of the amount such person was required to contribute.

In promulgating rules for the determination of fair and equitable reimbursement to the persons described in clauses (i) and (ii) for costs incurred with respect to a chemical substance or mixture, the Administrator shall, after consultation with the Attorney General and the Federal Trade Commission, consider all relevant factors, including the effect on the competitive position of the person required to provide reimbursement in relation to the person to be reimbursed and the share of the market for such substance or mixture of the person required to provide reimbursement in relation to the share of such market of the persons to be reimbursed. An order under this subparagraph shall, for purposes of judicial review, be considered final agency action.

(B) For purposes of subparagraph (A), the reimbursement period for any test data for a chemical substance or mixture is a period–

(i) beginning on the date such data is submitted in accordance with a rule promulgated under subsection (a) of this section, and

(ii) ending–

(I) five years after the date referred to in clause (i), or

(II) at the expiration of a period which begins on the date referred to in clause (i) and which is equal to the period which the Administrator determines was necessary to develop such data, whichever is later.

(4) (A) if the exemption under paragraph (2) of any person from the requirement to conduct tests and submit test data on a chemical substance or mixture is granted on the basis of the fact that test data is being developed by one or more persons pursuant to a rule promulgated under subsection (a) of this section, then (unless such person and the persons referred to in clauses (i) and (ii) agree on the amount and method of reimbursement) the Administrator shall order the person granted the exemption to provide fair and equitable reimbursement (in an amount determined under rules of the Administrator) –

(i) to each such person who is developing such test data, for a portion of the costs incurred by each such person in complying with such rule, and

(ii) to any other person who has been required under this subparagraph to contribute with respect to the costs of complying with such rule, for a portion of the amount such person was required to contribute.

In promulgating rules for the determination of fair and equitable reimbursement to the persons described in clauses (i) and (ii) for costs incurred with respect to a chemical substance or mixture, the Administrator shall, after consultation with the Attorney General and the Federal Trade Commission, consider the factors described in the second sentence of paragraph (3)(A). An order under this subparagraph shall, for purposes of judicial review, be considered final agency action.

(B) If any exemption is granted under paragraph (2) on the basis of the fact that one or more persons are developing test data pursuant to a rule promulgated under subsection (a) of this section and if after such exemption is granted the Administrator determines that no such person has complied with such rule, the Administrator shall (i) after providing written notice to the person who holds such exemption and an opportunity for a hearing, by order terminate such exemption, and (ii) notify in writing such person of the requirements of the rule with respect to which such exemption was granted.

(d) Notice

Upon the receipt of any test data pursuant to a rule under subsection (a) of this section, the Administrator shall publish a notice of the receipt of such data in the Federal Register within 15 days of its receipt. Subject to section 2613 of this title, each such notice shall (1) identify the chemical substance or mixture for which data have been received; (2) list the uses or intended uses of such substance or mixture and the information required by the applicable standards for the development of test data; and (3) describe the nature of the test data developed. Except as otherwise provided in section 2613 of this title, such data shall be made available by the Administrator for examination by any person.

(e) Priority list

(1) (A) There is established a committee to make recommendations to the Administrator respecting the chemical substances and mixtures to which the Administrator should give priority consideration for the promulgation of a rule under subsection (a) of this section. In making such a recommendation with respect to any chemical substance or mixture, the committee shall consider all relevant factors, including–

(i) the quantities in which the substance or mixture is or will be manufactured,

(ii) the quantities in which the substance or mixture enters or will enter the environment,

(iii) the number of individuals who are or will be exposed to the substance or mixture in their places of employment and the duration of such exposure,

(iv) the extent to which human beings are or will be exposed to the substance or mixture,

(v) the extent to which the substance or mixture is closely related to a chemical substance or mixture which is known to present an unreasonable risk of injury to health or the environment,

(vi) the existence of data concerning the effects of the substance or mixture on health or the environment,

(vii) the extent to which testing of the substance or mixture may result in the development of data upon which the effects of the substance or mixture on health or the environment can reasonably be determined or predicted, and

(viii) the reasonably foreseeable availability of facilities and personnel for performing testing on the substance or mixture.

The recommendations of the committee shall be in the form of a list of chemical substances and mixtures which shall be set forth, either by individual substance or mixture or by groups of substances or mixtures, in the order in which the committee determines the Administrator should take action under subsection (a) of this section with respect to the substances and mixtures. In establishing such list, the committee shall give priority attention to those chemical substances and mixtures which are known to cause or contribute to or which are suspected of causing or contributing to cancer, gene mutations, or birth defects. The committee shall designate chemical substances and mixtures on the list with respect to which the committee determines the Administrator should, within 12 months of the date on which such substances and mixtures are first designated, initiate a proceeding under subsection (a) of this section. The total number of chemical substances and mixtures on the list which are designated under the preceding sentence may not, at any time, exceed 50.

(B) As soon as practicable but not later than nine months after January 1, 1977, the committee shall publish in the Federal Register and transmit to the Administrator the list and designations required by subparagraph (A) together with the reasons for the committee's inclusion of each chemical substance or mixture on the list. At least every six months after the date of the transmission to the Administrator of the list pursuant to the preceeding[2] sentence, the committee shall make such previsions in the list as it determines to be necessary and shall transmit them to the Administrator together with the committee's reasons for the revisions. Upon receipt of any such revision, the Administrator shall publish in the Federal Register the list with such revision, the reasons for such revision, and the designations made under subparagraph (A). The Administrator shall provide reasonable opportunity to any interested person to file with the Administrator written comments on the committee's list, any revision of such list by the committee, and designations made by the committee, and shall make such comments available to the public. Within the 12-month period beginning on the date of the first inclusion on the list of a chemical substance or mixture designated by the committee under subparagraph (A) the Administrator shall with respect to such chemical substance or mixture either initiate a rulemaking proceeding under subsection (a) of this section or if such a proceeding is not initiated

2. So in original. Probably should be "preceding".

within such period, publish in the Federal Register the Administrator's reason for not initiating such a proceeding.

(2) (A) The committee established by paragraph (1)(A) shall consist of eight members as follows:

(i) One member appointed by the Administrator from the Environmental Protection Agency.

(ii) One member appointed by the Secretary of Labor from officers or employees of the Department of Labor engaged in the Secretary's activities under the Occupational Safety and Health Act of 1970 [29 U.S.C. 651 et seq.].

(iii) One member appointed by the Chairman of the Council on Environmental Quality from the Council or its officers or employees.

(iv) One member appointed by the Director of the National Institute for Occupational Safety and Health from officers or employees of the Institute.

(v) One member appointed by the Director of the National Institute of Environmental Health Sciences from officers or employees of the Institute.

(vi) One member appointed by the Director of the National Cancer Institute from officers or employees of the Institute.

(vii) One member appointed by the Director of the National Science Foundation from officers or employees of the Foundation.

(viii) One member appointed by the Secretary of Commerce from officers or employees of the Department of Commerce.

(B) (i) An appointed member may designate an individual to serve on the committee on the member's behalf. Such a designation may be made only with the approval of the applicable appointing authority and only if the individual is from the entity from which the member was appointed.

(ii) No individual may serve as a member of the committee for more than four years in the aggregate. If any member of the committee leaves the entity from which the member was appointed, such member may not continue as a member of the committee, and the member's position shall be considered to be vacant. A vacancy in the committee shall be filled in the same manner in which the original appointment was made.

(iii) Initial appointments to the committee shall be made not later than the 60th day after January 1, 1977. Not later than the 90th day after such date the members of the committee shall hold a meeting for the selection of a chairperson from among their number.

(C) (i) No member of the committee, or designee of such member, shall accept employment or compensation from any person subject to any requirement of this chapter or of any rule promulgated or order issued thereunder, for a period of at least 12 months after termination of service on the committee.

(ii) No person, while serving as a member of the committee, or designee of such member, may own any stocks or bonds, or have any pecuniary interest, of substantial value in any person engaged in the manufacture, processing, or distribution in commerce of any chemical substance or mixture subject to any requirement of this chapter or of any rule promulgated or order issued thereunder.

(iii) The Administrator, acting through attorneys of the Environmental Protection Agency, or the Attorney General may bring an action in the appropriate district court of the United States to restrain any violation of this subparagraph.

(D) The Administrator shall provide the committee such administrative support services as may be necessary to enable the committee to carry out its function under this subsection.

(f) Required actions

Upon the receipt of–

(1) any test data required to be submitted under this chapter, or

(2) any other information available to the Administrator, which indicates to the Administrator that there may be a reasonable basis to conclude that a chemical substance or mixture presents or will present a significant risk of serious or widespread harm to human beings from cancer, gene mutations, or birth defects, the Administrator shall, within the 180-day period beginning on the date of the receipt of such data or information, initiate appropriate action under section 2604, 2605, or 2606 of this title to prevent or reduce to a sufficient extent such risk or publish in the Federal Register a finding that such risk is not unreasonable. For good cause shown the Administrator may extend such period for an additional period of not more than 90 days. The Administrator shall publish in the Federal Register notice of any such extension and the reasons therefor. A finding by the Administrator that a risk is not unreasonable shall be considered agency action for purposes of judicial review under chapter 7 of title 5. This subsection shall not take effect until two years after January 1, 1977.

(g) Petition for standards for the development of test data

A person intending to manufacture or process a chemical substance for which notice is required under section 2604(a) of this title and who is not required under a rule under subsection (a) of this section to conduct tests and submit data on such substance may petition the Administrator to prescribe standards for the development of test data for such substance. The Administrator shall by order either grant or deny any such petition within 60 days of its receipt. If the petition is granted, the Administrator shall prescribe such standards for such substance within 75 days of the date the petition is granted. If the petition is denied, the Administrator shall publish, subject to section 2613 of this title, in the Federal Register the reasons for such denial.

(TSCA § 5)

Sec. 2604. Manufacturing and processing notices

(a) In general

(1) Except as provided in subsection (h) of this section, no person may–

(A) manufacture a new chemical substance on or after the 30th day after the date on which the Administrator first publishes the list required by section 2607(b) of this title, or

(B) manufacture or process any chemical substance for a use which the Administrator has determined, in accordance with paragraph (2), is a significant new use,

unless such person submits to the Administrator, at least 90 days before such manufacture or processing, a notice, in accordance with subsection (d) of this section, of such person's intention to manufacture or process such substance and such person complies with any applicable requirement of subsection (b) of this section.

(2) A determination by the Administrator that a use of a chemical substance is a significant new use with respect to which notification is required under paragraph (1) shall be made by a rule promulgated after a consideration of all relevant factors, including–

(A) the projected volume of manufacturing and processing of a chemical substance,

(B) the extent to which a use changes the type or form of exposure of human beings or the environment to a chemical substance,

(C) the extent to which a use increases the magnitude and duration of exposure of human beings or the environment to a chemical substance, and

(D) the reasonably anticipated manner and methods of manufacturing, processing, distribution in commerce, and disposal of a chemical substance.

(b) Submission of test data

(1) (A) If (i) a person is required by subsection (a)(1) of this section to submit a notice to the Administrator before beginning the manufacture or

processing of a chemical substance, and (ii) such person is required to submit test data for such substance pursuant to a rule promulgated under section 2603 of this title before the submission of such notice, such person shall submit to the Administrator such data in accordance with such rule at the time notice is submitted in accordance with subsection (a)(1) of this section.

(B) If–

(i) a person is required by subsection (a)(1) of this section to submit a notice to the Administrator, and

(ii) such person has been granted an exemption under section 2603(c) of this title from the requirements of a rule promulgated under section 2603 of this title before the submission of such notice, such person may not, before the expiration of the 90 day period which begins on the date of the submission in accordance with suchrule of the test data the submission or development of which was the basis for the exemption, manufacture such substance if such person is subject to subsection (a)(1)(A) of this section or manufacture or process such substance for a significant new use if the person is subject to subsection (a)(1)(B) of this section.

(2) (A) If a person–

(i) is required by subsection (a)(1) of this section to submit a notice to the Administrator before beginning the manufacture or processing of a chemical substance listed under paragraph (4), and

(ii) is not required by a rule promulgated under section 2603 of this title before the submission of such notice to submit test data for such substance, such person shall submit to the Administrator data prescribed by subparagraph (B) at the time notice is submitted in accordance with subsection (a)(1) of this section.

(B) Data submitted pursuant to subparagraph (A) shall be data which the person submitting the data believes show that–

(i) in the case of a substance with respect to which notice is required under subsection (a)(1)(A) of this section, the manufacture, processing, distribution in commerce, use, and disposal of the chemical substance or any combination of such activities will not present an unreasonable risk of injury to health or the environment, or

(ii) in the case of a chemical substance with respect to which notice is required under subsection (a)(1)(B) of this section, the intended significant new use of the chemical substance will not present an unreasonable risk of injury to health or the environment.

(3) Data submitted under paragraph (1) or (2) shall be made available, subject to section 2613 of this title, for examination by interested persons.

(4) (A) (i) The Administrator may, by rule, compile and keep current a list of chemical substances with respect to which the Administrator finds that the manufacture, processing, distribution in commerce, use, or disposal, or any combination of such activities, presents or may present an unreasonable risk of injury to health or the environment.

(ii) In making a finding under clause (i) that the manufacture, processing, distribution in commerce, use, or disposal of a chemical substance or any combination of such activities presents or may present an unreasonable risk of injury to health or the environment, the Administrator shall consider all relevant factors, including–

(I) the effects of the chemical substance on health and the magnitude of human exposure to such substance; and

(II) the effects of the chemical substance on the environment and the magnitude of environmental exposure to such substance.

(B) The Administrator shall, in prescribing a rule under subparagraph (A) which lists any chemical substance, identify those uses, if any, which the Administrator determines, by rule under subsection (a)(2) of this section, would constitute a significant new use of such substance.

(C) Any rule under subparagraph (A), and any substantive amendment or repeal of such a rule, shall be promulgated pursuant to the procedures specified in section 553 of title 5, except that (i) the Administrator shall give interested persons an opportunity for the oral presentation of data, views, or arguments, in addition to an opportunity to make written submissions, (ii) a transcript shall be kept of any oral presentation, and (iii) the Administrator shall make and publish with the rule the finding described in subparagraph (A).

(c) Extension of notice period

The Administrator may for good cause extend for additional periods (not to exceed in the aggregate 90 days) the period, prescribed by subsection (a) or (b) of this section before which the manufacturing or processing of a chemical substance subject to such subsection may begin. Subject to section 2613 of this title, such an extension and the reasons therefor shall be published in the Federal Register and shall constitute a final agency action subject to judicial review.

(d) Content of notice; publications in the Federal Register

(1) The notice required by subsection (a) of this section shall include–

(A) insofar as known to the person submitting the notice or insofar as reasonably ascertainable, the information described in subparagraphs (A), (B), (C), (D), (F), and (G) of section 2607(a)(2) of this title, and (B) in such form and manner as the Administrator may prescribe, any test data in the possession or control of the person giving such notice which are related to the effect of any manufacture, processing, distribution in commerce, use, or disposal of such substance or any article containing such substance, or of any combination of such activities, on health or the environment, and (C) a description of any other data concerning the environmental and health effects of such substance, insofar as known to the person making the notice or insofar as reasonably ascertainable.

Such a notice shall be made available, subject to section 2613 of this title, for examination by interested persons.

(2) Subject to section 2613 of this title, not later than five days (excluding Saturdays, Sundays and legal holidays) after the date of the receipt of a notice under subsection (a) of this section or of data under subsection (b) of this section, the Administrator shall publish in the Federal Register a notice which–

(A) identifies the chemical substance for which notice or data has been received;

(B) lists the uses or intended uses of such substance; and

(C) in the case of the receipt of data under subsection (b) of this section, describes the nature of the tests performed on such substance and any data which was developed pursuant to subsection (b) of this section or a rule under section 2603 of this title.

A notice under this paragraph respecting a chemical substance shall identify the chemical substance by generic class unless the Administrator determines that more specific identification is required in the public interest.

(3) At the beginning of each month the Administrator shall publish a list in the Federal Register of (A) each chemical substance for which notice has been received under subsection (a) of this section and for which the notification period prescribed by subsection (a), (b), or (c) of this section has not expired, and (B) each chemical substance for which such notification period has expired since the last publication in the Federal Register of such list.

(e) Regulation pending development of information

(1) (A) If the Administrator determines that–

(i) the information available to the Administrator is insufficient to permit a reasoned evaluation of the health and environmental effects of a chemical substance with respect to which notice is required by subsection (a) of this section; and

(ii) (I) in the absence of sufficient information to permit the Administrator to make such an evaluation, the manufacture, processing, distribution in commerce, use, or disposal of such substance, or any combination of such activities, may present an unreasonable risk of injury to health or the environment, or

(II) such substance is or will be produced in substantial quantities, and such substance either enters or may reasonably be anticipated to enter the environment in substantial quantities or there is or may be significant or substantial human exposure to the substance, the Administrator may issue a proposed order, to take effect on the expiration of the notification period applicable to the manufacturing or processing of such substance under subsection (a), (b), or (c) of this section, to prohibit or limit the manufacture, processing, distribution in commerce, use, or disposal of such substance or to prohibit or limit any combination of such activities.

(B) A proposed order may not be issued under subparagraph (A) respecting a chemical substance (i) later than 45 days before the expiration of the notification period applicable to the manufacture or processing of such substance under subsection (a), (b), or (c) of this section, and (ii) unless the Administrator has, on or before the issuance of the proposed order, notified, in writing, each manufacturer or processor, as the case may be, of such substance of the determination which underlies such order.

(C) If a manufacturer or processor of a chemical substance to be subject to a proposed order issued under subparagraph (A) files with the Administrator (within the 30-day period beginning on the date such manufacturer or processor received the notice required by subparagraph (B)(ii)) objections specifying with particularity the provisions of the order deemed objectionable and stating the grounds therefor, the proposed order shall not take effect.

(2) (A) (i) Except as provided in clause (ii), if with respect to a chemical substance with respect to which notice is required by subsection (a) of this section, the Administrator makes the determination described in paragraph (1)(A) and if–

(I) the Administrator does not issue a proposed order under paragraph (1) respecting such substance, or

(II) the Administrator issues such an order respecting such substance but such order does not take effect because objections were filed under paragraph (1)(C) with respect to it, the Administrator, through attorneys of the Environmental Protection Agency, shall apply to the United States District Court for the District of Columbia or the United States district court for the judicial district in which the manufacturer or processor, as the case may be, of such substance is found, resides, or transacts business for an injunction to prohibit or limit the manufacture, processing, distribution in commerce, use, or disposal of such substance (or to prohibit or limit any combination of such activities).

(ii) If the Administrator issues a proposed order under paragraph (1) (A) respecting a chemical substance but such order does not takeeffect because objections have been filed under paragraph (1)(C) with respect to it, the Administrator is not required to apply foran injunction under clause (i) respecting such substance if theAdministrator determines, on the basis of such objections, that the determinations under paragraph (1)(A) may not be made.

(B) A district court of the United States which receives an application under subparagraph (A)(i) for an injunction respecting a chemical substance shall issue such injunction if the court finds that–

(i) the information available to the Administrator is insufficient to permit a reasoned evaluation of the health and environmental effects of a chemical substance with respect to which notice is required by subsection (a) of this section; and

(ii) (I) in the absence of sufficient information to permit the Administrator to make such an evaluation, the manufacture, processing, distribution in commerce, use, or disposal of such substance, or any combination of such activities, may present an unreasonable risk of injury to health or the environment, or

(II) such substance is or will be produced in substantial quantities, and such substance either enters or may reasonably be anticipated to enter the environment in substantial quantities or there is or may be significant or substantial human exposure to the substance.

(C) Pending the completion of a proceeding for the issuance of an injunction under subparagraph (B) respecting a chemical substance, the court may, upon application of the Administrator made through attorneys of the Environmental Protection Agency, issue a temporary restraining order or a preliminary injunction to prohibit the manufacture, processing, distribution in commerce, use, or disposal of such a substance (or any combination of such activities) if the court finds that the notification period applicable under subsection (a), (b), or (c) of this section to the manufacturing or processing of such substance may expire before such proceeding can be completed.

(D) After the submission to the Administrator of test data sufficient to evaluate the health and environmental effects of a chemical substance subject to an injunction issued under subparagraph (B) and the evaluation of such data by the Administrator, the district court of the United States which issued such injunction shall, upon petition dissolve the injunction unless the Administrator has initiated a proceeding for the issuance of a rule under section 2605(a) of this title respecting the substance.

If such a proceeding has been initiated, such court shall continue the injunction in effect until the effective date of the rule promulgated in such proceeding or, if such proceeding is terminated without the promulgation of a rule, upon the termination of the proceeding, whichever occurs first.

(f) Protection against unreasonable risks

(1) If the Administrator finds that there is a reasonable basis to conclude that the manufacture, processing, distribution in commerce, use, or disposal of a chemical substance with respect to which notice is required by subsection (a) of this section, or that any combination of such activities, presents or will present an unreasonable risk of injury to health or environment before a rule promulgated under section 2605 of this title can protect against such risk, the Administrator shall, before the expiration of the notification period applicable under subsection (a), (b), or (c) of this section to the manufacturing or processing of such substance, take the action authorized by paragraph (2) or (3) to the extent necessary to protect against such risk.

(2) The Administrator may issue a proposed rule under section 2605(a) of this title to apply to a chemical substance with respect to which a finding was made under paragraph (1)–

(A) a requirement limiting the amount of such substance which may be manufactured, processed, or distributed in commerce,

(B) a requirement described in paragraph (2), (3), (4), (5), (6), or (7) of section 2605(a) of this title, or

(C) any combination of the requirements referred to in subparagraph (B).

Such a proposed rule shall be effective upon its publication in the Federal Register. Section 2605(d)(2)(B) of this title shall applywith respect to such rule.

(3) (A) The Administrator may–

(i) issue a proposed order to prohibit the manufacture, processing, or distribution in commerce of a substance with respect to which a finding was made under paragraph (1), or (ii) apply, through attorneys of the Environmental Protection Agency, to the United States District Court for the District of Columbia or the United States district court for the judicial district in which the manufacturer, or processor, as the case may be, of such substance, is found, resides, or transacts business for an injunction to prohibit the manufacture, processing, or distribution in commerce of such substance.

A proposed order issued under clause (i) respecting a chemical substance shall take effect on the expiration of the notification period applicable under subsection (a), (b), or (c) of this section to the manufacture or processing of such substance.

(B) If the district court of the United States to which an application has been made under subparagraph (A)(ii) finds that there is a reasonable basis to conclude that the manufacture, processing, distribution in commerce, use, or disposal of the chemical substance with respect to which such application was made, or that any combination of such activities, presents or will present an unreasonable risk of injury to health or the environment before a rule promulgated under section 2605 of this title can protect against such risk, the court shall issue an injunction to prohibit the manufacture, processing, or distribution in commerce of such substance or to prohibit any combination of such activities.

(C) The provisions of subparagraphs (B) and (C) of subsection (e)(1) of this section shall apply with respect to an order issued under clause (i) of subparagraph (A); and the provisions of subparagraph (C) of subsection (e)(2) of this section shall apply with respect to an injunction issued under subparagraph (B).

(D) If the Administrator issues an order pursuant to subparagraph (A) (i) respecting a chemical substance and objections are filed in accordance with subsection (e)

(1) (C) of this section, the Administrator shall seek an injunction under subparagraph (A)(ii) respecting such substance unless the Administrator determines, on the basis of such objections, that such substance does not or will not present an unreasonable risk of injury to health or the environment.

(g) Statement of reasons for not taking action

If the Administrator has not initiated any action under this section or section 2605 or 2606 of this title to prohibit or limit the manufacture, processing, distribution in commerce, use, or disposal of a chemical substance, with respect to which notification or data is required by subsection (a)(1)(B) or (b) of this section, before the expiration of the notification period applicable to the manufacturing or processing of such substance, the Administrator shall publish a statement of the Administrator's reasons for not initiating such action. Such a statement shall be published in the Federal Register before the expiration of such period. Publication of such statement in accordance with the preceding sentence is not a prerequisite to the manufacturing or processing of the substance with respect to which the statement is to be published.

(h) Exemptions

(1) The Administrator may, upon application, exempt any person from any requirement of subsection (a) or (b) of this section to permit such person to manufacture or process a chemical substance for test marketing purposes–

(A) upon a showing by such person satisfactory to the Administrator that the manufacture, processing, distribution in commerce, use, and disposal of such substance, and that any combination of such activities, for such purposes will not present any unreasonable risk of injury to health or the environment, and

(B) under such restrictions as the Administrator considers appropriate.

(2) (A) The Administrator may, upon application, exempt any person from the requirement of subsection (b)(2) of this section to submit data for a chemical substance. If, upon receipt of an application under the preceding sentence, the Administrator determines that–

(i) the chemical substance with respect to which such application was submitted is equivalent to a chemical substance for which data has been submitted to the Administrator as required by subsection (b)(2) of this section, and

(ii) submission of data by the applicant on such substance would be duplicative of data which has been submitted to theAdministrator in accordance with such subsection, the Administrator shall exempt the applicant from the requirement to submit such data on such substance. No exemption which is granted under this subparagraph with respect to the submission of data for a chemical substance may take effect before the beginning of the reimbursement period applicable to such data.

(B) If the Administrator exempts any person, under subparagraph (A), from submitting data required under subsection (b)(2) of this section for a chemical substance because of the existence of previously submitted data and if such exemption is granted during the reimbursement period for such data, then (unless such person and the persons referred to in clauses (i) and (ii) agree on the amount and method of reimbursement) the Administrator shall order the person granted the exemption to provide fair and equitable reimbursement (in an amount determined under rules of theAdministrator)–

(i) to the person who previously submitted the data on which the exemption was based, for a portion of the costs incurred by such person in complying with the requirement under subsection (b)(2) of this section to submit such data, and

(ii) to any other person who has been required under this subparagraph to contribute with respect to such costs, for a portion of the amount such person was required to contribute.

In promulgating rules for the determination of fair and equitable reimbursement to the persons described in clauses (i) and (ii) for costs incurred with respect to a chemical substance, the Administrator shall, after consultation with the Attorney General and the Federal Trade Commission, consider all relevant factors, including the effect on the competitive position of the person required to provide reimbursement in relation to the persons to be reimbursed and the share of the market for such substance of the person required to provide reimbursement in relation to the share of such market of the persons to be reimbursed. For purposes of judicial review, an order under this subparagraph shall be considered final agency action.

(C) For purposes of this paragraph, the reimbursement period for any previously submitted data for a chemical substance is a period–

(i) beginning on the date of the termination of the prohibition, imposed under this section, on the manufacture or processing of such substance by the person who submitted such data to the Administrator, and

(ii) ending–

(I) five years after the date referred to in clause (i), or

(II) at the expiration of a period which begins on the date referred to in clause (i) and is equal to the period which the Administrator determines was necessary to develop such data, whichever is later.

(3) The requirements of subsections (a) and (b) of this section do not apply with respect to the manufacturing or processing of any chemical substance which is manufactured or processed, or proposed to be manufactured or processed, only in small quantities (as defined by the Administrator by rule) solely for purposes of–

(A) scientific experimentation or analysis, or

(B) chemical research on, or analysis of such substance or another substance, including such research or analysis for the development of a product, if all persons engaged in such experimentation, research, or analysis for a manufacturer or processor are notified (in such form and manner as the Administrator may prescribe) of any risk to health which the manufacturer, processor, or the Administrator has reason to believe may be associated with such chemical substance.

(4) The Administrator may, upon application and by rule, exempt the manufacturer of any new chemical substance from all or part of the requirements of this section if the Administrator determines that the manufacture, processing, distribution in commerce, use, or disposal of such chemical substance, or that any combination of such activities, will not present an unreasonable risk of injury to health or the environment. A rule promulgated under this paragraph (and any substantive amendment to, or repeal of, such a rule) shall be promulgated in accordance with paragraphs (2) and (3) of section 2605(c) of this title.

(5) The Administrator may, upon application, make the requirements of subsections (a) and (b) of this section inapplicable with respect to the manufacturing or processing of any chemical substance (A) which exists temporarily as a result of a chemical reaction in the manufacturing or processing of a mixture or another chemical substance, and (B) to which there is no, and will not be, human or environmental exposure.

(6) Immediately upon receipt of an application under paragraph (1) or (5) the Administrator shall publish in the Federal Register notice of the receipt of such application. The Administrator shall give interested persons an opportunity to comment upon any such application and shall, within 45 days of its receipt, either approve or deny the application. The Administrator shall publish in the Federal Register notice of the approval or denial of such an application.

(i) "Manufacture" and "process" defined

For purposes of this section, the terms "manufacture" and "process" mean manufacturing or processing for commercial purposes.

(TSCA § 6)

Sec. 2605. Regulation of hazardous chemical substances and mixtures

(a) Scope of regulation

If the Administrator finds that there is a reasonable basis to conclude that the manufacture, processing, distribution in commerce, use, or disposal of a chemical substance or mixture, or that any combination of such activities, presents or will present an unreasonable risk of injury to health or the environment, the Administrator shall by rule apply one or more of the following requirements to such substance or mixture to the extent necessary to protect adequately against such risk using the least burdensome requirements:

(1) A requirement (A) prohibiting the manufacturing, processing, or distribution in commerce of such substance or mixture, or (B) limiting the amount of such substance or mixture which may be manufactured, processed, or distributed in commerce.

(2) A requirement–

(A) prohibiting the manufacture, processing, or distribution in commerce of such substance or mixture for (i) a particular use or (ii) a particular use in a concentration in excess of a level specified by the Administrator in the rule imposing the requirement, or

(B) limiting the amount of such substance or mixture which may be manufactured, processed, or distributed in commerce for (i) a particular use or (ii) a particular use in a concentration in excess of a level specified by the Administrator in the rule imposing the requirement.

(3) A requirement that such substance or mixture or any article containing such substance or mixture be marked with or accompanied by clear and adequate warnings and instructions with respect to its use, distribution in commerce, or disposal or with respect to any combination of such activities. The form and content of such warnings and instructions shall be prescribed by the Administrator.

(4) A requirement that manufacturers and processors of such substance or mixture make and retain records of the processes used to manufacture or process such substance or mixture and monitor or conduct tests which are reasonable and necessary to assure compliance with the requirements of any rule applicable under this subsection.

(5) A requirement prohibiting or otherwise regulating any manner or method of commercial use of such substance or mixture.

(6) (A) A requirement prohibiting or otherwise regulating any manner or method of disposal of such substance or mixture, or of any article containing such substance or mixture, by its manufacturer or processor or by any other person who uses, or disposes of, it for commercial purposes.

(B) A requirement under subparagraph (A) may not require any person to take any action which would be in violation of any law or requirement of, or in effect for, a State or political subdivision, and shall require each person subject to it to notify each State and political subdivision in which a required disposal may occur of such disposal.

(7) A requirement directing manufacturers or processors of such substance or mixture (A) to give notice of such unreasonable risk of injury to distributors in commerce of such substance or mixture and, to the extent reasonably ascertainable, to other persons in possession of such substance or mixture or exposed to such substance or mixture, (B) to give public notice

of such risk of injury, and (C) to replace or repurchase such substance or mixture as elected by the person to which the requirement is directed.

Any requirement (or combination of requirements) imposed under this subsection may be limited in application to specified geographic areas.

(b) Quality control

If the Administrator has a reasonable basis to conclude that a particular manufacturer or processor is manufacturing or processing a chemical substance or mixture in a manner which unintentionally causes the chemical substance or mixture to present or which will cause it to present an unreasonable risk of injury to health or the environment–

(1) the Administrator may by order require such manufacturer or processor to submit a description of the relevant quality control procedures followed in the manufacturing or processing of such chemical substance or mixture; and

(2) if the Administrator determines–

(A) that such quality control procedures are inadequate to prevent the chemical substance or mixture from presenting such risk of injury, the Administrator may order the manufacturer or processor to revise such quality control procedures to the extent necessary to remedy such inadequacy; or

(B) that the use of such quality control procedures has resulted in the distribution in commerce of chemical substances or mixtures which present an unreasonable risk of injury to health or the environment, the Administrator may order the manufacturer or processor to (i) give notice of such risk to processors or distributors in commerce of any such substance or mixture, or to both, and, to the extent reasonably ascertainable, to any other person in possession of or exposed to any such substance, (ii) to give public notice of such risk, and (iii) to provide such replacement or repurchase of any such substance or mixture as is necessary to adequately protect health or the environment.

A determination under subparagraph (A) or (B) of paragraph (2) shall be made on the record after opportunity for hearing in accordance with section 554 of title 5. Any manufacturer or processor subject to a requirement to replace or repurchase a chemical substance or mixture may elect either to replace or repurchase the substance or mixture and shall take either such action in the manner prescribed by the Administrator.

(c) Promulgation of subsection (a) rules

(1) In promulgating any rule under subsection (a) of this section with respect to a chemical substance or mixture, the Administrator shall consider and publish a statement with respect to–

(A) the effects of such substance or mixture on health and the magnitude of the exposure of human beings to such substance or mixture,

(B) the effects of such substance or mixture on the environment and the magnitude of the exposure of the environment to such substance or mixture,

(C) the benefits of such substance or mixture for various uses and the availability of substitutes for such uses, and

(D) the reasonably ascertainable economic consequences of the rule, after consideration of the effect on the national economy, small business, technological innovation, the environment, and public health.

If the Administrator determines that a risk of injury to health or the environment could be eliminated or reduced to a sufficient extent by actions taken under another Federal law (or laws) administered in whole or in part by the Administrator, the Administrator may not promulgate a rule under subsection (a) of this section to protect against such risk of injury unless the Administrator finds, in the Administrator's discretion, that it is in the public interest to protect against such risk under this chapter. In making such a finding the Administrator shall consider (i) all relevant aspects of the risk, as determined by the Administrator in the Administrator's discretion, (ii) a comparison of the estimated costs of complying with actions taken under this chapter and under such law (or laws), and (iii) the relative efficiency of actions under this chapter and under such law (or laws) to protect against such risk of injury.

(2) When prescribing a rule under subsection (a) the

Administrator shall proceed in accordance with section 553 of title 5 (without regard to any reference in such section to sections 556 and 557 of such title), and shall also (A) publish a notice of proposed rulemaking stating with particularity the reason for the proposed rule; (B) allow interested persons to submit written data, views, and arguments, and make all such submissions publicly available; (C) provide an opportunity for an informal hearing in accordance with paragraph (3); (D) promulgate, if appropriate, a final rule based on the matter in the rulemaking record (as defined in section 2618(a) of this title), and (E) make and publish with the rule the finding described in subsection (a) of this section.

(3) Informal hearings required by paragraph (2)(C) shall be conducted by the Administrator in accordance with the following requirements:

(A) Subject to subparagraph (B), an interested person is entitled–

(i) to present such person's position orally or by documentary submissions (or both), and

(ii) if the Administrator determines that there are disputed issues of material fact it is necessary to resolve, to present such rebuttal submissions and to conduct (or have conducted under subparagraph (B)(ii)) such cross-examination of persons as the Administrator determines (I) to be appropriate, and (II) to be required for a full and true disclosure with respect to such issues.

(B) The Administrator may prescribe such rules and make such rulings concerning procedures in such hearings to avoid unnecessary costs or delay. Such rules or rulings may include (i) the imposition of reasonable time limits on each interested person's oral presentations, and (ii) requirements that any cross-examination to which a person may be entitled under subparagraph (A) be conducted by the Administrator on behalf of that person in such manner as the Administrator determines (I) to be appropriate, and (II) to be required for a full and true disclosure with respect to disputed issues of material fact.

(C) (i) Except as provided in clause (ii), if a group of persons each of whom under subparagraphs (A) and (B) would be entitled to conduct (or have conducted) cross-examination and who are determined by the Administrator to have the same or similar interests in the proceeding cannot agree upon a single representative of such interests for purposes of cross-examination, the Administrator may make rules and rulings (I) limiting the representation of such interest for such purposes, and (II) governing the manner in which such cross-examination shall be limited.

(ii) When any person who is a member of a group with respect to which the Administrator has made a determination under clause (i) is unable to agree upon group representation with the other members of the group, then such person shall not be denied under the authority of clause (i) the opportunity to conduct (or have conducted) cross-examination as to issues affecting the person's particular interests if (I) the person satisfies the Administrator that the person has made a reasonable and good faith effort to reach agreement upon group representation with the other members of the group and (II) the Administrator determines that there are substantial and relevant issues which are not adequately presented by the group representative.

(D) A verbatim transcript shall be taken of any oral presentation made, and cross-examination conducted in any informal hearing under this subsection. Such transcript shall be available to the public.

(4) (A) The Administrator may, pursuant to rules prescribed by the Administrator, provide compensation for reasonable attorneys' fees, expert

witness fees, and other costs of participating in a rulemaking proceeding for the promulgation of a rule under subsection (a) of this section to any person–

(i) who represents an interest which would substantially contribute to a fair determination of the issues to be resolved in the proceeding, and

(ii) if–

(I) the economic interest of such person is small in comparison to the costs of effective participation in the proceeding by such person, or

(II) such person demonstrates to the satisfaction of the Administrator that such person does not have sufficient resources adequately to participate in the proceeding without compensation under this subparagraph.

In determining for purposes of clause (i) if an interest will substantially contribute to a fair determination of the issues to be resolved in a proceeding, the Administrator shall take into account the number and complexity of such issues and the extent to which representation of such interest will contribute to widespread public participation in the proceeding and representation of a fair balance of interests for the resolution of such issues.

(B) In determining whether compensation should be provided to a person under subparagraph (A) and the amount of such compensation, the Administrator shall take into account the financial burden which will be incurred by such person in participating in the rulemaking proceeding. The Administrator shall take such action as may be necessary to ensure that the aggregate amount of compensation paid under this paragraph in any fiscal year to all persons who, in rulemaking proceedings in which they receive compensation, are persons who either–

(i) would be regulated by the proposed rule, or

(ii) represent persons who would be so regulated,

may not exceed 25 per centum of the aggregate amount paid as compensation under this paragraph to all persons in such fiscal year.

(5) Paragraph (1), (2), (3), and (4) of this subsection apply to the promulgation of a rule repealing, or making a substantive amendment to, a rule promulgated under subsection (a) of this section.

(d) Effective date

(1) The Administrator shall specify in any rule under subsection (a) of this section the date on which it shall take effect, which date shall be as soon as feasible.

(2) (A) The Administrator may declare a proposed rule under subection (a) of this section to be effective upon its publication in the Federal Register and until the effective date of final action taken, in accordance with subparagraph (B), respecting such rule if–

(i) the Administrator determines that–

(I) the manufacture, processing, distribution in commerce, use, or disposal of the chemical substance or mixture subject to such proposed rule or any combination of such activities is likely to result in an unreasonable risk of serious or widespread injury to health or the environment before such effective date; and

(II) making such proposed rule so effective is necessary to protect the public interest; and

(ii) in the case of a proposed rule to prohibit the manufacture, processing, or distribution of a chemical substance or mixture because of the risk determined under clause (i)(I), a court has in an action under section 2606 of this title granted relief with respect to such risk associated with such substance or mixture.

Such a proposed rule which is made so effective shall not, for purposes of judicial review, be considered final agency action.

(B) If the Administrator makes a proposed rule effective upon its publication in the Federal Register, the Administrator shall, as expeditiously as possible, give interested persons prompt notice of such action, provide reasonable opportunity, in accordance with paragraphs (2) and (3) of subsection (c) of this section, for a hearing on such rule, and either promulgate such rule (as proposed or with modifications) or revoke it; and if such a hearing is requested, the Administrator shall commence the hearing within five days from the date such request is made unless the Administrator and the person making the request agree upon a later date for the hearing to begin, and after the hearing is concluded the Administrator shall, within ten days of the conclusion of the hearing, either promulgate such rule (as proposed or with modifications) or revoke it.

(e) Polychlorinated biphenyls

(1) Within six months after January 1, 1977, the Administrator shall promulgate rules to–

(A) prescribe methods for the disposal of polychlorinated biphenyls, and

(B) require polychlorinated biphenyls to be marked with clear and adequate warnings, and instructions with respect to their processing, distribution in commerce, use, or disposal or with respect to any combination of such activities.

Requirements prescribed by rules under this paragraph shall be consistent with the requirements of paragraphs (2) and (3).

(2) (A) Except as provided under subparagraph (B), effective one year after January 1, 1977, no person may manufacture, process, or distribute in commerce or use any polychlorinated biphenyl in any manner other than in a totally enclosed manner.

(B) The Administrator may by rule authorize the manufacture, processing, distribution in commerce or use (or any combination of such activities) of any polychlorinated biphenyl in a manner other than in a totally enclosed manner if the Administrator finds that such manufacture, processing, distribution in commerce, or use (or combination of such activities) will not present an unreasonable risk of injury to health or the environment.

(C) For the purposes of this paragraph, the term "totally enclosed manner" means any manner which will ensure that any exposure of human beings or the environment to a polychlorinated biphenyl will be insignificant as determined by the Administrator by rule.

(3) (A) Except as provided in subparagraphs (B), (C), and (D)–

(i) no person may manufacture any polychlorinated biphenyl after two years after January 1, 1977, and

(ii) no person may process or distribute in commerce any polychlorinated biphenyl after two and one-half years after such date.

(B) Any person may petition the Administrator for an exemption from the requirements of subparagraph (A), and the Administrator may grant by rule such an exemption if the Administrator finds that-

(i) an unreasonable risk of injury to health or environment would not result, and

(ii) good faith efforts have been made to develop a chemical substance which does not present an unreasonable risk of injury to health or the environment and which may be substituted for such polychlorinated biphenyl.An exemption granted under this subparagraph shall be subject to such terms and conditions as the Administrator may prescribe and shall be in effect for such period (but not more than 1 year from the date it is granted, except as provided in subparagraph (D)) as the Administrator may prescribe.

(C) Subparagraph (A) shall not apply to the distribution in commerce of any polychlorinated biphenyl if such polychlorinated biphenyl was sold for purposes other than resale before two and one half years after October 11, 1976.

(D) The Administrator may extend an exemption granted pursuant to subparagraph (B) that has not yet expired for a period not to exceed 60 days for the purpose of authorizing the Secretary of Defense and the Secretaries of the military departments to provide for the transportation into the customs territory of the United States of polychlorinated biphenyls generated by or under the control of the Department of Defense for purposes of their disposal, treatment, or storage in the customs territory of the United States if those polychlorinated biphenyls are already in transit from their storage locations but the Administrator determines, in the sole discretion of the Administrator, they would not otherwise arrive in the customs territory of the United States within the period of the original exemption. The Administrator shall promptly publish notice of such extension in the Federal Register.

(4) Any rule under paragraph (1), (2)(B), or (3)(B) shall be promulgated in accordance with paragraphs (2), (3), and (4) of subsection (c) of this section.

(5) This subsection does not limit the authority of the Administrator, under any other provision of this chapter or any other Federal law, to take action respecting any polychlorinated biphenyl.

(f) Mercury.

(1) Prohibition on sale, distribution, or transfer of elemental mercury by federal agencies. Except as provided in paragraph (2), effective beginning on the date of enactment of this subsection, no Federal agency shall convey, sell, or distribute to any other Federal agency, any State or local government agency, or any private individual or entity any elemental mercury under the control or jurisdiction of the Federal agency.

(2) Exceptions. Paragraph (1) shall not apply to—

(A) a transfer between Federal agencies of elemental mercury for the sole purpose of facilitating storage of mercury to carry out this Act; or

(B) a conveyance, sale, distribution, or transfer of coal.

(3) Leases of federal coal. Nothing in this subsection prohibits the leasing of coal.

(TSCA § 7)

Sec. 2606. Imminent hazards

(a) Actions authorized and required

(1) The Administrator may commence a civil action in an appropriate district court of the United States–

(A) for seizure of an imminently hazardous chemical substance or mixture or any article containing such a substance or mixture,

(B) for relief (as authorized by subsection (b) of this section) against any person who manufactures, processes, distributes in commerce, or uses, or disposes of, an imminently hazardous chemical substance or mixture or any article containing such a substance or mixture, or

(C) for both such seizure and relief.

A civil action may be commenced under this paragraph notwithstanding the existence of a rule under section 2603 of this title, 2604 of this title, 2605 of this title, or subchapter IV of this chapter or an order under section 2604 of this title or subchapter IV of this chapter, and notwithstanding the pendency of any administrative or judicial proceeding under any provision of this chapter.

(2) If the Administrator has not made a rule under section 2605(a) of this title immediately effective (as authorized by section 2605(d)(2)(A)(i) of this title) with respect to an imminently hazardous chemical substance or mixture, the Administrator shall commence in a district court of the United States with respect to such substance or mixture or article containing such substance or mixture a civil action described in subparagraph (A), (B), or (C) of paragraph (1).

(b) Relief authorized

(1) The district court of the United States in which an action under subsection (a) of this section is brought shall have jurisdiction to grant such temporary or permanent relief as may be necessary to protect health or the environment from the unreasonable risk associated with the chemical substance, mixture, or article involved in such action.

(2) In the case of an action under subsection (a) of this section brought against a person who manufactures, processes, or distributes in commerce a chemical substance or mixture or an article containing a chemical substance or mixture, the relief authorized by paragraph (1) may include the issuance of a mandatory order requiring (A) in the case of purchasers of such substance, mixture, or article known to the defendant, notification to such purchasers of the risk associated with it; (B) public notice of such risk; (C) recall; (D) the replacement or repurchase of such substance, mixture, or article; or (E) any combination of the actions described in the preceding clauses.

(3) In the case of an action under subsection (a) of this section against a chemical substance, mixture, or article, such substance, mixture, or article may be proceeded against by process of libel for its seizure and condemnation. Proceedings in such an action shall conform as nearly as possible to proceedings in rem in admiralty.

(c) Venue and consolidation

(1) (A) An action under subsection (a) of this section against a person who manufactures, processes, or distributes a chemical substance or mixture or an article containing a chemical substance or mixture may be brought in the United States District Court for the District of Columbia, or for any judicial district in which any of the defendants is found, resides, or transacts business; and process in such an action may be served on a defendant in any other district in which such defendant resides or may be found. An action under subsection (a) of this section against a chemical substance, mixture, or article may be brought in any United States district court within the jurisdiction of which the substance, mixture, or article is found.

(B) In determining the judicial district in which an action may be brought under subsection (a) of this section in instances in which such action may be brought in more than one judicial district, the Administrator shall take into account the convenience of the parties.

(C) Subpeonas[3] requiring attendance of witnesses in an action brought under subsection (a) of this section may be served in any judicial district.

(2) Whenever proceedings under subsection (a) of this section involving identical chemical substances, mixtures, or articles are pending in courts in two or more judicial districts, they shall be consolidated for trial by order of any such court upon application reasonably made by any party in interest, upon notice to all parties in interest.

(d) Action under section 2605

Where appropriate, concurrently with the filing of an action under subsection (a) of this section or as soon thereafter as may be practicable, the Administrator shall initiate a proceeding for the promulgation of a rule under section 2605(a) of this title.

(e) Representation

Notwithstanding any other provision of law, in any action under subsection (a) of this section, the Administrator may direct attorneys of the Environmental

---

3 So in original. Probably should be "Subpoenas".

Protection Agency to appear and represent the Administrator in such an action.

(f) "Imminently hazardous chemical substance or mixture" defined

For the purposes of subsection (a) of this section, the term "imminently hazardous chemical substance or mixture" means a chemical substance or mixture which presents an imminent and unreasonable risk of serious or widespread injury to health or the environment. Such a risk to health or the environment shall be considered imminent if it is shown that the manufacture, processing, distribution in commerce, use, or disposal of the chemical substance or mixture, or that any combination of such activities, is likely to result in such injury to health or the environment before a final rule under section 2605 of this title can protect against such risk.

(TSCA § 8)

Sec. 2607. Reporting and retention of information[4]

(a) Reports

(1) The Administrator shall promulgate rules under which–

(A) each person (other than a small manufacturer or processor) who manufactures or processes or proposes to manufacture or process a chemical substance (other than a chemical substance described in subparagraph (B)(ii)) shall maintain such records, and shall submit to the Administrator such reports, as the Administrator may reasonably require, and

(B) each person (other than a small manufacturer or processor) who manufactures or processes or proposes to manufacture or process–

(i) a mixture, or

(ii) a chemical substance in small quantities (as defined by the Administrator by rule) solely for purposes of scientific experimentation or analysis or chemical research on, or analysis of, such substance or another substance, including any such research or analysis for the development of a product,shall maintain records and submit to the Administrator reports but only to the extent the

4. Some copies of the TSCA statute contain, after this section (§ 8), The Asbestos Information Act of 1988, Pub. L. 100-577 (Oct. 31, 1988) 102 Stat. 2901, which provided for the submission of certain information by manufacturers of asbestos, and the publication of such information by EPA. The final obligation under that Act expired in 1989. That Act did not seem to be an amendment to TSCA, and in any event, since its obligations have expired, is only of historical interest.

Administrator determines the maintenance of records or submission of reports, or both, is necessary for the effective enforcement of this chapter.

The Administrator may not require in a rule promulgated under this paragraph the maintenance of records or the submission of reports with respect to changes in the proportions of the components of a mixture unless the Administrator finds that the maintenance of such records or the submission of such reports, or both, is necessary for the effective enforcement of this chapter. For purposes of the compilation of the list of chemical substances required under subsection (b) of this section, the Administrator shall promulgate rules pursuant to this subsection not later than 180 days after January 1, 1977.

(2) The Administrator may require under paragraph (1) maintenance of records and reporting with respect to the following insofar as known to the person making the report or insofar as reasonably ascertainable:

(A) The common or trade name, the chemical identity, and the molecular structure of each chemical substance or mixture for which such a report is required.

(B) The categories or proposed categories of use of each such substance or mixture.

(C) The total amount of each such substance and mixture manufactured or processed, reasonable estimates of the total amount to be manufactured or processed, the amount manufactured or processed for each of its categories of use, and reasonable estimates of the amount to be manufactured or processed for each of its categories of use or proposed categories of use.

(D) A description of the byproducts resulting from the manufacture, processing, use, or disposal of each such substance or mixture.

(E) All existing data concerning the environmental and health effects of such substance or mixture.

(F) The number of individuals exposed, and reasonable estimates of the number who will be exposed, to such substance or mixture in their places of employment and the duration of such exposure.

(G) In the initial report under paragraph (1) on such substance or mixture, the manner or method of its disposal, and in any subsequent report on such substance or mixture, any change in such manner or method.

To the extent feasible, the Administrator shall not require under paragraph (1), any reporting which is unnecessary or duplicative.

(3) (A)(i) The Administrator may by rule require a small manufacturer or processor of a chemical substance to submit to the Administrator such information respecting the chemical substance as the Administrator may

require for publication of the first list of chemical substances required by subsection (b) of this section.

(ii) The Administrator may by rule require a small manufacturer or processor of a chemical substance or mixture–

(I) subject to a rule proposed or promulgated under section 2603, 2604(b)(4), or 2605 of this title, or an order in effect under section 2604(e) of this title, or

(II) with respect to which relief has been granted pursuant to a civil action brought under section 2604 or 2606 of this title, to maintain such records on such substance or mixture, and to submit to the Administrator such reports on such substance or mixture, as the Administrator may reasonably require. A rule under this clause requiring reporting may require reporting with respect to the matters referred to in paragraph (2).

(B) The Administrator, after consultation with the Administrator of the Small Business Administration, shall by rule prescribe standards for determining the manufacturers and processors which qualify as small manufacturers and processors for purposes of this paragraph and paragraph (1).

(b) Inventory

(1) The Administrator shall compile, keep current, and publish a list of each chemical substance which is manufactured or processed in the United States. Such list shall at least include each chemical substance which any person reports, under section 2604 of this title or subsection (a) of this section, is manufactured or processed in the United States. Such list may not include any chemical substance which was not manufactured or processed in the United States within three years before the effective date of the rules promulgated pursuant to the last sentence of subsection (a)(1) of this section. In the case of a chemical substance for which a notice is submitted in accordance with section 2604 of this title, such chemical substance shall be included in such list as of the earliest date (as determined by the Administrator) on which such substance was manufactured or processed in the United States.

The Administrator shall first publish such a list not later than 315 days after January 1, 1977. The Administrator shall not include in such list any chemical substance which is manufactured or processed only in small quantities (as defined by the Administrator by rule) solely for purposes of scientific experimentation or analysis or chemical research on, or analysis of, such substance or another substance, including such research or analysis for the development of a product.

(2) To the extent consistent with the purposes of this chapter, the Administrator may, in lieu of listing, pursuant to paragraph (1), a chemical

substance individually, list a category of chemical substances in which such substance is included.

(c) Records

Any person who manufactures, processes, or distributes in commerce any chemical substance or mixture shall maintain records of significant adverse reactions to health or the environment, as determined by the Administrator by rule, alleged to have been caused by the substance or mixture. Records of such adverse reactions to the health of employees shall be retained for a period of 30 years from the date such reactions were first reported to or known by the person maintaining such records. Any other record of such adverse reactions shall be retained for a period of five years from the date the information contained in the record was first reported to or known by the person maintaining the record. Records required to be maintained under this subsection shall include records of consumer allegations of personal injury or harm to health, reports of occupational disease or injury, and reports or complaints of injury to the environment submitted to the manufacturer, processor, or distributor in commerce from any source. Upon request of any duly designated representative of the Administrator, each person who is required to maintain records under this subsection shall permit the inspection of such records and shall submit copies of such records.

(d) Health and safety studies

The Administrator shall promulgate rules under which the Administrator shall require any person who manufactures, processes, or distributes in commerce or who proposes to manufacture, process, or distribute in commerce any chemical substance or mixture (or with respect to paragraph (2), any person who has possession of a study) to submit to the Administrator–

(1) lists of health and safety studies (A) conducted or initiated by or for such person with respect to such substance or mixture at any time, (B) known to such person, or (C) reasonably ascertainable by such person, except that the Administrator may exclude certain types or categories of studies from the requirements of this subsection if the Administrator finds that submission of lists of such studies are unnecessary to carry out the purposes of this chapter; and

(2) copies of any study contained on a list submitted pursuant to paragraph (1) or otherwise known by such person.

(e) Notice to Administrator of substantial risks

Any person who manufactures, processes, or distributes in commerce as chemical substance or mixture and who obtains information which reasonably supports the conclusion that such substance or mixture presents a substantial risk of injury to health or the environment shall immediately inform the Administrator of such information unless such person has actual knowledge that the Administrator has been adequately informed of such information.

(f) "Manufacture" and "process" defined

For purposes of this section, the terms "manufacture" and "process" mean manufacture or process for commercial purposes.

(TSCA § 9)

Sec. 2608. Relationship to other Federal laws

(a) Laws not administered by the Administrator

(1) If the Administrator has reasonable basis to conclude that the manufacture, processing, distribution in commerce, use, or disposal of a chemical substance or mixture, or that any combination of such activities, presents or will present an unreasonable risk of injury to health or the environment and determines, in the Administrator's discretion, that such risk may be prevented or reduced to a sufficient extent by action taken under a Federal law not administered by the Administrator, the Administrator shall submit to the agency which administers such law a report which describes such risk and includes in such description a specification of the activity or combination of activities which the Administrator has reason to believe so presents such risk. Such report shall also request such agency–

(A) (i) to determine if the risk described in such report may be prevented or reduced to a sufficient extent by action taken under such law, and

(ii) if the agency determines that such risk may be so prevented or reduced, to issue an order declaring whether or not the activity or combination of activities specified in the description of such risk presents such risk; and

(B) to respond to the Administrator with respect to the matters described in subparagraph (A).Any report of the Administrator shall include a detailed statement of the information on which it is based and shall be published in the Federal Register. The agency receiving a request under such a report shall make the requested determination, issue the requested order, and make the requested response within such time as the Administrator specifies in the request, but such time specified may not be less than 90 days from the date the request was made. The response of an agency shall be accompanied by a detailed statement of the findings and conclusions of the agency and shall be published in the Federal Register.

(2) If the Administrator makes a report under paragraph (1) with respect to a chemical substance or mixture and the agency to which such report was made either–

(A) issues an order declaring that the activity or combination of activities specified in the description of the risk described in the report does not present the risk described in the report, or

(B) initiates, within 90 days of the publication in the FederalRegister of the response of the agency under paragraph (1), action under the law (or laws) administered by such agency to protect against such risk associated with such activity or combination of activities, the Administrator may not take any action under section 2605 or 2606 of this title with respect to such risk.

(3) If the Administrator has initiated action under section 2605 or 2606 of this title with respect to a risk associated with a chemical substance or mixture which was the subject of a report made to an agency under paragraph (1), such agency shall before taking action under the law (or laws) administered by it to protect against such risk consult with the Administrator for the purpose of avoiding duplication of Federal action against such risk.

(b) Laws administered by the Administrator

The Administrator shall coordinate actions taken under this chapter with actions taken under other Federal laws administered in whole or in part by the Administrator. If the Administrator determines that a risk to health or the environment associated with a chemical substance or mixture could be eliminated or reduced to a sufficient extent by actions taken under the authorities contained in such other Federal laws, the Administrator shall use such authorities to protect against such risk unless the Administrator determines, in the Administrator's discretion, that it is in the public interest to protect against such risk by actions taken under this chapter. This subsection shall not be construed to relieve the Administrator of any requirement imposed on the Administrator by such other Federal laws.

(c) Occupational safety and health

In exercising any authority under this chapter, the Administrator shall not, for purposes of section 653(b)(1) of title 29, be deemed to be exercising statutory authority to prescribe or enforce standards or regulations affecting occupational safety and health.

(d) Coordination

In administering this chapter, the Administrator shall consult and coordinate with the Secretary of Health and Human Services and the heads of any other appropriate Federal executive department or agency, any relevant independent regulatory agency, and any other appropriate instrumentality of the Federal Government for the purpose of achieving the maximum enforcement of this chapter while imposing the least burdens of duplicative requirements on those subject to the chapter and for other purposes. The Administrator shall, in the report required by section 2629 of this title, report annually to the

Congress on actions taken to coordinate with such other Federal departments, agencies, or instrumentalities, and on actions taken to coordinate the authority under this chapter with the authority granted under other Acts referred to in subsection (b) of this section.[5]

(TSCA § 10)

Sec. 2609. Research, development, collection, dissemination, and utilization of data[6]

(a) Authority

The Administrator shall, in consultation and cooperation with the Secretary of Health and Human Services and with other heads of appropriate departments and agencies, conduct such research, development, and monitoring as is necessary to carry out the purposes of this chapter. The Administrator may enter into contracts and may make grants for research, development, and monitoring under this subsection. Contracts may be entered into under this subsection without regard to section 3324(a) and (b) of title 31 and section 5 of title 41.

(b) Data systems

(1) The Administrator shall establish, administer, and be responsible for the continuing activities of an interagency committee which shall design, establish, and coordinate an efficient and effective system, within the Environmental Protection Agency, for the collection, dissemination to other Federal departments and agencies, and use of data submitted to the Administrator under this chapter.

(2) (A) The Administrator shall, in consultation and cooperation with the Secretary of Health and Human Services and other heads of appropriate departments and agencies design, establish, and coordinate an efficient and effective system for the retrieval of toxicological and other scientific data which could be useful to the Administrator in carrying out the purposes of this chapter. Systematized retrieval shall be developed for use by

5. For termination, effective May 15, 2000, of provisions in subsec.d) of this section relating to reporting certain coordinating actions annually to Congress in the report required by section 2629 of this title, see section 3003 of Pub. L. 104-66, as amended, set out as a note under section 1113 of Title 31, Money and Finance, and page 163 of House Document No. 103-7.

6. Grants awarded under this section are available for research, development, monitoring, public education, training, demonstrations, and studies, beginning in fiscal year 2000 and thereafter, see provisions of title III of Pub. L. 106-74, set out as a note under section 136r of Title 7, Agriculture.

all Federal and other departments and agencies with responsibilities in the area of regulation or study of chemical substances and mixtures and their effect on health or the environment.

(B) The Administrator, in consultation and cooperation with the Secretary of Health and Human Services, may make grants and enter into contracts for the development of a data retrieval system described in subparagraph (A). Contracts may be entered into under this subparagraph without regard to section 3324(a) and (b) of title 31 and section 5 of title 41.

(c) Screening techniques

The Administrator shall coordinate, with the Assistant Secretary for Health of the Department of Health and Human Services, research undertaken by the Administrator and directed toward the development of rapid, reliable, and economical screening techniques for carcinogenic, mutagenic, teratogenic, and ecological effects of chemical substances and mixtures.

(d) Monitoring

The Administrator shall, in consultation and cooperation with the Secretary of Health and Human Services, establish and be responsible for research aimed at the development, in cooperation with local, State, and Federal agencies, of monitoring techniques and instruments which may be used in the detection of toxic chemical substances and mixtures and which are reliable, economical, and capable of being implemented under a wide variety of conditions.

(e) Basic research

The Administrator shall, in consultation and cooperation with the Secretary of Health and Human Services, establish research programs to develop the fundamental scientific basis of the screening and monitoring techniques described in subsections (c) and (d) of this section, the bounds of the reliability of such techniques, and the opportunities for their improvement.

(f) Training

The Administrator shall establish and promote programs and workshops to train or facilitate the training of Federal laboratory and technical personnel in existing or newly developed screening and monitoring techniques.

(g) Exchange of research and development results

The Administrator shall, in consultation with the Secretary of Health and Human Services and other heads of appropriate departments and agencies, establish and coordinate a system for exchange among Federal, State, and local authorities of research and development results respecting toxic chemical substances and mixtures, including a system to facilitate and promote the development of standard data format and analysis and consistent testing procedures.

(TSCA § 11)

Sec. 2610. Inspections and subpoenas

(a) In general

For purposes of administering this chapter, the Administrator, and any duly designated representative of the Administrator, may inspect any establishment, facility, or other premises in which chemical substances, mixtures, or products subject to subchapter IV of this chapter are manufactured, processed, stored, or held before or after their distribution in commerce and any conveyance being used to transport chemical substances, mixtures, such products, or such articles in connection with distribution in commerce. Such an inspection may only be made upon the presentation of appropriate credentials and of a written notice to the owner, operator, or agent in charge of the premises or conveyance to be inspected. A separate notice shall be given for each such inspection, but a notice shall not be required for each entry made during the period covered by the inspection. Each such inspection shall be commenced and completed with reasonable promptness and shall be conducted at reasonable times, within reasonable limits, and in a reasonable manner.

(b) Scope

(1) Except as provided in paragraph (2), an inspection conducted under subsection (a) of this section shall extend to all things within the premises or conveyance inspected (including records, files, papers, processes, controls, and facilities) bearing on whether the requirements of this chapter applicable to the chemical substances, mixtures, or products subject to subchapter IV of this chapter within such premises or conveyance have been complied with.

(2) No inspection under subsection (a) of this section shall extend to–

(A) financial data,

(B) sales data (other than shipment data),

(C) pricing data,

(D) personnel data, or

(E) research data (other than data required by this chapter or under a rule promulgated thereunder), unless the nature and extent of such data are described with reasonable specificity in the written notice required by subsection (a) of this section for such inspection.

(c) Subpoenas

In carrying out this chapter, the Administrator may by subpoena require the attendance and testimony of witnesses and the production of reports, papers, documents, answers to questions, and other information that the Administrator deems necessary. Witnesses shall be paid the same fees and mileage that are paid witnesses in the courts of the United States. In the event of contumacy, failure, or refusal of any person to obey any such subpoena, any district court of the United States in which venue is proper shall have jurisdiction to order any such person to comply with such subpoena. Any failure to obey such an order of the court is punishable by the court as a contempt thereof.

(TSCA § 12)

Sec. 2611. Exports

(a) In general

(1) Except as provided in paragraph (2) and subsection (b) and (c) of this section, this chapter (other than section 2607 of this title)shall not apply to any chemical substance, mixture, or to an article containing a chemical substance or mixture, if–

(A) it can be shown that such substance, mixture, or article is being manufactured, processed, or distributed in commerce for export from the United States, unless such substance, mixture, or article was, in fact, manufactured, processed, or distributed in commerce, for use in the United States, and

(B) such substance, mixture, or article (when distributed in commerce), or any container in which it is enclosed (when so distributed), bears a stamp or label stating that such substance, mixture, or article is intended for export.

(2) Paragraph (1) shall not apply to any chemical substance, mixture, or article if the Administrator finds that the substance, mixture, or article will present an unreasonable risk of injury to health within the United States or to the environment of the United States. The Administrator may require, under section 2603 of this title, testing of any chemical substance or mixture exempted from this chapter by paragraph (1) for the purpose of determining whether or not such substance or mixture presents an unreasonable risk of injury to health within the United States or to the environment of the United States.

(b) Notice

(1) If any person exports or intends to export to a foreign country a chemical substance or mixture for which the submission of data is required under section 2603 or 2604(b) of this title, such person shall notify the Administrator of such exportation or intent to export and the Administrator shall furnish to the government of such country notice of the availability

of the data submitted to the Administrator under such section for such substance or mixture.

(2) If any person exports or intends to export to a foreign country a chemical substance or mixture for which an order has been issued under section 2604 of this title or a rule has been proposed or promulgated under section 2604 or 2605 of this title, or with respect to which an action is pending, or relief has been granted under section 2604 or 2606 of this title, such person shall notify the Administrator of such exportation or intent to export and the Administrator shall furnish to the government of such country notice of such rule, order, action, or relief.

(c) Prohibition on Export of Elemental Mercury.

(1) Prohibition. Effective January 1, 2013, the export of elemental mercury from the United States is prohibited.

(2) Inapplicability of Subsection (a). Subsection (a) shall not apply to this subsection.

(3) Report to Congress on mercury compounds.

(A) Report. Not later than one year after the date of enactment of the Mercury Export Ban Act of 2008, the Administrator shall publish and submit to Congress a report on mercuric chloride, mercurous chloride or calomel, mercuric oxide, and other mercury compounds, if any, that may currently be used in significant quantities in products or processes. Such report shall include an analysis of—

(i) the sources and amounts of each of the mercury compounds imported into the United States or manufactured in the United States annually;

(ii) the purposes for which each of these compounds are used domestically, the amount of these compounds currently consumed annually for each purpose, and the estimated amounts to be consumed for each purpose in 2010 and beyond;

(iii) the sources and amounts of each mercury compound exported from the United States annually in each of the last three years;

(iv) the potential for these compounds to be processed into elemental mercury after export from the United States; and

(v) other relevant information that Congress should consider in determining whether to extend the export prohibition to include one or more of these mercury compounds.

(B) Procedure. For the purpose of preparing the report under this paragraph, the Administrator may utilize the information gathering authorities of this title, including sections 10 and 11.

(4) Essential Use Exemption. (A) Any person residing in the United States may petition the Administrator for an exemption from the prohibition in

paragraph (1), and the Administrator may grant by rule, after notice and opportunity for comment, an exemption for a specified use at an identified foreign facility if the Administrator finds that—

(i) nonmercury alternatives for the specified use are not available in the country where the facility is located;

(ii) there is no other source of elemental mercury available from domestic supplies (not including new mercury mines) in the country where the elemental mercury will be used;

(iii) the country where the elemental mercury will be used certifies its support for the exemption;

(iv) the export will be conducted in such a manner as to ensure the elemental mercury will be used at the identified facility as described in the petition, and not otherwise diverted for other uses for any reason;

(v) the elemental mercury will be used in a manner that will protect human health and the environment, taking into account local, regional, and global human health and environmental impacts;

(vi) the elemental mercury will be handled and managed in a manner that will protect human health and the environment, taking into account local, regional, and global human health and environmental impacts; and

(vii) the export of elemental mercury for the specified use is consistent with international obligations of the United States intended to reduce global mercury supply, use, and pollution.

(B) Each exemption issued by the Administrator pursuant to this paragraph shall contain such terms and conditions as are necessary to minimize the export of elemental mercury and ensure that the conditions for granting the exemption will be fully met, and shall contain such other terms and conditions as the Administrator may prescribe. No exemption granted pursuant to this paragraph shall exceed three years in duration and no such exemption shall exceed 10 metric tons of elemental mercury.

(C) The Administrator may by order suspend or cancel an exemption under this paragraph in the case of a violation described in subparagraph (D).

(D) A violation of this subsection or the terms and conditions of an exemption, or the submission of false information in connection therewith, shall be considered a prohibited act under section 15, and shall be subject to penalties under section 16, injunctive relief under section 17, and citizen suits under section 20.

(5) Consistency with trade obligations. Nothing in this subsection affects, replaces, or amends prior law relating to the need for consistency with international trade obligations.

(6) Export of Coal. Nothing in this subsection shall be construed to prohibit the export of coal.

(TSCA § 13)

Sec. 2612. Entry into customs territory of the United States

(a) In general

(1) The Secretary of the Treasury shall refuse entry into the customs territory of the United States (as defined in general note of the Harmonized Tariff Schedule of the United States) of any chemical substance, mixture, or article containing a chemical substance or mixture offered for such entry if–

(A) it fails to comply with any rule in effect under this chapter, or

(B) it is offered for entry in violation of section 2604 of this title, 2605 of this title, or subchapter IV of this chapter, a rule or order under section 2604 of this title, 2605 of this title, or subchapter IV of this chapter, or an order issued in a civil action brought under section 2604 of this title, 2606 of this title or subchapter IV of this chapter.

(2) If a chemical substance, mixture, or article is refused entry under paragraph (1), the Secretary of the Treasury shall notify the consignee of such entry refusal, shall not release it to the consignee, and shall cause its disposal or storage (under such rules as the Secretary of the Treasury may prescribe) if it has not been exported by the consignee within 90 days from the date of receipt of notice of such refusal, except that the Secretary of the reasury may, pending a review by the Administrator of the entry refusal, release to the consignee such substance, mixture, or article on execution of bond for the amount of the full invoice of such substance, mixture, or article (as such value is set forth in the customs entry), together with the duty thereon. On failure to return such substance, mixture, or article for any cause to the custody of the Secretary of the Treasury when demanded, such consignee shall be liable to the United States for liquidated damages equal to the full amount of such bond. All charges for storage, cartage, and labor on and for disposal of substances, mixtures, or articles which are refused entry or release under this section shall be paid by the owner or consignee, and in default of such payment shall constitute a lien against any future entry made by such owner or consignee.

(b) Rules

The Secretary of the Treasury, after consultation with the dministrator, shall issue rules for the administration of subsection (a) of this section.

(TSCA § 14)

Sec. 2613. Disclosure of data

(a) In general

Except as provided by subsection (b) of this section, any information reported to, or otherwise obtained by, the dministrator (or any representative of the Administrator) under this chapter, which is exempt from disclosure pursuant to subsection (a) of section 552 of title 5 by reason of subsection (b)(4) of such section, shall, notwithstanding the provisions of any other section of this chapter, not be disclosed by the dministrator or by any officer or employee of the United States, except that such information–

(1) shall be disclosed to any officer or employee of the United tates–

(A) in connection with the official duties of such officer or employee under any law for the protection of health or the environment, or

(B) for specific law enforcement purposes;

(2) shall be disclosed to contractors with the United States and employees of such contractors if in the opinion of the dministrator such disclosure is necessary for the satisfactory performance by the contractor of a contract with the United tates entered into on or after October 11, 1976, for the performance of work in connection with this chapter and under such conditions as the Administrator may specify;

(3) shall be disclosed if the Administrator determines it necessary to protect health or the environment against an unreasonable risk of injury to health or the environment; or

(4) may be disclosed when relevant in any proceeding under this chapter, except that disclosure in such a proceeding shall be made in such manner as to preserve confidentiality to the extent practicable without impairing the proceeding.

In any proceeding under section 552(a) of title 5 to obtain information the disclosure of which has been denied because of the provisions of this subsection, the Administrator may not rely on section 552(b)(3) of such title to sustain the Administrator's action.

(b) Data from health and safety studies

(1) Subsection (a) does not prohibit the disclosure of–

(A) any health and safety study which is submitted under this chapter with respect to–

(i) any chemical substance or mixture which, on the date on which such study is to be disclosed has been offered for commercial distribution, or

(ii) any chemical substance or mixture for which testing is required under section 2603 of this title or for which notification is required under section 2604 of this title, and

(B) any data reported to, or otherwise obtained by, the dministrator from a health and safety study which relates to a chemical substance or mixture described in clause (i) or (ii) of subparagraph (A).

This paragraph does not authorize the release of any data which discloses processes used in the manufacturing or processing of a chemical substance or mixture or, in the case of a mixture, the release of data disclosing the portion of the mixture comprised by any of the chemical substances in the mixture.

(2) If a request is made to the Administrator under subsection (a) of section 552 of title 5 for information which is described in the first sentence of paragraph (1) and which is not information described in the second sentence of such paragraph, the dministrator may not deny such request on the basis of subsection (b)(4) of such section.

(c) Designation and release of confidential data

(1) In submitting data under this chapter, a manufacturer, processor, or distributor in commerce may (A) designate the data which such person believes is entitled to confidential treatment under subsection (a) of this section, and (B) submit such designated data separately from other data submitted under this chapter. A designation under this paragraph shall be made in writing and in such manner as the Administrator may prescribe.

(2) (A) Except as provided by subparagraph (B), if the Administrator proposes to release for inspection data which has been designated under paragraph (1)(A), the Administrator shall notify, in writing and by certified mail, the manufacturer, processor, or distributor in commerce who submitted such data of the intent to release such data. If the release of such data is to be made pursuant to a request made under section 552(a) of title 5, such notice shall be given immediately upon approval of such request by the Administrator. The Administrator may not release such data until the expiration of 30 days after the manufacturer, processor, or distributor in commerce submitting such data has received the notice required by this subparagraph.

(B) (i) Subparagraph (A) shall not apply to the release of information under paragraph (1), (2), (3), or (4) of subsection (a) of this section, except that the Administrator may not release data under paragraph (3) of subsection (a) of this section unless the Administrator has notified each manufacturer, processor, and distributor in commerce who submitted such data of such release.

Such notice shall be made in writing by certified mail at least 15 days before the release of such data, except that if the dministrator determines that the release of such data is necessary to protect against an imminent, unreasonable risk of injury to health or the environment, such notice may be made by such means as the Administrator determines will provide notice at least 24 hours before such release is made.

(ii) Subparagraph (A) shall not apply to the release of information described in subsection (b)(1) of this section other than information described in the second sentence of such subsection.

(d) Criminal penalty for wrongful disclosure

(1) Any officer or employee of the United States or former officer or employee of the United States, who by virtue of such employment or official position has obtained possession of, or has access to, material the disclosure of which is prohibited by subsection (a) of this section, and who knowing that disclosure of such material is prohibited by such subsection, willfully discloses the material in any manner to any person not entitled to receive it, shall be guilty of a misdemeanor and fined not more than $5,000 or imprisoned for not more than one year, or both. Section 1905 of title 18 does not apply with respect to the publishing, divulging, disclosure, or making known of, or making available, information reported or otherwise obtained under this chapter.

(2) For the purposes of paragraph (1), any contractor with the United States who is furnished information as authorized by subsection (a)(2) of this section, and any employee of any such contractor, shall be considered to be an employee of the United States.

(e) Access by Congress

Notwithstanding any limitation contained in this section or any other provision of law, all information reported to or otherwise obtained by the Administrator (or any representative of the Administrator) under this chapter shall be made available, upon written request of any duly authorized committee of the Congress, to such committee.

(TSCA § 15)

Sec. 2614. Prohibited acts

It shall be unlawful for any person to–

(1) fail or refuse to comply with (A) any rule promulgated or order issued under section 2603 of this title, (B) any requirement prescribed by

section 2604 or 2605 of this title, (C) any rule promulgated or order issued under section 2604 or 2605 of this title, or (D) any requirement of subchapter II of this chapter or any rule promulgated or order issued under subchapter I of this chapter;

(2) use for commercial purposes a chemical substance or mixture which such person knew or had reason to know was manufactured, processed, or distributed in commerce in violation of section 604 or 2605 of this title, a rule or order under section 2604 or 605 of this title, or an order issued in action brought under section 2604 or 2606 of this title;

(3) fail or refuse to (A) establish or maintain records, (B) submit reports, notices, or other information, or (C) permit access to or copying of records, as required by this chapter or a rule thereunder; or

(4) fail or refuse to permit entry or inspection as required by section 2610 of this title.

(TSCA § 16)

Sec. 2615. Penalties

(a) Civil

(1) Any person who violates a provision of section 2614 or 2689 of this title shall be liable to the United States for a civil penalty in an amount not to exceed $25,000 for each such violation.

Each day such a violation continues shall, for purposes of this subsection, constitute a separate violation of section 2614 or 2689 of this title.

(2) (A) A civil penalty for a violation of section section 2614 or 689 of this title shall be assessed by the Administrator by an order made on the record after opportunity (provided in accordance with this subparagraph) for a hearing in accordance with section 554 of title 5. Before issuing such an order, the Administrator shall give written notice to the person to be assessed a civil penalty under such order of the Administrator's proposal to issue such order and provide such person an opportunity to request, within 15 days of the date the notice is received by such person, such a hearing on the order.

(B) In determining the amount of a civil penalty, the Administrator shall take into account the nature, circumstances, extent, and gravity of the violation or violations and, with respect to the violator, ability to pay, effect on ability to continue to do business, any history of prior such violations, the degree of culpability, and such other matters as justice may require.

(C) The Administrator may compromise, modify, or remit, with or without conditions, any civil penalty which may be imposed under this subsection. The amount of such penalty, when finally determined, or the amount agreed upon in compromise, may be deducted from any sums owing by the United States to the person charged.

(3) Any person who requested in accordance with paragraph (2)(A) a hearing respecting the assessment of a civil penalty and who is aggrieved by an order assessing a civil penalty may file a petition for judicial review of such order with the United States Court of Appeals for the District of Columbia Circuit or for any other circuit in which such person resides or transacts business. Such a petition may only be filed within the 30-day period beginning on the date the order making such assessment was issued.

(4) If any person fails to pay an assessment of a civil penalty–

(A) after the order making the assessment has become a final order and if such person does not file a petition for judicial review of the order in accordance with paragraph (3), or

(B) after a court in an action brought under paragraph (3) has entered a final judgment in favor of the Administrator, the Attorney General shall recover the amount assessed (plus interest at currently prevailing rates from the date of the expiration of the 30-day period referred to in paragraph (3) or the date of such final judgment, as the case may be) in an action brought in any appropriate district court of the United States. In such an action, the validity, amount, and appropriateness of such penalty shall not be subject to review.

(b) Criminal

Any person who knowingly or willfully violates any provision of section 2614 or 2689 of this title, shall, in addition to or in lieu of any civil penalty which may be imposed under subsection (a) of this section for such violation, be subject, upon conviction, to a fine of not more than $25,000 for each day of violation, or to imprisonment for not more than one year, or both.

(TSCA § 17)

Sec. 2616. Specific enforcement and seizure

(a) Specific enforcement

(1) The district courts of the United States shall have jurisdiction over civil actions to–

(A) restrain any violation of section 2614 or 2689 of this title,

(B) restrain any person from taking any action prohibited by section 2604 of this title, 2605 of this title, or subchapter IV of this chapter, or by a rule or order under section 2604 of this title, 2605 of this title, or subchapter IV of this chapter,

(C) compel the taking of any action required by or under this chapter, or

(D) direct any manufacturer or processor of a chemical substance, mixture, or product subject to subchapter IV of this chapter manufactured or processed in violation of section 2604 of this title, 2605 of this title, or subchapter IV of this chapter, or a rule or order under section 2604 of this title, 2605 of this title, or subchapter IV of this chapter, and distributed in commerce, (i) to give notice of such fact to distributors in commerce of such substance, mixture, or product and, to the extent reasonably ascertainable, to other persons in possession of such substance, mixture, or product or exposed to such substance, mixture, or product, (ii) to give public notice of such risk of injury, and (iii) to either replace or repurchase such substance, mixture, or product, whichever the person to which the requirement is directed elects.

(2) A civil action described in paragraph (1) may be brought–

(A) in the case of a civil action described in subparagraph (A) of such paragraph, in the United States district court for the judicial district wherein any act, omission, or transaction constituting a violation of section 2614 of this title occurred or wherein the defendant is found or transacts business, or

(B) in the case of any other civil action described in such paragraph, in the United States district court for the judicial district wherein the defendant is found or transacts business.

In any such civil action process may be served on a defendant in any judicial district in which a defendant resides or may be found. Subpoenas requiring attendance of witnesses in any such action may be served in any judicial district.

(b) Seizure

Any chemical substance, mixture, or product subject to subchapter V of this chapter which was manufactured, processed, or distributed in commerce in violation of this chapter or any rule promulgated or order issued under this chapter or any article containing such a substance or mixture shall be liable to be proceeded against, by process of libel, for the seizure and condemnation of such substance, mixture, product, or article, in any district court of the United States within the jurisdiction of which such substance, mixture, product, or article is found. Such proceedings shall conform as nearly as possible to proceedings in rem in admiralty.

(TSCA § 18)

Sec. 2617. Preemption

(a) Effect on State law

(1) Except as provided in paragraph (2), nothing in this chapter shall affect the authority of any State or political subdivision of a State to establish or continue in effect regulation of any chemical substance, mixture, or article containing a chemical substance or mixture.

(2) Except as provided in subsection (b) of this section–

(A) if the Administrator requires by a rule promulgated under section 2603 of this title the testing of a chemical substance or mixture, no State or political subdivision may, after the effective date of such rule, establish or continue in effect a requirement for the testing of such substance or mixture for purposes similar to those for which testing is required under such rule; and

(B) if the Administrator prescribes a rule or order under section 2604 or 2605 of this title (other than a rule imposing a requirement described in subsection (a)(6) of section 2605 of this title) which is applicable to a chemical substance or mixture, and which is designed to protect against a risk of injury to health or the environment associated with such substance or mixture, no State or political subdivision of a State may, after the effective date of such requirement, establish or continue in effect, any requirement which is applicable to such substance or mixture, or an article containing such substance or mixture, and which is designed to protect against such risk unless such requirement (i) is identical to the requirement prescribed by the Administrator, (ii) is adopted under the authority of the Clean Air Act [42 U.S.C. 7401 et seq.] or any other Federal law, or (iii) prohibits the use of such substance or mixture in such State or political subdivision (other than its use in the manufacture or processing of other substances or mixtures).

(b) Exemption

Upon application of a State or political subdivision of a State the Administrator may by rule exempt from subsection (a)(2) of this section, under such conditions as may be prescribed in such rule, a requirement of such State or political subdivision designed to protect against a risk of injury to health or the environment associated with a chemical substance, mixture, or article containing a chemical substance or mixture if–

(1) compliance with the requirement would not cause the manufacturing, processing, distribution in commerce, or use of the substance, mixture, or article to be in violation of the applicable requirement under this chapter described in subsection (a)(2) of this section, and

(2) the State or political subdivision requirement (A) provides a significantly higher degree of protection from such risk than the requirement under this chapter described in subsection (a)(2) of this section and (B) does not, through difficulties in marketing, distribution, or other factors, unduly burden interstate commerce.

(TSCA § 19)

Sec. 2618. Judicial review

(a) In general

(1) (A) Not later than 60 days after the date of the promulgation of a rule under section 2603(a), 2604(a)(2), 2604(b)(4), 2605(a), 2605(e), or 2607 of this title, or under subchapter II or IV of this chapter, any person may file a petition for judicial review of such rule with the United States Court of Appeals for the District of Columbia Circuit or for the circuit in which such person resides or in which such person's principal place of business is located. Courts of appeals of the United States shall have exclusive jurisdiction of any action to obtain judicial review (other than in an enforcement proceeding) of such a rule if any district court of the United States would have had jurisdiction of such action but for this subparagraph.

(B) Courts of appeals of the United States shall have exclusive jurisdiction of any action to obtain judicial review (other than in an enforcement proceeding) of an order issued under subparagraph (A) or (B) of section 2605(b)(1) of this title if any district court of the United States would have had jurisdiction of such action but for this subparagraph.

(2) Copies of any petition filed under paragraph (1)(A) shall be transmitted forthwith to the Administrator and to the Attorney

General by the clerk of the court with which such petition was filed. The provisions of section 2112 of title 28 shall apply to the filing of the rulemaking record of proceedings on which the dministrator based the rule being reviewed under this section and to the transfer of proceedings between United States courts of appeals.

(3) For purposes of this section, the term "rulemaking record" means–

(A) the rule being reviewed under this section;

(B) in the case of a rule under section 2603(a) of this title, the finding required by such section, in the case of a rule under section 2604(b)(4) of this title, the finding required by such section, in the case of a rule under section 2605(a) of this title the finding required by section 2604(f) or 2605(a) of this title, as the case may be, in the case of a rule under section 605(a) of this title, the statement required by section 605(c)(1) of this title, and in the case of a rule under section 605(e) of this title, the findings required by paragraph (2)(B) or (3)(B) of such section, as the case may be[7] and in the case of a rule under subchapter IV of this chapter, the finding required for the issuance of such a rule;

(C) any transcript required to be made of oral presentations made in proceedings for the promulgation of such rule;

(D) any written submission of interested parties respecting the promulgation of such rule; and

(E) any other information which the Administrator considers to be relevant to such rule and which the Administrator identified, on or before the date of the promulgation of such rule, in a notice published in the Federal Register.

(b) Additional submissions and presentations; modifications

If in an action under this section to review a rule the petitioner or the Administrator applies to the court for leave to make additional oral submissions or written presentations respecting such rule and shows to the satisfaction of the court that such submissions and presentations would be material and that there were reasonable grounds for the submissions and failure to make such submissions and presentations in the proceeding before the Administrator, the court may order the Administrator to provide additional opportunity to make such submissions and presentations.

The Administrator may modify or set aside the rule being reviewed or make a new rule by reason of the additional submissions and presentations and shall file such modified or new rule with the return of such submissions and presentations. The court shall thereafter review such new or modified rule.

(c) Standard of review

(1) (A) Upon the filing of a petition under subsection (a)(1) of this section for judicial review of a rule, the court shall have jurisdiction (i) to grant appropriate relief, including interim relief, as provided in chapter 7 of title 5, and (ii) except as otherwise provided in subparagraph (B), to review such rule in accordance with chapter 7 of title 5.

(B) Section 706 of title 5 shall apply to review of a rule under this section, except that–

(i) in the case of review of a rule under section 2603(a), 2604(b)(4), 2605(a), or 2605(e) of this title, the standard for review prescribed by paragraph (2)(E) of such section 706 shall not apply

---

7. So in original. Probably should be followed by a comma.

and the court shall hold unlawful and set aside such rule if the court finds that the rule is not supported by substantial evidence in the rulemaking record (as defined in subsection (a)(3) of this section) taken as a whole;

(ii) in the case of review of a rule under section 2605(a) of this title, the court shall hold unlawful and set aside such rule if it finds that–

(I) a determination by the Administrator under section 605(c)(3) of this title that the petitioner seeking review of such rule is not entitled to conduct (or have conducted) cross-examination or to present rebuttal submissions, or

(II) a rule of, or ruling by, the Administrator under section 605(c)(3) of this title limiting such petitioner's cross-examination or oral presentations, has precluded disclosure of disputed material facts which was necessary to a fair determination by the Administrator of the rulemaking proceeding taken as a whole; and section 706(2)(D) shall not apply with respect to a determination, rule, or ruling referred to in subclause (I) or (II); and

(iii) the court may not review the contents and adequacy of–

(I) any statement required to be made pursuant to section2605(c)(1) of this title, or

(II) any statement of basis and purpose required by section 553(c) of title 5 to be incorporated in the rule except as part of a review of the rulemaking record taken as a whole.

The term "evidence" as used in clause (i) means any matter in the rulemaking record.

(C) A determination, rule, or ruling of the Administrator described in subparagraph (B)(ii) may be reviewed only in an action under this section and only in accordance with such subparagraph.

(2) The judgment of the court affirming or setting aside, in whole or in part, any rule reviewed in accordance with this section shall be final, subject to review by the Supreme Court of the nited States upon certiorari or certification, as provided in section 1254 of title 28.

(d) Fees and costs

The decision of the court in an action commenced under subsection

(a) of this section, or of the Supreme Court of the United States on review of such a decision, may include an award of costs of suit and reasonable fees for attorneys and expert witnesses if the court determines that such an award is appropriate.

(e) Other remedies

The remedies as provided in this section shall be in addition to and not in lieu of any other remedies provided by law.

(TSCA § 20)

Sec. 2619. Citizens' civil actions

(a) In general

Except as provided in subsection (b) of this section, any person may commence a civil action–

(1) against any person (including (A) the United States, and (B) any other governmental instrumentality or agency to the extent permitted by the eleventh amendment to the Constitution) who is alleged to be in violation of this chapter or any rule promulgated under section 2603, 2604, or 2605 of this title, or subchapter II or IV of this chapter, or order issued under section 2604 of this title or subchapter II or IV of this chapter to restrain such violation, or

(2) against the Administrator to compel the Administrator to perform any act or duty under this chapter which is not discretionary.

Any civil action under paragraph (1) shall be brought in the United tates district court for the district in which the alleged violation occurred or in which the defendant resides or in which the defendant's principal place of business is located. Any action brought under paragraph (2) shall be brought in the United States District Court for the District of Columbia, or the United States district court for the judicial district in which the plaintiff is domiciled. The district courts of the United States shall have jurisdiction over suits brought under this section, without regard to the amount in controversy or the citizenship of the parties. In any civil action under this subsection process may be served on a defendant in any judicial district in which the defendant resides or may be found and subpoenas for witnesses may be served in any judicial district.

(b) Limitation

No civil action may be commenced–

(1) under subsection (a)(1) of this section to restrain a violation of this chapter or rule or order under this chapter–

(A) before the expiration of 60 days after the plaintiff has given notice of such violation (i) to the Administrator, and (ii) to the person who is alleged to have committed such violation, or

(B) if the Administrator has commenced and is diligently prosecuting a proceeding for the issuance of an order under section 2615(a)(2) of this title to require compliance with this chapter or with such rule or order or if the Attorney General has commenced and is diligently prosecuting a civil action in a court of the United States to require compliance with this chapter or with such rule or order, but if such proceeding or civil action is commenced after the giving of notice, any person giving such notice may intervene as a matter of right in such proceeding or action; or

(2) under subsection (a)(2) of this section before the expiration of 60 days after the plaintiff has given notice to theAdministrator of the alleged failure of the Administrator to perform an act or duty which is the basis for such action or, in the case of an action under such subsection for the failure of the Administrator to file an action under section 2606 of this title, before the expiration of ten days after such notification.Notice under this subsection shall be given in such manner as the Administrator shall prescribe by rule.

(c) General

(1) In any action under this section, the Administrator, if not a party, may intervene as a matter of right.

(2) The court, in issuing any final order in any action brought pursuant to subsection (a) of this section, may award costs of suit and reasonable fees for attorneys and expert witnesses if the court determines that such an award is appropriate. Any court, in issuing its decision in an action brought to review such an order, may award costs of suit and reasonable fees for attorneys if the court determines that such an award is appropriate.

(3) Nothing in this section shall restrict any right which any person (or class of persons) may have under any statute or common law to seek enforcement of this chapter or any rule or order under this chapter or to seek any other relief.

(d) Consolidation

When two or more civil actions brought under subsection (a) of this section involving the same defendant and the same issues or violations are pending in two or more judicial districts, such pending actions, upon application of such defendants to such actions which is made to a court in which any such action is brought, may, if such court in its discretion so decides, be consolidated for trial by order (issued after giving all parties reasonable notice and opportunity to be heard) of such court and tried in–

(1) any district which is selected by such defendant and in which one of such actions is pending,

(2) a district which is agreed upon by stipulation between all the parties to such actions and in which one of such actions is pending, or

(3) a district which is selected by the court and in which one of such actions is pending. The court issuing such an order shall give prompt notification of the order to the other courts in which the civil actions consolidated under the order are pending.

(TSCA § 21)

Sec. 2620. Citizens' petitions

(a) In general

Any person may petition the Administrator to initiate a proceeding for the issuance, amendment, or repeal of a rule under section 2603, 2605, or 2607 of this title or an order under section 2604(e) or 2605(b)(2) of this title.

(b) Procedures

(1) Such petition shall be filed in the principal office of the Administrator and shall set forth the facts which it is claimed establish that it is necessary to issue, amend, or repeal a rule under section 2603, 2605, or 2607 of this title or an order under section 2604(e), 2605(b)(1)(A), or 2605(b)(1)(B) of this title.

(2) The Administrator may hold a public hearing or may conduct such investigation or proceeding as the Administrator deems appropriate in order to determine whether or not such petition should be granted.

(3) Within 90 days after filing of a petition described in paragraph (1), the Administrator shall either grant or deny the petition. If the Administrator grants such petition, the Administrator shall promptly commence an appropriate proceeding in accordance with section 2603, 2604, 2605, or 2607 of this title. If the Administrator denies such petition, the Administrator shall publish in the Federal Register the Administrator's reasons for such denial.

(4) (A) If the Administrator denies a petition filed under this section (or if the Administrator fails to grant or deny such petition within the 90-day period) the petitioner may commence a civil action in a district court of the United States to compel the Administrator to initiate a rulemaking proceeding as requested in the petition. Any such action shall be filed within 60 days after the Administrator's denial of the petition or, if the Administrator fails to grant or deny the petition within 90 days after filing the petition, within 60 days after the expiration of the 90-day period.

(B) In an action under subparagraph (A) respecting a petition to initiate a proceeding to issue a rule under section 2603, 2605, or 2607 of this title or an order under section 2604(e) or 2605(b)(2) of this title, the petitioner shall be provided an opportunity to have such petition considered by the court in a de novo proceeding. If the petitioner demonstrates to the satisfaction of the court by a preponderance of the evidence that–

(i) in the case of a petition to initiate a proceeding for the issuance of a rule under section 2603 of this title or an order under section 2604(e) of this title–

(I) information available to the Administrator is insufficient to permit a reasoned evaluation of the health and environmental effects of the chemical substance to be subject to such rule or order; and

(II) in the absence of such information, the substance may present an unreasonable risk to health or the environment, or the substance is or will be produced in substantial quantities and it enters or may reasonably be anticipated to enter the environment in substantial quantities or there is or may be significant or substantial human exposure to it; or

(ii) in the case of a petition to initiate a proceeding for the issuance of a rule under section 2605 or 2607 of this title or an order under section 2605(b)(2) of this title, there is a reasonable basis to conclude that the issuance of such a rule or order is necessary to protect health or the environment against an unreasonable risk of injury to health or the environment.[8] the court shall order the Administrator to initiate the action requested by the petitioner. If the court finds that the extent of the risk to health or the environment alleged by the petitioner is less than the extent of risks to health or the environment with respect to which the Administrator is taking action under this chapter and there are insufficient resources available to the Administrator to take the action requested by the petitioner, the court may permit the Administrator to defer initiating the action requested by the petitioner until such time as the court prescribes.

(C) The court in issuing any final order in any action brought pursuant to subparagraph (A) may award costs of suit and reasonable fees for attorneys and expert witnesses if the court determines that such an award is appropriate. Any court, in issuing its decision in an action brought to review such an order, may award costs of suit and reasonable fees for attorneys if the court determines that such an award is appropriate.

---

8. So in original. The period probably should be a semicolon.

(5) The remedies under this section shall be in addition to, and not in lieu of, other remedies provided by law.

(TSCA § 22)

Sec. 2621. National defense waiver

The Administrator shall waive compliance with any provision of this chapter upon a request and determination by the President that the requested waiver is necessary in the interest of national defense. The Administrator shall maintain a written record of the basis upon which such waiver was granted and make such record available for in camera examination when relevant in a judicial proceeding under this chapter. Upon the issuance of such a waiver, the Administrator shall publish in the Federal Register a notice that the waiver was granted for national defense purposes, unless, upon the request of the President, the Administrator determines to omit such publication because the publication itself would be contrary to the interests of national defense, in which event the Administrator shall submit notice thereof to the Armed Services Committees of the Senate and the House of Representatives.

(TSCA § 23)

Sec. 2622. Employee protection

(a) In general

No employer may discharge any employee or otherwise discriminate against any employee with respect to the employee's compensation, terms, conditions, or privileges of employment because the employee (or any person acting pursuant to a request of the employee) has–

(1) commenced, caused to be commenced, or is about to commence or cause to be commenced a proceeding under this chapter;

(2) testified or is about to testify in any such proceeding; or

(3) assisted or participated or is about to assist or participate in any manner in such a proceeding or in any other action to carry out the purposes of this chapter.

(b) Remedy

(1) Any employee who believes that the employee has been discharged or otherwise discriminated against by any person in violation of subsection (a) of this section may, within 30 days after such alleged violation occurs, file (or have any person file on the employee's behalf) a complaint with the Secretary of Labor (hereinafter in this section referred to as the "Secretary") alleging such discharge or discrimination. Upon receipt of such a complaint,

the Secretary shall notify the person named in the complaint of the filing of the complaint.

(2) (A) Upon receipt of a complaint filed under paragraph (1), the Secretary shall conduct an investigation of the violation alleged in the complaint. Within 30 days of the receipt of such complaint, the Secretary shall complete such investigation and shall notify in writing the complainant (and any person acting on behalf of the complainant) and the person alleged to have committed such violation of the results of the investigation conducted pursuant to this paragraph. Within ninety days of the receipt of such complaint the Secretary shall, unless the proceeding on the complaint is terminated by the Secretary on the basis of a settlement entered into by the Secretary and the person alleged to have committed such violation, issue an order either providing the relief prescribed by subparagraph (B) or denying the complaint. An order of the Secretary shall be made on the record after notice and opportunity for agency hearing. The Secretary may not enter into a settlement terminating a proceeding on a complaint without the participation and consent of the complainant.

(B) If in response to a complaint filed under paragraph (1) the Secretary determines that a violation of subsection (a) of this section has occurred, the Secretary shall order (i) the person who committed such violation to take affirmative action to abate the violation, (ii) such person to reinstate the complainant to the complainant's former position together with the compensation (including back pay), terms, conditions, and privileges of the complainant's employment, (iii) compensatory damages, and (iv) where appropriate, exemplary damages. If such an order issued, the Secretary, at the request of the complainant, shall assess against the person against whom the order is issued a sum equal to the aggregate amount of all costs and expenses (including attorney's fees) reasonably incurred, as determined by the Secretary, by the complainant for, or in connection with, the bringing of the complaint upon which the order was issued.

(c) Review

(1) Any employee or employer adversely affected or aggrieved by an order issued under subsection (b) of this section may obtain review of the order in the United States Court of Appeals for the circuit in which the violation, with respect to which the order was issued, allegedly occurred. The petition for review must be filed within sixty days from the issuance of the Secretary's order.

Review shall conform to chapter 7 of title 5.

(2) An order of the Secretary, with respect to which review could have been obtained under paragraph (1), shall not be subject to judicial review in any criminal or other civil proceeding.

(d) Enforcement

Whenever a person has failed to comply with an order issued under subsection (b)(2) of this section, the Secretary shall file a civil action in the United States district court for the district in which the violation was found to occur to enforce such order. In actions brought under this subsection, the district courts shall have jurisdiction to grant all appropriate relief, including injunctive relief and compensatory and exemplary damages.

(e) Exclusion

Subsection (a) of this section shall not apply with respect to any employee who, acting without direction from the employee's employer (or any agent of the employer), deliberately causes a violation of any requirement of this chapter.

(TSCA § 24)

Sec. 2623. Employment effects

(a) In general

The Administrator shall evaluate on a continuing basis the potential effects on employment (including reductions in employment or loss of employment from threatened plant closures) of–

(1) the issuance of a rule or order under section 2603, 2604, or 2605 of this title, or

(2) a requirement of section 2604 or 2605 of this title.

(b) Investigations

(1) Any employee (or any representative of an employee) may request the Administrator to make an investigation of–

(A) a discharge or layoff or threatened discharge or layoff of the employee, or

(B) adverse or threatened adverse effects on the employee's employment, allegedly resulting from a rule or order under section 2603, 2604, or 2605 of this title or a requirement of section 2604 or 2605 of this title. Any such request shall be made in writing, shall set forth with reasonable particularity the grounds for the request, and shall be signed by the employee, or representative of such employee, making the request.

(2) (A) Upon receipt of a request made in accordance with paragraph (1) the Administrator shall (i) conduct the investigation requested, and (ii) if requested by any interested person, hold public hearings on any matter

involved in the investigation unless the Administrator, by order issued within 45 days of the date such hearings are requested, denies the request for the hearings because the Administrator determines there are no reasonable grounds for holding such hearings. If the Administrator makes such a determination, the Administrator shall notify in writing the person requesting the hearing of the determination and the reasons therefor and shall publish the determination and the reasons therefor in the Federal Register.

(B) If public hearings are to be held on any matter involved in an investigation conducted under this subsection–

(i) at least five days' notice shall be provided the person making the request for the investigation and any person identified in such request,

(ii) such hearings shall be held in accordance with section 2605(c)(3) of this title, and

(iii) each employee who made or for whom was made a request for such hearings and the employer of such employee shall be required to present information respecting the applicable matter referred to in paragraph (1)(A) or (1)(B) together with the basis for such information.

(3) Upon completion of an investigation under paragraph (2), the Administrator shall make findings of fact, shall make such recommendations as the Administrator deems appropriate, and shall make available to the public such findings and recommendations.

(4) This section shall not be construed to require the Administrator to amend or repeal any rule or order in effect under this chapter.

(TSCA § 25)

Sec. 2624. Studies

(a) Indemnification study

The Administrator shall conduct a study of all Federal laws administered by the Administrator for the purpose of determining whether and under what conditions, if any, indemnification should be accorded any person as a result of any action taken by the Administrator under any such law. The study shall–

(1) include an estimate of the probable cost of any indemnification programs which may be recommended;

(2) include an examination of all viable means of financing the cost of any recommended indemnification; and

(3) be completed and submitted to Congress within two years from the effective date of enactment of this chapter.

The General Accounting Office shall review the adequacy of the study submitted to Congress pursuant to paragraph (3) and shall report the results of its review to the Congress within six months of the date such study is submitted to Congress.

(b) Classification, storage, and retrieval study

The Council on Environmental Quality, in consultation with the Administrator, the Secretary of Health and Human Services, the Secretary of Commerce, and the heads of other appropriate Federal departments or agencies, shall coordinate a study of the feasibility of establishing (1) a standard classification system for chemical substances and related substances, and (2) a standard means for storing and for obtaining rapid access to information respecting such substances. A report on such study shall be completed and submitted to Congress not later than 18 months after the effective date of enactment of this chapter.

(TSCA § 26)

Sec. 2625. Administration

(a) Cooperation of Federal agencies

Upon request by the Administrator, each Federal department and agency is authorized–

(1) to make its services, personnel, and facilities available (with or without reimbursement) to the Administrator to assist the Administrator in the administration of this chapter; and

(2) to furnish to the Administrator such information, data, estimates, and statistics, and to allow the Administrator access to all information in its possession as the Administrator may reasonably determine to be necessary for the administration of this chapter.

(b) Fees

(1) The Administrator may, by rule, require the payment of a reasonable fee from any person required to submit data under section 2603 or 2604 of this title to defray the cost of administering this chapter. Such rules shall not provide for any fee in excess of $2,500 or, in the case of a small business concern, any fee in excess of $100. In setting a fee under this paragraph, the Administrator shall take into account the ability to pay of the person required to submit the data and the cost to the Administrator of

reviewing such data. Such rules may provide for sharing such a fee in any case in which the expenses of testing are shared under section 2603 or 2604 of this title.

(2) The Administrator, after consultation with the Administrator of the Small Business Administration, shall by rule prescribe standards for determining the persons which qualify as small business concerns for purposes of paragraph (1).

(c) Action with respect to categories

(1) Any action authorized or required to be taken by the Administrator under any provision of this chapter with respect to a chemical substance or mixture may be taken by the Administrator in accordance with that provision with respect to a category of chemical substances or mixtures. Whenever the Administrator takes action under a provision of this chapter with respect to a category of chemical substances or mixtures, any reference in this chapter to a chemical substance or mixture (insofar as it relates to such action) shall be deemed to be a reference to each chemical substance or mixture in such category.

(2) For purposes of paragraph (1):

(A) The term "category of chemical substances" means a group of chemical substances the members of which are similar in molecular structure, in physical, chemical, or biological properties, in use, or in mode of entrance into the human body or into the environment, or the members of which are in some other way suitable for classification as such for purposes of this chapter, except that such term does not mean a group of chemical substances which are grouped together solely on the basis of their being new chemical substances.

(B) The term "category of mixtures" means a group of mixtures the members of which are similar in molecular structure, in physical, chemical, or biological properties, in use, or in the mode of entrance into the human body or into the environment, or the members of which are in some other way suitable for classification as such for purposes of this chapter.

(d) Assistance office

The Administrator shall establish in the Environmental Protection Agency an identifiable office to provide technical and other nonfinancial assistance to manufacturers and processors of chemical substances and mixtures respecting the requirements of this chapter applicable to such manufacturers and processors, the policy of the Agency respecting the application of such requirements to such manufacturers and processors, and the means and methods by which such manufacturers and processors may comply with such requirements.

(e) Financial disclosures

(1) Except as provided under paragraph (3), each officer or employee of the Environmental Protection Agency and the Department of Health and Human Services who–

(A) performs any function or duty under this chapter, and

(B) has any known financial interest (i) in any person subject to this chapter or any rule or order in effect under this chapter, or (ii) in any person who applies for or receives any grant or contract under this chapter, shall, on February 1, 1978, and on February 1 of each year thereafter, file with the Administrator or the Secretary of Health and Human Services (hereinafter in this subsection referred to as the "Secretary"), as appropriate, a written statement concerning all such interests held by such officer or employee during the preceding calendar year. Such statement shall be made available to the public.

(2) The Administrator and the Secretary shall–

(A) act within 90 days of January 1, 1977–

(i) to define the term "known financial interests" for purposes of paragraph (1), and

(ii) to establish the methods by which the requirement to file written statements specified in paragraph (1) will be monitored and enforced, including appropriate provisions for review by the Administrator and the Secretary of such statements; and

(B) report to the Congress on June 1, 1978, and on June 1 of each year thereafter with respect to such statements and the actions taken in regard thereto during the preceding calendar year.[9]

(3) The Administrator may by rule identify specific positions with the Environmental Protection Agency, and the Secretary may by rule identify specific positions with the Department of Health and Human Services, which are of a nonregulatory or nonpolicymaking nature, and the Administrator and the Secretary may by rule provide that officers or employees occupying such positions shall be exempt from the requirements of paragraph (1).

---

9. For termination, effective May 15, 2000, of provisions in subsec.(e)(2)(B) of this section relating to annual reports to Congress, see section 3003 of Pub. L. 104-66, as amended, set out as a note under section 1113 of Title 31, Money and Finance, and pages 93 and 164 of House Document No. 103-7.

(4) This subsection does not supersede any requirement of chapter 11 of title 18.

(5) Any officer or employee who is subject to, and knowingly violates, this subsection or any rule issued thereunder, shall be fined not more than $2,500 or imprisoned not more than one year, or both.

(f) Statement of basis and purpose

Any final order issued under this chapter shall be accompanied by a statement of its basis and purpose. The contents and adequacy of any such statement shall not be subject to judicial review in any respect.

(g) Assistant Administrator

(1) The President, by and with the advice and consent of the Senate, shall appoint an Assistant Administrator for Toxic Substances of the Environmental Protection Agency. Such Assistant Administrator shall be a qualified individual who is, by reason of background and experience, especially qualified to direct a program concerning the effects of chemicals on human health and the environment. Such Assistant Administrator shall be responsible for (A) the collection of data, (B) the preparation of studies, (C) the making of recommendations to the Administrator for regulatory and other actions to carry out the purposes and to facilitate the administration of this chapter, and (D) such other functions as the Administrator may assign or delegate.

(2) The Assistant Administrator to be appointed under paragraph (1) shall be in addition to the Assistant Administrators of the Environmental Protection Agency authorized by section 1(d) of Reorganization Plan No. 3 of 1970.

(TSCA § 27)

Sec. 2626. Development and evaluation of test methods

(a) In general

The Secretary of Health and Human Services, in consultation with the Administrator and acting through the Assistant Secretary for Health, may conduct, and make grants to public and nonprofit private entities and enter into contracts with public and private entities for, projects for the development and evaluation of inexpensive and efficient methods (1) for determining and evaluating the health and environmental effects of chemical substances and mixtures, and their toxicity, persistence, and other characteristics which affect health and the environment, and (2) which may be used for the development of test data to meet the requirements of rules promulgated under section 2603 of this title.

The Administrator shall consider such methods in prescribing under section 2603 of this title standards for the development of test data.

(b) Approval by Secretary

No grant may be made or contract entered into under subsection (a) of this section unless an application therefor has been submitted to and approved by the Secretary. Such an application shall be submitted in such form and manner and contain such information as the Secretary may require. The Secretary may apply such conditions to grants and contracts under subsection (a) of this section as the Secretary determines are necessary to carry out the purposes of such subsection. Contracts may be entered into under such subsection without regard to section 3324(a) and (b) of title 31 and section 5 of title 41.

(TSCA § 28)

Sec. 2627. State programs

(a) In general

For the purpose of complementing (but not reducing) the authority of, or actions taken by, the Administrator under this chapter, the Administrator may make grants to States for the establishment and operation of programs to prevent or eliminate unreasonable risks within the States to health or the environment which are associated with a chemical substance or mixture and with respect to which the Administrator is unable or is not likely to take action under this chapter for their prevention or elimination. The amount of a grant under this subsection shall be determined by the Administrator, except that no grant for any State program may exceed 75 per centum of the establishment and operation costs (as determined by the Administrator) of such program during the period for which the grant is made.

(b) Approval by Administrator

(1) No grant may be made under subsection (a) of this section unless an application therefor is submitted to and approved by the Administrator. Such an application shall be submitted in such form and manner as the Administrator may require and shall–

(A) set forth the need of the applicant for a grant under subsection (a) of this section,

(B) identify the agency or agencies of the State which shall establish or operate, or both, the program for which the application is submitted,

(C) describe the actions proposed to be taken under such program,

(D) contain or be supported by assurances satisfactory to the Administrator that such program shall, to the extent feasible, be integrated with other programs of the applicant for environmental and public health protection,

(E) provide for the making of such reports and evaluations as the Administrator may require, and

(F) contain such other information as the Administrator may prescribe.

(2) The Administrator may approve an application submitted in accordance with paragraph (1) only if the applicant has established to the satisfaction of the Administrator a priority need, as determined under rules of the Administrator, for the grant for which the application has been submitted. Such rules shall take into consideration the seriousness of the health effects in a State which are associated with chemical substances or mixtures, including cancer, birth defects, and gene mutations, the extent of the exposure in a State of human beings and the environment to chemical substances and mixtures, and the extent to which chemical substances and mixtures are manufactured, processed, used, and disposed of in a State.

(c) Annual reports

Not later than six months after the end of each of the fiscal years 1979, 1980, and 1981, the Administrator shall submit to the Congress a report respecting the programs assisted by grants under subsection (a) of this section in the preceding fiscal year and the extent to which the Administrator has disseminated information respecting such programs.

(d) Authorization

For the purpose of making grants under subsection (a) of this section, there are authorized to be appropriated $1,500,000 for each of the fiscal years 1982 and 1983. Sums appropriated under this subsection shall remain available until expended.

(TSCA § 29)

Sec. 2628. Authorization of appropriations

There are authorized to be appropriated to the Administrator for purposes of carrying out this chapter (other than sections 2626 and 2627 of this title and subsections (a) and (c) through (g) of section 2609 of this title) $58,646,000 for the fiscal year 1982 and $62,000,000 for the fiscal year 1983. No part of the funds appropriated under this section may be used to construct any research laboratories.

(TSCA § 29)

Sec. 2629. Annual report[10]

The Administrator shall prepare and submit to the President and the Congress on or before January 1, 1978, and on or before January 1 of each succeeding year a comprehensive report on the administration of this chapter during the preceding fiscal year.

Such reports shall include–

(1) a list of the testing required under section 2603 of this title during the year for which the report is made and an estimate of the costs incurred during such year by the persons required to perform such tests;

(2) the number of notices received during such year under section 2604 of this title, the number of such notices received during such year under such section for chemical substances subject to a rule, and a summary of any action taken during such year under section 2604(g) of this title;

(3) a list of rules issued during such year under section 2605 of this title;

(4) a list, with a brief statement of the issues, of completed or pending judicial actions under this chapter and administrative actions under section 2615 of this title during such year;

(5) a summary of major problems encountered in the administration of this chapter; and

(6) such recommendations for additional legislation as the Administrator deems necessary to carry out the purposes of this chapter.

Subchapter II - Asbestos Hazard Emergency Response

(TSCA § 201)

Sec. 2641. Congressional findings and purpose

(a) Findings

The Congress finds the following:

(1) The Environmental Protection Agency's rule on local educational agency inspection for, and notification of, the presence of friable asbestos-containing

---

10. For termination, effective May 15, 2000, of provisions in this section relating to submitting annual report to Congress, see section 3003 of Pub. L. 104-66, as amended, set out as a note under section 1113 of Title 31, Money and Finance, and page 163 of HouseDocument No. 103-7.

material in school buildings includes neither standards for the proper identification of asbestos-containing material and appropriate response actions with respect to friable asbestos-containing material, nor a requirement that response actions with respect to friable asbestos-containing material be carried out in a safe and complete manner once actions are found to be necessary. As a result of the lack of regulatory guidance from the Environmental Protection Agency, some schools have not undertaken response action while many others have undertaken expensive projects without knowing if their action is necessary, adequate, or safe.

Thus, the danger of exposure to asbestos continues to exist in schools, and some exposure actually may have increased due to the lack of Federal standards and improper response action.

(2) There is no uniform program for accrediting persons involved in asbestos identification and abatement, nor are local educational agencies required to use accredited contractors for asbestos work.

(3) The guidance provided by the Environmental Protection Agency in its "Guidance for Controlling Asbestos-Containing Material in Buildings" is insufficient in detail to ensure adequate responses. Such guidance is intended to be used only until the regulations required by this subchapter become effective.

(4) Because there are no Federal standards whatsoever regulating daily exposure to asbestos in other public and commercial buildings, persons in addition to those comprising the Nation's school population may be exposed daily to asbestos.

(b) Purpose

The purpose of this subchapter is–

(1) to provide for the establishment of Federal regulations which require inspection for asbestos-containing material and implementation of appropriate response actions with respect to asbestos-containing material in the Nation's schools in a safe and complete manner;

(2) to mandate safe and complete periodic reinspection of school buildings following response actions, where appropriate; and

(3) to require the Administrator to conduct a study to find out the extent of the danger to human health posed by asbestos in public and commercial buildings and the means to respond to any such danger.

(TSCA § 202)

Sec. 2642. Definitions

For purposes of this subchapter–

(1) Accredited asbestos contractor

The term "accredited asbestos contractor" means a person accredited pursuant to the provisions of section 2646 of this title.

(2) Administrator

The term "Administrator" means the Administrator of the Environmental Protection Agency.

(3) Asbestos

The term "asbestos" means asbestiform varieties of–

(A) chrysotile (serpentine),

(B) crocidolite (riebeckite),

(C) amosite (cummingtonite-grunerite),

(D) anthophyllite,

(E) tremolite, or

(F) actinolite.

(4) Asbestos-containing material

The term "asbestos-containing material" means any material which contains more than 1 percent asbestos by weight.

(5) EPA guidance document

The term "Guidance for Controlling Asbestos-Containing Material in Buildings", means the Environmental Protection Agency document with such title as in effect on March 31, 1986.

(6) Friable asbestos-containing material

The term "friable asbestos-containing material" means any asbestos-containing material applied on ceilings, walls, structural members, piping, duct work, or any other part of a building which when dry may be crumbled, pulverized, or reduced to powder by hand pressure. The term includes non-friable asbestos-containing material after such previously non-friable material becomes damaged to the extent that when dry it may be crumbled, pulverized, or reduced to powder by hand pressure.

(7) Local educational agency

The term "local educational agency" means–

(A) any local educational agency as defined in section 7801 of title 20,

(B) the owner of any private, nonprofit elementary or secondary school building, and

(C) the governing authority of any school operated under the defense dependents' education system provided for under the

Defense Dependents' Education Act of 1978 (20 U.S.C. 921 et seq.).

(8) Most current guidance document

The term "most current guidance document" means the Environmental Protection Agency's "Guidance for Controlling Asbestos-Containing Material in Buildings" as modified by the Environmental Protection Agency after March 31, 1986.

(9) Non-profit elementary or secondary school

The term "non-profit elementary or secondary school" means any elementary or secondary school (as defined in section 7801 of title 20) owned and operated by one or more nonprofit corporations or associations no part of the net earnings of which inures, or may lawfully inure, to the benefit of any private shareholder or individual.

(10) Public and commercial building

The term "public and commercial building" means any building which is not a school building, except that the term does not include any residential apartment building of fewer than 10 units.

(11) Response action

The term "response action" means methods that protect human health and the environment from asbestos-containing material.

Such methods include methods described in chapters 3 and 5 of the Environmental Protection Agency's "Guidance for Controlling Asbestos-Containing Materials in Buildings".

(12) School

The term "school" means any elementary or secondary school as defined in section 7801 of title 20.

(13) School building

The term "school building" means–

(A) any structure suitable for use as a classroom, including a school facility such as a laboratory, library, school eating facility, or facility used for the preparation of food,

(B) any gymnasium or other facility which is specially designed for athletic or recreational activities for an academic course in physical education,

(C) any other facility used for the instruction of students or for the administration of educational or research programs, and

(D) any maintenance, storage, or utility facility, including any hallway, essential to the operation of any facility described in subparagraphs (A), (B), or (C).

(14) State

The term "State" means a State, the District of Columbia, the Commonwealth of Puerto Rico, Guam, American Samoa, the Northern Marianas, the Trust Territory of the Pacific Islands, and the Virgin Islands.

(TSCA § 203)

Sec. 2643. EPA regulations

(a) In general

Within 360 days after October 22, 1986, the Administrator shall promulgate regulations as described in subsections (b) through (i) of this section. With respect to regulations described in subsections (b), (c), (d), (e), (f), (g), and (i) of this section, the Administrator shall issue an advanced notice of proposed rulemaking within 60 days after October 22, 1986, and shall propose regulations within 180 days after October 22, 1986. Any regulation promulgated under this section must protect human health and the environment.

(b) Inspection

The Administrator shall promulgate regulations which prescribe procedures, including the use of personnel accredited under section 2646(b) or (c) of this title and laboratories accredited under section 2646(d) of this title, for determining whether asbestos-containing material is present in a school building under the authority of a local educational agency. The regulations shall provide for the exclusion of any school building, or portion of a school building, if (1) an inspection of such school building (or portion) was completed before the effective date of the regulations, and (2) the inspection meets the procedures and other requirements of the regulations under this subchapter or of the "Guidance for Controlling Asbestos-Containing Materials in Buildings" (unless the Administrator determines that an inspection in accordance with the guidance document is inadequate). The regulations shall require inspection of any school building (or portion of a school building) that is not excluded by the preceding sentence.

(c) Circumstances requiring response actions

(1) The Administrator shall promulgate regulations which define the appropriate response action in a school building under the authority of a local educational agency in at least the following circumstances:

(A) Damage

Circumstances in which friable asbestos-containing material or its covering is damaged, deteriorated, or delaminated.

(B) Significant damage

Circumstances in which friable asbestos-containing material or its covering is significantly damaged, deteriorated, or delaminated.

(C) Potential damage

Circumstances in which–

(i) friable asbestos-containing material is in an area regularly used by building occupants, including maintenance personnel, in the course of their normal activities, and

(ii) there is a reasonable likelihood that the material or its covering will become damaged, deteriorated, or delaminated.

(D) Potential significant damage

Circumstances in which–

(i) friable asbestos-containing material is in an area regularly used by building occupants, including maintenance personnel, in the course of their normal activities, and

(ii) there is a reasonable likelihood that the material or its covering will become significantly damaged, deteriorated, or delaminated.

(2) In promulgating such regulations, the Administrator shall consider and assess the value of various technologies intended to improve the decision-making process regarding response actions and the quality of any work that is deemed necessary, including air monitoring and chemical encapsulants.

(d) Response actions

(1) In general

The Administrator shall promulgate regulations describing a response action in a school building under the authority of a local educational agency, using the least burdensome methods which protect human health and the environment. In determining the least burdensome methods, the Administrator shall take into account local circumstances, including occupancy and use patterns within the school building and short-and long-term costs.

(2) Response action for damaged asbestos

In the case of a response action for the circumstances described in subsection (c)(1)(A) of this section, methods for responding shall include methods identified in chapters 3 and 5 of the "Guidance for Controlling Asbestos-Containing Material in Buildings".

(3) Response action for significantly damaged asbestos

In the case of a response action for the circumstances described in subsection (c)(1)(B) of this section, methods for responding shall include methods identified in chapter 5 of the "Guidance for Controlling Asbestos-Containing Material in Buildings".

(4) Response action for potentially damaged asbestos

In the case of a response action for the circumstances described in subsection (c)(1)(C) of this section, methods for responding shall include methods identified in chapters 3 and 5 of the "Guidance for Controlling Asbestos-Containing Material inBuildings", unless preventive measures will eliminate the reasonable likelihood that the asbestos-containing material will become damaged, deteriorated, or delaminated.

(5) Response action for potentially significantly damaged asbestos

In the case of a response action for the circumstances described in subsection (c)(1)(D) of this section, methods for responding shall include methods identified in chapter 5 of the "Guidance for Controlling Asbestos-Containing Material in Buildings", unless preventive measures will eliminate the reasonable likelihood that the asbestos-containing material will become significantly damaged, deteriorated, or delaminated.

(6) "Preventive measures" defined

For purposes of this section, the term "preventive measures" means actions which eliminate the reasonable likelihood of asbestos-containing material becoming damaged, deteriorated, or delaminated, or significantly damaged[11] deteriorated, or delaminated (as the case may be) or which protect human health and the environment.

(7) EPA information or advisory

The Administrator shall, not later than 30 days after November 28, 1990, publish and distribute to all local education agencies and State Governors information or an advisory to–

(A) facilitate public understanding of the comparative risks associated with in-place management of asbestos-containing building materials and removals;

(B) promote the least burdensome response actions necessary to protect human health, safety, and the environment; and

11. So in original. Probably should be followed by a comma.

(C) describe the circumstances in which asbestos removal is necessary to protect human health.

Such information or advisory shall be based on the best available scientific evidence and shall be revised, republished, and redistributed as appropriate, to reflect new scientific findings.

(e) Implementation

The Administrator shall promulgate regulations requiring the implementation of response actions in school buildings under the authority of a local educational agency and, where appropriate, for the determination of when a response action is completed. Such regulations shall include standards for the education and protection of both workers and building occupants for the following phases of activity:

(1) Inspection.

(2) Response Action.[12]

(3) Post-response action, including any periodic reinspection of asbestos-containing material and long-term surveillance activity.

(f) Operations and maintenance

The Administrator shall promulgate regulations to require implementation of an operations and maintenance and repair program as described in chapter 3 of the "Guidance for Controlling Asbestos-Containing Materials in Buildings" for all friable asbestos-containing material in a school building under the authority of a local educational agency.

(g) Periodic surveillance

The Administrator shall promulgate regulations to require the following:

(1) An identification of the location of friable and non-friable asbestos in a school building under the authority of a local educational agency.

(2) Provisions for surveillance and periodic reinspection of such friable and non-friable asbestos.

(3) Provisions for education of school employees, including school service and maintenance personnel, about the location of and safety procedures with respect to such friable and non-friable asbestos.

(h) Transportation and disposal

The Administrator shall promulgate regulations which prescribe standards for transportation and disposal of asbestos-containing waste material to protect human health and the environment. Such regulations shall include such provisions related to the manner in which transportation vehicles are loaded

---

12. So in original. Probably should not be capitalized.

and unloaded as will assure the physical integrity of containers of asbestos-containing waste material.

(i) Management plans

(1) In general

The Administrator shall promulgate regulations which require each local educational agency to develop an asbestos management plan for school buildings under its authority, to begin implementation of such plan within 990 days after October 22, 1986, and to complete implementation of such plan in a timely fashion. The regulations shall require that each plan include the following elements, wherever relevant to the school building:

(A) An inspection statement describing inspection and response action activities carried out before October 22, 1986.

(B) A description of the results of the inspection conducted pursuant to regulations under subsection (b) of this section, including a description of the specific areas inspected.

(C) A detailed description of measures to be taken to respond to any friable asbestos-containing material pursuant to the regulations promulgated under subsections (c), (d), and (e) of this section, including the location or locations at which a response action will be taken, the method or methods of response action to be used, and a schedule for beginning and completing response actions.

(D) A detailed description of any asbestos-containing material which remains in the school building once response actions are undertaken pursuant to the regulations promulgated under subsections (c), (d), and (e) of this section.

(E) A plan for periodic reinspection and long-term surveillance activities developed pursuant to regulations promulgated under subsection (g) of this section, and a plan for operations and maintenance activities developed pursuant to regulations promulgated under subsection (f) of this section.

(F) With respect to the person or persons who inspected for asbestos-containing material and who will design or carry out response actions with respect to the friable asbestos-containing material, one of the following statements:

(i) If the State has adopted a contractor accreditation plan under section 2646(b) of this title, a statement that the person (or persons) is accredited under such plan.

(ii) A statement that the local educational agency used (or will use) persons who have been accredited by another State which has adopted a contractor accreditation plan under section 2646(b) of this title or is accredited pursuant to an Administrator-approved course under section 2646(c) of this title.

(G) A list of the laboratories that analyzed any bulk samples of asbestos-containing material found in the school building or air samples taken to detect asbestos in the school building and a statement that each laboratory has been accredited pursuant to the accreditation program under section 2646(d) of this title.

(H) With respect to each consultant who contributed to the management plan, the name of the consultant and one of the following statements:

(i) If the State has adopted a contractor accreditation plan under section 2646(b) of this title, a statement that the consultant is accredited under such plan.

(ii) A statement that the contractor is accredited by another State which has adopted a contractor accreditation plan under section 2646(b) of this title or is accredited pursuant to an Administrator-approved course under section 2646(c) of this title.

(I) An evaluation of resources needed to successfully complete response actions and carry out reinspection, surveillance, and operation and maintenance activities.

(2) Statement by contractor

A local educational agency may require each management plan to contain a statement signed by an accredited asbestos contractor that such contractor has prepared or assisted in the preparation of such plan, or has reviewed such plan, and that such plan is in compliance with the applicable regulations and standards promulgated or adopted pursuant to this section and other applicable provisions of law. Such a statement may not be signed by a contractor who, in addition to preparing or assisting in preparing the management plan, also implements (or will implement) the management plan.

(3) Warning labels

(A) The regulations shall require that each local educational agency which has inspected for and discovered any asbestos-containing material with respect to a school building shall attach a warning label to any asbestos-containing material still in routine maintenance areas (such as boiler rooms) of the school building, including–

(i) friable asbestos-containing material which was responded to by a means other than removal, and

(ii) asbestos-containing material for which no response action was carried out.

(B) The warning label shall read, in print which is readily visible because of large size or bright color, as follows:

"CAUTION: ASBESTOS. HAZARDOUS. DO NOT DISTURB WITHOUT PROPER TRAINING AND EQUIPMENT."

(4) Plan may be submitted in stages

A local educational agency may submit a management plan in stages, with each submission of the agency covering only a portion of the school buildings under the agency's authority, if the agency determines that such action would expedite the identification and abatement of hazardous asbestos-containing material in the school buildings under the authority of the agency.

(5) Public availability

A copy of the management plan developed under the regulations shall be available in the administrative offices of the local educational agency for inspection by the public, including teachers, other school personnel, and parents. The local educational agency shall notify parent, teacher, and employee organizations of the availability of such plan.

(6) Submission to State Governor

Each plan developed under this subsection shall be submitted to the State Governor under section 2645 of this title.

(j) Changes in regulations

Changes may be made in the regulations promulgated under this section only by rule in accordance with section 553 of title 5. Any such change must protect human health and the environment.

(k) Changes in guidance document

Any change made in the "Guidance for Controlling Asbestos-Containing Material in Buildings" shall be made only by rule in accordance with section 553 of title 5, unless a regulation described in this section dealing with the same subject matter is in effect. Any such change must protect human health and the environment.

(l) Treatment of Department of Defense schools

(1) Secretary to act in lieu of Governor

In the administration of this subchapter, any function, duty, or other responsibility imposed on a Governor of a State shall be carried out by the Secretary of Defense with respect to any school operated under the defense dependents' education system provided for under the Defense Dependents' Education Act of 1978 (20 U.S.C. 921 et seq.).

(2) Regulations

The Secretary of Defense, in cooperation with the Administrator, shall, to the extent feasible and consistent with the national security, take such action as may be necessary to provide for the identification, inspection, and management (including abatement) of asbestos in any building used by the Department of Defense as an overseas school for dependents of members of the Armed Forces. Such identification, inspection, and management (including abatement) shall, subject to the preceding sentence, be carried out in a manner comparable to the manner in which a local educational agency is required to carry out such activities with respect to a school building under this subchapter.

(m) Waiver

The Administrator, upon request by a Governor and after notice and comment and opportunity for a public hearing in the affected State, may waive some or all of the requirements of this section and section 2644 of this title with respect to such State if it has established and is implementing a program of asbestos inspection and management that contains requirements that are at least as stringent as the requirements of this section and section 2644 of this title.

(TSCA § 204)

Sec. 2644. Requirements if EPA fails to promulgate regulations

(a) In general

(1) Failure to promulgate

If the Administrator fails to promulgate within the prescribed period–

(A) regulations described in section 2643(b) of this title (relating to inspection);

(B) regulations described in section 2643(c), (d), (e), (f), (g), and (i) of this title (relating to responding to asbestos); or

(C) regulations described in section 2643(h) of this title (relating to transportation and disposal); each local educational agency shall carry out the requirements described in this section in subsection (b); subsections (c), (d), and (e); or subsection (f); respectively, in accordance with the Environmental Protection Agency's most current guidance document.

(2) Stay by court

If the Administrator has promulgated regulations described in paragraph (1)(A), (B), or (C) within the prescribed period, but the effective date of such regulations has been stayed by a court for a period of more than 30 days, a local educational agency shall carry out the pertinent requirements described in this subsection in accordance with the Environmental Protection Agency's most current guidance document.

(3) Effective period

The requirements of this section shall be in effect until such time as the Administrator promulgates the pertinent regulations or until the stay is lifted (as the case may be).

(b) Inspection

(1) Except as provided in paragraph (2), the local educational agency, within 540 days after October 22, 1986, shall conduct an inspection for asbestos-containing material, using personnel accredited under section 2646(b) or (c) of this title and laboratories accredited under section 2646(d) of this title, in each school building under its authority.

(2) The local educational agency may exclude from the inspection requirement in paragraph (1) any school building, or portion of a school building, if (A) an inspection of such school building (or portion) was completed before the date on which this section goes into effect, and (B) the inspection meets the inspection requirements of this section.

(c) Operation and maintenance

The local educational agency shall, within 720 days after October 22, 1986, develop and begin implementation of an operation and maintenance plan with respect to friable asbestos-containing material in a school building under its authority. Such plan shall provide for the education of school service and maintenance personnel about safety procedures with respect to asbestos-containing material, including friable asbestos-containing material.

(d) Management plan

(1) In general

The local educational agency shall–

(A) develop a management plan for responding to asbestos-containing material in each school building under its authority and submit such plan to the Governor under section 2645 of this title within 810 days after October 22, 1986,

(B) begin implementation of such plan within 990 days after October 22, 1986, and

(C) complete implementation of such plan in a timely fashion.

(2) Plan requirements

The management plan shall–

(A) include the elements listed in section 2643(i)(1) of this title, including an inspection statement as described in paragraph (3) of this section[13],

---

13. So in original. Probably should be "subsection,".

(B) provide for the attachment of warning labels as described in section 2643(i)(3) of this title,

(C) be prepared in accordance with the most current guidance document,

(D) meet the standard described in paragraph (4) for actions described in that paragraph, and

(E) be submitted to the State Governor under section 2645 of this title.

(3) Inspection statement

The local educational agency shall complete an inspection statement, covering activities carried out before October 22, 1986, which meets the following requirements:

(A) The statement shall include the following information:

(i) The dates of inspection.

(ii) The name, address, and qualifications of each inspector.

(iii) A description of the specific areas inspected.

(iv) A list of the laboratories that analyzed any bulk samples of asbestos-containing material or air samples of asbestos found in any school building and a statement describing the qualifications of each laboratory.

(v) The results of the inspection.

(B) The statement shall state whether any actions were taken with respect to any asbestos-containing material found to be present, including a specific reference to whether any actions were taken in the boiler room of the building. If any such action was taken, the following items of information shall be included in the statement:

(i) The location or locations at which the action was taken.

(ii) A description of the method of action.

(iii) The qualifications of the persons who conducted the action.

(4) Standard

The ambient interior concentration of asbestos after the completion of actions described in the most current guidance document, other than the type of action described in sections 2643(f) of this title and subsection (c) of this section, shall not exceed the ambient exterior concentration, discounting any contribution from any local stationary source. Either a scanning electron microscope or a transmission electron microscope shall be used to determine the ambient interior concentration. In the absence of reliable measurements, the ambient exterior concentration shall be deemed to be–

(A) less than 0.003 fibers per cubic centimeter if a scanning electron microscope is used, and

(B) less than 0.005 fibers per cubic centimeter if a transmission electron microscope is used.

(5) Public availability

A copy of the management plan shall be available in the administrative offices of the local educational agency for inspection by the public, including teachers, other school personnel, and parents. The local educational agency shall notify parent, teacher, and employee organizations of the availability of such plan.

(e) Building occupant protection

The local educational agency shall provide for the protection of building occupants during each phase of activity described in this section.

(f) Transportation and disposal

The local educational agency shall provide for the transportation and disposal of asbestos in accordance with the most recent version of the Environmental Protection Agency's "Asbestos Waste Management Guidance" (or any successor to such document).

(TSCA § 205)

Sec. 2645. Submission to State Governor

(a) Submission

Within 720 days after October 22, 1986 (or within 810 days if there are no regulations under section 2643(i) of this title), a local educational agency shall submit a management plan developed pursuant to regulations promulgated under section 2643(i) of this title (or under section 2644(d) of this title if there are no regulations) to the Governor of the State in which the local educational agency is located.

(b) Governor requirements

Within 360 days after October 22, 1986, the Governor of each State–

(1) shall notify local educational agencies in the State of where to submit their management plans under this section, and

(2) may establish administrative procedures for reviewing management plans submitted under this section.

If the Governor establishes procedures under paragraph (2), the Governor shall designate to carry out the reviews those State officials who are responsible for implementing environmental protection or other public health programs, or with authority over asbestos programs, in the State.

(c) Management plan review

(1) Review of plan

The Governor may disapprove a management plan within 90 days after the date of receipt of the plan if the plan–

(A) does not conform with the regulations under section 2643(i) of this title (or with section 2644(d) of this title if there are no regulations),

(B) does not assure that contractors who are accredited pursuant to this subchapter will be used to carry out the plan, or

(C) does not contain a response action schedule which is reasonable and timely, taking into account circumstances relevant to the speed at which the friable asbestos-containing material in the school buildings under the local educational agency's authority should be responded to, including human exposure to the asbestos while the friable asbestos-containing material remains in the school building, and the ability of the local educational agency to continue to provide educational services to the community.

(2) Revision of plan

If the State Governor disapproves a plan, the State Governor shall explain in writing to the local educational agency the reasons why the plan was disapproved and the changes that need to be made in the plan. Within 30 days after the date on which notice is received of disapproval of its plan, the local educational agency shall revise the plan to conform with the State Governor's suggested changes. The Governor may extend the 30-day period for not more than 90 days.

(d) Deferral of submission

(1) Request for deferral

A local educational agency may request a deferral, to May 9, 1989, of the deadline under subsection (a) of this section. Upon approval of such a request, the deadline under subsection (a) of this section is deferred until May 9, 1989, for the local educational agency which submitted the request. Such a request may cover one or more schools under the authority of the agency and shall include a list of all the schools covered by the request. A local educational agency shall file any such request with the State Governor by October 12, 1988, and shall include with the request either of the following statements:

(A) A statement–

(i) that the State in which the agency is located has requested from the Administrator, before June 1, 1988, a waiver under section 2643(m) of this title; and

(ii) that gives assurance that the local educational agency has carried out the notification and, in the case of a public school, public meeting required by paragraph (2).

(B) A statement, the accuracy of which is sworn to by a responsible official of the agency (by notarization or other means of certification), that includes the following with respect to each school for which a deferral is sought in the request:

(i) A statement that, in spite of the fact that the local educational agency has made a good faith effort to meet the deadline for submission of a management plan under subsection (a) of this section, the agency will not be able to meet the deadline. The statement shall include a brief explanation of the reasons why the deadline cannot be met.

(ii) A statement giving assurance that the local educational agency has made available for inspection by the public, at each school for which a deferral is sought in the request, at least one of the following documents:

(I) A solicitation by the local educational agency to contract with an accredited asbestos contractor for inspection or management plan development.

(II) A letter attesting to the enrollment of school district personnel in an Environmental Protection Agency-accredited training course for inspection and management plan development.

(III) Documentation showing that an analysis of suspected asbestos-containing material from the school is pending at an accredited laboratory.

(IV) Documentation showing that an inspection or management plan has been completed in at least one other school under the local educational agency's authority.

(iii) A statement giving assurance that the local educational agency has carried out the notification and, in the case of a public school, public meeting required by paragraph (2).

(iv) A proposed schedule outlining all significant activities leading up to submission of a management plan by May 9, 1989, including inspection of the school (if not completed at the time of the request) with a deadline of no later than December 22, 1988, for entering into a signed contract with an accredited asbestos contractor for inspection (unless such inspections are to be performed by school personnel), laboratory analysis of material from the school suspected of containing asbestos, and development of the management plan.

(2) Notification and public meeting

Before filing a deferral request under paragraph (1), a local educational agency shall notify affected parent, teacher, and employee organizations of its intent to file such a request. In the case of a deferral request for a public school, the local educational agency shall discuss the request at a public meeting of the school board with jurisdiction over the school, and affected parent, teacher, and employee organizations shall be notified in advance of the time and place of such meeting.

(3) Response by Governor

(A) Not later than 30 days after the date on which a Governor receives a deferral request under paragraph (1) from a local educational agency, the Governor shall respond to the local educational agency in writing by acknowledging whether the request is complete or incomplete. If the request is incomplete, the Governor shall identify in the response the items that are missing from the request.

(B) A local educational agency may correct any deficiencies in an incomplete deferral request and refile the request with the Governor. In any case in which the local educational agency decides to refile the request, the agency shall refile the request, and the Governor shall respond to such refiled request in the manner described in subparagraph (A), no later than 15 days after the local educational agency has received a response from the Governor under subparagraph (A).

(C) Approval of a deferral request under this subsection occurs only upon the receipt by a local educational agency of a written acknowledgment from the Governor that the agency's deferral request is complete.

(4) Submission and review of plan

A local educational agency whose deferral request is approved shall submit a management plan to the Governor not later than May 9, 1989. Such management plan shall include a copy of the deferral request and the statement accompanying such request.

Such management plan shall be reviewed in accordance with subsection (c) of this section, except that the Governor may extend the 30-day period for revision of the plan under subsection (c)(2) of this section for only an additional 30 days (for a total of 60 days).

(5) Implementation of plan

The approval of a deferral request from a local educational agency shall not be considered to be a waiver or exemption from the requirement under section 2643(i) of this title for the local educational agency to begin implementation of its management plan by July 9, 1989.

(6) EPA notice

(A) Not later than 15 days after July 18, 1988, the Administrator shall publish in the Federal Register the following:

(i) A notice describing the opportunity to file a request for deferral under this subsection.

(ii) A list of the State offices (including officials (if available) in each State as designated under subsection (b) of this section) with which deferral requests should be filed.

(B) As soon as practicable, but in no event later than 30 days, after July 18, 1988, the Administrator shall mail a notice describing the opportunity to file a request for deferral under this subsection to each local educational agency and to each State office in the list published under subparagraph (A).

(e) Status reports

(1) Not later than December 31, 1988, the Governor of each State shall submit to the Administrator a written statement on the status of management plan submissions and deferral requests by local educational agencies in the State. The statement shall be made available to local educational agencies in the State and shall contain the following:

(A) A list containing each local educational agency that submitted a management plan by October 12, 1988.

(B) A list containing each local educational agency whose deferral request was approved.

(C) A list containing each local educational agency that failed to submit a management plan by October 12, 1988, and whose deferral request was disapproved.

(D) A list containing each local educational agency that failed to submit a management plan by October 12, 1988, and did not submit a deferral request.

(2) Not later than December 31, 1989, the Governor of each State shall submit to the Administrator an updated version of the written statement submitted under paragraph (1). The statement shall be made available to local educational agencies in the State and shall contain the following:

(A) A list containing each local educational agency whose management plan was submitted and not disapproved as of October 9, 1989.

(B) A list containing each local educational agency whose management plan was submitted and disapproved, and which remains disapproved, as of October 9, 1989.

(C) A list containing each local educational agency that submitted a management plan after May 9, 1989, and before October 10, 1989.

(D) A list containing each local educational agency that failed to submit a management plan as of October 9, 1989.

(TSCA § 206)

Sec. 2646. Contractor and laboratory accreditation

(a) Contractor accreditation

A person may not–

(1) inspect for asbestos-containing material in a school building under the authority of a local educational agency or in a public or commercial building,

(2) prepare a management plan for such a school, or

(3) design or conduct response actions, other than the type of action described in sections 2643(f) and 2644(c) of this title, with respect to friable asbestos-containing material in such a school or in a public or commercial building, unless such person is accredited by a State under subsection (b) of this section or is accredited pursuant to an Administrator-approved course under subsection (c) of this section.

(b) Accreditation by State

(1) Model plan

(A) Persons to be accredited

Within 180 days after October 22, 1986, the Administrator, in consultation with affected organizations, shall develop a model contractor accreditation plan for States to give accreditation to persons in the following categories:

(i) Persons who inspect for asbestos-containing material in school buildings under the authority of a local educational agency or in public or commercial buildings.

(ii) Persons who prepare management plans for such schools.

(iii) Persons who design or carry out response actions, other than the type of action described in sections 2643(f) and 2644(c) of this title, with respect to friable asbestos-containing material in such schools or in public or commercial buildings.

(B) Plan requirements

The plan shall include a requirement that any person in a category listed in paragraph (1) achieve a passing grade on an examination and participate in continuing education to stay informed about current asbestos inspection and response action technology. The examination shall demonstrate the knowledge of the person in areas that the Administrator prescribes as necessary and appropriate in each of the categories. Such examinations may include requirements for knowledge in the following areas:

(i) Recognition of asbestos-containing material and its physical characteristics.

(ii) Health hazards of asbestos and the relationship between asbestos exposure and disease.

(iii) Assessing the risk of asbestos exposure through a knowledge of percentage weight of asbestos-containing material, friability, age, deterioration, location and accessibility of materials, and advantages and disadvantages of dry and wet response action methods.

(iv) Respirators and their use, care, selection, degree of protection afforded, fitting, testing, and maintenance and cleaning procedures.

(v) Appropriate work practices and control methods, including the use of high efficiency particle absolute vacuums, the use of amended water, and principles of negative air pressure equipment use and procedures.

(vi) Preparing a work area for response action work, including isolating work areas to prevent bystander or public exposure to asbestos, decontamination procedures, and procedures for dismantling work areas after completion of work.

(vii) Establishing emergency procedures to respond to sudden releases.

(viii) Air monitoring requirements and procedures.

(ix) Medical surveillance program requirements.

(x) Proper asbestos waste transportation and disposal procedures.

(xi) Housekeeping and personal hygiene practices, including the necessity of showers, and procedures to prevent asbestos exposure to an employee's family.

(2) State adoption of plan

Each State shall adopt a contractor accreditation plan at least as stringent as the model plan developed by the Administrator under paragraph (1), within 180 days after the commencement of the first regular session of the legislature of such State which is convened following the date on which the Administrator completes development of the model plan. In the case of a school operated under the defense dependents' education system provided for under the Defense Dependents' Education Act of 1978 (20 U.S.C. 921 et seq.), the Secretary of Defense shall adopt a contractor accreditation plan at least as stringent as that model.

(c) Accreditation by Administrator-approved course

(1) Course approval

Within 180 days after October 22, 1986, the Administrator shall ensure that any Environmental Protection Agency-approved asbestos training course is consistent with the model plan (including testing requirements) developed under subsection (b) of this section. A contractor may be accredited by taking and passing such a course.

(2) Treatment of persons with previous EPA asbestos training

A person who–

(A) completed an Environmental Protection Agency-approved asbestos training course before October 22, 1986, and

(B) passed (or passes) an asbestos test either before or after October 22, 1986, may be accredited under paragraph (1) if the Administrator determines that the course and test are equivalent to the requirements of the model plan developed under subsection (b) of this section. If the Administrator so determines, the person shall be considered accredited for the purposes of this subchapter until a date that is one year after the date on which the State in which such person is employed establishes an accreditation program pursuant to subsection (b) of this section.

(3) Lists of courses

The Administrator, in consultation with affected organizations, shall publish (and revise as necessary)–

(A) a list of asbestos courses and tests in effect before October 22, 1986, which qualify for equivalency treatment under paragraph (2), and

(B) a list of asbestos courses and tests which the Administrator determines under paragraph (1) are consistent with the model plan and which will qualify a contractor for accreditation under such paragraph.

(d) Laboratory accreditation

(1) The Administrator shall provide for the development of an accreditation program for laboratories by the National Institute of Standards and Technology in accordance with paragraph (2). The Administrator shall transfer such funds as are necessary to the National Institute of Standards and Technology to carry out such program.

(2) The National Institute of Standards and Technology, upon request by the Administrator, shall, in consultation with affected organizations–

(A) within 360 days after October 22, 1986, develop an accreditation program for laboratories which conduct qualitative and semi-quantitative analyses of bulk samples of asbestos-containing material, and

(B) within 720 days after October 22, 1986, develop an accreditation program for laboratories which conduct analyses of air samples of asbestos from school buildings under the authority of a local educational agency.

(3) A laboratory which plans to carry out any such analysis shall comply with the requirements of the accreditation program.

(e) Financial assistance contingent on use of accredited persons

(1) A school which is an applicant for financial assistance under section 505 of the Asbestos School Hazard Abatement Act of 1984 [20 U.S.C. 4014] is not eligible for such assistance unless the school, in carrying out the requirements of this subchapter–

(A) uses a person (or persons)–

(i) who is accredited by a State which has adopted an accreditation plan based on the model plan developed under subsection (b) of this section, or

(ii) who is accredited pursuant to an Administrator-approved course under subsection (c) of this section, and

(B) uses a laboratory (or laboratories) which is accredited under the program developed under subsection (d) of this section.

(2) This subsection shall apply to any financial assistance provided under the Asbestos School Hazard Abatement Act of 1984 [20 U.S.C. 4011 et seq.] for activities performed after the following dates:

(A) In the case of activities performed by persons, after the date which is one year after October 22, 1986.

(B) In the case of activities performed by laboratories, after the date which is 180 days after the date on which a laboratory accreditation program is completed under subsection (d) of this section.

(f) List of EPA-approved courses

Not later than August 31, 1988, and every three months thereafter until August 31, 1991, the Administrator shall publish in the Federal Register a list of all Environmental Protection Agency-approved asbestos training courses for persons to achieve accreditation in each category described in subsection (b)(1)(A) of this section and for laboratories to achieve accreditation. The Administrator may continue publishing such a list after August 31, 1991, at such times as the Administrator considers it useful. The list shall include the name and address of each approved trainer and, to the extent available, a list of all the geographic sites where training courses will take place. The Administrator shall provide a copy of the list to each State official on the list published by the Administrator under section 2645(d)(6) of this title and to each regional office of the Environmental Protection Agency.

(TSCA § 207)

Sec. 2647. Enforcement

(a) Penalties

Any local educational agency–

(1) which fails to conduct an inspection pursuant to regulations under section 2643(b) of this title or under section 2644(b) of this title,

(2) which knowingly submits false information to the Governor regarding any inspection pursuant to regulations under section 2643(i) of this title or knowingly includes false information in any inspection statement under section 2644(d)(3) of this title,

(3) which fails to develop a management plan pursuant to regulations under section 2643(i) of this title or under section 2644(d) of this title,

(4) which carries out any activity prohibited by section 2655 of this title, or

(5) which knowingly submits false information to the Governor regarding a deferral request under section 2645(d) of this title.[14]

is liable for a civil penalty of not more than $5,000 for each day during which the violation continues. Any civil penalty under this subsection shall be assessed and collected in the same manner, and subject to the same provisions, as in the case of civil penalties assessed and collected under section 2615 of this title. For purposes of this subsection, a "violation" means a failure to comply with respect to a single school building. The court shall order that any civil penalty collected under this subsection be used by the local educational agency for purposes of complying with this subchapter. Any portion of a civil penalty remaining unspent after compliance by a local educational agency is completed shall be deposited into the Asbestos Trust Fund established by section 4022 of title 20.

(b) Relationship to subchapter I of this chapter

A local educational agency is not liable for any civil penalty under subchapter I of this chapter for failing or refusing to comply with any rule promulgated or order issued under this subchapter.

(c) Enforcement considerations

(1) In determining the amount of a civil penalty to be assessed under subsection (a) of this section against a local educational agency, the Administrator shall consider–

(A) the significance of the violation;

---

14 So in original. The period probably should be a comma.

(B) the culpability of the violator, including any history of previous violations under this chapter;

(C) the ability of the violator to pay the penalty; and

(D) the ability of the violator to continue to provide educational services to the community.

(2) Any action ordered by a court in fashioning relief under section 2619 of this title shall be consistent with regulations promulgated under section 2643 of this title (or with the requirements of section 2644 of this title if there are no regulations).

(d) Citizen complaints

Any person may file a complaint with the Administrator or with the Governor of the State in which the school building is located with respect to asbestos-containing material in a school building.

If the Administrator or Governor receives a complaint under this subsection containing allegations which provide a reasonable basis to believe that a violation of this chapter has occurred, the Administrator or Governor shall investigate and respond (including taking enforcement action where appropriate) to the complaint within a reasonable period of time.

(e) Citizen petitions

(1) Any person may petition the Administrator to initiate a proceeding for the issuance, amendment, or repeal of a regulation or order under this subchapter.

(2) Such petition shall be filed in the principal office of the Administrator and shall set forth the facts which it is claimed establish that it is necessary to issue, amend, or repeal a regulation or order under this subchapter.

(3) The Administrator may hold a public hearing or may conduct such investigation or proceeding as the Administrator deems appropriate in order to determine whether or not such petition should be granted.

(4) Within 90 days after filing of a petition described in paragraph (1), the Administrator shall either grant or deny the petition. If the Administrator grants such petition, the

Administrator shall promptly commence an appropriate proceeding in accordance with this subchapter. If the Administrator denies such petition, the Administrator shall publish in the Federal Register the Administrator's reasons for such denial. The granting or denial of a petition under this subsection shall not affect any deadline or other requirement of this subchapter.

(f) Citizen civil actions with respect to EPA regulations

(1) Any person may commence a civil action without prior notice against the Administrator to compel the Administrator to meet the deadlines in

section 2643 of this title for issuing advanced notices of proposed rule-making, proposing regulations, and promulgating regulations. Any such action shall be brought in the district court of the United States for the District of Columbia.

(2) In any action brought under paragraph (1) in which the court finds the Administrator to be in violation of any deadline in section 2643 of this title, the court shall set forth a schedule for promulgating the regulations required by section 2643 of this title and shall order the Administrator to comply with such schedule. The court may extend any deadline (which has not already occurred) in section 2644(b), (c), or (d) of this title for a period of not more than 6 months, if the court-ordered schedule will result in final promulgation of the pertinent regulations within the extended period. Such deadline extensions may not be granted by the court beginning 720 days after October 22, 1986.

(3) Section 2619 of this title shall apply to civil actions described in this subsection, except to the extent inconsistent with this subsection.

(g) Failure to attain accreditation; penalty

Any contractor who–

(1) inspects for asbestos-containing material in a school, public or commercial building;

(2) designs or conducts response actions with respect to friable asbestos-containing material in a school, public or commercial building; or

(3) employs individuals to conduct response actions with respect to friable asbestos-containing material in a school, public or commercial building; and who fails to obtain the accreditation under section 2646 of this title, or in the case of employees to require or provide for the accreditation required, is liable for a civil penalty of not more than $5,000 for each day during which the violation continues, unless such contractor is a direct employee of the Federal Government.

(TSCA § 208)

Sec. 2648. Emergency authority

(a) Emergency action

(1) Authority

Whenever–

(A) the presence of airborne asbestos or the condition of friable asbestos-containing material in a school building governed by a local educational agency poses an imminent and substantial endangerment to human health or the environment, and

(B) the local educational agency is not taking sufficient action (as determined by the Administrator or the Governor) to respond to the airborne asbestos or friable asbestos-containing material, the Administrator or the Governor of a State is authorized to act to protect human health or the environment.

(2) Limitations on Governor's action

The Governor of a State shall notify the Administrator within a reasonable period of time before the Governor plans to take an emergency action under this subsection. After such notification, if the Administrator takes an emergency action with respect to the same hazard, the Governor may not carry out (or continue to carry out, if the action has been started) the emergency action.

(3) Notification

The following notification shall be provided before an emergency action is taken under this subsection:

(A) In the case of a Governor taking the action, the Governor shall notify the local educational agency concerned.

(B) In the case of the Administrator taking the action, the Administrator shall notify both the local educational agency concerned and the Governor of the State in which such agency is located.

(4) Cost recovery

The Administrator or the Governor of a State may seek reimbursement for all costs of an emergency action taken under this subsection in the United States District Court for the District of Columbia or for the district in which the emergency action occurred. In any action seeking reimbursement from a local educational agency, the action shall be brought in the United States District Court for the district in which the local educational agency is located.

(b) Injunctive relief

Upon receipt of evidence that the presence of airborne asbestos or the condition of friable asbestos-containing material in a school building governed by a local educational agency poses an imminent and substantial endangerment to human health or the environment–

(1) the Administrator may request the Attorney General to bring suit, or

(2) the Governor of a State may bring suit,to secure such relief as may be necessary to respond to the hazard.

The district court of the United States in the district in which the response will be carried out shall have jurisdiction to grant such relief, including injunctive relief.

(TSCA § 209)

Sec. 2649. State and Federal law

(a) No preemption

Nothing in this subchapter shall be construed, interpreted, or applied to preempt, displace, or supplant any other State or Federal law, whether statutory or common.

(b) Cost and damage awards

Nothing in this subchapter or any standard, regulation, or requirement promulgated pursuant to this subchapter shall be construed or interpreted to preclude any court from awarding costs and damages associated with the abatement, including the removal, of asbestos-containing material, or a portion of such costs, at any time prior to the actual date on which such material is removed.

(c) State may establish more requirements

Nothing in this subchapter shall be construed or interpreted as preempting a State from establishing any additional liability or more stringent requirements with respect to asbestos in school buildings within such State.

(d) No Federal cause of action

Nothing in this subchapter creates a cause of action or in any other way increases or diminishes the liability of any person under any other law.

(e) Intent of Congress

It is not the intent of Congress that this subchapter or rules, regulations, or orders issued pursuant to this subchapter be interpreted as influencing, in either the plaintiff's or defendant's favor, the disposition of any civil action for damages relating to asbestos. This subsection does not affect the authority of any court to make a determination in an adjudicatory proceeding under applicable State law with respect to the admission into evidence or any other use of this subchapter or rules, regulations, or orders issued pursuant to this subchapter.

(TSCA § 210)

Sec. 2650. Asbestos contractors and local educational agencies

(a) Study

(1) General requirement

The Administrator shall conduct a study on the availability of liability insurance and other forms of assurance against financial loss which are available to local educational agencies and asbestos contractors with respect to actions required under this subchapter. Such study shall examine the following:

(A) The extent to which liability insurance and other forms of assurance against financial loss are available to local educational agencies and asbestos contractors.

(B) The extent to which the cost of insurance or other forms of assurance against financial loss has increased and the extent to which coverage has become less complete.

(C) The extent to which any limitation in the availability of insurance or other forms of assurance against financial loss is the result of factors other than standards of liability in applicable law.

(D) The extent to which the existence of the regulations required by subsections (c) and (d) of section 2643 of this title and the accreditation of contractors under section 2646 of this title has affected the availability or cost of insurance or other forms of assurance against financial loss.

(E) The extent to which any limitation on the availability of insurance or other forms of assurance against financial loss is inhibiting inspections for asbestos-containing material or the development or implementation of management plans under this subchapter.

(F) Identification of any other impediments to the timely completion of inspections or the development and implementation of management plans under this subchapter.

(2) Interim report

Not later than April 1, 1988, the Administrator shall submit to the Congress an interim report on the progress of the study required by this subsection, along with preliminary findings based on information collected to that date.

(3) Final report

Not later than October 1, 1990, the Administrator shall submit to the Congress a final report on the study required by this subsection, including final findings based on the information collected.

(b) State action

On the basis of the interim report or the final report of the study required by subsection (a) of this section, a State may enact or amend State law to establish or modify a standard of liability for local educational agencies or asbestos contractors with respect to actions required under this subchapter.

(TSCA § 211)

Sec. 2651. Public protection

(a) Public protection

No State or local educational agency may discriminate against a person in any way, including firing a person who is an employee, because the person provided information relating to a potential violation of this subchapter to any other person, including a State or the Federal Government.

(b) Labor Department review

Any public or private employee or representative of employees who believes he or she has been fired or otherwise discriminated against in violation of subsection (a) of this section may within 90 days after the alleged violation occurs apply to the Secretary of Labor for a review of the firing or alleged discrimination. The review shall be conducted in accordance with section 660(c) of title 29.

(TSCA § 212)

Sec. 2652. Asbestos Ombudsman

(a) Appointment

The Administrator shall appoint an Asbestos Ombudsman, who shall carry out the duties described in subsection (b) of this section.

(b) Duties

The duties of the Asbestos Ombudsman are–

(1) to receive complaints, grievances, and requests for information submitted by any person with respect to any aspect of this subchapter,

(2) to render assistance with respect to the complaints, grievances, and requests received, and

(3) to make such recommendations to the Administrator as the Ombudsman considers appropriate.

(TSCA § 213)

Sec. 2653. EPA study of asbestos-containing material in public buildings

Within 360 days after October 22, 1986, the Administrator shall conduct and submit to the Congress the results of a study which shall–

(1) assess the extent to which asbestos-containing materials are present in public and commercial buildings;

(2) assess the condition of asbestos-containing material in commercial buildings and the likelihood that persons occupying such buildings, including service and maintenance personnel, are, or may be, exposed to asbestos fibers;

(3) consider and report on whether public and commercial buildings should be subject to the same inspection and response action requirements that apply to school buildings;

(4) assess whether existing Federal regulations adequately protect the general public, particularly abatement personnel, from exposure to asbestos during renovation and demolition of such buildings; and

(5) include recommendations that explicitly address whether there is a need to establish standards for, and regulate asbestos exposure in, public and commercial buildings.

(TSCA § 214)

Sec. 2654. Transitional rules

Any regulation of the Environmental Protection Agency under subchapter I of this chapter which is inconsistent with this subchapter shall not be in effect after October 22, 1986. Any advanced notice of proposed rulemaking, any proposed rule, and any regulation of the Environmental Protection Agency in effect before October 22, 1986, which is consistent with the regulations required under section 2643 of this title shall remain in effect and may be used to meet the requirements of section 2643 of this title, except that any such regulation shall be enforced under this chapter.

(TSCA § 215)

Sec. 2655. Worker protection

(a) Prohibition on certain activities

Until the local educational agency with authority over a school has submitted a management plan (for the school) which the State Governor has not disapproved as of the end of the period for review and revision of the plan under section 2645 of this title, the local educational agency may not do either of the following in the school:

(1) Perform, or direct an employee to perform, renovations or removal of building materials, except emergency repairs, in the school, unless–

(A) the school is carrying out work under a grant awarded under section 4014 of title 20; or

(B) an inspection that complies with the requirements of regulations promulgated under section 2643 of this title has been carried out in the school and the agency complies with the following sections of title 40 of the Code of Federal Regulations:

(i) Paragraphs (g), (h), and (i) of section 763.90 (response actions).

(ii) Appendix D to subpart E of part 763 (transport and disposal of asbestos waste).

(2) Perform, or direct an employee to perform, operations and maintenance activities in the school, unless the agency complies with the following sections of title 40 of the Code of Federal Regulations:

(A) Section 763.91 (operations and maintenance), including appendix B to subpart E of part 763.

(B) Paragraph (a)(2) of section 763.92 (training and periodic surveillance).

(b) Employee training and equipment

Any school employee who is directed to conduct emergency repairs involving any building material containing asbestos or suspected of containing asbestos, or to conduct operations and maintenance activities, in a school–

(1) shall be provided the proper training to safely conduct such work in order to prevent potential exposure to asbestos; and

(2) shall be provided the proper equipment and allowed to follow work practices that are necessary to safely conduct such work in order to prevent potential exposure to asbestos.

(c) "Emergency repair" defined

For purposes of this section, the term "emergency repair" means a repair in a school building that was not planned and was in response to a sudden, unexpected event that threatens either–

(1) the health or safety of building occupants; or

(2) the structural integrity of the building.

(TSCA § 216)

Sec. 2656. Training grants

(a) Grants

The Administrator is authorized to award grants under this section to nonprofit organizations that demonstrate experience in implementing and operating health and safety asbestos training and education programs for workers who are or will be engaged in asbestos-related activities (including State and local governments, colleges and universities, joint labor-management trust funds, and nonprofit government employee organizations) to establish and, or, operate asbestos training programs on a not-for-profit basis. Applications for grants under this subsection shall be submitted in such form and manner, and contain such information, as the Administrator prescribes.

(b) Authorization

Of such sums as are authorized to be appropriated pursuant to section 4021(a) of title 20 for the fiscal years 1991, 1992, 1993, 1994, and 1995, not more than $5,000,000 are authorized to be appropriated to carry out this section in each such fiscal year.

Subchapter III - Indoor Radon Abatement

(TSCA § 301)

Sec. 2661. National goal

The national long-term goal of the United States with respect to radon levels in buildings is that the air within buildings in theUnited States should be as free of radon as the ambient air outside of buildings.

(TSCA § 302)

Sec. 2662. Definitions

For purposes of this subchapter:

(1) The term "local educational agency" means–

(A) any local educational agency as defined in section 7801 of title 20;

(B) the owner of any nonprofit elementary or secondary school building; and

(C) the governing authority of any school operated pursuant to section 241 of title 20, as in effect before enactment of the Improving America's Schools Act of 1994, or successor authority, relating to impact aid for children who reside on Federal property.

(2) The term "nonprofit elementary or secondary school" has the meaning given such term by section 2642(8)[15]of this title.

(3) The term "radon" means the radioactive gaseous element and its short-lived decay products produced by the disintegration of the element radium occurring in air, water, soil, or other media.

(4) The term "school building" has the meaning given such term by section 2642(13) of this title.

(TSCA § 303)

Sec. 2663. EPA citizen's guide

(a) Publication

In order to make continuous progress toward the long-term goal established in section 2661 of this title, the Administrator of the Environmental Protection Agency shall, not later than June 1, 1989, publish and make available to the public an updated version of its document titled "A Citizen's Guide to Radon". The Administrator shall revise and republish the guide as necessary thereafter.

(b) Information included

(1) Action levels

The updated citizen's guide published as provided in subsection (a) of this section shall include a description of a series of action levels indicating the health risk associated with different levels of radon exposure.

(2) Other information

The updated citizen's guide shall also include information with respect to each of the following:

(A) The increased health risk associated with the exposure of potentially sensitive populations to different levels of radon.

(B) The increased health risk associated with the exposure to radon of persons engaged in potentially risk-increasing behavior.

(C) The cost and technological feasibility of reducing radon concentrations within existing and new buildings.

---

15. So in original. Probably should be section "2642(9)".

(D) The relationship between short-term and long-term testing techniques and the relationship between (i) measurements based on both such techniques, and (ii) the actions[16] levels set forth as provided in paragraph (1).

(E) Outdoor radon levels around the country.

(TSCA § 304)

Sec. 2664. Model construction standards and techniques

The Administrator of the Environmental Protection Agency shall develop model construction standards and techniques for controlling radon levels within new buildings. To the maximum extent possible, these standards and techniques should be developed with the assistance of organizations involved in establishing national building construction standards and techniques. The Administrator shall make a draft of the document containing the model standards and techniques available for public review and comment. The model standards and techniques shall provide for geographic differences in construction types and materials, geology, weather, and other variables that may affect radon levels in new buildings. The Administrator shall make final model standards and techniques available to the public by June 1, 1990. The Administrator shall work to ensure that organizations responsible for developing national model building codes, and authorities which regulate building construction within States or political subdivisions within States, adopt the Agency's model standards and techniques.

(TSCA § 305)

Sec. 2665. Technical assistance to States for radon programs

(a) Required activities

The Administrator (or another Federal department or agency designated by the Administrator) shall develop and implement activities designed to assist State radon programs. These activities may include, but are not limited to, the following:

(1) Establishment of a clearinghouse of radon related information, including mitigation studies, public information materials, surveys of radon levels, and other relevant information.

---

16. So in original. Probably should be "action".

(2) Operation of a voluntary proficiency program for rating the effectiveness of radon measurement devices and methods, the effectiveness of radon mitigation devices and methods, and the effectiveness of private firms and individuals offering radon-related architecture, design, engineering, measurement, and mitigation services. The proficiency program under this subparagraph shall be in operation within one year after October 28, 1988.

(3) Design and implementation of training seminars for State and local officials and private and professional firms dealing with radon and addressing topics such as monitoring, analysis, mitigation, health effects, public information, and program design.

(4) Publication of public information materials concerning radon health risks and methods of radon mitigation.

(5) Operation of cooperative projects between the Environmental

Protection Agency's Radon Action Program and the State's radon program. Such projects shall include the Home Evaluation Program, in which the Environmental Protection Agency evaluates homes and States demonstrate mitigation methods in these homes. To the maximum extent practicable, consistent with the objectives of the evaluation and demonstration, homes of low-income persons should be selected for evaluation and demonstration.

(6) Demonstration of radon mitigation methods in various types of structures and in various geographic settings and publication of findings. In the case of demonstration of such methods in homes, the Administrator should select homes of low-income persons, to the maximum extent practicable and consistent with the objectives of the demonstration.

(7) Establishment of a national data base with data organized by State concerning the location and amounts of radon.

(8) Development and demonstration of methods of radon measurement and mitigation that take into account unique characteristics, if any, of nonresidential buildings housing child care facilities.

(b) Discretionary assistance

Upon request of a State, the Administrator (or another Federal department or agency designated by the Administrator) may provide technical assistance to such State in development or implementation of programs addressing radon. Such assistance may include, but is not limited to, the following:

(1) Design and implementation of surveys of the location and occurrence of radon within a State.

(2) Design and implementation of public information and education programs.

(3) Design and implementation of State programs to control radon in existing or new structures.

(4) Assessment of mitigation alternatives in unusual or unconventional structures.

(5) Design and implementation of methods for radon measurement and mitigation for nonresidential buildings housing child care facilities.

(c) Information provided to professional organizations

The Administrator, or another Federal department or agency designated by the Administrator, shall provide appropriate information concerning technology and methods of radon assessment and mitigation to professional organizations representing private firms involved in building design, engineering, and construction.

(d) Proficiency rating program and training seminar

(1) Authorization

There is authorized to be appropriated not more than $1,500,000 for the purposes of initially establishing the proficiency rating program under subsection (a)(2) of this section and the training seminars under subsection (a)(3) of this section.

(2) Charge imposed

To cover the operating costs of such proficiency rating program and training seminars, the Administrator shall impose on persons applying for a proficiency rating and on private and professional firms participating in training seminars such charges as may be necessary to defray the costs of the program or seminars. No such charge may be imposed on any State or local government.

(3) Special account

Funds derived from the charges imposed under paragraph (2) shall be deposited in a special account in the Treasury. Amounts in the special account are authorized to be appropriated only for purposes of administering such proficiency rating program or training seminars or for reimbursement of funds appropriated to the Administrator to initially establish such program or seminars.

(4) Reimbursement of general fund

During the first three years of the program and seminars, the Administrator shall make every effort, consistent with the goals and successful operation of the program and seminars, to set charges imposed under paragraph (2) so that an amount in excess of operation costs is collected. Such excess amount shall be used to reimburse the General Fund of the Treasury for the full amount appropriated to initially establish the program and seminars.

(5) Research

The Administrator shall, in conjunction with other Federal agencies, conduct research to develop, test, and evaluate radon and radon progeny measurement methods and protocols. The purpose of such research shall be to assess the ability of those methods and protocols to accurately assess exposure to radon progeny.

Such research shall include–

(A) conducting comparisons among radon and radon progeny measurement techniques;

(B) developing measurement protocols for different building types under varying operating conditions; and

(C) comparing the exposures estimated by stationary monitors and protocols to those measured by personal monitors, and issue guidance documents that–

(i) provide information on the results of research conducted under this paragraph; and

(ii) describe model State radon measurement and mitigation programs.

(6) Mandatory proficiency testing program study

(A) The Administrator shall conduct a study to determine the feasibility of establishing a mandatory proficiency testing program that would require that–

(i) any product offered for sale, or device used in connection with a service offered to the public, for the measurement of radon meets minimum performance criteria; and

(ii) any operator of a device, or person employing a technique, used in connection with a service offered to the public for the measurement of radon meets a minimum level of proficiency.

(B) The study shall also address procedures for–

(i) ordering the recall of any product sold for the measurement of radon which does not meet minimum performance criteria;

(ii) ordering the discontinuance of any service offered to the public for the measurement of radon which does not meet minimum performance criteria; and

(iii) establishing adequate quality assurance requirements for each company offering radon measurement services to the public to follow.

The study shall identify enforcement mechanisms necessary to the success of the program. The Administrator shall report the findings of the study with recommendations to Congress by March 1, 1991.

(7) User fee

In addition to any charge imposed pursuant to paragraph (2), the Administrator shall collect user fees from persons seeking certification under the radon proficiency program in an amount equal to $1,500,000 to cover the Environmental Protection Agency's cost of conducting research pursuant to paragraph (5) for each of the fiscal years 1991, 1992, 1993, 1994, and 1995.

Such funds shall be deposited in the account established pursuant to paragraph (3).

(e) Authorization

(1) There is authorized to be appropriated for the purposes of carrying out sections 2663, 2664, and 2665 of this title an amount not to exceed $3,000,000 for each of fiscal years 1989, 1990, and 1991.

(2) No amount appropriated under this subsection may be used by the Environmental Protection Agency to administer the grant program under section 2666 of this title.

(3) No amount appropriated under this subsection may be used to cover the costs of the proficiency rating program under subsection (a)(2) of this section.

(TSCA § 306)

Sec. 2666. Grant assistance to States for radon programs

(a) In general

For each fiscal year, upon application of the Governor of a State, the Administrator may make a grant, subject to such terms and conditions as the Administrator considers appropriate, under this section to the State for the purpose of assisting the State in the development and implementation of programs for the assessment and mitigation of radon.

(b) Application

An application for a grant under this section in any fiscal year shall contain such information as the Administrator shall require, including each of the following:

(1) A description of the seriousness and extent of radon exposure in the State.

(2) An identification of the State agency which has the primary responsibility for radon programs and which will receive the grant, a description of the roles and responsibilities of the lead State agency and any other State agencies involved in radon programs, and description of the roles and

responsibilities of any municipal, district, or areawide organization involved in radon programs.

(3) A description of the activities and programs related to radon which the State proposes in such year.

(4) A budget specifying Federal and State funding of each element of activity of the grant application.

(5) A 3-year plan which outlines long range program goals and objectives, tasks necessary to achieve them, and resource requirements for the entire 3-year period, including anticipated State funding levels and desired Federal funding levels. This clause shall apply only for the initial year in which a grant application is made.

(c) Eligible activities

Activities eligible for grant assistance under this section are the following:

(1) Survey of radon levels, including special surveys of geographic areas or classes of buildings (such as, among others, public buildings, school buildings, high-risk residential construction types).

(2) Development of public information and educational materials concerning radon assessment, mitigation, and control programs.

(3) Implementation of programs to control radon in existing and new structures.

(4) Purchase by the State of radon measurement equipment or devices.

(5) Purchase and maintenance of analytical equipment connected to radon measurement and analysis, including costs of calibration of such equipment.

(6) Payment of costs of Environmental Protection Agency-approved training programs related to radon for permanent State or local employees.

(7) Payment of general overhead and program administration costs.

(8) Development of a data storage and management system for information concerning radon occurrence, levels, and programs.

(9) Payment of costs of demonstration of radon mitigation methods and technologies as approved by the Administrator, including State participation in the Environmental Protection Agency Home Evaluation Program.

(10) A toll-free radon hotline to provide information and technical assistance.

(d) Preference to certain States

Beginning in fiscal year 1991, the Administrator shall give a preference for grant assistance under this section to States that have made reasonable efforts to ensure the adoption, by the authorities which regulate building construction within that State or political subdivisions within States, of the model construction standards and techniques for new buildings developed under section 2664 of this title.

(e) Priority activities and projects

The Administrator shall support eligible activities contained in State applications with the full amount of available funds. In the event that State applications for funds exceed the total funds available in a fiscal year, the Administrator shall give priority to activities or projects proposed by States based on each of the following criteria:

(1) The seriousness and extent of the radon contamination problem to be addressed.

(2) The potential for the activity or project to bring about reduction in radon levels.

(3) The potential for development of innovative radon assessment techniques, mitigation measures as approved by the Administrator, or program management approaches which may be of use to other States.

(4) Any other uniform criteria that the Administrator deems necessary to promote the goals of the grant program and that the

Administrator provides to States before the application process.

(f) Federal share

The Federal share of the cost of radon program activities implemented with Federal assistance under this section in any fiscal year shall not exceed 75 percent of the costs incurred by the State in implementing such program in the first year of a grant to such State, 60 percent in the second year, and 50 percent in the third year. Federal assistance shall be made on the condition that the non-Federal share is provided from non-Federal funds.

(g) Assistance to local governments States may, at the Governor's discretion, use funds from grants under this section to assist local governments in implementation of activities eligible for assistance under paragraphs (2), (3), and (6) of subsection (c) of this section.

(h) Information

(1) The Administrator may request such information, data, and reports developed by the State as he considers necessary to make the determination of continuing eligibility under this section.

(2) Any State receiving funds under this section shall provide to the Administrator all radon-related information generated in its activities, including the results of radon surveys, mitigation demonstration projects, and risk communication studies.

(3) Any State receiving funds under this section shall maintain, and make available to the public, a list of firms and individuals within the

State that have received a passing rating under the Environmental Protection Agency proficiency rating program referred to in section 2665(a)(2) of this title. The list shall also include the address and phone number of such firms and individuals, together with the proficiency rating received by each. The Administrator shall make such list available to the public at appropriate locations in each State which does not receive funds under this section unless the State assumes such responsibility.

(i) Limitations

(1) No grant may be made under this section in any fiscal year to a State which in the preceding fiscal year received a grant under this section unless the Administrator determines that such State satisfactorily implemented the activities funded by the grant in such preceding fiscal year.

(2) The costs of implementing paragraphs (4) and (9) of subsection (c) of this section shall not in the aggregate exceed 50 percent of the amount of any grant awarded under this section to a State in a fiscal year. In implementing such paragraphs, a State should make every effort, consistent with the goals and successful operation of the State radon program, to give a preference to low-income persons.

(3) The costs of general overhead and program administration under subsection (c)(7) of this section shall not exceed 25 percent of the amount of any grant awarded under this section to a State in a fiscal year.

(4) A State may use funds received under this section for financial assistance to persons only to the extent such assistance is related to demonstration projects or the purchase and analysis of radon measurement devices.

(j) Authorization

(1) There is authorized to be appropriated for grant assistance under this section an amount not to exceed $10,000,000 for each of fiscal years 1989, 1990, and 1991.

(2) There is authorized to be appropriated for the purpose of administering the grant program under this section such sums as may be necessary for each of such fiscal years.

(3) Notwithstanding any other provision of this section, not more than 10 percent of the amount appropriated to carry out this section may be used to make grants to any one State.

(4) Funds not obligated to States in the fiscal year for which funds are appropriated under this section shall remain available for obligation during the next fiscal year.

(5) No amount appropriated under this subsection may be used to cover the costs of the proficiency rating program under section 2665(a)(2) of this title.

(TSCA § 307)

Sec. 2667. Radon in schools

(a) Study of radon in schools

(1) Authority

The Administrator shall conduct a study for the purpose of determining the extent of radon contamination in the Nation's school buildings.

(2) List of high probability areas

In carrying out such study, the Administrator shall identify and compile a list of areas within the United States which the Administrator determines have a high probability of including schools which have elevated levels of radon.

(3) Basis of list

In compiling such list, the Administrator shall make such determinations on the basis of, among other things, each of the following:

(A) Geological data.

(B) Data on high radon levels in homes and other structures nearby any such school.

(C) Physical characteristics of the school buildings.

(4) Survey

In conducting such study the Administrator shall design a survey which when completed allows Congress to characterize the extent of radon contamination in schools in each State. The survey shall include testing from a representative sample of schools in each high-risk area identified in paragraph (1) and shall include additional testing, to the extent resources are available for such testing. The survey also shall include any reliable testing data supplied by States, schools, or other parties.

(5) Assistance

(A) The Administrator shall make available to the appropriate agency of each State, as designated by the Governor of such State, a list of high risk areas within each State, including a delineation of such areas and any other data available to the Administrator for schools in that State. To assist such agencies, the Administrator also shall provide guidance and data detailing the risks associated with high radon levels, technical guidance and related information concerning testing for radon within schools, and methods of reducing radon levels.

(B) In addition to the assistance authorized by subparagraph (A), the Administrator is authorized to make available to the appropriate agency of each State, as designated by the Governor of such State, devices suitable for use by such agencies in conducting tests for radon within the schools under the jurisdiction of any such State agency. The Administrator is authorized to make available to such agencies the use of laboratories of the Environmental Protection Agency, or to recommend laboratories, to evaluate any such devices for the presence of radon levels.

(6) Diagnostic and remedial efforts

The Administrator is authorized to select, from high-risk areas identified in paragraph (2), school buildings for purposes of enabling the Administrator to undertake diagnostic and remedial efforts to reduce the levels of radon in such school buildings.

Such diagnostic and remedial efforts shall be carried out with a view to developing technology and expertise for the purpose of making such technology and expertise available to any local educational agency and the several States.

(7) Status report

On or before October 1, 1989, the Administrator shall submit to the Congress a status report with respect to action taken by the Administrator in conducting the study required by this section, including the results of the Administrator's diagnostic and remedial work. On or before October 1, 1989, the Administrator shall submit a final report setting forth the results of the study conducted pursuant to this section, including the results of the Administrator's diagnostic and remedial work, and the recommendations of the Administrator.

(b) Authorization

For the purpose of carrying out the provisions of paragraph (6) of subsection (a) of this section, there are authorized to be appropriated such sums, not to exceed $500,000, as may be necessary. For the purpose of carrying out the provisions of this section other than such paragraph (6), there are authorized to be appropriated such sums, not to exceed $1,000,000, as may be necessary.

(TSCA § 308)

Sec. 2668. Regional radon training centers

(a) Funding program

Upon application of colleges, universities, institutions of higher learning, or consortia of such institutions, the Administrator may make a grant or cooperative agreement, subject to such terms and conditions as the Administrator considers appropriate, under this section to the applicant for the purpose of establishing and operating a regional radon training center.

(b) Purpose of centers

The purpose of a regional radon training center is to develop information and provide training to Federal and State officials, professional and private firms, and the public regarding the health risks posed by radon and demonstrated methods of radon measurement and mitigation.

(c) Applications

Any colleges, universities, institutions of higher learning or consortia of such institutions may submit an application for funding under this section. Such applications shall be submitted to the Administrator in such form and containing such information as the Administrator may require.

(d) Selection criteria

The Administrator shall support at least 3 eligible applications with the full amount of available funds. The Administrator shall select recipients of funding under this section to ensure that funds are equitably allocated among regions of the United States, and on the basis of each of the following criteria:

(1) The extent to which the applicant's program will promote the purpose described in subsection (b) of this section.

(2) The demonstrated expertise of the applicant regarding radon measurement and mitigation methods and other radon-related issues.

(3) The demonstrated expertise of the applicant in radon training and in activities relating to information development and dissemination.

(4) The seriousness of the radon problem in the region.

(5) The geographical coverage of the proposed center.

(6) Any other uniform criteria that the Administrator deems necessary to promote the purpose described in subsection (b) of this section and that the Administrator provides to potential applicants prior to the application process.

(e) Termination of funding

No funding may be given under this section in any fiscal year to an applicant which in the preceding fiscal year received funding under this section unless the Administrator determines that the recipient satisfactorily implemented the activities that were funded in the preceding year.

(f) Authorization

There is authorized to be appropriated to carry out the program under this section not to exceed $1,000,000 for each of fiscal years 1989, 1990, and 1991.

(TSCA § 309)

Sec. 2669. Study of radon in Federal buildings

(a) Study requirement

The head of each Federal department or agency that owns a Federal building shall conduct a study for the purpose of determining the extent of radon contamination in such buildings. Such study shall include, in the case of a Federal building using a nonpublic water source (such as a well or other groundwater), radon contamination of the water.

(b) High-risk Federal buildings

(1) The Administrator shall identify and compile a list of areas within the United States which the Administrator, in consultation with Federal departments and agencies, determines have a high probability of including Federal buildings which have elevated levels of radon.

(2) In compiling such list, the Administrator shall make such determinations on the basis of, among other things, the following:

(A) Geological data.

(B) Data on high radon levels in homes and other structures near any such Federal building.

(C) Physical characteristics of the Federal buildings.

(c) Study designs

Studies required under subsection (a) of this section shall be based on design criteria specified by the Administrator. The head of each Federal department or agency conducting such a study shall submit, not later than July 1, 1989, a study design to the Administrator for approval. The study design shall follow the most recent Environmental Protection Agency guidance documents, including "A Citizen's Guide to Radon"; the "Interim Protocol for Screening and Follow Up: Radon and Radon Decay Products Measurements"; the "Interim Indoor Radon & Radon Decay Product Measurement Protocol"; and any other recent guidance documents. The study design shall include testing data from a representative sample of Federal buildings in each high-risk area identified in subsection (b) of this section. The study design also shall include additional testing data to the extent resources are available, including any reliable data supplied by Federal agencies, States, or other parties.

(d) Information on risks and testing

(1) The Administrator shall provide to the departments or agencies conducting studies under subsection (a) of this section the following:

(A) Guidance and data detailing the risks associated with high radon levels.

(B) Technical guidance and related information concerning testing for radon within Federal buildings and water supplies.

(C) Technical guidance and related information concerning methods for reducing radon levels.

(2) In addition to the assistance required by paragraph (1), the

Administrator is authorized to make available, on a cost reimbursable basis, to the departments or agencies conducting studies under subsection (a) of this section devices suitable for use by such departments or agencies in conducting tests for radon within Federal buildings. For the purpose of assisting such departments or agencies in evaluating any such devices for the presence of radon levels, the Administrator is authorized to recommend laboratories or to make available to such departments or agencies, on a cost reimbursable basis, the use of laboratories of the Environmental Protection Agency.

(e) Study deadline

Not later than June 1, 1990, the head of each Federal department or agency conducting a study under subsection (a) of this section shall complete the study and provide the study to the Administrator.

(f) Report to Congress

Not later than October 1, 1990, the Administrator shall submit a report to the Congress describing the results of the studies conducted pursuant to subsection (a) of this section.

(TSCA § 310)

Sec. 2670. Regulations

The Administrator is authorized to issue such regulations as may be necessary to carry out the provisions of this subchapter.

(TSCA § 311)

Sec. 2671. Additional authorizations

Amounts authorized to be appropriated in this subchapter for purposes of carrying out the provisions of this subchapter are in addition to amounts authorized to be appropriated under other provisions of law for radon-related activities.

Subchapter IV - Lead Exposure Reduction

(TSCA § 401)

Sec. 2681. Definitions

For the purposes of this subchapter:

(1) Abatement

The term "abatement" means any set of measures designed to permanently eliminate lead-based paint hazards in accordance with standards established by the Administrator under this subchapter.

Such term includes–

(A) the removal of lead-based paint and lead-contaminated dust, the permanent containment or encapsulation of lead-based paint, the replacement of lead-painted surfaces or fixtures, and the removal or covering of lead-contaminated soil; and

(B) all preparation, cleanup, disposal, and postabatement clearance testing activities associated with such measures.

(2) Accessible surface

The term "accessible surface" means an interior or exterior surface painted with lead-based paint that is accessible for a young child to mouth or chew.

(3) Deteriorated paint

The term "deteriorated paint" means any interior or exterior paint that is peeling, chipping, chalking or cracking or any paint located on an interior or exterior surface or fixture that is damaged or deteriorated.

(4) Evaluation

The term "evaluation" means risk assessment, inspection, or risk assessment and inspection.

(5) Friction surface

The term "friction surface" means an interior or exterior surface that is subject to abrasion or friction, including certain window, floor, and stair surfaces.

(6) Impact surface

The term "impact surface" means an interior or exterior surface that is subject to damage by repeated impacts, for example, certain parts of door frames.

(7) Inspection

The term "inspection" means (A) a surface-by-surface investigation to determine the presence of lead-based paint, as provided in section 4822(c) of title 42, and (B) the provision of a report explaining the results of the investigation.

(8) Interim controls

The term "interim controls" means a set of measures designed to reduce temporarily human exposure or likely exposure to lead-based paint hazards, including specialized cleaning, repairs, maintenance, painting, temporary containment, ongoing monitoring of lead-based paint hazards or potential hazards, and the establishment and operation of management and resident education programs.

(9) Lead-based paint

The term "lead-based paint" means paint or other surface coatings that contain lead in excess of 1.0 milligrams per centimeter squared or 0.5 percent by weight or (A) in the case of paint or other surface coatings on target housing, such lower level as may be established by the Secretary of Housing and Urban Development, as defined in section 4822(c) of title 42, or (B) in the case of any other paint or surface coatings, such other level as may be established by the Administrator.

(10) Lead-based paint hazard

The term "lead-based paint hazard" means any condition that causes exposure to lead from lead-contaminated dust, lead-contaminated soil, lead-contaminated paint that is deteriorated or present in accessible surfaces, friction surfaces, or impact surfaces that would result in adverse human health effects as established by the Administrator under this subchapter.

(11) Lead-contaminated dust

The term "lead-contaminated dust" means surface dust in residential dwellings that contains an area or mass concentration of lead in excess of levels determined by the Administrator under this subchapter to pose a threat of adverse health effects in pregnant women or young children.

(12) Lead-contaminated soil

The term "lead-contaminated soil" means bare soil on residential real property that contains lead at or in excess of the levels determined to be hazardous to human health by the Administrator under this subchapter.

(13) Reduction

The term "reduction" means measures designed to reduce or eliminate human exposure to lead-based paint hazards through methods including interim controls and abatement.

(14) Residential dwelling

The term "residential dwelling" means–

(A) a single-family dwelling, including attached structures such as porches and stoops; or

(B) a single-family dwelling unit in a structure that contains more than 1 separate residential dwelling unit, and in which each such unit is used or occupied, or intended to be used or occupied, in whole or in part, as the home or residence of 1 or more persons.

(15) Residential real property

The term "residential real property" means real property on which there is situated 1 or more residential dwellings used or occupied, or intended to be used or occupied, in whole or in part, as the home or residence of 1 or more persons.

(16) Risk assessment

The term "risk assessment" means an on-site investigation to determine and report the existence, nature, severity and location of lead-based paint hazards in residential dwellings, including–

(A) information gathering regarding the age and history of the housing and occupancy by children under age 6;

(B) visual inspection;

(C) limited wipe sampling or other environmental sampling techniques;

(D) other activity as may be appropriate; and

(E) provision of a report explaining the results of the investigation.

(17) Target housing

The term "target housing" means any housing constructed prior to 1978, except housing for the elderly or persons with disabilities (unless any child who is less than 6 years of age resides or is expected to reside in such housing for the elderly or persons with disabilities) or any 0-bedroom dwelling. In the case of jurisdictions which banned the sale or use of lead-based paint prior to 1978, the Secretary of Housing and Urban Development, at the Secretary's discretion, may designate an earlier date.

(TSCA § 402)

Sec. 2682. Lead-based paint activities training and certification

(a) Regulations

(1) In general

Not later than 18 months after October 28, 1992, the Administrator shall, in consultation with the Secretary of Labor, the Secretary of Housing and Urban Development, and the Secretary of Health and Human Services (acting through the Director of the National Institute for Occupational Safety and Health), promulgate final regulations governing lead-based paint activities to ensure that individuals engaged in such activities are properly trained; that training programs are accredited; and that contractors engaged in such activities are certified. Such regulations shall contain standards for performing lead-based paint activities, taking into account reliability, effectiveness, and safety. Such regulations shall require that all risk assessment, inspection, and abatement activities performed in target housing shall be performed by certified contractors, as such term is defined in section 4851b of title 42. The provisions of this section shall supersede the provisions set forth under the heading "Lead Abatement Training and Certification" and under the heading "Training Grants" in title III of the Act entitled

"An Act making appropriations for the Departments of Veterans Affairs and Housing and Urban Development, and for sundry independent agencies, commissions, corporations, and offices for the fiscal year ending September 30, 1992, and for other purposes", Public Law 102-139 [105 Stat. 765, 42 U.S.C. 4822 note], and upon October 28, 1992, the provisions set forth in such public law under such headings shall cease to have any force and effect.

(2) Accreditation of training programs

Final regulations promulgated under paragraph (1) shall contain specific requirements for the accreditation of lead-based paint activities training programs for workers, supervisors, inspectors and planners, and other individuals involved in lead-based paint activities, including, but not limited to, each of the following:

(A) Minimum requirements for the accreditation of training providers.

(B) Minimum training curriculum requirements.

(C) Minimum training hour requirements.

(D) Minimum hands-on training requirements.

(E) Minimum trainee competency and proficiency requirements.

(F) Minimum requirements for training program quality control.

(3) Accreditation and certification fees

The Administrator (or the State in the case of an authorized State program) shall impose a fee on–

(A) persons operating training programs accredited under this subchapter; and

(B) lead-based paint activities contractors certified in accordance with paragraph (1).

The fees shall be established at such level as is necessary to cover the costs of administering and enforcing the standards and regulations under this section which are applicable to such programs and contractors. The fee shall not be imposed on any State, local government, or nonprofit training program. The Administrator (or the State in the case of an authorized State program) may waive the fee for lead-based paint activities contractors under subparagraph (A) for the purpose of training their own employees.

(b) Lead-based paint activities

For purposes of this subchapter, the term "lead-based paint activities" means–

(1) in the case of target housing, risk assessment, inspection, and abatement; and

(2) in the case of any public building constructed before 1978, commercial building, bridge, or other structure or superstructure, identification of lead-based paint and materials containing lead-based paint, deleading, removal of lead from bridges, and demolition.

For purposes of paragraph (2), the term "deleading" means activities conducted by a person who offers to eliminate lead-based paint or lead-based paint hazards or to plan such activities.

(c) Renovation and remodeling

(1) Guidelines

In order to reduce the risk of exposure to lead in connection with renovation and remodeling of target housing, public buildings constructed before 1978, and commercial buildings, the Administrator shall, within 18 months after October 28, 1992, promulgate guidelines for the conduct of such renovation and remodeling activities which may create a risk of exposure to dangerous levels of lead. The Administrator shall disseminate such guidelines to persons engaged in such renovation and remodeling through hardware and paint stores, employee organizations, trade groups, State and local agencies, and through other appropriate means.

(2) Study of certification

The Administrator shall conduct a study of the extent to which persons engaged in various types of renovation and remodeling activities in target housing, public buildings constructed before 1978, and commercial buildings are exposed to lead in the conduct of such activities or disturb lead and create a lead-based paint hazard on a regular or occasional basis. The Administrator shall complete such study and publish the results thereof within 30 months after October 28, 1992.

(3) Certification determination

Within 4 years after October 28, 1992, the Administrator shall revise the regulations under subsection (a) of this section to apply the regulations to renovation or remodeling activities in target housing, public buildings constructed before 1978, and commercial buildings that create lead-based paint hazards. In determining which contractors are engaged in such activities, the Administrator shall utilize the results of the study under paragraph (2) and consult with the representatives of labor organizations, lead-based paint activities contractors, persons engaged in remodeling and renovation, experts in lead health effects, and others. If the Administrator determines that any category of contractors engaged in renovation or remodeling does not require certification, the Administrator shall publish an explanation of the basis for that determination.

(TSCA § 403)

Sec. 2683. Identification of dangerous levels of lead

Within 18 months after October 28, 1992, the Administrator shall promulgate regulations which shall identify, for purposes of this subchapter and the Residential Lead-Based Paint Hazard Reduction Act of 1992 [42 U.S.C. 4851 et seq.], lead-based paint hazards, lead-contaminated dust, and lead-contaminated soil.

(TSCA § 404)

Sec. 2684. Authorized State programs

(a) Approval

Any State which seeks to administer and enforce the standards, regulations, or other requirements established under section 2682 or 2686 of this title, or both, may, after notice and opportunity for public hearing, develop and submit to the Administrator an application, in such form as the Administrator shall require, for authorization of such a State program. Any such State may also certify to the Administrator at the time of submitting such program that the State program meets the requirements of paragraphs (1) and (2) of subsection (b) of this section. Upon submission of such certification, the State program shall be deemed to be authorized under this section, and shall apply in such State in lieu of the corresponding Federal program under section 2682 or 2686 of this title, or both, as the case may be, until such time as the Administrator disapproves the program or withdraws the authorization.

(b) Approval or disapproval

Within 180 days following submission of an application under subsection (a) of this section, the Administrator shall approve or disapprove the application.

The Administrator may approve the application only if, after notice and after opportunity for public hearing, the Administrator finds that–

(1) the State program is at least as protective of human health and the environment as the Federal program under section 2682 or 2686 of this title, or both, as the case may be, and

(2) such State program provides adequate enforcement.

Upon authorization of a State program under this section, it shall be unlawful for any person to violate or fail or refuse to comply with any requirement of such program.

(c) Withdrawal of authorization

If a State is not administering and enforcing a program authorized under this section in compliance with standards, regulations, and other requirements of this subchapter, the Administrator shall so notify the State and, if corrective action is not completed within a reasonable time, not to exceed 180 days, the Administrator shall withdraw authorization of such program and establish a Federal program pursuant to this subchapter.

(d) Model State program

Within 18 months after October 28, 1992, the Administrator shall promulgate a model State program which may be adopted by any State which seeks to administer and enforce a State program under this subchapter. Such model program shall, to the extent practicable, encourage States to utilize existing State and local certification and accreditation programs and procedures. Such program shall encourage reciprocity among the States with respect to the certification under section 2682 of this title.

(e) Other State requirements

Nothing in this subchapter shall be construed to prohibit any State or political subdivision thereof from imposing any requirements which are more stringent than those imposed by this subchapter.

(f) State and local certification

The regulations under this subchapter shall, to the extent appropriate, encourage States to seek program authorization and to use existing State and local certification and accreditation procedures, except that a State or local government shall not require more than 1 certification under this section for any lead-based paint activities contractor to carry out lead-based paint activities in the State or political subdivision thereof.

(g) Grants to States

The Administrator is authorized to make grants to States to develop and carry out authorized State programs under this section.

The grants shall be subject to such terms and conditions as the Administrator may establish to further the purposes of this subchapter.

(h) Enforcement by Administrator

If a State does not have a State program authorized under this section and in effect by the date which is 2 years after promulgation of the regulations under section 2682 or 2686 of this title, the Administrator shall, by such date, establish a Federal program for section 2682 or 2686 of this title (as the case may be) for such State and administer and enforce such program in such State.

(TSCA § 405)

Sec. 2685. Lead abatement and measurement

(a) Program to promote lead exposure abatement

The Administrator, in cooperation with other appropriate Federal departments and agencies, shall conduct a comprehensive program to promote safe, effective, and affordable monitoring, detection, and abatement of lead-based paint and other lead exposure hazards.

(b) Standards for environmental sampling laboratories

(1) The Administrator shall establish protocols, criteria, and minimum performance standards for laboratory analysis of lead in paint films, soil, and dust. Within 2 years after October 28, 1992, the Administrator, in consultation with the Secretary of Health and Human Services, shall establish a program to certify laboratories as qualified to test substances for lead content unless the Administrator determines, by the date specified in this paragraph, that effective voluntary accreditation programs are in place and operating on a nationwide basis at the time of such determination. To be certified under such program, a laboratory shall, at a minimum, demonstrate an ability to test substances accurately for lead content.

(2) Not later than 24 months after October 28, 1992, and annually thereafter, the Administrator shall publish and make available to the public a list of certified or accredited environmental sampling laboratories.

(3) If the Administrator determines under paragraph (1) that effective voluntary accreditation programs are in place for environmental sampling laboratories, the Administrator shall review the performance and effectiveness of such programs within 3 years after such determination. If, upon such review, the Administrator determines that the voluntary accreditation programs are not effective in assuring the quality and consistency of laboratory analyses, the Administrator shall, not more than 12 months thereafter, establish a certification program that meets the requirements of paragraph (1).

(c) Exposure studies

(1) The Secretary of Health and Human Services (hereafter in this subsection referred to as the "Secretary"), acting through the Director of the

Centers for Disease Control, (CDC), and the Director of the National Institute of Environmental Health Sciences, shall jointly conduct a study of the sources of lead exposure in children who have elevated blood lead levels (or other indicators of elevated lead body burden), as defined by the Director of the Centers for Disease Control.

(2) The Secretary, in consultation with the Director of the National Institute for Occupational Safety and Health, shall conduct a comprehensive study of means to reduce hazardous occupational lead abatement exposures. This study shall include, at a minimum, each of the following–

(A) Surveillance and intervention capability in the States to identify and prevent hazardous exposures to lead abatement workers.

(B) Demonstration of lead abatement control methods and devices and work practices to identify and prevent hazardous lead exposures in the workplace.

(C) Evaluation, in consultation with the National Institute of Environmental Health Sciences, of health effects of low and high levels of occupational lead exposures on reproductive, neurological, renal, and cardiovascular health.

(D) Identification of high risk occupational settings to which prevention activities and resources should be targeted.

(E) A study assessing the potential exposures and risks from lead to janitorial and custodial workers.

(3) The studies described in paragraphs (1) and (2) shall, as appropriate, examine the relative contributions to elevated lead body burden from each of the following:

(A) Drinking water.

(B) Food.

(C) Lead-based paint and dust from lead-based paint.

(D) Exterior sources such as ambient air and lead in soil.

(E) Occupational exposures, and other exposures that the Secretary determines to be appropriate.

(4) Not later than 30 months after October 28, 1992, the Secretary shall submit a report to the Congress concerning the studies described in paragraphs (1) and (2).

(d) Public education

(1) The Administrator, in conjunction with the Secretary of Health and Human Services, acting through the Director of the Agency for Toxic Substances and Disease Registry, and in conjunction with the Secretary of Housing and Urban Development, shall sponsor public education and outreach activities to increase public awareness of–

(A) the scope and severity of lead poisoning from household sources;

(B) potential exposure to sources of lead in schools and childhood day care centers;

(C) the implications of exposures for men and women, particularly those of childbearing age;

(D) the need for careful, quality, abatement and management actions;

(E) the need for universal screening of children;

(F) other components of a lead poisoning prevention program;

(G) the health consequences of lead exposure resulting from lead-based paint hazards;

(H) risk assessment and inspection methods for lead-based paint hazards; and

(I) measures to reduce the risk of lead exposure from lead-based paint.

(2) The activities described in paragraph (1) shall be designed to provide educational services and information to–

(A) health professionals;

(B) the general public, with emphasis on parents of young children;

(C) homeowners, landlords, and tenants;

(D) consumers of home improvement products;

(E) the residential real estate industry; and

(F) the home renovation industry.

(3) In implementing the activities described in paragraph (1), the Administrator shall assure coordination with the President's Commission on Environmental Quality's education and awareness campaign on lead poisoning.

(4) The Administrator, in consultation with the Chairman of the Consumer Product Safety Commission, shall develop information to be distributed by retailers of home improvement products to provide consumers with practical information related to the hazards of renovation and remodeling where lead-based paint may be present.

(e) Technical assistance

(1) Clearinghouse

Not later than 6 months after October 28, 1992, the Administrator shall establish, in consultation with the Secretary of Housing and Urban Development and the Director of the Centers for Disease Control, a

National Clearinghouse on Childhood Lead Poisoning (hereinafter in this section referred to as "Clearinghouse"). The Clearinghouse shall–

(A) collect, evaluate, and disseminate current information on the assessment and reduction of lead-based paint hazards, adverse health effects, sources of exposure, detection and risk assessment methods, environmental hazards abatement, and clean-up standards;

(B) maintain a rapid-alert system to inform certified lead-based paint activities contractors of significant developments in research related to lead-based paint hazards; and

(C) perform any other duty that the Administrator determines necessary to achieve the purposes of this chapter.

(2) Hotline

Not later than 6 months after October 28, 1992, the Administrator, in cooperation with other Federal agencies and with State and local governments, shall establish a single lead-based paint hazard hotline to provide the public with answers to questions about lead poisoning prevention and referrals to the Clearinghouse for technical information.

(f) Products for lead-based paint activities

Not later than 30 months after October 28, 1992, the President shall, after notice and opportunity for comment, establish by rule appropriate criteria, testing protocols, and performance characteristics as are necessary to ensure, to the greatest extent possible and consistent with the purposes and policy of this subchapter, that lead-based paint hazard evaluation and reduction products introduced into commerce after a period specified in the rule are effective for the intended use described by the manufacturer. The rule shall identify the types or classes of products that are subject to such rule. The President, in implementation of the rule, shall, to the maximum extent possible, utilize independent testing laboratories, as appropriate, and consult with such entities and others in developing the rules. The President may delegate the authorities under this subsection to the Environmental Protection Agency or the Secretary of Commerce or such other appropriate agency.

(TSCA § 406)

Sec. 2686. Lead hazard information pamphlet

(a) Lead hazard information pamphlet

Not later than 2 years after October 28, 1992, after notice and opportunity for comment, the Administrator of the Environmental Protection Agency, in consultation with the Secretary of Housing and Urban Development and with the Secretary of Health and Human Services, shall publish, and from time to time revise, a lead hazard information pamphlet to be used in connection with this subchapter and section 4852d of title 42. The pamphlet shall–

(1) contain information regarding the health risks associated with exposure to lead;

(2) provide information on the presence of lead-based paint hazards in federally assisted, federally owned, and target housing;

(3) describe the risks of lead exposure for children under 6 years of age, pregnant women, women of childbearing age, persons involved in home renovation, and others residing in a dwelling with lead-based paint hazards;

(4) describe the risks of renovation in a dwelling with lead-based paint hazards;

(5) provide information on approved methods for evaluating and reducing lead-based paint hazards and their effectiveness in identifying, reducing, eliminating, or preventing exposure to lead-based paint hazards;

(6) advise persons how to obtain a list of contractors certified pursuant to this subchapter in lead-based paint hazard evaluation and reduction in the area in which the pamphlet is to be used;

(7) state that a risk assessment or inspection for lead-based paint is recommended prior to the purchase, lease, or renovation of target housing;

(8) state that certain State and local laws impose additional requirements related to lead-based paint in housing and provide a listing of Federal, State, and local agencies in each State, including address and telephone number, that can provide information about applicable laws and available governmental and private assistance and financing; and

(9) provide such other information about environmental hazards associated with residential real property as the Administrator deems appropriate.

(b) Renovation of target housing

Within 2 years after October 28, 1992, the Administrator shall promulgate regulations under this subsection to require each person who performs for compensation a renovation of target housing to provide a lead hazard information pamphlet to the owner and occupant of such housing prior to commencing the renovation.

(TSCA § 407)

Sec. 2687. Regulations

The regulations of the Administrator under this subchapter shall include such recordkeeping and reporting requirements as may be necessary to insure the effective implementation of this subchapter. The regulations may be amended from time to time as necessary.

(TSCA § 408)

Sec. 2688. Control of lead-based paint hazards at Federal facilities

Each department, agency, and instrumentality of executive, legislative, and judicial branches of the Federal Government (1) having jurisdiction over any property or facility, or (2) engaged in any activity resulting, or which may result, in a lead-based paint hazard, and each officer, agent, or employee thereof, shall be subject to, and comply with, all Federal, State, interstate, and local requirements, both substantive and procedural (including any requirement for certification, licensing, recordkeeping, or reporting or any provisions for injunctive relief and such sanctions as may be imposed by a court to enforce such relief) respecting lead-based paint, lead-based paint activities, and lead-based paint hazards in the same manner, and to the same extent as any nongovernmental entity is subject to such requirements, including the payment of reasonable service charges. The Federal, State, interstate, and local substantive and procedural requirements referred to in this subsection include, but are not limited to, all administrative orders and all civil and administrative penalties and fines regardless of whether such penalties or fines are punitive or coercive in nature, or whether imposed for isolated, intermittent or continuing violations. The United States hereby expressly waives any immunity otherwise applicable to the United States with respect to any such substantive or procedural requirement (including, but not limited to, any injunctive relief, administrative order, or civil or administrative penalty or fine referred to in the preceding sentence, or reasonable service charge). The reasonable service charges referred to in this section include, but are not limited to, fees or charges assessed for certification and licensing, as well as any other nondiscriminatory charges that are assessed in connection with a Federal, State, interstate, or local lead-based paint, lead-based paint activities, or lead-based paint hazard activities program. No agent, employee, or officer of the United States shall be personally liable for any civil penalty under any Federal, State, interstate, or local law relating to lead-based paint, lead-based paint activities, or lead-based paint hazards with respect to any act or omission within the scope of his official duties.

(TSCA § 409)

Sec. 2689. Prohibited acts

It shall be unlawful for any person to fail or refuse to comply with a provision of this subchapter or with any rule or order issued under this subchapter.

(TSCA § 410)

Sec. 2690. Relationship to other Federal law

Nothing in this subchapter shall affect the authority of other appropriate Federal agencies to establish or enforce any requirements which are at least as stringent as those established pursuant to this subchapter.

(TSCA § 411)

Sec. 2691. General provisions relating to administrative proceedings

(a) Applicability

This section applies to the promulgation or revision of any regulation issued under this subchapter.

(b) Rulemaking docket

Not later than the date of proposal of any action to which this section applies, the Administrator shall establish a rulemaking docket for such action (hereinafter in this subsection referred to as a "rule"). Whenever a rule applies only within a particular State, a second (identical) docket shall be established in the appropriate regional office of the Environmental Protection Agency.

(c) Inspection and copying

(1) The rulemaking docket required under subsection (b) of this section shall be open for inspection by the public at reasonable times specified in the notice of proposed rulemaking. Any person may copy documents contained in the docket. The Administrator shall provide copying facilities which may be used at the expense of the person seeking copies, but the Administrator may waive or reduce such expenses in such instances as the public interest requires.

Any person may request copies by mail if the person pays the expenses, including personnel costs to do the copying.

(2) (A) Promptly upon receipt by the agency, all written comments and documentary information on the proposed rule received from any person for inclusion in the docket during the comment period shall be placed in the docket. The transcript of public hearings, if any, on the proposed rule shall also be included in the docket promptly upon receipt from the person who transcribed such hearings. All documents which become available after the proposed rule has been published and which the Administrator determines are of central relevance to the rulemaking shall be placed in the docket as soon as possible after their availability.

(B) The drafts of proposed rules submitted by the Administrator to the Office of Management and Budget for any interagency review process prior to proposal of any such rule, all documents accompanying such drafts, and all written comments thereon by other agencies and all written responses to such written comments by the Administrator shall be placed in the docket no later than the date of proposal of the rule. The drafts of the final rule submitted for such review process prior to promulgation and all such written comments thereon, all documents accompanying such drafts, and written responses thereto shall be placed in the docket no later than the date of promulgation.

(d) Explanation

(1) The promulgated rule shall be accompanied by an explanation of the reasons for any major changes in the promulgated rule from the proposed rule.

(2) The promulgated rule shall also be accompanied by a response to each of the significant comments, criticisms, and new data submitted in written or oral presentations during the comment period.

(3) The promulgated rule may not be based (in part or whole) on any information or data which has not been placed in the docket as of the date of such promulgation.

(e) Judicial review

The material referred to in subsection (c)(2)(B) of this section shall not be included in the record for judicial review.

(f) Effective date

The requirements of this section shall take effect with respect to any rule the proposal of which occurs after 90 days after October 28, 1992.

(TSCA § 412)

Sec. 2692. Authorization of appropriations

There are authorized to be appropriated to carry out the purposes of this subchapter such sums as may be necessary.

Subchapter V - Healthy High-Performance Schools

(TSCA § 501)

Sec. 2695. Grants for healthy school environments

(a) In general

The Administrator, in consultation with the Secretary of Education, may provide grants to States for use in–

(1) providing technical assistance for programs of the Environmental Protection Agency (including the Tools for Schools Program and the Healthy School Environmental Assessment Tool) to schools for use in addressing environmental issues; and

(2) development and implementation of State school environmental health programs that include–

(A) standards for school building design, construction, and renovation; and

(B) identification of ongoing school building environmental problems, including contaminants, hazardous substances, and pollutant emissions, in the State and recommended solutions to address those problems, including assessment of information on the exposure of children to environmental hazards in school facilities.

(b) Sunset

The authority of the Administrator to carry out this section shall expire 5 years after December 19, 2007.

(TSCA § 502)

Sec. 2695a. Model guidelines for siting of school facilities

Not later than 18 months after December 19, 2007, the Administrator, in consultation with the Secretary of Education and the Secretary of Health and Human Services, shall issue voluntary school site selection guidelines that account for–

(1) the special vulnerability of children to hazardous substances or pollution exposures in any case in which the potential for contamination at a potential school site exists;

(2) modes of transportation available to students and staff;

(3) the efficient use of energy; and

(4) the potential use of a school at the site as an emergency shelter.

(TSCA § 503)

Sec. 2695b. Public outreach

(a) Reports

The Administrator shall publish and submit to Congress an annual report on all activities carried out under this subchapter, until the expiration of authority described in section 2695(b) of this title.

(b) Public outreach

The Federal Director appointed under section 17092(a) of title 42 (in this subchapter referred to as the "Federal Director") shall ensure, to the maximum extent practicable, that the public clearinghouse established under section 17083(1) of title 42 receives and makes available information on the exposure of children to environmental hazards in school facilities, as provided by the Administrator.

(TSCA § 504)

Sec. 2695c. Environmental health program

(a) In general

Not later than 2 years after December 19, 2007, the Administrator, in consultation with the Secretary of Education, the Secretary of Health and Human Services, and other relevant agencies, shall issue voluntary guidelines for use by the State in developing and implementing an environmental health program for schools that–

(1) takes into account the status and findings of Federal initiatives established under this subchapter or subtitle C of title IV of the Energy Independence and Security Act of 2007 [42 U.S.C. 17091 et seq.] and other relevant Federal law with respect to school facilities, including relevant updates on trends in the field, such as the impact of school facility environments on student and staff–

(A) health, safety, and productivity; and

(B) disabilities or special needs;

(2) takes into account studies using relevant tools identified or developed in accordance with section 492 of the Energy Independence and Security Act of 2007 [42 U.S.C. 17122];

(3) takes into account, with respect to school facilities, each of–

(A) environmental problems, contaminants, hazardous substances, and pollutant emissions, including–

(i) lead from drinking water;

(ii) lead from materials and products;

(iii) asbestos;

(iv) radon;

(v) the presence of elemental mercury releases from products and containers;

(vi) pollutant emissions from materials and products; and

(vii) any other environmental problem, contaminant, hazardous substance, or pollutant emission that present or may present a risk to the health of occupants of the school facilities or environment;

(B) natural day lighting;

(C) ventilation choices and technologies;

(D) heating and cooling choices and technologies;

(E) moisture control and mold;

(F) maintenance, cleaning, and pest control activities;

(G) acoustics; and

(H) other issues relating to the health, comfort, productivity, and performance of occupants of the school facilities;

(4) provides technical assistance on siting, design, management, and operation of school facilities, including facilities used by students with disabilities or special needs;

(5) collaborates with federally funded pediatric environmental health centers to assist in on-site school environmental investigations;

(6) assists States and the public in better understanding and improving the environmental health of children; and

(7) takes into account the special vulnerability of children in low-income and minority communities to exposures from contaminants, hazardous substances, and pollutant emissions.

(b) Public outreach

The Federal Director and Commercial Director shall ensure, to the maximum extent practicable, that the public clearinghouse established under section 423 of the Energy Independence and Security Act of 2007 [42 U.S.C. 17083] receives and makes available-

(1) information from the Administrator that is contained in the report described in section 2695b(a) of this title; and

(2) information on the exposure of children to environmental hazards in school facilities, as provided by the Administrator.

(TSCA § 505)

Sec. 2695d. Authorization of appropriations

There are authorized to be appropriated to carry out this subchapter $1,000,000 for fiscal year 2009, and $1,500,000 for each of fiscal years 2010 through 2013, to remain available untisl expended.

Index

B

D

E

F

G

O

S

T